STAT BASICS

SECOND EDITION

With Applications for Science, Technology, Social Science and Business

F. SELCEN KILINC, PhD

Apex Consulting LLC, 2013
Richmond, Virginia, USA

Stat Basics

F. Selcen Kilinc, PhD, July 2010, October 2013

Stat Basics with Applications for Science & Technology, Social Science & Business, Second Edition

ISBN: 978-0-9827583-5-9

For a permission of using textbook materials, please send a written request to Apex, P.O.Box 5663, Richmond, VA 23220, or e-mail **sales@apexscientificconsulting.com** or call (804) 767-9020.

Additional resources can be accessed by visiting http://www.apexscientificconsulting.com.

Microsoft Excel is a registered trademark of Microsoft Corporation.

About the Author

Dr. F. Selcen Kilinc is a senior service fellow at Centers for Disease Control and Prevention (CDC)/ National Institute for Occupational Safety and Health (NIOSH)/ National Personal Protective Technology Laboratory (NPPTL) specializing in personal protective ensembles. She earned her Ph.D. degree from Auburn University, AL, U.S.A. She holds B.S. and M.S. degrees in Engineering, and an MBA degree. She taught statistics, statistical process control, and six-sigma for many years in different two universities. Before joining NPPTL, she worked as a senior engineer at DuPont Protection Technologies. She has more than 15 years of experience in data analysis in complex areas such as business research, quantitative reasoning, manufacturing and engineering technology, nonparametric applications, and design of experiments. She has published one book, four book chapters and numerous peer-reviewed papers. She extensively presented her research in national and international conferences. She has four patent applications filed in the area of antimicrobial fibers, slow release drug implants, and fabric tactile characterization. These areas require extensive analysis of both physical and business-related data. She has worked on several projects funded by NASA, USDA, and US Air Force in a variety of innovative topics in polymer science. She received "AATCC Research Award" in 2004 and "TAPPI-INDA International Nonwovens Technical Conference Best Paper and Presentation Award" in 2007. She is an active member of National Fire Protection Association (NFPA) and Technical Association of the Pulp and Paper Industry (TAPPI). She is currently the vice chair of 'Materials, Characterization, and Modeling Committee' of TAPPI.

Contents

Chapter 5: Probability Distributions
Part I: Probability Distributions for Discrete Variables

Chapter 6: Probability Distributions
Part II: Probability Distributions for Continuous Variables

Chapter 9: Inferential Statistics:
Hypothesis testing Using one population/one sample

Chapter 10: Inferential Statistics:
Hypothesis testing using two populations/two samples

Preface

Stat Basics is a statistics textbook that is designed and developed to provide students who are learning statistics for the first time with all the basic concepts of statistics. This new edition

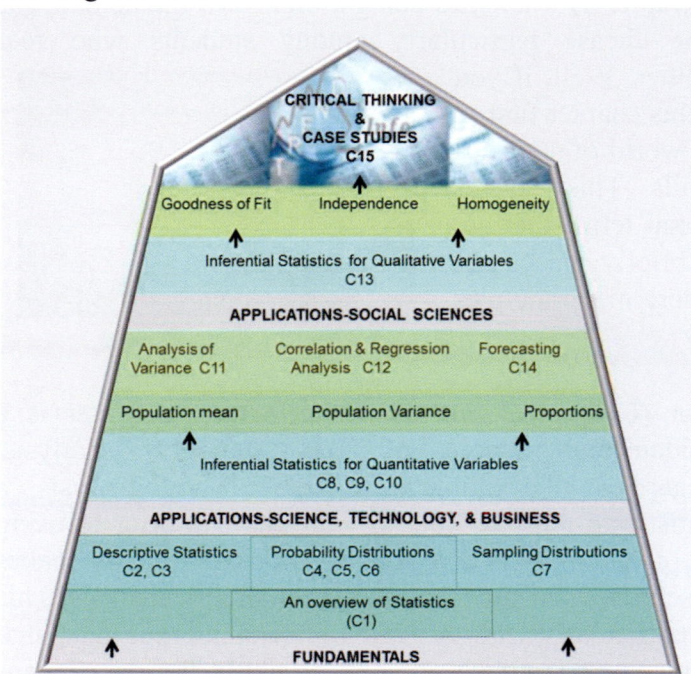

expands the knowledge base to cover more advanced topics. The ultimate goal of this book is to attract students and readers to use statistical tools in a multiplicity of applications such as business, politics, education, society, science, manufacturing, and quality control. Given the global economic pressure the world is experiencing now, students and people in the workforce need to understand that survival in any career will require analytical skills combined with good judgment. Regardless what career you will follow, statistics will always be your most valuable tool in understanding the dynamic changes surrounding you, carrying out important tasks, and making critical decisions that can make

or break your organization's prosperity. This textbook will take you into the world of statistics using a step-by-step format. It begins with a chapter of an overview of statistics. This chapter familiarizes the reader with common terms and applications of statistics without mathematical details. Chapters 2 through 7 cover all fundamental aspects of statistics (descriptive statistics, probability, sampling techniques, and sampling distributions). If you are in science, technology, or business majors, you will then need to understand inferential statistics for quantitative variables. These are covered in Chapters 8 through 10. Readers that will be involved in the area of research or product/service development will need to learn more advanced topics such as analysis of variance and regression analysis. These are covered in Chapters 11 and 12, respectively. If you have to deal with human aspects and social applications in your business, you will need to understand inferential statistics for qualitative variables. This topic is covered in many areas of the book including: Chapter 4 (contingency tables, and Bayes' theorem), Chapter 13 (goodness of fit, tests for independence, and tests for homogeneity), and Chapter 15 (critical thinking). Students in business and engineering will benefit a great deal from the coverage of forecasting in Chapter 14. Finally, a chapter is added on critical thinking in statistics and writing to learn (Chapter 15). The idea of this chapter was inspired by the opinions of the top scientists and statisticians who reviewed this textbook. In this regard, the author would like to express deep appreciation to the reviewers of this textbook who are members of many national and international organizations such as the American Society for Quality (ASQ, http://www.asq.org), the American Statistical Association (ASA, http://www.amstat.org), and the International Biometric Society (IBS, http://www.biometricsociety.org).

Subject Review

The contents of this book are divided into seven key subjects:

- ***An Overview of Basic Statistics (Chapter 1)***. Statistics being a branch of mathematics is often associated with anxiety or unease particularly among students who fear mathematics for one reason or another. Well, if you are one of those students then read this chapter first as it will take you on a journey to the world of statistics with minimum mathematical details. This chapter introduces key concepts and universal terms that are used among statisticians and briefly discusses common statistical tools, their underlying principles and their practical merits.

- ***Basic Statistics- Data Exploration (Chapter 2 and 3)***. Describing a data set is a fundamental aspect of any statistical analysis.

  Regardless the ultimate purpose of any analysis, a statistician must be able to read the data prior to using the data to reach any sort of conclusion. This makes descriptive statistics the foundation of any analysis. This is particularly true in view of the numerous data that humans deal with every day. Reading the data means understanding the boundaries of data and the data center. It also means detecting any abnormality in the data set. Chapter 2 will aim at describing the data numerically using measures of central tendency (mean, mode, and median), and measures of variability (range, standard deviation, and variance). Chapter 3 will aim at describing the data using graphical methods such as frequency distributions, box plots, stem and leaf plots, pie charts, bar charts, and scatter plots.

- ***Probability and Probability Distributions (Chapters 4, 5, and 6)***. Probability appears, to many, as an intuitive notion related to chance. Many things in everyday life such as stock price, lottery, surgery survival, weather, profit, success, and failure are random phenomena for which the outcome is uncertain. The concept of probability provides us with the idea on how to measure the chances of possible outcomes. Probability enables us to quantify uncertainty. In Chapter 4, basic probability rules are covered. In Chapters 5 and 6, the subjects of probability distributions for discrete and

  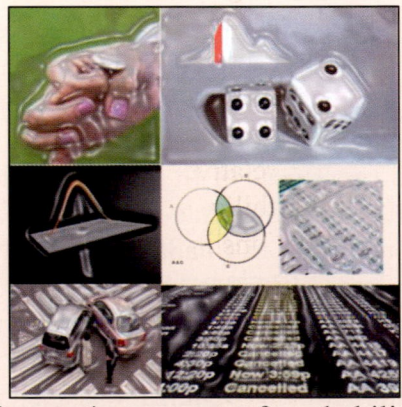

  continuous variables are discussed, respectively. The interesting aspect of probability distributions stems from the fact that it can be utilized to simulate variables following special patterns, leading to the concept of statistical simulation. This will be achieved using technology tools.

- ***Inferential Statistics- Estimation and Hypothesis Testing (Chapters 7 through 10)***. Estimation, commonly called statistical inference, is the process of making judgments about a population using sample properties. This is a form of inductive reasoning, or the bottom-up approach, in which the analyst begins with a small sample drawn from a population and uses sample descriptive statistics to estimate population parameters. In 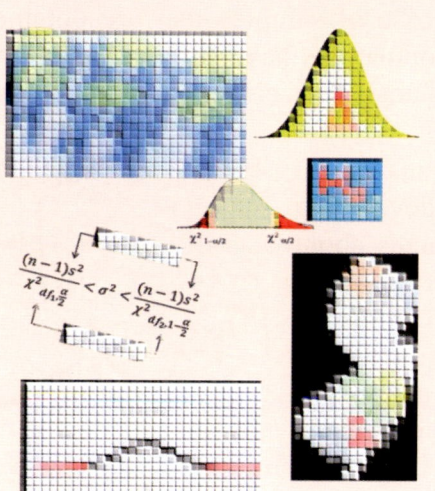 Chapter 7, the focus is on sampling techniques or the different ways to select a representative sample from a population. Also in this chapter, we discuss sampling distributions or the frequency distributions of sample means or proportions. These two subjects cannot be discussed to the full extent without discussion of the '*Central Limit Theorem,*' one of the most commonly used theorems in statistics. In Chapter 8, the focus is on establishing confidence intervals for estimating population means, proportions, and variances. In Chapters 9 and 10, the focus is shifted to the so-called '*hypothesis testing.*' This involves choosing between two opposing views or statements about the population. It may be perceived as a form of deductive reasoning, in which an analyst works from the more general information to the more specific one with the purpose being to decide whether the information about the population is true or false.

- ***System Analysis (Chapters 11 and 12)***. A system is generally defined as an entity which has multiple inputs and a response output of interest. The inputs are typically called '*independent variables*' and the output is called '*dependent or response variable.*' The characteristic associated with the response variable (say, income, profit, grade, or human weight) is primarily influenced by the variability in the input or independent variables. This variability is analyzed using the '*Analysis of Variance*' (Chapter 11)*,* in which the purpose is to isolate different sources of variability and determine the relative contribution of each source to the total  variability in the response variable. In Chapter 12, the focus is shifted to developing relationships between independent variables and the response variable using simple and multiple regression analysis. Software technology is used to perform these analyses.

- ***Qualitative Data Analysis (Chapter 13)***. This is a unique type of analysis used primarily in social statistics. Qualitative parameters are typically described by their frequencies or number of occurrences. For these qualitative data, we may wish to perform a hypothesis test about the frequency distribution of a qualitative (categorical) variable that has finitely

many possible values. In this regard, we perform the so-called 'goodness-of-fit' test, which is an inferential procedure used to determine whether a frequency distribution follows a specific pattern or fits a previously claimed distribution. We also discuss the relationships between qualitative variables that are described by cross frequencies in the form of a contingency table. The analysis used for handling contingency tables is called 'independence tests,' which is essentially a hypothesis test of the null hypothesis that the row and column variables are independent of each other. We also use the so-called 'homogeneity test' in which we consider the case of samples that are obtained from different populations, and test whether those populations have the same proportions of the characteristics being considered. This type of analysis is critical in social science.

- ***Forecasting (Chapter 14)***. Forecasting is a key analysis in business statistics. It is another way of developing relationships for the purpose of making statements about events whose outcomes have not yet been observed and it may happen in the future. Forecasting analysis requires the use of historic data to predict the direction of future trends. The independent variable used in forecasting analysis is always the time, t, or a function of time. The dependent variable is the parameter of interest, which can be of numerous types (e.g. sales, profits, revenues, etc.).

The World of Statistics in Words: Critical Thinking & Writing Assignments (Chapter 15). Throughout the different chapters of this book, the importance of interpretation and rationalization of results is emphasized. Indeed, no matter how simple or complicated an analysis can be, without good interpretation of results and knowledge-based rationalization, the efforts made will yield little benefits. In this closing chapter, the focus will be on the

subject of '*Writing-to-Learn*' in statistics and '*critical thinking.*' Many case studies of writing assignments are presented to assist students on how to approach different subjects and applications in the context of statistics.

New in the Second Edition

- **Learning objectives and Chapter Contents are presented at the beginning of each chapter.**

- **More focus on the different concepts of statistics.** Concepts are summarized in review boxes throughout the textbook

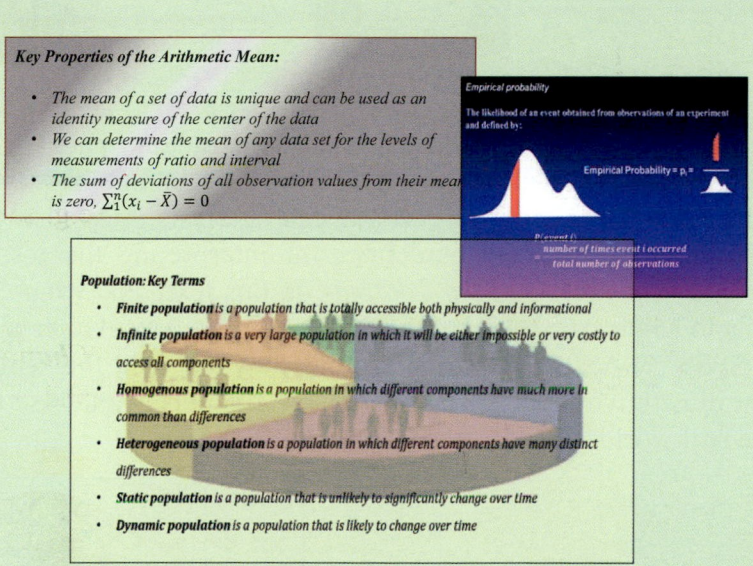

- **Three new chapters added.** Chapter 13: Statistical Tests with Qualitative Data, Chapter 14: Forecasting, and Chapter 15: The World of Statistics in Words. These chapters will allow the use of this textbook for more advanced statistics courses such as "Social Statistics," "Business Statistics," and "Statistics for Science and Technology."

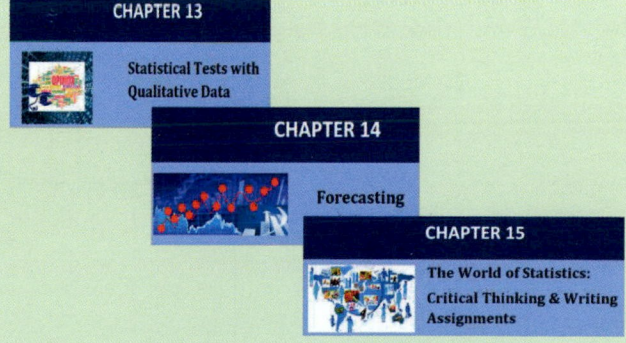

- **The addition of Bayes' theorem.** A complete section in Chapter 4 covers the Bayes' theorem. This is a critical concept in business and social statistics

- **The addition of new sampling techniques.** These include: probability sampling, non-probability sampling, and purposive sampling (Chapter 7)

- **More than 1000 review exercises.** These are the problems at the end of each chapter. Answers are provided to many selected problems for students and instructors

- **More than 300 working problems.** These are short problems provided at the end of each section. They closely follow the examples of the section. A work problem offers a quick review on the section before proceeding to the next section

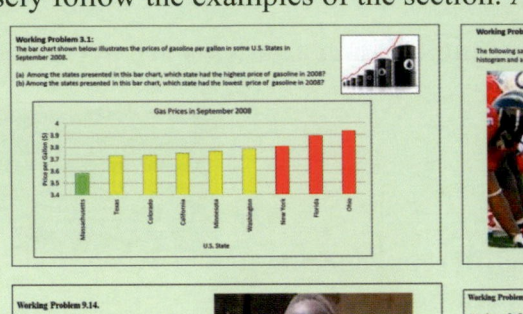

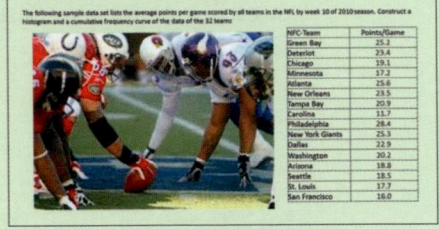

- **Test Bank**. This is available in the CD of Instructor's resources

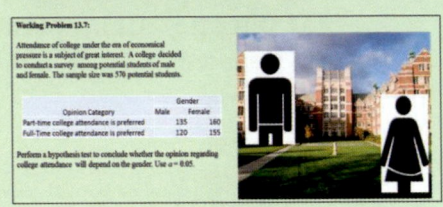

- **Emphasis on using technology**. *Statistics calculators are things of the past* as they mask the true merits of performing statistical analysis. Instructors who are still using these calculators should consider switching to data analysis technologies. Not only do these technologies provide all the tools to perform data analysis, they also provide all components of statistical reporting, and guidelines for interpreting the results. *Most statistics software programs provide standard outputs*. In this textbook, we use Microsoft Excel® Data Analysis to solve statistical problems of large data sets. Other technologies such as MegaStat®, SPSS®, SAS®, etc. can be used as they all yield the same forms of outputs with different illustrative capabilities. The key is: students should use technology to be prepared for the real world.

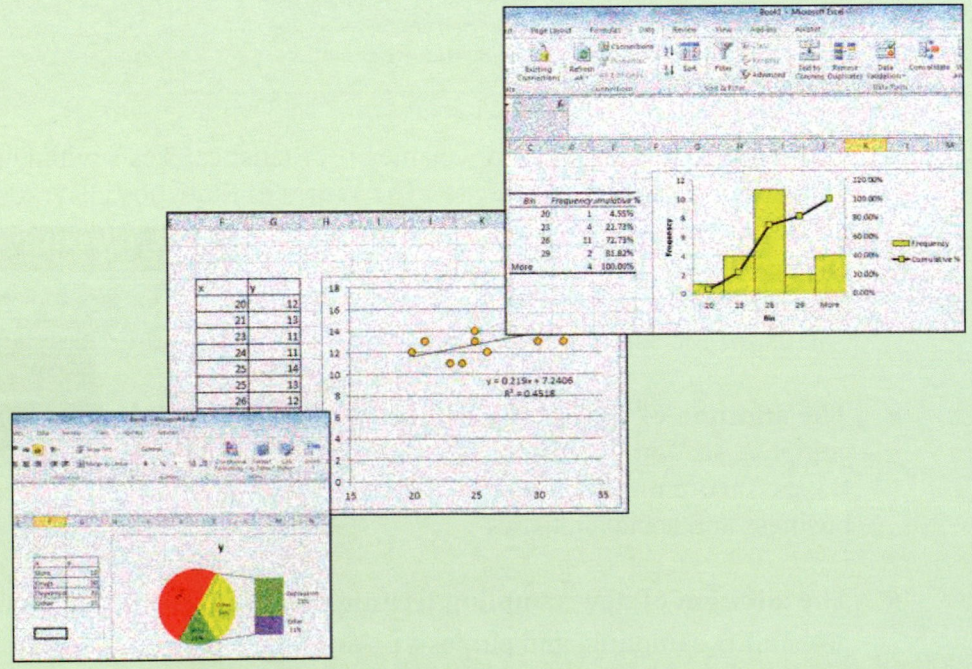

Different Ways to Utilize the Textbook:

(1)   Suggested contents for an Introduction to Statistics Course

Introduction to Statistics:

See CD for instructors

- **An Overview of Basic Statistics:**
  - Chapter 1

- **Descriptive Statistics:**
  - Chapter 2 (exclude sections 2.3.4, 2.4.2, and 2.5.2)
  - Chapter 3

- **Introduction to Probability:**
  - Chapter 4 (exclude Bayes' theorem)

- **Probability Distributions- Discrete and Continuous Variables**
  - Chapter 5 (sections 5.1 through 5.6, section 5.11).
  - Chapter 6 (Sections 6.1, 6.3, 6.4, 6.5, 6.6, and 6.8)

- **Sampling Techniques, Sampling distributions, Central Limit Theorem:**
  - Chapter 7

- **Inferential Statistics & Confidence Intervals:**
  - Chapter 8: Sections 8.1 to 8.4
  - Chapter 9: Sections 9.1 to 9.6
  - Chapter 10: Sections 10.1 to 10.5

- **Introduction to Correlation and Regression:**
  - Chapter 12- Sections 12.1 to 12.11

- **Introduction to the World of Statistics:**
  - Chapter 15 (all sections and case studies)

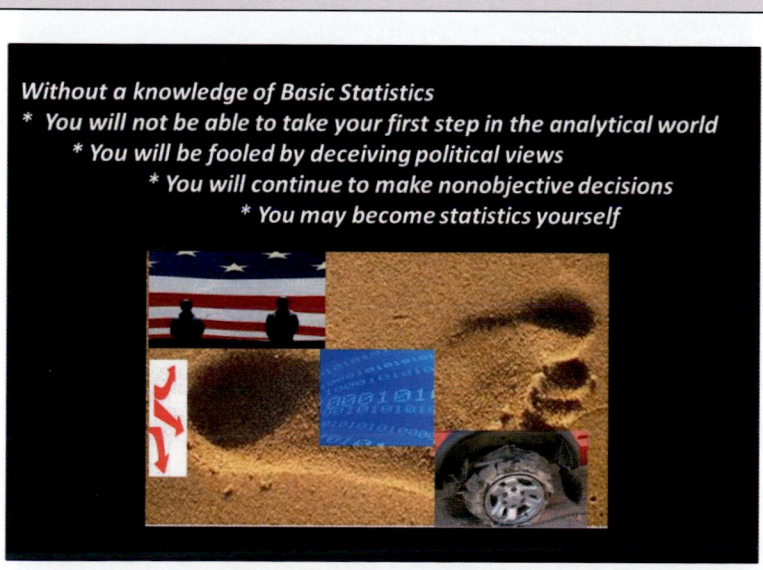

Without a knowledge of Basic Statistics
* *You will not be able to take your first step in the analytical world*
* *You will be fooled by deceiving political views*
* *You will continue to make nonobjective decisions*
* *You may become statistics yourself*

(2)　Suggested Contents for a Social Statistics Course

Social Statistics:

See CD for instructors

- **The importance of Statistics in Social Applications:**
  - Chapter 1

- **Descriptive Statistics:**
  - Chapter 2 (exclude sections 2.3.4, 2.4.2, and 2.5.2)
  - Chapter 3

- **Introduction to Probability:**
  - Chapter 4 with focus on the Contingency Table (section 4.8) and Bayes' theorem (section 4.14)

- **Probability Distributions- Discrete and Continuous Variables**
  - Chapter 5 (sections 5.1 through 5.6, section 5.11).
  - Chapter 6 (Sections 6.1, 6.3, 6.4, 6.5, 6.6, and 6.8)

- **Sampling and Surveying Techniques:**
  - Chapter 7 with focus on Planning (section 7.2.1), Establishing a sample structure (section 7.2.2), and Using a reliable database (7.2.3)
  - Chapter 7 with focus on sampling methods (random, 7.3.1, cluster, 7.3.3, and stratified, 7.3.4)

- **Inferential Statistics:**
  - Chapter 8: with focus on proportion (section 8.3.4), and the Chi-Square (χ^2) distribution (section 8.6.1)
  - Chapter 9: Hypothesis testing with focus on proportion (section 9.6), and the Chi-Square (χ^2) distribution (section 9.7)

- **Introduction to Correlation and Regression Analysis:**
  - Chapter 12- Sections 12.1 to 12.11

- **Statistical Tests with Qualitative Data:**
  - Chapter 13: Goodness of Fit (section 13.3, and Contingency Tables and Tests for Independence (Section 13.4)

- **The World of Statistics in Words:**
  - Chapter 15: with focus on social case studies

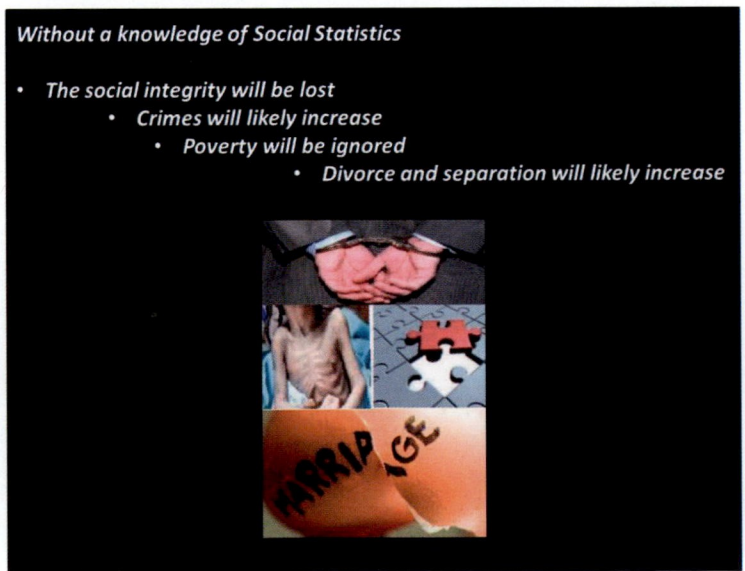

Without a knowledge of Social Statistics

- *The social integrity will be lost*
  - *Crimes will likely increase*
    - *Poverty will be ignored*
      - *Divorce and separation will likely increase*

(3) Suggested Contents for a Science, Technology, and Engineering Statistics Course

Science & Engineering Statistics:

See CD for instructors

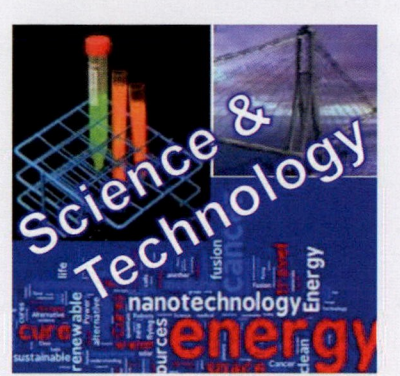

- **An Overview of Basic Statistics: Statistics in Science and Technology**
  - Chapter 1

- **Descriptive Statistics:**
  - Chapter 2 & Chapter 3

- **Probability:**
  - Chapter 4, Chapter 5, and Chapter 6

- **Sampling Techniques, Sampling distributions, and Central Limit Theorem:**
  - Chapter 7

- **Inferential Statistics:**
  - Chapter 8, Chapter 9, and Chapter 10

- **Analysis of Variance:**
  - Chapter 11

- **Correlation and Regression Analysis:**
  - Chapter 12

- **The World of Statistics in Words:**
  - Chapter 15: with focus on Science and Technology case studies

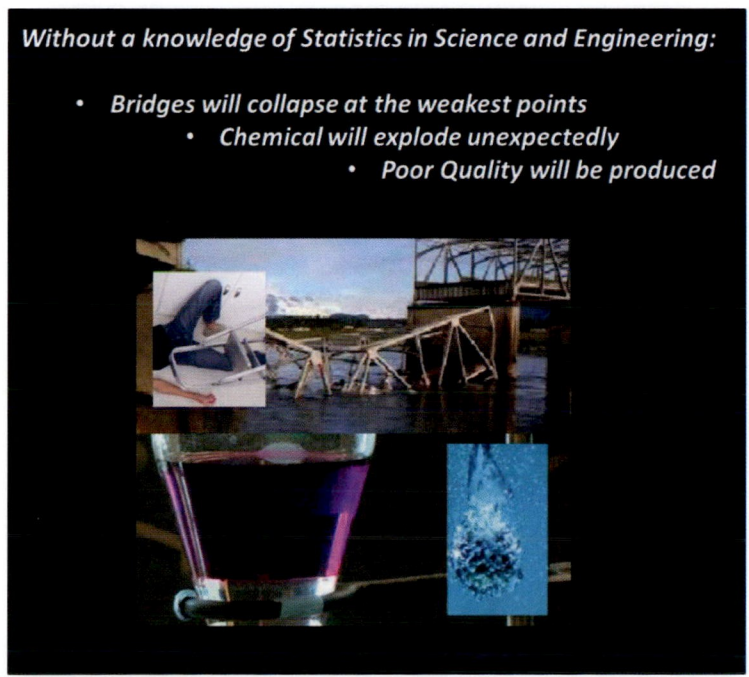

Without a knowledge of Statistics in Science and Engineering:

- *Bridges will collapse at the weakest points*
  - *Chemical will explode unexpectedly*
    - *Poor Quality will be produced*

(4)   Suggested Contents for a Business Statistics Course

Business Statistics:

See CD for instructors

- **An Overview of Basic Statistics-Statistics in Business and Economics:**
    - Chapter 1

- **Descriptive Statistics:**
    - Chapter 2 (with focus on **Geometric Mean, section 2.3.4)**
    - Chapter 3

- **Probability:**
    - Chapter 4, Chapter 5, and Chapter 6

- **Sampling Techniques, Sampling distributions, and Central Limit Theorem:**
    - Chapter 7

- **Inferential Statistics and Hypothesis Testing:**
    - Chapter 8
    - Chapter 9
    - Chapter 10

- **Analysis of Variance:**
    - Chapter 11

- **Correlation and Regression Analysis:**
    - Chapter 12

- **Forecasting with emphasis on Exponential Smoothing:**
    - Chapter 14

- **The World of Statistics in Words:**
    - Chapter 15 with focus on business case studies

Important Points to the Instructors

The classic outcomes of education have been based on:

- The mere acquisition and retention of information or knowledge using particular ways in which information is delivered and treated
- The mere possession of a set of skills so that people can continue to use them per their specific constraints

 These outcomes are useful as a first step in the education process. Given the condensed nature of most college courses and the limited time to cover all course contents, most students merely acquire these outcomes. Furthermore, students are often tested on the mere acquisition and the mere possession of information and skills. Unfortunately, these classic outcomes do not necessarily produce critical thinkers. Instead, and in the best case scenario, they often produce good instruction followers that can hardly think on their own.

Most cognitive Theories suggest the following key aspects:

- *Students learn best when they practice and perform on their own*
- *Knowledge tends to be specific to the context in which it is presented*
- *Learning involves making use of a piece of knowledge in a more meaningful sense, preferably with application to real situations*
- *Learning also involves integrating new knowledge with existing knowledge*
- *Learning becomes less efficient as the mental load increases.*
- *The true measure of a successful learning process stems from understanding contents in term of objectives and reflecting what we learn through thinking that goes beyond the learning contents*

As a result of the above points, teachers should summarize the key knowledge pieces before and after each chapter or topic; ask questions beyond the knowledge circle; invite questions and inputs from students, and progressively link different topics of the course to the relevant pieces of knowledge that represent the main theme of the objective structure of the course.

In order to achieve the maximum gain of learning and understanding statistics, it will be important to develop an appreciation among students of the rationale behind why and how statistics is used by the world, at large. Without proper perspective, statistics becomes a course of mathematical exercises in which students repeatedly perform addition, subtraction, multiplication, division, etc.

It is important that a statistics course be taught with full consideration of the aspect of critical thinking. Design your teaching methodology to accommodate critical thinking in every statistical subject. Given the limited time allocated for a course syllabus, this accommodation should be entirely based on students' efforts under the teacher's guidance. At the beginning of the course, students should be made aware of the different concepts of critical thinking. These include:

- Different people may think of a given issue differently depending on their background, knowledge base, and their style of thinking.
- Critical thinking is typically a self-motivated and self-driven process.
- When critical thinking is the task of a team, they should work together to develop an understanding of the concepts and principles that enable them to analyze, assess, and improve thinking.
- Key givens of critical thinkers are intellectual integrity, intellectual humility, intellectual civility, intellectual empathy, and intellectual sense of justice and confidence in reason.
- Critical thinking is not a steady-state or static process. In other words, no matter how skilled a person can be as thinker, he/she can always improve reasoning abilities and he/she will at times fall prey to mistakes in reasoning, human irrationality, prejudices, biases, distortions, uncritically accepted social rules and taboos, self-interest, and vested interest.
- It is important to consider the rights and needs of relevant others when you think critically.
- The Socratic principle is often referred to in critical thinking: 'The unexamined life is not worth living.'

Further Readings:

- Campbell, Stephen K. Flaws and Fallacies in Statistical Thinking. Prentice Hall (1974).
- Sofia D. Anastasiadou , Aikaterini Dimitriadou, What does Critical Thinking mean? A statistical data analysis of pre-service teachers' defining statements, International Journal of Humanities and Social Science Vol. 1 No. 7 [Special Issue –June 2011]
- Milo Schield, Statistical literacy: Thinking critically about statistics-The Inaugural issue of the Journal 'Of Significance,' Produced by the Association of Public Data Users (www.apdu.org)
- Jane M. Watson, Rosemary A. Callingham, Statistical Literacy: From Idiosyncratic to Critical Thinking, Curricular Development in Statistics Education, Sweden, 2004: Jane Watson, Rosemary Callingham (http://www.stat.auckland.ac.nz/~iase/publications/rt04/4.1_Watson&Callingham.pdf)
- Paul, R., & Elder, L. The miniature guide to critical thinking: Concepts and tools. Dillon Beach, CA: Foundation for Critical Thinking (2009)

Application Index: Examples, Working Problems, and Review Exercises Related to Specific Fields

Applications	Education	Human Health
	Key words: Education, teaching, learning, Community college, four-year college, professor, student, freshmen, sophomore, junior, senior, In-state tuition, out-state tuition, financial aid, etc.	Key words: weight loss, addiction, smoking, disease, body temperature, etc.
Examples	1.1, 1.2, 1.3, 1.4, 1.5, 1.6, 1.8, 1.9, 1.14, 1.15, 1.19, 2.13, 1.15, 3.11, 3.15, 3.18, 4.10, 4.18, 4.20, 5.13, 6.1, 6.5, 6.6, 6.9, 6.10, 6.14, 6.16, 7.4, 7.5, 7.14, 8.17, 8.18, 8.22, 8.24, 8.27, 10.1, 10.5	1.4, 1.7,3.9, 3.10, 4.11, 8.14, 10.2, 10.3, 10.6, 13.2, 13.6
Working problems	1.8, 1.9, 1.14, 1.15, 1.19, 2.21, 3.3, 3.14, 3.18, 3.19, 4.11, 5.15, 5.16, 5.18, 5.20, 6.2, 6.3, 6.12, 6.13, 7.7, 7.12, 7.13, 7.14, 7.15, 7.21, 8.7, 8.10, 8.20, 9.18, 9.19, 10.1, 10.11, 11.7, 11.8, 12.6, 12.8, 12.9, 12.10, 12.11, 12.12, 12.13, 12.14, 12.15, 12.16, 12.17	1.5, 1.6, 4.19, 4.29, 4.31, 4.32, 5.19, 6.4, 6.5, 7.11, 8.13, 9.11, 9.20, 10.4, 10.7, 11.6, 11.9, 11.10
Review Exercises	1.18, 1.23, 1.25, 1.32, 2.5, 2.7, 2.12, 2.14, 2.26, 2.27, 3.12, 3.13, 3.18, 3.19, 3.27, 3.28, 3.33, 3.34, 3.39, 3.40, 3.49, 3.50, 5.7, 5.8, 5.13, 5.14, 5.19, 5.27, 5.36, 6.4, 6.5, 6.6, 6.41, 7.14, 7.15, 7.16, 7.17, 7.22, 7.33, 7.34, 8.6, 8.9, 8.13, 8.14, 8.15, 8.16, 8.17, 8.20, 8.21, 8.24, 8.25, 8.26, 8.29, 8.60, 8.61, 8.73, 8.74, 8.83, 8.84, 9.1, 9.7, 9.9, 9.21, 9.23, 9.28, 9.31, 9.35, 9.39, 10.4, 10.18, 10.19, 10.20, 10.21, 10.22, 10.23, 10.24, 10.47, 11.14, 11.15, 11.16, 11.17, 11.18, 11.19, 11.23, 11.24, 11.25, 11.28, 11.30, 11.30, 11.32, 12.31, 12.37, 13.3, 13.5, 13.7, 13.8, 13.9, 13.10, 13.11	1.19, 1.22, 1.24, 3.47, 4.28, 4.30, 4.33, 4.42, 4.43, 4.44, 4.46, 4.47, 5.17, 5.26, 5.31, 5.32, 5.39, 6.38, 6.42, 7.29, 8.4, 8.5, 8.7, 8.8, 8.31, 8.32, 8.47, 8.65, 8.66, 8.68, 9.12, 9.60, 9.64, 10.9, 10.30, 10.34, 10.45, 10.56, 11.27, 11.31, 12.22, 12.35, 12.36, 13.1, 13.12

Applications	Science & Technology	Politics
	Key words: manufacturing, engineering, Testing, precision, accuracy, quality control	Key words: Governments, presidents, election, votes, inauguration, energy, jobs
Examples	1.3, 1.4, 1.8, 1.10, 3.7, 3.8, 3.24, 4.38, 5.8, 5.9, 5.10, 5.11, 5.14, 5.15, 5.16, 5.17, 6.13, 6.15, 6.18, 7.6, 7.21, 8.13, 8.25, 8.28, 9.1, 9.3, 9.4, 9.8, 9.9, 9.10, 9.12, 9.13, 9.14, 9.16, 10.4, 10.9, 11.4, 11.5, 11.6, 11.7, 11.9	4.10, 13.4
Working problems	3.15, 3.24, 4.27, 5.10, 5.11, 5.21, 6.7, 7.16, 7.19, 8.2, 8.6, 8.8, 8.11, 8.12, 8.19, 9.4, 9.5, 9.7, 9.12, 10.10, 11.1, 11.2, 13.2	7.4, 7.5, 9.16, 13.4, 13.5, 13.6, 13.7, 13.8, 13.9, 13.10, 13.11
Review Exercises	1.5, 3.42, 4.21, 4.27, 4.35, 4.37, 4.39, 4.48, 5.2, 5.6, 5.9, 5.18, 5.20, 5.22, 5.23, 5.24, 5.28, 5.29, 5.31, 5.32, 5.35, 6.10, 6.22, 6.23, 6.24, 6.25, 6.26, 6.28, 6.34, 6.37, 6.39, 6.40, 6.43, 6.45, 6.46, 7.9, 7.18, 7.19, 7.20, 8.30, 8.34, 8.44, 8.66, 8.85, 8.86, 8.87, 9.3, 9.14, 9.16, 9.18, 9.19, 9.20, 9.24, 9.25, 9.45, 9,46, 9.48, 9.49, 9.50, 9.51, 9.52, 9.61, 9.62, 9.70, 10.14, 10.15, 10.16, 10.17, 10.44, 10.48, 10.64, 10.66, 10.68, 11.9, 11.10, 11.11, 11.12, 11.29, 12.23	2.1, 2.16, 2.24, 3.1, 3.3, 3.4, 3.5, 3.6, 3.20, 4.11, 4.12, 4.13, 4.14, 4.15, 4.18, 5.33, 5.38, 7.31, 7.32, 8.48, 9.59, 9.60, 10.9, 10.18, 10.19, 10.20, 10.21, 10.22, 10.23, 10.24, 13.2, 13.4

Applications	Social Applications	Sports
	Ages, gender, time, household, workers, crimes, accidents on the job, guns, poverty, driving to work, heights, weights, dress codes, retirement	Football, basketball, NFL, points per game, touchdowns
Examples:	2.14, 3.2, 3.3, 3.5, 3.9, 3.13, 3.14, 3.19, 4.17, 4.20, 4.23, 4.26, 4.35, 4.36, 4.37, 5.3, 5.6, 5.7, 6.2, 6.3, 6.14, 6.17, 7.13, 7.15, 7.16, 7.18, 7.22, 7.23, 7.24, 7.25, 8.6, 8.8, 8.11, 8.15, 8.16, 8.21, 8.22, 8.23, 9.1, 9.2, 9.7, 9.8, 9.9, 9.13, 9.14, 10.9, 11.1, 11.2, 11.3, 11.8, 12.1, 12.4, 12.5, 12.7, 12.8, 12.9, 12.10, 12.11, 13.2, 13.5, 13.6,	3.1, 3.6, 8.2
Working problems:	3.4, 3.11, 3.20, 4.3, 4.4, 4.13, 4.18, 4.20, 4.21, 4.22, 4.23, 4.24, 5.4, 5.5, 5.6, 5.7, 5.8, 5.12, 5.14, 5.17, 5.22, 5.23, 7.5, 7.17, 8.2, 8.3, 8.4, 8.6, 8.14, 8.15, 8.16, 9.12, 10.5, 10.6, 10.7, 10.8, 10.9, 10.10, 10.11, 11.9, 11.10, 12.4, 12.5, 12.9, 12.10, 12.12, 12.13, 12.14, 12.15, 12.16, 13.2, 13.4, 13.5, 13.6, 13.7, 13.8, 13.9, 13.10, 13.11,	3.6, 3.8, 8.18
Review Exercises	1.27, 2.6, 2.13, 2.18, 2.20, 2.23, 3.6, 3.9, 3.31, 3.35, 3.41, 3.44, 3.45, 3.51, 4.7, 4.9, 4.10, 4.20, 4.24, 4.25, 4.26, 4.28, 4.29, 4.31, 4.32, 4.45, 4.49, 5.4, 5.5, 5.12, 5.15, 5.16, 5.17, 5.26, 5.30, 5.34, 5.38, 5.39, 5.42, 5.43, 6.2, 6.3, 6.8, 6.9, 6.24, 6.25, 6.26, 6.27, 6.28, 6.30, 6.41, 7.8, 7.23, 7.24, 7.25, 7.27, 7.28, 7.30, 8.3, 8.10, 8.11, 8.18, 8.19, 8.22, 8.23, 8.30, 8.33, 8.42, 8.43, 8.45, 8.68, 8.69, 8.70, 8.71, 8.72, 9.2, 9.14, 9.15, 9.17, 9.21, 9.23, 9.32, 9.33, 9.34, 9.36, 9.37, 9.38, 9.40, 9.41, 9.42, 9.43, 9.55, 9.56, 9.58, 9.61, 9.63, 9.64, 10.4, 10.5, 10.6, 10.7, 10.8, 10.9, 10.11, 10.13, 10.17, 10.18, 10.19, 10.20, 10.21, 10.22, 10.23, 10.24, 10.30, 10.54, 10,55, 10.56, 11.9, 11.26, 12.21, 12.27, 12.29, 12.30, 12.32, 12.33, 12.34, 12.37, 13.1, 13.2, 13.4, 13.6, 13.7, 13.12	2.23, 4.34, 7.21, 7.26, 8.2, 9.47

Applications	Quality control, engineering, and manufacturing
	Testing, precision, accuracy, inspection, quality assurance
Examples:	1.3, 1.4, 1.8, 1.10, 3.7, 3.8, 3.24, 4.38, 5.8, 5.9, 5.10, 5.11, 5.14, 5.15, 5.16, 5.17, 6.13, 6.15, 6.18, 7.6, 7.21, 8.13, 8.25, 8.28, 9.1, 9.3, 9.4, 9.8, 9.9, 9.10, 9.12, 9.13, 9.14, 9.16, 10.4, 10.9, 11.4, 11.5, 11.6, 11.7, 11.9
Working problems:	3.15, 3.24, 4.27, 5.10, 5.11, 5.21, 6.7, 7.16, 7.19, 8.2, 8.6, 8.8, 8.11, 8.12, 8.19, 9.4, 9.5, 9.7, 9.12, 10.10, 11.1, 11.2, 13.2
Review Exercises	1.5, 3.42, 4.21, 4.27, 4.35, 4.37, 4.39, 4.48, 5.2, 5.6, 5.9, 5.18, 5.20, 5.22, 5.23, 5.24, 5.28, 5.29, 5.31, 5.32, 5.35, 6.10, 6.22, 6.23, 6.24, 6.25, 6.26, 6.28, 6.34, 6.37, 6.39, 6.40, 6.43, 6.45, 6.46, 7.9, 7.18, 7.19, 7.20, 8.30, 8.34, 8.44, 8.66, 8.85, 8.86, 8.87, 9.3, 9.14, 9.16, 9.18, 9.19, 9.20, 9.24, 9.25, 9,46, 9.48, 9.49, 9.50, 9.51, 9.52, 9.61, 9.62, 9.70, 10.14, 10.15, 10.16, 10.17, 10.44, 10.48, 10.64, 10.66, 10.68, 11.9, 11.10, 11.11, 11.12, 11.29, 12.23

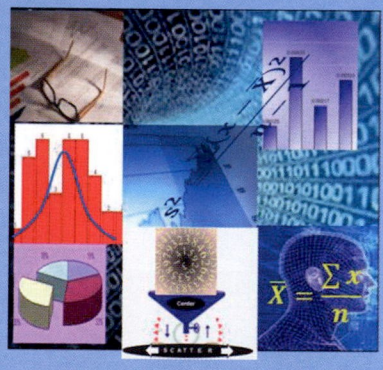

An Overview of Basic Statistics

After completing this chapter, students will become familiar with the following key terms:

- Statistics: Science & Art
- Numbers, Data, and Statistics
- Basic statistical terms such as:
    - Variables, Population, Sample
    - Statistic & Parameter
    - Precision & Accuracy
    - System & Process
    - Descriptive Statistics & Sampling Concepts
    - Different Sources of Variability
    - Different Types of Variables
    - The Levels of Measurements
    - The Normal Distribution
    - Inferential Statistics
    - The Meaning of Probability
    - The Meaning of Correlation and Regression
    - Different ways of Data Collection

CHAPTER 1

Statistics being a branch of mathematics is often associated with anxiety or unease particularly among students who fear mathematics for one reason or another. Well, if you are one of those students then read this chapter first as it will take you in a journey to the world of statistics with minimum mathematical details. This chapter introduces key concepts and universal terms that are used among statisticians, and briefly discusses common statistical tools, their underlying principles and their practical merits.

CHAPTER CONTENTS

1.1 Why should you learn statistics?

In dealing with many issues in our lives, we often fall short of solving problems as a result of our inability to face three major challenges: *variability*, *uncertainty*, and *subjectivity*. The best way to overcome these challenges is to follow objective procedures and use quantitative information. In this context, statistics is the science of dealing with these challenges. Globally, statistics is a key tool in governments' and organizations' activities. Examples of these activities are listed below.

- All governments around the world use statistics to measure and analyze key economic performances and activities including: population growth, environmental effects, educational progress, and medical care outcomes.
- Politicians use statistics to obtain people's opinions about important issues and to predict outcomes of elections for presidents, governors, and other elected officials.
- Colleges use statistics to measure student performance, teacher performance, enrollment, and passing rates.
- Media organizations use statistics to determine the popularity or the survival rate of television and radio shows.
- Businesses use statistics in all types of decision analysis including forecasting, inventory control, and project management.
- Manufacturers use statistics to monitor product quality, machine efficiency, and production variables.

The reason we need statistics is that we are living in a world of numbers, or more precisely a world of data. In this regard, it is useful to know the difference between *numbers, data,* and *statistics*:

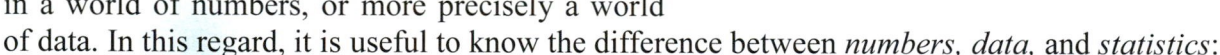

- *Numbers alone may not reveal much until they are identified by a variable*

- *Numbers are called data, only when they reflect clear information (meaning and units)*

- *Data, on the other hand, are called statistics when they reflect specific or descriptive measures of the event or the variable under study*

In today's information age, a given organization (business, education, manufacturing, or government) may be generating thousands or millions of numbers every day. These numbers become data when they are defined with narrative descriptions and identified with units. Without statistics, numbers will remain numbers, data will likely be scattered, and information will likely be unmanageable. When a flood of data is generated it becomes impossible to extract specific information and reach appropriate conclusions or decisions without the use of appropriate statistical tools. Indeed, *statistics can be considered as a vital tool to reduce the mass of data and increase useful information.*

In any career which you may choose, statistics will prove to be your powerful tool to meet many tasks and achieve many goals:

- A school teacher may use statistics to calculate the average grade or the range of grades of a test, compare the performances of different students, and examine the distribution of grades.

- A physician may use statistics to compare different medical treatments and reactions to medicines by different patients. Indeed, most of the medical information we have come to know have been a result of good statistical analyses using reliable data about medicine and medical treatments.

- An engineer may use statistics to determine the chance of failure of a construction or compare different material types for a specific design.

- An environmental scientist may use statistics to handle the numerous data describing plants, animals, pollution sources, and human activities.

- An economist may use statistics to determine economic growth rates, supply and demand, and household income.

- A social scientist may use statistics to determine distribution of gender and ethnic groups, unemployment

The History of Statistics

Somewhere in antiquity, the first uses of statistics were lost. Some suggest that the history of statistics can be traced back to the Ancient Egyptians based on the accomplishments this civilization made in engineering and science. However, the first documented trace of statistics is credited to the 17th Century John Graunt (1620–1674) who analyzed records of deaths in London in the early 1600s and was the first to perform detailed analysis for a massive amount of data using manual calculations. In the 18th century, Pierre Laplace (1749–1827) performed extensive probability analysis and Carl Friedrich Gauss (1777–1855) developed the familiar 'least-squares method' which is the basis for regression analysis as we know it today. These scientists are considered the first statisticians in history.

John Graunt
(1620–1674)

Pierre Laplace
(1749–1827)

Is economy improving?

This is a statistical question because you can't actually measure the entire economy and a slice or a sample of economic data can reveal virtually all information needed about the economy; but you need statistics to achieve this goal.

rates, crime rates, and attributes associated with households and human welfare.

- A businessman may use statistics to address many questions associated with potential markets, expected profits, and consumer behavior.

1.2 What is statistics?

Most definitions of statistics that you will find in textbooks, encyclopedias, and dictionaries will contain the word '*mathematics.*' Examples of these definitions are listed in Table 1.1. This word is rightfully incorporated in these definitions to imply that the power of statistics as a science stems from its solid mathematical foundation. However, there is a significant difference between mathematical statistics and applied statistics. Students who are learning mathematical statistics are being prepared to become professional mathematicians. Students who are learning applied statistics are being prepared to utilize the various mathematical tools of statistics in real-world applications.

Table 1.1 Definitions of statistics

Definition	Source
"The <u>mathematics</u> of the collection, organization, and interpretation of numerical data, especially the analysis of population characteristics by inference from sampling."	American Heritage Dictionary®
"A branch of <u>mathematics</u> dealing with the collection, analysis, interpretation, and presentation of masses of numerical data."	The Merriam-Webster's Collegiate Dictionary®
"The scientific application of <u>mathematical</u> principles to the collection, analysis, and presentation of numerical data."	The American Statistical Association (ASA, http://www.amstat.org/)

In general, *applied statistics* can be defined as:

> ### Applied Statistics:
>
> "The **<u>science</u>** and **<u>art</u>** of reading, describing, and manipulating <u>data</u>, which represents <u>variables</u> so that practical observations about a <u>population</u> can be made from a <u>sample</u> drawn from the population, and guidelines can be established to allow making conclusions with high levels of <u>precision</u> and <u>accuracy</u> about a certain <u>process</u> or a given <u>system</u>"

This definition consists of ten common terminologies that are often used by statisticians. These are: *science, art, data, variables, population, sample, precision, accuracy, process,* and *system.* Students who are studying statistics should become very familiar with these terminologies. In the following sections, we will discuss these terminologies in further detail.

1.3 Statistics: between science and art

In most statistical analyses, the association between science and art is a critical one. The 'science' aspect implies the mathematical language and the analytical tools required for reading, describing, and analyzing data. The 'art' aspect implies the need for using judgment and experience in understanding the nature of the process under consideration and in dealing with the outputs of data analysis. This aspect is very critical in dealing with cause and effects applications. It is well-known that *statistics does not provide causes and effects; it only yields analysis outcome based on the data used.* It is then your job to think of possible causes and effects. This is where the art of reading data and interpreting the results of the statistical analysis comes into play.

Does childhood vaccination harm children?

This represents a disturbing issue among many parents. Some activists propagate horror stories of children who seemed fine one day, got vaccinated, and then developed autism. Can these individual stories prove anything? This issue is also a statistical one but one has to be careful differentiating between correlation and causation.

To illustrate the above point, suppose you are trying to determine your performance in a biology course to find where you stand in comparison with other students. Suppose the class average is 85% and your grades on the four different tests are: 72, 79, 91, and 74. This yields an average of 79%. As a result, you will conclude that your mean grade is 6% below the class average. You will also notice that although you were able to earn an *A* in one of the exams (91%), your performance in other exams was consistently at the *C* level (72, 79, and 74). With the lowest grade being 72% and the highest being 91%, the range of your grades is 19%, which is a wide range. These statistical observations, though they reflect your true performance during the course, do not reveal any information about how you were able to achieve a 91% in one exam and why you were consistently at 70s on the other three exams. These are issues of causes and effects that statistics cannot reveal. Instead, statistics explores different dimensions of data that one can use to make a judgment or explore causes and effects. In this regard, and in view of the analysis outcomes, you may ask yourself a number of questions in searching for the causes:

- *Did I miss many classes?*
- *Did I make enough effort?*
- *Did I have poor study habits?*
- *Was it being sick during the semester?*
- *Was it being distracted by other things?*
- *If I achieve an A on one exam, why couldn't I achieve that on the other exams?*

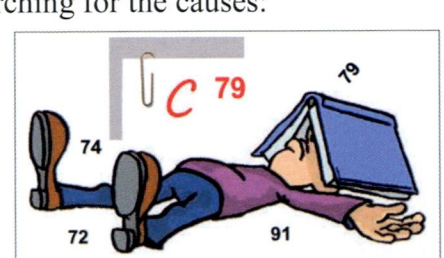

The above questions indicate the need to not only perform calculations and analysis, but also to interpret the outcomes of the analysis to obtain the ultimate benefits of statistics.

1.4 Numbers, data and statistics

Applied Statistics:

*"The <u>science</u> and <u>art</u> of reading, describing, and manipulating <u>**data**</u>, which represents <u>variables</u> so that practical observations about a <u>population</u> can be made from a <u>sample</u> drawn from the population, and guidelines can be established to allow making conclusions with high levels of <u>precision</u> and <u>accuracy</u> about a certain <u>process</u> or a given <u>system</u>"*

The next term that we should pay attention to in the above definition is '*data*.' This is the Latin plural of *datum*. In the United States, most popular newspapers, magazines, and technical journals, use the word 'data' synonymously with "information" and hence as a singular. For example, one may write: "the data *was* collected for the purpose of evaluating the education process." In Europe, particularly in Britain, it is used as a plural. For example, one may write: '*these* data show the ages of senior citizens.'

The most accepted meaning of the word data is '*factual information*'. The significance of this meaning is that data has to be collected carefully and it has to come from reliable and meaningful sources to be considered as factual information. Indeed, any good analysis should begin by questioning the validity and the reliability of the data used in the analysis.

In any statistical analysis, data is represented by numbers. As indicated earlier, the difference between data and numbers is that data are essentially numbers reflecting meaningful information. For example, consider the following numbers and attempt to guess what they mean:

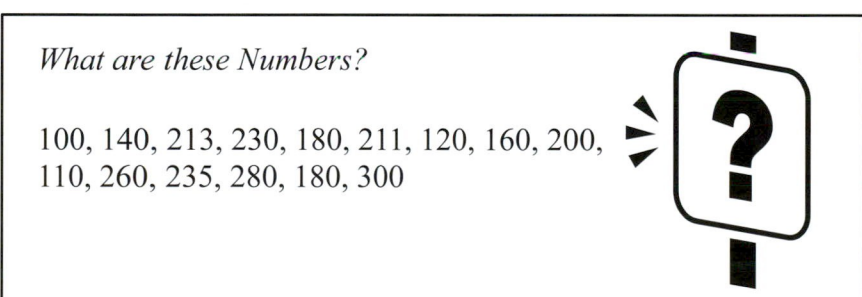

What are these Numbers?

100, 140, 213, 230, 180, 211, 120, 160, 200, 110, 260, 235, 280, 180, 300

You may make many guesses trying to figure out what these numbers represent, but the safest one would be that these are just numbers and they may mean many things. Now, suppose you are told that these numbers actually represent weights of a random sample of people. You can then start to feel the meaning of these numbers. You may even be able to rightfully guess that these weights are measured in pounds. Furthermore, you may be able to see that these are likely adult weights and that more than half of these weights are 200 pounds or greater.

As you can see from above, what was just considered as a set of numbers is now a set of data that carry useful information. The point to be emphasized here is that data should represent a set of observations or numbers that carry meaningful information. Therefore, it is important to examine the meaning of data and the units associated with the data (pounds, kilograms, seconds, meters, inches, etc.). It is also important to question the *validity* and the *reliability* of data. In the example above, the data of human weight are considered as valid data since they represent typical values of human weight. Reliability indicates the consistency of the measurements in association with some predetermined target value. The two key elements of reliability are precision and accuracy. These will be discussed shortly.

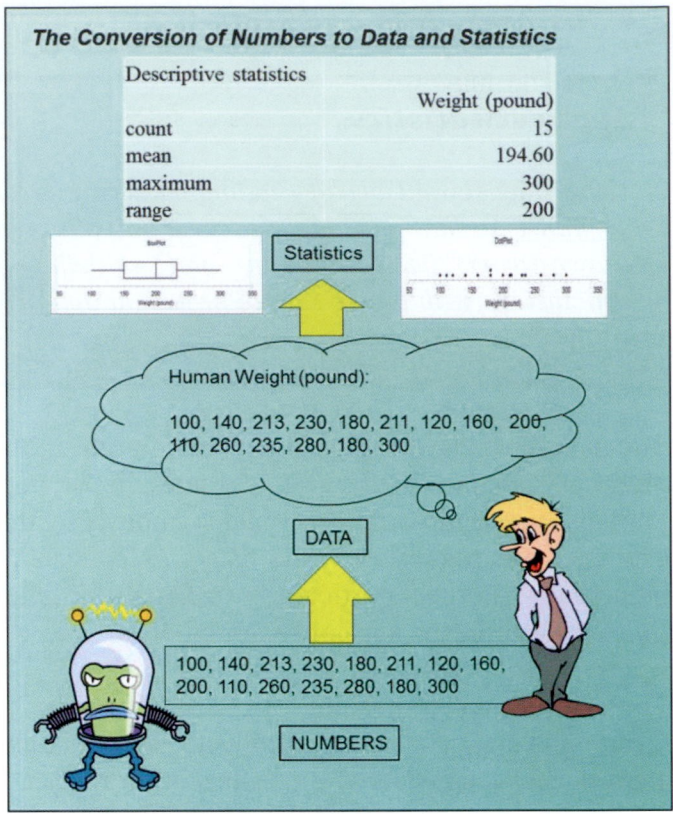

Although data provides a higher level of information than numbers, they can be massive, and scattered. This necessitates the conversion of data into statistics, which represent a summary of information in which data is represented by some descriptive measures such as the mean value and the range of data. For example, the above data set of human weight can be described by an average weight of 194.6 pounds. Since the minimum value is 100 pounds and the maximum value is 300 pounds, the range of weight values is 200 pounds. In Chapters 2 and 3, different types of descriptive statistics (numerical and graphical) will be discussed.

1.5 Constants and variables

> ### Applied Statistics:
>
> *"The <u>science</u> and <u>art</u> of reading, describing, and manipulating <u>data</u>, which represents* **<u>variables</u>** *so that practical observations about a <u>population</u> can be made from a <u>sample</u> drawn from the population, and guidelines can be established to allow making conclusions with high levels of <u>precision</u> and <u>accuracy</u> about a certain <u>process</u> or a given <u>system</u>"*

The next important term in our definition is '*variable*'. The antonym to variable is '*constant*'. In general, constants are represented by data that exhibit the same values. These are hardly found in the real world. Even with numbers that seem to be more or less equal, variability can be detected over a narrow range. For example, you can take your temperature repeatedly over a period of 20 minutes using a thermometer and find values such as 98°F, 98.2°F, 98.4°F, and 98.1°F. You may conclude that these values are more or less the same, but in reality they are different and they exhibit an average of 98.2°F and a range of 0.4°F.

Variables are represented by data that exhibit different values. For example, student grade in a given test is a variable since different students will have different grades that may range from, say 60% to 100% depending on their efforts in studying and preparing for the test. Similarly, people income is a variable since different people will have different incomes depending on their positions, experiences, years of service, education levels, etc. Other variables may be inherent in nature. These include: human height, human weight, skin color, etc. The point to be emphasized here is that variability is a fact of life and nothing is ever constant.

Many statisticians would like to think of statistics as the science of dealing with variability. Indeed, if everything in life was constant we would not need statistics. Consider these examples:

- You try hard to make an 'A' in each course you take, but the end result was A's, B's, and perhaps C's
- No two people are alike, not even twins
- A ceramic tile manufacturer tries to make all tiles identical to avoid mismatch, yet you open a box of tiles and you find some tiles exhibiting variation in thickness and areas
- The Coca Cola Company spends millions of dollars on automation to insure that all bottles of a certain size are filled equally, yet we find that some bottles are too full and other are below the normal weight
- You buy the same cell phone brand that your sister bought but yours may be slightly different or it may even have a problem or a defect

The above examples illustrate that no matter how hard we try to make things alike, variability is inevitable.

Variability is not always a negative thing; indeed it can be very positive. For example, we form a team of experts, each with a different background, to reach a solution to a complex problem involving many factors or multiple causes. Teachers are different in their style of teaching and this can have a positive impact on student's learning. We mix fibers of different characteristics to obtain a mixture of average desirable characteristics.

Statistics can assist in *determining the extent of variability* associated with any phenomenon. In Chapter 2, we will learn how some measures including the range and the variance can assist us in determining the extent of variability. Statistics can also help in determining the sources of variability. These issues are discussed throughout this book but the analysis that focuses on this issue in depth is the so-called 'analysis of variance' discussed in Chapter 11.

1.6 Population and sample

> ### Applied Statistics:
>
> "The <u>science</u> and <u>art</u> of reading, describing, and manipulating <u>data</u>, which represents <u>variables</u> so that practical observations about a **<u>population</u>** can be made from a **<u>sample</u>** drawn from the population, and guidelines can be established to allow making conclusions with high levels of <u>precision</u> and <u>accuracy</u> about a certain <u>process</u> or a given <u>system</u>"

The next terms in the above definition are '*population*' and '*sample.*' In statistics, a *population* implies a totality or a complete collection of things:

- The more than 315 million people living in the U.S. represents a population
- The more than 8 million people living in New York City represent a population
- All machines running in a factory represent a population
- All students attending a college represent a population

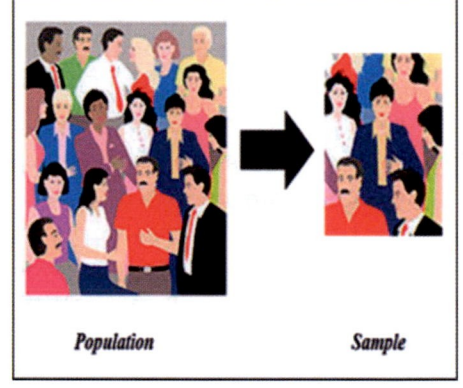

Population   **Sample**

Obviously, evaluation of the whole population can be very difficult if not impossible due to the immense effort required and/or the cost involved in evaluating every component in the population. As a result, we commonly draw a small representation called a '*sample*' from the population, test the sample, and estimate population measures from sample measures. Thus, a sample may represent few machines taken from a large factory, few people taken from a large town, or few students taken from a college campus.

The concept of population and sample is perhaps the most fascinating concept of statistics. Some may wonder if a small sample from a huge population could describe the whole population. The answer to this question is a sounding 'yes.' The key, however, is that *the sample must be a good representation of the population.* In order to achieve good representation, we have to understand the concepts and the procedures of sampling. This subject is covered in Chapter 7 of this book.

1.6.1 Deterministic inclusion vs. statistical inclusion

In selecting a sample from a population, it is important to understand the difference between *'deterministic inclusion'* and *'statistical inclusion.'* Deterministic inclusion means that all units, components, or people in a population must be tested and examined in order to reveal 100% of information about the population characteristic. Statistical inclusion, on the other hand, means that only a small portion of the population needs to be considered to reveal perhaps over 99% information about the population characteristic. If you find this hard to believe, think of a time during a presidential election in the U.S. when poll organizations gave us an estimation of election results that were virtually equal to the actual results, days or weeks before the actual election. You may think that they asked 100 million eligible voters (or 100% of the population) to get these results. Well, most organizations only select a sample of, as small as 1600 people at a time (0.0016 % of the population) to reveal almost a near perfect estimation of people's opinion. The key is that *each eligible voter in the whole population should have the same opportunity of being picked in the poll.* Few judgments should also be made such as avoiding decided or biased sectors of the population. This is the underlying concept of statistical inclusion as will be discussed in Chapter 7.

A population implies a totality or a complete collection of things (all students in a college, all people in a town, all machines in a factory, and so on)

A sample is a sub-collection of units or components selected from a population (few students from a college, few people from a town, and few machines from a factory, and so on)

A census is a collection of data from *every* member of the population (all students' grades, all people ages, and all machines' efficiencies, and so on)

Example 1.1: In a survey conducted by a community college of 5000 students, 800 students were selected randomly and asked if they are planning to transfer to a four-year university: 550 students said yes. Identify the population and the sample. Describe the data set.

Solution:

- The population consists of all students in the college (5000 students)
- The sample consists of all the students who were randomly selected (800 students)
- The percent of students saying 'yes' is 68.75% (or 100×550/800)

Working Problem 1.1:

Major television networks constantly monitor the popularity of their programs via asking some specialized organizations such as Nielsen company to sample the preferences of TV viewers.

(a) Suppose 1000 TV prime-time viewers selected randomly were asked if they watched a new talk-show, and 450 indicated they watched the show. Identify the population and the sample. Describe the data set.

(b) In another survey, suppose 1100 TV prime-time viewers selected randomly were asked if they watched the 2009 Super Ball on TV, and 999 indicated they watched the game. Identify the population and the sample. Describe the data set.

Answer: (a) Population: all potential TV prime-time viewers. The sample consists of all viewers who were randomly selected (1000 viewers). The actual data set consists of 450 who watched the new talk show (45%) and 550 (55%) who did not. (b) Population: all potential TV prime-time viewers. The sample consists of 1100 viewers who were randomly selected. The actual data set consists of 999 who watched the game (or 90%).

1.6.2 Statistic and parameter

In connection with the subject of population and sample, it is important to know that any measure describing a sample characteristic is called a *'statistic'* and any measure describing a population characteristic is called a *'parameter.'* These are universal terms that should be memorized in performing statistical analyses. A statistic is directly calculated from sample data and a parameter is either calculated from an entire population data or estimated from sample data. Figure 1.1 shows a conceptual illustration of a population from which a sample is taken randomly and examples of sample statistics and corresponding population parameters. Take note of the symbols used to denote the mean and standard deviation as they represent universal symbols used in most statistics books. This figure also illustrates the subject sequence that you should expect in the following chapters of this book. In Chapters 2 and 3, we will discuss the subject of descriptive statistics where we will be dealing with calculating sample statistics. In Chapters 8 through 10, we will discuss inferential statistics where we will be dealing with estimating population parameters.

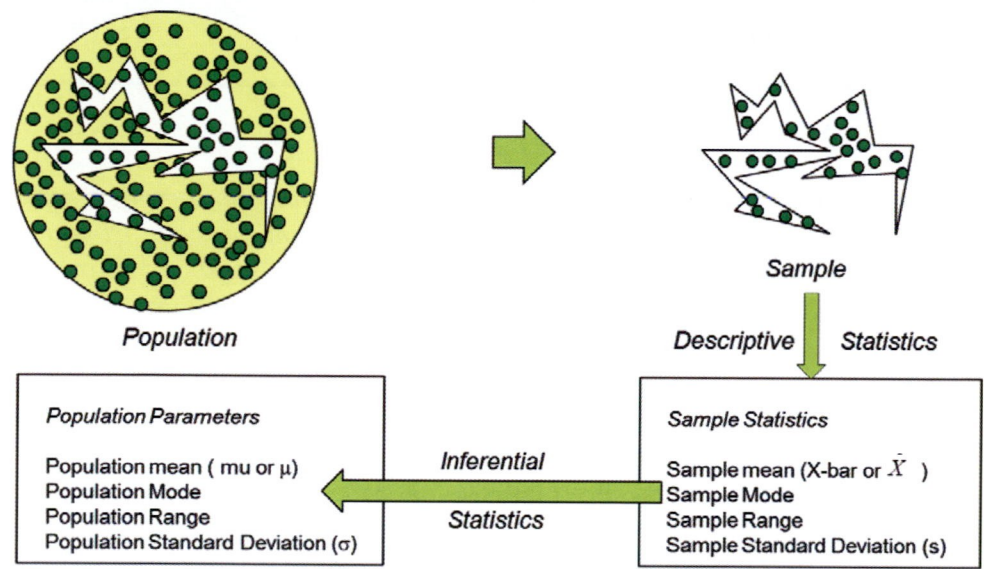

Figure 1.1. The Concept of Population and Sample

Example 1.2: Decide whether the numerical values given below describe a sample statistic or a population parameter.

(a) A sample of community college professors in the U.S. revealed that the average starting salary of a college professor is $52,000 and the range of salaries is $62,000.

(b) In a college survey of all freshmen students, it was revealed that 85% of the students were fresh out of the high school and 15% were students who graduated from high schools more than 5 years ago.

Solution:

(a) The average is a sample statistic and the range is a sample *statistic.*

(b) The proportion or percent of students is a *parameter* describing the population of freshmen students.

Working Problem 1.2:

Decide whether the numerical values given below describe a sample statistic or a population parameter.

(a) A company monitors its products prior to every shipping indicates that the percent of second-quality products is 2%

(b) New residents of apartment complex were asked if they like the landscaping surrounding the complex. Eighty five percent indicated that they like it

(c) The average salary of a group of 120 employees selected randomly from different divisions of a company was found to be $65,000

Answer: (a) Parameter, (b) parameter, (c) Statistic

1.7 Precision and accuracy

Applied Statistics:

*"The <u>science</u> and <u>art</u> of reading, describing, and manipulating <u>data</u>, which represents <u>variables</u> so that practical observations about a <u>population</u> can be made from a <u>sample</u> drawn from the population, and guidelines can be established to allow making conclusions with high levels of **<u>precision</u>** and **<u>accuracy</u>** about a certain <u>process</u> or a given <u>system</u>"*

We often use terms such as *'precision'* and *'accuracy'* in interpreting the outcomes of data analysis or in writing technical reports. We may also describe data as being accurate or precise. In the world of statistics, it will be important to use these terms appropriately. Therefore, it is important to know the difference between the two terms:

Accurate data set: A data set is said to be *accurate* when the measured values are very close to a target or a reference value

Precise data set: A data set is said to be precise when the measured values are close to each other

In the context of the above definitions, we may have one of the following four scenarios:

- *Inaccurate and imprecise data set*
- *Accurate but imprecise data set*
- *Precise but inaccurate data set*
- *Precise and accurate data set*

The example below illustrates these four scenarios.

Example 1.3: Suppose you are comparing the accuracy and the precision of four electronic scales by weighing a very fine polyester fiber using five measuring trials. This fiber was manufactured to exhibit a true weight of 10 microgram. A precision range was specified as a maximum difference of 1.5 microgram between fiber weights for a given fiber and a given electronic scale. The values obtained from the four electronic scales were as follow:

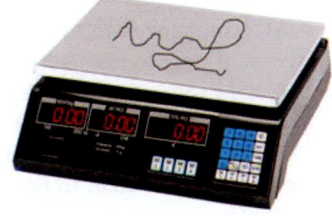

Electronic Scale *A*: 6.0, 6.5, 5.5, 6.2, 5.8
Electronic Scale *B*: 9.0, 9.0, 10.0, 11.0, 11.0
Electronic Scale *C*: 2.0, 6.0, 14.0, 2.5, 9.0
Electronic Scale *D*: 9.5, 9.7, 10.0, 10.2, 10.6

How would you describe the measures obtained by each of the four electronic scales in terms of accuracy and precision?

Solution:

By simply observing the data closely, we can see the following:

Electronic Scale *A:* the measures by this scale are very close to one another (6.0, 6.5, 5.5, 6.2, and 5.8) and the difference between the maximum and minimum value in the data set is less than 1.5 microgram (6.5-5.5 = 1.0). This means that the measures can be described as precise. However, these measures are far from the target value of 10 microgram as their average is only 6 microgram. This means that they are inaccurate.

Electronic Scale *B:* the measures by this scale (9.0, 9.0, 10.0, 11.0, and 11.0) are imprecise since they exhibit a difference of up to 2 microgram between the maximum value and the minimum value (11.0-9.0 = 2.0). However, the measures can be considered accurate since they are close to the target value of 10 microgram. Indeed, if you take the average of the five measures, it will give an exact 10 microgram.

Electronic Scale *C:* the measures by this scale (2.0, 6.0, 14.0, 2.5, and 9.0) are neither precise nor accurate. Can you tell why?

Electronic Scale *D:* the measures by this scale (9.5, 9.7, 10.0, 10.2, and 10.6) are both accurate and precise. Can you tell why?

Figure 1.2 illustrates the concept of accuracy and precision using a dart board in which the center represents the true or target value.

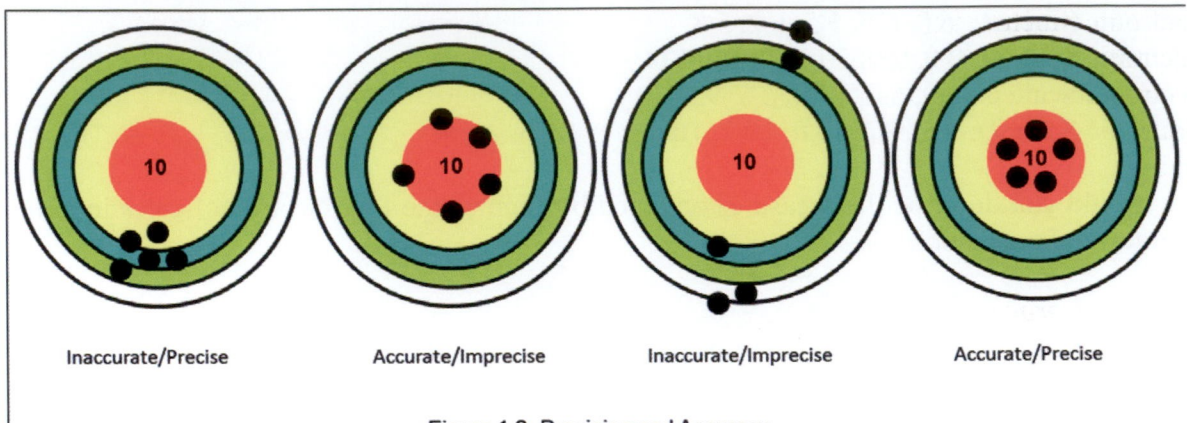

Figure 1.2. Precision and Accuracy

Working Problem 1.3:

Suppose a lab refrigerator holds a constant temperature of 38.0 °F. A temperature sensor is tested 10 times in the refrigerator. The threshold precision range is 1.5 °F. The temperatures from the test yield the following values of temperatures:

38.3   37.8   36.0   38.3   38.2   37.6   38.2   38.4   37.9   38.3   39.0

Describe these values in terms of precision and accuracy and explain your answer.

Answer:
Accurate but not precise. If you agree with this answer explain

---

1.8 Process and system

Applied Statistics:

*"The <u>science</u> and <u>art</u> of reading, describing, and manipulating <u>data</u>, which represents <u>variables</u> so that practical observations about a <u>population</u> can be made from a <u>sample</u> drawn from the population, and guidelines can be established to allow making conclusions with high levels of <u>precision</u> and <u>accuracy</u> about a certain **<u>process</u>** or a given **<u>system</u>**"*

Process and system are two common terms that are often used alternatively to describe the source of data or information. In performing statistical analysis, it will be important to distinguish between these two terms for the sake of better interpretation of the analysis outcome.

In general, the term '*process*' can be used to imply one or more of five basic elements: *machine, material, methodology, people, and environment*. For example, we may describe education as a process in which material implies course material (papers, books, etc.), machine implies media projector or computers, methodology implies the method of teaching (face-to-face, or distance learning), people implies teachers and students, and environment implies a class room or a laboratory (see Figure 1.3). On the other hand, the term 'system' is typically used when we are prepared to specify inputs and outputs. For example, a weaving machine is a system in which the input is the yarns, and the output is the fabric (see Figure 1.4).

- *A process* implies one or more of five basic elements: *machine, material, methodology, people, and environment*

- *A system* is an entity that has inputs and outputs

The significance of distinguishing a process from a system stems from the need for appropriate collection of data, adequate selection of the type of statistical analysis required, and meaningful interpretation of the analysis outcome. When data is generated from a process, the type of data may vary depending on the process elements under examination. For example, people may be associated with ages, years of experience, education, or rank. Material may be described by properties and amounts. A methodology may be classified using some codes such as '0' for face-to-face learning and '1' for distance learning. On the other hand, when the data is collected from a system, the objective is often to develop relationships between variables representing system inputs and variables representing system outputs. This subject will be discussed in detail in Chapter 12.

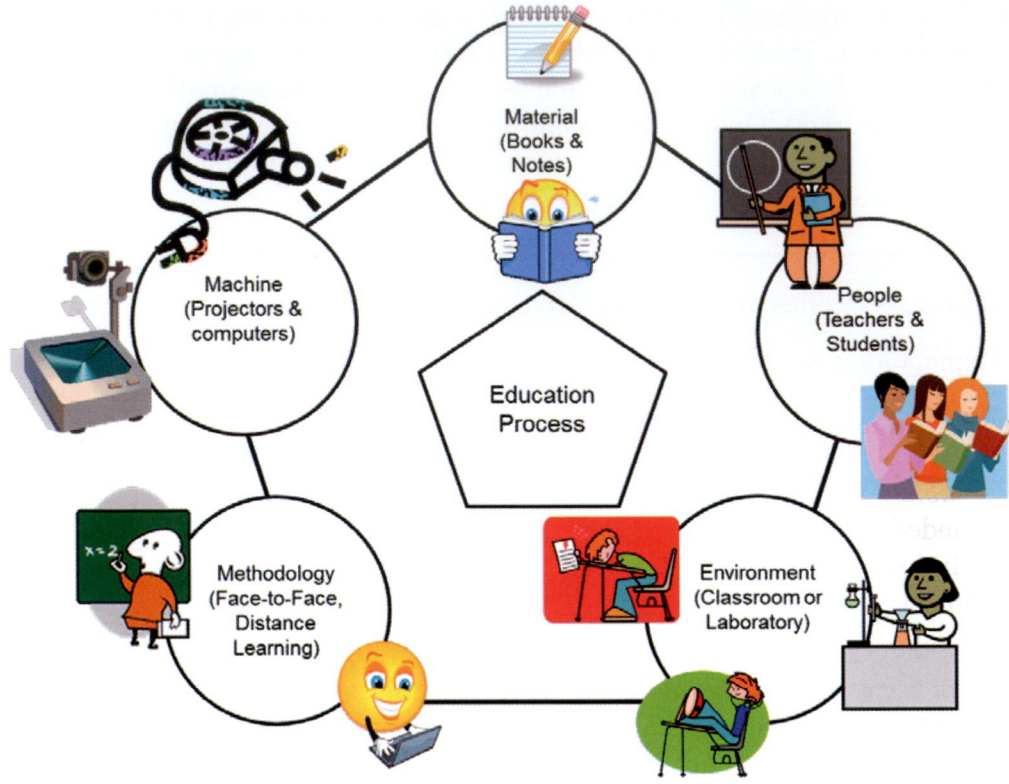

Figure 1.3 Example of a Process: The Education Process

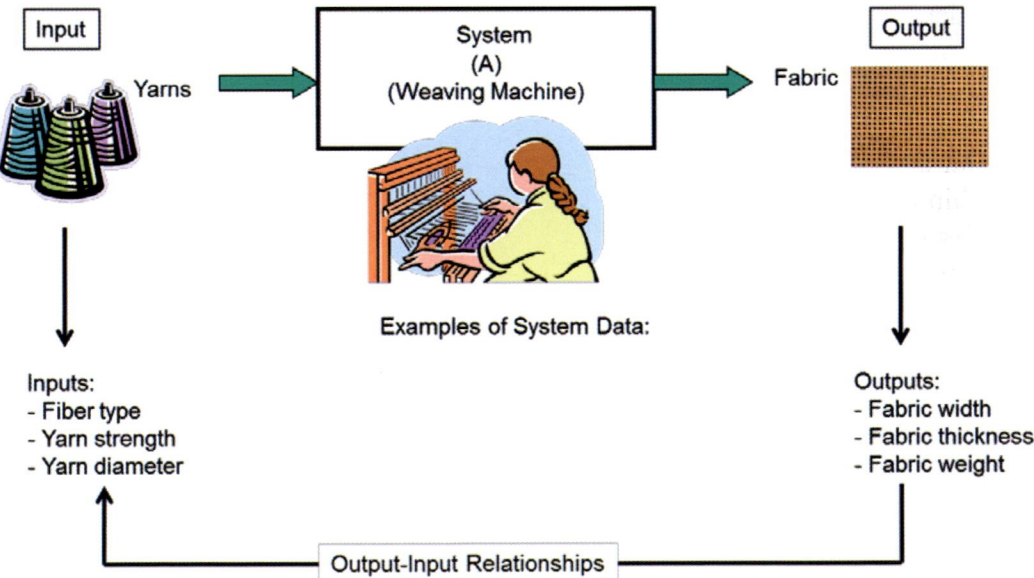

Figure 1.4 Example of a System: The Weaving Machine

Example 1.4: Discuss the following systems by specifying their inputs and outputs.

1. Pool table (billiards game) system
2. Spinning machine
3. Weight loss system
4. School system

Solution:

Obviously, this question can have many answers. It can also be the subject of a writing assignment.

(1) ***Pool table (billiards game) system-*** A system described by a table surrounded by borders within which colored balls are placed initially in a triangle arrangement. This is a unique system as the movement of any ball from its initial position at the start of the game will affect every other ball on the table. It is a system with boundaries as ball movements are constrained by the table borders. The input to this system is a kinetic energy transferred from the cue stick to the cue ball then transferred to other balls causing them to move. By the time all the balls are again at rest, the kinetic energy from the environment that initiated the process has been transformed by the laws of thermodynamics into heat, which has been dissipated and returned to the environment. The output of this system is the winner of the game determined by the player who pockets their balls. Note that an output of a system does not have to be of the same nature as the input.

(2) ***Spinning machine-*** A system that converts fibers into yarn. The input material is a fiber strand, which is linear but thick. The output material is a thinner strand with a desired diameter (the yarn). The system provides drawing to reduce the input strand diameter down to the yarn diameter, twisting to hold the fibers together in the yarn, and winding to form a yarn package.

(3) ***Weight loss system-*** A system in which the inputs are the weights of people suffering excessive weight and the outputs are the corresponding weights after some treatments have been implemented (for example, nutrition and/or exercise program).

(4) ***School system-*** This is a more complicated system as it consists of many subsystems and it has no well-defined boundaries. For simplicity, one can divide this system into two subsystems: technical subsystem, and administrative subsystem. The technical subsystem consists of faculty, department chairs, academic freedom policy statements, classrooms, and research laboratories. The inputs here include students, money, office supplies, books, and chemicals. The outputs include graduates, knowledge, and service. The administrative subsystem may consist of rules, regulations, department chairs, deans, budgets, presidents, and vice presidents. The inputs here include students, operating

costs, salaries, and office supplies, and the outputs include graduates, knowledge, and service. Note the overlapping between the two subsystems in terms of elements, inputs and outputs. However, each subsystem could have its unique structure and specific functions.

1.9 Descriptive statistics: how to describe data

The starting point in any statistical analysis is to read data using the language of statistics. As in any language where a sentence will not be understood or communicated without an organized sentence structure, the language of statistics uses the so called 'descriptive statistics' to establish an organized and meaningful display of data with the goal being to reduce the data, no matter how massive it may be, down to few statistics that can fully describe the entire data set and reveal important information. Another important reason for performing descriptive statistics is to detect any abnormality in the data that may result from data acquisition errors or mixing of data sets. For this reason, it is always a good practice to begin any statistical analysis by performing descriptive statistics. The following example illustrates the benefits of describing a data set.

Example 1.5: The four sets of data in Table 1.2 represent student grades of four statistics quizzes given to a class of 10 students. Describe each set of data by closely observing it and writing your comments.

Table 1.2 Grades of four quizzes

	1	2	3	4	5	6	7	8	9	10
Quiz 1	90	90	90	90	90	90	90	90	90	90
Quiz 2	82	86	78	30	88	82	79	77	81	99
Quiz 3	68	90	89	71	92	95	73	75	94	66
Quiz 4	82	76	85	88	95	86	84	87	96	78

Solution:
Given below is one descriptive scenario of each data set.
Quiz 1: all grades are identical; each student made a score of 90 on the first quiz
Quiz 2: most grades range from 77 to 88, but two grades seem exceptional, 30 and 99
Quiz 3: grades seem to be split into two groups: a group in the high 60s and low to mid 70s and another group in the high 80s or above
Quiz 4: grades seem to reflect typical quiz grades with few students making relatively low grades, 76 and 78; few students making high grades, 95 and 96; and the majority are in the intermediate range (82, 84, 85, 86, 87, 88). Table 1.3 highlights these observations.

Table 1.3 Grades of four quizzes-Observations

Quiz 1	90	90	90	90	90	90	90	90	90	90
Quiz 2	30	77	78	79	81	82	82	86	88	99
Quiz 3	66	68	71	73	75	89	90	92	94	95
Quiz 4	76	78	82	84	85	86	87	88	95	96

Now, if a teacher is looking at these four data sets of grades, he/she will also make the above quantitative descriptions but might add important qualitative descriptions that reflect a teacher's experience and judgment. A teacher's qualitative descriptive scenarios may be as follows:

Quiz 1: there is no way, that all students obtained the exact same grade; there must be a mistake!
Quiz 2: the extremely low grade value of 30 and the extremely high value of 99 represent two exceptions in this class (these are typically called outliers)
Quiz 3: this is a split class as half of the class has done poorly and the other has done very well
Quiz 4: these are normal and typical quiz grades

The above scenarios of quantitative and qualitative descriptions of data are fairly accurate. They also reflect the judgmental aspect of interpretation, which students have to train themselves to do. They are also unique to the type of data under consideration; meaning they cannot be generalized.

Obviously, the above descriptions were easily made due to the small number of observations of each data set. Descriptive statistics involve systematic analysis that is applicable to all type of data. In addition, they can be easily used for a large amount of data and still reveal accurate descriptions. The key outputs of descriptive statistics are numerical measures of data and graphical displays of data distribution.

1.9.1 Numerical descriptive statistics

Numerical descriptive statistics involve two key measures of a data set: (1) measures of data center (central tendency), and (2) measures of variability (or dispersion). These two measures combined can fully describe a set of data. The most common statistic describing the center of the data is the mean value, and the most common statistic describing the variability of the data is the range. The example below illustrates how to calculate these two measures.

Example 1.6: Determine the mean and the range of the following data of students' grades:

Grades	82	76	85	88	95	86	84	87	96	78

Solution:

The mean or the arithmetic mean of a set of data is calculated by calculating the sum of all individual values of the data set and dividing the sum by the number of observations:

$$Mean = \bar{X} = \frac{\sum_1^n x_i}{n} \qquad (1.1)$$

It is important that a student reads an equation when they see one. The above equation determines the mean, which usually takes the common symbol X-bar. The additive sum is always symbolized by Σ. Thus, $\sum_1^n x_i$ is the sum of individual n observations x_i (or $x_1 + x_2 + \cdots + x_n$). The mean of the above data set is obtained as follows:

$$Mean = \bar{X} = \frac{\sum_1^n x_i}{n} = \frac{82 + 76 + 85 + 88 + 95 + 86 + 84 + 87 + 96 + 78}{10} = 85.7$$

The range is calculated by subtracting the minimum observation from the maximum observation, or

$$Range = R = x_{maximum} - x_{minimum} \qquad (1.2)$$

For the above data set, the Range $R = 96\text{-}76 = 20$

In Chapter 2, we will introduce other measures of central tendency and dispersion.

Working Problem 1.4:

Calculate the mean and the range for the following data set of people income ($)

20,000, 22,000 ,28,000, 30,000, 27,000, 45,000, 50,000, 60,000

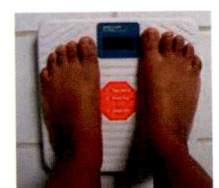

Answer: Mean = $35,250   Range = $40,000

Working Problem 1.5:

Calculate the mean and the range for the following data set of people weight (pound)

125, 145, 160, 155, 110, 95, 175, 158

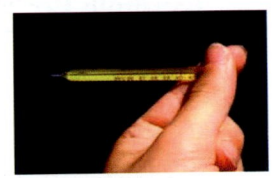

Answer: Mean = 140.375, Range = 80

Working Problem 1.6:

Calculate the mean and the range for the following data set of people temperature (F)

95.5, 98.0, 99.0, 96.5, 95.0, 97.0, 96.0, 98.0

Answer: Mean = 96.875 F, Range = 4 F

Working Problem 1.7:

Calculate the mean and range for the following data set of property taxes ($)
8100, 3500, 7000, 4200, 3000, 5000, 5100, 4000, 7500, 4800

Answer: Mean = $5220, Range = 5100

1.9.2 Graphical descriptive statistics: Histogram and frequency distribution

Another way to describe a set of data is by using a simple x-y graph in which the horizontal x-axis represents the values (or classes of values) of the variable and the vertical y-axis represents the number of observations corresponding to each value (or the frequency). This type of graph is generally called 'frequency distribution' or 'histogram'. For example, suppose the grades of 10 students on a test are as follows:

Observation #	1	2	3	4	5	6	7	8	9	10
Grades	75	65	90	75	90	75	65	90	75	100

We can construct a simple graph that illustrates the grades and their corresponding frequencies as shown below.

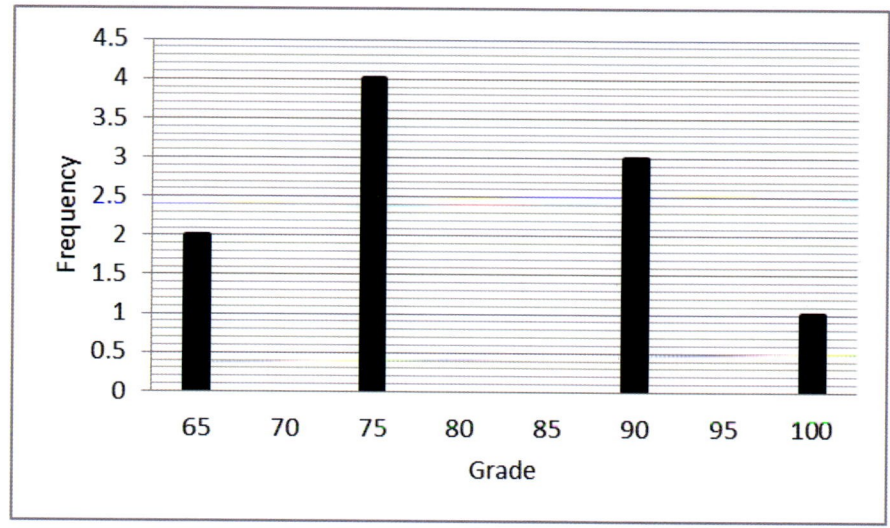

The above example illustrates a simple way to graph the frequency of data. In practice, a histogram is used for a large number of observations. In this case, the data is divided into classes of values and their corresponding frequencies are determined to form a histogram. The example below illustrates the benefits of using a frequency distribution or a histogram to describe a large set of data.

Example 1.7: Consider the data of Table 1.4, which represent the weights of a random sample of 60 young people (age 17 to 22). The amount of data here is much larger than that used in the above example, making it more difficult to attempt to observe each value or describe the data set. Describe this data set using a histogram.

Solution:
Descriptive statistics can assist a great deal in describing this set of data without having to examine each observation. Using the equations of mean and range discussed above, the mean of this set of data is 153.8 pounds, and the range is 173 pounds (minimum value = 110 pounds, and maximum value = 283). A histogram of this data is shown in Figure 1.5. Details of how a

histogram is constructed will be discussed in Chapter 3. At this point, what we need to know is that this histogram shows the percent of people at each class of weight.

Table 1.4 Data of human weight (lb) of a random sample of 60 people

n	Weight	n	Weight	n	Weight	n	Weight	N	Weight	n	Weight
1	146	11	145	21	144	31	153	41	127	51	146
2	145	12	157	22	267	32	162	42	145	52	159
3	147	13	148	23	151	33	144	43	137	53	157
4	120	14	155	24	143	34	160	44	160	54	144
5	187	15	158	25	161	35	110	45	141	55	159
6	157	16	195	26	148	36	142	46	154	56	162
7	143	17	142	27	240	37	155	47	152	57	157
8	117	18	154	28	128	38	145	48	149	58	149
9	170	19	160	29	136	39	150	49	125	59	283
10	138	20	160	30	110	40	136	50	139	60	154

As you can see in this histogram, the majority of people have a weight of about 145 pounds (this is called the *mode,* which corresponds to the highest bar). In addition, very few people have a weight above 230 pounds, which means that the large range of 173 pounds was largely due to those few high values. In Chapter 3, we introduce many more examples that illustrate how various types of information are obtained from a frequency distribution.

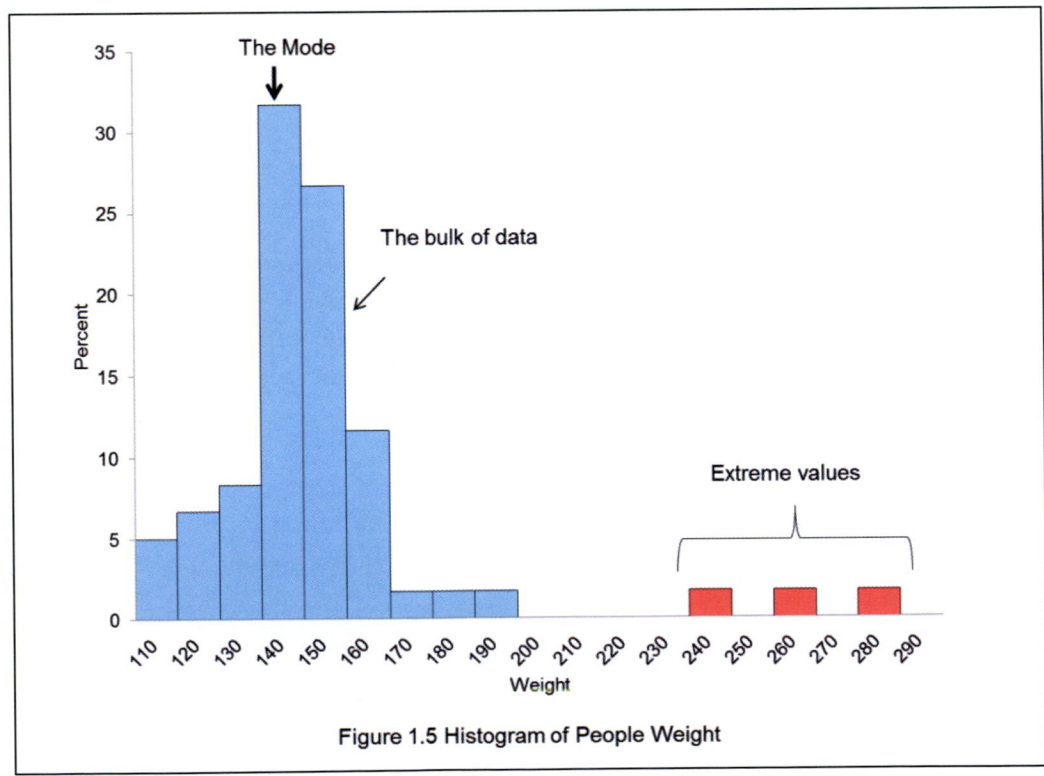

Figure 1.5 Histogram of People Weight

Working Problem 1.8:

Describe the following histogram of student grades

Answer:
- Grades range from 60 to 100%
- The majority of students made a grade of 75 (the highest bar midpoint)
- No one failed this class (<60)
- About 20% of students made an 'A'

Working Problem 1.9:

Describe the following histogram of student grades

Answer:
- Most Grades range from about 50 to 90%
- The majority of students made a grade of about 65% (the midpoint of the highest bar)
- 40% failed the course (<60)

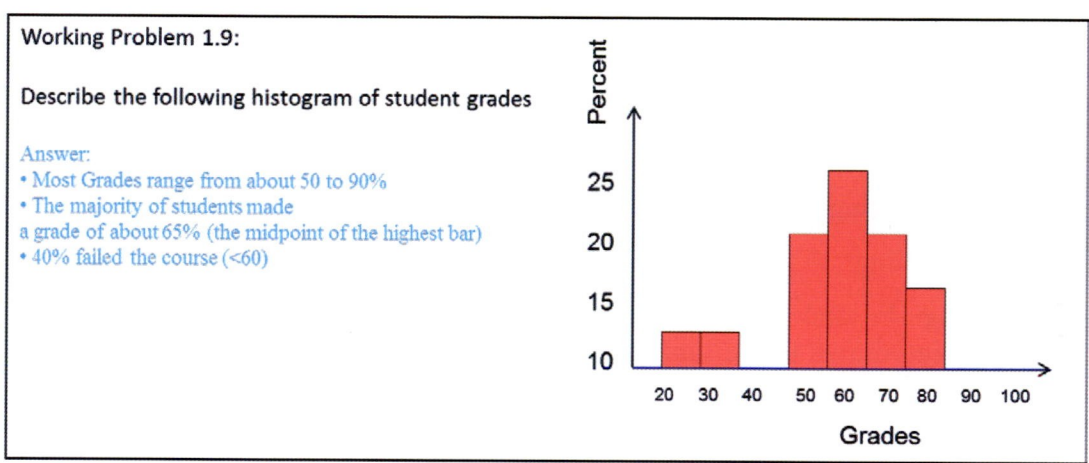

Key Points about Descriptive Statistics:

- *Any statistical analysis should begin by performing descriptive statistics*
- *Descriptive statistics represent a powerful tool of exploring data particularly when a large amount of data is analyzed*
- *The key elements of descriptive statistics are the measures of central tendency (e.g. the mean), and the measures of variability (e.g. the range).*
- *Using graphical descriptive statistics, data abnormality or data errors can be detected no matter how large the amount of data used...simply look at the bars far from the bulk of the histogram*

1.10 Sampling and sampling techniques

In section 1.6 we introduced the concept of sample and population. Selecting a representative sample from a population is a process called '*sampling.*' This process consists of the following two tasks:

1. Selecting a number of representative samples (say, k samples, each of size n) from a population using a technique suitable for the population under consideration and the purpose of testing
2. Testing the samples and listing sample data

As will be discussed in Chapter 7, many techniques can be used to collect a reliable sample from a population. The most common sampling techniques are:

- Random sampling

- Stratified sampling

- Cluster sampling

Random sampling- In random sampling, every element in the population will have the same opportunity of being drawn in the sample. For example, in a class room of 40 students, we can draw a representative sample of 10 students by writing each student name or identification number on a post card, shuffling the 40 cards, placing them in a box, and blindly withdraw 10 cards representing the sample. This is the physical approach to perform random sampling. In Chapter 7 we will discuss how to perform random sampling using Excel® data analysis.

Stratified sampling- In some situations, complete random sampling may not be possible due to the difficulty of accessing some portions of the population. In this case, we may use the so-called '*stratified sampling*'. In this approach, we simply divide the population into pre-specified categories, or strata, and draw samples from each category in random fashion and with size proportional to the category size in the population. This approach ensures that each category of the population is represented in the sample. For example, suppose we have a small city of a population of 100,000 people; 80,000 Caucasian, 15,000 African American, and 5,000 Hispanic. If these ethnic groups are intermingled in the city, we should then use stratified sampling to ensure that each group is represented in the sample and in proportional-weight allocated fashion. Accordingly, if the sample size is 100 people, 80 people should be selected randomly from the Caucasian group, 15 from the African American group, and 5 people from the Hispanic group. Figure 1.6 illustrates the differences between random sampling and stratified sampling.

Cluster Sampling- This is used when the population itself consists of natural or pre-designed clusters, with each cluster having its own unique features. For example, a company may have three or four factories in different areas producing the same product. In this case, a cluster sample should be a sample consisting of components from each factory or cluster.

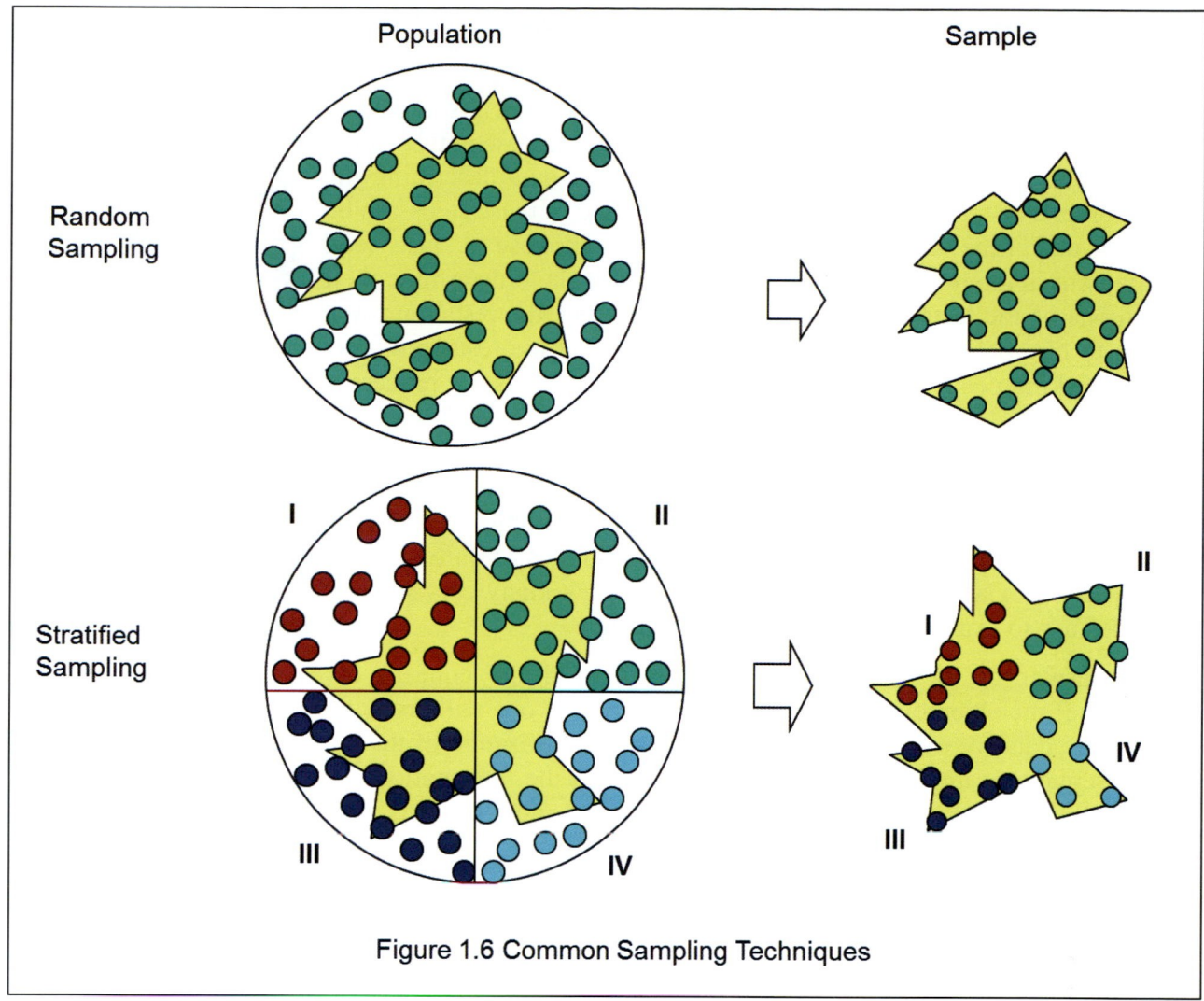

Population   Sample

Random Sampling

Stratified Sampling

Figure 1.6 Common Sampling Techniques

Example 1.8: A factory has 500 machines all of the same type and all produce the same product. Which sampling technique would you implement to test an important parameter such as machine efficiency? In another factory, three different types of machines were used all producing the same product, which sampling technique would you implement, and why?

Solution:

In the first case, it is obvious that the proper technique is random sampling since all machines are of the same type. In the second case, we may perform random sampling assuming that all machines are set alike and ignoring the fact that they are of different types. However, if different types of machines are likely to exhibit different performances (e.g. different efficiency or different product quality) we should then use stratified sampling to ensure that each type of machine will be included in the sample and in proportion to the number of machines of each type.

1.10.1 What is the appropriate sample size?

The question of sample size is a very practical one. As indicated earlier, sampling involves taking samples that are representative of the population and testing these samples to produce data describing the phenomena or the variable under study. Each one of these steps can be costly and time consuming. For example, suppose a fast food restaurant is interested in taking a sample of people to determine their opinions of the taste of a new recipe. In this case, the restaurant will  have to hire people for a part-time job to stand at the restaurant door with samples of the new recipe asking people to taste and get their opinions. This is a process that takes time and involves many tasks. The question is therefore, how many people should the restaurant survey? Not only is this a statistical question, it is also a cost question. In other situations, the sample components can be very expensive and the test can be destructive. For example, testing the collision and safety performance of automobiles requires total destruction of automobiles. In this situation, how many cars should we destroy to examine a car's safety performance?

The answer to the above questions stems from the concept of statistical inclusion discussed earlier. In general, no one will argue that the larger the sample, or the more data we can collect, the better the characterization of the population. However, a small representative sample can also yield virtually all the information we need; the question is *how small is small?* As we will find out in Chapter 8, how small is small or what is the minimum sample size will depend on key factors such as:

- How large do we want the difference between the sample mean and the population mean $(\bar{X} - \mu)$?

- What is the extent of variability in the population (range or variance)?

- How confident do we want to be in our estimation of the population parameter?

For the time being, obvious answers to the above questions are as follows:

- The smaller you want the difference between the sample mean and the population mean $(\bar{X} - \mu)$, the larger the sample size should be.

- The higher the variability in the population, the larger the sample size (i.e. the higher the range, the higher the sample size, n) should be.

- The more confident you want to have in your estimation of the population parameter, the larger the sample size should be.

In Chapter 8, we will address these questions using well-established analytical procedures. The key point to be emphasized is that sample size is often a cost-related issue and any analysis performed to determine the sample size should account for the cost factor through practical judgment.

1.11 What are the different sources of variability?

Recall our definition of applied statistics,

*"The science and art of reading, describing, and manipulating data representing **variables** …"*

Earlier, we discussed the differences between constants and variables and we came to realize that constants hardly exist in this world and virtually every situation or phenomenon in life involves variability or variables. The question now is *where does variability come from?*

In general, there are two types of variability in a process: *(i) inherent variability, and (ii) induced variability.* Inherent variability normally results from natural sources or from some form of limitation in any process element (material, machine, people, etc.). For example, humans are inherently different by virtue of their creation. This is a positive variability as no one can conceive a world with all human being alike in everything. Even twins are inherently different in so many aspects. Some statistics suggest that there are roughly over 120 million living human twins in the world today, and nearly 10 million of them are monozygotic twins  (twins derived from a single fertilized egg). Similarly, plants and animals exhibit inherent variability.

Induced variability is defined by the differences between things, which might otherwise be thought to be alike because they were produced under conditions, which were as nearly alike as it is possible to make them. This type of variability can be observed in products that are made to be identical (coffee makers, refrigerators, cars, etc.), yet they exhibit some differences resulting from human or manufacturing errors.

A good example of both inherent and induced types of variability is the production of ceramic tiles. A manufacturer producing ceramic tiles will set the machines and the manufacturing operations to produce the same dimensions of ceramic tiles every day, yet these tiles may encounter inherent variability in thickness, area, and even color due to chance or limitation in technology. In the absence of good quality control of the manufacturing process, gross defects may be encountered leading to significant differences in thickness or area. When these defects exceed pre-specified tolerances, they will be considered as induced variability.

Throughout the chapters of this book, many statistical tools will be introduced by which one can determine the extent of variability and distinguish between inherent and induced variability sources. Descriptive statistics represent the primary tool to determine the extent of variability using measures of dispersion such as the range, the standard deviation, and the variance. These will be discussed in detail in Chapter 2. In addition, histograms and frequency distributions can provide clear pictures of the extent of variability as will be discussed in Chapter 3. In Chapter 11, we will use the analysis of variance to distinguish between different sources of variability.

Working Problem 1.10:

Identify the following sources of variability as inherent or induced:

a. If one picks any boll of cotton from the field, one will not find two cotton fibers that are similar in length, diameter, or maturity.
Inherent (   )   Induced (   )

b. You open a box of water bottles and you find that some bottles are completely filled and some are half-empty
Inherent (   )   Induced (   )

c. At the workplace, you find some people performing better than other people of the same experience and background
Inherent (   )   Induced (   )

d. In a sample of natural soil aggregates taken from a certain area you find no two soil particles that are alike in size or texture.
Inherent (   )   Induced (   )

Answer: (a) Inherent, (b) Induced, (c) induced, (d) inherent

1.12 What are the different types of variables?

A variable represents a phenomenon or a characteristic of a process or system under investigation in which different elements are associated with different values. There are three main types of variables:

- *Continuous variables*
- *Discrete variables*
- *Special variables*

A continuous variable can take any value in a specified interval falling within its plausible range. In one sentence, continuous variables are variables whose sample spaces (or all possible outcomes) are intervals. For example, the diameter of a fine metal rod may take a value of 40, 40.25, 40.75 or 41 millimeters. These data imply continuity in the variable values. Similarly, variables such as students' grades, people's income, ages, material strength, thickness, length, temperature, concentration, and weight are all of the continuous variable type.

Discrete variables are variables whose sample spaces are sets of discrete points. They are associated with situations in which a count is made such as the count of pass or fail, stop or go, and good or bad. A discrete variable can take only integer values (e.g. 0, 1, 2, ...). Discrete variables are used in numerous applications. Educators use discrete variables such as the number of passing or failing students, the number of dropouts, and the number of absences. Engineers and manufacturers use discrete values to describe many parameters such as the number of defects, the number of rejects, and the number of machine failures.

Special variables are those that are not easily described in quantitative manner. This type of variable is typically initiated from nonnumeric sources. For example, when we describe the comfort resulting from wearing certain types of clothing, we may use terms such as smooth, flexible, harsh, rough, soft and stiff. In order to use statistics to describe the extent of comfort, we should first express these characterizations in some numeric format (e.g. establishing a numeric index). Depending on the structure of this format, the special variable can then be treated as a discrete or a continuous variable.

Specifying the variable as being continuous or discrete is critical for performing a reliable statistical analysis. In Chapters 5 and 6, we will discuss probability distributions for discrete and continuous variables, respectively. In Chapters 7 through 10, we will also discuss inferential statistics for both continuous variables and discrete variables.

Another way to classify variables is by dividing them into two main categories: *'quantitative'* and *'qualitative'* variables. Quantitative variables are those that can be measured numerically. These include income, weight, temperature, grades, etc. Qualitative variables are those that cannot be described numerically but may be converted into some kind of numerical codes depending on their natures. Categorical variables are just another name for qualitative variables. For example, when we categorize students as a freshman, a sophomore, a junior, or a senior, we are in essence using a qualitative variable. If we have to include these categories in a data set, it would be useful to associate them with some codes such as '1' for a freshman, '2' for a sophomore, '3' for a junior and '4' for a senior. This is a key step in dealing with these types of variables in a statistical analysis. Other qualitative variables include: color, taste, style, pain level, gender, race, and job position.

Working Problem 1.11:

Determine whether the following variables *are discrete or continuous. Explain your* reasoning.

1. The weights of football players in a team:
Discrete (   )   Continuous (   )

2. The number of defects in a shipment of cellular phones:
Discrete (   )   Continuous (   )

3. The number of passing students in a course:
Discrete (   )   Continuous (   )

4. Student grades in a course:
Discrete (   )   Continuous (   )

5. The speed at which different cars run on a highway:
Discrete (   )   Continuous (   )

Answer: 1. C, 2. D, 3. D, 4. C, 5. C

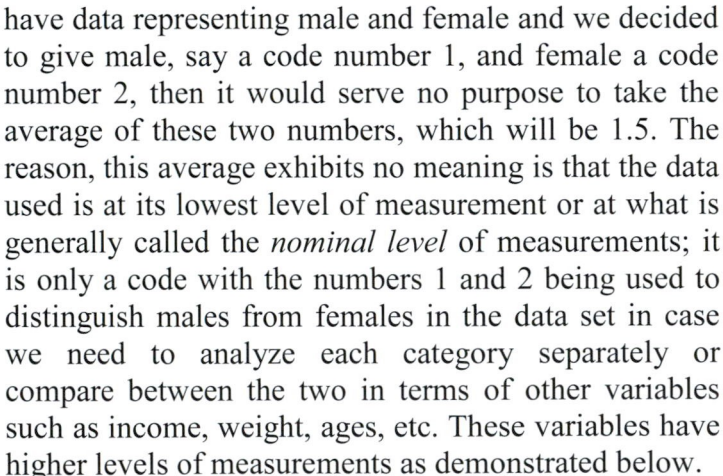

1.13 What are the levels of measurements?

Data can talk! Or data often try to tell us something. But, to what extent can data truly tell us what we need to know? The key to answering this question stems from the level of measurement of the data under consideration. In order to describe a variable we have to use associated data and in order to use the data in a meaningful way, we must realize the data level of measurement. For example, if we have data representing male and female and we decided to give male, say a code number 1, and female a code number 2, then it would serve no purpose to take the average of these two numbers, which will be 1.5. The reason, this average exhibits no meaning is that the data used is at its lowest level of measurement or at what is generally called the *nominal level* of measurements; it is only a code with the numbers 1 and 2 being used to distinguish males from females in the data set in case we need to analyze each category separately or compare between the two in terms of other variables such as income, weight, ages, etc. These variables have higher levels of measurements as demonstrated below.

In general, there are four basic levels of measurements as illustrated by the pyramid of Figure 1.7, where data resolution and meaningful aspects progressively increase as we move from the base of the pyramid to

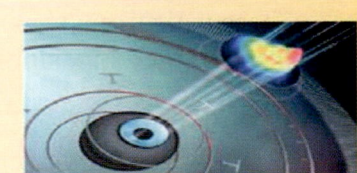

Key tips to figure out the level of measurement:

In order to avoid any confusion about what level of measurement a variable belongs to, we should begin by addressing the following key questions (*Michael Sullivan III, 2010, Statistics-Informed Decisions Using Data, Third Edition, Prentice Hall, Pearson Education, Inc.*):
•Does the variable simply categorize each individual? If so, the variable is nominal (e.g. gender)
•Does the variable categorize *and* allow ranking of each value of the variable? If so, the variable is ordinal (letter grade in your calculus class)
•Do differences in values of the variable have meaning, but a value of zero does not mean the absence of the quantity? If so, the variable is interval (e.g. temperature).
•Do ratios of values of the variable have meaning *and* there is a natural zero starting point? If so, the variable is ratio (e.g. human weight and number of hours you study every week)

the top. The lowest level is the *nominal measurement data*. At this level, variables are typically qualitative, mutually exclusive and exhaustive. They typically have no meaningful magnitude or logical order and we can do little with this type of data in terms of statistical analysis but they are useful for data organization and information management. Examples of nominal measurements include: eye or skin color, gender, people names, and religion.

Ordinal measurement level data are those used for sequencing or ranking. For example, you may wish to rate your professor after completing a statistics course according to a particular trait, say as excellent, very good, good, fair, and poor. Numbers assigned for these ratings may be: 0 (poor), 1(fair), 2(good), 3(very good), and 4(excellent). These numbers, though at equal distances, do not imply a rating magnitude; meaning, a rating of 4 is not twice as much a rating of 2. However, the order is meaningful as the higher the number the better the rating. Again, the data here are mutually exclusive and exhaustive.

Interval measurement level data exhibit all the characteristics of ordinal measurement data but in addition, the difference between values is constant. In other words, they exhibit constant increments that have some meaning. Temperature is the classic example of this type of measurements. Twenty degrees is certainly the same anywhere on the Fahrenheit temperature scale, but 60 degrees is not twice as hot as 30 degrees. Interval data measurement has no value-related zero. For example, on a temperature scale, zero Fahrenheit does not mean an absence of temperature or heat; it only implies cold and if we change the units to Celsius, this zero will roughly become -18 degrees. Again, interval measurement data is mutually exclusive, exhaustive, and equal differences in the variable are represented by equal differences in the measurements. Other examples of interval measurements include shoe sizes and IQ scores.

Ratio measurement level data represent the most commonly used data in practice. Virtually all quantitative data are essentially ratio data. They have meaningful magnitude, order, and ratios between numbers. The zero value of ratio measurements means an absence of the characteristic magnitude. These include: weight, length, strength, income, profit, area, etc.

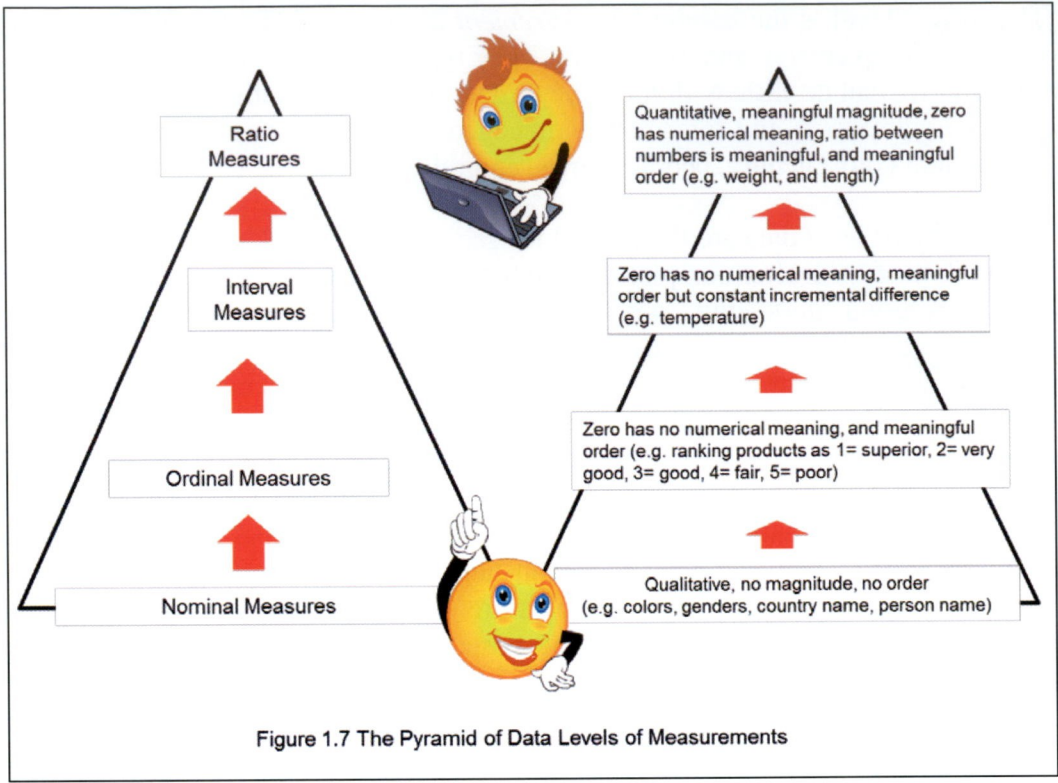

Figure 1.7 The Pyramid of Data Levels of Measurements

Example 1.9: What is the level of measurement for each of the following variables?

a. Your score on the first Math quiz
b. People's wages in a given business
c. Classification of students by gender
d. Ranking of education by K-12, community college, and four-year University
e. The number of hours you spend watching TV every week

Solution:

a. Interval   b. Ratio   c. Nominal   d. Ordinal   e. Ratio

Working Problem 1.12:

What is the level of measurement reflected by the following data?

(a) The ages of a sample of students entering first year of college:
18, 21, 19, 17, 16, 22, 21, 22, 23, 18, 18, 17, 19

(b) In a survey of 500 luxury-house owners (above $2million price), 200 were from California, 150 from New York, and 150 from Florida.

Answer:

a. Age is a ratio-scale variable. A 23-year-old is seven years older than a 16-year old
b. Answer yourself

Working Problem 1.13:

What is the level of measurement for each of the following variables?

a. Student scores in the first stat test
b. Waiting time (minutes) for a school bus
c. Classification of employee by gender
d. A ranking of students as freshman, sophomore, junior, and senior
e. The weight of football players

Attempt it yourself

1.14 What is a normal distribution?

A normal data set of a variable will typically have the following basic characteristics:

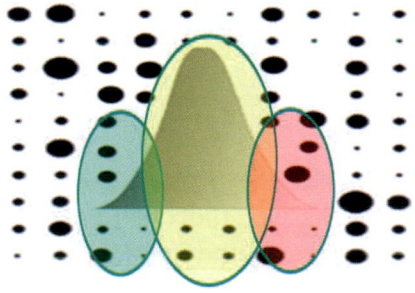

1. Relatively few components or elements will exhibit low values of the variable
2. Relatively few components or elements will exhibit high values of the variable
3. The majority of values will be in the middle

This data set will yield a distribution called 'the Gaussian' or the 'normal distribution.' In its ideal shape, the normal distribution is characterized by a symmetrical bell-shaped curve as shown in Figure 1.8. It has equal values of mean, mode, and median and they are all located at the center of the distribution. The normal distribution is fully described mathematically by two parameters: the mean of the data, and the standard deviation, which is a measure of the deviation of all values from the center. What students need to know at this point is the shape of the normal curve and how this shape relates to the distribution of values of a variable. It will also be useful that students begin to describe data by sketching a rough normal curve illustrating the variable values and their distribution. This point is illustrated in the following example.

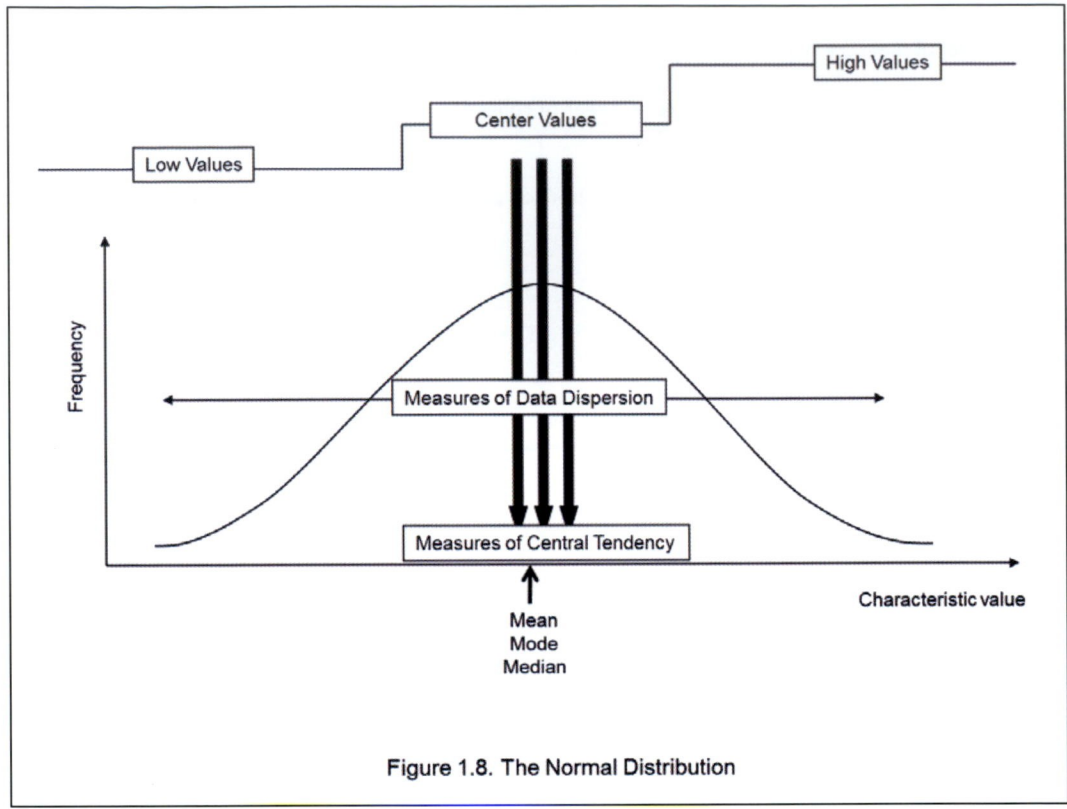

Figure 1.8. The Normal Distribution

Example 1.10: Figure 1.9 shows the distributions of the area of ceramic tiles of two types of tiles produced by two different suppliers. The tiles are advertised at the same price and with the same nominal specifications by the two suppliers. Describe the normal distributions of area for these two types of tiles.

Solution:

This example is provided without data, only the shapes of the distributions of the ceramic tile area, to assist students in describing a normal distribution. As you can see from the two distributions, both type *A* and type *B* tiles have the same mean value of area (same center). They also have the same mode (the most frequent value) as indicated by the peak of the curves. In addition, they both have the same median (This is the value right in the middle of all values). These are all measures of central tendency. The difference between the two distributions is in the width of the distribution; this reflects the variability or the dispersion in the data with the wider distribution indicating higher variability or larger range of values than the narrower distribution. Since it is important to buy tiles that are virtually identical in area (to avoid mismatch of tiles), type *A* should be the tiles of choice as they exhibit smaller variability in area than type *B* *(narrower distribution)*.

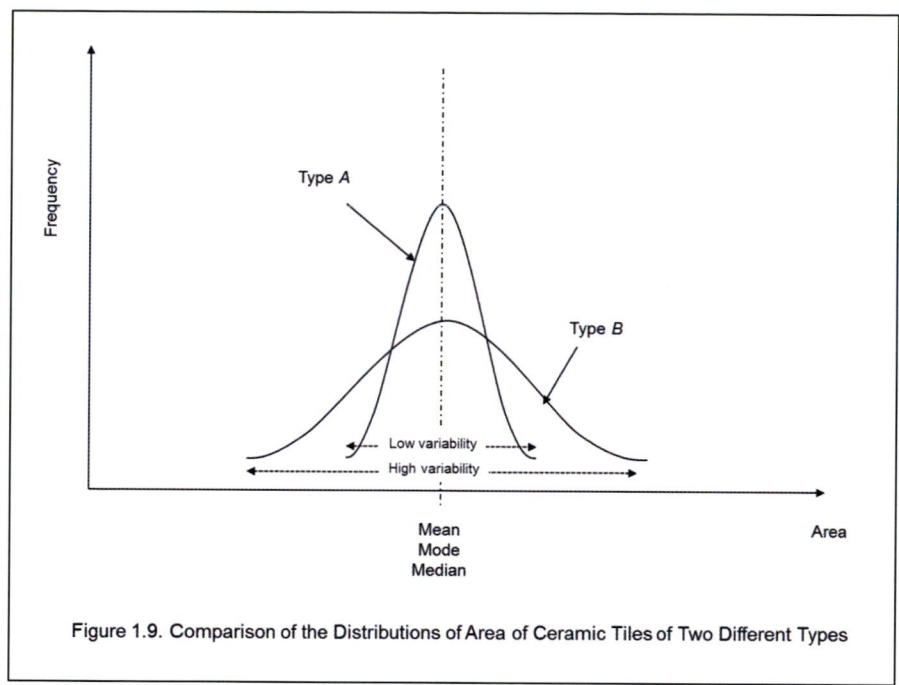

Figure 1.9. Comparison of the Distributions of Area of Ceramic Tiles of Two Different Types

The variable described in the above example represents the case of, *'nominal-the-best-variable;'* that is a variable, which should exhibit an exact value, not too low and not too high. Other variable types are the *'larger-the-better'* type, and the *'smaller-the-better-type.'* Figure 1.10 illustrates expected frequency distributions of these types of variables. Larger the better type variables include: student's grade, people's income, and machine efficiency (note the mode is at the high values). Smaller-the better type variables include: number of defects, car accidents, and number of failing students (note the mode is at the low values).

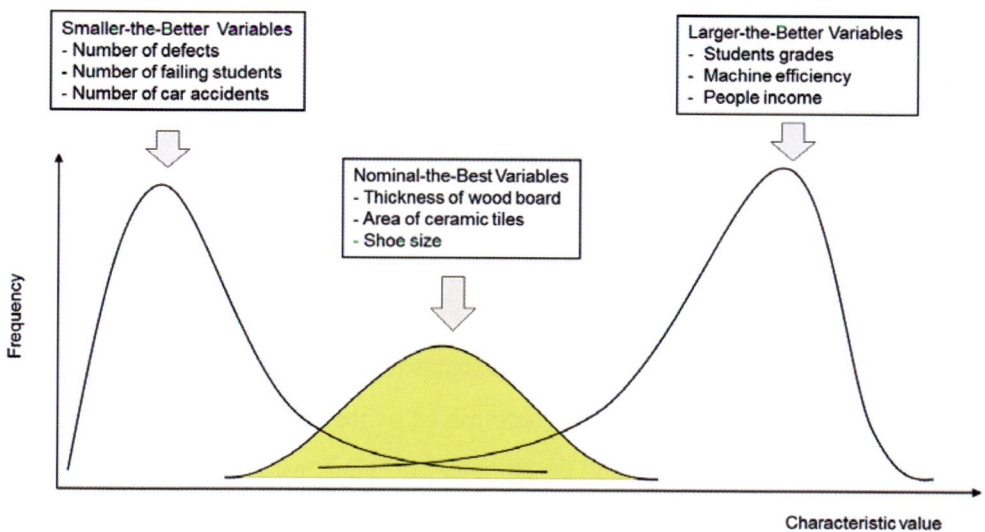

Figure 1.10. Distributions associated with Different Categories of Variables

1.15 Inferential statistics: how do you estimate population parameters from sample statistics?

One of the primary tools of statistics is *'inferential statistics'*. In practice, we often deal with a very large population of a process (machines, people, materials, etc.). Typically, our goal is to determine the performance of this population through examining one or more population parameters. For example, a company producing millions of electronic items, say smart phones wishes to examine important attributes such as picture resolution and audio performance. Since testing these attributes for the entire population of smart phones is time consuming and can be very costly, the company draws a random sample of a few smart phones from the population, tests the two attributes in the sample, produces sample data, and analyzes the data to determine key statistics such as the mean and the range. These systematic steps produce sample descriptive statistics. In doing so, the company's interest is not the sample per se but rather the whole population of electronic items from which the sample was drawn. In order to *estimate* population *parameters* from sample *statistics*, we use *'inferential statistics'*. This point was illustrated earlier in Figure 1.1.

In light of the above introduction, the problem of inferential statistics or estimation is essentially a problem of determining population parameters from sample statistics. In order to estimate a population parameter from a sample statistic, three basic criteria must be met:

Basic criteria of estimation:

- *A good point estimate or an estimator*: this is a sample statistic that estimates the value of the unknown corresponding population parameter. For example, the sample mean $\bar{X}$ is a good estimator of the population mean μ.

- *An interval estimate*: since one sample may give a mean value that is not exactly equivalent to the population mean, it will be important to provide an interval estimate of mean. For example, if the mean of a random sample of students' grades is 80, we say this is a point estimate of the mean of the entire population of students' grades but the interval estimate is, say 75 to 85. Another way to express this estimate is 80 ± 5 where 5 is the margin of error.

- *Confidence (%)*: when we establish an interval estimate, we should associate it with some confidence. This is largely determined by the risk we are willing to take in making our estimation, and the sample size. Thus, we say that the point estimate of the mean of students' grades of the entire population is 80; the interval estimate is from 75 to 85; with say a 95% or a 99% confidence.

Working Problem 1.14:

Using a random representative sample of 50 houses taken from Ocean County, NJ, the mean of property taxes was found to be $7000.
(1) Can this value be used to estimate the average property tax for all houses in Ocean County?
(a) Yes ....   (b) No ....

(2) What would you call the value of $7000:
(a) Point estimate ....   (b) Interval estimate .... (c) Confidence level

(3) If an estimation of property tax at 95% confidence yielded the following results:
            $7000 ± $1500
What is the margin of error?

Answer:
(1) a   (2) a   (3) ± $1500

Descriptive Statistics: *The analysis of determining sample statistics (e.g. mean and range)*

Inferential Statistics: *The analysis of estimating population parameters from sample statistics*

1.16 What is probability?

Most people use terms such as chance, likelihood, or probability to reflect the level of uncertainty about some events. Some of the common examples of using these terms are as follows:

- As you watch the news every day, you hear forecasters saying that there is a 70% chance of rain tomorrow.
- As you plan to enter a new business, an expert in the field tells you that the probability of making a profit in this business is only 0.4, or there is a 40% chance that you will make a profit.
- As you take a new course, you may be wondering about the likelihood of passing or failing the course.
- Your friend is undergoing a surgery and the physician is telling him that his chance of surviving the surgery is 95%.
- You hear it on health news all the time that a smoker has a greater chance of getting lung cancer than a nonsmoker.

These are all expressions of probability that we often hear or read about and they can affect our planning or intention to do or not to do things in life.

The general definition of probability is a value between zero and one, which reveals the relative possibility an event will occur. A probability of zero or close to zero implies that an event is very improbable to occur, and a probability of one or close to one gives us higher assurance that an event will occur. Between these two extremes, different values of probability will be expressed as a decimal such as 0.33, 0.7, or 0.50, as a fraction such as 1/3, 7/10, or 1/2, or as a percent such as 33.33%, 70%, or 50%.

Classically, probability is defined by the ratio of the number of particular target outcomes of an event to the number of all possible equally likely and mutually exclusive outcomes. For example, we know that in tossing a coin, the chance of a head being the outcome is 50% or, in the context of probability, we say that the probability of a head occurrence is 0.5. This value is a direct calculation from the classic definition of probability where the total number of possible outcomes in tossing a coin is 2 (a head or a tail), and the chance of head being one of the two outcomes is ½.

In Chapter 4 of this book, we will discuss all classic probability rules. We will also discuss empirical probability, which addresses real-world experiments from which useful probability values can be obtained. In Chapters 5 and 6, we address probability distributions for discrete and continuous variables, respectively. A probability distribution is a graphical representation of the probabilities of different possible outcomes from a certain experiment. These distributions can be used to simulate the behavior of some variables using key parameters unique for each probability distribution.

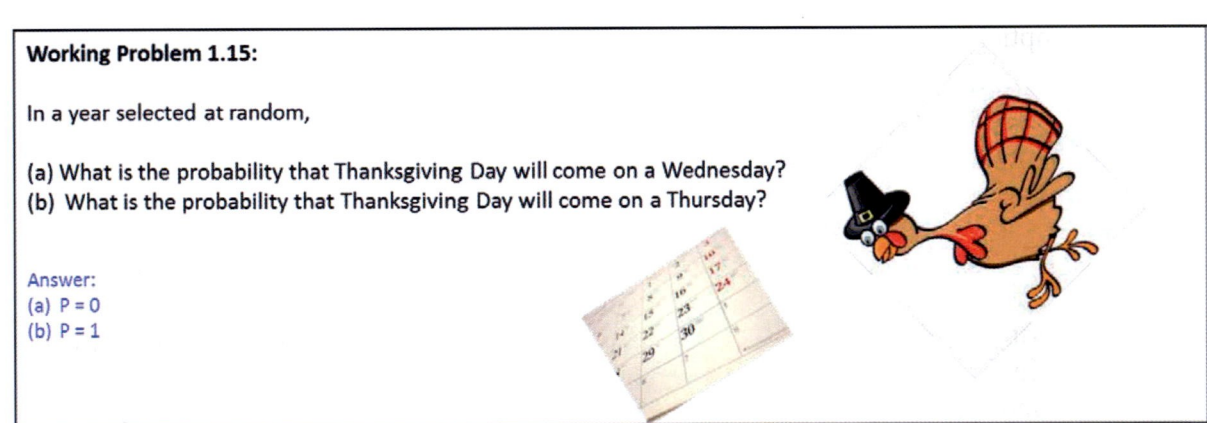

Working Problem 1.15:

In a year selected at random,

(a) What is the probability that Thanksgiving Day will come on a Wednesday?
(b) What is the probability that Thanksgiving Day will come on a Thursday?

Answer:
(a) P = 0
(b) P = 1

Working Problem 1.16:

If you draw a random card from a deck of 52 playing cards,
(a) What is the probability that you draw a 7?
(b) What is the probability you draw a heart?

Answer: P (drawing a 7) = $^4/_{52}$ = $^1/_{13}$

P (drawing a heart) = $^{13}/_{52}$ = $^1/_4$

1.17 Correlation and regression analysis

Earlier in this chapter, we introduced the terms process and system. When we deal with a system, one of the key statistical tools is the analysis of relationships between system's outputs and inputs, or the relationship between a response variable, and one or more independent variables. A relationship between variables may be driven by many practical questions such as:

- Is your grade influenced by the number of hours you study?

- Is there a relationship between the dollar value a business spends on advertising and the quantity of sales?

- Can we say that the larger the square footage of a house the larger the energy consumption?

- Do you consume more fuel when you drive faster?

- Is there a relationship between the level of education in a country and people's income?

To address these questions, you need correlation and regression analysis. Correlation analysis is the study of determining the strength of association between two variables. This strength is primarily determined by the shape of the relationship and the so-called *'coefficient of correlation,'* which is commonly denoted by *r*. This coefficient was developed by *Karl Pearson* in about 1900 and it describes the strength of association between two variables (interval or ratio levels). A correlation coefficient of zero means no association between the two variables; a value of 1.0 means perfect positive correlation; and a value of -1.0 means perfect negative correlation. Figure 1.11 illustrates different *x-y* relationships with associated values of coefficients of correlation.

Regression analysis aims at developing linear equations using the so-called *'least-squares method.'* A typical simple regression model will be as follows:

$$y = \beta_0 + \beta_1 x + \varepsilon \qquad (1.7)$$

where x is the independent variable, y is the dependent variable, β_0 and β_1 are called regression coefficients, and ε is an error term, which is typically assumed to have a normal distribution with mean zero. Regression analysis is performed to estimate the values of the regression coefficients using the least squares method. This method will be discussed in Chapter 12.

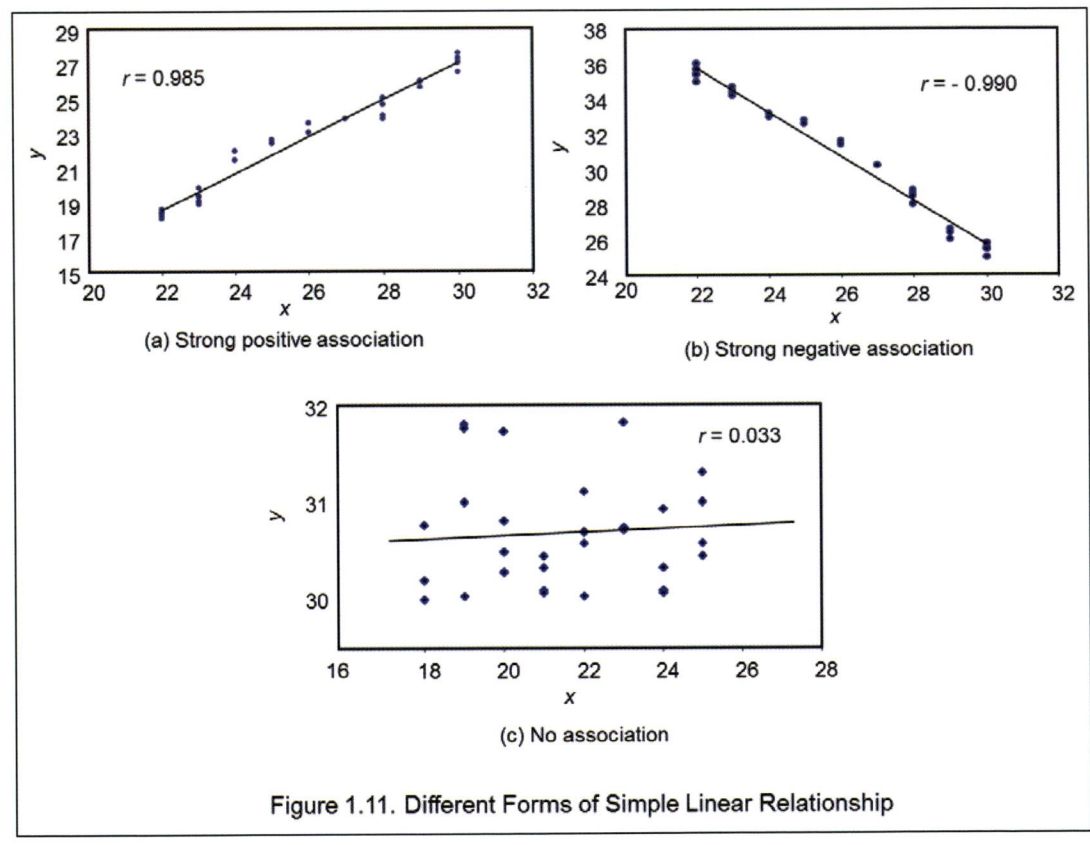

Figure 1.11. Different Forms of Simple Linear Relationship

Working Problem 1.17:

Prior to giving an exam, a teacher asked every student about the number of hours they study per week. He then tried to relate these hours to the students grades as shown below.
(a) Does this relationship reveals a perfect effect of study hours on student's grade? Explain.
(b) Why students studying same number of hours obtain different grades?

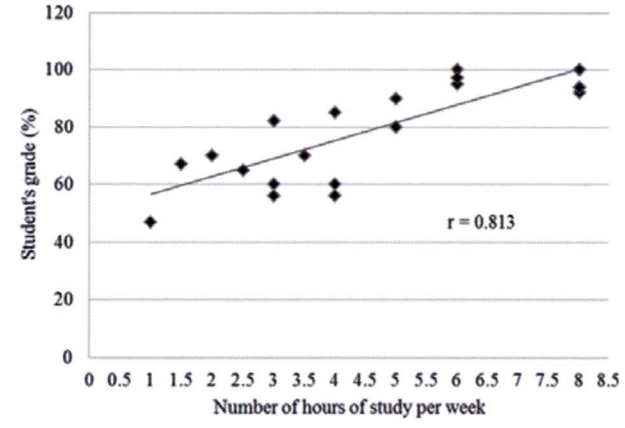

Answer: (a) No since a perfect relationship should have an r (coefficient of correlation) of one
(b) Due to other factors that may affect student's performance not included in this relationship
These include: study habits, number of absences, etc.

1.18 Collection of data

In order to perform any type of statistical analyses, we should collect appropriate data of the variable(s) in the process or the system under consideration. The task of data collection is twofold: (a) the choice of the appropriate data, and (b) the way by which data is collected. These two tasks are discussed below.

An appropriate data is the one which accurately describes the variable under consideration.

Different variables are associated with different data types. On the other hand, one variable can be described by two or more types of data. For example, if the variable under consideration is the value of houses in the marketplace, we will use the house market price ($) to determine this value. We may also use multiple data to determine this value including: the square feet of the house, the number of rooms, and the distance from the house to major areas in the city. Another example is business profit, which can be determined by calculating the values of profits for different business organizations. This may require knowledge of the revenues of these organizations and their costs (fixed and variable costs).

The way by which data is collected is another critical aspect in any statistical analysis as it can significantly influence both the cost and the reliability of the analysis. Generally, we can collect data in four different ways:

(a) From documented or published sources
(b) From an observational study
(c) From a survey
(d) From a designed experiment

Published Data-In today's information age, published data sources are numerous. These include social data, economic data, financial data, and political data. Many government organizations publish their data on routine basis. These include: the U.S. Census Bureau (http://www.census.gov/), World Bank data (http://data.worldbank.org/), and the U.S. Environmental Protection Agency (http://www.epa.gov/). The advantage of using published data is the low cost associated with the collection of this type of data, as it is often readily available at

no cost. The problem with this type of data is that it often deals with more general data type that may not pertain to the specific study under consideration. However, published data can provide immense useful information about trends and population dynamics. Using published data, we can obtain information about population growth, gender distribution, household income, energy consumption, etc.

Observational data is obtained by observing a process or a system at work and recording the data revealed by these observations. Examples of observation data include:

- Testing some material for some characteristics such as strength or weight and recording the data
- Monitoring some service departments and observing how customers are treated
- Monitoring student's performances in a National test and recording the grades
- Observing a collision test for some automobiles and recording the results

The advantage of observation method is that if we observe and record events, we will have a first-hand experience and it will not be necessary to rely on the willingness and ability of respondents to report accurately. The observation method also eliminates or reduces the bias effect resulting from obtaining data from a third party. Data collected by observation are, thus, more objective and generally more accurate. The main disadvantage of the observation method is the higher cost in comparison with the use of published data. In case of social experiments such as monitoring people's behavior, the observation method fails to provide accurate data about key variables such as people's attitudes and motivations. These variables require direct surveys and interviews with people. For example, one may observe consumers buying a certain product in massive numbers but without direct interviews the reasons for this buying behavior may be lost.

The **Survey method** is the technique of gathering data by asking questions to people who are thought to have desired information. Typically, a formal list of questionnaire is prepared to obtain consistent types of information. The data is collected from a respondent's opinion. As compared to other methods such as direct observation or experimentation, the survey method yields a broader range of information via multiple questions. Surveys are effective to produce information on socio-economic characteristics, consumer behaviors, attitudes, opinions, motives, and many other human-related aspects. They are also very useful in gathering information for planning product features, electing officials, advertising media, sales promotion, channels of distribution and other marketing variables.

The limitations experienced with the survey method include: the unwillingness of respondents to provide information due to privacy or confidentiality, the lack of qualification of some respondents leading to poor information or misleading data, human bias, and the choice of appropriate questionnaire wording.

In order to conduct a reliable survey, we should follow key guidelines including:

- Careful selection and phrasing of the survey questions
- Pre-determined ways to analyze the survey results
- The use of qualified personnel to conduct the surveys
- Good survey interpretation

The *designed experiment method* is used when highly controlled data is required. In this case, the data is collected in such a way that eliminates the existence of erroneous factors or uncontrollable noise. There are a number of experimental designs that are used in carrying out experiments. Examples of these include: completely randomized design (CRD), randomized block design (RBD), and factorial design.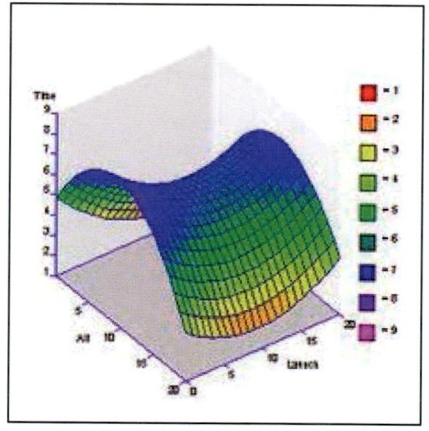

In a completely randomized design, after designing the experiment, the entire sampling selection is fully randomized. For example, suppose we have 6 people, 3 males and 3 females that are to be interviewed or tested. We may select to assign each person a letter or a number, and use a coin flip to determine a random sequence of sampling such as the following sequences:

$F_3, F_1, M_2, M_1, M_3, F_2$ or $M_1, F_1, F_3, M_3, M_2, F_2$ or $F_2, M_1, F_3, M_3, F_1, M_2$

In randomized block design (originated from agricultural research), several treatments of variables are applied to different blocks of land to determine their effects on parameters such as the yield of the crop or the quality of the harvested plant. Blocks are formed in such a manner that each block contains as many plots as a number of treatments so that one plot from each is selected at random for each treatment. The production of each plot is measured after the treatment is given. These data are then interpreted and inferences are drawn by using the analysis of variance technique so as to know the effect of various treatments like fertilizer type, harvesting time, etc. In Chapter 11, we discuss the analysis of variance in more detail.

Factorial design allows the experimenter to test two or more variables simultaneously. It also measures interaction effects of the variables and analyzes the impacts of each of the variables. Note that in a true experiment, randomization is essential so that the experimenter can infer cause and effect without any bias.

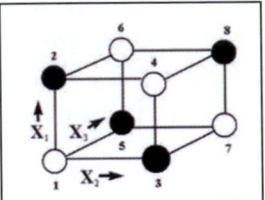

It is also important to distinguish between two types of data: *primary data* and *secondary data*. Primary data provides information directly related to the study in hand. Secondary data comes as supporting data that may be used as a reference or for comparative purposes. While primary data can be collected through direct observation, survey questionnaires, or designed experiments, the secondary data can be obtained through internal sources (these are within the organization) or external sources (these are outside the organization). Examples of primary data include students' grades in a particular course and in a given college. In this case, the national average of students' grades of this particular course is considered as secondary data.

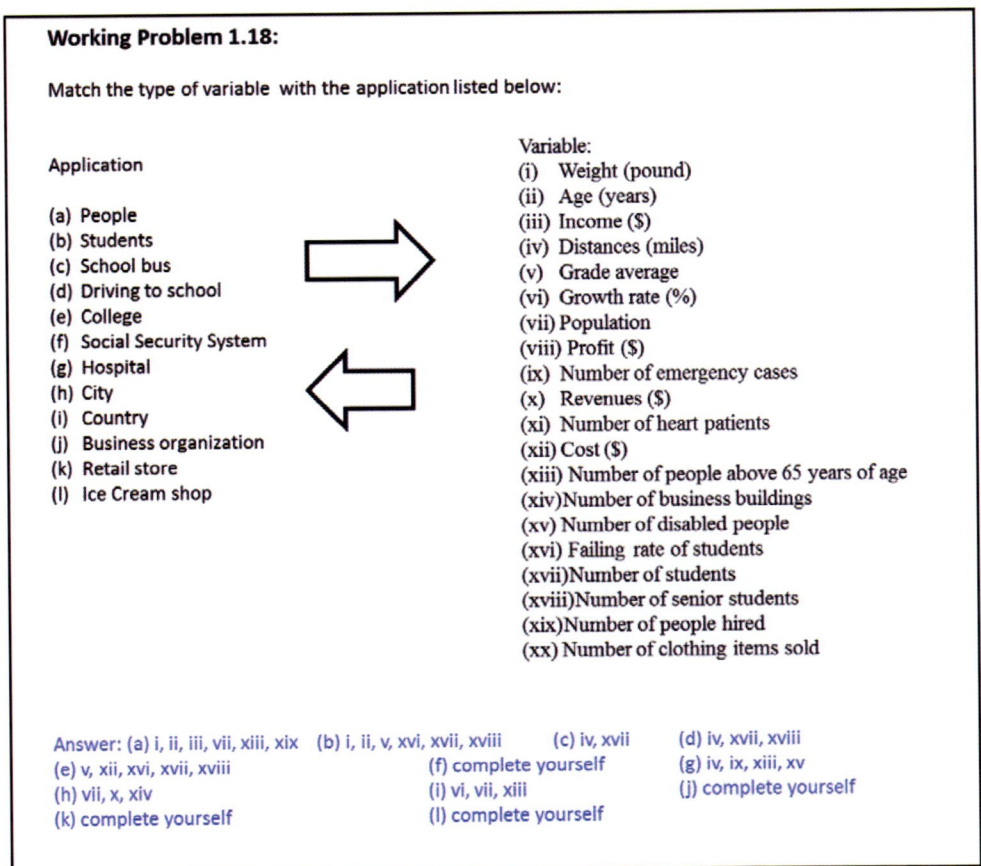

Working Problem 1.18:

Match the type of variable with the application listed below:

Application

(a) People
(b) Students
(c) School bus
(d) Driving to school
(e) College
(f) Social Security System
(g) Hospital
(h) City
(i) Country
(j) Business organization
(k) Retail store
(l) Ice Cream shop

Variable:
(i) Weight (pound)
(ii) Age (years)
(iii) Income ($)
(iv) Distances (miles)
(v) Grade average
(vi) Growth rate (%)
(vii) Population
(viii) Profit ($)
(ix) Number of emergency cases
(x) Revenues ($)
(xi) Number of heart patients
(xii) Cost ($)
(xiii) Number of people above 65 years of age
(xiv) Number of business buildings
(xv) Number of disabled people
(xvi) Failing rate of students
(xvii) Number of students
(xviii) Number of senior students
(xix) Number of people hired
(xx) Number of clothing items sold

Answer: (a) i, ii, iii, vii, xiii, xix (b) i, ii, v, xvi, xvii, xviii   (c) iv, xvii   (d) iv, xvii, xviii
(e) v, xii, xvi, xvii, xviii   (f) complete yourself   (g) iv, ix, xiii, xv
(h) vii, x, xiv   (i) vi, vii, xiii   (j) complete yourself
(k) complete yourself   (l) complete yourself

Working Problem 1.19:

Select the appropriate way of data collection for each of the following situations:

(a) Evaluating the effects of certain weight loss treatment on people weight
(b) Monitoring unemployment rate in the U.S.A. over the last 8 years
(c) Testing the opinions of an organization employees on a new medical insurance package
(d) Comparing road performances of a number of different sedan cars
(e) Determining the best U.S. state to live in upon retirement
(f) Determining the opinion of residents of a new subdivision on the landscaping of the surrounding areas
(g) Determining student's opinion on offering Sunday classes
(h) Determining the area of houses of the lowest property tax

Answer:

(a) Designed experiment
(b) Published data
(c) Do it yourself
(d) Observation data
(e) Do it yourself
(f) Do it yourself
(g) Survey data
(h) Do it yourself

1.19 Review Exercises

1.1: Observe the following numbers and select one of the answers describing the numbers (Note you may have more than one answer):
15, 25, 30, 35, 40, 45, 55, 65, 70

(a) The number of working hours per day by people in a textile factory ....
(b) The number of days, people can take as sick or personal leave per year ....
(c) The minimum wage per hour in McDonald's fast food restaurant ....

Answer: b

P1.2: The mean value and the range of data representing a sample of students' grades of a physics course offered in a college are called:

(a) Statistics ....
(b) Parameters ....
(c) All of the above ....

P1.3: The mean value and the range of data representing the population of all students' grades of a physics course offered in a college are called:

    (a) Statistics   …………

    (b) Parameters   …………

    (c) All of the above …………

Answer: b

P1.4: When the average age of football players at the college level is 20 year, how would you then describe the following data of student's age in a given college football team?
20, 20.5, 21, 20.8, 20.5, 19.8, 20, 19.75, 19.3, 20.2

        (a) Imprecise   …………

        (b) Inaccurate   …………

        (c) Precise and accurate …………

P1.5: When the area of a ceramic tile is manufactured to be of 75 square inch, how would you then describe the following data of area of a sample of ceramic tiles taken from this manufacturing line?
60, 59.5, 61, 58.9, 61.2, 60, 59.8, 61, 59.6, 60.8

        (a) Precise but inaccurate   …………

        (b) Accurate but imprecise   …………

        (c) Precise and accurate   …………

Answer: a

P1.6: What is the arithmetic mean of the following data of student grades?
82, 83, 94, 80, 76, 88, 72, 95, 90, 80

        (a) 87   ………..

        (b) 81   ………..

        (c) 84   ………..

        (d) None of the above ………..

P1.7: What is the range of the following data of student grades?
82, 83, 94, 80, 76, 88, 72, 95, 90, 80

        (a) 19   ………..

        (b) 23   ………..

        (c) 30   ………..

        (d) None of the above ………..

Answer: b

P1.8: How would you consider the number of rejects of a product?

        (a) A continuous variable   ………..

        (b) A discrete variable   ………..

(c) Neither continuous nor discrete ....

P1.9: How would you consider human weight?
     (a) A continuous variable ....
     (b) A discrete variable ....
     (c) Neither continuous nor discrete ....

Answer: a

P1.10: How would you consider people income?
     (a) A continuous variable ....
     (b) A discrete variable ....
     (c) Neither continuous nor discrete ....

P1.11: How would you consider your driving distance to school every day?
     (a) A continuous variable ....
     (b) A discrete variable ....
     (c) Neither continuous nor discrete ....

Answer: a

P1.12: The $\sum_1^4 x_i$ of the following data:
100, 105, 110, 102 is
     (a) 415 ....
     (b) 410 ....
     (c) 417 ....
     (d) None of the above ....

P1.13: The $\sum_1^4 x_i^2$ of the following data:
100, 105, 110, 102 is
     (a) 31201 ....
     (b) 43529 ....
     (c) 43127 ....
     (d) None of the above ....

Answer: b

P1.14: What is the level of measurement reflected by the following type of data?

(a) The age of students entering a community college
(b) A car race in which cars are identified as Car 1, Car 2, and Car 3

P1.15: Which of the following statements are true? (Check one)

I. Categorical variables are the same as qualitative variables.

II. Categorical variables are the same as quantitative variables.

III. Quantitative variables can be continuous variables.

(A) I Only ………

(B) II Only ………

(C) III Only ………

(D) I and II ………

(E) I and III ………

P 1.16: Which of the following is a discrete random variable?
I. The average height of a randomly selected group of boys.
II. The annual number of sweepstakes winners from New York City.
III. The number of U.S. presidential elections in the 20th century.

(A) I Only ………

(B) II Only ………

(C) III Only ………

(D) I and II ………

(E) II and III………

P1.17: For each of the following variables, determine the level of measurement.

(a) Gender
(b) Temperature
(c) Number of days during the past week that a college student ate at the college food center
(d) Letter grade earned in your Calculus course

Answer:
(a) Gender = nominal level
(b) Temperature = interval level
(c) Do it yourself
(d) Do it yourself

P1.18: Determine the mean, and range for the following four sets of data representing student grades of four consecutive physics quizzes (maximum points = 20) given to a class of 10 students. Interpret the results by comparing the grades in the four quizzes and express your opinion.

Test scores

	1	2	3	4	5	6	7	8	9	10
Quiz 1	20	20	20	20	20	20	20	20	20	20
Quiz 2	18	17	4	17	18	16	15	19	20	20
Quiz 3	8	7	19	18	17	8	6	20	18	19
Quiz 4	19	20	16	20	19	11	13	17	18	17

P1.19: The following data represents birth information in a given year of a random sample of mothers taken from Angel Hospital, the only hospital in Green Heaven City.

Mother age (year)	Baby gender	Mother weight gain (lb)	Baby weight at birth (lb)
16	M	22	7.5
18	M	23	8
21	F	40	9
24	M	18	6
26	M	23	6
30	F	25	7
32	F	30	8.5
35	F	26	7

(a) Identify the population
(b) Identify the sample
(c) Identify the variables
(d) Identify the measurement level of each variable

Answer:

(a) Population = all women giving birth at Angel Hospital in the given year
(b) Sample = Mothers selected or babies born in Angel Hospital = 8 mothers or babies
(c) Variables: mother age, baby gender, mother gain weight, baby weight
(d) Ratio: mother age, mother weight gain, baby weight
    Nominal: baby gender

P1.20: Classify the following variables into quantitative and qualitative variables:
(a) Weight of children 5 to 8 years old
(b) Skin color
(c) Driving distance to work
(d) Driving time to work
(e) Middle name
(f) Gender

P1.21: Suggest ways to handle the following outcomes in statistical analysis:
  (a) Pass or fail
  (b) Stop or go
  (c) Right or left
  (d) Young, middle, old
  (e) Dead or alive
  (f) Poor, fair, good, very good, excellent
  (g) Strongly disagree, disagree, agree, strongly agree

Answer:
  (a) Establish codes such as 0 for fail and 1 for pass
  (b) Do it yourself
  (c) Do it yourself
  (d) Establish codes such as 1, 2, and 3
  (e) Do it yourself
  (f) Do it yourself
  (g) Do it yourself

P1.22: The following data represents the frequency of weight gain during pregnancy of a random sample of women.

Weight Gain during to pregnancy (lb)	Percent of women
< 11	7.5
11-20	16.5
21-30	30
31-40	25
> 40	21

  (a) What is the weight gain during pregnancy that most women have?
  (b) What percent of women gain more than 30 pounds during pregnancy?
  (c) What percent of women gain less than 21 pounds during pregnancy?

P1.23: (Interact with your classmates):
  A. Your class is largely a representative sample of the students in your college. Count how many male and female in your class and make a rough estimate of the percent of male and female of students in the college population. Would you consider this as an accurate estimate? How confident are you that it is a good estimate? Explain.
  B. Go around the class, introduce yourself and ask other students about their heights. Form a column of data in Excel® spreadsheet representing the heights of the students in your class. Make sure you specify student gender (male or female). Calculate the mean and the range of the height data manually, or using Excel® Functions. Interpret the results.
  C. Using simple descriptive statistics: the mean as a measure of data center and the range as a measure of variability, compare the heights of male and female in your class and interpret the results.

D. In the above question, what types of measurement levels are the student gender and the student heights?

E. You asked the teacher of the class about your chance of making an *A*; the teacher answered, it is all up to you, but I had 12 students out of 35 passing with an *A* in this class when it was offered last semester. Assuming that students of last semester also represented a random sample of students, what is the chance of you not making an '*A*' in this class?

Answer: Questions in this problem will have varying answers. Below see how to use Excel functions in determining the mean and range using data from another class

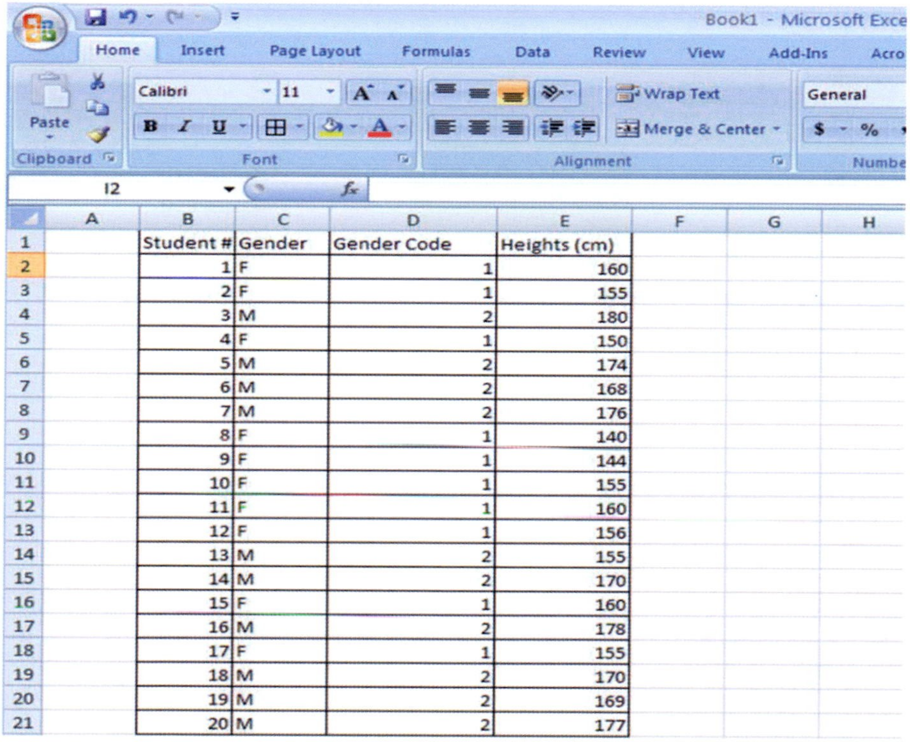

	A	B	C	D	E
1		Student #	Gender	Gender Code	Heights (cm)
2		1	F	1	160
3		2	F	1	155
4		3	M	2	180
5		4	F	1	150
6		5	M	2	174
7		6	M	2	168
8		7	M	2	176
9		8	F	1	140
10		9	F	1	144
11		10	F	1	155
12		11	F	1	160
13		12	F	1	156
14		13	M	2	155
15		14	M	2	170
16		15	F	1	160
17		16	M	2	178
18		17	F	1	155
19		18	M	2	170
20		19	M	2	169
21		20	M	2	177

Figure 1.12. Using Excel to perform statistical Functions:
Step 1: Insert your data in columns as shown in this portion of Excel Spread sheet

Student #	Gender	Gender Code	Heights (cm)
1	F	1	160
2	F	1	155
3	M	2	180
4	F	1	150
5	M	2	174
6	M	2	168
7	M	2	176
8	F	1	140
9	F	1	144
10	F	1	155
11	F	1	160
12	F	1	156
13	M	2	155
14	M	2	170
15	F	1	160
16	M	2	178
17	F	1	155
18	M	2	170
19	M	2	169
20	M	2	177
		Mean	162.6
		Minimum	140
		Maximum	180
		Range	40

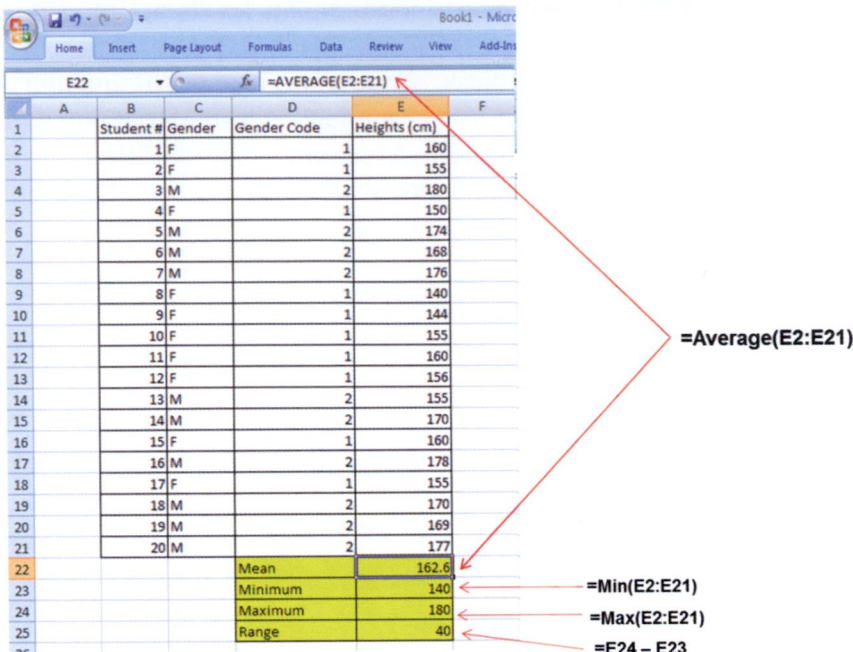

Figure 1.13. Using Excel to perform statistical Functions:
Step 2: Using Excel Function Codes (as shown) Calculate the Mean, Minimum, Maximum, and Range of Data

Student #	Gender	Gender Code	Heights (cm)
1	F	1	160
2	F	1	155
3	F	1	150
4	F	1	140
5	F	1	144
6	F	1	155
7	F	1	160
8	F	1	156
9	F	1	160
10	F	1	155
		Mean	153.5
		Minimum	140
		Maximum	160
		Range	20

Female Analysis

Student #	Gender	Gender Code	Heights (cm)
11	M	2	180
12	M	2	174
13	M	2	168
14	M	2	176
15	M	2	155
16	M	2	170
17	M	2	178
18	M	2	170
19	M	2	169
20	M	2	177
		Mean	171.7
		Minimum	155
		Maximum	180
		Range	25

Male Analysis

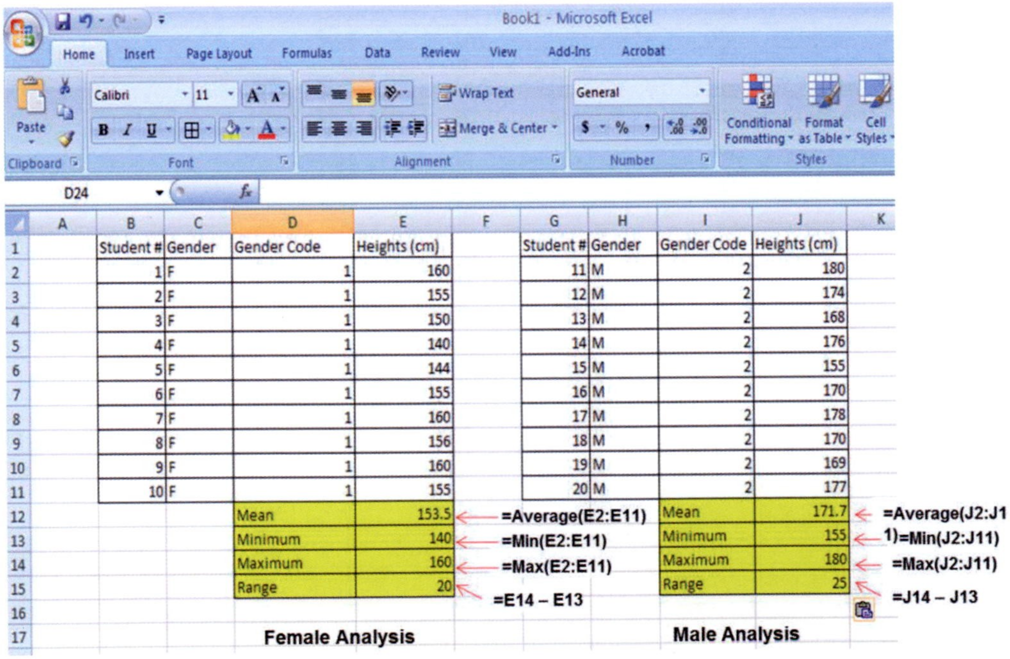

Figure 1.14. Using Excel to perform statistical Functions:
Step 3: You can divide the data into female and male using the gender code and calculate the Mean, Minimum, Maximum, and Range of each data set using Excel function codes

P1.24: Calculate the mean and the range of the following data set using Excel functions:

New born child weight (lb)	7.1	7.2	8.6	6.8	8.3	8.8	7.5	6.8	7.2	8.2

P1.25: Calculate the mean and the range of the following data set using Excel functions:

Ages of college freshmen (years)	18	17	22	21	20	20	18	19	17	16	18	19	18	17	20

P1.26: Select the appropriate way of data collection for each of the following situations:
    (a) Evaluating the safety performance of automobiles using collision tests
    (b) Monitoring gender distribution in different States in the U.S.A
    (c) Testing the opinions of an organization employees on the idea of working 4 days per week, with more hours per day, instead of the usual 5 days per week
    (d) Examining student's evaluation of a given class to teacher performance
    (e) Determining the performance of safety airbags using road test
Note:
Data can be collected using ways such as: from documented or published sources, from an observational study, from a survey, or from a designed experiment.

P1.27: Some Surveys indicate that about 13% of Americans are left-handed. Is this true for students at your class? If out of a random sample of 98 students, it was found that 15 are left-handed students.
    (a) What is the variable in question?
    (b) What is the population?
    (c) What is the sample?
    (d) What is the parameter?
    (e) What is the statistic?
Answer:
    (a) Inherent hand use
    (b) All students
    (c) Students
    (d) Number of left-handed people
    (e) Number of left-handed students

P1.28: In the following problems, determine which of the four levels of measurement (nominal, ordinal, interval, and ratio) is most appropriate.
    a. Nielsen ratings of TV shows
    b. Critic ratings of movies on a scale from 0 star to 5 stars
    c. Football player shirt numbers
    d. Voltage measurements from your home
    e. Years in which presidents were elected

P1.29: Carry out the following arithmetic operations:
a. Convert the fraction 3 to 8 to an equivalent percentage.
b. Convert 55% to an equivalent decimal.
c. What is 13% of 300?
d. Convert 0.188 to an equivalent percentage.
Answer:
  (a) 37.5%
  (b) Do it yourself
  (c) Do it yourself
  (d) 18.8%

P1.30: In a Gallup poll, 29% of 900 surveyed Internet users said that they spend 8 hours every day on the net. What is the actual number of people spending 8 hours every day on the net?

P1.31: Among 900 Internet users surveyed in a Gallup poll, 261 said that they spend 8 hours every day on the net. What is the percentage of responders who said they spend 8 hours every day on the net?
Answer:
  (a) 29%

P1.32: The class list below has all information for each student at the end of the semester, including their year in school, major, test grades, assignment grades, grade average in the class and final letter grade in the class.

Which of the variables in the list is: categorical (or qualitative), discrete quantitative; and continuous quantitative

Student ID #	Name	Term	Year	Major	Test 1	Test 2	Assig 1	Assig 2	Grade Avg.	Grade
48768	Michael Smith	Sp	1	Engin	77	77	19	20	81.1	B
28333	Susan Kear	Sp	1	Science	89	81	18	20	87	B
12764	John Anthony	Sp	2	Math	80	83	16	19	82.7	B
40006	Lisa Lakoon	Sp	2	Math	58	71	20	19	71.1	C
18988	Carla Thomas	Sp	2	Engin	91	88	20	19	91.1	A
55557	Shirley Land	Sp	1	Engin	78	73	16	17	76.9	C
......	......	......	......	......	......	......	......	......	......	......
40760	Lian Felda	Sp	1	Science	90	88	18	16	88.2	B
91888	Nancy Rogaan	Sp	2	Science	86	81	19	16	84.3	B
78008	Jacklyn Notaery	Sp	2	Math	89	88	12	15	84.3	B
38222	Simon Gans	Sp	2	Math	88	80	18	14	83.2	B
......	......	......	......	......	......	......	......	......	......	......
......	......	......	......	......	......	......	......	......	......	......

CHAPTER 2

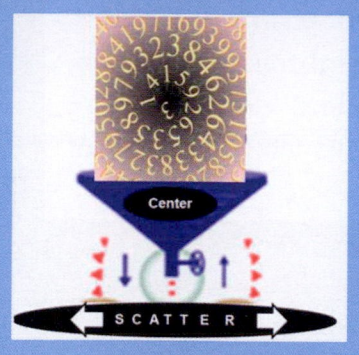

DESCRIPTIVE STATISTICS

Part I: Numerical Description

LEARNING OBJECTIVES

After completing this chapter, students will learn how to:

- *Calculate the measures of central tendency: Mean, Mode, Median, etc.*
- *Calculate the measures of dispersion or variability measures: Range, Standard Deviation, Variance, etc.*
- *Calculate combined measures*
- *Use Excel® Data Analysis to perform descriptive statistics*

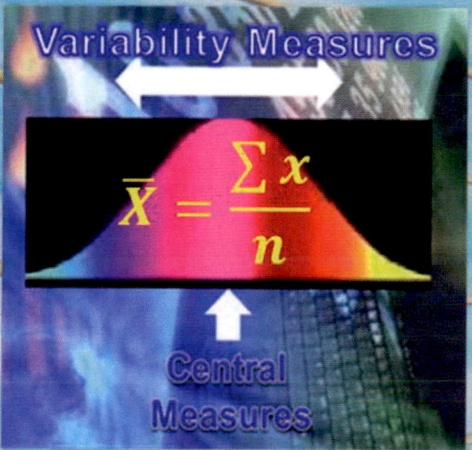

CHAPTER 2

In this chapter, we will learn how to describe a set of data using numerical methods. This is the first of two chapters that together will aim at providing methods of descriptive statistics. The key statistics discussed in this chapter are: (a) measures of central tendency (mean, mode, and median), and (b) measures of variability (range, standard deviation, and variance). In chapter 3, we discuss Part II of descriptive statistics, which is the use of graphical methods to display data and explore key statistics.

CHAPTER CONTENTS

2.1 What are the basic features of a data set?

A data set is a collection of data representing the values of a particular variable. Examples of data sets are given below.

Data Sets:

• *Students' grades in a calculus test (%):*

65, 85, 70, 75, 85, 80, 82, 85, 90, 78, 81, 82, 67, 80

• *Property tax of a sample of houses ($):*

$5000, $4500, $4000, $7200, $5000, $3800, $4100, $5000

• *Driving distance to work of a group of employees (miles):*

1.2, 2.0, 2.2, 15.0, 11.0, 5.0, 3.7, 4.9, 15.2, 16.0

• *Ages of all students in a college (years):*

18, 19, 21, ..., 22, 18, 19, 21

When a data set is being established, the following key questions should be addressed:

Data Set: Key Questions

- *Are the data qualitative or quantitative?*
- *What levels of measurement do the data exhibit? (nominal, ordinal, interval, or ratio)*
- *What is the source of data? (the population)*
- *What is the appropriate sampling technique that should be used to collect the samples? (e.g. random, stratified, or cluster)*
- *What is the appropriate sample size?*
- *In view of the purpose of the analysis, what statistical tools should be used?*

In Chapter 1, a brief review of the questions above was made. It is also important to recognize the form of data set to be analyzed. In this regard, data sets may be represented by one of three arrangements: *univariate*, *bivariate*, or *multivariate*. Figure 2.1 illustrates examples of these arrangements. Different data arrangements may require different types of statistical analysis as shown in Figure 2.1. In general, as more data dimensions are added to the data set, the analysis becomes more involved due to the need to coordinate data, compare data, and relate different variables in the data set.

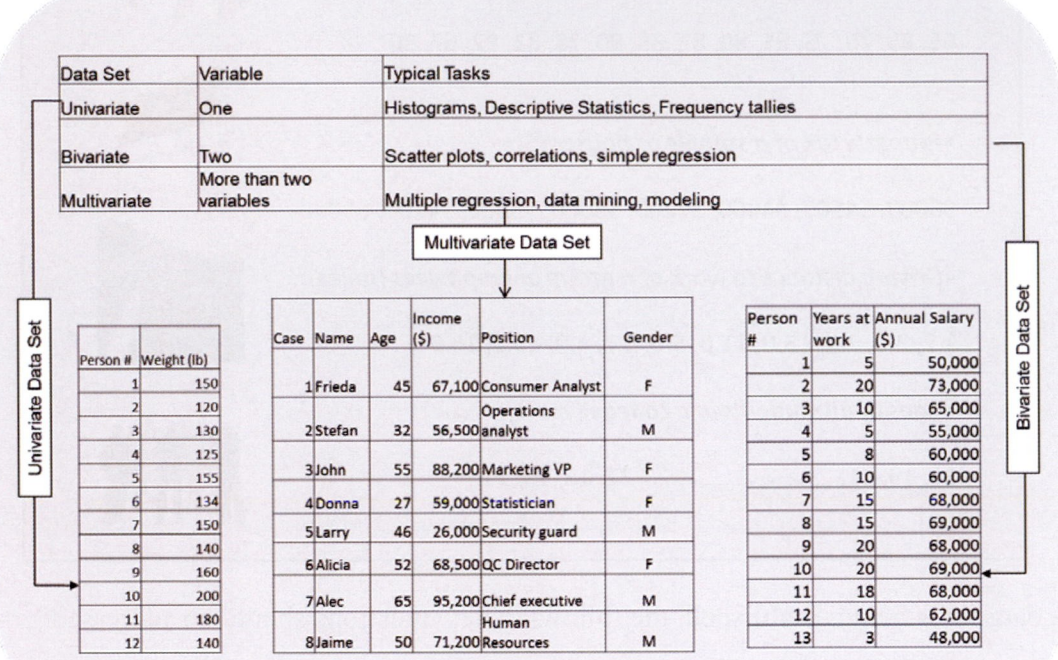

Figure 2.1 Different Arrangements of Data

A data set may also be classified on the basis of the sampling frequency. In this regard, two types of data structures can be considered: *cross-sectional data set*, and *time-series data set*. In a cross-sectional data set, all samples are collected at more or less the same point in time. In a time-series data set, samples are collected at specific intervals of time (e.g., weekly, monthly or quarterly). Figure 2.2 illustrates these two types of sample structure, and the common analyses used for the data collected in each type.

In practice, cross-sectional samples are normally large in size as they are typically used to take a snap shot at a population that is assumed to be more or less stable. An example of cross-sectional data may be the data of the prices of houses in a certain area collected in a given year. On the other hand, time-series samples are used for populations that encounter dynamic changes, periodic or seasonal. For example, the information on the quarterly revenue of a company is a time-series data set. Most of the data sets used in this book belong to the cross-sectional type. Chapter 14 will be entirely devoted to time-series data sets in the context of the subject of forecasting.

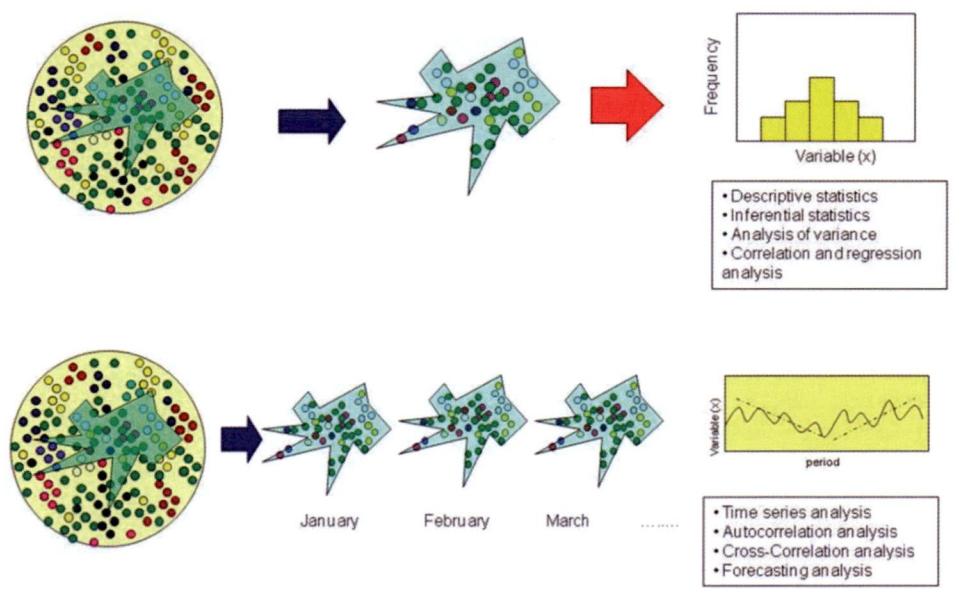

Figure 2.2 Cross-sectional and Time-series Data Sets

Working Problem 2.1:

Classify the following data sets as univariate, bivariate, or multivariate:

(a) ....   (b) ....   (c) ....

U.S. States Sales Tax (%)
0.0
4.0
6.0
6.0
2.9
0.0
4.0
4.0
6.0
4.0
8.3
7.0
7.0
6.0
6.0
5.5
5.0
0.0
7.0
5.0

State	Income Tax (%)	U.S. States Sales Tax (%)	Inheritance Tax (%)
Alaska	0.0	0.0	NO
Wyoming	0.0	4.0	No
Michigan	4.4	6.0	No
Pennsylvania	3.1	6.0	YES
Colorado	4.6	2.9	NO
Delaware	4.6	0.0	NO
Hawaii	1.4 to 11	4.0	NO
Georgia	1.0 to 6.0	4.0	NO
South Carolina	3.0 to 7.0	6.0	NO
Alabama	2.0 to 5.0	4.0	NO
California	1.25 to 10.55	8.3	NO
Rhode Island	3.75-9.9	7.0	NO
New Jersey	1.4 to 8.97	7.0	YES
Vermont	3.55-8.95	6.0	NO
Iowa	0.36 to 8.98	6.0	YES
Nebraska	2.56 to 6.84	5.5	Yes
Wisconsin	4.6 to 7.75	5.0	NO
Oregon	5.0 to 11.0	0.0	YES
Indiana	3.4	7.0	YES
North Dakota	1.84-4.86	5.0	NO

State Avergae Income Tax (%)	U.S. States Sales Tax (%)
0.0	0.0
0.0	4.0
4.4	6.0
3.1	6.0
4.6	2.9
4.6	0.0
6.2	4.0
3.5	4.0
5.0	6.0
3.5	4.0
5.6	8.3
6.8	7.0
5.2	7.0
6.3	6.0
4.6	6.0
4.7	5.5
6.2	5.0
8.0	0.0
3.4	7.0
3.4	5.0

http://portal.kiplinger.com/tools/slideshows/slideshow_pop.html?nm=TaxUnfriendlystatesBdress

(a) Univariate, (b) Multivariate, (c) Bivariate

61

Working Problem 2.2:

What is the level of measurement for each of the following variables: state, Income tax, sales tax, and inheritance tax. Why do some states have a wide range of income tax? Explain what is inheritance tax. What is the difference between inheritance tax and Estate tax?

State	Income Tax (%)	U.S. States Sales Tax (%)	Inheritance Tax (%)
Alaska	0.0	0.0	NO
Wyoming	0.0	4.0	No
Michigan	4.4	6.0	No
Pennsylvania	3.1	6.0	YES
Colorado	4.6	2.9	NO
Delaware	4.6	0.0	NO
Hawaii	1.4 to 11	4.0	NO
Georgia	1.0 to 6.0	4.0	NO
South Carolina	3.0 to 7.0	6.0	NO
Alabama	2.0 to 5.0	4.0	NO
California	1.25 to 10.55	8.3	NO
Rhode Island	3.75-9.9	7.0	NO
New Jersey	1.4 to 8.97	7.0	YES
Vermont	3.55-8.95	6.0	NO
Iowa	0.36 to 8.98	6.0	YES
Nebraska	2.56 to 6.84	5.5	Yes
Wisconsin	4.6 to 7.75	5.0	NO
Oregon	5.0 to 11.0	0.0	YES
Indiana	3.4	7.0	YES
North Dakota	1.84-4.86	5.0	NO

State = Nominal
Income tax, sales tax, inheritance tax = Ratio

http://portal.kiplinger.com/tools/slideshows/slideshow_pop.html?nm=TaxUnfriendlyStatesRetirees

---

Working Problem 2.3:

Identify the following data sets as 'Cross-Sectional Data' or 'Time-Series Data':

(a) Two weeks before the 56th quadrennial United States presidential election, which was held on November 4, 2008, a sample of people taking randomly from undecided states revealed that Democrat Barack Obama is expected to earn 54% of the popular votes and John McCain is expected to earn 46% of the votes

Cross Sectional (   )   Time-Series (   )

(b) A survey of 1000 students from a university of 10,000 students, revealed that 65% of the students do not prefer weekend classes

Cross Sectional (   )   Time-Series (   )

(c) The U.S. City average price per gallon of unleaded regular gasoline from 2000 to 2009 was as follow:

Year	Jan	Feb	Mar	Apr	May	Jun	Jul	Aug	Sep	Oct	Nov	Dec
2000	1.301	1.369	1.541	1.506	1.498	1.617	1.593	1.51	1.582	1.559	1.555	1.489
2001	1.472	1.484	1.447	1.564	1.729	1.64	1.482	1.427	1.531	1.362	1.263	1.131
2002	1.139	1.13	1.241	1.407	1.421	1.404	1.412	1.423	1.422	1.449	1.448	1.394
2003	1.473	1.641	1.748	1.659	1.542	1.514	1.524	1.628	1.728	1.603	1.535	1.494
2004	1.592	1.672	1.766	1.833	2.009	2.041	1.939	1.898	1.891	2.029	2.01	1.882
2005	1.823	1.918	2.065	2.283	2.216	2.176	2.316	2.506	2.927	2.785	2.343	2.186
2006	2.315	2.31	2.401	2.757	2.947	2.917	2.999	2.985	2.589	2.272	2.241	2.334
2007	2.274	2.285	2.592	2.86	3.13	3.052	2.961	2.782	2.789	2.793	3.069	3.02
2008	3.047	3.033	3.258	3.441	3.764	4.065	4.09	3.786	3.698	3.173	2.151	1.689
2009	1.787	1.928	1.949	2.056	2.265	2.631	2.543	2.627	2.574	2.561	2.66	2.621

http://data.bls.gov/cgi-bin/surveymost

Cross Sectional (   )   Time-Series (   )

(a) Cross sectional, (b) Cross sectional, (c) Time series

2.2 What are the different types of descriptive statistics?

In chapter 1, it was indicated that the starting point in any statistical analysis is to perform descriptive statistics. There are two types of descriptive statistics: (1) *numerical descriptive statistics*, and (2) *graphical descriptive statistics*. In this chapter, our focus will be on numerical descriptive statistics.

Numerical measures of descriptive statistics consist of two types:

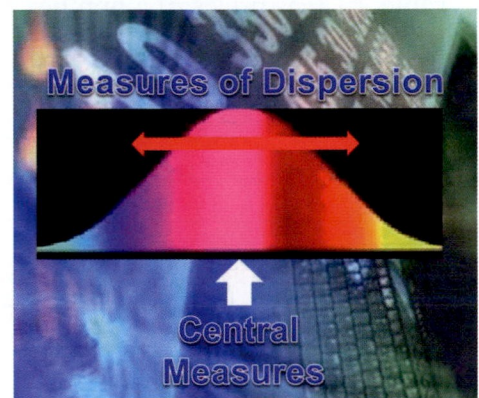

- Measures of central tendency (mean, median, and mode)
- Measures of dispersion (range, standard deviation, and variance)
- Combined measures (coefficient of variation, signal-to-noise ratio, and standardized variable)

These measures are discussed in the following sections.

2.3 What are the measures of central tendency?

Central tendency measures are those that describe the center of data. The most common measures of central tendency are:

- o *Arithmetic mean*
- o *Median*
- o *Mode*

In addition to these, other measures such as geometric mean and harmonic mean can also be used in some special applications.

2.3.1 Arithmetic Mean

For a sample data, the arithmetic mean is obtained from the following equation:

$$Mean = \bar{X} = \frac{sum\ of\ all\ observation\ values}{number\ of\ observations} = \sum_{1}^{n} x_i / n \qquad (2.1)$$

For a population data, the arithmetic mean is obtained from the following equation:

$$Mean = \mu = \frac{sum\ of\ all\ values}{number\ of\ observations} = \sum_{1}^{N} x_i / N \qquad (2.2)$$

It is important that you become familiar with the symbols used as they are universally accepted. These include: the mean of a sample, $\bar{X}$, the mean of a population, μ, the size of a sample, n, and the size of a population, N.

Example 2.1: Table 2.1 illustrates a comparison of gas prices in some U.S. states in September 2009 and September 2008. Determine the mean of gas prices ($ per gallon) for each year.

Table 2.1 Gas prices of a number of states in September 2008, and September 2009
http://www.eia.doe.gov

State	Sept- 2009	Sept-2008
California	3.099	3.750
Colorado	2.480	3.732
Florida	2.527	3.893
Massachusetts	2.597	3.582
Minnesota	2.452	3.765
New York	2.811	3.805
Ohio	2.411	3.933
Texas	2.404	3.729
Washington	2.947	3.785

Solution:

Using equation 2.1, we can determine the arithmetic mean for each year as follows:

For September 2009:

$$Mean = \bar{X} = \frac{\sum_1^n x_i}{n} = \frac{3.099 + 2.480 + 2.527 + \cdots + 2.947}{9}$$
$$= \$2.636\, per\, gallon$$

For September 2008:

$$Mean = \bar{X} = \frac{\sum_1^n x_i}{n} = \frac{3.750 + 3.732 + 3.893 + \cdots + 3.785}{9} = \$3.775\, per\, gallon$$

By comparison of the arithmetic means of the two years, one can see that the average price in 2009 was about $1.139 cheaper than that of 2008 during the month of September. This was good news to everyone particularly those who drove big SUVs or trucks. The results, however, do not tell us the cause of this drop. In searching for the cause of this significant drop, one may consult other sources that may partially or fully explain the trend. For example, a barrel of crude oil in this period in 2008 was about $105. In 2009, the price went down significantly and in September of 2009, it was only $69. Again, this may only represent a partial cause of the drop in gas price and one must also entertain other possible causes.

It is important that we understand the key properties of the arithmetic mean. These are as follows:

Key Properties of the Arithmetic Mean:

- *The mean of a set of data is unique and can be used as an identity measure of the center of the data*
- *We can determine the mean of any data set for the levels of measurements of ratio and interval*
- *The sum of deviations of all observation values from their mean is zero,* $\sum_1^n(x_i - \bar{X}) = 0$

Example 2.2: Determine the arithmetic mean of the following three values of student grades: 80, 40, and 30. Using the mean value, prove that $\sum_1^n(x_i - \bar{X}) = 0$.

Solution:

The arithmetic mean:

$$Mean = \bar{X} = \frac{\sum_1^n x_i}{n} = \frac{80 + 40 + 30}{3} = 50$$

$$\sum_1^3(x_i - \bar{X}) = (80 - 50) + (40 - 50) + (30 - 50) = 0$$

Working Problem 2.4:

Calculate the average value of the following data sets:

	Set 1	Set 2	Set 3
	21	252	126
	20	240	120
	21	252	126
	18	216	108
	19	228	114
	21	252	126
	22	264	132
	18	216	108
	20	240	120
	20	240	120

	Set 1	Set 2	Set 3
Mean	20	240	120

Working Problem 2.5:

The table below shows the annual gas prices in the U.S. from 1920 to 2012 before and after adjustment for inflation.

(a) What was the value of the dollar in 1920 compared to today?

(b) Calculate the average gas price before and after inflation adjustments from 1920 to 2012.

(c) Interpret the results

Year	Annual Gas Prices	Annual Gas Prices Adjusted for Inflation
1920	0.18	3.35
1930	0.17	2.6
1940	0.18	2.6
1950	0.3	2.48
1960	0.35	2.4
1970	0.4	1.97
1979	1.38	3.44
1999	1.5	1.44
2006	1.4	2.5
2009	2.35	3
2011	3.53	3.57
2012	3.77	3.77

(a) Based on the data of gas prices, in 1920, the gas price was 0.18, which is equivalent to $3.35. This means that the value of one dollar in 1920 was equivalent to (1×3.35/0.18 ≈ $18.6). This means that a household annual income of $10,000 in 1920 is equivalent to $186,000 of a today's household family. To answer this question more accurately, students can refer to different websites including:

http://inflationdata.com/inflation/inflation_Calculators/inflation_Rate_Calculator.asp

http://www.usinflationcalculator.com/inflation/historical-inflation-rates/

(b)

Annual Gas Prices	Annual Gas Prices Adjusted for Inflation
1.2925	2.76

Working Problem 2.6:

Calculate the mean for the following data set of minimum wage ($):

Wage($)	7	8	6	6	8	5	8	8	9	6

Important Facts about Minimum Wage in the U.S.A.   **Mean = 7.1**

President Obama highlighted the need to increase the federal minimum wage in his State of the Union address in 2013. Wages for U.S. workers, particularly low-wage workers, have eroded not just in recent years, but over several decades . This erosion has contributed to the growth of income inequality, leaving the economy less vibrant than if incomes were distributed more evenly. Raising the minimum wage and incorporating a system for automatic adjustment over time is key to reversing this erosion of low-wage workers' earnings, and would help combat growth of income inequality. See
http://www.epi.org/publication/bp357-federal-minimum-wage-increase/

2.3.2 Median

The median of a set of numbers arranged in order of magnitude is the middle value or the arithmetic mean of the two middle values.

Example 2.3: Calculate the median of the following data set:

14, 12, 14, 16, 15, 19, 17, 17, 17

Solution:
To determine the median, we first arrange the data in order of magnitude and find the middle value:

<u>12, 14, 14, 15</u>, 16, <u>17, 17, 17, 19</u>
Thus, the median is 16

Example 2.4: Calculate the median of the following data set:

8, 9, 10, 9, 8, 6, 11, 7, 12, 8

Solution:

To determine the median, we first arrange the data in order of magnitude:

<u>6, 7, 8, 8,</u> 8, 9, <u>9, 10, 11, 12</u>

We then find the middle value. Since this data set consists of an even number of observations, the middle values that split this data into an equal number of observations on both sides are 8 and 9. Thus, the median of this set of data is (8+9)/2 = 8.5

2.3.3 Mode

The mode is that value which occurs with the greatest frequency. The examples below illustrate how a mode is calculated.

Example 2.5: Calculate the mode of the following observations:

80, 87, 90, 82, 78, 74, 80, 77, 80, 91, 81, 80

Solution:

<u>80</u>, 87, 90, 82, 78, 74, <u>80</u>, 77, <u>80</u>, 91, 81, <u>80</u>
The mode of this set is 80.

Example 2.6: Calculate the mode of the following observations:

14	9	9	5	7	8	10	11	9	12	14	15	14

Solution:

5	7	8	**9**	**9**	**9**	10	11	12	**14**	**14**	**14**	15

This set exhibits no particular mode; instead it has two modes 9, and 14, and is called bimodal. Note that you should never take the average of two modes to calculate the unique mode of a data set.

Working Problem 2.7:

Calculate the median and the mode for the following data set of minimum wage ($):
7, 8, 6, 6, 8, 5, 6, 5, 8, 8

Answer:
Median =$6.5
Mode = $8

Working Problem 2.8:

Calculate the median and the mode of the following data sets:

Set 1	21	20	21	18	19	21	22	18	20	20
Set 2	252	240	252	216	228	252	264	216	240	240
Set 3	126	120	126	108	114	126	132	108	120	120

	Set 1	Set 2	Set 3
Median	20	240	120
Mode	No Mode	252	No Mode

Working Problem 2.9:

Find the arithmetic mean for each of the following data sets:

(a) Property tax of a random sample of 10 houses in Jersey City, New Jersey:

House ID	1	2	3	4	5	6	7	8	9	10
Annual Property Tax ($)	4800	12000	7000	8500	6000	12000	6000	7500	6000	6000

Mean $7580

(b) Gasoline Price in U.S.A. Per Gallon in 2009: http://data.bls.gov/cgi-bin/surveymost

Year	Jan	Feb	Mar	Apr	May	Jun	Jul	Aug	Sep	Oct	Nov	Dec
2009	1.787	1.928	1.949	2.056	2.265	2.631	2.543	2.627	2.574	2.561	2.66	2.621

Mean   2.350167

(c) Price of Chicken, fresh, whole, per lb. (453.6 gm) in 2010   http://data.bls.gov/cgi-bin/surveymost

Year	Jan	Feb	Mar	Apr	May	Jun	Jul	Aug	Sep	Oct
2010	1.265	1.265	1.231	1.23	1.259	1.239	1.28	1.254	1.276	1.302

Mean   1.2601

Working Problem 2.10:

Find the median and the mode for each of the following data sets:

(a) Property tax of a random sample of 10 houses in Jersey City, New Jersey:

House ID	1	2	3	4	5	6	7	8	9	10
Annual Property Tax ($)	4800	12000	7000	8500	6000	12000	6000	7500	6000	6000

Median = Do it yourself, Mode = $6000

(b) Gasoline Price in U.S.A. Per Gallon in 2009:   http://data.bls.gov/cgi-bin/surveymost

Year	Jan	Feb	Mar	Apr	May	Jun	Jul	Aug	Sep	Oct	Nov	Dec
2009	1.787	1.928	1.949	2.056	2.265	2.631	2.543	2.627	2.574	2.561	2.66	2.621

Median = $2.552, Mode = Do it yourself

(c) Price of Chicken, fresh, whole, per lb. (453.6 gm) in 2010   http://data.bls.gov/cgi-bin/surveymost

Year	Jan	Feb	Mar	Apr	May	Jun	Jul	Aug	Sep	Oct
2010	1.265	1.265	1.231	1.23	1.259	1.239	1.28	1.254	1.276	1.302

Median = Do it yourself, Mode = $1.265

69

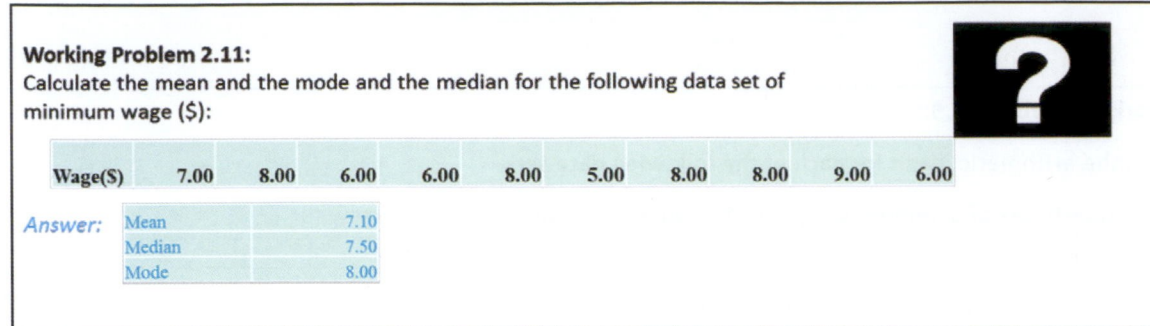

Working Problem 2.11:
Calculate the mean and the mode and the median for the following data set of minimum wage ($):

Wage($)	7.00	8.00	6.00	6.00	8.00	5.00	8.00	8.00	9.00	6.00

Answer:

Mean	7.10
Median	7.50
Mode	8.00

2.3.4 Geometric mean, G

The geometric mean is a different measure of central tendency that is commonly used *when the variable under consideration is likely to change over time or periodically*. It is used to find the average change over the entire period under study. Typical situations in which the geometric mean is useful include: population growth, quarterly or annual return on investment, and inflation. To calculate the geometric mean of x_1, x_2, ... x_n, we multiply them together and then find the nth root of this product:

$$G = \sqrt[n]{x_1 x_2 x_3 \, \dots \dots \, x_n} \qquad (2.3)$$

The reason for the name geometric is that this type of mean can be understood in the context of geometry. For example, the geometric mean of two values, a and b, $G = \sqrt{ab}$ is the side length of the square that has the same area as that of a rectangle with side lengths a and b. Suppose $a = 5$, and $b = 4$, then $A^2 = a.b = 20$. Thus, $A = G = \sqrt{ab} = \sqrt{20} = 4.4721$, which is the side length of a square of the same area ($A_{square} = 4.4721 \times 4.4721 = 20$).

Example 2.7: If the return on investment earned by a manufacturer of a sports car for four successive years was: 20 percent, 15 percent, -40 percent, and 100 percent. What is the geometric mean rate of return on investment?

Solution:

The value of 1.2 reflects a 20% return on investment (the original investment of 1.0 plus the return of 0.2); the value of 0.6 reflects a loss of 40% (the original investment of 1.0 less than the loss of 0.4); and the value of 2 reflects a gain of 100% (the original investment of 1.0 plus the return of 1). In business calculation, the total return in each period is typically reinvested in the next period, or it becomes the base for the next period. This makes the base for the second year 1.2, and the base for the third year (1.2)(1.15), and that for the fourth year (1.2)(1.15)(0.6) and so forth. Therefore, the geometric mean rate of return is:

$$G = \sqrt[n]{x_1 x_2 x_3 \, \dots \dots \, x_n} = \sqrt[4]{(1.2)(1.15)(0.6)(2)} = \sqrt[4]{1.656} = 1.1344$$

Accordingly, the average rate of return, which is essentially a compound annual growth rate is $(1.1344 - 1) \times 100 =)$ or 13.44%.

Note that if we calculated the classic arithmetic mean for the returns (20+15-40+100)/4 = 23.75%, we would have a substantially higher value than the geometric mean and this will overstate the true rate of return. Also note that this is the same as (1.2+1.15+0.6+2)/4 = 1.2375.

Example 2.8: Suppose the inflation rates for the last 5 years in a certain country are 5%, 4%, 2%, 8%, and 6%, respectively. What is the mean rate of inflation over this five-year period?

Solution:

At the end of the first year, the price index will be 1.05 times the price index at the beginning of the year; at the end of the second year, the price index will be (1.04)(1.05); at the end of the third year, the price index will be (1.02)(1.04)(1.05) and so on. Thus, the mean of 1.05, 1.04, 1.02, 1.08, and 1.06 is:

$$G = \sqrt[n]{x_1 x_2 x_3 \dots \dots x_n} = \sqrt[5]{(1.05)(1.04)(1.02)(1.08)(1.06)} = \sqrt[5]{1.275} = 1.0498$$

Accordingly, the average rate of inflation over the five-year period is 4.9%

Note that if we calculated the classic arithmetic mean for the annual inflations [(6+8+2+4+5)/5 − 5%], we would have a higher value than the geometric mean and this will overstate the true rate of inflation.

Working Problem 2.12:

The percent increase in sales for the last 4 years at X-L Company were:
9.91, 10.75, 13.12, 26.6

(a) Find the geometric mean percent increase.
(b) Find the arithmetic mean percent increase.
(c) Is the arithmetic mean equal to or greater than the geometric mean?

(a) $G = \sqrt[4]{1.991 \times 1.1075 \times 1.1312 \times 1.266} = 1.1491$

(b) Do it yourself
(c) Greater

2.4 What are the 'dispersion' or variability measures?

Dispersion or variability measures are those that describe the spread of data away from the center. The most common measures of central tendency are:

- o *Range*
- o *Mean deviation*
- o *Standard deviation*
- o *Variance*

2.4.1 Range

The range is the difference between the maximum and the minimum value of the x_i observations

$$Range = x_{max} - x_{min} \qquad (2.4)$$

Example 2.9: Calculate the range of the following set of data:

200, 205, 204, 202, 207, 208

Solution:
200, 205, 204, 202, 207, **208**

The Range = R = 208 - 200 = 8

Properties of range:

- The range represents the most commonly used statistic after the arithmetic mean
- It is simple as it relies on two values, the maximum value and the minimum value
- It is easy to understand: the higher the range, the higher the variability
- Since the range relies on two values (maximum and minimum), a mistake in any one of these two values or a presence of an outlier can result in a misleading value of range

---

2.4.2 Mean deviation

$$MD = \frac{1}{n}\sum_{1}^{n}|x_i - \overline{X}| \qquad (2.5)$$

Example 2.10: Calculate the mean deviation of the following ten observations of metal sheet thickness (*mm*):

83, 90, 70, 90, 90, 60, 70, 70, 90, 100

Solution:

We first calculate the mean value:

$$\bar{X} = (83 + 90 + 70 + 90 + 90 + 60 + 70 + 70 + 90 + 100) / 10 = 81.3 \; mm$$

We then create a table in which we calculate the deviation of each value from the mean value as shown in Table 2.2 below. This will lead to positive and negative values. The absolute values are those that ignore the sign and consider all values as positive.

Table 2.2 Calculation of mean deviation

Thickness (mm)	$(x_i - \bar{X})$	$|(x_i - \bar{X})|$
83	(83-81.3) =1.7	1.7
90	(90-81.3) = 8.7	8.7
70	(70-81.3) = -11.3	11.3
90	(90-81.3) = 8.7	8.7
90	(90-81.3) = 8.7	8.7
60	(60-81.3) = -21.3	21.3
70	(70-81.3) = -11.3	11.3
70	(70-81.3) = -11.3	11.3
90	(90-81.3) = 8.7	8.7
100	(100-81.3) = 18.7	18.7
Mean =$\bar{X}$ = 81.3	Sum = 0	Sum = 110.4

Mean Deviation = 110.4/10 = 11.04 *mm*

2.4.3 Standard deviation

When we analyze a sample data, the standard deviation, *s*, of the values $x_1, x_2, \ldots x_n$ is given by:

$$s = \sqrt{\frac{\sum_1^n (x_i - \bar{X})^2}{n}} \qquad (2.6)$$

For *n* < 30, we use (*n-1*) in the denominator to obtain a better estimate of the standard deviation of the population from which the sample data is taken.

For a population of size N, the standard deviation is given by:

$$\sigma = \sqrt{\frac{\sum_1^N (x_i - \mu)^2}{N}} \qquad (2.7)$$

It is important that you become familiar with the symbols used as they are universally accepted. These include: the standard deviation of a sample, s, the standard deviation of a population, σ, the size of a sample, n, and the size of a population, N.

Unlike the range which relies on two values, the standard deviation accounts for all the data points by measuring their deviations from the center point or the mean. In general, ***high values of standard deviation imply high variability*** in the values of the characteristic parameter being examined, and ***low standard deviation implies low variability***.

Example 2.11: Calculate the standard deviation of the following ten observations of metal sheet thickness (*mm*):

83, 90, 70, 90, 90, 60, 70, 70, 90, 100

Solution:

We first calculate the mean value:

$\bar{X}$ = (83 + 90 + 70 + 90 + 90 + 60 + 70 + 70 + 90 + 100) / 10 = 81.3 *mm*

We then create a table in which we calculate the deviation of each value from the mean value as shown in Table 2.3 below. This will lead to positive and negative values with a sum of zero. Therefore, we square each difference and sum up all difference squares.

Table 2.3 Calculation of standard deviation

Thickness (mm)	$(x_i - \bar{X})$	$(x_i - \bar{X})^2$
83	(83-81.3) =1.7	2.89
90	(90-81.3) = 8.7	75.69
70	(70-81.3) = -11.3	127.69
90	(90-81.3) = 8.7	75.69
90	(90-81.3) = 8.7	75.69
60	(60-81.3) = -21.3	453.69
70	(70-81.3) = -11.3	127.69
70	(70-81.3) = -11.3	127.69
90	(90-81.3) = 8.7	75.69
100	(100-81.3) = 18.7	349.69
Mean = 81.3	Sum = 0	Sum – 1492.1

Standard deviation:

$$s = \sqrt{\frac{\sum_1^n (x_i - \bar{X})^2}{n-1}} = \sqrt{\frac{1492.1}{9}} \approx 12.88mm$$

2.4.4 Variance

The variance of a set of data is the square of the standard deviation. In essence, it is the mean of the square deviations.

For a sample:

$$s^2 = \frac{\sum_1^n (x_i - \bar{X})^2}{n} \qquad (2.8)$$

For a population:

$$\sigma^2 = \frac{\sum_1^N (x_i - \mu)^2}{N} \qquad (2.9)$$

For the data in the above Example, since the standard deviation is 12.88, the variance is 165.8 mm^2.

Again, it is important that you become familiar with the symbols used as they are universally accepted. These include: the standard deviation of a sample, s^2, the standard deviation of a population, σ^2, the size of a sample, n, and the size of a population, N.

Properties of variance:

1. The variance represents the most commonly used statistic to indicate variability
2. The higher the variance, the higher the variability
3. Unlike the range, the variance takes into account all observation values. Therefore, it is less sensitive to outliers
4. One of the key differences between a variance and standard deviation is that we can use the variance to handle the net values of variability. This point will be illustrated in Chapter 11 under the subject of Analysis of Variance.
5. Variance values cannot be subtracted to determine variability. It can only be added. If $U = X \pm Y$, *Var* $(U) = Var$ $(X) + Var$ (Y). This is the principle of *analysis of variance* (Chapter 11)

Example 2.12: Suppose X and Y are independent random variables. The variance of X is 16; and the variance of Y is 9. Let $U = X - Y$.

What is the variance of U?

Solution:

The variance of U is equal to the variance of X plus the variance of Y:

$$Var(U) = Var(X - Y) = Var(X) + Var(Y) = 16 + 9 = 25$$

Also note that the standard deviation of U is equal to the square root of the variance, or 5.

Working Problem 2.13:

Calculate the values of minimum, maximum, range, standard deviation, and variance for each of the following data sets:

(a) Property tax of a random sample of 10 houses in Jersey City, New Jersey:

House ID	1	2	3	4	5	6	7	8	9	10
Annual Property Tax ($)	4800	12000	7000	8500	6000	12000	6000	7500	6000	6000

Mean	7580
Standard Deviation	2538.066
Sample Variance	6441778
Range	7200
Minimum	4800
Maximum	12000

(b) Gasoline Price in U.S.A. Per Gallon in 2009:

Year	Jan	Feb	Mar	Apr	May	Jun	Jul	Aug	Sep	Oct	Nov	Dec
2009	1.787	1.928	1.949	2.056	2.265	2.631	2.543	2.627	2.574	2.561	2.66	2.621

Mean	2.350167
Standard Deviation	0.331209
Sample Variance	0.109699
Range	0.873
Minimum	1.787
Maximum	2.66

(c) Price of Chicken, fresh, whole, per lb. (453.6 gm) in 2010

Year	Jan	Feb	Mar	Apr	May	Jun	Jul	Aug	Sep	Oct
2010	1.265	1.265	1.231	1.23	1.259	1.239	1.28	1.254	1.276	1.302

Mean	1.2601
Standard Deviation	0.022825
Sample Variance	0.000521
Range	0.072
Minimum	1.23
Maximum	1.302

Working Problem 2.14:

Question (1) Calculate the minimum, maximum, range, standard deviation, and variance for the following data set of minimum wage ($)

7, 8, 6, 6, 8, 5, 6, 5, 8, 8

Answer: Minimum = $5, Maximum =$8, Range = Do it yourself, Mean Deviation = Do it yourself, Standard deviation = $1.252, Variance = Do it yourself

Question (2): In two consecutive exams, the mean grade of the first test was 80 and the mean grade of the second test was 90. The standard deviation of grade of the first test was 6 and the standard deviation of grade of the second test was 8. Calculate the mean of the two tests and the variance of the two tests?

Mean = (80+90)/2 = 85
Variance (Exam 1 + Exam 2) = Var (Exam 1) + Var (Exam 2) = Complete

Working Problem 2.15

Calculate the range, standard deviation, and variance of the following data sets

Set 1	21	20	21	18	19	21	22	18	20	20
Set 2	252	240	252	216	228	252	264	216	240	240
Set 3	126	120	126	108	114	126	132	108	120	120

Answer:

	Set 1	Set 2	Set 3
Mean	20	240	120
Standard Error	0.421637	5.059644	2.529822
Median	20	240	120
Mode	21	252	126
Standard Deviation	1.333333	16	8
Sample Variance	1.777778	256	64
Range	4	48	24
Minimum	18	216	108
Maximum	22	264	132

2.5 What are combined descriptive measures?

Combined measures of descriptive statistics are those that combine the measures of central tendency and the measures of dispersion. Examples of these measures are given below.

2.5.1 Coefficient of variation (CV %)

This is expressed by the ratio of the standard deviation and the mean:

$$CV\% = \frac{s}{\bar{X}} 100 \qquad (2.10)$$

77

Where $\bar{X}$ = the arithmetic mean, and s = the standard deviation.

For the data of the metal sheet thickness, the coefficient of variation $CV\%$ is

$$CV\% = \frac{s}{\bar{X}} 100 = \frac{12.88}{81.30} \times 100 = 15.84\%$$

Working Problem 2.16:

Calculate the Coefficient of Variation (CV%) for the following data set of minimum wage ($):
7, 8, 6, 6, 8, 5, 6, 5, 8, 8

Answer:
C.V% = 18.69

Working Problem 2.17:

The three data sets shown in this table each has the same coefficient

Of variation of 6.667.

(a) Verify the above statement

(b) Explain why C.V% are the same

Set 1	Set 2	Set 3
21	252	126
20	240	120
21	252	126
18	216	108
19	228	114
21	252	126
22	264	132
18	216	108
20	240	120
20	240	120

2.5.2 Signal-to-noise ratio (S/N)

The signal-to-noise ratio is defined by:

$$\frac{S}{N} = 10\ log_{10}\left(\frac{\bar{X}^2}{s^2}\right) \qquad (2.11)$$

where $\bar{X}$ is the mean and s^2 is the variance.

The signal here is the target or the mean value, and the noise is the variability represented by the variance. For the data of metal sheet thickness,

$$\frac{S}{N} = 10\ log_{10}\left(\frac{\bar{X}^2}{s^2}\right) = 10\ log_{10}\left(\frac{81.3^2}{12.88^2}\right) = 16$$

2.5.3 Standardized variable (the z- score)

A standardized variable, or z-score, is a measure of the deviation from the mean by an individual value in units of the standard deviation:

$$z = \frac{x - \bar{X}}{s} \quad or \quad z = \frac{x - \mu}{\sigma} \qquad (2.12)$$

The above equation indicates that the z-score is a measure of how many standard deviation a variable value is above or below the mean value.

Example 2.13: An instructor who has been teaching statistics for twenty years has observed that the average grade of students is 88% and the standard deviation is 3%. After teaching the course for two classes, one in the fall semester of 2008 and one in the spring semester of 2009, the instructor found that the average grades were as follow:

Term	Mean Grade
Fall 2008	82%
Spring 2009	91%

How do these two semesters compare to the instructor's average over the period of twenty years?

Solution:

The standardized variable (z- score) is calculated for each semester as follows:

Term	Mean Grade	z-Score
Fall 2008	82%	$z_{82} = (82\text{-}88)/3 = \text{-}2$
Spring 2009	91%	$z_{91} = (91\text{-}88)/3 = 1$

From the above scores, you can conclude that the class's grade in the Fall of 2008 being 82% was 2 standard deviations below the teacher's mean grade, while the class's grade in the Spring of 2009 being 91% was 1 standard deviations above the teacher mean grade.

Example 2.14: The mean of a typical commute time of people living in Union City near Atlanta Georgia travelling to the CNN Center in downtown Atlanta is 40 minutes, with a standard deviation of 10 minutes. You asked four CNN employees who live in Union City about their commute time to the CNN Center, and you get the following answers: 38 minutes, 52 minutes, 58 minutes, and 40 minutes. Find the z-score that corresponds to each commute time. Interpret the difference in z-scores?

Solution:

The z-score that corresponds to each commute time can be calculated from the following equation:

$$z = \frac{t - \mu_t}{\sigma_t}$$

Where t is the actual commute time, μ_t is the mean of commute time, and σ_t is the standard deviation of commute time.

At t = 38 minutes, $z = \frac{38-40}{10} = -0.2$; at t = 52 minutes, $z = \frac{52-40}{10} = 1.2$; at t = 58 minutes,

$z = \frac{58-40}{10} = 1.8$; and at t = 40 minutes, $z = \frac{40-40}{10} = 0$

From the z-scores, you can conclude that a commute time of 38 minutes is 0.2 standard deviations below the mean; a commute time of 52 minutes is 1.2 standard deviations above the mean; a commute time of 58 minutes is 1.8 standard deviations above the mean; and a commute time of 40 minutes is zero standard deviation from the mean or equal to the mean.

Working Problem 2.18:

The average scoring points per game (PTG) up to week 10 in the 2010 NFL football season was 22 points and the standard deviation was 4 points. Using the z-score, compare the following 3 teams and determine which team had a relatively better scoring season:

San Francisco 16 PTG, New England 29 PTG, Pittsburgh 24 PTG

Answer:

San Francisco: z = (16-22)/4 = -1.5

New England: *Do it yourself*

Pittsburgh: *Do it yourself*

Working Problem 2.19:

The annual salaries of engineers in the U.S. automobile industry are normally distributed with a mean of $100,000 and a standard deviation of $10,000. What is the z-score for the income x of an auto-engineer who earns $85,000 annually? And for an auto-engineer who earns $105,000 annually?

Answer:

For x = $85,000, z = (x-m)/s = (85,000 – 100,000)/10,000 = -1.5

For x = $105,000, *Do it yourself*

The z of -1.5 indicates that an annual salary of $85,000 is one and half standard deviation below the mean

Working Problem 2.20:

The annual salaries of U.S. state governors are normally distributed with a mean of $135,450 and a standard deviation of $36,530. If in 2007, the Arkansas governor made $85,000 annual salary, and the California governor made $206,000. Compare the annual salaries of these two governors using the z-score.

Arnold Schwarzenegger   Mike Beebe
(California)   (Arkansas)

Answer:

For Arkansas governor: $x = \$85,000$, Do it yourself

For California governor: $x = \$206,000$, $z = (x-m)/s = (206,000 - 135,450)/36,530 = 1.931$

The z of 1.931 indicates that the annual salary of the California governor of $206,000 was 1.931 standard deviation above the governor's mean salary.

2.6 The Use of software programs for performing descriptive statistics

Software programs available for performing statistical analysis are numerous. In this book, we use Microsoft Excel® Data Analysis. You may also use Excel®-supporting programs such as Mega-Stat®. Students may also use other software programs as most of these programs produce standard analysis outputs. Students should keep in mind that this textbook does not teach Excel®, only the use of data analysis tools in Excel®. In other words, it is assumed that students have basic computer and Excel® skills.

Example 2.15: The cost of getting your education can be very significant and it is likely to increase every year. In most states, this increase ranges from 5% to 15% annually. Therefore, many students and parents decide on schools that are cost efficient or the ones that offer good financial aid to students. The data in Table 2.4 represents a survey of some universities using the following attributes: in-state tuition, out-state tuition, total cost- tuition plus room and living, and financial aid- the average financial aid package available to students.

    (a) Using numerical descriptive statistics determine the mean, the mode, and the median of in-state tuition and out-state tuition.

    (b) Using numerical descriptive statistics, determine the mean, the mode, and the median of student total cost of education and financial aid.

Table 2.4 Data on education costs in different U.S. state colleges (http://www.ordoludus.com/costs.php, 2006)

School	In-State Tuition	Out-of-State Tuition	Total Cost ($)	Financial Aid ($)
Georgia Institute of Technology	$4,648	$18,990	$25,792	$8,222
University of Tennessee	$5,290	$16,060	$21,270	$6,954
University of Mississippi	$4,320	$9,744	$14,442	$7,532
University of Kentucky	$5,812	$12,798	$18,027	$7,861
Louisiana State University	$4,515	$12,815	$19,145	$8,006
University of Florida	$3,094	$16,579	$22,839	$10,566
University of Virginia	$7,133	$23,877	$30,266	$13,449
University of South Carolina	$7,314	$18,956	$25,039	$9,501
University of North Carolina	$4,515	$18,313	$24,903	$9,687
University of Georgia	$4,628	$16,848	$23,224	$7,320
University of Alabama	$4,864	$13,516	$18,540	$7,980
University of California (UCLA)	$6,504	$24,324	$36,252	$13,462
North Dakota State University	$5,264	$12,545	$17,675	$5,487
Florida State University	$3,208	$16,340	$23,118	$8,269

In this example, we will use Excel[®] 'Data Analysis' to perform descriptive statistics. In most Excel[®] packages, Data Analysis has to be added as it is not one of the default menus. To add Data Analysis in Excel[®] 2010, refer to Appendix 2.A at the end of this chapter. For newer versions of Microsoft[®] Office, please check the help menu associated with these versions.

Using Excel[®] to perform statistical analysis involves few systematic steps that you will become familiar with throughout this book.

Using the file in which the data in question is presented we take the following steps:

Step 1: Click on Data (Figure 2.3)

Step 2: Click on Data Analysis (Figure 2.3)

Steps 3 and 4: Select 'Descriptive Statistics' and Click 'OK' (Figure 2.4). This will display the 'Descriptive Statistics' Menu shown in Figure 2.5.

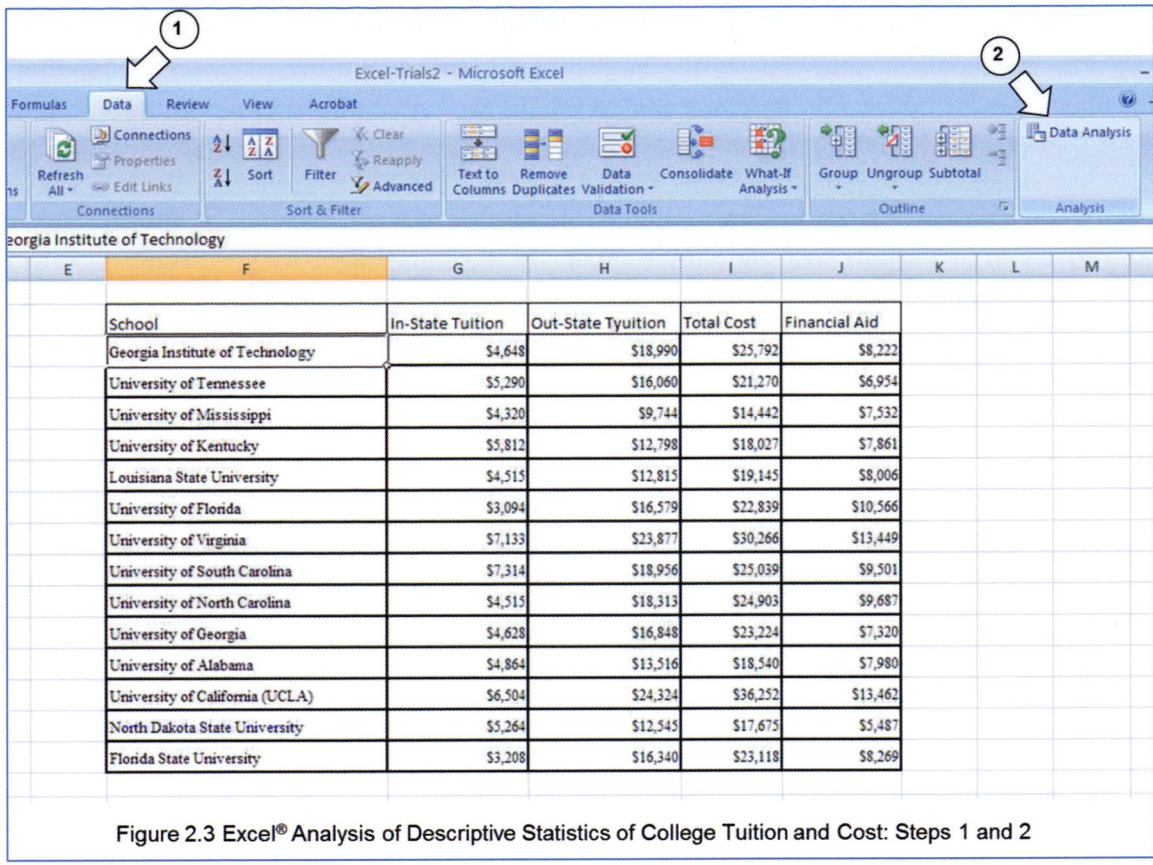

Figure 2.3 Excel® Analysis of Descriptive Statistics of College Tuition and Cost: Steps 1 and 2

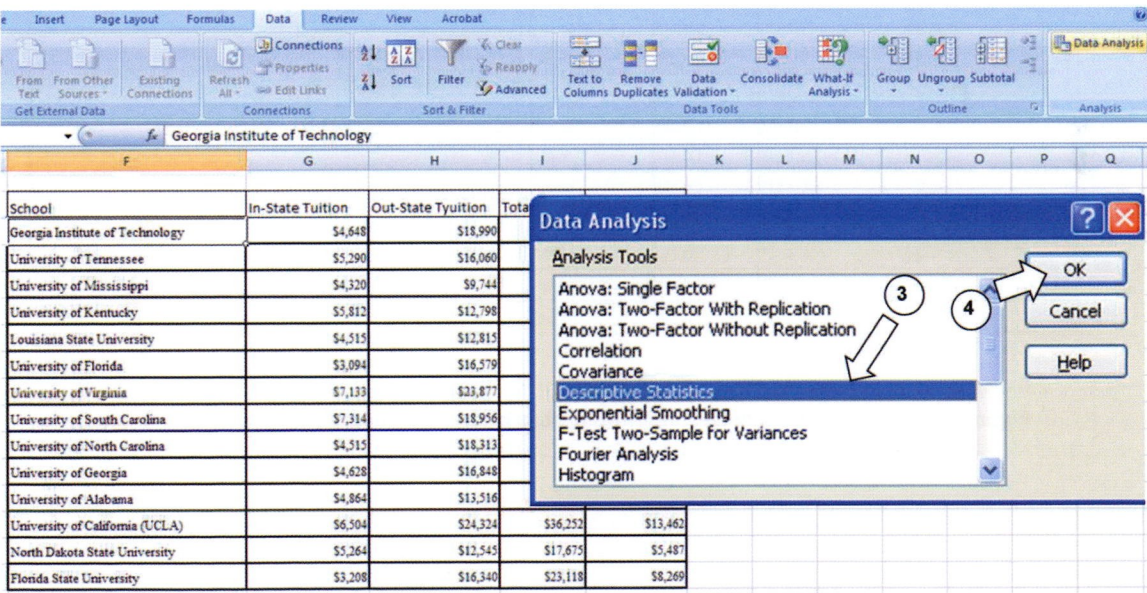

Figure 2.4 Excel® Analysis of Descriptive Statistics of College Tuition and Cost: Steps 3 and 4

Step 5: Select the Input Range, which is the column of data to be analyzed. As shown in Figure 2.5, the input range is the data of In-State Tuition, or cells G2:G16. Since you have a label in

Cell G2, Check 'label in first raw' box. Check 'Summary Statistics'. You may also check '*k*th largest' and *k*th smallest' and specify the largest and smallest number of observations that you would like to set as thresholds for your analysis. This will give you the maximum value of the smallest four observations, and the minimum value of the largest 4 observations.

Step 6: Click 'OK' to obtain the final output, which will appear in a different Excel® Sheet (see Figure 2.6). You can also make the output appear in the same sheet by specifying a cell in the output range window.

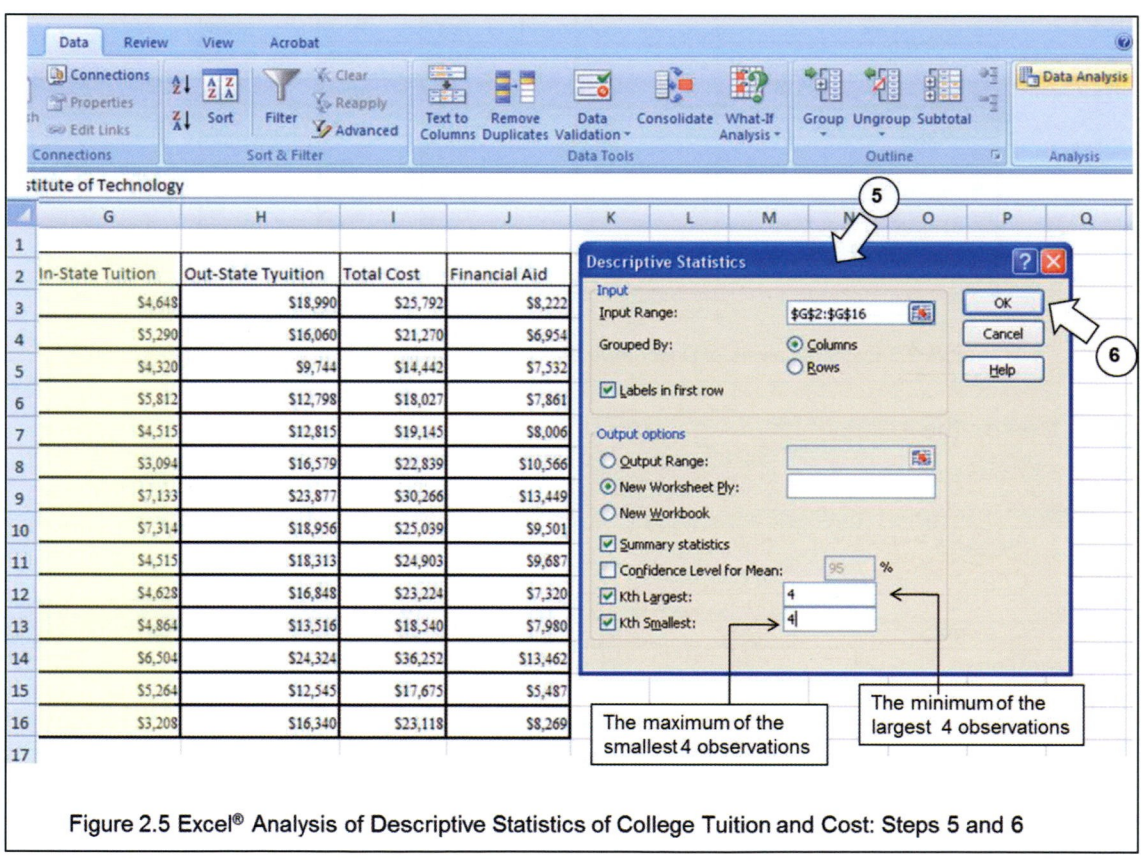

Figure 2.5 Excel® Analysis of Descriptive Statistics of College Tuition and Cost: Steps 5 and 6

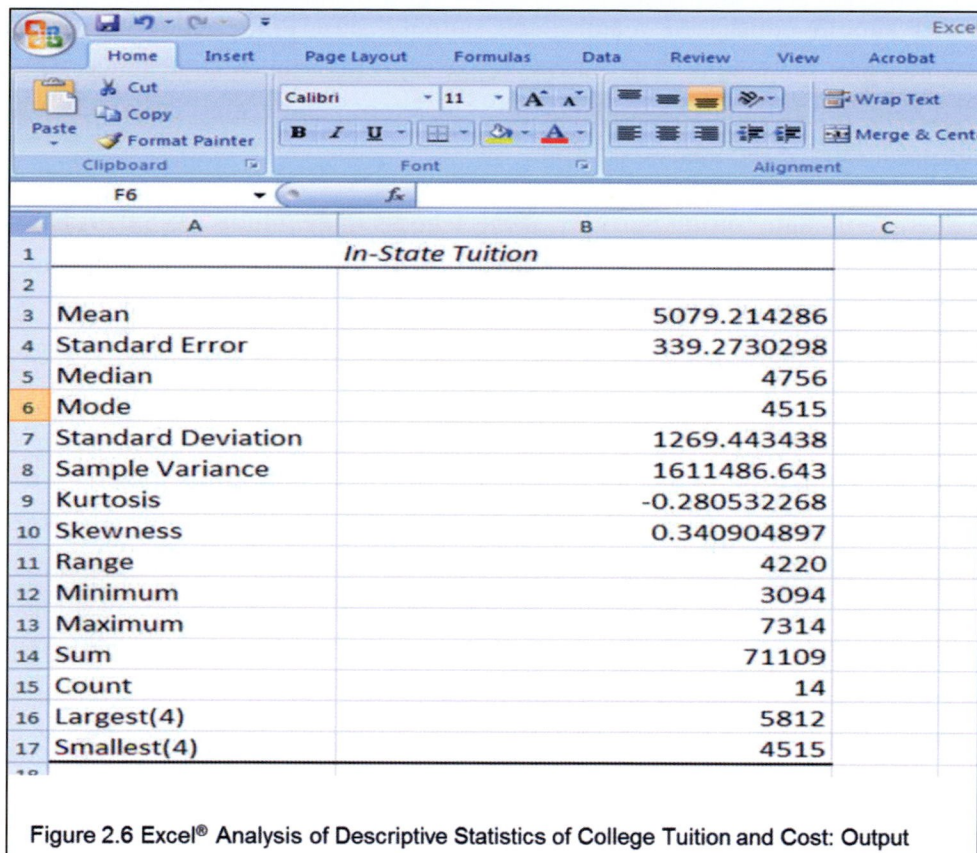

Figure 2.6 Excel® Analysis of Descriptive Statistics of College Tuition and Cost: Output

The output of the above analysis is shown in Table 2.5 for all the variables in the data set of Table 2.4 obtained by following the same steps as described above and changing the input range in Excel® 'Descriptive Analysis' to analyze the variable in question.

Table 2.5 Outputs of descriptive statistics for tuition, cost, and financial aid

Statistic	In-State Tuition ($)	Out-State Tuition ($)	Total Cost ($)	Financial Aid ($)
Mean	5079	16550	22895	8878
Median	4756	16460	22979	8114
Mode	4515	None	None	None
Standard Deviation	1269.44	4196.51	5602.14	2297.84
Sample Variance	1611486.64	17610692.25	31383983.67	5280083.14
Range	4220	14580	21810	7975
Minimum	3094	9744	14442	5487
Maximum	7314	24324	36252	13462
Count	14	14	14	14
Largest(4)	5812	18956	25039	9687
Smallest(4)	4515	12815	18540	7532

The true effort should consist of reading the outputs, describing what we understand, and attempting to interpret the results. The following points reflect these key aspects of analysis and they are listed here as guidelines to students since different people may have different reads and different interpretations of the analysis output.

- The average in-state tuition per year of the schools under study is $5,079. However, some schools can be as low as $3,094 (University of Florida) and some can be as high as $7,314 (University of South Carolina). The median of in-state tuition is $4,756. The mode of in-state tuition is $4,515; that is what most schools in this set charge for in-state tuition.

- The average out-of-state tuition of the schools under study is $16,550. However, some schools can be as low as $9,744 (University of Mississippi) and some can be as high as $24,324 (University of California). The median of out-state tuition is $16,460. The mode of out-state tuition is not well-defined as there may be more than one mode involved.

- The average total cost of the schools under study is $22,895. However, some schools can be as low as $14,442 (University of Mississippi) and some can be as high as $36,252 (University of California). The median of total cost is $22,979. The mode of total cost is not well-defined as there may be more than one mode involved.

- The average financial aid of the schools under study is $8,878. However, some schools can be as low as $5,487 (North Dakota State University) and some can be as high as $13,462 (University of California). The median of financial aid is $8,114. The mode of financial aid is not well-defined as there may be more than one mode involved.

- You may also set thresholds for a certain variable of interest, say total cost, by specifying the maximum of the smallest four universities, and the minimum of the largest four universities. For total cost, the maximum of the smallest four universities is $18,540 (University of Alabama), and the minimum of the largest four universities is $25,039 (University of South Carolina).

As you can see from the above points, the guidelines to describe and interpret analysis outputs will depend on the key questions that one wishes to address in the analysis application. Examples of these questions are as follows:

Q1: *Which school will be associated with the lowest total cost of education?*

University of Mississippi

Q2: *Which school will be associated with the largest financial aid for education?*

University of California

Q3: *Which school(s) will have the lowest total cost and the highest financial aid?*

This question may not be easy to answer if there is a positive association between total cost and financial aid (i.e. the higher the cost, the higher the financial aid). Unfortunately, this is normally the case for most schools as shown in Figure 2.7. In this case, you may have to make a compromising choice such as University of Kentucky, University of Mississippi, and University of Alabama.

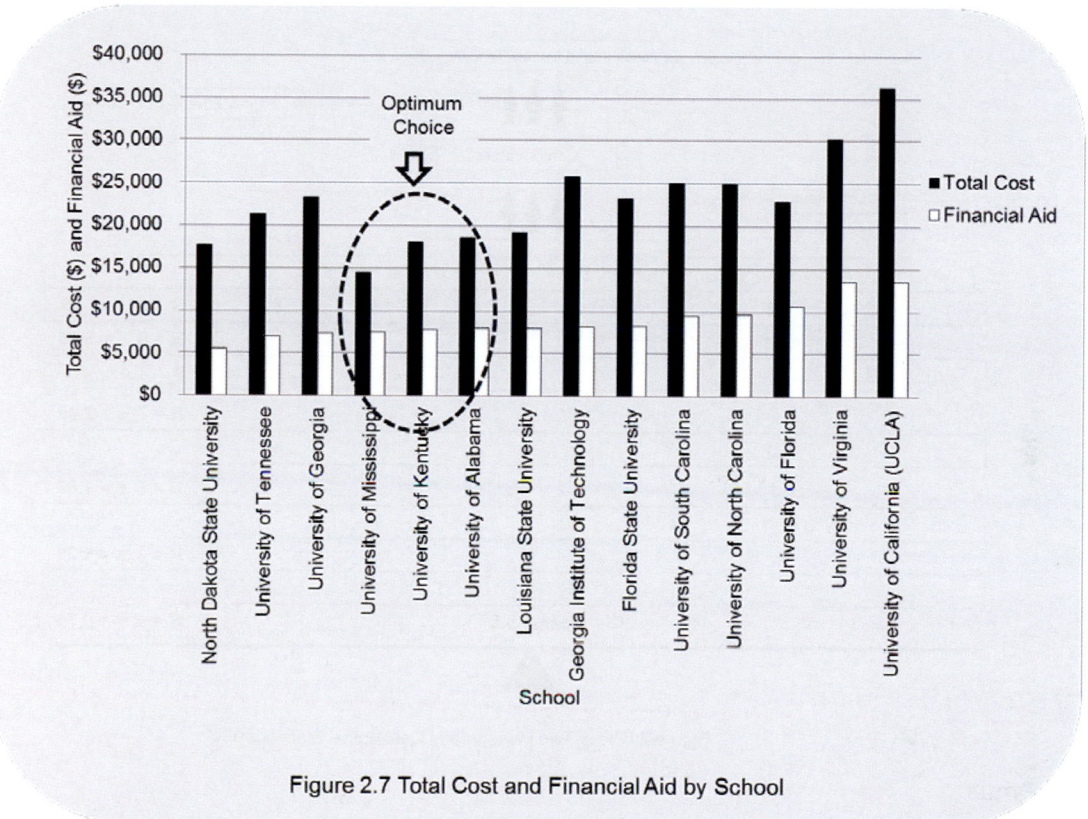

Figure 2.7 Total Cost and Financial Aid by School

2.7 Why two measures of descriptive statistics?

In the above sections, we introduced two types of descriptive statistics: measures of central tendency, and measures of dispersion or variability. The main reason we need both measures of descriptive statistics is to allow full description of a data set. For example, if we only rely on the mean value to describe a set of data, the following different data sets will all yield the same mean value of 5.5 despite the substantial difference between them particularly in relation to variability:

(a) 1,2,3,4,5,6,7,8,9,10
(b) 2,3,4,5,6,7,8,9
(c) 3,4,5,6,7,8
(d) 4,5,6,7
(e) 5,6

The values of the range of the above data sets are: (a) 9, (b) 7, (c) 5, (d) 3, and (e) 1, and the values of the standard deviation are: (a) 3.03, (b) 2.45, (c) 1.87, (d) 1.29, and (e) 0.71. These differences are illustrated in Figure 2.8.

In light of this simple example, it follows that relying on the mean value alone may mask a great deal of information. More seriously, it may result in an unfair comparison between data sets.

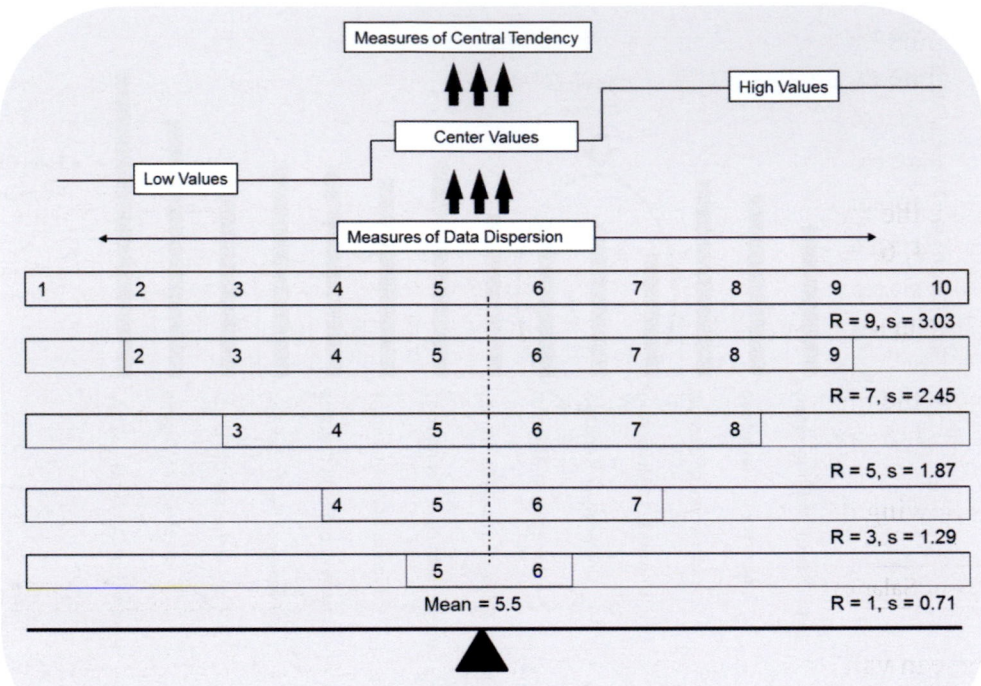

Figure 2.8 Why Two Measures of Descriptive Statistics?

Working Problem 2.21:

The following data sets represents students grades in three different classes taking the same course. Using descriptive statistics, calculate mean, median, standard deviation, variance, and range for each data set and discuss the needs for both measures of central tendency and measures of variability

Class A	Class B	Class C
60	65	70
65	70	75
70	75	80
75	80	85
80	85	90
85	90	
90	95	
95		
100		

Answer:

	Class A	Class B	Class C
Mean	80	80	80
Median	80	80	80
Standard Deviation	13.69306	10.80123	7.905694
Sample Variance	187.5	116.6667	62.5
Kurtosis	-1.2	-1.2	-1.2
Skewness	0	0	0
Range	40	30	20
Minimum	60	65	70
Maximum	100	95	90

2.8 Review Exercises

P2.1: The following data represents the ages (years) of a sample of U.S. States Governors in 2008:

50	58	55	43	47	37	62	60	58	45
68	57	55	58	46	53	56	48	42	45

- Determine the mean, mode, and median of U.S. states governor's age
- Determine the range, standard deviation, and variance of U.S. states governor's age

Answer: Mean = 52.15, median = 54, mode = 58, standard deviation = 7.86, range = 31

P2.2: Compute the mean, and the range of the following sample values:
6, 3, 5, 7, 6, 9, 4, 6, 5, 10.

P2.3: For the data set 6, 3, 5, 7, 6, 9, 4, 6, 5, 10, show that $\sum_1^{10}(x_i - \bar{X}) = 0$

P2.4: Compute the median and the mode of the following sample values:
6, 3, 5, 7, 6, 9, 4, 6, 5, 10.

P2.5: The following data represents a sample of annual salaries of professors in a college:

Annual Professor Salaries ($)	45000	55000	65000	60000	48000	45000	55000	39000	46000	55000

a. The mean value of annual salary is

$51,300 --------- $48,210 -------- $60,111 -------- $51,289 --------

b. The range value of annual salary is

$18,100 --------- $26,900 --------- $26,000 --------- $19,000 ---------

c. The mode of annual salary is

$48,000 --------- $46,000 --------- $55,000 --------- $65,000 ---------

d. The median of annual salary is

$51,500 --------- $51,210 --------- $51,600 --------- $58,300 ---------

P2.6: The following data represents a sample of number of people per household:

2	4	5	6	2	1	2	3	1	2
2	4	1	5	1	2	4	4	3	2
2	4	2	2	4	3	3	2	8	4
1	2	2	5	3	4	3	2	5	3

89

a. The mean value of household number is

2 -------   3 -------   5 -------   4.5 -------

b. The range value of household number is

5 -------   3 -------   7 -------   4 -------

c. The mode of household number is

5 -------   3 -------   2 -------   4 -------

d. The median of household number is

5 -------   3 -------   7 -------   4 -------

P2.7: The following data represents a sample of exam scores:

Exam Scores (%)	65	55	80	72	70	85	55	54	65	75	80	72	89

a. The mean value of exam score is

70.54------   71.34 ------   76.65 ------   70.23 ------

b. The range value of exam score is

45 ------   30 ------   35 ------   40 ------

c. The mode of exam score is

55 ------   62 ------   65 ------   80 ------

d. The median of exam score is

58 ------   72 ------   70 ------   80 ------

P2.8: For the data set 6, 3, 5, 7, 6, 9, 4, 6, 5, 10 compute $\sum_1^{10}(x_i - \bar{X})^2$

P2.9: For the data set 6, 3, 5, 7, 6, 9, 4, 6, 5, 10,

The standard deviation is:
2.1435 ------- 2.1318 ------- 2.1545 ------- 2.3216 -------

P2.10: For the data set 6, 3, 5, 7, 6, 9, 4, 6, 5, 10,

The variance is:

4.5946 ------- 4.4619 ------- 5.3898 ------- 4.5445 -------

P2.11: For the data set 6, 3, 5, 7, 6, 9, 4, 6, 5, 10 show how the variance and standard deviation are computed from $\sum_1^{10}(x_i - \bar{X})^2$
Answer: Variance = 4.5444, Standard deviation = 2.1318

P2.12: The following data represents a sample of annual salaries of professors in a college:

Annual Salary ($)	45000	55000	65000	60000	48000	45000	55000	39000	46000	55000

(a) The standard deviation of annual salary is

$7986.795 ------- $7988.215 ------- $7886.333 ------- $7986.210 -------

(b) The variance value of annual salary is

$62788888.89 ------- $61788888.89 -------- $63788888.89 ------- $60788888.89 -------

P2.13: The following data represents a sample of number of people per household:

2	4	5	6	2	1	2	3	1	2
2	4	1	5	1	2	4	4	3	2
2	4	2	2	4	3	3	2	8	4
1	2	2	5	3	4	3	2	5	3

(a) The standard deviation value of household number is

1.567 ------ 1.845 ------ 1.536 ------ 1.789 ------

(b) The variance value of household number is

2.567 ------ 2.645 ------ 2.456 ------ 2.359 ------

P2.14: The following data represents a sample of exam scores (%):

65	55	80	72	70	85	55
54	65	75	80	72	89	

(a) The standard deviation value of exam scores is

11.4427 ------ 11.3420 ------- 12.2341 ------- 10.7888 -------

(b) The variance value of exam scores is

149.67 ------- 128.641 ------- 130.94 ------ 116.39 -------

91

P2.15: The table below shows wages of a sample of workers of a textile company.
Wages of factory workers

Factory worker ID	Wage ($)/hr	Gender	Factory worker ID	Wage ($)/hr	Gender
88	4.4	F	565	6.6	F
109	23.5	M	364	19	M
504	19	F	17	21.6	M
77	21.1	M	156	19	M
415	31.8	M	26	16.2	F
388	12.4	F	65	29	M
179	20.2	M	88	18.2	M
14	19	F			

(a) Compute the mean, the median, and the mode of wages
(b) Compute the minimum, maximum, range, standard deviation, and variance of wages.
(c) Compute the mean, the median, and the mode of wages of male and those of female
(d) Compute the minimum, maximum, range, standard deviation, and variance of wages of male and those of female
(e) Do you see a difference between male and female wages? Why?

Answer: Mean = 18.733, mode = 19, median = 19, range = 27.4, std. dev. = 7.144
For male and female, do it yourself

P2.16: For the data shown in the table below of U.S. States Governors annual salaries in 2007.

(a) Compute the mean, the median, and the mode of salaries.
(b) Compute the minimum, maximum, range, standard deviation, and variance of salaries.
(c) Explain why there is a wide range of governor salary in the U.S.

Governors salaries (2007) (http://www.stateline.org/live/details/story)

State	Governor Salary ($)	State	Governor Salary ($)
Michigan	177,000	Maine	70,000
Pennsylvania	164,396	Texas	115,345
Georgia	135,281	Alabama	112,895
Mississippi	122,160	Alaska	125,000
California	206,500	North Carolina	130,629
Florida	132,932	Arkansas	85,000
New York	179,000	Iowa	130,000
South Carolina	106,078	New Jersey	175,000

P2.17: A car salesman was working for a car dealer for ten years. A year ago he was told that his monthly sales performance averaged $30,000 (about 2 cars per month) with a standard deviation of $5000. As a result, he decided to move to a new car dealership where he thought he could do better. In the first month of this year, he made $50,000 in sales. Using the standardized variable (z-score), do you believe he should continue in this business or try another car dealership?

P2.18: Using Excel® Software Program, calculate the mean, mode, median, range, standard deviation, and variance of the following data set of ages of mine workers:

Ages of mine workers

Age (years)	Age (years)	Age (years)	Age (years)	Age (years)
29.7	39.7	31.1	32.6	36.9
31.3	23.4	30.6	29.2	34.1
39.4	34.7	34.6	23.4	30.5
23.2	30.3	34.7	26.1	32.7
24.9	33.3	20.5	37	35.1
35.2	32.8	23	22.1	30.2
22.6	32.8	29.3	11.7	32.7
38.2	19.3	33.8	29.4	31.1
35.4	31	41.7	33.3	38.3
30.8	35.4	33.5	38.5	26.8
28.4	30.3	32.5	28.9	28.2
42.9	27.5	27	24.4	36.4
16.8	27.1	30.5	25.9	30
33.6	37	34.4	26.6	26.9
29	25.6	23.3	37.9	22.4
25.9	32.6	30.7	23.1	30.7
29.2	17.6	37.1	28.6	29.3
22.2	32.4	16.9	30.6	24
30.1	21.6	26.6	30.2	27.7
36.4	32	30.4	33.2	34.4

P2.19: Using Excel® Software Program, calculate the mean, mode, median, range, standard deviation, and variance of the following data set of property taxes:

				Property Taxes					
$5,228	$5,896	$5,157	$6,493	$5,676	$5,926	$4,662	$7,584	$4,715	$6,538
$6,134	$5,311	$6,300	$5,346	$6,776	$6,050	$2,704	$6,694	$7,011	$7,062
$5,666	$5,693	$6,318	$5,251	$4,355	$4,524	$7,687	$6,852	$5,376	$4,656
$8,275	$3,550	$6,600	$6,355	$3,483	$2,638	$3,780	$5,939	$6,848	$7,345
$7,249	$5,243	$5,983	$4,583	$7,667	$5,777	$5,281	$7,454	$9,097	$8,229
$7,007	$7,532	$5,546	$5,567	$6,215	$6,392	$4,088	$5,738	$3,522	$8,060
$5,101	$6,046	$5,201	$6,550	$4,252	$4,289	$5,943	$5,415	$6,381	$5,667
$3,851	$6,179	$8,620	$5,709	$7,054	$8,725	$6,672	$2,982	$4,015	$6,950
$8,685	$7,320	$5,162	$3,064	$6,239	$5,612	$8,074	$6,266	$5,720	$5,370
$7,286	$3,480	$7,061	$5,064	$5,637	$4,868	$7,187	$4,560	$7,022	$4,983

Answer: Mean = 5889.46, median = 5911, range = 6459, std. deviation = 1405.22

P2.20: Using Excel® Software Program, calculate the mean, mode, median, range, standard deviation, and variance of the following data set of number of accidents on the job of welding factory per year:

Accidents/year									
8	6	6	8	7	7	5	5	6	5
6	5	7	7	6	6	7	8	6	6
6	7	7	7	5	5	7	7	7	5
6	7	7	7	7	5	8	5	6	9
6	7	4	7	7	6	7	5	6	6
7	5	6	7	6	6	6	6	6	6
7	5	5	7	6	5	5	7	6	5
8	7	6	6	7	6	7	6	4	7
5	6	5	6	6	4	6	6	7	5
5	5	5	7	5	6	6	7	5	6

P2.21: The U.S. Energy Information Administration collects data on residential energy consumption and expenditures. Results are published in the document *Residential Energy Consumption Survey: Consumption and Expenditures*. The following table gives one year's energy consumptions for a sample of 30 households in the South. Data are in millions of BTUs. Calculate the mean, mode, median, range, standard deviation, and variance. Interpret the results.

Residential energy consumption

n	BTU(millions)	n	BTU(millions)	n	BTU(millions)	n	BTU(millions)
1	102	16	129	9	112	24	70
2	151	17	135	10	111	25	119
3	111	18	145	11	80	26	38
4	78	19	87	12	90	27	106
5	54	20	50	13	85	28	56
6	129	21	107	14	108	29	50
7	130	22	55	15	113	30	133
8	45	23	88				

Answer: Mean = 95.567, median = 104, mode = 111, range = 113, std. dev. = 32.3

P2.22: The following data represents residential energy consumption and expenditures in two different cities in the U.S.A. in millions of BTUs. Calculate the mean, mode, median, range, standard deviation, and variance for each city. Compare the two cities energy consumption.

Residential energy consumption of two cities

n	BTU(millions)-City A	n	BTU(millions)-City B
1	102	1	76
2	151	2	45
3	111	3	111
4	78	4	55
5	54	5	54
6	129	6	58
7	130	7	70
8	45	8	45
9	112	9	58
10	111	10	80
11	102	11	75
12	111	12	66
13	120	13	54
14	108	14	69
15	113	15	71
16	129	16	80
17	135	17	59
18	145	18	83
19	87	19	87
20	50	20	50

P2.23: From a random sample taken by the ESPN, the age of the players on the major league baseball teams in 2005 was as follows.

Age of the players on the major league baseball teams

27.6	28.9	28.9	30.9	30.3	29.1
29.4	29.9	28.7	29.7	31.5	30.8
29.5	28.9	31.9	30.3	29.8	29.6
30.1	32	31.7	31.3	30.7	32
30.4	30.8	30.4	33.7	35	32.8

Calculate the mean, mode, median, range, standard deviation, and variance of age of the players on the major league baseball teams. Interpret the results and determine if you believe this age is suitable for this sport and why?
Answer: Mean = 30.6, median = 30.4, mode = 28.9, range = 7.4, std. dev. = 1.572

P2.24: The following data represents the age of U.S. presidents at the time of inauguration from George Washington to Barack Obama. Calculate the mean, mode, median, range, standard deviation, and variance of U.S. president age. Determine the z-score for Obama's age at inauguration in reference to the overall mean of president's age.

Ages of U.S. presidents at the time of inauguration

President	Age	President	Age	President	Age	President	Age
G. Washington	57	B. Harrison	55	Z. Taylor	64	D. Eisenhower	62
J. Adams	61	G. Cleveland	55	M. Fillmore	50	J. Kennedy	43
T. Jefferson	57	W. McKinley	54	F. Pierce	48	L. Johnson	55
J. Madison	57	T. Roosevelt	42	J. Buchanan	65	R. Nixon	56
J. Monroe	58	W. Taft	51	A. Lincoln	52	G. Ford	61
J. Q. Adams	57	W. Wilson	56	A. Johnson	56	J. Carter	52
A. Jackson	61	W. Harding	55	U. Grant	46	R. Reagan	69
M. Van Buren	54	C. Coolidge	51	R. Hayes	54	G. Bush	64
W. Harrison	68	H. Hoover	54	J. Garfield	49	W. Clinton	46
J. Tyler	51	F. Roosevelt	51	C. Arthur	50	G. W. Bush	54
J. Polk	49	H. Truman	60	G. Cleveland	47	Barack Obama	48

P2.25: A national achievement test is administered annually to 3rd graders. The test has a mean score of 100 and a standard deviation of 15. If Sandra's z-score is 1.20, what was her score on the test? (A) 100 ....   (B) 112 ……...   (C) 118 ………

P2.26: The results of a physics test given to 20 students are as shown below. Calculate the mean and standard deviation of grades. Assuming that the mean and standard deviation of this sample represent good estimates of the student's population calculate the z-score corresponding to each grade.

Grades of 20 students

Student #	Grades	Student #	Grades
1	57	11	70
2	77	12	85
3	75	13	85
4	70	14	58
5	67	15	63
6	85	16	74
7	62	17	64
8	72	18	51
9	78	19	76
10	86	20	65

P2.27: In an attempt to grade on the curve, the physics instructor who obtained the grades below decided to increase the grade average of the class from 71% to 80%, meanwhile reduce the variability or the standard deviation from 10.2 down to 2.75. Using the z-score, show how the instructor can achieve these new values.

Grades of 20 students

Student #	Grades	Student #	Grades	Student #	Grades	Student #	Grades
1	57	6	85	11	70	16	74
2	77	7	62	12	85	17	64
3	75	8	72	13	85	18	51
4	70	9	78	14	58	19	76
5	67	10	86	15	63	20	65

APPENDIX 2.A
Steps to add data analysis to Microsoft Excel® 2010

Step 1: Click on File

Step 2: Click on Excel® Options

Step 3: Go to Adds-In

See Figure 2.A.1

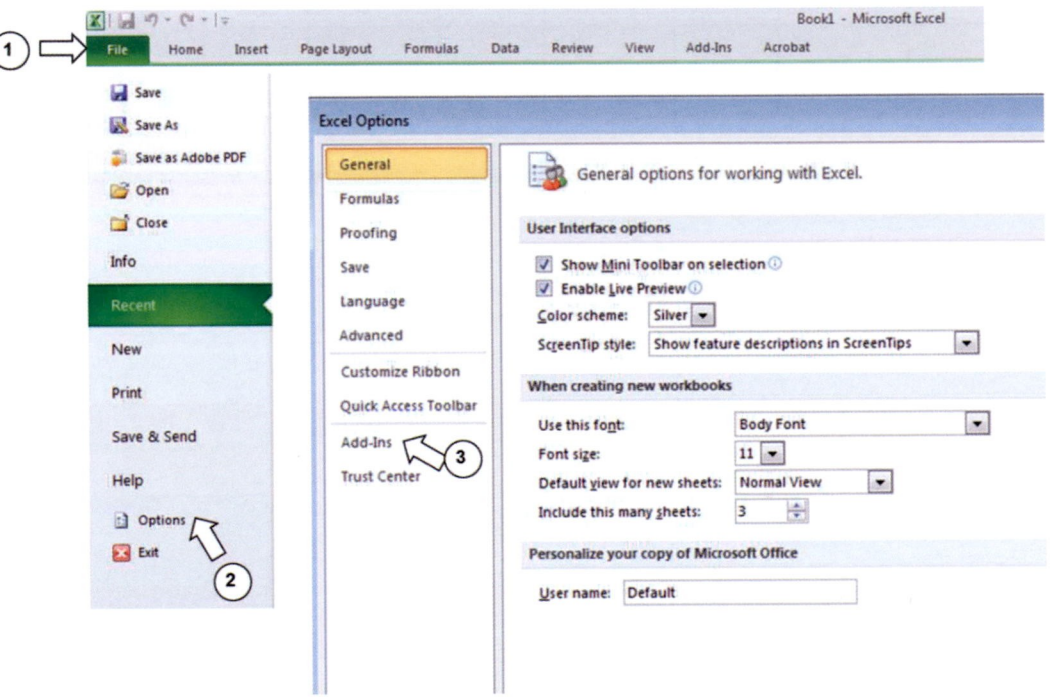

Figure 2.A.1 Data Analysis Add-In-Steps 1, 2, 3
- Go to File ⟶ Options ⟶ Add-Ins

Step 4: Click on Analysis ToolPack

Step 5: Click on Go

See Figure 2.A.2

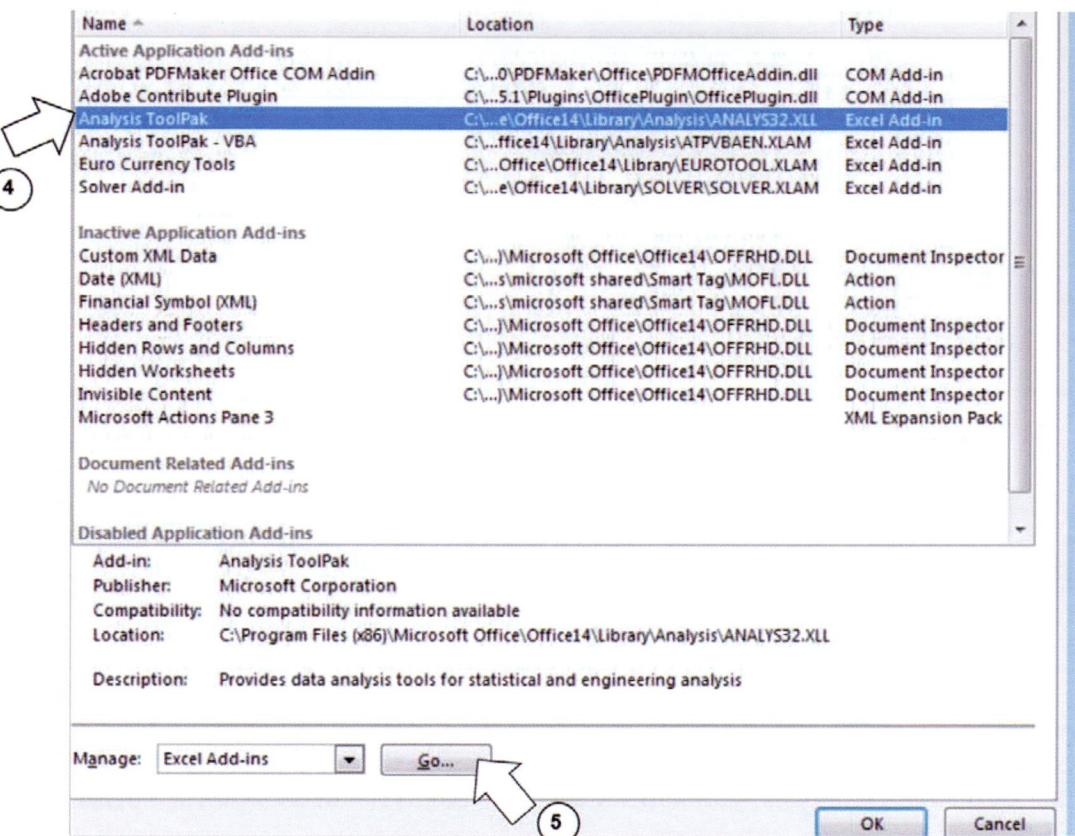

Figure 2.A.2 Data Analysis Add-In-Steps 4 and 5

Step 6: Go to Add-Ins Menu

Step 7: Click OK

This will add Data Analysis to Excel Data Menu

See Figure 2.A.3

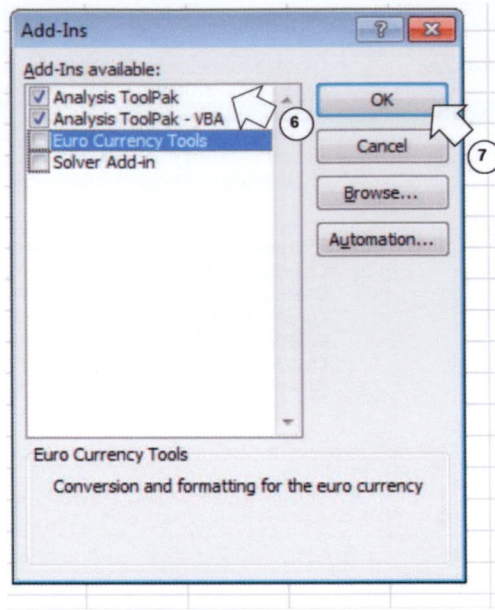

Figure 2.A.3 Data Analysis Add-In-Steps 6 and 7

Step 8: Click on Data, you should see Data Analysis

Step 9: Click on Data Analysis, you will see the Data Analysis menu as shown below

See Figure 2.A.4

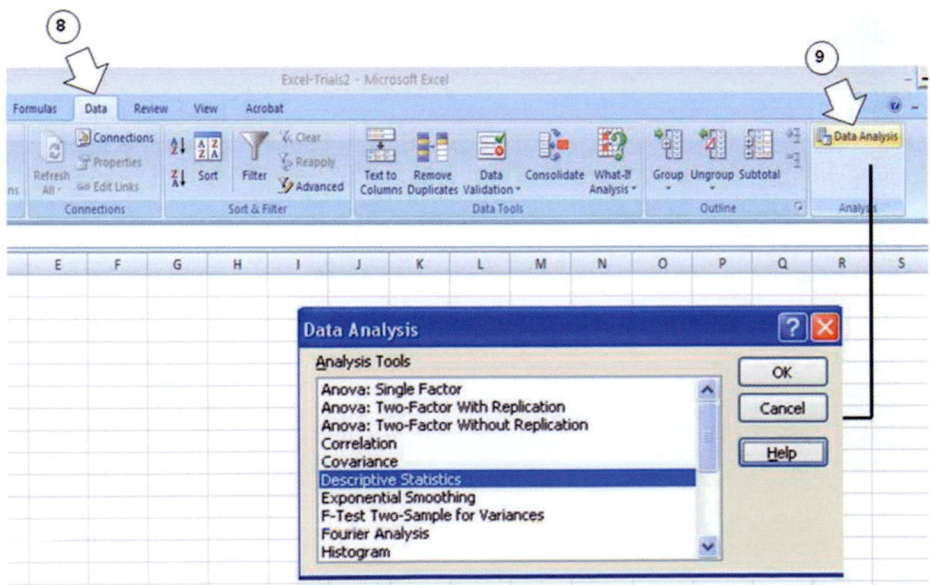

Figure 2.A.4 Data Analysis Add-In-Steps 8 and 9

CHAPTER 3

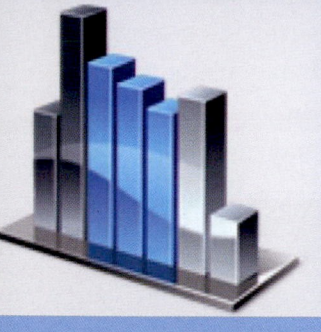

DESCRIPTIVE STATISTICS

Part I: Graphical Description

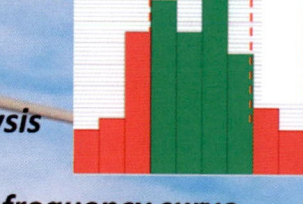

After completing this chapter, students will be able to:

- *Construct a histogram manually and using Excel® Data Analysis*
- *Construct a cumulative frequency curve*
- *Obtain useful information from a histogram or a cumulative frequency curve*
- *Describe the shape of the frequency distribution*
- *Calculate the weighted mean and standard deviation*
- *Learn how to use Chebyshev's theorem*
- *Use the empirical rule*

 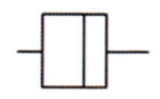

CHAPTER 3

In Chapter 2, we learned how to describe a set of data using numerical measures such as the measures of central tendency (mean, mode, and median) and the measures of dispersion (range, standard deviation, and variance). We also learned about some combined measures such as the coefficient of variation and the z-score. In this chapter, we will learn how to picture data using many graphical methods. As you will see throughout the chapter, there are many methods of graphing data with the common goal being to make the data easier to understand, describe, and explore.

CHAPTER CONTENTS

3.1 Raw data and processed data

In general, raw data is data recorded in a sequence in which they are collected without any effort to identify, organize, sort, manipulate, or analyze it. Any one of these four actions will convert raw data into processed (or more meaningful) data. Examples of raw data are given below.

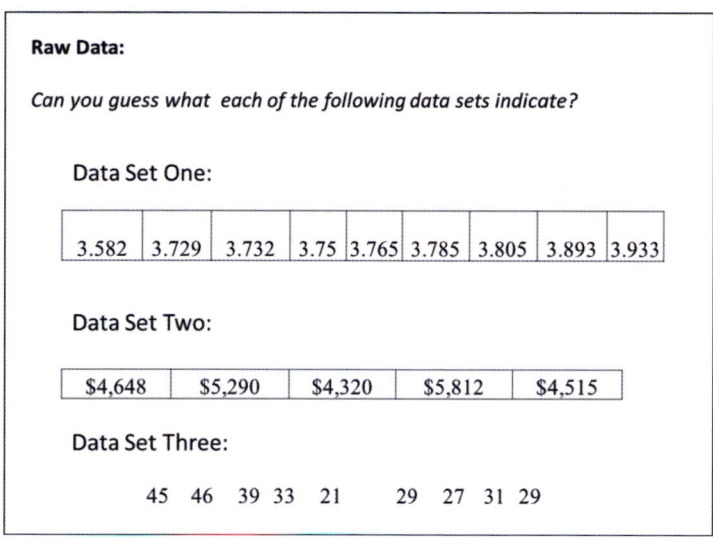

Raw Data:

Can you guess what each of the following data sets indicate?

Data Set One:

3.582	3.729	3.732	3.75	3.765	3.785	3.805	3.893	3.933

Data Set Two:

$4,648	$5,290	$4,320	$5,812	$4,515

Data Set Three:

45 46 39 33 21   29 27 31 29

It will be difficult to obtain any useful information from a set of raw data such as the ones described above. In order to process these data sets (make them useful to use), the first step is to identify the values presented in each data set by labeling them and identifying their units as shown below.

Processed Data:

Data Set One:

State	Massachusetts	Texas	Colorado	California	Minnesota	Washington	New York	Florida	Ohio
Gas Prices ($) in 2008	3.582	3.729	3.732	3.75	3.765	3.785	3.805	3.893	3.933

Data Set Two:

School	Georgia Institute of Technology	University of Tennessee	University of Mississippi	University of Kentucky	Louisiana State University
In-State Tuition (2006)	$4,648	$5,290	$4,320	$5,812	$4,515

103

Data Set Three:

Quarterback	Aaron Rodgers	Drew Brees	Tom Brady	Peyton Manning	Ben Roethlisberger	Eli Manning	Philip Rivers	Tony Romo	Matt Ryan
Number of Touchdowns in 2012 Regular NFL Season	45	46	39	33	21	29	27	31	29

In addition to identifying data by labels and units, the data may be arranged in such a way that will make it easier to obtain useful information. In some situations, we may have to sort the data in some order to reveal the relative magnitudes sorted by some criteria. In other situations, we may have to divide data into categories or classes so that we can compare the values associated with these categories. These manipulation procedures will depend on the nature of the data and the type of analysis used. In Chapter 2, we discussed one way to convert raw data into processed data using numerical descriptive statistics. In this chapter, the focus will be on graphic displays to describe and explore data.

3.2 Bar chart and pie chart

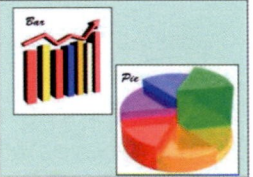

Graphic displays can assist in converting raw data into processed data by exploring the information revealed by the data via a visual aid, which people can understand without the need for a long list of data or mathematical details. Two examples of simple graphic displays are the bar chart and the pie chart.

The bar chart is an *x-y* chart in which the *x*-axis represents values of a quantitative variable or labels of a qualitative variable and the *y*-axis represents the corresponding values depicted by the heights of the bars.

The pie chart is a circle divided into wedge-shaped pieces that represent areas proportional to the frequencies or relative frequencies.

Example 3.1: The data in Table 3.1 illustrates the average points scored per game for eight NFL teams throughout 10 games in the 2010 season. Construct a bar chart to compare the performance of the eight teams. What teams had the highest points per game and what teams had the lowest points per game?

Table 3.1 Average points per game of eight NFL teams throughout 10 games in 2010 season

Team	Average Points/Game	Team	Average Points/Game
Atlanta	25.6	Pittsburgh	23.5
New England	28.9	Philadelphia	28.4
Baltimore	23.3	Green Bay	25.2
New York Jets	23.8	New Orleans	23.5

Solution:

Figure 3.1 shows the bar chart with the x-axis representing the teams' names, and the heights of the bars representing the average score per game for each team. Key information revealed by this bar chart:

- Among the eight teams displayed in the bar chart, the New England Patriots and the Philadelphia Eagles were the two teams that had the highest average points per game after 10 games of the 2010 NFL season.
- Baltimore Ravens and Pittsburgh Steelers had the lowest average points per game.

The bar chart can also be constructed using Excel® spreadsheet as shown in the steps of Figures 3.2 and 3.3. For additional information on how you construct charts on Excel® spreadsheet, students can consult Microsoft help associated with Excel® spreadsheet.

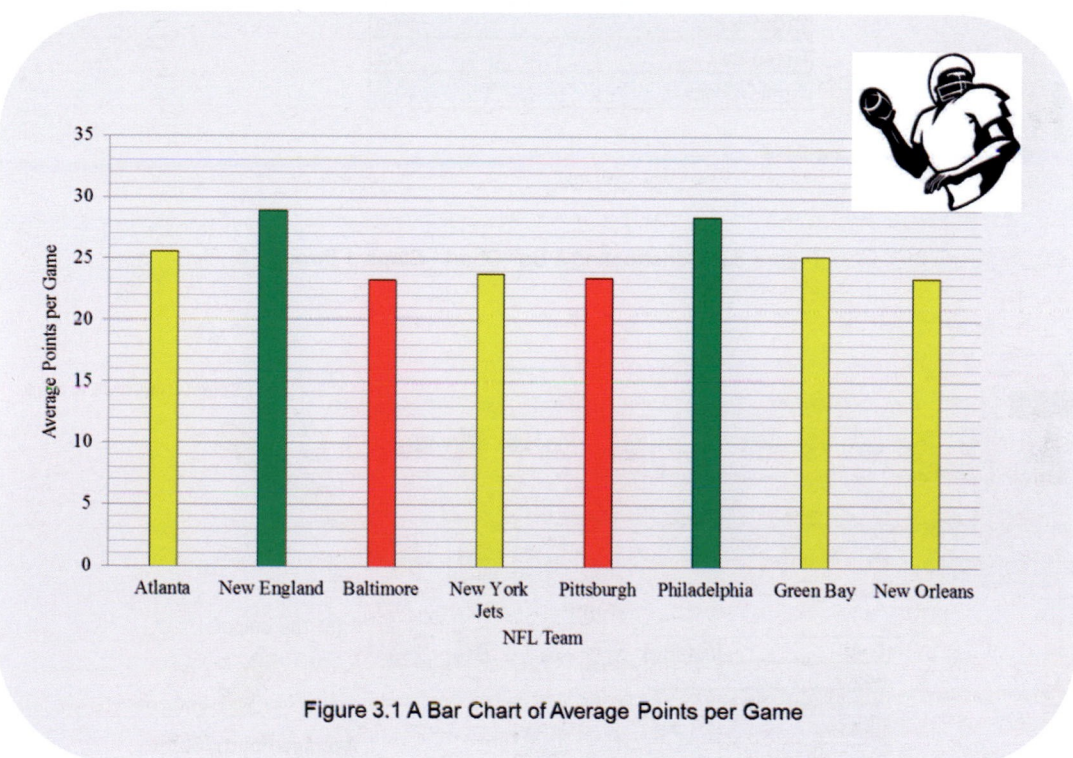

Figure 3.1 A Bar Chart of Average Points per Game

105

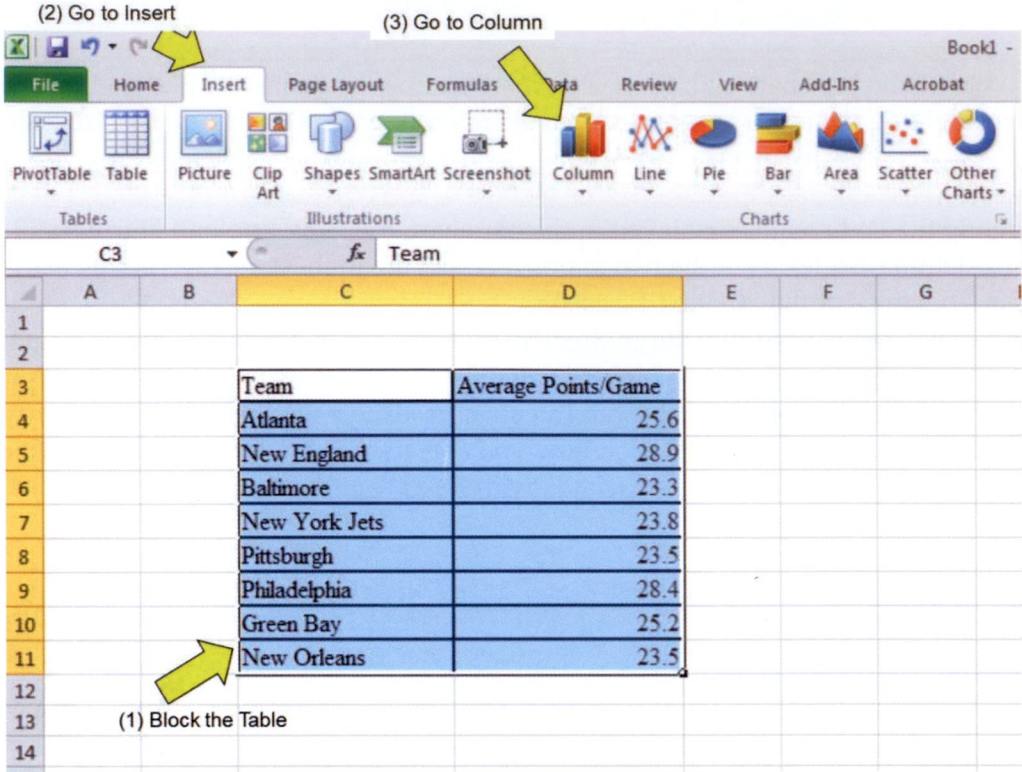

Figure 3.2 Constructing a Bar Chart –Steps 1 through 3

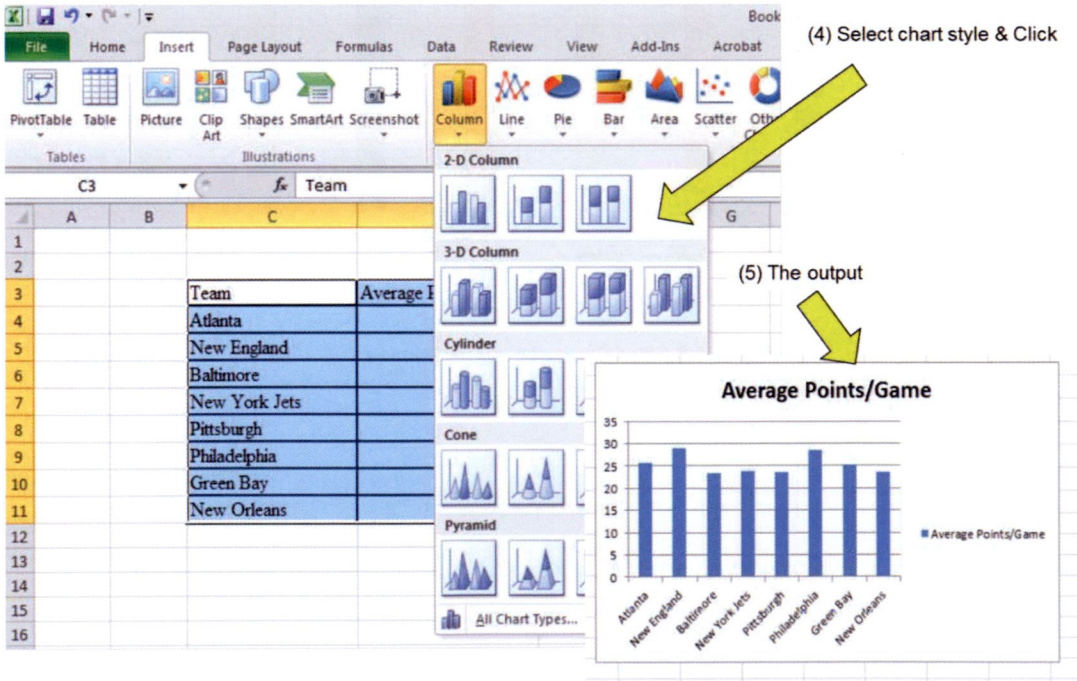

Figure 3.3 Constructing a Bar Chart –Steps 4 and 5

Example 3.2: The data in Table 3.2 illustrates the percentage of cause of death among U.S. residents in the age range of 18 to 24 in the year 2004. Construct a pie chart illustrating the causes of death percentage. What is the related cause of death that most effects this age range of U.S. residents?

Table 3.2 Percent of death incidents and their causes

Cause of death	Percent
Car Accidents	89
Fire arms	2
Poison	4
Other	5

Solution:

As shown in Figure 3.4, this pie chart is represented by a circle divided into wedge-shaped pieces with areas representing the percent of each cause. Key information revealed by this bar chart includes:

- The largest percentage contributing to cause of death in young residents is death by car accident (89%)
- The least percentage contributing to cause of death in young residents is death by fire arm

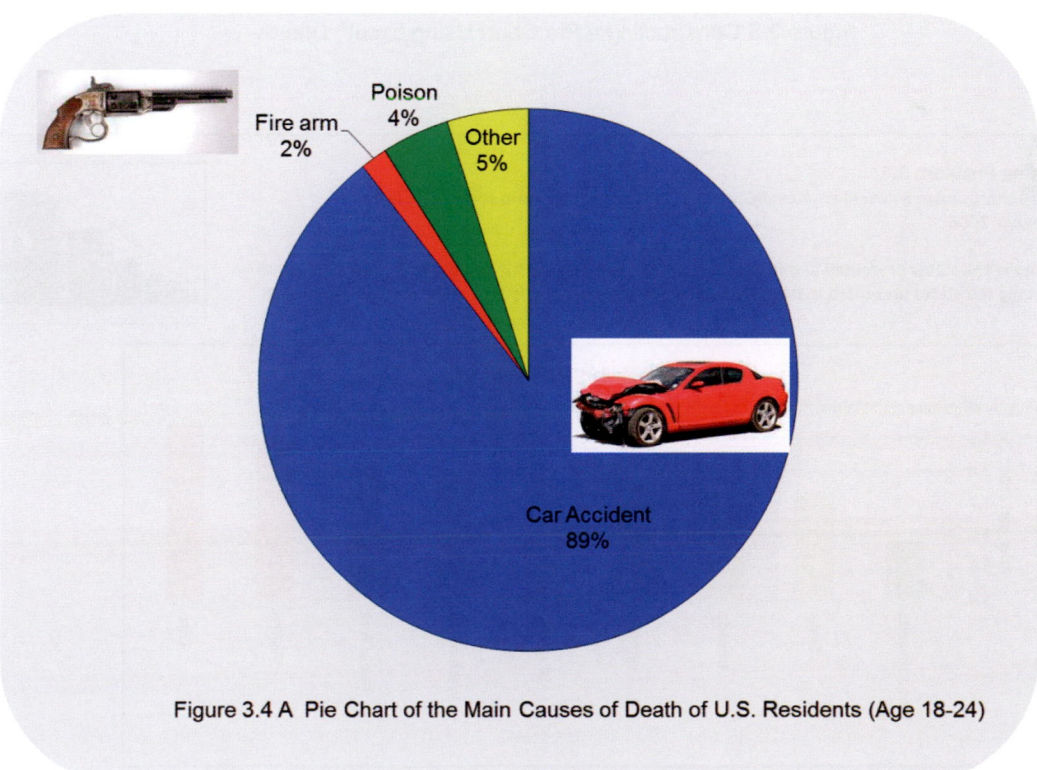

Figure 3.4 A Pie Chart of the Main Causes of Death of U.S. Residents (Age 18-24)

107

The pie chart can also be constructed using Excel® spreadsheet as shown in the steps of Figure 3.5.

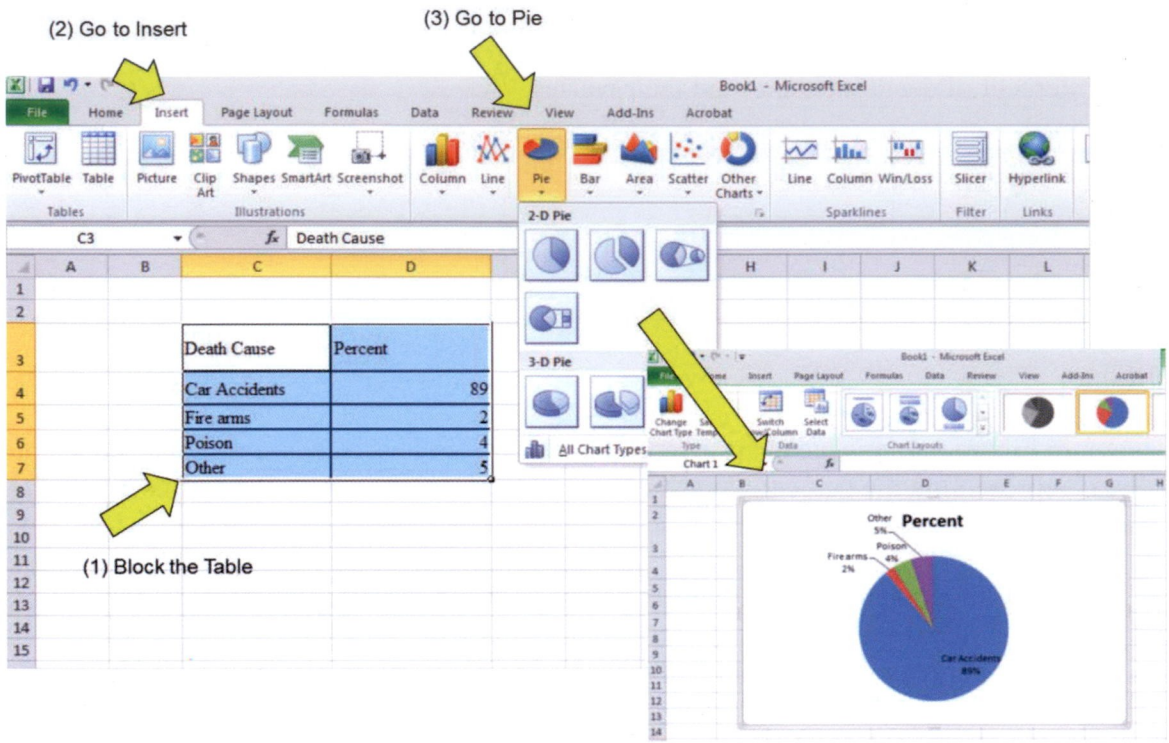

Figure 3.5 Constructing a Pie Chart Using Excel® Charts

Working Problem 3.1:

The bar chart shown below illustrates the prices of gasoline per gallon in some U.S. States in September 2008.

(a) Among the states presented in this bar chart, which state had the highest price of gasoline in 2008?
(b) Among the states presented in this bar chart, which state had the lowest price of gasoline in 2008?

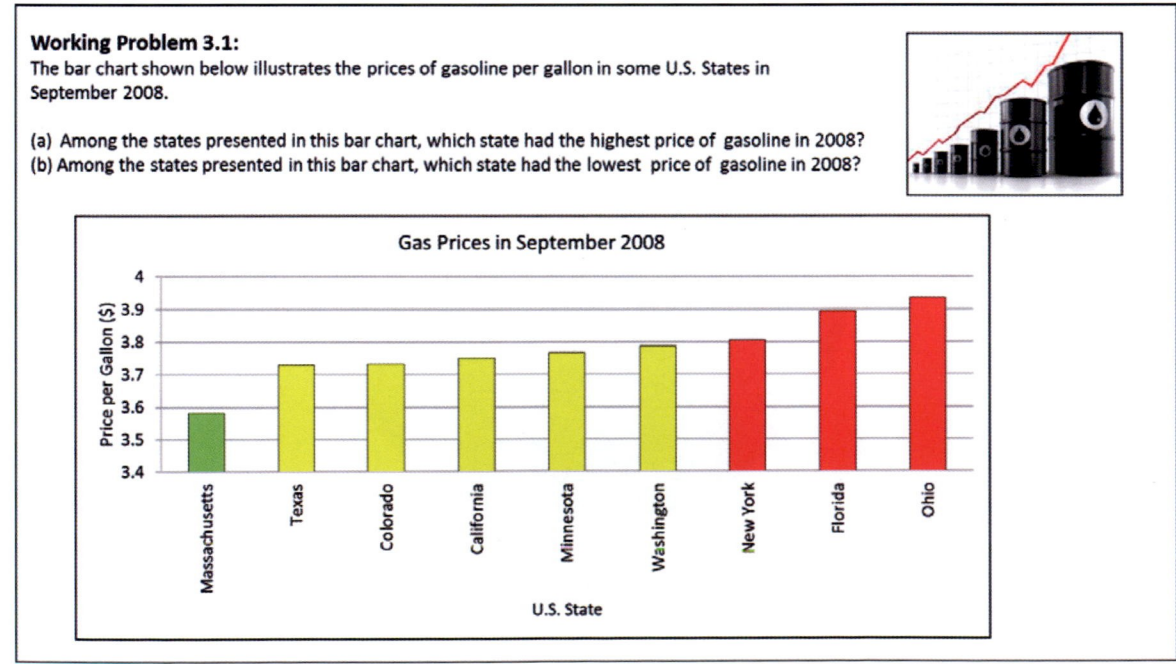

Working Problem 3.2:

(a) Using Excel® charts, construct two bar charts for the price of gasoline per gallon for September 2008 and September 2009 using the data in the Table below

(b) Using Excel® charts, construct a bar chart of the difference in gasoline per gallon between September 2008 and September 2009 using the data in the Table below

Gas prices of a number of states in September 2008, and September 2009

http://www.eia.doe.gov

State	Sept- 2009	Sep-2008
California	3.099	3.750
Colorado	2.480	3.732
Florida	2.527	3.893
Massachusetts	2.597	3.582
Minnesota	2.452	3.765
New York	2.811	3.805
Ohio	2.411	3.933
Texas	2.404	3.729
Washington	2.947	3.785

Working Problem 3.3:

The bar chart shown below illustrates the In-State tuition of some U.S. Universities (2006)

(a) Which university charges the highest in-state tuition?

(b) Which university charges the lowest in-state tuition?

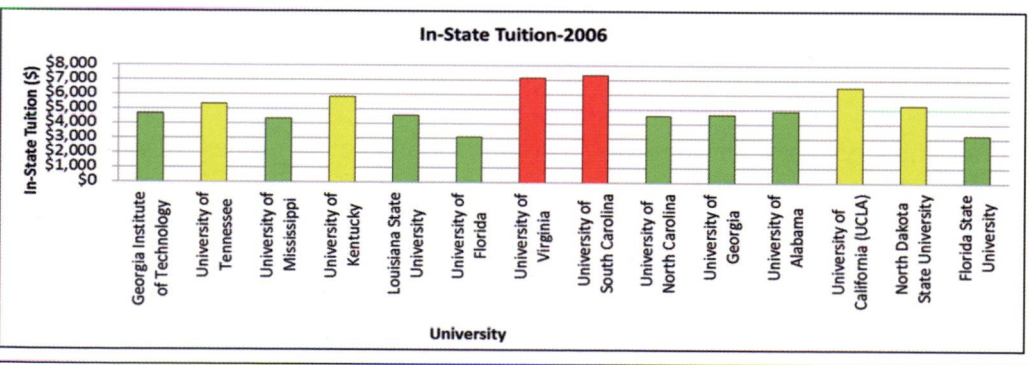

109

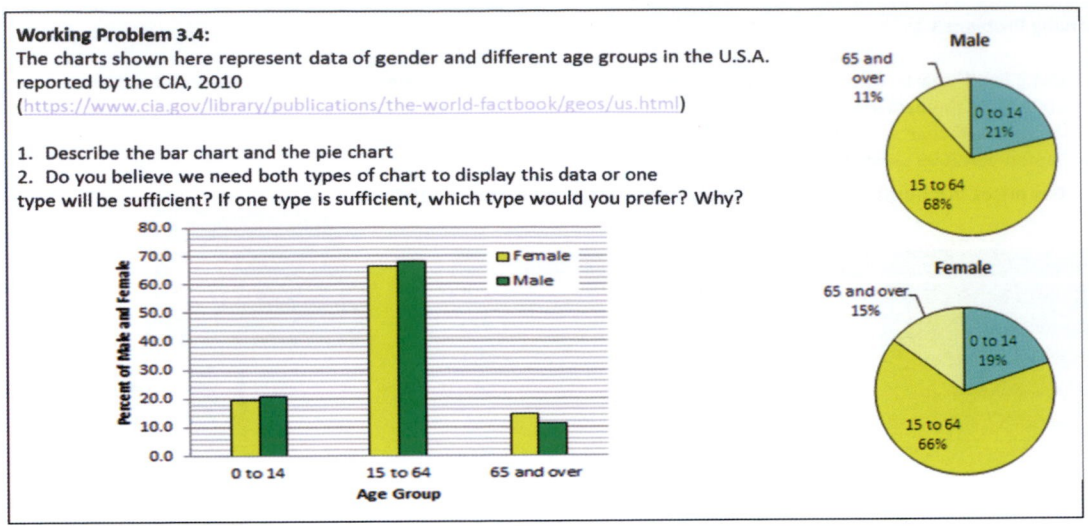

3.4 What is a histogram or a frequency distribution?

As discussed in chapter 1, a histogram or a frequency distribution is a simple *x-y* graph in which the horizontal *x*-axis represents the values (or classes of values) of the variable and the vertical *y*-axis represents the number of observations corresponding to each value (or the frequency). The underlying concept of a histogram or a frequency distribution is to divide the data set into consecutive categories or classes of equal ranges, count the number of observations belonging to each class, and construct a two-dimensional graph in which the horizontal axis consists of the classes of values of the variable under study and the vertical axis consists of the frequency or the number of observations corresponding to each class represented by the heights of the bars. For this reason, a frequency distribution is considered as a form of grouping data into mutually exclusive classes or categories showing the frequency in each.

To demonstrate the key characteristics of a histogram, suppose the grades of students were divided into five classes, each of 10 points grade intervals. If the minimum grade point is 50 and the maximum grade point is 100, this will yield 5 classes (50/5 = 10 points) as shown below.

Classes of student grade
50 to 60
60 to 70
70 to 80
80 to 90
90 to 100

110

Each class can be represented by the center of the class or the midpoint as shown below.

Classes of student grade	Mid-Point
50 to 60	55
60 to 70	65
70 to 80	75
80 to 90	85
90 to 100	95

At this point, we need to know how many students scored points in each class. This is the frequency of data as shown below. Note the use of '<' to avoid counting a student grade twice.

Classes of student grade	Mid-point (x)	Number of students (y, frequency)
50 to < 60	55	4
60 to < 70	65	6
70 to < 80	75	12
80 to < 90	85	9
90 to < 100	95	4

Using the data in the above table, we can now construct the histogram of students' grades as shown below. Note that each class is represented in the histogram by a bar, the height of which is the frequency. Also note the midpoint of each class.

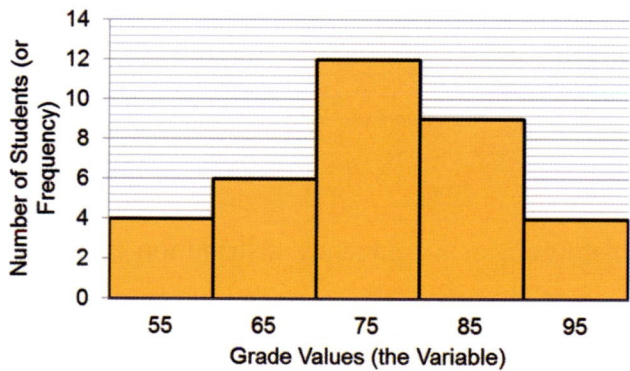

From the histogram above, important information can be obtained:

- How many students took the test? Add up the heights of the bar (4+6+12+9+4 = 35 students)
- Approximately, what are the minimum and maximum grades, or what is the range? 95-55 = 40 points
- What grade did the majority of students earn (the Mode)? ≈75 points
- Approximately, how many students failed the test (<60%)? 4 students

111

- Approximately, how many students passed the test with a grade of a C (70%) or more?
  25 students
- Approximately, what percent of the students earned an "A" (or above 90%)?($100 \times \frac{4}{35} \approx$
  11.43%)

The reason the information above represents approximate values is that a histogram will always be associated with a loss of complete data resolution depending on the number of classes used. The only way to avoid a loss of data resolution would be to examine all individual observations in the data set, which can be very difficult particularly if there is a large amount of data. As will be seen in the next section, the higher the number of classes, or the smaller the class width, the better the data resolution, and the more accurate the information obtained.

3.4.1 How do we construct a histogram?

In order to construct a histogram, we should form the so-called 'frequency table' in which we tally the data and show the values and the frequency in each class. The example below illustrates how a histogram is constructed.

Example 3.3: Consider the data of the work commute shown in Table 3.3. This data was taken from a random sample of employees working in a large retail store in New York City. Construct a frequency distribution (histogram).

Table 3.3 Values of work commute distances (miles)

55	50	47	50	55	81	80	98
62	38	67	70	60	69	78	39
70	65	99	55	64	89	85	65
75	56	75	50	100	68	95	85
50	30	60	66	85	79	85	70

Solution:

In order to construct a histogram or a frequency distribution of this data, we follow the basic steps described below.

Step 1: Find the minimum and the maximum values of the data set: minimum = 30 and maximum = 100. This gives you an idea about the span or the range of the entire data set, which is 70 miles (100-30).

Step 2: The number of classes is roughly determined by the range divided by the class width. For example, if the class width is 10 miles, the number of classes will be 70/10 = 7 classes. Commonly, the minimum number of classes used is 5. Note that, the more classes used, the higher the resolution of data display.

112

Step 3: In this step we form the first column of the frequency Table, which represents the classes of data. It is recommended that the first class should begin at a value below the actual minimum value of the data set, say 25, and the upper limit of the last class should by greater than the maximum value of the data set, say 105. This is typically recommended to cover the entire range of data and avoid missing observations in the frequency count. The upper value of each class begins with the notation of 'less than, <' to avoid double counting of the upper values in two consecutive classes.

Classes
25 to < 35
35 to < 45
45 to < 55
55 to < 65
65 to < 75
75 to < 85
85 to < 95
95 to <105

Step 4: We form the second column of the frequency table, which is the mid-point of each class. This step is significant as it indicates that each class will be represented by one point, which is the point in the middle of the class. It also indicates that the 40 observations that we began the analysis with is now reduced to few values of 7 or 8 midpoints.

Classes	Mid-Points
25 to < 35	30
35 to < 45	40
45 to < 55	50
55 to < 65	60
65 to < 75	70
75 to < 85	80
85 to < 95	90
95 to <105	100

Step 5: This step shows that each class should be associated with a weight or a frequency value depending on the number of observations in the original data set that fall within the class. We count the number of observations in each class and place the count in the third column labeled 'frequency.' Note that the total frequency is 40, which is the total number of observations.

55	50	47	50	55	81	80	98
62	38	67	70	60	69	78	39
70	65	99	55	64	89	85	65
75	56	75	50	100	68	95	85
50	30	60	66	85	79	85	70

Table 3.4 shows the results of the above steps. Figure 3.6 shows the histogram produced by the above steps with the *x*-axis being the midpoints of class values (column 2 of Table 3.4) and the vertical axis being the frequency values (column 3 of Table 3.4).

113

Table 3.4 Frequency tables of driving-to-work distance

Classes	Mid-Points	Frequency
25 to < 35	30	1
35 to < 45	40	2
45 to < 55	50	5
55 to < 65	60	8
65 to < 75	70	9
75 to < 85	80	6
85 to < 95	90	5
95 to <105	100	4
		Total = 40

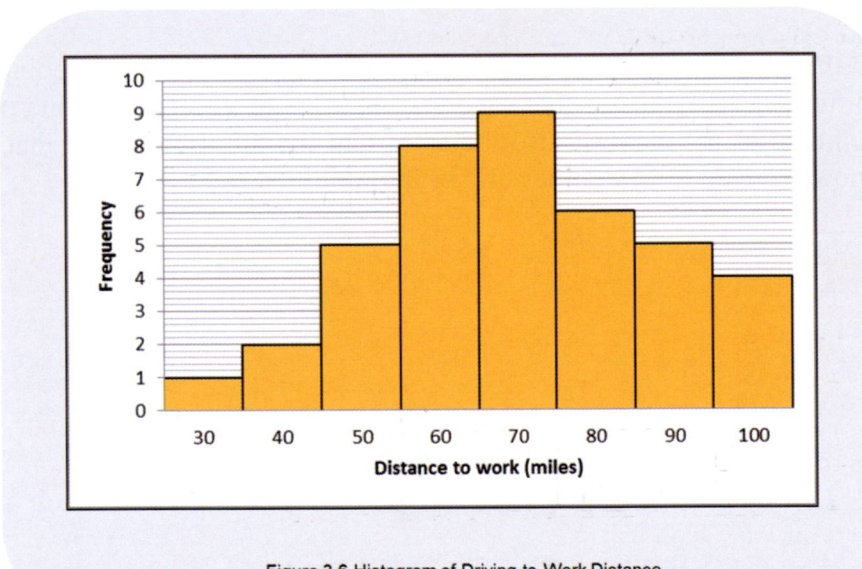

Figure 3.6 Histogram of Driving-to-Work Distance

3.4.2 What is a relative frequency distribution?

The absolute number of observations corresponding to a certain class or interval can be converted into a relative frequency value or a fraction of the total frequency using the following expression:

$$Relative\ Frequency = \frac{frequency\ of\ the\ ith\ class}{total\ frequency} = \frac{f_i}{\sum_1^k f_i} \qquad (3.1)$$

where f_i is the frequency of the ith class, k is the number of classes, and $\sum_1^k f_i$ is the sum of all frequencies.

We can also obtain the percent relative frequency by multiplying the relative frequency by 100:

$$Relative\ Frequency\ (\%) = 100 \times \frac{frequency\ of\ the\ ith\ class}{total\ frequency} = 100 \times \frac{f_i}{\sum_1^k f_i} \qquad (3.2)$$

Example 3.4: Using the data of work commute distances in miles shown in Table 3.3, construct a relative frequency distribution.

Solution:

Table 3.5 shows the relative frequencies and the percent relative frequencies for different distance-to-work categories or classes. Note that the sum of relative frequencies is 1 and the sum of percent relative frequencies is 100. Also note that using the relative frequency or percent relative frequency instead of the absolute frequency will not alter the shape of the frequency distribution, only the values on the vertical axis as shown in Figure 3.7.

Table 3.5 Relative frequency and percent relative frequency values

Classes	Mid-Points (x)	Frequency (F)	Relative Frequency (RF)	Percent Relative Frequency $(RF\,\%)$
25 to < 35	30	1	(1/40) or 0.025	0.025×100 = 2.5%
35 to < 45	40	2	(2/40) or 0.050	0.050×100 = 5.0%
45 to < 55	50	5	0.125	12.5
55 to < 65	60	8	0.200	20
65 to < 75	70	9	0.225	22.5
75 to < 85	80	6	0.150	15
85 to < 95	90	5	0.125	12.5
95 to <105	100	4	0.100	10
		Total = 40	1.0	100

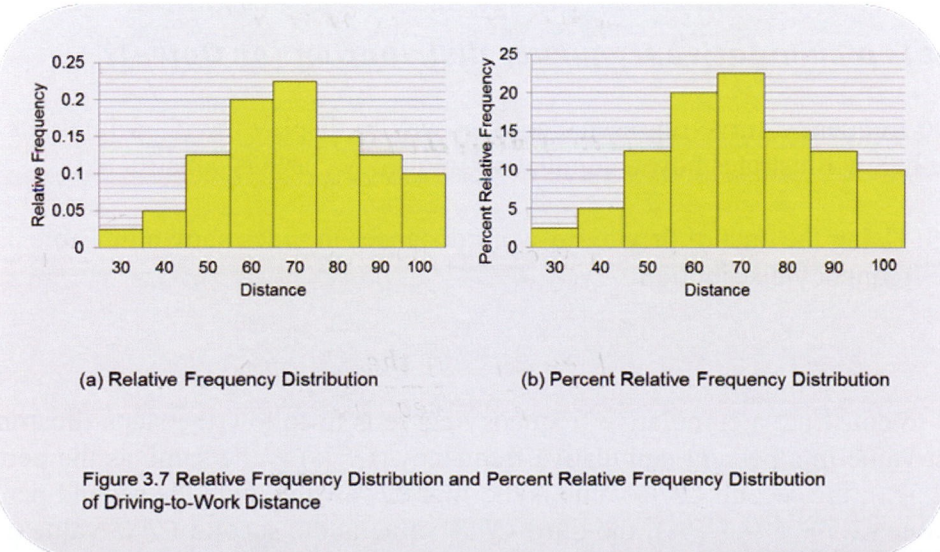

(a) Relative Frequency Distribution   (b) Percent Relative Frequency Distribution

Figure 3.7 Relative Frequency Distribution and Percent Relative Frequency Distribution of Driving-to-Work Distance

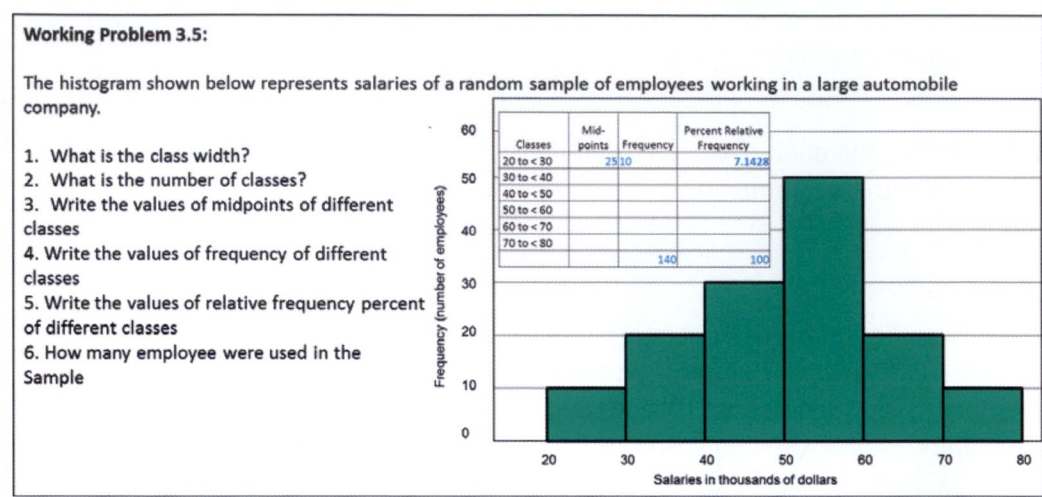

Working Problem 3.5:

The histogram shown below represents salaries of a random sample of employees working in a large automobile company.

1. What is the class width?
2. What is the number of classes?
3. Write the values of midpoints of different classes
4. Write the values of frequency of different classes
5. Write the values of relative frequency percent of different classes
6. How many employee were used in the Sample

Classes	Mid-points	Frequency	Percent Relative Frequency
20 to < 30	25	10	7.1428
30 to < 40			
40 to < 50			
50 to < 60			
60 to < 70			
70 to < 80			
		140	100

Working Problem 3.6:

The following sample data set lists the number of touchdowns scored by all teams in the NFL by week 10 of 2010 season. Construct a frequency distribution that has eight classes.

Team	Touchdowns	Team	Touchdowns
Atlanta	27	Tennesse	28
New England	42	Washington	21
Baltimore	26	Miami	15
New York Jets	28	Houston	28
Pittsburgh	27	Seattle	18
Philadelphia	32	St. Louis	18
Green Bay	30	Cleveland	21
New Orleans	30	Dallas	31
Indianapolis	31	Minnesota	20
New York Giants	31	San Francisco	18
Tampa Bay	25	Denver	26
Chicago	20	Buffalo	27
Kansas City	29	Arizona	22
San Diego	34	Cincinnati	25
Jacksonville	25	Deteriot	30
Oakland	24	Carolina	10

3.4.3 What is a cumulative frequency distribution (or Ogive)?

A cumulative frequency curve represents another way to display the class intervals of the data. The example below illustrates how a cumulative frequency curve is constructed.

Example 3.5: Using the data of driving-to-work distances in miles shown in Table 3.3, construct a cumulative frequency distribution.

Solution:

One method to construct a cumulative frequency curve is to follow the steps illustrated in Table 3.6. The first value in a percent cumulative frequency ($CF\%$) is the same as the percent relative frequency (2.5%); the second $CF\%$ value is the first $CF\%$ value plus the second percent relative frequency value (2.5 + 5 = 7.5%); the third $CF\%$ value is the second $CF\%$ value plus the third percent relative frequency value (7.5 + 12.5 = 20%); and so on to reach the cumulative total of 100.

When a cumulative curve is constructed, the horizontal axis should consist of the upper values of the different classes (in this example, 35, 45, 55, 65, 75, 85, 95, and 105). Figure 3.8 shows the cumulative frequency curve of this example. A cumulative frequency curve constructed using the method above can provide direct information of the percent of data observations exhibiting values less than a certain value, x_o, or $p(x < x_o)$. Note how the percent of employees driving less than 75 miles is directly obtained from the curve by drawing a vertical line from the x-axis at 75 that intersects with the curve at a point determining the percentage of employees, which is 62.5%.

Table 3.6 Cumulative frequency of students' grades

Classes	Mid-Points (x)	Frequency (F)	Relative Frequency (RF)	Percent Relative Frequency (RF %)	Percent Cumulative Frequency (CF%)
25 to < 35	30	1	0.025	2.5	2.5
35 to < 45	40	2	0.050	5	7.5
45 to < 55	50	5	0.125	12.5	20
55 to < 65	60	8	0.200	20	40
65 to < 75	70	9	0.225	22.5	62.5
75 to < 85	80	6	0.150	15	77.5
85 to < 95	90	5	0.125	12.5	90
95 to <105	100	4	0.100	10	100
		Total = 40	1	100	

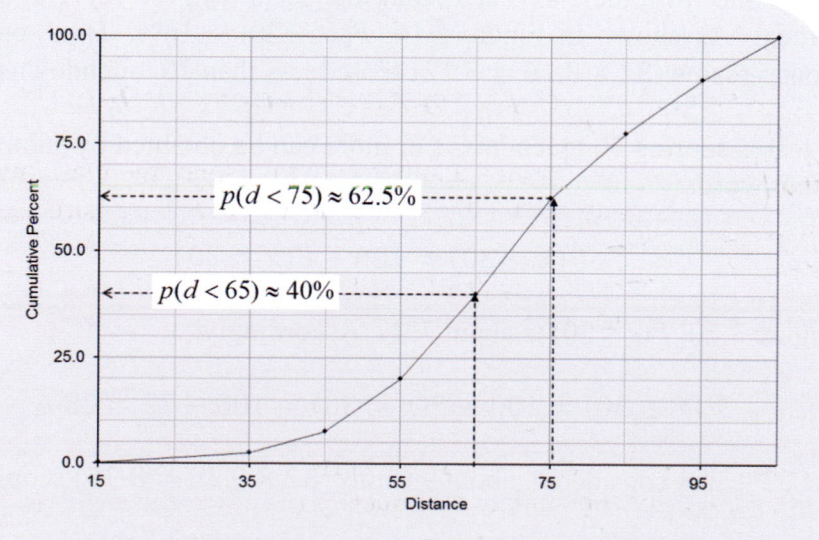

Figure 3.8 Cumulative Frequency Distribution of Driving-to-Work Distance

117

Example 3.6: The cumulative frequency distribution of touchdowns scored by 32 NFL teams after the tenth week of the 2010 season is shown in Figure 3.9.

(a) How many teams scored less than 20 touchdowns?
(b) How many teams scored 30 touchdowns or more?

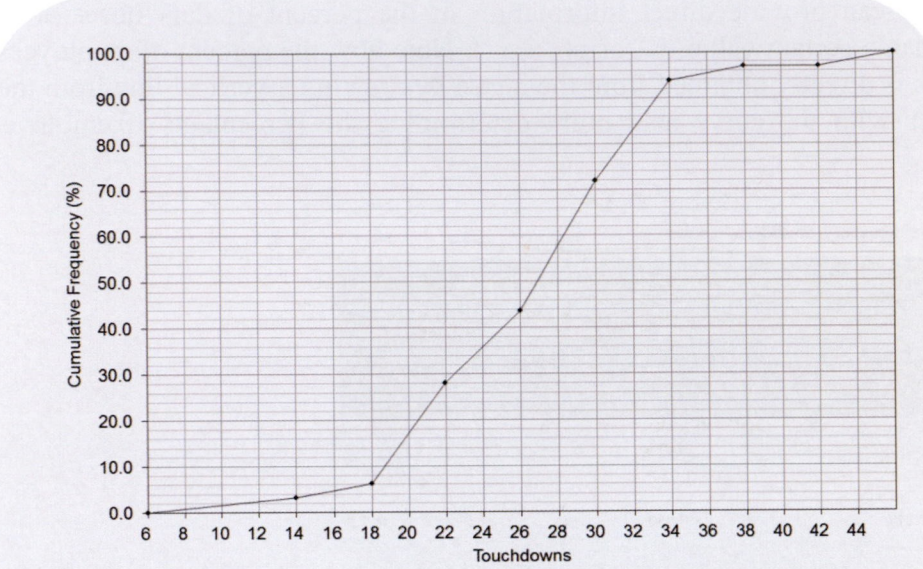

Figure 3.9 Cumulative frequency distribution of touchdowns of the NFL teams after the tenth week of 2010 season

Solution:

As discussed earlier, a value of $P(x < x_0)$ is directly obtained from the cumulative curve by drawing a vertical line from the x-axis at x_0 that intersects with the curve at a point determining the desired percent. As shown in Figure 3.10, $P(x < 20) \approx 16\%$. Thus, out of the 32 teams considered, about 5 teams ($32 \times 0.16 = 5.12$) scored less than 20 touchdowns.

The percent of teams scoring 30 touchdowns or more can be obtained by subtracting $P(x < 30)$ from 100. In other words:

$$P(x \geq 30) = 100 - P(x < 30)$$

As shown in Figure 3.10, $P(x < 30)$ is about 72%. Accordingly:

$$P(x \geq 30) = 100 - P(x < 30) = 100 - 72 = 28\%$$

Thus, out of the 32 teams considered, about 9 teams ($32 \times 0.28 = 8.96$) scored 30 touchdowns or more.

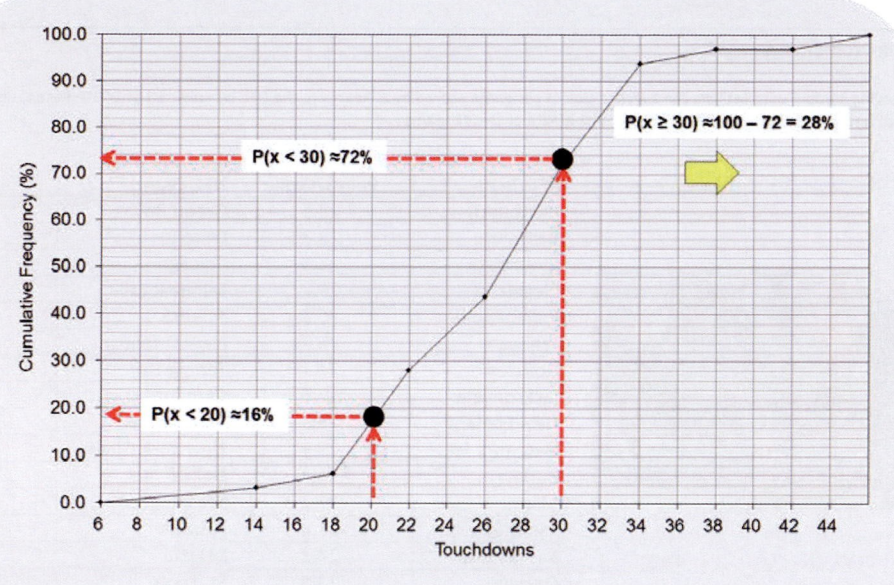

Figure 3.10 Cumulative frequency distribution of touchdowns of the NFL teams after the tenth week of 2010 season

Working Problem 3.7:

Complete the frequency table below and construct the cumulative frequency curve that corresponds to the histogram shown below, which represents salaries of a random sample of employees working in a large automobile company.

Classes	Mid-points	Frequency	Relative Frequency (%)	Cumulative Frequency	Cumulative Frequency (%)
20 to < 30	25	10			
30 to < 40	35	20			
40 to < 50					
50 to < 60					
60 to < 70					
70 to < 80					

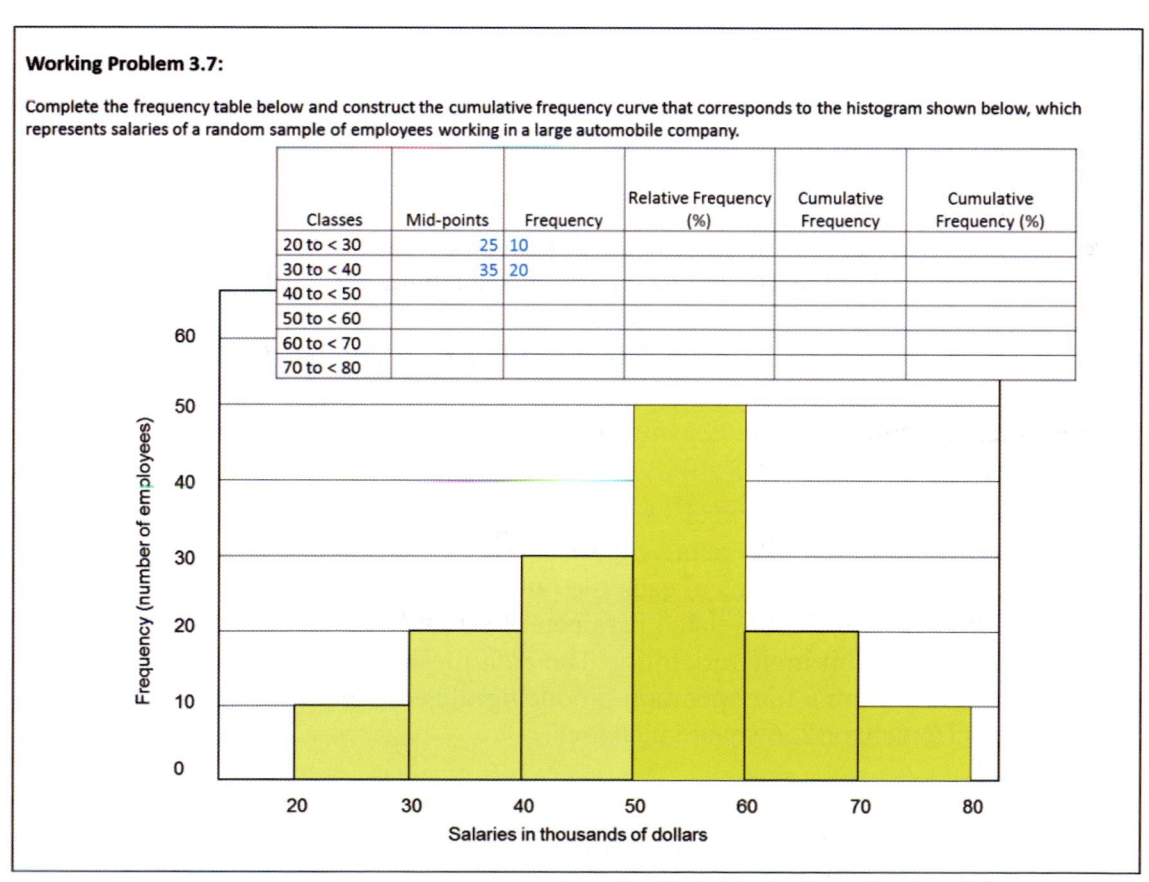

Working Problem 3.8:

The following sample data set lists the average points per game scored by all teams in the NFL by week 10 of 2010 season. Construct a histogram and a cumulative frequency curve of the data of the 32 teams

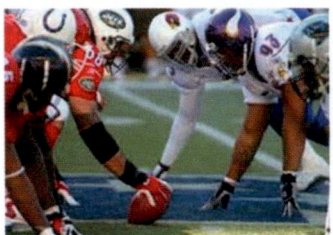

AFC-Team	Points/Game	NFC-Team	Points/Game
Pittsburgh	23.5	Green Bay	25.2
Baltimore	23.3	Deteriot	23.4
Cincinnati	21.5	Chicago	19.1
Cleveland	19.2	Minnesota	17.2
Indianapolis	26.8	Atlanta	25.6
Tennesse	25.7	New Orleans	23.5
Houston	24.4	Tampa Bay	20.9
Jacksonville	22.0	Carolina	11.7
New England	28.9	Philadelphia	28.4
New York Jets	23.8	New York Giants	25.3
Buffalo	21.3	Dallas	22.9
Miami	17.2	Washington	20.2
San Diego	27.4	Arizona	18.8
Kansas City	24.3	Seattle	18.5
Oakland	23.8	St. Louis	17.7
Denver	21.7	San Francisco	16.0

3.5 Using Excel® Data Analysis for constructing frequency distributions: Case study: Ceramic tile area

When software programs are used to construct a histogram, we should be aware that different programs may use different procedures to produce a frequency distribution or a cumulative frequency distribution. It is important, therefore to interpret the distributions produced in the context of the approach or the method used. When Excel® data analysis is used, a class is defined by $> a$ to $a + w$  where a is the lower value of a class, and w is the class width. In MegaStat®, a class is defined by a to $< a + w$ where a is the lower value of a class, and w is the class width. In the above examples, we used the method utilized in MegaStat®. In this section, we will use the method utilized in Excel® data analysis to give students a different perspective of how frequency distributions can be constructed.

Example 3.7: To illustrate how Excel® can be used to construct a histogram or a frequency distribution, we will use data of ceramic tile area. This is a critical parameter as nearly every tiling job requires perfect dimensions of each tile (area and thickness) for smooth installation and straight clean cuts. It is also a cost-related parameter as waste of tiles can be a potential problem when tile dimensions exhibit high variability. The data in Table 3.7 represents a sample of 100 tiles selected randomly from a tile operation producing tiles of consistent thickness and nominal dimensions of 16x16 inch, or 256 square inch area.

As indicated in Chapter 2, when we use Excel® data analysis, data has to be arranged in one column as shown in Figure 3.11. It is always useful to begin the analysis by performing numerical descriptive statistics using the procedure discussed in Chapter 2. Figure 3.12 illustrates this procedure.

Table 3.7 Values of ceramic tile areas

258.5	255.0	255.5	256.4	256.6	258.4	257.2	257.4	256.3	259.5
255.7	254.9	256.1	254.5	253.3	257.9	259.1	256.8	257.7	255.1
254.1	255.5	256.5	256.1	255.0	255.9	255.1	254.6	255.1	255.1
255.4	254.3	258.5	256.3	255.6	256.5	257.5	253.8	256.2	256.1
256.2	255.7	257.1	256.7	256.1	257.4	255.0	256.2	254.6	257.0
255.5	256.9	255.8	254.7	256.2	256.9	256.4	255.6	254.8	255.6
257.3	256.8	256.0	254.9	256.0	256.2	257.7	252.7	255.6	255.5
253.9	256.3	255.4	256.1	256.0	254.0	257.8	252.7	256.4	256.6
255.5	255.6	255.1	256.6	254.5	255.4	254.1	256.0	256.9	256.9
254.6	254.8	256.3	255.5	256.4	253.8	254.8	254.6	255.4	255.2

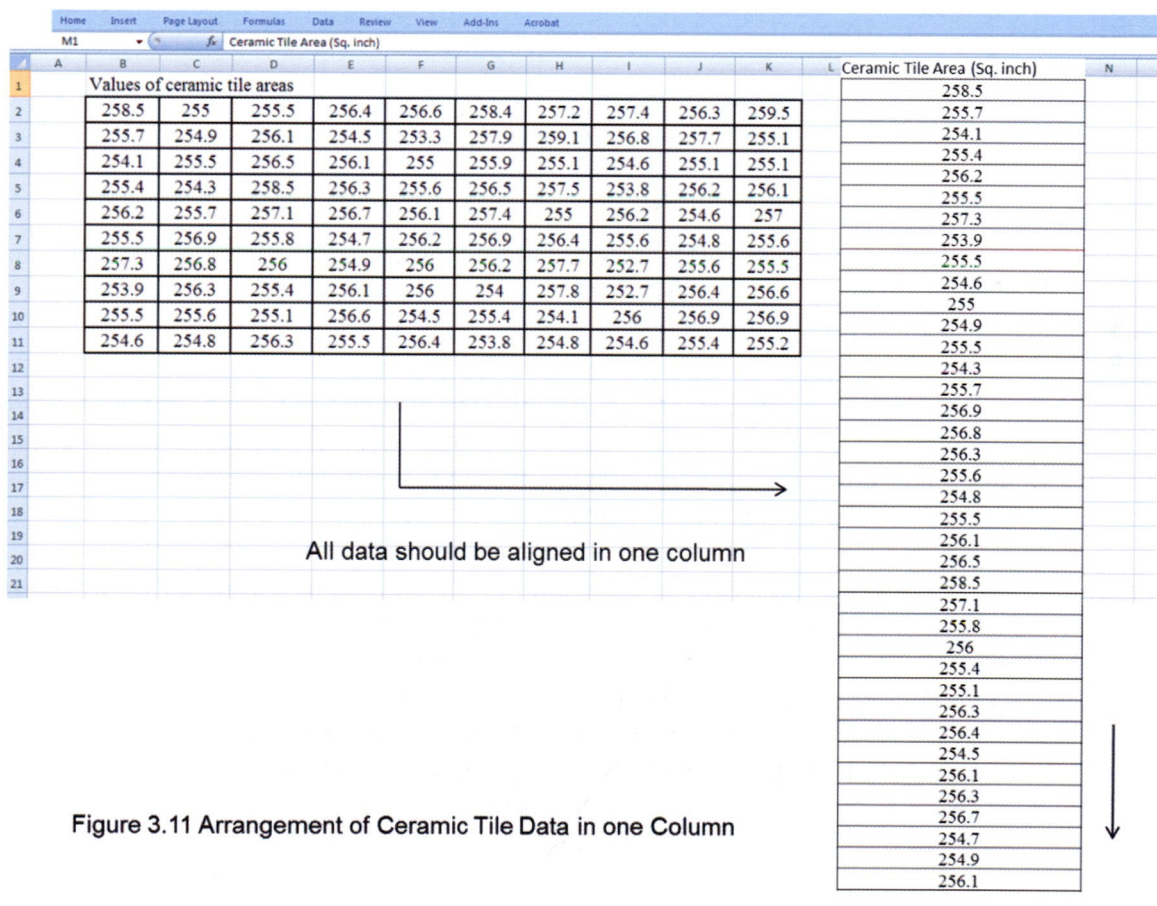

Figure 3.11 Arrangement of Ceramic Tile Data in one Column

121

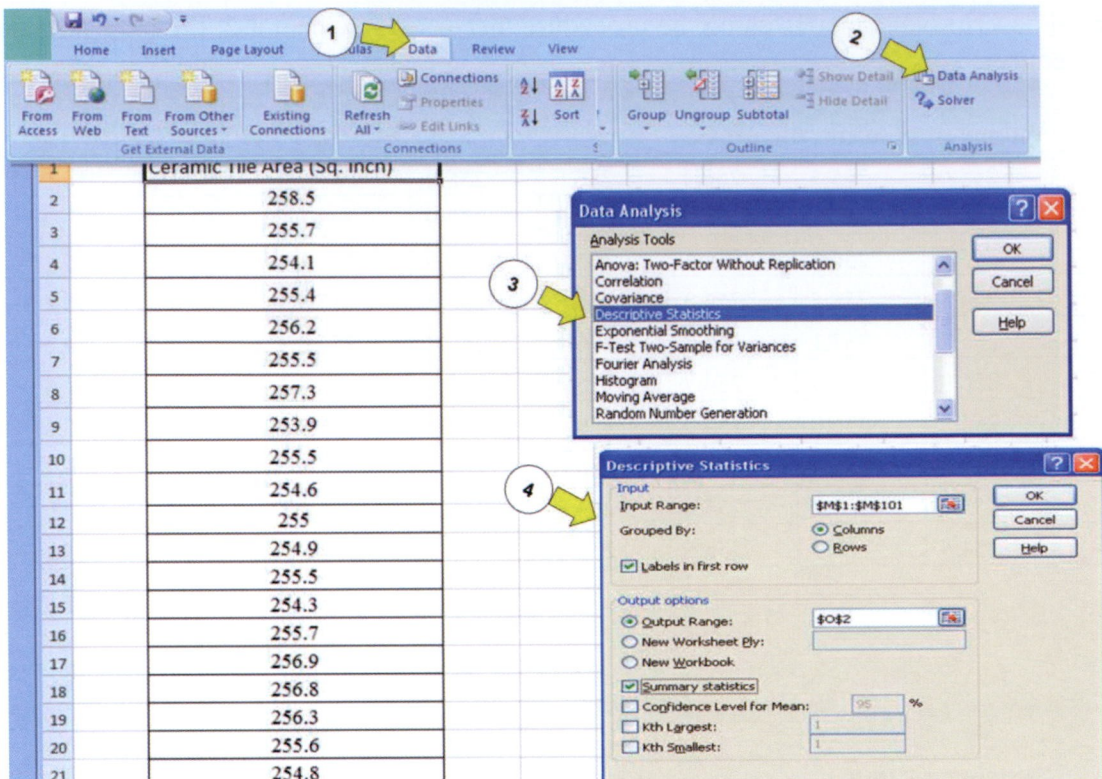

Figure 3.12 Using Excel® to perform Descriptive Statistics of Ceramic Tile Data

Interpretation of descriptive statistics should be made in view of the type of variable under consideration. In this example, the variable is the area of ceramic tile, which is a ratio level of measurement and follows the pattern of *'nominal-the-best.'* This means that the area has to be exact and not more or less than the nominal target value of 256 square inches. As can be seen in Figure 3.13, the mean area is 255.87 square inches, the median is 255.95 square inches, and the mode is 255.5 square inches. These central measures indicate that the target value is largely met. Values of the mean, the median, and the mode are approximately equal. This is a sign that the frequency distribution will be largely symmetrical.

Evaluating the variability measures reveals that ceramic tile area suffers high variability as some tiles exhibit an area of as low as 252.7 and some as high as 259.5. This difference yields a range of 6.8 square inch (259.5 – 252.7). A standard deviation of 1.272 indicates that the variability in ceramic tile area is not zero; that is despite the serious attempt during manufacturing to make all ceramic tiles of the exact same area. These observations call for constructing a frequency distribution to closely examine the extent of variability and its associated frequency.

	L	M	N	O	P	Q
1		Ceramic Tile Area (Sq. inch)				
2		258.5		*Ceramic Tile Area (Sq. inch)*		
3		255.7				
4		254.1		Mean	255.87	
5		255.4		Standard Error	0.13	
6		256.2		Median	255.95	
7		255.5		Mode	255.5	
8		257.3		Standard Deviation	1.272	
9		253.9		Sample Variance	1.618	
10		255.5		Kurtosis	0.487	
11		254.6		Skewness	0.181	
12		255		Range	6.8	
13		254.9		Minimum	252.7	
14		255.5		Maximum	259.5	
15		254.3		Sum	25587.4	
16		255.7		Count	100	
17		256.9				
18		256.8				
19		256.3				
20		255.6				

Figure 3.13 Excel® Output of Descriptive Statistics of Ceramic Tile Data

Using Excel® data analysis, a histogram or frequency distribution can be constructed as follows:

Step 1: *Determine the class width by preparing a bin range* (see Figure 3.14). Bin numbers represent the intervals that you want the histogram tool to use. Excel® counts the number of data points in each data bin. A data point is included in a particular bin if the number is greater than the lowest bound and equal to or less than the highest bound for the data bin ($> a$ to $a + w$) where a is the lower value of a class, and w is the class width. If you omit the bin range, Excel® creates a set of evenly distributed bins between the minimum and maximum values of the input data. In this example, you may select to begin with a convenient number such as 252 (since the minimum area is 252.7) and end with a convenient number such as 260 (since the maximum area is 259.5).

Step 2: *Go to Data Analysis* (see Figure 3.15)

Step 3: Select Histogram (see Figure 3.15)

Step 4: In the Histogram Tool, *select the data column as the input range, and the bin-range column as bin range* (see Figure 3.16). Specify an output, check 'Chart Output' and 'Cumulative Percentage,' and click Ok.

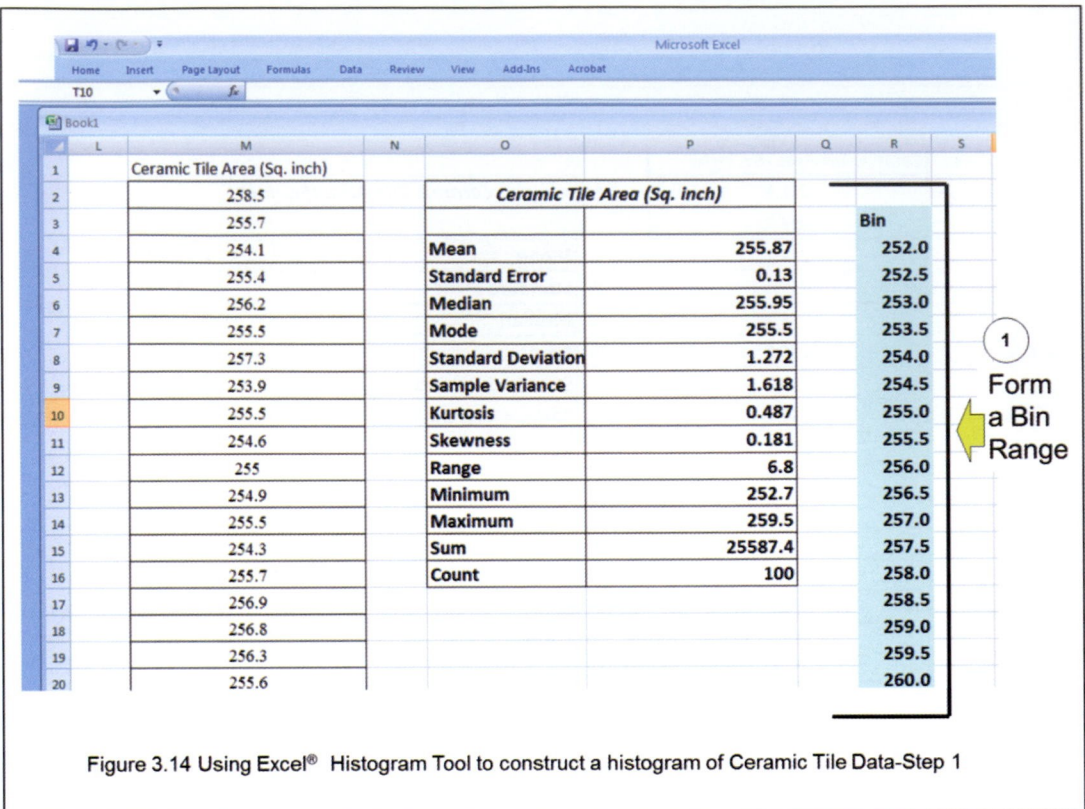

Figure 3.14 Using Excel® Histogram Tool to construct a histogram of Ceramic Tile Data-Step 1

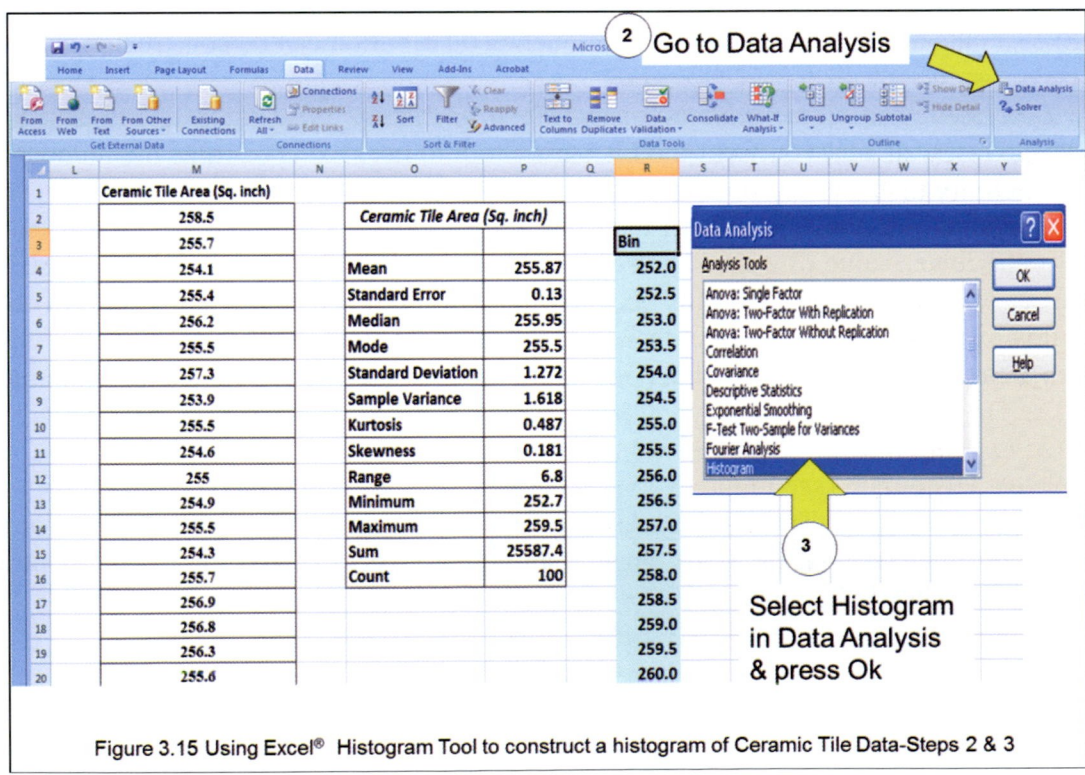

Figure 3.15 Using Excel® Histogram Tool to construct a histogram of Ceramic Tile Data-Steps 2 & 3

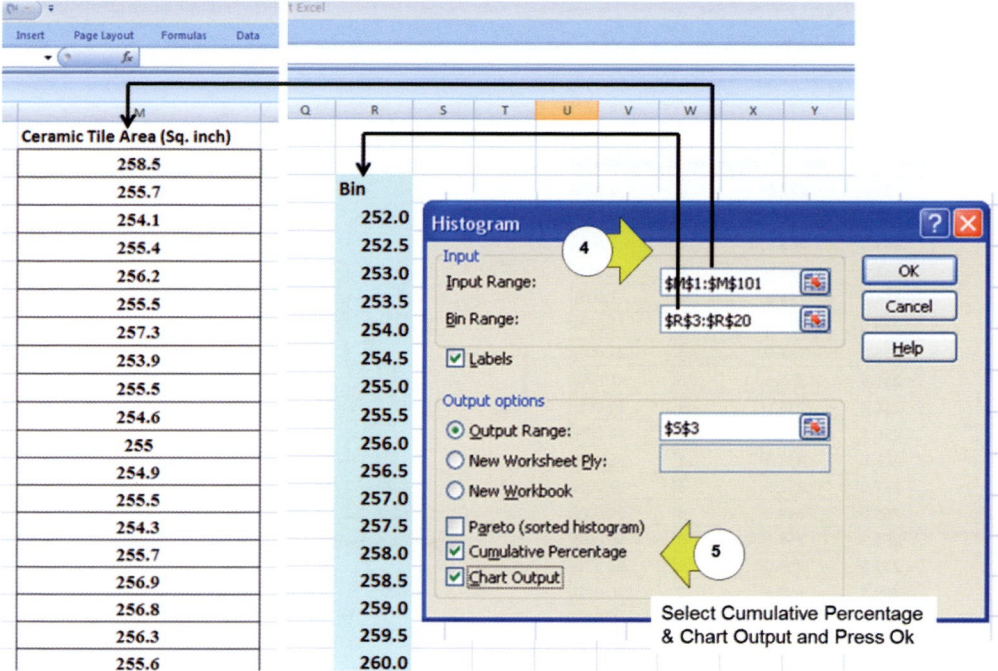

Figure 3.16 Using Excel® Histogram Tool to construct a histogram of Ceramic Tile Data-Steps 4 & 5

The steps above produce the output shown in Figure 3.17 (after some customization). Note that the histogram and the cumulative curve are presented in the same graph. Use Excel® - Help to further manipulate the graphs or to separate the histogram from the cumulative curve. You may also wish to convert the frequency distribution to a relative frequency distribution or a percent relative frequency distribution. This will require Excel® calculations to create new columns of relative frequency and percent relative frequency. In addition, it will require using Excel® graphic capability to construct the distributions. Again, these are systematic and simple steps that you can do yourself or with the support of Excel® -Help.

In order to accurately interpret Excel® Histogram output, it is important that you know that the bin-range values are indeed the upper boundaries of the classes. Table 3.8 illustrates the classes corresponding to each bin-range value. One of the reasons Excel® uses this approach is to allow graphing the histogram superimposed with the cumulative curve. If you wish to separate the two graphs, you will need to copy the entire graph to another area of the spread sheet. You can then go to the first graph and delete the cumulative curve (click on it and press delete). This will leave you with the histogram alone. In the second graph, delete the histogram (click on it and press delete). This will leave you with the cumulative curve alone. A histogram produced by Excel® will normally have gaps between bars (by default). To close these gaps and produce a histogram similar to the one in Figure 3.17 click on the bars and go to '*format data series*' then '*gap width*' and close the gap by moving the slide to '*No gap.*' These steps are shown in Figure 3.18. The next example shows how to make use of the information revealed by a histogram or a cumulative frequency curve.

125

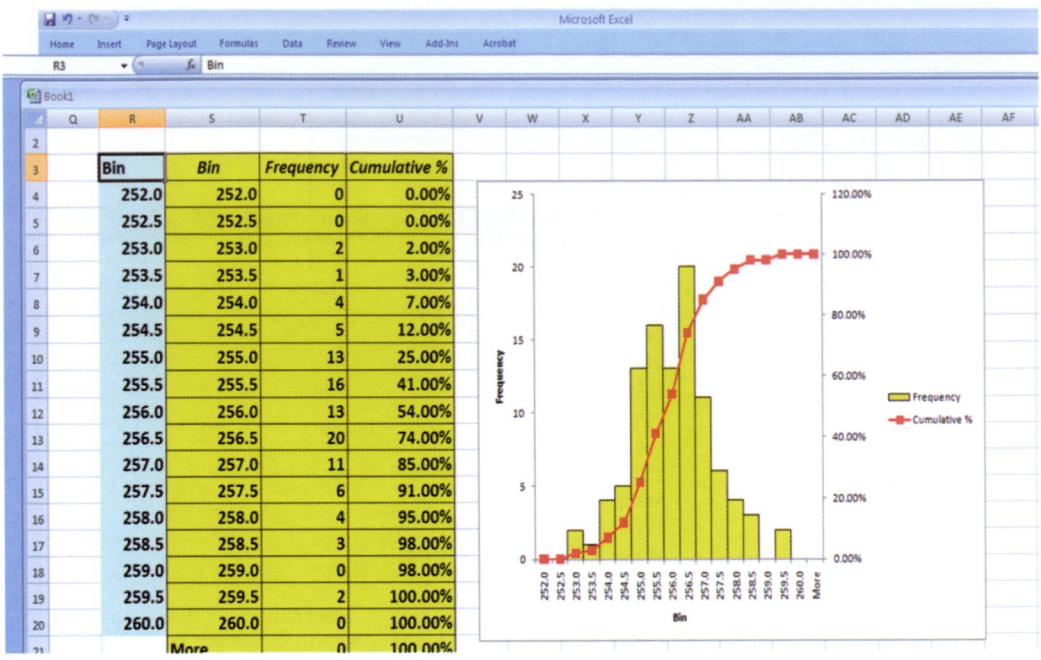

Figure 3.17 Excel® Histogram Output of Ceramic Tile Data

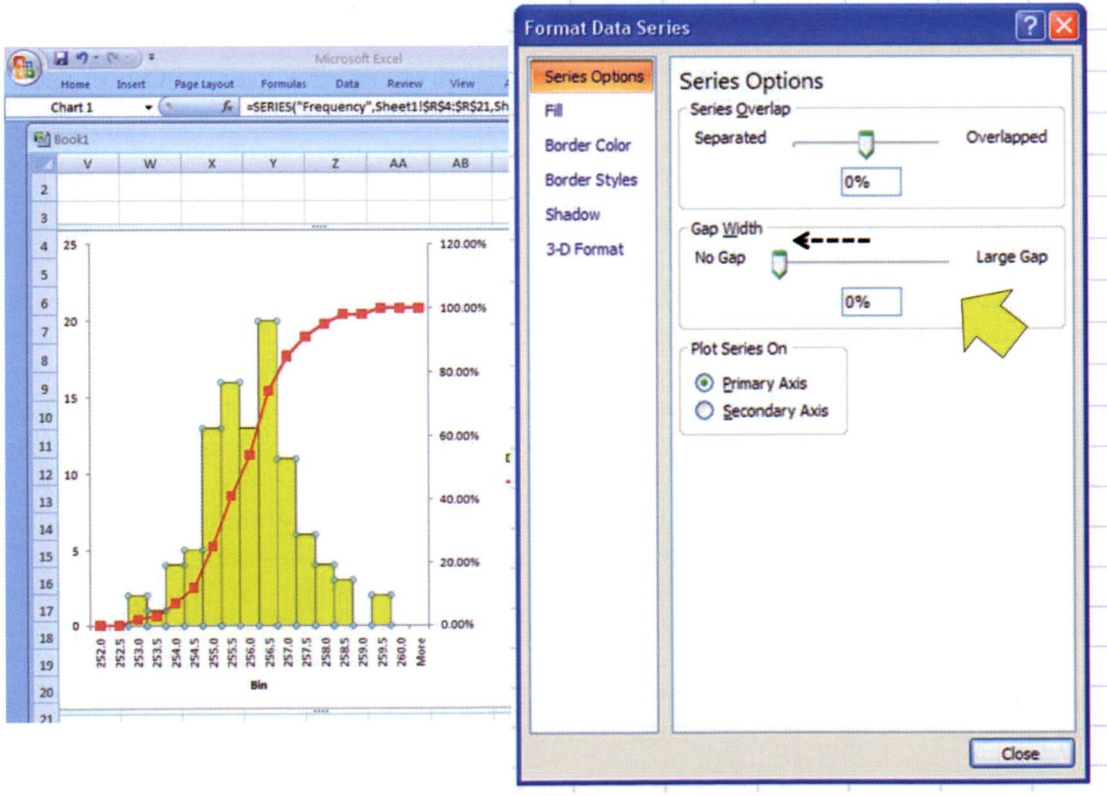

Figure 3.18 Closing the gap between bars in Excel® Histogram Output

Table 3.8 Classes corresponding to each bin-range value in Excel® Output

Classes	Bin	Frequency	Cumulative %
> 251.5 to 252	252	0	0.00%
> 252 to 252.5	252.5	0	0.00%
> 252.5 to 253	253	2	2.00%
> 253 to 253.5	253.5	1	3.00%
> 253.5 to 254	254	4	7.00%
> 254 to 254.5	254.5	5	12.00%
> 254.5 to 255	255	13	25.00%
> 255 to 255.5	255.5	16	41.00%
> 255.5 to 256	256	13	54.00%
> 256 to 256.5	256.5	20	74.00%
> 256.5 to 257	257	11	85.00%
> 257 to 257.5	257.5	6	91.00%
> 257.5 to 258	258	4	95.00%
> 258 to 258.5	258.5	3	98.00%
> 258.5 to 259	259	0	98.00%
> 259 to 259.5	259.5	2	100.00%
> 259.5 to 260	260	0	100.00%

Example 3.8: Suppose in the tile area example discussed above, a consumer would like to purchase tiles of the following specifications: target = 256 square inches, tolerance = 256 ± 1. In other words, the consumer has a plan to use tiles of area of 256 square inches, but he is willing to tolerate tiles ranging in area from 255 to 257 square inches. Using the frequency distribution determine what percent of tiles will meet these specifications?

Solution:

The frequency distribution of tile area is shown in Figure 3.19. Using this distribution, one can mark the area of the specified values and the area where tiles will be rejected for failing to meet the specifications. In this sense, the histogram will provide a rough idea on the quantity of tiles that fall within the specified limits and those that will be rejected for not meeting specifications (any value below 255 or above 257). In order to get quantitative estimates of the quantities of tiles that fall within the specified limits and those that will be rejected for not meeting specifications, the cumulative frequency curve should be used as discussed below.

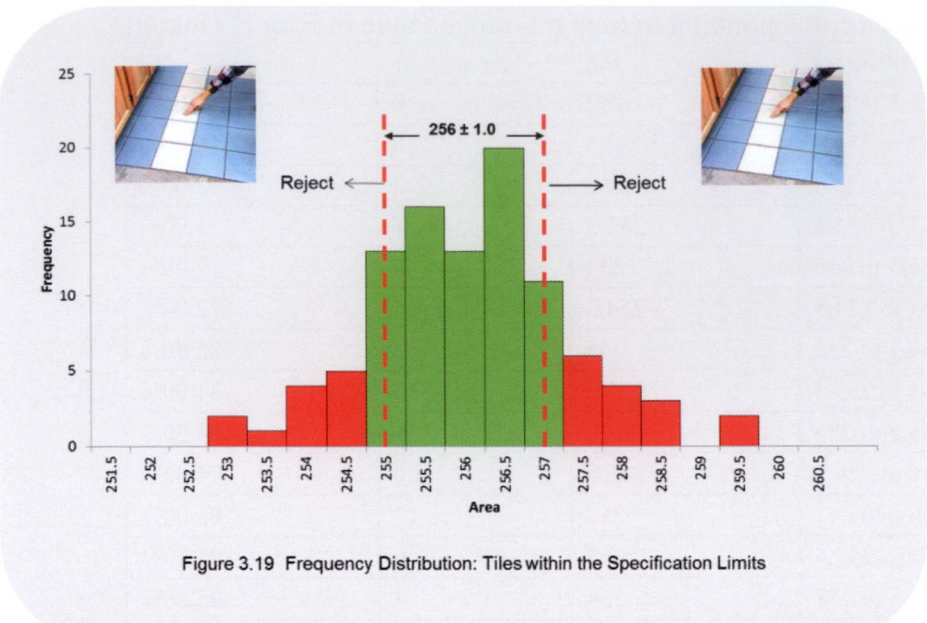

Figure 3.19 Frequency Distribution: Tiles within the Specification Limits

As shown in Figure 3.20, the point of intersection of the vertical line at the area value of 255 square inch, and the horizontal line is at 25% cumulative frequency. This gives the percent of tiles of less than or equal 255 square inches. The point of intersection of the vertical line at the area value of 257 square inches, and the horizontal line is at 85% cumulative frequency. This gives the percent of tiles of less than or equal 257 square inches. The required percent is then calculated by:

$$p(255 \leq x \leq 257) = p(x \leq 257) - p(x \leq 255) = 0.85 - 0.25 = 0.60 \; or \; 60\%$$

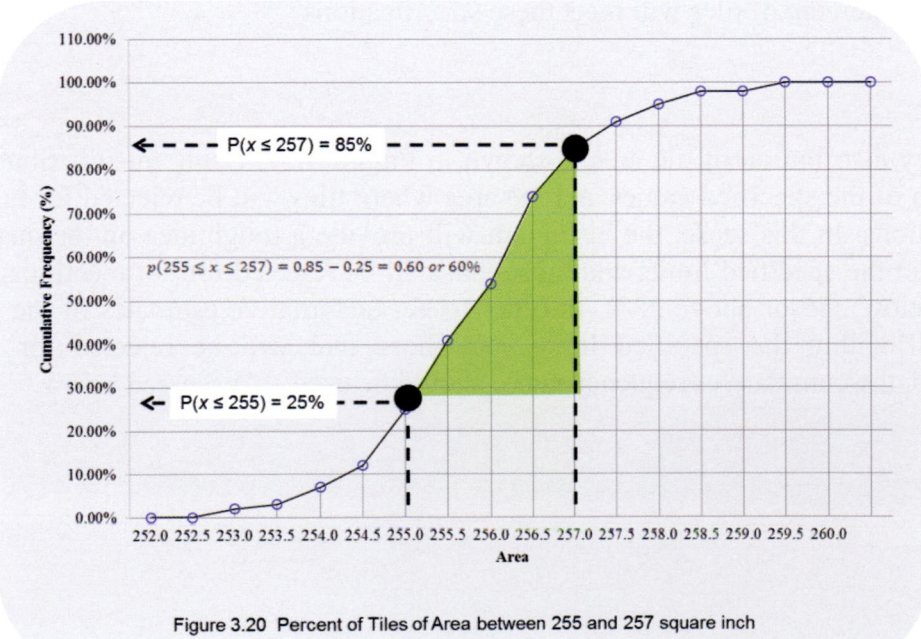

Figure 3.20 Percent of Tiles of Area between 255 and 257 square inch

To this point, we discussed two methods of constructing a histogram and a cumulative frequency curve: the common method (section 3.4.1) and Excel method (section 3.5). To avoid any confusion, we summarize these two methods in the illustration below. Students can use either method to construct frequency distributions.

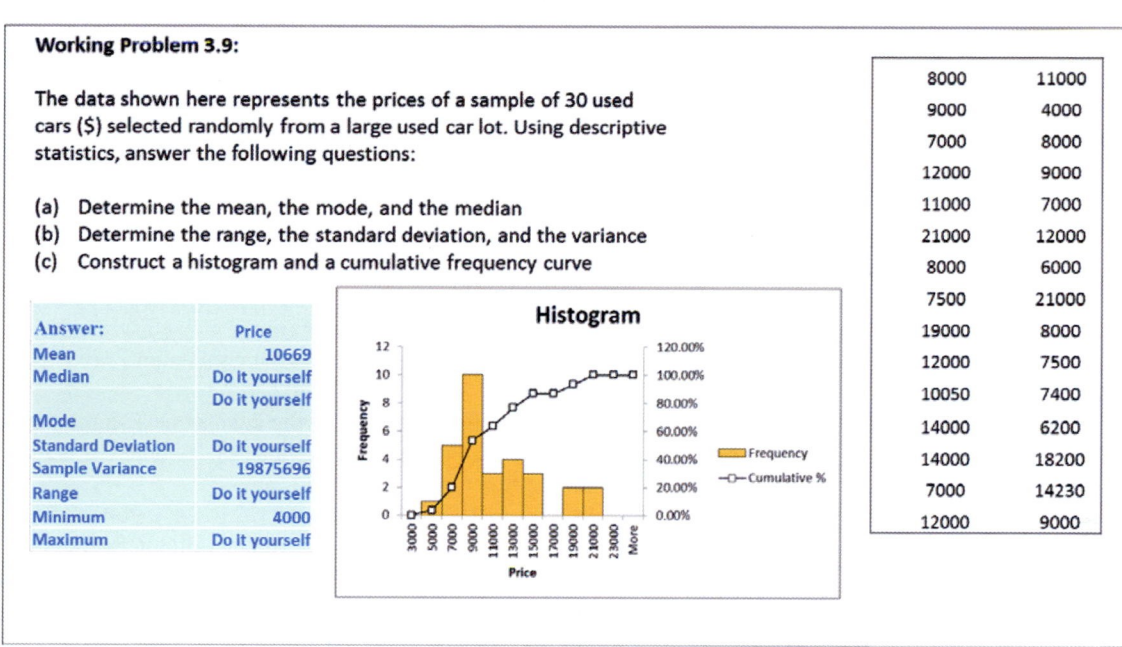

Working Problem 3.9:

The data shown here represents the prices of a sample of 30 used cars ($) selected randomly from a large used car lot. Using descriptive statistics, answer the following questions:

(a) Determine the mean, the mode, and the median
(b) Determine the range, the standard deviation, and the variance
(c) Construct a histogram and a cumulative frequency curve

Answer:	Price
Mean	10669
Median	Do it yourself
	Do it yourself
Mode	
Standard Deviation	Do it yourself
Sample Variance	19875696
Range	Do it yourself
Minimum	4000
Maximum	Do it yourself

8000	11000
9000	4000
7000	8000
12000	9000
11000	7000
21000	12000
8000	6000
7500	21000
19000	8000
12000	7500
10050	7400
14000	6200
14000	18200
7000	14230
12000	9000

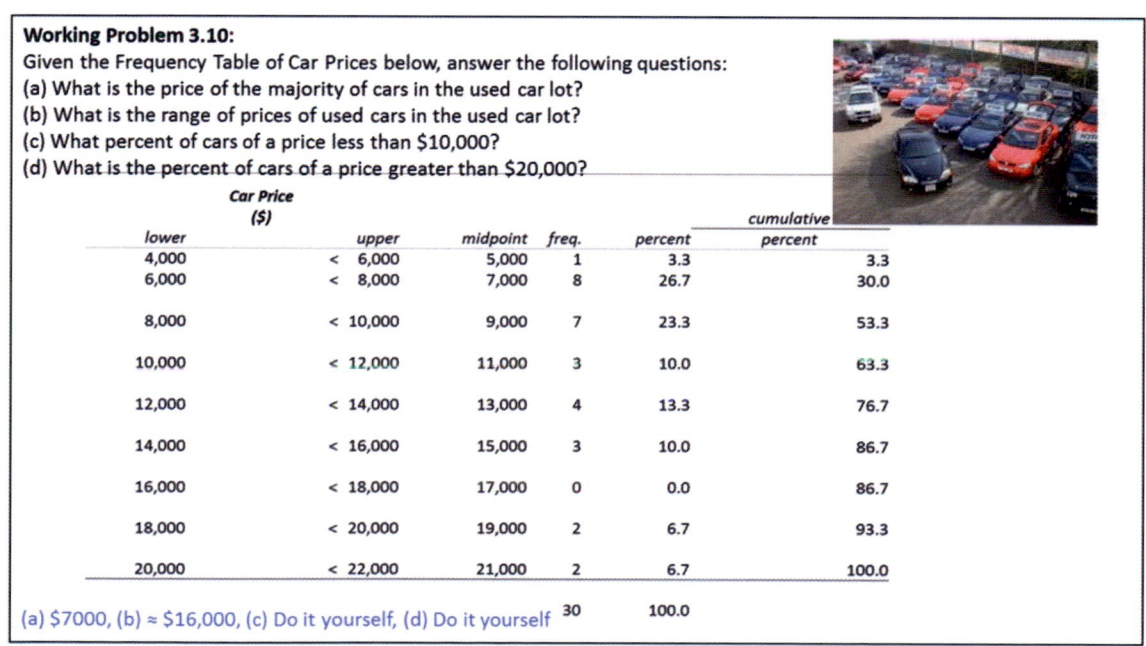

Working Problem 3.10:

Given the Frequency Table of Car Prices below, answer the following questions:
(a) What is the price of the majority of cars in the used car lot?
(b) What is the range of prices of used cars in the used car lot?
(c) What percent of cars of a price less than $10,000?
(d) What is the percent of cars of a price greater than $20,000?

Car Price ($) lower		upper	midpoint	freq.	percent	cumulative percent
4,000	<	6,000	5,000	1	3.3	3.3
6,000	<	8,000	7,000	8	26.7	30.0
8,000	<	10,000	9,000	7	23.3	53.3
10,000	<	12,000	11,000	3	10.0	63.3
12,000	<	14,000	13,000	4	13.3	76.7
14,000	<	16,000	15,000	3	10.0	86.7
16,000	<	18,000	17,000	0	0.0	86.7
18,000	<	20,000	19,000	2	6.7	93.3
20,000	<	22,000	21,000	2	6.7	100.0
				30	100.0	

(a) $7000, (b) ≈ $16,000, (c) Do it yourself, (d) Do it yourself

Illustration 3.1:

Key tips for constructing a histogram and a cumulative frequency curve-By Example:

1. Determine the minimum, the maximum, and the range of the data set.

18	20	Max = 23	21	16
19	18	20	22	19
19	20	21	Min =16	18
20	20	20	22	20
21	19	21	23	22

2. Decide on the number of classes to include in the histogram. The minimum number of classes should be 5 but it can be more than 5 depending on the extent of data resolution required. In this illustration we use 5 classes

3. Find the class width by dividing the range by the number of classes (range = 7, class width = 7/5 = 1.4). If this is not a convenient class width, you may alter it to make it convenient, say class width of '2'.

4. Find the first class lower limit. This may be the minimum value of the data set or a slightly lower convenient value, say 14 (note it is 2 points less than the minimum value of 16, where 2 is the class width). Add the class width to obtain the first class (14 to 16).

5. Proceed to list the other classes ('16 to 18', '18 to 20', '20 to 22', and '22 to 24'). Note that the upper limit of the final class '24' can be slightly higher than the maximum value in the data set '23'.

6. Classes must be mutually exclusive. No value should be counted in two classes. To avoid an overlap, you can use one of the following two methods:

Excel® Method

Class	Bin
> 14 to 16	16
> 16 to 18	18
> 18 to 20	20
> 20 to 22	22
> 22 to 24	24

Common Method

Class	Mid-Point
14 to < 16	15
16 to < 18	17
18 to < 20	19
20 to < 22	21
22 to < 24	23

7. Now, you are ready to determine the frequency, or the number of observations belonging to each class. Note that the two methods described above will yield different frequency values:

Excel® Method

Class	Bin	frequency
> 14 to 16	16	2
> 16 to 18	18	3
> 18 to 20	20	11
> 20 to 22	22	7
> 22 to 24	24	2
		Total = 25

Common Method

Class	Mid-Point	frequency
14 to < 16	15	0
16 to < 18	17	2
18 to < 20	19	7
20 to < 22	21	11
22 to < 24	23	5
		Total = 25

Illustration 3.1 (cont'd):

Key tips for constructing a histogram and a cumulative frequency curve-By Example:

8. Be aware that the two methods will yield slightly different histograms as shown below. It is important, therefore, to interpret a histogram on the basis of the way it was constructed.

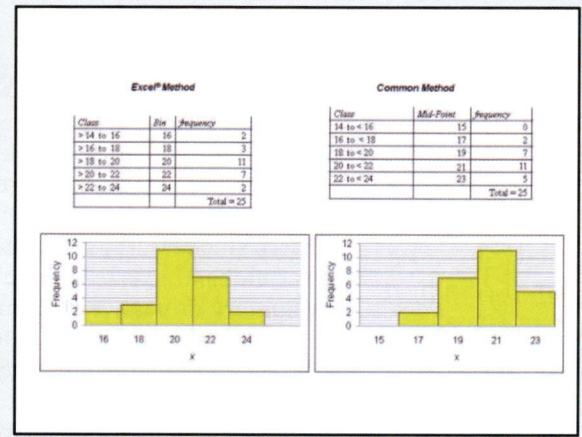

9. Construct a percent relative frequency column
10. Use the percent relative frequency column to construct the percent cumulative frequency column
11. In a cumulative frequency chart, the horizontal axis consists of upper class boundaries, and the vertical axis represents the cumulative frequencies.
12. Plot points that represent the upper class boundaries and their corresponding cumulative frequencies. Connecting these points by line segments will yield the cumulative frequency curve.
13. If you use Excel® method, you will be able to directly obtain the value of $P(x \leq x_o)$ by drawing a vertical line from the x-axis at x_o that intersect with the curve at a point determining the percent $P(x \leq x_o)$.
14. If you use the common method, you will be able to directly obtain the value of $P(x < x_o)$ by drawing a vertical line from the x-axis at x_o that intersect with the curve at a point determining the percent $P(x < x_o)$.

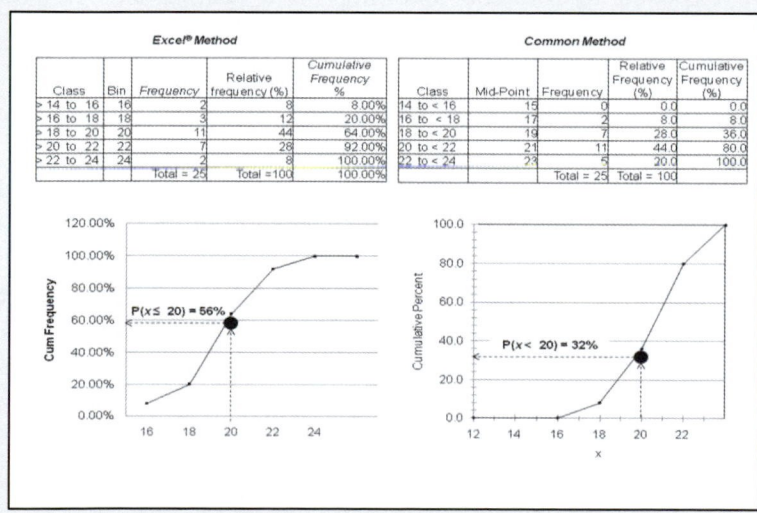

131

3.6 Comparing frequency distributions- The case of second-hand smokers

When two or more frequency distributions are compared, it is critical that they should be constructed of identical class width and they should both cover the entire range of data. Violation of these requirements will result in meaningless comparison and misleading information. The example below illustrates this point.

Example 3.9: Children represent the primary target of many studies on second-hand smoke. In this regard, the important variable to be considered is *the level of blood cotinine in the body*. Cotinine is an alkaloid found in tobacco and is also a metabolite of nicotine. The word "cotinine" is an anagram of '*nicotine*' and it is a chemical that forms inside the body following exposure to nicotine, an ingredient in all tobacco products and a component of Environmental Tobacco Smoke (ETS). Following nicotine exposures, cotinine can usually be detected in the blood for at least 1 to 2 days. The

What is Secondhand Smoke?
Secondhand smoke is a mixture of the smoke given off by the burning end of a cigarette, pipe, or cigar, and the smoke exhaled by smokers. Secondhand smoke is also called environmental tobacco smoke (ETS) and exposure to secondhand smoke is sometimes called involuntary or passive smoking. Secondhand smoke contains more that 4,000 substances, several of which are known to cause cancer in humans or animals. One of the common health risks to children is Asthma. This is the most common chronic childhood disease affecting 1 in 13 school aged children on average. Exposure to secondhand smoke can cause new cases of asthma in children who have not previously shown symptoms. Exposure to secondhand smoke can trigger asthma attacks and make asthma symptoms more severe.
http://www.epa.gov/smokefre/healtheffects.html

data in Table 3.9 represents values of blood cotinine level in two random samples representing children ages 4 to 17. The first set (unexposed children) represents children who were not exposed to tobacco smoking on a regular basis. The second set (exposed children) represents children who were exposed to tobacco smoking on a regular basis. Blood cotinine level is measured in *nanogram per millimeter* (*ng/ml*).

- Determine the mean, the mode, the median, the range, the standard deviation, and the variance for each data set
- Construct a histogram and a cumulative frequency curve for each data set
- According to the Center for Disease Control and Prevention, non-smokers exposed to low levels of ETS typically have blood cotinine concentrations less than 1 *ng/ml*. What percent of the unexposed children has a blood cotinine level of more than 1 *ng/ml*? What percent of the exposed children has a blood cotinine level of more than 1 *ng/ml*?

Table 3.9 Blood-cotinine levels for two groups of children

Cotinine levels of unexposed children (ng/ml)	Cotinine levels of exposed children (ng/ml)	Cotinine levels of unexposed children (ng/ml)	Cotinine levels of exposed children (ng/ml)
0.54	1.88	0.44	1.78
0.62	1.57	0.4	2.04
0.65	2.13	0.55	1.93
0.49	2.61	0.35	2.44
0.51	2.25	0.8	2.4
0.48	2.02	0.33	1.91
0.39	1.65	0.6	1.74
0.63	2	1.1	1.63
0.6	4	0.51	2.2
0.43	1.77	0.41	1.61
0.39	2.21	0.51	1.97
0.5	1.53	0.42	3.5
0.45	2.17	1.2	1.78
0.57	2.21	0.61	1.81
0.38	1.41	0.48	2.23

Solution:

Table 3.10 lists the values of descriptive statistics for the unexposed and the exposed children. These values reveal the following information:

- The mean value of blood-cotinine level found in the unexposed children is 0.545 *ng/ml* and that found in the exposed children is 2.079 *ng/ml*. This is roughly a stunning 282% increase in blood-cotinine level ($100 \times (2.079 - 0.545)/0.545$).
- For each data set, the mean ≈ the mode ≈ the median. This is typically a result of data symmetry or a normal distribution.
- Variability measures such as the range, the standard deviation, and the variance for the exposed children are substantially greater than the corresponding measures for the unexposed children.

Table 3.10 Comparison of blood-cotinine (ng/ml) for the two groups of children

Statistic	Unexposed children	Exposed children
Mean	0.545	2.079
Median	0.505	1.985
Mode	0.51	2.21
Standard Deviation	0.195	0.542
Sample Variance	0.03799	0.29398
Range	0.87	2.59

133

The histograms and cumulative frequency curves constructed for the two data sets are shown in Figures 3.21. These were constructed using Excel® histogram data analysis tool as described in the previous section. Note that the bin range for each data set was the same (class width = 0.25 ng/ml) despite the differences in the data range of each set. This is to allow meaningful comparison between the frequency distributions of the two data sets.

The output of the Excel® histogram tool analysis can also be customized to provide better exploration of the data. Figures 3.22 and 3.23 illustrate the histograms and the cumulative frequency distributions, respectively. Note that the graphs for the data of unexposed and exposed children were superimposed to allow meaningful comparison. This can be achieved using Excel® graphing methods. The frequency tables leading to these graphs are combined in Table 3.11.

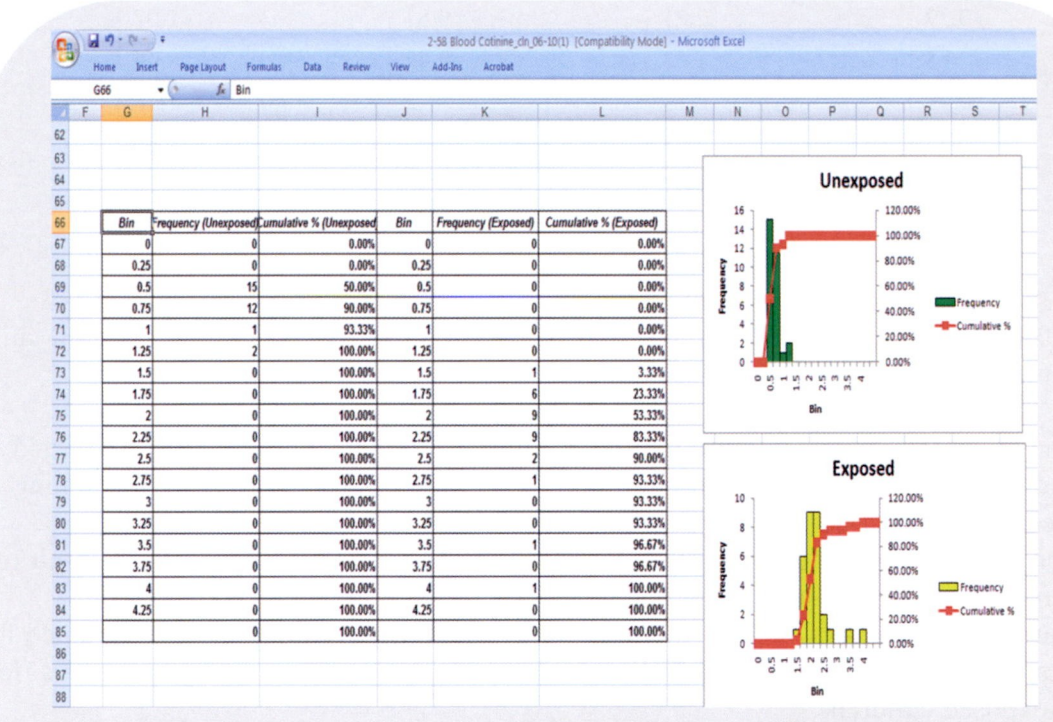

Figure 3.21 Outputs of Excel® Histogram Analysis Tool for blood-cotinine (*ng/ml*)

Table 3.11 Frequency table of blood-cotinine (ng/ml)-Excel® Data Analysis

Classes	Bin	Frequency (Unexposed)	Cumulative % (Unexposed)	Bin	Frequency (Exposed)	Cumulative % (Exposed)
> - 0.25 to 0.00	0	0	0.00%	0	0	0.00%
> 0.00 to 0.25	0.25	0	0.00%	0.25	0	0.00%
> 0.25 to 0.50	0.5	15	50.00%	0.5	0	0.00%
> 0.50 to 0.75	0.75	12	90.00%	0.75	0	0.00%
> 0.75 to 1.0	1	1	93.33%	1	0	0.00%
> 1.00 to 1.25	1.25	2	100.00%	1.25	0	0.00%
> 1.25 to 1.500	1.5	0	100.00%	1.5	1	3.33%
> 1.500 to 1.75	1.75	0	100.00%	1.75	6	23.33%
> 1.75 to 2.00	2	0	100.00%	2	9	53.33%
> 2.00 to 2.25	2.25	0	100.00%	2.25	9	83.33%
> 2.25 to 2.50	2.5	0	100.00%	2.5	2	90.00%
> 2.50 to 2.75	2.75	0	100.00%	2.75	1	93.33%
> 2.75 to 3.00	3	0	100.00%	3	0	93.33%
> 3.00 to 3.25	3.25	0	100.00%	3.25	0	93.33%
> 3.25 to 3.50	3.5	0	100.00%	3.5	1	96.67%
> 3.50 to 3.75	3.75	0	100.00%	3.75	0	96.67%
> 3.75 to 4.00	4	0	100.00%	4	1	100.00%
> 4.00 to 4.25	4.25	0	100.00%	4.25	0	100.00%

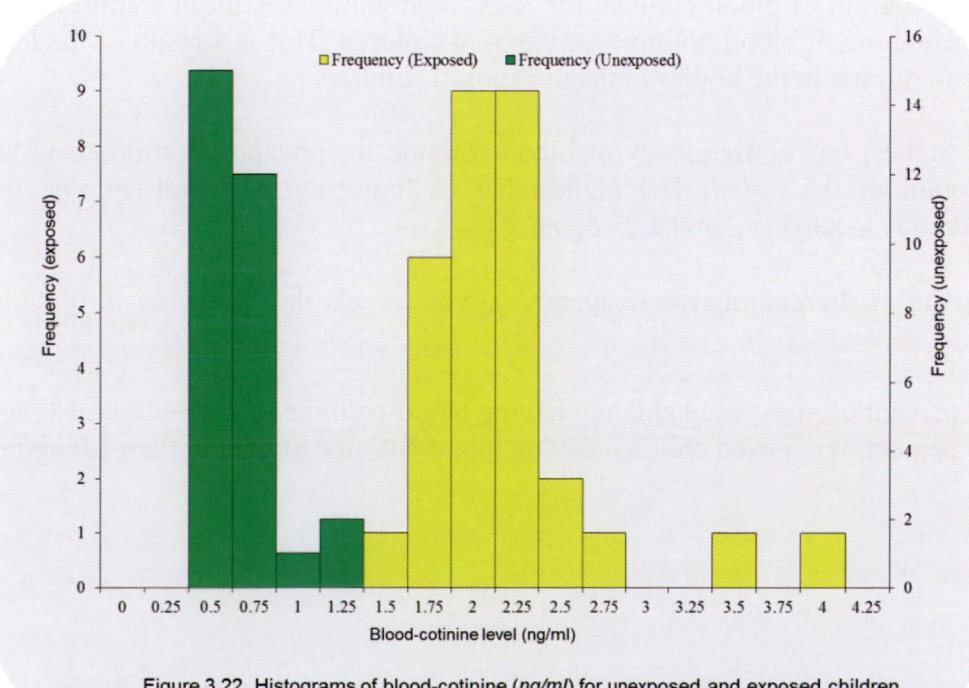

Figure 3.22 Histograms of blood-cotinine (*ng/ml*) for unexposed and exposed children

135

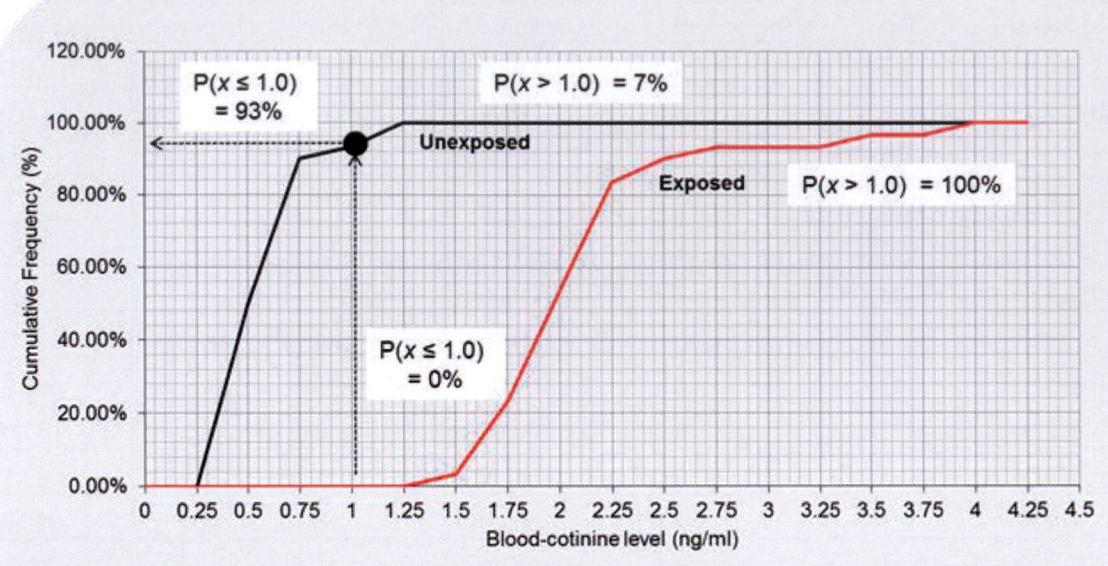

Figure 3.23 Cumulative Frequency Curves of blood-cotinine (*ng/ml*) for unexposed and exposed children Calculation of P($x \leq 1.0$)

Comparison of the histograms of the exposed and unexposed children reveals the following information:

- The histogram of blood-cotinine for unexposed children is located entirely to the left of the histogram of blood-cotinine for exposed children. This is a result of the low values of blood-cotinine in the bodies of the unexposed children.

- The highest bar of frequency of blood-cotinine for unexposed children is located at a midpoint of 0.5 *ng/ml*. The highest bar of frequency of blood-cotinine for exposed children is located at 2 and 2.25 *ng/ml*.

Comparison of the cumulative frequency curves reveals the following information (Figure 3.23):

- The percent of unexposed children having blood-cotinine of greater than 1.0 *ng/ml* is 7%.
- The percent of exposed children having blood-cotinine of greater than 1.0 *ng/ml* is 100%.

Example 3.10: In the example above, what percent of the unexposed children has a blood cotinine level of more than 2 *ng/ml*? What percent of the exposed children has a blood cotinine level of more than 2 *ng/ml*?

Solution:

The answer to this question is illustrated in Figure 3.24.

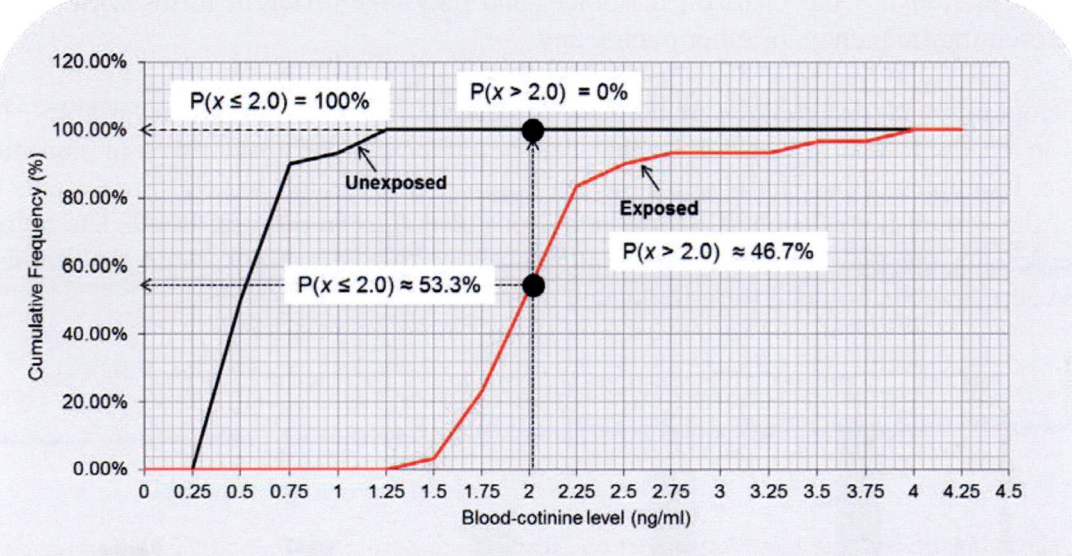

Figure 3.24 Cumulative Frequency Curves of blood-cotinine (*ng/ml*) for unexposed and exposed children Calculation of P(x ≤ 2.0)

Working Problem 3.11:

This histogram was constructed using the Excel® Method. It illustrates the distribution of ages of the top 98 billionaires in the world as of 2011.

(a) Roughly determine the number of billionaires that are 40 years of age or younger (2 billionaires)
(b) Roughly determine the number of billionaires that are 50 years of age or younger (13 billionaires)
(c) Roughly determine the number of billionaires that are 60 years of age or younger (36 billionaires)
(d) Roughly determine how many billionaires that are older than 70 (40 billionaires)
(e) Interpret the descriptive statistics of the ages of top billionaires

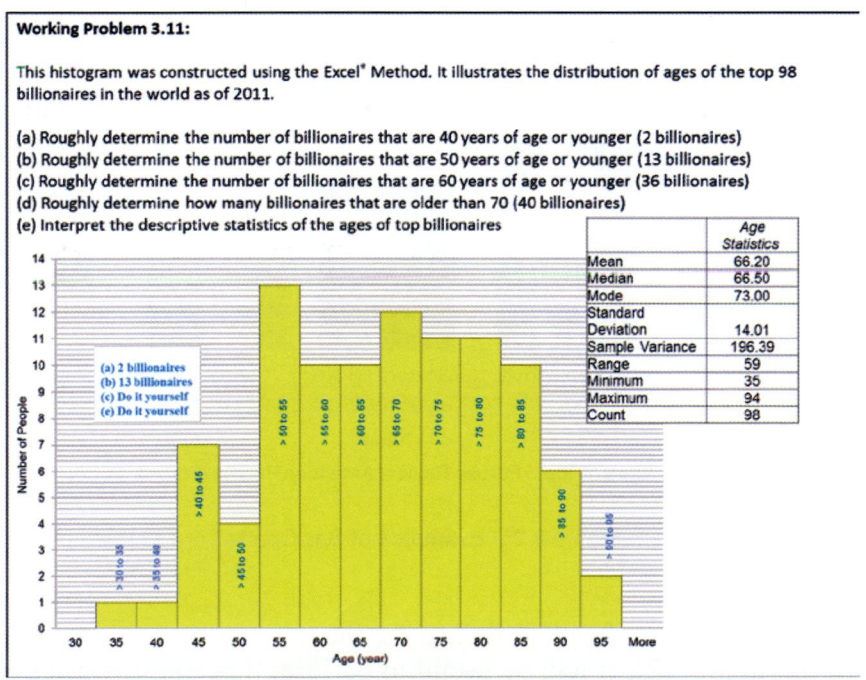

3.7 Bar chart versus histogram: The net worth of billionaires

Earlier in this chapter, we discussed the bar chart and defined it as an x-y chart in which the x-axis represents values of a quantitative variable or labels of a qualitative variable and the y-axis represents the corresponding values depicted by bars. We then defined a histogram or a frequency distribution as a graph resulting from grouping data into mutually exclusive classes of values and displaying frequencies or the number of observations for each class. In essence, a histogram is a bar chart, which reflects the frequencies of equally spaced classes of values of the variable under study. A bar chart on the other hand may take different forms with the vertical axes representing frequency, or other parameters.

Both histograms and bar charts can be used for qualitative or quantitative variables, but bar charts can be used with arrangements that can be either mutually exclusive or non-mutually exclusive. Examples of bar charts are shown in Figure 3.25. The top bar chart represents the net worth of the United States' richest people in billions of dollars in the year 2009. The bottom bar chart represents the ages of those same billionaires in the year 2009. With the limited data involved here, there is no need for a frequency distribution.

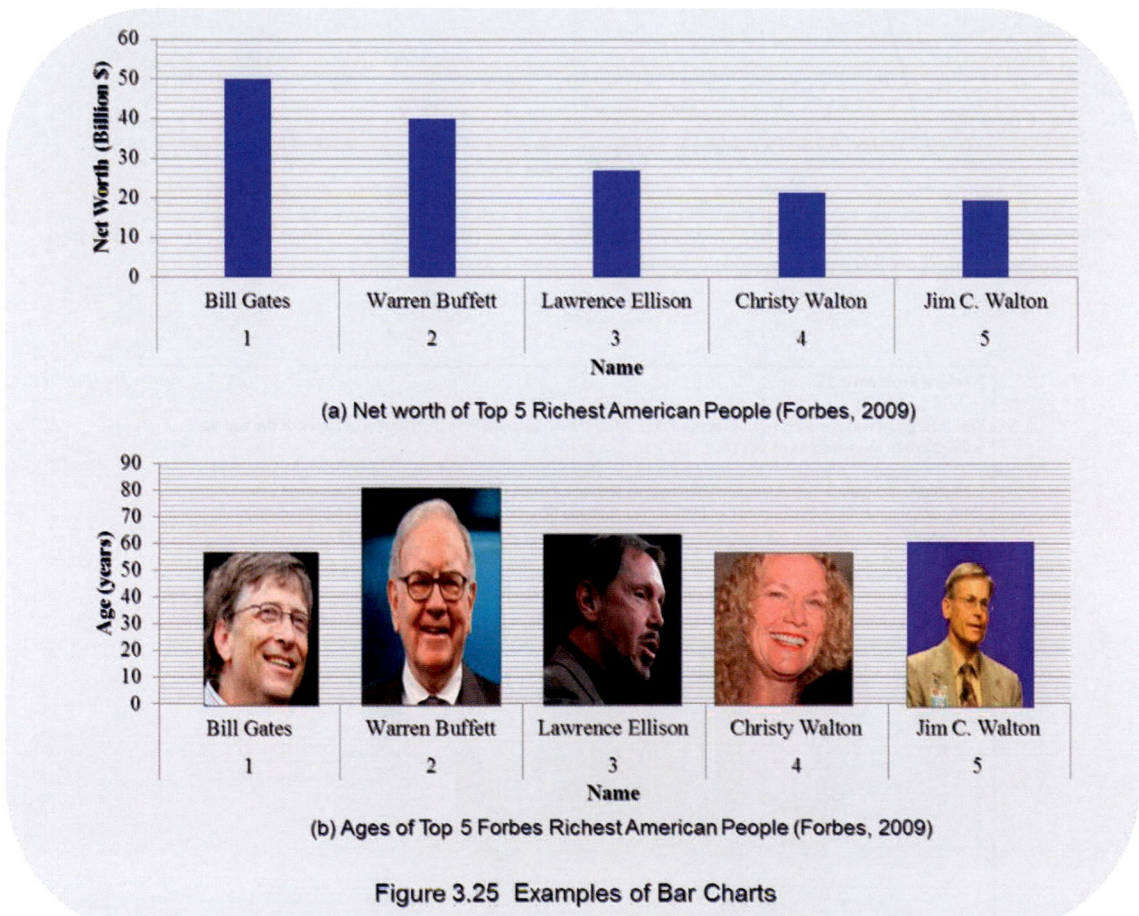

(a) Net worth of Top 5 Richest American People (Forbes, 2009)

(b) Ages of Top 5 Forbes Richest American People (Forbes, 2009)

Figure 3.25 Examples of Bar Charts

When the objective, on the other hand, is to analyze the net worth of the top 100 billionaires in the world (shown in Table 3.12), it will be useful to perform this analysis using a histogram and a cumulative frequency curve as shown in Figures 3.26. The classes and the frequency values associated with these data are illustrated in Table 3.13. Note how only very few have a net worth of over $25 billion and how the majority of billionaires have a net worth of $5 to $6 billion dollars. Also note from the cumulative frequency curve of Figure 3.26 that the percentage of billionaires making more than $10 billion dollars is 38%.

Table 3.12 Data of net worth (billion $) of the top 100 billionaires in the world

$5.70	$17.60	$13.40	$10.50	$6.00	$11.00	$22.00	$6.80	$9.00	$8.10
$5.70	$17.60	$13.30	$5.00	$7.60	$11.00	$18.30	$6.70	$9.00	$8.00
$5.70	$17.60	$13.20	$4.40	$6.00	$21.50	$17.80	$6.50	$8.50	$8.00
$5.60	$16.50	$13.00	$3.50	$6.00	$19.50	$6.30	$6.30	$8.20	$10.00
$5.50	$16.20	$7.00	$3.40	$5.20	$19.30	$6.30	$10.50	$8.20	$10.00
$12.30	$16.00	$7.00	$9.00	$5.20	$18.80	$6.20	$10.10	$5.50	$9.90
$12.00	$50.00	$7.00	$9.00	$5.20	$7.80	$6.10	$10.00	$5.50	$9.50
$12.00	$40.00	$7.00	$9.00	$5.00	$7.80	$6.00	$10.00	$5.40	$14.50
$12.00	$35.00	$7.00	$9.00	$5.00	$7.70	$5.40	$5.20	$5.00	$14.00
$11.00	$22.50	$7.00	$9.00	$5.00	$6.00	$5.30	$5.20	$5.00	$14.00

Table 3.13 Frequency table of net worth (billion $) of the top 100 billionaires in the world

Lower		Upper	Mid-point	Frequency	Relative Frequency (%)	Cumulative Frequency (%)
2	<	4	3	2	2	2
4	<	6	5	22	22	24
6	<	8	7	23	23	47
8	<	10	9	15	15	62
10	<	12	11	10	10	72
12	<	14	13	8	8	80
14	<	16	15	3	3	83
16	<	18	17	7	7	90
18	<	20	19	4	4	94
20	<	22	21	1	1	95
22	<	24	23	2	2	97
24	<	26	25	0	0	97
26	<	28	27	0	0	97
28	<	30	29	0	0	97
30	<	32	31	0	0	97
32	<	34	33	0	0	97
34	<	36	35	1	1	98
36	<	38	37	0	0	98
38	<	40	39	0	0	98
40	<	42	41	1	1	99
42	<	44	43	0	0	99
44	<	46	45	0	0	99
46	<	48	47	0	0	99
48	<	50	49	0	0	99
50	<	52	51	1	1	100

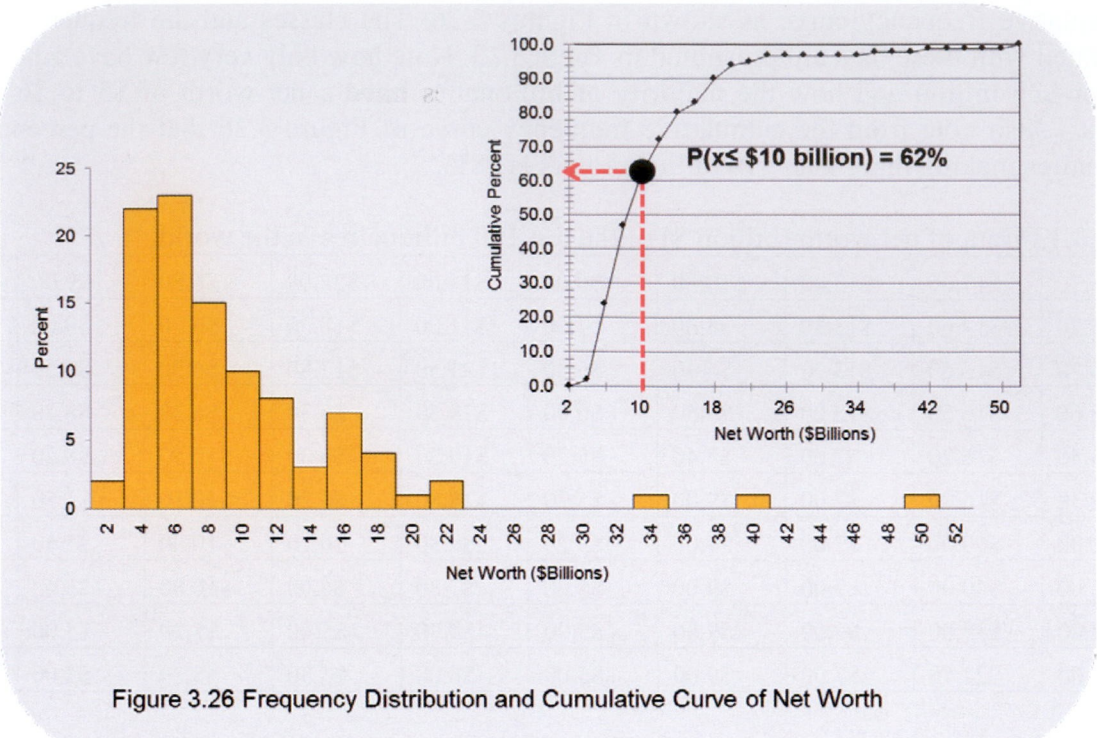

Figure 3.26 Frequency Distribution and Cumulative Curve of Net Worth

3.8 The shape of the frequency distribution

In general, common shapes that a frequency distribution may take are as follows (see Figure 3.27):

- Symmetrical shape
- Positively skewed
- Negatively skewed
- Steep (positive kurtosis)
- Flat (negative kurtosis)
- Bimodal or multimodal

A symmetrical (unimodal) shape (Figure 3.27.a) will have equal values of mean, median, and mode. These three statistics are located at the center of the distribution and data values are evenly spread around these values. A symmetrical shape is usually generated from a large amount of data and it is to be expected for variables that follow *'nominal-the-best'* patterns. These include data of dimensions such as thickness of wood boards or areas of ceramic tiles.

A data set that is skewed to the right is known as positively skewed. The distribution of this type of data is shown in Figure 3.27.b and it is characterized by a single peak with data values extended to the right of the peak rather than to the left of the peak. For this shape, the mean value is larger than the median and the skewness index, to be defined shortly, is positive. This type of distribution is often generated from data representing practical situations such as a challenging

140

exam in which the majority of students performed poorly (low scores) and only few performed well. It also simulates large corporate salaries, where the majority of workers are making low or middle salary rates while only a few are making top dollar. S*maller-the-better* variables such as accidents on the job per month, car accidents, defects, and rejects should ideally follow a positively skewed distribution.

A data set that is skewed to the left is known as negatively skewed. The distribution of this type of data is shown in Figure 3.27.c and it is characterized by a single peak with data values extended to the left of the peak rather than to the right of the peak. For this shape, the mean value is smaller than the median and the skewness index, to be defined shortly, is negative. This type of distribution is often generated from data representing practical situations such as the grades of an easy exam in which the majority of students performed well (high scores) and only few performed poorly. *Larger-the-better* variables such as operating efficiency, economic growth rate, people's income, health, and working performance indexes should ideally follow a negatively skewed distribution.

A data set that has a steep peak with values to the right and to the left close to the center will produce the distribution shown in Figure 3.27.d. This distribution is known to have a positive kurtosis index as will be defined shortly. A data set that has an extended uniform and flat shape will produce the distribution shown in Figure 3.27.e. This distribution is known to have a negative kurtosis index as will be defined shortly. A bimodal or multimodal distribution will have two or more peaks (see Figure 3.27.f). This is often the case when there is a potential mix of samples coming from different populations.

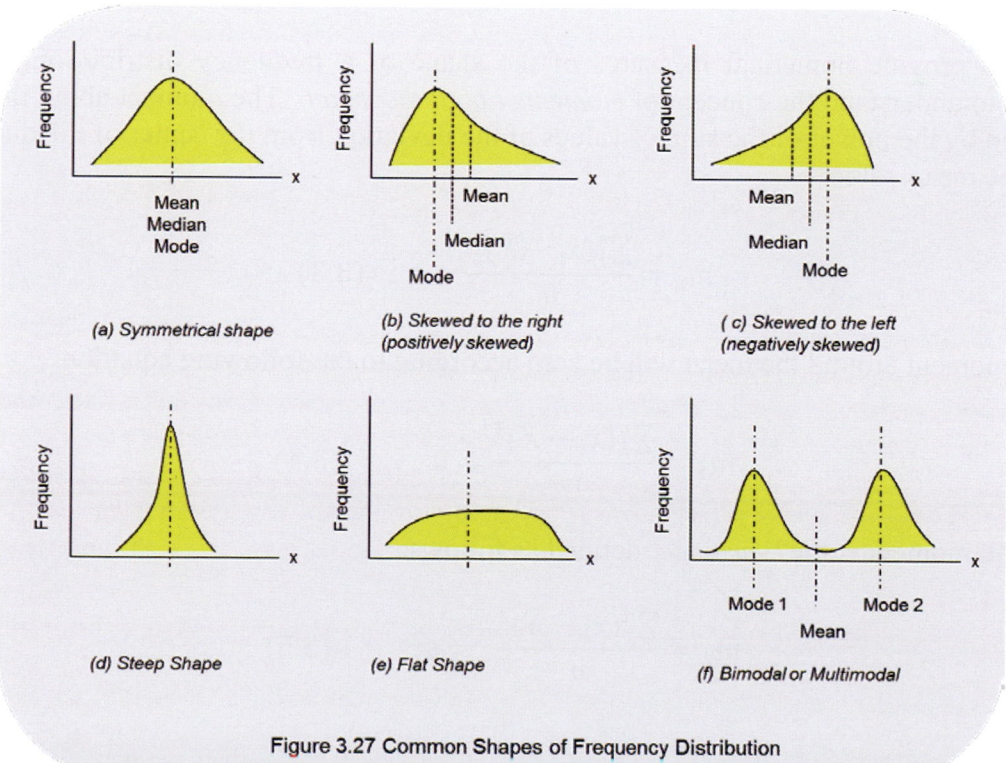

Figure 3.27 Common Shapes of Frequency Distribution

141

Working Problem 3.12:

Describe each of the histograms below by determining a variable that may follow the shape of each histogram. For the following variables, which histogram will ideally represent its values:

- Income
- Number of failing students
- Property tax
- Waiting time for school bus

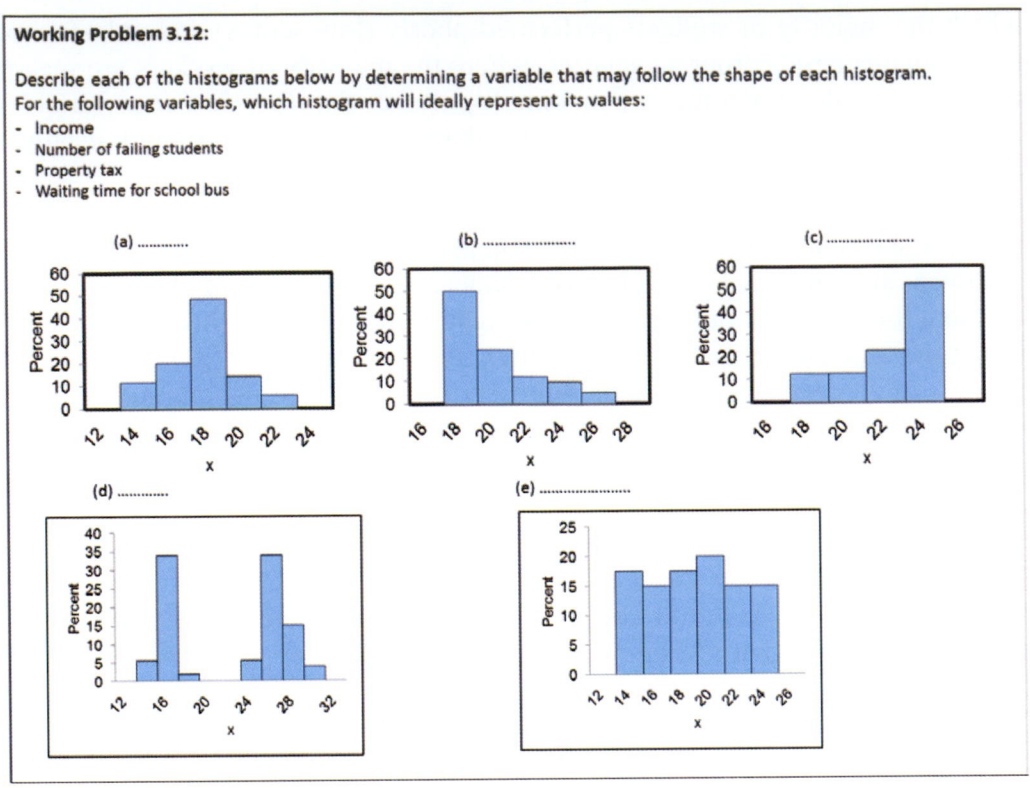

3.9 Moments about the mean

In order to provide numerical measures of the shape of a frequency distribution, it will be important to understand the concept of *moments about the mean*. The moment about the mean is determined by the power of the sum of values of the deviation from the center of the distribution, or from the mean value:

$$m_r = \frac{\sum_1^n (x_i - \bar{X})^r}{n} \qquad (3.3)$$

The first moment around the mean will be zero according to the following equation:

$$m_1 = \frac{\sum_1^n (x_i - \bar{X})^1}{n} = 0 \qquad (3.4)$$

The second moment is the '*variance*' defined as follows:

$$m_2 = \frac{\sum_1^n (x_i - \bar{X})^2}{n} = s^2 \qquad (3.5)$$

The third moment is called 'skewness,' which is calculated as follows:

$$m_3 = \frac{\sum_1^n (x_i - \bar{X})^3}{n} = skewness \qquad (3.6)$$

As illustrated in Figure 3.27, skewness is a measure of the symmetry of the data distribution around the mean. Figure 3.27.b shows a positively skewed distribution, and Figure 3.27.c shows a negatively-skewed distribution.

The fourth moment is called 'kurtosis,' which is calculated as follows:

$$m_4 = \frac{\sum_1^n (x_i - \bar{X})^4}{n} = kurtosis \qquad (3.7)$$

Kurtosis is a measure of the relative shape of the middle and the tails of the data distribution. In other words, it is a measure of flatness and/or peakness in relation to the normal distribution. Figure 3.27.d and 3.27.e show positive and negative kurtosis, respectively.

In practice, the skewness is determined by the following index:

$$Skewness\ Index = \frac{n}{(n-1)(n-2)} \sum_1^n \left(\frac{x_i - \bar{X}}{s}\right)^3 \qquad (3.8)$$

This index is used by Excel® data analysis (under descriptive statistics).

Another way to determine the skewness is by using Pearson's coefficient of skewness (named after the English statistician Karl Pearson 1857-1936):

$$SK = \frac{3(\bar{X} - Median)}{s} \qquad (3.9)$$

The value of SK ranges from -3 to 3 for most frequency distributions. When $SK > 0$, the data will be skewed to the right. When $SK < 0$, the data will be skewed to the left. When $SK = 0$, the data will be symmetrical.

Kurtosis is determined by the following equation:

$$Kurtosis\ Index = \frac{n(n+1)}{(n-1)(n-2)(n-3)} \sum_1^n \left(\frac{x_i - \bar{X}}{s}\right)^4 - \frac{3(n-1)^2}{(n-2)(n-3)} \qquad (3.10)$$

This index is used by Excel® data analysis (under descriptive statistics).

Example 3.11: Using manual calculations and the Excel® descriptive statistics tool, determine the skeweness and the kurtosis of the following data set of ages of college students.

Table 3.14 Ages of college students

20	19	19	18	20	23
19	18	18	18	21	24
18	20	18	19	21	24
19	20	18	19	22	25
18	20	18	19	22	25
20	19	18	20	22	26
19	19	18	20	23	26

Solution:

The skewness of this data can be determined by first calculating the mean and the standard deviation as discussed in Chapter 2. The mean of the above data is:

$$Mean = \bar{X} = \frac{\sum_1^n x_i}{n} = \frac{20 + 19 + 18 + \cdots + +26 + 26}{42} = 20.29$$

The standard deviation is:

$$s = \sqrt{\frac{\sum_1^n (x_i - \bar{X})^2}{n}} = \sqrt{\frac{(20 - 29.29)^2 + (19 - 29.29)^2 + \cdots + (26 - 29.29)^2}{42}} = 2.402$$

Accordingly, the skewness index can be calculated as follows:

$$Skewness\ Index = \frac{n}{(n-1)(n-2)} \sum_1^n \left(\frac{x_i - \bar{X}}{s}\right)^3$$

$$= \frac{42}{(41)(40)} \left[\frac{(20 - 20.29)^3}{(2.402)^3} + \frac{(19 - 20.29)^3}{(2.402)^3} + \cdots \frac{(26 - 20.29)^3}{(2.402)^3}\right] = 1.087$$

The median (the middle value of the data set) is 19.5. Using the Pearson's coefficient of skewness:

$$SK = \frac{3(\bar{X} - Median)}{s} = \frac{3(20.29 - 19.5)}{2.402} = 0.987$$

Since $SK > 0$, we conclude that the data are skewed to the right.

The Kurtosis of this data set can be determined by the following equation:

$$Kurtosis\ Index = \frac{n(n+1)}{(n-1)(n-2)(n-3)}\sum_{1}^{n}\left(\frac{x_i - \bar{X}}{s}\right)^4 - \frac{3(n-1)^2}{(n-2)(n-3)} =$$

$$\frac{42(42+1)}{(42-1)(42-2)(42-3)}\left[\frac{(20-20.29)^4}{(2.402)^3} + \cdots + \cdots \frac{(26-20.29)^4}{(2.402)^3}\right] - \frac{3(42-1)^2}{(42-2)(42-3)}$$

$$= 0.129$$

The above calculations can be made using Excel® descriptive statistics tool as discussed in Chapter 2. The output of this analysis is shown in Table 3.15.

Table 3.15 Descriptive statistics (Excel® Descriptive Statistics output)

Mean	20.29
Median	19.5
Mode	18
Standard Deviation	2.402
Sample Variance	5.770
Kurtosis	0.129
Skewness	1.087

In conclusion, the data has a positive skew of 1.087 and a positive kurtosis of 0.129. The histogram of the data is shown in Figure 3.28. The frequency distribution depicted by this histogram indicates a positive skew.

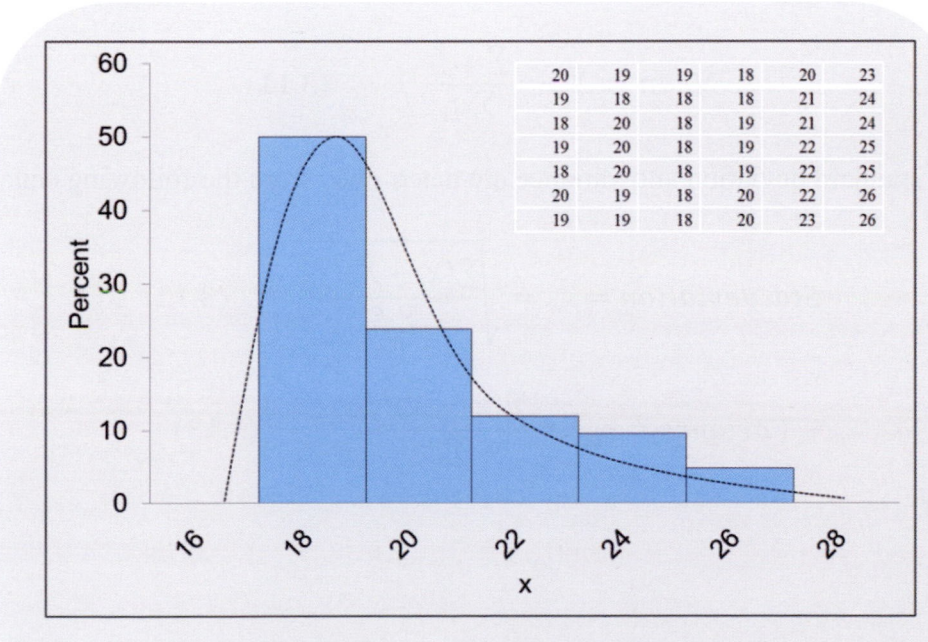

Figure 3.28 Frequency Distribution of Student's Age

Working Problem 3.13 (review of key points of Chapters 2 & 3):

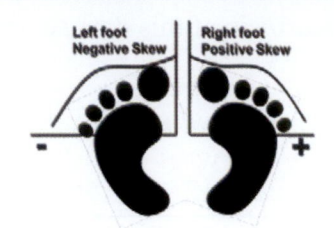

For each of the following three data sets:
(a) Determine the mean, the mode, the median, the range, the standard deviation, and the variance?
(b) Determine the skeweness and the kurtosis
(c) Construct the histogram and the cumulative frequency
(d) Compare the shapes of the frequency distributions of the three data sets in the context of skeweness and kurtosis

Data Set A:

14	17	19	18	21
14	17	19	18	21
15	17	19	18	22
15	17	19	18	22
16	18	20	18	18
16	18	20	18	18
16	18	20	18	18

Data Set B:

20	21	23	24	25
19	21	23	24	25
18	22	23	24	25
19	22	24	25	25
18	22	24	25	25
20	23	24	25	25
19	23	24	25	25
20	23	24	25	25

Data Set C:

22	16	24	19	22
21	14	23	22	19
22	16	21	20	19
19	17	24	14	16
24	14	14	14	24
14	24	24	20	22
20	21	15	21	20
19	16	19	16	18

3.10 The weighted mean and standard deviation

The use of frequency distributions leads to the issue of how to perform numerical descriptive statistics for grouped data. In other words, if the data available is already grouped with associated weight or frequency, how can we determine their mean value and standard deviation? In general, if x_i is the variable value, and f_i is the weight or frequency associated with the variable value, the weighed mean is determined by:

$$Mean = \bar{X}_w = \frac{\sum x_i f_i}{\sum f_i} \qquad (3.11)$$

The weighted standard deviation and variance are determined from the following equations:

$$Std.\, deviation = s_w = \sqrt{\frac{\sum (x_i - \bar{X})^2 f_i}{\sum f_i}} \qquad (3.12)$$

$$Variance = s_w{}^2 = \frac{\sum (x_i - \bar{X})^2 f_i}{\sum f_i} \qquad (3.13)$$

146

Example 3.12: Suppose you had a party with 20 guests in attendance. You went to McDonald's restaurant and bought five Big Mac meals for $6 each, eight happy meals for $2.50 each, and seven grilled chicken meals for $5.50 each. How much did you pay and what is the average price per meal? What is the variance of the meal price?

Solution:

The data given in this example and associated calculations are presented in the following frequency table:

Table 3.16 Calculations of mean and variance of grouped data

Price (x)	Frequency (f_i)	$x_i f_i$	$(x_i - \bar{X})$	$(x_i - \bar{X})^2$	$f_i(x_i - \bar{X})^2$
6.0	5	30.0	1.575	2.481	12.405
2.5	8	20.0	-1.925	3.706	29.648
5.5	7	38.5	1.075	1.156	8.092
Sum	$n = 20$	88.5			50.145

The total you paid will be $88.5 (5×6.0 + 8×2.5 + 7×5.5).

The average price per meal is:

$$\bar{X}_w = \frac{\sum x_i f_i}{\sum f_i} = \frac{5 \times 6 + 8 \times 2.5 + 7 \times 5.5}{20} = \frac{88.5}{20} = \$4.425$$

Using the calculations in Table 3.16:

$$Std.\,deviation = s_w = \sqrt{\frac{\sum (x_i - \bar{X})^2 f_i}{\sum f_i}} = \sqrt{\frac{50.145}{19}} = \$1.625 \quad and \quad s_w{}^2 = 2.641$$

Note, we used the sum minus 1 since the total frequency, n is less than 30.

Working Problem 3.14:

In a stat test, 4 students earned 75/100, 24 students earned 85/100, and 12 students earned 95/100. What are the mean, standard deviation, and variance of the grades?

Answer: Calculations of mean and variance of grouped data

Grade (x)	Frequency (f_i)	xf	$(x - \bar{X})$	$(x - \bar{X})^2$	$f(x - \bar{X})^2$
75	4	300	-12	....	576
85	...	......	-2	4	96
....	12	1140	8	64	....
	Sum = 40	Sum 3480			......

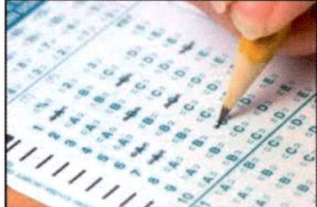

Mean =	87
Variance	36.00
Std. Dev	6.00

Working Problem 3.15:

The Seno car body shop pays its hourly employees $10.50, $15.00, or $20.00 per hour. There are 26 hourly employees, 14 of which are paid at the $10.50 rate, 10 at the $15.00 rate, and 2 at the $20.00 rate.

- What is the mean hourly rate paid?
- What is the standard deviation?
- What is the variance?

Answer:

Calculations of mean and variance of grouped data

Price (x)	Frequency (f_i)	xf	$(x - \bar{X})$	$(x - \bar{X})^2$	$f(x - \bar{X})^2$
.....	....	......	-2.46154	....	....
15	10	......	....	4.155325	41.55325
20	....	40	7.038462	....	....
	26	......			....
		Mean =	12.96154		
		Variance	9.02		
		Std. Dev	3.00		

Working Problem 3.16:

Use the frequency distribution shown in the table to Determine the mean, standard deviation and variance of the property tax value for the sample of 50 houses.

Tax ($)	Frequency (f_i)
6000	6
7000	8
8000	16
9000	11
10000	5
11000	4

Mean	8260
Variance	1912400
std dev	1382.89551

3.11 What is Chebyshev's theorem?

As indicated earlier, a small standard deviation for a set of values indicates that these values are located close to the mean. On the other hand, a large standard deviation reveals that the observations are widely scattered about the mean. The Russian mathematician *P. L. Chebyshev* (1821–1894) developed a theorem that allows us to determine the minimum proportion of the values that lie within a specified number of standard deviations of the mean. This theorem states:

"In a frequency distribution of data, the proportion of the values that lie within k standard deviations of the mean is at least $1-1/k^2$, where k is any constant greater than one"

This means that at least three of four values, or 75 percent, must lie between the mean plus two standard deviations and the mean minus two standard deviations. This relationship holds regardless of the shape of the distribution. Further, at least eight of nine values, or 88.9 percent, will lie between plus three standard deviations and minus three standard deviations of the mean, and at least 24 of 25 values, or 96 percent, will lie between plus and minus five standard deviations of the mean.

Example 3.13: Figure 3.29 shows the frequency distributions of annual salary between professors at two different colleges. As you can see in this figure, both colleges share the same average annual salary, but college *B* had twice the standard deviation, which is reflected in a much wider distribution than that of college *A*.

(a) Using the case of College '*A*' frequency distribution shown in Figure 3.29, where the mean of professors' salaries is $80,000, and the standard deviation is $10,000, answer the following questions:

- At least what percent of the salaries lie within plus and minus 2.0 standard deviations of the mean?
- At least what percent of the salaries lie within plus and minus 3.0 standard deviations of the mean?

(b) Using the case of College 'B' frequency distribution shown in Figure 3.29, where the mean of professors' salaries is $80,000, and the standard deviation is $20,000, answer the following questions:

- At least what percent of the salaries lie within plus and minus 2.0 standard deviations of the mean?
- At least what percent of the salaries lie within plus and minus 3.0 standard deviations of the mean?

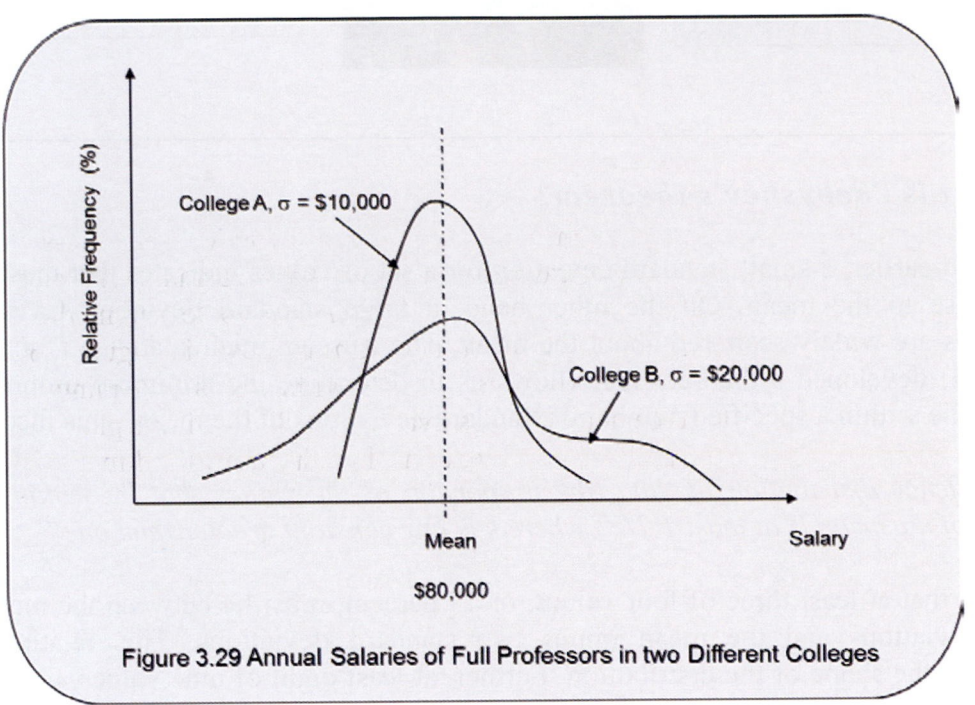

Figure 3.29 Annual Salaries of Full Professors in two Different Colleges

Solution:

(a) For College A,

- At $\pm 2.0\sigma$, $1 - \frac{1}{k^2} = 1 - \frac{1}{2^2} = 0.75$, which means that at least 75% of the salaries lie within plus 2.0 standard deviations and minus 2.0 standard deviations of the mean (or $60,000 to $100,000).

- At $\pm 3.0\sigma$, $1 - \frac{1}{k^2} = 1 - \frac{1}{3^2} = 0.8888$, which means that at least 89% of the salaries lie within plus 3.0 standard deviations and minus 3.0 standard deviations of the mean (or $50,000 to $110,000).

(b) For College B, attempt to do it yourself

150

Working Problem 3.17:

In remodeling your home, you used many contractors that were paid hourly an average wage of $50. The standard deviation of wages was $15.

- At least what percent of the wages lie within plus 2 standard Deviations and minus 2 standard deviations of the average wage?

- At least what percent of the wages lie within plus 3 standard deviations and minus 3 standard deviations of the average wage?

3.12 What is the empirical rule?

The Chebyshev's theorem is applied for any frequency distribution regardless its shape. In Chapter 1, the normal distribution was introduced as a bell-shaped symmetrical distribution. For this type of distribution, we can use the so-called '*empirical rule*' to determine the proportion of the values that lie within k standard deviations of the mean as shown in Figure 3.30. According to this rule, 68.26 percent of the observations will lie within plus and minus one standard deviation of the mean; 95.44 percent of the observations will lie within plus and minus two standard deviations of the mean; and 99.74 percent will lie within plus and minus three standard deviations of the mean.

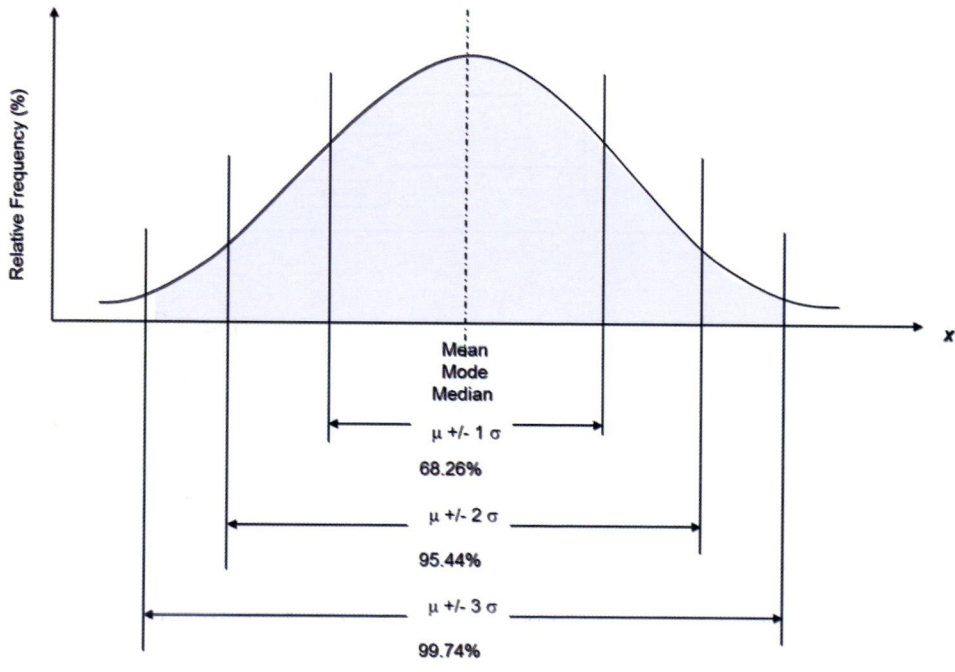

Figure 3.30 The Empirical Rule

151

Example 3.14: Using the empirical rule, answer part (a) of Example 3.13 assuming that College '*A*' frequency distribution of salary can be approximated by a normal distribution.

Solution:

The percent of salaries within the range of the mean plus and minus 2 standard deviation, $\mu \pm 2\sigma = 80,000 \pm 20,000$ (or from \$60,000 to \$100,000) is 95.44%.

The percent of salaries within the range of the mean plus and minus 3 standard deviation, $\mu \pm 3\sigma = 80,000 \pm 30,000$ (or from \$50,000 to \$110,000) is 99.74%.

Working Problem 3.18:

A course average grade is typically 80%, and the standard deviation of grade is 5%. Assuming that the grade value has bell-shaped symmetrical distribution:

(a) What percent of students will make '*C*' grade or lower (C = 70%)
(b) What percent of students will make '*B*' grade or better (B = 80%)
(c) What percent of students will make '*A*' grade or better (A = 90%)

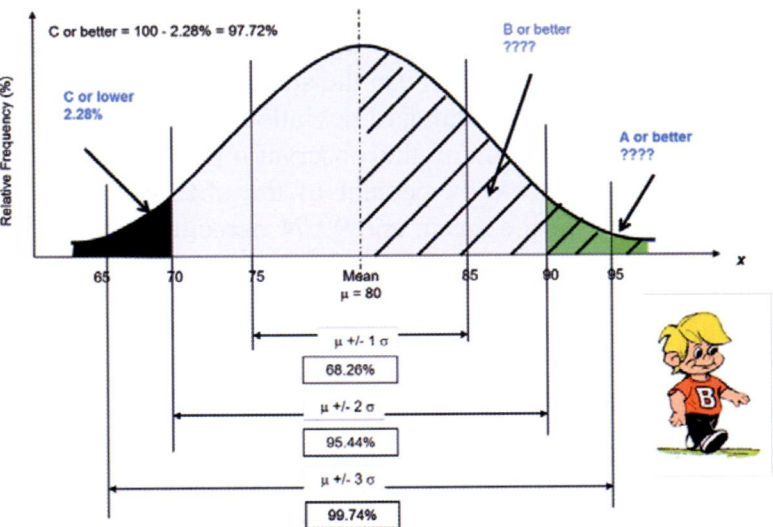

Working Problem 3.19:

A course average grade is typically 75%, and the standard deviation of grade is 2.5%. Assuming that the grade value has bell-shaped symmetrical distribution:

- What percent of students will make '*C*' grade or lower (C = 70%)
- What percent of students will make '*B*' grade or better (B = 80%)
- What percent of students will make '*A*' grade or better (A = 90%)

Answer:
Follow the procedure of the previous working problem and do it yourself

Working Problem 3.20:

Heights of men have a bell-shaped distribution with a mean of 176 cm and a standard deviation of 7 cm. Using the empirical rule, what is the approximate percentage of men:

a. 169 cm and 183 cm?
b. 155 cm and 197 cm?
c. Taller than 190?

Answer: (a) 68.26%, (b) 99.74%, (c) 2.28%

3.13 Other forms of graphical displays of data

Bar charts, pie charts and histograms are among the most commonly used graphical representations of data. In addition, there are other ways to display and explore data that can be useful for many applications. These include:

- *Dot plot*
- *Stem and leaf plot*
- *Box plot*
- *Scatter plot*

For a small number of observations, these plots can easily be constructed manually. For a large number of observations, specialized software programs should be used.

3.13.1 Dot plot

A *dot plot* represents a form of frequency distributions in which no classes or groups are used. Instead, each observation in the data set is represented by a dot that can be seen on the dot plot along the horizontal axis to indicate the value of data. When we have many observations of the same value or observations that are too close to be shown individually, the dots are stacked on top of each other. This provides an illustration of the frequency distribution. In practice, dot plots are used for small data sets and when individual values are of high significance.

Example 3.15: Suppose you are searching for an apartment for rent near your college and a random sample of apartments have the following monthly rent ($):

500, 500, 400, 400, 350, 350, 400, 400, 500, 500, 500, 500, 600, 600, 600, 700, 700

Construct a dot plot to illustrate the frequency distribution of apartment rent.

Solution:

Students can easily construct the dot plot for this problem manually. Alternatively, they may use MegaStat® program, which works in conjunction with Excel and in the same manner as Excel data analysis. Figure 3.31 illustrates the MegaStat® menu of descriptive statistics in which you can see all types of plots. The dot plot produced by this analysis is shown in Figure 3.32.

153

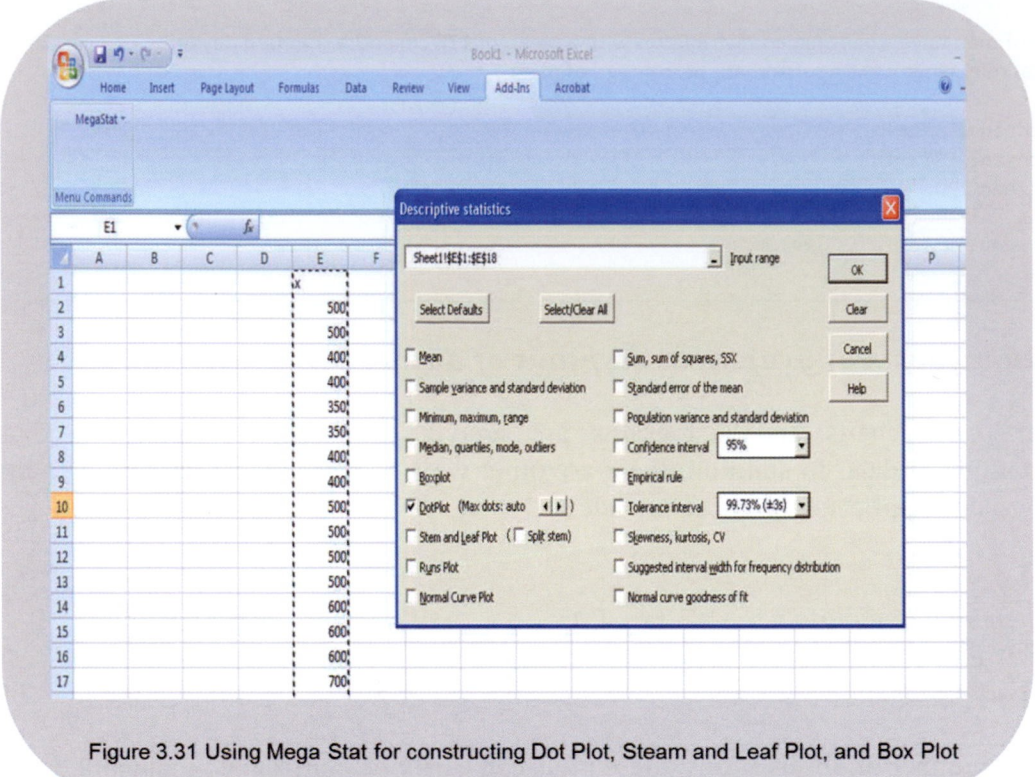

Figure 3.31 Using Mega Stat for constructing Dot Plot, Steam and Leaf Plot, and Box Plot

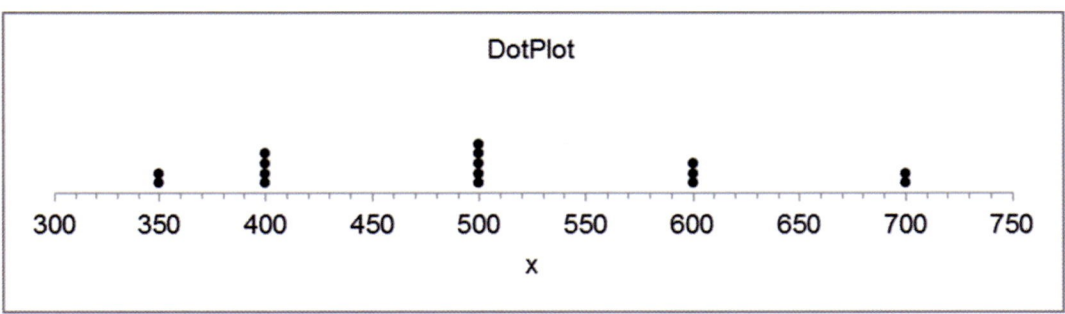

Figure 3.32 Dot Plot of Apartments Rents

3.13.2 Stem and leaf plot

A '*stem-and-leaf plot*' represents a simple method to represent the frequency of a small data set. In this case, each stem defines a group of the partitioned frequency distribution, and the values represented by the leaves fall between the lower and upper limits for a given stem. The leaves of the stem and leaf plot form a picture of the frequency distribution that has virtually a shape identical to that of the histogram with the same grouping; the only difference being that the actual numerical values of the variable are preserved. The example below illustrates the difference between a histogram and a stem-and-leaf diagram.

Example 3.16: An engineer takes 10 sample groups of composite plates, each of 10 plates and measures the area of each plate (mm^2). The reported values are shown in Table 3.17, and corresponding descriptive statistics are listed in Table 3.18.

Table 3.17 Area values of composite plates (mm^2)

G1	G2	G3	G4	G5	G6	G7	G8	G9	G10
119	128	133	135	139	140	143	203	149	211
120	129	133	135	139	140	143	147	150	153
122	130	133	136	139	142	144	147	150	198
123	130	134	137	139	142	144	147	150	153
124	130	134	137	139	142	144	147	152	190
126	131	135	137	139	142	144	147	152	155
126	131	135	137	139	142	198	148	152	215
128	131	135	137	140	142	145	148	152	156
128	131	135	139	140	143	211	149	152	159
128	132	135	139	140	143	147	149	152	160

Table 3.18 Descriptive statistics of composite plate area

Statistics	Value
Mean	144.30
Median	140.24
Mode	198
Standard Deviation	18.68
Sample Variance	348.78
Range	96.35
Minimum	118.65
Maximum	215

The stem and leaf plot of the area data is shown in Figure 3.33. Note the high degree of resolution associated with the stem-and-leaf diagram, not only can we see the extent of the frequency of different classes or values, but we also can see what values are available within each class. For example, at the bottom of the plot, the stem represents the highest base value, 21 and the leaf is represented by 1, 1, 5 to represent the observations 211, 211, and 215 (light-shaded in Table 3.17). The top stem at 11 has the leaf of 9 to represent the value 119 (dark shaded area in Table 3.17).

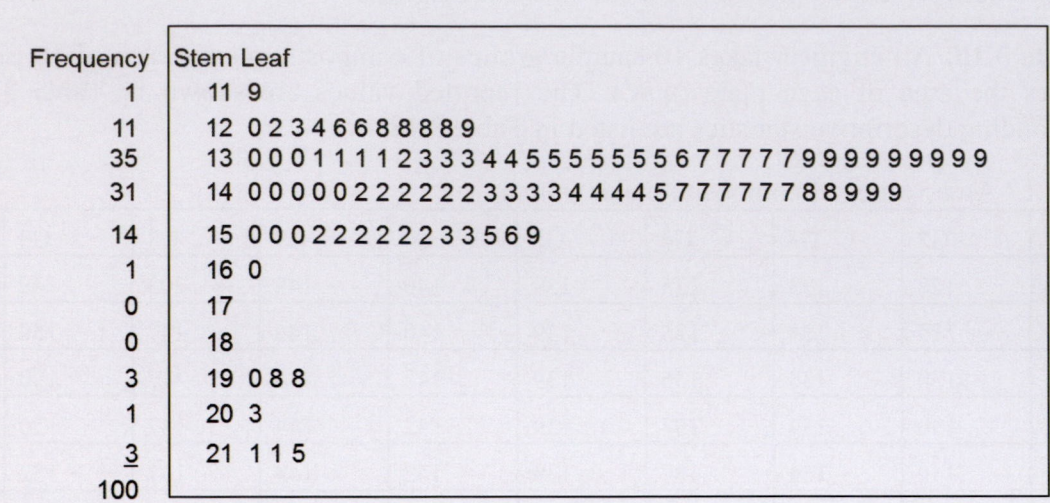

Figure 3.33 Stem and Leaf Plot of Plate Area

3.13.3 Box plot (data percentiles)

A set of data can be divided into percentiles with the desired percentile obtained from the following equation:

$$l_p = \frac{p}{100}(n+1) \qquad (3.14)$$

where l_p represents the location of a certain percentile, p is the required percentile, and n is the number of observations in the data set.

A box plot uses the above equation to display the percentiles of data as demonstrated by the example below.

Example 3.17: Using the data of property tax shown in Table 3.19, determine the lower quartile, the median, and the upper quartile of tax property.

Table 3.19 Data of property tax of a sample of houses in Monmouth County, New Jersey

6121	7748	7094
8419	7828	8390
8452	8289	7178
7141	6644	7886
8461	7963	7914

156

Solution:

The first step to determine the percentiles is to arrange the data from the lowest to the highest value as shown in Table 3.20.

Table 3.20 Data of property tax sorted

n	Annual property tax ($)
1	6121
2	6644
3	7094
4	7141
5	7178
6	7748
7	7828
8	7886
9	7914
10	7963
11	8289
12	8390
13	8419
14	8452
15	8461

The locations of the lower quartile, median, and upper quartile of the data are:

$l_{25} = \frac{25}{100}(15 + 1) = 4$ (or 4th observation)

$l_{50} = \frac{50}{100}(15 + 1) = 8$ (or 8th observation)

$l_{75} = \frac{75}{100}(15 + 1) = 12$ (or 12th observation)

Accordingly, the lower quartile is the 4th observation, or $7141, the median is the 8th observation, or $7886, and the upper quartile is the 12th observation, or $8390. A box plot of the above data is shown in Figure 3.34. It shows the median, the lower quartile, the upper quartile, the minimum value and the maximum value of the data set.

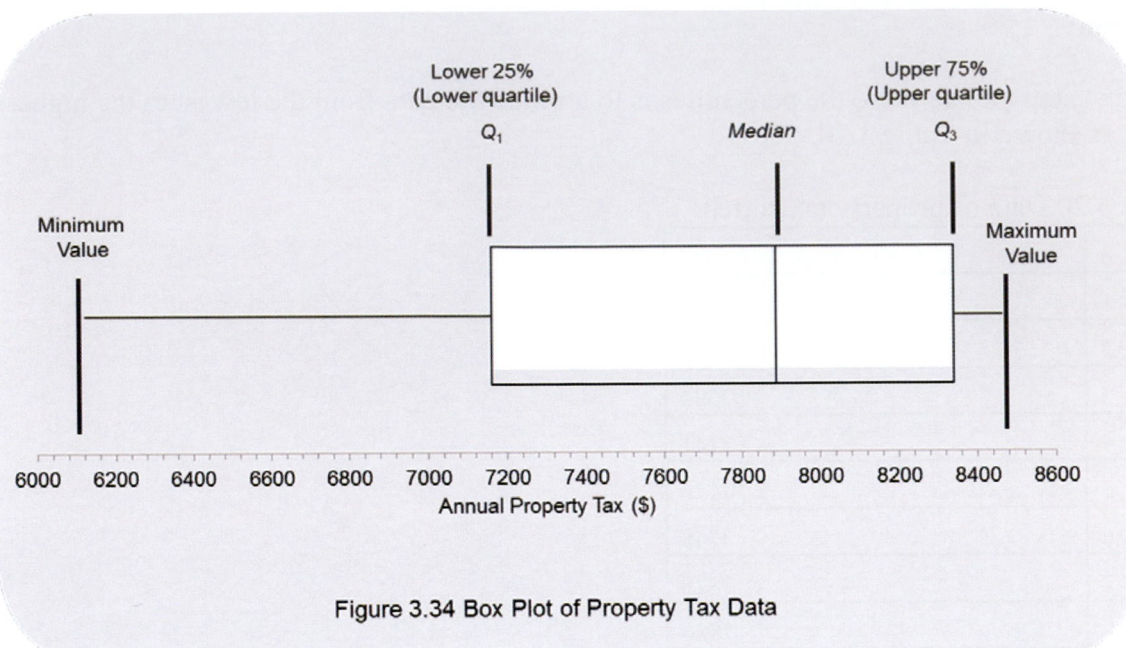

Figure 3.34 Box Plot of Property Tax Data

Working Problem 3.21:

Listed below are the property taxes ($) paid by a sample of 15 houses in Montgomery, Alabama, in 2009:

2000	1500	1800	1050	2000	2050	1800	1670	1800	1400	2800	950	1800	1200	1300

- Locate the median, the first quartile, and the third quartile for the property taxes.
- Construct a steam and leaf plot
- Construct a histogram
- Construct a box plot

Answer:

Descriptive statistics	Property Tax
1st quartile	1,350.00
median	1,800.00
3rd quartile	1,900.00
interquartile range	550.00

Stem and Leaf plot for Property Tax

stem unit = 1000

leaf unit = 100

Frequency	Stem Leaf
1	0 9
4	1 0 2 3 4
6	1 5 6 8 8 8 8
3	2 0 0 0
1	2 8
15	

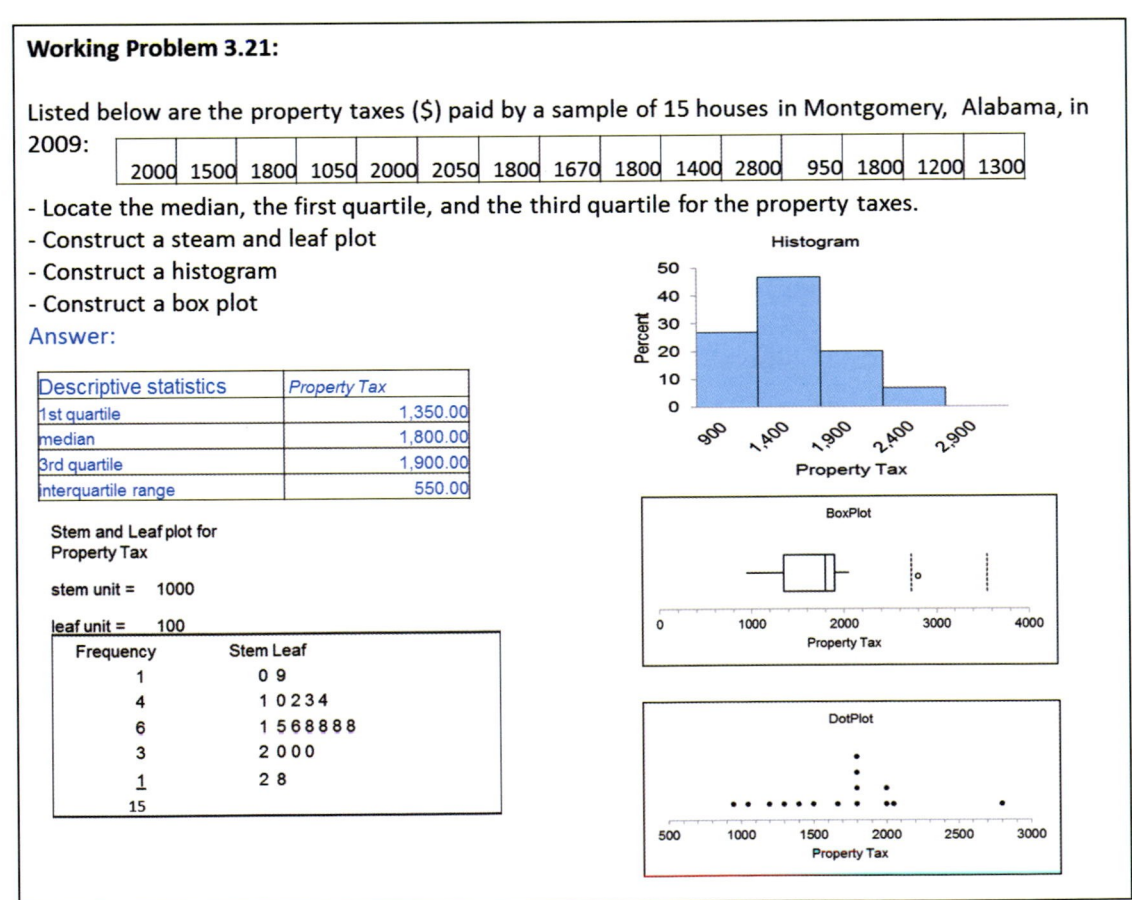

Working Problem 3.22:

For each of he following three data sets:
(a) Determine mean, median, mode, range, standard deviation, skewness, and kurtosis for each data set
(b) Construct histogram, dot plot, and box plot
(c) Using these graphs, explain how each graph reveals a different type of information
(d) Compare the three data sets using histogram, dot plot, and box plot

Answer:
Complete the answer

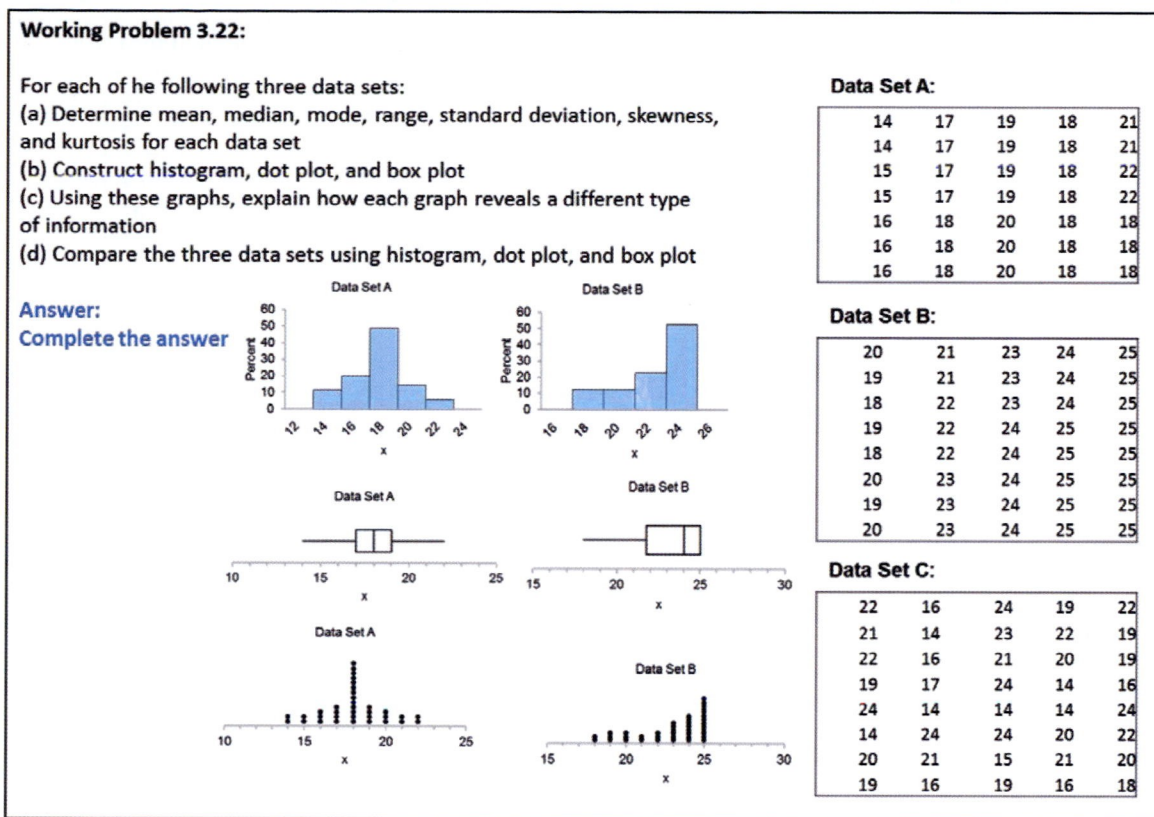

Data Set A:

14	17	19	18	21
14	17	19	18	21
15	17	19	18	22
15	17	19	18	22
16	18	20	18	18
16	18	20	18	18
16	18	20	18	18

Data Set B:

20	21	23	24	25
19	21	23	24	25
18	22	23	24	25
19	22	24	25	25
18	22	24	25	25
20	23	24	25	25
19	23	24	25	25
20	23	24	25	25

Data Set C:

22	16	24	19	22
21	14	23	22	19
22	16	21	20	19
19	17	24	14	16
24	14	14	14	24
14	24	24	20	22
20	21	15	21	20
19	16	19	16	18

3.13.4 Scatter plot

A scatter plot represents a relationship between two variables. It provides a visual measure of how an independent variable may affect a dependent or response variable. The example below demonstrates how a scatter plot can be constructed.

Example 3.18: Suppose a teacher wonders if the number of hours a student studies for the course will affect the student's grade. Using a random sample of 20 students, each student was asked about how many hours per week he/she studies and prepares for the course assignments and exams. The teacher then matched the students' replies with their grades as shown in Table 3.21. Construct a scatter plot of the relationship between the number of hours studied and the student's grade.

Table 3.21 Data of student's study time and corresponding test grades

Number of hours of study per week	Grade (out of 100%)	Number of hours of study per week	Grade (out of 100%)
4	81	7	88
7	72	7	75
6	85	8	81
5	75	8	95
7	90	7	87
8	90	6	97
1	60	3	75
1	45	6	65
5	89	5	85
6	88	3	80

Solution:

The scatter plot can be constructed manually using the number of hours of study as the x-variable and the corresponding grade as the y-variable. It can also be made using Excel® graphing as shown in Figures 3.35 through 3.37.

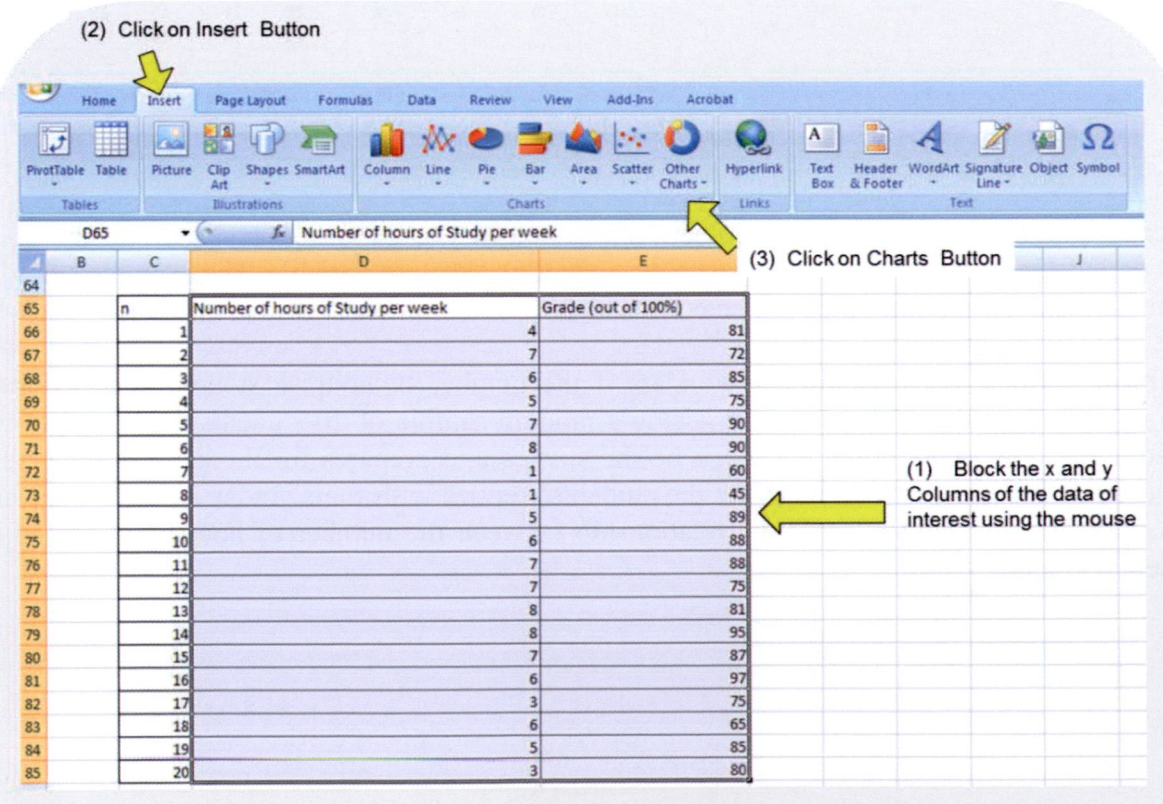

Figure 3.35 Developing a Scatter Plot Using Excel® Program-Steps 1 through 3

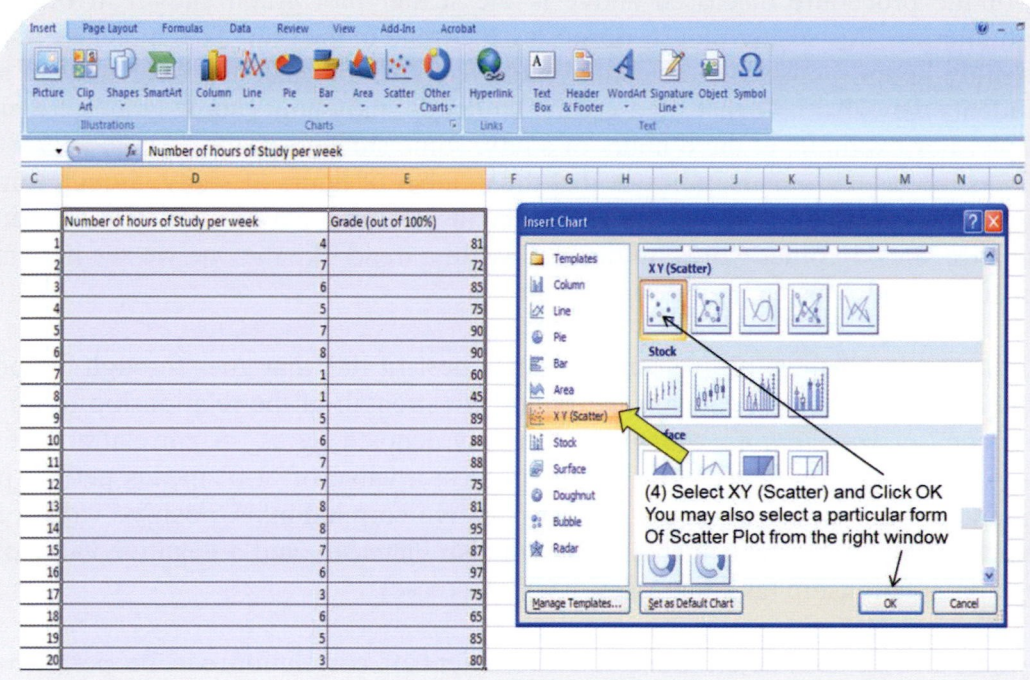

Figure 3.36 Developing a Scatter Plot Using Excel® Program- Step 4

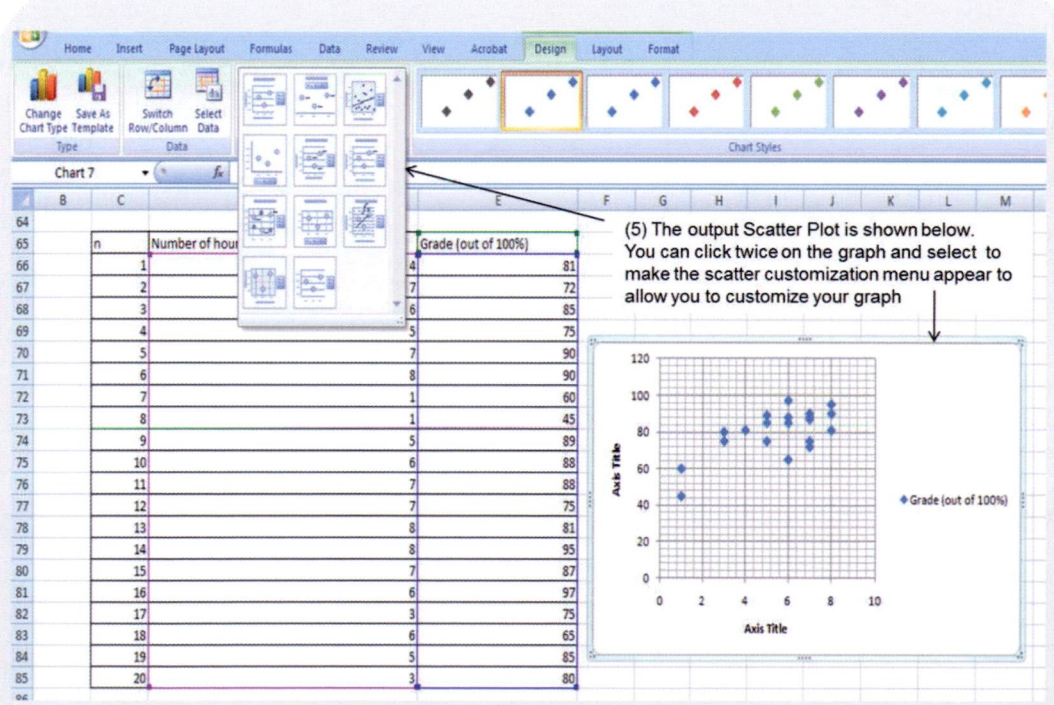

Figure 3.37 Developing a Scatter Plot Using Excel® Program- Step 5

The result of the procedure discussed above is the scatter plot graph shown in Figure 3.37. Students can interpret this scatter plot by observing the trend in the plot. This indicates that as the number of study hours increases, a student's grade tends to increase approximately in a linear fashion. Students may also note that for a given number of study hours some grades are high and others are low. For example, at the 6 hours of study, some students made as high as 97% while others made as low as 65%. This indicates that the number of hours of study, though important, is not the only factor affecting the grade and other factors may play a role (e.g. student study habit, attendance, etc). In other words, in the real world a trend like the one we see here may not be a perfect straight line; instead it is a scatter plot.

As we will discuss in Chapter 12, we can generate a best-fit line that goes through the points to represent the average trend. We can also determine the strength of the relationship using the so-called *'coefficient of correlation,'* which is commonly denoted by *'r.'* A correlation coefficient of '0' means no association between the two variables; a value of '1.0' means perfect positive correlation; and a value of '-1.0' means perfect negative correlation. A positive value of *r* will imply a positive relationship (as *x* increases, *y* will also increase), and a negative value of *r* will imply a negative relationship (as *x* increases, *y* will decrease).

Drawing a best-fit line and determining the coefficient of correlation can be performed in a matter of seconds using Excel® graphing capabilities. Figures 3.38 and 3.39 illustrate the basic steps to develop a best-fit line and produce its equation and the measure of the relationship strength, or the coefficient of correlation. Students can perform these analyses until they learn more about their fundamentals in Chapter 12.

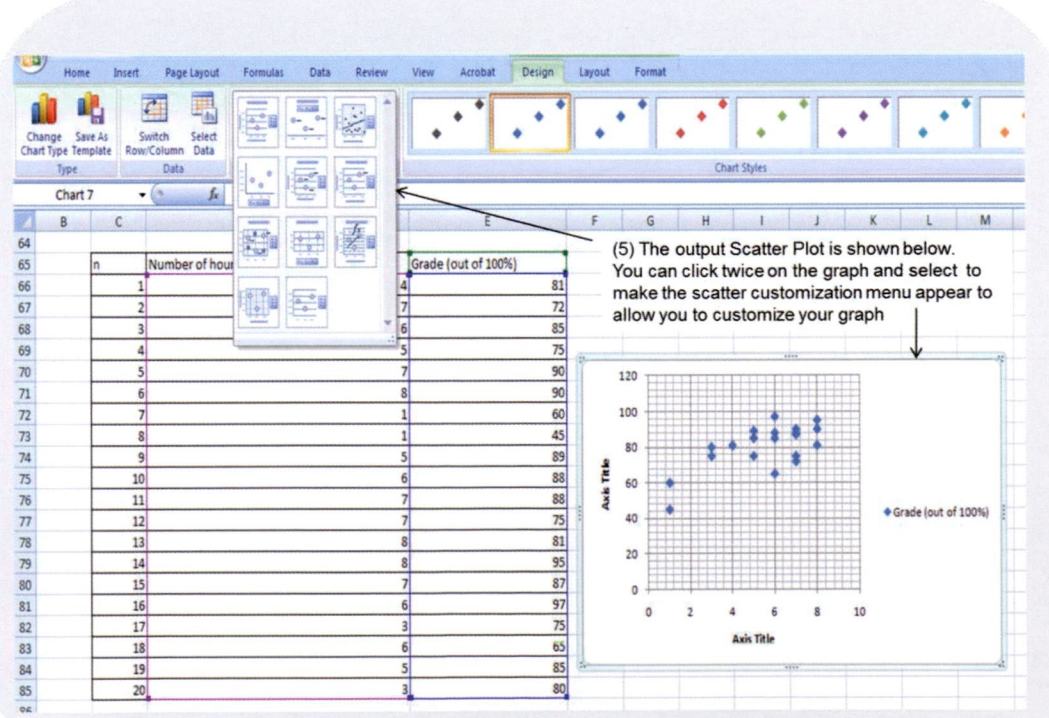

Figure 3.37 Developing a Scatter Plot Using Excel® Program- Step 5

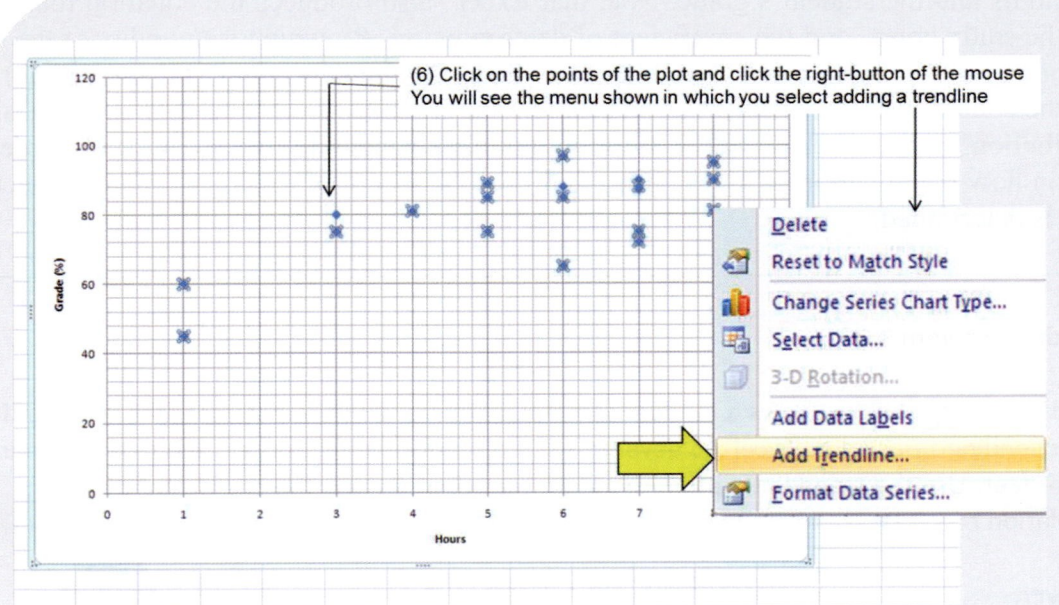

(6) Click on the points of the plot and click the right-button of the mouse You will see the menu shown in which you select adding a trendline

Figure 3.38 Developing a Scatter Plot Using Excel Program- Step 6: Adding a Trend Line

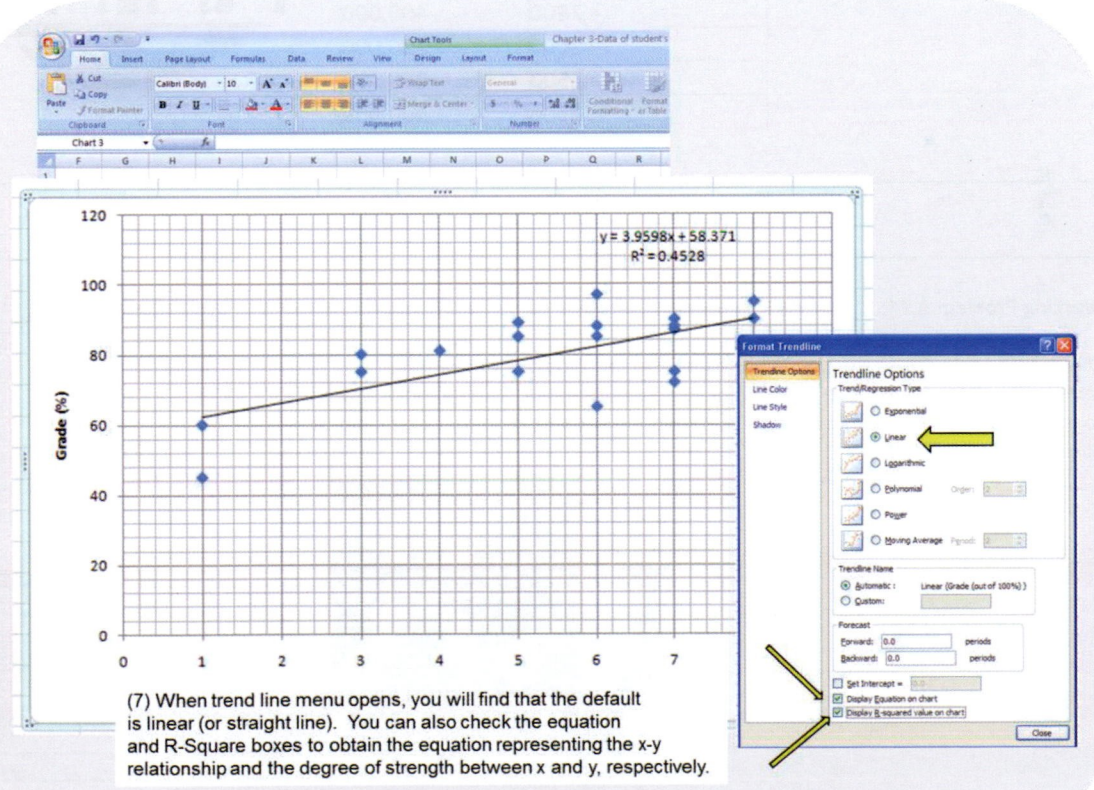

(7) When trend line menu opens, you will find that the default is linear (or straight line). You can also check the equation and R-Square boxes to obtain the equation representing the x-y relationship and the degree of strength between x and y, respectively.

Figure 3.39 Developing a Scatter Plot Using Excel Program- Step 7: Trend Line Menu

The trend line, shown in Figure 3.39 shows that there is a linear relationship between the number of study hours and the student's grade. Note that Excel® also produces the equation relating the grade to the study hours, and the coefficient of determination, R^2, which is an index of the extent of contribution of the independent variable (study hours) to the dependent variable (grade). This index is the square of the coefficient of correlation and it ranges from 0 to 1, in which 0 means no contribution, and 1 means 100% contribution. In Chapter 12, we will provide detailed analysis on how the equation was developed and how the extent of the association between two variables is determined.

Working Problem 3.23:

The data in table below shows a random sample of houses with their square feet areas and corresponding prices. Use Excel® to develop a scatter plot relating house price to the area in square feet. Use the trend line option to obtain the equation and the coefficient of correlation r.

Answer:

y = 104.19x + 97074
R² = 0.7548, r = 0.869

House Square Feet	House Price ($)
3200	410,000
3600	440,000
2600	400,000
2000	260,000
3000	425,000
2800	400,000
2000	280,000
2500	380,000
2500	400,000

Working Problem 3.24:

The data in table shows the points per game and touch downs of a random sample of college teams. Use Excel® to develop a scatter plot relating touchdowns to points/game. Use trendline option to obtain the equation and the coefficient of correlation r.

Answer:
y = 0.4774x + 10.417
R² = 0.8406
r = 0.917

TDs	Points/Game
27	23.5
26	23.3
25	21.5
21	19.2
31	26.8
28	25.7
28	24.4
25	22
42	28.9
28	23.8
27	21.3
15	17.2
34	27.4
29	24.3
24	23.8
26	21.7

3.14 What is an outlier?

In using statistical graphing, it is important to look for outliers. In general, an outlier is a data observation that seems to not belong to the family of data under consideration. A data observation may deviate significantly from the data set due to some exceptional situation or due to data error. For example, a test is given to 10 students and the results are as follows: 75, 80, 88, 20, 90, 82, 79, 80, 83, and 90. Although the value of 20 is plausible it seems to be  exceptionally low compared to the family of data. This makes the value of 20 in this data set an outlier. In other cases, we may not know the reason why an outlier is presented in the data set. The key, however, is to detect it, particularly when we are dealing with a massive amount of data.

Statistically, an outlier is a value that is inconsistent with the family of data under evaluation. Examples of outliers include:

- A value of $1 million within a data set of a company's annual wages in which the plausible range is from $40,000 to $220,000
- A value of 5000 pounds in a data set of people's weight
- A value of 102 in a data set of people's ages
- A value of 13 years old in a data set of college students' age

Normally, an outlier is detected via descriptive statistics (minimum, maximum, range, box plot, frequency distribution, dot plot, etc.). You may also detect an outlier in a scatter plot, i.e. An 'A' grade for a student who studies zero hours per week. Another rule used for detecting outliers is based on defining an outlier *as a value that is more than 1.5 times the inter-quartile range smaller than the lower quartile and larger than the upper quartile*. This is illustrated in the following example.

Example 3.19: Detect outliers in the following data set of monthly accidents on the job during a year evaluation in a firm of 100 people.

Table 3.22 Accidents on the job

Month	Accidents/month
January	3
February	4
March	1
April	2
May	1
June	2
July	3
August	15
September	2
October	1
November	3
December	2

The analysis of the above data set can be performed manually. We can also use MegaStat® as shown in Figure 3.40. Note how an outlier is quite apparent in the box plot and the dot plot (the extreme point to the right).

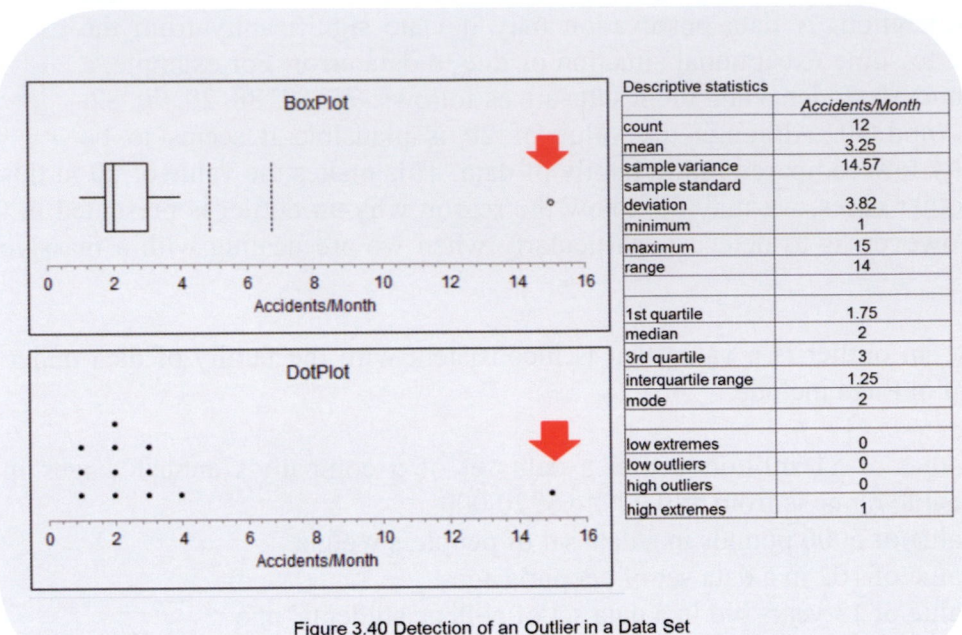

Figure 3.40 Detection of an Outlier in a Data Set

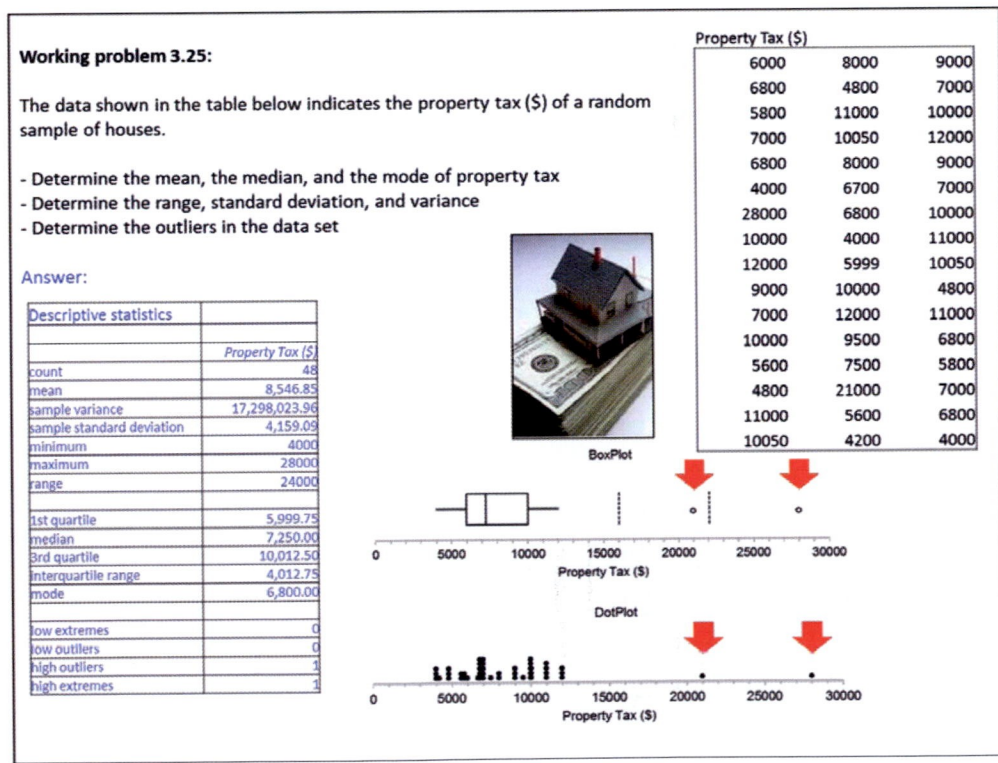

166

3.15 Review Exercises

P3.1: In 2009, Energy Information Administration (EIA, http://www.eia.gov/) data showed 37% of the nation's energy came from petroleum, 21% from coal, and 25% from natural gas. Nuclear power supplied 9% and renewable energy supplied 8%, which was mainly from hydroelectric dams although other renewables are included such as wind power, geothermal and solar energy. Construct a pie chart showing these sources of energy.

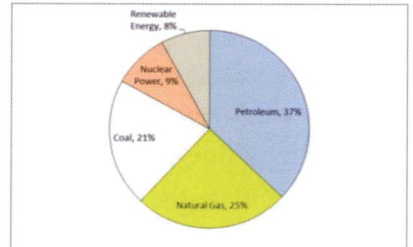

P3.2:The data below represents the 20 Highest-Paid CEOs ($ Millions) according to CNN-Money, (http://money.cnn.com/galleries/2011/news/1104/gallery.top_ceo_pay/index.html), 2009-2010. CEO's salaries are typically based on two sources of income: cash compensation and stock and options.

(a) What is the level of measurement of each of the variables in the table?

(b) Construct a bar graph illustrating CEOs total income in descending order

(c) Calculate the mean, mode, median, range, and variance of total CEO income

(d) Why do you believe that different COEs make different incomes?

CEO	Company	Cash compensation ($ million)	Stock and options ($ million)	Total ($ million)
Philippe P. Dauman	Viacom (VIAB)	$14	$70.50	$84.50
Ray R. Irani	Occidental Petroleum	$35.90	$40.30	$76.20
Lawrence J. Ellison	Oracle (ORCL)	$8.20	$61.90	$70.10
Michael D. White	DIRECTV (DTV)	$5.70	$27.20	$32.90
John F. Lundgren	Stanley Black & Decker	$6	$26.60	$32.60
Brian L. Roberts	Comcast (CMCSA)	$16.90	$11.20	$28.10
Robert A. Iger	Walt Disney (DIS)	$16.30	$11.80	$28.10
Alan Mulally	Ford Motor	$11.50	$15	$26.50
Samuel J. Palmisano	I.B.M.	$11.90	$13.30	$25.20
David N. Farr	Emerson Electric	$3.90	$19.10	$23.00
Howard Schultz	Starbucks	$5	$16.70	$21.70
William C. Weldon	Johnson & Johnson	$14.10	$7.50	$21.60
Louis C. Camilleri	Philip Morris International	$10.10	$10.60	$20.70
Randall L. Stephenson	AT&T	$7	$13.20	$20.20
Miles D. White	Abbott Laboratories	$6.40	$13.60	$20.00
George W. Buckley	3M	$7.90	$11.80	$19.70
Louis Chenevert	United Technologies	$7.30	$12.20	$19.50
Robert P. Kelly	Bank of New York Mellon	$7	$12.40	$19.40
Muhtar Kent	Coca-Cola	$8.40	$10.80	$19.20
Robert J. Stevens	Lockheed Martin	$12.10	$7.10	$19.20

P3.3: College students are interested to know the average annual salary of a certain job in careers that they might align their educations with. There are many sources from which average salaries can be obtained. The following data represents average values of annual salaries of sales representatives of different categories. The data is dated December 25, 2011 (http://www.simplyhired.com/a/salary/home)

(a) Sort the data from the lowest annual salary to the highest annual salary.
(b) Plot a line or a bar graph of the sorted data and interpret the graph
(c) Calculate the mean, the median, the range, the standard deviation, and the variance of the average salary.
(d) Interpret the results

Sales person category	Average annual salary
sales representative	$48,000
account executive	$54,000
legal secretary	$43,000
administrative assistant	$30,000
account manager	$45,000
sales manager	$63,000
director of sales	$115,000
regional sales manager	$118,000
insurance sales agent	$160,000
inside sales	$32,000
sales associate	$28,000
outside sales representative	$52,000

Answer:
(c)

	Average annual salary
Mean	65666.667
Median	???
Standard Deviation	???
Sample Variance	???
Range	???
Minimum	28000
Maximum	160000
Count	12

P3.4: The following data represents average values of annual salaries of different nurses. The data is dated December 25, 2011 (http://www.simplyhired.com/a/salary/home)

1. Sort the data from the lowest annual salary to the highest annual salary
2. Plot a line or a bar graph of the sorted data and interpret the graph
3. Calculate the mean, the median, the range, the standard deviation, and the variance of the average salary.
4. Interpret the results

Nurse category	Average annual salary
Registered nurse	$50,000
Nursing assistant	$27,000
Licensed practical nurse	$29,000
Clinical nurse	$48,000
Public health nurse	$46,000
Nurse practitioner	$60,000
Practical nurse	$32,000
RN	$38,000
Staff nurse	$47,000
Nurse specialist	$54,000
Director of nursing services	$62,000
Nurse consultant	$61,000

P3.5: The following data represents average values of annual salaries of different engineers. The data is dated December 25, 2011 (http://www.simplyhired.com/a/salary/home)

1. Sort the data from the lowest annual salary to the highest annual salary
2. Plot a line a graph of the sorted data and interpret the graph
3. Calculate the mean, the median, the range, and standard deviation of the average salary.

Engineering category	Average annual salary
Mechanical engineer	$63,000
Electrical engineer	$63,000
Software engineer	$75,000
Civil engineer	$58,000
General engineer	$74,000
Electronics engineer	$72,000
Systems engineer	$77,000
Manufacturing engineer	$54,000
Network engineer	$67,000
Project engineer	$62,000
Process engineer	$58,000
Environmental engineer	$59,000

Answer:

	Average annual salary
Mean	???
Median	63000
Mode	???
Standard Deviation	7685.09
Sample Variance	???
Range	???

P3.6: The table below lists the sizes of the top ancestry groups in the U.S. in 2011 (http://www.census.gov/compendia/statab/cats/population.html)

Ancestry group	Number of People in each Ancestry group
Russian	3,163,084
European	3,197,273
Scotch-Irish	3,570,427
Swedish	4,347,703
Norwegian	4,642,526
Dutch	5,023,846
Scottish	5,847,063
French (except Basque)	9,411,789
Polish	10,091,056
Italian	18,085,336
American	18,699,411
English	27,657,961
Irish	36,915,155
German	50,707,758

(a) Construct a bar chart to illustrate the number of people in each ancestry group.

(b) Given that at the time this data was collected, the U.S. population was 389,674,835, construct a bar chart of the percent of people in each ancestry group with respect to the U.S. population

P3.7: Give a practical example that can best be represented by each of the frequency distributions shown below, and assign typical values for the variable. For example, a symmetrical (normal distribution) may represent annual income with few at low values (say, below $30,000) and few at very high annual income (say, $300,000), and the bulk of the population is in-between.

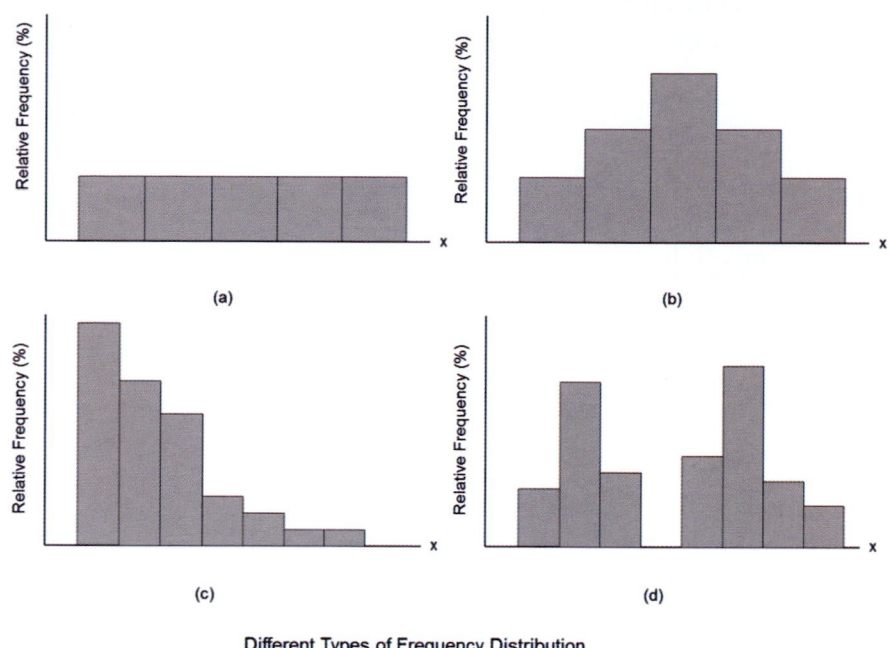

(a)

(b)

(c)

(d)

Different Types of Frequency Distribution

P3.8: The two frequency distributions shown below represent annual property tax in one of the townships in the State of New Jersey for the years 2001 and 2008. Answer the following questions:

1. What are the minimum and maximum values of annual property tax charged for 2001 and 2008?
2. What are the mean values of annual property tax charged for 2001 and 2008?
3. What are the values of annual property tax charged to most homes for 2001 and 2008?
4. Do you believe that the two frequency distributions below are fully comparable? If your answer is No, explain why?

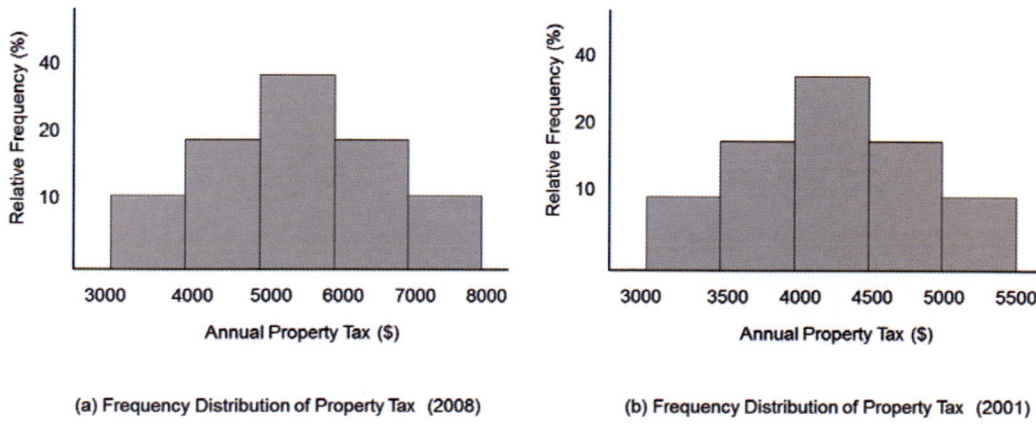

(a) Frequency Distribution of Property Tax (2008)

(b) Frequency Distribution of Property Tax (2001)

Frequency Distributions of Property Tax for Years 2008 and 2001

P3.9: The following frequency table reports the number of employees in a company, earning frequent flyer miles (in thousands) during the first half of 2008.

Frequent flyer data

Frequent flyer miles (×1000)	Number of employees
0 to < 5	10
5 to < 10	22
10 to < 15	55
15 to < 20	821
20 to < 25	8

- How many employees were evaluated?
- What is the midpoint of the 4th class?
- Construct a histogram
- Interpret the outcome

Answer:
How many employees were evaluated? 916
What is the midpoint of the 4th class? 17500

P3.10: For each of the following data sets,
   (a) Calculate the mean, the mode, the range, and the standard deviation
   (b) Construct a histogram for each data set
   (c) Construct a cumulative frequency curve for each data set

Data Set A:	80	42	78	81	80	88	62	85	79	84	87	72	42	80	82
Data Set B:	92	89	34	41	33	60	32	32	31	46	40	32	35	32	50
Data Set C:	59	66	45	76	74	48	55	67	65	85	68	66	86	75	58

P3.11: For each of the following data sets, calculate the skewness and kurtosis

Data Set A:	80	42	78	81	80	88	62	85	79	84	87	72	42	80	82
Data Set B:	92	89	34	41	33	60	32	32	31	46	40	32	35	32	50
Data Set C:	59	66	45	76	74	48	55	67	65	85	68	66	86	75	58

Answer:

	Data Set A	Data Set B	Data Set C
Kurtosis	??	2.0479	??
Skewness	-1.6943	1.7398	??

172

P3.12: Shown below is a boxplot of the student grades of a statistics course. What do the values of 20, 60, 80, 90, and 100 tell us?

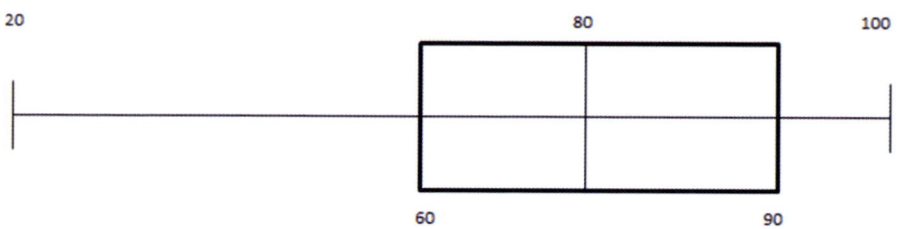

P3.13: Using the boxplot shown below, what are the values of the lowest grade, the first quartile Q1, the second quartile Q2 (or median), the third quartile Q3, and the maximum? Are there any outliers? What are the values of these outliers?

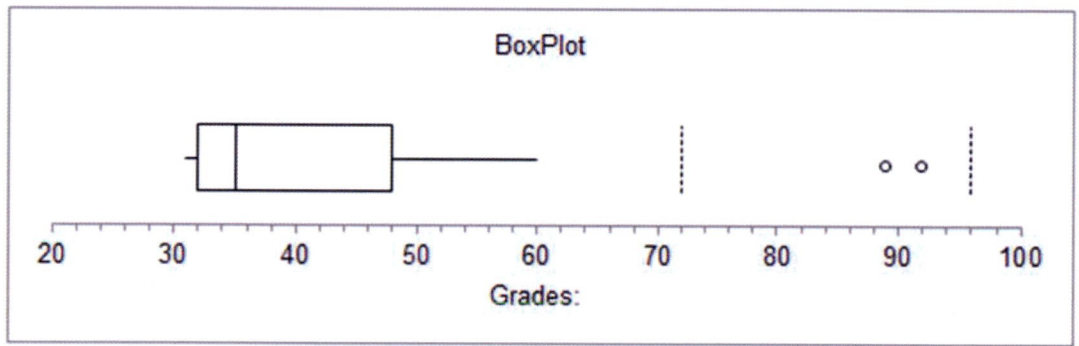

P3.14: For each of the following data sets, construct a box plot and determine the lower quartile, the median, and the upper quartile, the minimum and the maximum. Detect any outlier in any of the data sets.

Data Set A:	80	42	78	81	80	88	62	85	79	84	87	72	42	80	82
Data Set B:	92	89	34	41	33	60	32	32	31	46	40	32	35	32	50
Data Set C:	59	66	45	76	74	48	55	67	65	85	68	66	86	75	58

P3.15: For each of the following data sets, construct a dot plot

Data Set A:	80	42	78	81	80	88	62	85	79	84	87	72	42	80	82
Data Set B:	92	89	34	41	33	60	32	32	31	46	40	32	35	32	50
Data Set C:	59	66	45	76	74	48	55	67	65	85	68	66	86	75	58

P3.16: Suppose you are in search for a minimum-wage job to help through school. After searching for a while, you found several jobs in your area that pay the hourly wages shown below.

- Perform numerical descriptive statistics to determine measures of central tendency and measures of variability
- Construct histogram, relative frequency diagram, cumulative frequency curve, dot plot, steam and leaf plot, and a box plot for the hourly wage data.

Hourly wage data ($)

Company #	Hourly Wages ($)	Company #	Hourly Wages ($)
1	9.3	16	7.0
2	8.6	17	9.7
3	7.5	18	7.4
4	8.8	19	8.4
5	8.9	20	10.8
6	7.4	21	8.1
7	7.8	22	10.9
8	8.2	23	9.2
9	10.3	24	10.8
10	10.0	25	11.5
11	11.2	26	8.2
12	10.1	27	6.3
13	8.9	28	9.3
14	7.1	29	10.7
15	8.0	30	5.4

P3.17: Using the plots you constructed in the previous question, answer the following questions.
1. What is the hourly wage paid by most jobs?
2. What is the lower quartile, median, and upper quartile of hourly wage data?
3. What is percent of jobs paying less than $7.50 per hour?
4. What is percent of jobs paying more than or equal $10 per hour?
Answer:
   (1) The Mode = $9.30/hr, (2) Median = 8.850, (3) about 23%, (4) about 30%

P3.18: In a four-hour math test, a teacher wanted to evaluate the actual time taken by different students to finish the test. Some teachers like to collect this type of data to judge student's efficiency in solving problems or the extent of challenge the test may pose on students. The data shown below represent the time in minutes spent by each student from the moment the test paper was received by the student to the time it was submitted to the teacher.

(a) Using descriptive statistics what was the time used by most students to finish the test?
(b) Did the teacher plan the test appropriately to meet the time requirement?
(c) How many students finished the test in less than half of the time allocated for the test?
(d) How many students needed more time than that allocated for the test?

174

(e) How many students finished the test within the last hour of the test?

Data on time (min) used by students in a four-hour math test

Student ID	Time of test (min)	Student ID	Time of test (min)
1012	185	1100	190
2022	180	1255	200
2122	182	1000	180
1116	182	2010	195
1271	210	2110	230
1016	216	1104	200
1387	176	1259	225
1900	174	4326	200
7235	186	2789	210
5462	172	3244	210
2468	218	1108	228
1004	170	1263	220
2014	224	1008	195
2114	165	2018	225
1008	166	2118	190
1017	162	1112	190
2475	160	1267	188

P3.19: In another four-hour math test by the same teacher in the previous problem but in a different class, the time data were as shown below.

(a) Using descriptive statistics what was the time used by most students to finish the test?
(b) How many students finished the test in less than half of the time allocated for the test?
(c) How many students needed more time than the time allocated for the test?
(d) How many students finished the test within the last hour of the test?

Data on time (min) used by students in a four-hour math test

Student ID	Time of test (min)	Student ID	Time of test (min)	Student ID	Time of test (min)	Student ID	Time of test (min)
1112	145	1200	190	1108	166	2218	200
2122	225	1355	200	1117	238	1212	228
2222	174	1100	240	2575	160	1367	188
1216	142	2110	237	2214	210	2118	55
1371	200	2210	160	2568	218	1208	50
1116	55	1204	240	1104	240	1363	240
1487	235	1359	225	2114	224	1108	195
2000	94	4426	200	5562	172	3344	58
7335	86	2889	210				

175

P3.20: The table below shows data of home prices in one of the largest U.S. Cities, represented in a frequency format

- Calculate the relative frequencies (%) and the cumulative frequencies (%)
- Construct the relative frequency distribution and the cumulative frequency curve
- What is the percent of houses of price less than $200,000?

Home price data

Classes	Mid-Point	Frequency
110000 - < 130000	120000	20
130000 - < 150000	140000	25
150000 - < 170000	160000	38
170000 - < 190000	180000	49
190000 - < 210000	200000	89
210000 - < 230000	220000	80
230000 - < 250000	240000	99
250000 - < 270000	260000	65
270000 - < 290000	280000	55
290000 - < 310000	300000	35
310000 - < 330000	320000	30
330000 - < 350000	340000	22

P3.21: For the frequency data in the table below, calculate the mean and the standard deviation of home prices.

Home price data

Classes	Mid-Point	Frequency
110000 - < 130000	120000	20
130000 - < 150000	140000	25
150000 - < 170000	160000	38
170000 - < 190000	180000	49
190000 - < 210000	200000	89
210000 - < 230000	220000	80
230000 - < 250000	240000	99
250000 - < 270000	260000	65
270000 - < 290000	280000	55
290000 - < 310000	300000	35
310000 - < 330000	320000	30
330000 - < 350000	340000	22

Answer: Mean = 230378.91, Variance = 2846479160

176

P3.22: The statistics shown below represent the mean and standard deviation of revenues and profit of some of the top 100 companies in the U.S (2009, http://money.cnn.com/magazines/fortune/fortune500/2009/full_list/).

	Revenues (millions$)	Profit (millions$)
Mean	58992	2983
Std. Dev.	17617	4224

1. Using the Empirical Rule, what percent of the companies having revenues falling between $6141 million and $111,843 million and what percent of companies encountering loss/profit falling between -$9689 million and $15655 million?
2. Using the Empirical Rule, what percent of the companies having revenues falling between $23758 million and $94226 million and what percent of companies encountering loss/profit falling between -$5465 million and $11431 million?
3. What percent of companies make more than $15655 million profit?
4. What percent of companies make less than $41375 million revenues?

P3.23: An auto rental company wanted to reach its maximum rental capacity of 10,000 cars during the weekends. One option was to reduce the weekend rate to encourage more people to rent. In order to determine what rate the company should use, data of a sample of historical weekend daily rental rates and the corresponding demand was collected. This data is shown in the table below.

Weekend daily rates ($)	Rental Demand during weekend (number of cars rented)	Weekend daily rates ($)	Rental Demand during weekend (number of cars rented)
40	5000	31	5500
30	5800	44	6900
25	7100	17	6200
16	9300	20	6000
42	4800	40	5800
18	7100	21	7800
32	5700	16	8900
26	6100	42	5320
44	3600	20	8400
16	7800	28	5900
29	7000	18	8500
16	9700	35	4298
18	9990	24	7300
38	5060		

Using Excel®, develop a scatter plot describing the relationship between the weekend daily rate and the rental demand. Write the equation relating the weekend daily rate to the rental demand. What is the strength of the relationship between the weekend daily rate and the rental demand.

What is the weekend daily rental rate that you think the company should use to reach its maximum rental capacity?

P3.24: A restaurant decided to offer home delivery service to deliver meals to surrounding areas. In the first month of delivery service, the frequencies of daily orders were as shown in the table below.

Lower		upper	midpoint	Frequency	Percent relative percent	Cumulative percent
6	<	8		2		
8	<	10		3		
10	<	12		1		
12	<	14		0		
14	<	16		2		
16	<	18		1		
18	<	20		3		
20	<	22		4		
22	<	24		5		
24	<	26		4		
26	<	28		3		
28	<	30		1		
30	<	32		1		

(a) How many deliveries were made during the first month?
(b) Complete the frequency table

P3.25: Using the delivery frequency data in the above problem,

- Construct a relative frequency distribution
- Construct a cumulative frequency curve
- How many days in which more than 10 deliveries were made?

P3.26: The data shown below represent the annual wages given by two different firms to factory supervisors:

Wages in Firm A ($)	Wages in Firm B ($)	Wages in Firm A ($)	Wages in Firm B ($)
29363	34035	39034	35606
39535	31466	33363	33632
38587	31027	29784	37682
36103	29679	29864	35320
34304	38730	34093	29587
43698	33258	39914	30293
32119	33979	40139	29658
37081	32870	22099	30544
40069	33578	37759	36973
44344	33946	35928	32826
36377	28985	36832	37557
43284	33640	30786	25704
43229	35110	33870	29079
29988	34993	35884	32816
32308	31458	40703	30827
37747	32321	28414	31136
32830	30939	30870	34792
26695	31492	34301	34860

- Determine the mean, mode, median of wages of each firm
- Determine the range, standard deviation, and variance
- Determine the skewness and kurtosis
- Construct a frequency distribution and a cumulative frequency curve for each firm
- Using the cumulative frequency curves, what is the percent of supervisors in each firm that make $30,000 or less? What is the percent of supervisors in each firm that make more than $40,000?
- Construct a dot plot for each firm
- Construct a box plot and determine the lower quartile (Q_1), upper quartile (Q_3), and the interquartile ($Q_3 - Q_1$)

P3.27: The descriptive statistics displayed below were obtained for three sets of data representing three different sections of students who took the same statistics test. Evaluate the numerical outputs shown below with the objective being to discuss the key differences between the test results of the three sections.

Statistic	Section A
Mean	74.8
Median	80
Mode	80
Standard deviation	14.722
Sample variance	216.7
Kurtosis	1.889
Skewness	-1.694
Range	46
Minimum	42
Maximum	88
Sum	1122
Count	15
1st quartile	75.00
3rd quartile	83.00
Inter-quartile range	8.00

Statistic	Section B
Mean	45.3
Median	35
Mode	32
Standard deviation	20.130
Sample variance	405.2
Kurtosis	2.048
Skewness	1.740
Range	61
Minimum	31
Maximum	92
Sum	679
Count	15
1st quartile	32.00
3rd quartile	48.00
Inter-quartile range	16.00

Statistic	Section C
Mean	66.2
Median	66
Mode	66
Standard deviation	11.983
Sample variance	143.6
Kurtosis	-0.400
Skewness	-0.066
Range	41
Minimum	45
Maximum	86
Sum	993
Count	15
1st quartile	58.50
3rd quartile	74.50
Inter-quartile range	16.00

P3.28: The graphical descriptive statistics displayed below were obtained for three sets of data representing three groups of students who took the same statistics test.

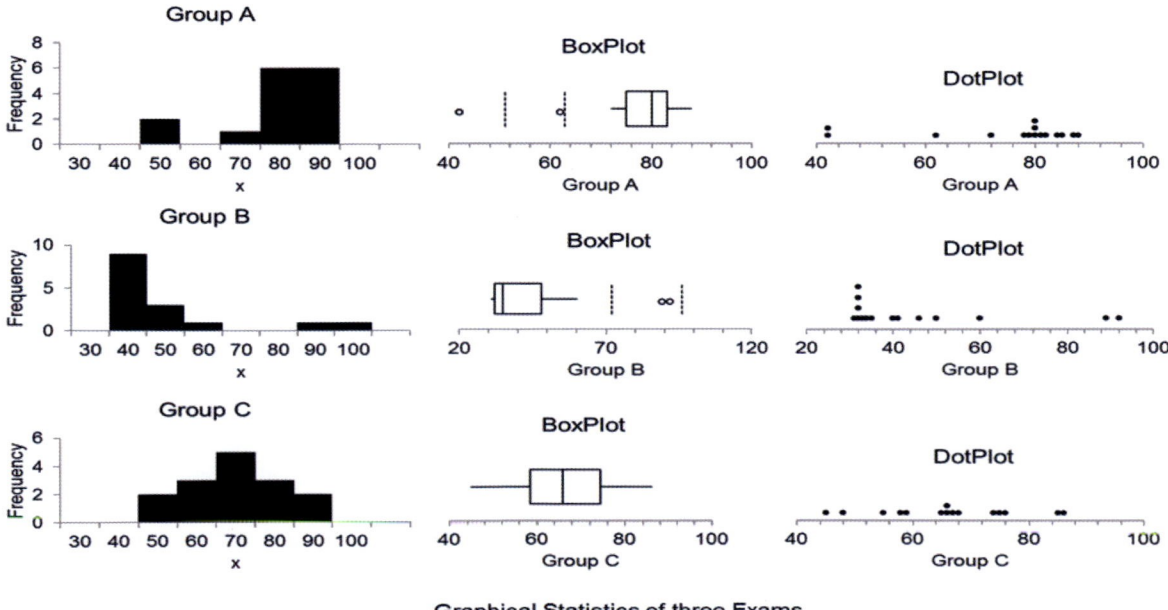

Graphical Statistics of three Exams

180

Evaluate the graphical displays with the objective being to discuss the key differences between the test results of the three student groups. Do you detect any outliers in these data?

P3.29: Calculate the mean, mode, median of the following data of annual income ($):

n	Annual Income ($)
1	20000
2	21000
3	20000
4	22000
5	22000
6	20000
7	20000
8	19000
9	18000
10	23000

Answer: Mean = 20500, Median = 20000, Mode = 20000

P3.30: Calculate the range, minimum, maximum, standard deviation, and variance of the following data of annual income ($):

n	Annual Income ($)
1	20000
2	21000
3	20000
4	22000
5	22000
6	20000
7	20000
8	19000
9	18000
10	23000

P3.31: Calculate the mean, mode, and median of the following data of children weight in the age range 8 to 12

n	1	2	3	4	5	6	7	8	9	10
Weights (pound)	80	90	110	80	110	110	85	86	95	110

Answer: Mean = 95.6, Median = 92.5, Mode = 110

P3.32: Calculate the standard deviation, the variance, the range, the minimum, and the maximum of the following data of children weight in the age range 8 to 12

n	1	2	3	4	5	6	7	8	9	10
Weights (pound)	80	90	110	80	110	110	85	86	95	110

P3.33: Calculate the mean, the mode, and the median of grades of the following student quizzes

Quiz #	1	2	3	4	5
Quiz Grade (Scale 1 to 4)	2	2	3	3	4

Answer: Mean = 2.8, Median = 3, No Mode

P3.34: Calculate the mean, mode, and median of grades of the following student quizzes

Quiz #	1	2	3	4	5
Quiz Grade (Scale 1 to 4)	2	2	2	3	4

A = 4, B = 3, C =2, D =1, and F = 0

P3.35: Calculate the mean, mode, median, standard deviation, variance, and range of the following data of hourly wage

Employee #	1	2	3	4	5	6	7	8	9	10	11	12	13	14	15	16	17	18	19	20
Hourly Wage ($)	8	5.5	5.5	3.5	2	4	4.5	7	7.5	7	8	7.5	6.5	6	6	5.5	5.5	6	4	8

Answer: Mean = 5.875, Mode = 5.5, Variance = 2.734, Range = 6

P3.36: Construct a frequency distribution, a relative frequency distribution, a percent relative frequency distribution, and a cumulative frequency distribution of the following data of hourly wage. Describe the distributions. Estimate the mode and the range of data from the frequency distribution.

Employee #	Hourly Wage ($)	Employee #	Hourly Wage ($)
1	8	11	8
2	5.5	12	7.5
3	5.5	13	6.5
4	3.5	14	6
5	2	15	6
6	4	16	5.5
7	4.5	17	5.5
8	7	18	6
9	7.5	19	4
10	7	20	8

182

P3.37: Construct a cumulative frequency distribution of the following data of hourly wage. Estimate the percent of workers making less than or equal $7.

Employee #	Hourly Wage ($)	Employee #	Hourly Wage ($)
1	8	11	8
2	5.5	12	7.5
3	5.5	13	6.5
4	3.5	14	6
5	2	15	6
6	4	16	5.5
7	4.5	17	5.5
8	7	18	6
9	7.5	19	4
10	7	20	8

P3.38: Calculate the weighted average and the weighted variance of the following data of used car prices

Price ($)	Frequency
8,000	10
12,000	14
14,000	8
16,000	3

P3.39: Describe the following frequency distribution of ages of students attending community colleges in the context of the variable under consideration, modes, ranges, possible patterns, outliers, and merits

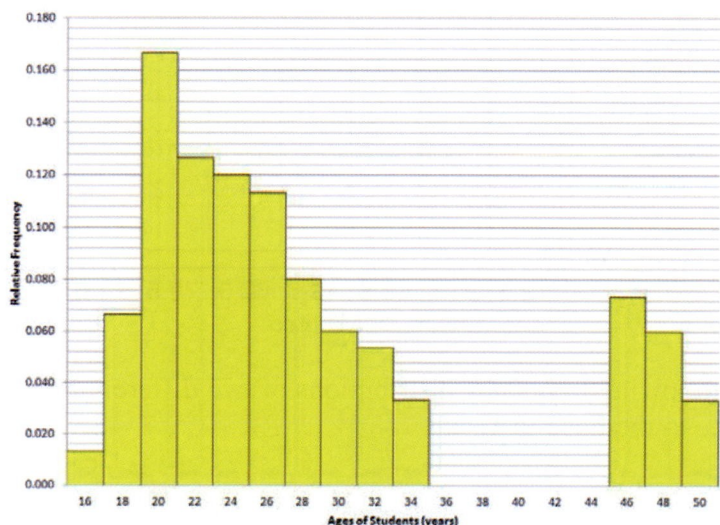

183

P3.40: Describe the following frequency distribution of ages of students attending four-year colleges in the context of the variable under consideration, modes, ranges, possible patterns, outliers, and merits

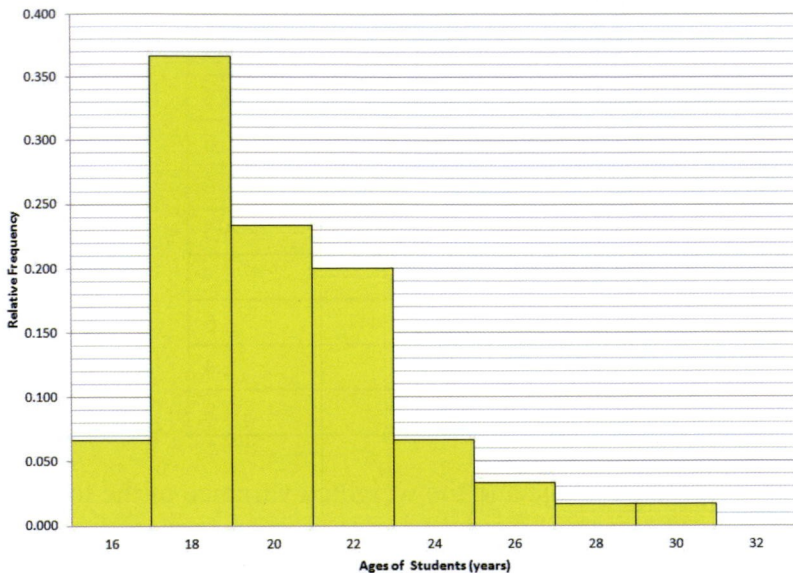

P3.41: Describe the following frequency distributions of time spent on cell phone text-messaging every day in the context of the variable under consideration, modes, ranges, possible patterns, outliers, and merits

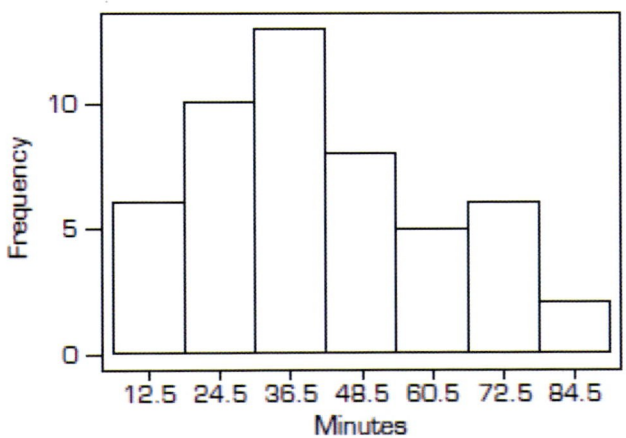

P3.42: Describe the following frequency distributions of two different brands of TV to be compared in reference to the Ease-to-Use.

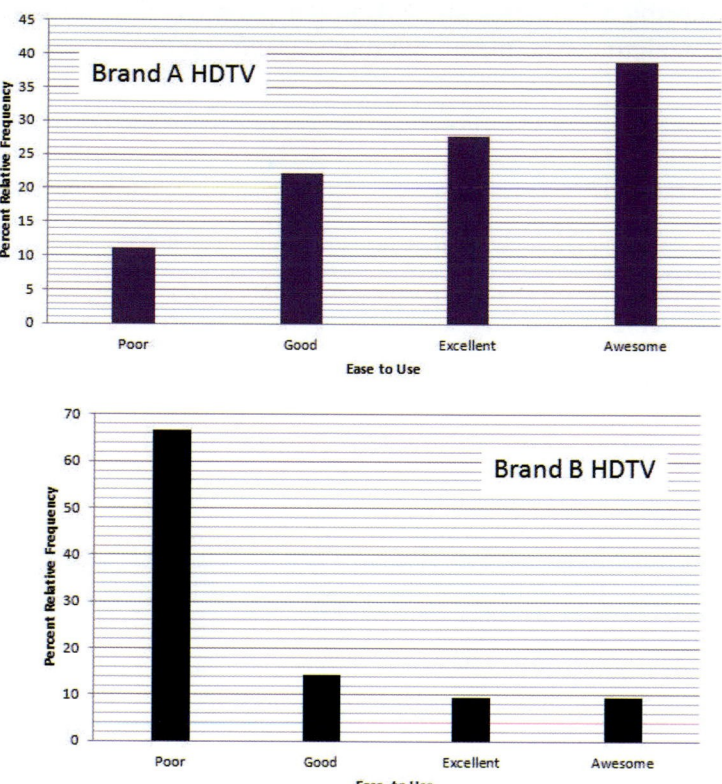

P3.43: For the following data set of house prices ($), determine the mean, the mode, the median, the range, the standard deviation, and the variance.

House Price ($)	200,000	180,000	167,000	150,000	149,000	190,000	189,000	188,000	185,000	201,000

P3.44: For the following data set of driving time from Newark, NJ, to Raleigh, NC (hr), determine the mean, the mode, the median, the range, the standard deviation, and the variance.

Driving Time (hr)	8	8.5	9	7.5	7.5	8	8.5	9	9.5	8.5

P3.45: For the following data set of waiting time for a school bus (minutes), determine the mean, the mode, the median, the range, the standard deviation, and the variance.

Waiting Time (minutes)	17	12	15	20	14	16	15	18	16	15

P3.46: A restaurant is serving a 21-ounce steak. Using a sample of 20 steaks, the following data of weight was obtained. Calculate the mean, the median, the standard deviation, the median, and the variance.

Weight (ounce)			
18	18	21	20
19	18	21	20
19	20	20	18
20	20	18	19
19	20	20	17

P3.47: The data listed below represents pulse rates (beats per minute) of two samples; one for females and the other for males.

(a) Using descriptive statistics, compare the two samples
(b) Construct a frequency distribution of the pulse rates of females and males
(c) Compare the two frequency distributions for the pulse rates.
(d) Construct dot plots of the pulse rates of females and males
(e) Construct box plots of the pulse rates of females and males
Note: when frequency distributions are to be compared, class widths should be made identical

Pulse rates (beats per minute)

Females PR	Females PR	Females PR	Females PR	Males PR	Males PR	Males PR	Males PR
76	76	76	80	72	72	72	72
72	72	68	88	56	88	56	68
72	88	72	60	68	72	84	64
88	60	96	64	64	64	88	56
80	72	64	80	60	72	56	64
60	68	80	88	68	60	64	60
72	64	76	80	60	88	56	64
88	68	76	72	60	76	56	84
72	68	76	64	56	60	60	76
64	80	80	80	84	96	64	84
			64				88

Answer:

	Females PR		Males PR
Mean	??		69.073
Median	72		64
Mode	72		??
Standard Deviation	8.857		??
Sample Variance	??		128.820
Range	??		40

186

P3.48: The Insurance Institute for Highway Safety conducted tests with crashes of new cars traveling at 6 mi/h. The total cost of the damages was found for a simple random sample of the tested cars and listed below. Calculate the mean, the mode, the median, the standard deviation, and the variance.

Car #	Damage Cost ($)	Car #	Damage Cost ($)
1	$7,778	6	$8,888
2	$7,658	7	$5,980
3	$7,777	8	$8,882
4	$8,100	9	$7,865
5	$6,800	10	$8,785

P3.49: The letter grade system works as follows: A = 4; B = 3; C = 2; D = 1; F = 0. Suppose a student obtained the following letter grades in 8 consecutive quizzes: A, B, B, C, C, D, and F, F. Compute the grade point average (GPA) and round the result with two decimal places. If C is the minimum letter grade for this student to pass the course, did this student pass the course?

P3.50: The letter grade system works as follows: A = 4; B = 3; C = 2; D = 1; F = 0. Suppose a student obtained the following letter grades in 5 consecutive quizzes: A, B, C, A, and C. Compute the grade point average (GPA) and round the result with two decimal places. If C is the minimum letter grade for this student to pass the course, did this student pass the course?

P3.51: Listed below is the annual income of highest-paid women reported by CNN-Money http://money.cnn.com/galleries/2011/news/1104/gallery.top_ceo_pay/index.html

(a) What is the level of measurement of each variable in the table
(b) Construct a bar chart of annual income
(c) Calculate the mean, mode, median, range, standard deviation, and variance of annual income
(d) Based on your readings, explain the reason for the wide difference in annual income

187

Name	Company	Annual Income ($Million)
Carol Bartz	President & CEO- Yahoo	$47.20
Safra Catz	President- Oracle (ORCL)	$36.40
Carrie Cox	Former EVP and President, Global Pharmaceuticals	$23
Irene Rosenfeld	Chairman and CEO Kraft Foods (KFT)	$22.10
Wellington J. Denahan-Norris	Vice Chairman, Chief Investment Officer and COO-Annaly Capital Management (NLY)	$21.60
Pamela H. Patsley	Chairman and CEO Moneygram International (MGI)	$17.90
Susan M. Ivey	Chairman, President and CEO Reynolds American (RAI)	$16.20
Martine A. Rothblatt	Chairman and CEO United Therapeutics (UTHR)	$15.80
Carol M. Meyrowitz	President and CEO TJX Companies (TJX)	$14.80
Indra Nooyi	Chairman and CEO PepsiCo (PEP)	$14.20
Angela Braly	President and CEO WellPoint (WLP)	$13.10
Brenda Barnes	Former Chairman and CEO Sara Lee (SLE)	$11.50
Linda Chen	President of Wynn International Marketing Wynn Resorts (WYNN)	$11.20
Patricia Woertz	Chairman, President and CEO Archer Daniels Midland (ADM)	$11.00
Kim Sinatra	General Counsel and Secretary Wynn Resorts (WYNN)	$10.50
Mary Callahan Erdoes	CEO, Asset Management JPMorgan Chase (JPM)	$10.40
Nancy Wysenski	EVP and Chief Commercial Officer Vertex Pharmaceuticals (VRTX)	$10.20
Jackwyn Nemerov	Executive Vice President Polo Ralph Lauren (RL)	$10.10
Ursula Burns	CEO Xerox (XRX)	$9.90
Martha Stewart	Founder and Chief Editorial, Media and Content Officer Martha Stewart Living Omnimedia (MSO)	$9.70

Answer:

Name = Nominal-qualitative

Company = Nominal-qualitative

Annual Income = Ratio- quantitative

	Annual Income ($Million)
Mean	16.84
Median	13.65
Standard Deviation	??
Sample Variance	93.95
Range	37.5

CHAPTER 4

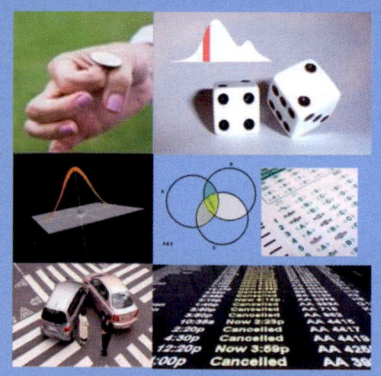

Introduction to Probability

LEARNING OBJECTIVES

- After completing this chapter, students will learn how to:

- *Use basic probability rules to determine the chances of events*
- *Construct a Venn diagram and a tree diagram*
- *Interpret subjective probability*
- *Use classic probability rules*
- *Use empirical probability rules*
- *Construct a contingency table and determine all probability components (marginal, union, and conditional)*
- *Determine probabilities of dependent and independent events*
- *Use counting rules*
- *Use Bayes' theorem*

CHAPTER 4

In Chapters 2 and 3, the focus was on descriptive statistics; we described data sets numerically and graphically for the sake of revealing important information that may shed some light not only on the sample components but also on the population from which the sample is withdrawn. In this chapter, the focus is shifted to the subject of probability which is considered by all statisticians as the mathematical backbone of statistics. We will learn about basic probability rules. We will also discuss the use of contingency tables to determine marginal, union, and conditional probabilities. Finally, we will discuss the Bayes' theorem of probability.

CHAPTER CONTENTS

4.1 What is probability?

Most people use terms such as chance, likelihood, or probability to reflect the level of uncertainty about some issues or events. Examples in which these terms may be used are as follows:

- As you watch the news every day, you hear forecasters saying that the chance of rain tomorrow is 70% or 80%.
- As you plan to enter a new business, an expert in the field tells you that the probability of making a first-year profit in this business is only 0.4, or there is a 40% chance that you will make a profit.
- As you take a new course, you may be wondering about the likelihood of passing or failing the course.
- Your friend is undergoing a surgery and the physician is telling him that his chance of surviving is 99%.

- You hear it on health news all the time that a smoker has a much greater chance of suffering lung cancer than a nonsmoker does.

These are all expressions of probability that we often hear or read and they can affect our planning or intention to do or not to do things in life.

On the theoretical side, *probability is a numerical index of the likelihood that a certain event will occur*. It is a value between zero and one, which reveals the relative possibility that an event will occur. A probability of zero or close to zero implies that an event is impossible or very improbable to occur, and a probability of one or close to one gives us high certainty that an event will occur. Between these two extremes, different values of probability are expressed as a decimal such as 0.20, 0.90, or 0.5, or as a fraction such as 1/5, 9/10, or 1/2. Note that both ways of expression can easily be expressed in percent (20%, 90%, or 50%).

Working problem 4.1:

In a year selected at random,

(a) What is the probability that Thanksgiving Day will come on a Wednesday?
(b) What is the probability that Thanksgiving Day will come on a Thursday?

Answer:
(a) Thanksgiving Day always falls on the fourth Thursday in November of each year. This makes it impossible for Thanksgiving to be on a Wednesday. Thus,
P(Thanksgiving Day will come on a Wednesday) = 0
(b) Do it yourself

4.2 Experiment, outcome, event, and sample Space

The discussion of probability should begin by introducing four basic terms that are often used in the context of probability: experiment, outcome, event, and sample space. These terms are defined below.

191

An Experiment:

- A pre-planned procedure for the sake of producing data to reveal useful results
- In the context of probability, when the term 'experiment' is used it typically indicates a trial that can result in only one of several possible outcomes
- Tossing a coin or rolling a die is considered an experiment
- Testing a student in a certain subject is considered an experiment

An Outcome:

- An outcome is the result of a single trial of an experiment
- A head turning in tossing a coin is an outcome
- When you roll a fair die and get the number '5' this is considered an outcome.
- A student earning a 'C' on a test is an outcome

An Event:

- An event is the collection of one or more outcomes of an experiment.
- An even number resulting from rolling a fair die is an event
- Getting a result of heads both times when tossing a coin twice is an event
- Half of your students passing a test with a 'C' grade is an event

A Sample space:

- All possible outcomes taken together represent the *'sample space'* for the experiment.
- The sample space resulting from tossing a coin once is {*H* and *T*}
- The sample space resulting from rolling a die once is {1, 2, 3, 4, 5, and 6}
- The sample space resulting from grading a course is {*A*, *B*, *C*, *D*, and *F*}

Example 4.1: In rolling a six-sided die,

- What is an experiment?
- What is an outcome?
- What is an event?
- What is a sample space?

Solution:

Rolling a six-sided die is the experiment. A number such as 1, 2, 3, 4, 5, or 6 is the outcome. Specifying a certain combination, such as odd or even number will be an event. The sample space for this experiment is $S = \{1, 2, 3, 4, 5, 6\}$.

Example 4.2: In the process of rolling a pair of fair dice,

- What is an experiment?
- What is an outcome?
- What is an event?
- What is a sample space?

Solution:

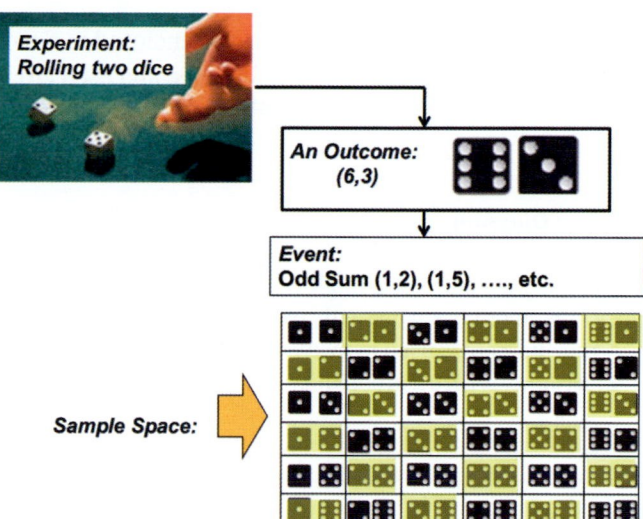

The experiment in this example is rolling a pair of fair dice. A possible outcome of this experiment is the combination (6,3). An event can be the observation of odd sum such as (2,1), (4,1), (6,1), (1,2), (3,2), (5,2), etc.

The sample space of this experiment is as follows:

S = {(1,1), (1,2), (1,3), (1,4), (1,5), (1,6), (2,1), (2,2), (2,3), (2,4), (2,5), (2,6), (3,1), (3,2), (3,3), (3,4), (3,5), (3,6), (4,1), (4,2), (4,3), (4,4), (4,5), (4,6), (5,1), (5,2), (5,3), (5,4), (5,5), (5,6), (6,1), (6,2), (6,3), (6,4), (6,5), (6,6)}.

Table 4.1 illustrates some examples of experiments, outcomes, and sample spaces.

Table 4.1 Examples of experiments, outcomes, events, and sample spaces

Experiment	Examples of outcomes	Examples of event	Examples of sample space
Rolling a die once	1, 2, 3, 4, 5, or 6	Odd number	S = {1, 2, 3, 4, 5, 6}
Taking a test	A, B, C, D, or F	Test performance	S = {A, B, C, D, F}
Selecting an age	Old, middle, or young	Age category	S = {old, middle, young}
Birth	Male or female	Gender	S = {male, female}
Tossing a coin twice	$(H, H), (H, T), (T, H)$, or (T, T)	Two heads	S = {$(H, H), (H, T), (T, H), (T, T)$}

4.3 The Venn diagram and the tree diagram

Events can be displayed graphically using common methods such as the Venn diagram or the tree diagram. The Venn diagram was named after its pioneer J. Venn (1835–1888) an English logician who developed it to provide a graphical display of the outcomes of an experiment. In this diagram, letters such as A, B, C, D, are used to represent outcomes or events. The sample space is depicted as a rectangle (may be other shapes), and the various events are drawn as circles inside the rectangle. In a tree diagram, each outcome is represented by a branch of a tree to separate events and provide a flowchart of event sequence.

The Venn Diagram:

- A picture representing events as circles enclosed in a rectangle
- The rectangle represents the sample space and each circle represents an event

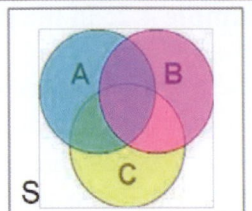

The Tree Diagram:

- This diagram starts at a single node, with branches emanating to additional nodes, which represent mutually exclusive decisions or events
- A tree diagram is used in many applications related to strategic decisions involving uncertainty where a probability flowchart is required.

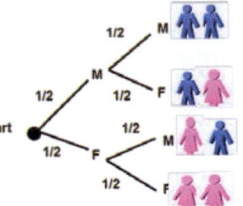

Example 4.3: Display the Venn diagram and the tree diagram of the experiment of tossing a coin twice.

Solution:
In this experiment, the following sample space represents all possible outcomes:
$S = \{HH, TT, HT, TH\}$.

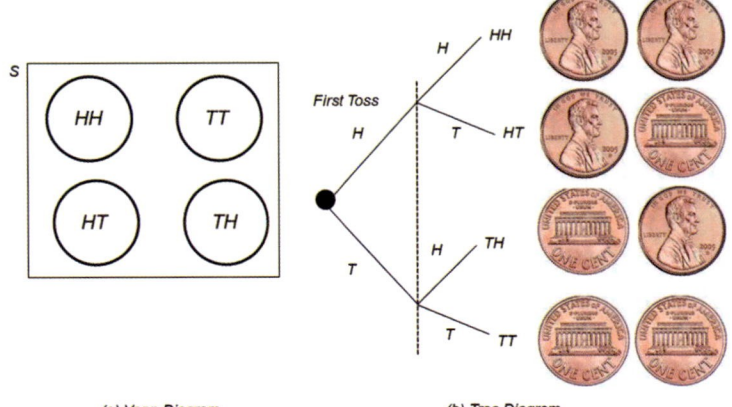

(a) Venn Diagram   (b) Tree Diagram

Working problem 4.2:

A box has 10 cards labeled 0, 1, 2, 3, 4, 5, 6, 7, 8, or 9.
'A' represents the event "choose a number less than 3," and
'B' represents the event "choose a number greater than 5."

Draw a Venn diagram illustrating these events

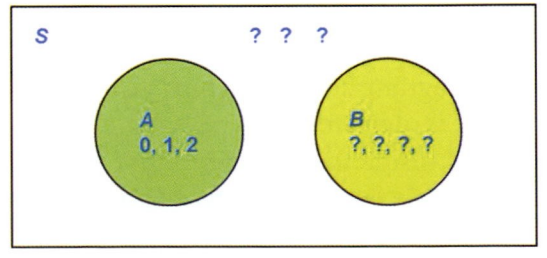

Working Problem 4.3:

Assuming that in birth, boys and girls are equally likely and that the gender of any child is not influenced by the gender of any other child. Draw a tree diagram illustrating all possibilities associated with a couple that has three children.

Answer:

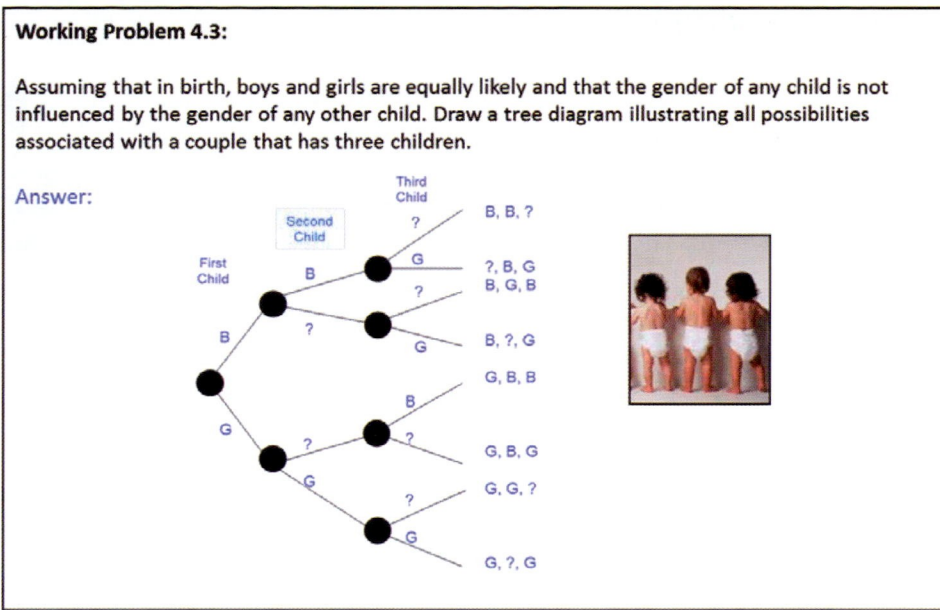

4.4 Mutually exclusive events and collectively exhaustive events

When events are mutually exclusive, the occurrence of one event results in other events not occurring at the same time. For example, tossing a coin once results in one of two mutually exclusive events, a head or a tail. Items inspected for shipping can either be good or bad, resulting in mutually exclusive events of passing or failing. Other events may be collectively exhaustive, which means that at least one of the events must occur when an experiment is conducted. For example, in the six possible outcomes of rolling a die, any outcome will be either odd or even. This makes the set collectively exhaustive.

4.5 Different types of probability

Probability is commonly divided into two types:

(1) Subjective probability
(2) Objective probability

Subjective probability is defined as the likelihood of a particular event estimated on the basis of some expert judgment, individual intuition, or some general information. Objective probability is defined as the relative possibility of occurrence of an event defined either by the ***classic law of probability***, or by using ***empirical means***. These two types of probability are discussed in the following sections.

195

4.5.1 Subjective probability

In the absence of well-defined sample space, and when past data does not exist, the chance of an event outcome may be arrived at subjectively. For example, an economist may decide to evaluate a number of opinions on the direction of the state of economy and speculate that there is a high chance that the stock market will collapse in a year. He/she may even go further by specifying a 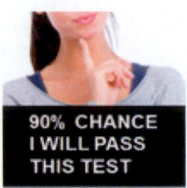 chance of, say 60%, of this collapse. Many politicians, economists, and sports analysts speculate on future events and assign chances or probabilities solely on the basis of general evaluation, expert opinions, short-term or long-term trends, or even random guesses.

Examples of subjective probability are as follows:

1. The likelihood that the University of Florida will win the National college football championship next year is 0.6, or 60% chance.
2. The probability that Google will acquire Yahoo within the next 10 years is 0.1, or 10%.
3. You may guess that the chance of earning an *A* in the statistics class you are currently taking is 0.5, or 50% chance.
4. You may speculate that the likelihood that your business will begin to earn profit in the second year of its initiation is 80%.
5. A company may speculate that the chance that a new product will sweep the market is 90%.

Note that these are statements about probabilities of events that have not yet occurred. As a result, they are associated with minimum or no degree of certainty. The extent of believing in some of these probabilities will depend on the reliability of the source of information and the expertise involved.

4.5.2 Objective probability

Objective probability is based on data from either a well-defined experiment with a well-defined sample space, or from a well-defined experiment but with partially defined sample space. When the sample space is well-defined and outcomes are equally likely, the classic law of probability can be used to estimate probabilities associated with the events. For example, the sample space of rolling a fair die is {1, 2, 3, 4, 5, and 6}. This makes the chance of occurrence of any of these outcomes a 1/6 since we have a total of 6 outcomes. This value will always be the same for rolling a fair die.

In practice, we often rely on data that are unique to the experiment under consideration. In this case, we can estimate an empirical probability. For example, suppose a teacher often gives an '*A*' grade to 20% of the students in his classes. This means that if you take this teacher's class, you will have a 20% chance of earning an '*A*'. It is important to point out that this value may not hold all the time and certainly will not hold for other teachers teaching the same course. This uncertainty is a direct result of the absence of a complete sample space. However, it represents the best value of probability given the partial sample space available. This point will be clarified further by examples in the next sections.

4.5.2.1 Classic probability

The classic probability of an event, A, is determined by the ratio between the number of favorable outcomes, m, and the total number of possible outcomes, n:

$$P(A) = \frac{number\ of\ favorable\ outcomes}{total\ number\ of\ outcomes} = \frac{m}{n} \qquad (4.1)$$

The underlying assumption of this definition is that the different outcomes of an experiment are equally likely. The probability of non-occurrence of the event A is called the probability of failure of occurrence and is denoted by:

$$P(A') = q(A) = P(not\ A) = \frac{(n-m)}{n}$$

$$or\ P(A') = 1 - p(A) = 1 - \frac{m}{n} \qquad (4.2)$$

where p = the probability of the occurrence of event A, q = the probability of the nonoccurrence of event A, and $q = 1 - p$.

For an event A, the probability will lie between 0 and 1, or

$$0 \leq P(A) \leq 1 \qquad (4.3)$$

The sum of probabilities in a given experiment will always equal one.

$$\sum P(A_i) = 1 \qquad (4.4)$$

Example 4.4: If a coin is tossed once, what is the probability of a head (H) outcome? What is the probability of a non-head outcome? What is the sum of probabilities?

Solution:

Since tossing a coin will result in one of two outcomes, namely: head (H) and tail (T), then

$$P(Head) = P(H) = \frac{number\ of\ favorable\ outcomes}{total\ number\ of\ outcomes} = \frac{1}{2}$$

The probability of non-occurrence of the heads outcome is called the probability of failure of occurrence and is denoted by:

$$P(H') = q(H) = P(not\ H) = \frac{(n-m)}{n} = 1 - p(A) = 1 - \frac{1}{2} = \frac{1}{2}$$

Note that the probability lies between 0 and 1, or $0 \leq P(A) \leq 1$

The sum of probabilities in this experiment is

$$\sum P = P(H) + P(H') = P(H) + P(T) = \frac{1}{2} + \frac{1}{2} = 1$$

Example 4.5: In an experiment of rolling a die, find the probability of obtaining an odd number in one roll of a die. What is the probability of obtaining a number less than 4?

Solution:

The total number of possible outcomes of this experiment is 6, and the sample space is $S = \{1, 2, 3, 4, 5, 6\}$. If A is the event that an odd number is observed on the die, the number of favorable outcomes will be 3, or $\{1, 3, 5\}$. Accordingly,

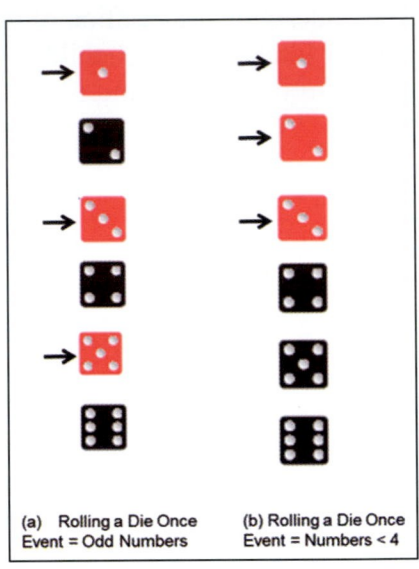

(a) Rolling a Die Once
Event = Odd Numbers

(b) Rolling a Die Once
Event = Numbers < 4

$$P(A = odd\ outcome) = \frac{3}{6} = \frac{1}{2} = 0.5$$

The probability of obtaining a number less than 4 involves three outcomes, namely $\{1, 2, 3\}$. Accordingly,

$$P(rolling\ a\ number\ less\ than\ 4) = \frac{3}{6} = \frac{1}{2}$$

Try to solve these questions yourself:

-   What is the probability of obtaining an even number in one roll of a die?
-   What is the probability of rolling a number less than 6?
-   What is the probability of rolling a number more than 5?

As you try these problems, you should realize that the key to solving a classic probability question is through knowledge of all possible outcomes of an experiment, or sample space.

Example 4.6: If a pair of fair dice is rolled,

    (a) What is the probability of rolling a sum of two?
    (b) What is the probability of rolling a sum of seven?
    (c) What is the probability of rolling a sum of four?

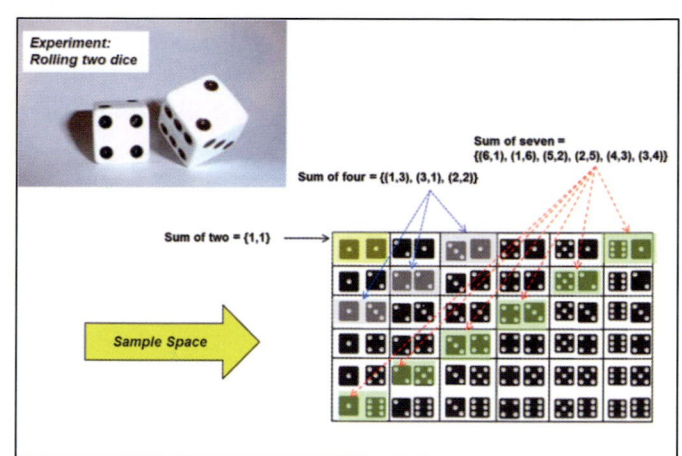

Solution:

$$P(A) = P(roll\ a\ sum\ of\ two) = \frac{1}{36}$$

$$P(B) = P(roll\ a\ sum\ of\ seven) = \frac{6}{36} = \frac{1}{6}$$

$$P(C) = P(roll\ a\ sum\ of\ four) = \frac{3}{36} = \frac{1}{12}$$

Example 4.7: If E is the event of heads coming up in tossing a coin twice and G is the event of odd numbers coming up in rolling a six-sided die once:

  - What are the outcomes of these two events?
  - Calculate $P(E)$, $P(G)$, $P(E')$, and $P(G')$
  - Draw a Venn diagram illustrating these events

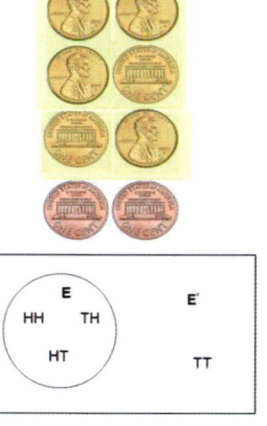

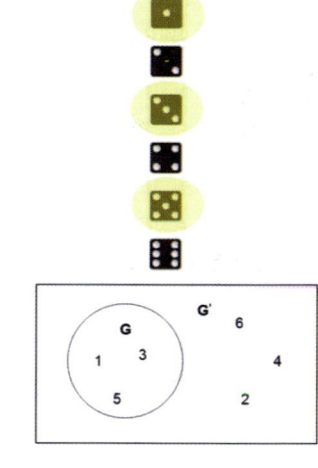

(a) Tossing a Coin Twice

(b) Rolling a die once

Solution:

In tossing a coin twice, the sample space is S = {HH, HT, TH, TT}, E = {HH, HT, TH} then E' = {TT}, $P(E)$ =3/4, and $P(E') = 1/4$

In rolling a die once, the sample space is S = {1, 2, 3, 4, 5, 6}, G = {1, 3, 5}, then G' = {2, 4, 6}, $P(G)$ = 3/6, and $P(G') = 3/6$

Example 4.8: In the experiment of rolling a pair of ordinary dice, answer the following questions:

    (a) What is the probability that both dice show the same face?
    (b) What is the probability that a sum of four is rolled?

(a) Rolling two balanced dice: Event = Doubles

Solution:

To answer these questions, we have to identify the sample space for rolling a pair of dice.

(a) The total number of possible outcomes of this experiment is 36. The number of times doubles (same face) are rolled is 6, or {(1,1), (2,2), (3,3), (4,4), (5,5), (6,6)}. Thus, the probability of doubles is:

$$P(A) = \frac{number\ of\ favorable\ outcomes}{total\ number\ of\ outcomes} = \frac{6}{36} = 0.167$$

(b) The number of times a sum of 4 will come up is 3, or {(1,3), ((3,1), (2,2)}. Thus, the probability of a sum of 4 is:

$$P(B) = \frac{Number\ of\ favorable\ outcomes}{Total\ number\ of\ outcomes}$$
$$= \frac{3}{36} = \frac{1}{12} = 0.083$$

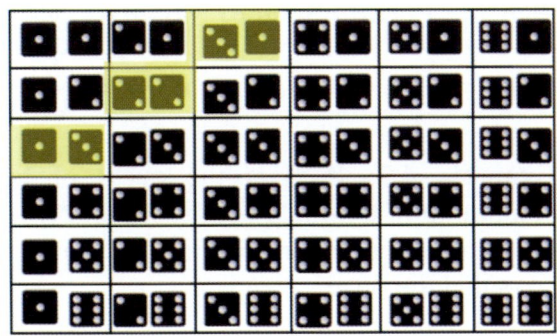

(b) Rolling two balanced dice: Event = Sum of 4

Example 4.9: In the previous example, what is the probability that the two faces will have different numbers?

Solution:

Since the probability that the two dice will have the same face is $P(A) = 6/36$. The complement event is that the two faces are different. The probability of this event is given by

$$P(A') = 1 - P(A) = 1 - \frac{6}{36} = \frac{5}{6}$$

Working Problem 4.4:

Assuming that in birth, boys and girls are equally likely and that the gender of any child is not influenced by the gender of any other child.

What is the probability that when a couple has 3 children, they will have exactly 2 girls?
What is the probability that when a couple has 3 children, they will have one or more girls?
What is the probability that when a couple has 3 children, they will have no boys?
What is the probability that when a couple has 3 children, they will have no girls?

P(2 girls) = 3/8=0.375
P (one or more girls) = P(1 G, 2G, or 3G) = 7/8 = 0.875
P(no boys) = P (all girls) = 1/8 = 0.125
P(no girls) = P (all boys) = 1/8 = 0.125

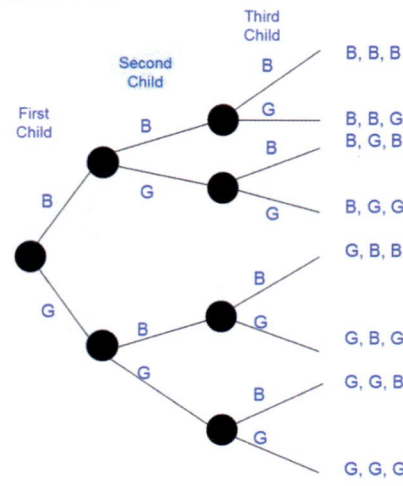

Working problem 4.5:

A box has 10 cards labeled 0, 1, 2, 3, 4, 5, 6, 7, 8, or 9.
A represents the event "choose a number less than 3," and
B represents the event "choose a number greater than 5."

- What is P(A)?
- What is P(B)?

Answer:

Using the Venn Diagram below:

P (A) = (3/10) = 0.3
P(B) = ????

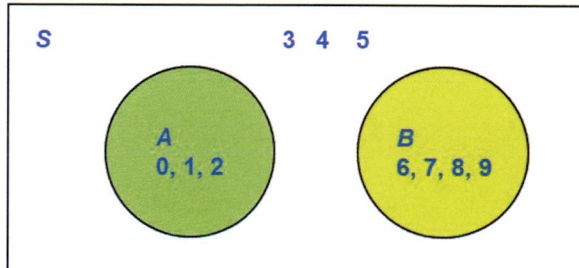

Working problem 4.6:

According to 2012 statistics (http://usgovinfo.about.com/od/consumerawareness/a/congestion.htm) , traffic congestion costs Americans $63.1 billion a year and it is only getting worse, according to a new report from the Texas Transportation Institute (TTI). Factoring in today's rising fuel prices adds another $1.7 billion per year.

You drive to school every day and traffic can be a problem, what is the probability that you will be late to your class tomorrow?
What is the probability that you will be late to your class tomorrow if instead you ride a motorcycle?

Answer: Multiple answers

Working problem 4.7:

In drawing one card from a standard 52-card deck,
(a) What is the probability the card will be a queen?
(b) Which approach to probability did you use to answer this Question?

Answer:
(a) P (Queen) = 4/52 = 0.0769
(b) Answer yourself

Working problem 4.8:

You roll a six-sided die. Find the probability of the following events:
(1) Event A: rolling a 2
(2) Event B: rolling a 6
(3) Event C: rolling a 9
(4) Event D: rolling less than 5

Answer:
P(A) = 1/6 ≈ 0.167
P(B) = ??
P(C) = ??
P(D) = 4/6 ≈ 0.667

Working problem 4.9:

You roll a pair of ordinary dice. Find the probability of the following events:
(1) Event A: rolling a sum of 2
(2) Event B: rolling a sum of 6
(3) Event C: rolling a sum of 9
(4) Event D: rolling less than a sum of 5

Answer:

Use the sample space shown here to answer the above questions

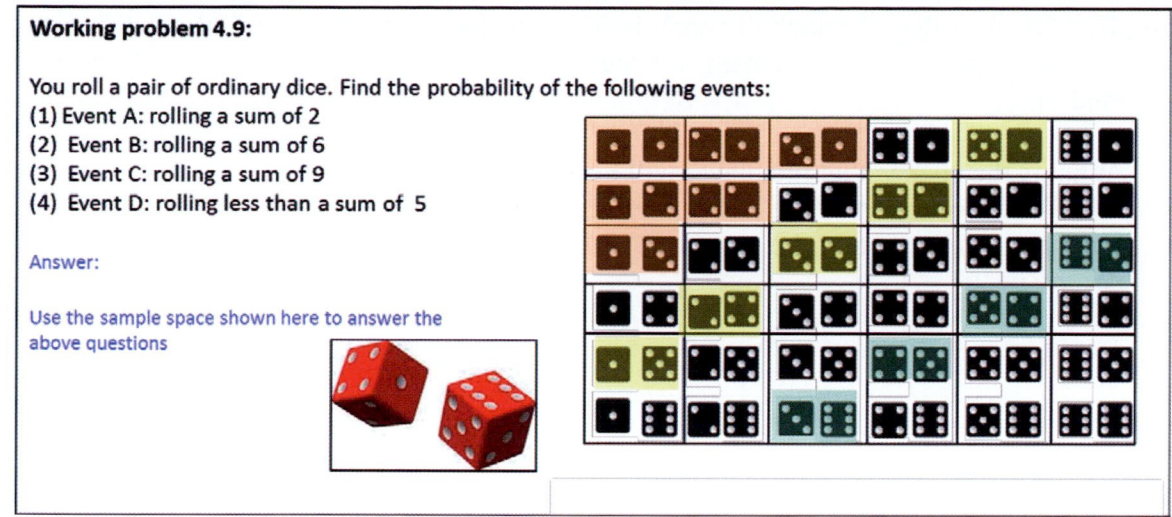

4.5.2.2 Empirical probability

In chapter 3, we discussed the relative frequency distribution and we defined a relative frequency by:

$$Relative\ frequency = \frac{frequency\ of\ class\ i}{total\ frequency} = \frac{f_i}{\sum_1^k f_i} \qquad (4.5)$$

where f_i is the frequency of the ith class, k is the number of classes, and $\sum_1^k f_i$ is the sum of all frequencies.

The above equation is essentially a probability expression as it describes the relative occurrence of an event (or a class of values) as a fraction of the sum of all possible frequencies. Empirical probability is typically calculated from a relative frequency. Indeed, the above equation can be expressed in probability terms as follows:

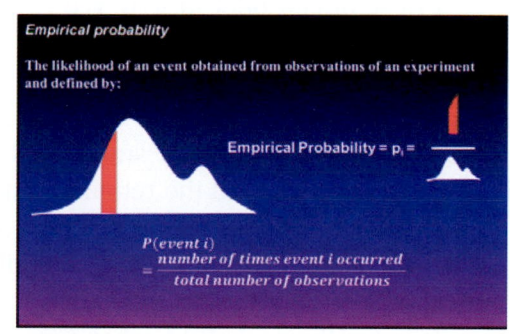

$$P(event\ i) = \frac{number\ of\ times\ event\ i\ occurred}{total\ number\ of\ observations} \qquad (4.6)$$

Unlike the classic probability which is associated with a well-defined total number of possible outcomes of an experiment, empirical probability is associated with a number of possible outcomes that may vary depending on the experiment under consideration and the number of experimental trials attempted.

Example 4.10: A college basketball coach is trying to form a team from 190 equally qualified players. Seventy players are freshmen, 60 are sophomores, and 60 are seniors. If he picks a player randomly:

- What is the chance that the player will be a freshman?
- What is the chance that the player will be a sophomore?
- What is the chance that the player will be a senior?

Student level	Number of students (f_i)
Freshman	70
Sophomores	60
Seniors	60
Total	$\sum f_i = 190$

Solution:

Student level	Number of students (f_i)	Relative Frequency (probability)
Freshman	70	$70/190 \approx 0.368$
Sophomore	60	$60/190 \approx 0.316$
Senior	60	$60/190 \approx 0.316$
Total	$\sum f_i = 190$	$\sum p_i = 1$

- P(a freshman) = 70/190 = 0.368   or 36.8%
- P(a sophomore) = 60/190 = 0.316   or 31.6%
- P(a senior) = 60/190 = 0.316   or 31.6%

Example 4.11: In a recent CNN poll, 2000 adult Americans were selected randomly to ask whether secondhand tobacco smoke is harmful. 1450 said secondhand smoke is harmful, 300 said it is not harmful, and the remainder had no opinion. Based on the results of this survey.

- What is the probability that a randomly selected adult American believes that secondhand smoke is harmful?
- What is the probability that a randomly selected adult American believes that secondhand smoke is not harmful?
- What is the probability that a randomly selected adult American will have no opinion about secondhand smoke?

Solution:

Adult opinion	Number of students (f_i)	P(event i)
Secondhand smoke is harmful	1450	0.725
Secondhand smoke is not harmful	300	0.150
No opinion	250	0.125
Total	$\sum f_i = 2000$	$\sum p_i = 1$

- The probability that a randomly selected adult American believes that secondhand smoke is harmful = 0.725 or 72.5%

- The probability that a randomly selected adult American believes that secondhand smoke is not harmful = 0.150 or 15%

- The probability that a randomly selected adult American will have no opinion about secondhand smoke = 0.125 or 12.5%

These results indicate that the majority of people believe that secondhand smoke is harmful.

What is secondhand smoke?

Secondhand smoke (SHS) is also known as environmental tobacco smoke (ETS). SHS is a mixture of 2 forms of smoke that come from burning tobacco:

(a) Side-stream smoke – the smoke that comes from the end of a lighted cigarette, pipe, or cigar and

(b) Mainstream smoke – the smoke that is exhaled by a smoker

Even though we think of these as the same, they aren't. The side-stream smoke has higher concentrations of cancer-causing agents (carcinogens) than the mainstream smoke. And, it contains smaller particles than mainstream smoke, which make their way into the body's cells more easily.

When non-smokers are exposed to SHS it is called *involuntary smoking* or *passive smoking*. Non-smokers who breathe in SHS take in nicotine and other toxic chemicals just like smokers do. The more SHS you are exposed to, the higher the level of these harmful chemicals in your body.

http://www.cancer.org/Cancer/CancerCauses/TobaccoCancer/secondhand-smoke

Working problem 4.10:

The data in the Table below represent the results of a survey in which a random sample of people were asked about their best TV show category.
(a) What is the probability that a randomly selected individual will only watch sports events
(b) What is the probability that a randomly selected individual will only watch movies
(c) What is the probability that a randomly selected individual will only watch political news
(d) What is the probability that a randomly selected individual will not watch movies

TV show category	Number of people
Sports shows only	780
Business News Only	220
Political news only	100
Movies	900
Total	2000

Answer:

P(only watch sports events) = 0.39
P(only watch movies) = ??
P(only watch political news) = 0.05
P(will not watch movies) = ??

TV show category	Number of people	Pi
Sports shows only	780	0.39
Business News Only	220	???
Political news only	100	0.05
Movies	900	???
Total	2000	1

Working problem 4.11:

A survey of a random sample of 250 students at the Evergreen college revealed the following majors:

Major	Number of students
Business	67
Engineering	61
Environmental science	47
Nursing	75
Total	250

Suppose we select a student at random and ask for his/her major.
- What is the chance that the student will be a nursing major?
- What is the chance that the student will be an engineering major?
- What is the chance that the student will not be an environmental science major?

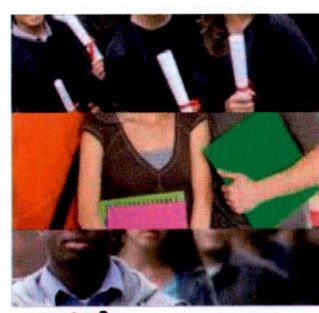

Answer:
Complete the table below and answer the questions.

Major	Number of students	Pi
Business	67	0.268
Engineering	61	??
Environmental science	??	0.188
Nursing	??	0.3
Total	250	1

4.6 What is the law of large numbers (probability stabilization)?

The law of large numbers indicates that as the number of trials of a probability experiment increases, the proportion with which a certain outcome is observed gets closer to the actual probability of the outcome. In other words, if an experiment is repeated many times in identical fashion, the probability of an event obtained from this experiment and determined by the relative frequency of the event occurrence will become stable and approach the actual probability. The Examples below illustrate this law.

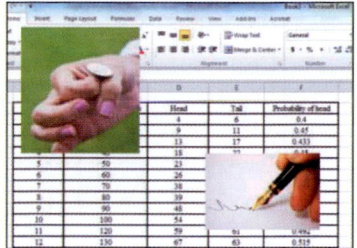

Example 4.12: In an earlier example, we found that the probability that a head will turn up in a single toss of a coin is 0.5. In practical terms, if this is true then tossing a coin a hundred times should result in 50 heads and 50 tails. Suppose you want to test this argument for yourself by tossing a fair coin many times and listing the number of times a head comes up. If you make this attempt, you will likely obtain values similar to those in Table 4.2. As you can see in this table, values of empirical probability will fluctuate around the 0.5 and ultimately become 0.5 as the number of trials becomes larger. This point is also illustrated in Figure 4.1.

Table 4.2 Repeated coin tossing trials

Trial #	Total number of tosses	Head	Tail	Probability of head
1	10	4	6	0.400
2	20	9	11	0.450
3	30	13	17	0.433
4	40	18	22	0.450
5	50	23	27	0.460
6	60	26	34	0.433
7	70	38	32	0.543
8	80	39	41	0.488
9	90	48	42	0.533
10	100	54	46	0.540
11	120	59	61	0.492
12	130	67	63	0.515
13	140	72	68	0.514
14	150	74	76	0.493
15	160	82	78	0.513
16	170	84	86	0.494
17	180	88	92	0.489
18	190	94	96	0.495
19	200	101	99	0.505
20	300	151	149	0.503
21	400	200	200	0.500
22	500	249	251	0.498

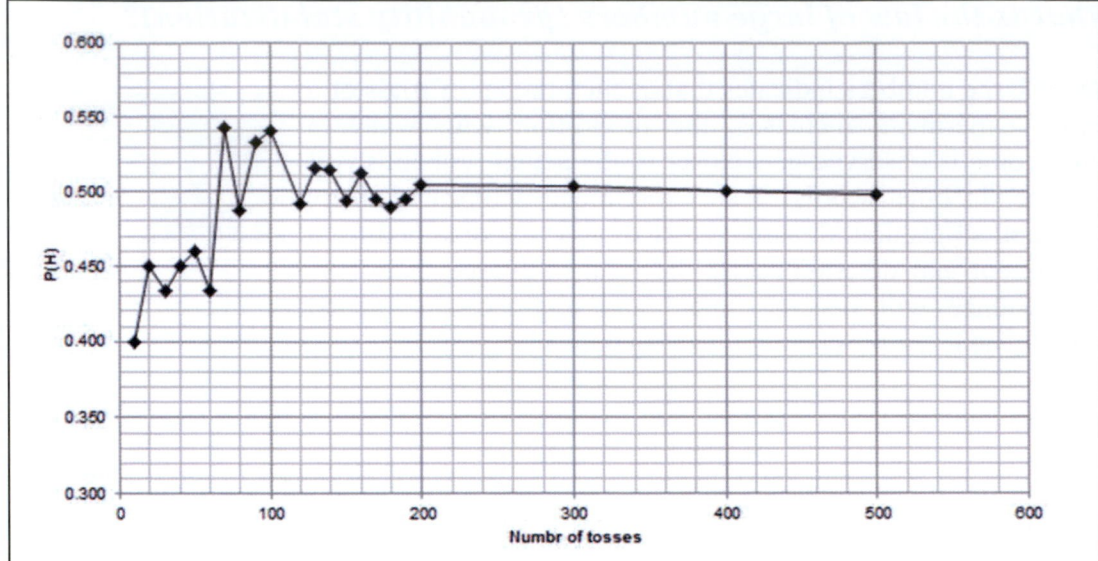

Figure 4.1 Stabilization of Empirical Probability (The Law of Large Numbers)-Coin Tossing Example

Working problem 4.12:

If the event is a number '5' turning in rolling a die, simulate rolling a die for 1000 times with increments of 100 and explain how the law of large numbers will prevail.

Answer:
This problem may have multiple answers one of which is shown below. A student can try to make his/her simulation and produce a different answer. The key in all answers is whether the law of large numbers prevail.

Number of trials	Number of 5 turning	P(x =5)
100	15	0.150
200	28	0.140
300	54	0.180
400	36	0.090
500	80	0.160
600	99	0.165
700	116	0.166
800	133	0.166
900	150	0.167
1000	167	0.167

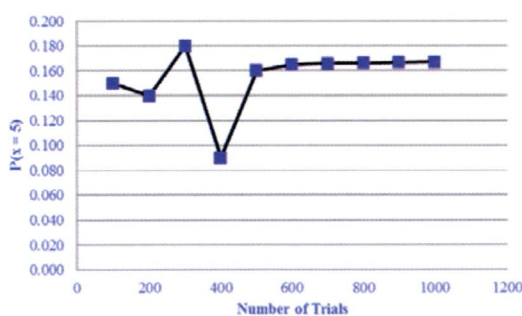

Working problem 4.13 :

The data in the Table below was taken from the U.S. Census Bureau report titled "HINC-01. Selected Characteristics of Households, by Total Money Income in 2005"
(http://www.census.gov/hhes/www/cpstables/032010/hhinc/new01_001.htm)

Income	Households (thousands)
Under $20,000	24,559
$20,000 to < $40,000	26,904
$40,000 to < $60,000	20,026
$60,000 to < $80,000	14,535
$80,000 to < $100,000	9,362
Above $100,000	7,813

Income	Households (thousands)	Probability
Under $20,000	24,559	0.237977
$20,000 to < $40,000	??????	0.2607
$40,000 to < $60,000	20,026	?????2
$60,000 to < $80,000	14,535	0.140844
$80,000 to < $100,000	9,362	0.090718
Above $100,000	?????	0.075708
Total	103,199	1

If a U.S. family is selected at random, Determine

(a) The probability that the family selected has an annual income of less than $40,000
(b) The probability that the family selected has an annual income of $40,000 to less than $80,000
(c) The probability that the family selected has an annual income of more than $100,000

(a) ?

Answer:
Complete the relative distribution table and answer the questions

(b) 0.335

(c) ?

4.7 Relationships between events

In this section, we determine the probability of a combination of events, say event *A* and event *B*. In this regard, a number of key questions should be addressed:

- *What is the probability of the occurrence of event A and event B together?* **P(A&B)**

- *What is the probability of the occurrence of event A or event B?* **P(A or B)**

- *What is the probability of the occurrence of event A, given event B has occurred?* **P(A| B)**

- *Are events A and B dependent or independent?*

4.7.1 Events union

The relationship between two events, say *A* and *B*, can be demonstrated using the Venn diagram as shown in Figure 4.2. In this regard, three types of event relationships may be considered:

- Union of two mutually exclusive events (*A* or *B*) as shown in Figure 4.2.a
- Union of two non-mutually exclusive events (*A* or *B*) as shown in Figure 4.2.b.
- Coexistence of events (*A & B*) as shown in Figure 4.2.c.

209

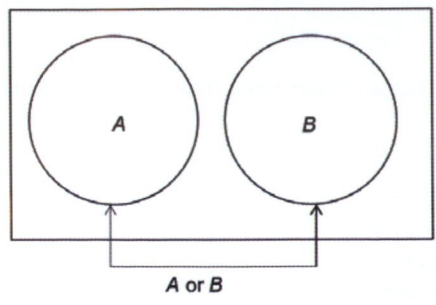 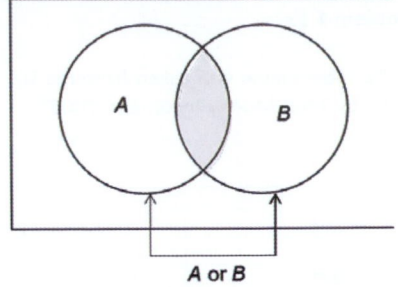

(a) Union Event (mutually exclusive events)   (b) Union (non-mutually exclusive)

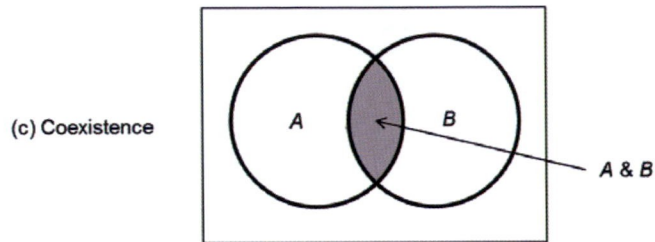

Figure 4.2 Union and Coexistence of Events

The probability that event A or B will occur is $P(A\ or\ B)$ and it is determined by:

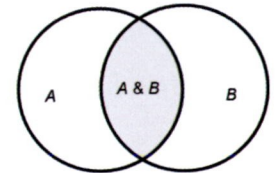

$$P(A\ or\ B) = P(A) + P(B) - P(A\ and\ B) \qquad (4.7)$$

This addition rule can be extended to accommodate more than two events

$$P(A\ or\ B\ or\ C) = P(A) + P(B) + P(C) - P(A\ \&\ B) - P(A\&C) - P(B\&C) + P(A\&B\&C)$$

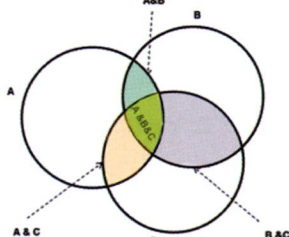

When events are mutually exclusive (i.e. when one event occurs, none of the other events can occur at the same time), the probability of one or the other outcomes occurring will equal to the sum of their probabilities:

$$P(A\ or\ B) = P(A) + P(B) \qquad (4.8)$$

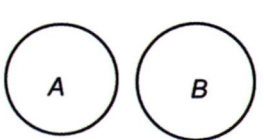

Note that this rule can also be expanded to any number of mutually exclusive outcomes:

$$P(A\ or\ B\ or\ C) = P(A) + P(B) + P(C) \qquad (4.9)$$

Example 4.13: A box has 10 cards each labeled 0, 1, 2, 3, 4, 5, 6, 7, 8, and 9. Let '*A*' represents the event "choose a number less than 3," and '*B*' represents the event "choose a number greater than 5."

(a) What is *P(A)*?
(b) What is *P(B)*?
(c) What is *P(A and B)*?
(d) What is *P(A or B)*?

Solution:

$A = \{0, 1, 2\}$ = 3 outcomes out of 10
$B = \{6, 7, 8, 9\}$ = 4 outcomes out of 10
$P(A) = (3/10) = 0.3$
$P(B) = (4/10) = 0.4$

$P(A \& B) = 0$ (*A* and *B* are mutually-exclusive events)
$P(A \text{ or } B) = P(A) + P(B) = 0.3 + 0.4 = 0.7$

Example 4.14: Using the sample space of rolling a die twice, suppose *A* is the event that the total is 4, *B* is the event that the total is 3:

- Define the outcomes of these events
- Compute *P(A)*, *P(B)*, and *P(A or B)*

Solution:

		First Roll					
		1	2	3	4	5	6
	1	2	3	4	5	6	7
Second	2	3	4	5	6	7	8
Roll	3	4	5	6	7	8	9
	4	5	6	7	8	9	10
	5	6	7	8	9	10	11
	6	7	8	9	10	11	12

$A = \{(1,3), (3,1), (2,2)\}$, $B = \{(2,1), (1,2)\}$

The probabilities of these outcomes are:

$P(A) = 3/36$,
$P(B) = 2/36$, and
$P(A \text{ or } B) = P(A) + P(B) = 3/36 + 2/36 = 5/36$

Example 4.15: Using the sample space in the previous example, determine the probability that the sum in rolling a pair of dice is either 7 or 11.

Solution:

		First Roll					
		1	2	3	4	5	6
	1	2	3	4	5	6	7
Second	2	3	4	5	6	7	8
Roll	3	4	5	6	7	8	9
	4	5	6	7	8	9	10
	5	6	7	8	9	10	11
	6	7	8	9	10	11	12

If D = the event of 7 and E is the event of 11, then D = {(1,6), (2,5), (3,4), (4,3), (5,2), (6,1)}, and E = {(5,6), (6,5)}. The probabilities of D or E are:

$P(D) = 6/36,$
$P(E) = 2/36,$ and
$P(D \text{ or } E) = P(D) + P(E) = 6/36 + 2/36 = 8/36 = 2/9$

Example 4.16: Suppose a card is selected randomly from an ordinary deck of 52 playing cards. What is the probability that the card selected is either a spade or a face card?

Solution:

Let A = the event that the card selected is a spade, B = the event that the card selected is a face card, and A & B = the event that the card is both spade and face. Event A consists of 13 spades, event B consists of 12 face cards, and event (A & B) consists of three spades that are face cards:

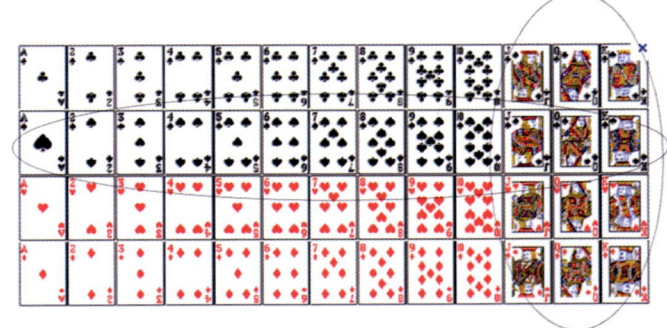

$P(A \text{ or } B) = P(A) + P(B) - P(A \text{ and } B)$
$P(A) = 13/52, P(B) = 12/52,$ and $P(A \text{ and } B) = 3/52$
$P(A \text{ or } B) = 13/52 + 12/52 - 3/52 = 22/52 = 0.423$

Alternatively, we can use the classic law of probability as follows:

Suppose C = the event that the card is selected is either one of the 13 spade cards (including the 3 spade face cards) or one of the other face cards (9 non-spade face cards), $P(C) = m/n = (13+9)/52 = 22/52 = 0.423$

Working problem 4.14:

A box has 10 cards. Each is labeled 0, 1, 2, 3, 4, 5, 6, 7, 8, or 9.
'A' represents the event "choose a number less than 7," and
'B' represents the event "choose a number greater than 5."

- What is P(A)?
- What is P(B)?
- What is P(A or B)?

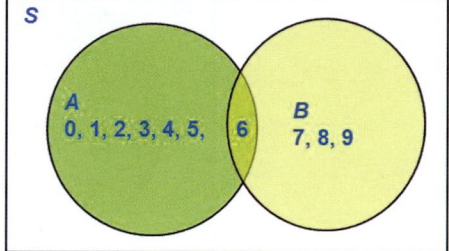

Answer:
P (A) = (7/10) = 0.7
P(B) = (4/10) = 0.4
P(A or B) = P(A) + P(B) − P(A&B)
= ????

Working problem 4.15:

A box has 10 cards. Each is labeled 0, 1, 2, 3, 4, 5, 6, 7, 8, or 9.
C represents the event "choose a number less than or equal 3," and
D represents the event "choose a number greater than or equal 5."

- Draw a Venn diagram illustrating these events
- What Is P(C)?
- What is P(D)?
- What is P (C & D)?
- What is P(C or D)?

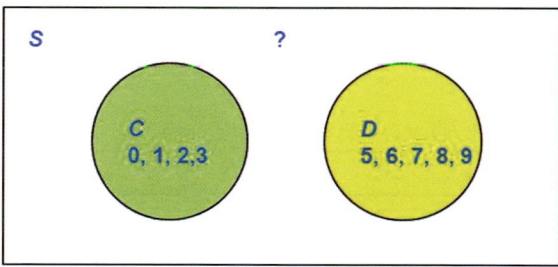

Answer:
P (C) = (4/10) = 0.4
P(D) = (5/10) = 0.5
P(C & D) = ??
P(C or D) = ??

Working problem 4.16:

A box has 10 cards. Eeach is labeled 0, 1, 2, 3, 4, 5, 6, 7, 8, or 9.
E represents the event "choose a number less than or equal 5," and
F represents the event "choose a number greater than or equal 4."

- Draw a Venn diagram illustrating these events
- What is P(E)?
- What is P(F)?
- What is P(E or F)?

Answer:
P (E) = (6/10) = 0.6
P(F) = (6/10) = 0.6
P(E & F) = ??
P(E or F) = ??

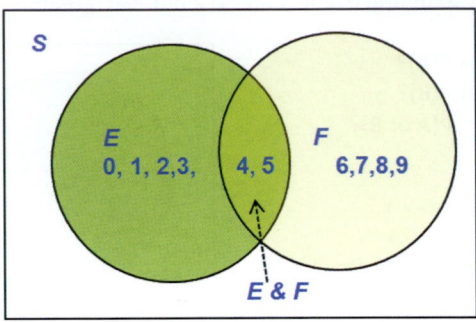

Working problem 4.17:

For the experiment of selecting a card randomly from a deck of 52 cards:
B = The event the card selected is a king,
C = The event the card selected is a heart
D = The event the card selected is a face card
What is P(not D)?
What is P(B & C) ?
What is P(B or C)?
What is P(C & D)?

Answer:
P(not D) = 40/52, P (B & C) = ??, P(B or C) = ??, P(C & D) = ??

Working problem 4.18 :

The data in the Table below was taken from the U.S. Census Bureau report titled "HINC-01. Selected Characteristics of Households, by Total Money Income in 2005"
(http://www.census.gov/hhes/www/cpstables/032010/hhinc/new01_001.htm)

Income	Households (thousands)
Under $20,000	24,559
$20,000 to < $40,000	26,904
$40,000 to < $60,000	20,026
$60,000 to < $80,000	14,535
$80,000 to < $100,000	9,362
Above $100,000	7,813

If a U.S. family is selected at random, Determine
- What is the probability that the family has an annual income of under $20,000
- What is the probability that the family has an annual income of under $60,000
- What is the probability that the family selected has an annual income of less than $40,000 or less than $80,000?

Answer:
P(x < $20,000) = 0.2379, P(x < $60,000) = ?????
- The probability that the family selected has an annual income of less than $40,000 or less than $80,000 = ?????

Income	Households (thousands)	Probability
Under $20,000	24,559	0.237977
$20,000 to < $40,000	26,904	???
$40,000 to < $60,000	20,026	???
$60,000 to < $80,000	14,535	0.140844
$80,000 to < $100,000	???	0.090718
Above $100,000	7,813	???
	103,199	1

4.8 The contingency table

A contingency table is a tabulated form used to classify observations according to two identifiable characteristics. It is a cross tabulation that simultaneously summarizes the frequencies of occurrences of two events of interest. Using a contingency table, we can calculate all sorts of probability including marginal probability, union probability, and conditional probability. We can also determine independency of events. The examples below illustrate the meaning of a contingency table.

Example 4.17: In a survey about whether people would like to have a long dating relationship prior to marriage, 200 people were asked if they like, dislike, or have no opinion. 45 were male and 155 were female. The results of this survey were as follows:

	Like	Dislike	No Opinion
Male	20	15	10
Female	60	45	50

Construct a contingency table showing the two classifications and associated frequencies.

Solution:

	Like	Dislike	No Opinion	Total
Male	20	15	10	45
Female	60	45	50	155
Total	80	60	60	200

Since the number of males is not equal to the number of females in the sample, it will be useful to convert the absolute frequency values in the above table to probability values or percent frequencies values as shown below.

	Like	Dislike	No Opinion	Total
Male	0.1	0.075	0.05	0.225
Female	0.3	0.225	0.25	0.775
Total	0.4	0.300	0.30	1.00

	Like	Dislike	No Opinion	Total
Male	10%	7.5%	5%	22.5%
Female	30%	22.5%	25%	77.5%
Total	40%	30%	30%	100%

Example 4.18: In a qualifying test for college mathematics courses conducted by a college, 1000 students took the test. Out of the 1000 students, 400 students were male, 350 students were under 22 years of age, and 180 students were male under 22 years of age. If a student is selected at random,

   (a) What is the chance that the student is male?
   (b) What is the chance that the student is female?
   (c) What is the chance that the student is under 22 years of age?
   (d) What is the chance that the student is ≥ 22 of age?

(e) What is the chance that the student is male and under 22 years of age?
(f) What is the chance that the student is female and ≥ 22 of age?
(g) What is the chance that the student is either male or under 22 years of age?
(h) What is the chance that the student is either female or ≥ 22 of age?

Solution:

In this type of problem, it will be useful to summarize the experiment by constructing a contingency table as shown in Table 4.3 and fill in the missing data. This will provide the full sample space of this experiment. We then convert this table into an event table (Table 4.4) then a probability table (Table 4.5).

Table 4.3 Qualifying test data

	Under 22 (U)	≥ 22 of age (O)	Total
Male (M)	180	220	400
Female (F)	170	430	600
Total	350	650	1000

Table 4.4 Possible outcomes of qualifying test

	U	O
M	(M,U)	(M, O)
F	(F,U)	(F, O)

Table 4.5 Marginal and union probabilities of qualifying test

	U (Under 22)	O (≥ 22 of age)	Total
M (Male)	0.18	0.22	0.4
F (Female)	0.17	0.43	0.6
Total	0.35	0.65	1

Marginal probabilities:

We may consider one characteristic at a time:

Gender: the student selected can be a male, or a female (mutually exclusive)
Age: under 22 or ≥ 22 of age (mutually exclusive)

This will result in four simple events that are associated with **_'marginal probabilities'_** or **_'simple probabilities.'_** They are called marginal probabilities because they are calculated by dividing the corresponding row margins (totals for the rows) or column margins (totals for the columns) by the grand total. Calculations of marginal probabilities are presented below. These can be obtained directly from Table 4.5.

(a) Let M = the event that the student is male, $P(M) = \frac{400}{1000} = 0.4$

216

(b) Let F = the event that the student is female, $P(F) = \frac{600}{1000} = 0.6$

(c) Let U = event the student is under 22 years of age, $P(U) = \frac{350}{1000} = 0.35$

(d) Let O = event the student is $\geq$ 22 of age, $P(O) = \frac{650}{1000} = 0.65$

Union probabilities:

(e) Let C = the event that the student is male and under 22 years of age, $P(C) = P(M \text{ and } U) = \frac{180}{1000} = 0.18$

(f) Let D = the event that the student is female and $\geq$ 22 of age, $P(D) = P(F \text{ and } O) = \frac{430}{1000} = 0.43$

(g) The chance that the student is either male or under 22 years of age

$$P(M \text{ or } U) = P(M) + P(U) - P(M \text{ and } U) = 0.4 + 0.35 - 0.18 = 0.57$$

(h) The chance that the student is either female or $\geq$ 22 of age

$$P(F \text{ or } O) = P(F) + P(O) - P(F \text{ and } O) = 0.6 + 0.65 - 0.43 = 0.82$$

Working problem 4.19:

In a typical pregnancy test, possible outcomes are as follow:

	Results = Positive	Results = Negative
Woman is pregnant	True Positive	False Negative
Woman is not pregnant	False Positive	True Negative

- **False positive:** Incorrect test results - *a woman tests pregnant* when she is not actually pregnant
- **False negative:** Incorrect test results- a woman tests not pregnant when she is actually pregnant
- **True positive:** Correct test- a woman test pregnant when she is actually pregnant
- **True negative:** Correct test- a woman test not pregnant when she is not actually pregnant

Note that the accuracy of pregnancy tests may be affected by many factors including: (a) period after conception (more reliable when taken at least two weeks after conception), and (b) different types of tests may have different levels of accuracy

200 women were randomly selected for a pregnancy test from a population of women who are concerned whether they are pregnant. The results of the tests were as follows:

	Results = Positive	Results = Negative
Woman is pregnant	170	10
Woman is not pregnant	6	14

Assuming that one woman is randomly selected from the 200 women included in the test trial,
(1) What is the probability of selecting a woman who is pregnant?
(2) What is the probability of selecting a woman who is not pregnant?
(3) What is the probability of selecting a woman who test positive?
(4) What is the probability of selecting a woman who test negative?
(5) What is the probability of selecting a woman who is pregnant and test positive?
(6) What is the probability of selecting a woman who is not pregnant and test negative?
(7) What is the probability of selecting a woman who is pregnant or test positive?
(8) What is the probability of selecting a woman who is pregnant or test negative?
(9) What is the probability of selecting a woman who is not pregnant or test positive?
(10) What is the probability of selecting a woman who is not pregnant or test negative?

Answer:

1	2	3	4	5	6	7	8	9	10
0.9	0.1	??	0.12	??	0.07	??	0.97	??	??

Working problem 4.20:

According to a sample of size 100 taken by the U.S. Federal Bureau of Investigation in Crime in the United States, in 2008, 72 of the people arrested were male, 14 were under 18 years of age, and 12 were males under 18 years of age. If a person arrested that year is selected at random,

- What is the probability that that the person is male? P(M) = ?
- What is the probability that that the person is female? P(F) = ?
- What is the probability that that the person is under 18? P(U) = ?
- What is the probability that that the person is ≥ 18 years old ? P(O) = ?
- What is the probability that that the person is male and ≥ 18 years old ? P(M & O) = ?
- What is the probability that that the person is female and under 18? P(F&U) = ?
-What is the probability that that the person is male and under ? P (M&U) = ?
- What is the probability that that the person is either male or under 18? P(M or U) = ?
- What is the probability that that the person is either female or under 18? P(F or U) = ?
- What is the probability that that the person is either male or ≥ 18 years old ? P(M or O) = ?

Answer:

	Under 18 years	≥ 18 years	Total
Male	12	??	72
Female	??	26	28
Total	14	??	100

P (M) = ??
P (F) = ??
P (U) = ??
P (O) = ??
P (M & O) = 0.6
P (F & U) = ??
P (M&U) = ??

	Under 18 years	≥ 18 years	Total
Male	0.12	??	0.72
Female	??	0.26	0.28
Total	0.14	??	1

P(M or U) = P(M) + P(U) - P(M&U) = 0.74
P(F or U) = P(F) + P(U) - P(F&U) = ??
P(M or O) = P(M) + P(O) - P(M&O) = ???

4.9 Conditional probability

Conditional Probability:

The probability of a particular event (A) occurring, given that another event (B) has occurred

$$P(A|B) = \frac{P(A\&B)}{P(B)} \qquad (4.10)$$

Example 4.19: In example 4.18,

(a) What is the probability that the person is under 22 given that he is a male?
(b) What is the probability that the person is a female given that she is ≥ 22 of age?

Solution:

$$P(U|M) = \frac{P(U\&M)}{P(M)} = \frac{0.18}{0.4} = 0.45$$
$$P(F|O) = \frac{P(F\&O)}{P(O)} = \frac{0.43}{0.65} = 0.662$$

218

Working problem 4.21:

According to reports by the U.S. Federal Bureau of Investigation on Crime in the United States, in 2008, 72.0% of the people arrested were male, 14% were under 18 years of age, and 12% were males under 18 years of age. If a person arrested that year is selected at random,

- What is the probability that that the person is a male given that the person is ≥ 18 of age? P(M|O) = ?
- What is the probability that that the person is a female given that the person is under 18? P(F|U) = ?

Answer:

	Under 18 years	Over 18 years	Total
Male	12	??	72
Female	??	26	??
Total	14	??	100

	Under 18 years	Over 18 years	Total
Male	0.12	??	0.72
Female	??	0.26	??
Total	0.14	??	1

P (M) = 0.72
P (F) = 0.28

P (U) = ??
P (O) = ??

P (F & U) = 0.02
P (M&U) = ??

P(M|O) = P(M&O)/P(O)= ??
P(F|U) = P(F&U)/P(U)= 0.142857

Example 4.20: In a public school system, the issue of dress code was brought up as a result of some violations. Three hundred students categorized by gender were asked about their opinion on this issue. Table 4.6 gives a two-way classification (contingency table) of the responses of students. If a student is selected randomly from these 300 students:

(a) What is the probability that the student will agree with dress code or has no opinion?
(b) What is the probability that the student is female or will agree with dress code?
(c) What is the probability that the student is male or will agree with dress code?
(d) What is the probability that the student will agree with dress code, given that the student is male?

Table 4.6 Survey results of students regarding dress code

	Agree	Disagree	No-opinion	Total
Male	80	30	10	120
Female	60	105	15	180
Total	140	135	25	300

Solution:

Events:
Let A = the event of students agreeing with dress code
Let D = the event of student disagreeing with dress code
Let N = the event of students of no opinion.
Let M = the event of students being male

Let F = the event of students being female

Tables 4.7 and 4.8 illustrate the different possible outcomes, and corresponding simple probabilities, respectively.

Table 4.7 Possible outcomes of survey results of dress code

	A	D	N
M	(M,A)	(M,D)	(M,N)
F	(F,A)	(F,D)	(F,N)

Table 4.8 Marginal probabilities of survey results of students regarding dress code

	Agree (A)	Disagree (D)	No-opinion (N)	Total
Male (M)	0.267	0.100	0.033	0.400
Female (F)	0.200	0.350	0.050	0.600
Total	0.467	0.450	0.083	1

Marginal probability:

In this example, we have two-way classification: one is based on gender, and the other is based on opinion. Suppose one student is selected at random from these 300 students. This student may be classified either on the basis of gender alone or on the basis of opinion alone. If only one characteristic is considered at a time, the student selected can be a male, a female, in favor, against, or of no opinion. The probability of each of these five characteristics or events is called '***marginal probability***' or '***simple probability.***' These probabilities are called marginal probabilities because they are calculated by dividing the corresponding row margins (totals for the rows) or column margins (totals for the columns) by the grand total. Calculations of marginal probabilities are presented below.

Probability of a student agreeing with dress code:

$$P(A) = \frac{140}{300} = 0.467$$

Probability of a student disagreeing with dress code:

$$P(D) = \frac{135}{300} = 0.450$$

Probability of a student of no opinion of dress code:

$$P(N) = \frac{25}{300} = 0.083$$

Probability of a student being male:

$$P(M) = \frac{120}{300} = 0.400$$

Probability of a student being female:

$$P(F) = \frac{180}{300} = 0.600$$

In view of the above calculations, marginal probability is defined as the probability of a single event without consideration of any other event. In solving probability problems involving multiple classifications, it is always recommended that students begin by calculating the marginal probabilities. Table 4.8 illustrates all marginal probabilities. Note that the sum of all marginal probabilities must be one, which is a good way to verify the correctness of your calculations.

Union probability (the rule of addition), P(A&B) and P(A or B):

Union probabilities are those derived directly from the rule of addition discussed earlier. The calculations below illustrate the use of addition rule to calculate union probabilities.

(1) The probability that a randomly selected student will agree with dress code or has no opinion (A or N):

The events A and N are mutually exclusive. According to the addition rule,

$$P(A \text{ or } N) = P(A) + P(N) = 0.467 + 0.083 = 0.55$$

(2) The probability that a randomly selected student is a female or will agree with dress code (F or A)

$$P(F \text{ or } A) = P(F) + P(A) - P(F \text{ and } A) = 0.600 + 0.467 - 0.200 = 0.867$$

(3) The probability that a randomly selected student is a male or will agree with dress code (M or A)

$$P(M \text{ or } A) = P(M) + P(A) - P(M \text{ and } A) = 0.400 + 0.467 - 0.267 = 0.600$$

Conditional probability, P(B|A):

If A and B are two events, then the conditional probability of B given A (or the probability of B given that A has already occurred) is $P(B|A)$. The probability of co-occurrence of A and B, $P(A$ and $B)$ is determined by $P(A \text{ and } B) = P(A)P(B|A)$. Accordingly, the conditional probability is expressed by:

$$P(B|A) = \frac{P(A\&B)}{P(A)}$$

The probability $P(agree|male)$ or $P(A|M)$ is the conditional probability that a randomly selected student agrees with the dress code, given that this student is a male. Based on the information that the student selected is a male, we can infer that the student selected must be one of the 120 males and, hence, must belong to the first row of Table 4.6. Therefore, we are concerned only with the first row of that table.

	Agree	Disagree	No-Opinion	Total
Male	80	30	10	120

$$P(A|M) = \frac{P(A\&M)}{P(M)} = \frac{\frac{80}{300}}{\frac{120}{300}} = \frac{80}{120} = 0.667$$

Other scenarios of conditional probability are illustrated by the tree diagram shown in Figure 4.3.

Note that $P(Male\ and\ Agree)$ or $P(M and\ A)$ can be determined by:

$$P(M\ and\ A) = P(M)P(A|M) = (0.4)(0.667)$$
$$= 0.267$$

4.10 Independent versus dependent events

Two events are said to be **independent** if the occurrence of one does not affect the occurrence of the other. In general, A and B are independent events if $P(A|B) = P(A)$ and $P(B|A) = P(B)$.

Example 4.21: In the previous example of student's opinion of dress code, given in Table 4.6:

- Are events "Male (M)" and "Disagree with Dress Code (D)" independent?

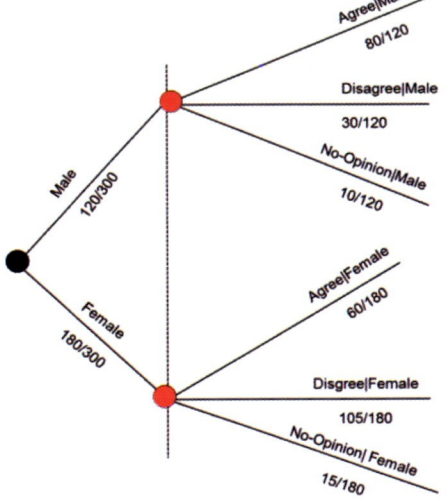

Figure 4.3 Illustration of Conditional Probability-Dress Code

Solution:

Events M and D are independent events if $P(M|D) = P(M)$

Since $P(M|D) = \frac{30}{135} = 0.222$, $P(M) = \frac{120}{300} = 0.400$

Therefore, the two events are dependent.

Example 4.22: In the example of student's opinion of dress code, given in Table 4.6, are events "Female (F)" and "Disagree with Dress Code (D)" independent?

Solution:

Events F and D are independent events if $P(F|D) = P(F)$. Since $P(F|D) = \frac{105}{135} = 0.778$ and $P(F) = \frac{180}{300} = 0.600$, the two events are dependent.

4.11 Multiplication rule (dependent events), P(AB)

The probability of the intersection of two events is called joint probability, or $P(A\&B)$. As indicated earlier, this probability is obtained by multiplying the marginal probability of one event by the conditional probability of the second event, $P(A \ and \ B) = P(A)P(B|A)$. This is called the multiplication rule $P(A \ and \ B)$ and it can also be denoted by $P(A \cap B) or \ P(AB)$.

Example 4.23: In a survey by a company regarding an optional retirement package, employees were divided into two groups according to their working experience: Junior (5 to 10 years of working experience) and Senior (above 10 years working experience). Table 4.9 illustrates the opinion on this package.

Table 4.9 Survey results of retirement package

	Approve (A)	Disapprove (B)	Total
Senior (S)	16	40	56
Junior (J)	22	22	44
Total	38	62	100

If one of these employees is selected at random, what is the probability that this employee is a junior and approves the retirement package?

Solution:

This question can be immediately answered as follows: $P(J\&A) = \frac{22}{100} = 0.22$

In applying the rule of multiplication: $P(A \ and \ J) = P(J)P(A|J)$

Notice that there are 44 juniors among 100 employees. Hence, the probability that a junior is selected is $P(J) = \frac{44}{100} = 0.440$, the conditional probability $P(A|J) = \frac{22}{44} = 0.500$. Accordingly, $P(A \ and \ J) = P(J)P(A|J) = 0.44 \times 0.5 = 0.22$

223

Example 4.24: Suppose in a box of 30 smart phones (SP), 3 smart phones are typically defective. If two smart phones are selected randomly in consecutive order from the box:

- What is the probability of selecting a defective smart phone followed by another defective smart phone?
- What is the probability of selecting a defective smart phone followed by a second defective smart phone, and followed by a third defective smart phone?

Note that the selection is made without replacement.

Solution:

$$P(first\ SP\ is\ defective) = P(SP_1) = \frac{3}{30}$$

$$P(SP_2|SP_1) = \frac{2}{29}$$

This is because after the first SP was found to be defective, only 2 defective SPs remained in the box. Using the rule of multiplication of dependent events,

$$P(SP_1 and\ SP_2) = P(SP_1)P(SP_2|SP_1) = \left(\frac{3}{30}\right)\left(\frac{2}{29}\right) = \left(\frac{6}{870}\right) = 0.0069$$

The probability of selecting a defective SP followed by a second defective SP, and followed by a third defective SP can be determined by extending the rule of multiplication as follows:

$$P(A\ and\ B\ and\ C) = P(A)P(B|A)P(C|(A\ and\ B))$$

$$P(SP_1\ and\ SP_2\ and\ SP_3) = P(SP_1)P(SP_2|SP_1)P(SP_3|SP_1\ and\ SP_2) =$$

$$\left(\frac{3}{30}\right)\left(\frac{2}{29}\right)\left(\frac{1}{28}\right) = \left(\frac{6}{24360}\right) = 0.0002463$$

4.12 Multiplication rule (independent events)

When the two events A and B are independent, then

$$P(A) = P(A|B)\ and\ P(B) = P(B|A)$$

Since $P(A\ and\ B) = P(A)P(B|A)$
$P(A\ and\ B) = P(A)P(B)$

Example 4.25: In one of the hotels, a wake-up system was used to wake up hotel guests. The chance that this wake-up system fails to activate is 0.01. Suppose the Hotel uses two wake-up systems, a primary one and a backup one. What is the probability that both systems will fail to activate?

Solution:

In this example, the two wake-up systems are independent and the activation of one will have no effect on the activation of the other. Let A = the first wake-up system fails to activate, and B = the second wake-up system fails to activate. Thus,

$$P(A \text{ and } B) = P(A)P(B) = (0.01)(0.01) = 0.0001$$

Note how the use of a backup system reduced the chance of failure immensely.

Example 4.26: A survey by a large company revealed that 70 percent of its employees bought a new optional dental insurance offered through a special deal made for the company. If two employees are selected at random, what is the probability that both employees bought this optional dental insurance?

Solution:

The probability that the first employee bought the optional dental insurance is 0.70, or $P(D_1)$ = 0.7. The probability that a second employee bought the optional dental insurance is also 0.70, or $P(D_2)$ = 0.70. Since the company has a large number of employees, we may assume that D_1 and D_2 are independent. Accordingly,

$$P(D_1 \text{ and } D_2) = P(D_1)P(D_2) = (0.70)(0.70) = 0.49$$

Working problem 4.22:

In a company's committee for organizational structure, 23% of the members are female and 12% of the females are top executives. What is the probability that a randomly selected member of the committee is a female top executive?

Answer: Let F = event the member selected is a female, T = event the member selected is top executive.
The event that the member is a female top executive is (F & T)
P(F) = 0.23
Since 12% of females are top executives, P(T|F) = 0.12
Applying the general rule of multiplication:
P(F & T) = P(F). P(T|F)= (0.23)(0.12) = 0.0276
This means that about 2.8% of the members are female executives

Working problem 4.23:

According to the U.S. Department of Justice, Office of Justice Programs, *Bureau of Justice Statistics, about 15% of Federal* law enforcement officers are female and 85% are male. Two federal law enforcement officers were selected at random from a group of 40 officers. The first officer is not returned to the group (sampling without replacement). Find the probability that the first officer selected is female and the second is male.

Answer: Let F = event the first officer selected is female, M = event the second officer selected is male
P(F then M) = ?
P(F then M) = P(F). P(M|F)
P(F) = 6/40 = 0.15
P(M|F) = P(second officer is male, given that the first officer is female) = 34/39 = 0.872
Applying the multiplication rule:
P(F then M) = P(F). P(M|F) = (0.15) (0.872) = 0.1308
Accordingly, when officers are randomly selected from the
Group, the probability is 0.1308 that the first officer is female and the second is male.

Working problem 4.24:

According to the U.S. Department of Justice, Office of Justice Programs, *Bureau of Justice Statistics, about 15% of Federal* law enforcement officers are female (F) and 85% are male (M). Two federal law enforcement officers were selected at random from a group of 40 officers. The first officer is not returned to the group (sampling without replacement
Using a tree-diagram:
Determine P(F&F), P(F&M), P(M&F), and P(M&M)
Answer:

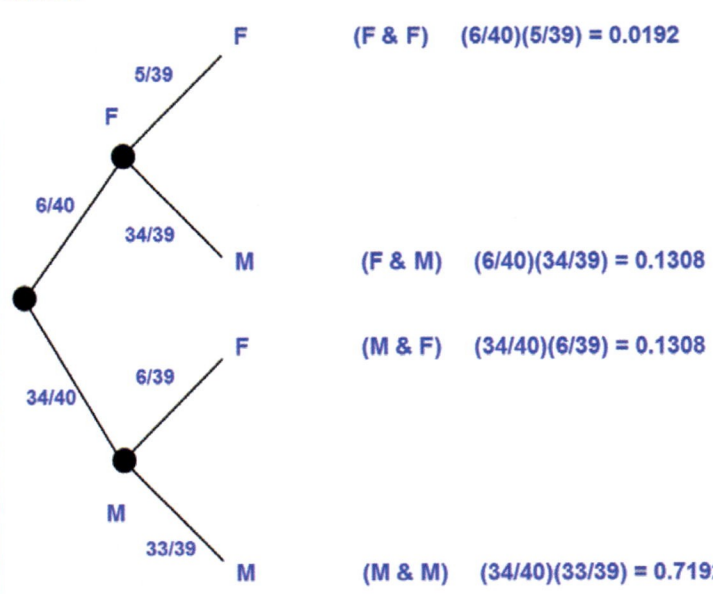

F   (F & F)   (6/40)(5/39) = 0.0192

M   (F & M)   (6/40)(34/39) = 0.1308

F   (M & F)   (34/40)(6/39) = 0.1308

M   (M & M)   (34/40)(33/39) = 0.7192

Working problem 4.25:

Two cards are selected in sequence from a standard deck. Find the probability that the second card is a queen, given that the first card is a king. (Assume that the king is not replaced.)

Answer:
Since the first card is a king and is not replaced, the remaining deck has 51 cards, 4 of which are queen. Accordingly,
P(Q|K) = 4/51 = 0.078

Working problem 4.26:

Consider the experiment of randomly selecting one card from a deck of 52 playing cards.
a. Determine whether the event of selecting a king is independent of the event of selecting a face.
b. Determine whether the event of selecting a king is independent of the event of selecting a heart.

Answer: Let F = event a face card is selected, K = event a king is selected, and H = event a heart is selected.
(a) P(K) = 4/52 = ??
K is independent of F if P(K|F) = P(K)
Face = 12 (4 jacks, 4 kings, and 4 queens)
P(K|F) = (4/12) = ??
Since P(K|F) ≠ P(K)
Then K and F are dependent.
(b) K is independent of H if P(K|H) = P(K)
13 hearts
 P(K|H) = ???
Complete the answer.

4.13 Counting rules

In dealing with probability problems, counting is one of the key aspects. In most simple experiments, counting is an easy task. For example, the total number of possible outcomes in tossing a coin is 2, and the total number of possible outcomes in rolling a die is 6. When the experiment is more complex, we use some rules to count the total number of possible outcomes. These rules include: multiplication counting, permutation counting, and combination counting.

Counting Rules- Multiplication:

The multiplication counting is used when there are *m* ways of doing one thing and *n* ways of doing another thing. In this case, there are $m \times n$ ways of doing both.

Example 4.27: If you have 5 shirts and 8 sweaters, how many shirt and sweater outfit can you wear?

The answer is very simple, $5 \times 8 = 40$

Example 4.28: In a sea-food restaurant, for the same price of $27 the menu allows you to order shrimp, fish, or crab legs with your choice of single or double (for two) orders. How many different arrangements of meals and sizes can you order?

Total possible arrangements = $(m)(n) = (3)(2) = 6$

Working problem 4.27:

A construction company offers 4 different basement models:

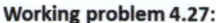

Model A:
Up to 800 sq. ft. of living space including ceiling, ½ " Drywall & ceiling, R13 insulation

Model B:
Up to 1500 sq. ft. of living space including ceiling, ½ " Drywall & ceiling, R 13 insulation, 5x7 Bathroom

Model C:
Up to 2000 sq. ft. of living space including ceiling, ½ " Drywall & ceiling, R 13 insulation, complete laminate flooring, 5x7 Bathroom

Model D:
Up to 2500 sq. ft. of living space including ceiling, ½ " Drywall & ceiling, R 13 insulation, complete laminate flooring, game room area, bar, 5x7 Bathroom

Each model is provided in three different finish levels
(good, L_1, very good L_2, and excellent finish L_3)
Draw a tree diagram showing all possibilities.
How many choices are there for the selection of a basement, including both model and finish?

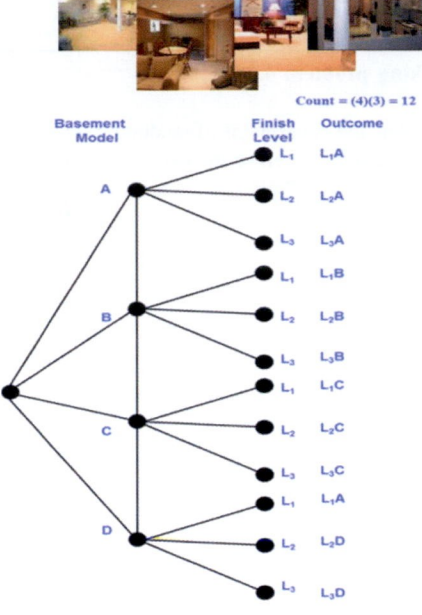

Working problem 4.28:

A company established identification pass codes to its employees to enter its research laboratories. Each consist of three digits followed by three letters.
a. How many different pass codes are possible?
b. How many possibilities are there for pass codes in which no letter or digit is repeated?

Answer:
a. Each digit is associated with 10 possibilities (0, 1, 2, ..., 9) and each letter is associated with 26 possibilities (A, B, C, ...X, Y, Z). Thus,
The number of different pass codes possible = (10)(10)(10) (26)(26)(26)= 17,576,000
b. In this case, each digit is associated with 10 possibilities (0, 1, 2, ..., 9) and each letter is associated with 26 possibilities (A, B, C, ...X, Y, Z).
However, for each possibility for the first digit, there are 9 corresponding possibilities for the second digit since the
second digit cannot be the same as the first. For each possibility for the first two digits, there are 8 corresponding possibilities for the third digit since the third digit cannot be the same as either the first or the second.
Similarly, for each possibility for the first letter, there are 25 corresponding possibilities for the second letter since the second letter cannot be the same as the first. For each possibility for the first two letters, there are 24 corresponding possibilities for the third letter since the third letter cannot be the same as either the first or the second Thus,
The number of different pass codes possible = (26)(25)(24)(10)(9)(8) =
= 11,323,000

Working problem 4.29:
One of the most commonly used terms in criminal investigations is the so-called "DNA". DNA, or deoxyribonucleic acid. It is the fundamental building block for an individual's entire genetic makeup. DNA consists of two long polymers of simple units called nucleotides, with backbones made of sugars and phosphate groups joined by ester bonds. These two strands run in opposite directions to each other and are therefore anti-parallel. Attached to each sugar is one of four types of molecules called bases. It is the sequence of these four bases along the backbone that encodes information. This information is read using the genetic code, which specifies the sequence of the amino acids within proteins. The code is read by copying stretches of DNA into the related nucleic acid RNA, in a process called transcription. Nucleobases (or nucleotide bases/nitrogenous bases) are the parts of DNA and RNA that may be involved in pairing). The primary nucleobases are cytosine (C), guanine (G), adenine (A), and thymine (T), and uracil (U). They are usually simply called bases in genetics. Because A, G, C, and T appear in the DNA, these molecules are called DNA-bases; A, G, C, and U are called RNA-bases. For this example, let us consider the DNA bases, A, G, C, and T. Suppose one of these four bases must be selected three times to form a linear triplet, how many different triplets are possible? Note that all four bases can be selected for each of the three components of the triplet.

Answer:
There are 4 possibilities for each of the three components making up the triplet, so the number of different possibilities is (4)(4)(4) = 64
The 64 cases could be listed as AAA, AAG, A... T T

Factorials:

The product of the first m positive integers is called m factorial and is denoted $m!$. The way to handle a factorial is as follows:

$$m! = m(m-1)(m-2) \cdots \cdots 2 \cdot 1 \qquad (4.11)$$

It should be noted that $0! = 1$ and $1! = 1$.

Example 4.29: Determine $3!$, $6!$, and $20!/9!$

$$3! = 3(2)(1) = 6$$

$$6! = 6(5)(4)(3)(2)(1) = 720$$

$$\frac{20!}{9!} = \frac{20(19)(18)(17)(16)(15)(14)(13)(12)(11)(10)(9!)}{9!} = 6704425728000$$

Working problem 4.30:

Determine the following:
(a) 5!
(b) 4!
(c) (5!)(6!)/(11!)
(d) 8!/(3!)(5!)
(e) (6!)(4!)/(3!)(2!)

Answer:
(a) 5! = 120
(b) 4! = Do it yourself
(c) (5!)(6!)/(11!) = (5)(4)(3)(2)(1)6!/(11)(10)(9)(8)(7)(6!) = 0.002164502
(d) 8!/(3!)(5!) = Do it yourself
(e) (6!)(4!)/(3!)(2!) = Show how = 1440

Counting Rules – Permutation:

A permutation is any ***ordered*** arrangement of *r* objects selected from a collection of *n* objects. The number of possible permutations of *r* objects that can be formed from a collection of *m* objects is expressed by:

$$n^P r = \frac{n!}{(n-r)!} \qquad (4.12)$$

This reads "*n* permute *r*", where *r* is the number of objects selected and *n* is the total number of objects.

Terms such as permutations, arrangements, or sequences, are used to imply that order is taken into account in the sense that different orderings of the same items are counted separately. For example, the letters *A, B, C* can be arranged six different ways: *ABC, ACB, BAC, BCA, CAB,* and *CBA*. Thus,

$$n^P r = \frac{n!}{(n-r)!} = 3^P 3 = \frac{3!}{(3-3)!} = \frac{3 \times 2 \times 1}{1} = 6$$

Shortly, we will refer to combinations, which do not count such arrangements separately. In the following example, we are asked to find the total number of different sequences that are possible. This calls for the use of the permutations rule.

Example 4.30: Four mechanical components (C1, C2, C3, and C4) are to be assembled into a machine. In how many different ways can they be assembled?

$$nPr = 4^P4 = \frac{n!}{(n-r)!} = \frac{4!}{(4-4)!} = \frac{4 \times 3 \times 2 \times 1}{0!} = 24$$

Example 4.31: For the five letters v, w, x, y, z, list all possible permutations of three letters. How many possible permutations of three letters that can be formed from the collection of five letters?

vwx	vwy	vwz	vxy	vxz	vyz	wxy	wxz	wyz	xyz
vxw	vyw	vzw	vyx	vzx	vzy	wyx	wzx	wzy	xzy
wvx	wvy	wvz	xvy	xvz	yvz	xwy	xwz	ywz	yxz
wxv	wyv	wzv	xyv	xzv	yzv	xyw	xzw	yzw	yzx
xvw	yvw	zvw	yvx	zvx	zvy	ywx	zwx	zwy	zxy
xwv	ywv	zwv	yxv	zxv	zyv	yxw	zxw	zyw	zyx

$$nPr = 5^P3 = \frac{n!}{(n-r)!} = \frac{5!}{(5-3)!} = \frac{5 \times 4 \times 3 \times 2 \times 1}{2 \times 1} = 60$$

Another way to solve this problem is by $n_1 \cdot n_2 \cdot n_3 = 5 \cdot 4 \cdot 3 = 60$

Working problem 4.31:

In a weight-loss program using a new medical treatment, a pharmaceutical research organization called for 50 volunteers. The way the organization operates is by taking 5 volunteers, treat them and assess the effectiveness of the weight loss treatment. These five volunteers are treated in sequence to allow modification or termination of treatment in case of adverse side effects. How many different sequences of 5 subjects are possible?

$$nPr = \frac{n!}{(n-r)!} = 50^P5 = \frac{50!}{(50-5)!} = \frac{50 \times 49 \times 48 \times 47 \times 46 \times 45!}{45!} = 254251200$$

Counting Rules – Combination:

In some situations, when we select a few elements from a large number of distinct elements, we don't care about the ordering of the chosen elements; we care only which elements are selected. For example, we may not care which letters come first, second, and third in the previous example. Each distinct set of letters that can be selected, without regard to order, is called a combination. In this case, the number of combinations of r letters from a set of 5 letters can be obtained using the following expression:

$$nCr = \frac{n!}{r!\,(n-r)!} \qquad (4.13)$$

Using the above expression, we must have a total of *n* different items available. We must select *r* of the *n* items (without replacement). We must consider rearrangements of the same items to be the same. (The combination *xyz* is the same as *zyx*). Accordingly, the combinations of 3 letters from the 5 letters in the previous example will be:

$$n^C r = \frac{n!}{r!\,(n-r)!}$$

$$or \; 5^C 3 = \frac{5!}{3!\,(5-3)!} = \frac{5 \times 4 \times 3 \times 2 \times 1}{3 \times 2 \times 1(2 \times 1)} = 10 \; combinations$$

These combinations are: *vwx, vwy, vwz, vxy, vxz, vyz, wxy, wxz, wyz, and xyz*

Example 4.32: In a statistics test, each student is required to select three questions out of 6 to answer. What is the number of question combinations?

The number of combinations of questions in this case is:

$$n^C r = \frac{n!}{r!\,(n-r)!} = 6^C 3 = \frac{6!}{3!\,(6-3)!} = \frac{6 \times 5 \times 4 \times 3 \times 2 \times 1}{3 \times 2 \times 1(3 \times 2 \times 1)} = 20$$

Example 4.33: A bookstore was trying to attract more people to read science fiction books. It made an offer in which purchasing one science fiction book at regular price will allow getting 2 free science fiction books from a collection of 100 books. How many possibilities does the customer have for the selection of the two free books?

$$n^C r = \frac{n!}{r!\,(n-r)!} = 100^C 2 = \frac{100!}{2!\,(100-2)!} = \frac{100 \times 99 \times 98!}{(2 \times 1)(98!)} = 4950$$

Working problem 4.32:

In a weight-loss program using a new medical treatment, a pharmaceutical research organization called for 50 volunteers. The way the organization operates is by taking 5 volunteers, treat them and assess the effectiveness of the weight loss treatment. These five volunteers are treated all at once to allow group comparisons. How many different treatment groups are possible?

Answer:
Because order does not count, the number of combinations of r = 5 people selected from the 50 volunteers are determined by:

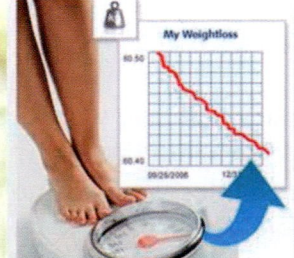

$$n^C r = \frac{n!}{r!\,(n-r)!} = 50^C 5 = \frac{50!}{5!\,(50-5)!} = \frac{50 \times 49 \times 48 \times 47 \times 46 \times 45!}{(5 \times 4 \times 3 \times 2 \times 1)(45!)} = 2118760$$

4.14 Bayes' theorem

The Bayes' theorem was formulated by Laplace based on some thoughts proposed by Reverend Thomas Bayes, an English Presbyterian minister in the 18th century. According to *Bayes*, a probability value should be revised when additional information becomes available. In this context, the terms *prior probability* and *posterior probability* are commonly used:

Prior probability is an initial probability value obtained before additional information becomes available

Posterior probability is a probability value determined by revising the prior probability using additional information that becomes available

Rev. Thomas Bayes
(1702-1761)

BAYES' THEOREM:
The probability of event A, given that event B has **_subsequently_** occurred, is

$$P(A_i|B) = \frac{P(A_i)P(B|A_i)}{P(A_1)P(B|A_1) + P(A_2)P(B|A_2)} \quad (4.14)$$

A_i refers to either event A_1 or A_2.

The examples below illustrate some applications in which the Bayes' theorem can be used effectively to reveal more precise probabilities based on new information obtained.

Example 4.34: In Italy, 49% of the adults are males (51% females). One Italian adult is randomly selected for a survey involving interest in watching soccer games regularly on TV.

a. Find the prior probability that the selected person is a male.
b. Suppose it was later learned that 80% of Italian males watch soccer on regular basis, whereas only 18% of Italian females watch soccer on regular basis. Use this additional information to find the probability that the selected subject is a male?

Solution:

Let M = male, M' = female or not male, S = watch soccer regularly, S' = does not watch soccer regularly. Before using the added information, we know that 49 % of the adults are males (51% females). Thus, $P(M) = 0.49$.

Using the additional information, we have the following:

$P(M) = 0.49$, $P(M') = 0.51$, $P(S|M) = 0.80$, $P(S|M') = 0.18$

233

Using Bayes' theorem:

The probability of event A, given that event B has subsequently occurred, is

$$P(A_i|B) = \frac{P(A_i)P(B|A_i)}{P(A_1)P(B|A_1) + P(A_2)P(B|A_2)}$$

A_i refers to either event A_1 or A_2.

Accordingly,

$$P(M|S) = \frac{P(M)P(S|M)}{P(M)P(S|M) + P(M')P(S|M')} = \frac{0.49 \times 0.80}{0.49 \times 0.80 + 0.51 \times 0.18} = \frac{0.392}{0.4838} = 0.81$$

Thus, before we knew the survey subject watched soccer, there was a 0.49 probability that the survey subject was male. However, after learning that the subject watches soccer on regular basis, we revised the probability to 0.81. This means that there is 81% chance that soccer watching respondent is a male.

Example 4.35: Suppose 5 percent of the U.S. citizens make more than $500,000 per year in income. If we select a person from the U.S.A. at random,

- What is the *prior probability* that the person selected earns more than $500,000 annually?
- What is the *prior probability* that the person selected earns $500,000 or less annually?

Solution:

Let A_1 refer to 'making more than $500,000 annual income.' Based on the information we have, if we select a person from the U.S.A., the probability the individual chosen earns more than $500,000 is 0.05, or $P(A_1) = 0.05$. This is the prior probability. It is given this name because no empirical data was collected to determine it; only subjective estimation. The prior probability that the person selected earns $500,000 or less annually is $P(A_2) = 1 - P(A_1) = 1 - 0.05 = 0.95$.

Example 4.36: Suppose in the above example, new information was released, which indicates that 80% of the people owning houses with a worth of over $1 million dollar (B) are also making over $500,000 annually (A₁). Thus, the probability that a person will own a house of over $1 million given that the person makes more than $500,000 per year income, $P(B|A_1) = 0.8$. Another piece of information was that the probability a person who actually does not earn more than $500,000 annually (A₂) will own a house of over $1 million is $P(B|A_2)$ is 0.15. Note that these values are determined subjectively. If we select a person who owns a house of over $1 million (B), what is the probability the person actually makes more than $500,000 per year in income (*posterior probability*)?

Solution:

This is a posterior probability. In symbolic form, we want to know $P(A_1|B)$, which is interpreted as:

P(a person owning a house of over $1million makes more than $500,000 per year income)

$$P(A_i|B) = \frac{P(A_i)P(B|A_i)}{P(A_1)P(B|A_1) + P(A_2)P(B|A_2)}$$

$$P(A_1|B) = \frac{P(A_1)P(B|A_1)}{P(A_1)P(B|A_1) + P(A_2)P(B|A_2)}$$

$$= \frac{(0.05)(0.80)}{(0.05)(0.8) + (0.95)(0.15)} = \frac{0.04}{0.1825} = 0.2192$$

In summary, if a person is selected at random from the U.S. population, the probability that he/she will make more than $500,000 is 0.05. If the person owns a house of over $1 million, the prior probability will now be adjusted and increased about threefold, from 0.05 to 0.2192 or 21.92%. This is the posterior probability. Table 4.10 provides a summary of the above calculations.

Table 4.10 Stepwise Solution to Bayes' theorem Applications-Income Example

Event A_i	Prior Probability $P(A_i)$	Conditional Probability $P(B|A_i)$	Joint Probability $P(A_i \& B)=$ $P(A_i) \times P(B|A_i)$	Posterior Probability $P(A_i|B)$
A_1, makes >$500,000	0.05	0.80	$(0.05\times0.8) = 0.04$	$(0.04/0.1825)=$ 0.219
A_2, makes ≤ $500,000	0.95	0.15	$(0.95\times0.15) = 0.1425$	$(0.1425/0.1825)=$ 0.781
			$P(B)= 0.1825$	$\sum p = 1$

Example 4.37: A knitting manufacturer of high-fashion garments, purchases a specialty fancy yarn, called Super-Cotton-Modal from three different spinners (or yarn suppliers): Buhlar-QY, Texmax, and Frontier-Y. Thirty percent of the yarns are purchased from Buhlar-QY, twenty percent from Texmax, and the remaining fifty percent from Frontier-Y. Based on the manufacturer's historical experience, the three suppliers have different rates of defective yarns: 3% for Buhlar-QY, 5% for Texmax, and 4% for Frontier-Y. Typically, when yarn shipments arrive, they are placed in a conditioned warehouse and not inspected or otherwise identified by the yarn supplier. Later, a knitter selects a yarn set for knitting and finds it defective. What is the probability that it was manufactured by Texmax yarn supplier?

Solution:

Prior probability: $P(A_1=$ Buhler QY$) = 0.3$, $P(A_2=$ Texmax$) = 0.2$, $P(A_3=$ Frontier$) = 0.5$
Looking at the Texmax's quality record, it has the highest defect rate of the three yarn suppliers. Now that we have found a defective yarn set, we suspect that $P(A_2 | B)$ is greater than $P(A_2)$.

Note that $P(B|A_2) = 0.05$. Table 4.11 illustrates the calculations of prior and posterior probabilities.

Table 4.11 Stepwise Solution to Bayes' theorem Applications-Yarn Example

Event A_i	Prior Probability $P(A_i)$	Conditional Probability $P(B|A_i)$	Joint Probability $P(A_i \& B)=$ $P(A_i) \times P(B|A_i)$	Posterior Probability $P(A_i|B)$
A_1, Buhlar-QY	0.3	0.03	0.009	(0.009/0.039)= 0.2308
A_2, Texmax	0.2	0.05	0.01	(0.01/0.039)= 0.2564
A_3, Frontier-Y	0.5	0.04	0.02	(0.02/0.039)= 0.5128
		$P(B) =$	0.039	1

$$P(A_2|B) = \frac{P(A_2)P(B|A_2)}{P(A_1)P(B|A_1) + P(A_2)P(B|A_2) + P(A_3)P(B|A_3)}$$

$$P(A_2|B) = \frac{(0.2)(0.05)}{(0.3)(0.03) + (0.2)(0.05) + (0.5)(0.04)}$$

$$= \frac{0.01}{0.009 + 0.01 + 0.02} = \frac{0.01}{0.039} = 0.2564$$

Example 4.38: In the previous example, use a tree diagram to illustrate all prior and posterior probabilities associated with this problem?

Solution:

As was shown in the solution of the previous example, looking at the Texmax's quality record, it has the highest defect rate of the three yarn suppliers. Now that we have found a defective yarn set, we suspect that $P(A2 | B)$ is greater than $P(A2)$. That is, we expect the revised probability to be greater than 0.20. But how much greater? Bayes' theorem can give us the answer via a supporting tree diagram as shown below. In examining this diagram, we need to move from right to left instead of left to right. We have a defective yarn set, and we want to determine the likelihood that it was purchased from Texmax yarn supplier. We first look at the joint probabilities as relative frequencies out of 1,000 yarn cones. For example, the likelihood of a defective yarn cone that was produced by Buhlar-QY is 0.009. So of 1,000 yarn cones we would expect to find 9 defective cones produced by Buhlar- QY. We observe that in 39 of 1,000 cases the yarn cones selected for assembly will be defective, found by 9 +10 + 20. Of these 39 defective chips, 10 were produced by Texmax. Thus, the probability that the defective yarn cone was purchased from Texmax is $10/39 = 0.2564$. We have now determined the revised probability of $P(A2 | B)$. Before we found the defective chip, the likelihood that it was purchased from

Texmax was 0.20. This likelihood has been increased to 0.2564. The tree diagram showing all probabilities is shown below.

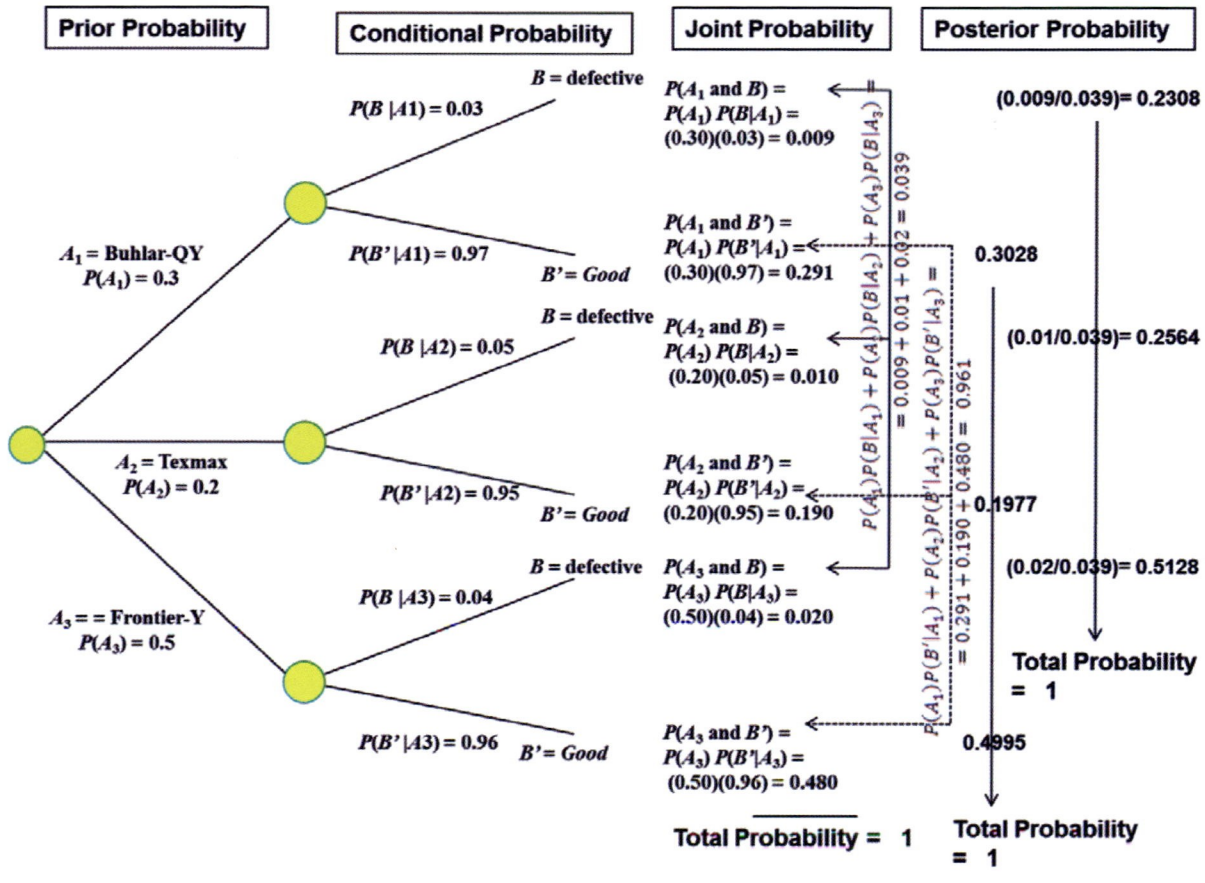

4.15 Review Exercises

P4.1: When two balanced dice are rolled, find the probability that
   a. The sum is 1.
   b. The sum is 11.
   c. The sum is 12 or less.
Answer: (a) 0, (b) 0.056, (c) = 1.0

P4.2: A coin is tossed four times.
   - What are all possible outcomes?
   - Determine the probabilities of the following events:
A = event exactly two heads are tossed
B = event the first two tosses are tails
C = event the first toss is heads
D = event all four tosses come up the same

P4.3: Determine the following probability values (note: some can be determined subjectively):
a. You have a 50-50 chance of passing this course
b. There is a very high chance of snow tomorrow
c. You have absolutely no chance of making a million dollar this year
d. There is a chance of high winds tomorrow
e. It will definitely become morning at 6 am
f. You have two chances in twenty of being correct
Answer: a. 0.5, b. 0.9, c. 0, d. 0.7, e. 1.0, f. 0.1

P4.4:
a. What is the probability that death will occur?
b. What is the probability that you will graduate after failing all classes?
c. A sample space consists of 20 separate events that are equally likely. What is the probability of each?
d. On a true/false test, what is the probability of answering a question correctly if you make a random guess?
e. On a multiple-choice test with four possible answers for each question, what is the probability of answering a question correctly if you make a random guess?

P4.5: If the probability of an event is approximately zero based on empirical results; does this mean the event is impossible to occur?
Answer: No- as another experiment may reveal different probability value

P4.6: Why do you think a probability value should range from 0 to 1?

P4.7: Each year heart attacks kill more than 150,000 Americans, nearly half of them are women. If the population in the U.S.A. in 2010 is 308745538, and assuming that the population will not change significantly for the following 5 years:
(a) What is the probability that a person selected randomly from the U.S. population will have a heart attack in 2015?
(b) What is the chance that a person selected randomly will have a heart attack and will be a female in 2015?
Answer: (a) $(4.858 \times 10^{-4})100 = 0.049\%$, (b) $(2.43 \times 10^{-4})100 = 0.024\%$

P4.8: One card is selected from a standard deck.
- Compute the probability that the card is a king
- Compute the probability that the card is a king or a queen
- Compute the probability that the card is a king, or queen, or a jack
- Compute the probability that the card is a king, or a diamond
- Compute the probability that the card is either a spade or a face card

P4.9: According to 2010 Census Data (http://quickfacts.census.gov/qfd/states/00000.html), there are 40.14 million persons 65 year old or older in the U.S.A population. In a random sample of U.S.A. people, what is the probability of finding a person that is 65 year old or older?
Answer: U.S.A. Population (2010) = 308745538, P (persons over 65 years) = 0.13 or 13%

P4.10: According to 2010 Census Data (http://quickfacts.census.gov/qfd/states/00000.html), there are 151.902805 million male persons in the U.S.A population. In a random sample of U.S.A. people, what is the probability of finding a female person?

P4.11: The United Nations Security Council (UNSC) consists of 5 veto-wielding permanent members: China (C), France (F), Russia (R), United Kingdom (UK), and United States (US). A veto by any one of these five members will prevent an adoption of a proposal submitted to the UNSC, even if it has received the "yes" vote of all other members. Draw a tree diagram describing all possible votes by the permanent members of the UNSC

Answer: 32 outcomes should be displayed

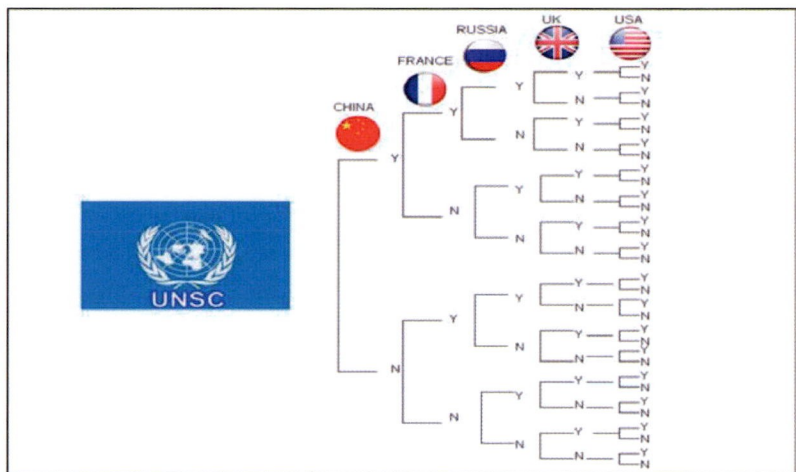

P4.12: For the above problem, and for a given resolution presented to the UNSC,
- What is the probability that no UNSC permanent member will veto a resolution?
- What is the probability that all UNSC permanent members will veto a resolution?
- What is the probability that one UNSC permanent member will veto a resolution?
- What is the probability that two UNSC permanent member will veto a resolution?
- What is the probability that three UNSC permanent member will veto a resolution?
- What is the probability that four UNSC permanent member will veto a resolution?

P 4.13: The United Nations Security Council (UNSC) consists of 5 veto-wielding permanent members: China (C), France (F), Russia (R), United Kingdom (UK), and United States (US). A veto by any one of these five members will prevent an adoption of a proposal submitted to the UNSC, even if it has received the "yes" vote of all other members.

For a given resolution presented to the UNSC,
- What is the probability that less than two UNSC permanent members will veto a resolution?
- What is the probability that two or less UNSC permanent members will veto a resolution?
- What is the probability that less than three UNSC permanent members will veto a resolution?
- What is the probability that three or less UNSC permanent members will veto a resolution?

- What is the probability that less than four UNSC permanent members will veto a resolution?
- What is the probability that four or less UNSC permanent members will veto a resolution?

Answer: 0.1875, 0.50, 0.50, 0.8125, 0.8125, 0.96875

P4.14: In the United Nations Security Council (UNSC), up to 2005, the 5 veto-wielding permanent members used veto 261 times. China (ROC/PRC) has used its veto 6 times; France 18 times; Russia/USSR 123 times; the United Kingdom 32 times; and the United States 82 times. Suppose a new resolution is presented to the UNSC, based on the history of veto,

- What is the probability that the U.S. will use the veto against the resolution?
- What is the probability that the U.S. or U.K will use the veto against the resolution?
- What is the probability that the China or France will use the veto against the resolution?
- Interpret the results

P4.15: Following the previous problem of the UNSC, if you know that the majority of Russian/Soviet vetoes were in the first ten years of the Council's existence (1946 to 1956) and since 1984, China and France have vetoed three resolutions each; Russia/USSR four; the United Kingdom ten; and the United States 43. Using only the data since 1984, and suppose a new resolution is presented to the UNSC,

- What is the probability that the U.S. will use the veto against the resolution?
- What is the probability that the U.S. or U.K will use the veto against the resolution?
- What is the probability that the China or France will use the veto against the resolution?
- Compare these results with those from the previous problem and explain the differences.

Answer: 0.6825 (or 68.25%), 0.8412 (or 84.12%), 0.0952 (or 9.52%)

P4.16: Which of the following numbers could be the probability of an event?
0.40, 1.2, -0.5, 0.01, 1.75

P4.17: Suppose we randomly select two students from a mathematics class and asked whether the student selected were members of the Math-Club or Not. Write all the outcomes for this experiment. Draw the Venn and tree diagrams for this experiment.

Answer: The sample space in this case is: S = {*MM, MN, NM, NN*}

P4.18: According to 2010 Census Data (http://quickfacts.census.gov/qfd/states/00000.html), there are 20.068 million children under 5 years of age in the U.S.A population. In a random sample of U.S. families, what is the probability of finding a child under the age of 5 years?

P4.19: In a group of 1000 people, 210 have travelled using airways at least once. Suppose one of these 1000 people is selected at random. What is the probability that the person has travelled using airways at least once?

Answer: 0.21

P4.20: A trucking company was keeping track of highway accidents that occurred to its trucks since the start of its business five years ago. In its 680 trips, only 3 trips were associated with highway accidents. What is the probability that a future trip is successfully completed without accidents? By the time this company finishes its 1000 trips, how many trips do you believe will be problematic?

P4.21: A food product was tested in the market to evaluate its acceptance using a survey involving 250 people. The survey feedback consisted of three key replies: 'like it', 'dislike it', and 'not sure'. The company would sell the product if people's opinion was in favor. Based on the outcome of the survey shown in the table below, what is the chance that the product will be sold in the market? What is the probability that a randomly selected person will either like the new food product or will be unsure?

Survey of opinion of a food product

Opinion	Number of people, frequency, f
Like it	110
Dislike it	80
Not sure	60

Answer: 0.44, 0.68

P4.22: A company tracking its employee wages in a given year obtained the data in the table below from a random sample of 350 employees. If the company randomly selects another employee, what is the probability that this person will have an income of less than $45,000? What is the probability that the employee will have an income in the range from $75,000 to less than $95,000?

Survey of employee wages

Wage ($)	Number of people , frequency, f
15000 to < 25000	30
25000 to < 35000	28
35000 to < 45000	42
45000 to < 55000	55
55000 to < 65000	60
65000 to < 75000	73
75000 to < 85000	44
85000 to < 95000	18

P4.23: Suppose a market research organization wishes to survey the interest of using a certain wireless phone system by gender (male and female). Two types of wireless systems are surveyed: Type A and Type B. This survey is summarized in the table below.

Contingency table of wireless system preference by gender

	Male (M)	Female (F)
Type A	135	120
Type B	115	180

If a person is selected at random,

    (a) What is the probability that this person will be a male?

    (b) What is the probability that this person will be a female?

    (c) What is the probability that this person will not prefer Type A wireless system?

    (d) What is the probability that this person will be a male and prefer Type A wireless system?

    (e) What is the probability that this person will be a male and prefer Type B wireless system?

    (f) What is the probability that this person will be a female and prefer Type A wireless system?

    (g) What is the probability that this person will be either a male or prefer Type A wireless system?

    (h) What is the probability that this person will be either a female or prefer Type A wireless system?

    (i) What is the probability that this person will be a male given that prefers Type A wireless system?

    (j) What is the probability that this person will be a female given that prefers Type A wireless system?

Answer: 0.455, 0.545, 0.536, 0.245, 0.209, 0.218, 0.674, 0.791, 0.528, 0.4698

P4.24: The table below provides the percent distribution of U.S. household by type in 2007 (Source: Census Bureau, Current Population Survey. Annual Social and Economic Supplement (2007) http://www.census.gov/prod/2009pubs/p20-561.pdf)

Household by Type	Percent
Married couples with children	22.4
Married couples without children	28.3
Other family households	16.8
Men living alone	11.7
Women living alone	15.2
Other nonfamily households	5.6

If a household is selected randomly:

    - What is the chance that the household will be a married couple without children?

    - What is the chance that the household will be a married couple with children?

    - What is the chance that the household will be a woman living alone?

    - What is the chance that the household will be a married couple without or with children?

    - What is the chance that the household will be a woman living alone or a man living alone?

P4.25: The table below shows the percent distribution of U.S. household by the number of persons in a household in 2007 [Source: Census Bureau, Current Population Survey. Annual Social and Economic Supplement (2007), http://www.census.gov/prod/2009pubs/p20-561.pdf]

Household	Percent	Probability
1 person	26.8	0.268
2 people	33.3	0.333
3 people	16.2	0.162
4 people	13.9	0.139
5 people or more	9.8	0.098
Total	100	1

If a household is selected randomly:
- What is the chance that the household will consist of one person?
- What is the chance that the household will consist of two persons?
- What is the chance that the household will consist of three or more persons?

Answer: 0.268, 0.333, 0.399)

P4.26: The chart shown below represents the distribution of U.S. living arrangements of fathers and mothers in 2007.[Source: Census Bureau, Current Population Survey. Annual Social and Economic Supplement (2007) http://www.census.gov/prod/2009pubs/p20-561.pdf]

	Alone with child under 18	With child and another adult	With child's other parent
Father	4	3	94
Mother	18	9	74

If a person is picked randomly:
- What is the chance that the person will be a father living alone with a child under 18?
- What is the chance that the person will be a father living with a child and another adult?
- What is the chance that the person will be a mother living with a child's other parent?
- What is the chance that the person will be a mother living alone with a child under 18 or with child and another adult?

P4.27: The data in the table below describes the ages of management staff and their positions in a large retail store.

	Vice president (P1)	Division director (P2)	Store manager (P3)	Store supervisor (P4)
Under 30 (A1)	0	1	3	4
30-39 (A2)	0	3	10	12
40-49 (A3)	2	10	43	50
50-59 (A4)	3	12	45	55
60 & over (A5)	4	13	10	5

Suppose an individual is selected randomly from the management staff, determine the following:
- The probability that this individual is a vice president?
- The probability that this individual is a store manager?
- The probability that this individual is a store supervisor?
- The probability that this individual is of age 40 to 49?
- The probability that this individual is of age 60 and over?
- The probability that this individual is of age less than 50?
- The probability that this individual is a vice president and of age 60 and over?
- The probability that this individual is a store manager and of age 40 to 49?
- The probability that this individual is a vice president or of age 60 and over?
- The probability that this individual is a division director and of age 50 to 59?
- The probability that this individual is of age 60 and over given that the individual is a vice president?
- The probability that this individual is of age 40 to 49 given that the individual is a vice president?
- The probability that this individual is of age 40 to 49 given that the individual is division director?

Answer: 0.0316, 0.3895, 0.4421, 0.3684, 0.1123, 0.4842, 0.0140, 0.1509, 0.1299, 0.0421, 0.44444, 0.2215, 0.2566

P4.28: RMS *Titanic* was the largest passenger steamship in the world. On April 14[th]1912, and in a journey from Southampton, England to New York City, she struck an iceberg and sank. 1517 of the 2,227 people on board died, making this accident one of the deadliest peacetime maritime disasters in history. The high casualty rate when the ship sank was due in part to the fact that, although complying with the regulations of the time, the ship carried lifeboats for only 1,178 people. Data on the survivals and dead people is shown in the table below.

	Men (M)	Women (W)	Boys (B)	Girls (G)
Died (D)	1360	104	35	18
Survived (S)	332	320	30	28

(a) Assuming that the lack of lifeboats was the primary reason for the shortage of survivals, what is the probability that a person on the ship selected randomly would have survived?
(b) Using the value of probability obtained from problem (a) and the corresponding probability of survival based on the actual data, to what extent do you believe that lack of lifeboats was the primary reason for the shortage of survivals
(c) Some eyewitnesses of the Titanic disaster speculated that another cause of the low survival rate was the presence of many children and women on the ship. Using marginal, joint, and conditional probability rules, determine whether you agree with this speculation or not.

P4.29: An insurance company routinely surveys people by gender to determine the percent of smokers among male and female for life insurance adjustment purposes. In a large sample of 3190, the company obtained the following results:

	Smoking	Not smoking
Male	1600	440
Female	300	850

Using marginal, joint, and conditional probability rules, determine which gender should be charged higher life insurance and why.

Answer: Male

P4.30: A health department in one of the developing countries gathered information about smoking in relation to gender and age using a sample of 4000 people. The department obtained the following data.

	Smoking (S)	Not smoking (N)
Male under 50 year age (MU)	500	800
Male over 50 year age (MO)	250	500
Female under 50 year age (FU)	220	850
Female over 50 year age (FO)	80	800

Using marginal, joint, and conditional probability rules, determine the gender and the age in which smoking represents a serious issue?

P4.31: The data shown below provides information about the marital status of people by gender using a sample of 13950 people representing a small town in the State of Alabama.

	Single (S)	Married (Ma)	Widowed (W)	Divorced (D)	Separated (Sp)
Male (M)	500	1000	200	3000	2200
Female (F)	350	1200	600	2800	2100

If a person from this town was selected randomly,

- What is the chance that this person is a female and widowed?
- What is the chance that this person is a male and separated?
- What is the chance that this person is either a female or single?
- What is the chance that this person is either a male or single?
- What is the chance that this person is either a male or separated?
- What is the chance that this person is either a female or separated?
- What is the chance that this person is divorced given that he is a male?
- What is the chance that this person is widowed given that she is a female?
- What is the chance that this person is married given that she is a female?
- What is the chance that this person is married given that he is a male?
- What is the chance that this person is either divorced or separated?
- What is the chance that this person is either widowed or single?

- What is the chance that this person is single given that she is a female?
- What is the chance that this person is single given that he is a male?

P4.32: The data in the table below represent the results of a survey in a random sample of people who were asked about the best type of food they would prefer

Food type	Frequency
Mexican	120
Italian	105
Chinese	180
Indian	86
Lebanese	46
American	65

(a) Estimate the probability that a randomly selected individual will prefer Italian food
(b) Estimate the probability that a randomly selected individual will prefer either Italian or Mexican food
(c) Estimate the probability that a randomly selected individual will prefer Lebanese food
(d) Estimate the probability that a randomly selected individual will prefer either Mexican or Indian food

P4.33: According to a study by a private health insurance company in which a random sample of 1000 people was selected from a large U.S. city to test if they were smokers or not and whether they have lung disease or not. The study revealed that 290 people were smokers, 90 people in the sample have lung disease. Among those having lung disease, 70 people are smokers.

	Lung Disease	No Lung Disease	Total
Smoker	70		290
Non-smoker			
Total	90		1000

Let S = the event a person is a smoker, N = the event a person is a non-smoker, L = the event a person has a lung disease, and M = the event a person has no lung disease

What is $P(S)$?, What is $P(N)$? , What is $P(L)$?, What is $P(M)$? , What is $P(S\&L)$?, What is $P(S\&M)$? , What is $P(N\&L)$?, What is $P(N\&M)$? , What is $P(S\ or\ L)$? , What is $P(S\ or\ M)$?, What is $P(N\ or\ L)$? , What is $P(N\ or\ M)$? , What is $P(L|S)$)?, What is the probability that a randomly selected smoker has lung disease?
Answer: $P(S) = 0.29$, $P(N) = 0.71$, $P(L) = 0.09$, $P(M) = 0.91$, $P(S\&L) = 0.07$, $P(S\&M) = 0.22$, $P(N\&L) = 0.02$, $P(N\&M) = 0.69$, $P(SorL) = 0.31$, $P(SorM) = 0.98$, $P(NorL) = 0.78$, $P(Nor\ M) = 0.93$, $P(L|S) = 0.2414$, $P(M|S) = 0.7586$, $P(S|L) = 0.7777$, $P(S|M) = 0.2418$, $P(L|N) = 0.0282$, $P(S|L) = 0.7777$, $P(S|M) = 0.2418$, $P(L|S) = 0.241$, Using the Bayes' theorem: $P(L|S) = 0.2412$

P4.34: The Colonial high school football team plays 90 percent of its games at night and 10 percent during the day. The team wins 60 percent of their night games and 90 percent of their day games. If they won the game yesterday, what is the probability the game was played at night?

P4.35: On its route, a truck delivery company must include five cities. How many different routes are possible, assuming that it does not matter in which order the cities are included in the routing?
Answer: 120

P4.36: A national survey organization has developed 15 questions designed to rate the performance of top executives in the United States. The organization will select 10 of these questions. How many different arrangements are there for the order of the 10 selected questions?

P4.37: A tire company found that using accelerated- rubbing service life tests, 95 percent of the newly manufactured tires lasted 3 years before becoming road hazardous.
a. If a person purchased four of these tires, what is the probability all four tires would operate properly for at least 3 years?
b. Using letters to represent the four tires, write an equation to show how you arrived at the answer to part a.
Answer: 0.8145, P(A & B & C & D) = P(A) P(B) P(C) P(D)

P.38: A study involving a random sample of 300 clothing retail stores revealed the following annual revenue values:

Revenue ($Million)	Number of retail stores
Under $2 million	180
$2 million to under $5 million	70
$5 million or more	50

1. What is the probability a particular clothing retail store selected at random will have $5 million or more in annual revenue?
2. What is the probability a particular clothing retail store selected at random will have revenue ranging from $2 million to under $5 million in annual revenue?
3. What is the chance that a retail store selected randomly will have either revenue under $2 million, or revenue of $5 million or more? What rule of probability was used to calculate this probability?

P4.39: A wireless phone service company revealed that, on average, two percent of the millions of calls serviced by the company may encounter signal corruption issues (defective). Suppose the company's quality control department selects three phone calls randomly, and inspect signal quality. What is the probability that exactly one of these three phone calls is defective?
Answer: B = a selected phone call signal is defective, G = a selected phone call signal is good, P(B) = 0.02 and P(G) = 0.98, P(BGG or GBG, or GGB) = 0.057

P3.40: Using the counting rule of combination, find the following values:
$_{100}C_1, _{100}C_0, _{100}C_{100}, _6C_3, _8C_2, _{20}C_8$

P3.41: A teacher who has 60 students in his class is trying to form 6 teams each of 10 students. How many combinations of students can he select randomly?
Answer: 75.3940 billion

P 4.42: Some estimates suggest that about 5% of the population of Egypt has hepatitis C (an infectious disease affecting the liver, caused by the hepatitis C virus, HCV).
- What is the prior probability that an individual chosen randomly from Egypt will have hepatitis C?
- What is the prior probability that an individual chosen randomly from Egypt will not have hepatitis C?

P 4.43: Suppose now the way to detect the hepatitis C in Egypt in an individual is facing some degree of uncertainty or inaccuracy because of a number of health-care problems and social limitations. Let B denote the event 'test shows hepatitis C is present.' Suppose historical evidence showed that if a person actually has the disease, the probability that the test will indicate the presence of the disease is 0.90. What is $P(B|A_1)$? Suppose the probability that for a person who actually does not have hepatitis C, the test used will reveal the disease is present is 0.15. What is $P(B|A_2)$?
Answer: $P(B|A_1) = 0.9, P(B|A_2) = 0.15$

P 4.44: Now, let us randomly select a person from Egypt and perform the test on him or her. Suppose the test results indicate hepatitis C is present. What is the probability the person actually has the disease hepatitis C?

P4.45: The data shown below represents five countries from South America. The second column is the percent of population in 2010 with respect to the five countries, and the third column is the percent of population below poverty line (Early 2000s). If a person is selected randomly from South America, what is the probability that the person is living below the poverty line? Or based on the information given, what is the percentage of South American residents that live under poverty line.

Country	Population	Percent of population below poverty line (early 2000s)
Argentina	10.4	45.4
Brazil	49.8	38.7
Chile	4.5	18.7
Mexico	29.3	39.4
Venezuela	6	48.6

P4.46: The following table shows the effect of wearing a helmet on head injury of bike riding in a certain area and over a period of one year

	Head Injury (HI)	No Head Injury (NHI)
With Helmet (WH)	90	600
Without Helmet (NH)	400	2000

(a) If one of the subjects is randomly selected, find the probability of selecting someone with a head injury.
(b) If one of the subjects is randomly selected, find the probability of selecting someone who had a head injury or wore a helmet.
(c) If one of the subjects is randomly selected, find the probability of selecting someone who wore a helmet and was injured.
(d) If two different study subjects are randomly selected, find the probability that they both wore helmets.
(e) If one of the subjects is randomly selected, find the probability of selecting someone who did not wear a helmet, given that the subject had head injuries.

P4.47: The following table shows the effect of wearing a helmet on head injury of motorcycle riding on a certain highway and over a period of one year

	Head Injury (HI)	No Head Injury (NHI)
With Helmet (WH)	1000	3000
Without Helmet (NH)	2200	1200

(a) If one of the subjects is randomly selected, find the probability of selecting someone with a head injury.
(b) If one of the subjects is randomly selected, find the probability of selecting someone who had a head injury or wore a helmet.
(c) If one of the subjects is randomly selected, find the probability of selecting someone who wore a helmet and was injured.
(d) If two different study subjects are randomly selected, find the probability that they both wore helmets.
(e) If one of the subjects is randomly selected, find the probability of selecting someone who did not wear a helmet, given that the subject had head injuries.

P4.48: On January 1, 2005, the bar codes put on retail products were changed so that they now represent 13 digits instead of 12. How many different products can now be identified with the new bar codes?

P4.49: In a CNN poll, Internet users were asked if they want to live to be 100. There were 6000 responses of "yes," and 3800 responses of "no."
(a) What percentage of responses were "yes"?
(b) Based on the poll results, what is the probability of randomly selecting someone who does not want to live to be 100?

(c) What term is used for this type of sampling method, and is this sampling method suitable?
Answer: 61.2%, 0.388

P4.50: One of the State lottery games is called "Pick 3 lottery". In this game, you pay $2 to select a sequence of three digits, such as 211. If you select the same sequence of three digits that are drawn, you win and collect $500.
    a. How many different selections are possible?
    b. What is the probability of winning?
    c. If you buy one lottery and win, what is your net profit?
    d. Find the expected value.

P4.51: Find 3!, 4!, 5!, and 6!
Answer: 6, 24, 120, 720

P4.52: A permutation is one of the different arrangements of a group of items where order matters. When $AB \neq BA$. Given 3 people, Baily, Mike and Susan, how many different ways can these three people be arranged where order matters?

P4.53: Given 4 people, Baily, Mike, Sue and Alan, how many different ways can these four people be arranged where order matters. Illustrate the arrangement.
Answer: 24

P4.54: Suppose we have 4 people, Baily, Mike, Sue and Alan. Suppose we want to take these four people and arrange them in groups of three at a time where order matters. How many ways by which once can arrange 4 items taken 3 at a time when order matters? Demonstrate these arrangements.

P4.55: Find the number of ways to arrange 6 items in groups of 4 at a time where order matters
Answer: 360

P4.56: A combination is one of the different arrangements of a group of items where order does not matter. When order does not matter $AB = BA$. Given 3 people, Baily, Mike and Susan, how many different ways can these three people be arranged where order does not matters?

P4.57: Suppose we want to take four people, Baily, Mike, Susan and Alan, and arrange them in groups of three at a time where order does not matter. What are all the possible arrangements and how many?
Answer: 4

P4.58: Find the number of ways to take 4 people and place them in groups of 3 at a time where order does not matter.

P4.59: Find the number of ways to take 20 objects and arrange them in groups of 5 at a time where order does not matter
Answer: 15,504

P4.60: Is the State Lotteries a combination or a permutation? Do you think the numbers on a ticket have to be in the same order as the order in which they became the winning numbers? In other words, let us say the winning numbers rolled out of the machine in the order of say 1,2,3,4,5,6. Do the numbers on your ticket have to be in this same order to win? Or will any order such as 2,3,1,5,6,4 also be a winning ticket?

APPENDIX 4.1:
Sets and set operations

The concept of mathematical set represents the foundation of the probability theory. In this appendix, we only review some of the basic rules of the set theory, particularly those related to probability theory. More details on set theory and operations can be found in numerous books.
A set is typically denoted by a capital letter A, B, or C and it is basically a collection of objects, called members or elements of the set denoted by small letters a, b, or c. An element "a" belonging to a set "A" is denoted by $\in A$. On the other hand, an element c that does not belong to the set A is denoted by $c \notin A$. Typically, we use a set to describe all the outcomes of a certain event. For example, the set describing rolling an ordinary die is denoted by $\{1, 2, 3, 4, 5,$ and $6\}$.

A subset is only a portion of a set. For example, if each element of a set U also belongs to a set V we consider U a subset of V. This operation is denoted by $U \subset V$ (meaning, U is contained in V), or $V \supset U$ (meaning, V contains U). In the example of rolling an ordinary die, $A \subset B$ when A is $\{1, 2, 5\}$ and B is $\{1, 2, 3, 4, 5, 6\}$. When $U \subset V$ and $V \subset U$ we call U and V equal, or $U = V$. This means that U and V have exactly the same elements.

One of the common concepts of the set theory is the universe of discourse (briefly called universe set, u). A universe set contains all possible elements and is typically graphically represented by a rectangle. A null set ϕ is an empty set and it can be considered as a subset of any set. In Table A4.1, common set operations and rules are summarized. These operations explain many of the rules associated with the probability theory.

Table A4.1 Common operations used in the set theory

Operation	Description	Rules
[1] *Union*	The set of all elements belonging to either A or B or both A and B is called the union of A and B	$A \cup B =$ all shaded area *Rules:* $A \cup B = B \cup A$ $A \cup B(B \cup C) = (A \cup B) \cup C = A \cup B \cup C$
[2] *Intersection*	The set of all elements which belong to both A and B is called the intersection of A and B	$A \cap B =$ middle dark area *Rules:* $A \cap B = B \cap A$ $A \cap (B \cap C) = (A \cap B) \cap C = A \cap B \cap C$ $A \cap (B \cup C) = (A \cap B) \cup (A \cap C)$ $A \cup (B \cap C) = (A \cup B) \cap (A \cup C)$
[3] *Disjoint Sets*	Disjoint sets A and B are in the same universe but with no intersection	$A \cap B = \varphi$

252

Table A4.1 (Cont'd) Common operations used in the set theory

Operation	Description	Rules
[4] *Difference*	The difference of A and B implies the set consisting all elements of A which do not belong to B	$A - B$ = Shaded Area
[5] *Complement*	*IF* $B \subset A$, we call A-B the complement of B relative to A and is denoted by $B_A{}'$	$B_{A'}$ = Shaded Area *Rules:* $A - B = A \cap B'$ *If* $A \subset B$, *then* $A' \supset B'$ *or* $B' \supset A'$ $(A \cup B)' = A' \cap B'$ $(A \cap B)' = A' \cup B'$

CHAPTER 5

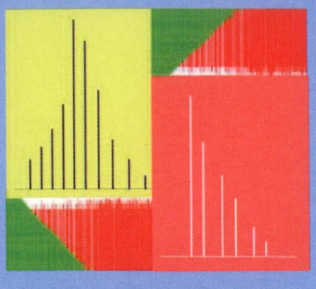

Probability distributions
Part I: Discrete Variables

LEARNING OBJECTIVES

After completing this chapter, students will be able to:

- *Understand the meaning of a probability distribution*
- *Understand the difference between discrete and continuous probability distributions*
- *Use the binomial distribution to determine probabilities*
- *Use the Poisson distribution to determine probabilities*
- *Simulate variables following probability distributions of discrete variables*

CHAPTER 5

In Chapter 4, we introduced basic concepts of probability. In this chapter, we will turn our attention to the "probability distribution". This is defined as a relative frequency distribution which provides the entire range of values of an experimental outcome. A probability distribution can be used to describe the likelihood of future outcomes or events. In this chapter, the focus is on probability distributions for discrete variables. In chapter 6, the attention will be shifted to probability distributions for continuous variables. The interesting aspect of probability distribution stems from the fact that it can be utilized to simulate variables following special patterns, leading to the concept of statistical simulation as will be seen in this chapter

CHAPTER CONTENTS

5.1 What is a probability distribution?

In Chapter 4, we introduced key probability terms such as experiment, outcome, and event. We also indicated that any given statistical experiment can have several outcomes. When an experiment is conducted, it is impossible to predict which of the many possible outcomes will actually occur and at what frequency. As a result, we have to make decisions under uncertain conditions. A probability distribution can help us making these decisions.

In general, a probability distribution is a relative frequency distribution of all possible outcomes of an experiment. Recall in chapter 4, we determined empirical probabilities from a relative frequency distribution similar to the one in Figure 5.1.a, which shows probabilities associated with different income levels. We also used a contingency table to determine joint probabilities such as the ones illustrated in Figure 5.1.b, in which the joint probabilities in a pregnancy test are listed. These types of plots represent forms of probability distributions. We can also construct a probability distribution based on knowledge of the probable patterns of the variable under consideration, and the parameters controlling these patterns. These points will be thoroughly demonstrated in the examples of this chapter.

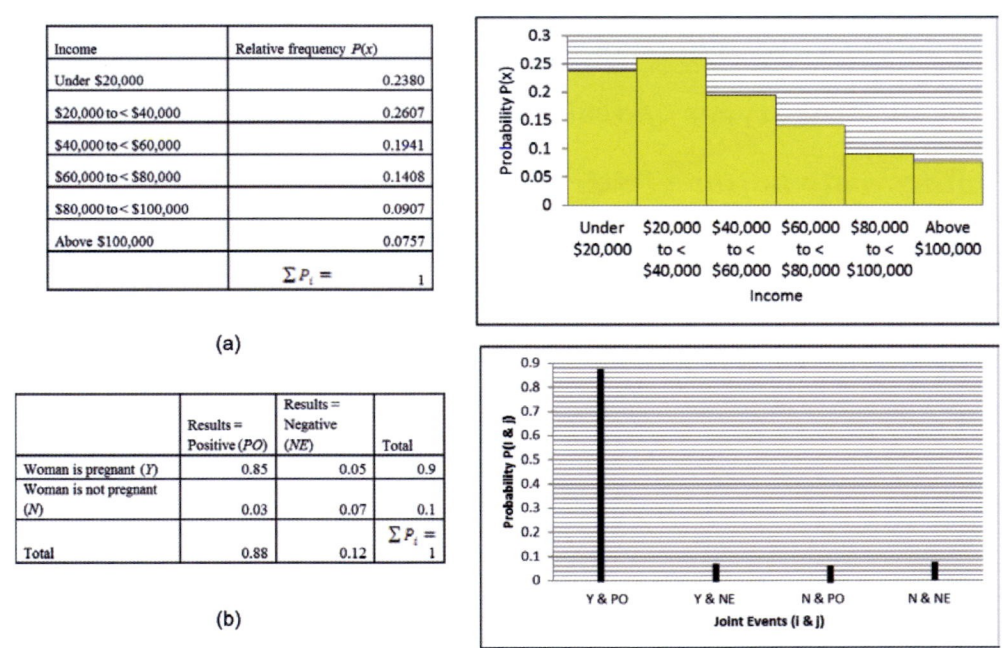

(a)

(b)

Figure 5.1 Examples of Probability Distributions

The need for probability distributions stems from the fact that the classic definition of probability requires that the total number of independent trials of the experiment be finite. For example, the experiment of tossing a coin twice yields exactly 4 outcomes, and the experiment of rolling a pair of dice yields exactly 36 outcomes. In practice, a finite number of trials are often not enough to obtain a stabilized probability. In addition, the problem with the classic definition of probability is that the words 'equally likely' are often ambiguous. Since these words seem to be synonymous with 'equally probable,' the definition is circular because we are essentially defining probability in terms of itself.

5.2 What are the different types of probability distribution?

As discussed in Chapter 1, a discrete variable can take only integer values (e.g. 0, 1, and 2). Examples of situations involving discrete variables include: (a) tossing a coin (*H* or *T*), (b) inspection of a product (pass or fail), (c) the number of defects in a product (say, 5 or 8, not 5.5), and (d) the number of students passing a course (say, 20 or 25, not 23.6). A continuous variable can take any value in a specified interval falling within its plausible range. For example, the diameter of a fine metal rod may take a value of 40, 40.25, 40.75 or 41 millimeter, and human weight may take values of 120 pounds, 155 pounds, or 165.8 pounds. These data imply continuity of the variable values.

Probability distributions can be classified into two main types: probability distributions of discrete variables, and probability distributions of continuous variables. Figure 5.2 illustrates the difference between these two types of distribution. As can be seen in Figure 5.2.a, a probability distribution of a discrete variable is represented by separated needles of heights indicating the values of probabilities, $P(x_i)$, corresponding to different values of *x*. Examples of probability distributions of discrete variables include the *'binomial distribution'* and the *'Poisson distribution.'* These distributions are discussed in the following sections. Figure 5.2.b shows a probability distribution of a continuous variable, which is represented by adjacent bars of heights indicating the values of probabilities, $P(x_i)$, corresponding to different values of *x*. Examples of probability distributions of continuous variables include the *'uniform distribution'* and the *'normal distribution.'* These distributions will be discussed Chapter 6.

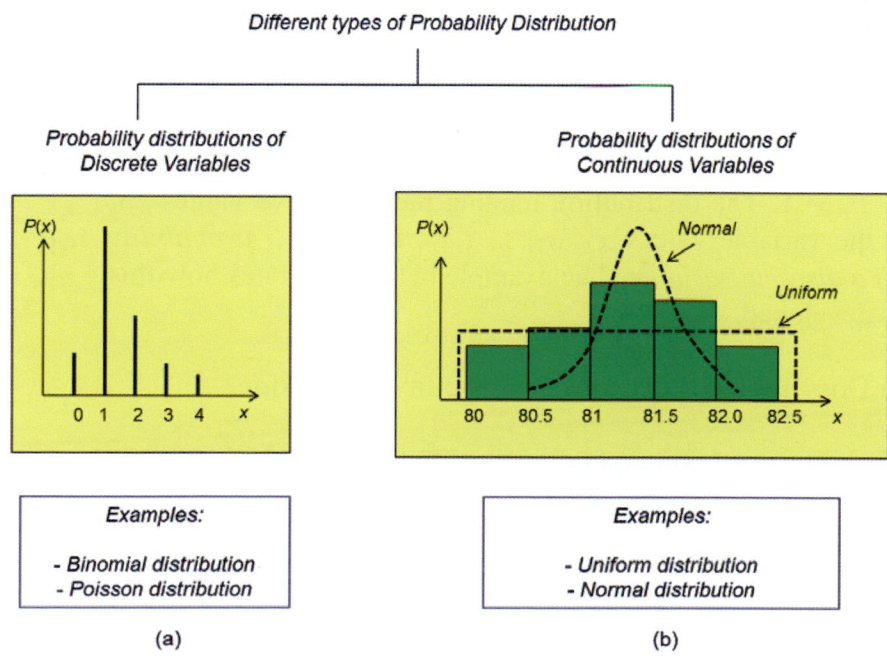

Figure 5.2 Discrete and Continuous Probability Distributions

Random variable:
A variable is a characteristic that varies from one component of a population to another. It becomes a random variable when its values vary randomly or by chance.

Discrete random variable:
This is a variable that can take only integer values (e.g. 0, 1, and 2)

Continuous random variable:
This is a variable that can take any value in a specified interval falling within its plausible range (e.g. 5, 5.6, 8.8, 10, and 12.4)

Working problem 5.1:

Decide whether the following random variables x are discrete or continuous. Explain your answer

1. Human height
2. Human weight
3. Temperature
4. Number of graduating students
5. Number of students in a stat class
6. House area in square feet
7. The number of eggs that a hen lays in a day
8. The number of emergency room patients in one day in a hospital

Answer: (3) Continuous, (8) Discrete.

5.3 The probability distribution of discrete variables

Suppose a variable x can assume a discrete set of values x_1, x_2, ..., x_n with respective relative frequencies (or probabilities) P_1, P_2, ..., P_n where $P_1 + P_2 + ... + P_n = 1$. The distribution relating the respective values P_1, P_2, ..., P_n to the variable values x_1, x_2, ..., x_n, is called *a probability distribution of a discrete variable*. The example below illustrates how this distribution is developed.

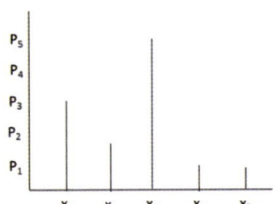

Example 5.1: Does Table 5.1 describe a probability distribution?

Table 5.1 probabilities $p(x)$ corresponding to a random variable x

x	$P(x)$
0	0.15
1	0.20
2	0.05
3	0.25
4	0.25
5	0.30
6	0.10

Solution:

- All probability values here are less than one, which satisfies the condition: $0 \leq P(x) \leq 1$
- However, the sum of probabilities $\sum P(x) = 1.3$, which is not equal to one.

Because the sum requirement is not satisfied, we conclude that Table 5.1 does not describe a probability distribution.

Example 5.2: In an experiment in which two coins are tossed, what are the possible outcomes? If the outcome of interest is 'head,' what are the probabilities of zero head, one head, and two heads? Construct a probability distribution illustrating this experiment.

Solution:

Table 5.2 shows all possible outcomes associated with tossing two coins. Table 5.3 illustrates the probability values associated with the number of heads. The discrete probability distribution resulting from this experiment is shown in Figure 5.3.

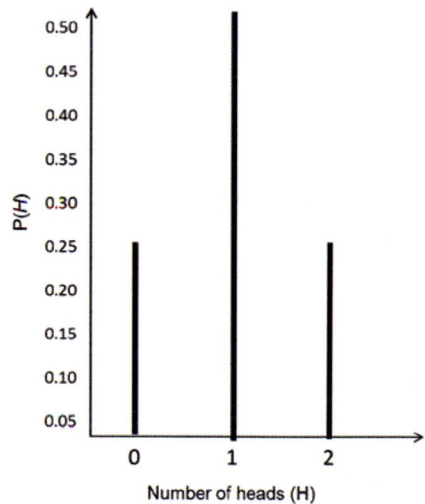

Figure 5.3 Discrete Probability Distribution of number of heads in tossing two coins

Table 5.2 Outcomes resulting from tossing two coins

Possible outcomes	x = number of heads	P(x)
T, T	0	1/4
T, H	1	1/4
H, T	1	1/4
H, H	2	1/4

Table 5.3 Probability values associated with the number of heads

x = number of heads	P(x)
0	1/4
1	1/2
2	1/4
	$\sum P_i = 1$

Example 5.3: In a survey conducted by a real-estate broker, houses in a certain city were classified by the number of bedrooms available. The results of this survey are shown in Table 5.4. The first column represents the number of bedrooms, and the second column represents the number of houses. Construct a probability distribution representing this survey.

Table 5.4 Number of houses classified by the number of bedrooms per house

Number of bedrooms per house (x)	Number of houses
1	200
2	310
3	330
4	600
5	450
6	110

Solution:

Assuming that the data is large enough to represent a finite population, we can calculate the relative frequency or the probability corresponding to each value of x or the number of bedrooms as shown in Table 5.5. The discrete probability distribution corresponding to this survey is shown in Figure 5.4.

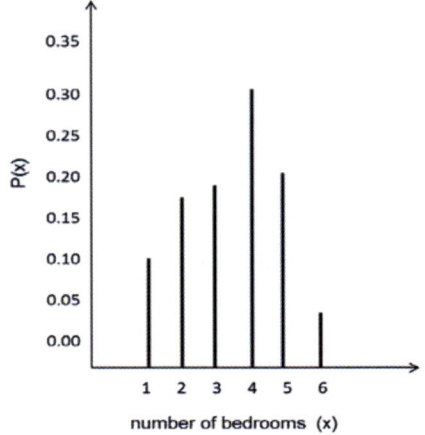

Figure 5.4 Discrete Probability Distribution of number of bedrooms

Table 5.5 Probabilities of houses classified by the number of bedrooms per house

Bedrooms per house (x)	Number of houses	$P(x)$
1	200	200/2000 = 0.1
2	310	310/2000= 0.155
3	330	0.165
4	600	0.3
5	450	0.225
6	110	0.055
Total	2000	$\sum P_i = 1$

Working problem 5.2:

Decide whether the following distributions of a discrete random variable x are probability distributions. Explain your reasoning

(a)

X	P(X)
0	0.12500
1	0.37500
2	0.37500
3	0.12500

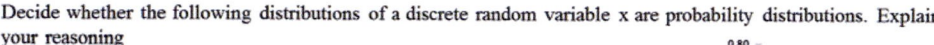

(b)

X	P(X)
0	0.69444
1	0.27778
2	0.02778

(c)

X	P(X)
0	0.30000
1	0.60000
2	0.20000

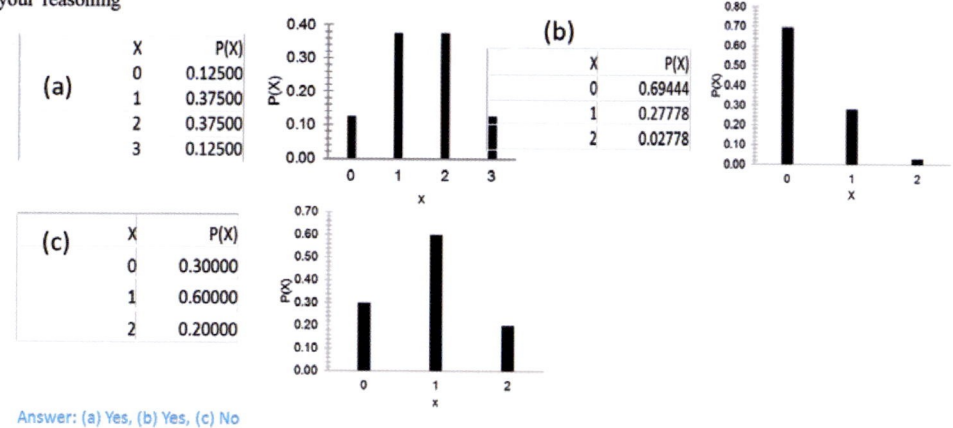

Answer: (a) Yes, (b) Yes, (c) No

Working problem 5.3:

(a) Does $P(x) = x/6$, where x can be 0, 1, or 5 determine a probability distribution? Explain why?

(b) Does $P(x) = x/5$, where x can be 0 or 1, 2, or 3 *determine a probability distribution? Explain why?*

(c) Does $P(x) = x/3$, where x can be 0 or 1, or 2 *determine a probability distribution? Explain why?*

Answer: (a) Yes, (b) No, (c) Yes

Working problem 5.4:

In a survey conducted by a Real-Estate broker, houses in a certain city were classified by the number of bathrooms available. The results of this survey are shown below. The first column represents the number of bathrooms, and the second column represents the number of houses. Construct a probability distribution representing this survey.

Number of bathrooms per house	Number of houses
1	400
1.5	840
2	330
2.5	920
3	360
3.5	420

Answer:

Number of bathrooms per house	Number of houses	P(x)
1	400	???
1.5	840	0.256881
2	330	???
2.5	920	0.281346
3	360	0.110092
3.5	420	???
	3270	1

Note that values such as 1.5, 2.5. and 3.5 represent categorical measures and not continuous variable measures.

5.4 The mean and standard deviation of the probability distribution of discrete variables

The mean of a discrete random variable x (also called the expected value of x) is expressed by:

$$\mu = E(x) = \sum x\,P(x) \qquad (5.1)$$

The reason the mean is called 'the expected value' is that the mean in an experiment represents the average value that we would expect to get if the experimental trials could continue indefinitely. The expected value represents a key parameter in many applications associated with *decision theory,* which is used in many applications including the stock market.

The standard deviation of a discrete variable x is expressed by:

$$\sigma = \sqrt{\sum [(x-\mu)^2 . P(x)]} = \sqrt{\sum x^2 P(x) - \mu^2} \qquad (5.2)$$

Note the similarity between the above equations and those used to calculate weighted mean and standard deviation discussed earlier in Chapter 3 (section 3.10).

Example 5.4: For the data of Table 5.6, calculate the mean and standard deviation of the discrete variable representing the number of bedrooms per house.

Using equation 5.1, we can calculate $xP(x)$ for each x value as shown in Table 5.6. This calculation yields a mean value or an expected value of about 3.56 bedrooms (roughly 4 bedrooms):

$$\mu = \sum x\,P(x) = (1 \times 0.1) + (2 \times 0.155) + \cdots + (6 \times 0.055) = 3.56$$

Table 5.6 Calculations of mean of a discrete variable

Bedrooms per house (x)	Number of houses	$P(x)$	$xP(x)$
1	200	(200/2000) = 0.1	(1×0.1) = 0.1
2	310	0.155	0.31
3	330	0.165	0.495
4	600	0.3	1.2
5	450	0.225	1.125
6	110	0.055	0.33
	Total = 2000	$\sum P(x_i) = 1$	$\sum x_i P(x_i) = 3.56$

To calculate the standard deviation we first calculate $x^2 P(x)$ for each x value as shown in Table 5.7.

Table 5.7 Calculations of standard deviation of a discrete variable

Number of rooms (x)	Number of houses	$P(x)$	x^2	$x^2P(x)$
1	200	(200/2000) = 0.1	(1×1) =1	(1×0.1) = 0.1
2	310	0.155	4	0.62
3	330	0.165	9	1.485
4	600	0.3	16	4.8
5	450	0.225	25	5.625
6	110	0.055	36	1.98
	2000	$\sum P(x_i) = 1$		$\sum x_i^2 P(x_i) = 14.61$

We then use equation 5.2 to calculate the standard deviation as follows:

$$\sigma = \sqrt{\sum x^2 P(x) - \mu^2} = \sqrt{14.61 - (3.56)^2} = 1.392$$

Example 5.5: A person plans to invest a $100,000. An investment consultant offered this person five investment packages, the return of each will depend on whether the economy next year will be fair or good. The table below lists the anticipated return on each investment.

Table 5.8 Investment options

Investment	Fair	Good
Currency exchange (Ce)	1000	6000
Mutual Funds (M)	-1000	9000
Regular Saving (S)	4000	6000
Certificate of deposit (C)	4500	7200
Real Estate (R)	11000	14000

Suppose that, according to the investment consultant, next year's economy has a 30% chance of being good and a 70% chance of being fair.

a. Determine the probability distribution of each random variable Ce, M, S, C, and R
b. Determine the expected value of each random variable.
c. Which investment has the best expected payoff? Which has the worst?

Solution:

    a. Different probability distributions are listed below
    b. Expected value $E(x) = \sum x_i P(x_i)$
       Example: $E(Ce) = \sum Ce_i P(Ce_i) = 1000 \times 0.7 + 6000 \times 0.3 = \$2500$

Ce	P(Ce)
1000	0.7
6000	0.3
Expected Value	2500

S	P(S)
4000	0.7
6000	0.3
Expected Value	4600

M	P(M)
-1000	0.7
9000	0.3
Expected Value	2000

C	P(C)
4500	0.7
7200	0.3
Expected Value	5310

R	P(R)
11000	0.7
14000	0.3
Expected Value	11900

c. The investment that has the best expected payoff is Real Estate and the investment that has the worst payoff is the mutual fund.

Working Problem: 5.5

In a survey conducted by a real-estate broker, houses in a certain city were classified by the number of full bathrooms available. The results of this survey are shown in the table below. If a house is picked from this area randomly:

(a) What is the chance that it will have 3 bathrooms?

(b) What is the chance that it will have less than 3 bathrooms?

Frequency of houses by the number of full bathrooms

Number of full bathrooms per house	Number of houses
1	45
2	410
3	320
4	38
5	12

Answer: (a) *0.388*, (b) *0.552*

Working Problem: 5.6

In a survey conducted by a real-estate broker, houses in a certain city were classified by the number of full bathrooms available. The results of this survey are shown in the table below.

- Calculate the mean number of bathrooms per house

- Calculate the standard deviation of the number of bathrooms per house.

Frequency of houses by the number of full bathrooms

Number of full bathrooms per house	Number of houses
1	45
2	410
3	320
4	38
5	12

Answer:

Mean = 2.469, Standard deviation = 0.7332

Working problem 5.7:

A person plans to invest a $100,000. An investment consultant offered this person five investment packages the return of each will depend on whether the economy next year will be fair or good. The table below lists the anticipated return on each investment.

Investment	Fair	Good
Mutual Funds (M)	6000	9000
Regular Saving (S)	2500	3000
Certificate of deposit (C)	5500	5500
Real Estate (R)	9000	15000

According to the investment consultant, next year's economy has a 45% chance of being good and a 55% chance of being fair.

a. Determine the probability distribution of each random variable M, S, C, and R
b. Determine the expected value of each random variable.
c. Which investment has the best expected payoff? Which has the worst?

Answer:

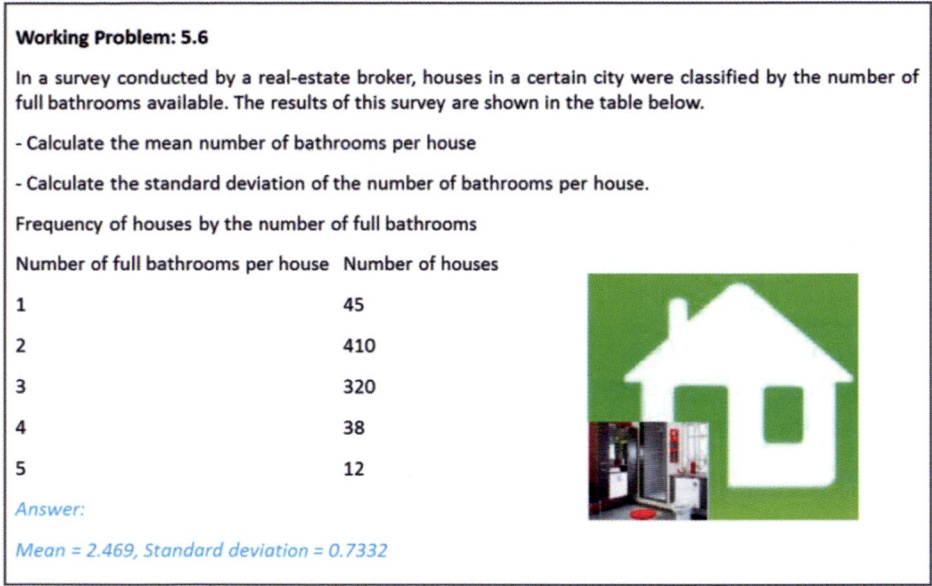

M	P(M)
6000	??
9000	0.45
Expected Value	??

C	P(C)
	??
5500	0.55
Expected Value	5500

S	P(S)
??	0.55
3000	0.45
Expected Value	2725

R	P(R)
9000	??
15000	0.45
Expected Value	??

5.5 The binomial distribution

A binomial distribution is a probability distribution used to model discrete variables, or variables that can be described by observations placed in only one of two mutually exclusive categories, such as good or bad, fail or pass, stop or go, etc. The distribution associated with example 5.2 in which the experiment involved the tossing of two coins, shown in Figure 5.3, is essentially a binomial distribution described by two parameters: the number of trials n, and the probability p. In that case, $n = 2$ and $p = 0.5$.

In practice, the binomial distribution is widely used to determine the probability that an outcome will occur x times in n trials of an experiment. In this case, the variable x must be a discrete random variable and each repetition of the experiment must result in one of two possible outcomes. Statistically, if p is the probability that an event will happen in any single trial and $q =$

$1 - p$, is the probability that it will fail to happen, then the probability that the event will happen exactly x times in n trials (i.e. x successes and n-x failures) is given by:

$$P(x) = f(x|n) = \binom{n}{x} p^x (1 - p)^{n-x}$$

or

$$P(x) = \frac{n!}{x! \, (n - x)!} \, p^x \, (1 - p)^{n-x} \qquad (5.3)$$

$$x = 0,1,2,3,4, \dots, n$$

Note that the main parameters of the binomial distribution are n and p. Knowledge of the values of these two parameters will allow us to completely simulate a variable following a binomial distribution.

The mean and variance of a binomial distribution are:

$$\mu = np \qquad (5.4)$$
$$\sigma^2 = np(1 - p) \qquad (5.5)$$

In summary, basic characteristics of the binomial distribution are as follows:

(1) The binomial distribution is the most appropriate probability distribution for sampling from an infinitely large population, where p represents the probability of occurrence of a particular outcome, and x represents the number of occurrences in a random number of trials, n. Examples of variables that are best approximated by a binomial distribution include success and failure in business, passing or failing a course, product defects, rejected items, and heads or tails in tossing a coin. In other words, each trial has two and only two outcomes.
(2) In a binomial experiment, there are n identical trials. In other words, the given experiment is repeated n times, where n is a positive integer.
(3) Each repetition of a binomial experiment is called a trial or a Bernoulli trial (after Jacob Bernoulli).
(4) The probability of occurrence of an event is denoted by p and that of failure of occurrence by q or (1-p).
(5) Binomial trials are independent. This means that the outcome of one trial does not affect the outcome of the next trial or any other trial.

The shape of the binomial distribution depends strictly on the values of its two parameters, n and p. In general, as n increases, the binomial distribution will tend to be more symmetrical. In addition, when $p = 0.5$, the distribution also becomes symmetrical. Figure 5.5 illustrates these two points using binomial distributions of different values of n and p.

266

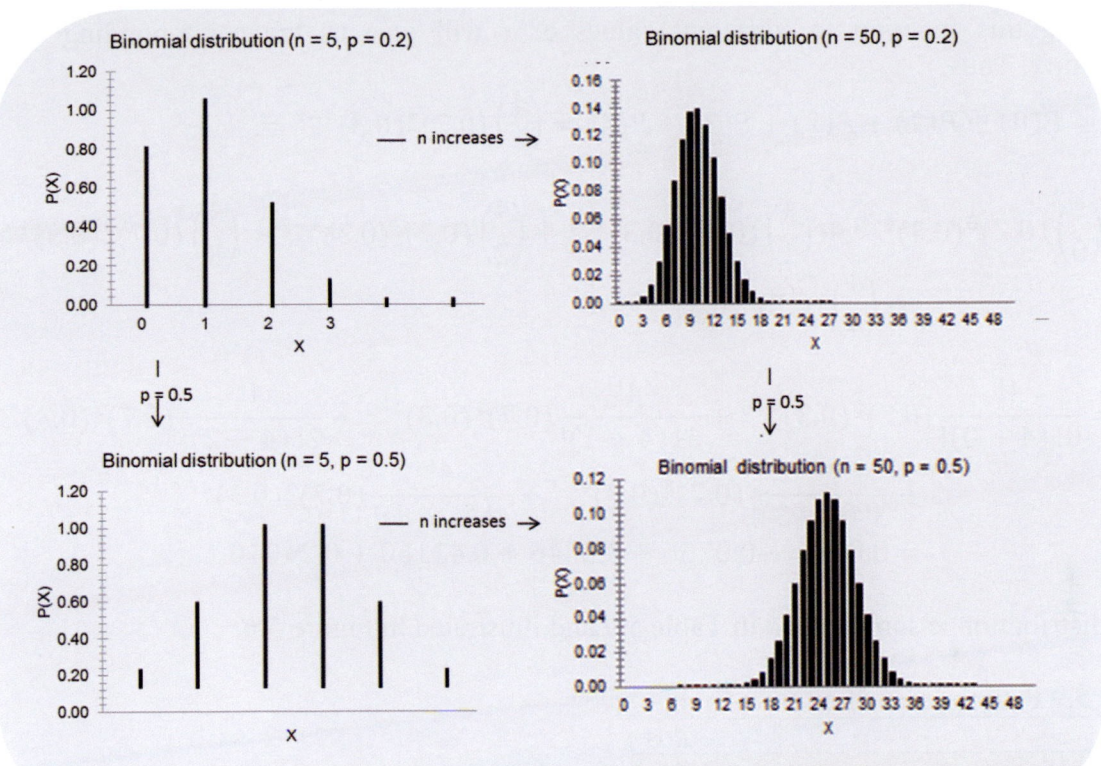

Figure 5.5 Binomial Distributions at Different values of p and n

Example 5.6: There are four flights daily from Atlantic City Airport, New Jersey, to Atlanta Airport, Georgia, via Air Tran Airline. Suppose the probability that any flight arrives on time is 0.70.

- Construct a binomial distribution of the random variable 'number of on-time arrivals.'
- What is the probability that none of the flights will arrive on time tomorrow?
- What is the probability that exactly two of the flights will be on time?

Solution:

If we are willing to assume that the variable arrival time follows a binomial distribution (a fair assumption), we can construct this distribution using equation 5.3, given the two parameters n and p. In symbols, the x variable is described as a variable which follows a binomial distribution with parameters n and p, or $x \sim b(n, p)$ or $x \sim b(4, 0.7)$.

$$P(x) = f(x|n) = \binom{n}{x} p^x (1-p)^{n-x} = \binom{4}{x} (0.7)^x (0.3)^{4-x}$$

$$x = 0,1,2, \ldots \text{ and } \binom{n}{x} = \frac{n!}{x!(n-x)!}$$

267

Resolving this function for different values of x will give us the corresponding values of probability. Thus,

$$P(x) = P(0) + P(1) + P(2) + P(3) + P(4) = \binom{4}{x}(0.7)^x(0.3)^{4-x} =$$

$$\binom{4}{0}(0.7)^0(0.3)^{4-0} + \binom{4}{1}(0.7)^1(0.3)^{4-1} + \binom{4}{2}(0.7)^2(0.3)^{4-2} + \binom{4}{3}(0.7)^3(0.3)^{4-3}$$

$$+ \binom{4}{4}(0.7)^4(0.3)^{4-4} =$$

$$= \frac{4!}{0!\,(4-0)!}(0.7)^0(0.3)^{4-0} + \frac{4!}{1!\,(4-1)!}(0.7)^1(0.3)^{4-1} + \frac{4!}{2!\,(4-2)!}(0.7)^2(0.3)^{4-2}$$

$$+ \frac{4!}{3!\,(4-3)!}(0.7)^3(0.3)^{4-3} + \frac{4!}{4!\,(4-4)!}(0.7)^4(0.3)^{4-4}$$

$$= 0.0081 + 0.0756 + 0.2646 + 0.41160 + 0.24010$$

This distribution is summarized in Table 5.9 and illustrated in Figure 5.6.

Table 5.9 Probabilities of on time flights

x	$P(x)$
0	0.00810
1	0.07560
2	0.26460
3	0.41160
4	0.24010

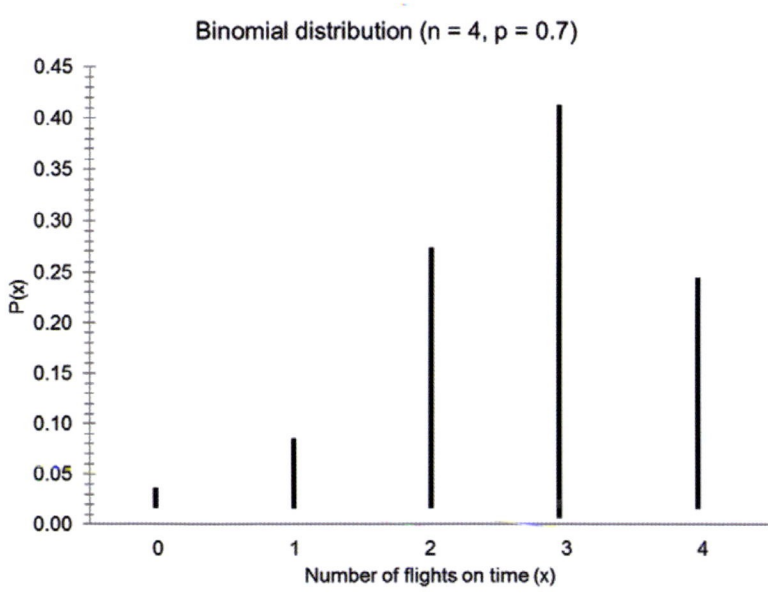

Figure 5.6 Binomial Distributions of flight on-time arrivals

The probability that none of the flights will arrive on time tomorrow = $P(x=0) = 0.0081$

The probability that exactly two of the flights will be on time = $P(x=2) = 0.26460$ (about 26% chance that exactly two flights will be on time)

Example 5.7: Using the results of Example 5.6, what is the expected value of arrival on time, and what is the extent of variation (variance)?

Solution:

$n = 4, p = 0.7$

$$Expected\ value = \mu = np = 4 \times 0.7 = 2.8$$

$$\sigma^2 = np(1-p) = 4 \times 0.7(0.3) = 0.84$$

Working problem 5.8:

There are three flights daily from Charlotte, NC , to New York, NY (JFK), via U.S. Air . Suppose the probability that any flight arrives late is 0.10.
(a) Construct a binomial probability distribution of flight arrival
(b) What is the expected value and the variance?
(c) What is the probability that none of the flights are late today?
(d) What is the probability that exactly one of the flights is late today?
(e) What is the probability that exactly two of the flights are late today?

Answer:

(b) 0.300, 0.270
(c) 0.72900
(d) 0.2430
(e) 0.02700

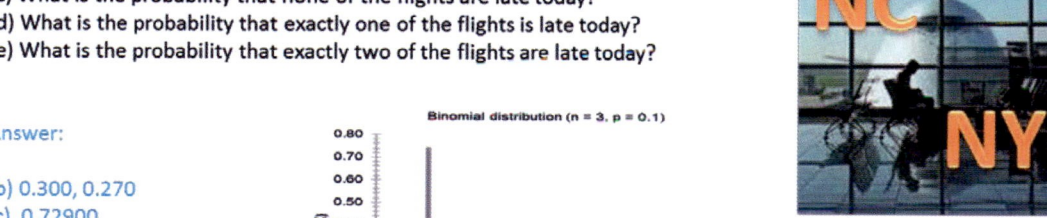

Working problem 5.9:

For the experiment of tossing a coin 6 times, construct a binomial probability distribution.
(a) What is the expected value and the variance?
(b) What is the probability that 2 heads will turn up?
(c) What is the probability that five heads will turn up?
(d) What is the probability that no heads will turn up?

Answer:
(a) 3.00 & 1.5
(b) 0.343775
(c) 0.09375
(d) 0.01563

Binomial distribution (n = 6, p = 0.5)

Example 5.8: A garment manufacturer produces thousands of shirts per day. On average, 1.0% of the shirts do not conform to first quality specifications. Every day, the manufacturer selects a random sample of 500 shirts and classifies through inspection, each shirt in the sample as conforming or nonconforming. If we let x be the random variable representing the number of nonconforming items in the sample, construct a binomial distribution of this variable.

Solution:

If we are willing to assume that the variable shirt defect follows a binomial distribution, we can construct this distribution using equation 5.3, and the two parameters n and p. In symbols, the x variable is described as $x \sim b(n, p)$ or $x \sim b(500, 0.01)$.

$$P(x) = f(x|n) = \binom{n}{x} p^x (1-p)^{n-x} = \binom{500}{x} (0.01)^x (0.99)^{500-x}$$

$x = 0, 1, 2, \ldots$

Resolving this function for different values of x will give us the corresponding values of probability. Thus,

$$P(x) = P(0) + P(1) + P(2) + \cdots = \binom{500}{x} (0.01)^x (0.99)^{500-x} =$$

$$\binom{500}{0}(0.01)^0(0.99)^{500-0} + \binom{500}{1}(0.01)^1(0.99)^{500-1} + \binom{500}{2}(0.01)^2(0.99)^{500-2} + \cdots$$

$$= 0.0066 + 0.0332 + 0.0836 + 0.1401 + 0.1760 + \cdots$$

More values of the probability at different x values are listed in Table 5.10. This distribution is illustrated in Figure 5.7. Note that the distribution is largely symmetrical as a result of using a large sample size n.

Table 5.10 Values of binomial probabilities at $n = 500$, and $p = 0.01$

x	P(x)
0	0.00657
1	0.03318
2	0.08363
3	0.14023
4	0.17600
5	0.17635
6	0.14696
7	0.10476
8	0.06521
9	0.03601
10	0.01786
11	0.00804
12	0.00331
13	0.00125
14	0.00044
15	0.00014
16	0.00004
17	0.00001
18	0.00000
19	0.00000

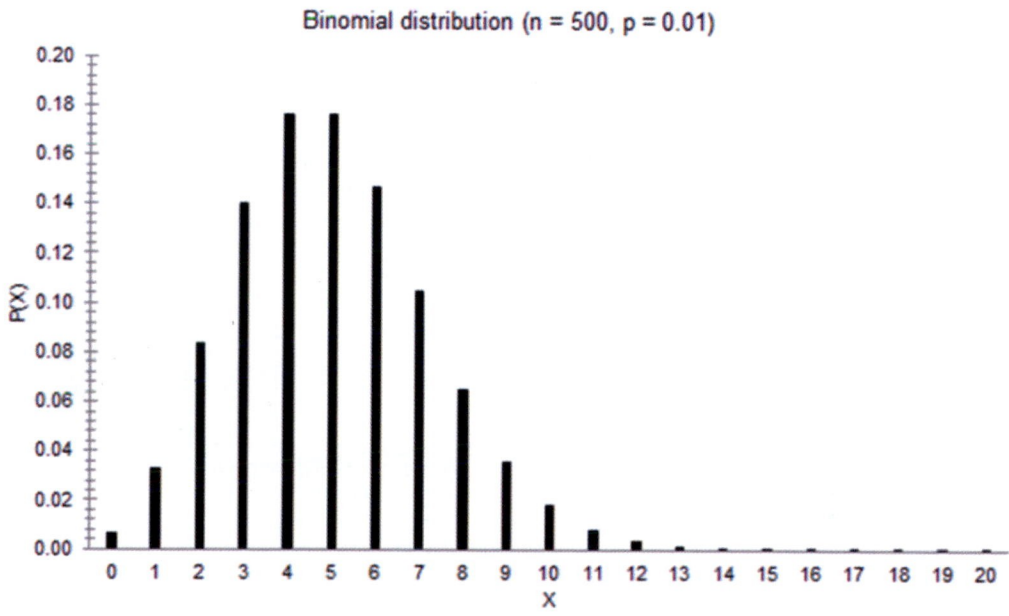

Figure 5.7 Binomial Distributions at $p = 0.01$ and $n = 500$

Example 5.9: In the above example:

- What are the expected value and the variance?
- What is the probability that less than two nonconforming shirts will be found randomly in a set of 500 shirts?
- What is the probability that less than 5 nonconforming shirts will be found randomly in a set of 500 shirts?
- What is the probability that more than three nonconforming shirts will be found randomly in a set of 500 shirts?

Solution:

At $n = 500$, $p = 0.01$, *Expected value* $= \mu = np = 500 \times 0.01 = 5$, and
$\sigma^2 = np(1 - p) = 500 \times 0.01(0.99) = 4.95$

- The probability that less than two nonconforming shirts will be found randomly in a set of 500 shirts: $P(x < 2) = P(0) + P(1) = 0.00657 + 0.03318 = 0.03975$

- The probability that less than 5 nonconforming shirts will be found randomly in a set of 500 shirts: $P(x < 5) = P(0) + P(1) + P(2) + P(3) + P(4) = 0.00657 + 0.03318 + 0.08363 + 0.14023 + 0.17600 = 0.43961$

- The probability that more than three nonconforming shirts will be found randomly in a set of 500 shirts: $P(x>3) = 1 - P(x \le 3) = 1 - [P(0) + P(1) + P(2) + P(3)] = 1 - [0.00657 + 0.03318 + 0.08363 + 0.14023] = 0.73638$

Working problem 5.10: A manufacturer of electromagnetic combined clutch-brake units used for automobiles finds that on average 1.2% of the units fails at high-speed accelerated test. This finding represents historical value based on routine inspection of 100 units daily. If we let x be the random variable representing the number of failing brake units,

- Construct a binomial distribution of this variable
- Determine the expected value and the variance of failure of brakes

Answer:

Binomial distribution

Expected value = 1.200
Variance = 1.186
Std. dev. = 1.089

		n = 100
		p = 0.012
	x	P(x)
	0	0.29902
	1	0.36318
	2	0.21835
	3	0.08663
	4	0.02552
	5	0.00595
	6	0.00114
	7	0.00019
	8	0.00003
	9	0.00000
	10	0.00000
	11	0.00000
	12	0.00000

Binomial distribution (n = 100, p = 0.012)

Working problem 5.11:

A manufacturer of electromagnetic combined clutch-brake units used for automobiles finds that on average 1.2% of the units fails at high-speed accelerated test. This finding represents historical value based on routine inspection of 100 units daily. If we let x be the random variable representing the number of failing brake units:
- What is the probability that exactly one brake unit will fail? 0.36318
- What is the probability that less than two brake units will fail? $P(0) + P(1) = 0.29902 + 0.36318 = 0.66219$
- What is the probability that more than 4 brake units will fail? $1 - P(x \le 4) =$
$= 1 - [P(0) + P(1) + P(2) + P(3) + P(4)] = 1 - [0.29902 + 0.36318 + 0.21835 + 0.08663 + 0.02552] = 0.00731$

Answer:

Binomial distribution (n = 100, p = 0.012)

Binomial distribution		
	n	100
	p	0.012
	x	P(x)
	0	0.29902
	1	0.36318
	2	0.21835
	3	0.08663
	4	0.02552
	5	0.00595
	6	0.00114
	7	0.00019
	8	0.00003
	9	0.00000
	10	0.00000
	11	0.00000
	12	0.00000

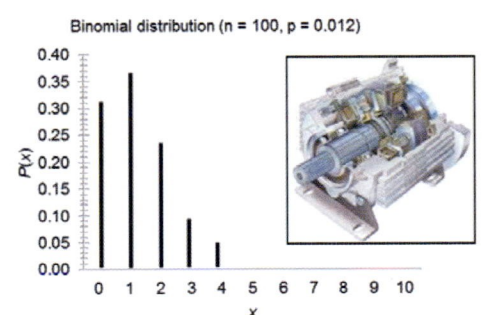

Example 5.10: Two percent of all laptop computers produced by a large electronic company are classified as second quality due to some minor defects. Routinely, the quality control department would inspect 3 laptops from the production line randomly. In one of these inspections,

- What is the probability that exactly one of these three laptops will be classified as second?
- What is the probability that at least 2 of the three laptops will be classified as seconds?
- What is the mean and variance of the binomial distribution associated with this experiment?

Solution:

Using the binomial formula, we can compute the probability values in question. In this case, the selection of a good laptop will be denoted 'G' and the selection of a second quality laptop will be denoted 'S.' The binomial parameters are: $n = 3$ and probability of second quality $= p = 0.02$.

- The probability that exactly one of these three laptops will be classified as second can be determined from:

$$P(x = 1) = \binom{n}{x} p^x (1-p)^{n-x} = \binom{3}{1} (0.02)^1 (0.98)^2 = 0.0576$$

273

- The probability that at least 2 of the three laptops will be classified as seconds can be determined from:

-

$$P(x \geq 2) = \binom{n}{x} p^x (1-p)^{n-x} = P(2) + P(3) =$$

$$= \binom{3}{2}(0.02)^2(0.98)^1 + \binom{3}{3}(0.02)^3(0.98)^0 = 0.00118 + 0.00001 = 0.00119$$

The Binomial distribution associated with the experiment in this example is shown in Figure 5.8.

The mean and variance of this distribution are:

$$\mu = np = 3 \times 0.02 = 0.06$$
$$\sigma^2 = np(1-p) = 3 \times 0.02 \times 0.98 = 0.0588$$

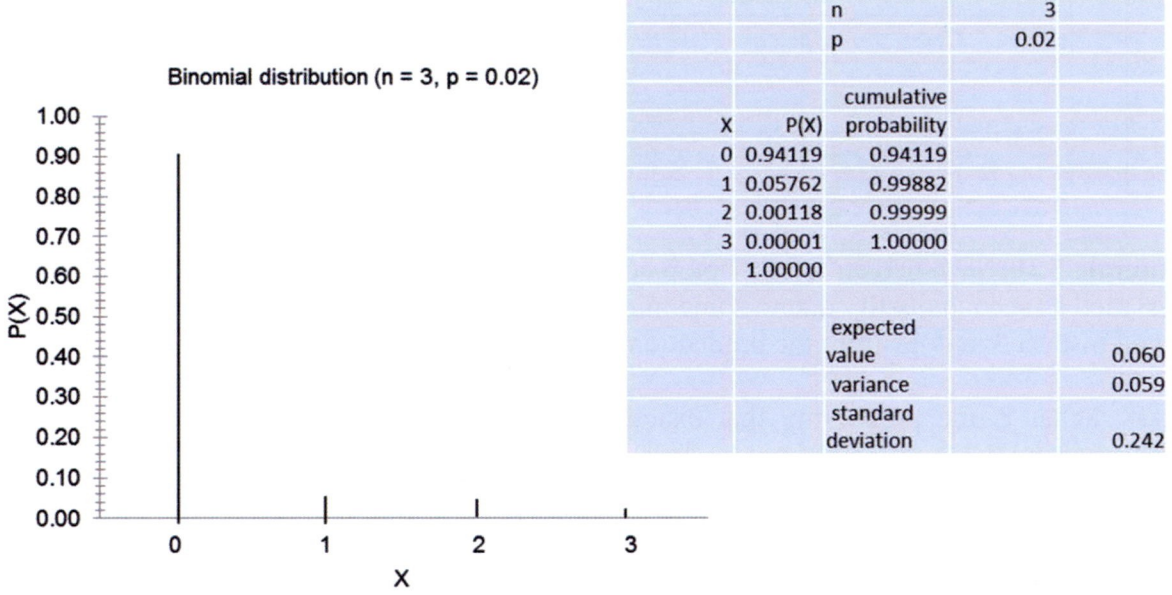

		n	3
		p	0.02
		cumulative	
X	P(X)	probability	
0	0.94119	0.94119	
1	0.05762	0.99882	
2	0.00118	0.99999	
3	0.00001	1.00000	
	1.00000		
		expected value	0.060
		variance	0.059
		standard deviation	0.242

Figure 5.8 Binomial Distributions at $p = 0.02$ and $n = 3$

Example 5.11: If 15% of the bolts produced by a machine are defective, what is the probability that out of the three bolts selected at random, (a) zero bolts will be defective, (b) one bolt will be defective, and (c) less than two bolts will be defective?

Solution:

$p = 0.15$, $1-p = 0.85$

$$P(x = 0) = \binom{3}{0}(0.15)^0(0.85)^3 = 0.614$$

274

$$P(x = 1) = \binom{3}{1}(0.15)^1(0.85)^2 = 0.325$$

$$P(x < 2) = P(x = 0) + P(x = 1) = 0.614 + 0.325 = 0.939$$

The binomial distribution associated with the experiment in this example is shown in Figure 5.9.

The mean and variance of this distribution are:

$$\mu = np = 3 \times 0.15 = 0.45$$
$$\sigma^2 = np(1 - p) = 3 \times 0.15 \times 0.85 = 0.3825$$

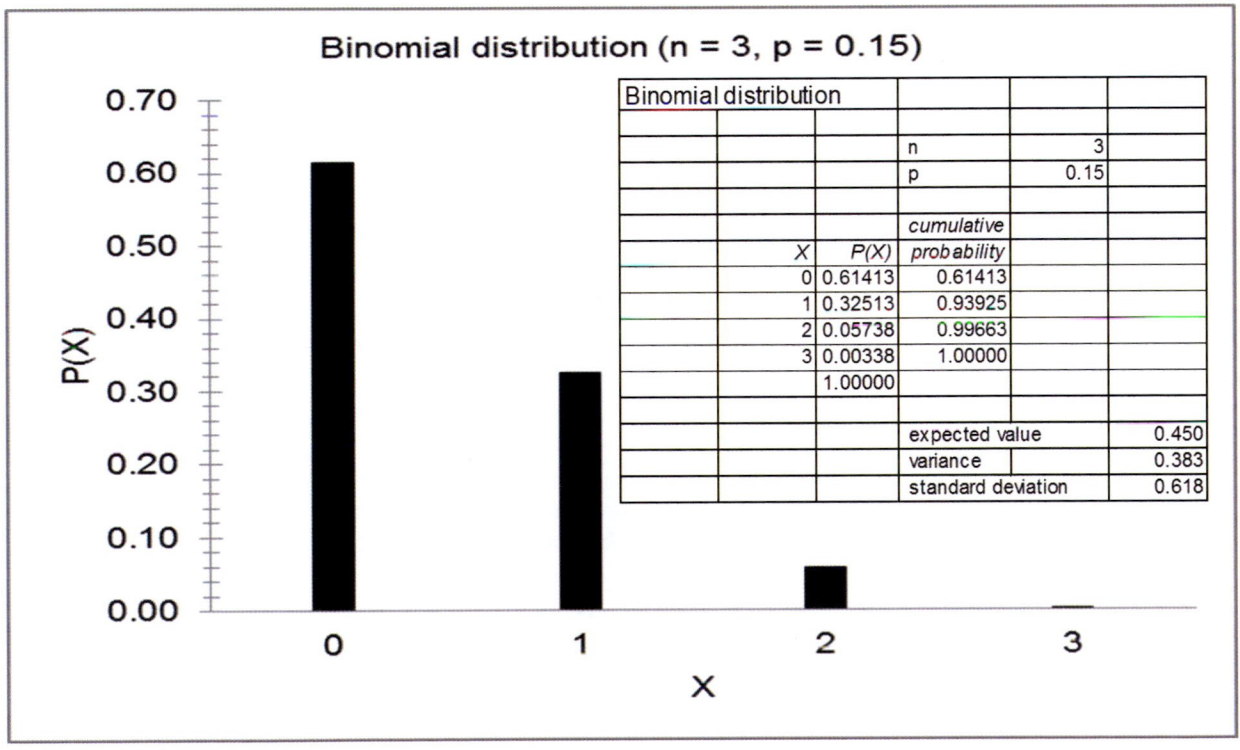

Figure 5.9 Binomial Distributions at $p = 0.15$ and $n = 3$

Working Problem 5.12:

There are five bus trips from JFK Airport to Newark Airport.
Suppose the probability that any bus arrives late is 0.20.

- Construct a binomial distribution describing the random event of bus late a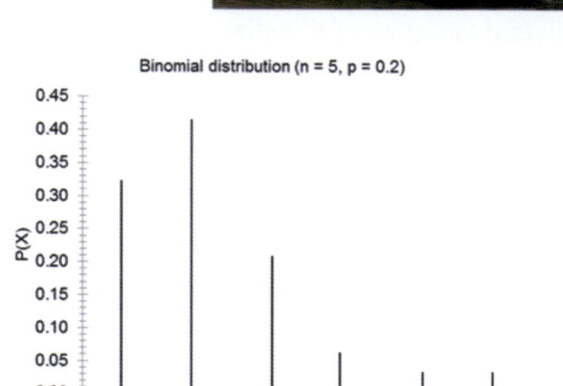

- Calculate the mean and the variance

Answer:
Binomial distribution

n	5	n	
p	0.2	p	
		cumulative	
X	P(X)	probability	
0	0.32768	0.32768	
1	0.40960	0.73728	
2	0.20480	0.94208	
3	0.05120	0.99328	
4	0.00640	0.99968	
5	0.00032	1.00000	
	1.00000		
	1.000	expected value	
	0.800	variance	
		standard	
	0.894	deviation	

Binomial distribution (n = 5, p = 0.2)

Working Problem 5.13:

There are five bus trips from JFK Airport to Newark Airport.
Suppose the probability that any bus arrives late is 0.20.

(a) What is the probability that none of the bus trips will be late today?
(b) What is the probability that one of the bus trips will be late today?

Answer:
Find the answers from the Table

Binomial distribution

		5	n
		0.2	p
			cumulative
X		P(X)	probability
0		0.32768	0.32768
1		0.40960	0.73728
2		0.20480	0.94208
3		0.05120	0.99328
4		0.00640	0.99968
5		0.00032	1.00000
		1.00000	
		1.000	expected value
		0.800	variance
			standard
		0.894	deviation

The Binomial Probability Distribution: Review

- In practice, the binomial distribution is widely used to determine the probability that an outcome will occur x times in n performances of an experiment.
- The binomial formula:

$$P(x) = f(x|n) = \binom{n}{x} p^x (1-p)^{n-x}$$

$$x = 0,1,2,3,4, \ldots., n$$

- The mean and variance of a binomial distribution are:

$$\mu = np \ \& \ \sigma^2 = np(1-p)$$

In summary, basic characteristics of the binomial distribution are as follows:

1. The binomial distribution is the most appropriate probability distribution for sampling from an infinitely large population, where p represents the fraction of defective or nonconforming items in the population, x represents the number of nonconforming items found in a random sample of n items. x and p both refer to the *same* category (success, pass, etc.)

2. The two parameters that fully identify a binomial probability function are n and p.

3. In a binomial experiment, there are n identical trials. In other words, the given experiment is repeated n times, where n is a positive integer.

4. Each repetition of a binomial experiment is called a trial or a Bernoulli trial (after Jacob Bernoulli).

5. Each trial has two and only two outcomes (*success or failure, pass or fail, heads or tails*, etc.).

6. The probability of success is denoted by p and that of failure by q or (1-p).

7. Binomial trials are independent. This means that the outcome of one trial does not affect the outcome of the next trial or any other trial.

8. When sampling without replacement, events can be treated as if they were independent if the sample size is no more than 5% of the population size (n ≤ 0.05 N)

9. The shape of the binomial distribution depends strictly on the values of its two parameters, n and p. In general, as n increases, the binomial distribution will tend to be more symmetrical. In addition, when $p = 0.5$, the distribution also becomes symmetrical. Figure 5.5 illustrates these two points using binomial distributions of different values of n and p.

Working problem 5.14

Based on a worldwide mortality statistics, there is about 60% chance that a person aged 30 will be alive at age 70.
Suppose that five people aged 30 are selected at random
(a) Find the probability that the number alive at age 70 will be exactly two
(b) Find the probability that the number alive at age 70 will be at most two
(c) Find the probability that the number alive at age 70 will be at least three
(d) Find the probability that the number alive at age 70 will be none
(e) Determine the probability distribution of the number alive at age 70
(f) Determine the expected value and the variance of the number alive at age 70

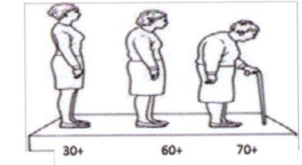

Answer:
Binomial distribution
Find the answers from the table below

n	5
p	0.6
X	P(X)
0	0.01024
1	0.07680
2	0.23040
3	0.34560
4	0.25920
5	0.07776
	1.00000
expected value	3.000
variance	1.200
standard deviation	1.095

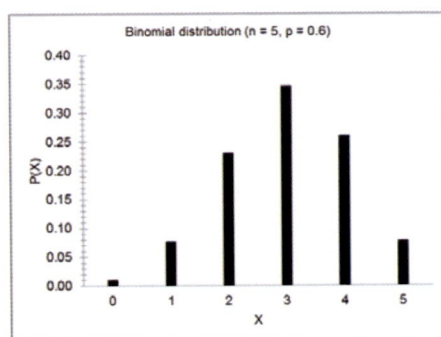

Binomial distribution (n = 5, p = 0.6)

Working problem 5.15:

In a multiple-choice exam of 20 questions, 5 possible answers were assigned for each question and only one answer is correct. If a student is answering these questions randomly, would this represent a binomial experiment? If the answer is 'yes', formulate the probability function
- What are the values of the two parameters, n and p of the binomial distribution? Calculate the expected value and the variance.
- What is your chance to answer exactly 2 questions correctly?
- What is your chance to answer less than 3 questions correctly?
- What is your chance to answer more than 15 questions correctly?

Answer:
This experiment fully satisfies the binomial model. The reasons are:
A fixed number of trials = $n = 20$
The trials are independent (the answer of one question is independent of the answer of another question)
Each trial is associated with two outcomes, correct or wrong
Each trial is associated with fixed probability $p = 1/5$, since the chance of a correct answer is one out of five.
Thus, the probability remains constant

$n = 20, p = 0.20$ $P(x) = \dfrac{20!}{x!\,(20-x)!}(0.20)^x(0.80)^{20-x}$
$x = 0,1,2,3,4,\dots,20$

Binomial distribution		
	n	20
	p	0.2
	X	P(X)
	0	0.01153
	1	0.05765
	2	0.13691
	3	0.20536
	4	0.21820
	5	0.17456
	6	0.10910
	7	0.05455
	8	0.02216
	9	0.00739
	10	0.00203
	11	0.00046
	12	0.00009
	13	0.00001
	14	0.00000
	15	0.00000
	16	0.00000
	17	0.00000
	18	0.00000
	19	0.00000
	20	0.00000
		1.00000
expected value		4.000
variance		3.200
standard deviation		1.789

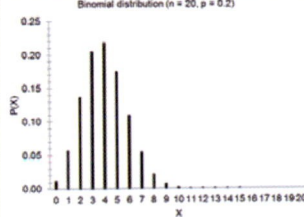

Binomial distribution (n = 20, p = 0.2)

Working problem 5.16:

In a multiple-choice exam of 60 questions, 4 possible answers were assigned for each question and only one answer is correct. A student made a serious attempt at the first 40 questions. This student typically answer multiple-choice tests with a rate of success of about 80%.

(a) How many questions will this student be expected to answer correctly out of the first 40 questions?

(b) If the same student then attempted to answer the remaining 20 questions randomly. Would you consider his attempts as a binomial experiment? If the answer is 'yes", what is the expected number of questions that this student will answer correctly out of these 20 questions? Estimate the total number of questions that this student can answer correctly, and predict his letter grade?

Note:

$G \geq 90 = A, 80 \leq G < 90 = B$

$70 \leq G < 80 = C, 60 \leq G < 70 = D$

expected value	5.000
variance	3.750
standard deviation	1.936

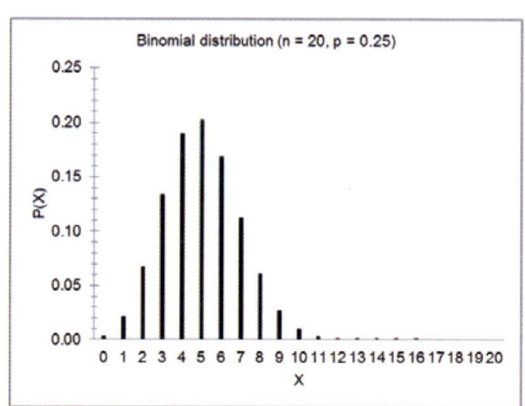

5.6 Using Microsoft Excel® to perform binomial distribution analysis

In the above examples, we used manual calculations to determine the probability values associated with a discrete variable following a binomial distribution. In this section we use Excel® to perform these calculations.

In example 5.11, 15% of the bolts produced by a machine are defective, and the question was about the probability that out of the three bolts selected at random (a) zero bolts will be defective, (b) one bolt will be defective, and (c) less than two bolts will be defective? The parameters of this binomial distribution are $p = 0.15$, and $n = 3$. Using Microsoft Excel® Functions, we follow these steps (Figures 5.10 and 5.11):

1. Go to Excel® Spreadsheet
2. Click on insert function '*fx*'
3. Select 'Statistical' from the 'select a category' drop down list box
4. Select 'BINOMDIST' from the 'Select a function' list
5. Click OK
6. To answer Part (a) of this Example, type 0 in the Number's window, and 3 in the Trials Window, 0.15 in the Probability's window, and False in the 'Cumulative' Window.
7. You should be able to see the value of the $P(x = 0)$ on the function arguments window as illustrated in Figure 5.11, or you can Click Ok and the probability value will be displayed.

Figure 5.12 illustrates how the rest of the questions are answered. Note how we use 'FALSE' in the 'Cumulative' Window for getting the exact probability value (i.e. $P(x = 0)$ or $P(x = 1)$), or 'TRUE' for getting cumulative probability

$$P(x < 2) = P(x = 0) + P(x = 1) = 0.614 + 0.325 = 0.939$$

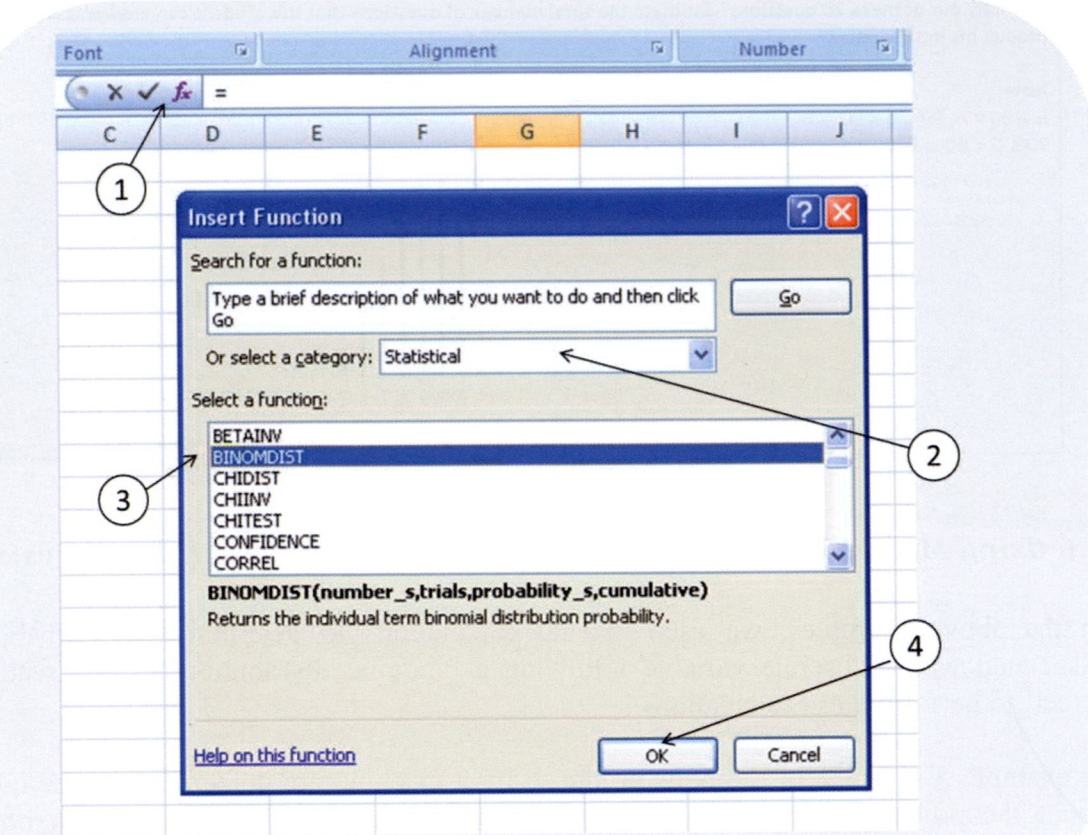

Figure 5.10 Using Excel® to Perform Binomial Distributions Analysis: Steps 1 through 4

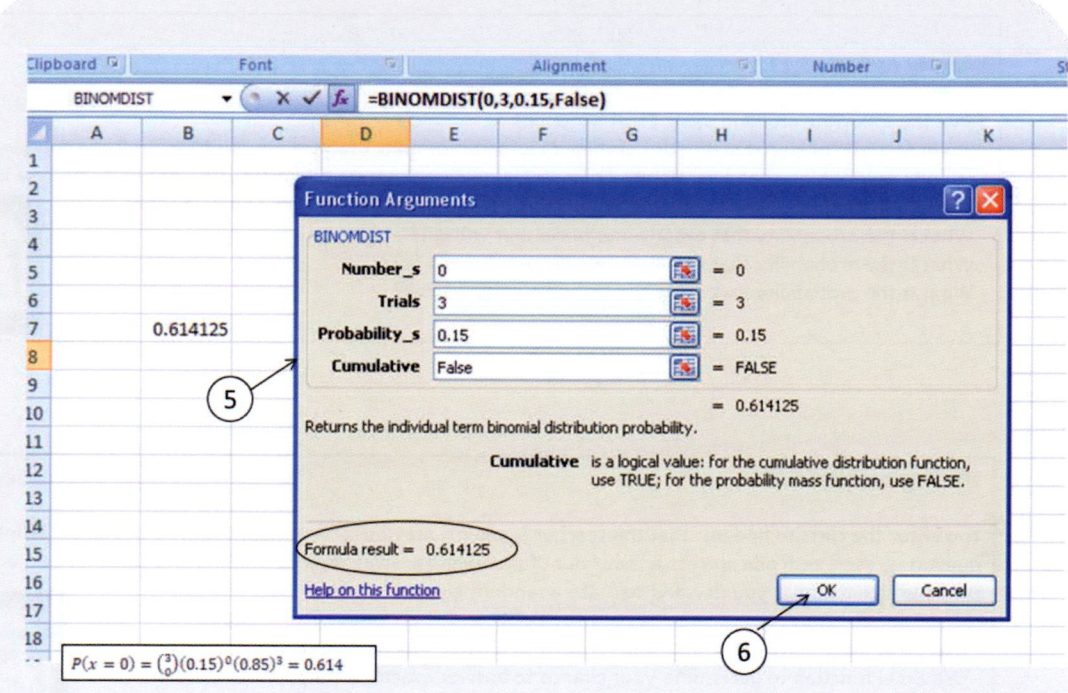

Figure 5.11 Using Excel® to Perform Binomial Distributions Analysis: Steps 5 and 6

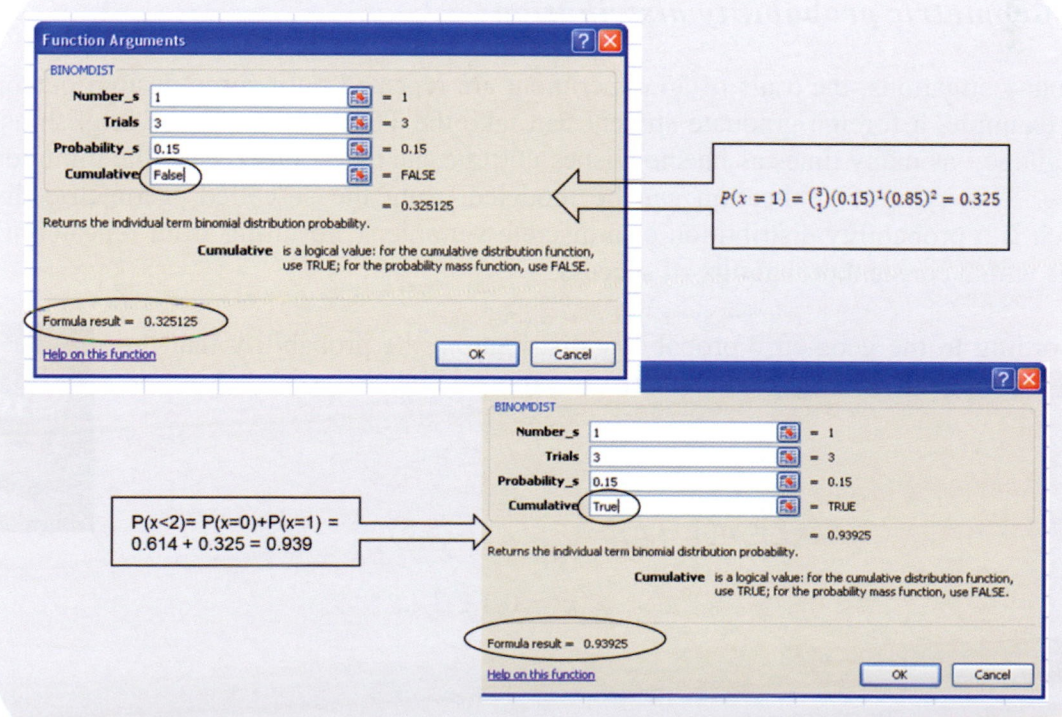

Figure 5.12 Using Excel® to Perform Binomial Distributions Analysis: False & True Options

Working problem 5.17:

Solve the following problem using Excel Functions
A manufacturer of electromagnetic combined clutch-brake units used for automobiles finds that on average 1.2% of the units fails at high-speed accelerated test. This finding represents historical value based on routine inspection of 100 units daily. If we let x be the random variable representing the number of failing brake units:
- What is the probability that exactly one brake unit will fail?
- What is the probability that less than two brake units will fail?
- What is the probability that more than 4 brake units will fail?

Working problem 5.18:

You enter the class to find out that the teacher is given a previously unannounced quiz of eight multiple-choice questions, each with one correct answer out of possible 4 answer choices (A, B, C, and D). Since you were not prepared for the quiz, you decided to make a random guess.

- Use Excel function to determine your chance to answer exactly 3 questions correctly?
- Use Excel function to determine your chance to answer exactly 2 questions correctly?
- Use Excel function to determine your chance to answer no questions correctly?

5.7 Geometric probability distribution

In many situations, the trials of an experiment are repeated until some desired outcome occurs. For example, a foreign graduate student can take the TOEFL or 'Test of English as a Foreign Language,' as many times as he/she wishes until he/she meets or exceeds the minimum required score. This type of application can be modeled using the so-called 'geometric distribution,' which is a probability distribution of a discrete variable, x, resulting from repeated independent trials with a constant probability of success.

According to the geometric probability distribution, the probability that the first success will occur in trial number x is expressed by:

$$P(x) = p(1-p)^{x-1} \qquad (5.6)$$

$$x = 0,1,2,3, \dots$$

Example 5.12: Suppose from past data, it is known that the chance of meeting the minimum score of the TOEFL test is 0.25.What is the probability that a student will meet the required minimum score on the second or third trial?

Solution:

At $p = 0.25$, $x = 2$, $P(x) = p(1 - p)^{x-1}$, and $P(2) = 0.25(0.75)^{2-1} = 0.1875$

At $p = 0.25$, $x = 3$, $P(x) = p(1 - p)^{x-1}$, and $P(3) = 0.25(0.75)^{3-1} = 0.141$

Since these are independent trials, the probability that a student will meet the required minimum score on the second or third trial is:

$$P(x = second\ or\ third\ trial) = P(2) + P(3) = 0.1875 + 0.1410 = 0.329$$

Working problem 5.19:

From experience, an anti-smoking organization knows that the chance of convincing smokers to quit smoking is 0.20. In a large campaign conducted during the smoke-out day, find the probability that the organization's first smoker to quit will occur on its fourth or fifth attempt to convince smokers to give up this destructive habit.

Answer: 0.18432

5.8 Hypergeometric probability distribution

Recall that one of the key characteristics of the binomial distribution is that the trials should be independent. This is the reason why the probabilities of success or failure remain constant in a binomial experiment. Typically, this situation occurs when a sample is drawn from an *infinite population*, or when it is withdrawn with replacement from a finite population. When a sample is drawn without replacement from a finite population, the assumption of independent trials becomes inaccurate as each trial is likely to influence the outcome of the next one. In this case, the trials are indeed not independent and we cannot use the binomial distribution. Instead, we use the so-called '*hypergeometric*' probability distribution defined by the following expression:

$$P(x) = \frac{S^C x\ (N - S)^C (n - x)}{N^C n} \qquad (5.7)$$

where $P(x)$ = the probability of x successes in n trials, N = total number of elements in the population, S = number of successes in the population, $N-S$ = number of failures in the population, n = number of trials (sample size), x = number of successes in n trials, and $n - x$ = number of failures in n trials

The key features of a hypergeometric distribution are as follows:

- The outcome of any trial is classified into one of two mutually exclusive categories, namely: success or failure.
- The random variable is the number of successes in a fixed number of trials
- Trials are not independent.
- The sample is assumed to be taken from a finite population without replacement leading to a change in the probability of success for each trial.

Example 5.13: The Mathematics Department in Keytown College has 16 full-time faculty members, with 12 tenured faculty members and 4 non-tenured faculty members. The Department is planning to select three of these 16 faculty members to serve on the college educational planning committee. If three faculty members are randomly selected out of the 16 faculty members, what is the probability that all three faculty members will be tenured?

Solution:

This problem seems to be solvable using the binomial distribution with $n = 16$, and p(tenured) = 0.75, or $q = 0.25$. At $p = 0.75$, $q = 1 - p = 0.25$

$$P(x = 3) = \binom{16}{3}(0.75)^3(0.25)^{13} = 0.00000352$$

This means that using the binomial approach, there is almost a zero chance of selecting 3 faculty members that are all tenured.

A close examination of the problem scenario will reveal that we are dealing with a finite population of faculty members (16 members). Drawing one faculty member without replacement will certainly influence the independency aspect of the trail and will make the probability of tenured or non-tenured not constant. For this reason, we use the hypergeometric distribution:

$$P(x) = \frac{S^C x \ (N-S)^C(n-x)}{N^C n}$$

N = total number of elements in the population = 16, S = number of successes in the population (in this case we will let success be tenured) = 12, $N - S$ = number of failures in the population = 4, n = number of trials (sample size) = 3, x = number of successes in n trials = 3, and $n - x$ = number of failures in n trials = 0

$P(x)$ = the probability of x tenured faculty in n trials can be obtained as follows:

$$P(x) = \frac{S^C x \ (N-S)^C(n-x)}{N^C n} = \frac{12^C 3 \ 4^C 0}{16^C 3} = \frac{12!}{3! \ (12-3)!} \frac{4!}{0! \ (4)!} \frac{3! \ (16-3)!}{16!}$$
$$= 0.393$$

Note that there is a substantial difference between this value and the previous value of 0.00000352 as a result of accounting for the dependency of trials. The hypergeometric distribution associated with this problem is shown in Figure 5.13.

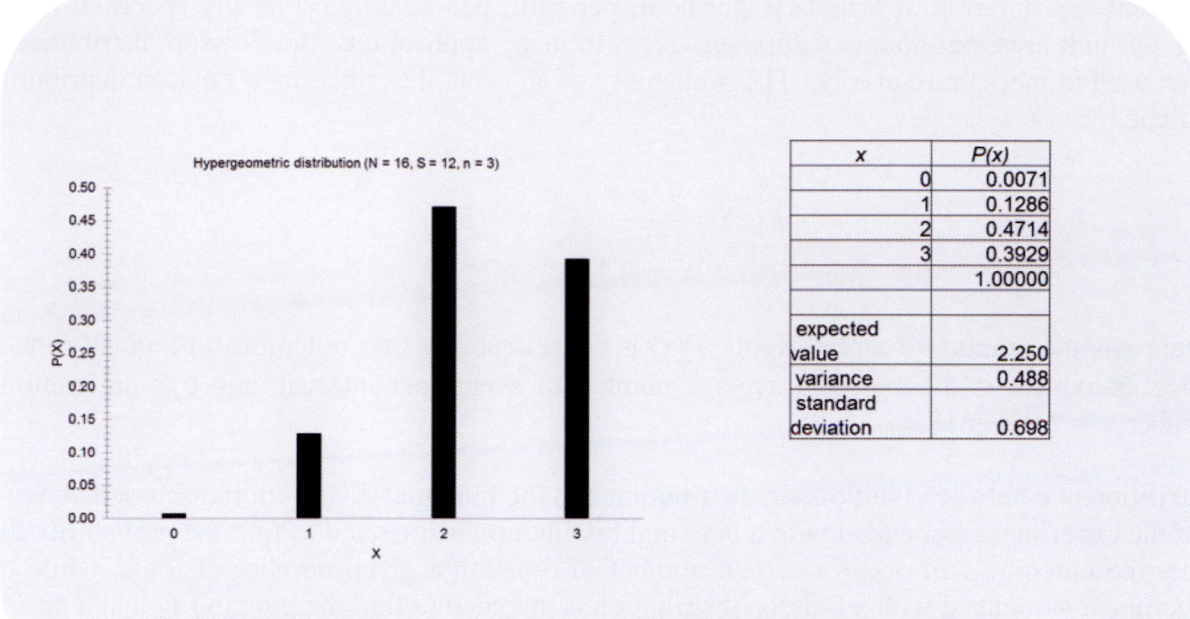

x	P(x)
0	0.0071
1	0.1286
2	0.4714
3	0.3929
	1.00000

expected value	2.250
variance	0.488
standard deviation	0.698

Figure 5.13 Hypergeometric Distribution of Tenured Faculty Committee selection

Working problem 5.20:

A college has 60 faculty members. Fifteen of these are non-tenured and forty five are tenured. If five faculty members are selected randomly to attend a conference, what is the probability that three of the five faculty members are non-tenured?

Answer:

Hypergeometric distribution

60	N, population size	
	S, number of possible	
15	occurrences	
5	n, sample size	

X	P(X)	cumulative probability
0	0.22370	0.22370
1	0.40921	0.63292
2	0.27281	0.90573
3	0.08248	0.98820
4	0.01125	0.99945
5	0.00055	1.00000
	1.00000	
	1.250	expected value
	0.874	variance
	0.935	standard deviation

285

5.9 Poisson probability distribution

The Poisson distribution was named after the French mathematician Simeon D. Poisson (1781 – 1840). It is a probability distribution used for modeling discrete variables with the concern being with the number of events occurring during a given time or space interval. The interval may represent any duration of time (e.g. per hour, per shift, per week, etc.) or any specified region (e.g. per unit area, per box, per shipment, etc.). In many applications, the Poisson distribution is often used to model rare events. The probability of an event described by a Poisson distribution is given by:

$$P(x) = \frac{\lambda^x e^{-\lambda}}{x!} \qquad (5.8)$$
$$x = 0,1,2,3, \dots$$

where x is the number of target events, $P(x)$ is the probability of x outcomes in a given time or space interval, λ is the expected average number of events per interval, and e is an irrational number, $e = 2.7182818$.

The difference between the Poisson distribution and the binomial distribution discussed above is that the experiment associated with a binomial distribution is intended to find the probability that a desired outcome will occur a certain number of times in a given number of trials; while the experiment associated with a Poisson distribution is intended to find the probability that a desired outcome will occur a certain number of times within a given unit of time or space. Because of this difference, the binomial distribution is associated with two parameters, n and p and the Poisson distribution is associated with only one parameter, λ, or the expected number of outcomes per time or space interval.

The mean and variance of the Poisson distribution are given by:

$$\mu = \lambda = np \qquad (5.9)$$

$$\sigma^2 = \lambda = np \qquad (5.10)$$

where n is the total number of events, p is the probability that each event will occur in an interval, and λ is as defined before and it can take a fractional value.

Note that equations 5.9 and 5.10 indicate that the mean of the Poisson distribution is equal to its variance. In practice, this feature is very important. Events that have mean values approximately equal to their variances are commonly called Poisson events.

Example 5.14: The mean number of accidents on the job per year at a certain company is 3. Assuming that a Poisson distribution can best represent this random variable, determine the probability that in any given year four accidents will occur at this company? Construct the Poison distribution describing this variable. What is the mean and variance of this distribution?

Solution:

The Poisson distribution associated with the experiment in this example is shown in Figure 5.14. This distribution is manually developed using different values of x and corresponding probability values as follows:

$$at\ x = 0, \quad P(0) = \frac{\lambda^x e^{-\lambda}}{x!} = \frac{3^0 \times e^{-3}}{0!} = 0.0498$$

$$at\ x = 1, \quad P(1) = \frac{\lambda^x e^{-\lambda}}{x!} = \frac{3^1 \times e^{-3}}{1!} = 0.1494$$

$$at\ x = 2, \quad P(2) = \frac{\lambda^x e^{-\lambda}}{x!} = \frac{3^2 \times e^{-3}}{2!} = 0.224$$

$$\dots \dots \dots \dots \dots \dots \dots \dots$$

$$at\ x = 7, \quad P(7) = \frac{\lambda^x e^{-\lambda}}{x!} = \frac{3^7 \times e^{-3}}{7!} = 0.0216$$

$$P(x = 4) = \frac{\lambda^x e^{-\lambda}}{x!} = \frac{3^4 \times e^{-3}}{4!} = \frac{81 \times 0.0498}{4 \times 3 \times 2 \times 1} = 0.168$$

The mean and variance of this distribution are:

$$\mu = \lambda = 3$$
$$\sigma^2 = \lambda = 3$$

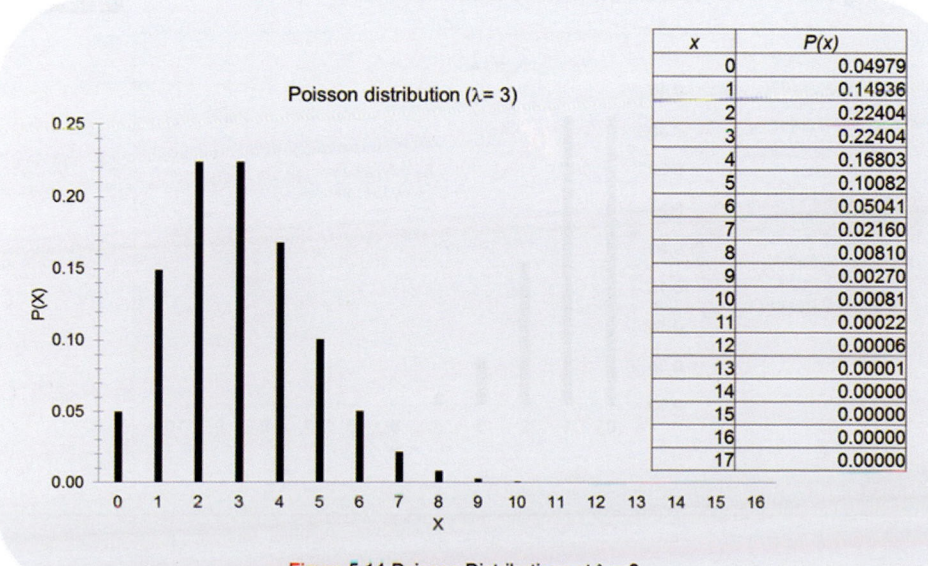

x	P(x)
0	0.04979
1	0.14936
2	0.22404
3	0.22404
4	0.16803
5	0.10082
6	0.05041
7	0.02160
8	0.00810
9	0.00270
10	0.00081
11	0.00022
12	0.00006
13	0.00001
14	0.00000
15	0.00000
16	0.00000
17	0.00000

Figure 5.14 Poisson Distributions at λ = 3

287

The Poisson Probability Distribution: Review

- It is a probability distribution used for modeling discrete variables with the concern being with the number of events occurring during a given time or space interval
- The probability of an event described by a Poisson distribution is given by:

$$P(x) = \frac{\lambda^x e^{-\lambda}}{x!}$$
$$x = 0,1,2,3,4,\ldots\ldots,n$$

- The mean and variance of the Poisson distribution are given by:

$$\mu = \lambda = np$$
$$\sigma^2 = \lambda = np$$

- The only parameter required to fully describe a Poisson distribution is λ
- The occurrences of the random variable, x, must be *random*
- The occurrences must be *independent* of each other
- In a binomial distribution, the possible values of the random variable x are 0, 1, 2, ..., n, but a Poisson distribution has possible x values of 0, 1, 2, ... with no upper limit.

Siméon Denis Poisson (1781-1840)

Working problem 5.21:

The mean number of on-site accidental deaths per a period of five years in an electric-service company is 1.0. Assuming that a Poisson distribution can best represent this random variable, determine the probability that in any given five-year period, three on-site accidental deaths will occur? Construct the Poison distribution describing this variable. What is the mean and variance of this distribution?

Answer:

X	P(X)
0	0.36788
1	0.36788
2	0.18394
3	0.06131
4	0.01533
5	0.00307
6	0.00051
7	0.00007
8	0.00001
9	0.00000
10	0.00000

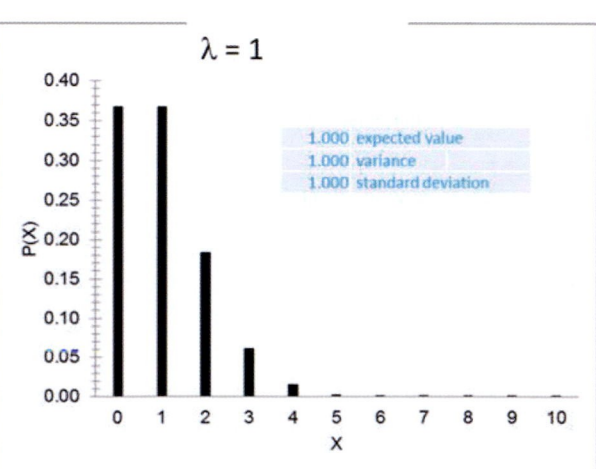

1.000 expected value
1.000 variance
1.000 standard deviation

5.10 Using Microsoft Excel® to perform Poisson analysis

In the above example, we used manual calculations to determine the probability values associated with a discrete variable following a Poisson distribution. We can also use Microsoft Excel® Functions to perform Poisson analysis as illustrated by the example below.

Example 5.15: Suppose the average number of machine breakdowns per week is one, $\lambda = 1$. What is the probability of having 2 breakdowns in the coming week?

Solution:

One way to perform this analysis more efficiently is to use Microsoft Excel® Functions. In this case, we follow these steps (Figures 5.15 through 5.18):

1. Go to Excel® Spreadsheet.
2. Click on insert function '*fx*'
3. Select 'Statistical' from the 'select a category' drop down list box
4. Select POISSON from the 'Select a function' list- Click OK.
5. To answer this question, type 2 at the 'X' window, 1 in Mean window, and False in the Cumulative Window.
6. You should be able to see the value of the $P(x = 2)$ as illustrated in Figure 5.16, or you can click Ok and the value will be presented.
7. See Figure 5.17 for how to do the other problems in the above example using Excel®.

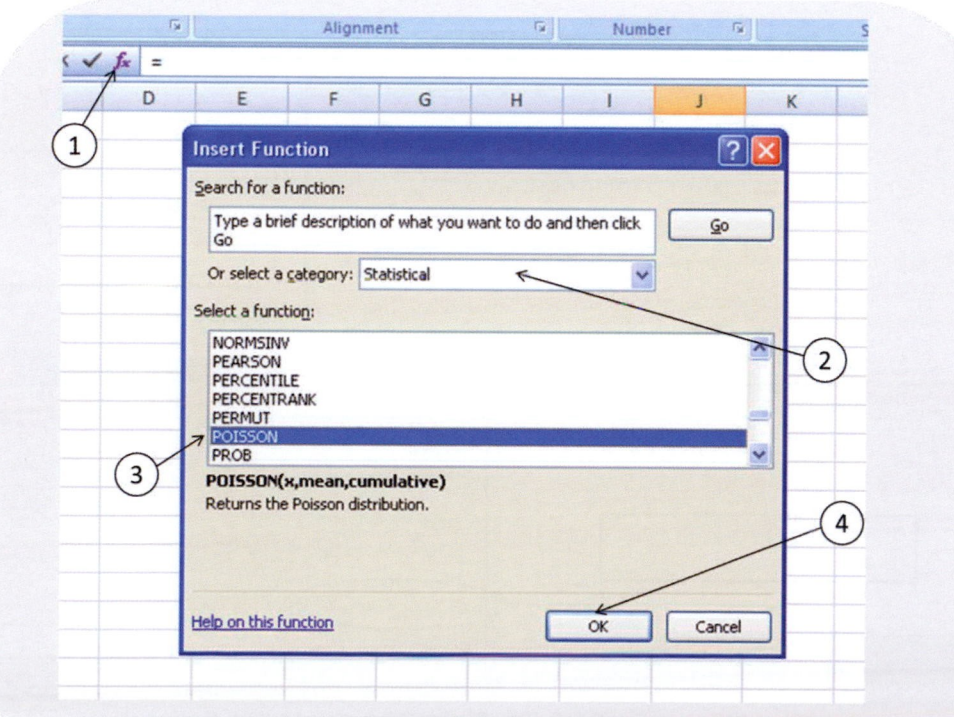

Figure 5.15 Using Excel® to Perform Poisson Distributions Analysis: Steps 1 through 4

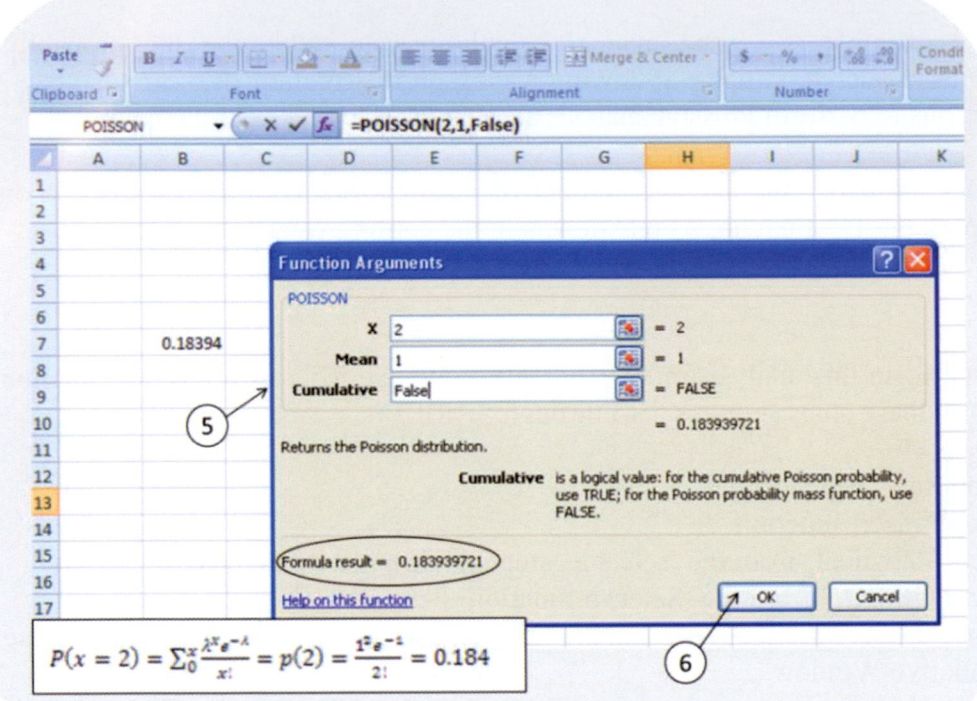

Figure 5.16 Using Excel® to Perform Poisson Distributions Analysis: Steps 5 and 6

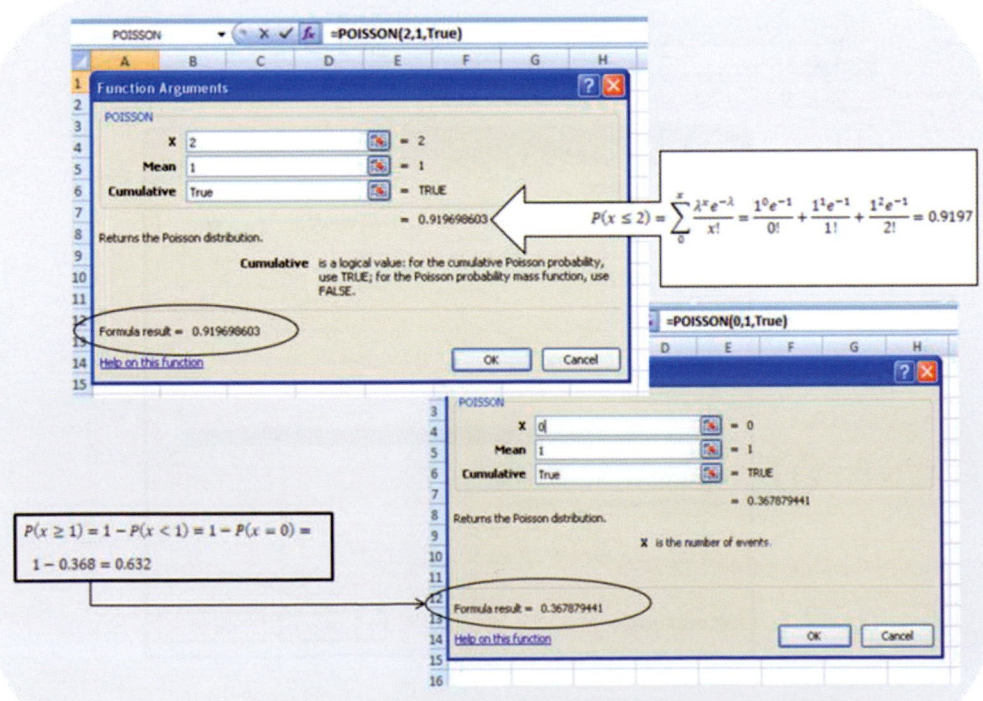

Figure 5.17 Using Excel® to Perform Poisson Distributions Analysis: $P(x \leq 2)$ & $P(x \geq 1)$

Working problem 5.22:

The mean number of car accidents in Peachtree street in Atlanta, Georgia is 3 per month. Assuming that a Poisson distribution can best represent this random variable, determine the probability that in any given month, 5 or more car accidents will occur? Construct the Poison distribution describing this variable. What is the mean and variance of this distribution?

Answer:

Poisson distribution

		mean rate of occurrence =3
	x	P(x)
	0	0.04979
	1	0.14936
	2	0.22404
	3	0.22404
	4	0.16803
	5	0.10082
	6	0.05041
	7	0.02160
	8	0.00810
		0.99620
	expected value	3.000
	variance	3.000
	standard deviation	1.732

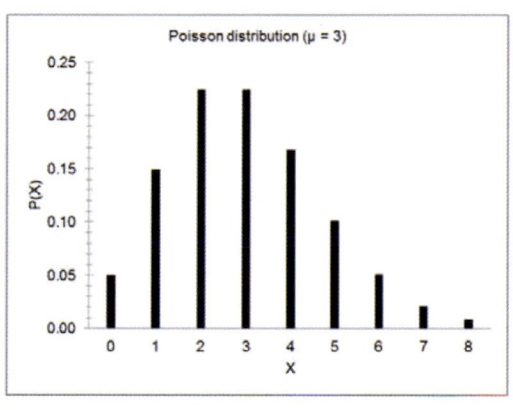

Poisson distribution (μ = 3)

Working Problem 5.23:

Assume on-time flight per week is a rare situation for a particular airline. Suppose on average, this number is about 2. Construct a Poisson distribution of this random variable.
(a) What is the expected value and variance of the number of on-time flights per week? (2 & 2)
(b) What is the chance that the number of on-time flights per week will exceed 5?

Answer:
(a) (2&2)
(b) $P(x>5) = 1-p(x<=5) =$ 0.01656

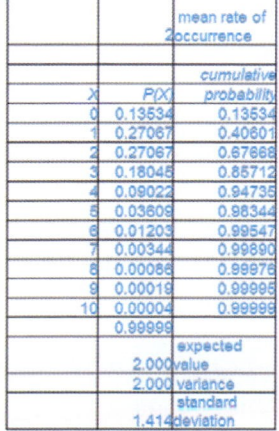

Poisson Distribution

X	P(X)	mean rate of occurrence 2 cumulative probability
0	0.13534	0.13534
1	0.27067	0.40601
2	0.27067	0.67668
3	0.18045	0.85712
4	0.09022	0.94735
5	0.03609	0.98344
6	0.01203	0.99547
7	0.00344	0.99890
8	0.00086	0.99976
9	0.00019	0.99995
10	0.00004	0.99999
	0.99999	
	2.000	expected value
	2.000	variance
	1.414	standard deviation

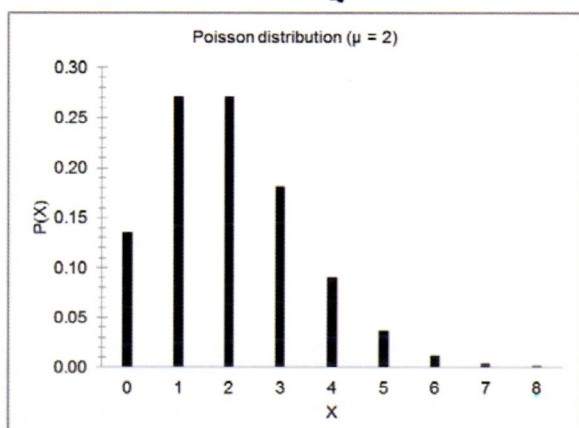

Poisson distribution (μ = 2)

291

5.11 Simulation of probability distributions of discrete variables

Many software programs have tools that allow us to determine probabilities and construct probability distributions. In this section, we demonstrate the use of Microsoft Excel® in simulating binomial and Poisson distributions using some examples.

The underlying concept of statistical simulation is to generate ***random numbers*** representing values of a random variable (x), which has a pattern following a binomial or a Poisson distribution. In order to generate these random numbers, we should know the parameters of the distribution. Recall that the binomial distribution is associated with two parameters, n and p, and the Poisson distribution is associated with one parameter λ. Using reliable values of these parameters will allow us to simulate probability distributions from virtual experiments.

Example 5.16: Suppose a manufacturer typically finds 2% defects in hard drive units produced for personal computers. Generate a binomial distribution of nonconforming hard drives that simulates the inspection trials of these hard drives using a trial set each of 400 hard drives.

Solution:

Generating a distribution simply means simulating an experiment describing the random variable in question. In this example, the experiment is to inspect 400 hard drives, say on a daily basis, and to find the number of nonconforming hard drives. In the real world, this will takes many days of inspection and sorting of the non-conforming units. Using computer simulation, we can perform this experiment in a matter of seconds provided that we use reliable values of the distribution parameters, n and p.

As indicated earlier, the binomial distribution is fully characterized by two parameters, n and p. In this example, $n = 400$, and $p = 0.02$. Using Excel® 'Data Analysis,' we select 'Random Number Generation' as shown in Figure 5.18.

In the 'Random Number Generation' menu, we follow these steps:

- Type 1 in the window 'Number of Variables.' This means we have one variable, which is the number of defects
- Type an appropriate number, say 500 or1000, in the window 'Number of Random Numbers.' This number simulates the number of trials (in this example, each trial involves inspection of 400 units).
- Select 'binomial' from the pull-down menu. This will prompt you to insert the values of the parameters of the binomial distribution, $p = 0.02$, $n = 400$. Then select an output area.
- You may prepare a label called defects under which you can specify your output as shown in Figure 5.19.

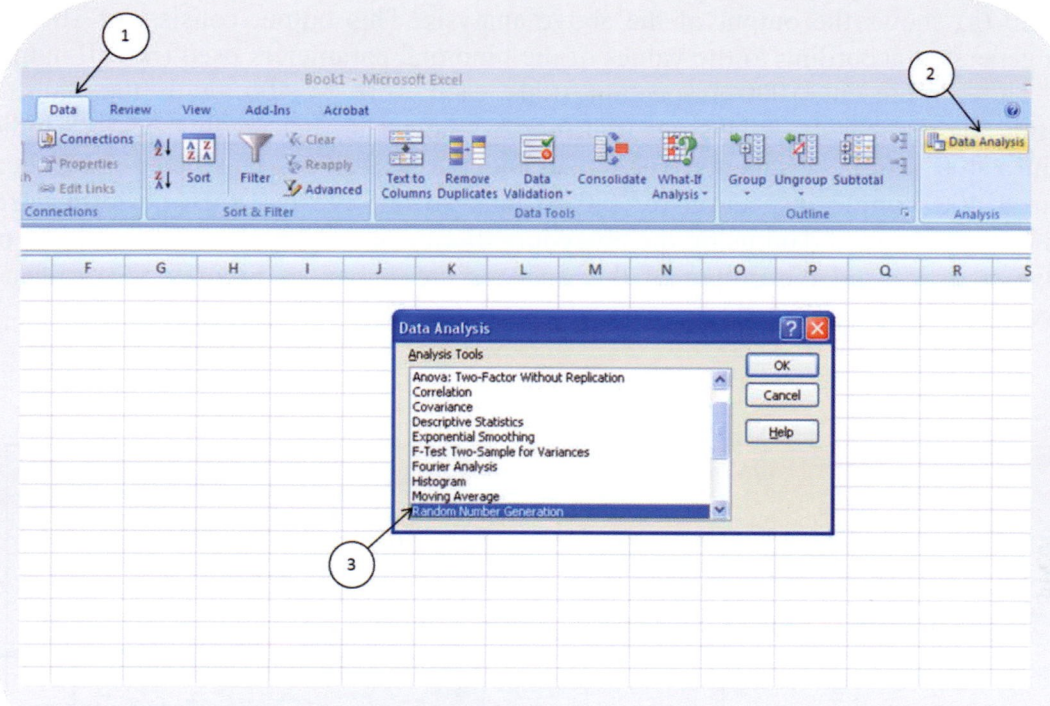

Figure 5.18 Using Excel® to Simulate Binomial Distribution-Steps 1 through 3

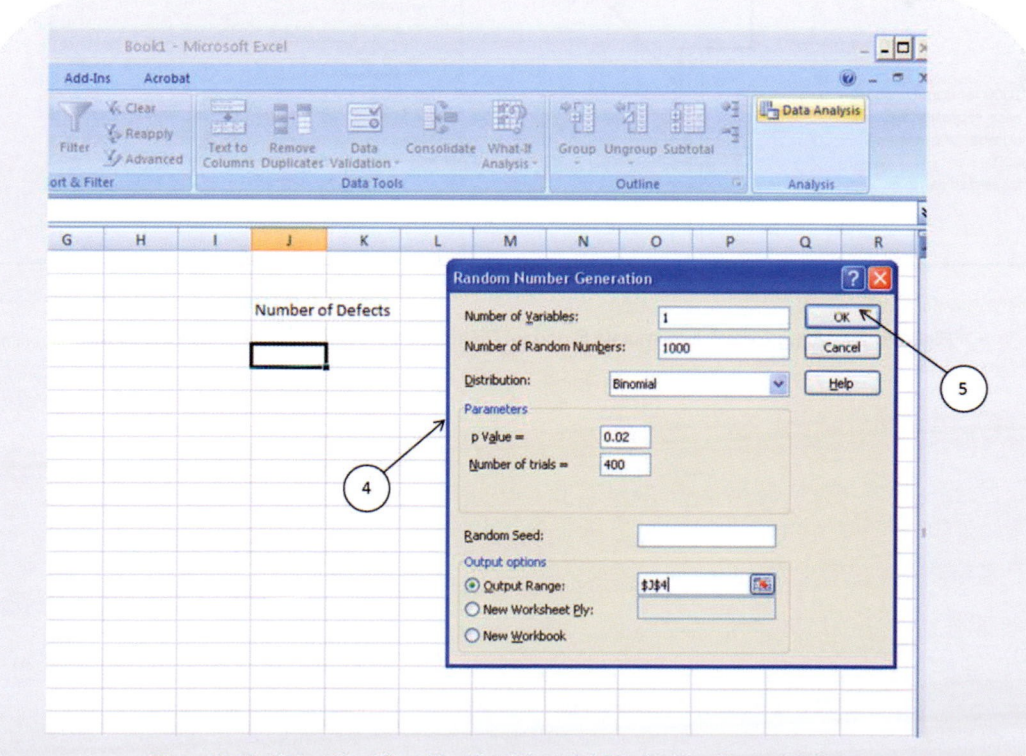

Figure 5.19 Using Excel® to Simulate Binomial Distribution-Steps 4 & 5

Figure 5.20 (a) shows the output of the above analysis. This output consists of 1000 random numbers generated according to the values of the binomial parameters used (not all numbers are shown). These represent 1000 inspection trials each of $n = 400$, with the value shown representing the number of defects per trial. For example, the first reading being 8 indicates 8 defects in a 400 sample inspection (or 0.02), and the second reading being 10 indicates 10 defects in a 400 sample inspection (or 0.025), and so on. We can then perform descriptive statistics to the generated data using the procedure discussed in Chapter 2. The steps to perform descriptive statistics and the output of this analysis are shown in Figures 5.20 (b) and 5.21, respectively.

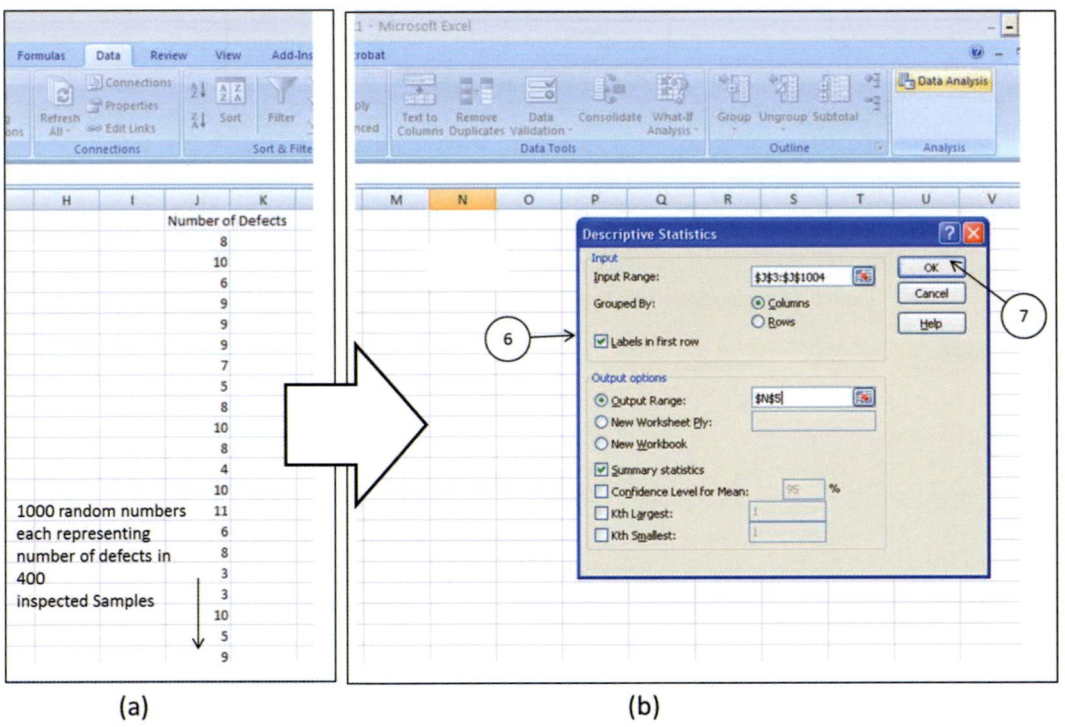

(a)   (b)

Figure 5.20 Using Excel® to Simulate Binomial Distribution-Descriptive Statistics: Steps 6 & 7

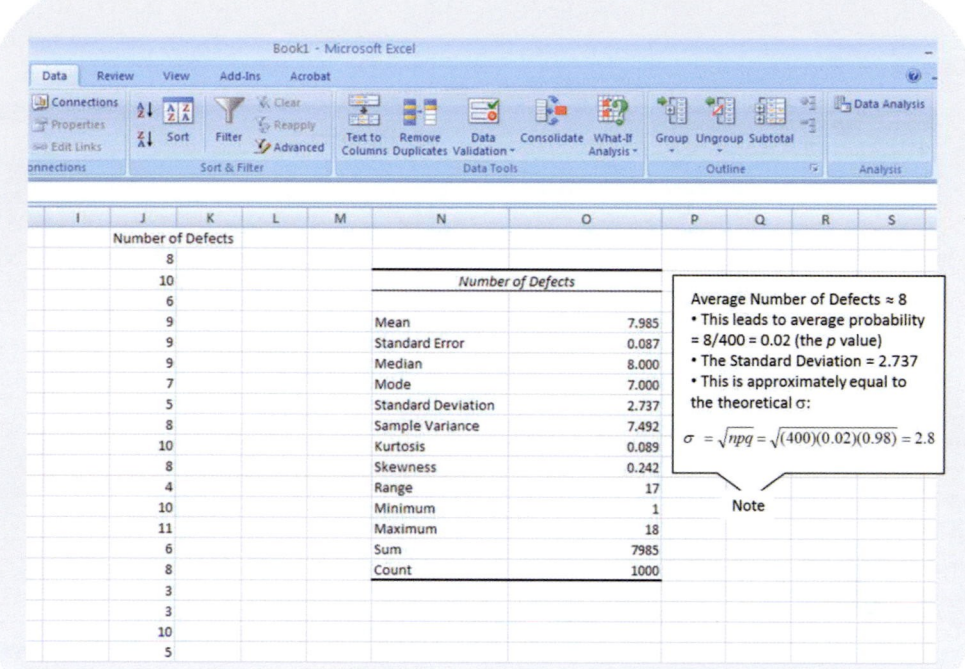

Figure 5.21 Output of Descriptive Statistics of Binomial Data

To construct a probability distribution, we first construct a histogram using the procedure discussed in Chapter 3 (see Figures 5.22 through 5.24). Since the variable in question is a discrete one, the bin range in this case should consist of integer values bounded by the minimum and maximum values obtained from the output of descriptive statistics.

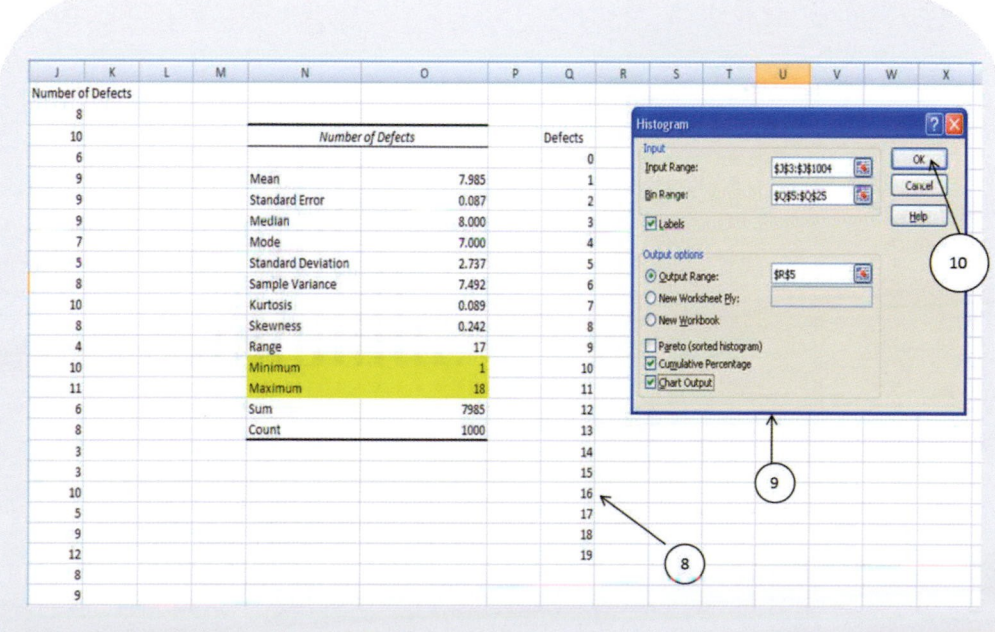

Figure 5.22 Using Excel® to Construct a Binomial Probability Distribution of the Simulated Data: Steps 8-10

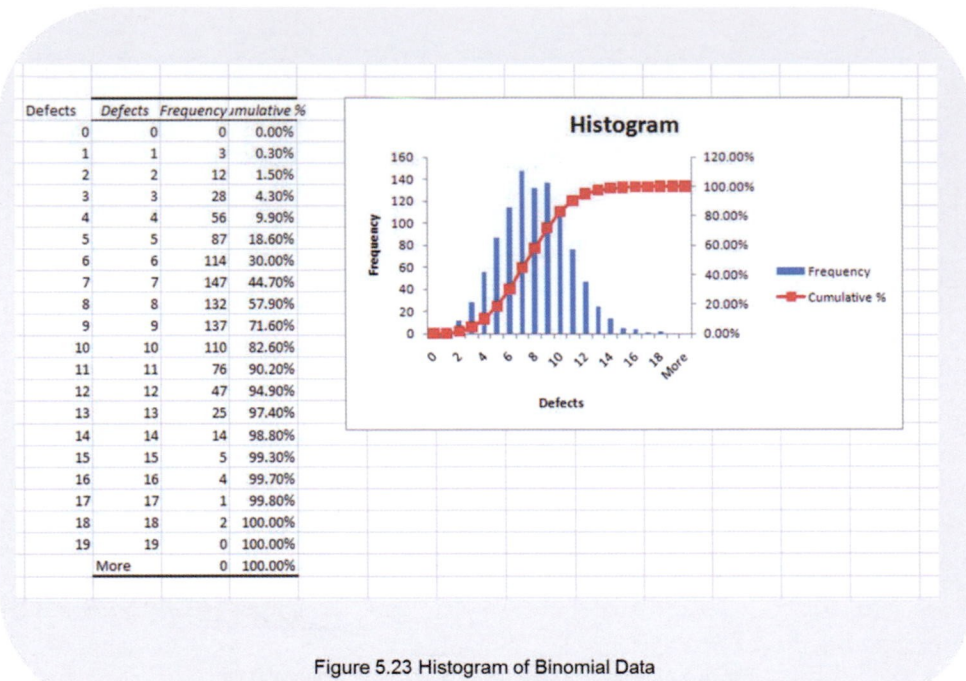

Figure 5.23 Histogram of Binomial Data

We can then convert the histogram into a probability distribution by calculating the relative frequencies corresponding to different frequencies (column 5 in the table of Figure 5.24) and plot a graph relating the mid points to the relative frequency, or $p(x)$.

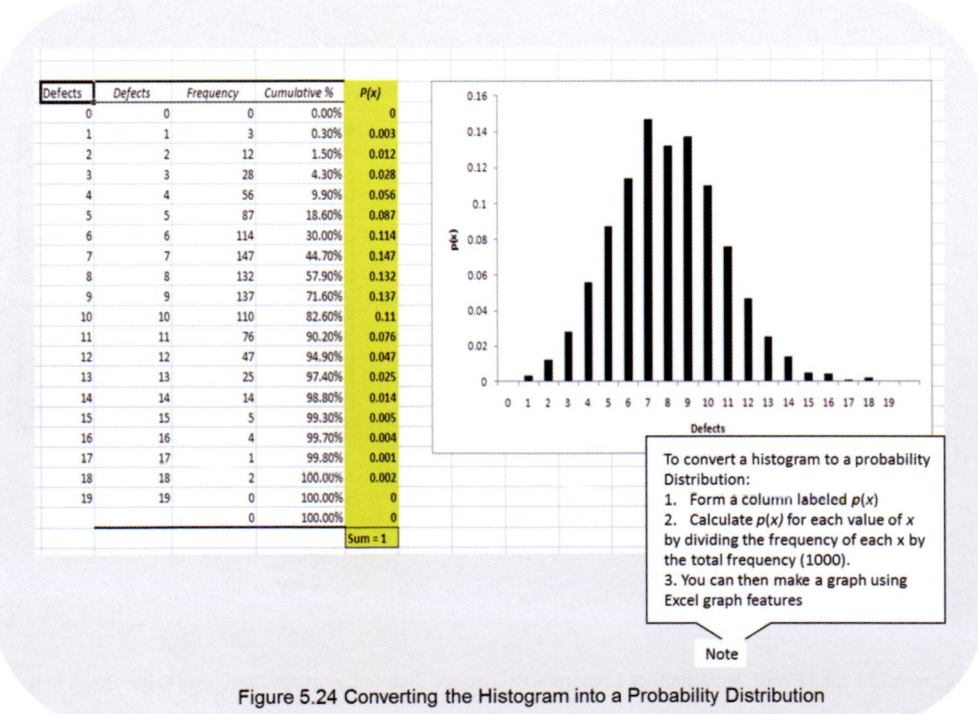

Figure 5.24 Converting the Histogram into a Probability Distribution

Example 5.17: A company producing notebook computers historically finds an average of 1.2 defects per shipment. Use Excel® Data Analysis to simulate the probability distribution of defects. Assume that shipment size is more or less constant.

Solution:

Assuming a Poisson distribution, we can simulate this variable using Microsoft Excel® Data Analysis and a similar procedure to the one discussed in the above example. As indicated earlier, a Poisson distribution is fully described by the parameter λ. In this case, $\lambda = 1.2$. We first go to 'Data Analysis,' and 'Random Number Generation.' We generate, say 1000 random numbers, select 'Poisson' as the distribution, and input the Poisson parameter $\lambda = 1.2$ as shown in Figure 5.25. When we specify an output area and press OK, 1000 random numbers following a Poisson distribution will be generated.

For the randomly generated data we can perform descriptive statistics and construct a histogram using the same steps of the previous example (see Figures 5.26 and 5.27). We can then convert the histogram into a probability distribution by calculating the relative frequencies corresponding to different frequencies (column 5 in the table of Figure 5.27) and plot a graph relating the mid points to the relative frequency, or $P(x)$.

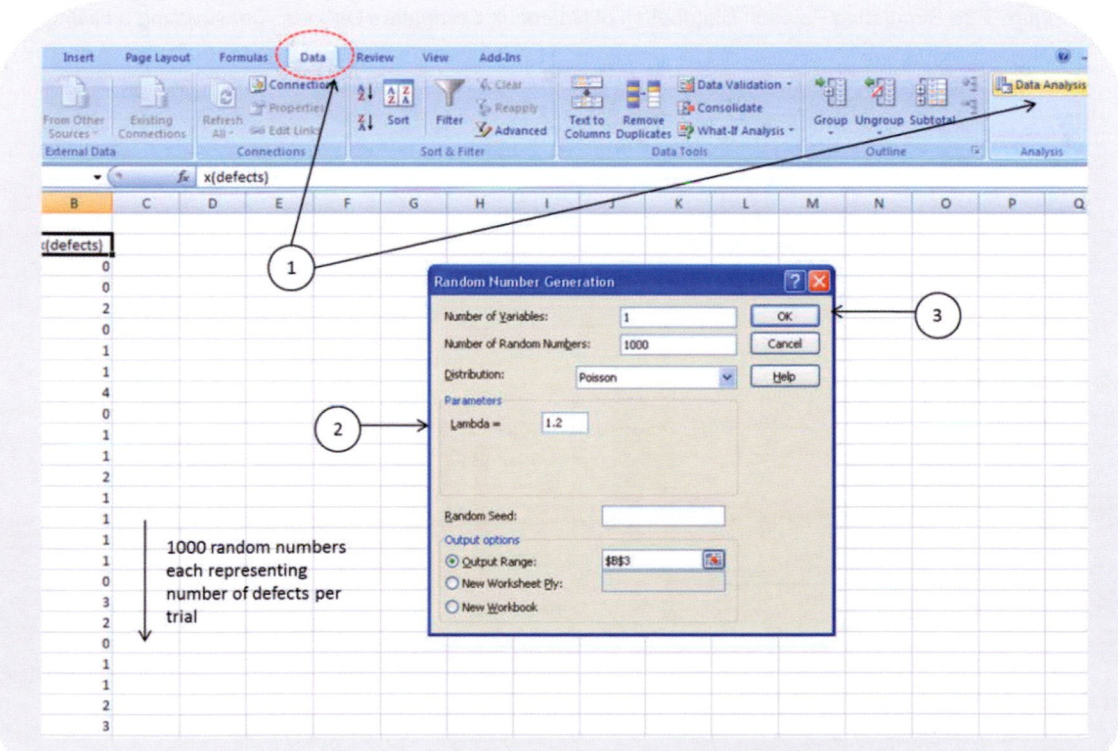

Figure 5.25 Simulating Poisson Distribution of Notebook Computers Defects: Steps 1, 2, and 3

297

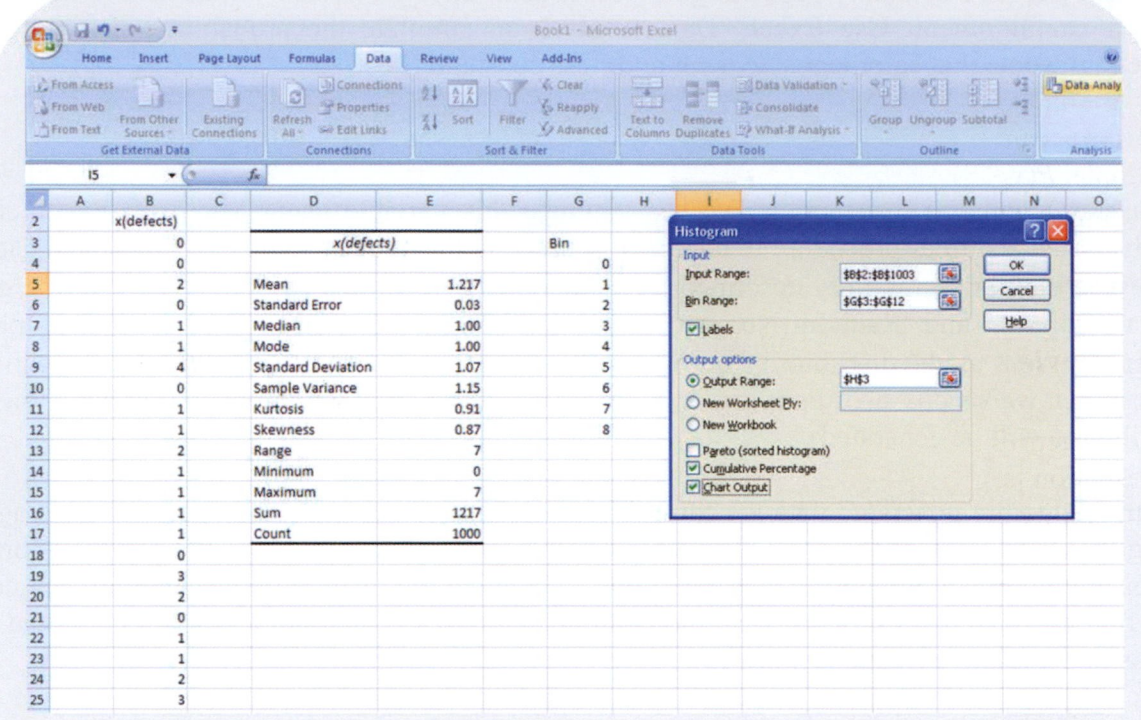

Figure 5.26 Simulating Poisson Distribution of Notebook Computers Defects: Constructing a Histogram

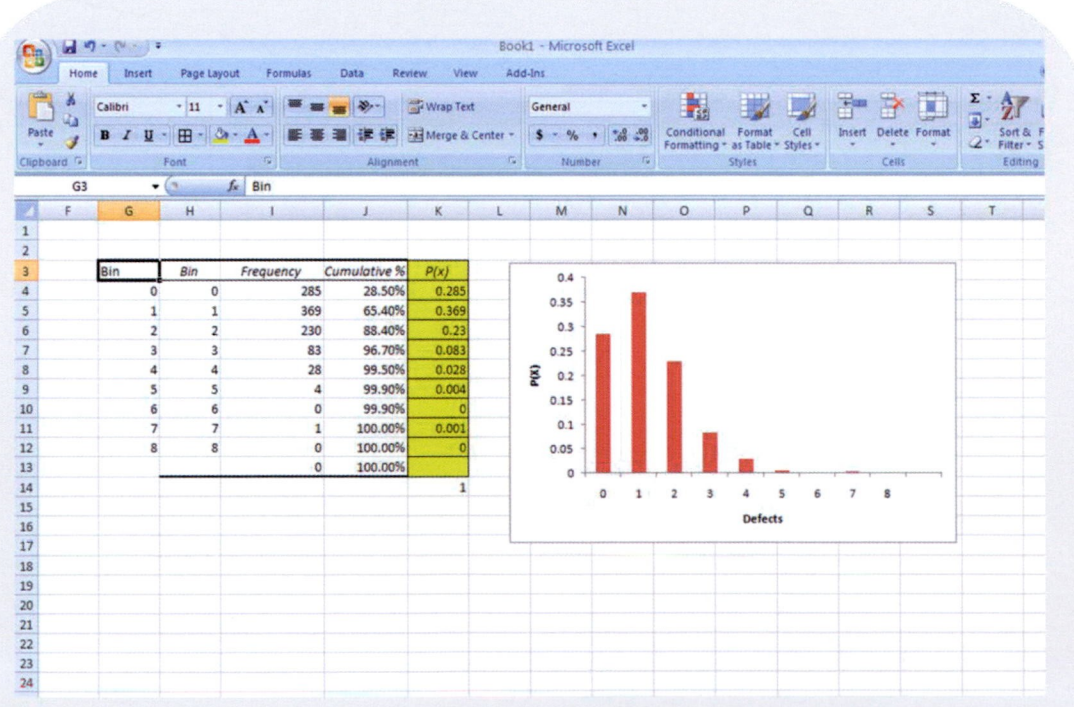

Figure 5.27 Simulating Poisson Distribution of Notebook Computers Defects: Constructing a Probability Distribution

The above procedure simulates a situation in which 1000 sample units were inspected, and the output numbers are the number of nonconforming notebooks found in each sample. In other words, the output of this analysis actually represents randomly generated values of the variable x, or the number of nonconforming notebooks. Note that using the Poisson distribution of Figure 5.27 one can determine the probability of nonconforming notebooks at any value of x. For example, $P(x \leq 3)$ represents the sum of the heights of the bars of the distribution at x values of 3, 2, 1, and 0, which is about 0.967 (or 0.083+0.230+0.369+0.285).

5.12 Review Exercises

P5.1: Determine whether a probability distribution is given. In those cases where a probability distribution is not described, identify the requirements that are not satisfied. In those cases where a probability distribution is described, find its mean (the expected value) and standard deviation.

(a)

x	P(x)
0	0.03125
1	0.15625
2	0.3125
3	0.3125
4	0.15625
5	0.03125

(b)

x	P(x)
0	0.2401
1	0.4116
2	0.2646
3	0.0756
4	0.0081

(c)

x	P(x)
0	0.00073
1	0.0102
2	0.05953
3	0.18522
4	0.32414
5	0.30253
6	0.11765

(d)

x	P(x)
0	0.32768
1	0.40960
2	0.13200
3	0.01110

(e)

x	P(x)
0	0.32768
1	0.15625
2	0.3125
3	0.05953
4	0.32414
5	0.03125

Answer: (a) Yes, (b) Yes, (c) Yes, (d) No, (e) No

P5.2: The following table lists the number of times a knitting machine stops accidentally every day expressed in probability form:

Probability of machine stops

Machine stops/day	Probability
0	0.30
1	0.25
2	0.24
3	0.21

- Find the mean number of stops per day for this machine
- Explain the meaning of the expected value of knitting stops

P5.3: In an experiment in which four coins are tossed, how many possible outcomes are expected? What are these outcomes? If the outcome of interest is 'head,' what are the probabilities of zero head, one head, two heads, three heads, and four heads? Construct a probability distribution illustrating this experiment.

Answer:

x	0	1	2	3	4
P(x)	0.0625	0.25	0.375	0.25	0.0625

P5.4: In a survey conducted by a real-estate broker, houses in a certain city were classified by the number of full bathrooms available. The results of this survey are shown in the table below. The first column represents the number of bathrooms, and the second column represents the number of houses. Construct a probability distribution representing this survey. If a house is picked from this area randomly, what is the chance that it will have 3 bathrooms? What is the chance that it will have less than 3 bathrooms?

Frequency of houses by the number of full bathrooms

Number of full bathrooms per house	1	2	3	4	5
Number of houses	45	410	320	38	12

P5.5: For the data of problem P5.4, calculate the mean and standard deviation of the discrete variable representing the number of bathrooms per house.
Answer: 2.472, 0.732

P5.6: A DVD manufacturer produces thousands of DVDs per day. On average, 2.0% of the DVDs do not conform to first quality specifications. Every day, an automatic inspection system selects a random sample of 1000 DVDs and classifies, through laser inspection, each DVD in the sample as conforming or nonconforming. Construct a binomial distribution of this variable. You may use Excel® to construct the distribution.

P5.7: The probability that a student passes a particular remedial mathematic course with a minimum of C grade is 0.60. Typically, a student who fails this course has to take it many times until he/she passes with a C-grade (the minimum grade required for passing).

   - What is the probability that a student will pass the course in the second trial?
   - What is the probability that a student will pass the course in the third or fourth trial?
Answer: 0.24, 0.1344

P5.8: In evaluating student attendance in a large history class, it was found that the mean number of a student failure to attend the class per week was 2 (the number of absences). Assuming that a Poisson distribution can best represent this variable, determine the probability that in any given week selected randomly, five absences will occur in this class? What is the probability that in any given week, less than three absences will be encountered? Determine the mean and variance of the Poisson distribution.

P5.9: Suppose in a bottling company, the average percentage of overfilled bottles is 1%. Find the probability that in a sample of 10 bottles chosen at random exactly one bottle will be overfilled? Calculate this probability using a binomial and a Poisson distribution.
Answer: Binomial (0.09135), Poisson (0.0905)

P5.10: Given the data in Problem 5.9, use Excel® or other software programs to construct a binomial and a Poisson distribution and compare the results.

P5.11: If the delay record of an airline company due to reasons unrelated to weather is assumed to follow a Poisson distribution with a mean value 0.5 per month.

300

- What is the probability of finding 2 delays per month?
- What is the probability of finding at most 2 delays per month?
- What is the probability of finding at least one delay per month?

Answer: 0.0758, 0.986, 0.393

P5.12: Thirty flights take off daily from Atlanta Airport, Georgia to Newark Airport, New Jersey via Delta Airline. Suppose the probability that any flight will be nonstop is 0.40.
- Construct a binomial probability distribution
- Calculate the expected value and the variance
- What is the probability that none of the flights will be nonstop?
- What is the probability that exactly three flights will be nonstop?

P5.13: In a multiple-choice exam of 100 questions, 4 possible answers were assigned for each question and only one answer is correct. If a student is answering these questions randomly, explain why this can be considered as a binomial experiment?

Answer: a fixed number of trials $= n = 100$; independent trials (the answer of one question is independent of the answer of another question); each trial is associated with two outcomes, correct or wrong; and each trial is associated with fixed probability $p = 1/4$, since the chance of a correct answer is one out of four.

P5.14: In Problem 5.13, what are the values of the two parameters, n and p of the binomial distribution? Calculate the expected value and the variance. What is the chance to answer exactly 20 questions correctly? What is the chance to answer exactly 30 questions correctly?

P5.15: Based on some social studies on marriage in a European country, it was revealed that the probability that one will be successful in his/her marriage is 0.40.

(a) What is the name of the discrete probability distribution used to solve this problem?
(b) Find the probability that for a person who married multiple times, his/her true success will be in the second marriage.
(c) Find the probability that for a person who married multiple times, his/her true success will be in the third marriage.
(d) Find the probability that for a person who married multiple times, his/her true success will occur in the second or third marriage.

Answer: (a) Geometric (b) $P(x) = p(1-p)^{x-1}$ $P(2) = (0.4)(1-0.4)^{2-1} = 0.24$ (c) 0.144, (d) 0.384

P5.16: Based on some social studies on marriage in an African country, it was revealed that the probability that one will be successful in his/her marriage is 0.65.

(a) What is the name of the discrete probability distribution used to solve this problem?
(b) Find the probability that for a person who married multiple times, his/her true success will be in the second marriage.
(c) Find the probability that for a person who married multiple times, his/her true success will be in the third marriage.

301

(d) Find the probability that for a person who married multiple times, his/her true success will occur in the second or third marriage.

P5.17: From experience, an anti-smoking organization knows that the chance of convincing smokers to quit smoking is 0.40. What is the name of the discrete probability distribution used to solve this problem? In a large campaign conducted during the smoke-out day, find the probability that the organization's first smoker to quit will occur on its fourth or fifth trial.
Answer: Geometric, 0.13824

P5.18: In soft-tech Company there are 60 employees in the programming staff. Forty of these belong to Microsoft partnership organization and twenty do not. If five employees are selected randomly for a cooperative project with Microsoft, what is the probability that four of the five selected for the committee belong to the Microsoft partnership organization.
Hint: This is a hypergeometric distribution problem.

P5.19: A college has 80 faculty members. Twenty of these are non-tenured and sixty are tenured. If ten faculty members are selected randomly to attend a conference, what is the probability that eight of the ten faculty members are non-tenured?
Answer: This is a hypergeometric distribution problem
The population in this case is the 80 faculty members. A faculty member can be selected for attending the conference only once. Hence, the sampling is done without replacement. Thus, the probability of selecting a non-tenured faculty, for example, changes from one trial to the next. The hypergeometric distribution is appropriate for determining the probability. In this problem: N is 80, the number of employees, S is 20, the number of non-tenured faculty, x is 8, the number of non-tenured faculty selected, and n is 10, the number of faculty selected. (0.00014)

P5.20: The mean number of on-site accidental deaths per year in an electric-service company is 0.2. Assuming that a Poisson distribution can best represent this random variable, determine the probability that in any given year, one on-site accidental death will occur? Construct the Poison distribution describing this variable. What is the mean and variance of this distribution?

P5.21: A fast-food restaurant tried to extend breakfast service from 10 am to 10:30 am to allow more customers, particularly those who wake up late, to be served breakfast. From past experience, the restaurant found that on average, the number of people showing up for breakfast service from 10:00 am to 10:30 am is only 3 people. What advice would you give this restaurant? To assist you in this task, the restaurant will allow the service to be extended if they can maintain more than 4 customers coming for breakfast service in this period. What is the chance that the restaurant will maintain more than 4 customers during the added period? What is the chance that the restaurant will maintain more than 7 customers during the added period?
Answer: 0.18474, 0.01190

P5.22: Suppose historically a machine producing bolts yields a rate of 10% defective bolts. Find the probability that in a sample of 10 bolts chosen at random exactly two will be defective? Calculate this probability using Binomial and Poisson distributions.

P5.23: If the number of some type of metal defects is assumed to follow a Poisson distribution with a mean value 1 per 1000 square yard.
   (a) What is the probability of finding 2 defects?

302

(b) What is the probability of finding at most 2 defects?
(c) What is the probability of finding at least 1 defect?
Answer: 0.184, 0.920, 0.632

P5.24: Suppose a new knitting machine used by a mill only fails to operate one time every 10 hours. This leads to a failure rate, λ, of 0.1 failure per hour. What is the probability of two failures occurring randomly per one hour?

P5.25: Using Excel Random Number Generation tool, generate a probability distribution of the last two digits of a telephone number. Each digit has the same chance of being randomly generated. Find the mean and standard deviation and describe the shape of the probability histogram.
Answer: Use Excel Random Number Generation, Uniform Distribution, Min = 0, and Max = 9. Generate 1000 number

P5.26: According to the U.S. National Center for Health Statistics in *Vital Statistics of the United States*, there is roughly an 80% chance that a person aged 20 will be alive at age 65. Suppose that three people aged 20 are selected at random.

- Find the probability that the number alive at age 65 will be
a. exactly two.   b. at most two.   c. at most one   d. at least one.
- Construct the binomial probability distribution
- Determine the mean and the standard deviation of the binomial distribution

P5.27: A professor of statistics plans to give a surprise test consisting of 4 multiple-choice questions, each with 5 possible answers (a, b, c, d, e), one of which is correct. Suppose a student who was not prepared for the test makes random guesses. What is the probability that the student will have exactly 3 correct answers to the 4 questions? Is this a situation that can be represented by a binomial distribution? If the answer is yes, what are the values of p, n, and q? If the answer is yes, what is the mean and variance of the binomial distribution?
Answer: Yes, 0.02560, $\mu = 3.2$, $\sigma^2 = 0.64$

P5.28: A fast food chain has a famous sandwich with a recognition rate of 95% among customers. Assuming that we randomly select 10 people:
  a. The probability that exactly 5 of the 10 people recognize the sandwich
  b. The probability that exactly 9 of the 10 people recognize the sandwich
  c. The probability that the number of people who recognize the sandwich is more than 3
  d. Construct the probability distribution
  e. Determine the mean and the standard deviation

P5.29: One percent of all external hard drives manufactured by a large electronics company are defective. Five external hard drives are randomly selected from the production line of this company. The selected hard drives are inspected to determine whether each of them is defective or good. Is this experiment a binomial experiment? Explain why?
Answer: Yes, $p = 0.01$, $n = 5$

P5.30: At one of the major express delivery services in the U.S., providing an efficient delivery to customers is a top priority of the management. The company guarantees all packages will arrive within the specified time to the specified destination. It is known from past data that despite all efforts, 3% of the packages mailed through this company do not arrive at their destinations within the specified time. Suppose a customer mails 10 packages through this express delivery service on a certain day.

(a) Find the probability that exactly one of these 10 packages will not arrive at its destination within the specified time.
(b) Find the probability that at most one of these 10 packages will not arrive at its destination within the specified time.

P5.31: Rex Hospital keeps records of emergency room (ER) traffic. Those records indicate that the number of patients arriving between 5:00 P.M. and 8:00 P.M. has a Poisson distribution with parameter $\lambda = 4$. Determine the probability that, on a given day, the number of patients who arrive at the emergency room between 5:00 P.M. and 8:00 P.M. will be

a. exactly four.
b. at most two.
c. between four and 10, inclusive.
d. Obtain a table of probabilities for the random variable x, the number of patients arriving between 5:00 P.M. and 6:00 P.M. Stop when the probabilities become zero to three decimal places.
e. Use part (d) to construct a probability distribution for x.
f. Identify the shape of the probability distribution of x.
g. Determine the mean and the variance of x.
Answer: 0.19537, 0.23810, 0.56369, mean = 4.0, Variance = 4.0

P5.32: Rex Hospital keeps records of emergency room (ER) traffic. Those records indicate that the number of patients arriving between 3:00 A.M. and 8:00 A.M. has a Poisson distribution with parameter $\lambda = 1.5$. Determine the probability that, on a given day, the number of patients who arrive at the emergency room between 3:00 A.M. and 8:00 A.M. will be

a. exactly four.
b. at most two.
c. between four and 10, inclusive.
d. Obtain a table of probabilities for the random variable x, the number of patients arriving between 5:00 A.M. and 6:00 A.M. Stop when the probabilities become zero to three decimal places.
e. Use part (d) to construct a probability distribution for x.
f. Identify the shape of the probability distribution of x.
g. Determine the mean and the variance of x.

P5.33: In analyzing hits by a certain bomb during a war, an air force may divide an area into a number of regions of fixed areas and determine the total number of bombs. Suppose an air force divided an area into 40 regions, each of 10 square miles, with the intention being to bomb the combined area with 15 bombs.

    A. If a region is randomly selected, find the probability that it was hit exactly one time
    B. If a region is randomly selected, find the probability that it was hit at most one time
    C. If a region is randomly selected, find the probability that it was hit at least two times
    D. Based on the probability values found in part (a), part (b), and part (c), how many of the 40 regions are expected to be hit exactly twice?
    E. Construct a Poisson distribution
    F. Find the mean and variance

P5.34: On average, a household receives 2 telemarketing phone calls per week. Using the Poisson distribution formula, what is the probability that a randomly selected household will receive exactly one telemarketing phone calls during a given week? Construct the probability distribution associated with this variable and determine its mean and standard deviation.

P5.35: A drink vending machine in a large mall breaks down an average of three times per month. Using the Poisson probability distribution formula, find the probability that during the next month this machine will have (a) exactly two breakdowns (b) at most one breakdown. Construct the probability distribution and determine the mean and standard deviation.
Answer: 0.22404, 0.19915, 3.0, 3.0

P5.36: An educational organization conducted a study to determine whether there were significant differences in passing rates in college algebra admission test between students admitted freshly out of the high school and adult students who have been away from schools for at least 10 years after high school. It was found that the passing rate was 94% for students admitted freshly out of the high school.

(A) If 10 of the students admitted freshly out of the high school are randomly selected, find the probability that at least 9 of them passed college algebra admission test
(B) Would it be unusual to randomly select 10 students from the students admitted freshly out of the high school and get only 7 that passed? Why or why not?

P5.37: A television station broadcast an interview with the president of the U.S.A. and received a share of 22, meaning that among the TV sets in use, 22% were tuned to that interview (based on data from Nielsen Media Research). An advertiser wants to obtain a second opinion by conducting its own survey, and a pilot survey begins with 20 households having TV sets in use at the time of the interview.

    a. Find the probability that none of the households are tuned to the interview
    b. Find the probability that at least one household is tuned to the interview
    c. Find the probability that at most one household is tuned to the interview
    d. If at most one household is tuned to the interview, does it appear that the 22% share value is wrong? Why or why not?
Answer: (a) 0.00695, (b) 0.993, (c) 0.0461, (d) Yes. With a 22 share, there is a very small chance of getting at most one household turned to the interview, so it appears that the share is not 22.

P5.38: Each year, the U.S. Department of Energy publishes an *Annual Energy Review* that includes per capita energy consumption (in millions of Btu) for each of the 50 states. If you calculate the mean of these 50 values, does the result represent the mean per capita energy consumption for the total population from all 50 states combined? If it is not, explain how you would use those 50 values to calculate the mean per capita energy consumption for the total population from all 50 states combined.

P5.39: According to data from the American Medical Association, 10% of the people are left-handed.
  (A) If three people are randomly selected, find the probability that they are all left-handed.
  (B) If three people are randomly selected, find the probability that at least one of them is left-handed.
Answer: (A) 0.001, (B) 0.271

P5.40: When a balanced coin is tossed three times, how many equally likely outcomes can be obtained? What are these outcomes? If x denote the total number of heads obtained in the three tosses, would you consider x as a continuous or a discrete random variable? What are the possible values of x? What is $P(x=2)$? What is $P(x<2)$? What is $P(x>2)$?

P5.41: Determine the values of:
$(a) \binom{7}{3}$ $(b) \binom{5}{5}$ $(c) \binom{20}{4}$ $(d) \binom{5}{3}$
Answer: 35, 1, 4845, 10

P5.42: A private transportation company normally runs twenty city bus trips from downtown Atlanta to Atlanta Airport. Suppose the chance that any bus arrives late is 0.15. What is the probability that none of the buses will be late today? What is the probability that at least one bus will be late today? What is the probability that more than two busses will be late today? What is the probability that three busses or less will be late today?

P5.43: During holidays, package delivery encounters some delay that is often inevitable due to the high mass of delivery. An express delivery company defines delay as any delivery that is one day or more after the specified delivery date. This company finds that during Christmas, the rate of delay is 3%. Suppose a family mails 10 packages through this express delivery company. What is the probability that exactly one of the 10 packages will be delayed? What is the probability that at most one of the 10 packages will be delayed? In solving this problem, use the binomial function.
Answer: 0.228, 0.965

P5.44: Solve the previous problem using Poisson distribution.

CHAPTER 6

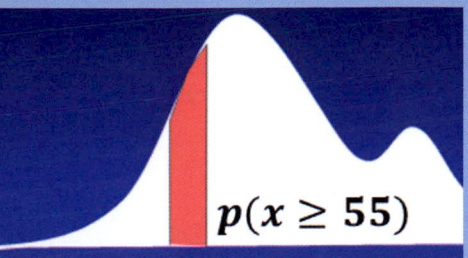

$p(x \geq 55)$

Probability Distributions
Part II: Continuous Variables

After completing this chapter, students will be able to:

- *Understand the meaning of a probability distribution of a continuous variable*
- *Determine probabilities associated with a uniform distribution*
- *Determine probabilities associated with a normal distribution*
- *Simulate variables following a uniform or a normal distribution*

APEX®

CHAPTER 6

In Chapter 5, we discussed probability distributions for discrete variables. In this chapter, we discuss probability distributions for continuous variables. A continuous variable is a variable that can take any value in a specified interval falling within its plausible range. Examples of continuous variables include: people income, student grades, human weight, home market values, material strength, and operational costs. The two key distributions discussed in this Chapter are: the uniform distribution and the normal distribution.

CHAPTER CONTENTS

6.1 What is a probability distribution for continuous variables?

In chapter 5, we introduced probability distributions and divided them into two main types: probability distributions for discrete variables and probability distributions for continuous variables. We also introduced probability distributions for discrete variables such as the binomial and the Poisson distribution. In this chapter, we turn our attention to probability distributions for continuous variables. Recall that a continuous variable can take any value in a specified interval falling within its plausible range. For example, the diameter of a fine metal rod may take a value of 40, 40.25, 40.75 or 41 millimeters, and human weight may take a value of 120 pounds, 155 pounds, or 165.8 pounds. These data imply continuity in the variable values. Therefore, variables of this type are called continuous variables.

A probability distribution for a continuous variable is a relative frequency distribution of a large amount of data, representing all possible outcomes of values of a continuous variable. The following example illustrates the concept of a probability distribution.

Example 6.1: Suppose 5000 students took a course on statistics in a college over the last 5 years and the results of their grades are displayed by the frequency distribution of Table 6.1.

Table 6.1 Frequency distribution of students' grades in a statistics course

Student grades (%)	Number of students (frequency, f)
20 to < 30	16
30 to < 40	20
40 to < 50	98
50 to < 60	256
60 to < 70	1490
70 to < 80	1675
80 to < 90	1111
90 to < 100	334
	N − 5000

The frequency distribution of the data in Table 6.1 is shown in Figure 6.1. We can also calculate the relative frequency for each class, as discussed in Chapter 3, and construct a relative frequency distribution as shown in Figure 6.2. This distribution virtually simulates all grade categories and their possible relative frequencies. On this ground, it can be considered as a probability distribution of student's grades.

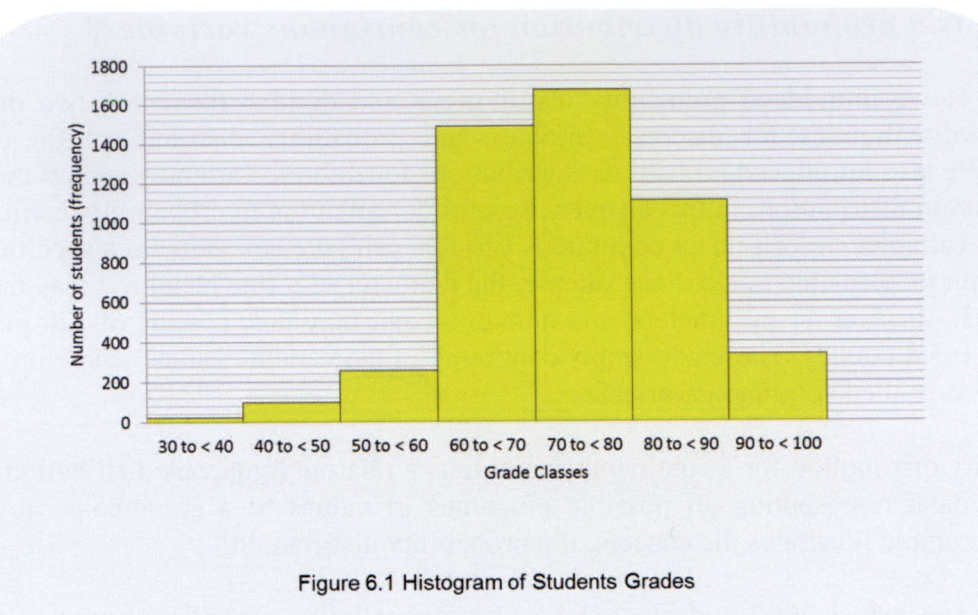

Figure 6.1 Histogram of Students Grades

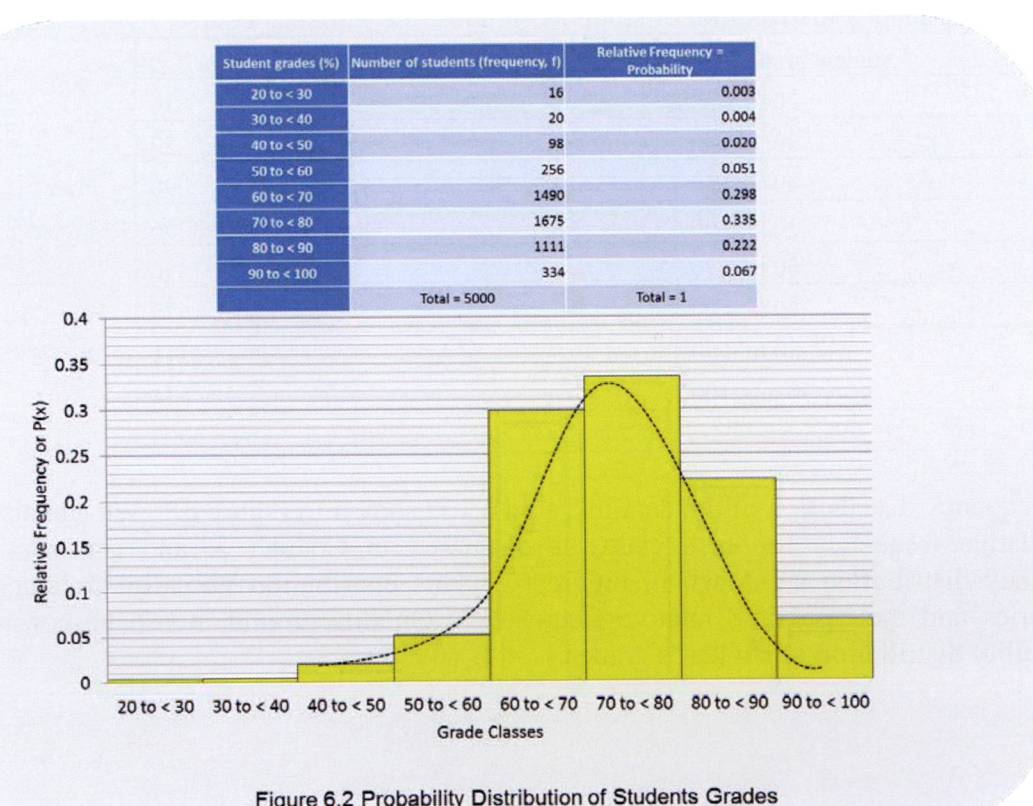

Student grades (%)	Number of students (frequency, f)	Relative Frequency = Probability
20 to < 30	16	0.003
30 to < 40	20	0.004
40 to < 50	98	0.020
50 to < 60	256	0.051
60 to < 70	1490	0.298
70 to < 80	1675	0.335
80 to < 90	1111	0.222
90 to < 100	334	0.067
	Total = 5000	Total = 1

Figure 6.2 Probability Distribution of Students Grades

In order to calculate the mean (or the expected value) and the variance of students' grades, we should determine the midpoints of the different classes, and the relative frequency of probability values, or $P(x)$ as shown in Table 6.2. A key characteristic of a probability distribution of a continuous variable is that the area under the probability distribution curve is equal to one. This is a direct result of the fact that the sum of relative frequencies (or probabilities) always equals to one as shown in column 4, Table 6.2.

Table 6.2 Calculations of probability values of students' grades

Student grades (%)	Mid-point (x)	Number of students (frequency, f)	Relative frequency, or $P(x)$
20 to < 30	25	16	0.0032
30 to < 40	35	20	0.0040
40 to < 50	45	98	0.0196
50 to < 60	55	256	0.0512
60 to < 70	65	1490	0.2980
70 to < 80	75	1675	0.3350
80 to < 90	85	1111	0.2222
90 to < 100	95	334	0.0668
		$n = 5000$	Sum = 1

The mean value of the variable x can be obtained from:

$$\mu = \sum x\,P(x) \qquad (6.1)$$

As indicated earlier, the mean is a typical value used to represent the central location of a probability distribution. The mean of a probability distribution is also referred to as its **expected value**. It is a weighted average where the possible values of a random variable are weighted by their corresponding probabilities of occurrence.

The standard deviation can be obtained from:

$$\sigma = \sqrt{\sum [(x - \mu)^2 . P(x)]} = \sqrt{\sum x^2 P(x) - \mu^2} \qquad (6.2)$$

Accordingly,

$$\mu = \sum x\,P(x) = 0.08 + 0.14 + \cdots + 18.89 + 6.35 \approx 73.7$$

$$\sigma^2 = \sum (x - \mu)^2 . P(x) = 7.57 + 5.97 + \cdots + 28.64 + 30.46 \approx 129.4$$

Table 6.3 illustrates the different steps followed to perform these calculations.

311

Table 6.3 Calculations of mean and standard deviation of students' grades

Student grades (%)	Mid-point (x)	Number of students-(frequency, f)	Relative frequency $p(x)$	$x \cdot p(x)$	$(x-\mu)^2$	$p(x) \cdot (x-\mu)^2$
20 to < 30	25	16	(16/5000 = 0.0032)	(25×0.0032 = 0.08)	$(25-73.7)^2$ = 2366.43	(0.0032×2366.43 = 7.57)
30 to < 40	35	20	0.0040	0.14	1493.51	5.97
40 to < 50	45	98	0.0196	0.88	820.59	16.08
50 to < 60	55	256	0.0512	2.82	347.67	17.8
60 to < 70	65	1490	0.2980	19.37	74.75	22.28
70 to < 80	75	1675	0.3350	25.13	1.83	0.61
80 to < 90	85	1111	0.2222	18.89	128.91	28.64
90 to < 100	95	334	0.0668	6.35	455.99	30.46
		N= 5000	Sum= 1	Mean, $\mu = \sum x\,P(x) = 0.08 + 0.14 + 0.88 + \cdots + 6.35) \approx 73.7$		Variance = $\sigma^2 = \sum P(x)(x-\mu)^2 = 7.57 + 5.97 + 16.08 + \cdots + 30.46 \approx 129.4$

The example above demonstrates how a probability distribution of a continuous variable can be developed. In the following sections, we discuss two main types of probability distributions of continuous variables: the uniform distribution and the normal distribution. These distributions are used in many practical applications.

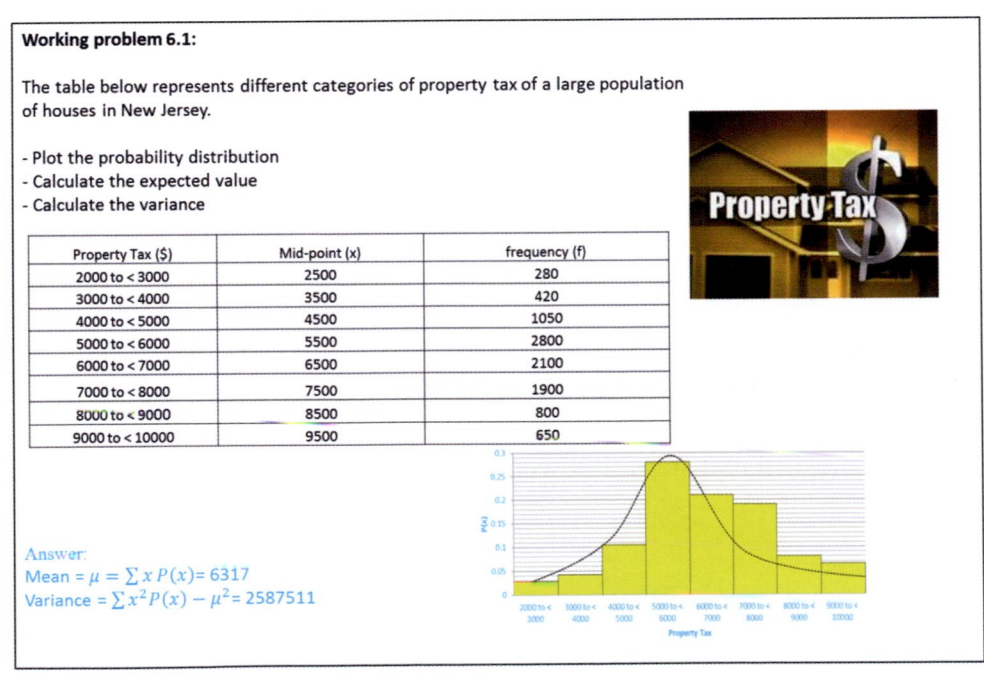

Working problem 6.1:

The table below represents different categories of property tax of a large population of houses in New Jersey.

- Plot the probability distribution
- Calculate the expected value
- Calculate the variance

Property Tax ($)	Mid-point (x)	frequency (f)
2000 to < 3000	2500	280
3000 to < 4000	3500	420
4000 to < 5000	4500	1050
5000 to < 6000	5500	2800
6000 to < 7000	6500	2100
7000 to < 8000	7500	1900
8000 to < 9000	8500	800
9000 to < 10000	9500	650

Answer:
Mean = $\mu = \sum x\,P(x)$ = 6317
Variance = $\sum x^2 P(x) - \mu^2$ = 2587511

6.2 The uniform probability distribution for continuous variables

The simplest type of probability distributions for continuous variables is the uniform distribution. Ideally, the uniform distribution is rectangular in shape as a result of the fact that different data classes exhibit the same probability. The distribution is fully defined by two parameters: the minimum and the maximum value of a variable. Mathematically, the uniform distribution is expressed by the following function:

$$P(x) = \frac{1}{b-a} \qquad (6.3)$$

$$if \ a \le x \le b, and \ x = 0 \ elsewhere$$

Figure 6.3 shows a typical shape of a uniform distribution. Note that the minimum value is 'a' and the maximum value is 'b.' The height of the distribution is constant (1/b-a), which reflects a uniform frequency over the entire range of the variable value. Also note that the area under the curve is one, or $(b-a) \times \frac{1}{b-a}$.

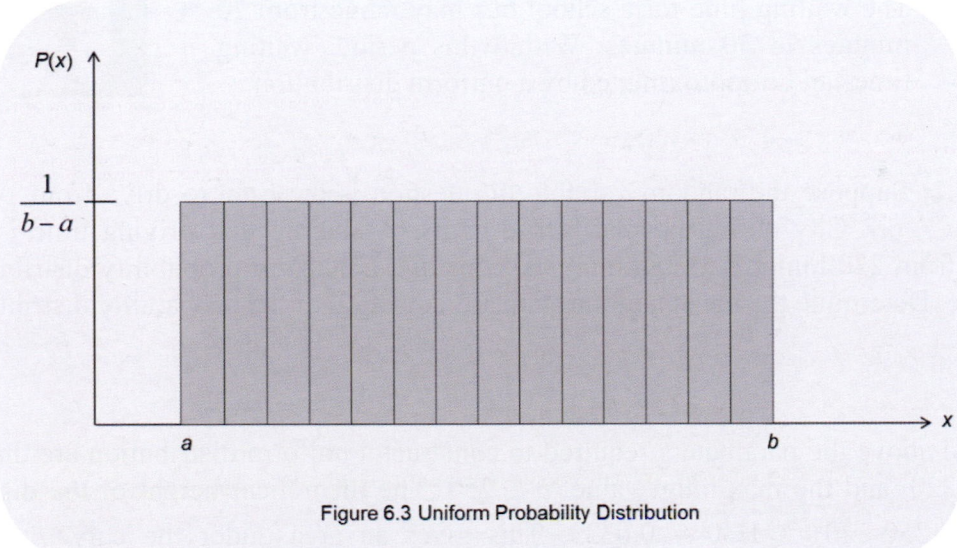

Figure 6.3 Uniform Probability Distribution

It should be noted that a uniform distribution can also be used to model discrete variables.

The mean and standard deviation of the uniform distribution are obtained from the following equations:

$$\mu = \frac{a+b}{2} \qquad (6.4)$$

$$\sigma = \sqrt{\frac{(b-a)^2}{12}} \qquad (6.5)$$

Examples of variables following a uniform distribution:

- The time to fly via a commercial airliner from one airport to another, say from Raleigh, North Carolina, to Atlanta, Georgia. This time may range from 55 minutes to 65 minutes. If you monitor the flying time for many commercial flights it will follow more or less a uniform distribution constrained by these two values.
- The time a student takes to finish a one-hour standard test may range from 50 minutes to 60 minutes. Within this interval, the variable can best be approximated by a uniform distribution.
- The time to deliver a pizza to a certain location in town may range from 20 minutes to 30 minutes from the time the delivery person leaves the store. Within this interval, the variable can best be approximated by a uniform distribution.
- The waiting time for a school bus may range from 20 minutes to 30 minutes. Within this period, waiting time can be approximated by a uniform distribution.

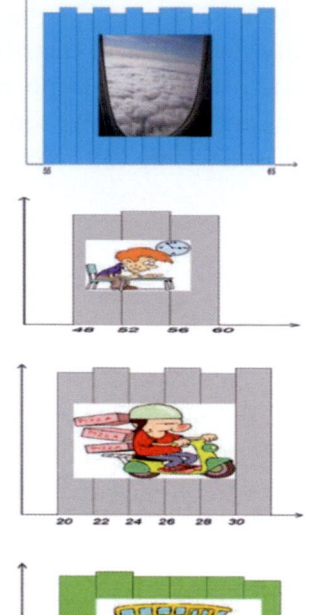

Example 6.2: Suppose the random variable in question is the time to drive from Washington, DC, to New York City during normal traffic hours. Assuming that driving time is uniformly distributed from 220 minutes to 250 minutes, construct a uniform probability distribution of the driving time. Determine the mean and the standard deviation of the probability distribution.

Solution:

As indicated above the parameters required to construct a uniform distribution are the minimum value, $a = 220$, and the maximum value, $b = 250$. The theoretical height of the distribution is $1/(b\text{-}a) = 1/(250\text{-}220) = 1/30 = 0.0333$. This gives an area under the curve $A = \frac{1}{30}(250 - 220) = 1$. Figure 6.4.a shows the shape of the uniform distribution of the driving time. Note that the distribution takes a rectangular shape with a minimum value of 220 and a maximum value of 250. The height of the distribution is constant and it represents a probability of 0.0333. The mean value is:

$$\mu = \frac{a + b}{2} = \frac{220 + 250}{2} = 235 \ minutes$$

The standard deviation of the distribution is

$$\sigma = \sqrt{\frac{(b - a)^2}{12}} = \sqrt{\frac{(250 - 220)^2}{12}} = 8.66 \ (\approx 9 \ minutes)$$

314

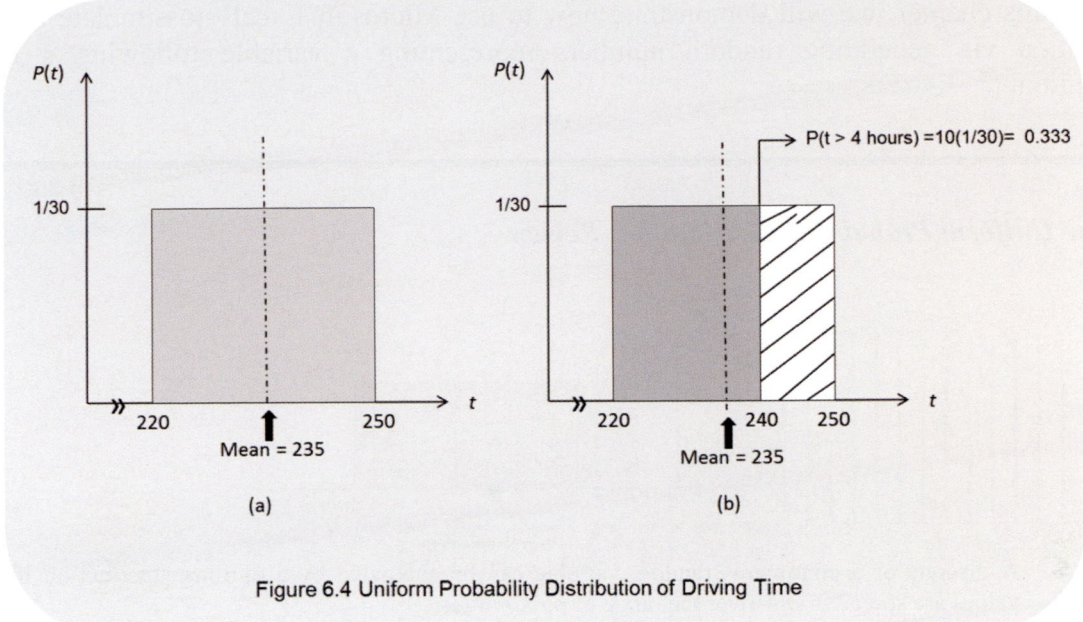

Figure 6.4 Uniform Probability Distribution of Driving Time

Example 6.3: Using the uniform distribution of the above example, answer the following questions:

1. On average, how long will it take a person typically to drive from Washington, DC, to New York City during normal traffic hours?
2. What is the chance that a person may spend more than 4 hours on the road driving from Washington, DC, to New York City during normal traffic hours?
3. What is the probability that a person will make the trip from Washington, DC, to New York City during normal traffic hours in less than 2 hours?

Solution:

1. The average driving time will indicate the typical drive time for a person from Washington, DC, to New York City during normal traffic hours:

$$\mu = \frac{a + b}{2} = \frac{220 + 250}{2} = 235 \; (or \; three \; hours \; and \; 55 \; minutes)$$

2. The probability a person may spend more than 4 hours on the road driving from Washington, DC, to New York City during normal traffic hours is shown by the dashed area of Figure 6.4.b. This area is 0.333. This may translate to about 33% chance of exceeding 4 hours of driving time between the two cities.

3. The probability a person will make the trip from Washington, DC, to New York City during normal traffic hours in less than 2 hours is zero as this value is outside the uniform distribution limits.

315

Later in this chapter, we will demonstrate how to use Microsoft Excel® to simulate a uniform distribution via generating random numbers representing a variable following a uniform distribution.

The Uniform Probability Distribution: Review

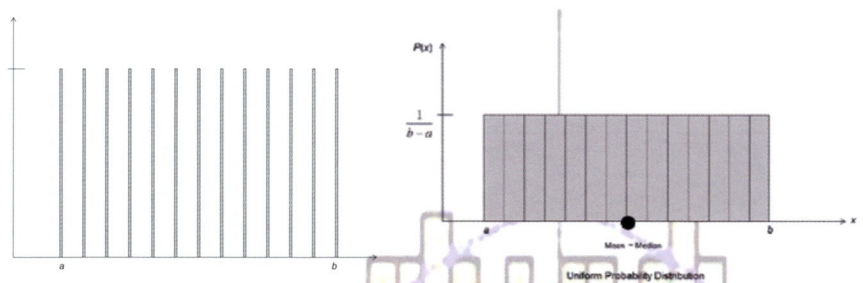

- A discrete or a continuous random variable can be simulated by a uniform distribution if its values are spread *evenly* over the range of possibilities.
- The uniform distribution is ideally rectangular in shape as a result of the fact that different data classes exhibit the same frequency or relative frequency.
- The distribution is fully defined by two parameters: the minimum and the maximum value of a variable. Mathematically, the uniform distribution is expressed by the following function:

$$P(x) = \frac{1}{b - a}$$
$$if \ a \leq x \leq b, and \ x = 0 \ elsewhere$$

- The mean and standard deviation of the uniform distribution are obtained from the equations:

$$\mu = \frac{a+b}{2} \qquad \& \quad \sigma = \sqrt{\frac{(b-a)^2}{12}}$$

- A uniform distribution has either no peaks or infinitely many peaks, depending on how you look at it. In any case, we do not classify a uniform distribution according to modality.

Working problem 6.2:

Your teacher is often late to the class. Let the random variable x represent the time from when the class is supposed to start until the time the teacher shows up. In addition, suppose that your teacher could be on time for some classes or up to 15 minutes late, with all intervals between 0 and 15 being equally likely. Construct a probability distribution for the random continuous variable, x. Determine the mean and the standard deviation?

Answer:
Mean = 7.5 minutes
Std. dev. = 4.33

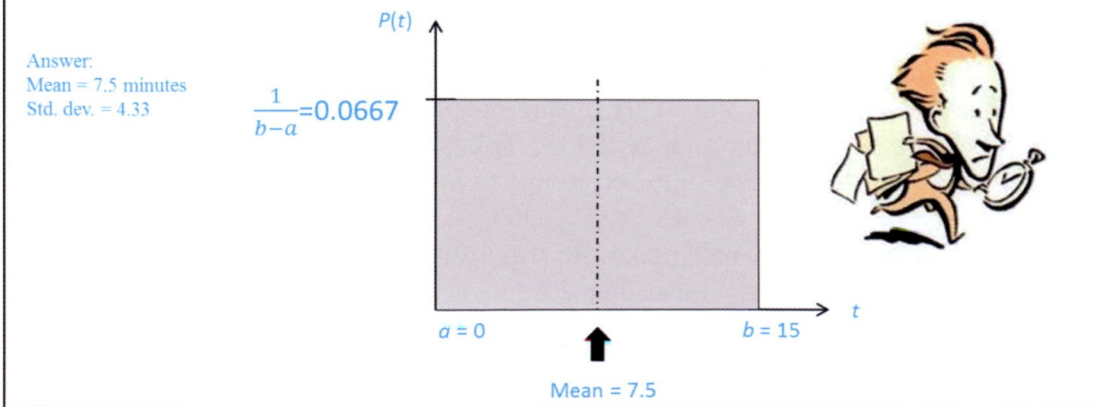

Working problem 6.3:

Your teacher is always late to the class. Let the random variable x represent the time from when the class is supposed to start until the teacher shows up. In addition, suppose that your teacher could be on time for some classes or up to 15 minutes late, with all intervals between 0 and 15 being equally likely.

- What is the probability that the teacher will arrive within 5 minutes from the start of the class?

- What is the probability that the teacher will arrive in more than 10 minutes from the start of the class?

$P(t \leq 5) = 0.3335$
$P(t > 10) = 0.3335$

$$\frac{1}{b-a} = \frac{1}{15-0} = 0.0667$$

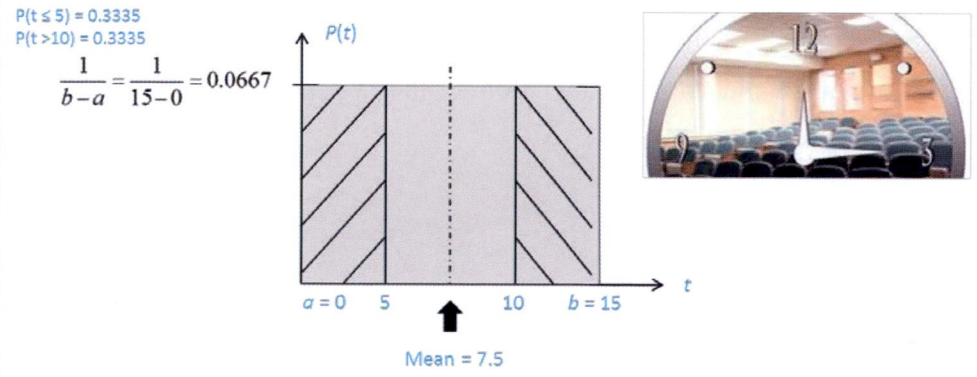

Mean = 7.5

Working problem 6.4:

Waiting period to see your eye doctor can be considered as a random variable x representing the time from signing in to the time you actually see the doctor. Suppose that your doctor could see you as soon as you sign in ($x = 0$) or up to 30 minutes late ($x = 30$) with all intervals between 0 and 30 being equally likely. Construct a probability distribution for the random continuous variable, x. Determine the mean and the standard deviation?

Answer:
Mean = 15 minute
Std. Dev. = 8.66 minutes

Working problem 6.5:

Waiting period to see your eye doctor can be considered as a random variable x representing the time from signing in to the time you actually see the doctor. Further suppose that your doctor could see you as soon as you sign in ($x = 0$) or up to 30 minutes late ($x = 30$) with all intervals between 0 and 30 being equally likely.

- What is the probability that your eye doctor will see you between 10 and 20 minutes?
- What is the probability that your eye doctor will see you in less than 5 minutes?

Answer:
What is the probability that your eye doctor will see you between 10 and 20 minutes?
$P(10 \leq t \leq 20) = (10)(0.0333) = 0.333$

$$\frac{1}{b-a} = \frac{1}{30-0} = 0.0333$$

What is the probability that your eye doctor will see you in less than 5 minutes
$P(t < 5) = (5)(0.0333) = 0.1665$

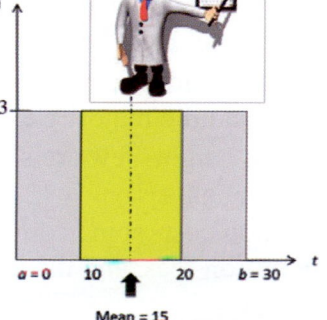

Mean = 15

6.3 The normal distribution

The normal distribution is considered by most statisticians as the distribution that can simulate the random behavior of virtually all continuous variables. The mathematical function of the normal distribution is:

$$P(x) = \frac{1}{\sigma\sqrt{2\pi}} e^{-(x-\mu)^2/2\sigma^2} \qquad (6.6)$$

$$-\infty \leq x \leq \infty$$

where μ and σ are the mean and standard deviation, or the two parameters of the normal distribution.

As shown in Figure 6.5, a normal distribution is bell-shaped and perfectly symmetrical. It also has equal values of mean, mode, and median. But, why is the distribution called 'normal?' In the last half of the nineteenth century, many researchers discovered that it is quite usual, or 'normal' for a variable to have a distribution

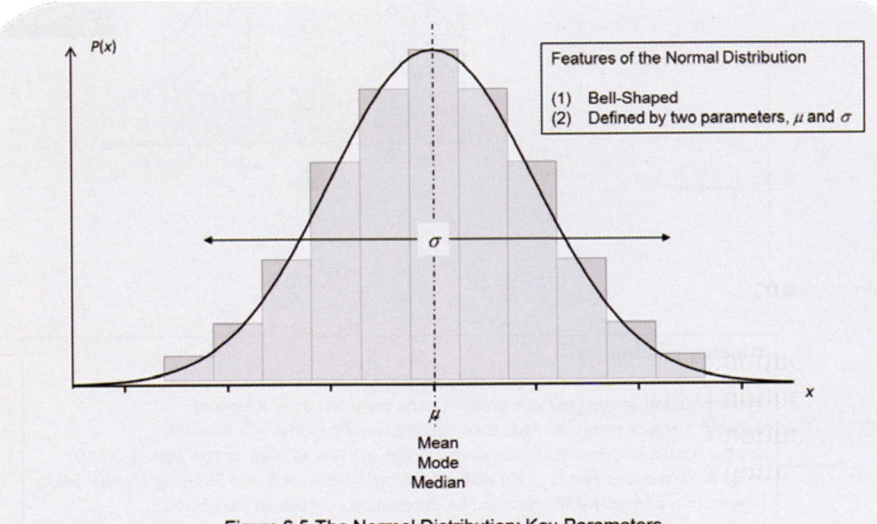

Figure 6.5 The Normal Distribution: Key Parameters

shaped like that of Figure 6.5. With the British statistician Karl Pearson leading the way, such a distribution began to be referred to as a *normal distribution*. It is also called 'Gaussian distribution' after Johann Carl Friedrich Gauss, the German mathematician who developed the normal function.

Examples of random variables following a normal distribution include:

- People's income in a given nation- few earn low income, few earn high income, and the majority earns middle income.
- Students' grades in a course- few earn low grades, few earn high grades, and the majority earns middle grades.
- People's height- few are short, few are tall, and the majority is of middle heights.
- Education cost- some colleges charge small tuition fees, some charge high tuition fees, and the majority charges tuition fees in between.

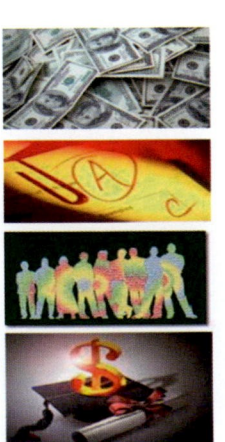

Example 6.4: Given the three normal distributions A, B, and C below:

- Which normal curve has the greatest mean and which has the lowest mean?
- Which normal curve has the greatest standard deviation and which has the lowest standard deviation?

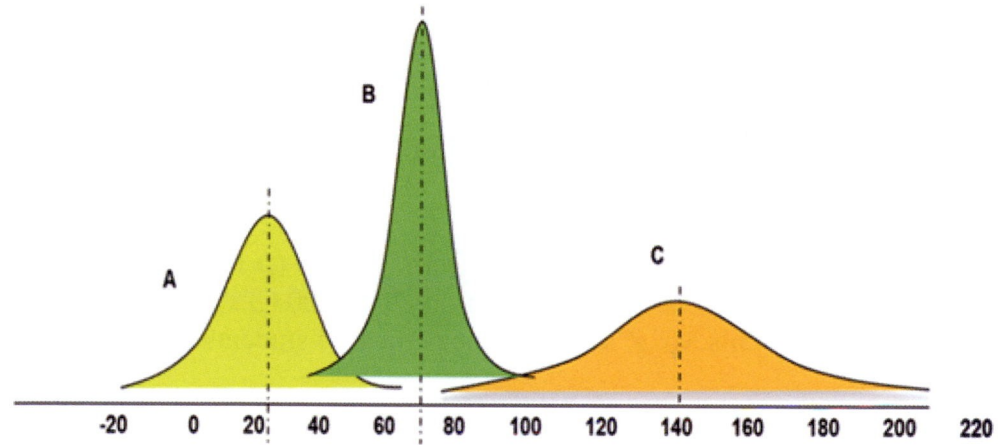

Solution:

Distribution C has a higher mean value than those of distributions B and A
Distribution B has a higher mean value than distribution A
Distribution C is the most spread out distribution. Therefore, it has the largest standard deviation.
Distribution B is the least spread out distribution. Therefore, it has the lowest standard deviation.

Example 6.5: Mr. Z is teaching a course of statistics in a community college. The grades of the population of students taught by this instructor over a number of years are represented by the normal distribution shown in Figure 6.6. Describe the pattern of this instructor's grading.

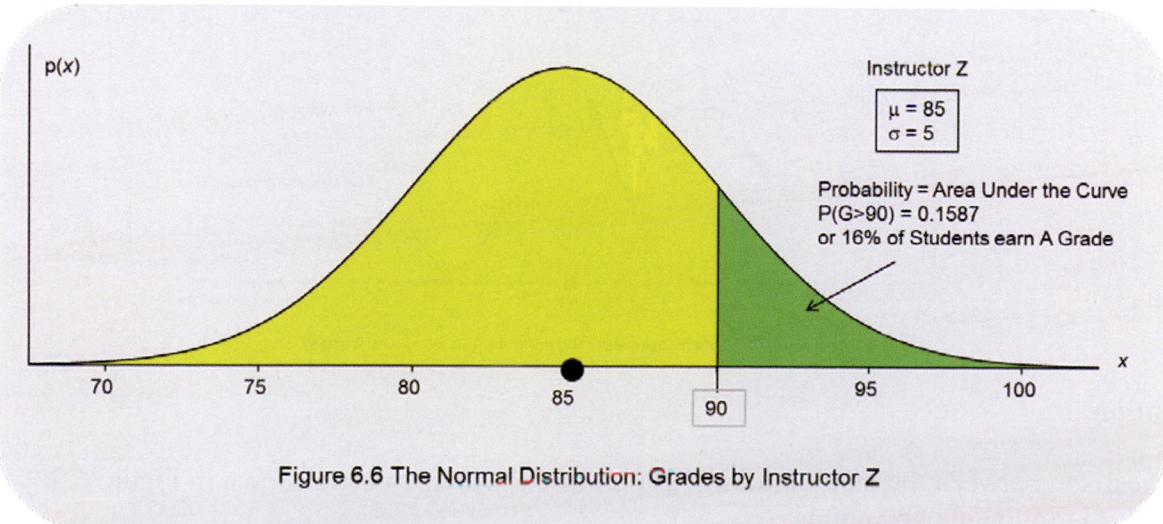

Figure 6.6 The Normal Distribution: Grades by Instructor Z

Solution:

This example provides a good illustration of how to describe a normal distribution. As seen in Figure 6.6, the grades given by Mr. Z follow a normal distribution with mean of 85 and a standard deviation of 5. This means that Mr. Z's average grade is a *B* and also most of his students earn a *B* grade (the mode).

Recalling the empirical rule in Chapter 3, one can also conclude that:

-   About 68.26 % of Mr. Z's class earns grades from 80 to 90 ($\mu \pm 1\sigma$). The percent of students earning below 80 is 15.87% (or (100 - 68.26)/2), and the percent of students earning above 90 is also 15.97%
-   About 95.44% of Mr. Z's class earn grades from 75 to 95 ($\mu \pm 2\sigma$)
-   About 99.74% of Mr. Z's class earn grades from 70 to 100 ($\mu \pm 3\sigma$)
-   Virtually, no student fails Mr. Z's class as the percent of students earning less than 70% is zero.

Example 6.6: Suppose we want to compare the grades of Mr. Z with those of another instructor, Mr. W who is teaching the same course for a different group of students. The grades of the populations of students taught by the two instructors are represented by the two normal distributions shown in Figure 6.7. Describe the two distributions and compare the grades by the two instructors.

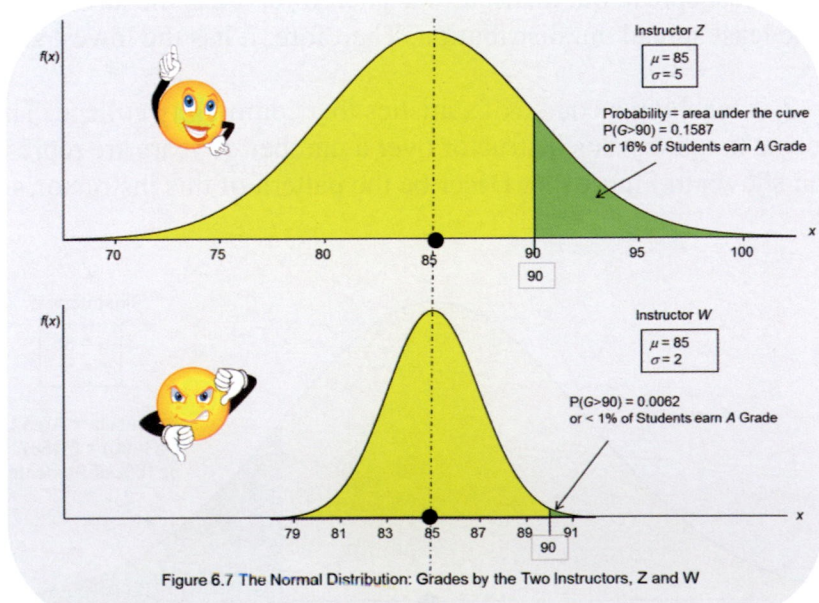

Figure 6.7 The Normal Distribution: Grades by the Two Instructors, Z and W

Solution:

Comparison between the distributions of grades of the two instructors shown in Figure 6.7 reveals the following key points:

-   The grades of the two instructors follow a normal distribution

- The two distributions have the same mean value of 85; they both have the same mode, and the same median, but they have different values of standard deviation (5 and 2, respectively)
- The majority of students who are taking the course with both instructors (the mode) earn a *B* grade.
- Grades given by instructor Z seem to cover a wider range of values by virtue of the higher standard deviation of 5 than those given by instructor W (standard deviation of only 2). Using the empirical rule, the two instructors hardly fail any student and instructor Z gives more *A* grades ($\approx$16%) than instructor W (less than 1%).

Working Problem 6.6:

Given the three normal distributions A, B, and C below:
- Which normal curve has the greatest mean and which has the lowest mean?
- Which normal curve has the greatest standard deviation and which has the lowest standard deviation?
Answer: Do it yourself

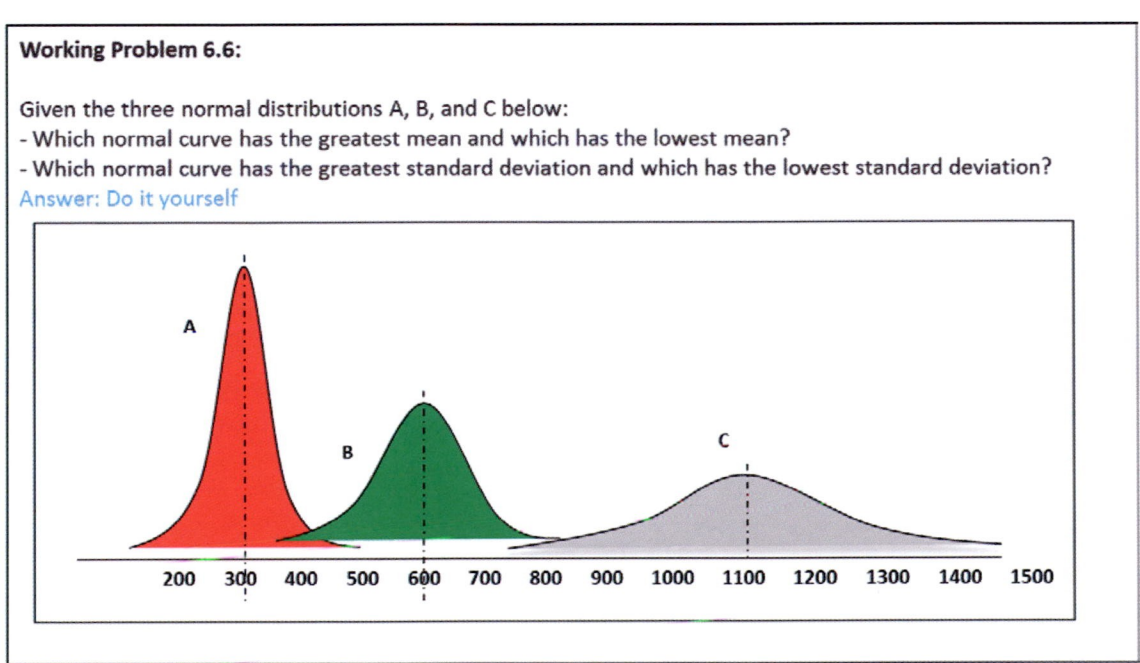

Working Problem 6.7:

The two normal distributions below describe the area (cm²) of ceramic tiles produced by two manufacturers A & B:
- Compare the mean and the variability of the two distributions
- Which manufacturer should you buy ceramic tiles from? Why

Answer:
Do it yourself

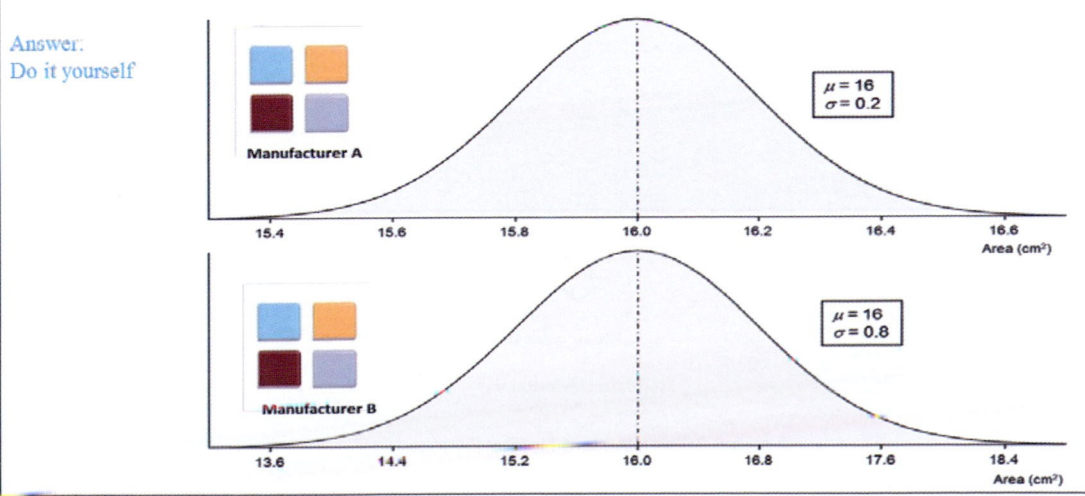

6.4 The standard normal distribution

A normal distribution having a mean value of zero and a standard deviation of one is said to be a standard normal distribution (see Figure 6.8). The idea of a standard normal distribution came about as a result of the need for a more simplified normal function that can be easily integrated to obtain the area under the normal curve. This simplification is achieved by moving the center of the normal distribution to the origin (at $x = 0$), via transforming the variable x to a new variable z, defined by $z = (x - \mu)/\sigma$. Common names of the z statistics are the z score, the standard normal deviate, the standard normal value, or the normal deviate. This transformation leads to the following standard normal function:

$$P(z) = \frac{1}{\sqrt{2\pi}} e^{-\frac{z^2}{2}} \qquad (6.7)$$

$$-\infty \leq z \leq \infty$$

where the mean value of the variable z is 0 and the standard deviation of the variable z is 1.

Note that the empirical rule, discussed in Chapter 3, can be used for the standard normal distribution with 68.26 percent of the observations falling within plus and minus one of the mean; 95.44 percent of the observations falling within plus and minus two of the mean; and 99.74 percent falling within plus and minus three of the mean. These values are shown in Figure 6.8.

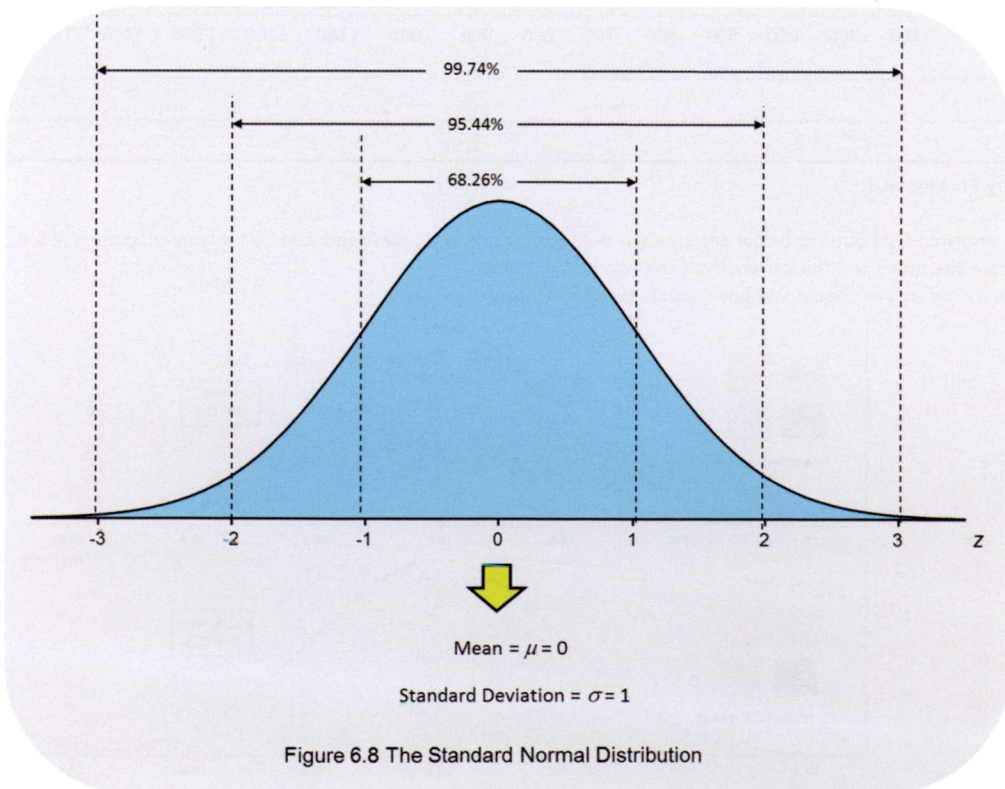

Figure 6.8 The Standard Normal Distribution

The basic properties of the standard normal distribution curve are as follows:

- The total area under the standard normal curve is one.
- The standard normal curve extends indefinitely in both directions ($-\infty \leq z \leq \infty$).
- The standard normal curve is symmetric about 0.
- Almost all the area under the standard normal curve lies between values of z of -3.4 and 3.4.
- Areas under the standard normal curve can be obtained from special tables such as the ones shown in Appendix 6.A.
- The construction of this table is illustrated in Figure 6.9. The first column of the table represents the z values, the first row of the table represents the complementary decimals of z values, and the four-decimal-place numbers in the body of the table give the area under the standard normal curve from $-\infty$ to z. Another form of the table in which the area presented is from the origin 0 to some z value is shown in Appendix 6.B.

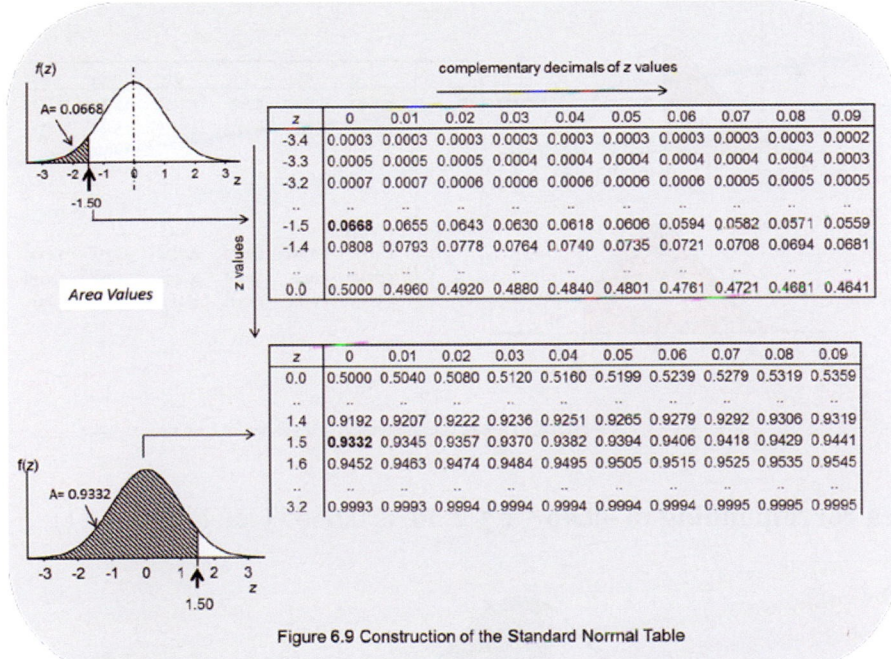

Figure 6.9 Construction of the Standard Normal Table

Example 6.7: Find the area under the standard normal curve for the following z values:

(a) $0 \leq z \leq 1.5$
(b) $-0.46 \leq z \leq 2.30$
(c) $0.80 \leq z \leq 2.0$

Solution:

In answering these types of questions, it is highly recommended that the student get used to sketching a standard normal curve ($\mu = 0$, $\sigma = 1$) and roughly locate the values of z on the horizontal axis (see Figure 6.10).

(a) **Area corresponding to $0 \leq z \leq 1.5$:** to determine the area under the curve between $z = 0$ and $z = 1.5$, we use the Table in Appendix 6.A. In order to get the required area we can first find the area at $z = 1.5$. This is by proceeding downward under column marked z until entry 1.5 is reached. Then we continue right to column marked 0. The result is 0.9332. This is the entire area from $z = -\infty$ to $z = 1.5$. Since we need the area in the region $0 \leq z \leq 1.5$, we have to subtract the area from $z = -\infty$ to $z = 0$ as shown in Figure 6.10. We should know that this area is 0.5, but we can also get it from the table at $z = 0$. The required area under the curve is therefore $(0.9332 - 0.5000)$, or 0.4332. This solution is illustrated in Figure 6.10.

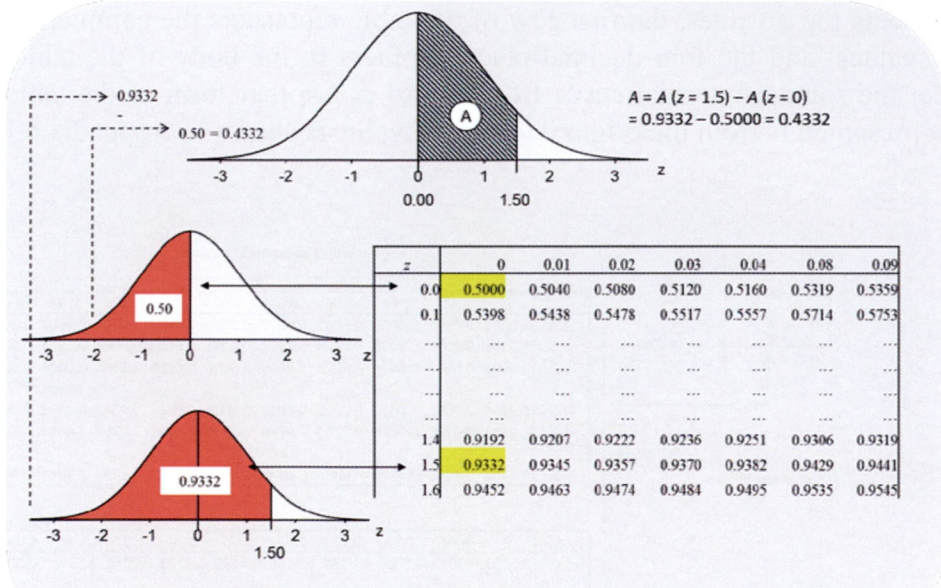

Figure 6.10 Areas Corresponding to z values: $0 \leq z \leq 1.5$

(b) **Area corresponding to $-0.46 \leq z \leq 2.30$** is 0.6665 (see Figure 6.11)

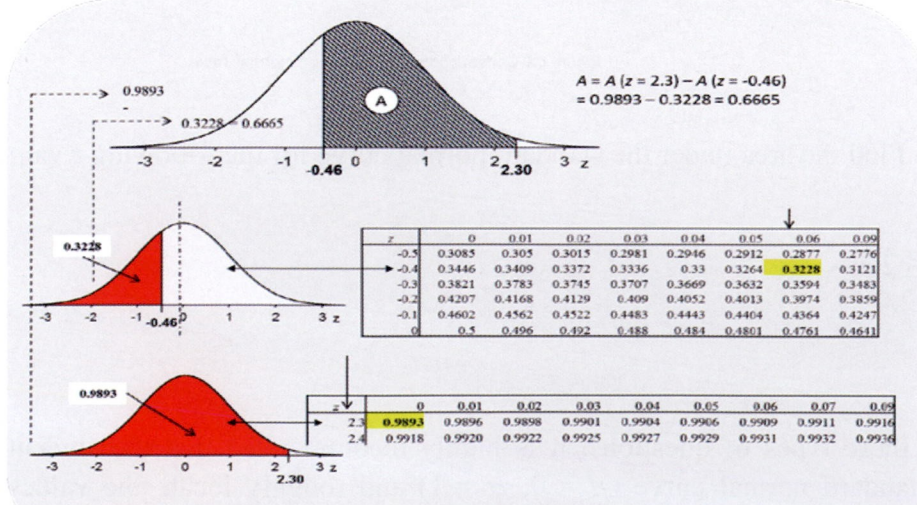

Figure 6.11 Areas Corresponding to z values: $-0.46 \leq z \leq 2.30$

(c) **Area corresponding to $0.80 \leq z \leq 2.0$** is 0.1891 (see Figure 6.12)

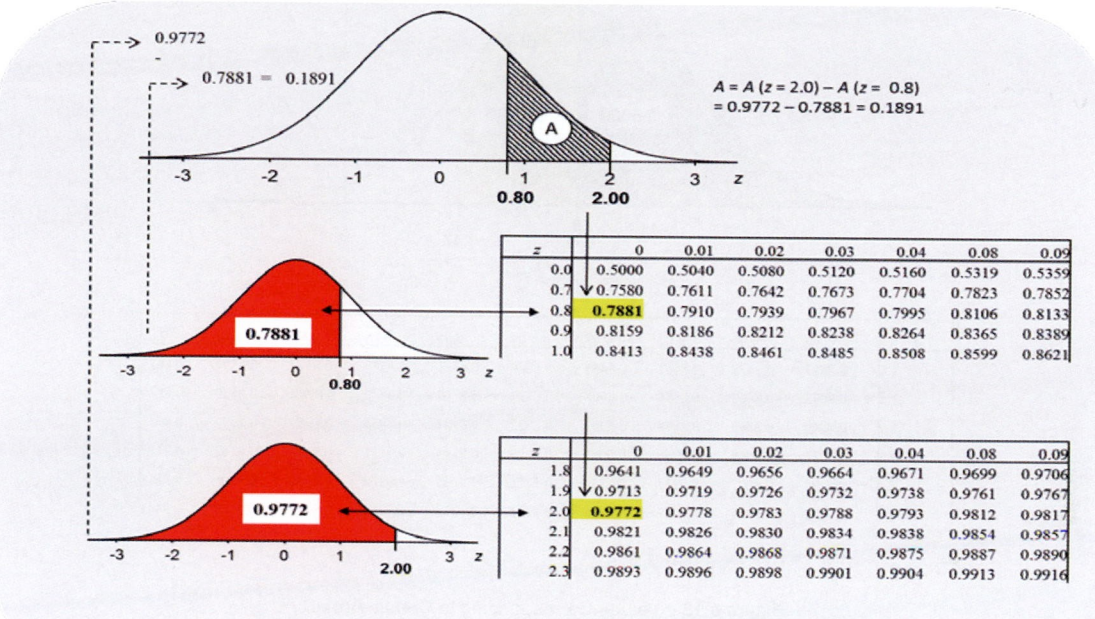

Figure 6.12 Areas Corresponding to z values: $0.80 \leq z \leq 2.0$

Example 6.8: Determine the value(s) of z in the following cases:

(a) Area under the normal curve between 0 and z is 0.3790.

(b) Area under the normal curve to left of z is 0.6100.

Solution:

(a) **Area under the normal curve between 0 and z is 0.3790:** To solve this question, we sketch the standard normal curve as shown in Figure 6.13. Adding the area of 0.3790 to half of the area of the normal curve (0.5) yields a total area of 0.879. Locating this area in the body of standard normal table and tracking the value of z corresponding to this area will yield the answer of $z = 1.17$.

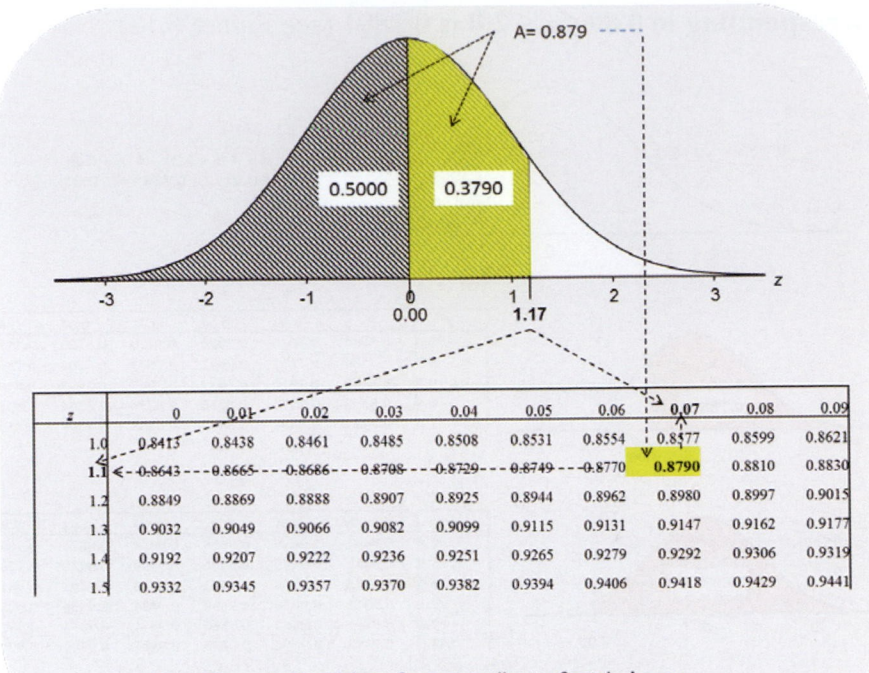

Figure 6.13 z Values Corresponding to Certain Areas:
z value for Area of 0.3790 under the normal curve between 0 and z is 1.17

(b) **Area under the normal curve to left of z is 0.6100:** Sketching the standard normal curve and identifying the area 0.6100 will yield the answer to this question $z = 0.28$ from the standard normal table as shown in Figure 6.14.

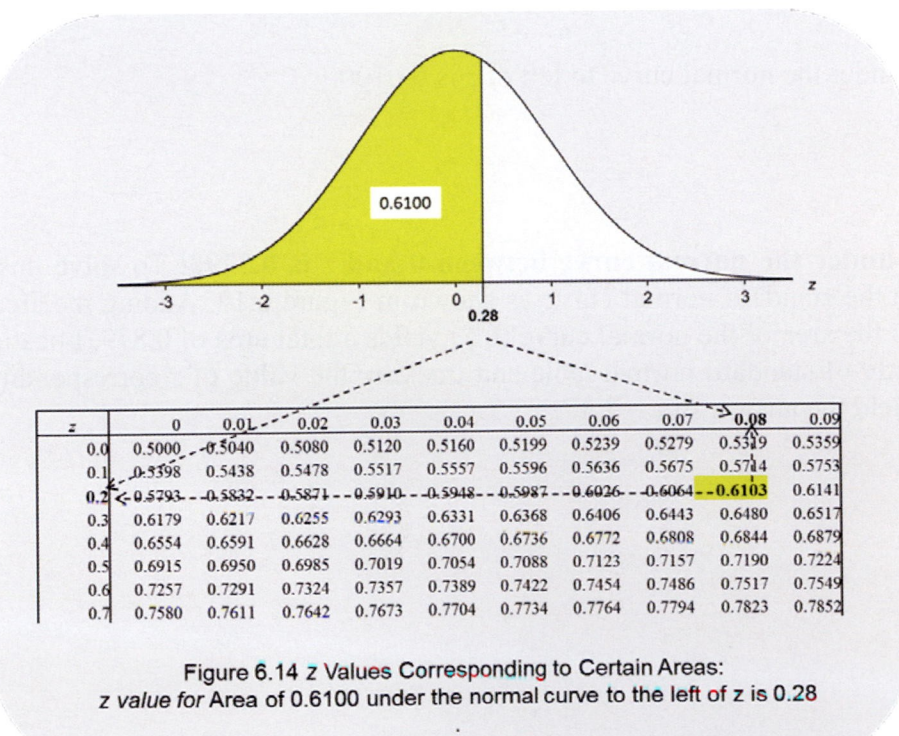

Figure 6.14 z Values Corresponding to Certain Areas:
z value for Area of 0.6100 under the normal curve to the left of z is 0.28

Example 6.9: The mean value of course grades in a large population of students is 85, and the standard deviation is 5, assuming that the grade follows a normal distribution, determine the z values corresponding to the following grades:

(a) Grade = x = 75
(b) $80 \leq x \leq 90$
(c) $75 \leq x \leq 95$
(d) $70 \leq x \leq 100$

Solution:

(a) At x = 75, $z = (x-\mu)/\sigma = (75-85)/5 = -2$
(b) $80 \leq x \leq 90$ yields $(80-85)/5 \leq z \leq (90-85)/5$, or $-1 \leq z \leq +1$
(c) $75 \leq x \leq 95$ yields $(75-85)/5 \leq z \leq (95-85)/5$, or $-2 \leq z \leq +2$
(d) $70 \leq x \leq 100$ yields $(70-85)/5 \leq z \leq (100-85)/5$, or $-3 \leq z \leq +3$

Example 6.10: The mean value of course grades in a large population of students is 85, and the standard deviation is 5, assuming that the grade follows a normal distribution, what percent of students made the following grades?

(a) $80 \leq x \leq 90$
(b) $75 \leq x \leq 95$
(c) $70 \leq x \leq 100$
(d) $x \geq 73$
(e) $x \leq 84$

Solution:

Using the empirical rule,

(a) $80 \leq x \leq 90$ yields $(80-85)/5 \leq z \leq (90-85)/5$, or $-1 \leq z \leq +1$ and this corresponds to 68.26% of the students' grades.
(b) $75 \leq x \leq 95$ yields $(75-85)/5 \leq z \leq (95-85)/5$, or $-2 \leq z \leq +2$ and this corresponds to 95.44% of the students' grades.
(c) $70 \leq x \leq 100$ yields $(70-85)/5 \leq z \leq (100-85)/5$, or $-3 \leq z \leq +3$ and this corresponds to 99.74% of the students' grades.
(d) In order to determine the area or percent of students earning larger than or equal to 73 ($x \geq 73$), we have to refer to the standard normal table. In this case, we calculate the corresponding z value, $z \geq (73-85)/5$ or $z \geq -2.4$. As illustrated in Figure 6.15, the area to the left of -2.4 is 0.0082 and the required area $P(z \geq -2.4)$ is 0.9918 (or 1- 0.0082). Thus, the percent of students earning larger or equal to 73 is 99.18%.

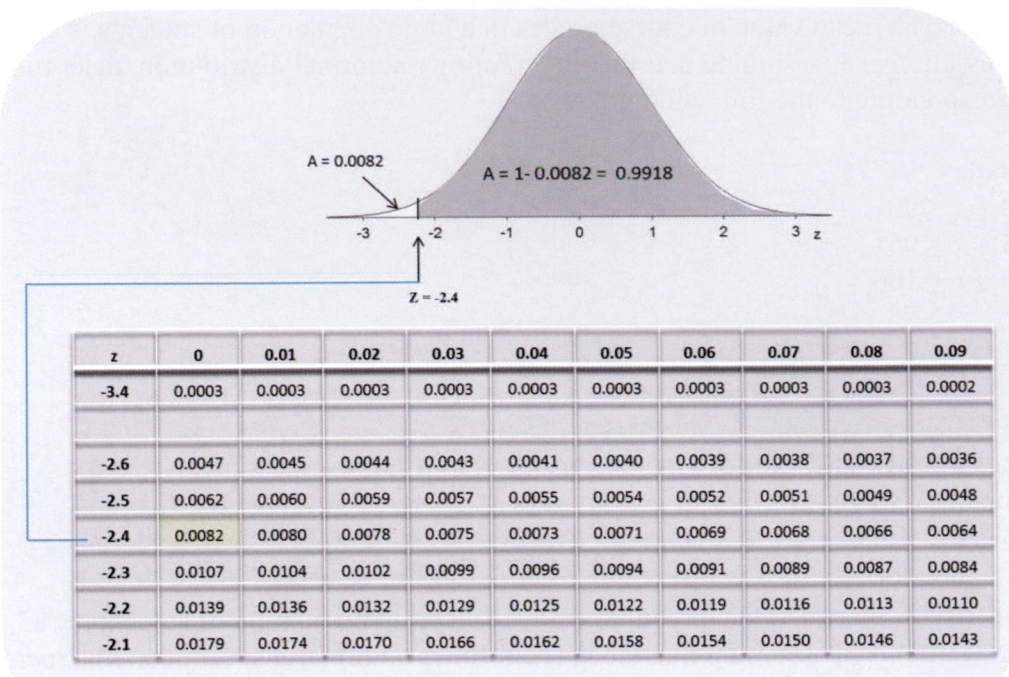

Figure 6.15 Areas Corresponding to z values: $z \geq -2.4$

(e) To determine the area corresponding to $x \leq 84$ we have to refer to the standard normal table. In this case, we calculate the corresponding z value, $z \leq (84-85)/5$ or $z \geq -0.2$. As illustrated in Figure 6.16, the area to the left of -0.2 is 0.4207 and the required area $P(z \leq -0.2)$ is 0.4207. Thus, the percent of students earning less than 84% is 42.07%.

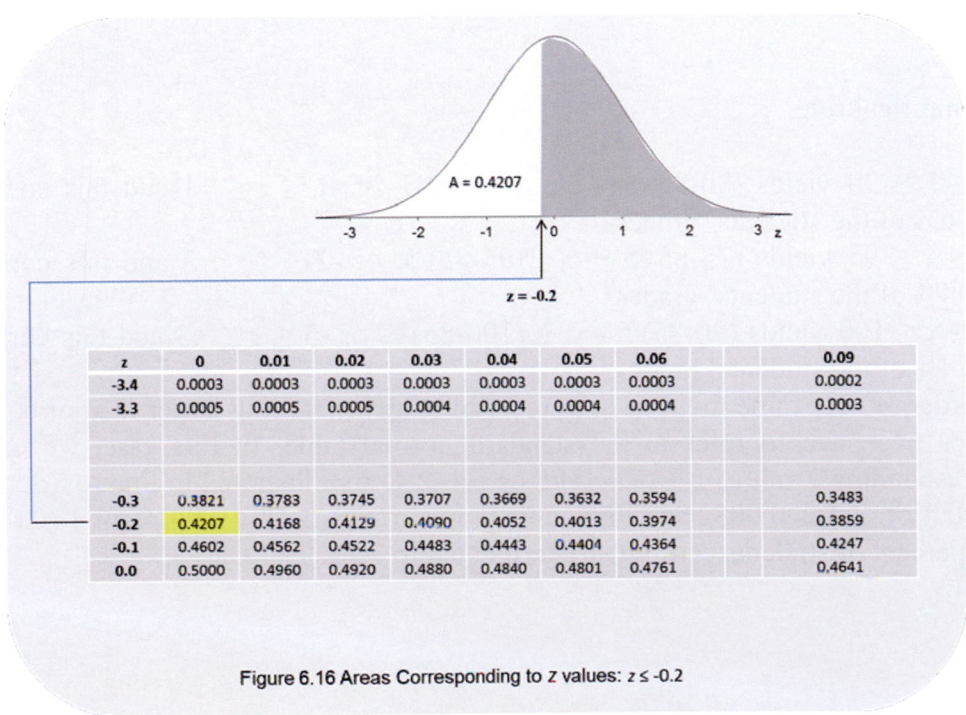

Figure 6.16 Areas Corresponding to z values: $z \leq -0.2$

Working Problem 6.8: For the three normal distributions shown below, find the values of z corresponding to the values of x in the circles

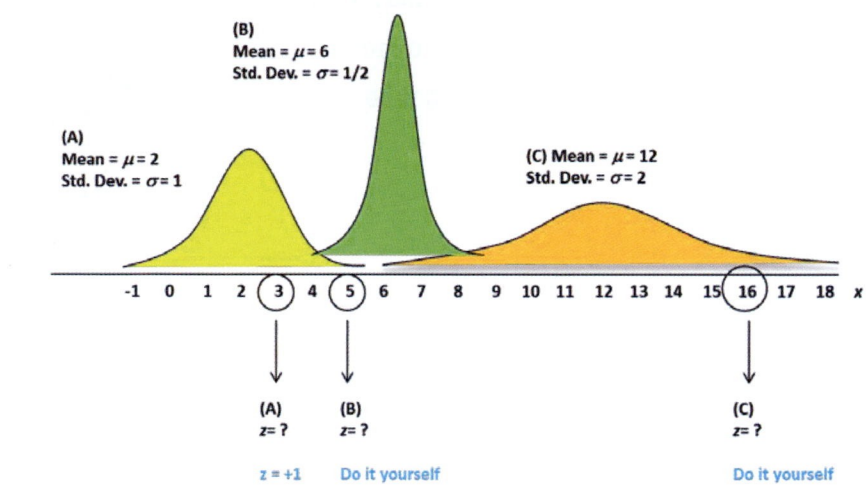

Working Problem 6.9:

Find the area under the standard normal curve for the following z values:

(a) $0 \leq z \leq 1.0$
(b) $-2 \leq z \leq 2$
(c) z < 3

Answer:
(a) 0.3413
(b) Do it yourself
(c) Do it yourself

Working Problem 6.10:

Find the area under the standard normal curve for the following z values:

(a) $-\infty \leq z \leq 1.3$
(b) $-1 \leq z \leq 1.3$
(c) z > -3.2

Answer:
(a) 0.9032
(b) 0.7445
(c) Do it yourself

Working Problem 6.11:

Determine the value(s) of z in the following cases:

(a) Area under the normal curve between $-\infty$ and z is 0.100.

(b) Area under the normal curve to right of z is 0.8100.

(c) Area under the normal curve to left of z is 0.7100

Answer:

(a) -1.28

(b) Do it yourself

(c) Do it yourself

Working Problem 6.12:

The three normal distributions shown below represent the grades of pre-algebra course of students obtained in three different semesters...

- Describe and compare the performances of students in the three semester

- What percent of students earning ≤70%) in each semester

Answer:

(a) At $x = 70$, $z = (70-75)/5 = -1$

15.87%

(b) Do it yourself

(c) Do it yourself

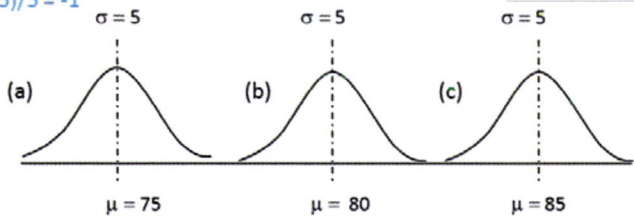

Working Problem 6.13:

The three normal distributions shown below represent the grades of pre-algebra course of students obtained in three different semesters...

- Describe and compare the performances of students in the three semester

- What percent of students made at least B (≥ 80%) in each semester

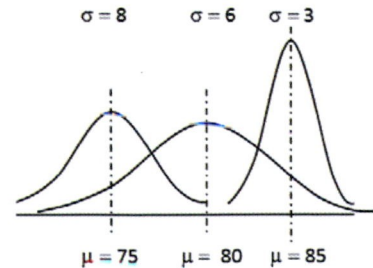

Answer:

Do it yourself

6.5 The z_α notation

The z_α notation is an important tool that students will become very familiar with when we discuss inferential statistics (Chapters 8 through 10). This notation indicates the z-score that has an area α under the standard normal distribution curve to the right of z. The examples below will familiarize the student with the z_α notation using values of α that are commonly utilized in the analysis of inferential statistics.

Example 6.11: Find the z_α values for the following cases:

(a) $\alpha = 0.01$
(b) $\alpha = 0.05$
(c) $\alpha = 0.10$

Using the same procedures we used in the above examples, the answers to this question are illustrated in Figure 6.17.

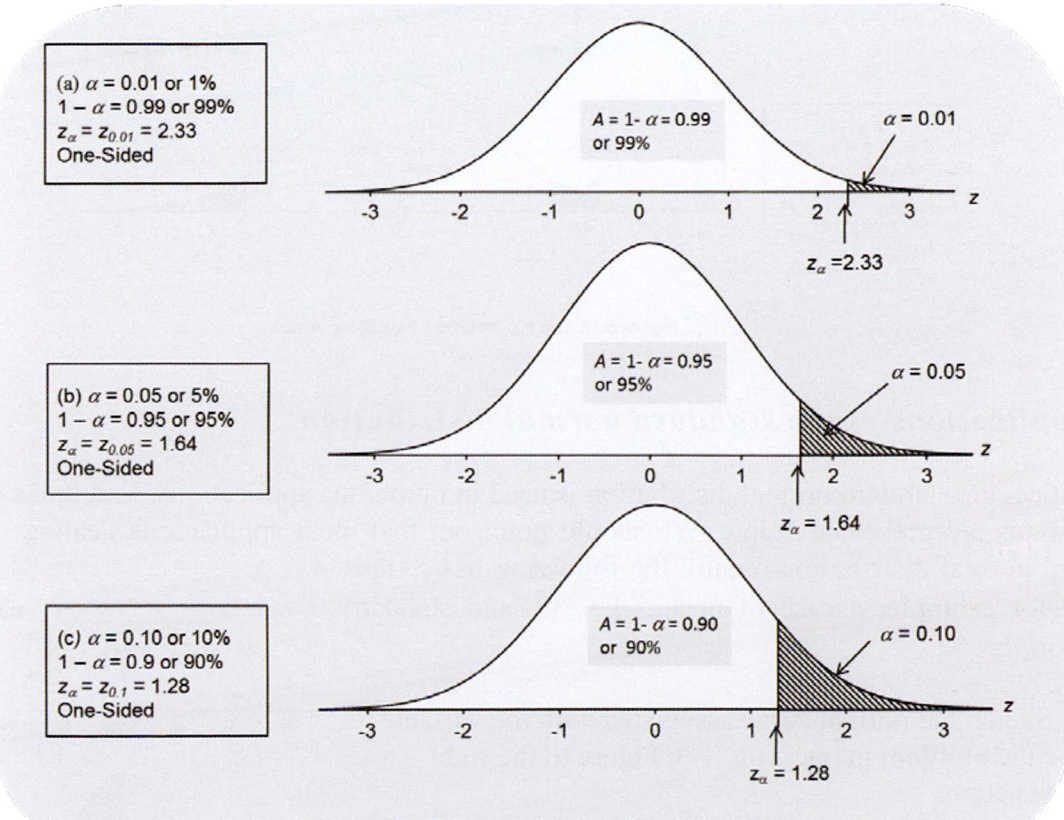

Figure 6.17 The z_α Notation-One Sided Areas

331

Example 6.12: Find the $z_{\alpha/2}$ values for the following cases:

(a) $\alpha/2 = 0.005$
(b) $\alpha/2 = 0.025$
(c) $\alpha/2 = 0.05$

The answers to the above question are illustrated in Figure 6.18.

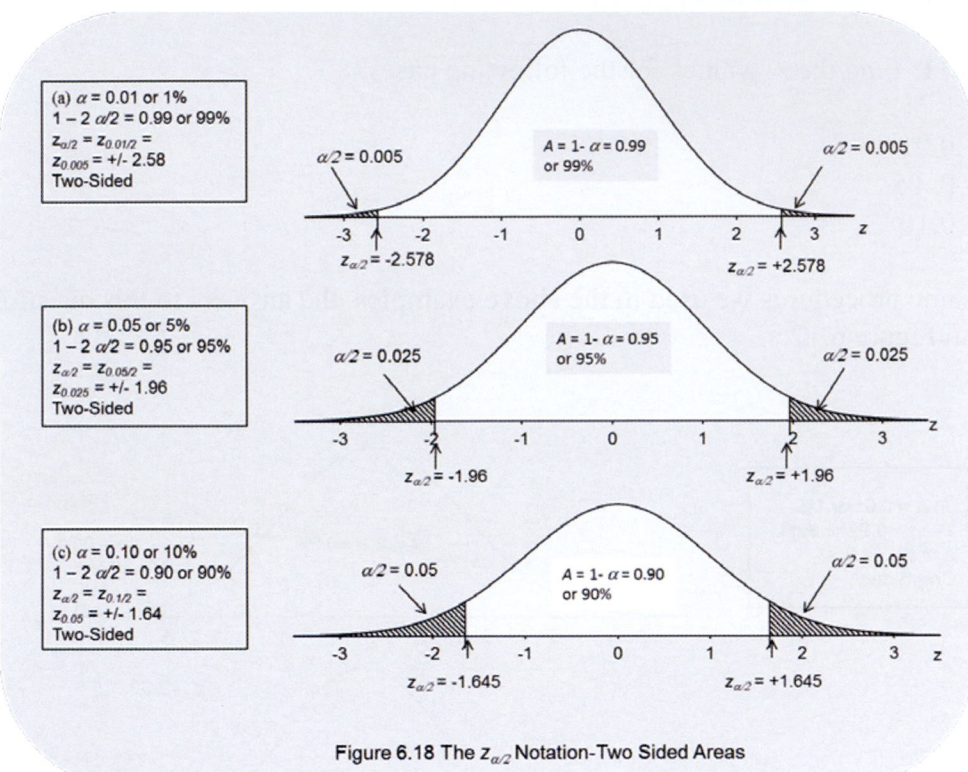

Figure 6.18 The $z_{\alpha/2}$ Notation-Two Sided Areas

6.6 Applications of the standard normal distribution

In practice, the standard normal distribution is used in numerous applications. Examples of these applications are presented below. We should point out that most applications dealing with the standard normal distribution require the following basic steps (using, for example, a case of mean, $\mu = 80$, and standard deviation, $\sigma = 5$):

Step 1: Sketch the normal curve associated with the variable to describe the problem in question. The Figure to the right shows this curve.

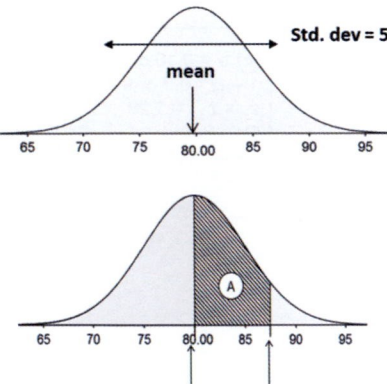

Step 2: Shade the region of interest and mark its delimiting *x*-value(s). Suppose the region of interest is from $x = 80$ to $x = 87.5$.

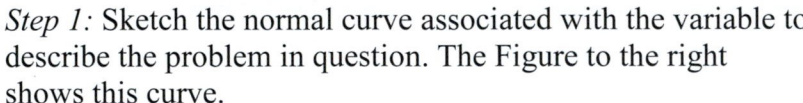

332

Step 3: Calculate the *z*-score(s) corresponding to the *x* values: $= (x - \mu)/\sigma$.

$$At\ x = 80, z = \frac{(x - \mu)}{\sigma} = \frac{80 - 80}{5} = 0$$

$$At\ x = 87.5, z = \frac{(x - \mu)}{\sigma} = \frac{87.5 - 80}{5} = 1.5$$

Step 4: Use the standard normal distribution table to find the area under the standard normal curve delimited by the *z*-scores (0 and 1.5). As shown below, this area is 0.4332.

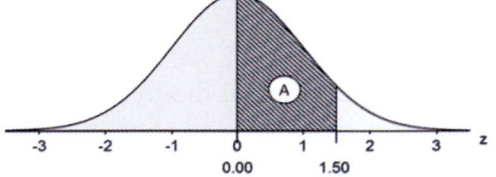

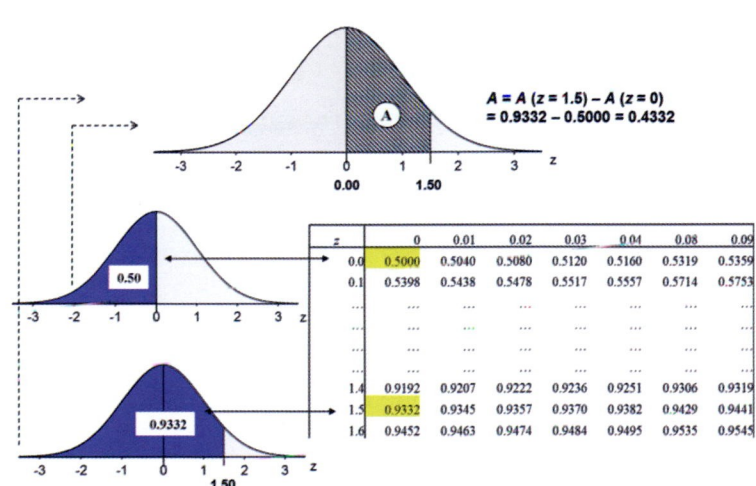

Step 5: Express the findings in terms of *x* values.
In this example: the percent of values ranging from 80 to 87.5 is 43.32%

Example 6.13: The Thermoscale Company produces digital thermometers that have a 0°C midpoint, which is the reading expected at the freezing point of water. In actual testing of a large number of thermometers, the temperature at freezing points fluctuates around the 0°C from negative values (below 0°C) to positive values (above 0°C). The temperature follows a normal distribution with a mean value of 0°C and a standard deviation of 1°C. If one thermometer is randomly selected, find the probability that, at the freezing point of water, the reading is more than -1.2°C. What is the probability that, at the freezing point of water, the reading is less than 0.5°C?

Solution:

With a mean value $\mu = 0$ and a standard deviation $\sigma = 1$, this is a standard normal distribution. Using the normal table in Appendix 6-A, we can find the area $P(z \leq -1.2)$, which is 0.1151 as shown below. This yields value of $P(z > -1.2)$ of 0.8849 (or 1- 0.1151). This answer means that the chance that the reading at the freezing point of water will be more than -1.2°C is 0.8849 or about 88.5%.

z	0	0.01	0.02	0.03	0.04
-1.4	...	...	...	...	...
-1.3	0.0968	0.0951	0.0934	0.0918	...
-1.2	**0.1151**	0.1131	0.1112	0.1093	...
-1.1	0.1357	0.1335	0.1314	0.1292	...

The probability that, at the freezing point of water, the reading is less than 0.5°C can be obtained using the normal table in Appendix 6-A, we can find the area $P(z < 0.5)$, which is 0.6915 as shown below. This answer means that the chance that the reading at the freezing point of water will be less than 0.5°C is 0.6915 or about 69.15%. Figure 6.19 illustrates the answers of this example.

z	0	0.01	0.02	0.03	...	...
0.0	0.5000	0.5040	0.5080	0.5120	...	...
...	...	...	...	...	...	...
0.5	**0.6915**	0.6950	0.6985	0.7019	...	...
0.6	0.7257	0.7291	0.7324	0.7357	...	...

The results obtained in this example indicate that there is a 57.64% chance that at the freezing point, a randomly selected digital thermometer produced by this company may give a reading ranging from -1.2 °C to 0.5 °C. Students need to verify this point.

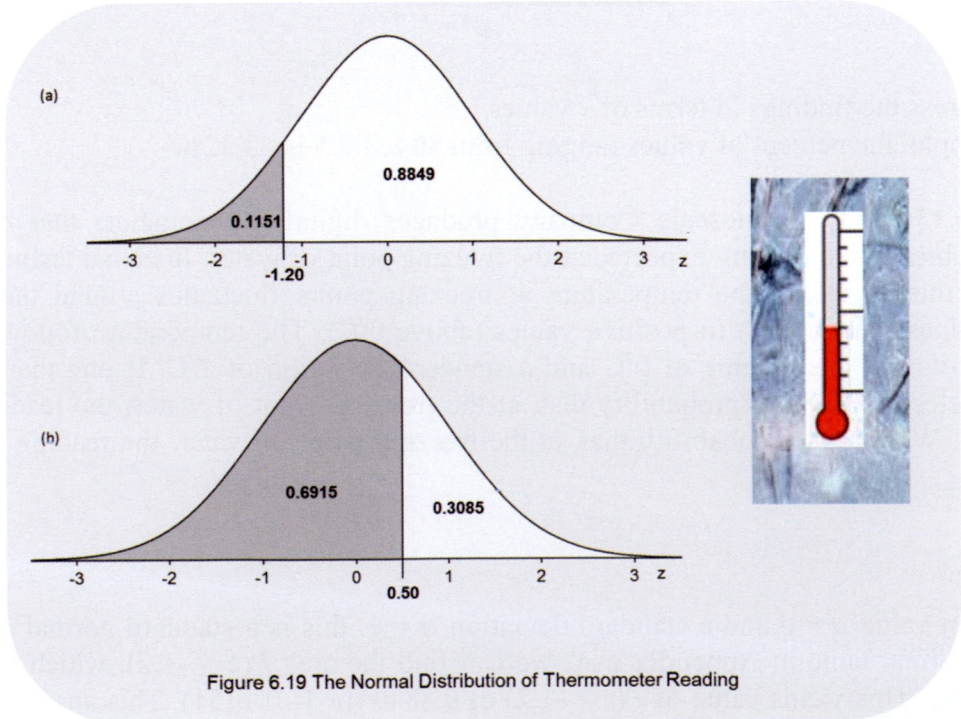

Figure 6.19 The Normal Distribution of Thermometer Reading

334

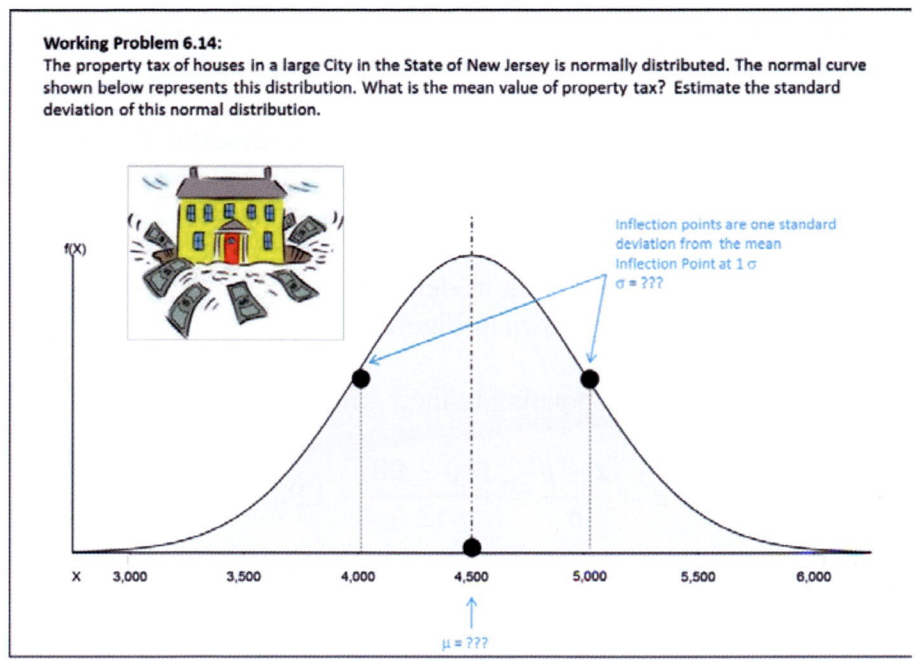

Working Problem 6.14:
The property tax of houses in a large City in the State of New Jersey is normally distributed. The normal curve shown below represents this distribution. What is the mean value of property tax? Estimate the standard deviation of this normal distribution.

Example 6.14: According to the controversial 2002 book titled '*IQ and the Wealth of Nations*' written by Richard Lynn, and Tatu Vanhanen (Praeger/Greenwood Publication, Westport, Connecticut, London, 2002) the average IQ (Intelligence Quotient) test score of the world was 88 and the standard deviation was 12. The criteria in Table 6.4 typically describe one's intelligence with respect to IQ score:

Table 6.4 IQ criteria (http://iq-test.learninginfo.org/iq04.html)

IQ	Description
130+	Very superior
120-129	Superior
110-119	High average
90-109	Average
80-89	Low average
70-79	Borderline
Below 70	Extremely low

- Estimate the percent of people in the world with intelligences that are considered above average or better (IQ ≥ 110)?
- Estimate the percent of people in the world with intelligences that are considered average (IQ = 90-109)?

335

Solution:

Calculation of the percent of people in the world with intelligences that are considered above average or better (IQ ≥ 110) can be made as follows:

Step 1: Sketch the normal curve associated with the variable to describe the problem in question Assuming that IQ score world-wide is normally distributed with an average of 88 and standard deviation of 12, we sketch the normal distribution as shown in Figure 6.20.a.

Step 2: Shade the region of interest and mark its delimiting x-value(s)
The area corresponding to IQ ≥ 110 is shown in Figure 6.20.b

Step 3: Calculate the z-score(s) corresponding to the x values using $z = (x - \mu)/\sigma$

$$z = \frac{x - \mu}{\sigma} = \frac{110 - 88}{12} = 1.833$$

Step 4: Use the Standard Normal Distribution Table to find the area under the standard normal curve delimited by the z-score(s) as shown in Figure 6.20.c.
From the Standard Normal Distribution Table of Appendix 6.A, the area to the left of $z = 1.833$ is 0.9664. This means that the area to the right, which is the desired area, is 0.0336 (1- 0.9664).
Step 5: Express the findings in terms of x values

- The percent of people in the world with intelligences that are considered above average or better (IQ ≥ 110) is 3.4%.

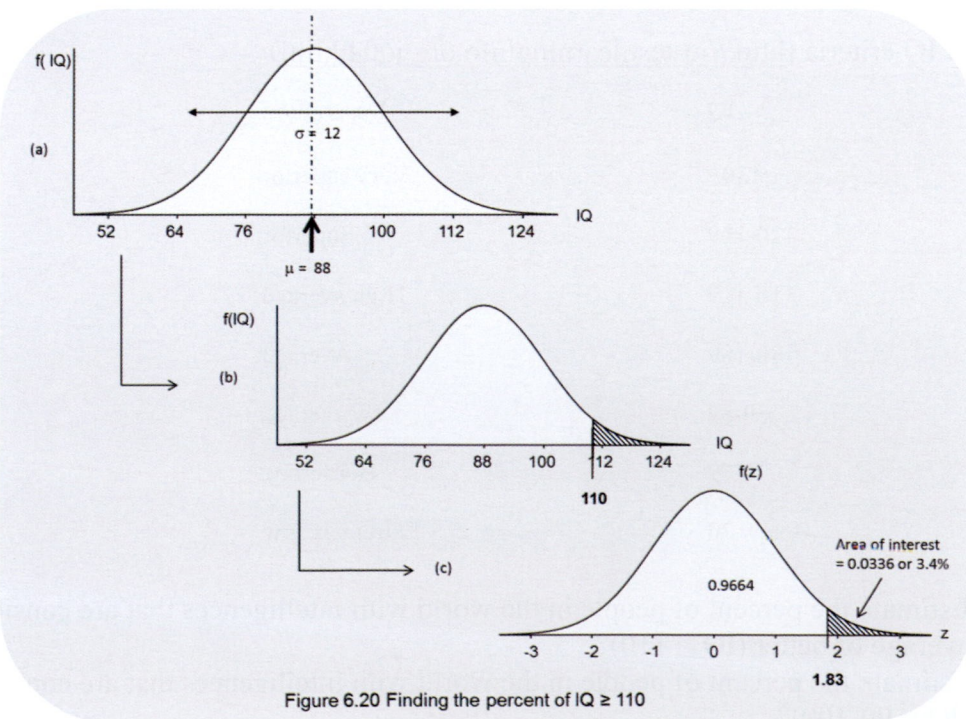

Figure 6.20 Finding the percent of IQ ≥ 110

Calculation of the percent of people in the world with intelligences that are considered average (IQ = 90-109) can be made as follows:

Step 1: Sketch the normal curve associated with the variable to describe the problem in question Assuming that IQ score world-wide is normally distributed with an average of 88 and standard deviation of 12, we sketch the normal distribution as shown in Figure 6.21.a.
Step 2: Shade the region of interest and mark its delimiting x-value(s)
- The area corresponding to $90 \leq IQ \geq 109$ is shown in Figure 6.21.b

Step 3: Calculate the z-score(s) corresponding to the x values using $z = (x - \mu)/\sigma$

$$z_{90} = \frac{x - \mu}{\sigma} = \frac{90 - 88}{12} = 0.167$$

$$z_{109} = \frac{x - \mu}{\sigma} = \frac{109 - 88}{12} = 1.750$$

Step 4: Use the Standard Normal Distribution Table to find the area under the standard normal curve delimited by the z-score(s) as shown in Figure 6.21.c.
From the Standard Normal Distribution Table of Appendix 6.A, the area to the left of $z = 1.75$ is 0.9599 and the area to the left of $z = 0.167$ is 0.5679. The area of interest is the difference between these two areas as shown in Figure 6.21.c, which is 0.3920 (0.9599-0.5679).
Step 5: Express the findings in terms of x values
- The percent of people in the world with intelligences that are considered average or in the range $90 \leq IQ \leq 109$ is 39.2%

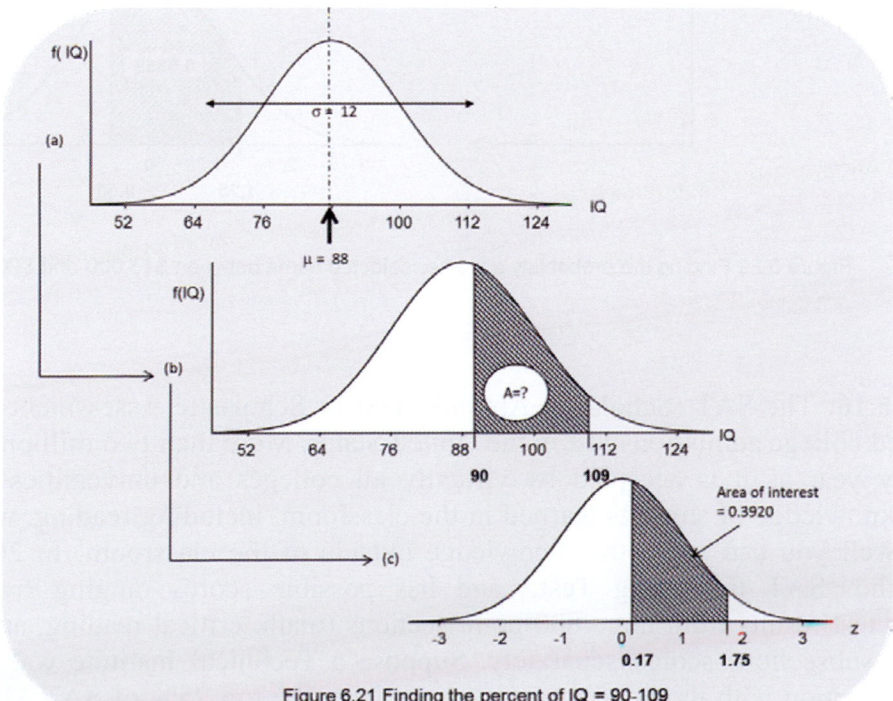

Figure 6.21 Finding the percent of IQ = 90-109

337

Example 6.15: A sewing mill pays workers by the quantity of garments they make. The average annual pay per worker is $18,000 and the standard deviation is $4000. Find the probability that a worker selected randomly earns between $13,000 and $20,000.

Solution:

The probability that a worker selected randomly earns between $13,000 and $20,000 is calculated using steps similar to those in the previous example. As can be seen in Figure 6.22, this probability is 0.5859. This result implies that about 58.6% of the workers earn wages between $13,000 and $20,000.

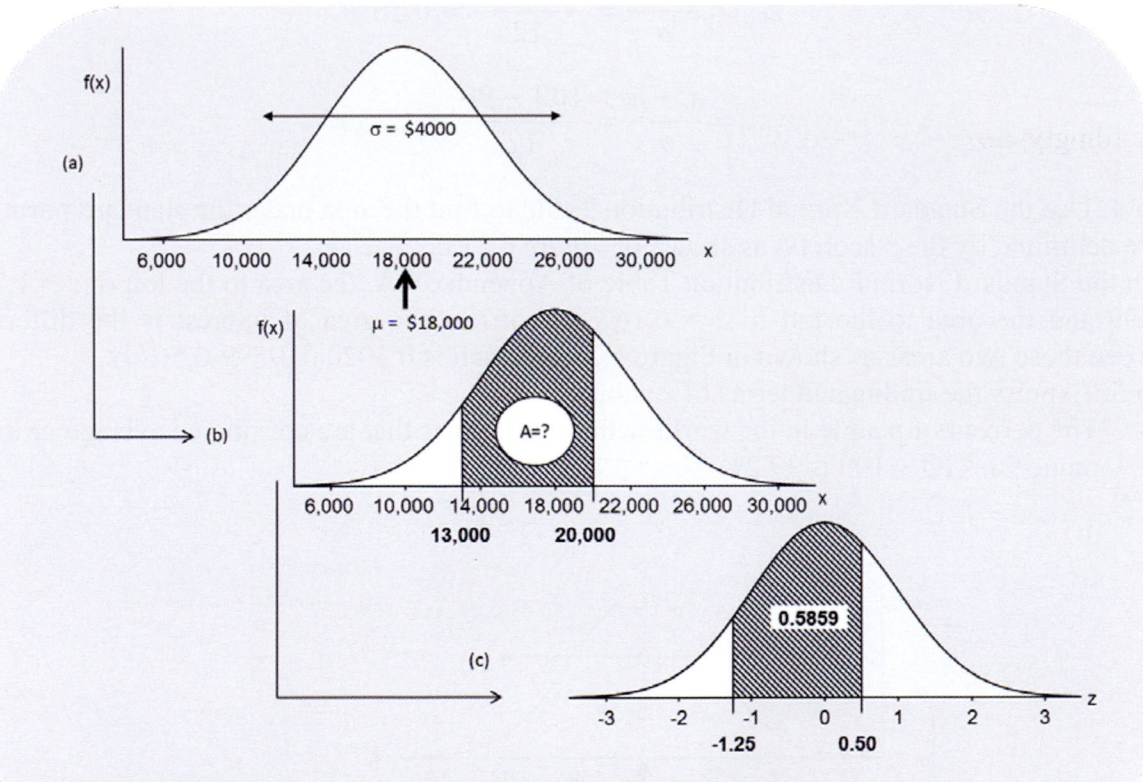

Figure 6.22 Finding the probability a worker selected earns between $13,000 and $20,000

Example 6.16: The SAT (Scholastic Aptitude Test or Scholastic Assessment Test) is the most widely used college admissions test in the United States. More than two million students take the SAT every year as it is accepted by virtually all colleges and universities in the U.S.A. It measures knowledge of subjects learned in the classroom, including reading, writing, and math, and how well you can apply that knowledge outside of the classroom. In 2005, the test was renamed the 'SAT Reasoning Test,' and has possible scores ranging from 600 to 2400 combining test results from three 800-point sections (math, critical reading, and writing), along with other subsections scored separately. Suppose a Technical Institute was interested in the SAT-Math section with the hope to get students from the top 25% of SAT-Math scores. In the

338

State in which this Institute is located, the average score in the SAT-Math section was 550, and the standard deviation was 30. What would be the score that this Institute would accept from the State?

Solution:

This problem is different from the previous problems in that, you are given the area under the curve and you are required to determine the *x* value associated with this area. Again, we begin by sketching the normal distribution curve as shown in Figure 6.23.a. We then go to the Standard Normal Distribution Table and look for the 0.75 area. This gives us a *z* value of 0.67 (Figure 6.22.b). The *x*-value corresponding to 0.67 *z* value is

$$0.67 = (x - 550)/30$$
$$x = 570.1$$

Accordingly, this Institute will take students scoring 570 or better in the SAT-Math section.

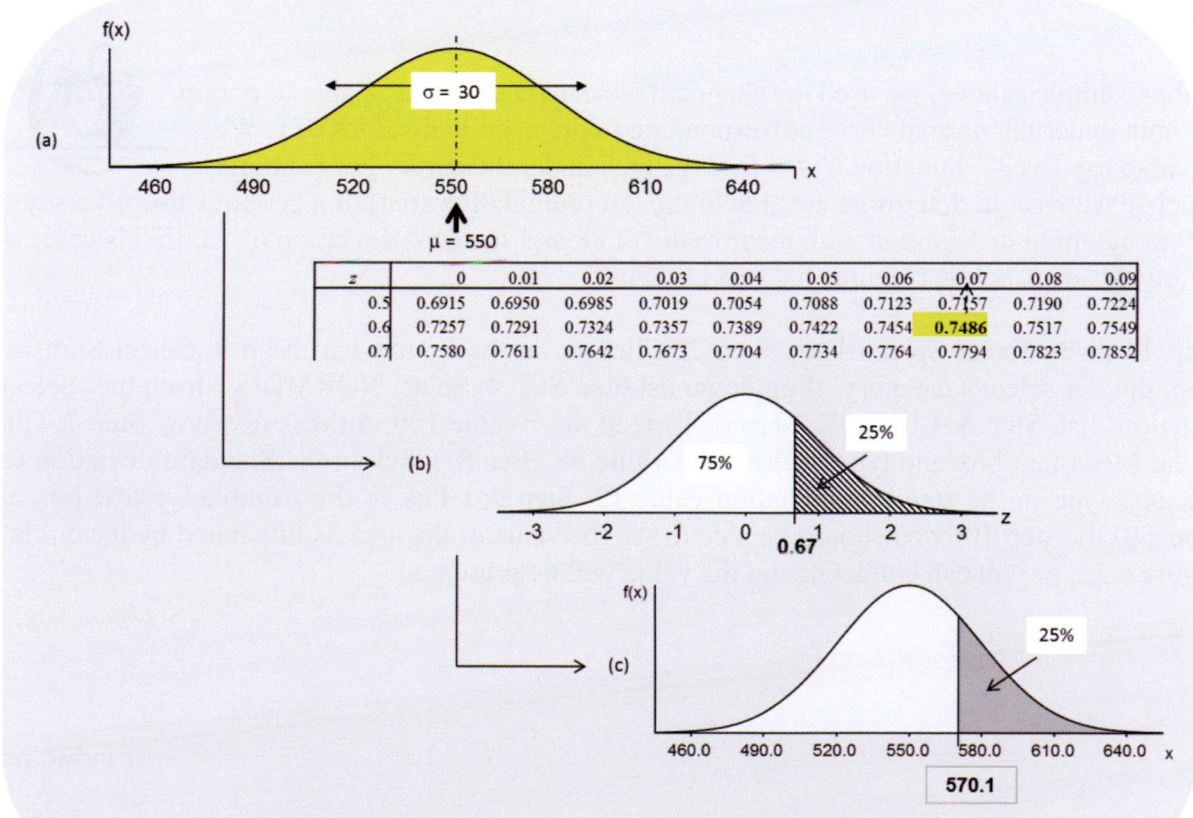

Figure 6.23 Finding the scores of the top 25% of Students taking the SAT

Working Problem 6.15:

The weekly gross income of restaurant assistant managers follows a normal distribution

with a mean of $1,000 and a standard deviation of $100. The variation in the weekly

income of assistant managers is a result of managers getting a commission in addition

to their weekly salary.

(a) What are the z values for the income of assistant managers earning between $900 and $1,100 weekly? What is the percent of assistant managers earning this range of income?
(b) What are the z values for the income of assistant managers earning between $800 and $1,200 weekly? What is the percent of assistant managers earning this range of income?
(c) What are the z values for the income of assistant managers earning between $700 and $1,100 weekly? What is the percent of assistant managers earning this range of income?
(d) What is the z value for the income of assistant managers earning less than $860 weekly? What is the percent of assistant managers earning this range of income?
(e) What is the z value for the income of assistant managers earning more than $1,050 weekly? What is the percent of assistant managers earning this range of income?

Answer: (a) -1, +1, 68.26%, (b) Do it yourself, (c) -3, +1, 84%, (d) Do it yourself, (e) Do it yourself

6.7 Using Microsoft Excel® to find the area under the normal distribution curve

In the examples above, we used the Standard Normal Distribution Table to obtain the area under the normal curve corresponding to pre-specified values of x. We can also use Excel® Function (f_x) to find the area under the curve. For example, suppose we wish to determine the area to the left (cumulative area) of a certain value of x, say 109 in a normal distribution with mean value of 88 and standard deviation of 12. In this case, we follow the steps below (Figures 6.24 and 6.25):

Step 1: Go to Excel Spreadsheet. Step 2: Click fx on the button bar. Step 3: Select Statistical from the 'Or select a category' drop down list box. Step 4: Select NORMDIST from the 'Select a function' list. Step 5: Click OK. Step 6: Type in the x value 109 in the X text box. Step 7: Click in the Mean text box and type in the mean value 88. Step 8: Click in the Standard deviation text box and type in the standard deviation value 12. Step 9: Click in the Cumulative text box and type TRUE. Step 10: You should be able to see the value of the area as illustrated by the circle in Figure 6.25, or you can Click Ok and the value will be presented.

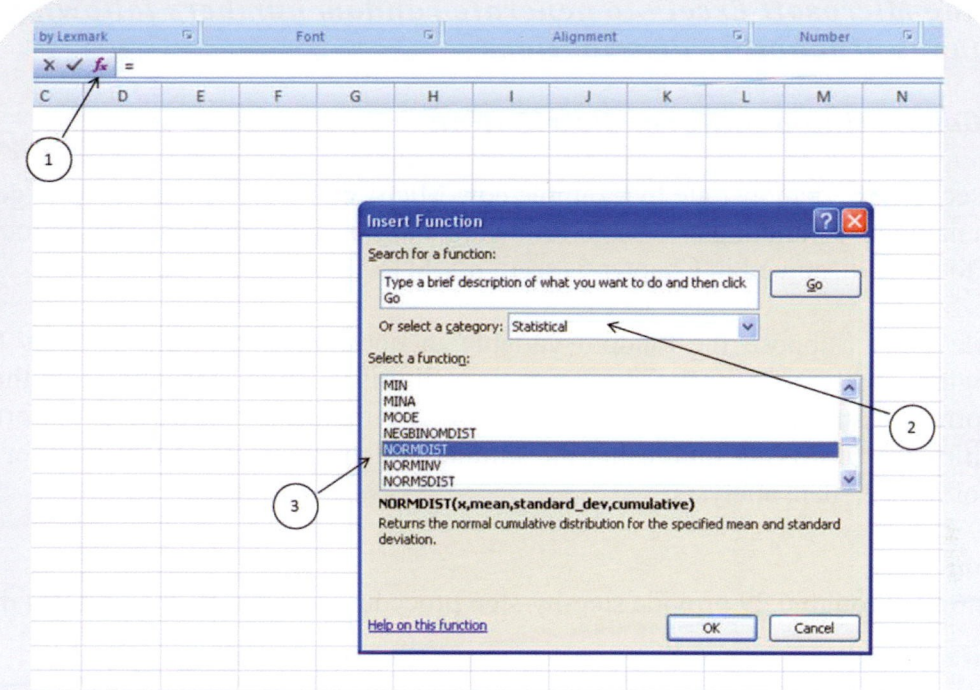

Figure 6.24 Finding the Area Under the Normal Distribution Curve Using Excel® Functions: Steps 1 to 3

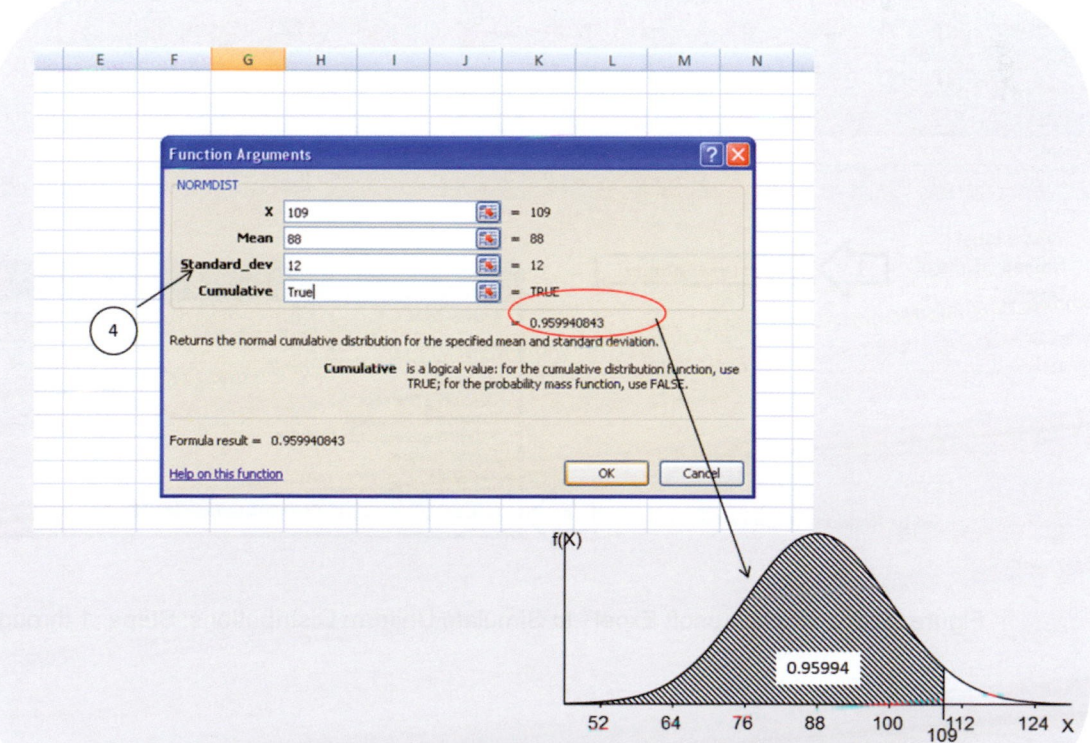

Figure 6.25 Finding the Area Under the Normal Distribution Curve Using Excel® Functions . Step 4

341

6.8 Using Microsoft Excel® to generate random numbers following continuous probability distributions

6.8.1 Generating a uniform distribution

In this section, we demonstrate by example how Microsoft Excel® can be used to generate random numbers simulating a variable following a uniform distribution. These procedures are similar to those discussed in Chapter 5 (section 5.11).

Example 6.17: Suppose the random variable in question is the time it takes to drive from Washington, DC to New York City during normal traffic hours. Assuming that the driving time is uniformly distributed from 220 minutes to 250 minutes; construct a uniform probability distribution of the driving time using the simulation technique of random number generation of Microsoft Excel® data analysis.

Solution:
Figures 6.26 through 6.29 provide step-by-step procedure to simulate the uniform distribution.

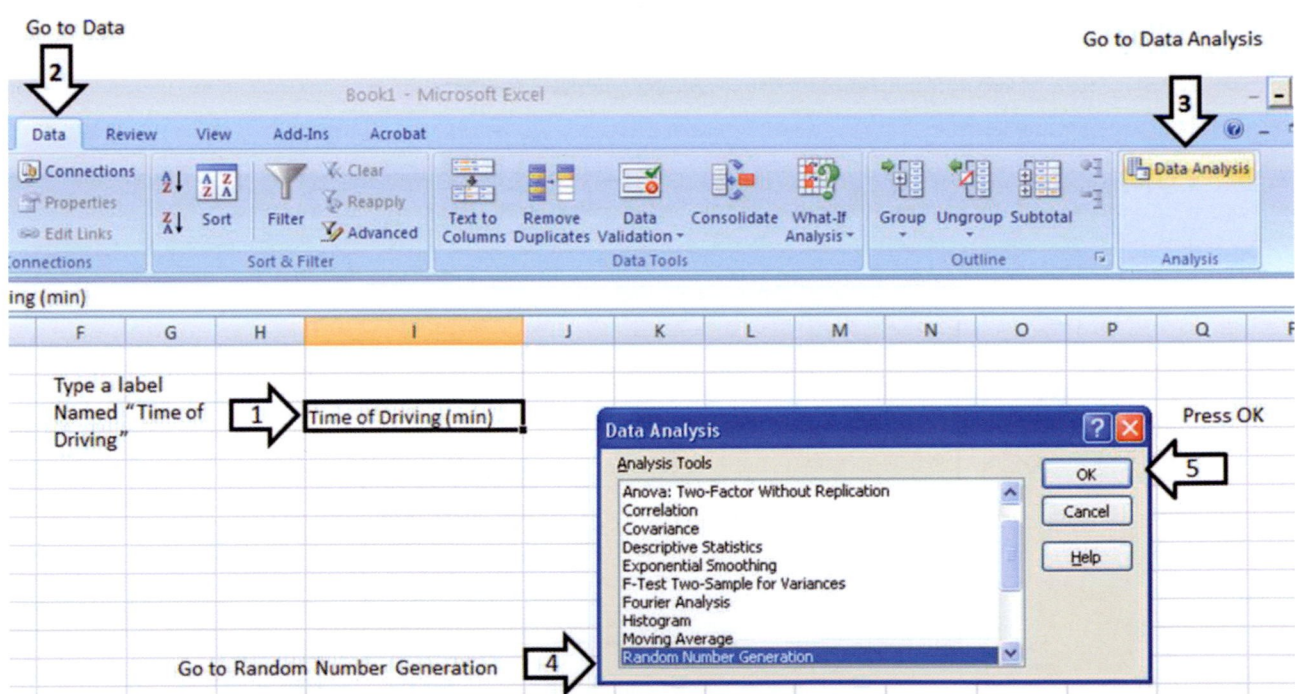

Figure 6.26 Using Microsoft Excel® to Simulate Uniform Distributions: Steps 1 through 5

342

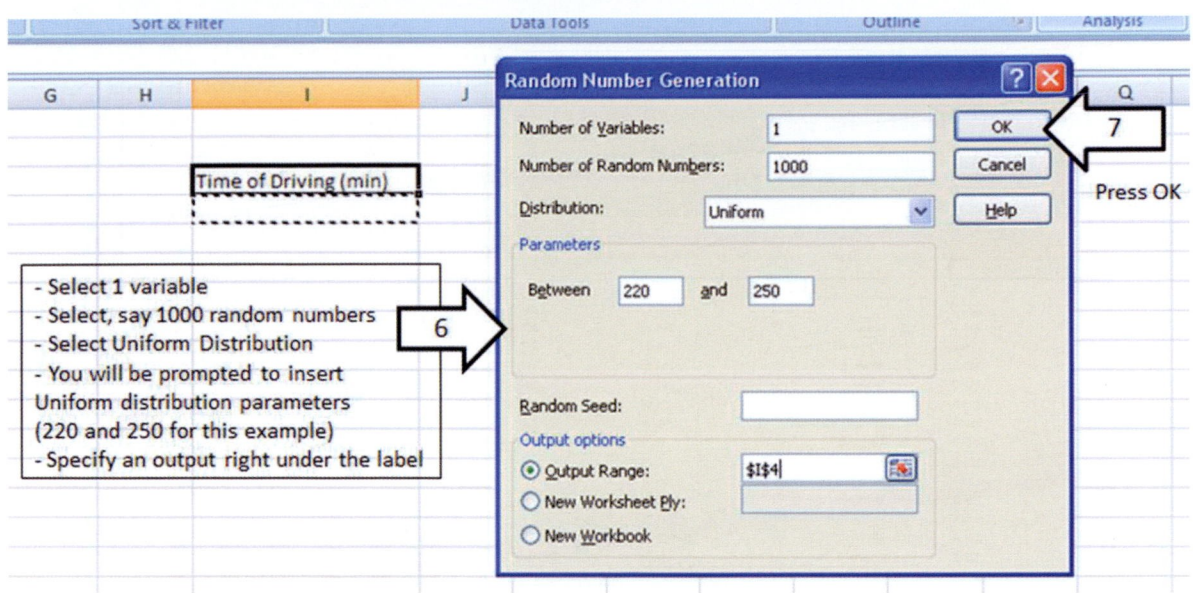

Figure 6.27 Using Microsoft Excel® to Simulate Uniform Distributions: Steps 6 and 7

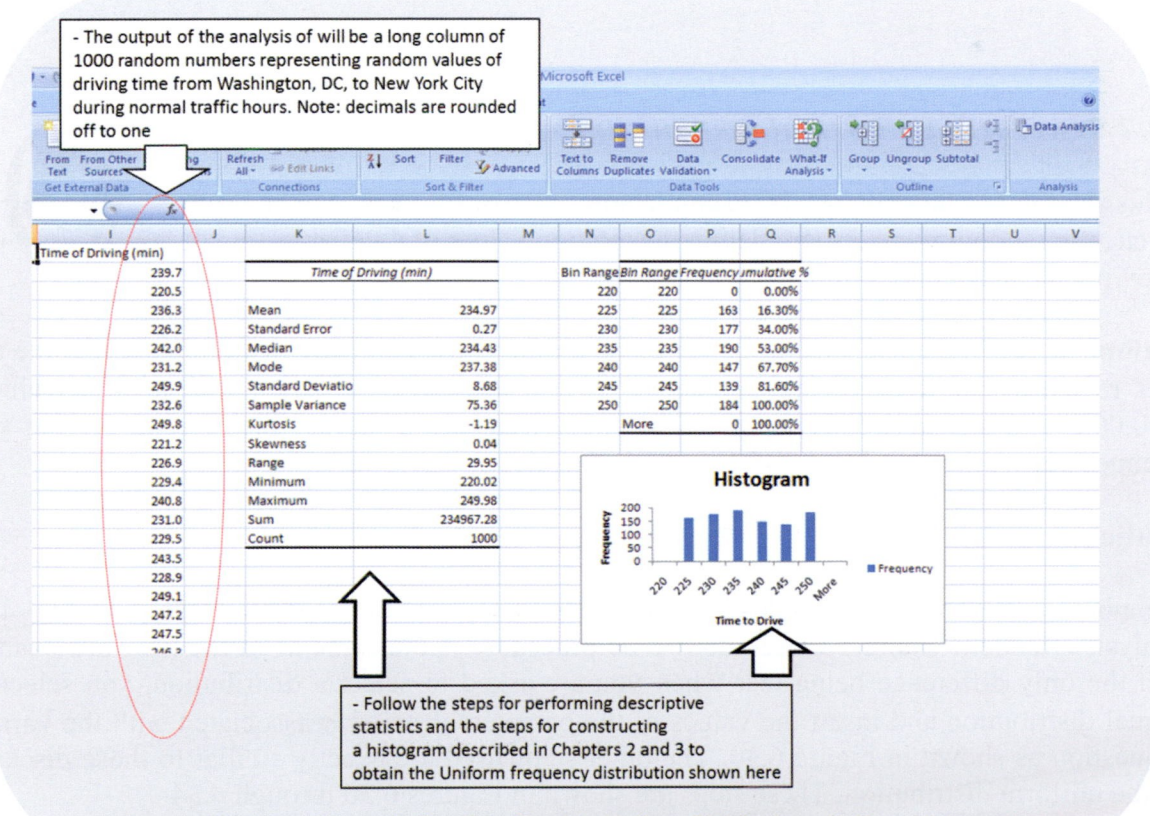

Figure 6.28 Using Microsoft Excel® to Simulate Uniform Distributions: Uniform Histogram

343

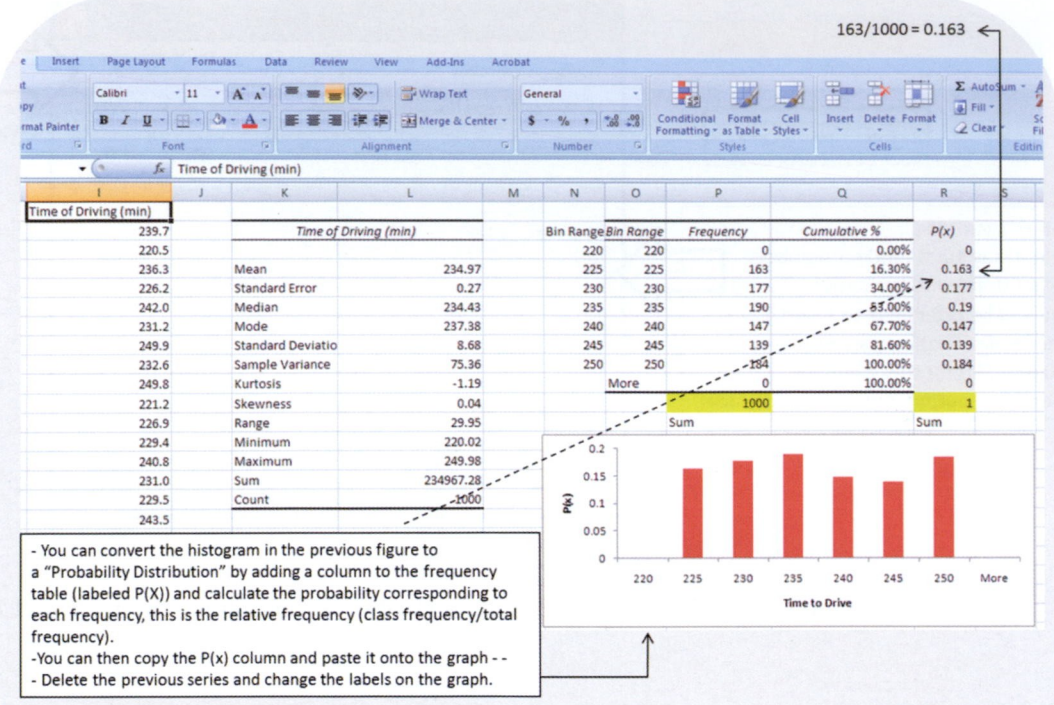

Figure 6.29 Using Microsoft Excel® to Simulate Uniform Distributions: Uniform Probability Distribution

6.8.2 Generating a normal distribution

In this section, we demonstrate by example how Microsoft Excel® can be used to generate random numbers simulating the random values of a variable following a normal distribution.

Example 6.18: In the analysis of the net income of a textile company, it was found that the total sales revenues per week of the company follows a normal distribution with a mean value of $100,000, and a standard deviation of $15,000. Generate a normal distribution for the sales revenues per week using Microsoft Excel® data analysis.

Solution:

The normal distribution for sales revenues per week can be generated using Excel® Data Analysis (Random Number Generation). The procedure is the same as in the previous example with the only difference being that when you are asked to select a distribution, you select the normal distribution and insert the values of the parameters μ and σ associated with the variable in question as shown in Figure 6.30. The other steps used are exactly similar to those discussed for the uniform distribution. These steps are shown in Figures 6.30 through 6.34.

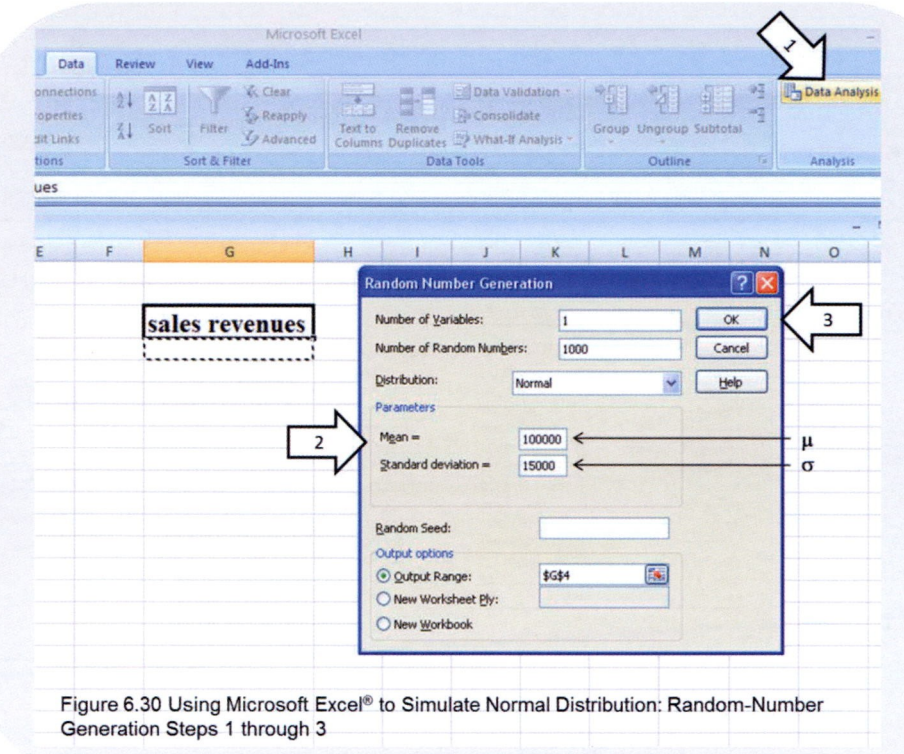

Figure 6.30 Using Microsoft Excel® to Simulate Normal Distribution: Random-Number Generation Steps 1 through 3

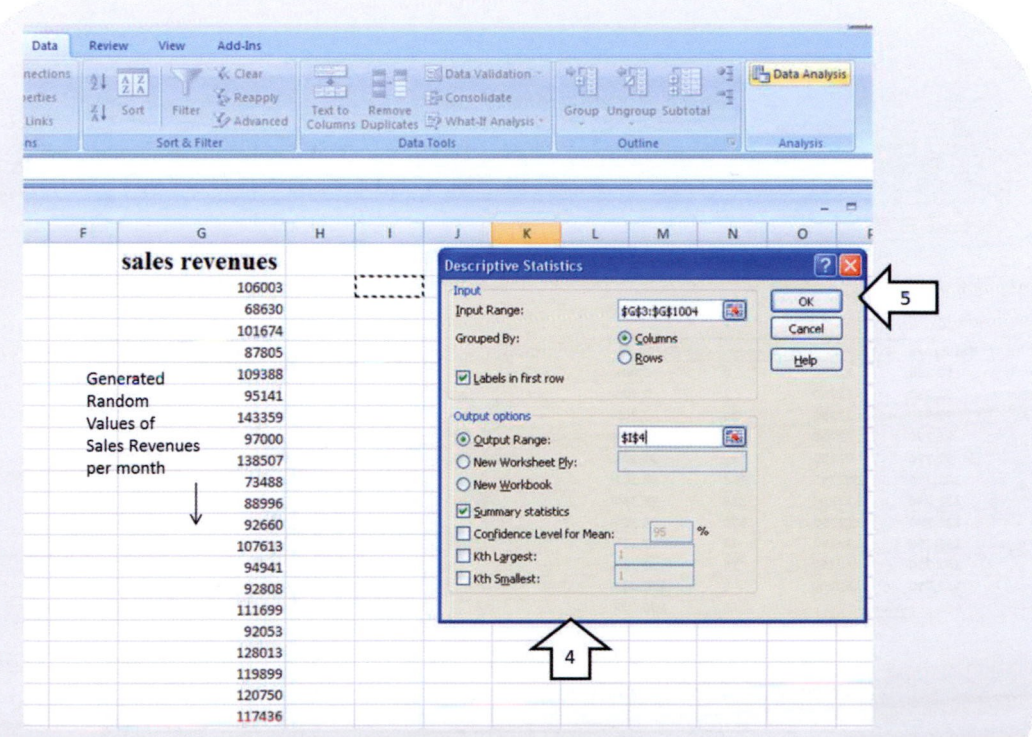

Figure 6.31 Using Microsoft Excel® to Simulate Normal Distribution: Descriptive Statistics Steps 4 and 5

345

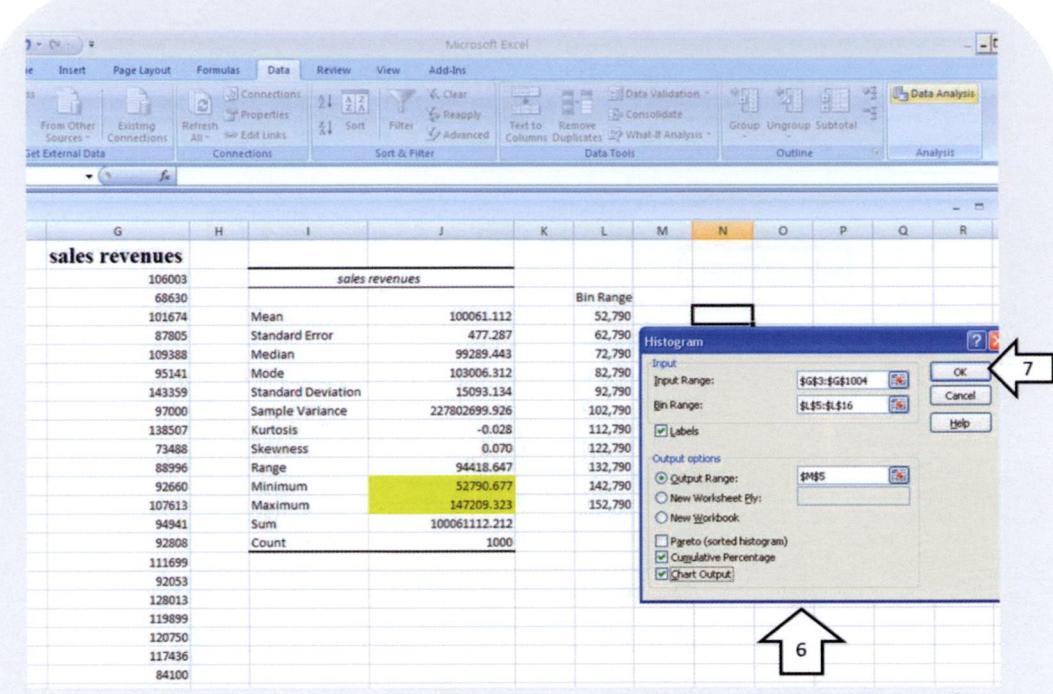

Figure 6.32 Using Microsoft Excel® to Simulate Normal Distribution: Histogram-Steps 6 and 7

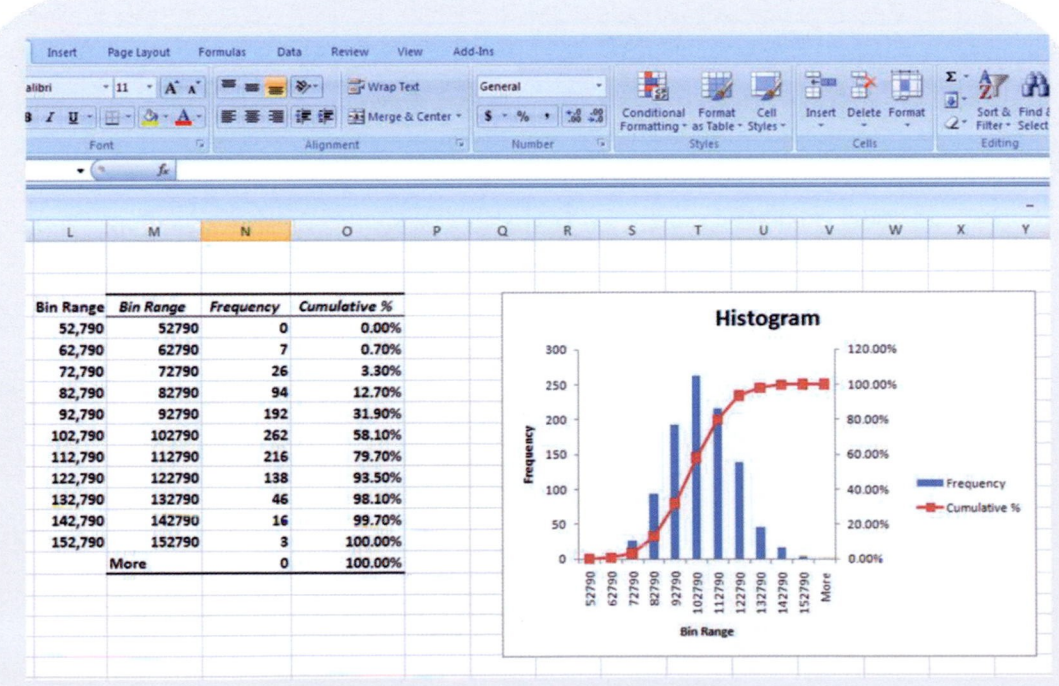

Figure 6.33 Using Microsoft Excel® to Simulate Normal Distribution: Histogram of Sales Revenues

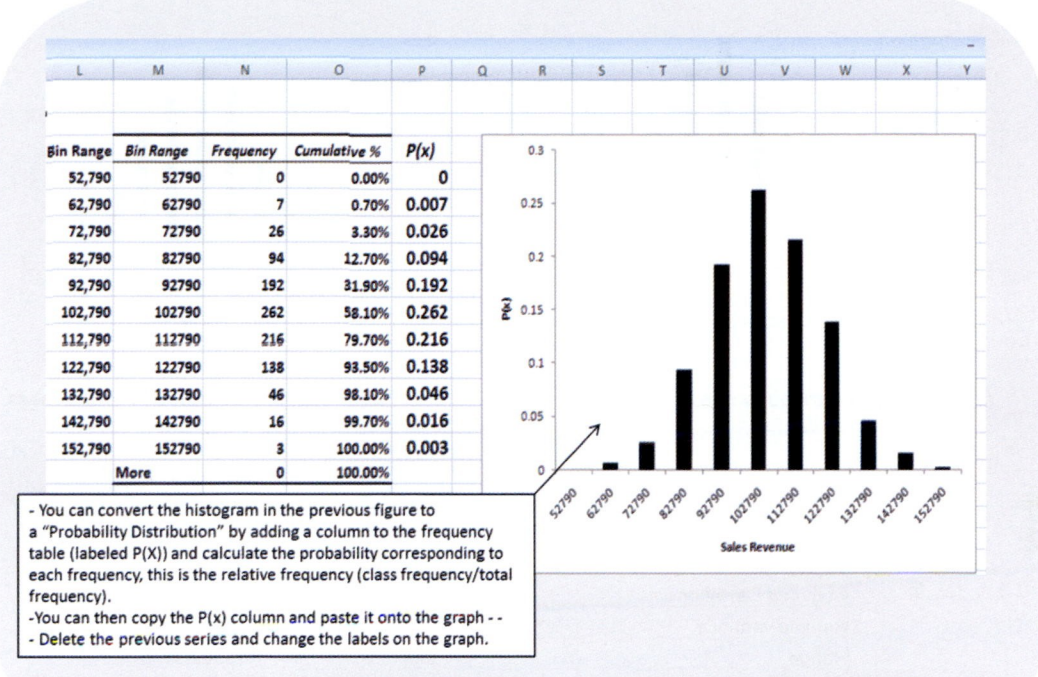

Figure 6.34 Using Microsoft Excel® to Simulate Normal Distribution: Probability Distribution

Example 6.19: For the same company in the above example, if the total expenses per week also follows a normal distribution with a mean value of $60,000 and standard deviation of $18,000. Generate a normal distribution of weekly expenses. Compare this distribution with that of the sales revenue produced in the previous example.

Solution:

Following the same procedures discussed above we can generate a normal distribution for the weekly expenses. Figure 6.35 shows two distributions; one for weekly revenues and one for weekly expenses and associated descriptive statistics of the two variables. As you can see in the table in this figure, the company earns average revenue of $100,061 and spends average expenses of $60,073. Assuming no other costs are encountered, the average company's net profit is:

Net profit = Revenues – Expenses = 100,061 – 60,073 = $39,988 ≈ $40,000

Note that for both distributions, mean ≈ mode ≈ median. This indicates the existence of approximately symmetrical (or normal distributions).

347

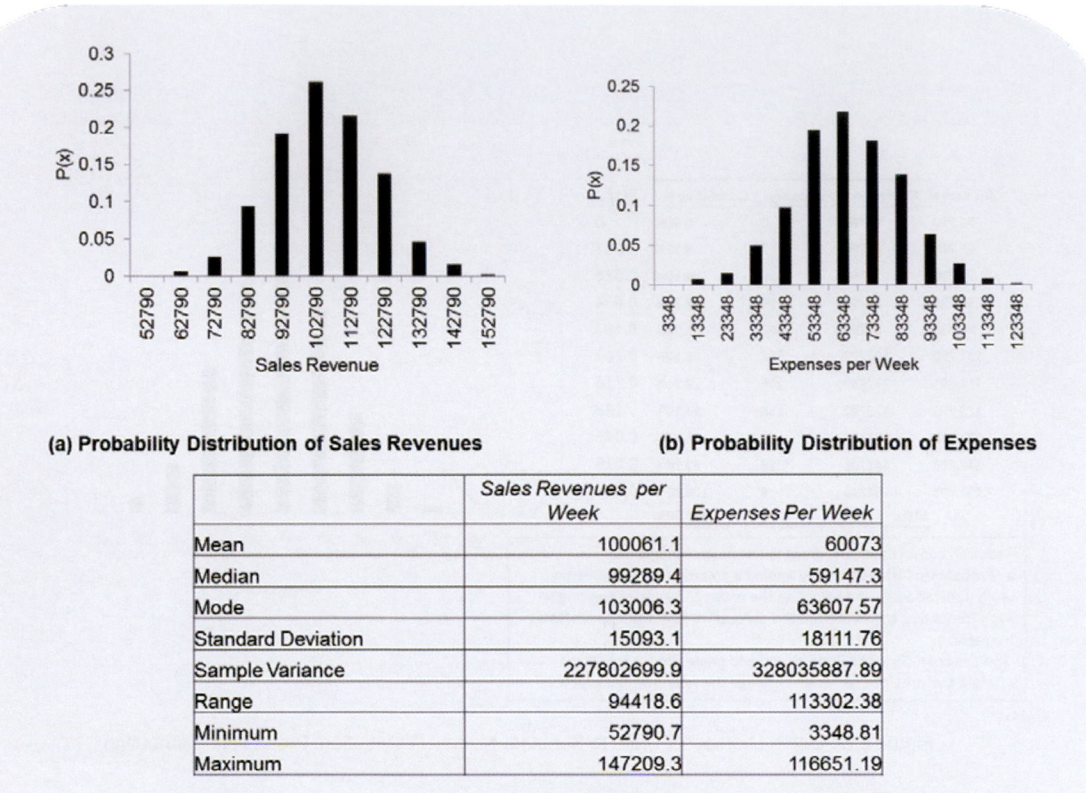

(a) Probability Distribution of Sales Revenues

(b) Probability Distribution of Expenses

	Sales Revenues per Week	Expenses Per Week
Mean	100061.1	60073
Median	99289.4	59147.3
Mode	103006.3	63607.57
Standard Deviation	15093.1	18111.76
Sample Variance	227802699.9	328035887.89
Range	94418.6	113302.38
Minimum	52790.7	3348.81
Maximum	147209.3	116651.19

Figure 6.35 Normal Probability Distributions of Sales Revenues and Expenses

Example 6.20: In the above two examples, we simulated normal probability distributions of weekly sales revenues and weekly expenses using Excel® Data Analysis. Recall that sales revenues per week of the company follow a normal distribution with a mean value of $100,000, and a standard deviation of $15,000, and the total expenses per week follow a normal distribution with a mean value of $60,000 and a standard deviation of $18,000. The net profit (income) of the company is roughly determined by the difference between the sales revenues and the expenses. A positive difference will imply a gain and a negative difference will imply a loss. What is the probability that this company will suffer a loss?

Solution:

The probability of loss is determined by the area of overlap between the normal distribution of sales revenue and the normal distribution of expenses in which expenses are larger than sales revenues, or $P_{loss} = P(expenses > Sales\ revenues)$. This area is illustrated in Figure 6.36.

348

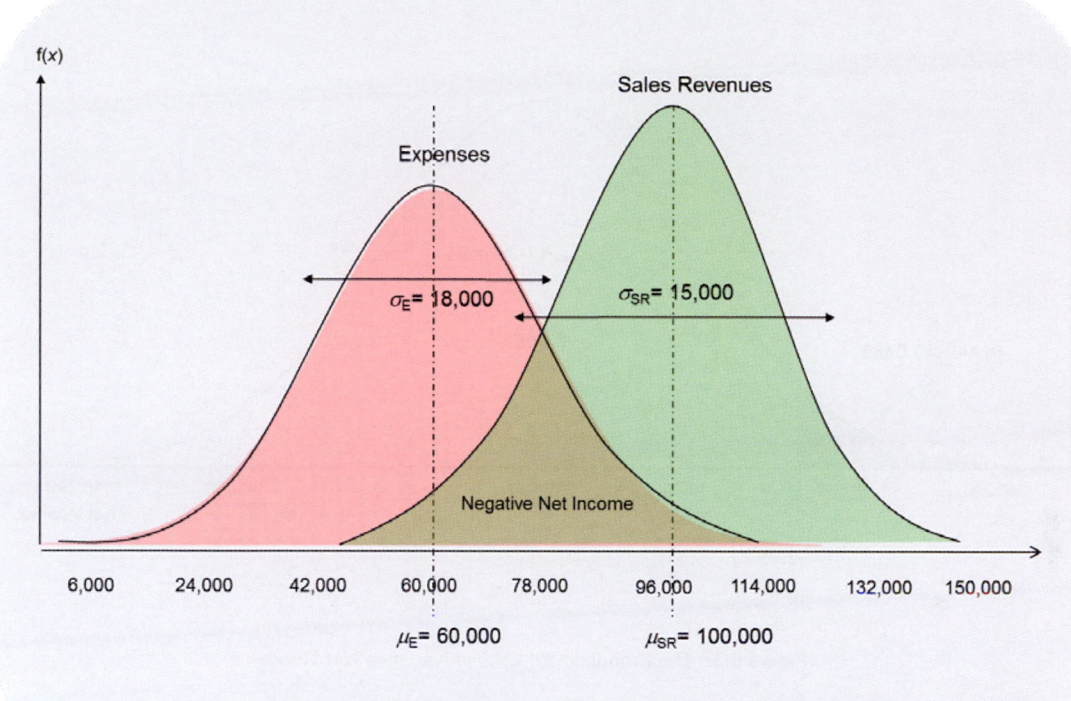

Figure 6.36 Normal Distributions of Expenses and Sales Revenues

A simple approach to determine the value of the probability of loss is by generating a normal distribution of the net income (profit) or the difference between sales revenues (*SR*) and expenses (*E*). The parameters of this distribution are as follows:

$$\mu_{net\ income} = \mu_{(SR-E)} = \mu_{SR} - \mu_E = 100,000 - 60,000 = \$40,000$$

$$\sigma_{net\ income} = \sqrt{\sigma^2_{SR} + \sigma^2_B} = \sqrt{15,000^2 + 18,000^2} = \$23431$$

Now, we can generate a normal distribution of the net income using Excel® Data Analysis-Random Number Generation. This distribution is shown in Figure 6.37. As can be seen in this distribution, the area of loss is the area to the left of zero. In this area, the sales revenue is less than the total expenses. At $x = 0$, $z = (0-40,000)/23,431 = -1.71$. As can be seen in Figure 6.37, the probability of loss or negative net income is $P(x< 0) = P(z< -1.71)$ is 0.0436 or there is a 4.4% chance that the company will suffer a loss.

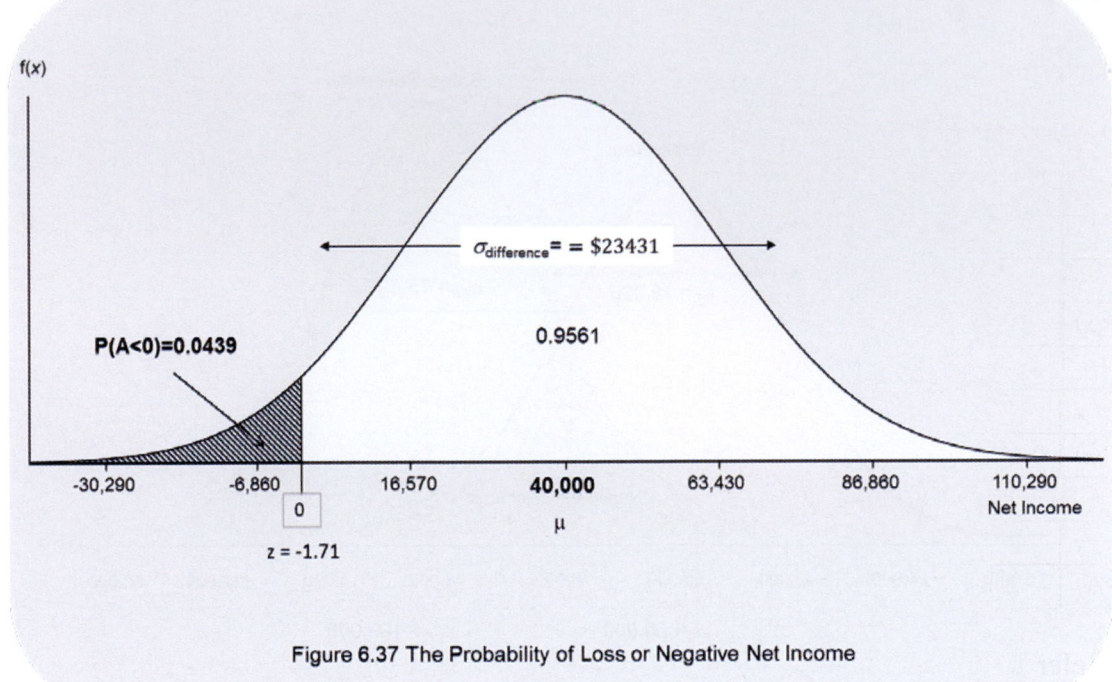

Figure 6.37 The Probability of Loss or Negative Net Income

Note that in the above example we used a simple operation to calculate the mean and standard deviation of the difference of two independent variables. Examples of other operations of this sort are shown in Table 6.5.

Table 6.5 Expressions of mean and standard deviation of some functions

Algebraic function	Mean, $\bar{Q}$	Std. deviation (σ_Q)
Q = Constant = C	C	0
$Q = Cx$	$C\bar{X}$	$C\sigma_x$
$Q = x + C$	$\bar{x} + C$	σ_x
$Q = x \pm y$	$\bar{x} \pm \bar{y}$	$\sqrt{\sigma^2_x + \sigma^2_y}$
$Q = xy$	$\bar{x}\bar{y}$	$\sqrt{\bar{y}^2\sigma^2_x + \bar{x}^2\sigma^2_y}$
$Q = x/y$	$\bar{x}/\bar{y}$	$\dfrac{\sqrt{\bar{y}^2\sigma^2_x + \bar{x}^2\sigma^2_y}}{\bar{y}^2}$
$Q = 1/x$	$1/\bar{x}$	$\dfrac{\sigma_x}{\bar{x}^2}$

6.9 Review Exercises

P6.1: Determine whether each of the following distributions is a uniform distribution:

(a)

x	7	10	13	16	19
$P(x)$	0.3	0.3	0.3	0.3	0.3

(b)

x	4	5	6	7	8
$P(x)$	0.2	0.2	0.2	0.2	0.2

(c)

x	1	2	3	4	5	6
$P(x)$	0.166667	0.166667	0.166667	0.166667	0.166667	0.166667

(d)

x	1	2	3	4	5	6	7
$P(x)$	0.15	0.15	0.15	0.15	0.15	0.15	0.15

P6.2: Refer to the continuous uniform distribution depicted below. Assume that the variable x (say bus trip time) is between 5 hours and 8 hours. Find the probability that a randomly selected time is (a) greater than 6 hours, and (b) between 6 and 7 hours.

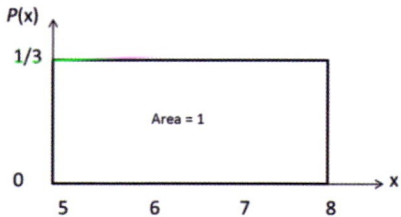

P6.3: In a statistics course, the instructor always gives a 15 minute small quiz to students every week. Typically, students spend about 10 to 14 minutes to finish the quiz. This can be modeled by a uniform distribution with the probability density function shown below. What is the probability that a student will spend at most 11 minutes to finish the quiz? What is the probability that a student will spend 12 minutes or less to finish the quiz? Select one of the following answers for these two questions, respectively:

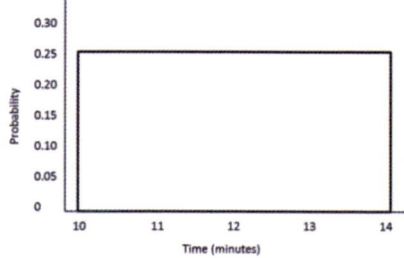

 (a) 0.25; 0.5 0

 (b) 0.75; 0.50

 (c) 0.50; 0.50

 (d) Can't be determined from the given information

P6.4: Refer to the continuous uniform distribution depicted below. Assume that the variable x (say human weight) is between 123.0 and 125.0 pounds. Find the probability that a randomly selected weight is (a) greater than 124.0 pounds, and (b) between 123.2 volts and 124.7 volts

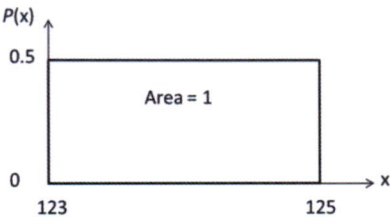

Answer: 0.5, 0.75

P6.5: In a statistics course, the instructor always gives a 15 minute small quiz to students every week. Typically, students spend from 10 minutes to 14 minutes to finish the quiz. This can be modeled by a uniform distribution with the probability density function shown below. What is the probability that a student will spend at least 15 minutes to finish the quiz? What is the probability that a student will spend at most 5 minutes to finish the quiz? Select one of the following answers for these two questions, respectively:

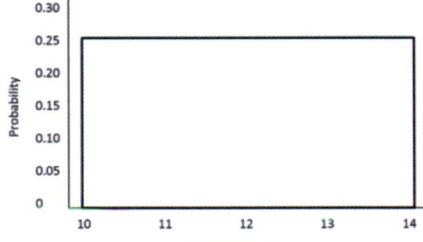

    (a) 0.25; 0
    (b) 0; 0.50
    (c) 1.0; 0
    (d) None of the above

P6.6: A uniform distribution is defined over the interval from 4 to 6.
a. What are the values for a and b?
b. What is the mean of this uniform distribution?
c. What is the standard deviation?
d. Show that the total area is 1.00.
e. Find the probability of a value more than 5.
f. Find the probability of a value between 4 and 5.
Answer:
    a.   b = 6, a = 4
    b. $\mu = (a + b)/2 = (4 + 6)/2 = 5$
    c.   *Do it yourself*
    d.   Area $= \frac{1}{(6-4)}(6 - 4)) = 1$
    e.   *Do it yourself*
    f.   *Do it yourself*

P6.7: In a statistics course, the instructor always gives a 15 minute small quiz to students every week. Typically, students spend from 10 minutes to 14 minutes to finish the quiz. This can be modeled by a uniform distribution with the probability density function shown below. What is the probability that a student will spend at least 13 minutes to finish the quiz? And what is the probability that a student will spend 13 minutes or less to finish the quiz?

(a) 0.25; 0.5 0

(b) 0.25; 0.75

(c) 0.50; 0.50

(d) Can't be determined from the given information

P6.8: Air Tran Airlines reports the flight time from Atlanta Airport, GA to Newark Airport, NJ is 2 hours. Suppose the actual flying time is uniformly distributed between 110 and 130 minutes.
a. Show a graph of the continuous probability distribution.
b. What is the mean flight time?
c. What is the variance of the flight times?
d. What is the probability the flight time is less than 120 minutes?
e. What is the probability the flight takes more than 115 minutes?

P6.9: Suppose the random variable in question is the time for a commercial aircraft to fly from JFK Airport in New York City to Cairo Airport in Egypt. Assuming that flying time is uniformly distributed from 10 hours to 12 hours, construct a uniform probability distribution of the flying time. What are the mean and the standard deviation of flying time? What is the probability that the flying time from JFK Airport in New York City to Cairo Airport in Egypt is less than 11.5 hours? Interpret the results.
Answer: 11, 0.577, 0.75

P6.10: The amount of soda drink in 12-ounce cans is uniformly distributed between 11.96 ounces and 12.05 ounces.
a. What is the mean amount per can?
b. What is the standard deviation amount per can?
c. What is the probability of selecting a can of cola and finding it has less than 12 ounces?
d. What is the probability of selecting a can of cola and finding it has more than 11.98 ounces?
e. What is the probability of selecting a can of cola and finding it has more than 11.00 ounces?

P6.11: When we refer to a 'normal' distribution, does the word 'normal' have the same meaning as in ordinary language, or does it have a special meaning in statistics? What exactly is a normal distribution?
Answer: Read section 6.3

P6.12: Explain how a normal probability function is converted into a standard normal probability function. What are the mean and the variance of a *standard* normal probability distribution?

P6.13: The distribution of students' grades is a normal distribution with a mean of 70 and a standard deviation of 5. What are the values of the mean and standard deviation after all grades have been standardized by converting them to z scores.
Answer: 0, 1

P6.14: Find the area of the shaded region for the following standard normal distributions

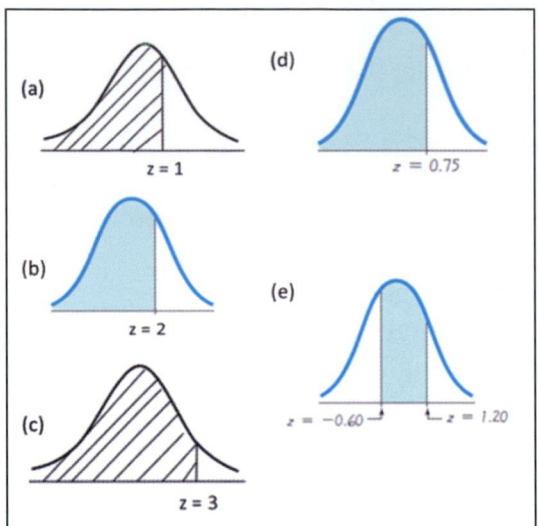

P6.15: Find the indicated z score for the standard normal distributions shown below

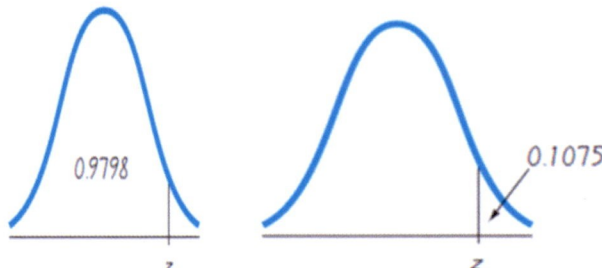

Answer: 2.05, 1.24

P 6.16: For the problems given below, draw a sketch of the standard normal distribution, and find the probability of each reading

(a) Between -3.0 and -1.0, (b) Less than 3.55, (c) Greater than -1.75, (d) Greater than 2.22, (e) Less than -1.5, (f) Less than 1.23, (g) Between 0.50 and 1.00, (h) Between -1.20 and 1.95, (i) Between -2.50 and 5.00, (j) Greater than 0

P6.17: Find the indicated area under the curve of the standard normal distribution, then convert it to a percentage to fill in the blank.
- About _____% of the area is between z = -2 and z = 2
- About _____% of the area is greater than z = -1
- About _____% of the area is between z = -1 and z = 1
- About _____% of the area is less than z = 3
- About _____% of the area is between z = -3 and z = 3
- About _____% of the area is greater than z = 2
Answer: 95.44%, 84.13%, 68.26%, 99.87%, 99.74%, 2.28%

354

P6.18: Find the following x values for a variable that is normally distributed with a mean of 100 and a standard deviation of 15

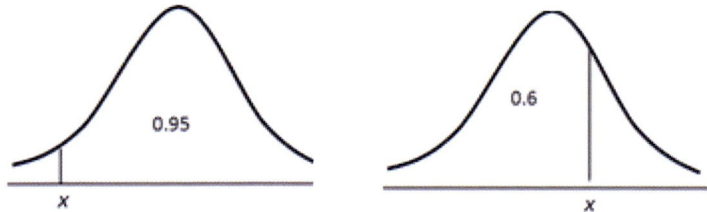

P6.19: Find the area of the shaded region for a variable that is normally distributed with a mean of 100 and a standard deviation of 15

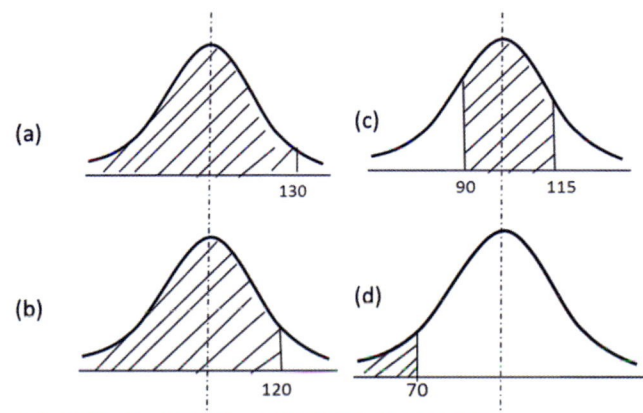

Answer: (a) 0.9772, (b) 0.9082, (c) 0.5899, (d) 0.0228

P6.20: Determine the value(s) of z in the following cases:
(a) Area under the normal curve between - ∞ and z is 0.100.
(b) Area under the normal curve to right of z is 0.8100.
(c) Area under the normal curve to left of z is 0.7100

P6.21:
    (a) Find the z-score that corresponds to a cumulative area of 97.5%
    (b) Find the z-score that corresponds to a cumulative area of 99.5%
    (c) Find the z-score that corresponds to a cumulative area of 36.32%
    (d) Find the z-score that corresponds to a cumulative area of 89.25%
Answer: (a) 1.9, (b) 2.58, (c) -0.35, (d) 1.24

P6.22: A furniture company designs office chairs with the main design objective being to make office chairs wide enough to fit 95% of people. A survey of many people revealed that the average desired width of an office chair is 18 inches, with a standard deviation of 1.5 inches. Find values of chair width of 95 percent of the seats to be manufactured.

P6.23: A furniture company designs theater seats, with the main design objective being to make theater seats wide enough to fit 98% of people. A survey of many people revealed that the average desired width of a theater seat is 20 inches, with a standard deviation of 0.75 inches. Find values of chair width of 98 percent of the seats to be manufactured.

P6.24: A survey indicates that people drive their cars an average 6 years before buying another car with a standard deviation of 1.2 year. A car owner is selected at random.
1. Find the probability that he/she will drive it for a period between 3 years and 4 years?
2. Find the probability that he/she will drive it for less than 4 years?

P6.25: A survey indicates that during shopping customers in Wal-Mart stay in the store an average of 1 hour with a standard deviation of 10 minutes. If the length of shopping time can be assumed to follow a normal distribution, answer the following questions:
   (a) What is the chance that a random shopper will stay over 2 hours at Wal-Mart?
   (b) What is the chance that a random shopper will stay less than 30 minutes at Wal-Mart?
   (c) What is the chance that a random shopper will stay less than 40 minutes at Wal-Mart?
   (d) What is the chance that a random shopper will stay between 30 minutes to 50 minutes at Wal-Mart?
Answer: (a) 0, (b) 0.0013, (c) 0.0228, (d) 0.1574

P6.26: The worker's wage per hour in a textile factory follows a normal distribution with a mean of $20.0 and a standard deviation of $4.0.
a. Compute the z value associated with a wage of $25.0.
b. What percent of the worker's population makes between $20.0 and $25.0?
c. What percent of the worker's population makes less than $18.0?

P6.27: The worker's hourly wage in a large retail store follows a normal distribution with a mean of $20.5 and a standard deviation of $3.50. If we select a worker at random, what is the probability the worker earns: a. Between $20.50 and $24.00 per hour? b. More than $24.00 per hour?, c. Less than $19.00 per hour?
Answer: (a) 0.3413, (b) 0.1587, (c) 0.3336

P6.28: The ages of top management in a large organization follows a normal distribution with a mean value of 50 years and a standard deviation of 4 years.
a. Compute the probability of age between 44.0 and 55.0.
b. Compute the probability of age greater than 55.0.
c. Compute the probability of age between 52.0 and 55.0.

P6.29: A variable following a normal distribution with a mean value of 7 and a variance of 0.01.
a. What is the probability that the variable will have a value between 7.10 and 7.25?
b. What is the probability that that the variable will have a value of 7.25 or more?
c. What is the probability that the variable will have a value between 6.80 and 7.25?
Answer: a. 0.1525, b. 0.0062, c. 0.9710

P6.30: Suppose the random variable in question is the driving time from Raleigh, NC to Washington, DC during normal traffic hours. Assuming that driving time is uniformly distributed from 210 minutes to 240 minutes, construct a uniform probability distribution of the driving time using the simulation technique of random number generation of Microsoft Excel® data analysis.

P6.31: In the analysis of the net income of a fast-food restaurant, it was found that the total sales revenues per month of the restaurant follows a normal distribution with a mean value of $70,000, and a standard deviation of $6,000. Generate a normal distribution for the sales revenues per month using Excel® data analysis.
Answer: Use the steps described in section 6.8.2 for solving this problem.

P6.32: For the same fast-food restaurant in the above problem, if the total cost of operating the restaurant per month also follows a normal distribution with a mean value of $30,000 and standard deviation of $12,000. Generate a normal distribution of monthly expenses using Excel® data analysis.

P6.33: Using the data obtained from the above two problems, simulate the net income of the restaurant using Excel® data analysis. What is the probability that this restaurant will suffer a loss?
Answer: Use the steps described in section 6.8.2 for solving this problem.

P6.34: A tech-support department in an organization finds that call times follow a normal distribution with mean value of 15 minutes and a standard deviation of 3.5 minutes. What is the probability that a random tech-support call is: (a) more than 20 minutes, (b) 20 minutes or less, (c) between 10 and 12 minutes?

P6.35: Assume that the mean monthly salary of the management staff in a large retail store is $2,100 and the standard deviation is $250. What is the salary of the lowest 3 percent of the management staff?
Answer: $1630 (2100-1.88×250)

P6.36: A variable x follows a normal distribution with mean value of 50 and standard deviation of 4. Determine the value of x below which 95% of the observations will occur.

P6.37: The amount of soda drink dispensed by a bottling machine is normally distributed with mean of 7 ounces per cup and standard deviation of 0.1 ounce per cup. How much soda is dispensed in the largest 1 percent of the cups?
Answer: ≈ 7.0

P6.38: Birth weights in the United States are normally distributed with a mean of 3420g (7.5398 pound) and a standard deviation of 495g (1.09 pound). If a hospital plans to set up special observation conditions for the lightest 2% of babies, what weight is used for the cutoff separating the lightest 2% from the others?
a. Find the standard z score with a cumulative area to its left of 0.6700.
b. Find the standard z score with a cumulative area to its right of 0.9960.

P6.39: A company manufactures thermometers that are supposed to give readings of 0 C at the freezing point of water. Tests on a large sample of these instruments reveal that at the freezing point of water, some thermometers give readings below 0 and some give readings above 0. Assume that the mean reading is 0 C and the standard deviation of the readings is 1.00 C. Also assume that the readings are normally distributed. If one thermometer is randomly selected,

  (a) Find the temperature separating the bottom 95% from the top 5% (or find the temperature corresponding to P_{95}, the 95th percentile).
  (b) find the temperatures separating the bottom 2.5% and the top 2.5%

P6.40: In designing seats to be installed in commercial aircraft, engineers want to make the seats wide enough to fit 98% of all males. Keep in mind that accommodating 100% of males may require very wide seats that would take more space and will be expensive. Some publications suggest that men have hip breadths that are normally distributed with a mean of 14.4 in. and a standard deviation of 1.0 in. Find P_{98}, That is, find the hip breadth of men that separates the bottom 98% from the top 2%.

P6.41: Assume that adults have IQ scores that are normally distributed with a mean of 100 and a standard deviation of 15
  a) Find the probability that a randomly selected adult has an IQ that is less than 115
  b) Find the probability that a randomly selected adult has an IQ between 90 and 110
  c) Find P_{20} which is the IQ score separating the bottom 20% from the top 80%
  d) Find the IQ score separating the top 15% from the others
Answer: (a) 0.8413, (b) 0.4972, (c) 87.4, (d) 115.6

P6.42: Assume human body temperatures are normally distributed with a mean of 98.2°F and a standard deviation of 0.62°F.

  (a) A hospital uses 100.6°F as the lowest temperature considered to be a fever. What percentage of normal and healthy persons would be considered to have a fever? Does this percentage suggest that a cutoff of 100.6°F is appropriate?
  (b) Physicians want to select a minimum temperature for requiring further medical tests. What should that temperature be, if we want only 5.0% of healthy people to exceed it?

P6.43: The sitting height (from seat to top of head) of drivers must be considered in the design of a new car model. Suppose men have sitting heights that are normally distributed with a mean of 36.0 in. and a standard deviation of 1.4 in. Engineers have provided plans that can accommodate men with sitting heights up to 38.8 in., but taller men cannot fit. If a man is randomly selected,
  (a) Find the probability that he has a sitting height less than 40.2 in.
  (b) Find the probability that he has a sitting height less than 38.8 in.
  (c) Based on that result, is the current engineering design feasible?

P6.44: A financial advisor recommended that you invest in Japa Electronic common stock. He thinks that it has a 0.4 chance of generating a 10% return, a 0.3 chance of generating a 25% return, and a 0.1 chance of generating a 45% return. The catch is it may also be associated with a loss of 15% with a chance of 0.2. If you decided to go for this investment, what would be your expected return?

P6.45: A large company is planning to launch a new product in the market. However, the company is not sure about the state of the economy and its impact on the return on the capital investment associated with this new product. A key analysis in this regard is the expected return and risk. Since the new product can come in three different versions, each is associated with a different capital investment, the company formed three teams each is involved in an independent project to determine which project generates the highest expected return. The analysis in each project made in the context of the chance of economic change is shown in the table below.

State of Economy	Probability of Occurrence	Project 1	Project 2	Project 3
Downward (Recession)	0.6	4	6	7
No Change (Stable)	0.3	5	7	8
Upward (booming)	0.1	12	14	16

a. Determine each project's expected return and variability in return
b. Which project yields the highest expected return and lowest risk?

P6.46: Suppose that a structural member is subjected to a static load that develops a normal stress distribution over the member of mean μ_{str} and standard deviation σ_{str}. The material from which the structural member is made has a yield strength that also exhibits a normal distribution of mean μ_{yield} and standard deviation σ_{yield}. From historical records the following information was obtained: $\mu_{str} = 30$ ksi, $\sigma_{str} = 8$ ksi, $\mu_{yield} = 40$ ksi, $\sigma_{yield} = 6$ ksi. Generate normal distributions for the stress and the yield strength.

P6.47: From the results of the above problem you will find that the distribution of loading stress and that of the material yield strength overlaps. From a design viewpoint, this overlaps creates a great deal of concern since it implies that some stress values will actually be greater than the yield strength of material, which can lead to failure of the structural member. Determine the probability that the stress will exceed the yield strength (or the probability that the member will fail).

Statistical Tables are key sources to find the values of many important statistics and the corresponding areas under the distribution curve. Examples of these sources are listed below:

http://www.statsoft.com/textbook/distribution-tables/

http://web.abo.fi/fak/mnf/mate/kurser/statistik1/StaTable.pdf

http://faculty.vassar.edu/lowry/tabs.html

http://facultyweb.berry.edu/vbissonnette/tables/tables.html

APPENDIX 6.A: Statistical Tables

Cumulative Normal Distribution

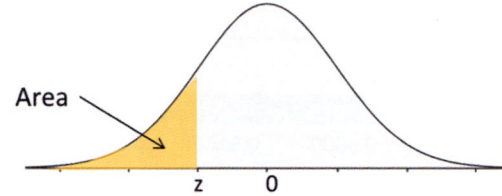

Area

z   0

z	0	0.01	0.02	0.03	0.04	0.05	0.06	0.07	0.08	0.09
-3.6	0.0002	0.0002	0.0001	0.0001	0.0001	0.0001	0.0001	0.0001	0.0001	0.0001
-3.5	0.0002	0.0002	0.0002	0.0002	0.0002	0.0002	0.000	0.000	0.0002	0.0002
-3.4	0.0003	0.0003	0.0003	0.0003	0.0003	0.0003	0.0003	0.0003	0.0003	0.0002
-3.3	0.0005	0.0005	0.0005	0.0004	0.0004	0.0004	0.0004	0.0004	0.0004	0.0003
-3.2	0.0007	0.0007	0.0006	0.0006	0.0006	0.0006	0.0006	0.0005	0.0005	0.0005
-3.1	0.0010	0.0009	0.0009	0.0009	0.0008	0.0008	0.0008	0.0008	0.0007	0.0007
-3.0	0.0013	0.0013	0.0013	0.0012	0.0012	0.0011	0.0011	0.0011	0.0010	0.0010
-2.9	0.0019	0.0018	0.0018	0.0017	0.0016	0.0016	0.0015	0.0015	0.0014	0.0014
-2.8	0.0026	0.0025	0.0024	0.0023	0.0023	0.0022	0.0021	0.0021	0.0020	0.0019
-2.7	0.0035	0.0034	0.0033	0.0032	0.0031	0.0030	0.0029	0.0028	0.0027	0.0026
-2.6	0.0047	0.0045	0.0044	0.0043	0.0041	0.0040	0.0039	0.0038	0.0037	0.0036
-2.5	0.0062	0.0060	0.0059	0.0057	0.0055	0.0054	0.0052	0.0051	0.0049	0.0048
-2.4	0.0082	0.0080	0.0078	0.0075	0.0073	0.0071	0.0069	0.0068	0.0066	0.0064
-2.3	0.0107	0.0104	0.0102	0.0099	0.0096	0.0094	0.0091	0.0089	0.0087	0.0084
-2.2	0.0139	0.0136	0.0132	0.0129	0.0125	0.0122	0.0119	0.0116	0.0113	0.0110
-2.1	0.0179	0.0174	0.0170	0.0166	0.0162	0.0158	0.0154	0.0150	0.0146	0.0143
-2.0	0.0228	0.0222	0.0217	0.0212	0.0207	0.0202	0.0197	0.0192	0.0188	0.0183
-1.9	0.0287	0.0281	0.0274	0.0268	0.0262	0.0256	0.0250	0.0244	0.0239	0.0233
-1.8	0.0359	0.0351	0.0344	0.0336	0.0329	0.0322	0.0314	0.0307	0.0301	0.0294
-1.7	0.0446	0.0436	0.0427	0.0418	0.0409	0.0401	0.0392	0.0384	0.0375	0.0367
-1.6	0.0548	0.0537	0.0526	0.0516	0.0505	0.0495	0.0485	0.0475	0.0465	0.0455
-1.5	0.0668	0.0655	0.0643	0.0630	0.0618	0.0606	0.0594	0.0582	0.0571	0.0559
-1.4	0.0808	0.0793	0.0778	0.0764	0.0749	0.0735	0.0721	0.0708	0.0694	0.0681
-1.3	0.0968	0.0951	0.0934	0.0918	0.0901	0.0885	0.0869	0.0853	0.0838	0.0823
-1.2	0.1151	0.1131	0.1112	0.1093	0.1075	0.1056	0.1038	0.1020	0.1003	0.0985
-1.1	0.1357	0.1335	0.1314	0.1292	0.1271	0.1251	0.1230	0.1210	0.1190	0.1170
-1.0	0.1587	0.1562	0.1539	0.1515	0.1492	0.1469	0.1446	0.1423	0.1401	0.1379
-0.9	0.1841	0.1814	0.1788	0.1762	0.1736	0.1711	0.1685	0.1660	0.1635	0.1611
-0.8	0.2119	0.2090	0.2061	0.2033	0.2005	0.1977	0.1949	0.1922	0.1894	0.1867
-0.7	0.2420	0.2389	0.2358	0.2327	0.2296	0.2266	0.2236	0.2206	0.2177	0.2148
-0.6	0.2743	0.2709	0.2676	0.2643	0.2611	0.2578	0.2546	0.2514	0.2483	0.2451
-0.5	0.3085	0.3050	0.3015	0.2981	0.2946	0.2912	0.2877	0.2843	0.2810	0.2776
-0.4	0.3446	0.3409	0.3372	0.3336	0.3300	0.3264	0.3228	0.3192	0.3156	0.3121
-0.3	0.3821	0.3783	0.3745	0.3707	0.3669	0.3632	0.3594	0.3557	0.3520	0.3483
-0.2	0.4207	0.4168	0.4129	0.4090	0.4052	0.4013	0.3974	0.3936	0.3897	0.3859
-0.1	0.4602	0.4562	0.4522	0.4483	0.4443	0.4404	0.4364	0.4325	0.4286	0.4247
0.0	0.5000	0.4960	0.4920	0.4880	0.4840	0.4801	0.4761	0.4721	0.4681	0.4641

Cumulative Normal Distribution

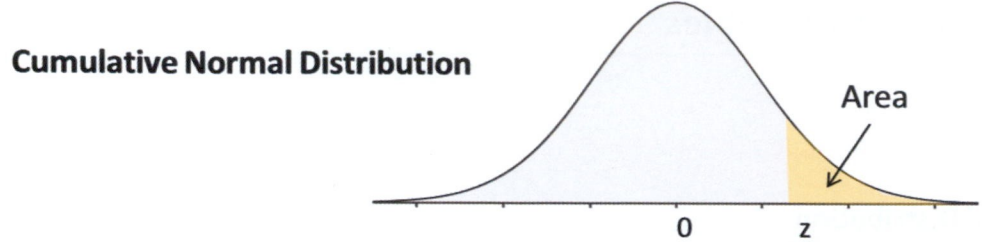

Area

0   z

z	0	0.01	0.02	0.03	0.04	0.05	0.06	0.07	0.08	0.09
0.0	0.5000	0.5040	0.5080	0.5120	0.5160	0.5199	0.5239	0.5279	0.5319	0.5359
0.1	0.5398	0.5438	0.5478	0.5517	0.5557	0.5596	0.5636	0.5675	0.5714	0.5753
0.2	0.5793	0.5832	0.5871	0.5910	0.5948	0.5987	0.6026	0.6064	0.6103	0.6141
0.3	0.6179	0.6217	0.6255	0.6293	0.6331	0.6368	0.6406	0.6443	0.6480	0.6517
0.4	0.6554	0.6591	0.6628	0.6664	0.6700	0.6736	0.6772	0.6808	0.6844	0.6879
0.5	0.6915	0.6950	0.6985	0.7019	0.7054	0.7088	0.7123	0.7157	0.7190	0.7224
0.6	0.7257	0.7291	0.7324	0.7357	0.7389	0.7422	0.7454	0.7486	0.7517	0.7549
0.7	0.7580	0.7611	0.7642	0.7673	0.7704	0.7734	0.7764	0.7794	0.7823	0.7852
0.8	0.7881	0.7910	0.7939	0.7967	0.7995	0.8023	0.8051	0.8078	0.8106	0.8133
0.9	0.8159	0.8186	0.8212	0.8238	0.8264	0.8289	0.8315	0.8340	0.8365	0.8389
1.0	0.8413	0.8438	0.8461	0.8485	0.8508	0.8531	0.8554	0.8577	0.8599	0.8621
1.1	0.8643	0.8665	0.8686	0.8708	0.8729	0.8749	0.8770	0.8790	0.8810	0.8830
1.2	0.8849	0.8869	0.8888	0.8907	0.8925	0.8944	0.8962	0.8980	0.8997	0.9015
1.3	0.9032	0.9049	0.9066	0.9082	0.9099	0.9115	0.9131	0.9147	0.9162	0.9177
1.4	0.9192	0.9207	0.9222	0.9236	0.9251	0.9265	0.9279	0.9292	0.9306	0.9319
1.5	0.9332	0.9345	0.9357	0.9370	0.9382	0.9394	0.9406	0.9418	0.9429	0.9441
1.6	0.9452	0.9463	0.9474	0.9484	0.9495	0.9505	0.9515	0.9525	0.9535	0.9545
1.7	0.9554	0.9564	0.9573	0.9582	0.9591	0.9599	0.9608	0.9616	0.9625	0.9633
1.8	0.9641	0.9649	0.9656	0.9664	0.9671	0.9678	0.9686	0.9693	0.9699	0.9706
1.9	0.9713	0.9719	0.9726	0.9732	0.9738	0.9744	0.9750	0.9756	0.9761	0.9767
2.0	0.9772	0.9778	0.9783	0.9788	0.9793	0.9798	0.9803	0.9808	0.9812	0.9817
2.1	0.9821	0.9826	0.9830	0.9834	0.9838	0.9842	0.9846	0.9850	0.9854	0.9857
2.2	0.9861	0.9864	0.9868	0.9871	0.9875	0.9878	0.9881	0.9884	0.9887	0.9890
2.3	0.9893	0.9896	0.9898	0.9901	0.9904	0.9906	0.9909	0.9911	0.9913	0.9916
2.4	0.9918	0.9920	0.9922	0.9925	0.9927	0.9929	0.9931	0.9932	0.9934	0.9936
2.5	0.9938	0.9940	0.9941	0.9943	0.9945	0.9946	0.9948	0.9949	0.9951	0.9952
2.6	0.9953	0.9955	0.9956	0.9957	0.9959	0.9960	0.9961	0.9962	0.9963	0.9964
2.7	0.9965	0.9966	0.9967	0.9968	0.9969	0.9970	0.9971	0.9972	0.9973	0.9974
2.8	0.9974	0.9975	0.9976	0.9977	0.9977	0.9978	0.9979	0.9979	0.9980	0.9981
2.9	0.9981	0.9982	0.9982	0.9983	0.9984	0.9984	0.9985	0.9985	0.9986	0.9986
3.0	0.9987	0.9987	0.9987	0.9988	0.9988	0.9989	0.9989	0.9989	0.9990	0.9990
3.1	0.9990	0.9991	0.9991	0.9991	0.9992	0.9992	0.9992	0.9992	0.9993	0.9993
3.2	0.9993	0.9993	0.9994	0.9994	0.9994	0.9994	0.9994	0.9995	0.9995	0.9995
3.3	0.9995	0.9995	0.9995	0.9996	0.9996	0.9996	0.9996	0.9996	0.9996	0.9997
3.4	0.9997	0.9997	0.9997	0.9997	0.9997	0.9997	0.9997	0.9997	0.9997	0.9998
3.5	0.9998	0.9998	0.9998	0.9998	0.9998	0.9998	0.9998	0.9998	0.9998	0.9998
3.6	0.9998	0.9998	0.9999	0.9999	0.9999	0.9999	0.9999	0.9999	0.9999	0.9999

APPENDIX 6.B Standard Normal Distribution Table: $P(0 \text{ to } z)$

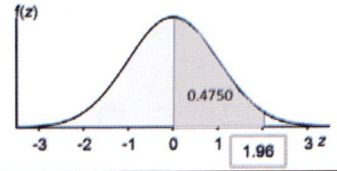

z	0	0.01	0.02	0.03	0.04	0.05	0.06	0.07	0.08	0.09
0.0	0.0000	0.0040	0.0080	0.0120	0.0160	0.0199	0.0239	0.0279	0.0319	0.0359
0.1	0.0398	0.0438	0.0478	0.0517	0.0557	0.0596	0.0636	0.0675	0.0714	0.0753
0.2	0.0793	0.0832	0.0871	0.0910	0.0948	0.0987	0.1026	0.1064	0.1103	0.1141
0.3	0.1179	0.1217	0.1255	0.1293	0.1331	0.1368	0.1406	0.1443	0.1480	0.1517
0.4	0.1554	0.1591	0.1628	0.1664	0.1700	0.1736	0.1772	0.1808	0.1844	0.1879
0.5	0.1915	0.1950	0.1985	0.2019	0.2054	0.2088	0.2123	0.2157	0.2190	0.2224
0.6	0.2257	0.2291	0.2324	0.2357	0.2389	0.2422	0.2454	0.2486	0.2517	0.2549
0.7	0.2580	0.2611	0.2642	0.2673	0.2704	0.2734	0.2764	0.2794	0.2823	0.2852
0.8	0.2881	0.2910	0.2939	0.2967	0.2995	0.3023	0.3051	0.3078	0.3106	0.3133
0.9	0.3159	0.3186	0.3212	0.3238	0.3264	0.3289	0.3315	0.3340	0.3365	0.3389
1.0	0.3413	0.3438	0.3461	0.3485	0.3508	0.3531	0.3554	0.3577	0.3599	0.3621
1.1	0.3643	0.3665	0.3686	0.3708	0.3729	0.3749	0.3770	0.3790	0.3810	0.3830
1.2	0.3849	0.3869	0.3888	0.3907	0.3925	0.3944	0.3962	0.3980	0.3997	0.4015
1.3	0.4032	0.4049	0.4066	0.4082	0.4099	0.4115	0.4131	0.4147	0.4162	0.4177
1.4	0.4192	0.4207	0.4222	0.4236	0.4251	0.4265	0.4279	0.4292	0.4306	0.4319
1.5	0.4332	0.4345	0.4357	0.4370	0.4382	0.4394	0.4406	0.4418	0.4429	0.4441
1.6	0.4452	0.4463	0.4474	0.4484	0.4495	0.4505	0.4515	0.4525	0.4535	0.4545
1.7	0.4554	0.4564	0.4573	0.4582	0.4591	0.4599	0.4608	0.4616	0.4625	0.4633
1.8	0.4641	0.4649	0.4656	0.4664	0.4671	0.4678	0.4686	0.4693	0.4699	0.4706
1.9	0.4713	0.4719	0.4726	0.4732	0.4738	0.4744	0.4750	0.4756	0.4761	0.4767
2.0	0.4772	0.4778	0.4783	0.4788	0.4793	0.4798	0.4803	0.4808	0.4812	0.4817
2.1	0.4821	0.4826	0.4830	0.4834	0.4838	0.4842	0.4846	0.4850	0.4854	0.4857
2.2	0.4861	0.4864	0.4868	0.4871	0.4875	0.4878	0.4881	0.4884	0.4887	0.4890
2.3	0.4893	0.4896	0.4898	0.4901	0.4904	0.4906	0.4909	0.4911	0.4913	0.4916
2.4	0.4918	0.4920	0.4922	0.4925	0.4927	0.4929	0.4931	0.4932	0.4934	0.4936
2.5	0.4938	0.4940	0.4941	0.4943	0.4945	0.4946	0.4948	0.4949	0.4951	0.4952
2.6	0.4953	0.4955	0.4956	0.4957	0.4959	0.4960	0.4961	0.4962	0.4963	0.4964
2.7	0.4965	0.4966	0.4967	0.4968	0.4969	0.4970	0.4971	0.4972	0.4973	0.4974
2.8	0.4974	0.4975	0.4976	0.4977	0.4977	0.4978	0.4979	0.4979	0.4980	0.4981
2.9	0.4981	0.4982	0.4982	0.4983	0.4984	0.4984	0.4985	0.4985	0.4986	0.4986
3.0	0.4987	0.4987	0.4987	0.4988	0.4988	0.4989	0.4989	0.4989	0.4990	0.490

CHAPTER 7

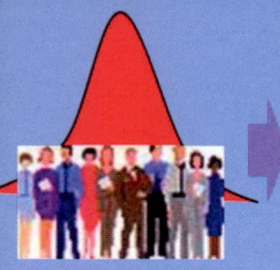 

Sampling Techniques & sampling distributions

After completing this chapter, students will be able to:

- *Plan for a representative sample*
- *Estimate sampling error*
- *Perform sampling techniques: Random, Stratified, and Cluster Sampling*
- *Understand the concept of a Sampling Distribution*
- *Understand the Central Limit Theorem*

CHAPTER 7

This chapter takes us to the world of sampling, which is *the driving force of all statistical analyses*. It should be realized by now that the effectiveness of any statistical analysis is derived from the data used. Indeed, no matter how detailed or how lengthy the analysis you perform, it will all depend on the accuracy of data and the credibility of data source. It is important, therefore, that the analyst questions the source of data and oversees the techniques used to gather and organize data. In most statistical applications, the primary source of data is a *sample* drawn from a large *population*. A sample is a representation of the whole population and therefore a great deal of effort should be made to make sure that the sample selected truly reflects the parent population without any bias. In this regard, the method of sampling and the nature of sampling distribution represent critical issues. In addition, it is important to understand the concept of sampling distribution and the Central-Limit-Theorem. These concepts are discussed in detail in this chapter.

CHAPTER CONTENTS

7.1 Sampling theory

As indicated in Chapter 1, sampling is the process of taking representative samples from a large population for the sake of gaining accurate and precise information about the population. The sampling theory represents an analysis of the relationship existing between a population and the samples drawn from the population. As we will see in chapters 8 and 9, understanding the sampling theory can assist in three basic applications:

- Estimating unknown *population parameters* from corresponding *sample statistics*
- Evaluating the differences between the same parameters of two populations, through comparison of statistics of samples selected from each population
- Testing hypotheses about some variables in a population using sample statistics

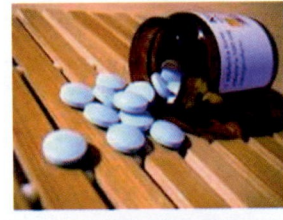

In practice, many questions can be answered through understanding the sampling theory. Examples of these questions are as follows:

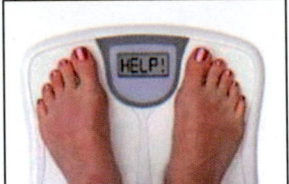

- What medical treatment is more suitable for a particular disease?
- What weight-loss program is more effective?
- What investment is likely to generate higher profit?
- What raw material should we use?
- Which car is safe to drive?
- Which process is running better?
- Which design will meet the intended function of a product?
- What testing technique should we utilize?
- Did a particular problem occur due to random variation or due to assignable causes?

These questions are answered through performing appropriate sampling techniques, determining sample statistics, and estimating population parameters from sample statistics. This process is called *inferential statistics* and it will be discussed in depth in chapter 8. In this chapter, our focus will be on sampling principles, sampling techniques, and sampling distributions.

7.2 Sample/population relationship

In the context of probability, a population implies all possible outcomes of an experiment. In practice, a population implies a totality of things or the entire universe of the objects in question. Since statistics works with data, this definition is associated with the values of the variable of interest of these objects. In other words, we should distinguish between the *physical population* and the *statistical population*. A physical population represents a description of the actual population and the nature of its members. A statistical population represents a description of the variable of interest associated with the population. In order to assist you in making this distinction, consider the following examples:

Populations & Samples:

- New York City with more than 10 million people living in the city represents a *physical population*. The age of all people living in the city represents a *statistical population*.

-

- All machine units in a factory represent a *physical population*. The efficiency values of different machines represent a *statistical population*.

- All students attending a college represent a *physical population*. Grades of these students represent a *statistical distribution*.

Since we have to rely on a sample to describe a whole population, it is important that the sample truly reflects the population from which it is withdrawn. In this regard, a representative sample should be defined as the sample in which each item in the parent population has an equal chance of being represented in the sample. In other words, a good sample is a true reflection of the population from which it is withdrawn. The basic steps required for selecting a representative sample are:

1. *Planning*
2. *Establishing a sample structure*
3. *Using a reliable database*

7.2.1 Planning

Planning consists of addressing three key questions related to three key sampling issues. These questions are:

- *Population size-* Is the population finite or infinite?
- *Population integrity-* Is the population homogenous or heterogeneous?
- *Population expected change-* Is the population static (exhibits no or little change over time) or dynamic (exhibits significant change over time)?

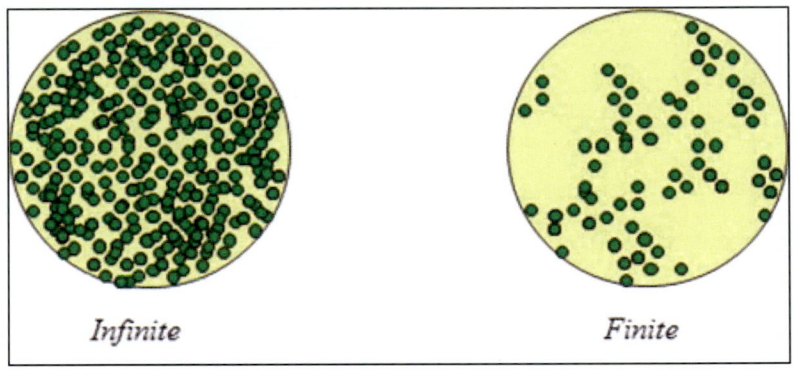

7.2.1.1 Population size

This is a key aspect of sampling. In this regard, two types of population may be considered: *finite population* and *infinite population*. A large city consisting of millions of people living in the city is considered as an infinite population. A small region of the city such as the downtown area may be considered as a finite population. Similarly, students attending a large university may be considered as an infinite population, while students in a department or college within the university may be considered as a finite population. As you can see from these examples,

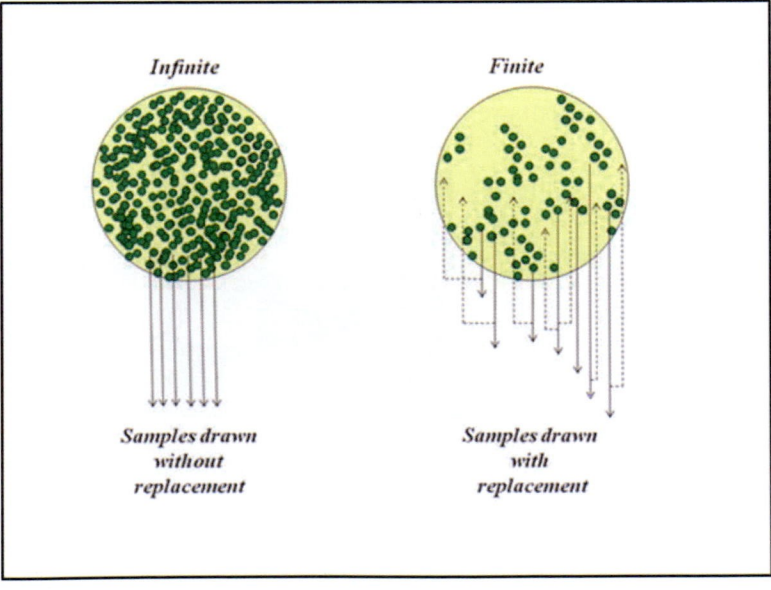

considering a population as finite or infinite represents a judgment of the relative size of the population. From an analytical viewpoint, we may define *a finite population as a population of members that are entirely accessible either via their identification numbers or names, or via other criteria.*

The issue of population size represents a practical problem in most statistical applications. In many situations, we need to justify the use of a small sample rather than the whole population. Dealing with an infinite population is both costly and time-consuming. For example, surveying a large city consisting of millions of people by conducting a census may take a great deal of resources. This task can be achieved with high degree of accuracy by taking an appropriate sample of relatively small size. In addition, the time consumed in conducting a census may be so long that by the time it is completed the results may be less useful or even obsolete due to changes in the population.

In the context of sampling, when the population is infinite, sampling is typically performed without replacement. In other words, a sample component that is drawn from the population is not returned back to the population. When the population is finite, it is possible to perform sampling with replacement (i.e. components are returned back to the population and are subject to be drawn again). Theoretically, a finite population in which sampling is made with replacement can be considered as an infinite population, since the population will never be exhausted by this method of sampling.

Example 7.1: Determine whether you would consider the following populations finite or infinite:
  a. Students taking a particular statistics course in a given semester and in a particular college
  b. Working staff in the U.S. Whitehouse
  c. People living in a subdivision in Atlanta, Georgia
  d. People living in Chicago, Illinois

Solution:

  a. Finite population
  b. Finite population
  c. Finite population
  d. Infinite population

7.2.1.2 Population integrity

In the context of population integrity, two main types of population can be considered: *homogenous* and *heterogeneous*. A homogenous population typically consists of components that are assumed to be alike or have many attributes in common. For example, a population of students

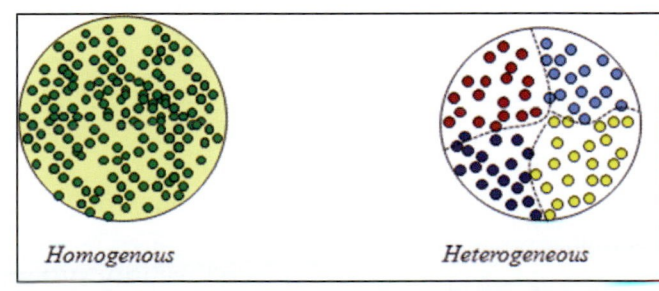

Homogenous   Heterogeneous

369

graduating from college, which is likely to exhibit many common attributes (e.g. age range, degree level, and potential job status), can be considered as a homogenous population. A heterogeneous population typically consists of components that are different in many attributes. For example, a population of people representing different nationalities is considered as a heterogeneous population. Each one of these two types of population will require a different sampling technique. For the homogenous population, we can perform random sampling in which each component in the population has the same chance of being selected. For the heterogeneous population, it may be more useful to perform *stratified sampling as* will be discussed shortly.

Example 7.2: Determine whether you would consider the following populations homogenous or heterogeneous:

    a. Dishwashers of the same model produced by a manufacturer
    b. People living in the newly independent South of Sudan
    c. People living in China Town, NY City
    d. People visiting Manhattan, NY City daily
    e. Tourists visiting the great pyramids of Egypt every year

Solution:

    a. Homogenous
    b. Homogenous
    c. Homogenous
    d. Heterogeneous
    e. Heterogeneous

7.2.1.3 Population expected change

This is a key aspect of sampling. We often have to deal with populations that undergo dynamic (or over time) changes in many attributes including opinion, size, integrity, and division. For example, during an election year, people's opinion of a candidate may continuously change as a result of an election campaign's efforts, political debates, conventions, 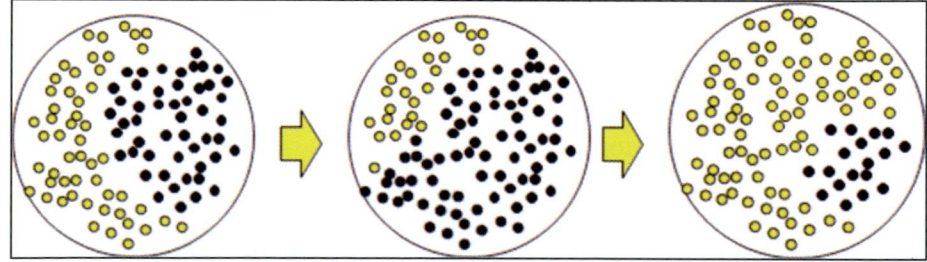 etc. In this case, samples have to be regularly withdrawn to reflect the changes in the population.

Example 7.3: Determine whether you would consider the following populations static or dynamic:
    a. People's opinion of the social security system in the U.S.A. over the last 10 years
    b. Automatic machines used to assemble car parts in an auto-manufacturing facility

c. Voters' opinions in a Mayoral election over a year period

Solution:

a. Dynamic
b. Static
c. Dynamic

Key Terms:

- **Finite population** *is a population that is totally accessible both physically and informational*

- **Infinite population** *is a very large population in which it will be either impossible or very costly to access all components*

- **Homogenous population** *is a population in which different components have much more in common than differences*

- **Heterogeneous population** *is a population in which different components have many distinct differences*

- **Static population** *is a population that is unlikely to significantly change over time*

- **Dynamic population** *is a population that is likely to change over time*

Working problem 7.1:

Mark the following populations as finite or infinite:

	Finite	Infinite
1. New York City population	Finite ( )	Infinite ( )
2. The U.S. population	Finite ( )	Infinite ( )
3. The Department of Civil Engineering in MIT	Finite ( )	Infinite ( )
4. FBI employee	Finite ( )	Infinite ( )
5. Students taking pre-algebra course in a Community College	Finite ( )	Infinite ( )
6. Employees in a WalMart Store	Finite ( )	Infinite ( )
7. Employees of all WalMart stores	Finite ( )	Infinite ( )

Answer: 1. I, 2. I, 3. F, 4. I, 5. F, 6. F, 7. I

Working problem 7.2:

Mark the following populations as homogenous or heterogeneous:

1. 2008 graduates from Harvard University
Homogenous ( )   Heterogeneous ( )

2. People celebrating New Year's eve in Times Square (NY City)
Homogenous ( )   Heterogeneous ( )

3. United Nation employees
Homogenous ( )   Heterogeneous ( )

4. Cars displayed for sales in a large used car lot
Homogenous ( )   Heterogeneous ( )

Answer: 1. Homogenous, 2. Heterogeneous, 3. Do it yourself, 4. Do it yourself

---

Working problem 7.3:

Mark the following populations as static or dynamic population:

1. The population of eligible voters during an election year
Static ( )   Dynamic ( )

2. Merchandises in a large fashion store
Static ( )   Dynamic ( )

3. People living in an apartment complex
Static ( )   Dynamic ( )

4. People flying via Atlanta Airport every week
Static ( )   Dynamic ( )

Answer: 1. D, (2) Do it yourself, (3) S, (4) Do it yourself

7.2.2 Establishing a Sample Structure

The reliability of any inferences about a population will primarily depend on the sample collected and the data obtained from it. This means that the sample must represent a good cross section of the parent population under study, and the data obtained from testing or surveying the sample should be reliable. The issue of sample structure addresses a number of key factors that contribute to the appropriateness of a sample and the reliability of the sample data. These factors are:

1. Sample data sources
2. Sampling frequency
3. Sample randomization

372

4. Sample size and sample replication
5. The distribution of the parent population

7.2.2.1 Sample data source

In general, there are three main sources of data: *pre-existing data*, *survey data* and *experimental data*. Pre-existing data may consist of an organization's internal records that have been collected over time or data from external records such as the United Nation's data on global statistics (http://unstats.un.org/unsd/databases.htm), or data from the Bureau of Labor Statistics (http://www.bls.gov). Survey data is collected by gathering people's opinions on some issues such as the likeability of some products in the marketplace, the political candidate they would vote for, or their needs and wants regarding critical services including health care or education. Experimental data is collected from pre-designed experiments in which the factors influencing a response variable are selected carefully to reach a target decision such as at what speed a machine or car should run in order to achieve optimum performance or maximum fuel efficiency.

In all categories of data sources, data may be classified as *census data* or *sample data*. Census data represents values of the variable of interest collected from the entire population. In other words, they include every member of the population. In practice, census data is not frequently used because of the cost and the length of time involved in collecting this type of data. In many situations, collecting data requires destructive testing which is inconceivable to perform for the entire population. For example, an automaker producing thousands of cars every week is required to test the safety of these cars. This commonly involves a destructive test in which cars are impacted to destruction. Can you imagine an automaker destroying hundreds of cars to test their safety? Obviously, this will be very costly and unnecessary. The alternative in this case is to take a small representative sample from the population, test it, produce sample data, determine the *statistics* of the variable of interest and ultimately estimate the *parameters* of the parent population.

In light of the above discussion, it is clear that all sources of data require the existence of physical sample components that are used to generate the data. These components may be represented by people being surveyed to obtain opinions, students being tested to obtain grades, machines being examined to generate performance measures, or products being inspected to determine their quality status. The knowledge of sample source will largely determine how the sample will be accessed and evaluated. In some situations, the issue of sample source may face logistical and production obstacles. For instance, suppose the samples to be considered are products produced by different machines. In this case, should we delay production and stop all the machines to take samples? Or should we wait until machines are stopped for periodic maintenance before we can take samples? The first option will allow a perfectly representative sample, but it may not be practical. The second option will likely create bias since randomization may be violated. In other situations, the issue of sample sources may face legal obstacles. For instance, when a new medical treatment is being examined, the common question is whether it should be applied to humans or animals. The first choice may be risky to humans, and the second one may be upsetting to animal right advocates.

From a statistical viewpoint, it is important to divide samples into two main categories: observational samples, and experimental samples. These are discussed below.

7.2.2.1.1 Observational sampling: Retrospective and prospective sampling

Sampling can typically be performed in two types of studies: *retrospective* and *prospective* studies. In retrospective studies, we collect data about the variable of interest from historical records obtained from samples that were collected in the past. For example, a retrospective study of weight loss treatments might work backwards to determine which treatments were associated with the best results of weight loss. Such a retrospective study requires subjects who had undergone the treatments and subjects that did not have the treatments. This approach makes the study directly related to the subjects being examined and not the general population. For example, we may discover from past record samples that a particular treatment associated with a certain routine exercise had resulted in optimum weight loss. We may also discover that the samples taken were not fully representative of the target population or suffered some bias; these are issues that should be resolved in future sampling. Indeed, it is always advisable to consider historical data (or retrospective sampling) prior to selecting new samples.

In prospective studies we go forward in time by taking samples that we anticipate will have potential causative effects on the variable under study. For example, we may take samples of people who are about to undergo weight loss treatments and samples of people who do not use weight loss treatments for the sake of comparison. In this case, we should limit our study to certain groups of people which may be determined by age, gender, or race. This will eliminate a great deal of noise from the observational sampling procedure.

> **Retrospective sample:** *A sample selected from historical records or past data*
>
> **Prospective sample:** *A sample, which is planned ahead of time and intended to be taken from groups that perhaps share common factors*

Example 7.4: Classify the following samples as retrospective and prospective and explain why?
   a. A random sample of grades taken from students in the last 5 year record.
   b. A random sample of grades intended to be taken from students who will complete the upcoming semester's midterm.

Solution:

   a. This sample is based on a retrospective approach as it relies on data that has been collected in the past
   b. This sample is based on a prospective approach and it can be designed in view of the outcome of the retrospective sample.

7.2.2.1.2 Experimental sampling

The above approaches are based on simple observations of samples and associated characteristics without any intention to change or control sample components. Experimental sampling is based on establishing a design of experiment in which specific factors are deliberately selected. For example, a sample of students may be selected to represent freshmen, sophomore, and senior students. In addition, the experiment may adhere to students in a certain discipline (i.e. business or engineering). It is important to warn that experimental sampling may be affected by the so-called *confounding*. This is the case when effects of variables are so mixed that the individual effects of the variables cannot be identified or isolated. For example, failing to design the sample by assuring the presence of male and female in proportional-weight allocation may result in a loss of important information related to the effect of gender on student's performance.

> **Confounding** is a consequence of confusing variable effects or overlooking variables that can have significant effects on the output of the analysis

Example 7.5: Suppose we are collecting a sample of 1000 people who graduated from business school to examine their placement in certain jobs, which of the following approaches may create confounding:

1. Failure to specify the year of graduation
2. Failure to specify the school or the business program from which students have graduated
3. Failure to specify gender (male vs. female)

Solution:

Specifying the year of graduation will minimize confounding as it will provide information about the effect of the number of years since graduation on job placement. Confounding will be created by failure to specify the school or the business program from which students have graduated as this may mask whether the quality (reputation and accreditation) of the program has any effect on placement. Confounding will also be created by failure to specify gender (male vs. female) as this may mask the effect of gender on placement.

Working Problem 7.4:

Suppose we are collecting a sample of 500 eligible voters during governor election of one of the U.S. States, would you perform observational sampling or experimental sampling, and why?

Answer:
This question is somewhat subjective...
Both options should be on the table. However, if we already know that some areas are largely decided, we may elect to disregard these areas and Focus on the undecided areas...This will make sampling more experimental

Do you have a different opinion from this one?

375

Working Problem 7.5:

Suppose we are using experimental sampling for collecting a sample of 500 eligible voters during governor election of one of the U.S. States. What are the factors that you believe can lead to confounding and how to avoid them?

Answer may include: age, gender, financial status, and location

Working Problem 7.6:

Suppose a weight-loss program is designed to treat 1000 people that have obesity problems. If an early study of this program indicated that it has side effects including stomach problems and laziness. This early study showed that these side effects occurred only for people 40 years or older. In planning for a *prospective study, what would be the factors that should be considered in the samples selected to avoid confounding?*

Answer may include: age and gender. Think of other factors

7.2.2.2 Sample frequency

Sampling frequency is the issue of how often we should take a sample. In this regard, two categories of samples may be considered (see Figure 7.1): (a) a snap-shot sample or a cross-sectional sample, and (b) a periodic sample. A snap-shot sample is typically a large sample drawn from a population for a one-time evaluation of population parameters. This approach assumes that the population undergoes little or no change for a significant period of time. A snapshot sample is typically large and inclusive as the goal is normally to evaluate the whole population, perhaps once every year, or when changes are made that warrant evaluation. For example, a large organization may take a large sample of employees at one point of time to survey their opinions of the organization's employment benefits.

If the source population is likely to undergo changes over time, periodic samples should be taken. The size and the extent of inclusiveness of a periodic sample will depend primarily on the anticipated shift in values of the population characteristic that we are trying to evaluate. If we anticipate that the population characteristic may change daily (e.g. airline flight delay, or stock value) then daily samples should be taken. On the other hand, if we anticipate quarterly or semiannual changes (e.g. college enrollment, or seasonal retailer performance, etc.) then samples should be drawn in correspondence to these periods. This concept represents the basis for *rational subgroups* in *Statistical Process Control* (*SPC*).

In practice, drawing a line between taking a snap-shot or a periodic sample requires some judgment. For example, a factory operating hundreds of machines that are nominally set equally, may take a sample of machines and evaluate their performance (e.g. efficiency, production rate, etc.) once every year assuming that machine settings will not change over this period. The same factory may also decide to take periodic samples of randomly selected machines in anticipation of possible periodic changes due to pre-scheduled maintenance or changes in machine parts.

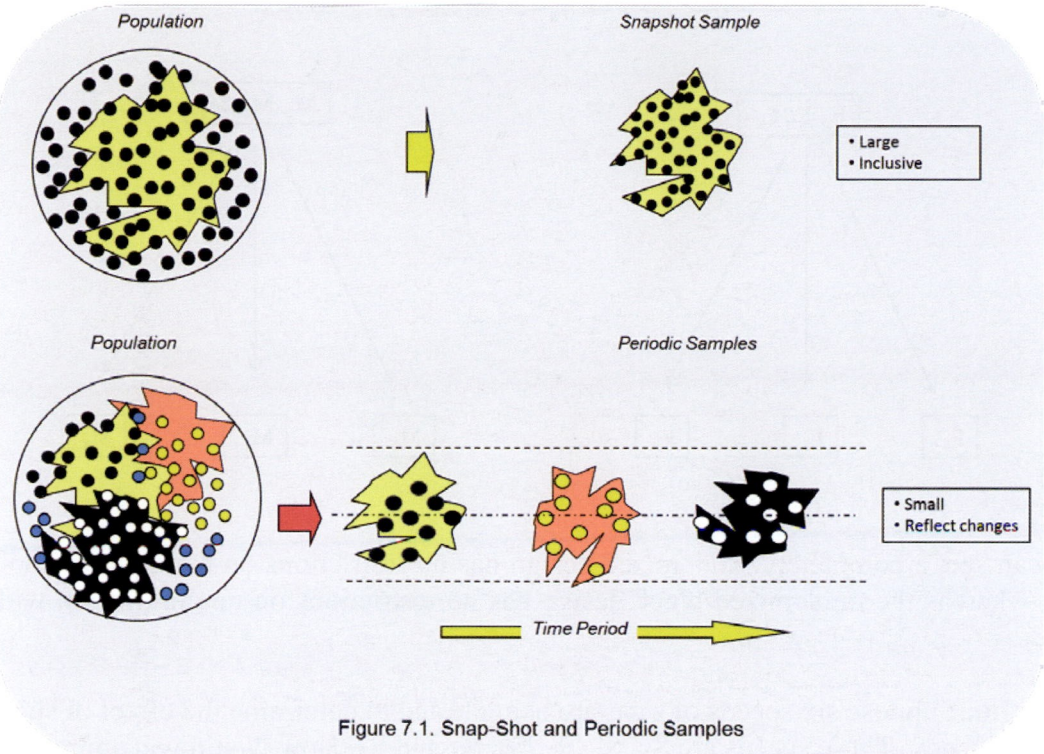

Figure 7.1. Snap-Shot and Periodic Samples

7.2.2.3 Sample randomization

Basically, a representative sample is a sample that should be based on random selection of different components from the parent population. The use of experimental sampling often gives the perception that randomization will be violated as a result of attempts to control the sample selection process. It is important, therefore, that experimental sampling should not come at the expense of randomization as this is the foundation of any sampling approach. In chapter 11, we will discuss how to randomize an experiment in the context of the analysis of variance. In general, one approach of random selection is the so-called *completely randomized design*. In this approach, after designing the experiment, the entire sampling selection is fully randomized. For example, suppose we have 6 people, 3 males and 3 females that are to be interviewed or tested. We may select to assign each person a letter or a number, and use a coin flip to determine a random sequence of sampling such as the following sequences:

$F_3, F_1, M_2, M_1, M_3, F_2$ or $M_1, F_1, F_3, M_3, M_2, F_2$ or $F_2, M_1, F_3, M_3, F_1, M_2$

Note that M and F stands for male and female, and the suffix numbers 1, 2, and 3 represent the person's identification.

Another approach of randomization is the so-called randomized block design. In this approach, we form blocks such as a block of males and another block of females; then within each block we flip a coin to determine which male or female in each block to select.

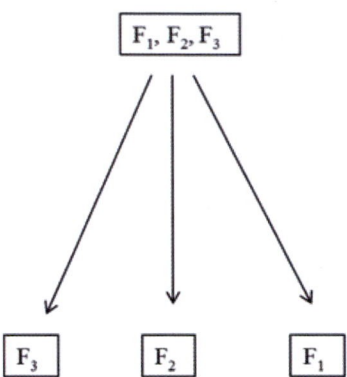 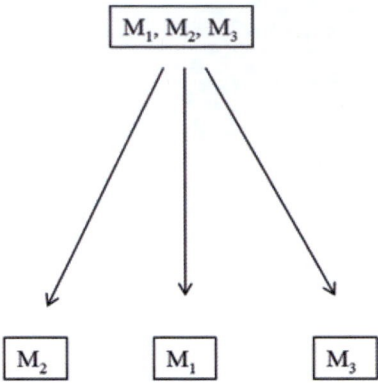

As you can see, a completely randomized design has no restrictions on the entire randomization process, whereas the randomized block design has no restrictions on randomization within each block.

Example 7.6: Suppose six speeds of a car are being tested to determine the effect of speed on the car fuel efficiency. These speeds are S_1, S_2, S_3, S_4, S_5 and S_6. How would you approach using these speed settings to conduct your experiment?

Solution:

In this case, we should implement completely randomized design. Examples of speed sequence can be as follows:

$S_5, S_2, S_3, S_1, S_4, S_6$ or $S_1, S_2, S_4, S_6, S_5, S_3$ or $S_3, S_1, S_6, S_4, S_5, S_2$

Working Problem 7.7:

Suppose an evaluator plans to observe 5 Math classes over the next 5 weeks to determine teachers' performances in the classes. These classes are identified by the following sections: S_{01}, S_{02}, S_{03}, S_{04}, and S_{05}. How would you approach the way the evaluator should pick the sections to obtain a fair and unbiased evaluation?

Answer: In this case, the evaluator should use completely randomized design. Examples of section sequence can be as follows:
$S_{01}, S_{05}, S_{03}, S_{02}$, and S_{04} or $S_{02}, S_{01}, S_{05}, S_{03}$, and S_{04} or $S_{05}, S_{02}, S_{03}, S_{01}$, and S_{04} ......Try other solutions

7.2.2.4 Sample size and sample replication

The minimum sample size required is a key aspect in any sampling process. In Chapter 8, we will discuss this aspect in greater detail. In the context of sample size, or how large a sample should be, it is important that we distinguish between *'deterministic inclusion'* and *'statistical inclusion.'* Deterministic inclusion means that all units, components, or people in a population must be tested and examined in order to reveal 100% information about the population. In other words, the sample size should be equal to the population size to obtain 100% information about the population. Statistical inclusion, on the other hand, means that only a small portion of the population needs to be considered to reveal immense information about the population. The key to appropriate statistical inclusion is that *each member in the whole population should have the same opportunity of being selected in the sample.* The general rule of thumb is that samples should be large enough so that noise or variability of the characteristic under consideration is accounted for. They should also be large enough so that components of extreme characteristic values can be included.

Taking replicates or repetitions is a common practice in most sampling techniques. This is particularly true when we anticipate a great deal of within-sample variability. In this case, more samples from the same category are taken, or experiments are repeated to assure and confirm reproducibility of effects. Additional experiments or samples may also be taken to verify previously obtained results that seem to be somewhat out of the norm.

7.2.2.5 The shape of the frequency distribution of the parent-population

Knowledge of the anticipated frequency distribution of the parent population can provide very useful guidelines of how samples should be selected and the appropriate sampling technique. Figure 7.2 shows examples of shapes of population frequency distribution. In most situations, the variable under consideration will come from a population that is normally distributed (e.g. income, student's grade, age, cost, revenue, etc.). As indicated in chapter 6, a normal distribution is bell-shaped, symmetrical, and has similar values of mean, mode, and median. A sample taken from this type of distribution should reflect the symmetrical nature of the parent-population's distribution and should consist of low and high values that are symmetrically distributed around the center of the population as well as bulk or middle values. Later in this chapter, we will discuss the Central Limit theorem, which provides many guidelines for the relationship between sample statistics and population parameters for this type of distribution.

Other parent-population distributions may be uniform, asymmetrical or highly skewed, bimodal, or multi-modal. These types of distributions require special efforts to make sure that the sample is reflective of the nature of the parent population. For example, suppose we are interested in people's annual income in a certain town in which a majority of the people are living under poverty. Since the parent-population distribution is expected to be extremely biased to low income, extraordinary efforts should be made to take a sample which represents a cross section of all members of the population. In practice, people living under poverty are typically difficult to access by virtue of their isolation from society and their lack of participation in social activities. This is a factor that should also be taken into consideration in sampling planning.

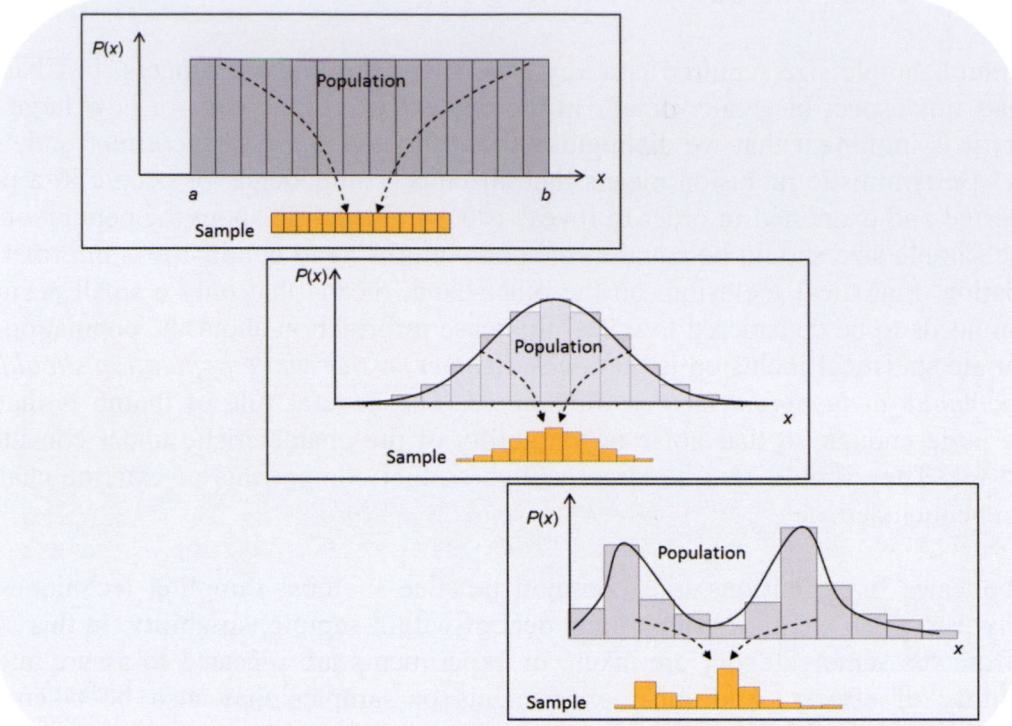

Figure 7.2. Sample Reflection of the Parent Population

7.2.3 Using reliable database: sampling and non-sampling errors

Depending on the purpose of the analysis, samples should be selected to provide the data intended for the study. This means that possible ambiguity in the data should be carefully examined and eliminated. We also should understand that a difference between sample mean and population mean is inevitable as it is impossible to have a sample that is perfectly in agreement with the population. The key however is our judgment of the extent of this difference and its causes. In this regard, two types of errors should be recognized when sampling is being conducted: *(a) sampling error*, and *(b) non-sampling error*.

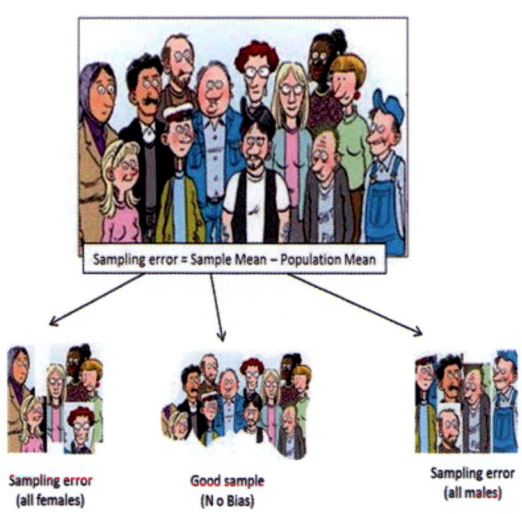

Sampling error is committed when there is a difference between the data of the sample and the data of the parent population obtained (if a census can be conducted). This error is difficult to detect since accessing a complete population data is nearly impossible in most situations. It is also an error that is difficult to avoid, because samples drawn from the population are likely to yield different values by virtue of the inherent variability in the population, or the law

380

of chance. In general, sampling error is measured by the difference between the sample mean and the population mean:

$$Sampling\ error = \bar{X} - \mu \qquad (7.1)$$

The non-sampling error results from human mistakes in performing sampling and it can be attributed to many reasons related to the issues discussed in the above sections. It can also be attributed to errors in data collection, recording, and tabulation.

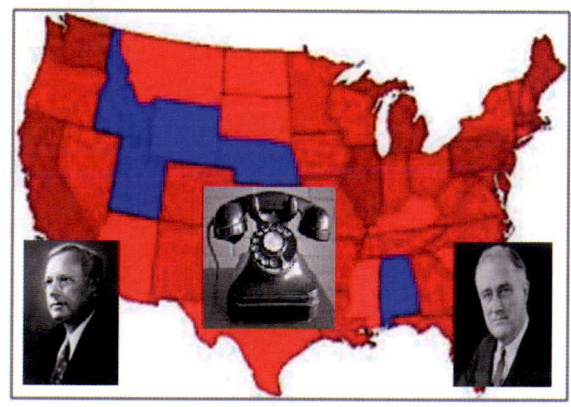

Unfortunately, non-sampling errors are often detected when the results or the conclusions obtained from the analysis turn out to be unrealistic or different from the anticipated or the actual results. Perhaps, the best example to demonstrate this error is the U.S. presidential opinion poll conducted by the magazine Literary Digest in 1936. In this poll, the Literary Digest poll predicted that Franklin D. Roosevelt would lose to Alf Landon, whereas Roosevelt actually won in a landslide victory. This incorrect prediction was largely a result of a drastic bias. In reaching this prediction, the *Literary Digest* ballots were sent to magazine subscribers as well as to registered car owners and those who used telephones. On the heels of the Great Depression, this group included disproportionately more wealthy people, who were Republicans. But the real flaw in the *Literary Digest* poll is that it resulted in a voluntary response sample. In the same election, three different polling pioneers, George Gallup, Elmo Roper, and Archibald Crossley correctly predicted Roosevelt's victory and thus launched scientific public opinion polling due to its great popularity. They used the quota method of sampling, in which individual members of the sample are chosen in accordance with a quota so as to roughly match the national population on factors such as geographical regions within the country, urban versus rural residence, sex, age, race, and socioeconomic status. However, the problem with the quota method of sampling was that the interviewers were allowed discretion in choosing the individual respondents within the quota categories. This discretion introduces a possible source of bias, because the resulting sample can largely omit some types of people, such as those who are difficult to contact.

The quota method continued to be used after the 1936 election and until 1948 where it was abandoned in election applications after the 1948 presidential election, in which the underdog, Harry Truman, defeated Thomas E. Dewey, who was heavily favored to win in the opinion polls. Since then election polls have been conducted using random sampling or selective non-random sampling as will be explained shortly.

Most non-sampling errors can be avoided by following the basic steps discussed above, namely: planning, establishing a sample structure, and using a reliable database.

Example 7.7: Suppose an organization typically pays its salesmen an average annual commission of $50,000 with a standard deviation of $3000. These are considered population data since they are based on internal records collected over many years. A consultant for the organization took a sample of 5 salesmen that he thought represented the organization's population of salesmen and found the following values of annual commission:

$46,000, $51,000, $50,000, $48,000, $53,000
What is the sampling error?

Solution:

The mean of the sample is:

$$Mean = \bar{X} = \frac{\sum_1^n x_i}{n} = \frac{46,000 + 51,000 + 50,000 + 48,000 + 53,000}{5} = \$49600/year$$

Since the anticipated mean value is $50,000, then
the sampling error $= \bar{X} - \mu = 49,600 - 50,000 = -\$400$.

Note that the negative sign here indicates that the error was toward the lower side of values or below the population mean.

Example 7.8: For the same organization of the above example, suppose the consultant took another sample which exhibits the following commission values:

$45,000, $49,000, $50,000, $51,000, $44,000

If the organization has established $400 as the maximum acceptable sampling error, what is the non-sampling error?

Solution:

The mean of this sample is

$$Mean = \bar{X} = \frac{\sum_1^n x_i}{n} = \frac{45,000 + 49,000 + 50,000 + 51,000 + 44,000}{5} = \$47,800/year$$

The difference between the sample mean and the population mean is

$$\bar{X} - \mu = 47,800 - 50,000 = -\$2200$$

By the organization's threshold of the maximum acceptable sampling error, this difference between the population mean and the sample mean does not represent a pure sampling error and the sample selected may have suffered a bias or a non-sampling error. Since we already know the anticipated sampling error to be $400, the non-sampling error is:

$$\text{Nonsampling error} = -2200 - (-400) = -\$1800$$

Note that the negative sign here indicates that the error was toward the lower side of values or below the population mean.

Example 7.9: For the same organization in the above example, suppose the organization decided not to take a sample and only relied on its population data, can you tell the organization what is the sales commission made by most of its salesmen?

Solution:

This example is intended to link previous information you learned in this course with present information. Recall that according to the empirical rule discussed in chapters 3 and 6, and assuming that salesmen's commission follows a normal distribution, about 99.74% of the organization's salesmen make a commission within $\mu \pm 3\sigma$. For this organization, population information indicates that the average annual commission is $50,000 and the standard deviation is $3000. This means that 99.74% of the organization's salesmen make a commission within $\mu \pm 3\sigma = 50,00 \pm 9000$. In other words, most salesmen make commissions ranging from $41,000 and $59,000.

Sampling error is committed when there is a difference between the data of a representative sample and the data of the parent population obtained if a census can be conducted.

Non-sampling error results from human mistakes in performing sampling and it can be attributed to errors in data collection, recording, and tabulation.

Working Problem 7.8:

Suppose an organization typically spends on average $25,000 per employee in annual benefits with a standard deviation of $5,000. If the organization took a random sample of 5 employees that it thought it represents a good cross section of its population of employee and found the following values of benefits:

$25,000, $20,000, $30,000, $30,000, $21,000

What is the sampling error?

Answer: $200

Working Problem 7.9:

Suppose an organization typically spends on average $25,000 per employee in annual benefits with a standard deviation of $5,000. If the organization took a random sample of 5 employees that it thought it represents a good cross section of its population of employee and found the following values of benefits:

$20,000, $21,000, $32,000, $33,000, $32,000

Also, suppose that the sampling error is known to be $200.

What is the non-sampling error?

Answer: $2400

Working Problem 7.10:

Suppose an organization typically spends on average $25,000 per employee in annual benefits with a standard deviation of $5,000. If the organization decided not to take a sample and only rely on its population data, can you tell the organization what is the annual benefits made by most of its employees?

Answer: $10,000 to $40,000

7.3 Sampling techniques

In practice, there are many ways to perform sampling and they all aim at selecting components or items from a population that largely represent the population. As shown in Figure 7.3, there are two main categories of samples: (a) probability sampling, and (b) non-probability sampling. A probability sampling is any method of sampling that utilizes some form of random selection. In other words, it involves a selection among participants or population components randomly and based on some probability. In terms of planning, probability sampling requires setting up some process or procedure that assures that the different units in the population have either equal probabilities of being selected in the sample (random sampling) or a probability based on proportional-weight allocation (stratified sampling) of different categories in the population. A non-probability sampling is a method of sampling that does not involve random selection; instead it relies on a great deal of judgment for convenience or for meeting some purposes. In the context of outcome, the differences between these two categories of sampling may be summarized as follows:

- With probability sampling, we should know the odds or probability that we have represented the population appropriately. This is important in performing good inferential statistics for estimating population parameters from sample statistics as will be discussed in Chapter 8. The problem with some probability sampling methods is that they are not always practically feasible as will be discussed later.
- With non-probability sampling, a convenient (rapid and less costly) sample can be selected, but it may or may not fully represent the entire population. This may lead to a bias in our estimation of population parameters from sample statistics.

In Appendix 7.A, definitions and examples of different sampling techniques are presented. In the following sections, we focus on the most commonly used methods of sampling; namely: random sampling, cluster sampling, and stratified sampling. These methods belong to the category of probability sampling. Figure 7.4 illustrates the basic concepts of these three sampling methods.

7.3.1 Simple random sampling

In random sampling, subjects are randomly drawn from the parent population to form a sample. The most common method of sampling is simple random sampling. In this method, every component in the population has the same chance of being selected in the sample. By definition, any value of the member characteristic in the population will have the same opportunity to be represented in the sample. If the population is of a finite size N, and we require a random sample of n members, this sample will be selected randomly from the $\binom{N}{n}$ distinct possible samples, in each of which no population member is included more than once. Such a sample can be obtained sequentially by drawing members from the population one at a time without replacement so that at each stage every remaining member of the population has the same probability of being chosen.

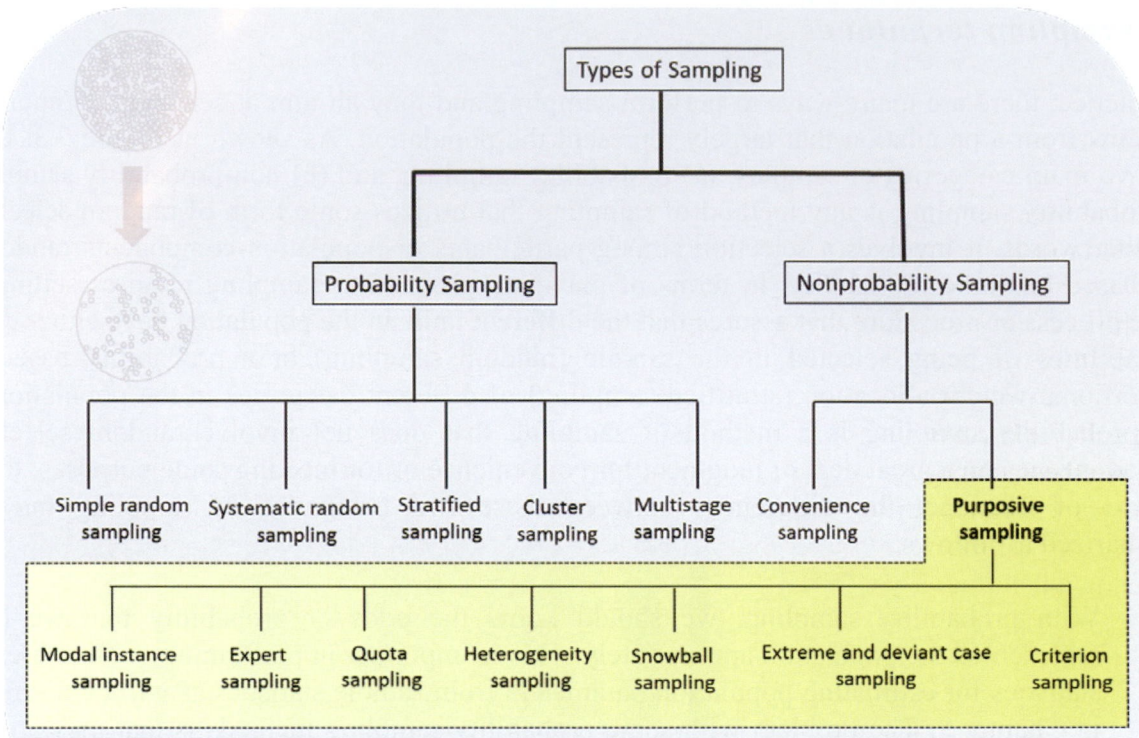

Figure 7.3 Different Types of Sampling-See Definitions & Examples in Appendix 7.A

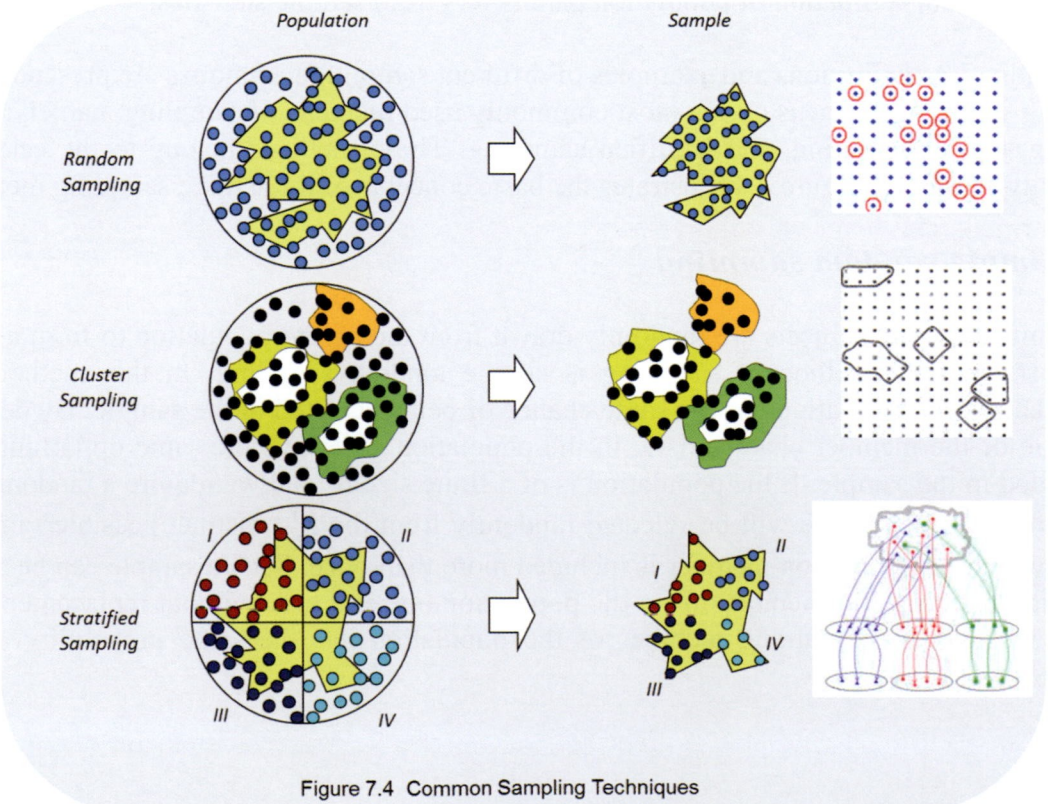

Figure 7.4 Common Sampling Techniques

Example 7.10: Imagine a big basket of green and red grapes. Can you estimate the percent of green grapes?

Solution:

If we are interested in what percent are green, we will not need to count all of the grapes in the basket to estimate this. Grabbing a few grapes randomly and counting just those that are green will give us a reasonable estimate.

Example 7.11: Now, just to make it more difficult, suppose these grapes are of different sizes, with the green grapes significantly larger than the red grapes. Can we still estimate the percent of green grapes by grabbing a handful of grapes randomly?

Solution:

A simple random sample requires that each component in the population should have the same chance of being picked. Since the green grapes are significantly larger than the red ones, we are more likely going to grab numbers of green and red grapes that are not proportional to the total numbers in the whole basket. If that happens, then random sampling cannot be achieved fully as it can result in overestimating the percent of one type of grapes over the other.

7.3.2 Systematic random sampling

The key feature of random sampling is that it should be done non-systematically to assure pure randomness. In situations where the population is very large, a *systematic random sampling* may be performed. This is achieved by randomly selecting one member from the first k members. Then every kth member, starting with the first selected member, is included in the sample. The example below illustrates how to take a systematic random sample.

Example 7.12: Suppose from a company population of 60,000 employees we wish to take a random sample of 200 employees. Explain how to take a simple random sample and a systematic random sample from this population.

Solution:

If we can access all members of the entire population all at once, a simple random sample can be taken. The use of software programs can be very useful in obtaining a simple random sample as will be discussed later in this chapter. We may also arrange the 60,000 employees in some order say alphabetically or by employee identification number to take a systematic random sample. Since the sample size is 200, the ratio of population to sample size is 60,000/200 = 300. Based on this ratio, we can select one employee from the first 300 employees in the arranged list at random. Suppose this member was the number 180th employee in the list of 300, we should then select every 180th from every 300 employees in the list. This will result in employees in the sample with numbers 180, 480, 780, 1080, and so on.

7.3.3 Cluster sampling

In cluster sampling, we divide the population up into a set of different coherent areas. We then randomly select areas to assess and randomly select subjects in the selected areas. The key point here is that the different coherent areas should be naturally occurring and not artificially made. Its main use is in market research where the total population is divided into samples or groups; a sample of the groups is randomly selected. After this process, relevant and required data from all the elements of all the groups is collected. In some situations, instead of collecting information from each group, information can be collected from a sub-sample of the elements.

Example 7.13: Select one of the States in the United States of America and demonstrate how you would select a cluster sample of households in the state.

Solution:

For this type of application, it is important to begin with a map of the state displaying all counties. In this example, we select the State of New Jersey as shown below. Here counties are considered as the different clusters in the state. In this State, there are 21 counties that together contain 566 municipalities. We may select say 7 counties (clusters) randomly. We may then consider the municipalities in each county as another cluster and select a random sample of municipalities from each

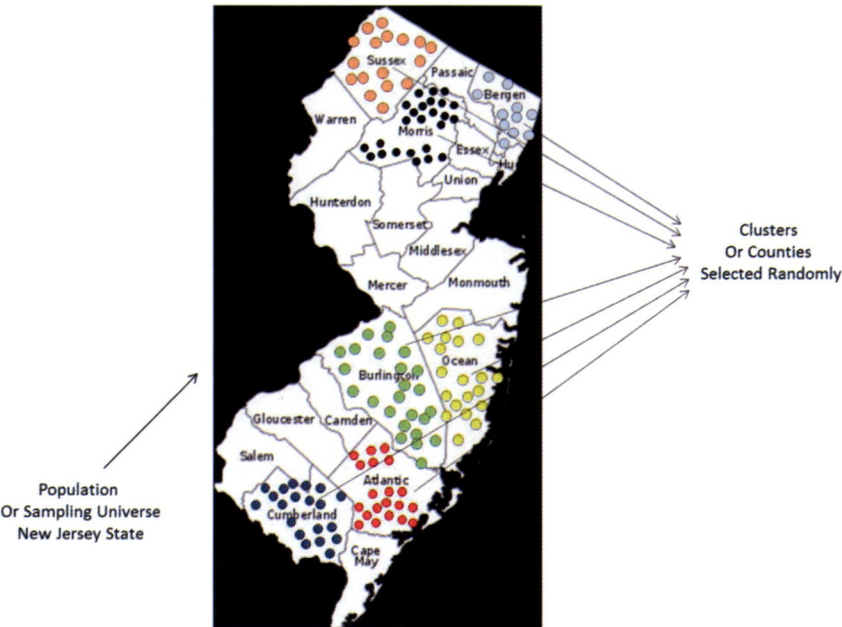

county. Finally, we can select a random sample of households from each sub-cluster.

7.3.4 Stratified random sampling

Stratified sampling is used when the population under consideration is heterogeneous with distinct categories forming the population, and when we are interested in making sure that each category of the population is represented in the sample. In this case, different components of the sample are selected randomly from the different categories or strata.

In stratified sampling, members belonging to a certain category or stratum within the population should be picked randomly and should be represented in the sample in numbers proportional to the relative frequency of their category in the population. Accordingly, a stratified sample should satisfy the condition that the probability of the presence of a member from a certain category in the sample is equivalent to N_i/N, where N_i is the size of category i in the population, and N is the population size. For a sample size, n, the number of sample members, n_i, belonging to a certain category i is given by:

$$n_i = n\left(\frac{N_i}{N}\right) \qquad (7.2)$$

Example 7.14: Suppose we have a finite population of 3000 students representing a population of a small college. 1400 students are female and 1600 are male. If a stratified sample of 25 students is selected from this population in a proportional-weight allocated fashion, how many students would you select in the sample from each gender?

Solution:

Following equation 7.2,

$N = 3000$, $n = 25$, $N_m = 1600$, and $N_f = 1400$

$$n_i = n\left(\frac{N_i}{N}\right)$$

$$n_m = n\left(\frac{N_m}{N}\right) = 25\left(\frac{1600}{3000}\right) = 13.333$$

$$n_f = n\left(\frac{N_f}{N}\right) = 25\left(\frac{1400}{3000}\right) = 11.666$$

In general, decimals should be rounded off to obtain a true number of elements. This means that the number of males in the sample will be 13 students and the number of females in the sample will be 12 students. This leads to a total of 25 students. In practice, we may need to round up to assure having larger sample.

Example 7.15: Suppose we have a finite population of 1000 people representing the population of a small city. 240 of those people are Caucasian females, 260 are Caucasian males, 210 are African American females, and 290 people are African American males.

    (a) Explain how to select a random sample of 100 people from this population.
    (b) Explain how to select a stratified sample of 100 people from this population.

Solution:

In order to select a random sample of 100 people from this population, we can have everyone's identification number typed on a card, shuffle the 1000 cards, and put them all in a box from which we withdraw a blind sample of 100 cards that will represent a random sample of 100 people.

In order to select a stratified sample, we should make sure that we have 4 sets of post cards each assigned for one of the four categories. Accordingly, we will need 4 boxes. In the first box, we should have 240 cards representing the identification numbers of Caucasian females (*FW*); in the second box 260 cards representing the identification numbers of Caucasian males (*MW*); in the third box, 210 cards representing the identification numbers of African American females (*FB*); and in the fourth box, 290 cards representing the identification numbers of African American males (*MB*). We can then go to each box and blindly select a sub-sample representing the group of interest in proportional-weight allocated fashion using equation 7.2. The numbers of people selected from each box are as follows:

$$Box\ 1(FW):\ n_{FW} = n\left(\frac{N_{FW}}{N}\right) = 100\left(\frac{240}{1000}\right) = 24$$

$$Box\ 2(MW):\ n_{MW} = n\left(\frac{N_{MW}}{N}\right) = 100\left(\frac{260}{1000}\right) = 26$$

$$Box\ 3(FB):\ n_{FB} = n\left(\frac{N_{FB}}{N}\right) = 100\left(\frac{210}{1000}\right) = 21$$

$$Box\ 4(MB):\ n_{MB} = n\left(\frac{N_{MB}}{N}\right) = 100\left(\frac{290}{1000}\right) = 29$$

Note that if you add the number of people of all categories in the sample, the sum will be 100 (24+26+21+29).

Working Problem 7.11:

Suppose an organization that has 10 divisions wishes to determine the opinion of its employees on a new health-care benefit program. What would be the appropriate sampling technique?

Answer:
1. Random Sample
- If all employees of different divisions are accessible (via names or identification number), and if different divisions can be treated as equally important, a random sample can be selected in which, each employee in the entire organization will have the same chance of being selected
2. Cluster Sample
Because each division can be treated as a subgroup (or a cluster), taking a random sample from each division will yield a cluster sample.
3. Stratified Sample
Because employees in different divisions are categorized by the division task (e.g. manufacturing division, finance division, marketing division, etc.) , we may consider using stratified sampling for some categories

Working Problem 7.12:

Suppose we have a finite population of 1000 students representing a population of the college of business in a university. 350 of those students are freshman, 260 are sophomore, and 210 are junior, and 180 are seniors. If you were to select a stratified random sample of 100 students from this population, what is number of students from each category should you select?

Answer: 35 (F), 26 (So), 21 (J), 18 (Se)

Working Problem 7.13:

Suppose we have a finite population of 1150 students representing a population of the college of business in a university. 400 of those students are freshman, 310 are sophomore, and 235 are junior, and 205 are seniors. If you were to select a stratified random sample of 100 students from this population, what is number of students from each category should you select?

Answer:

35 (F), 27 (So), 20 (J), 18 (Se)

7.4 Using Microsoft Excel® to select random samples

For finite populations, we can use Microsoft Excel® to select random samples provided that identification numbers of population elements are known and listed. The steps required to perform sampling using Microsoft Excel® are listed below by example.

Example 7.16: Suppose we have a finite population of 1000 people representing a population of a small city. 240 of those people are Caucasian females, 260 are Caucasian males, 210 are African American females, and 290 people are African American males. Select a random sample of 32 people from the population of 1000 people using Microsoft Excel®.

Solution:

Assume the identification numbers of the people in this population are in consecutive order as shown in Table 7.1.

Table 7.1 Identification numbers and categories of city population

People ID #	Category	People ID #	Category	People ID #	Category	People ID #	Category
1	FW	241	MW	501	FB	711	MB
2	FW	242	MW	502	FB	712	MB
3	FW	243	MW	503	FB	713	MB
4	FW	244	MW	504	FB	714	MB
...	...	...	...	...	...	...	...
...	...	...	...	...	...	...	...
234	FW	494	MW	704	FB	994	MB
235	FW	495	MW	705	FB	995	MB
236	FW	496	MW	706	FB	996	MB
237	FW	497	MW	707	FB	997	MB
238	FW	498	MW	708	FB	998	MB
239	FW	499	MW	709	FB	999	MB
240	FW	500	MW	710	FB	1000	MB

In order to select a random sample, we use the following steps:

- Arrange all data in two parallel columns (one for identification number and the other for category).
- Go to 'Data,' 'Data Analysis,' and select 'Sampling' as shown in Figure 7.5.
- In the Input Range, we specify the cells covering all the identification numbers including the label (check the label box).
- Excel® provides two sampling options: random and periodic (see Figure 7.6). In this example, we select random sampling.
- The window labeled 'Number of Samples' implies the number of members in a sample. In our example, we need to select 32 random members. We can do that by typing 32 as the number of samples indicating that we need to select a random sample of size 32 as shown in Figure 7.6.
- We then specify where we wish to place the output results by going to the Output Range window and clicking on a blank cell and allow enough space on the spreadsheet for displaying the results.
- We may also display the results on a new worksheet by bypassing the Output Range window and checking the box at the New Worksheet Ply.

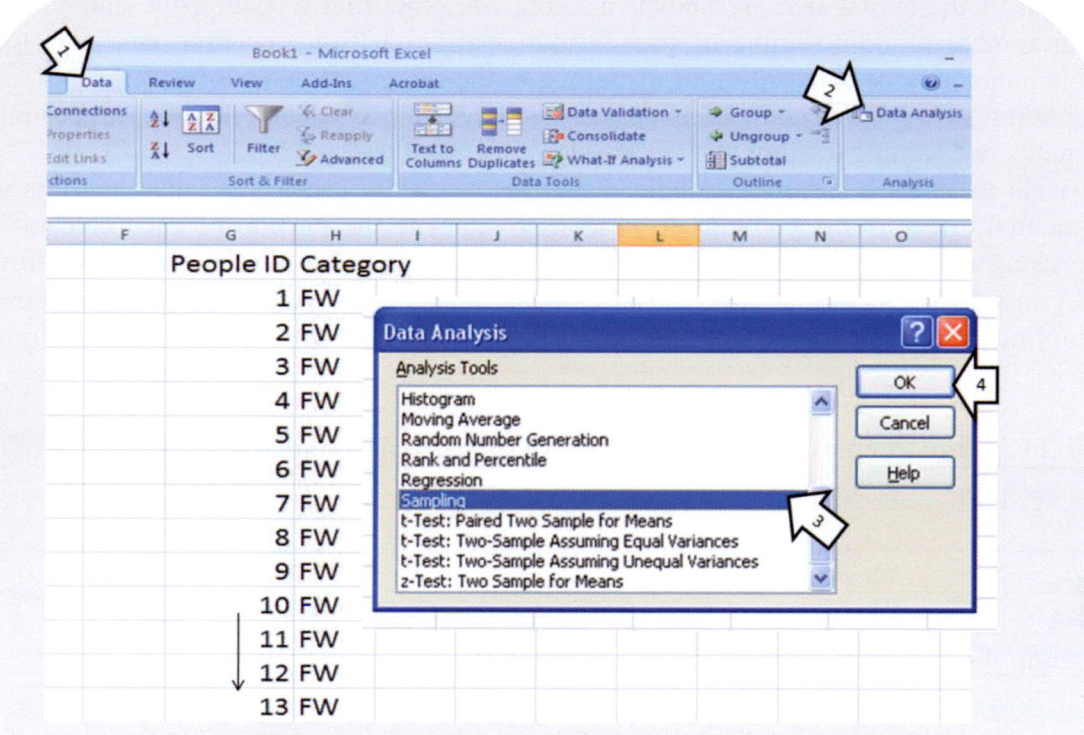

Figure 7.5 Using Microsoft Excel® for Performing Random Sampling: Steps 1 through 4

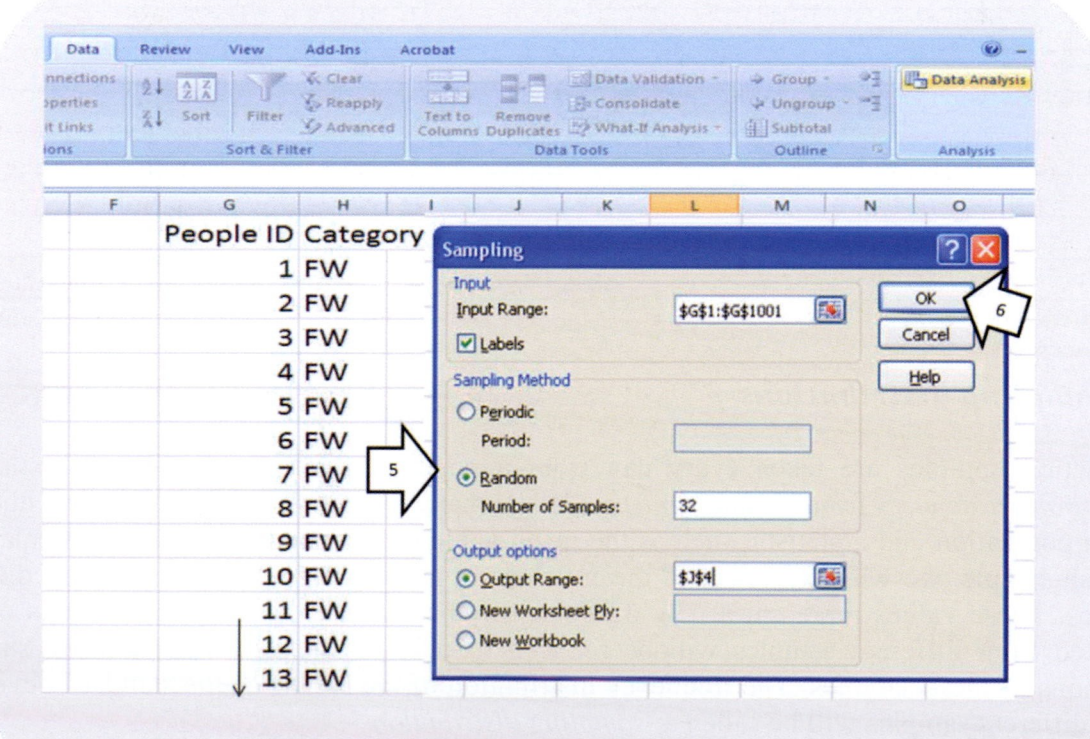

Figure 7.6 Using Microsoft Excel® for Performing Random Sampling: Steps 5 and 6

The output of the above steps is shown in Table 7.2. Note that repeating the above steps will result in another random sample of size 32 that is different from the first one. Also note that some elements may be selected more than once in the same sample as a result of this sampling method being with replacement. In this case, you may want to select a slightly larger number of components in a sample to allow the discarding of repeated ones.

If you wish to select a stratified sample, you cannot directly use Excel$^®$ data analysis without some manual effort. What you can do is to first calculate the portion of each category in the sample using equation 7.2, and use Excel$^®$ data analysis to select a random sample from each category in proportion-weight allocated fashion. In other words, you will repeat the above steps by sampling randomly from each category the number of components required from each category.

Table 7.2 Random samples generated by Microsoft Excel$^®$: Two random samples each of $n = 32$

Sample 1		Sample 2	
3	333	622	604
341	570	670	778
904	273	307	629
496	21	347	6
793	501	551	362
87	997	485	238
783	523	772	309
812	753	202	176
375	271	497	834
144	412	985	100
306	499	717	692
884	870	6	336
46	160	362	845
601	693	887	69
896	33	879	135
120	898	116	809

7.5 Sampling distributions

In practice, samples are taken every day from a population for the purpose of estimating *population parameters* from *sample statistics*. When many representative samples are withdrawn from a population and a statistic such as the mean value or the standard deviation is calculated for each sample, we will have a set of mean values or a set of standard deviations of different samples. These values represent a new data set. In other words, the massive amounts of data collected from different samples will be reduced to only the mean values and the standard deviations of these samples. The frequency distribution of the means or the standard deviations of the different samples will be called a '*sampling distribution.*'

To demonstrate the concept of sampling distributions, suppose the data in the big circle shown in Figure 7.7 represents the ages of a finite population of, say 2000 salesmen ($N = 2000$) in a large organization. Because of the extensive travel that the organization expects from its salesmen, the organization maintains an average age of 40 years in different sales divisions. This is considered as the population mean, μ. The standard deviation of age of this population, σ_x is about 3.0 (the suffix x implies standard deviation of individual values of age). We use the suffix x here to indicate that this is the standard deviation of all x values or the individual values of age of all salesmen in the population.

Suppose the organization takes k samples (say 50 samples) from different divisions each of size n (say 5) to examine their performances in association with the average age of each sample. This will yield a new set of data representing 50 mean values of the samples collected as shown in the right side of Figure 7.7. If we take the mean value of sample means (the average of averages, $\bar{\bar{X}}$), we should obtain a value that is approximately identical to the mean of the population ($\bar{\bar{X}} = \mu$). Note that the standard deviation of the samples mean values $\sigma_{\bar{X}}$ is 1.4, which is smaller than the standard deviation of the whole population, σ_x ($= 3.0$). This key point will be discussed shortly.

If the organization decided to construct a frequency distribution using the 50 values of sample means, this would be considered as the *sampling distribution of mean values*. Both the frequency distribution of population age (individual values) and the corresponding frequency distribution of sample means (sampling distribution) are superimposed in Figure 7.8. Note how the two distributions share the same center or mean value. Also note how narrow the sampling distribution is in comparison with the population distribution. These features represent the essence of the ***central limit theorem*** that will be discussed shortly.

The example above simply demonstrates the concept of sampling distribution. It follows that the frequency distribution or the histogram of the mean values of samples is the sampling distribution of sample means. Similarly, we can have a sampling distribution for the standard deviation or the variance as will be discussed later. The following examples illustrate the concept of sampling distribution in the real world using the classic case of sampling distribution of sample means.

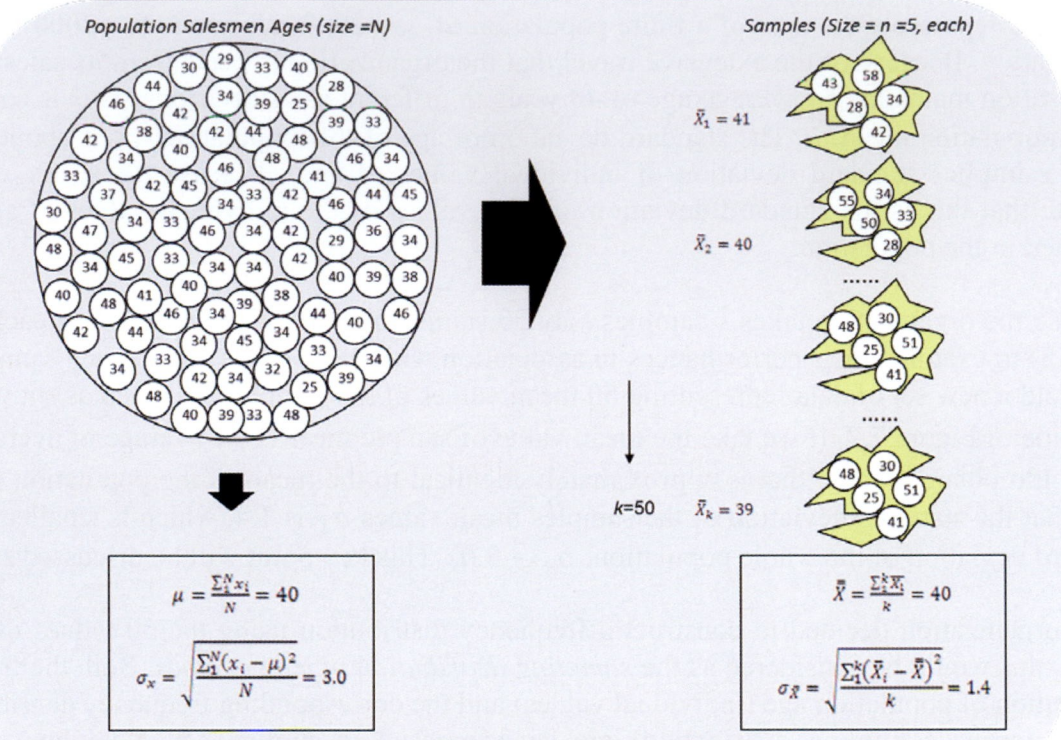

Figure 7.7 The concept of Sampling Distribution: (1) Population and Samples

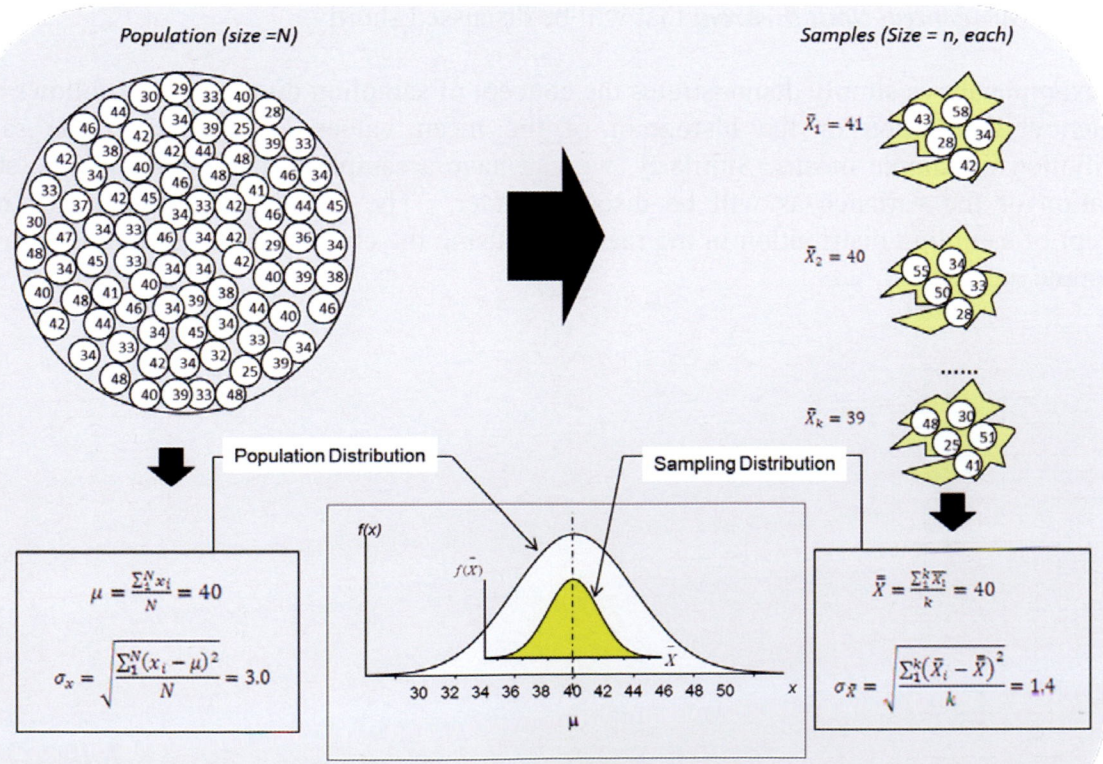

Figure 7.8 The concept of Sampling Distribution: (2) Population and Sampling Distributions

Example 7.17: A large biotech and pharmaceutical company located in the State of New Jersey is interested in the distance driven by its employee's to-and-from work every day in order to decide whether it will be beneficial to provide transportation means to its employees. Over a forty-day period, the company collected daily random samples from its employees, each day taking ten random employees aside and asking them about the distance they drive to work. The data collected is shown in Table 7.4. In its planning for this option, the company established a minimum distance of 40 miles and a maximum distance of 60 miles to justify its decision to offer transportation service as only employees driving distances in this range will benefit from this service.

(a) Perform descriptive statistics for the entire data set collected.
(b) Construct a frequency distribution for the entire data set collected.
(c) Based on the pre-specified distance established by the company, what percent of the employees will benefit from this service?

Table 7.4 Distances driven by 40 samples of company employees (miles)

Employee Identification																			
1	2	3	4	5	6	7	8	9	10	11	12	13	14	15	16	17	18	19	20
38	42	38	41	52	34	38	50	37	31	40	33	51	41	43	40	50	48	35	51
39	37	35	40	38	37	43	40	47	37	41	36	41	52	34	52	38	41	43	31
42	34	38	46	44	40	42	40	29	40	43	36	34	32	43	35	32	37	30	32
40	36	43	32	32	40	47	40	32	41	45	43	31	34	44	51	40	37	37	37
38	36	42	51	34	35	45	39	41	39	44	39	40	44	35	31	44	41	47	29
35	36	37	44	43	41	40	42	43	30	37	40	48	35	42	44	34	31	38	42
44	33	35	44	41	52	45	42	40	45	37	52	32	48	35	46	41	40	36	33
41	36	40	32	32	48	39	44	41	41	44	36	45	36	36	43	36	38	44	45
41	39	43	45	33	42	44	31	32	45	38	39	52	41	37	42	37	44	44	47
46	33	52	42	40	36	34	46	47	38	32	41	38	42	38	36	37	37	43	36

Employee Identification																			
21	22	23	24	25	26	27	28	29	30	31	32	33	34	35	36	37	38	39	40
34	45	35	35	43	39	49	44	39	37	37	36	37	32	37	45	40	49	41	31
41	44	38	44	44	38	37	39	45	33	42	40	40	36	42	31	40	45	43	54
36	32	35	43	41	38	43	48	45	44	50	40	35	33	38	43	39	40	42	39
44	36	37	45	43	35	33	42	40	37	42	46	36	38	44	41	42	35	36	41
42	40	40	38	42	43	39	40	31	36	50	43	41	32	35	41	39	33	37	42
41	38	41	41	39	35	42	40	47	46	35	37	41	36	42	34	49	41	37	31
36	36	35	41	44	38	32	39	34	35	33	40	37	36	35	41	37	50	41	33
39	42	40	35	42	44	47	38	41	51	36	44	48	42	44	40	40	45	38	40
42	41	39	48	42	36	39	33	41	42	38	41	51	42	41	40	40	38	38	46
37	30	39	52	41	35	39	40	42	41	36	43	39	43	42	49	33	44	44	45

Solution:

The large amount of data collected can be considered as population data since it was collected over a period of time and it covered almost the entire population of employees. In order to answer the above questions, we can calculate the population mean and standard deviation as follows:

$$Mean = \mu_x = \frac{\sum_1^N x_i}{N} = \frac{38 + 39 + 42 + \cdots + 40 + 46 + 45}{400} = 39.9 \; miles$$

$$\sigma_x{}^2 = \frac{\sum_1^N (x_i - \mu)^2}{N} = \frac{(38 - 39.9)^2 + (39 - 39.9)^2 + \ldots\ldots + (45 - 39.9)^2}{400} = 24.8$$

$$\sigma_x = \sqrt{\sigma_x{}^2} = \sqrt{24.8} = 4.98 \; miles$$

More parameters of the population can be calculated using Excel® data analysis-descriptive statistics as described in Chapter 2. In addition, you can construct a histogram or a frequency distribution of all data using Excel® data analysis-histogram as described in Chapter 3. Figure 7.9 shows the frequency distribution of distance of the entire population and associated statistics.

Based on the pre-specified distance established by the company, the percent of the employees that will benefit from the transportation service is $P(40 \le x \le 60)$. Typically, this is obtained from the cumulative frequency curve as follows:

$$P(40 \le x \le 60) = P(x \le 60) - P(x \le 40)$$

Note that since no value in the data set was greater than 60, this problem can be treated as $P(x > 40)$. This probability or percent can be obtained roughly from the histogram or directly from the cumulative frequency curve:

$P(x > 40) = 100 - P(x \le 40) = 100 - 54.5 = 45.5\%$.

This means that about 45.5% of the employees will benefit from the company's proposed transportation service.

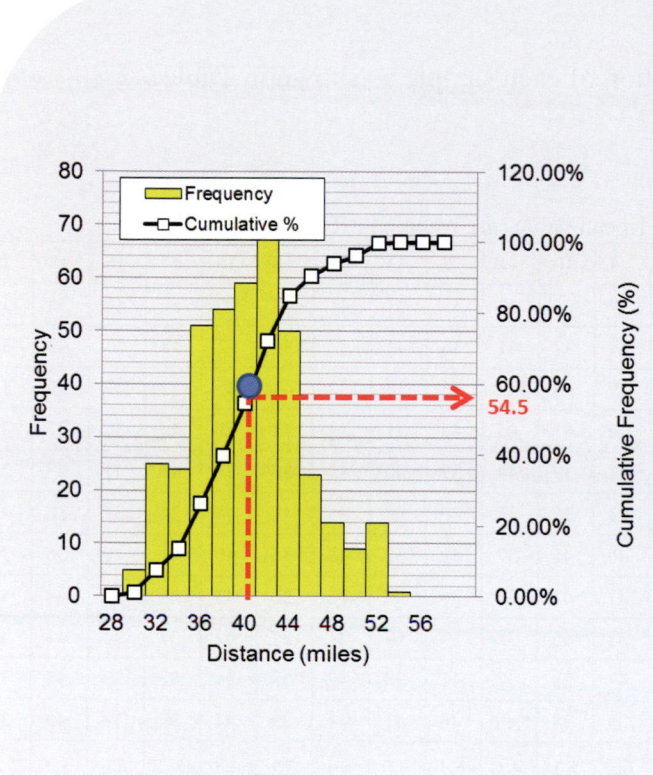

Mid-Points	Frequency	Cumulative %
28	0	0.00%
30	5	1.25%
32	25	7.50%
34	24	13.50%
36	51	26.25%
38	54	39.75%
40	59	54.50%
42	71	72.25%
44	50	84.75%
46	23	90.50%
48	14	94.00%
50	9	96.25%
52	14	99.75%
54	1	100.00%
56	0	100.00%
58	0	100.00%

Population Parameters	
Mean	39.9
Median	40.0
Mode	41.0
Standard Deviation	4.98
Sample Variance	24.80
Range	25
Minimum	29
Maximum	54
Count	400

Figure 7.9 Frequency Distribution of Driving Distances of a Finite Population of 400 Employees

Example 7.18: In the example above, suppose instead of analyzing the entire data set of the finite population, the company decided to only consider the sample statistics, particularly the values of samples averages. As a result, the company calculated the mean value of each sample.

We should point out that these forms of arrangement of data represent the common way of how organizations manage their data on a daily basis. They typically collect daily samples, generate data associated with these samples, and determine sample statistics. Over time, individual observations will largely reflect the whole population, and sample statistics will provide useful sampling distributions of mean or standard deviation.

The question now is how is the data from sample statistics different from the entire population data? The answer to this question is the key to understanding the concept of sampling distribution.

Solution:

1. Calculate the mean and standard deviation of each sample as shown in Table 7.5.

Table 7.5 Statistics of sample data of distance (mean values are rounded off)

Sample #	1	2	3	4	5	6	7	8	9	10	11	12	13	14	15	16	17	18	19	20
	38	42	38	41	52	34	38	50	37	31	40	33	51	41	43	40	50	48	35	51
	39	37	35	40	38	37	43	40	47	37	41	36	41	52	34	52	38	41	43	31
	42	34	38	46	44	40	42	40	29	40	43	36	34	32	43	35	32	37	30	32
	40	36	43	32	32	40	47	40	32	41	45	43	31	34	44	51	40	37	37	37
	38	36	42	51	34	35	45	39	41	39	44	39	40	44	35	31	44	41	47	29
	35	36	37	44	43	41	40	42	43	30	37	40	48	35	42	44	34	31	38	42
	44	33	35	44	41	52	45	42	40	45	37	52	32	48	35	46	41	40	36	33
	41	36	40	32	32	48	39	44	41	41	44	36	45	36	36	43	36	38	44	45
	41	39	43	45	33	42	44	31	32	45	38	39	52	41	37	42	37	44	44	47
	46	33	52	42	40	36	34	46	47	38	32	41	38	42	38	36	37	37	43	36
Mean	40	36	40	42	39	41	42	41	39	39	40	40	41	41	39	42	39	39	40	38
Standard deviation	3.2	2.7	5.1	5.9	6.5	5.7	3.9	5	6.3	5.1	4.1	5.3	7.6	6.4	3.9	6.8	5.2	4.6	5.3	7.5
Sample #	21	22	23	24	25	26	27	28	29	30	31	32	33	34	35	36	37	38	39	40
	34	45	35	35	43	39	49	44	39	37	37	36	37	32	37	45	40	49	41	31
	41	44	38	44	44	38	37	39	45	33	42	40	40	36	42	31	40	45	43	54
	36	32	35	43	41	38	43	48	45	44	50	40	35	33	38	43	39	40	42	39
	44	36	37	45	43	35	33	42	40	37	42	46	36	38	44	41	42	35	36	41
	42	40	40	38	42	43	39	40	31	36	50	43	41	32	35	41	39	33	37	42
	41	38	41	41	39	35	42	40	47	46	35	37	41	36	42	34	49	41	37	31
	36	36	35	41	44	38	32	39	34	35	33	40	37	36	35	41	37	50	41	33
	39	42	40	35	42	44	47	38	41	51	36	44	48	42	44	40	40	45	38	40
	42	41	39	48	42	36	39	33	41	42	38	41	51	42	41	40	40	38	38	46
	37	30	39	52	41	35	39	40	42	41	36	43	39	43	42	49	33	44	44	45
Mean	39	38	38	42	42	38	40	40	41	40	40	41	40	37	40	41	40	42	40	40
Standard deviation	3.3	4.9	2.3	5.4	1.5	3.2	5.5	3.9	4.9	5.6	6	3.1	5.2	4.2	3.5	5.1	4	5.6	2.8	7.3

2. List the mean and standard deviation of each sample as shown in Table 7.6.

400

Table 7.6 Summary of sample statistics (with actual mean values)

Sample #	Mean	Standard deviation	Sample #	Mean	Standard deviation
1	40.4	3.2	21	39.2	3.3
2	36.2	2.7	22	38.4	4.9
3	40.3	5.1	23	37.9	2.3
4	41.7	5.9	24	42.2	5.4
5	38.9	6.5	25	42.1	1.5
6	40.5	5.7	26	38.1	3.2
7	41.7	3.9	27	40	5.5
8	41.4	5	28	40.3	3.9
9	38.9	6.3	29	40.5	4.9
10	38.7	5.1	30	40.2	5.6
11	40.1	4.1	31	39.9	6
12	39.5	5.3	32	41	3.1
13	41.2	7.6	33	40.5	5.2
14	40.5	6.4	34	37	4.2
15	38.7	3.9	35	40	3.5
16	42	6.8	36	40.5	5.1
17	38.9	5.2	37	39.9	4
18	39.4	4.6	38	42	5.6
19	39.7	5.3	39	39.7	2.8
20	38.3	7.5	40	40.2	7.3

3. Calculate the overall mean and the variance of the sample means:

$$Mean = \mu_{\bar{X}} = \frac{\sum_1^k \bar{X}}{k} = \frac{40.4 + 36.2 + 40.3 + \cdots + 42 + 39.7 + 40.2}{40} = 39.9 \, miles$$

$$\sigma_{\bar{X}}^2 = \frac{\sum_1^k (x_i - \mu)^2}{k} = \frac{(40.4 - 39.9)^2 + (36.2 - 39.9)^2 + \ldots + (40.2 - 39.9)^2}{40} = 1.9$$

$$\sigma_{\bar{X}} = \sqrt{\sigma_{\bar{X}}^2} = \sqrt{1.9} = 1.38 \, miles$$

As expected, the above results indicate that the mean of the sample means is identical to the mean of the entire data calculated earlier. The standard deviation of sample means on the other hand being 1.38 is much smaller than that of the entire population, 4.98 (calculated in the previous example). In other words, the standard deviation of sample means is less than that of the whole population, or $\sigma_{\bar{X}} < \sigma_x$.

These findings confirm what we discussed earlier regarding sampling distribution. We can also construct a histogram of the sample means as shown in Figure 7.10, which will be the sampling distribution of means. As you can see in this Figure, the sampling distribution shares the same mean as that of the parent distribution but it exhibits a narrower width as a result of the smaller standard deviation. We will let the student estimate what percent of the employees will benefit from the transportation service using the pre-specified distance established by the company, but this time from the sampling distribution. The key point of this exercise is to realize how much information was lost by dealing with a sampling distribution instead of the whole population distribution and whether this will influence the decision of the company of providing a transportation service to its employees.

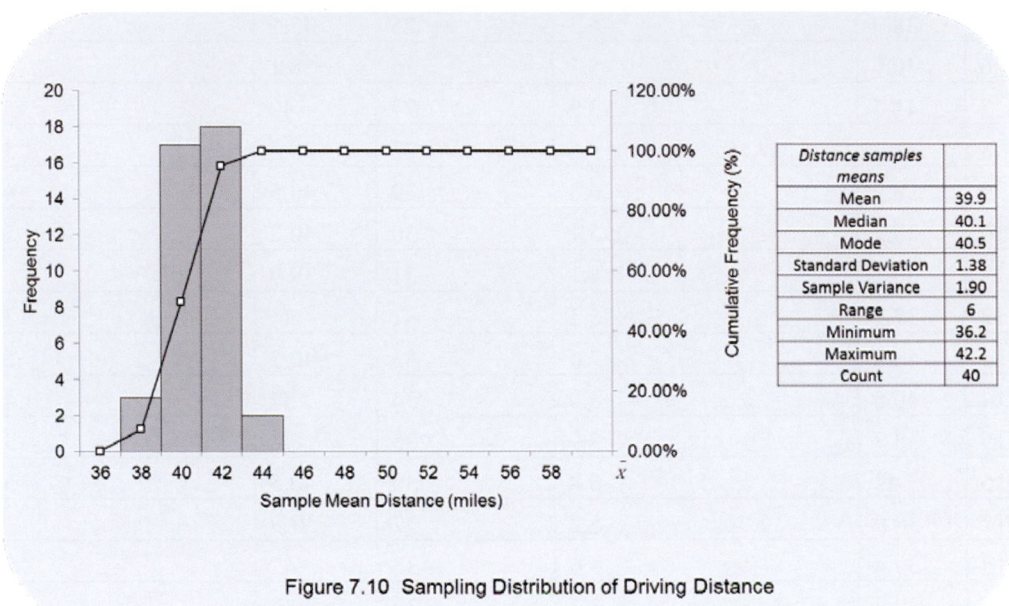

Distance samples means	
Mean	39.9
Median	40.1
Mode	40.5
Standard Deviation	1.38
Sample Variance	1.90
Range	6
Minimum	36.2
Maximum	42.2
Count	40

Figure 7.10 Sampling Distribution of Driving Distance

Working Problem 7.14:

The data shown in the Table below represent the grades of a finite population of 100 students:

(a) Calculate the overall mean and the overall standard deviation

(b) Construct a histogram of student grades

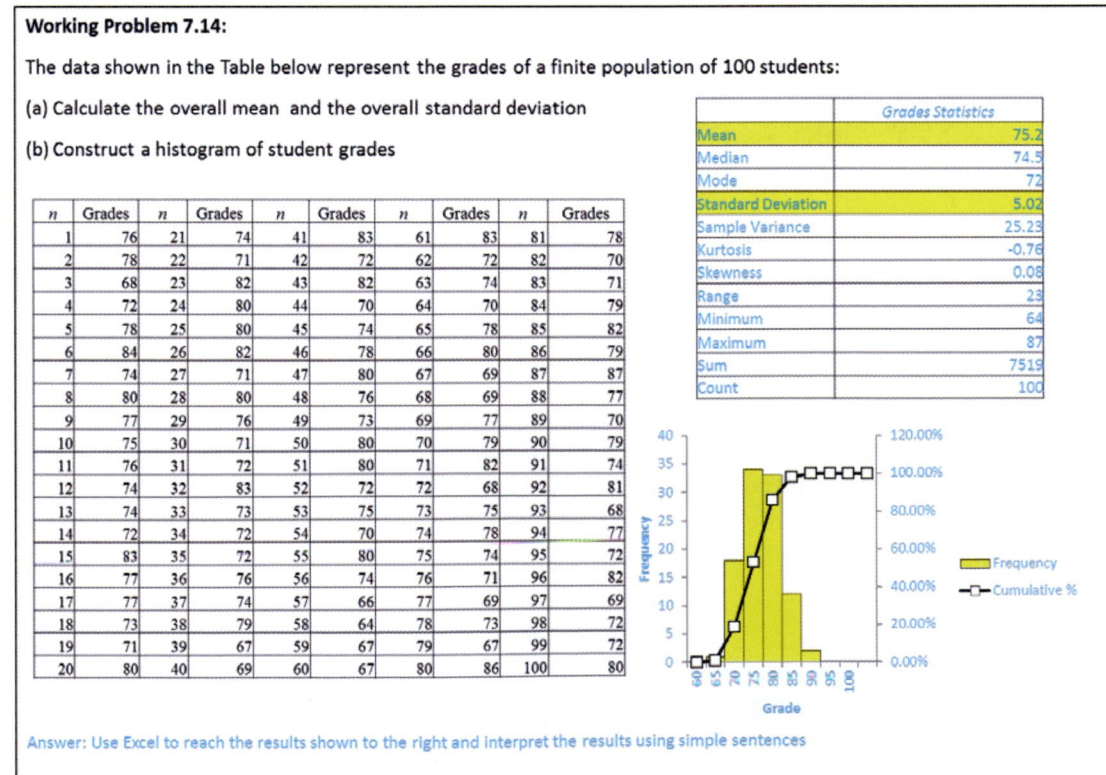

	Grades Statistics
Mean	75.2
Median	74.5
Mode	72
Standard Deviation	5.02
Sample Variance	25.23
Kurtosis	-0.76
Skewness	0.08
Range	23
Minimum	64
Maximum	87
Sum	7519
Count	100

n	Grades	n	Grades	n	Grades	n	Grades	n	Grades
1	76	21	74	41	83	61	83	81	78
2	78	22	71	42	72	62	72	82	70
3	68	23	82	43	82	63	74	83	71
4	72	24	80	44	70	64	70	84	79
5	78	25	80	45	74	65	78	85	82
6	84	26	82	46	78	66	80	86	79
7	74	27	71	47	80	67	69	87	87
8	80	28	80	48	76	68	69	88	77
9	77	29	76	49	73	69	77	89	70
10	75	30	71	50	80	70	79	90	79
11	76	31	72	51	80	71	82	91	74
12	74	32	83	52	72	72	68	92	81
13	74	33	73	53	75	73	75	93	68
14	72	34	72	54	70	74	78	94	77
15	83	35	72	55	80	75	74	95	72
16	77	36	76	56	74	76	71	96	82
17	77	37	74	57	66	77	69	97	69
18	73	38	79	58	64	78	73	98	72
19	71	39	67	59	67	79	67	99	72
20	80	40	69	60	67	80	86	100	80

Answer: Use Excel to reach the results shown to the right and interpret the results using simple sentences

7.6 The Central Limit theorem

Earlier in this chapter we discussed the practical aspects associated with the sample-population relationship and in the previous section, we discussed how a sampling distribution is different from the distribution of the parent distribution. These concepts are best described using the so-called 'Central Limit Theorem.'

The Central Limit Theorem consists of three unique rules that collectively represent the foundation of estimation or inferential statistics, which will be discussed in Chapter 8. These rules are as follows:

1. If the variable, x, in the parent population follows a normal distribution, then the sample mean, $\bar{X}$, of samples taken from this population will also follow a normal distribution (Figure 7.11.a). In other words, if the parent population distribution is normal, the sampling distribution of means will also be a normal distribution.

2. If the variable, x, in the parent population does not follow a normal distribution, then the sample mean, $\bar{X}$, can still be approximated by a normal distribution particularly when the sample size is large (Figures 7.11.b and 7.11.c). In general, the larger the sample size, the more normal the sampling distribution will become. Statistically speaking, a sample is considered large when it has 30 or more members ($n \geq 30$). A small sample will have $n < 30$.

3. The sampling distribution of sample means will have a mean value equal to the parent population mean, and a variance equal to $1/n$ times the variance of the population:

$$\mu_{\bar{X}} = \mu_x \qquad (7.3)$$

$$\sigma_{\bar{X}} = \frac{\sigma_x}{\sqrt{n}} \qquad (7.4)$$

Recall that in the examples of the previous section, we denoted the standard deviation of the sampling distribution of the sample means by $\sigma_{\bar{X}}$. This is known as the 'standard error of mean.'

It is also important to point out that when sampling is done without replacement from a finite population, the standard error will be determined from the following equation:

$$\sigma_{\bar{X}} = \sqrt{\frac{N-n}{N-1}} \, \frac{\sigma_x}{\sqrt{n}} \qquad (7.5)$$

where n is the sample size, N is the population size, σ_x is the standard deviation of population values.

In practice, equation 7.4 is used more frequently than equation 7.5. One of the reasons is that N is typically very large compared to n, or the ratio n/N is typically very small in most practical applications. Mathematically, the smaller the n/N ratio, the closer the value of $\sigma_{\bar{X}}$ calculated from equation 7.4 to that calculated from equation 7.5. It should be noted that if we draw samples from a finite population without replacement the n/N ratio will progressively increase since the finite population will be progressively exhausted.

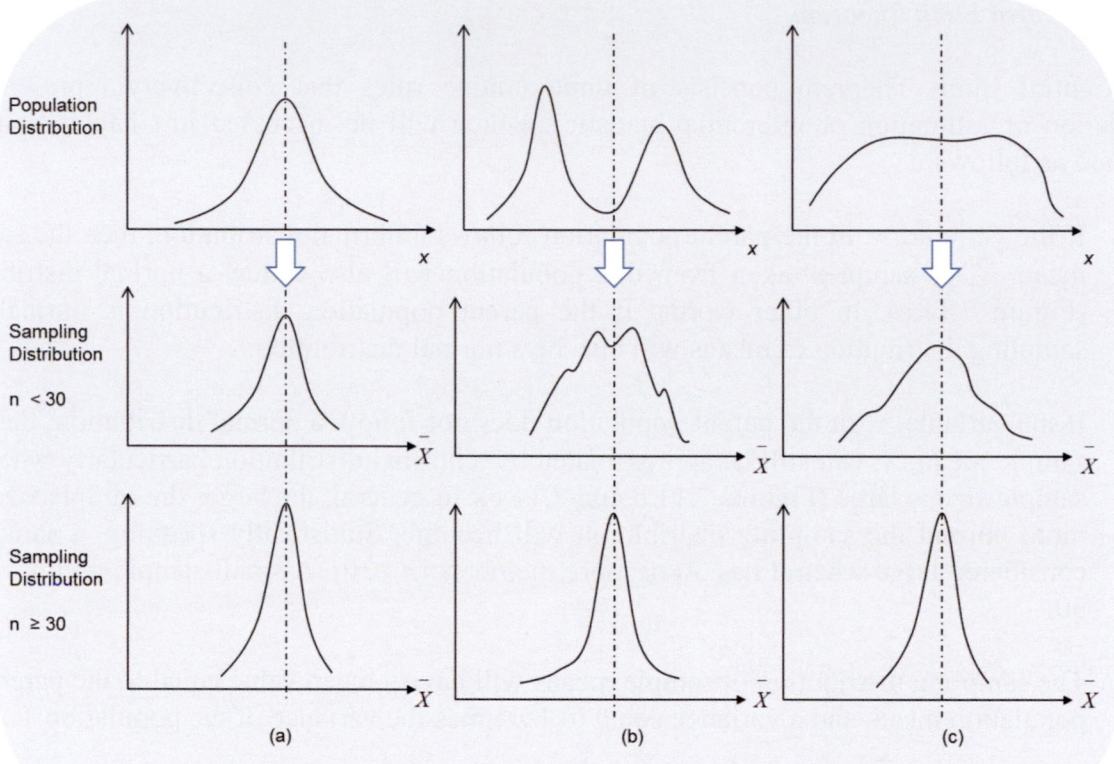

Figure 7.11 Parent Population and Sampling Distributions at Different Sample Sizes

Example 7.19: Using the data in Examples 7.17 and 7.18, verify the plausibility of the Central Limit Theorem.

Solution:

It is important to note that the samples in Example 7.17 are of small size $n = 10$. Normally, the Central Limit Theorem is more valid for samples of sample size $n \geq 30$. Nevertheless, we can still examine the plausibility of the theorem.

According to the analysis performed in Example 7.17, the parent population of distance largely follows a normal distribution as evident by the shape of the distribution (see Figure 7.9). The analysis performed in Example 7.18 revealed that the sampling distribution approximately follows a normal distribution (see Figure 7.10). Accordingly, the first aspect of the Central Limit theorem is satisfied. This point is illustrated in Figure 7.12.

404

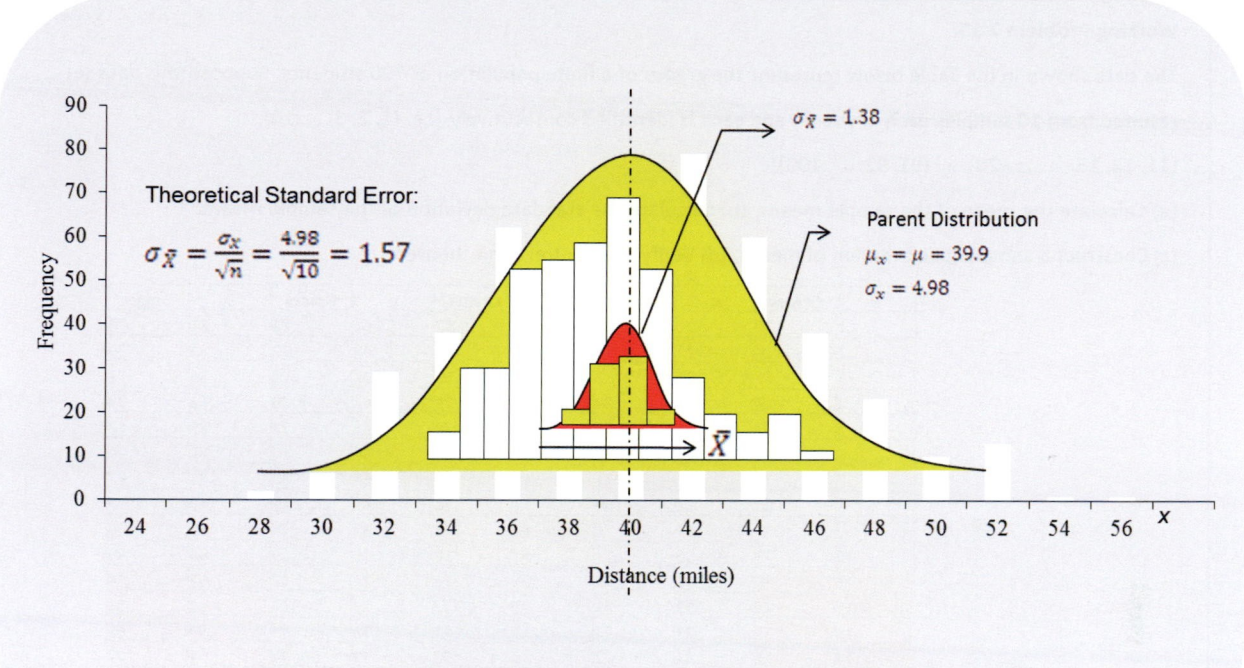

Figure 7.12 Parent and Sampling Distributions of Driving Distance

We can also see from the analysis of the data in Examples 7.17 and 7.18 that the mean of the sampling distribution equals to the mean of the parent population:

$$\mu_{\bar{X}} = \mu_x = 39.9$$

The standard deviation of the sampling distribution was 1.38. Following the Central Limit Theorem, this should equal:

$$\sigma_{\bar{X}} = \frac{\sigma_x}{\sqrt{n}} = \frac{4.98}{\sqrt{10}} = 1.57$$

This value is at a difference of 0.19 from the actual value of the standard deviation of mean (1.38). This is largely due to the small sample size used. We can also use equation 7.5 to yield the following value:

$$\sigma_{\bar{X}} = \sqrt{\frac{N-n}{N-1}}\frac{\sigma_x}{\sqrt{n}} = \sqrt{\frac{400-10}{400-1}}\frac{4.98}{\sqrt{10}} = \sqrt{\frac{390}{399}}\frac{4.98}{\sqrt{10}} = 0.9887\frac{4.98}{3.162} = 1.557$$

Working Problem 7.15:

The data shown in the Table below represent the grades of a finite population of 100 students. Suppose this data set resulted from 10 samples each of size 10 and each is identified consecutively (i.e. (1, 2, 3, ...10),

(11, 12, 13, ...20), ... (91, 92, ...100))

(a) Calculate the mean of the sample means, (b) Calculate the standard deviation of the sample means

(c) Construct a sampling distribution of means, (d) Verify the Central Limit theorem

n	Grades	n	Grades	n	Grades	n	Grades	n	Grades
1	76	21	74	41	83	61	83	81	78
2	78	22	71	42	72	62	72	82	70
3	68	23	82	43	82	63	74	83	71
4	72	24	80	44	70	64	70	84	79
5	78	25	80	45	74	65	78	85	82
6	84	26	82	46	78	66	80	86	79
7	74	27	71	47	80	67	69	87	87
8	80	28	80	48	76	68	69	88	77
9	77	29	76	49	73	69	77	89	70
10	75	30	71	50	80	70	79	90	79
11	76	31	72	51	80	71	82	91	74
12	74	32	83	52	72	72	68	92	81
13	74	33	73	53	75	73	75	93	68
14	72	34	72	54	70	74	78	94	77
15	83	35	72	55	80	75	74	95	72
16	77	36	76	56	74	76	71	96	82
17	77	37	74	57	66	77	69	97	69
18	73	38	79	58	64	78	73	98	72
19	71	39	67	59	67	79	67	99	72
20	80	40	69	60	67	80	86	100	80

7.7 Standard normal sampling distribution

In Chapter 6, we defined the standard normal distribution as a normal distribution with mean zero and standard deviation one, which results from the conversion of the x value to a z value using the following mathematical transformation:

$$z = \frac{x - \mu_x}{\sigma_x}$$

For a sampling distribution of mean values, the standard normal distribution results from the conversion of $\bar{X}$ to a z value using the following mathematical transformation:

$$z = \frac{\bar{X} - \mu_{\bar{X}}}{\sigma_{\bar{X}}} = \frac{\bar{X} - \mu_{\bar{X}}}{\frac{\sigma_x}{\sqrt{n}}} \qquad (7.6)$$

Note the similarity of the transformation equation as x in the first equation was replaced by $\bar{X}$; μ_x was replaced by $\mu_{\bar{X}}$ and σ_x was replaced by $\sigma_{\bar{X}}$ (or $\frac{\sigma_x}{\sqrt{n}}$). Figure 7.13 illustrates the difference between the transformation to a standard normal distribution for individual values x and for average values $\bar{X}$. The above equation assumes that the population standard deviation, σ_x is known. In situations where it is unknown, and the sample size is large (n ≥ 30), we can use the sample standard deviation, s_x, as an estimate of the population standard deviation σ_x, and determine the z-statistic by the following equation:

$$z = \frac{\bar{X} - \mu_{\bar{X}}}{\frac{\sigma_x}{\sqrt{n}}} \approx \frac{\bar{X} - \mu_{\bar{X}}}{\frac{s_x}{\sqrt{n}}} \qquad (7.7)$$

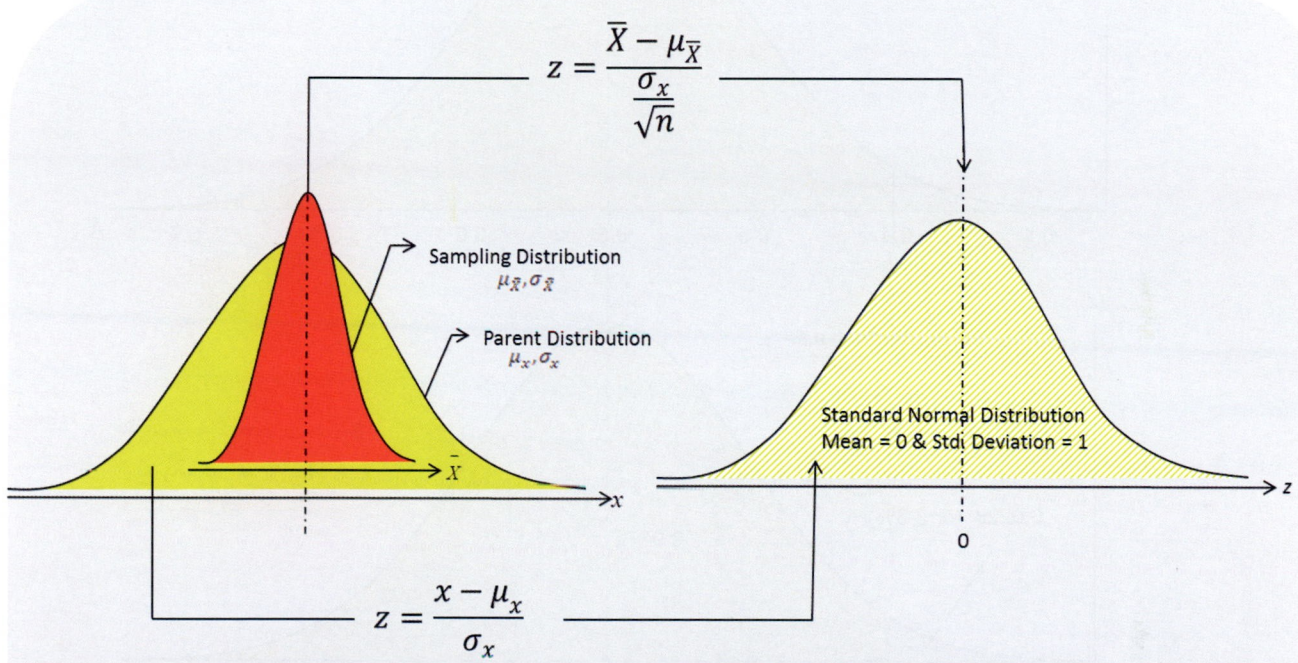

Figure 7.13 The conversion from a parent population distribution and a sampling distribution to a standard normal distribution using z-statistic

Example 7.20: A company producing wood boards takes a random sample of 40 boards from each shipment and measure the thickness of each board. Using the mean values of these samples a sampling distribution was constructed, which has a mean value of 0.5 inches, and standard deviation of 0.05 inches. What is the probability that a shipment of wood boards will have a mean value of thickness less than 0.4 inches?

Solution:

Using the z-score transformation, at $\mu_{\bar{X}} = 0.5$, and standard error, $\sigma_{\bar{X}} = 0.05$, and for a mean value $\bar{X} = 0.4$,

$$z = \frac{\bar{X} - \mu_{\bar{X}}}{\sigma_{\bar{X}}} = \frac{0.4 - 0.5}{0.05} = -2$$

Using the Standard Normal Table in Appendix 6.A, the area to the left of $z = -2$ is 0.0228 (see Figure 7.14). This means that there is about 2.3% chance of a shipment of wood boards having a mean value of thickness of less than 0.4 inches.

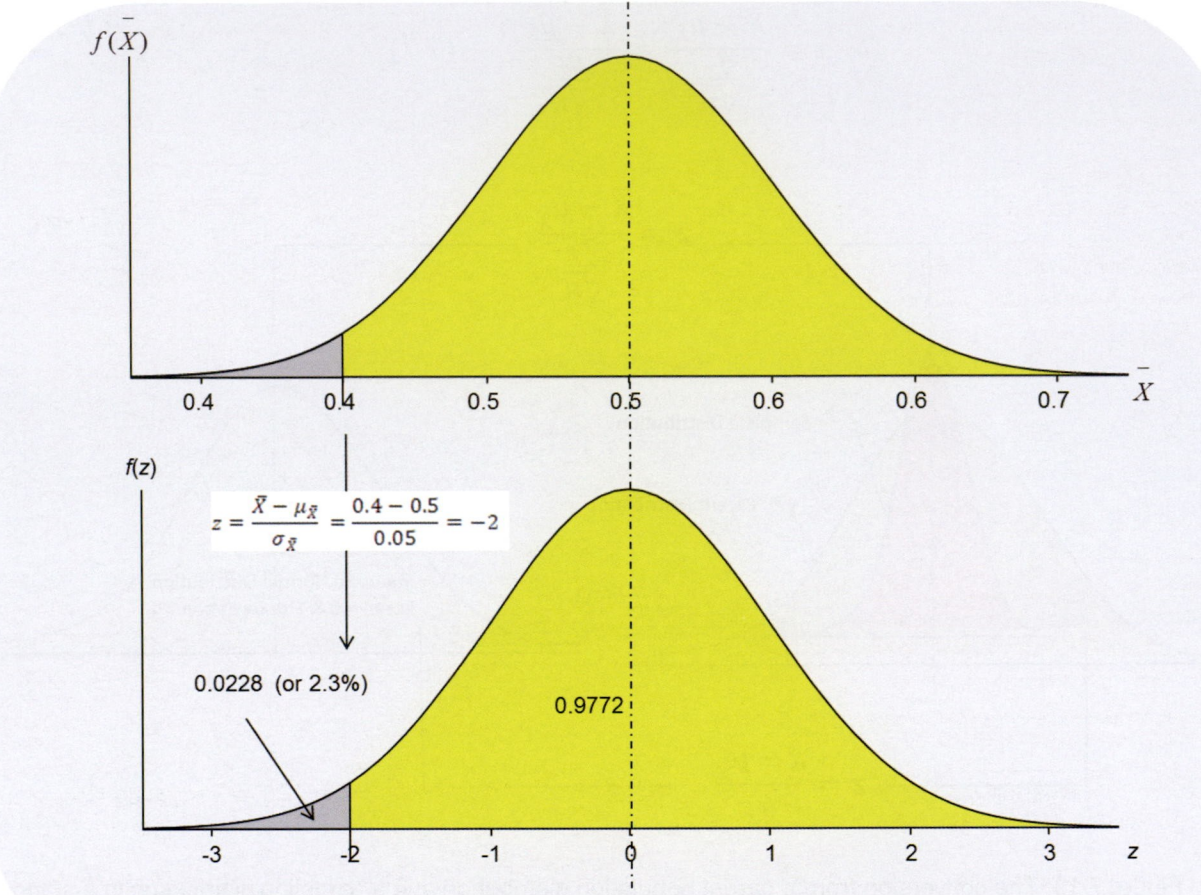

Figure 7.14 Percent of Wood Board of Mean Thickness of less than 0.4 inch

---

Working Problem 7.16:

A company producing wood boards takes a random sample of 40 boards from each shipment and measure the thickness of the wood board. Using the mean values of these samples a sampling distribution was constructed, which has a mean value of 0.5 inch, and standard deviation of 0.05 inch. what is the probability that a shipment of wood boards will have a mean thickness value between 0.45 and 0.55 inch?

Answer:
Follow the procedure in the example above. $\bar{X} = 0.45$ $\qquad z = \dfrac{\bar{X} - \mu_{\bar{x}}}{\sigma_{\bar{x}}} = \dfrac{0.45 - 0.5}{0.05} = -1$

$\bar{X} = 0.55$ $\qquad z = \dfrac{\bar{X} - \mu_{\bar{x}}}{\sigma_{\bar{x}}} = \dfrac{0.55 - 0.5}{0.05} = 1$

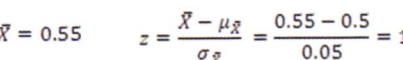

Area = 0.6826
You may also use the empirical rule discussed in Chapters 3 and 6.

Working Problem 7.17:

A company interested in the medical cost of its employees takes a random sample of 30 people from each division and determine the medical cost of the employee. Using the mean values of these samples a sampling distribution was constructed, which has a mean value of $20,000. From past record, the standard deviation of medical cost is found to be $10000. What is the probability that a randomly selected division of the company will have an average medical cost of over $25,000?

Answer: 0.0031

Working Problem 7.18:

Hourly wages for employees in a chain of a fast-food restaurant have a mean of $12 and a standard deviation of $2. Random samples of 30 employees are drawn from this population, and the mean of each sample is determined. Determine the mean and standard error of the mean of the sampling distribution. Then sketch a graph of the sampling distribution of sample means.

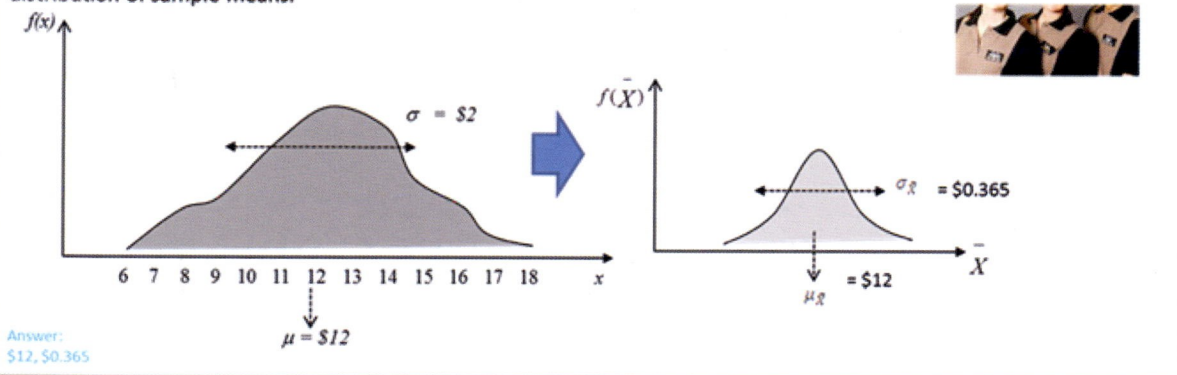

Answer:
$12, $0.365

Working Problem 7.19:

Based on many samples, each of 20 tech-support employees taken randomly from a large service company, the times spent on the phone for tech support have a mean value of 30 minutes and a standard deviation is 1.5 minutes.

(a) Based on the sampling distribution, what is the chance that a random group of tech-support employees will spend on average more than 20 minutes in tech-support?

(b) What is the chance that a tech-support employee taken randomly from the entire population of tech-support employees will spend more than 20 min. in tech support

Answer:

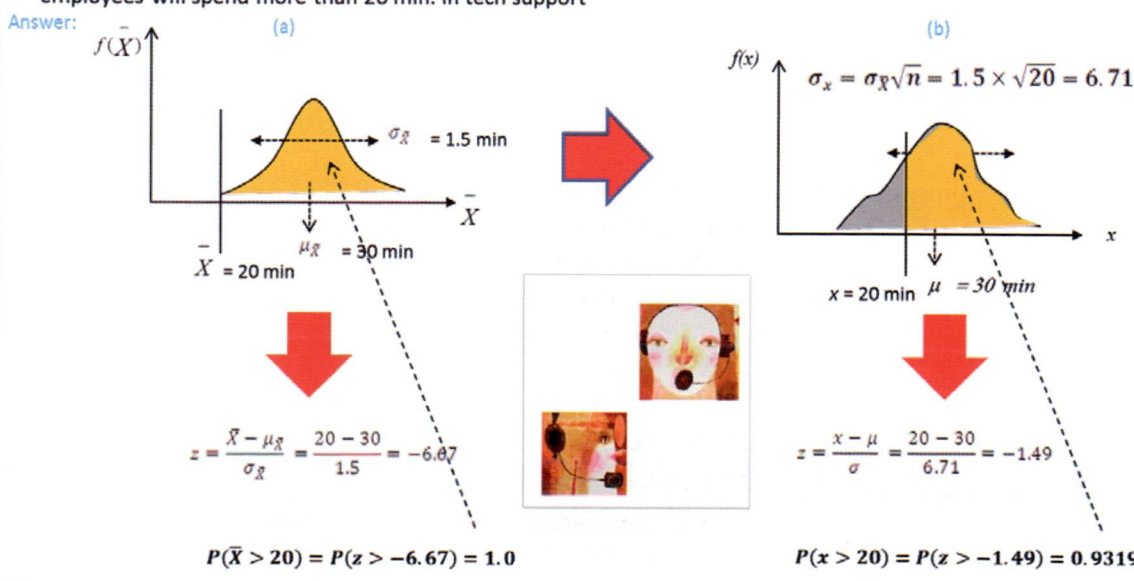

$$z = \frac{\bar{X} - \mu_{\bar{x}}}{\sigma_{\bar{x}}} = \frac{20 - 30}{1.5} = -6.67$$

$$P(\bar{X} > 20) = P(z > -6.67) = 1.0$$

$$\sigma_x = \sigma_{\bar{x}}\sqrt{n} = 1.5 \times \sqrt{20} = 6.71$$

$$z = \frac{x - \mu}{\sigma} = \frac{20 - 30}{6.71} = -1.49$$

$$P(x > 20) = P(z > -1.49) = 0.9319$$

The Central Limit Theorem: Key Points

- The parent population of a random variable x will have a distribution of some shape with a mean μ and standard deviation σ

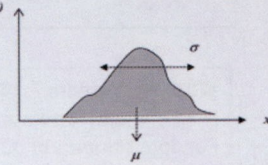

- Selecting random samples from this population each of size n and calculating the mean value of each sample $\bar{X}_i$ will result in a new data set consisting of mean values of these samples

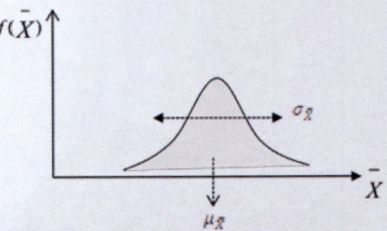

- The frequency distribution of the mean values of different samples is called the *sampling distribution of mean*
- If the original parent distribution is normal, the sampling distribution will be normal
- As sample size, n, increases (≥ 30), the sampling distribution will approach the normal shape (symmetrical, bell-shaped)
- In both cases, the sampling distribution will have a mean value $\mu = \mu_x = \mu_{\bar{x}}$ and a standard deviation $\sigma_{\bar{x}} = \frac{\sigma_x}{\sqrt{n}}$. The statistic $\sigma_{\bar{x}}$ is called the *standard error*

7.8 The Normal approximation to a binomial distribution

In Chapter 5, the binomial distribution was introduced with its key parameters p and n. When we deal with proportions, a sufficiently large sample is achieved when np and nq are both greater than 5. In this case, the variable x can be approximated by a normal distribution, with mean value μ, and a standard deviation σ, where:

$$\mu = np \ \& \ \sigma = \sqrt{npq} \qquad (7.8)$$

where p = the probability of success (occurrence), q is the probability of failure (nonoccurrence), and n is the sample size. Note that $p = 1 - q$.

The example below illustrates the above point.

Example 7.21: For the binomial experiment given below, can you determine if it is possible to use the normal approximations? If so, determine the mean and standard deviation.

Food security refers to the availability of food and one's access to it. A household is considered food-secure when its occupants do not live in hunger or fear of starvation. In 2008, 14.6 percent of U.S. households fell into the food-insecure category at some point during the year—the highest rate since the Department of Agriculture started recording stats in 1995 (http://www.ers.usda.gov/Briefing/FoodSecurity/).

The experiment consists of randomly selecting 40 households in the United States to determine if they indeed suffer food insecurity. Calculate the mean value.

Solution:

$n = 40$, $p = 0.146$, $q = 0.854$, $np = 5.84$, and $nq = 34.16$
Both np and nq are greater than 5. Thus, we can use the normal approximation

$$\mu = np = 40 \times 0.146 = 5.84 \ \& \ \sigma = \sqrt{npq} = \sqrt{40 \times 0.146 \times 0.854} = 2.23$$

Example 7.22: Fifty-five percent of married people in the U.S. express dissatisfaction with their marriage life. If we randomly select 15 married people in the United States and ask each if he or she is satisfied with their marriage. What is the probability that 10 or fewer than 10 of them respond no?

Solution:
$n = 15, p = 0.55, and \ q = 0.45$
$\mu = np = 15 \times 0.55 = 8.25 \ \& \ \sigma = \sqrt{npq}$
$\qquad \qquad = \sqrt{15 \times 0.55 \times 0.45} = 1.93$
$P(x \leq 10) = ?$
$z = \dfrac{x - \mu}{\sigma} = \dfrac{10 - 8.25}{1.93} = 0.91$
$P(x \leq 10) = 0.82$

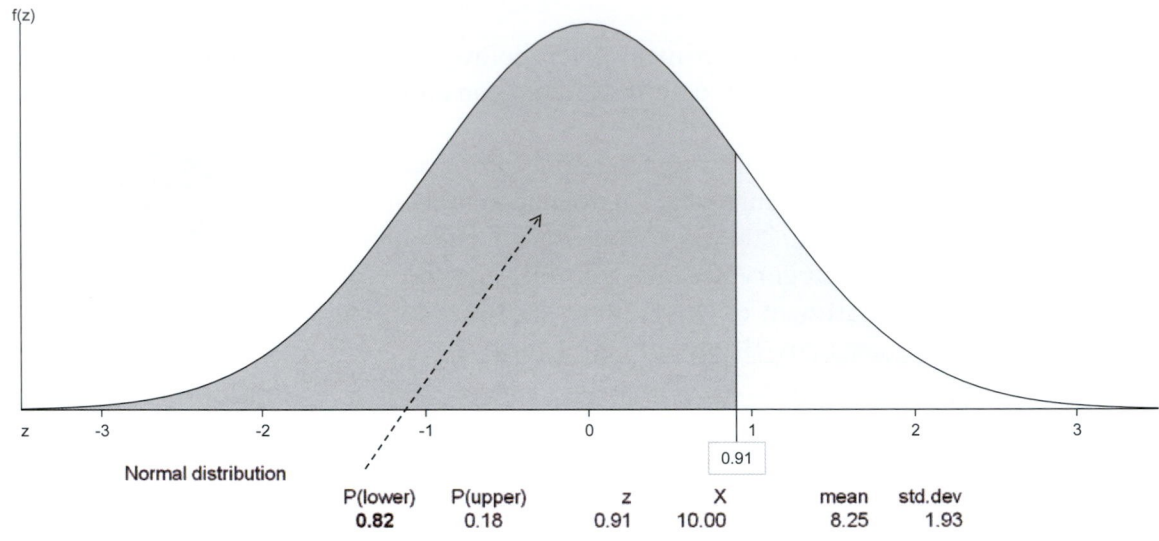

P(lower)	P(upper)	z	X	mean	std.dev
0.82	0.18	0.91	10.00	8.25	1.93

7.9 Sampling distribution of proportions: The Central Limit theorem for proportions

We can construct a sampling distribution of proportion using the same concepts as discussed above. In this case, the sample proportion is the random variable. Concepts such as the sampling error and the Central Limit theorem can be applied to proportions as illustrated in the examples below.

Example 7.23: Suppose a total of 10,000 adults live in a city and 2500 of them own a new car. A random sample of 250 adults was selected from this city, and it was found that 80 of them own new cars. Calculate the proportion of adults who own new cars in the population and in the sample. Assuming the difference is due to chance alone, determine the sampling error.

Solution:

For the population of adults in this city,
N = Population size = 10,000
N_i = Adults in the population who own new cars = 2500
The proportion of all adults in this city who own new cars is:

$$\mu_p = \frac{N_i}{N} = \frac{2500}{10000} = 0.25$$

n = Sample size = 250
n_i = Adults in the sample who own new cars = 80
The sample proportion is:

$$\hat{p} = \frac{n_i}{n} = \frac{80}{250} = 0.32$$

The sampling error is obtained from:

$$Sampling\ error = \hat{p} - \mu_p = 0.32 - 0.25 = 0.07$$

Note that if we take repeated samples and calculate $\hat{p}$ for each sample, the frequency distribution of $\hat{p}$ will represent the sampling distribution of proportions.

Example 7.24: Suppose from the same city of the above example, 40 representative samples were withdrawn each of 250 people and the number of adults owning a new car in each sample was counted. The results of this counting are shown in Table 7.7 along with the proportion of each sample. Construct a sampling distribution of proportion and discuss its characteristics.

Table 7.7 Samples of adults and proportion of new car owners

Sample No.	Number of Adults tested	Number of Adults owning a new car	p	Sample No.	Number of Adults tested	Number of Adults owning a new car	p
1	250	59	0.236	21	250	65	0.26
2	250	60	0.24	22	250	66	0.264
3	250	54	0.216	23	250	60	0.24
4	250	67	0.268	24	250	59	0.236
5	250	56	0.224	25	250	50	0.2
6	250	68	0.272	26	250	57	0.228
7	250	57	0.228	27	250	55	0.22
8	250	65	0.26	28	250	71	0.284
9	250	68	0.272	29	250	68	0.272
10	250	55	0.22	30	250	73	0.292
11	250	66	0.264	31	250	69	0.276
12	250	62	0.248	32	250	61	0.244
13	250	58	0.232	33	250	56	0.224
14	250	67	0.268	34	250	74	0.296
15	250	58	0.232	35	250	52	0.208
16	250	67	0.268	36	250	62	0.248
17	250	65	0.26	37	250	61	0.244
18	250	68	0.272	38	250	63	0.252
19	250	52	0.208	39	250	67	0.268
20	250	63	0.252	40	250	59	0.236

Solution:

The sampling distribution of proportions is the frequency distribution of $\hat{p}$. This distribution is shown in Figure 7.15. The characteristics of this distribution can be obtained by observing and examining the distribution and performing descriptive statistics on the $\hat{p}$ values as shown in Table 7.8.

Table 7.8 Descriptive statistics of sample proportions

$\hat{p}$	Value of statistic
Mean & Median	0.248
Mode	0.268
Standard Deviation	0.024
Range	0.096
Count	40

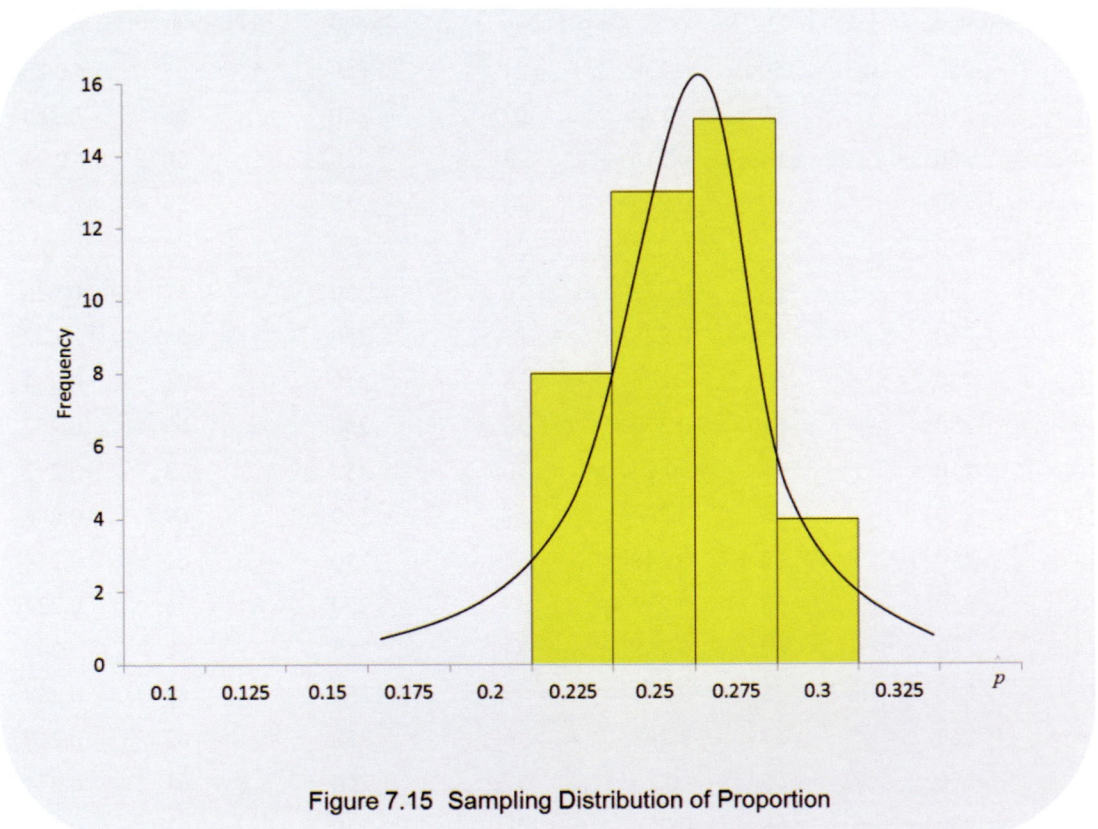

Figure 7.15 Sampling Distribution of Proportion

In theory, the mean and the standard deviation of the sampling distribution of proportions are derived from the characteristics of the binomial distribution and they are as follows:

$$\mu_p = p \qquad (7.9)$$

414

$$\sigma_p = \sqrt{\frac{p(1-p)}{n}} = \sqrt{\frac{pq}{n}} \qquad (7.10)$$

where p = population proportion, $q = 1 - p$, n = sample size

Recall that the sample size is 250 and the population mean is 0.25. Theoretically,

$$\mu_p = p = 0.25$$

$$\sigma_p = \sqrt{\frac{p(1-p)}{n}} = \sqrt{\frac{0.25(0.75)}{250}} = 0.0274$$

Note that from Table 7.8, the mean of the sampling proportion distribution is 0.248 and the standard deviation obtained from the sampling distribution is 0.024, which is different from the theoretical value calculated above. Again, repeated samples can lead to closer agreement between the two values.

We should also point out that the above formula for standard deviation is valid when $n/N \leq 0.05$, where N is the population size. In our example, $n/N = 0.25$, which is much greater than 0.05.

If n/N is greater than 0.05, then

$$\sigma_p = \sqrt{\frac{p(1-p)}{n}} \sqrt{\frac{N-n}{N-1}} \qquad (7.11)$$

The term

$$\sqrt{\frac{N-n}{N-1}}$$

is called the *finite population correction factor.*

For our example,

$$\sigma_{\hat{p}} = \sqrt{\frac{p(1-p)}{n}} \sqrt{\frac{N-n}{N-1}} = \sqrt{\frac{0.25(0.75)}{250}} \sqrt{\frac{10000-250}{10000-1}} = 0.027$$

Working problem 7.20:

For the binomial experiments given below, can you determine if it is possible to use the normal approximations?

1. Thirty-five percent of the people in the United States own a new car. If we randomly select 20 people in the United States to determine if they indeed have new cars

    1. $n = 20$, $p = 0.35$, $q = 0.65$, $np = 7$, and $nq = 13$
    Both np and nq are greater than 5. Thus, we can use the normal approximation

    $\mu = np = 7.0$ $\qquad$ $\sigma = \sqrt{npq} = \sqrt{20 \times 0.35 \times 0.65} = 2.13$

2. Five percent of people in Beverly-Hills, California own assets exceeding one million dollar. If we randomly select 50 people from Beverley Hills to see if their assets exceed a million dollar

   2. $n = 50$, $p = 0.05$, $q = 0.95$, $np = 2.5$, and $nq = 47.5$
   Since $np < 5$ we can not use the normal approximation

Working problem 7.21:

Suppose in a survey of the U.S. College students, 30% expressed dissatisfaction with the way developmental courses are taught in college. In a random sample taken by a college consisting of 1000 students, what would be the mean and the standard deviation of the samples proportions? Describe the shape of the sampling distribution.

Answer:

According to the survey, the proportion of the population of students who are dissatisfied is $p = 0.3$, and $q = 0.7$. The values of np and nq are 300 and 700, respectively. Since they both are greater than 5, we can apply the Central Limit theorem to describe the sampling distribution of proportions of unsatisfied students. In this case, the distribution will largely be normal with the following values of mean and standard deviation:

$$\mu_{\hat{p}} = p = 0.3 \qquad \sigma_{\hat{p}} = \sqrt{\frac{p(1-p)}{n}} = \sqrt{\frac{0.3(0.70)}{1000}} = 0.014$$

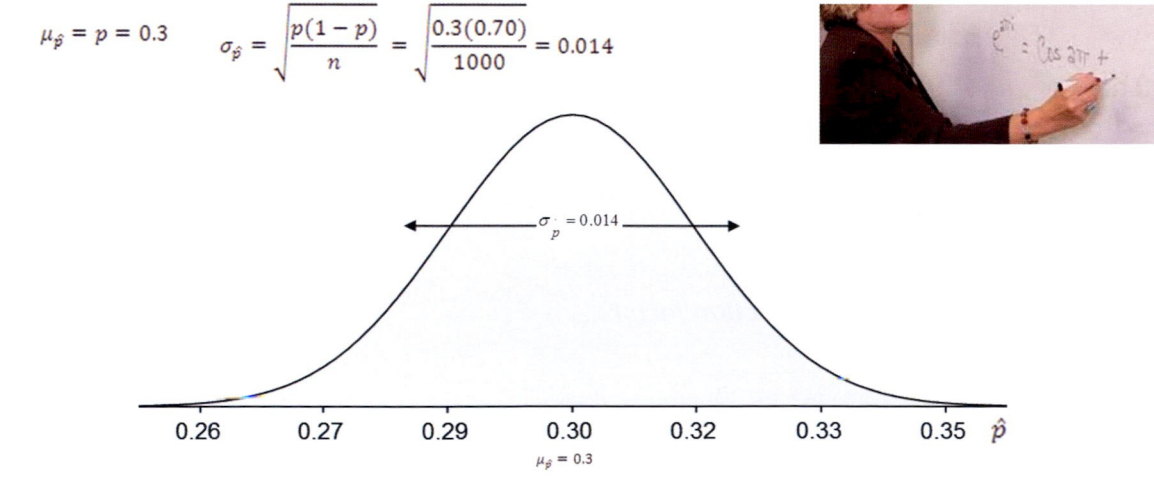

Sampling Distribution of Proportion at mean value of 0.3 and Standard Deviation 0.014

7.10 Review Exercises

P7.1: Determine whether you would consider the following populations finite or infinite:

    a. Students taking a particular biology course in a given semester and in a particular college
    b. Working staff in the U.S. Congress
    c. People living in a large subdivision in Raleigh, NC
    d. People living and visiting New York City, daily

Answer:
    (a) Finite, (b) Do it yourself, (c) Finite, (d) Do it yourself

P7.2: Determine whether you would consider the following populations homogenous or heterogeneous:
    a. Refrigerators of the same model produced by a manufacturer
    b. People living in Alaska
    c. People living in the Hispanic community
    d. Tourists visiting Disney World

P7.3: Determine whether you would consider the following populations static or dynamic:
    a. People opinions of a presidential candidate over 12 month period
    b. Daily weather condition
    c. Number of people visiting a mall during week days

Answer:
    a. Do it yourself, b. Dynamic, c. Do it yourself

P7.4: List two reasons why samples can be taken with replacement and without replacement?

P7.5:
a. What is a simple random sample?
b. What is a voluntary response sample, and why is it generally unsuitable for statistical purposes?
Answer: (a) see Chapter' contents. (b) A voluntary sample is a sample obtained in such a way that the members in the sample volunteer to be selected in the sample. This type creates biased results.

P7.6: A student in the class listed the names of all other students when he surveyed a simple random sample of them. Although this is a simple random sample, are the results likely to be representative of the general population of all the students in the college? Why or why not?

P7.7: For a study in which subjects are treated with a new drug and then observed, is the study observational or is it an experimental?
Answer: Experimental

P7.8: Twelve percent of Americans leave their cars unlocked while they are shopping. These results are based on 4000 responses from 65,000 questionnaires that were mailed.
    a. What is wrong with this survey?

b. As stated, the value of 12% refers to all Americans, so is that 12% a statistic or a parameter? Explain.

c. Does the survey constitute an observational study or an experiment?

P7.9: According to 2011 data, Wal-Mart Stores, Inc., (NYSE: WMT) serves customers and members more than 200 million times per week at more than 9,700 retail units under 69 different banners in 28 countries. With fiscal year 2011 sales of $419 billion, Walmart employs more than two million associates worldwide. A vice president plans to conduct a survey to study the numbers of shares held by Wal-Mart individual stockholders.

a. Is the number of shares held by stockholders discrete or continuous?

b. Identify the level of measurement (nominal, ordinal, interval, or ratio) for the numbers of shares held by stockholders.

c. If the survey is conducted by calling 600 randomly selected stockholders in each of the 50 United States, what type of sampling (random, systematic, convenience, stratified, cluster) is being used?

d. If a sample of 600 stockholders is obtained, and the average (mean) number of shares is calculated for this sample, is the result a statistic or a parameter?

e. What is wrong with gauging stockholder views about employee benefits by mailing a questionnaire that Wal-Mart stockholders could complete and mail back?

Answer: a. Discrete, b. Do it yourself, c. Stratified, d. Do it yourself

e. The mailed responses would be a voluntary response sample; those with strong opinions about the topic would be more likely to respond, so the results would not be likely to reflect the true opinions of the population of all stockholders.

P7.10: If you look at an unfamiliar crowd of people and visually select a sample of 30 individuals for a survey, this sample is an example of

a) simple random sample

b) stratified sample

c) unbiased sample

d) biased sample

P7.11: Suppose an organization typically spends on average $25,000 per employee in annual benefits with a standard deviation of $1,000. If the organization took a random sample of 5 employees that it thought it represents a good cross section of its population of employee and found the following values of benefits:

$25,000, $15,000, $35,000, $30,000, $19,000

What is the sampling error?

Answer: $200

P7.12: For the same organization of problem P7.11, suppose that the organization mistakenly took a sample that was biased to the high benefits and found that the benefit values are as follows:

$25,000, $25,000, $38,000, $31,000, $29,000

What is the non-sampling error?

P7.13: Consider the following analytical studies. Which method of sampling would you use to collect data for each study? Explain your reasoning.

1. A study on how the number of study hours per week affect student's grade
2. A study on how course type makes a difference in student's grade
3. A study of the effect of garlic on preventing heart attacks
4. A study on the effect of location in a city on house prices
5. A study on the effect of State and County on the amount of property tax
6. A study of the effect of ethnic background on job performance
7. A study of the effect of race on crime rate

Answer: 1. Random 2. Do it yourself. 3. Random 4. Cluster 5. Cluster 6. Do it yourself 7. Stratified

P7.14: In a university population of 30,000 students, suppose we wish to take a random sample of 150 students to evaluate their financial aid status. Explain how to take a simple random sample and a systematic random sample from this population.

P7.15: Suppose we have a finite population of 5000 students representing a population of the college of business in a university. Suppose 1850 of those students are freshman, 1650 are sophomore, and 1000 are junior, and 500 are seniors. If you were to select a stratified random sample of 120 students from this population, what is number of students from each category should you select?

Answer: 44, 40, 24, 12

P7.16: Suppose we have a finite population of 1000 students representing a population of the college of business in a university. Suppose 350 of those students are freshman, 260 are sophomore, and 210 are junior, and 180 are seniors. If you were to select a stratified random sample of 110 students from this population, what is number of students from each category should you select?

P7.17: A University decided to test random samples of freshmen students to examine their ability in reading and writing. The University took 20 samples each of 30 students and reported the results as shown in the table below.

- Calculate the mean of each sample
- Construct a sampling distribution and describe the distribution
- Calculate the mean and standard deviation of the sampling distribution
- If the criterion to by-pass developmental English courses in the University is for a student to obtain a score in this test of 80% or more, what is the percent of students that are likely to take developmental English courses?
- Suppose the entire data set roughly represents the whole population, verify the Central Limit theorem.
- Suppose the University decided to use the entire data set to estimate the percent of students that are likely to take developmental English courses, what would be the percent in this case? How is this value different from the estimation from the sampling distribution? What is your interpretation of this difference?

Students' grades in English entry tests

n	S1	S2	S3	S4	S5	S6	S7	S8	S9	S10
1	82.0	75.7	79.3	83.5	77.8	77.2	83.1	77.4	82.9	80.9
2	69.5	84.0	80.7	78.5	79.5	75.5	71.3	77.1	79.6	78.0
3	80.6	78.8	82.1	73.1	85.6	87.0	76.5	74.5	80.4	77.0
4	75.9	75.7	80.3	82.1	71.4	77.6	75.9	79.1	78.2	75.6
5	83.1	89.2	78.6	75.0	79.8	74.9	76.8	83.8	78.0	78.7
6	78.4	79.8	86.9	82.0	78.3	80.2	85.6	75.5	87.3	73.5
7	94.5	74.0	88.1	82.2	77.5	78.8	79.8	81.9	77.6	66.4
8	79.0	74.7	79.9	77.1	81.0	81.3	79.3	79.8	73.7	86.2
9	92.8	78.7	72.5	79.4	77.8	80.2	75.0	68.3	78.8	72.0
10	71.2	83.2	85.9	81.0	77.1	78.0	83.1	81.9	79.3	81.1
11	76.3	81.2	85.7	84.2	83.2	79.7	89.0	80.7	74.9	86.2
12	77.6	78.2	85.7	75.7	76.7	84.8	81.8	80.2	73.2	86.8
13	82.5	81.6	80.5	85.1	72.0	77.7	76.7	81.5	89.4	81.6
14	78.3	90.0	76.2	85.3	73.9	75.2	83.3	84.7	74.2	85.8
15	77.6	80.1	81.7	68.4	79.9	73.9	70.3	85.2	76.0	77.2
16	83.9	80.3	68.9	77.9	78.1	71.9	74.6	83.1	87.2	74.3
17	77.4	70.8	80.6	79.0	76.3	84.2	83.7	87.8	79.6	77.1
18	89.3	76.3	90.0	75.4	77.2	82.8	85.2	74.6	79.1	81.3
19	86.6	83.5	86.2	84.0	79.2	79.2	80.1	78.4	79.2	78.0
20	86.9	79.9	74.2	72.7	78.6	81.3	86.7	83.3	77.3	78.1
21	85.8	85.2	76.2	74.2	83.0	78.7	87.0	75.0	84.1	75.4
22	74.7	87.4	85.7	70.8	80.7	82.9	82.3	81.3	78.4	86.0
23	72.1	74.7	80.6	77.0	83.1	78.7	77.7	90.3	72.6	79.0
24	75.7	87.8	82.7	82.0	75.3	80.9	78.7	84.9	73.3	84.3
25	81.4	77.9	69.6	81.4	80.0	80.3	78.3	79.9	89.0	77.8
26	94.0	91.8	75.9	82.2	77.3	78.9	82.5	84.3	77.6	77.8
27	68.9	78.7	77.4	79.8	87.4	80.5	72.1	83.0	79.7	76.5
28	82.4	86.5	78.9	76.9	78.8	74.8	77.3	85.6	79.8	76.5
29	77.7	76.5	76.4	76.8	71.2	82.3	71.6	82.5	73.7	74.2
30	79.8	71.6	85.0	84.4	84.8	81.9	79.8	91.0	79.8	74.6

Students' grades in English entry tests (Cont'd)

n	S11	S12	S13	S14	S15	S16	S17	S18	S19	S20
1	82.0	80.9	77.7	87.1	81.5	73.6	79.0	78.5	83.1	75.8
2	77.5	81.5	80.0	69.6	82.1	77.1	84.9	81.4	79.3	86.3
3	81.3	72.6	76.4	70.6	75.6	86.1	84.1	79.4	88.6	90.6
4	85.3	80.4	87.4	81.7	92.8	70.6	75.9	79.0	84.0	86.6
5	79.7	79.9	80.9	84.3	84.8	69.4	87.1	75.7	84.0	86.5
6	81.6	82.4	83.2	76.5	84.3	78.3	70.4	87.2	74.2	73.7
7	75.5	73.7	82.8	86.5	76.7	76.8	75.5	84.9	75.8	87.8
8	85.1	82.2	81.7	87.2	85.9	82.4	70.2	80.6	90.0	81.6
9	76.9	79.6	90.2	80.3	78.1	85.0	85.6	76.8	77.2	66.8
10	73.0	74.2	74.1	75.4	80.0	77.7	84.9	80.4	86.3	71.8
11	92.2	85.0	74.1	88.1	90.3	83.2	73.9	76.7	81.1	79.4
12	87.3	81.9	81.4	82.3	79.2	76.9	75.7	83.4	73.2	83.8
13	80.0	86.2	88.2	76.8	86.2	86.3	78.7	85.8	71.2	77.3
14	91.7	72.4	75.0	74.3	88.1	75.6	79.3	77.4	84.2	80.8
15	79.1	81.8	77.5	78.1	77.8	83.0	85.8	75.9	76.5	85.7
16	77.3	82.1	81.3	81.2	82.2	79.4	85.7	81.9	81.1	77.0
17	87.5	84.5	83.6	80.9	77.8	69.2	78.5	77.5	80.9	81.0
18	80.1	83.7	84.8	84.1	77.7	78.5	81.5	81.0	86.7	74.7
19	74.6	85.4	78.2	78.2	83.9	82.9	77.5	85.1	78.2	79.3
20	75.4	82.0	86.3	77.4	80.6	74.6	80.7	83.5	71.9	82.1
21	83.4	85.5	80.7	86.0	87.8	85.2	85.5	79.7	74.1	89.9
22	88.7	81.9	78.2	79.0	83.9	79.3	76.3	81.8	74.2	82.7
23	73.4	91.6	77.8	71.0	80.1	71.4	79.3	82.0	72.2	76.4
24	78.2	81.0	81.8	84.6	76.3	86.1	82.6	75.7	76.9	85.1
25	75.6	78.8	78.7	75.7	85.2	81.7	76.6	70.2	80.0	86.0
26	79.7	77.4	79.6	79.4	81.8	78.6	74.8	75.7	71.0	75.6
27	84.6	80.8	81.4	77.9	86.0	72.8	87.7	75.0	84.6	78.0
28	88.0	76.9	79.6	83.9	71.1	85.0	74.1	92.4	79.6	75.2
29	76.1	75.9	80.4	79.8	75.8	81.4	77.7	78.5	78.9	85.4
30	82.0	75.7	79.2	83.8	81.0	66.8	84.9	83.8	83.5	82.8

Answer: Do it yourself following examples 7.18 and 7.19 in this chapter

P7.18: A company producing solid metal rods takes a random sample of 30 rods from each shipment and measure the diameter of metal rods. Using the mean values of these samples a sampling distribution was constructed, which has a mean value of 1 cm, and standard deviation of 0.1 cm. What is the probability that a shipment of metal rods will have a mean value of diameter between 0.7 cm and 1.3 cm?

P7.19: A company producing solid metal rods takes a random sample of 30 rods from each shipment and measure the diameter of metal rods. Using the mean values of these samples a

sampling distribution was constructed, which has a mean value of 1 cm, and standard deviation of 0.1 cm. What is the probability that a shipment of metal rods will have a mean value of diameter of less than 0.85 cm?
Answer: 0.0668

P7.20: A factory interested in evaluating annual labor cost takes random samples of 40 factory workers from each operation and determine their wages and benefits. Using the mean values of these samples a sampling distribution was constructed, which has a mean value of $32,000. From past record, the standard deviation of labor cost is found to be $12000. What is the probability that a randomly selected operation of the factory will have an average labor cost exceeding $36000?

P7.21: Samples were taken from a population of football players to determine the average weight (pounds). The average values of these samples were as follow:

Sample #	Sample size	Mean
1	30	205
2	30	200
3	30	200
4	30	201
5	30	200
6	30	203
7	30	201
8	30	200
9	30	200
10	30	205
11	30	200
12	30	200

(a) Using the Central Limit Theorem, what is the best estimate of the mean weight of the population of the football players
(b) Using the Central Limit Theorem, what is the best estimate of the standard deviation of weight of the population of the football players

Answer: 201.25 pounds, $\sigma_{\bar{x}} = \frac{\sigma_x}{\sqrt{n}}$, $\sigma_x = 1.9598 \times \sqrt{30} = 10.7344$ pounds

P7.22: A college takes a random sample of 30 different class sections of students taking the same statistics course but by different teachers. Using the mean values of these samples a sampling distribution was constructed, which has a mean value of 82%, and standard deviation of 4%. What is the probability that a class section of students taking the same course will have a mean value of grade of less than 75%?

P7.23: Forty two percent of people in the United States reported that they visited Disney World in Florida in the last 15 years. We randomly select 200 people in the United States and ask each if he or she visited Disney World in the last 15 years. What is the probability that greater than 100 will say they did?
Answer: 0.01

P7.24: According to some estimates, 50% of the people in America are female. If a random sample of 30 people is selected, what is the probability that 19 of them will be female? Use the binomial distribution and the normal approximation to the binomial distribution and compare the two solutions.

P7.25: Forty eight percent of married people in Europe express dissatisfaction with their marriage life. If we randomly select 20 married people in Europe and ask each if he or she is satisfied with their marriage. What is the probability that 10 or fewer than 10 of them respond no? Use the binomial distribution and the normal approximation to the binomial distribution and compare the two solutions.
Answer: $P(x \leq 10) = 0.657$, $P(x \leq 10) = P(z \leq 0.179) = 0.5714$. This difference will decrease as n increases.

P7.26: Fifty percent of football players retire before the age of 35. If we randomly select 200 football players and ask about their intention to retire before the age of 35, what is the probability that 90 or fewer than 90 of them will retire?

P7.27: A gondola lift (or a cable car) is a type of aerial lift, which is supported and propelled by cables from above. It consists of a loop of steel cable that is strung between two stations, sometimes over intermediate supporting towers. The cable is driven by a bullwheel in a terminal, which is typically connected to an engine or electric motor. Suppose one gondola lift has a nominal maximum capacity of 12 people, each averaging 167 pounds (or a maximum of 2004 pounds) as indicated on a sign posted on the gondola. Most data suggest that men tend to weigh more than women. Accordingly, the gondola managers would consider a worst case scenario as having 12 passengers who are all men. Given that men's weights are normally distributed with a mean of 172 pounds and a standard deviation of 29 pounds (National Health Interview Survey, http://www.cdc.gov/nchs/nhis/about_nhis.htm).

a. Find the probability that if an individual man is randomly selected, his weight will be greater than 167 pounds.
b. Find the probability that 12 randomly selected men will have a mean that is greater than167 pounds
c. Does the gondola appear to have the correct weight limit? Why or why not?
Answer: (a) 0.567, (b) 0.7257, (c) Do it yourself

P7.28: A gondola lift (or a cable car) is a type of aerial lift, which is supported and propelled by cables from above. It consists of a loop of steel cable that is strung between two stations, sometimes over intermediate supporting towers. The cable is driven by a bullwheel in a terminal, which is typically connected to an engine or electric motor. Suppose one gondola lift has a nominal maximum capacity of 12 people, each averaging 167 pounds (or a maximum of 2004 pounds) as indicated on a sign posted on the gondola. Most data suggest that men tend to weigh more than women. Accordingly, the gondola managers would consider a worst case scenario as having 12 passengers who are all men. Suppose a group of professional football players is planning to take a trip to the mountain where this gondola lift is used. This group has an average weight of 248 pounds and standard deviation of 90 pounds.

(a) Find the probability that 12 randomly selected football players will have a mean that is greater than 167 pounds
(b) What would be a reasonable average number of those players to ride the gondola lift?

P7.29: The weights of men are normally distributed with a mean of 172 pounds and a standard deviation of 29 pounds.
  a. Find the probability that if an *individual* man is randomly selected, his weight will be greater than 170 pounds.
  b. Find the probability that *20 randomly selected men* will have a mean weight that is greater than 170 pound

Answer: (a) 52.75%, (b) 62.11%

P7.30: Thirty-eight percent of people in the United States reported that they visited Disney World in Florida in the last 5 years. We randomly select 200 people in the United States and ask each if he or she visited Disney World in the last 5 years. What is the probability that greater than 70 will say they did?

P7.31: A survey made in 2010 reports that 95% of the people in Libya did not want Muammar al-Gaddafi as their president. If we randomly select 300 people from different areas of Libya and ask each whether he or she did not want Muammar al-Gaddafi as their president. (a) What is the probability that more than 295 will say yes? (b) What is the probability that more than half of the people will say no?

Answer: (a) 0.004 (b) Do it yourself

P7.32: According to a survey by a poll organization, 50% of the people in the State of Georgia, U.S.A. agree with allowing citizens to carry automatic guns. Let $\hat{p}$ be the proportion of Georgians in a random sample of 1000 who agree. Find the mean and standard deviation of $\hat{p}$ and describe the shape of its sampling distribution.

P7.33: In 2007, some statistics revealed that the population of professors in the State of Alabama has an average annual salary of $80,000 and a standard deviation of $10,000. The distribution of professor's salary is a normal distribution. If a random sample of 40 professors was taken in that year and it was found that it has a mean value of $70,000.
  (a) What is the sampling error?
  (b) What does the sign of the sampling error mean?
  (c) What is the standard error?
  (d) Using the empirical rule discussed in Chapter 3 and 6, do you believe this sample to be representative of the population? Justify your Yes or No answer.
  (e) Based on your answer of part (d) do you believe the sampling error calculated in part (a) is a pure sampling error or it may involve non-sampling error?

P7.34: In a survey of the State of Georgia high school students, 25% prefers a dress code in high schools. In a random sample of size 600 taken by a poll organization from different high schools in the State of Georgia, what would be the mean and the standard deviation of the sample proportion?

Appendix 7.A Different Methods of Sampling
1. Probability Sampling

Sampling Category	Definition	Examples
Simple random sampling	In random sampling, subjects are randomly drawn from the parent population to form a sample. Every component in the population has the same chance of being selected in the sample	Selecting 100 people randomly from a football stadium during a National football game by drawing a blind sample of 100 ticket numbers from all the tickets purchased.
Systematic random sampling	In systematic random sampling, one unit is selected randomly. Additional elementary units are then selected at evenly spaced intervals until the desired number of units is obtained.	Suppose from a company population of 60,000 employees we wish to take a systematic random sample of 200 employees. In this case, we can arrange the 60,000 employees in some order say alphabetically or by employee identification number. Since the sample size is 200, the ratio of population to sample size is 60,000/200 = 300. Based on this ratio, we can select one employee from the first 300 employees in the arranged list at random. Suppose this member was number 180th in the 300 employee list, we should then select every 180th from every 300 employees in the list. This will result in employees in the sample with numbers 180, 480, 780, 1080, and so on.
Stratified sampling	In stratified sampling, a population is divided into different categories (or strata) based on some characteristic of the variable under consideration. A stratified sample is then obtained by selecting a separate simple random sample from each population stratum. It assists in analyzing population subgroups of interest.	We're interested in the retention rate of different students' groups: freshmen (F), junior (J), sophomore (So), and senior (S) in a certain college. Assume the population of students can be divided into these four groups: F = 36%, J = 26%, So = 22%, S = 16%. In a stratified sample of 100 students (n=100), we can randomly select 36 freshmen, 26 junior, 22 sophomore, and 16 senior. This will result in enough students in each subgroup to make meaningful inferences.
Cluster sampling	In cluster sampling, specific categories or regions in the population are considered for the sake of saving time, effort, and cost. In cluster sampling, the whole population is first divided into groups called clusters. A random sample of clusters is selected and finally a random sample of elements from each of the selected clusters is selected.	Suppose we are interested in surveying the population of a State consisting of many counties. In this case, we can take samples from different counties treating those counties as clusters. Within each cluster, we may have sub-clusters represented by small and large cities from which we can continue to sample.
Multistage sampling	In this method, a combination of different methods of probability sampling is used.	Suppose we are interested in students' performance in a certain State. We can begin by using cluster sampling to select certain schools, and then doing random samples or stratified sampling (by student ethnic background) within each school.

426

2. Non-Probability Sampling

Sampling Category	Definition	Examples
Convenience sample	In convenience sampling, more convenient elementary units are chosen from a population for observation.	Use a sample of clients of a certain hospital to evaluate client's satisfaction Use 'people on the street' to interview for a TV talk show Interviewing people coming out of a movie theater about their opinion of the movie Note: The problem with all of these types of samples is that we have no evidence that they are representative of the entire population. It is important, therefore not to generalize and make sure to mention how the sample was selected and potential bias issues.
Purposive sampling	In purposive sampling, a sample of one or more specific predefined groups is selected	We are interested in evaluating how some students reach excellence in their performance. We select students that have 'A' or 'B' average grades. We interested in machine's efficiency, we select a sample of machines that only exhibit poor running performance Note: This type of sampling may yield quick results related to the purpose of sampling, but it cannot be generalized.

3. Different types of Purposive Sampling

Sampling Category	Definition	Examples
Modal instance sampling	In modal instance sampling, the most frequent case, or the 'typical' case is sampled.	* We are interested in people who can drive. This is a group that is characterized by age (say, 18 years old or above). We can select our samples from this group. * We are interested in specific voters such as democrats, republicans, or independent, we then go where those voters are concentrated and take a random sample from their population * Note: The problem with modal instance sampling is that it looks into the majority of a certain group without paying attention to some of the variability that may exist among the group. For cxample, we may select a sample of drivers of 18 years old or older but ignore the gender or the education. Inferences in this case should focus only on the specific mode.
Sampling Category	In expert sampling, an expert group or a panel of experts is selected to get their opinion on some issues	We are interested in evaluating why a product is not performing well in the marketplace. In this case, we may rely on a sample of market analysts who can help us in this matter.

Sampling Category	Definition	Examples
Heterogeneity sampling	In heterogeneity sampling, sampling is made to include all opinions or views, but not representing these views proportionately.	* Sampling for evaluation of the extent of diversity in the population may involve all ethnic groups regardless their proportions in the population * Sampling students of different nationalities regardless the proportion of each nationality in the population under consideration
Snowball sampling	In snowball sampling, someone who meets the criteria for inclusion in our study is initially selected. This person is then asked to recommend others who he/she may know who also meet the criteria, and so on.	* We are interested in the population of people who smoke Marijuana regularly and are willing to reveal their addiction. We may not find many people who are willing to reveal this information directly. In this case, we begin with one or few and ask them to refer us to more people. * Note: This method does not lead to representative samples and it may be the best method available for reaching populations that are inaccessible or hard to find.
Extreme and deviant case sampling	This type of sampling is used to evaluate extreme or unusual cases of the phenomenon of interest.	* Studying exceptionally intelligent students require taking a sample from those students * Evaluating the reasons for people who become so wealthy despite their poor upbringing will require selecting a sample from those people.
Criterion sampling	In this sampling, we set a certain criteria and select all cases that meet that criteria	* All men seven feet tall or taller * All women who exceeds 300 pound in weight

428

CHAPTER 8

Inferential Statistics: confidence intervals

After completing this chapter, students will be able to:

- *Establish a confidence interval on the population mean*
- *Determine the minimum sample size required for reliable estimation*
- *Establish a confidence interval on population proportion*
- *Establish confidence intervals on variance*
- *Using software programs to perform estimation*

CHAPTER 8

In Chapter 7, we learned about *sampling techniques*, *sampling distributions* and *the Central Limit theorem*. These aspects represent the gateways to the world of inferential statistics. Inferential statistics is a collection of methods that are used to estimate population parameters from sample statistics. It involves performing descriptive statistics, setting criteria for estimation, and reaching conclusions about population parameters. The two major activities of inferential statistics are the establishment of confidence intervals of population parameters (introduced in this chapter) and hypothesis testing (introduced in the next two chapters). Determining the minimum sample size required for a statistical study is a critical aspect in numerous practical applications. This aspect will be also discussed in this chapter.

CHAPTER CONTENTS

8.1 Inferential statistics-basic steps

One of the main learning objectives of statistics is to be able to estimate the parameters of a large population using the statistics of a small sample. Inferential statistics is a collection of methods that aim at revealing important information about population parameters from the statistics obtained from samples withdrawn from the population. There are two basic elements of inferential statistics: (1) *estimation*, and (2) *test of hypothesis*. These two elements represent two sides of the same coin as they both require the reliance on sample statistics to estimate or verify the values of population parameters. In practice, performing estimation involves the following steps (see Figure 8.1):

- *We select a sample of size n from a population of size N*
- *We test the sample and generate sample data, x_i values*
- *We determine sample statistics such as sample mean ($\overline{X}$) and standard deviation, s*
- *We use sample statistics to estimate population parameters such as population mean, μ, and standard deviation, σ*
- *We draw conclusions about population parameters*

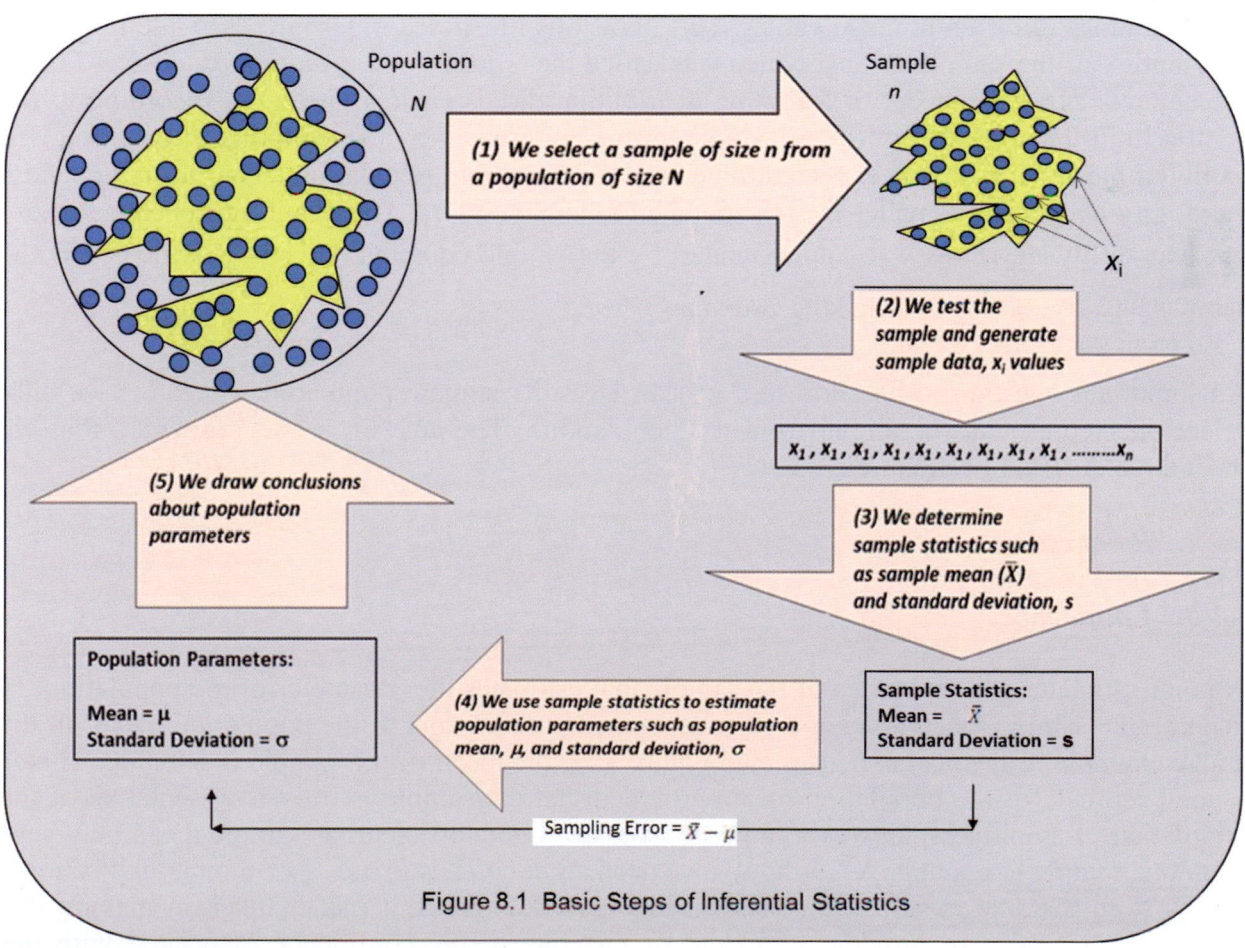

Figure 8.1 Basic Steps of Inferential Statistics

8.2 Estimation of Population Mean

The problem of estimation is simply a problem of determining population parameters from sample statistics. The most common application is the estimation of a population mean, μ from sample mean, $\bar{X}$. For example, suppose we are trying to estimate the mean of employee annual medical costs in a large company. If the entire record of the employee medical expenses is inaccessible, we can then take a representative sample from the company's population to determine the average expenses and the variability in medical cost. Suppose we took a sample of 40 employees and found that the average annual medical expenses of this sample was $30,000. If this sample is truly representative of the company population then we have a good reason to believe that the sample mean will closely approximate the population mean of medical expenses. This means that the company's population may have a mean value of $30,000. In general, this is called a point estimate of population mean. In the real world we often find that this type of analysis ends at this point. As we will see in this chapter, the mean of the sample is only a point estimate of the population mean and we need more criteria to be able to fully estimate the population mean.

In the context of inferential statistics, and as indicated above, the mean value of the sample is called the '*point estimate*' of the population mean. If we take another representative sample, we may have a different mean value, and if we repeat the sampling process many times we will have many samples of different mean values. This point was illustrated in Chapter 7 by the frequency distribution of the sample means, which was called the '*sampling distribution of means.*' Figure 8.2 summarizes the concept of sampling distribution discussed in Chapter 7. According to the central limit theorem, the profile of sample means represented by the sampling distribution will exhibit a mean value that is expected to be equal to the parent population mean, $\mu_{\bar{X}} = \mu_x$, and a variability $\sigma_{\bar{X}}$ which is smaller than the population variability σ_x. The relationship between these two variability measures was approximated by the simple equation: $\sigma_{\bar{X}} = \frac{\sigma_x}{\sqrt{n}}$, where n is the sample size. $\sigma_{\bar{X}}$, or $\frac{\sigma_x}{\sqrt{n}}$, is called the '*standard error.*'

An important question to be addressed is 'can we still estimate population's mean if we only select one representative sample from the population?' The answer is 'yes' provided that we meet three criteria of estimation, namely:

1. *Point estimate*
2. *Interval estimate*
3. *Confidence*

A point estimate is the statistics of the sample that estimates the parameter of the population. In general, the sample mean is a good point estimate (or estimator) of the population mean. In the above example of medical expenses (see Figure 8.2), the mean of the sample is $30,000. This is a good estimate of the population mean, provided that the sample is truly representative of the population of employees. However, a point estimate is not sufficient, as sample mean may vary from one sample to another. Accordingly, we need an interval estimate say, an interval of sample means from $29,000 to $31,000 as shown in Figure 8.2. Since a risk is taken in making this estimation, we need to provide the extent of this risk or the confidence associated with our estimation, by saying, for example, '*we are confident that our estimate of the mean medical cost is $30,000, with an interval from $29,000 to $31,000 in 95% of the time, or with a 5% risk.*' In the discussion below, we will demonstrate by example how these values are calculated to meet the criteria of full estimation of population mean.

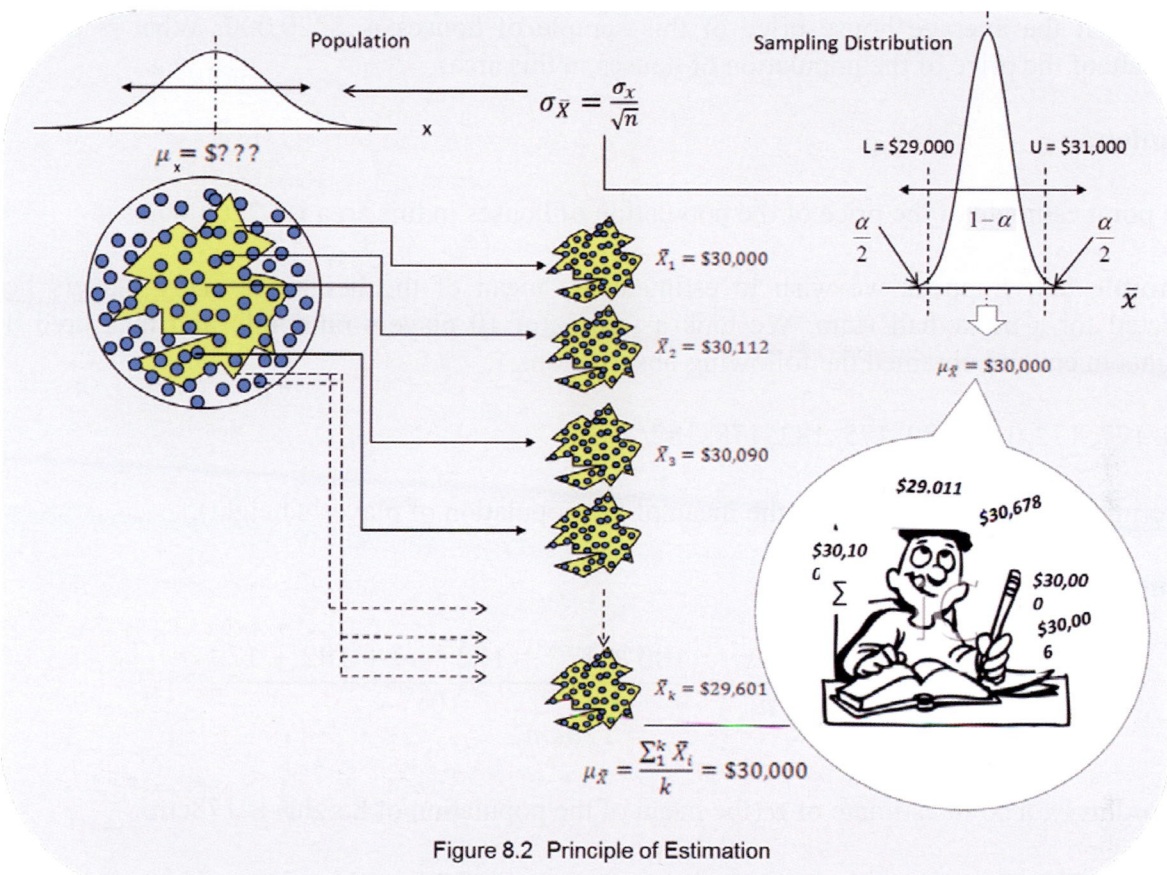

Figure 8.2 Principle of Estimation

8.2.1 Point estimate-The expected value

As indicated above, a point estimate or an estimator is the sample statistic that is used to estimate the value of the unknown population parameter. A good point estimate should be unbiased and it should have a low standard error. The sample mean $\bar{X}$ is a good estimator of the population mean μ. For example, if a sample of metal sheets was tested for strength, the average strength based on the sample data will be a good estimate of the mean of the strength of the population from which the sample was drawn, provided that the sample is truly representative of the parent population.

We may classify an estimator or a point estimate as an unbiased or a biased estimator. In general, the sample mean is a good estimator of the population mean. In statistical terms, we say that the sample mean is an unbiased estimate of the population mean if the expected value of the sample mean is equal to the population mean, that is if:

$$E(\bar{X}) = \mu \qquad (8.1)$$

433

The concept of sampling distribution, discussed in chapter 7, tells us that we can obtain better estimates of the population mean from the mean of the sampling distribution or the frequency distribution of the means of samples, $\mu_{\bar{X}} = \mu_x$.

Example 8.1: A real estate agent collected a random sample of houses in a certain area and found that the average house price of this sample of houses is $220,000. What is the point estimate of the price of the population of houses in this area?

Solution:

The point estimate of the price of the population of houses in this area is $220,000.

Example 8.2: Suppose we wish to estimate the mean of the height of many players being selected for a basketball team. We took a sample of 10 players randomly and measured their heights in cm and obtained the following observations:

180, 177, 172, 181, 180, 175, 182, 178, 182, 173

Determine a point estimate of μ (the mean of the population of player's height).

Solution:

$$Mean = \bar{X} = \frac{\sum_1^n x_i}{n} = \frac{180 + 177 + 172 + \cdots + 182 + 173}{10}$$
$$= 178cm$$

Accordingly, a point estimate of μ (the mean of the population of height) is 178cm.

Example 8.3: Suppose we wish to estimate the mean of the prices of houses in a certain area from a sample of 36 houses (see Table 8.1). What is the point estimate of the population of houses in this area?

Solution:

To determine a point estimate of the population mean we calculate the sample mean as follows:

$$Mean = \bar{X} = \frac{\sum_1^n x_i}{n} = \frac{216,254 + 228,133 + 230,843 + \cdots + 239,238 + 212,996}{36}$$
$$= \$222,522$$

Accordingly, a point estimate of μ (the mean of the population of house prices) is $222,522.

Table 8.1 Houses prices of a 36 house sample

House #	Price ($)	House #	Price ($)	House #	Price ($)	House #	Price ($)
1	216,254	10	229,499	19	203,701	28	230,383
2	228,133	11	234,333	20	207,196	29	235,111
3	230,843	12	234,016	21	225,742	30	240,335
4	244,418	13	214,230	22	217,892	31	227,623
5	207,822	14	216,224	23	204,812	32	209,455
6	236,399	15	225,479	24	229,788	33	235,485
7	218,516	16	198,514	25	228,956	34	224,768
8	233,733	17	221,562	26	225,342	35	239,238
9	222,529	18	222,782	27	176,666	36	212,996

8.2.2. Interval estimate and confidence interval

In addition to assigning a point estimate or a single value to a population parameter, we also need to assign an interval around the point estimate. The interval estimate of a population is a statement of two values between which we have some confidence that the parameter value will fall. For estimating the population mean, the general form of an interval estimate is as follows:

$$L < \mu < U \qquad (8.2)$$

With $\bar{X}$ being the point estimate, interval estimates are described as follows:

$$\bar{X} - E < \mu < \bar{X} + E \qquad (8.3)$$

$$or\ \mu = \bar{X} \pm E \qquad (8.4)$$

In the above expression E is called *the margin of error* associated with estimation.

In light of the above expressions, an interval estimation of a parameter is the interval between the upper, U, and the lower, L, value that includes the true value of the parameter with some probability. The probability that the population mean, μ, falls within a certain interval is expressed as follows:

$$P(L < \mu < U) = 1 - \alpha \qquad (8.5)$$

435

where L and U are the lower and upper limits of the interval, and α is the risk area as shown in Figure 8.2.

The above type of confidence interval is suitable for estimating parameters that are desired to meet a target value (not too high and not too low).

The interval estimate of equation 8.3 or 8.4 is called a *two-sided estimate*. When the interest is of extremely low or extremely high values, a *one-sided confidence interval* is established. Interval estimates associated with one-sided situations are expressed as follows:

$$\bar{X} - E < \mu \qquad (8.6)$$

or

$$\mu < \bar{X} + E \qquad (8.7)$$

In this case, the probabilities that the population mean, μ, is greater than a certain value, L, or lower than a certain value U are expressed as follows:

$$P(L < \mu) = 1 - \alpha \ \& \ P(\mu < U) = 1 - \alpha \qquad (8.8)$$

8.3 Estimation of population mean: Special conditions

8.3.1 Population standard deviation, σ, is known or large sample (n ≥ 30)

When the population standard deviation is known or when the sample is large ($n \geq 30$), the interval estimate is determined from the following expression:

Two-sided interval estimate:

$$\bar{X} - E < \mu < \bar{X} + E$$

The value of E represents the difference between the population mean and the sample mean. In order to explain how this value is determined we need to recall the Central Limit theorem discussed in Chapter 7. According to this theory, we can find that the underlying assumption of estimating a population mean from a sample is that when a variable, x, is normally distributed with mean (μ) and standard deviation (σ_x), then the means of the samples of size, n, will also be normally distributed with mean (μ) and standard deviation ($\sigma_x/\sqrt{n}$). Using the Central Limit theorem, the z score can be modified to express values associated with sample means as follows:

$$z = \frac{\bar{X} - \mu_{\bar{X}}}{\sigma_{\bar{X}}} = \frac{\bar{X} - \mu_{\bar{X}}}{\frac{\sigma_x}{\sqrt{n}}} \qquad (8.9)$$

where $\mu_{\bar{X}}$ = the mean of all samples' means = the population mean = μ, $\bar{X}$ = sample mean, σ_x = population standard deviation, n = sample size, and $\frac{\sigma_x}{\sqrt{n}}$ is called the standard error

Rearranging the above equation will lead to the expression used to estimate the population mean.

$$\bar{X} - z_{\alpha/2}\sigma_{\bar{X}} < \mu < \bar{X} + z_{\alpha/2}\sigma_{\bar{X}}$$

$$or \; \mu = \bar{X} \pm z_{\alpha/2}\sigma_{\bar{X}} \qquad (8.10)$$

where $\sigma_{\bar{X}}$ is the standard error, or $\frac{\sigma}{\sqrt{n}}$, n is the sample size, and E is the margin of error.

One-sided interval estimate:

$$\bar{X} - z_{\alpha}\sigma_{\bar{X}} < \mu \qquad (8.11)$$

or

$$\mu < \bar{X} + z_{\alpha}\sigma_{\bar{X}} \qquad (8.12)$$

Example 8.4: Use the following information to find the margin of error E.
Factory workers' monthly earnings: $n = 64$, sample *mean* = \$2800, population standard deviation $\sigma = \$120$, and 95% confidence.

Solution:

$$\mu = \bar{X} \pm z_{\alpha/2}\sigma_{\bar{X}}$$

$$\mu = 2800 \pm z_{\alpha/2}\frac{120}{\sqrt{64}}$$

At 95% confidence, the z value is 1.96. This value can be found from the standard normal table (Appendix 6.A, Chapter 6). You may also refer to the z_{α} notation in section 6.5, Chapter 6 (repeated in Figures 8.3 and 8.4 for convenience).

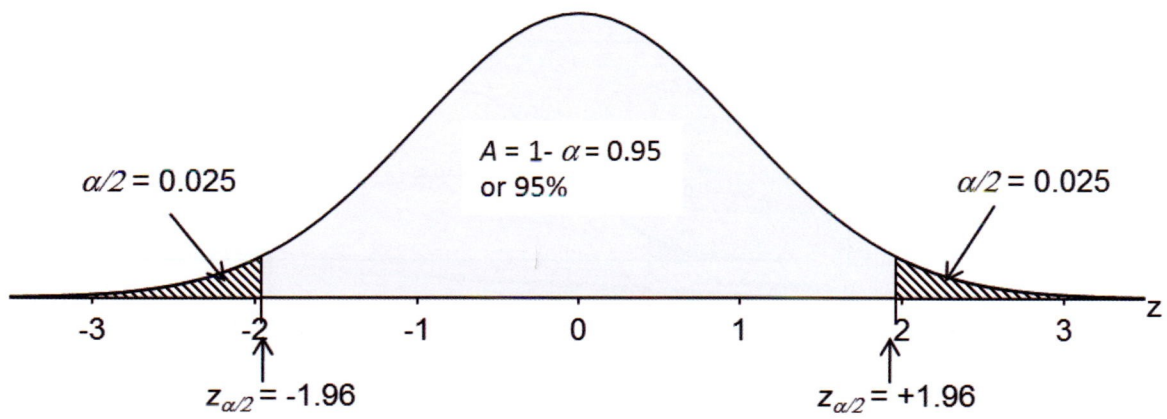

Accordingly,
$$\mu = 2800 \pm 1.96\frac{120}{\sqrt{64}} = 2800 \pm 29.4$$
Thus, the margin of error E is 29.4.

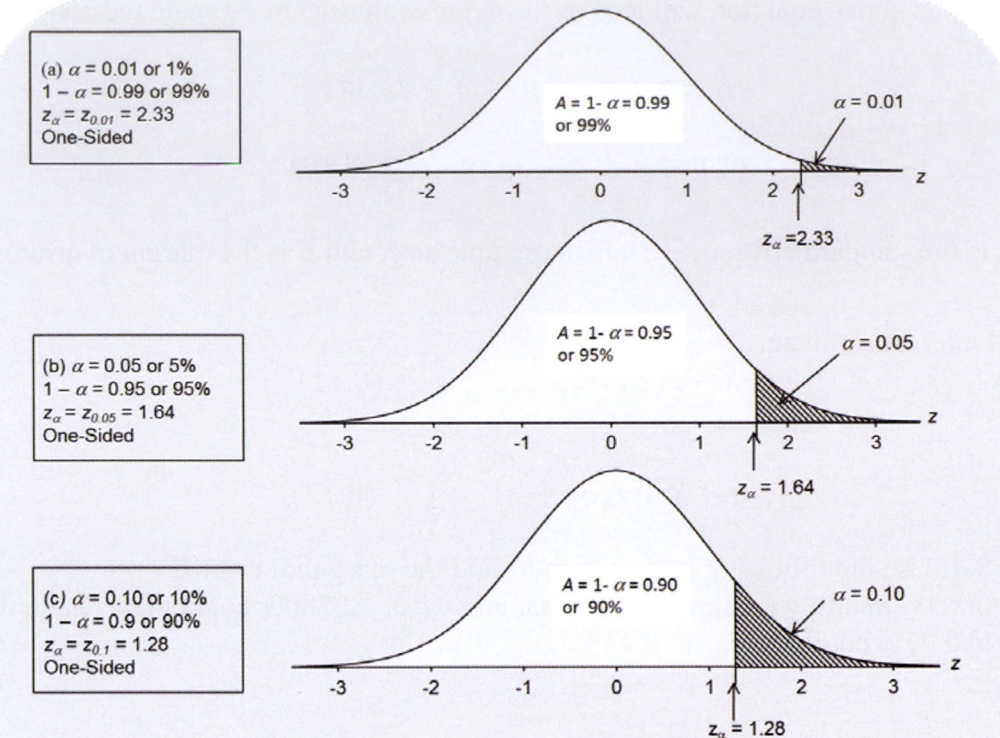

Figure 8.3 The z_α Notation-One Sided Areas

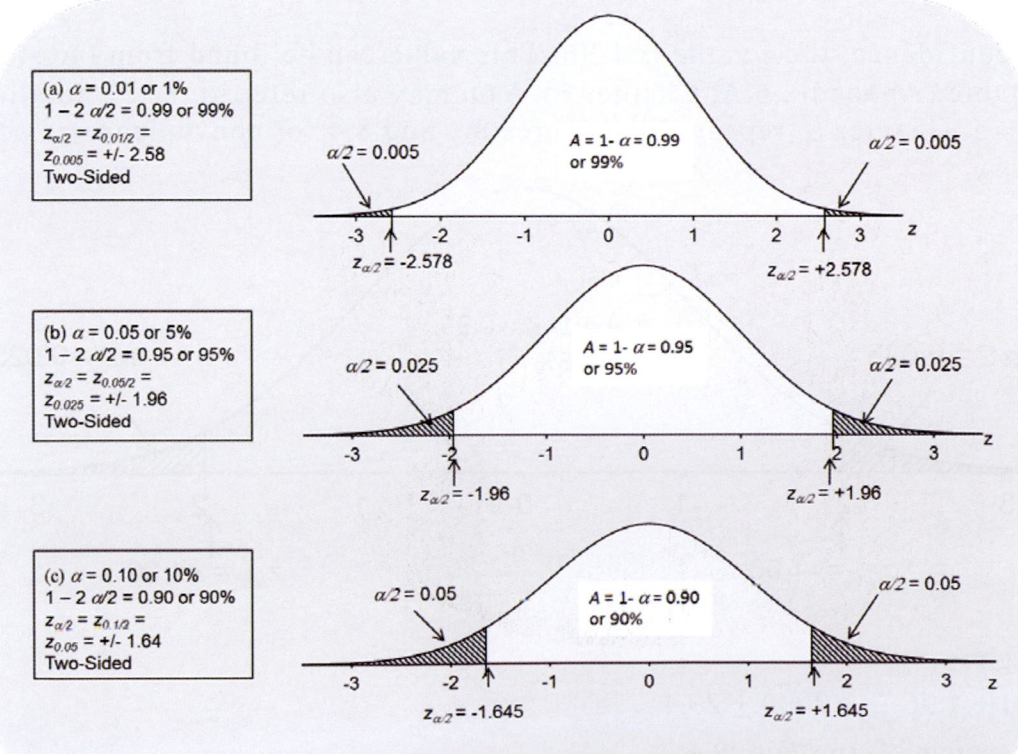

Figure 8.4 The $z_{\alpha/2}$ Notation-Two Sided Areas

Example 8.5: A real estate agent collected a random sample of 20 houses in a certain area and found that the average house price of this sample of houses is $220,000. If the standard deviation of the population of house prices in this area is known to be $15,000, establish an interval estimate of the price of house population at a 95% confidence level?

Solution:

The point estimate of the price of the population of houses in this area is $\bar{X} = \$220,000$. The interval estimate of the price of the population of houses in this area is:

$$\bar{X} - z_{\alpha/2}\sigma_{\bar{X}} < \mu < \bar{X} + z_{\alpha/2}\sigma_{\bar{X}}$$

$$\bar{X} - z_{\alpha/2}\frac{\sigma}{\sqrt{n}} < \mu < \bar{X} + z_{\alpha/2}\frac{\sigma}{\sqrt{n}}$$

$$220,000 - z_{\alpha/2}\frac{15,000}{\sqrt{20}} < \mu < 220,000 + z_{\alpha/2}\frac{15,000}{\sqrt{20}}$$

$$or\ \mu = 220,000 \pm z_{\alpha/2}\frac{15,000}{\sqrt{20}}$$

At 95% confidence, the z value is 1.96.

Accordingly,

$$220,000 - 1.96\frac{15,000}{\sqrt{20}} < \mu < 220,000 + 1.96\frac{15,000}{\sqrt{20}}$$

$$220,000 - 6574.04 < \mu < 220,000 + 6574.04$$

$$213,425.96 < \mu < 226,574.04$$

$$or\ \mu = 220,000 \pm 6574.04$$

Example 8.6: Suppose 50 people were selected randomly from a small town population for the purpose of estimating the average age of people in town. Age values are shown in Table 8.2. The population standard deviation of the ages is known to be 14 years. Find a 95% and a 99% confidence interval for the mean age, μ, of all people in town.

Table 8.2 People age values

Person ID	Age (years)	Person ID	Age (years)	Person ID	Age (years)	Person ID	Age (years)	Person ID	Age (years)
1	61	11	56	21	33	31	33	41	29
2	24	12	56	22	31	32	56	42	34
3	37	13	48	23	39	33	40	43	19
4	20	14	23	24	41	34	46	44	30
5	64	15	45	25	34	35	48	45	45
6	18	16	36	26	33	36	20	46	47
7	18	17	40	27	23	37	46	47	29
8	18	18	28	28	48	38	21	48	53
9	37	19	15	29	24	39	71	49	15
10	62	20	44	30	29	40	26	50	42

Solution:

The point estimate of people's age is:

$$Mean = \bar{X} = \frac{\sum_1^{50} x_i}{n} = \frac{61 + 24 + 37 + \cdots + 53 + 15 + 42}{50} = 36.7$$

The point estimate $= \bar{X} = 36.7$, $n = 50$, and population standard deviation $= \sigma = 14$

The two-sided interval estimate is:

$$\bar{X} - z_{\alpha/2}\sigma_{\bar{X}} < \mu < \bar{X} + z_{\alpha/2}\sigma_{\bar{X}}$$

The standard deviation of the population (σ_x) is known and the sample size is large ($n \geq 30$), therefore, we use the standard deviation of the population (σ_x). At 95% confidence level, the $z_{\alpha/2}$ of interest will be $z_{0.025}$ and $z_{0.025} = 1.96$. The confidence interval estimate is calculated as follows:

$$36.7 - 1.96\frac{14}{\sqrt{50}} < \mu < 36.7 + 1.96\frac{14}{\sqrt{50}}$$
$$36.7 - 3.88 < \mu < 36.7 + 3.88$$

or $32.82 < \mu < 40.58$

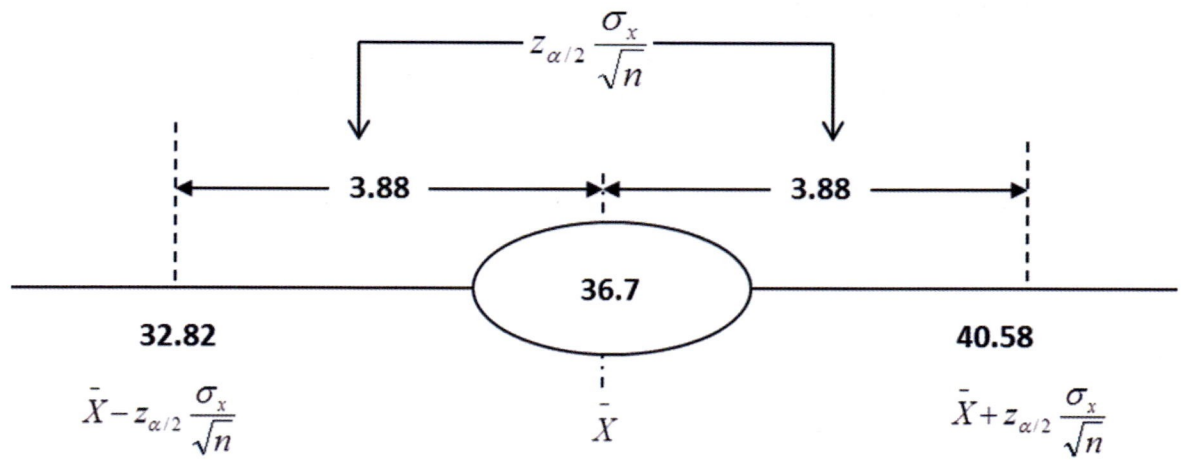

Accordingly, the 95% confidence interval for μ would be from 32.82 to 40.58. In other words, we could be 95% confident that the mean age, μ, of all people in town is somewhere between 32.82 and 40.58.

At 99% confidence level, the $z_{\alpha/2}$ of interest will be $z_{0.005}$ (see Figure 8.4.a) and $z_{0.005} = 2.58$.

$$\bar{X} - z_{\frac{\alpha}{2}}\sigma_{\bar{X}} < \mu < \bar{X} + z_{\frac{\alpha}{2}}\sigma_{\bar{X}}$$

$$36.7 - z_{0.005}\frac{14}{\sqrt{50}} < \mu < 36.7 + z_{0.005}\frac{14}{\sqrt{50}}$$

$$36.7 - 2.58\,\frac{14}{\sqrt{50}} < \mu < 36.7 + 2.58\,\frac{14}{\sqrt{50}}$$

$$36.7 - 5.11 < \mu < 36.7 + 5.11$$

or $31.59 < \mu < 41.81$

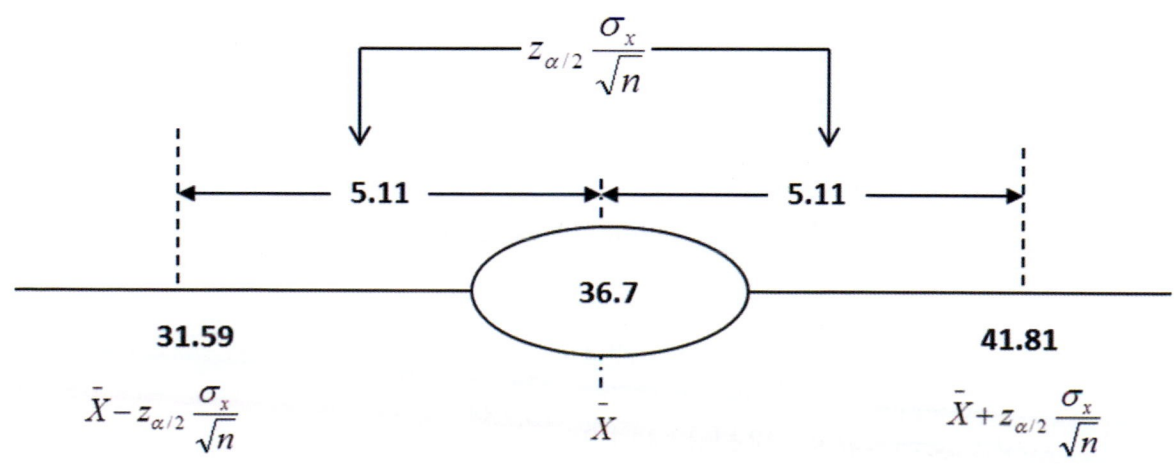

Accordingly, the 99% confidence interval for μ would be from 31.59 to 41.81. In other words, we could be 99% confident that the mean age, μ, of all people in town is somewhere between 31.59 and 41.81. Note how the confidence interval at 99% confidence level is wider than that at 95% confidence level. Can you explain why?

Example 8.7: For the sample data of house prices given in Example 8.3, the point estimate of the population mean is $222,522. Using the same data, establish a 95% confidence interval on the population mean?

Solution:

The point estimate $= \bar{X} = 222,522, n = 36$, and the standard deviation of the sample data $=$

$$s = \sqrt{\frac{\sum_1^n (x_i - \bar{X})^2}{n}}$$

$$= \sqrt{\frac{(216,254 - 222,522)^2 + (228,133 - 222,522)^2 + \cdots .. + (212,996 - 222,522)^2}{36}}$$

$$= \$13,734$$

The two-sided interval estimate is:

$$\bar{X} - z_{\alpha/2}\sigma_{\bar{X}} < \mu < \bar{X} + z_{\alpha/2}\sigma_{\bar{X}}$$

$$or\ \mu = \bar{X} \pm z_{\alpha/2}\sigma_{\bar{X}}$$

The standard deviation of the population (σ_x) is unknown and the sample size is large ($n \geq 30$), therefore we can use the standard deviation of the sample, s, or $13,734.

Accordingly,

$$\bar{X} - z_{\frac{\alpha}{2}}s_{\bar{X}} < \mu < \bar{X} + z_{\frac{\alpha}{2}}s_{\bar{X}}$$

$$222,522 - z_{0.025}\frac{13,734}{\sqrt{36}} < \mu < 222,522 + z_{0.025}\frac{13,734}{\sqrt{36}}$$

Again, the problem is narrowed down to finding the value of $z_{0.025}$. This can be obtained from the standard normal table (Appendix 6.A). You may also use the graphs of Figure 8.4 to aid you in getting your z values. As can be seen in Figure 8.4.b, at 95% confidence, $z_{\alpha/2} = z_{0.025} = 1.96$. Therefore, the 95% confidence interval estimate is:

$$222,522 - 1.96\frac{13,734}{\sqrt{36}} < \mu < 222,522 + 1.96\frac{13,734}{\sqrt{36}}$$

$$222{,}522 - 4486.44 < \mu < 222{,}522 + 4486.44$$

$$or \ \mu = \bar{X} \pm z_{\frac{\alpha}{2}} \sigma_{\bar{x}}$$

$$\mu = 222{,}522 \pm 4486.44$$
$$or \ 218{,}036 < \mu < 227{,}008$$

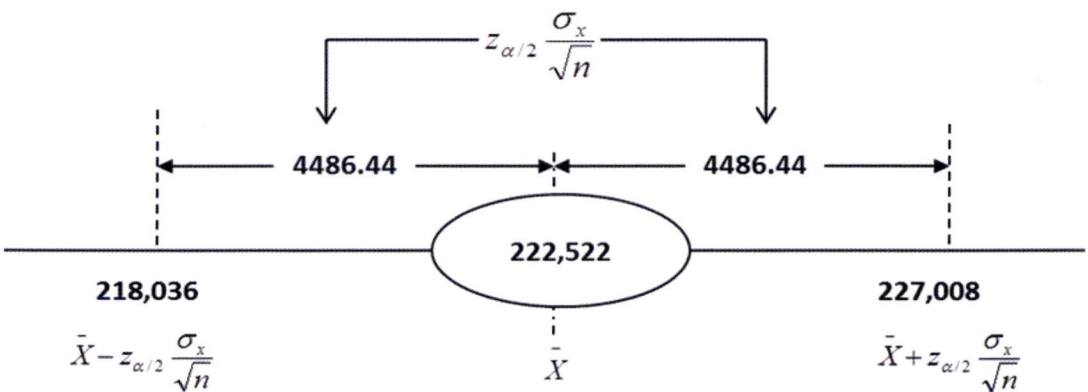

You can see that the interval estimate is expressed in different ways to allow multiple ways of interpreting the results. Examples of ways to interpret the above results are as follows:

- The mean value of the population of house prices is estimated to be on average $222,522 but it can be a plus or minus $4486.44 from this point estimate in 95% of the time.
- The mean value of the population of house prices is estimated to fall between $218,036 and $227,008 in 95% of the time.
- We could be 95% confident that the mean price, μ, of all houses is somewhere between $218,036 and $227,008.

Working problem 8.1:

The following data represents the annual salaries (in thousands) of a random sample of administrators taken from a company. Use the data to determine the point estimate of the population mean salary, μ, of all administrators.

63.8	64.4	55.2	52.9	59.9	58.2	51.6	68.9	58.6
63.1	69.4	59.7	53.7	62.7	57.7	51.5	45.3	68.9
45.9	52.5	67.2	55.1	60.3	60.0	51.9	47.3	49.7
52.0	72.7	72.8	56.6	70.5	53.9	66.4	59.8	73.9

Answer: $59.278 thousand

Working Problem 8.2:

Use the following information to find the margin of error E.

Factory workers' monthly earnings: $n = 64$, sample *mean* = $2800,

Population Standard deviation $\sigma = 120, and 99% confidence.

Answer: $38.7

Working Problem 8.3:

The following data represents the annual salaries (in thousands) of a random sample of administrators taken from a company. If the population standard deviation of annual salary is $7200

a. Identify the distribution of the variable, $\bar{X}$ *that is, the sampling distribution* of the sample mean for samples of size 36.

b. Use part (a) to show that 95.44% of all samples of 36 administrators have the property that the interval from $\bar{X} - 2400$ *to* $\bar{X} + 2400$ *contains* μ.

63.8	64.4	55.2	52.9	59.9	58.2	51.6	68.9	58.6
63.1	69.4	59.7	53.7	62.7	57.7	51.5	45.3	68.9
45.9	52.5	67.2	55.1	60.3	60.0	51.9	47.3	49.7
52.0	72.7	72.8	56.6	70.5	53.9	66.4	59.8	73.9

Answer:

$$\mu = \mu_{\bar{X}} \qquad \sigma_{\bar{X}} = \frac{\sigma}{\sqrt{n}} = 7200/\sqrt{36} = 1200$$

b. The empirical rule states that, for a normally distributed variable, 95.44% of all possible observations lie within two standard deviations to either side of the mean. Applying this rule to the variable x *and referring to part (a)*, we see that 95.44% of all samples of 36 new mobile homes have mean prices within $2 \cdot 1200 = 2400$ of μ.

Working Problem 8.4

Suppose the mean of property taxes of 32 randomly selected houses in a large city is $8688.44, and the population standard deviation of property taxes is $3300.14, estimate the property tax of this city at 95%.

Answer: $7,545 to $9,832 at 95% confidence

Working Problem 8.5

Suppose the mean of property taxes of 32 randomly selected houses in a large city is $8688.44, and the population standard deviation of property taxes is $3300.14, estimate the property tax of this city at 99%.

Answer: $7,185.732 to $10191.148 at 99% confidence

Working problem 8.6:

In an analysis made by the U.S. Bureau of Labor statistics, fifty people in the civilian labor force were randomly selected to determine their ages. The results of this sample are shown below. Find a 95% confidence interval for the mean age, μ, of all people in the civilian labor force. Assume that the population standard deviation of the ages is 12.1 years.

43	37	28	35	37
22	58	49	29	30
32	34	45	38	19
33	16	19	21	62
27	31	33	24	43
51	37	65	57	26
34	40	42	43	41
28	39	26	38	60
33	32	33	31	34
35	29	42	40	38

Answer: 33.0 to 39.8

Key points of estimation:

1. *Confidence interval (CI):* An interval of numbers obtained from a point estimate of a parameter. In example 8.7, the confidence interval is from $218,036 to $227,008. It can also be defined as a range (or an interval) of values used to estimate the true value of a population parameter.

2. *Confidence level:* The extent of confidence that the parameter lies in the confidence interval or the probability that the confidence interval contains the parameter in question. In the above example, the confidence level is 95%. It can also be defined as the probability $1 - \alpha$ (often expressed as the equivalent percentage value, such as 95%) that is the proportion of times that the confidence interval actually does contain the population parameter, assuming that the estimation process is repeated a large number of times. The confidence level is also called the *degree of confidence,* or the *confidence coefficient.*

3. *Confidence-interval estimate:* This consists of both the confidence level and confidence interval.

4. $\sigma_{\bar{X}} = \frac{\sigma_x}{\sqrt{n}}$, where $\sigma_{\bar{X}}$ is the standard error, and σ_x is the population standard deviation. When σ_x is unknown and the sample is large ($n \geq 30$), we can use s (sample standard deviation) instead of σ_x.

5. The values of z_α or $z_{\alpha/2}$ are obtained from the standard normal table (Appendix 6.A-Chapter 6). Recall the z_α-notation discussed in Chapter 6.

8.3.2 What is the minimum sample size (n) we should use to estimate μ?

One of the practical questions that we often face is '*how much should we test*' or '*what is the minimum sample size (n) we should use to estimate population mean,* μ?' This question is a result of the fact that sampling and testing are costly tasks and they require planning, finding appropriate samples, testing each sample, and producing meaningful data. In addition, many tests are destructive in nature, which multiplies the cost and makes it impossible to test but few sample units. In this regard, imagine that you have to address the following questions:

- *How many cars should we destroy in an impact test to evaluate safety features?*
- *How many auto-safety airbags should we test to evaluate deployment performance?*
- *How many people should we test for a new experimental weight-loss treatment?*
- *How many computers should we inspect before we deliver a large shipment to a big retailer?*

The question of how much should we test cannot be addressed in the absolute terms of accuracy and precision as this would mean testing the whole population, which is virtually impossible in

445

most situations. Indeed, the question of how much we should test is the wrong question to ask. Instead, the question should be phrased as follows:

How much should we test this particular characteristic so that our sample average, $\bar{X}$, lies within a certain tolerance, E, from the population average, μ, in 95% or 99% of the time?

Example: If we know that the average income of people in a small town is likely to be $60,000, the appropriate question will then be:

How many people should we survey (asking them about their income) so that the people's sample average, $\bar{X}$, lies within, say $5000, E, from the population average income, μ, in 95% or 99% of the time?

As you can see, in order to estimate the appropriate sample size, the margin of error, E, and the confidence level should be known in advance. It will also be beneficial to know the standard deviation of the population as discussed below.

The answer to the sample size question stems from the estimation expression we used earlier (equation 8.10). Rearranging this equation can yield an expression of the minimum sample size n.

$$or\ \mu = \bar{X} \pm z_{\alpha/2}\ \sigma_{\bar{X}}$$

$$\mu = \bar{X} \pm z_{\frac{\alpha}{2}} \frac{\sigma_x}{\sqrt{n}}$$

$$E = \pm z_{\alpha/2} \frac{\sigma_x}{\sqrt{n}}$$

$$n = \left(\frac{z \cdot \sigma_x}{E}\right)^2 \qquad (8.13)$$

The equation above provides a general expression of the minimum sample size. The use of this equation assumes that we have some knowledge of the tolerance, E, the confidence level, and the population variance, σ_x^2. The type of parameter under consideration dictates the tolerance or the difference between sample mean and population mean. For example, a company producing a composite component that will be used in a spaceship may assume a tolerance of its strength of approximately zero because of the high level of safety and durability required. In this case, the sample size will be very large, approaching the population size. On the other hand, a company producing a mop yarn used for making cleaning towels would care less about the tolerance in yarn strength and it may assume a large magnitude of tolerance. In this case, the tolerance will be large and the sample size may be very small.

The population variability is often known from past data or historical records. In the absence of such information, one can take a series of representative large samples and estimate the population variance from sample variance.

In any case, the sample size should be stated in the context of ***maximum sampling error***, primarily dictated by the tolerance, E. This point will be illustrated by example shortly.

446

Example 8.8: If the standard deviation of the IQ of the population of math professors is known to be 20 and we want to estimate the mean IQ score for the population of math professors. How many math professors must be randomly selected for IQ tests if we want a 95% confidence that the sample mean is within 3 IQ points of the population mean?

Solution:

Using a 95% confidence, and given the standard deviation, σ of 20, and the tolerance E of 3, the minimum sample size is calculated as follow:

$$z_{\alpha/2} = 1.96, E = 3, \sigma = 20$$

$$n = \left[\frac{z_{\alpha/2} \cdot \sigma}{E}\right]^2 = \left[\frac{1.96 \times 20}{3}\right]^2 = 170.738 \approx 171$$

Example 8.9: A real estate broker was interested in the property tax paid for houses in his sales area. He took a random sample of 40 houses and found that the mean of the annual property tax of these houses is $4000 and the standard deviation is $1000. Estimate the population mean of annual property tax at 95% confidence level. What is the sampling error? What is the minimum sample size required to reduce this sampling error down to half of its current value?

Solution:

At a 95% confidence level, the confidence interval will be as follows:

$$or \; \mu = \bar{X} \pm z_{\frac{\alpha}{2}}\sigma_{\bar{x}} \quad or \quad \mu = 4000 \pm 1.96\frac{1000}{\sqrt{40}}$$

$$or \quad \mu = 4000 \pm 309.9$$

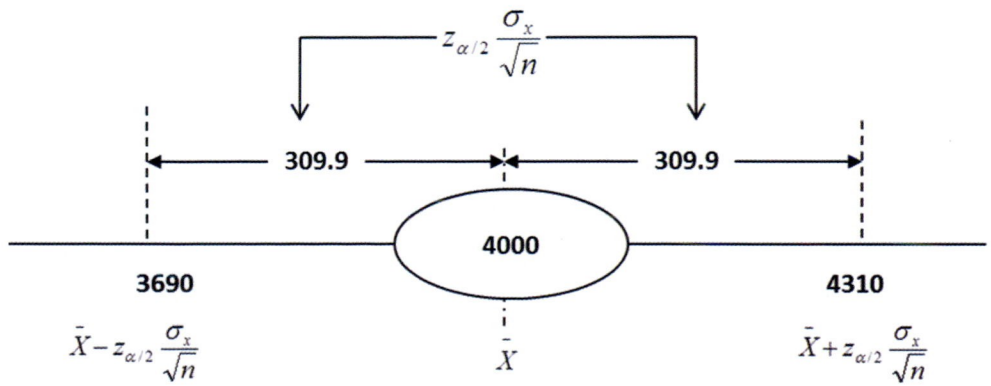

This yields a 95% confidence interval of 4000 ± 309.9. This confidence interval means that in 95% of the time property tax will be between $3690 and $4310. The maximum sampling error is calculated as follows:

$$Maximum \; sampling \; error = 100\left(\frac{E}{\bar{X}}\right) = 100\left(\frac{309.9}{4000}\right) = 7.75\%$$

Thus, the sample size of 40 is associated with a sampling error of 7.75%. If we are satisfied with the 7.75% sampling error, we need to test no more. If we are not satisfied, we should establish a new allowable sampling error and calculate the corresponding sample size. The minimum sample size required for reducing this sampling error down to half its current value, or 3.875% is calculated as follows:

At 3.875% sampling error, E value is $155 (3.875×4000/100). In other words, instead of a tolerance E of ± $309.9, the new tolerance will be ± $155. In this case, we use the expression of sample size:

$$n = \left(\frac{z \cdot \sigma}{E}\right)^2 = \left(\frac{1.96 \times 1000}{155}\right)^2 \approx 160$$

This result means that to reduce the sampling error down to 3.875%, we will need a minimum sample size of 160.

Working Problem 8.7:

If the standard deviation of grades of a population of students taking a biology course is known to be 8 and we want to estimate the mean grade for the whole population of students. How many grades must be randomly selected for this evaluation if we want a 95% confidence that the sample mean is within 2 points of the population mean?

Answer: 62

Working Problem 8.8:

A yarn manufacturer normally tests 36 specimens for yarn strength. Using a random sample of this size, he found that the mean strength is 65 lb and the standard deviation is 9 lb. Estimate the population mean of yarn strength at 95% confidence level. What is the sampling error? What is the minimum sample size required to reduce this sampling error down to half its current value?

Answer: 62.060 to 67.940, 144

8.3.3 Population standard deviation, σ, is unknown and small sample (n < 30)

In practice, we are often faced with a situation where we can only use a small sample from a population. In addition, the population standard deviation is unknown. Two common examples of this situation are:

- When the experiment is too expensive or when the test is destructive as in the case of the collision test of cars required to measure their safety.
- When a new product is being developed and only few models of the product are available for testing.

When the sample is small but the standard deviation of the population is known, we can use the methods in the previous section to estimate population mean. On the other hand, when the standard deviation of the population is unknown and the sample is small, we may have to rely on the standard deviation of the sample, s, and we may have to be satisfied with a small sample size ($n < 30$). If the variable of the parent population can be approximated by a normal distribution, the sampling distribution of sample means of small samples will be called the t distribution (or Studentized distribution). Some of the characteristics of this distribution are discussed in Appendix 8.B.1. The variable of this distribution is called the t-statistic and it is defined by the following equation:

$$t = \frac{\bar{X} - \mu_{\bar{X}}}{\frac{s_x}{\sqrt{n}}} \qquad (8.14)$$

where $\bar{X}$ = sample mean, $\mu_{\bar{X}}$ = population mean, s_x = sample standard deviation, n = sample size, and $s_x/\sqrt{n}$ is called the standard error.

Note the similarity between the t statistic expressed by the above equation and the z statistic expressed by equation 8.9. In both equations, the numerator is exactly the same ($z = \frac{\bar{X} - \mu_{\bar{X}}}{\frac{\sigma_x}{\sqrt{n}}}$). The difference is in the denominator where σ_x in equation 8.9 is replaced by s_x in equation 8.14.

Basic properties of the t distribution are as follows:

- The t-distribution is bell shaped and symmetric about the mean.
- The total area under the t-curve is one, or 100%.
- The mean of the t distribution is equal to zero and its standard deviation is $\sqrt{df/(df-2)}$, where df is the degree of freedom or n-1.
- There is a different t-distribution for each sample size. In other words, a particular t-distribution is typically identified by its number of degrees of freedom, $df = n$-1.
- As the degree of freedom, n-1, increases (approaching 30), the t-distribution approaches the standard normal distribution (see Figure 8.5).

Similar to the standard normal distribution, we use a special table for the t-distribution to determine the t values at critical areas or confidence levels. This table is presented in Appendix 8.A, Table I. It is used to determine the critical area to the right (from $t = t_{n-1,\alpha}$ to infinity) or the t-value corresponding to this area. In this table, the first column represents the degrees of freedom ($df = n$-1). The first row represents the critical area α or $\alpha/2$, and the t values represent the body of the table.

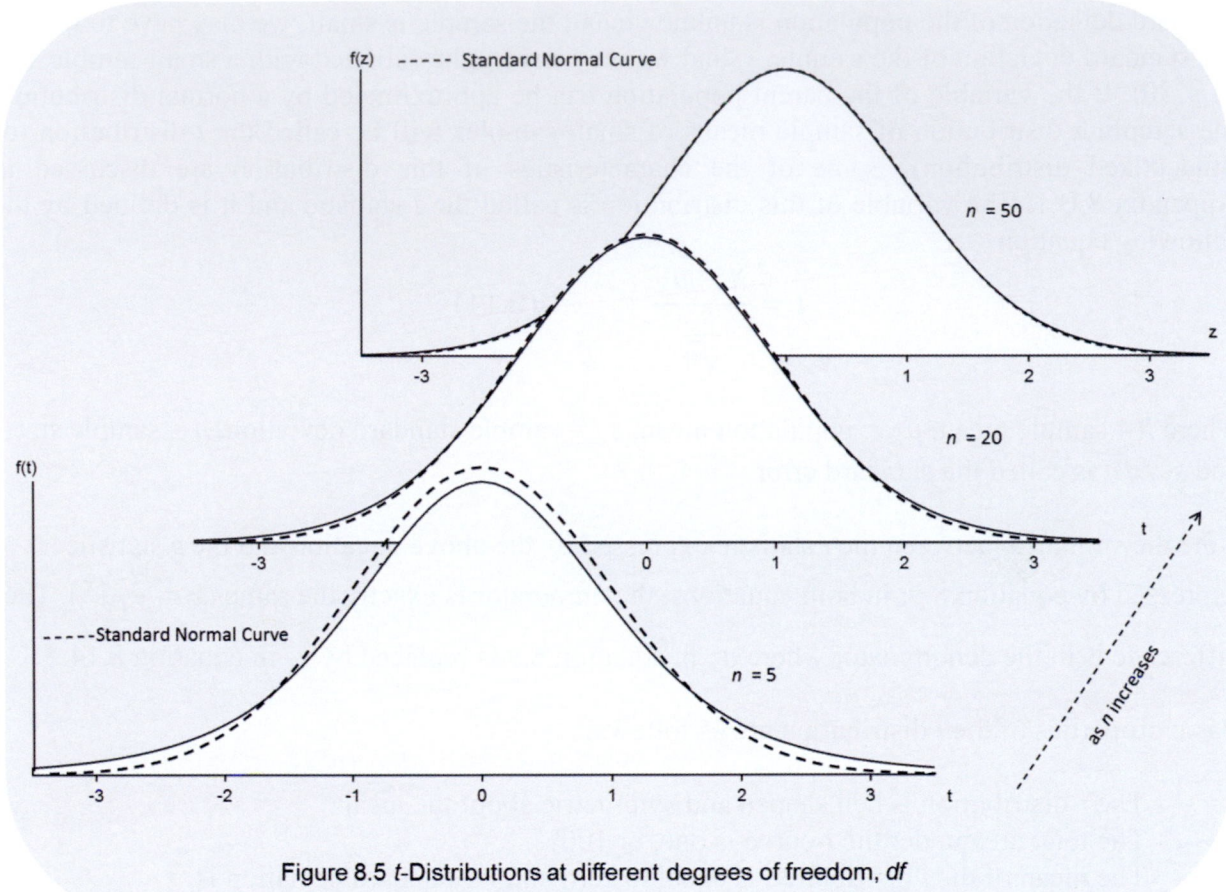

Figure 8.5 *t*-Distributions at different degrees of freedom, *df*

8.3.3.1 Finding the critical value-The t-table

In order to construct a confidence interval for small samples, we need to determine the *t* value at a certain confidence and for a given degree of freedom. The principle of finding the critical value is similar to that used for the standard normal distribution. To find the critical *t* value for a confidence interval, let 1- α be the confidence level expressed as a decimal. The critical value is then $t_{\alpha/2}$ because the area under the *t*-curve between -$t_{\alpha/2}$ and $t_{\alpha/2}$ is 1- α as shown in Figure 8.6. The critical *t*-value can be found from the *t*-Table by finding the row corresponding to the given degree of freedom (the first column in the table), and the column corresponding to the desired confidence level. The *t* values are listed in the body of the table. The examples below illustrate how the *t* values are found from the *t* Table.

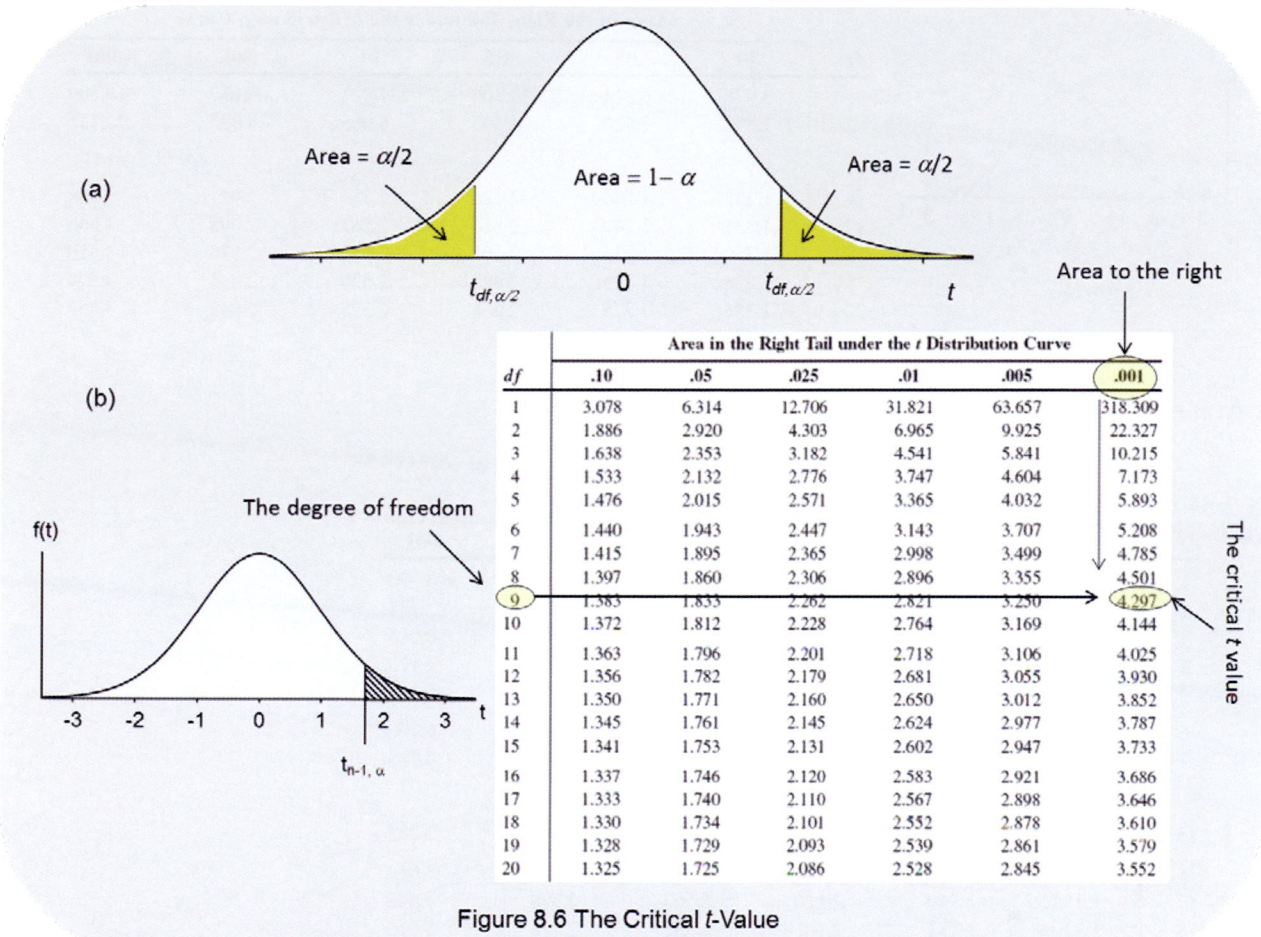

Figure 8.6 The Critical *t*-Value

Example 8.10: Find the value of *t* for the following cases:

    (a) Sample size 20 and 0.005 area in the right tail of a *t*-distribution curve
    (b) Sample size 17 and 0.05 area in the right tail of a *t*-distribution curve
    (c) Sample size 21 and 0.025 area in the right tail of a *t*-distribution curve

Solution:

Solutions to the above questions are illustrated in Figure 8.7. In any case, you find the *df* in the *t*-Table, and the area. At the point of crossing lines from these two values you can find the *t* value as shown below.

At $n = 20$, $df = 20-1 = 19$, $\alpha = 0.005$, $t = 2.861$

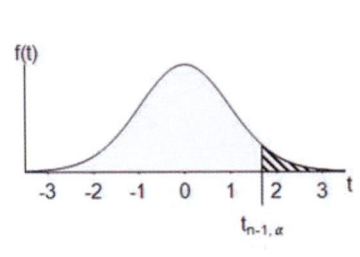

	Area in the Right Tail under the *t* Distribution Curve					
df	.10	.05	.025	.01	.005	.001
1	3.078	6.314	12.706	31.821	63.657	318.309
2	1.886	2.920	4.303	6.965	9.925	22.327
16	1.337	1.746	2.120	2.583	2.921	3.686
17	1.333	1.740	2.110	2.567	2.898	3.646
18	1.330	1.734	2.101	2.552	2.878	3.610
19	1.328	1.729	2.093	2.539	2.861	3.579
20	1.325	1.725	2.086	2.528	2.845	3.552

At $n = 17$, $df = 17-1 = 16$, $\alpha = 0.05$, $t = 1.746$

	Area in the Right Tail under the *t* Distribution Curve					
df	.10	.05	.025	.01	.005	.001
1	3.078	6.314	12.706	31.821	63.657	318.309
2	1.886	2.920	4.303	6.965	9.925	22.327
3	1.638	2.353	3.182	4.541	5.841	10.215
4	1.533	2.132	2.776	3.747	4.604	7.173
5	1.476	2.015	2.571	3.365	4.032	5.893
6	1.440	1.943	2.447	3.143	3.707	5.208
7	1.415	1.895	2.365	2.998	3.499	4.785
15	1.341	1.753	2.131	2.602	2.947	3.733
16	1.337	1.746	2.120	2.583	2.921	3.686
17	1.333	1.740	2.110	2.567	2.898	3.646
18	1.330	1.734	2.101	2.552	2.878	3.610
19	1.328	1.729	2.093	2.539	2.861	3.579
20	1.325	1.725	2.086	2.528	2.845	3.552

At $n = 21$, $df = 21-1 = 20$, $\alpha = 0.025$, $t = 2.086$

	Area in the Right Tail under the *t* Distribution Curve					
df	.10	.05	.025	.01	.005	.001
1	3.078	6.314	12.706	31.821	63.657	318.309
2	1.886	2.920	4.303	6.965	9.925	22.327
3	1.638	2.353	3.182	4.541	5.841	10.215
4	1.533	2.132	2.776	3.747	4.604	7.173
5	1.476	2.015	2.571	3.365	4.032	5.893
15	1.341	1.753	2.131	2.602	2.947	3.733
16	1.337	1.746	2.120	2.583	2.921	3.686
17	1.333	1.740	2.110	2.567	2.898	3.646
18	1.330	1.734	2.101	2.552	2.878	3.610
19	1.328	1.729	2.093	2.539	2.861	3.579
20	1.325	1.725	2.086	2.528	2.845	3.552

Working Problem 8.9:

Find the value of t for 10, 15 and 60 degrees of freedom and 0.005 area in the right tail of a t distribution curve.

Answer:

3.169, 2.947, 2.66

8.3.3.2 The confidence interval for unknown σ and a small sample

In light of the above discussion, when the population standard deviation is unknown and the sample is small, the interval estimate is determined from the following expression:

Two-sided Interval Estimate:

$$\bar{X} - E < \mu < \bar{X} + E$$

$$\bar{X} - t_{df,\alpha/2}s_{\bar{X}} < \mu < \bar{X} + t_{df,\alpha/2}s_{\bar{X}}$$

$$or \ \mu = \bar{X} \pm t.s_{\bar{X}}$$

$$or \ \mu = \bar{X} \pm t\frac{s}{\sqrt{n}} \qquad (8.15)$$

One-sided Interval Estimate:

$$\bar{X} - t_{df,\alpha}s_{\bar{X}} < \mu \ \& \ \mu < \bar{X} + t_{df,\alpha}s_{\bar{X}} \qquad (8.16)$$

$s_{\bar{X}} = \frac{s}{\sqrt{n}}$, where $s_{\bar{X}}$ is called the standard error, and s is the sample standard deviation. The values of $t_{df,\alpha/2}$ or $t_{df,\alpha}$ are obtained from the t-Table (Table 8.A.I, Appendix 8.A). Some of the characteristics of the t-distribution are discussed in Appendix 8.B.I.

Example 8.11: Suppose a random sample of 16 students was selected from a college to measure their heights. The sample mean was 150 cm, and the standard deviation was 10 cm. Find a 95% confidence interval for the mean height of students assuming that student height is approximately normally distributed.

Solution:

Since the sample size is small (<30), and the population standard deviation is unknown, we use the t-statistic to estimate μ. In this case, $n = 16$, $df = 15$, $\bar{X} = 150 \ cm$, and $s = 10$ cm. At 95% confidence interval, we have a two-sided estimation with a risk of 5%; 2.5% (or $\alpha/2 = 0.025$) on each side.

$$\bar{X} - t_{df,\alpha/2}s_{\bar{X}} < \mu < \bar{X} + t_{df,\alpha/2}s_{\bar{X}}$$

$$150 - t_{df,\alpha/2}\frac{10}{\sqrt{16}} < \mu < 150 + t_{df,\alpha/2}\frac{10}{\sqrt{16}}$$

At $df = 15$, and $\alpha/2 = 0.025$, $t_{15, 0.025} = 2.131$ (see below)

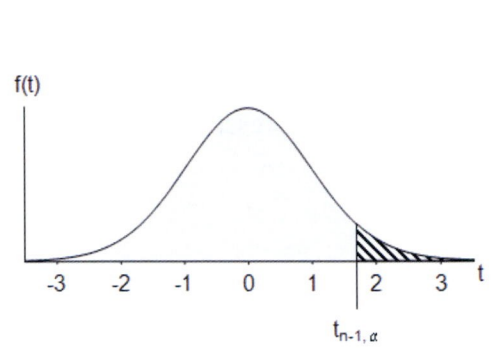

	Area in the Right Tail under the *t* Distribution Curve					
df	.10	.05	.025	.01	.005	.001
1	3.078	6.314	12.706	31.821	63.657	318.309
2	1.886	2.920	4.303	6.965	9.925	22.327
3	1.638	2.353	3.182	4.541	5.841	10.215
4	1.533	2.132	2.776	3.747	4.604	7.173
5	1.476	2.015	2.571	3.365	4.032	5.893
6	1.440	1.943	2.447	3.143	3.707	5.208
7	1.415	1.895	2.365	2.998	3.499	4.785
8	1.397	1.860	2.306	2.896	3.355	4.501
9	1.383	1.833	2.262	2.821	3.250	4.297
10	1.372	1.812	2.228	2.764	3.169	4.144
11	1.363	1.796	2.201	2.718	3.106	4.025
12	1.356	1.782	2.179	2.681	3.055	3.930
13	1.350	1.771	2.160	2.650	3.012	3.852
14	1.345	1.761	2.145	2.624	2.977	3.787
15	1.341	1.753	2.131	2.602	2.947	3.733

Thus,

$$150 - 2.131\frac{10}{\sqrt{16}} < \mu < 150 + 2.131\frac{10}{\sqrt{16}}$$

$$150 - 5.328 < \mu < 150 + 5.328$$

$$144.672 < \mu < 155.328$$

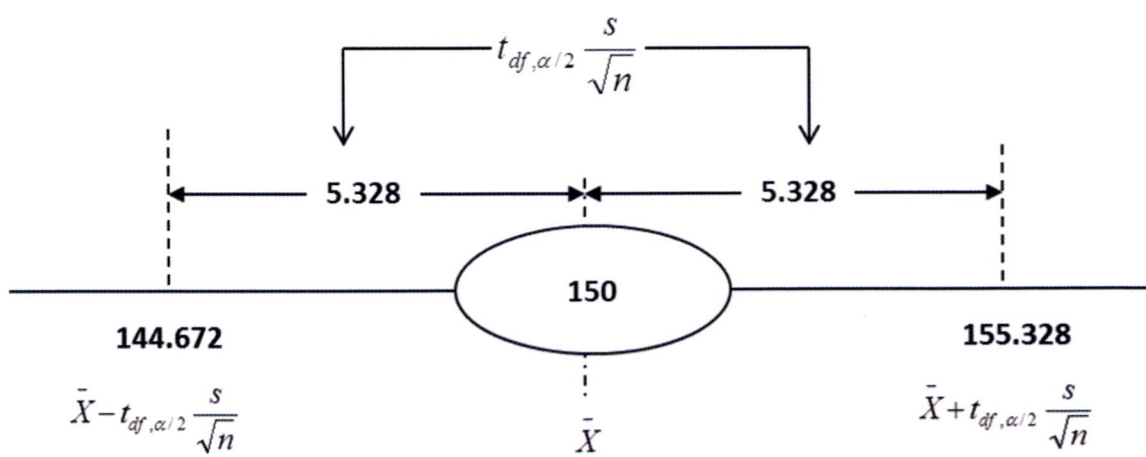

Accordingly, the 95% confidence interval for μ would be from 144.672 *cm* to 155.328 *cm*. In other words, we could be 95% confident that the mean height, μ, of all students is somewhere between 144.672 *cm* and 155.328 *cm*.

454

Example 8.12: In order to estimate property tax in a small town, a random sample of 27 houses was selected. The sample mean of property tax was $4000 per year, and the standard deviation was $650. Find a 99% confidence interval for the mean value of property tax in the house population assuming that property tax follows approximately a normal distribution.

Solution:

Since the sample size is small (<30), and the population variance is unknown, $n = 27$, $df = 26$, $\bar{X} = \$4000$, and $s = \$650$, we can use the *t*-distribution to estimate the population mean:

The 99% confidence interval in this case is:

$$\bar{X} - t_{df,\alpha/2} s_{\bar{X}} < \mu < \bar{X} + t_{df,\alpha/2} s_{\bar{X}}$$

$$4000 - t_{df,\alpha/2} \frac{650}{\sqrt{27}} < \mu < 4000 + t_{df,\alpha/2} \frac{650}{\sqrt{27}}$$

At $df = 26$, and $\alpha/2 = 0.005$, $t_{26,\,0.005} = 2.779$. Thus,

$$4000 - 2.779 \frac{650}{\sqrt{27}} < \mu < 4000 + 2.779 \frac{650}{\sqrt{27}}$$

$$4000 - 347.6 < \mu < 4000 + 347.6$$

$$3652.4 < \mu < 4347.6$$

Accordingly, the 99% confidence interval for μ would be approximately from $3652.4 to $4347.6. In other words, we could be 99% confident that the mean property tax, μ, of all houses in town is somewhere between $3652.4 and $4347.6.

Example 8.13: A company making metal bars wishes to estimate the mean weight of the metal bar population. The company used only 10 bars and found the values of weight of these bars to be as shown in Table 8.3. Find a 99% confidence interval for the mean bar weight of the population assuming that the variable bar weight follows approximately a normal distribution.

Table 8.3 Values of bar weight

Bar weights (pounds)	2.2	2.4	2.1	1.9	2.3	2.2	2.3	2.3	2.3	2.1

Solution:

$$Mean = \bar{X} = \frac{\sum_1^n x_i}{n} = \frac{2.2 + 2.4 + 2.1 + \cdots + 2.3 + 2.1}{10} = 2.21 \; lbs$$

$$s = \sqrt{\frac{\sum_1^n (x_i - \bar{X})^2}{n-1}} = \sqrt{\frac{(2.2 - 2.21)^2 + (2.4 - 2.21)^2 + \ldots + (2.1 - 2.21)^2}{9}} = 0.145 \; lbs$$

$$\bar{X} - t_{df,\alpha/2} s_{\bar{X}} < \mu < \bar{X} + t_{df,\alpha/2} s_{\bar{X}}$$

At $df = 9$, and $\alpha/2 = 0.005$, $t_{9, 0.005} = 3.25$

$$\bar{X} - t_{9,0.005}\frac{s}{\sqrt{n}} < \mu < \bar{X} + t_{9,0.005}\frac{s}{\sqrt{n}}$$

$$2.21 - 3.25\ \frac{0.145}{\sqrt{10}} < \mu < 2.21 + 3.25\ \frac{0.145}{\sqrt{10}}$$

$$2.21 - 0.149 < \mu < 2.21 + 0.149$$

$$2.061 < \mu < 2.359$$

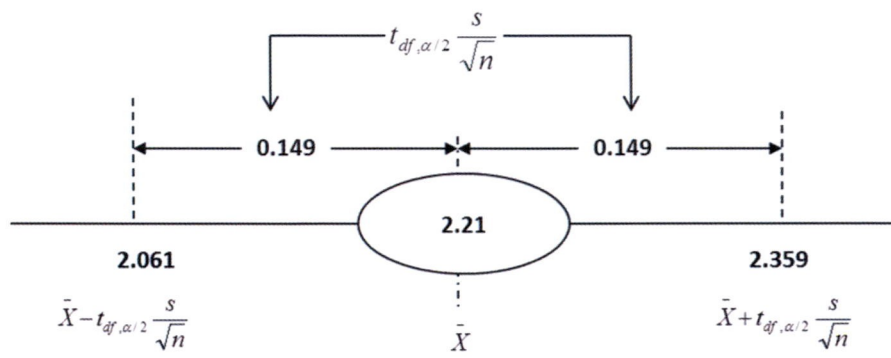

Accordingly, the 99% confidence interval for μ would be approximately from 2.061 pounds to 2.359 pounds. In other words, we could be 99% confident that the mean bar weight of the population, μ, is somewhere between 2.061 pounds and 2.359 pounds.

Working Problem 8.10:

Suppose that a random sample of 22 students was selected to evaluate their grades. The sample mean is 78%, and the standard deviation is 7%. Find a 95% confidence interval for the mean grade of students assuming that student grade is approximately normally distributed.

Confidence interval - mean

95% confidence level
78 mean
Std. Dev. = 7
n= 22
2.080 t (df = 21)
3.104 half-width
81.104 upper confidence limit
74.896 lower confidence limit

Working Problem 8.11:

A metal rod manufacturer wishes to investigate the consistency in the diameter of the rods. A sample of 10 rods taken randomly revealed a sample mean of 0.32 inch with a standard deviation of 0.09 inch.

a. Construct a 95 percent confidence interval for the population mean.
b. Construct a 99 percent confidence interval for the population mean
c. Compare the two answers and discuss the difference

Assume that the population is normally-distributed

Answer:

Confidence interval - mean

95% confidence level
0.384 upper confidence limit
0.256 lower confidence limit

Confidence interval - mean

99% confidence level
0.412 upper confidence limit
0.228 lower confidence limit

Estimation of population mean: Summary

(1) Population standard deviation, σ_x, is known or Large sample (n ≥ 30)

$$\bar{X} - z_{\alpha/2}\sigma_{\bar{X}} < \mu < \bar{X} + z_{\alpha/2}\sigma_{\bar{X}} \qquad (A)$$

where $\sigma_{\bar{X}} = \frac{\sigma_x}{\sqrt{n}}$ Note that $E = z_{\alpha/2}\sigma_{\bar{X}}$ is the margin of error

(2) The minimum sample size (n) we should use to estimate μ

$$n = \left(\frac{z \cdot \sigma_x}{E}\right)^2$$

(3) Population Standard Deviation, σ_x is Unknown and Small Sample (n < 30)

$$\bar{X} - t_{df,\alpha/2}s_{\bar{X}} < \mu < \bar{X} + t_{df,\alpha/2}s_{\bar{X}} \qquad (B)$$

where $s_{\bar{X}} = \frac{s}{\sqrt{n}}$, $E = t_{df,\alpha/2}\sigma_{\bar{X}}$ is the margin of error

The number of **degrees of freedom (df)** for a collection of sample data is the number of sample values that can vary after certain restrictions have been imposed on all data values. For one sample, it is equal to sample size minus 1, or *n-1*.

Basic Steps:

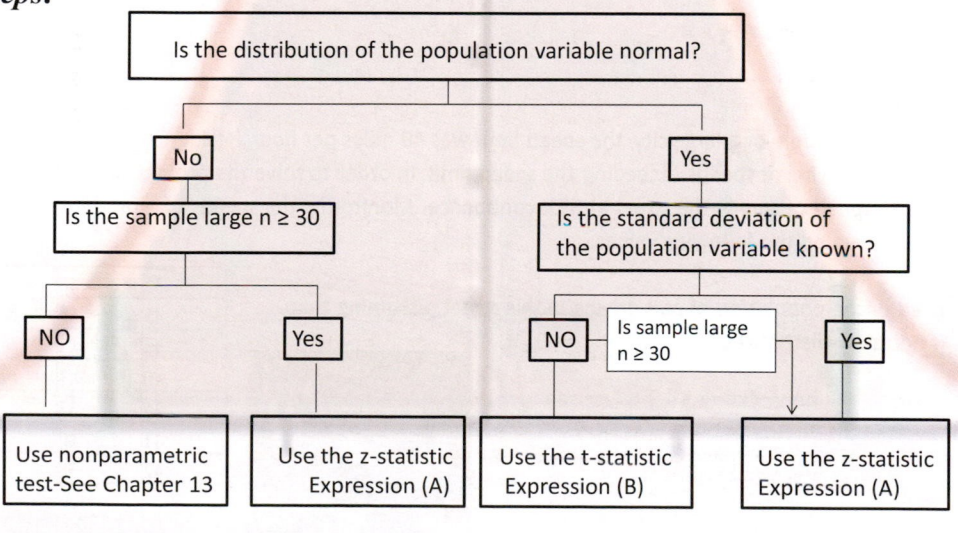

Working Problem 8.12:

A metal rod manufacturer wishes to investigate the consistency in the diameter of the rods. A sample of 10 rods taken randomly revealed a sample mean of 0.32 inch with a standard deviation of 0.09 inch.

Construct a 90 percent confidence interval for the population mean.

Assume that the population is normally-distributed

Answer:

Do it yourself

Working problem 8.13:

In a random sample of 24 people, the measurements of body temperature revealed an average of 98.20°F, and the standard deviation was 0.7°F.

- Use this sample to find best point estimate of the population mean m of all body temperatures.
- Establish a confidence interval at 95%

Assume that the population is normally distributed

Answer:

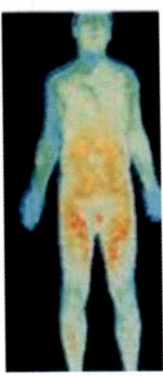

98.496 upper confidence limit

97.904 lower confidence limit

Working Problem 8.14:

In a narrow street in the middle of a large city, the speed limit was 40 miles per hour. Residents living around this street complained about cars driving at speeds exceeding the speed limit. In order to solve the problem the city decided to estimate the average speed of cars in the street at 99% confidence. Monitoring the speeds of a random sample of cars driving in the street revealed the following values:

Estimate the speed of the population of cars driving in this street, assuming that the car speed is normally-distributed

35	40	45
45	50	37
44	43	35
40	43	56
35	33	36
41	40	40
42	38	40

Answer:

44.213 upper confidence limit

37.507 lower confidence limit

8.3.4 Estimation of population proportion

Using the concepts presented in Chapter 5 about the binomial distribution, and the central limit theorem discussed in Chapter 7, we can estimate population proportions using the following expressions:

(a) Two-sided confidence interval for the proportion, p, of a population:

$$\hat{p} - z_{\alpha/2}\sigma_p < p < \hat{p} + z_{\alpha/2}\sigma_p$$
$$p = \hat{p} \pm z_{\alpha/2}\sigma_p$$

$$\hat{p} - z_{\alpha/2}\sqrt{\frac{\hat{p}(1-\hat{p})}{n}} < p < \hat{p} + z_{\alpha/2}\sqrt{\frac{\hat{p}(1-\hat{p})}{n}} \qquad (8.17)$$

where $\hat{p}$ = sample proportion, $p = \mu_p$ = the proportion of population, σ_p = population standard deviation, n = sample size, and $\sqrt{\frac{\hat{p}(1-\hat{p})}{n}}$ = standard error

(b) One-sided confidence interval for the proportion, p, of a population:

$$\hat{p} - z_{\alpha}\sqrt{\frac{\hat{p}(1-\hat{p})}{n}} < p \qquad (8.18)$$

$$p < \hat{p} + z_{\alpha}\sqrt{\frac{\hat{p}(1-\hat{p})}{n}} \qquad (8.19)$$

The minimum sample size for proportion inspection is obtained from the following formula:

$$n = \hat{p}(1-\hat{p})\left(\frac{z}{E}\right)^2 \qquad (8.20)$$

Note that

$$Maximum\ sampling\ error\ (\%) = 100\left(\frac{E}{\hat{p}}\right) \qquad (8.21)$$

Example 8.14: In a poll of 1500 randomly selected people in the U.S., 44% said they take vitamins and other dietary supplements on regular basis. Estimate the population proportion of U.S. adults who take vitamins and other dietary supplements on regular basis at 95% confidence. What is the standard error for the estimate of the proportion of all people in the U.S. who take vitamins and other dietary supplements on a regular basis?

Solution:

$\hat{p}$ = sample proportion = 0.44, n = sample size =1500, $\sqrt{\frac{\hat{p}(1-\hat{p})}{n}}$ = standard error = $\sqrt{\frac{0.44(1-0.44)}{1500}}$ = 0.0128

459

At 95% confidence, $z = 1.96$

$$\hat{p} - z_{\alpha/2}\sqrt{\frac{\hat{p}(1-\hat{p})}{n}} < p < \hat{p} + z_{\alpha/2}\sqrt{\frac{\hat{p}(1-\hat{p})}{n}}$$

$$0.44 - 1.96\sqrt{\frac{0.44(1-0.44)}{1500}} < p < 0.44 + 1.96\sqrt{\frac{0.44(1-0.44)}{1500}}$$

$$0.44 - 0.025 < p < 0.44 + 0.025$$
$$0.415 < p < 0.465$$

Thus, with a 95% confidence, we can estimate that on average the proportion of all people in the U.S. who take vitamins and other dietary supplements on regular basis is 0.44 but it may range from 0.415 to 0.465 (or roughly 41.5% to 46.5%).

Example 8.15: A large company surveyed a representative random sample of 200 of its employees regarding the addition of extended dental insurance. The result of this survey revealed that 160 of the employees prefer the new dental plan. Estimate the company population proportion of employees that will prefer the new dental plan at 95% confidence.

Solution:

n = Sample size = 200, n_i = Employee in agreement with the new plan = 160

The sample proportion is: $\hat{p} = \frac{n_i}{n} = \frac{160}{200} = 0.8$

At 95% confidence, $z_{\alpha/2} = z_{0.025} = 1.96$

$$\hat{p} - z_{\alpha/2}\sigma_p < p < \hat{p} + z_{\alpha/2}\sigma_p$$

$$\hat{p} - z_{\alpha/2}\sqrt{\frac{\hat{p}(1-\hat{p})}{n}} < p < \hat{p} + z_{\alpha/2}\sqrt{\frac{\hat{p}(1-\hat{p})}{n}}$$

$$0.8 - 1.96\sqrt{\frac{0.8(1-0.8)}{200}} < p < 0.8 + 1.96\sqrt{\frac{0.8(1-0.8)}{200}}$$
$$0.8 - 0.0554 < p < 0.8 + 0.0554$$

$$0.745 < p < 0.855$$

Thus, with a 95% confidence, we can estimate that on average the proportion of all employees in the company who will prefer the new dental plan is 0.80 but it may range from 0.745 to 0.855 (or roughly 74.5% to 85.5%).

Example 8.16: Solve the above problem at a 99% confidence.

Solution:

At 99% confidence, $z_{\alpha/2} = z_{0.005} = 2.58$

$$0.8 - 2.58\sqrt{\frac{0.8(1-0.8)}{200}} < p < 0.8 + 2.58\sqrt{\frac{0.8(1-0.8)}{200}}$$

$$0.8 - 0.07297 < p < 0.8 + 0.07297$$

$$0.727 < p < 0.873$$

Note how the confidence interval increased as a result of using a higher confidence level.

Example 8.17: A sample of 500 students in a large university was surveyed regarding the addition of classes on the weekends. The result of the survey revealed that 120 students would attend weekend classes. Establish a 99% confidence on the acceptance by the student population of these new classes.

Solution:

n = sample size = 500, n_i = students in agreement with weekend classes = 120. The sample proportion is:

$$\hat{p} = \frac{n_i}{n} = \frac{120}{500} = 0.24$$

At 99% confidence, $z_{\alpha/2} = z_{0.005} = 2.58$

$$\hat{p} - z_{\alpha/2}\sigma_p < p < \hat{p} + z_{\alpha/2}\sigma_p$$

$$\hat{p} - z_{\alpha/2}\sqrt{\frac{\hat{p}(1-\hat{p})}{n}} < p < \hat{p} + z_{\alpha/2}\sqrt{\frac{\hat{p}(1-\hat{p})}{n}}$$

$$0.24 - 2.58\sqrt{\frac{0.24(1-0.24)}{500}} < p < 0.24 + 2.58\sqrt{\frac{0.24(1-0.24)}{500}}$$

$$0.24 - 0.0493 < p < 0.24 + 0.0493$$

$$0.191 < p < 0.289$$

This means that the 99% confidence interval of the student population approval proportion is from 19.1% to 28.9.

Example 8.18: In the example above, calculate the maximum sampling error. What is the sample size required to reduce this sampling error down to 10%?

Solution:

At a 99% confidence level, the confidence interval is: $p = 0.24 \pm 0.0493$
The maximum sampling error is:

$$Maximum\ sampling\ error = 100\left(\frac{E}{\hat{p}}\right) = 100\left(\frac{0.0493}{0.24}\right) = 20.54\%$$

Thus, the sample size of 500 is associated with a sampling error of 20.54%. The minimum sample size required for reducing this sampling error down to only 10% is calculated as follows:

At 10% sampling error, E value is 0.024 $(or\ 10(\frac{0.24}{100}))$. In other words, instead of a tolerance E of ± 0.0493, the new tolerance will be ± 0.024. In this case, we use the expression of sample size:

$$n = \hat{p}(1 - \hat{p})\left(\frac{Z}{E}\right)^2$$

$$n = 0.24(1 - 0.24)\left(\frac{2.58}{0.024}\right)^2 \approx 2108$$

The above result indicates that to reduce the sampling error down to 10%, the sample size must be increased from 500 to 2108 (or more than four times the current size).

Working Problem 8.15:

A large company surveyed a representative random sample of 600 people of its employee regarding a new retirement package. The result of this survey revealed that 235 of employee prefer the new retirement plan. Estimate the employee population proportion that would agree to the new retirement plan at 95% confidence.

Answer: Perform the calculations required to verify the answer below

Confidence interval - proportion

0.431 upper confidence limit
0.353 lower confidence limit

Working Problem 8.16:

A large company surveyed a representative random sample of 600 people of its employee regarding a new retirement package. The result of this survey revealed that 235 of employee prefer the new retirement plan. Calculate the maximum sampling error. What is the sample size required to reduce this sampling error down to half its value?

Answer:

The maximum sampling error is 9.96%

$n \approx 2408$

How to determine the sample size n if we do not know the value of $\hat{p}$?

The formula $n = \hat{p}(1 - \hat{p}) \left(\frac{z}{E}\right)^2$ assumes that we know the value of $\hat{p}$ in advance. In order to know p we should know n (since $\hat{p} = \frac{n_i}{n}$), which is what we are trying to calculate in the first place. What if we do not know the value of $\hat{p}$? In this case, we may follow one of two approaches:

(1) We may determine a preliminary value of $\hat{p}$, perhaps based on an initial study or early data

(2) We may start with a $\hat{p}$ value of 0.5. When $\hat{p} = 0.5$, the maximum value of $\hat{p}(1 - \hat{p}) = 0.25$ is obtained. Using the maximum value will give us the largest possible value of n for a given confidence level and a given margin of error E. Thus, $n = 0.25 \left(\frac{z}{E}\right)^2$

8.3.5 Correction for finite population: Finite-population correction factor

In the above sections, estimation was made based on the assumption that the population is very large or infinite. When a sample of size n is withdrawn from a finite population of size N, we should make the following correction to the standard error of the sample means and proportions:

Standard error for sample means:

$$\sigma_{\bar{X}} = \frac{\sigma_x}{\sqrt{n}} \sqrt{\frac{N - n}{N - 1}} \qquad (8.22)$$

where $\sigma_{\bar{X}}$ = the standard error, σ_x = the standard deviation of population, n = sample size, N is population size, and $\sqrt{\frac{N-n}{N-1}}$ is the correction factor.

In this case, the standard error for proportions is:

$$\sigma_p = \sqrt{\frac{\hat{p}(1 - \hat{p})}{n}} \sqrt{\frac{N - n}{N - 1}} \qquad (8.23)$$

where $\hat{p}$ = sample proportion, n = sample size, N = population size, and $\sqrt{\frac{N-n}{N-1}}$ is the correction factor.

Example 8.19: Calculate the correction factor for a finite population at sample size n of 100, and the following population sizes 200 and 1000. What is the effect of population size on the correction factor?

Solution:

The correction factor is $\sqrt{\frac{N-n}{N-1}}$

At $n = 100$, and $N = 200$, $\sqrt{\frac{N-n}{N-1}} = \sqrt{\frac{200-100}{200-1}} \approx 0.709$

At $n = 100$, and $N = 1000$, $\sqrt{\frac{N-n}{N-1}} = \sqrt{\frac{1000-100}{1000-1}} \approx 0.949$

The results indicate that as the population size increases, the correction factor increases approaching a value of 1.

Example 8.20: Calculate the correction factor for a finite population at a population size N of 1000, and samples n of 100 and 600. What is the effect of sample size on the correction factor?

Solution:

The correction factor is $\sqrt{\frac{N-n}{N-1}}$

At $n = 100$, and $N = 1000$, $\sqrt{\frac{N-n}{N-1}} = \sqrt{\frac{1000-100}{1000-1}} \approx 0.949$

At $n = 600$, and $N = 1000$, $\sqrt{\frac{N-n}{N-1}} = \sqrt{\frac{1000-600}{1000-1}} \approx 0.633$

As the sample size decreases, the correction factor increases approaching a value of 1.

Example 8.21: In a small town of only 600 people, a survey was made using a random sample of 200 people regarding annexing the town to an adjacent city. Eighty people agreed to the annexation action. Estimate the population proportion that would agree to the annexation at 95% confidence.

Solution:

n = Sample size = 200, n_i = People in agreement = 80. The sample proportion is:

$$\hat{p} = \frac{n_i}{n} = \frac{80}{200} = 0.4$$

At 95% confidence, $z_{\alpha/2} = z_{0.025} = 1.96$, the confidence interval on proportion is:

$$\hat{p} - z_{\alpha/2}\sigma_p < p < \hat{p} + z_{\alpha/2}\sigma_p$$

Since this is a finite population, we should use a correction factor to calculate σ_p:

$$\sigma_p = \sqrt{\frac{\hat{p}(1-\hat{p})}{n}} \sqrt{\frac{N-n}{N-1}} = \sqrt{\frac{0.4(1-0.4)}{200}} \sqrt{\frac{600-200}{600-1}} = 0.0346 \times 0.817 = 0.0283$$

$$\hat{p} - z_{\alpha/2}\sigma_p < p < \hat{p} + z_{\alpha/2}\sigma_p$$

$$0.40 - 1.96 \times 0.0283 < p < 0.40 + 1.96 \times 0.0283$$
$$0.40 - 0.0555 < p < 0.40 + 0.0555$$

$$0.3445 < p < 0.4555$$

This means that the 95% confidence interval of the town population approval proportion is from about 34.5% to about 45.5%. As a result, it is likely that the town will not approve the annexing action. Note that if we overlook the correction factor, our 95% estimation will be:

$$\hat{p} - z_{\alpha/2}\sigma_p < p < \hat{p} + z_{\alpha/2}\sigma_p$$

$$\hat{p} - z_{\alpha/2}\sqrt{\frac{\hat{p}(1-\hat{p})}{n}} < p < \hat{p} + z_{\alpha/2}\sqrt{\frac{\hat{p}(1-\hat{p})}{n}}$$

$$0.4 - 1.96\sqrt{\frac{0.4(1-0.4)}{200}} < p < 0.4 + 1.96\sqrt{\frac{0.4(1-0.4)}{200}}$$

$$0.4 - 0.068 < p < 0.4 + 0.068$$

$$0.332 < p < 0.468$$

Working Problem 8.17 :

To illustrate the effect of population and sample sizes on estimation, calculate the correction factors for finite population at different values of population size and sample size and develop a table of these factors. What is your conclusion regarding the effects of population and sample size on the correction factor?

Answer: Possible answer is as shown in the Table below. Complete the Table or develop a new one with different values of *n* and *N*.

n	N = 1000	N = 2000	N = 3000	N = 4000	N = 5000	N = 6000	N = 7000	N = 8000	N = 9000	N = 10000
100	0.949158	0.974923	0.983356	0.987544	0.990049	0.991714	0.992902	0.993792	0.994484	0.995037
200	0.894875	0.948921	0.966253	0.974801	0.979894	0.983274	0.985681	0.987483	0.988881	0.989999
300	....	....	....	....	....	....	....	....	....	....
400	....	....	....	....	....	....	....	....	....	....
500	....	....	....	....	....	....	....	....	....	....
600	....	....	....	....	....	....	....	....	....	....
700	....	....	....	....	....	....	....	....	....	....
800	0.447437	0.77479	0.856492	0.894539	0.916607	0.931027	0.941191	0.948743	0.954574	0.959214
900	0.316386	0.741805	0.8368	0.880451	0.905629	0.922031	0.93357	0.942131	0.948736	0.953987
1000	0	0.707284	0.816633	0.866134	0.894517	0.912947	0.925886	0.935473	0.942861	0.948731

Working Problem 8.18:

In a social club of 800 members, a survey was made using a random sample of 200 members regarding the addition of a bowling alley at an extra membership fee of $50 per year. 130 members agreed to this addition. Estimate the member population proportion that would agree to the addition at 99% confidence. Perform estimation with and without corrections for finite population and compare the answers.

Answer:
Without: $0.56299 < p < 0.73701$
With: $0.5746 < p < 0.7754$
As you can see, ignoring the correction factor will result in a wider tolerance and a more relaxed estimation for the same confidence level. This is a result of the larger standard error when correction is ignored.

8.4 Using software programs to perform estimation

Most of the analyses presented in this chapter can be performed using many commercial software programs and self-explanatory procedures. In this section, we discuss some examples in which Microsoft Excel® is used.

Example 8.22: The data in Table 8.4 represents the ages of a sample of students selected randomly from a college population. Assuming the variable age is normally-distributed; find a 95% and 99% confidence interval on student age in the college population.

Table 8.4 Students Ages

Student no.	Student's age	Student no.	Student's age
1	20	11	22
2	21	12	23
3	19	13	25
4	20	14	25
5	21	15	23
6	18	16	22
7	17	17	21
8	17	18	20
9	19	19	20
10	21	20	20

The step-by-step solution to find a 95% confidence interval using Microsoft Excel® Data Analysis is shown in Figures 8.7 through 8.9. These steps are summarized below.
Step 1: Go to Microsoft Excel® 'Data Analysis,' and select 'Descriptive Statistics'
Step 2: Press 'Ok'
Step 3: Assign the input range, which is the column of student age data.
Step 4: Assign a confidence level (95% is the default)
Step 5: Press 'Ok'

Figure 8.9 shows the output resulting from the above steps. Note the cell titled 'Confidence Level (95%)' giving a value of 1.042. This value is the margin of error of the estimation. Using this value and the mean value (the two shaded cells), you can establish the 95% confidence interval as illustrated in Figure 8.9.

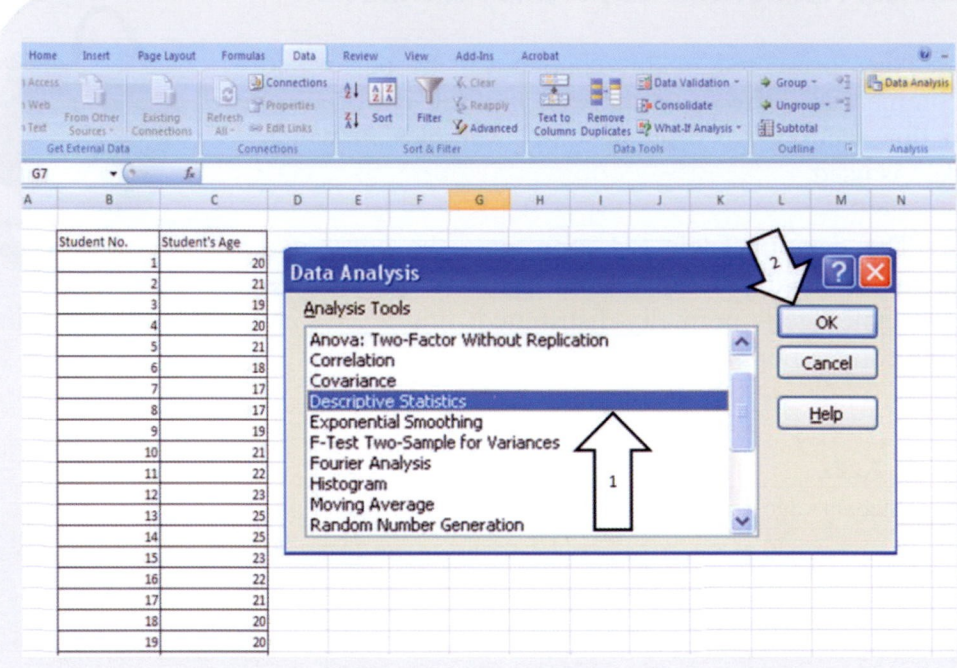

Figure 8.7 Using Excel® to perform estimation analysis- Steps 1 & 2

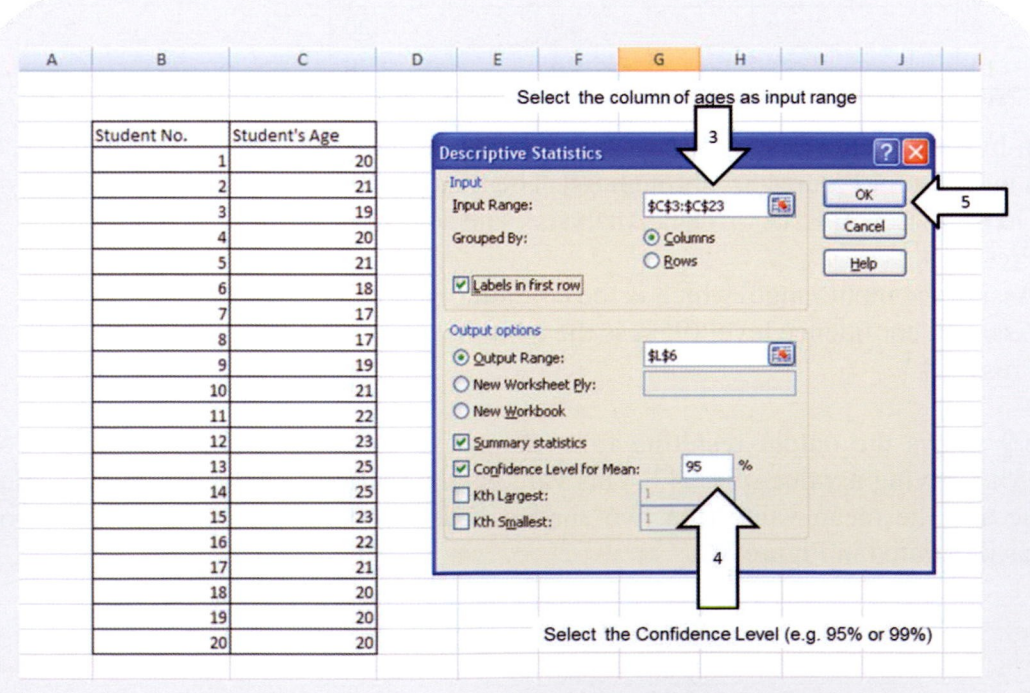

Figure 8.8 Using Excel® to perform estimation analysis- Steps 3,4,and 5

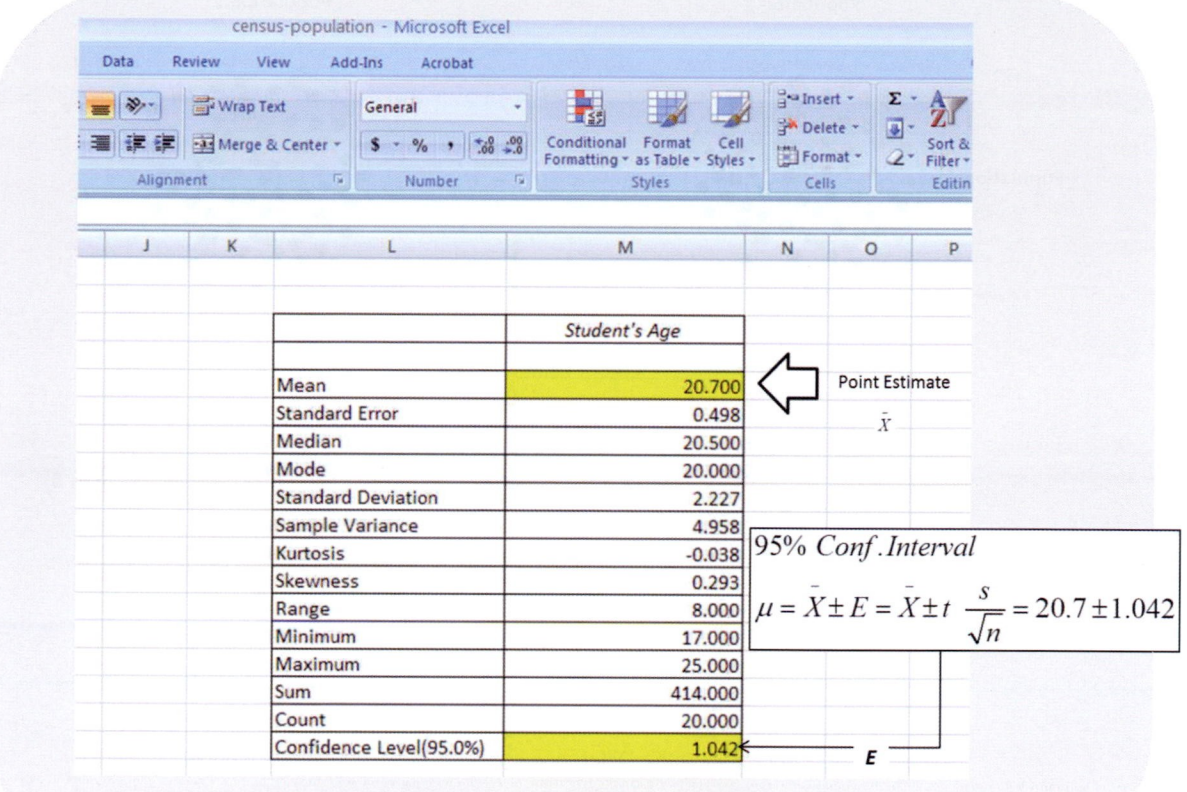

Figure 8.9 Using Excel® to perform estimation analysis: Output

8.5 Confidence intervals of the difference between two means

8.5.1 Case I: Population variances known

In many practical situations, we are required to estimate the difference between the means of two populations, $'\mu_1 - \mu_2.'$ The point estimate in this case is the sample mean difference, $'\bar{X}_1 - \bar{X}_2'$, and the general formula for estimating the population mean will be as follows:

$$\mu_1 - \mu_2 = (\bar{X}_1 - \bar{X}_2) \pm E \qquad (8.24)$$

where E is the margin of error.

In light of the above equation, it will be important to draw a sample from each of the two populations, determine the mean and standard deviation of the variable in each sample, and use these statistics to estimate the difference in population means as shown in Figure 8.10.

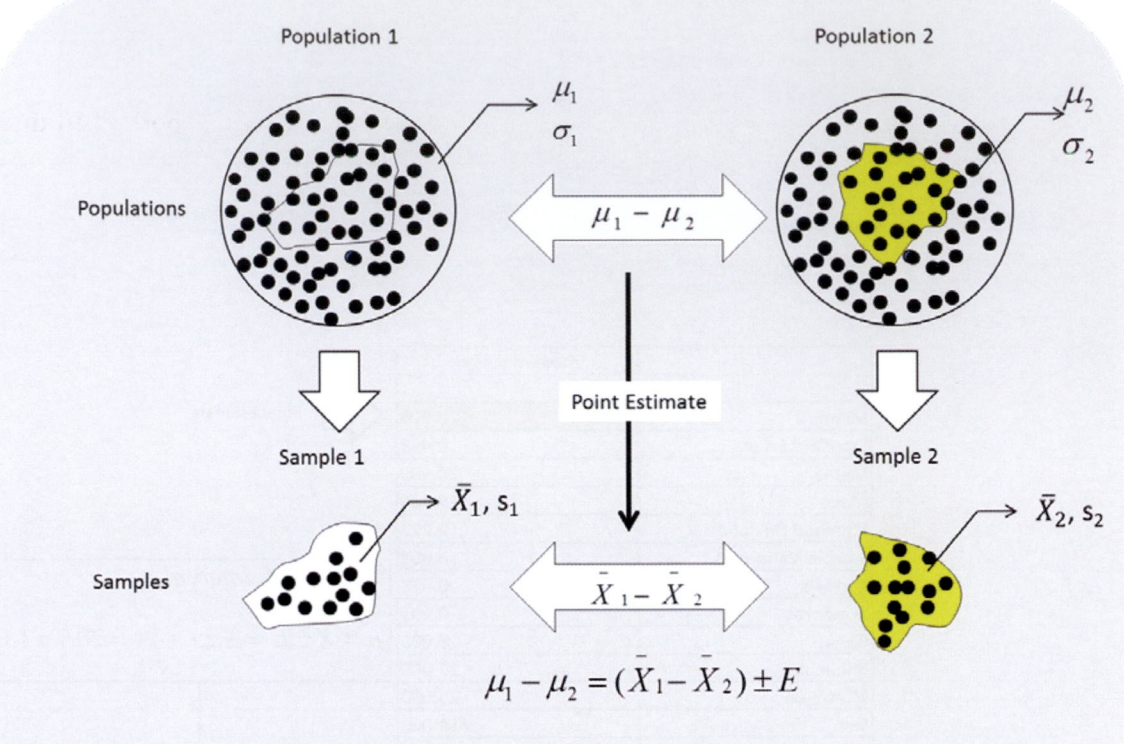

Figure 8.10 Estimation of the Difference between Two Populations Means

If the variances of the two populations, σ_1^2 and σ_2^2, are known, the confidence interval on the difference between population means is given by:

Two-Sided:

$$\mu_1 - \mu_2 = (\bar{X}_1 - \bar{X}_2) \pm z_{\alpha/2}\sqrt{\frac{\sigma_1^2}{n_1} + \frac{\sigma_2^2}{n_2}}$$

or

$$(\bar{X}_1 - \bar{X}_2) - z_{\alpha/2}\sqrt{\frac{\sigma_1^2}{n_1} + \frac{\sigma_2^2}{n_2}} < \mu_1 - \mu_2 < (\bar{X}_1 - \bar{X}_2) + z_{\alpha/2}\sqrt{\frac{\sigma_1^2}{n_1} + \frac{\sigma_2^2}{n_2}} \qquad (8.25)$$

One-Sided:

$$(\bar{X}_1 - \bar{X}_2) - z_{\alpha}\sqrt{\frac{\sigma_1^2}{n_1} + \frac{\sigma_2^2}{n_2}} < \mu_1 - \mu_2 \qquad (8.26.\,a)$$

$$\mu_1 - \mu_2 < (\bar{X}_1 - \bar{X}_2) + z_{\alpha}\sqrt{\frac{\sigma_1^2}{n_1} + \frac{\sigma_2^2}{n_2}} \qquad (8.26.\,b)$$

where $\bar{X}_1$ = the mean of the sample from the first population, $\bar{X}_2$ = the mean of the sample from the second population, n_1 = the size of the sample from the first population, n_2 = the size of the sample from the second population, $\sigma_1{}^2$ = variance of the first population, and $\sigma_2{}^2$ = variance of the second population

Before proceeding with the applications of the above estimation, it will be important to discuss the underlying concepts of the confidence interval of mean difference. Suppose you have two populations that you are withdrawing samples from for the sake of comparing the two population means. A key question is what would be the characteristics of the sampling distribution of the mean difference?

When the samples are large, and according to the Central Limit theorem, the sampling distribution of mean difference will follow a normal distribution with mean value and standard deviation expressed as follow:

$$\mu_{\bar{X}_1 - \bar{X}_2} = \mu_{\bar{X}_1} - \mu_{\bar{X}_2} = \mu_1 - \mu_2 \tag{8.27}$$

$$\sigma_{\bar{X}_1 - \bar{X}_2} = \sqrt{\sigma_{\bar{X}_1}{}^2 + \sigma_{\bar{X}_2}{}^2} = \sqrt{\frac{\sigma_1{}^2}{n_1} + \frac{\sigma_2{}^2}{n_2}} \tag{8.28}$$

Figure 8.11 illustrates the above points. Note that $\sigma_{\bar{X}_1 - \bar{X}_2}$ is the standard error or the standard deviation of the mean difference.

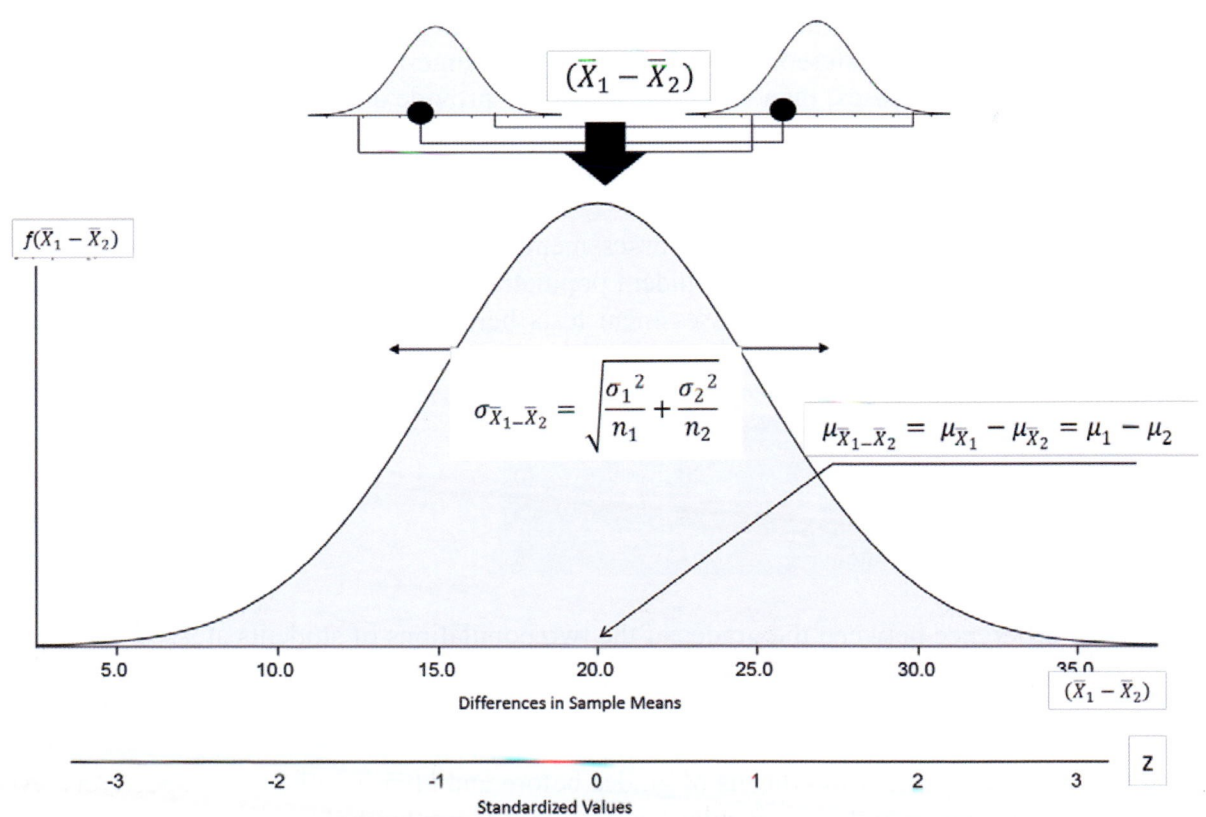

Figure 8.11 Sampling Distribution of Mean Differences

Example 8.23: Two cities were compared with respect to property taxes. From City A, a random sample of 200 houses was selected and it was found that the average property tax was $5400. From City B, a random sample of 300 houses was selected and it was found that the average property tax was $4200. If it is known that the population standard deviations for property tax of these two cities are $400 and $900 respectively, establish a 95% confidence interval on the difference between these two population means.

Solution:

Let μ_A and μ_B be the population means of property tax of the two cities. Also let σ_A and σ_B be the population standard deviations of property tax of the two towns. Since σ_A and σ_B are known, we estimate the difference using the following equation:

$$\mu_A - \mu_B = (\bar{X}_A - \bar{X}_B) \pm z_{\alpha/2} \sqrt{\frac{\sigma_A^2}{n_A} + \frac{\sigma_B^2}{n_B}}$$

$$\mu_A - \mu_B = (5400 - 4200) \pm 1.96 \sqrt{\frac{400^2}{200} + \frac{900^2}{300}}$$

$$\mu_A - \mu_B = 1200 \pm 115.96$$

The above results indicate that the property tax in City A is significantly higher than that of City B with an estimated point difference of $1200 or with a range from $1084 to $1316. If the two cities have comparable houses, then living in city B will provide an annual relief of property tax of over $1000. Other factors should be considered before one decides to live in the second city. These may include: schools, closeness to work, environment, etc.

Example 8.24: As a result of changing the assessment mechanism of a social statistics course, it was important to compare the grades of student populations before and after the change. Using a sample of 40 students who took the assessment tests before and after the change, the average results were as follow:

	Before	After
n	40	40
Average Score	85	80
Standard deviation	5	5

Estimate the difference between the grades of the two populations of students at 99% confidence.

Solution:

Let μ_B and μ_A be the population means of grades before and after the change, respectively. Also let σ_B and σ_A be the population standard deviations of grades before and after the change, respectively. We estimate the difference using the following equation:

$$\mu_A - \mu_B = (\bar{X}_A - \bar{X}_B) \pm z_{\alpha/2} \sqrt{\frac{\sigma_A^2}{n_A} + \frac{\sigma_B^2}{n_B}}$$

Since σ_B and σ_A are unknown, we can use the samples standard deviations instead, s_B and s_A

$$\mu_A - \mu_B = (80 - 85) \pm 2.58 \sqrt{\frac{5^2}{40} + \frac{5^2}{40}}$$

$$\mu_A - \mu_B = 5 \pm 2.885$$

Working Problem 8.19:

Two manufacturing organizations, A and B, making the same product were compared with respect to the annual salaries of manufacturing workers. From organization A, a random sample of 150 workers was selected and it was found that the average annual salary was 25,000. From Organization B, a random sample of 100 workers was selected and it was found that the average annual salary was also $25,000 . If it is known that the population standard deviations of annual salary of these two organizations are $2000 and $5000, respectively, establish a 95% confidence interval on the difference between these two population means.

Answer:

The range of difference between the two organizations is from -1030.94 to + 1030.94 in 95% of the workers.

8.5.2 Case II: Population variances unknown

When the variances of the two populations, σ_1^2 and σ_2^2 are unknown, we assume that the characteristics of the two populations are normally distributed. In this case, the confidence intervals on the mean difference are:

Two-Sided:

$$(\bar{X}_1 - \bar{X}_2) - t_{(df,\frac{\alpha}{2})} \, S_p \sqrt{\frac{1}{n_1} + \frac{1}{n_2}} < \mu_1 - \mu_2$$

$$< (\bar{X}_1 - \bar{X}_2) + t_{(df,\frac{\alpha}{2})} \, S_p \sqrt{\frac{1}{n_1} + \frac{1}{n_2}} \qquad (8.29)$$

where $\bar{X}_1$ = the mean of the sample from the first population, $\bar{X}_2$ = the mean of the sample from the second population, n_1= the size of the sample from the first population, n_2= the size of the sample from the second population, df = the degree of freedom = n_1+n_2-2, $t_{df,\,\alpha/2}$ = the t-value at $\alpha/2$ and degree of freedom df, and S_p = pooled standard deviation

One-Sided:

$$(\bar{X}_1 - \bar{X}_2) - t_{(df,\propto)} \ S_p \sqrt{\frac{1}{n_1} + \frac{1}{n_2}} < \mu_1 - \mu_2 \ \& $$

$$\mu_1 - \mu_2 < (\bar{X}_1 - \bar{X}_2) + t_{(df,\propto)} \ S_p \sqrt{\frac{1}{n_1} + \frac{1}{n_2}} \qquad (8.30)$$

The pooled standard deviation, S_p, is given by:

$$S_p = \sqrt{\frac{(n_1 - 1)s_1{}^2 + (n_2 - 1)s_2{}^2}{n_1 + n_2 - 2}} \qquad (8.31)$$

where n_1= the size of the sample from the first population, n_2= the size of the sample from the second population, $s_1{}^2$ = variance of the first sample, $s_2{}^2$ = variance of the second sample. Note that we find the *t* value at degrees of freedom *df* of $n_1 + n_2$ -2 from the t-Table in Table 8.A.I, Appendix 8.A.

Example 8.25: The absorption capacity of soil material is defined by the maximum amount of water that will soak into the aggregate pores. Suppose a civil engineer is in a position to estimate the difference between the mean values of the maximum absorption capacity of two different soft soils say, limestone and dolomite. Summary of the statistics associated with each soil type is given below.

Statistic	Limestone	Dolomite
Mean	$\bar{X}_1 = 0.9$	$\bar{X}_2 = 1.1$
Standard deviation	$s_1 = 0.03$	$s_2 = 0.09$
n	$n_1 = 10$ tests	$n_2 = 10$ tests

Determine the confidence interval on the difference at 99% confidence level.

Solution:

This example represents a classic case of small sample with unknown population means and variances. Accordingly, we use the case for population variances unknown to estimate the mean difference. In this case, we assume that the populations of the two soil types have a common variance, and calculate the pooled standard deviation as follows:

$$S_p = \sqrt{\frac{(n_1 - 1)s_1{}^2 + (n_2 - 1)s_2{}^2}{n_1 + n_2 - 2}} = \sqrt{\frac{(9)(0.03)^2 + (9)(0.09)^2}{18}} = 0.06708$$

At a 99% confidence, $t_{df,\,\alpha/2} = t_{18,0.005} = 2.878$ (Appendix 8.A). Note that the degree of freedom, $df = n_1 + n_2 - 2 = 10 + 10 - 2 = 18$. The confidence interval on the difference between the means of the two populations is:

$$(\bar{X}_1 - \bar{X}_2) - t_{(df,\frac{\alpha}{2})}\, S_p \sqrt{\frac{1}{n_1} + \frac{1}{n_2}} < \mu_1 - \mu_2 < (\bar{X}_1 - \bar{X}_2) + t_{(df,\frac{\alpha}{2})}\, S_p \sqrt{\frac{1}{n_1} + \frac{1}{n_2}}$$

$$(1.1 - 0.9) - 2.878\,(0.06708)\sqrt{\frac{1}{10} + \frac{1}{10}} < \mu_1 - \mu_2$$

$$< (1.1 - 0.9) + 2.878\,(0.06708)\sqrt{\frac{1}{10} + \frac{1}{10}}$$

$$0.113663 < \mu_1 - \mu_2 < 0.286337$$

This example illustrates that the difference in the absorption capacity between the two soil types may be as low as 0.114 or as high as 0.286 in 99% of the time.

Working Problem 8.20:

Establish a 99% confidence interval on the difference between two quiz grades represented by the statistics shown below.

Statistics of Two Quiz Grades

Statistic	Quiz 1	Quiz 2
Mean	81%	85%
Std. Dev	$s_1 = 2$	$s_2 = 5$
n	$n_1 = 20$	$n_2 = 20$

Answer: Sp = 3.808, $0.744 < \mu_1 - \mu_2 < 7.256$

8.6 Confidence intervals on variance or standard deviation
8.6.1. The Chi-Square (χ^2) distribution

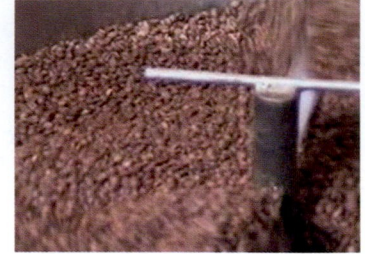

In the sections above, we discussed the methods of establishing confidence intervals of population mean, proportion, and mean difference. In some situations, we may wish to establish confidence intervals of a measure of dispersion or variability such as the variance or standard deviation. Examples of this type of analysis include:

- When we deal with mixing problems of coffee or fibers we would be more concerned about the mix homogeneity or the mix variance.

- Social mixing and team formations are associated with characteristics that require estimation of their variability.

- Teaching students of a wide range of qualification (by virtue of age, years since high-school graduation, etc.) requires estimation of the variability in the performance of those students (variability in grade, retention, years in school, etc.).

The most common way to establish a confidence interval on variance or standard deviation is to use the Chi-square χ^2 distribution (pronounced 'kigh;' rhymes with sky). Basic properties of this distribution are listed below.

Basic Properties of Chi-Square (χ^2) Distribution

- The chi-squared (χ^2) distribution is an asymmetrical distribution that has a shape determined by the degree of freedom
- As the number of degree of freedom increases, the chi-square distribution becomes more nearly symmetric. Degree of freedom = n -1
- The total area under a χ^2-curve equals 1.
- A χ^2-curve starts at 0 on the horizontal axis and extends indefinitely to the right, approaching, but never touching, the horizontal axis as it does so.
- A χ^2-curve is right skewed.

The χ^2-distribution has a special shape represented by a right-skewed curve for low values of sample size and it becomes more symmetrical as the sample size or degree of freedom increases. Figure 8.12 illustrates a number of Chi-Square distributions varied in shape by the degree of freedom (n-1). Table 8.A.II, Appendix 8.A provides values of $\chi^2_{df,\alpha}$ at different degrees of freedom and areas. Some of the characteristics of this distribution are discussed in Appendix 8.B.II. The example below illustrates how the χ^2 values are determined.

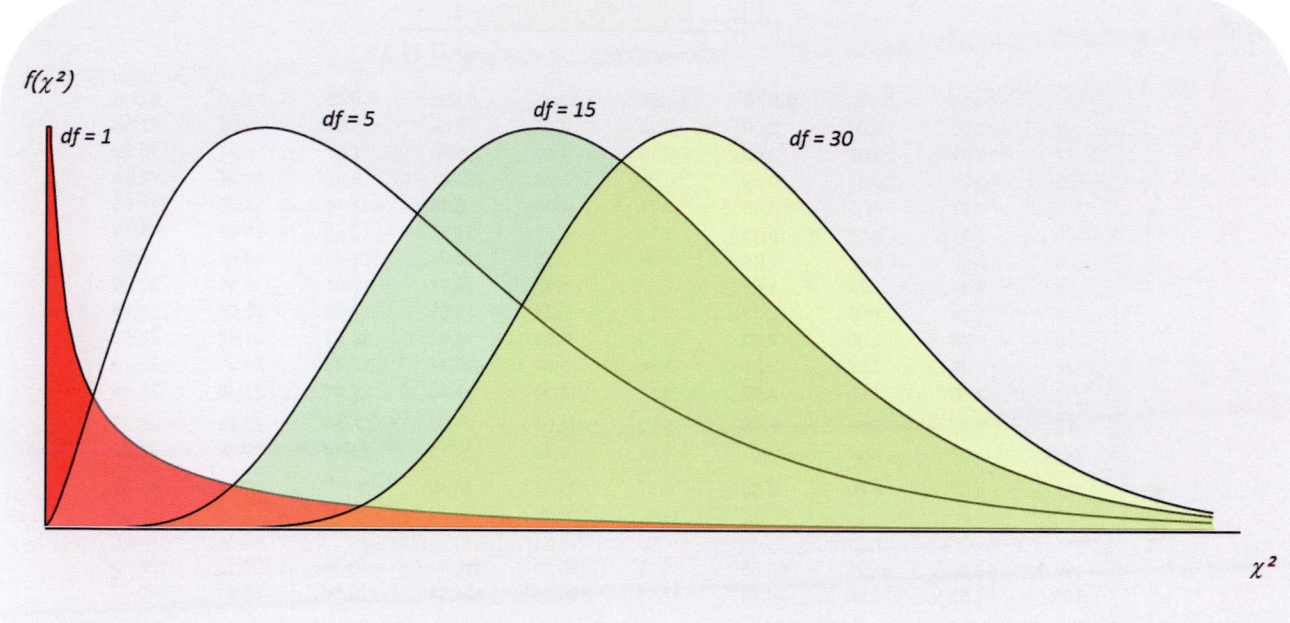

Figure 8.12 χ^2 Distributions at different Degrees of Freedom

Example 8.26: Find the critical values of χ^2 that separate the middle 95% of the chi-square distribution from the 2.5% area in each tail, assuming 12 degrees of freedom.

Solution:

Figure 8.13 presents the χ^2 that with 12 degrees of freedom and shows the locations of the critical values. The χ^2 Table is constructed as follows:

- The values of the area in the right tail of the χ^2 distribution first row are listed in the first row.
- The values of the degree of freedom are listed in the first column
- The values of χ^2 are listed in the body of the table.

The critical values of χ^2 that separate the middle 95% of the chi-square distribution from the 2.5% area in each tail are found by locating the value of 12 degrees of freedom in the first column, then going to the right to locate the χ^2 value under 0.975 (4.40) and the of χ^2 under 0.025 (23.34). In other words, the χ^2 are found at the intersection of the row corresponding to 12 degrees of freedom and the columns corresponding to 0.975 and 0.025.

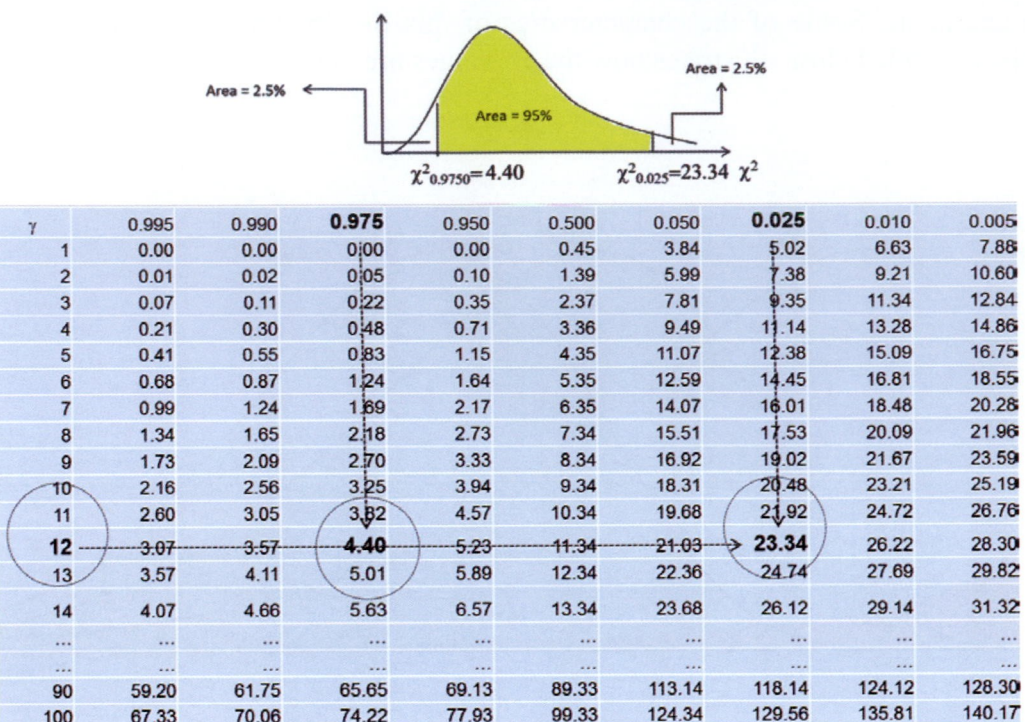

γ	0.995	0.990	**0.975**	0.950	0.500	0.050	**0.025**	0.010	0.005
1	0.00	0.00	0.00	0.00	0.45	3.84	5.02	6.63	7.88
2	0.01	0.02	0.05	0.10	1.39	5.99	7.38	9.21	10.60
3	0.07	0.11	0.22	0.35	2.37	7.81	9.35	11.34	12.84
4	0.21	0.30	0.48	0.71	3.36	9.49	11.14	13.28	14.86
5	0.41	0.55	0.83	1.15	4.35	11.07	12.38	15.09	16.75
6	0.68	0.87	1.24	1.64	5.35	12.59	14.45	16.81	18.55
7	0.99	1.24	1.69	2.17	6.35	14.07	16.01	18.48	20.28
8	1.34	1.65	2.18	2.73	7.34	15.51	17.53	20.09	21.96
9	1.73	2.09	2.70	3.33	8.34	16.92	19.02	21.67	23.59
10	2.16	2.56	3.25	3.94	9.34	18.31	20.48	23.21	25.19
11	2.60	3.05	3.82	4.57	10.34	19.68	21.92	24.72	26.76
12	3.07	3.57	**4.40**	5.23	11.34	21.03	**23.34**	26.22	28.30
13	3.57	4.11	5.01	5.89	12.34	22.36	24.74	27.69	29.82
14	4.07	4.66	5.63	6.57	13.34	23.68	26.12	29.14	31.32
...	...	...	...	...	...	...	...	...	...
...	...	...	...	...	...	...	...	...	...
90	59.20	61.75	65.65	69.13	89.33	113.14	118.14	124.12	128.30
100	67.33	70.06	74.22	77.93	99.33	124.34	129.56	135.81	140.17

Figure 8.13 Chi-Squared values at df = 12

Working problem 8.21:
This working problem will help students practicing finding the values of χ^2 at different areas and different degrees of freedom.
Q1: Find the critical values for a 95% confidence interval using the χ^2 distribution with 18 degrees of freedom.
Q2: Find the critical values for a 99% confidence interval using the χ^2 distribution with 25 degrees of freedom.
Q3: Find the critical values for a 95% confidence interval using the χ^2 distribution with 2 degrees of freedom.

Answer: Q1: 8.23, 31.53, Q2: 10.52, 46.93, Q3: 0.05, 7.38

8.6.2. The use of Chi-Square (χ^2) distribution for establishing confidence intervals on variance or standard deviation

Confidence intervals for variances and standard deviations follow a different pattern than those discussed earlier for means and proportions. In case of means and proportions, we were required to determine a point estimate, a critical value, and a standard error value. In case of variances or standard deviations, we are required to establish a point estimate and two critical values. The point estimate is the sample variance, s^2, and the critical values come from the χ^2 distribution as discussed above. Figure 8.14 illustrates these differences.

The key condition for establishing confidence on the population variance is the assumption of normality; that is the characteristic in the parent population follows a normal distribution. The simplest way to establish confidence on the variance is to collect a random sample of size, n, calculate the sample variance, s^2, and find the critical values , $\chi^2_{1-\alpha/2}$ and , $\chi^2_{\alpha/2}$ using the χ^2

distribution with $n-1$ degrees of freedom. Given these values, we compute the lower and upper confidence bounds:

Lower bound $= \dfrac{(n-1)s^2}{\chi^2_{\frac{\alpha}{2}}}$

Upper bound $= \dfrac{(n-1)s^2}{\chi^2_{1-\frac{\alpha}{2}}}$

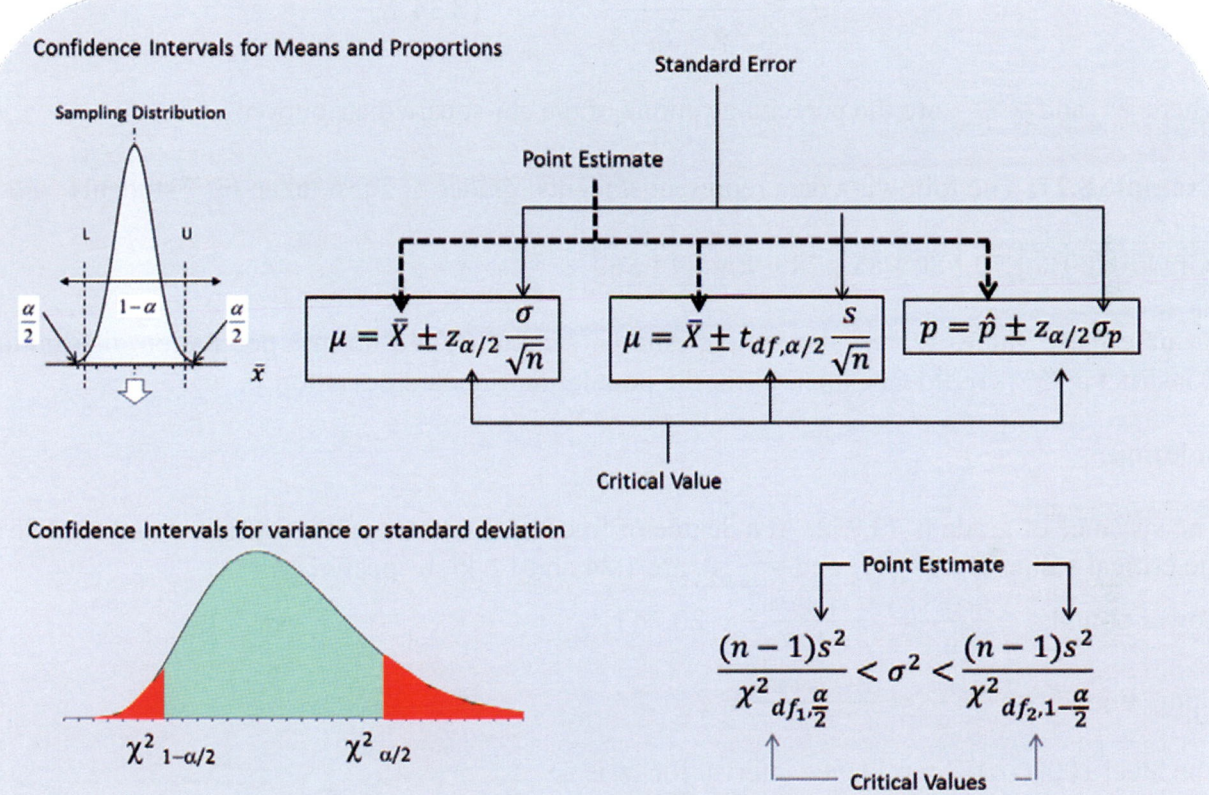

Figure 8.14 Differences between Confidence Intervals for Means and Confidence Intervals for Variances

The level $100(1-\alpha)\%$ confidence interval for σ^2 is

$$\frac{(n-1)s^2}{\chi^2_{\frac{\alpha}{2}}} < \sigma^2 < \frac{(n-1)s^2}{\chi^2_{1-\frac{\alpha}{2}}} \qquad (8.32)$$

The level $100(1-\alpha)\%$ confidence interval for σ is

$$\sqrt{\frac{(n-1)s^2}{\chi^2_{\frac{\alpha}{2}}}} < \sigma < \sqrt{\frac{(n-1)s^2}{\chi^2_{1-\frac{\alpha}{2}}}} \qquad (8.33)$$

479

Where n = sample size, s^2 = sample variance, σ^2 = population variance

The lower and upper (1- α) % confidence interval on the variance is given by:

$$\frac{(n-1)s^2}{\chi^2_{\alpha}} < \sigma^2 \qquad (8.34.\,a)$$

$$\sigma^2 < \frac{(n-1)s^2}{\chi^2_{1-\alpha}} \qquad (8.34.\,b)$$

where χ^2_{α} and $\chi^2_{1-\alpha}$ are the percentage points of the chi-square distribution.

Example 8.27: The following data represent students' grades of a test taken by 7 students

Grades/100%	70	80	85	78	90	89	86

Assume these values represent a simple random sample from a normal population distribution. Construct a 95% confidence interval for the population standard deviation σ.

Solution:

The variance of grade is 49.952. At a degree of freedom 7 - 1 = 6, and a confidence level of 95%, the critical values are $\chi^2_{0.975}$ and $\chi^2_{0.025}$ are 1.24 and 14.45, respectively.

Lower bound = $\frac{(n-1)s^2}{\chi^2_{\frac{\alpha}{2}}} = \frac{(7-1)49.952}{14.45} = 20.741$

Upper bound = $\frac{(n-1)s^2}{\chi^2_{1-\frac{\alpha}{2}}} = \frac{(7-1)49.952}{1.24} = 241.7$

The level $100(1-\alpha)\%$ confidence interval for σ^2 is

$$\frac{(n-1)s^2}{\chi^2_{\frac{\alpha}{2}}} < \sigma^2 < \frac{(n-1)s^2}{\chi^2_{1-\frac{\alpha}{2}}}$$

$$or\ 20.741 < \sigma^2 < 241.29$$

The confidence interval for σ is $4.554 < \sigma < 15.53$

Example 8.28: The following data represents percent values of polyester fiber in a cotton/polyester blend.

Percent of Polyester in the blend:

42	45	38	43	41	40	38	44	41	30	40	40	42	37	44	42	39	38	39	40

Assume these values represent a simple random sample from a normal population distribution. Construct a 99% confidence interval for the population standard deviation σ.

Solution:

The variance of grade is 10.660. At a degree of freedom 20 - 1 = 19, and a confidence level of 99%, the critical values are $\chi^2_{0.995}$ and $\chi^2_{0.005}$ are 6.84 and 38.58, respectively.

Lower bound $= \dfrac{(n-1)s^2}{\chi^2_{\frac{\alpha}{2}}} = \dfrac{(20-1)10.660}{38.58} = 5.25$

Upper bound $= \dfrac{(n-1)s^2}{\chi^2_{1-\frac{\alpha}{2}}} = \dfrac{(20-1)10.660}{6.84} = 29.61$

The level $100(1-\alpha)\%$ confidence interval for σ^2 is

$$\frac{(n-1)s^2}{\chi^2_{\frac{\alpha}{2}}} < \sigma^2 < \frac{(n-1)s^2}{\chi^2_{1-\frac{\alpha}{2}}}$$
$$or \; 5.25 \; < \sigma^2 < 29.61$$

The confidence interval for σ is
$$2.29 \; < \sigma < 5.44$$

Before you start solving problems review this:

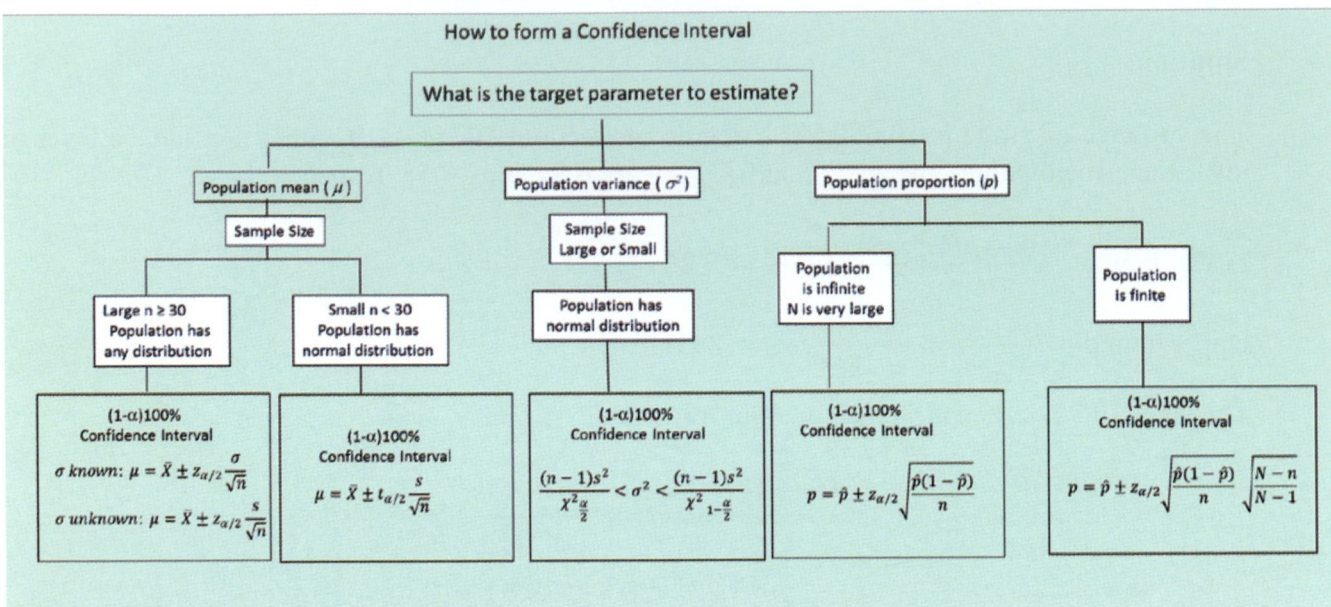

How to form a Confidence Interval

What is the target parameter to estimate?

Population mean (μ)

Sample Size

Large n ≥ 30
Population has
any distribution

Small n < 30
Population has
normal distribution

(1-α)100%
Confidence Interval

σ known: $\mu = \bar{X} \pm z_{\alpha/2}\dfrac{\sigma}{\sqrt{n}}$

σ unknown: $\mu = \bar{X} \pm z_{\alpha/2}\dfrac{s}{\sqrt{n}}$

(1-α)100%
Confidence Interval

$\mu = \bar{X} \pm t_{\alpha/2}\dfrac{s}{\sqrt{n}}$

Population variance (σ^2)

Sample Size
Large or Small

Population has
normal distribution

(1-α)100%
Confidence Interval

$\dfrac{(n-1)s^2}{\chi^2_{\frac{\alpha}{2}}} < \sigma^2 < \dfrac{(n-1)s^2}{\chi^2_{1-\frac{\alpha}{2}}}$

Population proportion (p)

Population
is infinite
N is very large

(1-α)100%
Confidence Interval

$p = \hat{p} \pm z_{\alpha/2}\sqrt{\dfrac{\hat{p}(1-\hat{p})}{n}}$

Population
Is finite

(1-α)100%
Confidence Interval

$p = \hat{p} \pm z_{\alpha/2}\sqrt{\dfrac{\hat{p}(1-\hat{p})}{n}}\sqrt{\dfrac{N-n}{N-1}}$

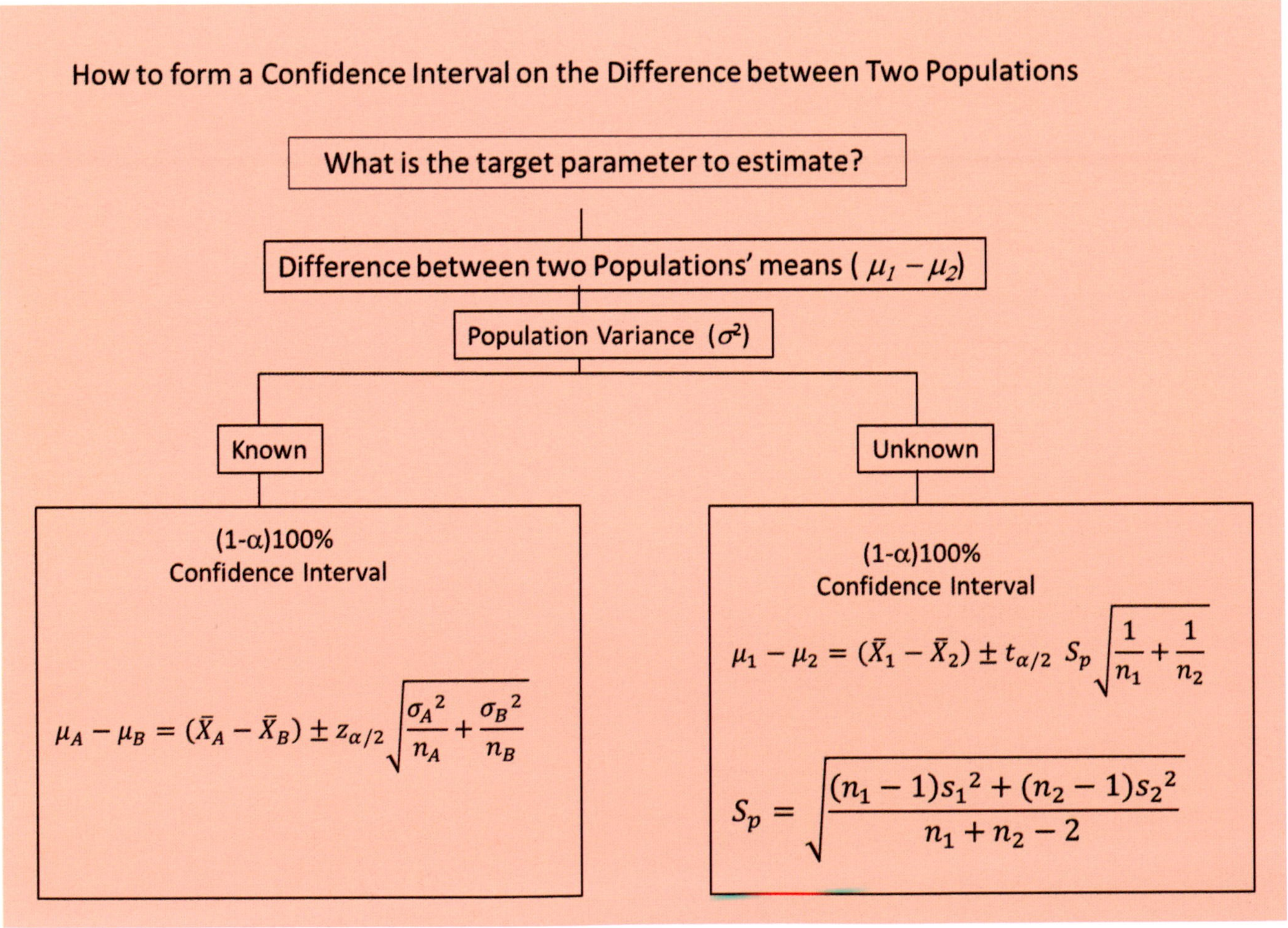

How to form a Confidence Interval on the Difference between Two Populations

What is the target parameter to estimate?

Difference between two Populations' means ($\mu_1 - \mu_2$)

Population Variance (σ^2)

Known

(1-α)100%
Confidence Interval

$$\mu_A - \mu_B = (\bar{X}_A - \bar{X}_B) \pm z_{\alpha/2}\sqrt{\dfrac{\sigma_A^2}{n_A} + \dfrac{\sigma_B^2}{n_B}}$$

Unknown

(1-α)100%
Confidence Interval

$$\mu_1 - \mu_2 = (\bar{X}_1 - \bar{X}_2) \pm t_{\alpha/2}\, S_p\sqrt{\dfrac{1}{n_1} + \dfrac{1}{n_2}}$$

$$S_p = \sqrt{\dfrac{(n_1-1)s_1^2 + (n_2-1)s_2^2}{n_1 + n_2 - 2}}$$

8.7 Review Exercises

P8.1: A real estate agent collected a random sample of houses in a certain area and found that the average house price of this sample of houses is $350,000. What is the point estimate of the price of the population of houses in this area?
Answer: $350,000

P8.2: Suppose we wish to estimate the mean of the weight of many players being selected for a football team. We took a sample of 10 players randomly and measured their weights in pounds and obtained the following observations:

160	168	200	145	180	220	210	176	210	220

   (a) Determine the mean, the mode, the median, the range, the standard deviation and the variance of the data.
   (b) Determine a point estimate of μ (the mean of the population of player's weight).

P8.3: Suppose we wish to estimate the mean of the property tax of houses in a certain area from a sample of 32 houses with the values listed below. What is the point estimate of the population of houses in this area?

Property tax of a 32 house sample

House #	Annual Tax ($)	House #	Annual Tax ($)	House #	Annual Tax ($)	House #	Annual Tax ($)
1	18000	9	4300	17	5600	25	2900
2	12000	10	8000	18	8200	26	11300
3	7000	11	7100	19	10300	27	10250
4	6500	12	12000	20	6500	28	7000
5	7200	13	11000	21	12900	39	5200
6	12000	14	10200	22	11000	30	6890
7	12100	15	11000	23	2800	31	7210
8	8000	16	8000	24	4580	32	11000

Answer: $8688.44

P8.4: Body temperatures taken for a random sample of 300 people yielded an average of 98.0°F, and standard deviation of 0.50°F, Use this sample to find the best point estimate and interval estimate of the population mean of all body temperatures at 95% confidence.

P8.5: Body temperatures taken for a random sample of 300 people yielded an average of 98.0°F, and standard deviation of 0.50°F, Use this sample to find the best point estimate and interval estimate of the population mean of all body temperatures at 99% confidence.
Answer: 97.926, 98.074

P8.6: Suppose thirty students were selected randomly from a college for the purpose of estimating the average grade of a Math assessment test of the whole college. The data of grade values are shown below. Assuming the grade of the parent population is normally distributed. Find a 95% and a 99% confidence interval for the mean grade, μ, of all students.

Student grade values of assessment test

Student ID	Grade (%)	Student ID	Grade (%)	Student ID	Grade (%)
1	88	11	56	21	90
2	77	12	76	22	89
3	68	13	91	23	71
4	80	14	82	24	80
5	81	15	80	25	80
6	82	16	80	26	69
7	77	17	73	27	92
8	72	18	72	28	88
9	70	19	61	29	87
10	62	20	79	30	70

P8.7: Body temperatures taken for a random sample of 500 people yielded an average of 98.2°F, and standard deviation of 0.65°F, Use this sample to find the best point estimate and interval estimate of the population mean of all body temperatures at 95% confidence.
Answer: 98.143, 98.257

P8.8: Body temperatures taken for a random sample of 500 people yielded an average of 98.2°F, and standard deviation of 0.65°F, Use this sample to find the best point estimate and interval estimate of the population mean of all body temperatures at 90% confidence.

P8.9: Assume that we want to estimate the mean IQ score for the population of statistics' professors. How many statistics professors must be randomly selected for IQ tests if we know that the standard deviation of IQ is 12 and we want 95% confidence that the sample mean is within 3 IQ points of the population mean?
Answer: 63 (after rounding up)

P8.10: Assume that we want to estimate the mean IQ score for the population of statistics professors. How many statistics professors must be randomly selected for IQ tests if we know that the standard deviation of IQ is 15 and we want 99% confidence that the sample mean is within 2 IQ points of the population mean?

P8.11: Assume that we want to estimate the mean IQ score for the population of statistics professors. How many statistics professors must be randomly selected for IQ tests if we Know that the standard deviation of IQ is 15 and we want 90% confidence that the sample mean is within 2 IQ points of the population mean?
Answer: 153 (after rounding up)

P8.12: Use the given confidence level and sample data to find (a) the margin of error E and (b) a confidence interval for estimating the population of

   a. Salaries of science professor: 95% confidence, $n = 300$, $\bar{X} = \$60{,}000$ and $\sigma = \$15{,}000$
   b. Property tax: 99% confidence, $n = 26$, $\bar{X} = \$6{,}000$ and $\sigma = \$1500$
   c. Male height: 90% confidence, $n = 20$, $\bar{X} = 160\ cm$ and $\sigma = 4\ cm$
   d. Baby at birth weight: 95% confidence, $n = 22$, $\bar{X} = 6\ lb$ and $\sigma = 0.6\ lb$
   e. Grades in a statistics course: 99% confidence, $n = 111$, $\bar{X} = 79$ and $\sigma = 5$

P8.13: Use the given confidence level and sample data to find (a) the margin of error E and (b) a confidence interval for estimating the population of salaries of science professor: 99% confidence, $n = 200$, $\bar{X} = \$60{,}000$ and $\sigma = \$15{,}000$
Answer: 57267.920, 62732.080

P8.14: Use the given confidence level and sample data to find (a) the margin of error E and (b) a confidence interval for estimating the population of salaries of science professor: 90% confidence, $n = 200$, $\bar{X} = \$60{,}000$ and $\sigma = \$15{,}000$

P8.15: Use the given confidence level and sample data to find (a) the margin of error E and (b) a confidence interval for estimating the population of ages of college students up to the junior year: 99% confidence, $n = 600$, $\bar{X} = 21$ and $\sigma = 1.4$
Answer: 20.853, 21.147

P8.16: Use the given confidence level and sample data to find (a) the margin of error E and (b) a confidence interval for estimating the population of ages of college students up to the junior year: 95% confidence, $n = 300$, $\bar{X} = 21$ and $\sigma = 3$

P8.17: Use the given confidence level and sample data to find (a) the margin of error E and (b) a confidence interval for estimating the population of ages of college students up to the junior year: 90% confidence, $n = 100$, $\bar{X} = 21$ and $\sigma = 2.4$
Answer: 20.605, 21.395

P8.18: Use the given confidence level and sample data to find (a) the margin of error E and (b) a confidence interval for estimating the population of times between text-messaging by young people in the age of 15 to 18: 95% confidence, $n = 100$, $\bar{X} = 12\ minutes$ and $\sigma = 2\ minutes$

P8.19: Use the given confidence level and sample data to find (a) the margin of error E and (b) a confidence interval for estimating the population of times between text-messaging by young people in the age of 15 to 18: 99% confidence, $n = 100$, $\bar{X} = 12\ minutes$ and $\sigma = 3\ minutes$
Answer: 0.773, 11.227, 12.773

P8.20: Use the given confidence level and sample data to find (a) the margin of error E and (b) a confidence interval for estimating the population of starting salary of college students graduating with an engineering degree: 95% confidence, $n = 200$, $\bar{X} = \$65{,}000$ and $\sigma = \$4000$

P8.21: Use the given confidence level and sample data to find (a) the margin of error E and (b) a confidence interval for estimating the population of starting salary of college students graduating with an engineering degree: 99% confidence, $n = 300$, $\bar{X} = \$65,000$ and $\sigma = \$7000$
Answer: 1041.009, 63958.991, 66041.009

P8.22: Use the given margin of error, confidence level, and population standard deviation to find the minimum sample size required to estimate an unknown population mean of minimum wage per hour in the U.S.A.: Margin of error = $0.5, confidence level = 95%, standard deviation, $\sigma = \$1$

P8.23: Use the given margin of error, confidence level, and population standard deviation to find the minimum sample size required to estimate an unknown population mean of minimum wage per hour in the U.S.A.: Margin of error = $0.5, confidence level = 99%, standard deviation, $\sigma = \$1$
Answer: 27

P8.24: Use the given margin of error, confidence level, and population standard deviation to find the minimum sample size required to estimate an unknown population mean of students' grades in pre-algebra course in a College: Margin of error = 3%, confidence level = 95%, standard deviation, $\sigma = 5\%$

P8.25: Use the given margin of error, confidence level, and population standard deviation to find the minimum sample size required to estimate an unknown population mean of students' grades in pre-algebra course in a College: Margin of error = 1%, confidence level = 95%, standard deviation, $\sigma = 5\%$
Answer: 97(after rounding up)

P8.26: Use the given margin of error, confidence level, and population standard deviation to find the minimum sample size required to estimate an unknown population mean of students' grades in pre-algebra course in a College: Margin of error = 1%, confidence level = 99%, standard deviation, $\sigma = 5\%$

P8.27: A sample of 65 observations is taken from a normal population with a standard deviation of 8. The sample mean is 80.
   (a) Determine the 95 percent confidence interval for the population mean.
   (b) Determine the 99 percent confidence interval for the population mean.
   (c) Compare the answers of (a) and (b) and interpret the difference
   Answer: (a) 78.055, 81.945, (b) 77.444, 82.556

P8.28: A sample of 49 observations is taken from a normal population with a standard deviation of 10. The sample mean is 55.
   (a) Determine the 95 percent confidence interval for the population mean.
   (b) Determine the 99 percent confidence interval for the population mean
   (c) Compare the answers of (a) and (b) and interpret the difference

P8.29: The following data represent the grades of a random sample of students taken from a large population of students who took the same biology course.

75.6	79.7	88.1	74.4
85.3	82.5	80.7	73.8
83.3	82.6	77.7	74.5
80.1	83.8	78	77.1
82.6	76.1	78.4	77.9
84.1	90.7	81.2	79.7
84.9	80.4	85.7	80.9
84.1	81.7	78.4	81.7
82.3	84.9	80.4	80.7
78.8	78.8	83.9	80.7

- Determine a 90% confidence interval on the population grade
- Determine a 95% confidence interval on the population grade
- Determine a 99% confidence interval on the population grade

Answer:

upper confidence limit	lower confidence limit
81.864	79.946
82.047	79.763
82.406	79.404

P8.30: In order to estimate employee time-to-work arrival delays in minutes, a random sample of 40 employees was monitored and values of delay to arrive to work were recorded as shown below. According to the human resources department, the standard deviation of delay is 10 minutes. Given that the time delay is normally distributed, estimate the mean of delay time at 95% and 99% confidence levels.

Delay-to-arrive time values

Employee #	Time Delay (min)	Employee #	Time Delay (min)	Employee #	Time Delay (min)	Employee #	Time Delay (min)
1	10	11	0	21	0	31	5
2	5	12	8	22	7	32	2
3	2	13	3	23	14	33	18
4	13	14	6	24	10	34	32
5	12	15	1	25	8	35	21
6	12	16	2	26	20	36	15
7	14	17	0	27	13	37	12
8	10	18	8	28	18	38	4
9	2	19	5	29	7	39	5
10	4	20	5	30	5	40	17

P8.31: In a random sample of 106 people, the measurements of body temperature revealed an average of 98.20°F, and the standard deviation was 0.62°F. Use this sample to find best point estimate of the population mean μ of all body temperatures.
Answer: $98.2°F$

P8.32: In a random sample of 106 people, the measurements of body temperature revealed an average of 98.20°F, and the standard deviation was 0.62°F. Use this sample to find best interval estimate at 90%, 95%, and 99% confidence levels.

P8.33: If the standard deviation of the IQ of the population of Science professors is known to be 15 and we want to estimate the mean IQ score for the population of science professors. How many science professors must be randomly selected for IQ tests if we want confidence that the sample mean is within 2 IQ points of the population mean? Use a 95% confidence.
Answer: 217

P8.34: A wood board manufacturer normally tests 50 boards for thickness uniformity. Using a random sample of this size, he found that the mean thickness is 1.2 cm and the standard deviation is 0.2 cm. Estimate the population mean of wood board thickness at 95% confidence level. What is the sampling error? What is the minimum sample size required to reduce this sampling error down to half its current value?

P8.35: Find the value of t for 16 degrees of freedom and .05 area in the right tail of a t distribution curve
Answer: $t = 1.746$

P8.36: Find the value of t for sample size 18 and .005 area in the right tail of a t distribution curve

P8.37: Find the value of t for 10, 15, 20, 25, 30, and 40 degrees of freedom and .025 area in the right tail of a t distribution curve. Interpret the value of t statistic as the degrees of freedom increase in comparison with the standard normal distribution or z-statistic.

P8.38: Find the value of t for 5, 20 and 30, and 50 degrees of freedom and 0.025 area in the right tail of a t distribution curve. Do you notice a change as the degrees of freedom increase? Explain.

P8.39: Suppose that a random sample of 22 students was selected to evaluate their grades. The sample mean is 78%, and the standard deviation is 7%. Find a 95% confidence interval for the mean grade of students assuming that student grade is approximately normally distributed.
Answer: 74.896, 81.104

P8.40: A metal rod manufacturer wishes to investigate the consistency in the diameter the rods. A sample of 20 rods taken randomly revealed a sample mean of 0.30 inch with a standard deviation of 0.06 inch.

    a. Construct a 95 percent confidence interval for the population mean.
    b. Construct a 99 percent confidence interval for the population mean
    c. Compare the two answers and discuss the difference

P8.41: In a random sample of 16 people, the measurements of body temperature revealed an average of 98 °F, and the standard deviation was 0.66°F. Use this sample to find best interval estimate at 90%, 95%, and 99% confidence levels.

Answer:

upper confidence limit	lower confidence limit
98.289	97.711
98.352	97.648
98.486	97.514

P8.42: In a narrow street of two-lane in the middle of Atlanta, Georgia, the speed limit was 40 miles per hour. Residents living around this street complained about the high speed of this street. In order to solve the problem the city decided to estimate the speed of cars in the street at 99% confidence. Monitoring the speeds of a random sample of cars driving on the street revealed the following values:

30   35   44   45   50   52   36   38   45   44

Estimate the speed of the population of cars driving on this street, assuming that the car speed is normally-distributed.

P8.43: In a narrow street of two-lane in the middle of Atlanta, Georgia, the speed limit was 40 miles per hour. Residents living around this street complained about the high speed of this street. In order to solve the problem the city decided to estimate the speed of cars in the street at 99% confidence. Monitoring the speeds of a random sample of cars driving on the street revealed the following values:

30   35   44   45   50   52   36   38   45   44

Estimate the speed of the population of cars driving on this street, assuming that the car speed is normally-distributed and given the value of 5 miles/hr as the standard deviation of the population.

Answer:
45.973   upper confidence limit
37.827   lower confidence limit

P8.44: A company making wood boards wishes to estimate the mean of the board thickness of its entire production. The company used only 18 boards and it found the values of thickness shown below. Find a 95% confidence interval for the mean board thickness of the population assuming that the variable thickness follows approximately a normal distribution.

Thickness values of wood boards

Thickness (inch)	
0.2	0.22
0.25	0.27
0.18	0.25
0.26	0.24
0.31	0.18
0.22	0.27
0.19	0.22
0.18	0.21
0.23	0.22

P8.45: A large company surveyed a representative random sample of 600 people of its employee regarding a new retirement package. The result of this survey revealed that 235 of employee prefer the new retirement plan. Estimate the employee population proportion that would agree to the new retirement plan at 99% confidence.

Answer:

Confidence interval - proportion

99%	confidence level
0.3917	proportion
600	n
2.576	z
0.051	half-width
0.443	upper confidence limit
0.340	lower confidence limit

P8.46: In the above problem, calculate the maximum sampling error. What is the sample size required to reduce this sampling error down to 5%? Do this problem at 99% confidence.

P8.47: A sample of 1000 employees in a large organization was surveyed regarding the addition of vision-insurance package to their health plan. The result of the survey revealed that 890 employees agree to obtain this package. Establish a 95% confidence on the acceptance by the employee population of this package.

Answer: $0.87061 < p < 0.90939$

P8.48: In a poll of 700 randomly selected people in the U.S.A that are 50 years or older, 20% said they would prefer a complete overhauling of the Social Security System. Estimate the population proportion of U.S. of 50 years or older who would prefer a complete overhauling of the Social Security System. Use 95% and 99% confidence levels and compare the results.

P8.49: For the following cases, calculate the margin of error and the lower and upper confidence interval values

$n =$	700
$\hat{p} =$	0.2
95% Confidence	
Std. Error	
$\sqrt{\dfrac{\hat{p}(1-\hat{p})}{n}}$	
Margin of Error	
Lower Interval Value	
Higher Interval Value	

$n =$	500
$\hat{p} =$	0.3
95% Confidence	
Std. Error	
$\sqrt{\dfrac{\hat{p}(1-\hat{p})}{n}}$	
Margin of Error	
Lower Interval Value	
Higher Interval Value	

$n =$	1000
$\hat{p} =$	0.5
95% Confidence	
Std. Error	
$\sqrt{\dfrac{\hat{p}(1-\hat{p})}{n}}$	
Margin of Error	
Lower Interval Value	
Higher Interval Value	

Answer: The answer below is only for the first case. Do the other two cases yourself

$n =$	700
$\hat{p} =$	0.2
95% Confidence	1.96
Std. Error $\sqrt{\dfrac{\hat{p}(1-\hat{p})}{n}}$	0.015119
Margin of Error	0.029632
Lower Interval Value	0.170368
Higher Interval Value	0.229632

P8.50: For the following cases, calculate the margin of error and the lower and upper confidence interval values

$n =$	700
$\hat{p} =$	0.2
95% Confidence	
Std. Error	
$\sqrt{\dfrac{\hat{p}(1-\hat{p})}{n}}$	
Margin of Error	
Lower Interval Value	
Higher Interval Value	

$n =$	500
$\hat{p} =$	0.3
95% Confidence	
Std. Error	
$\sqrt{\dfrac{\hat{p}(1-\hat{p})}{n}}$	
Margin of Error	
Lower Interval Value	
Higher Interval Value	

$n =$	1000
$\hat{p} =$	0.5
95% Confidence	
Std. Error	
$\sqrt{\dfrac{\hat{p}(1-\hat{p})}{n}}$	
Margin of Error	
Lower Interval Value	
Higher Interval Value	

P8.51: For the following cases, calculate the margin of error and the lower and upper confidence interval values

$n =$	900
$\hat{p} =$	0.1
95% Confidence	
Std. Error $\sqrt{\dfrac{\hat{p}(1-\hat{p})}{n}}$	
Margin of Error	
Lower Interval Value	
Higher Interval Value	

$n =$	700
$\hat{p} =$	0.9
95% Confidence	
Std. Error $\sqrt{\dfrac{\hat{p}(1-\hat{p})}{n}}$	
Margin of Error	
Lower Interval Value	
Higher Interval Value	

$n =$	700
$\hat{p} =$	0.6
95% Confidence	
Std. Error $\sqrt{\dfrac{\hat{p}(1-\hat{p})}{n}}$	
Margin of Error	
Lower Interval Value	
Higher Interval Value	

Answer: The answer below is only for the first case. Do the other two cases yourself

$n =$	900
$\hat{p} =$	0.1
95% Confidence	1.96
Std. Error $\sqrt{\dfrac{\hat{p}(1-\hat{p})}{n}}$	0.01
Margin of Error	0.0196
Lower Interval Value	0.0804
Higher Interval Value	0.1196

P8.52: For the following cases, calculate the margin of error and the lower and upper confidence interval values

$n =$	900
$\hat{p} =$	0.1
95% Confidence	
Std. Error $\sqrt{\dfrac{\hat{p}(1-\hat{p})}{n}}$	
Margin of Error	
Lower Interval Value	
Higher Interval Value	

$n =$	700
$\hat{p} =$	0.9
95% Confidence	
Std. Error $\sqrt{\dfrac{\hat{p}(1-\hat{p})}{n}}$	
Margin of Error	
Lower Interval Value	
Higher Interval Value	

$n =$	700
$\hat{p} =$	0.6
95% Confidence	
Std. Error $\sqrt{\dfrac{\hat{p}(1-\hat{p})}{n}}$	
Margin of Error	
Lower Interval Value	
Higher Interval Value	

P8.53: For the following cases, calculate the margin of error and the lower and upper confidence interval values

$n =$	2000
$\hat{p} =$	0.2
95% Confidence	
Std. Error $\sqrt{\dfrac{\hat{p}(1-\hat{p})}{n}}$	
Margin of Error	
Lower Interval Value	
Higher Interval Value	

$n =$	1700
$\hat{p} =$	0.2
95% Confidence	
Std. Error $\sqrt{\dfrac{\hat{p}(1-\hat{p})}{n}}$	
Margin of Error	
Lower Interval Value	
Higher Interval Value	

$n =$	800
$\hat{p} =$	0.4
95% Confidence	
Std. Error $\sqrt{\dfrac{\hat{p}(1-\hat{p})}{n}}$	
Margin of Error	
Lower Interval Value	
Higher Interval Value	

Answer: The answer below is only for the first case. Do the other two cases yourself

$n =$	2000
$\hat{p} =$	0.2
95% Confidence	1.96
Std. Error $\sqrt{\dfrac{\hat{p}(1-\hat{p})}{n}}$	0.008944
Margin of Error	0.017531
Lower Interval Value	0.182469
Higher Interval Value	0.217531

P8.54: For the following cases, calculate the margin of error and the lower and upper confidence interval values

$n =$	2000
$\hat{p} =$	0.2
95% Confidence	
Std. Error $\sqrt{\dfrac{\hat{p}(1-\hat{p})}{n}}$	
Margin of Error	
Lower Interval Value	
Higher Interval Value	

$n =$	1700
$\hat{p} =$	0.2
95% Confidence	
Std. Error $\sqrt{\dfrac{\hat{p}(1-\hat{p})}{n}}$	
Margin of Error	
Lower Interval Value	
Higher Interval Value	

$n =$	800
$\hat{p} =$	0.4
95% Confidence	
Std. Error $\sqrt{\dfrac{\hat{p}(1-\hat{p})}{n}}$	
Margin of Error	
Lower Interval Value	
Higher Interval Value	

P8.55: Calculate the correction factor for finite population at sample size n of 200, and the following population sizes 1000 and 5000. What is the effect of population size on the correction factor?
Answer:
At $n = 200$, and $N = 1000$, CF = 0.894875
At $n = 200$, and $N = 5000$, CF = 0.979894
As the population size increases, the correction factor increases approaching a value of 1.

P8.56: Calculate the correction factor for finite population at sample size n of 100, and the following population sizes 2000 and 9000. What is the effect of population size on the correction factor?

P8.57: Calculate the correction factor for finite population at a population size N of 10000, and samples n of 100 and 600. What is the effect of sample size on the correction factor?
Answer:
At $n = 100$, and $N = 10000$, CF ≈ 0.995037
At $n = 600$, and $N = 10000$, ≈ 0.969584
As the sample size decreases, the correction factor increases approaching a value of 1.

P8.58: Calculate the correction factor for finite population at a population size N of 10000, and samples n of 200 and 900. What is the effect of sample size on the correction factor?

P8.59: Using the graph shown below, discuss the effects of sample size and population size on the correction factor for finite population.

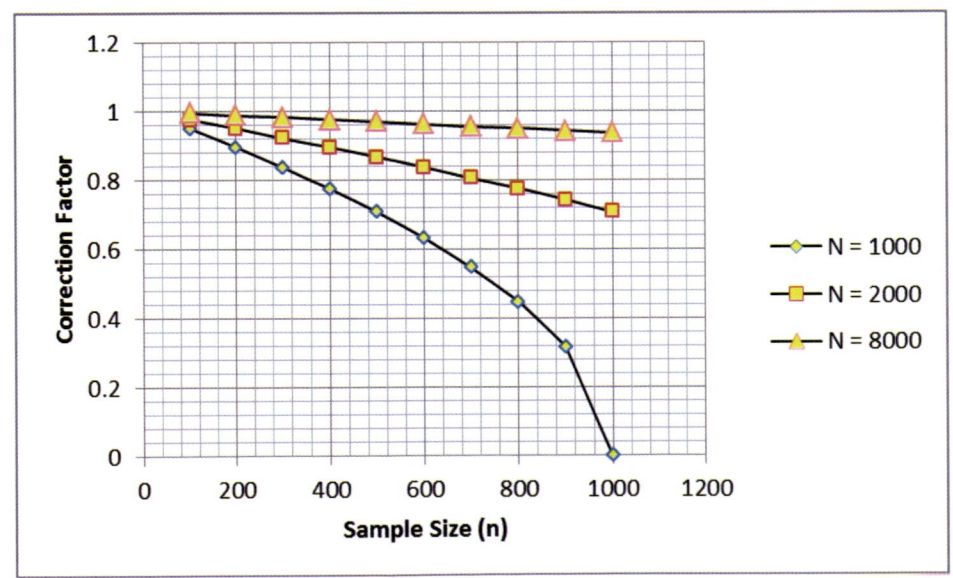

P8.60: From a population of 1000 students who took college statistics course, 200 students were asked if they feel the course was useful in helping them in writing better reports and term papers. Only 70 students replied yes. Estimate the student population proportion that would answer yes to this question at 95% confidence.

494

P8.61: From a population of 1000 students who took college statistics course, 200 students were asked if they feel the course was useful in helping them in writing better reports and term papers. Only 70 students replied yes. Estimate the student population proportion that would answer yes to this question at 99% confidence.
Answer:
$0.272 < p < 0.425$

P8.62: For the following cases, calculate the correction factor for finite populations, margin of error and the lower and upper confidence interval values

$N =$	1000
$n =$	100
$\hat{p} =$	0.3
95% Confidence	
Uncorrected Std. Error	
Correction Factor	
Margin of Error	

$N =$	1000
$n =$	200
$\hat{p} =$	0.3
95% Confidence	
Uncorrected Std. Error	
Correction Factor	
Margin of Error	

$N =$	1000
$n =$	300
$\hat{p} =$	0.3
95% Confidence	
Uncorrected Std. Error	
Correction Factor	
Margin of Error	

P8.63: For the following cases, calculate the correction factor for finite populations, margin of error and the lower and upper confidence interval values

$N =$	1000
$n =$	100
$\hat{p} =$	0.3
99% Confidence	
Uncorrected Std. Error	
Correction Factor	
Margin of Error	

$N =$	1000
$n =$	200
$\hat{p} =$	0.3
99% Confidence	
Uncorrected Std. Error	
Correction Factor	
Margin of Error	

$N =$	1000
$n -$	300
$\hat{p} =$	0.3
99% Confidence	
Uncorrected Std. Error	
Correction Factor	
Margin of Error	

Answer: The answer below is only for the first case. Do the other two cases yourself

$N =$	1000
$n =$	100
$\hat{p} =$	0.3
99% Confidence	2.58
Uncorrected Std. Error $\sqrt{\dfrac{\hat{p}(1 - \hat{p})}{n}}$	0.045826
Correction Factor $\sqrt{\dfrac{N - n}{N - 1}}$	0.949158
Margin of Error	0.112219

P8.64: For the following cases, calculate the correction factor for finite populations, margin of error and the lower and upper confidence interval values

$N =$	1000
$n =$	100
$\hat{p} =$	0.3
90% Confidence	
Uncorrected Std. Error $$\sqrt{\frac{\hat{p}(1-\hat{p})}{n}}$$	
Correction Factor $$\sqrt{\frac{N-n}{N-1}}$$	
Margin of Error	

$N =$	1000
$n =$	200
$\hat{p} =$	0.3
90% Confidence	
Uncorrected Std. Error $$\sqrt{\frac{\hat{p}(1-\hat{p})}{n}}$$	
Correction Factor $$\sqrt{\frac{N-n}{N-1}}$$	
Margin of Error	

$N =$	1000
$n =$	300
$\hat{p} =$	0.3
90% Confidence	
Uncorrected Std. Error $$\sqrt{\frac{\hat{p}(1-\hat{p})}{n}}$$	
Correction Factor $$\sqrt{\frac{N-n}{N-1}}$$	
Margin of Error	

P8.65: In an organization of 1000 employees, a survey was made using a random sample of 300 people regarding prohibiting smoking in the parking lots of the organization buildings. 210 people agreed to prohibit smoking in the parking lots of the organization buildings. Estimate the population proportion that would agree to prohibit smoking in the parking lots of the organization buildings at 95% confidence. Perform estimation with and without corrections for finite population and compare the answers.
Answer:
$0.648 < p < 0.752$
$0.6566 < p < 0.7434$

P8.66: A random sample of 300 nurses in a large hospital was surveyed regarding working extra hours daily. The result of the survey revealed that 120 nurses agree to work extra hours. Establish a 95% confidence on the acceptance by the nurse population of working overload.

P8.67: A random sample of 20 houses was taken from a large city to estimate the property tax of the house population. The mean value of annual property tax was $6400, and the standard deviation was $800. Find a 95% confidence interval. Use the z and the t statistic and compare the two answers.
Answer:
Using the z-value: 6049.4, 6750.6
Using the *t*-value: 6025.588, 6774.412

P8.68: Two weight loss clubs, *A* and *B*, were compared with respect to overall performance. From club *A*, a random sample of 100 people was selected and it was found that the average weight loss over a one month period was 20 pounds. From club *B*, a random sample of 100 people was selected and it was found that the average weight loss over a one month period was 26 pounds. If it is known that the population standard deviations for weight loss of these two clubs are 4 pound and 7 pound, respectively, establish a 95% confidence interval on the difference between these two population means.

P8.69: In a comparative study between two highways with regard to the driving speed, the following results were obtained:

Highway A	Highway B
$\bar{X}_A = 51 \: miles/hr$	$\bar{X}_B = 55 \: miles/hr$
$Variance = 64$	$Variance = 9$
$n_A = 10$	$n_B = 12$

Establish a 95% confidence on the difference of speed on these two highways.
Answer: $-9.1893 < \mu_1 - \mu_2 < 1.1893$

P8.70: For the above problem, establish a 99% confidence on the difference of speed on these two highways

Highway A	Highway B
$\bar{X}_A = 51 \: miles/hr$	$\bar{X}_B = 55 \: miles/hr$
$Variance = 64$	$Variance = 9$
$n_A = 10$	$n_B = 12$

P8.71: Two cities were compared with respect to property taxes. From City A, a random sample of 200 houses was selected and it was found that the average property tax was $7000. From City B, a random sample of 200 houses was selected and it was found that the average property tax was $5000. If it is known that the population standard deviations for property tax of these two cities are $500 and $400 respectively, establish a 95% confidence interval on the difference between these two population means.
Answer: $\mu_A - \mu_B = 2000 \pm 88.74$

P8.72: Two cities were compared with respect to property taxes. From City A, a random sample of 200 houses was selected and it was found that the average property tax was $7000. From City B, a random sample of 200 houses was selected and it was found that the average property tax was $5000. If it is known that the population standard deviations for property tax of these two cities are $500 and $400 respectively, establish a 99% confidence interval on the difference between these two population means.

P8.73: As a result of changing the assessment mechanism of a biology course, it was important to compare the grades of student populations before and after the change. Using a sample of 50 students who took the assessment tests before and after the change, the average results were as follow:

	Before	After
N	50	50
Average Score	80	75
Standard deviation	5	5

Estimate the difference between the grades of the two populations of students at 99% confidence.
Answer: $\mu_A - \mu_B = 5 \pm 2.58$

P8.74: For the above problem, estimate the difference between the grades of the two populations of students at 95% confidence.

P8.75: Find the critical values for a 95% confidence interval using the χ^2 distribution with 10 degrees of freedom.
Answer: 3.25, 20.48

P8.76: Find the critical values for a 95% confidence interval using the χ^2 distribution with 18 degrees of freedom.

P8.77 Find the critical values for a 99% confidence interval using the χ^2 distribution with 25 degrees of freedom.
Answer: 10.52, 46.93

P8.78: Find the critical values for a 95% confidence interval using the χ^2 distribution with 2 degrees of freedom.

P8.79: Find the critical values for a 95% confidence interval using the χ^2 distribution with 100 degrees of freedom.
Answer: 74.22, 129.56

P8.80: Find the critical values for a 99% confidence interval using the χ^2 distribution with 2 degrees of freedom.

P8.81: Find the critical values for a 99% confidence interval using the χ^2 distribution with 80 degrees of freedom.
Answer: 51.17, 116.32

P8.82: Find the critical values for a 99% confidence interval using the χ^2 distribution with 90 degrees of freedom.

P8.83: The following data represent students' grades of a test taken by 20 students

Grade	65	68	80	89	90	98	55	50	67	84	86	77	74	82	94	90	69	70	80	90

Assume these values represent a simple random sample from a normal population distribution. Construct a 95% confidence interval for the population variance σ^2.
Answer:

82.883	confidence interval 99.% lower
467.243	confidence interval 99.% upper

P8.84: The following data represent students' grades of a test taken by 20 students

Grade	65	68	80	89	90	98	55	50	67	84	86	77	74	82	94	90	69	70	80	90

Assume these values represent a simple random sample from a normal population distribution. Construct a 90% confidence interval for the population variance σ^2.

P8.85: The following data represent percent values of polyester fiber in a cotton/polyester blend.

Percent of Polyester in the blend

P%	51	50	55	50	50	50	52	51	51	52	50	51	49	50	48	52	51	50	47	50

Assume these values represent a simple random sample from a normal population distribution. Construct a 99% confidence interval for the population variance σ^2.
Answer:
  Variance   2.684
  1.322   confidence interval 99.% lower
  7.452   confidence interval 99.% upper

P8.86: The following data represent percent values of polyester fiber in a cotton/polyester blend.

Percent of Polyester in the blend

P%	51	50	55	50	50	50	52	51	51	52	50	51	49	50	48	52	51	50	47	50

Assume these values represent a simple random sample from a normal population distribution. Construct a 90% confidence interval for the population variance σ^2.

P8.87: Determine a 95% confidence interval on σ^2 for the data in the table below
Values of Metal Plates Thickness (cm)

Observation No.	Thickness	Observation No.	Thickness	Observation No.	Thickness	Observation No.	Thickness
1	4.04	11	3.87	21	3.99	31	3.85
2	3.98	12	4.16	22	4	32	4
3	4.01	13	4.05	23	3.73	33	4.02
4	3.99	14	3.98	24	3.95	34	3.78
5	3.84	15	4.05	25	4.06	35	4.13
6	3.93	16	3.85	26	4.17	36	4.13
7	4.11	17	4.14	27	4.13	37	3.9
8	4.02	18	3.81	28	3.95	38	3.91
9	4.08	19	3.96	29	3.94	39	4.01
10	3.95	20	4.34	30	3.93	40	3.97

Answer: $0.09726 \leq \sigma \leq 0.1516$

APPENDIX 8.A
Table 8.A.1

Critical Values for the t-distribution

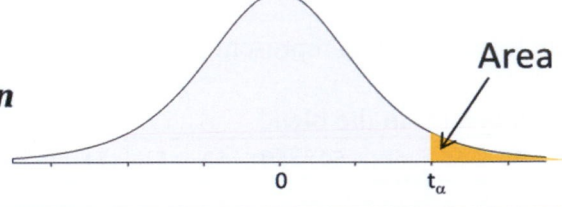

Area

Area in the Right Tail									
γ \ α	0.40	0.25	0.10	0.05	0.025	0.01	0.005	0.0025	0.001	0.0005
1	0.325	1.000	3.078	6.314	12.706	31.821	63.657	127.32	318.31	636.62
2	0.289	0.816	1.886	2.920	4.303	6.965	9.925	1.4.089	23.326	31.598
3	0.277	0.765	1.638	2.353	3.182	4.541	5.841	7.453	10.213	12.924
4	0.271	0.741	1.533	2.132	2.776	3.747	4.604	5.598	7.173	8.610
5	0.267	0.727	1.476	2.015	2.571	3.365	4.032	4.773	5.893	6.869
6	0.265	0.727	1.440	1.943	2.447	3.143	3.707	4.317	5.208	5.959
7	0.263	0.711	1.415	1.895	2.365	2.998	3.499	4.019	4.785	5.408
8	0.262	0.706	1.397	1.860	2.306	2.896	3.355	3.833	4.501	5.041
9	0.261	0.703	1.383	1.833	2.262	2.821	3.250	3.690	4.297	4.781
10	0.260	0.700	1.372	1.812	2.228	2.764	3.169	3.581	4.144	4.587
11	0.260	0.697	1.363	1.796	2.201	2.718	3.106	3.497	4.025	4.437
12	0.259	0.695	1.356	1.782	2.179	2.681	3.055	3.428	3.930	4.318
13	0.259	0.694	1.350	1.771	2.160	2.650	3.012	3.472	3.852	4.221
14	0.258	0.692	1.345	1.761	2.145	2.624	2.977	3.326	3.787	4.140
15	0.258	0.691	1.341	1.753	2.131	2.602	2.947	3.286	3.733	4.073
16	0.258	0.690	1.337	1.746	2.120	2.583	2.921	3.252	3.686	4.015
17	0.257	0.689	1.333	1.740	2.110	2.567	2.898	3.222	3.646	3.965
18	0.257	0.658	1.330	1.734	2.101	2.552	2.878	3.197	3.610	3.922
19	0.257	0.688	1.328	1.729	2.093	2.539	2.861	3.174	3.579	3.883
20	0.257	0.687	1.325	1.725	2.086	2.528	2.845	3.153	3.552	3.850
21	0.257	0.686	1.323	1.721	2.080	2.518	2.831	3.135	3.527	3.819
22	0.256	0.686	1.321	1.717	2.074	2.508	2.819	3.119	3.505	3.792
23	0.256	0.685	1.419	1.714	2.069	2.500	2.807	3.104	3.485	3.767
24	0.256	0.685	1.318	1.711	2.064	2.492	2.797	3.091	3.467	3.745
25	0.256	0.684	1.316	1.708	2.060	2.485	2.787	3.078	3.450	3.725
26	0.256	0.684	1.315	1.706	2.056	2.479	2.779	3.067	3.435	3.707
27	0.256	0.684	1.314	1.703	2.052	2.473	2.771	3.057	3.421	3.690
28	0.256	0.683	1.313	1.701	2.048	2.467	2.763	3.047	3.408	3.674
29	0.256	0.683	1.311	1.699	2.045	2.462	2.756	3.038	0.330	3.659
30	0.256	0.683	1.310	1.697	2.042	2.457	2.750	3.030	3.385	3.646
40	0.255	0.681	1.303	1.684	2.021	2.423	2.704	2.971	3.307	3.551
60	0.254	0.679	1.296	1.671	2.000	2.390	2.660	2.915	3.232	3.460
120	0.254	0.677	1.289	1.658	1.980	2.358	2.617	2.860	3.160	3.373
∞	0.253	0.674	1.282	1.645	1.960	2.326	2.576	2.807	3.090	3.291

Table 8.A.II

Critical Values for the χ^2-distribution

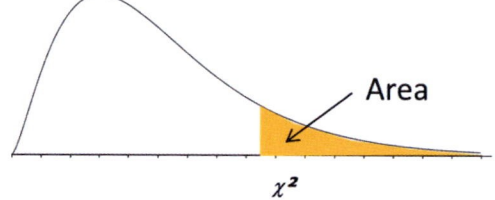

Area

χ^2

	Area in Right Tail								
DF = γ	0.995	0.990	0.975	0.950	0.500	0.050	0.025	0.010	0.005
1	0.00	0.00	0.00	0.00	0.45	3.84	5.02	6.63	7.88
2	0.01	0.02	0.05	0.10	1.39	5.99	7.38	9.21	10.60
3	0.07	0.11	0.22	0.35	2.37	7.81	9.35	11.34	12.84
4	0.21	0.30	0.48	0.71	3.36	9.49	11.14	13.28	14.86
5	0.41	0.55	0.83	1.15	4.35	11.07	12.38	15.09	16.75
6	0.68	0.87	1.24	1.64	5.35	12.59	14.45	16.81	18.55
7	0.99	1.24	1.69	2.17	6.35	14.07	16.01	18.48	20.28
8	1.34	1.65	2.18	2.73	7.34	15.51	17.53	20.09	21.96
9	1.73	2.09	2.70	3.33	8.34	16.92	19.02	21.67	23.59
10	2.16	2.56	3.25	3.94	9.34	18.31	20.48	23.21	25.19
11	2.60	3.05	3.82	4.57	10.34	19.68	21.92	24.72	26.76
12	3.07	3.57	4.40	5.23	11.34	21.03	23.34	26.22	28.30
13	3.57	4.11	5.01	5.89	12.34	22.36	24.74	27.69	29.82
14	4.07	4.66	5.63	6.57	13.34	23.68	26.12	29.14	31.32
15	4.60	5.23	6.27	7.26	14.34	25.00	27.49	30.58	32.80
16	5.14	5.81	6.91	7.96	15.34	26.30	28.85	32.00	34.27
17	5.70	6.41	7.56	8.67	16.34	27.59	30.19	33.41	35.72
18	6.26	7.01	8.23	9.39	17.34	28.87	31.53	34.81	37.16
19	6.84	7.63	8.91	10.12	18.34	30.14	32.85	36.19	38.58
20	7.43	8.26	9.59	10.85	19.34	31.41	34.17	37.57	40.00
25	10.52	11.52	13.12	14.61	24.34	37.65	40.65	44.31	46.93
30	13.79	14.95	16.79	18.49	29.34	43.77	46.98	50.89	53.67
40	20.71	22.16	24.43	26.51	39.34	55.76	59.34	63.69	66.77
50	27.99	29.71	32.36	34.76	49.33	67.50	71.42	76.15	79.49
60	35.53	37.48	40.48	43.19	59.33	79.08	83.30	88.38	91.95
70	43.28	45.44	48.76	51.74	69.33	90.53	95.02	100.42	104.22
80	51.17	53.54	57.15	60.39	79.33	101.88	106.63	112.33	116.32
90	59.20	61.75	65.65	69.13	89.33	113.14	118.14	124.12	128.30
100	67.33	70.06	74.22	77.93	99.33	124.34	129.56	135.81	140.17

APPENDIX 8.B Sampling Distributions and Properties

APPENDIX 8.B.I: The t-Distribution

The t-distribution is named after its pioneer Gosset, who published his analysis under the pseudonym of 'Student' during the early part of the 20th century. This distribution is based on the assumption that the characteristic values x follow a normal distribution. Theoretically, t is defined by:

$$t = \frac{(\bar{X} - \mu)}{s/\sqrt{n}}$$

Where $\bar{X}$ and s are the sample mean and standard deviation, respectively, n is the sample size, and μ is the population mean.

Experimentally, the t-distribution can be obtained by collecting samples of size n drawn from a normally-distributed (or approximately normal) population with mean μ, computing t statistic using the sample mean and sample standard deviation and constructing the relative frequency distribution of t values. Mathematically, this distribution takes the following form:

$$f(t) = \frac{Y_o}{\left(1 + \frac{t^2}{n-1}\right)^{n/2}} = \frac{Y_o}{\left(1 + \frac{t^2}{\gamma}\right)^{(\gamma+1)/2}}$$

where Y_o is a constant depending on the sample size, n, such that the total area under the curve is one, and the constant $\gamma = (n\text{-}1)$ is called the degree of freedom.

In the above equation, we introduced the term degree of freedom. The value of this term for the t distribution is $n\text{-}1$ or the sample size minus one. In general, the number of degrees of freedom of a statistic is defined as the number of independent observations in the sample (or the sample size) minus the number k of population parameters that should be estimated from sample observations. Since the parameter we are estimating is the population mean, μ, $k = 1$ and $\gamma = n\text{-}1$.

The t-distribution is basically a normal distribution with mean $\mu = 0$ and standard deviation $\sigma = \sqrt{\gamma/(\gamma - 2)}$ for $\gamma > 2$. Indeed, for large values of γ or n ($n \geq 30$), the above equation approaches the standardized normal curve: $f(t) = \frac{1}{\sqrt{2\pi}} e^{-t^2/2}$.

APPENDIX 8.B.II: The Chi-Square χ^2-Distribution

The χ^2-distribution has a total area under the curve equals one. The curve starts at zero on the horizontal axis and extends indefinitely to the right, approaching, but never touching, the horizontal axis as it does so. Commonly, a χ^2-curve is right skewed. In practice, the χ^2-distribution can be obtained by collecting samples of size n drawn from a normal (or approximately normal) population with standard deviation σ, computing ☐☐χ^2-statistic using the sample standard deviation and constructing the relative frequency distribution of χ^2 values. In this case, χ^2 is defined by $\chi^2 = \frac{ns^2}{\sigma^2}$. This means that

$$\chi^2 = \frac{ns^2}{\sigma^2} = \frac{(x_1 - \bar{X})^2 + (x_2 - \bar{X})^2 + \cdots + (x_n - \bar{X})^2}{\sigma^2}$$

Mathematically, the χ^2-distribution is expressed by the following frequency function:

$$f(\chi^2) = Y_o(\chi^2)^{\frac{1}{2}(\gamma-2)}e^{-\frac{1}{2}\chi^2} = Y_o\chi^{(\gamma-2)}e^{-\frac{1}{2}\chi^2}$$

where $\gamma = n-1$ is the number of degrees of freedom, and Y_o is a constant depending on γ such that the total area under the curve is one. A unique feature of the χ^2-distribution is that it is skewed with mean $\mu = n$, and variance $\sigma^2 = 2n$.

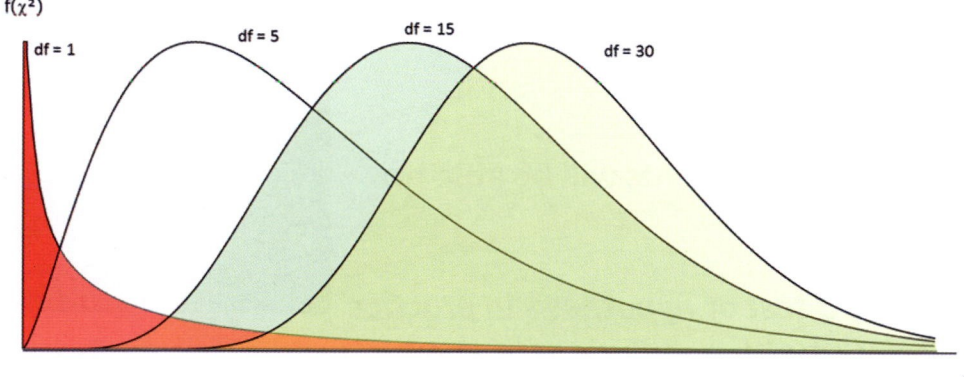

CHAPTER 9

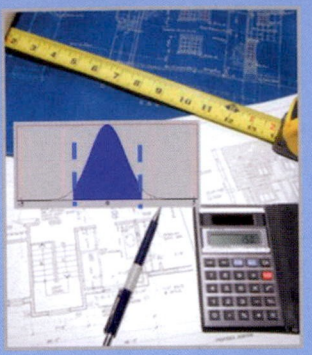

Inferential Statistics: Hypothesis testing using one population/one sample

LEARNING OBJECTIVES

After completing this Chapter students will be able to:

$H_0: \mu = \mu_0$
$H_1: \mu \neq \mu_0$

$g(t|H_0)$

$H_0: \mu = \mu_0$
$H_1: \mu \neq \mu_0$

$g(t|H_1)$

α

Accept H_0 Reject H_0

- *Understand the merits of a test of hypothesis in practice*
- *Test hypotheses associated with populations of known standard deviation*
- *Test hypotheses associated with populations of unknown standard deviation*
- *Test hypothesis of population proportions*
- *Test hypothesis of a population variance*

APEX®

CHAPTER 9

In this chapter we turn our attention to the subject of hypothesis testing. This is a different form of inferential statistics in which you will be required to make decisions regarding accepting or rejecting a contention or claimed value of a population parameter using a sample selected from the population. Hypothesis testing is a standard procedure that is commonly used by professionals in numerous fields and different disciplines. This subject will be covered over two chapters starting with this chapter in which we adhere to one population and one sample. In Chapter 10, we will deal with two populations and two samples.

CHAPTER CONTENTS

9.1 What is hypothesis testing?

A hypothesis is a contention based on preliminary observations of what appear to be facts, which may or may not be true. ***The test of hypothesis compares the contention with the collected facts.*** If these facts can be shown to agree with the contention, the contention is retained; that is the hypothesis is accepted with some confidence. If the contention and facts do not agree, the contention is discarded; that is the hypothesis is rejected with some confidence.

In order to understand the concept of hypothesis testing, let us discuss scenarios of some applications and try to make decisions regarding the claim of each application.

Scenario One: Student Retention

Suppose we want to test a claim by Professor Hardy who has been teaching physics for many years, that the average student retention in her physics courses exceeds 70%. One way to test this claim is to take a random sample of a few classes taught by Professor Hardy in the past and examine the retention rate in these classes. Suppose we looked at 10 random samples of classes taught by her in the past and we found the values of retention rates shown in Figure 9.1. What would be our decision? Do we accept the teacher's claim or reject it?

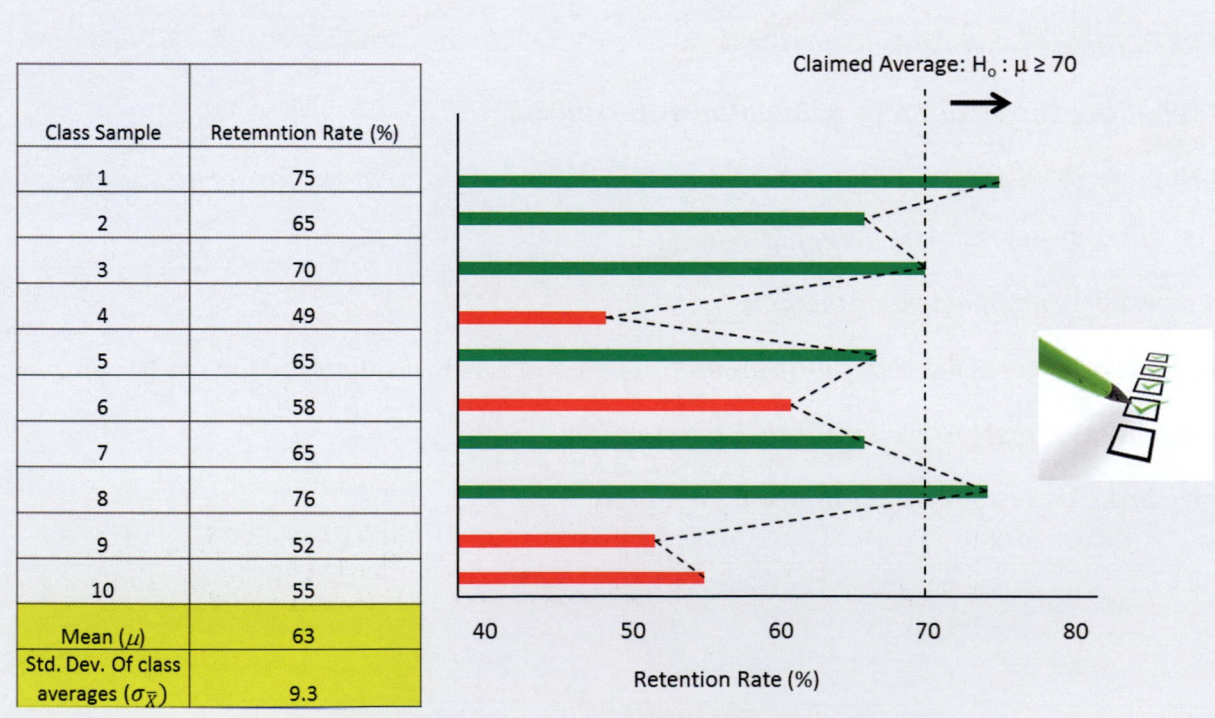

Class Sample	Retemntion Rate (%)
1	75
2	65
3	70
4	49
5	65
6	58
7	65
8	76
9	52
10	55
Mean (μ)	63
Std. Dev. Of class averages ($\sigma_{\overline{x}}$)	9.3

Claimed Average: $H_o : \mu \geq 70$

Figure 9.1 Scenario One: Testing the Claim of Student's Retention

Decision:

Examining the values of retention rate shown in Figure 9.1 reveals that only two classes out of the 10 random classes selected exceeded 70% retention. Furthermore, many classes had retention rates of less than 65%. As a result, we may conclude that Professor Hardy has a retention rate of less than 70% and we should reject her claim. Are we correct in making this conclusion?

Using the concept of central limit theorem (Chapter 7), if these samples of classes are truly representative of the population of Professor Hardy's classes, and the size of each class is more or less the same, then: $\mu \approx 63 \; and \; \sigma_{\bar{x}} = 9.3$. by converting these to z values to find the probability p(retention < 70%), this will lead to more than 77% of her classes with retention rates less than 70% as shown below (see Chapter 7, section 7.7). Does this support our conclusion of rejecting Professor Hardy's claim?

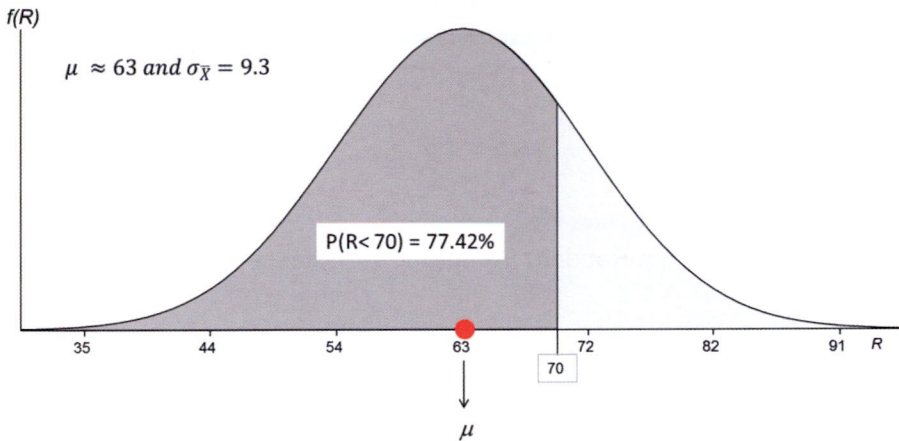

Scenario Two: **Student grades**

Suppose we want to test a claim by a teacher that the average grade of his students' population in the physics course he teaches is 80%. We looked at 10 random samples of classes that this teacher taught in the past and we found the values of average grades shown in Figure 9.2. What would be our decision? Do we accept the teacher's claim or reject it?

507

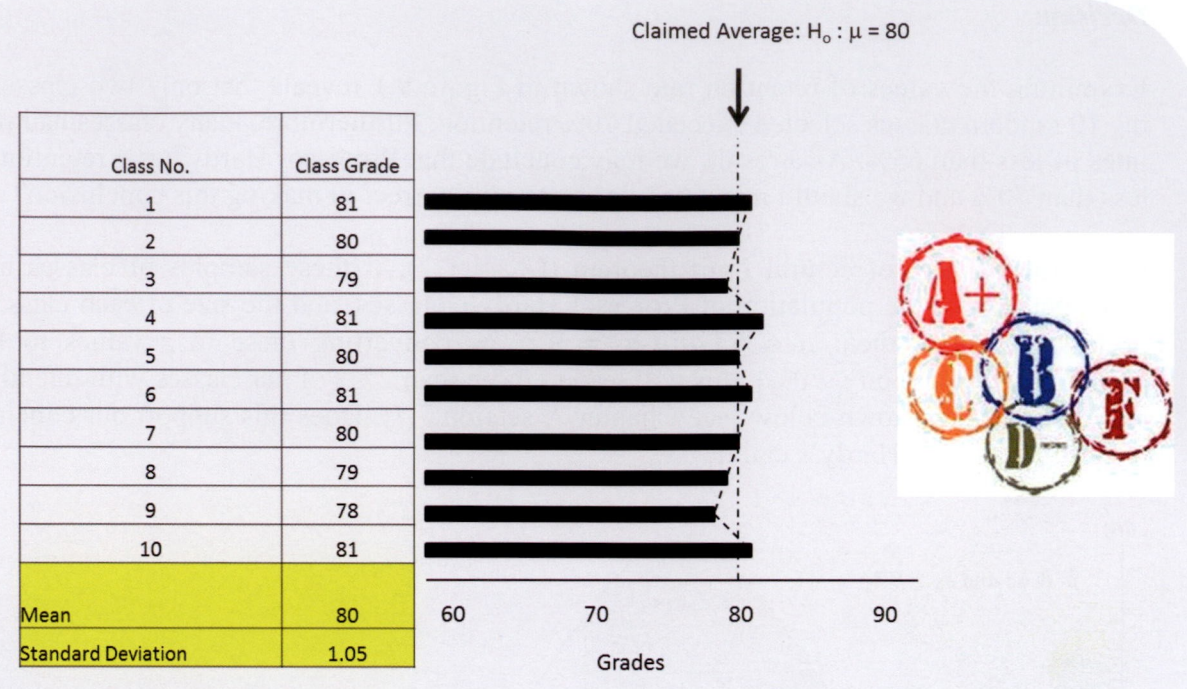

Figure 9.2 Teacher's Average Grades in a Random Sample of Ten Classes-Consistency

Decision:

The data in Figure 9.2 reveals high consistency of students' grades with values very close to 80%. The overall average grade is also 80%. This may lead us to believe that the teacher's claim is true. If these samples of classes are truly representative of the students' population of this professor then population mean (μ) is 80 and $\sigma_{\bar{X}}$ is 1.05. Using the empirical rule, this will lead to 99.74% of classes with grades within $\pm 3\sigma_{\bar{X}}$, or between 76.85% and 83.15%. Given this interval, do we still accept the teacher's claim?

Scenario Three: Student grades

Suppose that another teacher claims that the grade average of his students in the biology course he teaches is 80%. We looked at 10 random samples of classes that this teacher taught in the past and we found the values of average grades shown in Figure 9.3. What would be our decision? Do we accept the teacher's claim or reject it?

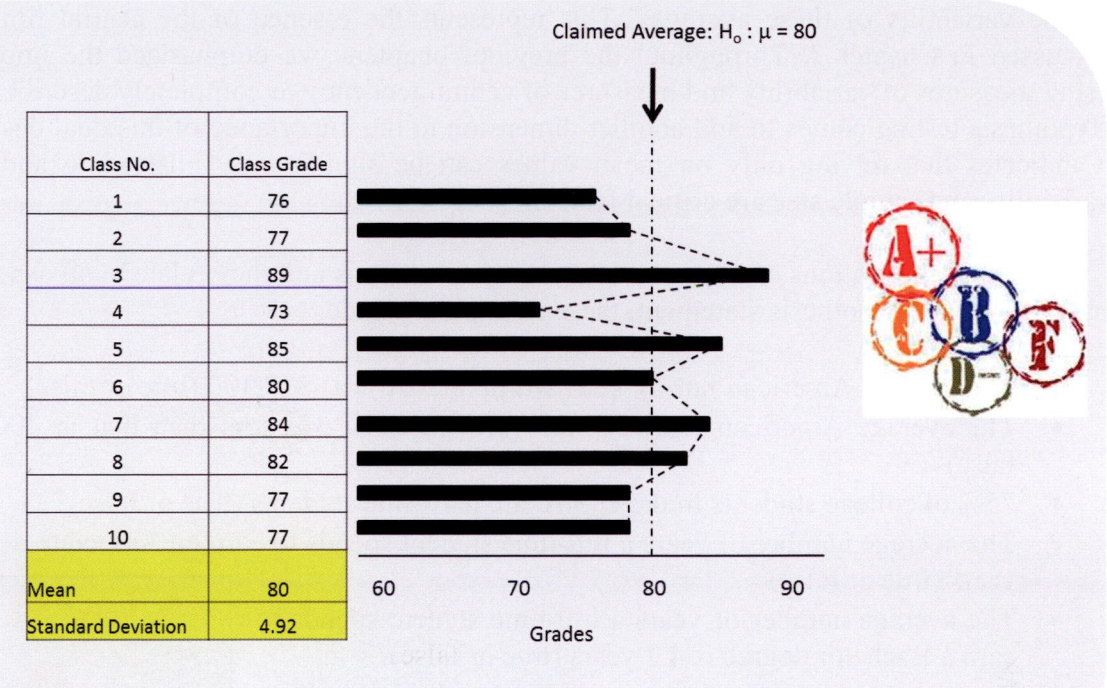

Claimed Average: $H_o : \mu = 80$

Class No.	Class Grade
1	76
2	77
3	89
4	73
5	85
6	80
7	84
8	82
9	77
10	77
Mean	80
Standard Deviation	4.92

Figure 9.3 Teacher's Average Grades in a Random Sample of Ten Classes-Inconsistency

Decision:

Examining the values in Figure 9.3 may lead us to doubt that this teacher's average grade is truly 80%; that is despite the fact that his overall average is indeed 80%. The reason for the doubt stems from the high variability between class grades. As you can see, he gave some classes an average of as low as 73% and some as high as 89%. If these samples of classes are truly representative of the population of this professor then population mean (μ) is 80 and $\sigma_{\bar{X}}$ is 4.92. Using the empirical rule, this will lead to 99.74% of his classes with grades within $\pm 3\sigma_{\bar{X}}$, or between 65.24% and 94.76%. Given this wide interval, do we still reject the teacher's claim?

The three case scenarios described above demonstrate the need for a more systematic way to test claims. When we are faced with a situation in which variability prevails, our judgment of the average value of the population associated with this situation should be based not only on the averages of samples taken from the population, but also

NEW YORK (CNNMoney)
The average American family's net worth dropped almost 40% between 2007 and 2010, according to a triennial study released Monday by the Federal Reserve. The stunning drop in median net worth -- from $126,400 in 2007 to $77,300 in 2010 -- indicates that the recession wiped away 18 years of savings and investment by families.

http://money.cnn.com

509

on the variability of these averages. This represents the essence of the central limit theorem discussed in Chapter 7. Throughout the previous chapters, we emphasized the importance of using measures of variability and measures of central tendency to completely describe a data set. Hypothesis testing comes to add another dimension to the importance of this dual description as it indicates that relying only on mean values can be significantly misleading and that both variability and sample size are critical factors.

Examples of applications of hypothesis testing are numerous and they relate to all aspects of life. In the form of a hypothesis statement, these examples include:

- The average American family's net worth in 2010 was $77,300 (true or false)
- The average American family's net worth in 2010 was less than that in 2007 (true or false)
- 75% of college students in the U.S.A. are part-time students (true or false)
- The average number of years a full-time student spends to earn an Associate degree is 3.8 years (true or false)
- The average number of years a full-time student spends to earn a Bachelor degree is 4.7 years (true or false)
- Part-time students spend more years than full-time students to earn an Associate or a Bachelor degree in the U.S.A. (true or false)

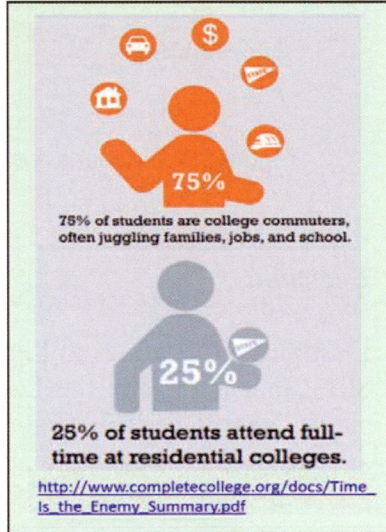

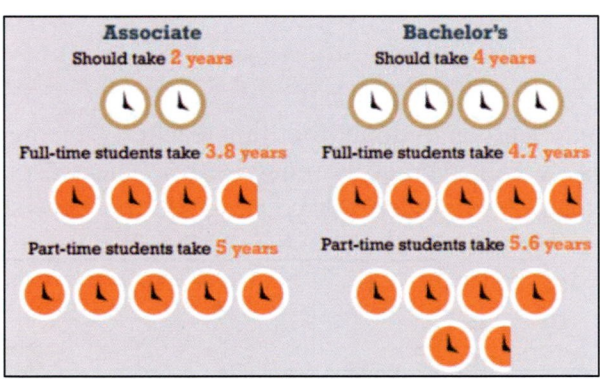

- The average weight of an NFL football player is 250 pounds (true or false)
- The average height of an NFL football player is 6 feet (true or false)

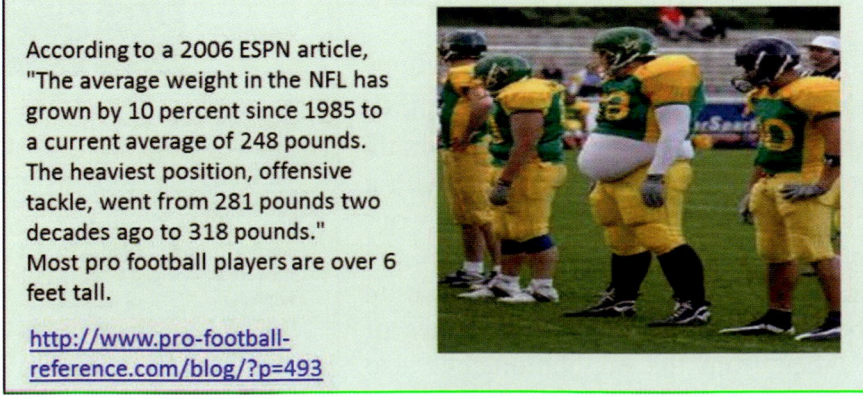

510

9.2 Formatting a hypothesis test

A hypothesis test is commonly formatted as follows:

$$H_o: \mu = \mu_o$$
$$H_1: \mu \neq \mu_o$$

H_o is called the null hypothesis. It is a claim (or statement) about a population parameter that is assumed to be true until it is declared false. In this case, the claim is that the population's mean value is μ_o. H_1 is called the alternative hypothesis and it implies that the average of the population variable may not be equal μ_o. Since this is a case of equal or not equal, it is called a **two-sided (or two-tailed) hypothesis test**.

The primary form of a null hypothesis is $H_o: \mu = \mu_o$. However, we may use other forms such as $H_o: \mu \leq \mu_o$ or $H_o: \mu \geq \mu_o$.

The corresponding forms an alternative hypothesis may take are as follows:

$$(1)\ H_1: \mu \neq \mu_o$$

$$(2)\ H_1: \mu > \mu_o$$

$$(3)\ H_1: \mu < \mu_o$$

The complete statement of a hypothesis test can take the following formats:

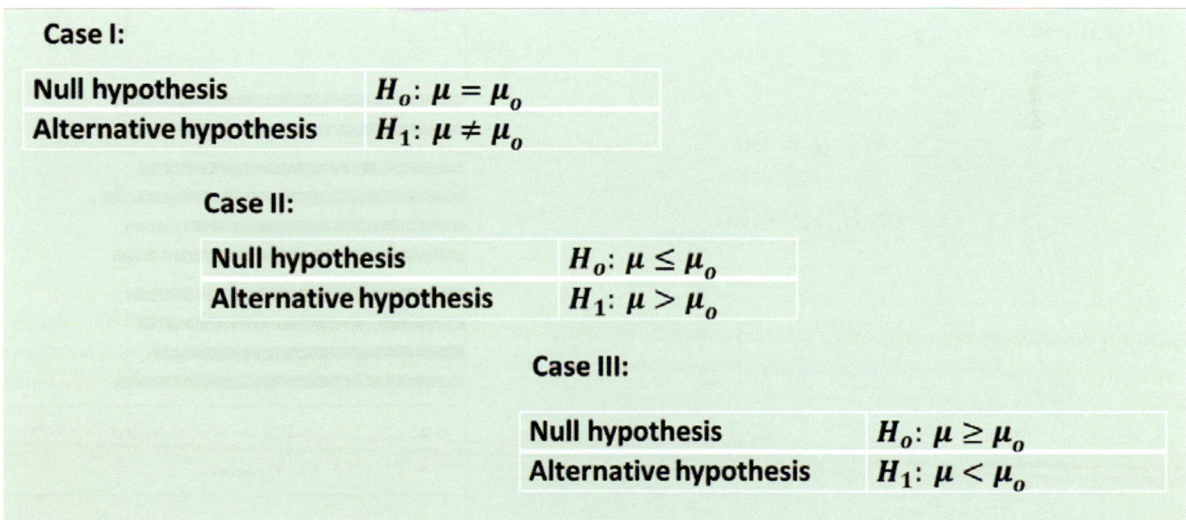

Case I:

Null hypothesis	$H_o: \mu = \mu_o$
Alternative hypothesis	$H_1: \mu \neq \mu_o$

Case II:

Null hypothesis	$H_o: \mu \leq \mu_o$
Alternative hypothesis	$H_1: \mu > \mu_o$

Case III:

Null hypothesis	$H_o: \mu \geq \mu_o$
Alternative hypothesis	$H_1: \mu < \mu_o$

The key to a good test of hypothesis is to understand that our target is once again to **test a claim via estimating population parameters using a representative sample** so that we can make a decision on whether we accept or reject the claim.

Using the case scenarios discussed earlier, we can format the hypothesis tests as follow:

Scenario One: Student retention

In order to test whether Professor Hardy's retention rate exceeds 70%, we can use one of the formats in the side graph. The analysis will then focus on whether to reject or accept the null hypothesis

$$H_o: \mu = 70$$
$$or \ H_o: \mu \geq 70$$

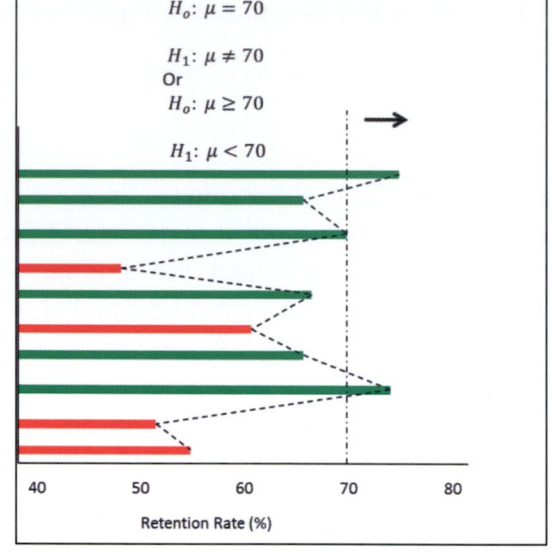

Scenario Two & Three: Student grades

In order to test the claim by a teacher that the grade average of his students is 80%, we can use one of the formats in the side graph. The analysis will then focus on whether to reject or accept the null hypothesis

$$H_o: \mu = 80$$

$$or \ H_o: \mu \leq 80$$

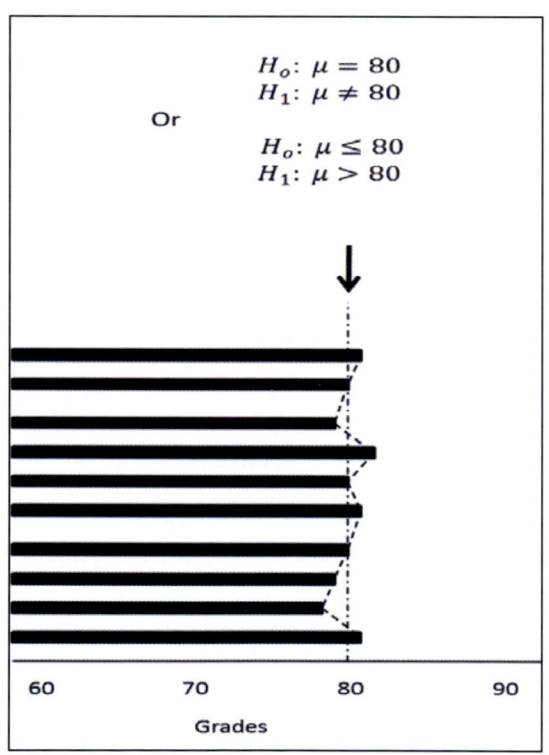

9.3 What are the basic steps of hypothesis testing?

The basic steps associated with performing a hypothesis test are illustrated in Figure 9.4. These steps are discussed below.

Step 1: *Identify and define the characteristic under consideration and state the hypothesis*
Step 2: *Select a sample from the population and determine sample statistics*
Step 3: *Select the level of significance or the extent of error*
Step 4: *Identify and use an appropriate test statistic*
Step 5: *Follow appropriate decision rules to reject or accept the null hypothesis*

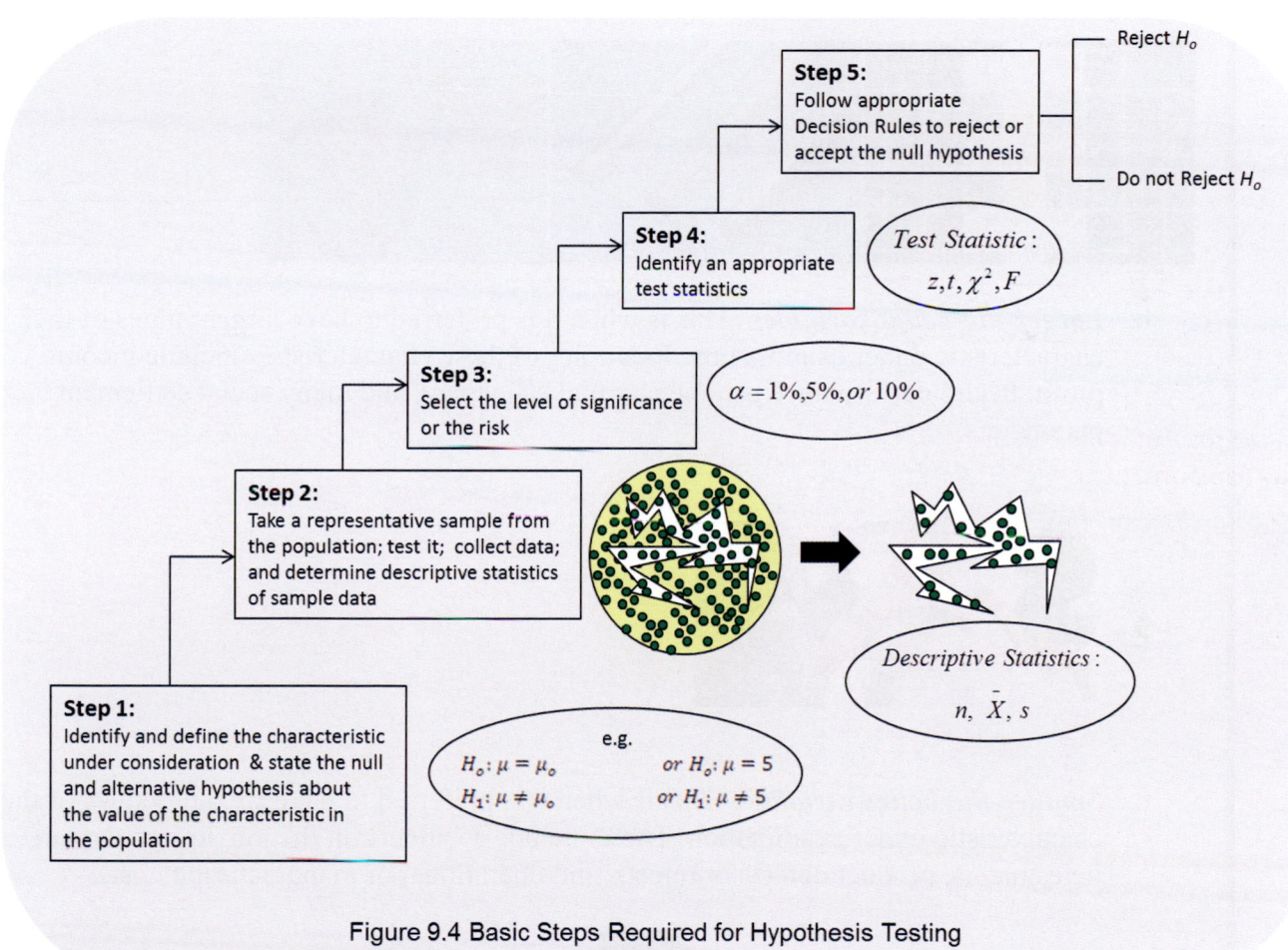

Figure 9.4 Basic Steps Required for Hypothesis Testing

Step 1: *Identifying and defining the characteristic under consideration and stating the hypothesis*

The first step is to state a hypothesis. In order to appropriately state the test of hypothesis, it is important to define and identify the characteristic or the variable under consideration. In this regard, it is important to classify the variable as one of the following three categories described below.

Variable Categories:

a. ***Nominal-the-best variables-*** This is when the average value of the characteristic should be exact (not too high and not too low). Most dimensional characteristics such as length, thickness, area, and volume follow this category. Other variables that follow this category include percent of chemicals in the human body and the number of people required for a specific task.

b. ***Larger-the-better variables-*** This is when it is preferred to have larger values of the characteristic under examination. Examples of these characteristics include income, profit, health performance parameters, fuel efficiency, and many social settlement parameters.

c. ***Smaller-the-better variables-*** This is when it is preferred to have smaller values of the characteristic under examination. These include accidents on the job, loss in market investments, product defects or rejects, and operational or manufacturing costs.

The test of hypothesis should be formatted in accordance to the variable category. For example, if a claim is made that a rod diameter is 5 cm, we should keep in mind that this is a nominal-the-best variable. In this case, a two-sided test will make perfect sense. In other words, the statement about the population should reflect a target of an exact value or a value with minimum tolerance. This statement will be as follow:

$$H_o: \mu = 5$$

$$H_1: \mu \neq 5$$

In the above form of hypothesis test, μ is the actual population mean (which we do not know), and μ_o is the claimed value of the population mean (which we try to verify).

Suppose, on the other hand, the variable was the annual profit expected from a certain investment, which is claimed to be $50,000. In this case, the variable category is larger-the-better, and the hypothesis test may be formatted as follows:

$$H_o: \mu \geq \$50,000$$

$$H_1: \mu < \$50,000$$

If the variable was one of the smaller-the-better, say percent defects in a product, claimed to be not more than 3%, the hypothesis test may be formatted as follows:

$$H_o: \mu \leq 3\%$$

$$H_1: \mu > 3\%$$

Step 2: *Selecting a sample and determining sample statistics*

Since the goal is to evaluate a hypothesis regarding a population parameter, we take a representative sample from the population, test it, collect relevant data, and determine its descriptive statistics such as the mean and the standard deviation($\bar{X}, s$). It is important to note that all aspects of sampling discussed in Chapter 7 should be considered in this step.

Step 3: *Selecting the level of significance or the extent of error*

When testing a hypothesis, we use a sample withdrawn from the population. No matter how representative this sample is, there is a chance that we may be making some errors. In this regard, two types of errors should be considered:

TYPE I ERROR: If the null hypothesis H_o is rejected when it is true, then a type I error has occurred. This type of error may result in taking actions that are not necessary (over-control thinking), or it may result in unnecessary modification of a process.

515

TYPE II ERROR: If the null hypothesis H_o is not rejected when it is false, then a type II error has occurred. This may lead to an opposite action to that of type I error or under-control.

In statistical terms, we define the probabilities of these two types of errors as follows:

- $\alpha = P$ (type I error) $= P\{$reject $H_o \mid H_o$ is true$\}$
- $\beta = P$ (type II error) $= P\{$fail to reject $H_o \mid H_o$ is false$\}$

The dynamics of these two types of errors are displayed below.

	Reality	
Decision	H_o True	H_o False
Reject H_o	Type I error	Correct decision
Don't reject H_o	Correct decision	Type II error

The mathematical determination of Type I and Type II errors is discussed in Appendix 9.A under the subject of the power of a hypothesis test.

Example 9.1: A director of human resources of a large company wants to determine whether the mean driving-to-work distance of his population of employees is greater than 30 miles. He will perform a hypothesis test with the following null and alternative hypothesis:

$$H_o: \mu = 30$$
$$H_1: \mu \neq 30$$

a. Suppose that the true mean is $\mu = 30$, and the director rejects H_o. Is this a Type I error, a Type II error, or a correct decision?
b. Suppose that the true mean is $\mu = 35$, and the director rejects H_o. Is this a Type I error, a Type II error, or a correct decision?
c. Suppose that the true mean is $\mu = 35$, and the director does not reject H_o. Is this a Type I error, a Type II error, or a correct decision?

Solution:

a. The true mean is $\mu = 30$. Thus, H_o is true. Since the director rejects H_o, this is a Type I error.
b. The true mean is $\mu = 35$. Thus, H_o is false. Since the director rejects H_o, this is a correct decision.
c. The true mean is $\mu = 35$. Thus, H_o is false. Since the director does not reject H_o, this is a Type II error.

The selection of a significance level of a test of hypothesis should be based on the fact that *the maximum allowable chance of making a type I error is determined by the level of significance (α), or the level of confidence (1-α).* By deciding the level of significance at a certain value, say 0.05 (or 5%), we essentially mean that we wish to maintain the chance of type I error at 5% or less. In other words, we wish to place the chance of rejecting a true H_o when it is true at only 5%. For a fixed sample size, the smaller we specify the significance level, α, the larger the probability, β, of not rejecting a false null hypothesis while it is false. Therefore, we must always consider a trade-off assessment of the risks involved in committing both types of errors and use that assessment as a method for balancing type I and type II error probabilities. In Appendix 9.A of this Chapter, specific guidelines and ways to calculate type I and type II errors are discussed.

Example 9.2: In 2004, a Family organization conducted a survey about the time housewives spend watching TV every day. The organization found that the average number of hours spent by housewives watching TV was 5 hours/day. If we want to test this today to see if this time has changed, what would be the format of the hypothesis test, and how can we assign type I error associated with the test?

Solution:

This is an example of a two-tailed test. In this case, there are two possible decisions:

1. The mean time spent watching television by housewives has not changed since 2004, that is, currently $\mu = 5$
2. The mean time spent watching television by housewives has changed since 2004, that is, currently $\mu \neq 5$

These two possible decisions can be formatted as follows:

$$H_o: \mu = \mu_o \qquad or \; H_o: \mu = 5$$
$$H_1: \mu \neq \mu_o \qquad or \; H_1: \mu \neq 5$$

This two-tailed test is described in Figure 9.5. As you can see in this Figure, we have to make a decision about whether we reject or fail to reject the null hypothesis, H_o. Sketching the problem the way it is demonstrated in Figure 9.5 is a key step toward reaching an appropriate decision. Here we can see that we assigned a risk (or type I error) of α, which should be divided on the two tails giving $\alpha/2$ for each tail. This is a result of the use of a two-tailed test to handle this problem. Since the total area under the normal curve is one, the area of no rejection should be 1 - α. In the following steps, we will see how to reach the decision of rejecting or not rejecting a null hypothesis. Note that the normal curve here represents the average values $\bar{X}$ of the number of hours spent in watching TV.

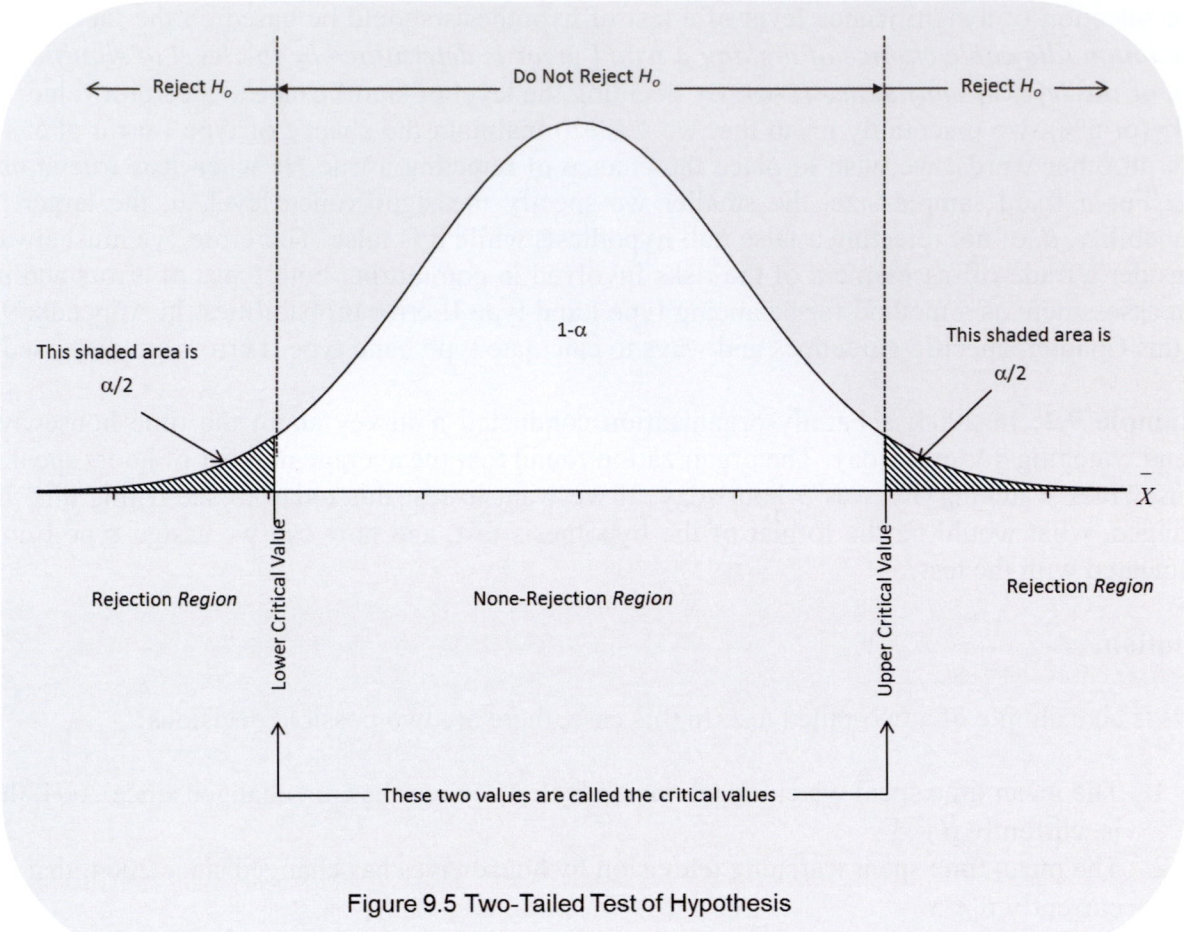

Figure 9.5 Two-Tailed Test of Hypothesis

Example 9.3: Suppose we are concerned about the consistency in a thin metal rod diameter manufactured by a metal factory that claims that the average diameter is 5 mm. what would be the format of the hypothesis test? Explain how type I or type II error may occur for this hypothesis and discuss their impacts.

Solution:

In this case, the hypothesis test can be formatted as follows:

$$H_o: \mu = 5$$
$$H_1: \mu \neq 5$$

According to the definitions of type I and type II errors, a type I error occurs if the conclusion is to reject H_o or $d = 5$ mm, while it is actually true. In this case, the supplier may have to make readjustments and perhaps a re-design of the whole metal rod manufacturing process. This is an over control approach. A type II error occurs if the conclusion is to accept H_o or $d = 5$ mm, while it is actually false. In this case, the supplier will take no action, and the company buying the rods will discover the problem during assembly, which can be very costly. This is an under control approach.

Working Problem 9.1 :
A hypothesis test is formatted as follows:
H_o: $\mu = 50$
H_1: $\mu \neq 50$

The true value of μ is 80, and H_o is rejected. Is this a Type I error, a Type II error, or a correct decision?
Answer: Correct decision

Working Problem 9.2:
A hypothesis test is formatted as follows:
H_o: $\mu \leq 10$
H_1: $\mu > 10$
The true value of μ is 10, and H_o is not rejected. Is this a Type I error, a Type II error, or a correct decision?
Answer: Do it yourself

Working Problem 9.3:
A hypothesis test is formatted as follows:
H_o: $\mu \geq 12$
H_1: $\mu < 12$
The true value of μ is 12, and H_o is rejected. Is this a Type I error, a Type II error, or a correct decision?
Answer: Do it yourself

Example 9.4: A new Coke bottle is designed to have 20 ounces of Coke. Although the actual net weights may deviate slightly from 20 ounces and vary from one bottle to another, the company insists that the mean net weight of the bottles is 20 ounces. As a result, the quality assurance department periodically performs a hypothesis test to decide whether the bottling machines are working properly, that is, to decide whether the mean net weight of all bottles is 20 ounces.
a. Format the null hypothesis for the hypothesis test.
b. Format the alternative hypothesis for the hypothesis test.
c. Classify the hypothesis test as two tailed, left tailed, or right tailed.

Solution
Let μ denote the mean net weight of all bottles.

a. The null hypothesis is that the bottling machine is working properly; that is the mean net weight, μ, of all bottles *equals* 20 ounces, or

$$H_o: \mu = 20 \text{ ounces}$$

b. The alternative hypothesis is that the bottling machine is not working properly; that is the mean net weight, μ, of all bottles is *different from* 20 ounces. or

$$H_a: \mu \neq 20 \text{ ounces}$$

519

c. This hypothesis test is two tailed because the variable under consideration is nominal-the-best variable.

Example 9.5: Write the claim as a mathematical sentence. State the null and alternative hypotheses, and identify which represents the claim.
1. A college claims that the overall grade point average of its students is 3.0
2. A manufacturer claims that the percent defects of the produced units is less than 2.5%
3. A bottling company claims that the mean weight of its bottles is greater than 14 ounces.

Solution:

1. The claim 'the overall grade point average of its students is 3.0' can be written as
$H_o: \mu = 3.0$ (Claim)
$H_1: \mu \neq 3.0$

2. A manufacturer claims that the percent defects of the produced units is less than 2.5% can be written as
$H_o: p \geq 0.025$ (or $\geq 2.5\%$)
$H_1: p < 0.025$ (Claim)

3. A bottling company claims that the mean weight of its bottles is greater than 14 oz. can be written as
$H_o: \mu \leq 14$
$H_1: \mu > 14$ (Claim)

Working Problem 9.4:

Write the claim as a mathematical sentence. State the null and alternative hypotheses, and identify which represents the claim.
1. A manufacturer claims that the area of the ceramic tiles it produces (8x8 or 64 cm²)
2. A manufacturer claims that the percent defects of the produced units is less than 3%
3. A bottling company claims that the mean weight of its bottles is greater than 16oz.

Answer:
$H_o: \mu = 64.0$ (Claim)
$H_1: \mu \neq 64.0$
2. Do it yourself
3. Do it yourself

Working Problem 9.5:

A factory claims that the percent rejects of the engines it manufactures is 1%. A quality control inspector wanted to test this claim by performing a hypothesis test to determine whether the factory's claim is true.
(a) Format this hypothesis
(b) When will a type I or type II error occur? Which is more serious?

Answer:
(a)
H_o: P = 0.01 (Claim)
H_1: P ≠ 0.01
(b) Do it yourself

Step 4: *Identify and use an appropriate test statistic*

In Chapter 8, we discussed a number of statistics suitable for establishing a confidence interval on population parameters. These include: z, t, and χ^2. The test statistic can be any one of these depending on the parameter under claim and the information provided about the population. A test statistic is a value, determined from sample statistics, which is used to determine whether to reject or accept the null hypothesis. Expressions used to determine these statistics will be presented in the following sections. For example, in a situation where population variance is known, or the sample is large, the suitable test statistic to test a hypothesis about population mean would be:

$$z_O = \frac{\bar{X} - \mu_o}{\sigma_{\bar{X}}} = \frac{\bar{X} - \mu_o}{\frac{\sigma_x}{\sqrt{n}}} \qquad (9.1)$$

where $\bar{X}$ = sample mean, μ_o = the claimed population mean, σ_x = population standard deviation, and n = sample size

Step 5: *Follow appropriate decision rules to reject or accept the null hypothesis*

Understanding the decision rule of whether to reject or accept the null hypothesis requires good knowledge of the underlying principle of hypothesis testing. This principle is illustrated using the example of metal rod diameter discussed above. In this example, the test of hypothesis is in the following format:

$$H_o: \mu = 5$$
$$H_1: \mu \neq 5$$

In order to make an appropriate decision to reject or accept a null hypothesis, it will be important to consider the following points:

a. If the claimed value, μ_o, represents the true mean of the population and we know the population standard deviation σ, then selecting samples from this population of size n will result in a sampling distribution with mean, $\mu_{\bar{X}}$, and standard deviation, $\sigma_{\bar{X}}$ or $\frac{\sigma_x}{\sqrt{n}}$. Suppose we know that the population standard deviation of metal rod diameter is 0.8 mm.

Also suppose the metal factory took a sample of 100 rods to test the null hypothesis. If the value of 5 *mm* is the true mean and assuming the means of the samples follow a normal distribution, then the mean of the sampling distribution will be $\mu_{\bar{X}} = \mu_x = 5\,mm$, and the standard deviation will be $\sigma_{\bar{X}}\ or\ \frac{\sigma_x}{\sqrt{n}} = \frac{0.8}{\sqrt{100}} = 0.08$. Note that μ_x and σ_x are the mean and the standard deviation of the parent population, respectively.

b. At a certain confidence level, say 95% (i.e. $z = 1.96$), any sample taken from this population should have a mean value falling within $\mu = \mu_{\bar{X}} \pm z.\sigma_{\bar{X}} = \mu_{\bar{X}} \pm z.\frac{\sigma_x}{\sqrt{n}} =$ $5 \pm 1.96(0.08)$ in 95% of the time. In other words, any sample we take from the population should have a mean value in the range from 4.843 to 5.157 (or a corresponding z value from -1.96 to 1.96) in 95% of the time for the null hypothesis to be accepted.

c. Now, suppose the mean of the sample selected, $\bar{X}$, turned out to be 5.2 *mm*. This means that we have to reject the null hypothesis $H_o: \mu = 5$ since it is outside the range at 95% confidence (4.843 to 5.157). Using the standard normal distribution, if this sample did belong to the claimed population, the test z-statistic ($z_o = \frac{\bar{X}-\mu_o}{\sigma_{\bar{X}}} = \frac{5.2-5}{\frac{0.8}{\sqrt{100}}} = 2.5$) should have been within the $\pm$ 1.96. But it is not and we express that as a test statistic value z_o falling in the rejection area as illustrated in Figure 9.6.

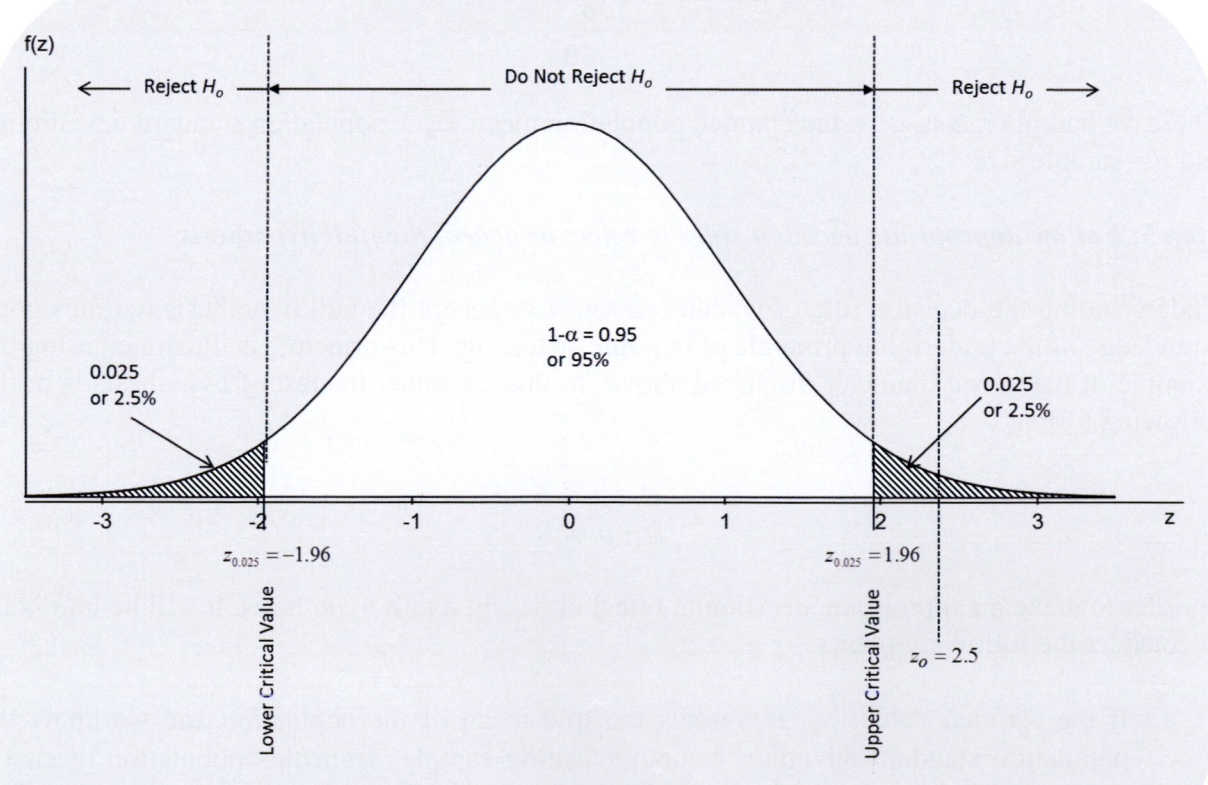

Figure 9.6 The Concept of Rejection Rules in Hypothesis Testing

In general, there are two approaches to determine if we should reject a null hypothesis. The classic approach is called the *'critical region'* approach. The second approach is called the *'p-value'* approach.

Critical Region:

As discussed above, the critical region approach requires that the rejection/acceptance procedure should consist of four tasks:
- Determine the test statistics, say z_o or t_o
- Decide on type I error, α
- Find the corresponding appropriate critical value ($z_{a/2}$ or $t_{df,\ a/2}$) at the selected type I error from statistics tables
- Compare the test statistic (z_o or t_o) with the critical $z_{a/2}$ or $t_{df,\ a/2}$ value to see if z_o or t_o is in the rejection region, which will result in a rejection of the null hypothesis (see Figures 9.5 and 9.6).

P-Value:

The *p*-value approach to set the rejection/acceptance rule will consist of four tasks:
- Determine the test statistics, say z_o or t_o
- Calculate the *p*-value associated with the test statistic.
- Decide on type I error, α
- Compare the *p*-value with type I error to make a decision.

The examples below will illustrate the use of these two approaches. These examples will be associated with different conditions of sample size and information about the population's standard deviation. Note that these conditions follow the conditions presented in Chapter 8 for establishing confidence intervals.

9.4 Hypothesis tests for a population mean, μ, when σ is known (or for large samples, n≥30)

9.4.1. Using the critical region method

Table 9.1 and Figure 9.7 summarize the procedures to perform hypothesis tests for a population mean when σ is known or when the sample size is large using the critical region approach. The critical values can be found in APPENDIX 6.A, Standard Normal Distribution Table, Chapter 6. Some of the critical values that are commonly used in hypothesis testing are listed in Table 9.2.

Table 9.1 Hypothesis tests for population mean-σ is known (or n $\geq$ 30)-critical region method

Test	Null hypothesis	Alternative hypothesis	Test statistic	Critical statistic	Reject When
Two-sided	$H_o: \mu = \mu_o$	$H_1: \mu \neq \mu_o$		$z_{\alpha/2}$	z_o is in the rejection region (See Table 9.2)
One-sided-left	$H_o: \mu \geq \mu_o$	$H_1: \mu < \mu_o$	$z_o = \dfrac{\bar{X} - \mu_o}{\dfrac{\sigma_x}{\sqrt{n}}}$	z_α	
One-sided-right	$H_o: \mu \leq \mu_o$	$H_1: \mu > \mu_o$		z_α	

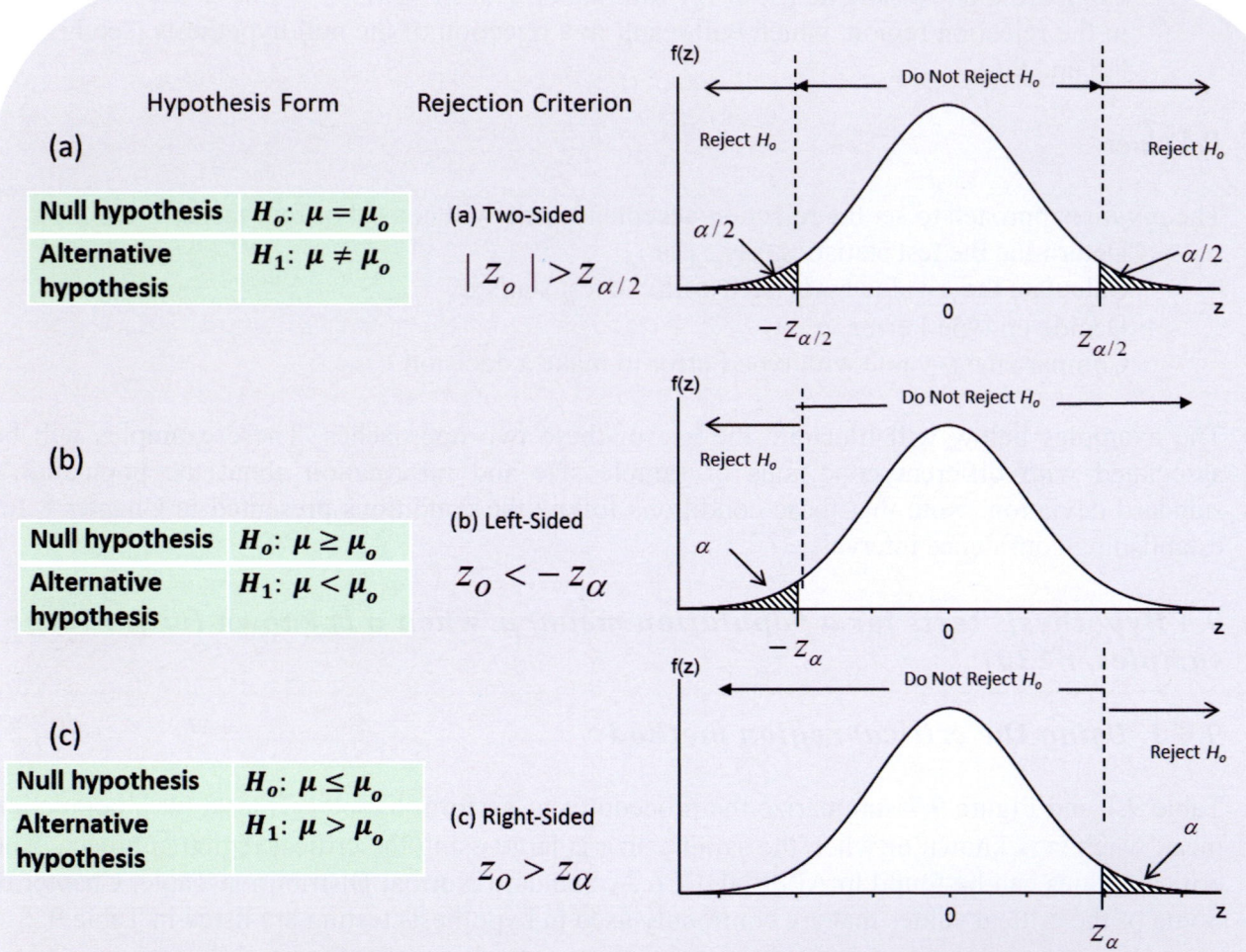

Figure 9.7 Critical Region Approach: Rejection Rules for Hypothesis Testing: Population Variance Known/Large Sample

Table 9.2 Rejection regions for selected values of α

α	Alternative Hypothesis H_1		
	Left-tailed $(H_1: \mu < \mu_o)$ Reject if:	Right-tailed $(H_1: \mu > \mu_o)$ Reject if:	Two-tailed $H_1: \mu \neq \mu_o)$ Reject if:
0.1	$z_o < -1.282$	$z_o > 1.282$	$z_o < -1.645$ or $z_o > 1.645$
0.05	$z_o < -1.645$	$z_o > 1.645$	$z_o < -1.960$ or $z_o > 1.960$
0.01	$z_o < -2.326$	$z_o > 2.326$	$z_o < -2.576$ or $z_o > 2.576$

Example 9.6: Determine the z-statistic, the critical z value, and make appropriate decision for the hypothesis test of the following cases:

(a) $\bar{X} = 80, \sigma = 5, n = 40, Claimed\ value = 82, \alpha = 0.05, H_o: \mu = \mu_o,\ H_1: \mu \neq \mu_o$
(b) $\bar{X} = 50, \sigma = 8, n = 60, Claimed\ value = 52,, \alpha = 0.01, H_o: \mu = \mu_o,\ H_1: \mu > \mu_o$
(c) $\bar{X} = 82, \sigma = 5, n = 40, Claimed\ value = 84,, \alpha = 0.10, H_o: \mu = \mu_o,\ H_1: \mu < \mu_o$

Solution:

(a) $\bar{X} = 80, \sigma = 5, n = 40, Claimed\ value = 82,, \alpha = 0.05$

$$H_o: \mu = 82,\ \ H_1: \mu \neq 82$$

$$z_o = \frac{\bar{X} - \mu_o}{\frac{\sigma_x}{\sqrt{n}}} = \frac{80 - 82}{\frac{5}{\sqrt{40}}} = -2.5298, at\ \alpha = 0.05, z_{\frac{\alpha}{2}} = 1.96, -1.96$$

Using the criteria in Table 9.2, we reject when $z_o < -1.96$ or $z_o > 1.96$. Accordingly, H_o should be rejected. Note that following the procedures discussed in Chapter 8 ($\bar{X} - z_{\alpha/2}\sigma_{\bar{X}} < \mu < \bar{X} + z_{\alpha/2}\sigma_{\bar{X}}$), we can also determine the confidence interval to verify our conclusion. In this case, the confidence interval is from 78.45 to 81.55. This means that the claimed value is outside this range and we should reject the null hypothesis.

(b) $\bar{X} = 50, \sigma = 8, n = 60, Claimed\ value = 52,, \alpha = 0.01, H_o: \mu = \mu_o,\ H_1: \mu > \mu_o$

$$H_o: \mu = 52,\ \ H_1: \mu > 52$$

$$z_o = \frac{\bar{X} - \mu_o}{\frac{\sigma_x}{\sqrt{n}}} = \frac{50 - 52}{\frac{8}{\sqrt{60}}} = -1.94, at\ \alpha = 0.01, z_\alpha = 2.326$$

Using the criteria in Table 9.2, we reject when $z_o > z_\alpha$. Accordingly, H_o should not be rejected.

(c) $\bar{X} = 82, \sigma = 5, n = 40, Claimed\ value = 84,, \alpha = 0.10, H_o: \mu = \mu_o,\ H_1: \mu < \mu_o$

$$H_o: \mu = 84 , \quad H_1: \mu < 84$$

$$z_o = \frac{\bar{X} - \mu_o}{\frac{\sigma_x}{\sqrt{n}}} = \frac{82 - 84}{\frac{5}{\sqrt{40}}} = -2.529, \, at \, \alpha = 0.1, z_\alpha = -1.282$$

Using the criteria in Table 9.2, we reject when $z_o < z_\alpha$. Accordingly, H_o should be rejected.

Example 9.7: An insurance company is concerned about its current policy rates. Those rates were originally set on the basis that the average claim amount was $1,700. Now, it is believed that the true mean may actually be higher than this. Using a randomly selected sample of 60 claims, the mean was found to be $1,900. Historically, the standard deviation of claims is found to be $400. At 5% risk, test the hypothesis that the insurance company should be concerned about the current rates.

Solution:

Step 1: *Identifying and defining the characteristic under consideration and stating the hypothesis*
Step 2: *Selecting a sample and determining sample statistics*
Step 3: *Selecting the level of significance or the extent of error*
Step 4: *Identify and use an appropriate test statistic*
Step 5: *Follow appropriate decision rules to reject or accept the null hypothesis*

Step 1: *Identifying and defining the characteristic under consideration and stating the hypothesis*

The characteristic under consideration is average claim amount. The hypothesis test format is:

$H_o: \mu = 1700$
$H_1: \mu \neq 1700$

Step 2: *Selecting a sample and determining sample statistics*
$n = 60, \bar{X} = \$1900, \sigma = \$400$

Step 3: *Selecting the level of significance or the extent of error*
$\alpha = 0.05$, with two-tailed test, $\alpha = 0.025$.

Step 4: *Identify and use an appropriate test statistic*

$$z_o = \frac{\bar{X} - \mu_o}{\frac{\sigma_x}{\sqrt{n}}} = \frac{1900 - 1700}{\frac{400}{\sqrt{60}}} = 3.87$$

526

Step 5: *Follow appropriate decision rules to reject or accept the null hypothesis*

As shown below, at $\alpha = 0.05$, $\alpha/2 = 0.025$, $z = 1.96$, we reject the null hypothesis since z_o is in the reject region ($z_o > z_{\alpha/2}$). Note that following the procedures discussed in Chapter 8 ($\bar{X} - z_{\alpha/2}\sigma_{\bar{x}} < \mu < \bar{X} + z_{\alpha/2}\sigma_{\bar{x}}$), we can also determine the confidence interval to verify our conclusion. In this case, the confidence interval is from 1,798.79 to 2,001.21. This means that the claimed value is outside this range and we should reject the null hypothesis.

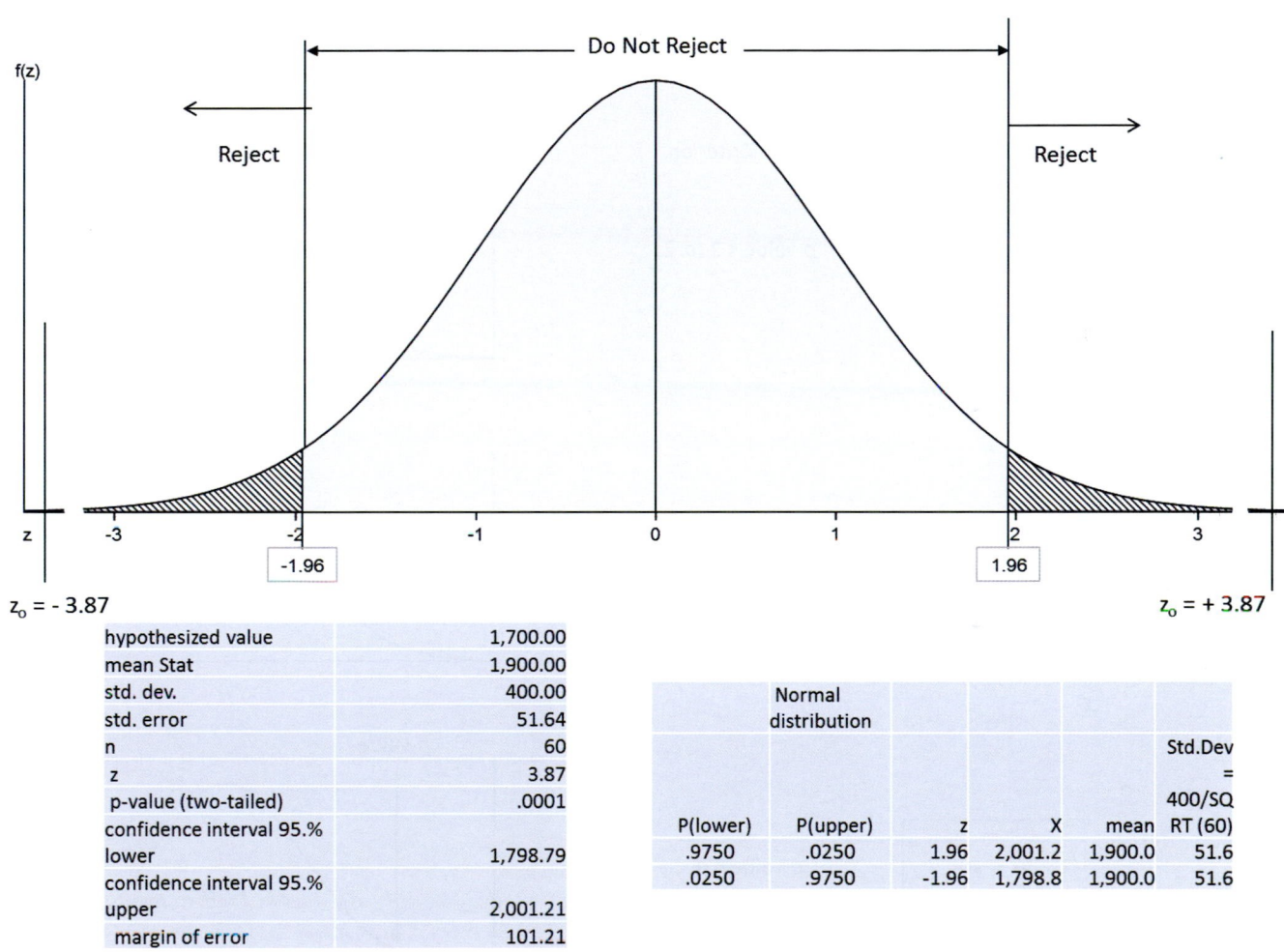

hypothesized value	1,700.00
mean Stat	1,900.00
std. dev.	400.00
std. error	51.64
n	60
z	3.87
p-value (two-tailed)	.0001
confidence interval 95.% lower	1,798.79
confidence interval 95.% upper	2,001.21
margin of error	101.21

	Normal distribution					Std.Dev = 400/SQ
P(lower)	P(upper)	z	X	mean	RT (60)	
.9750	.0250	1.96	2,001.2	1,900.0	51.6	
.0250	.9750	-1.96	1,798.8	1,900.0	51.6	

9.4.2. Using the p-value method

Table 9.3 and Figure 9.8 summarize the procedures to perform hypothesis tests for a population mean when σ is known or when the sample size is large using the *p*-value approach.

Table 9.3 Hypothesis tests for population mean- σ is known (or large sample)-p-value method

Test	Null hypothesis	Alternative hypothesis	Test statistic	Reject when
Two-sided	$H_o: \mu = \mu_o$	$H_1: \mu \neq \mu_o$		
One-sided-left	$H_o: \mu \geq \mu_o$	$H_1: \mu < \mu_o$	$z_0 = \dfrac{\bar{X} - \mu_o}{\dfrac{\sigma_x}{\sqrt{n}}}$	$p\text{-}value < \alpha$
One-sided-right	$H_o: \mu \leq \mu_o$	$H_1: \mu > \mu_o$		

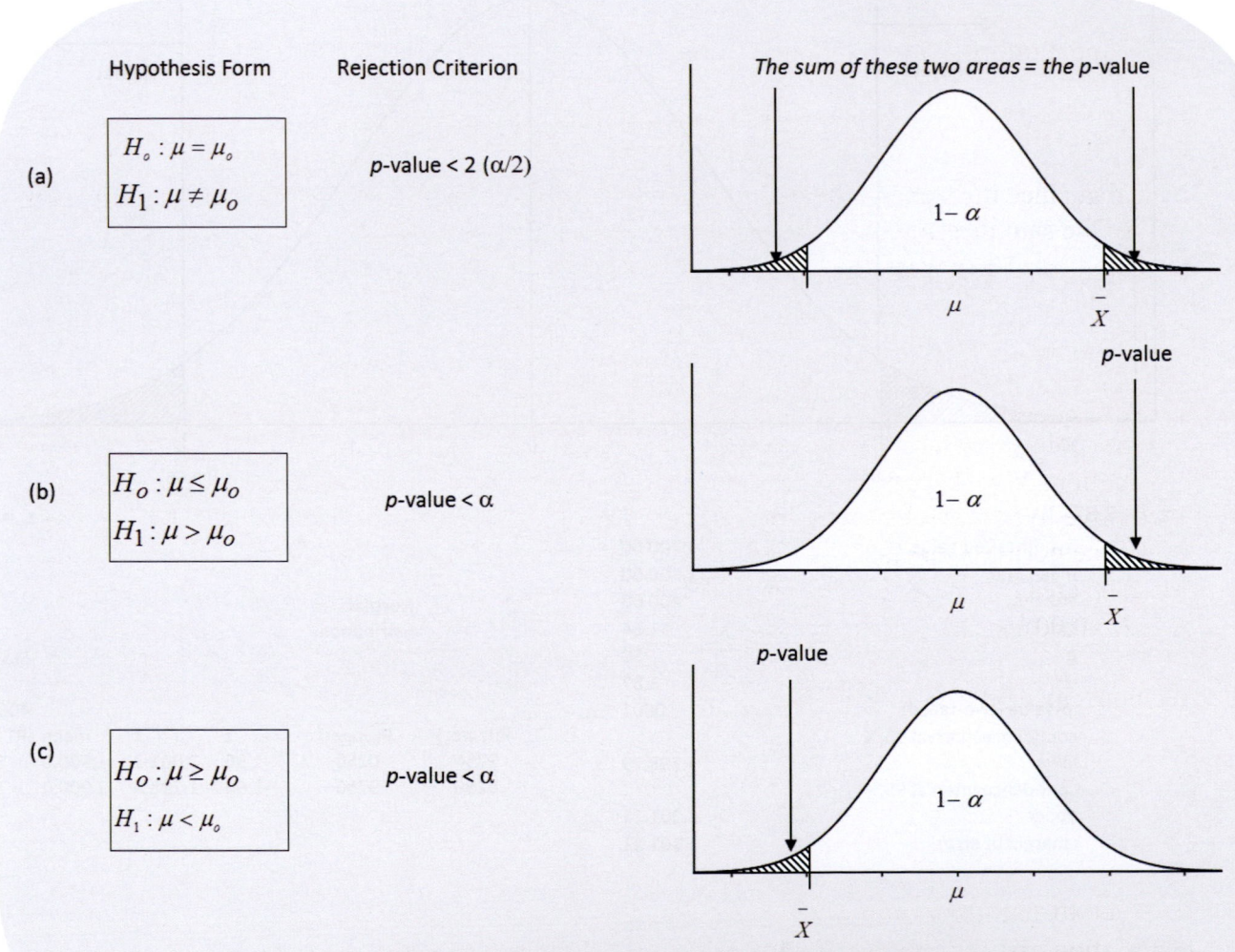

Figure 9.8 p-Value Approach: Rejection Rules for Hypothesis Testing: Population Variance Known/Large Sample

528

Example 9.8: A company with a large number of employees located in New York City is thinking about providing transportation means for its employees who live within some distances from the company's headquarter. The company is willing to arrange transportation buses for its employees if the average driving distance-to-work by the employees is about 80 miles. Using a sample of 50 employees selected randomly, the company found that the average driving distance-to-work is 85 miles and the standard deviation is 16 miles. Assist this company in making this decision using hypothesis testing at 99% confidence level.

Solution:

Using the Critical Region Approach:

The sample information is as follows:

$$\bar{X} = 85, n = 50, \sigma \approx s = 16$$

Note that since the standard deviation of the population is unknown, and the sample size is large, we use the sample standard deviation, s, as an approximation of the population's standard deviation, σ. The hypothesis test we would like to perform is:

$$H_o: \mu = 80$$
$$H_1: \mu \neq 80$$

At this point, we have to be willing to assume that the sampling distribution is a normal distribution. We also need to decide on type I error, in this case $\alpha = 0.01$. The sign $\neq$ in the alternative hypothesis indicates that the test is two-tailed with two rejection regions, one in each tail of the normal sampling distribution curve. Because the total area of both rejection regions is 0.01, the area of the rejection region in each tail is 0.005 (or $\alpha/2 = 0.005$). The corresponding $z_{\alpha/2}$ at $\alpha/2 = 0.005$ is 2.575 ($z_{0.005} = 2.58$).

We now calculate the test statistic:

$$z_o = \frac{\bar{X} - \mu_o}{\frac{\sigma_x}{\sqrt{n}}} = \frac{85 - 80}{16/\sqrt{50}} = 2.209$$

In order to use the critical region approach, it will be useful to sketch the standard normal distribution and roughly locate the $z_{\alpha/2}$ (or $z_{0.005}$) value and the z_o value to realize their relative positions. As can be seen in the normal graph, the value of z_o does not fall within the rejection region. Accordingly, H_o is not rejected since z_o falls within the do-not reject area (-2.58 to + 2.58). In other words the criterion of rejection, $|z_o| > z_{\alpha/2}$, is not met. Therefore, we fail to reject the null hypothesis that the mean distance is 80 miles. As a result, we would report to the company's headquarter that the sample results do not support a value different from 80 miles and that the company should offer the transportation service.

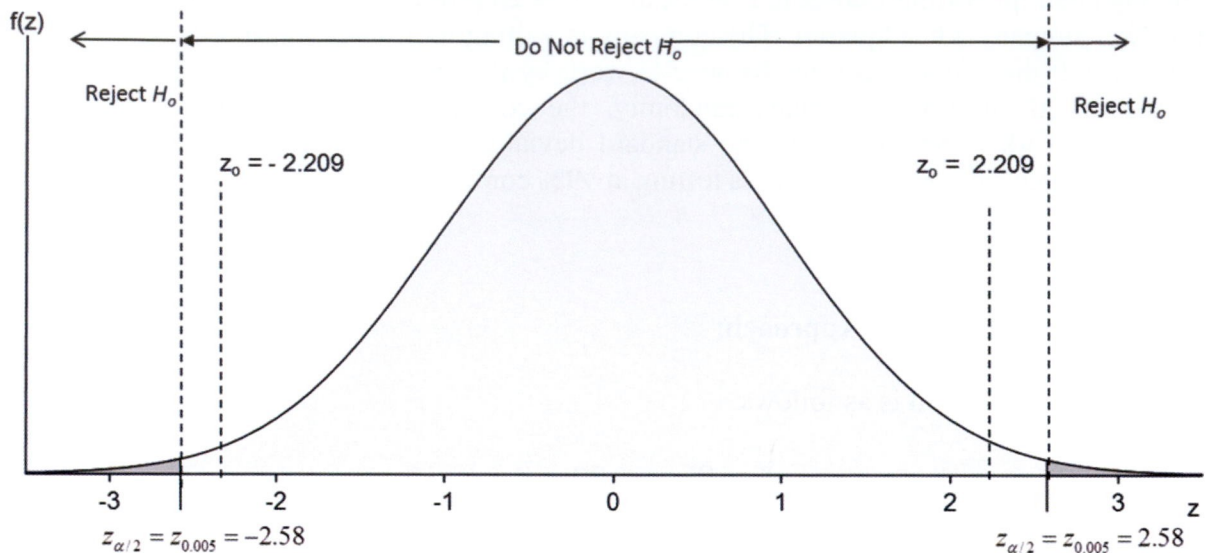

As indicated earlier, and as a way to verify your answer, you can always perform estimation on the mean value of the population, as discussed in chapter 8, and see whether it agrees with your conclusion. In this example, we can use the following equation:

$$\mu = \bar{X} \pm z_{\frac{\alpha}{2}}\sigma_{\bar{X}} \quad or \quad \mu = 85 \pm 2.58\frac{16}{\sqrt{50}}$$

or $79.16 < \mu < 90.84$

The above estimation reveals that a value of μ_o of 80 falls within the estimated range of μ. For this reason, we fail to reject the null hypothesis: $H_o: \mu = 80$

Solution using the *p*-value Approach:

The basis for the *p*-value approach is that a decision of whether to reject a null hypothesis can be made by determining whether the probability corresponding to the standardized test statistic is less than the desired level of significance. This approach results in the same conclusion as the critical region approach. Let us illustrate this using this example.

The sample information is as follows:

$\bar{X} = 85, n = 50, \sigma \approx s = 16$

Again, the hypothesis test we would like to perform is:

$$H_o: \mu = 80$$
$$H_1: \mu \neq 80$$

Assuming a normal sampling distribution, and at a significance level of 0.99 the total area of both rejection regions is 0.01, and the area of the rejection region in each tail is 0.005 (or $\alpha/2 = 0.005$).

Again, we calculate the test statistic:

$$z_o = \frac{\bar{X} - \mu_o}{\frac{\sigma_x}{\sqrt{n}}} = \frac{85 - 80}{16/\sqrt{50}} = 2.209$$

At this point, we calculate the p-value corresponding to this z_o value or actually to the $\bar{X}$ value by looking into the normal table (Appendix 6.A, Chapter 6). We find that at z_o value of 2.209, the area is 0.0136, leading to a p-value of 0.0272 (2×0.0136), which is larger than the 0.01 significance level. Thus, we fail to reject the null hypothesis that the mean distance is 80 miles. See the graph below for illustration.

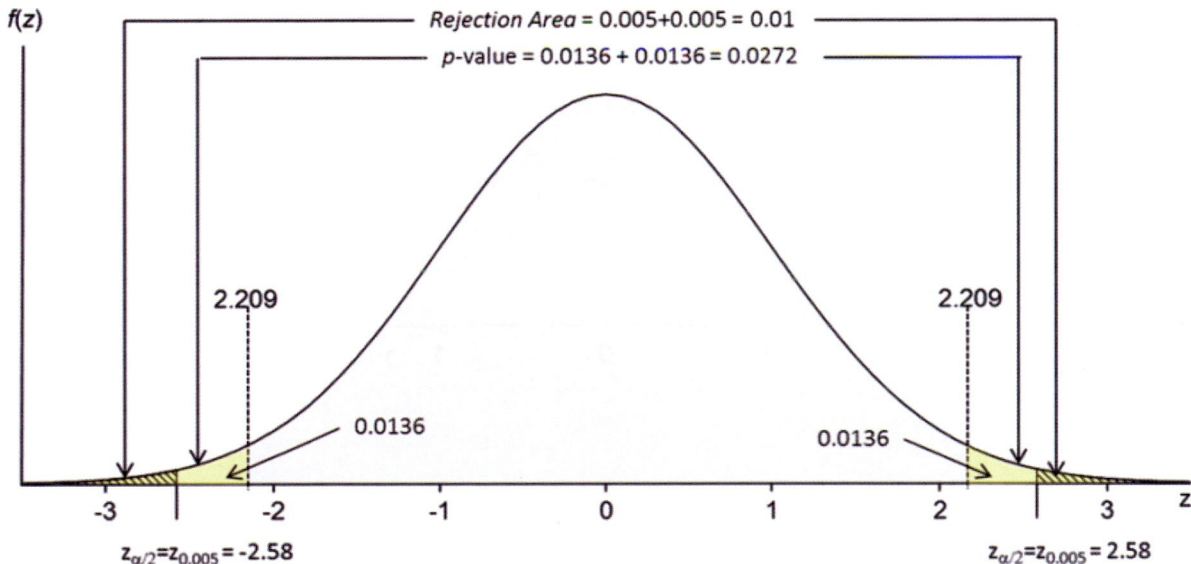

Example 9.9: In Example 9.8, suppose the company was more concerned about whether the average distance is greater than 80 miles. What type of hypothesis test should you use to assist the company making its decision? Perform the test of hypothesis at 1% type I error.

Solution:

In this case, a more appropriate format of the hypothesis test will be as follows:

$$H_o: \mu \leq 80 \ (desired)$$
$$H_1: \mu > 80 \ (concern)$$

Again, we calculate the test statistic as follows:

$$z_o = \frac{\bar{X} - \mu_o}{\frac{\sigma_x}{\sqrt{n}}} = \frac{85 - 80}{16/\sqrt{50}} = 2.209$$

At a one-tailed test and a risk of committing type I error of 1%, the total area of rejection regions is 0.01. At this area, the critical value z_α or $z_{0.01}$ is 2.33. Accordingly, the value of z_o does not fall within the rejection region. Accordingly, H_o is not rejected since z_o falls within the do-not reject area (< 2.33). In other words the criterion of rejection $z_o > z_\alpha$ is not met. Therefore, we fail to reject the null hypothesis that the mean distance is less than or equal to 80 miles. The critical region and the test statistic associated with this test are shown below.

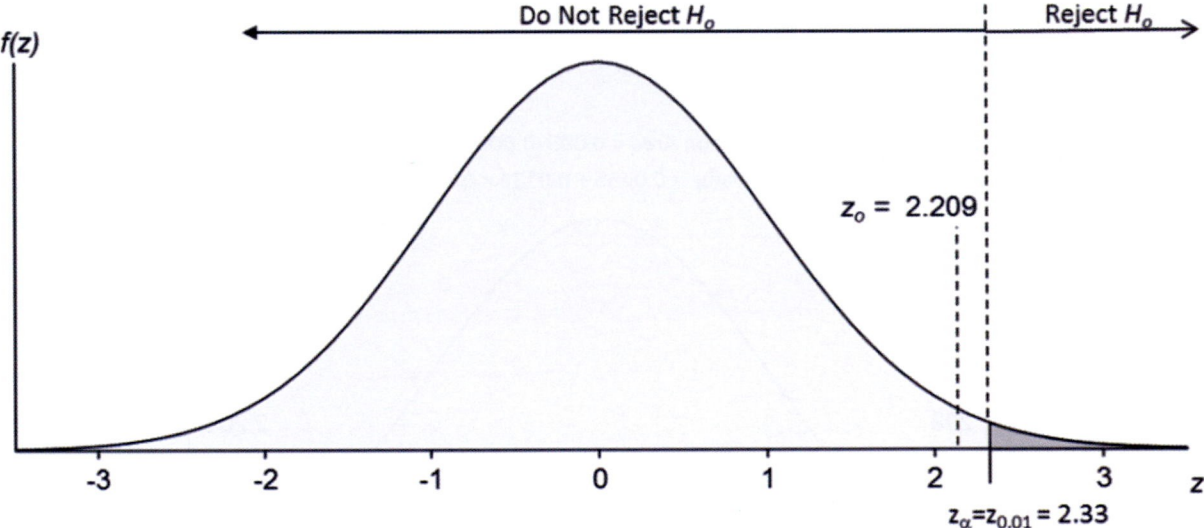

Using the p-value approach, we find that at z_o value of 2.209, the area is 0.0136 (APPENDIX 6.A Standard Normal Distribution Table, Chapter 6), which is larger than the 0.01 risk level. Thus, we fail to reject the null hypothesis that the mean distance is less than or equal to 80 miles. This supports our conclusion in the previous example.

Example 9.10: A new Coke bottle is designed to hold 20 ounces of Coke. Although the actual net weights may deviate slightly from 20 ounces and vary from one bottle to another, the company insists that the mean net weight of the bottles is 20 ounces. As a result, the quality assurance department periodically performs a hypothesis test to decide whether the bottling machines are working properly, that is, to decide whether the mean net weight of all bottles is 20 ounces. Using a sample of 25 bottles, values of bottle weight were found to be as shown in Table 9.4.

Table 9.4 Data of weight of Coke in ounces

19	18.5	19	20.5	20
21	19	20	20	20
20	21	20	20.5	18
20	19	20	20	19
20	19.5	20	19	20

Assuming that the net weights are normally distributed, and given that the population standard deviation of all such weights is 0.5 ounces, does the data provide sufficient evidence to conclude that the bottling machine is not working properly? In answering this question:

a. State the null and alternative hypotheses for the hypothesis test
b. Discuss the logic of this hypothesis test
c. Identify the distribution of the variable $\bar{X}$; that is, the sampling distribution of the sample mean for samples of size 25
d. Obtain a precise criterion for deciding whether to reject the null hypothesis in favor of the alternative hypothesis at 5% type I error
e. Apply the criterion in part (d) to the sample data and state the conclusion

Solution

Let μ denote the mean net weight of all bottles.
    a.   The null and alternative hypotheses are

Ho: $\mu = 20$ ounces (the bottling machine is working properly)
Ha: $\mu \neq 20$ ounces (the bottling machine is not working properly).

    b.   Basically, the logic of this hypothesis test is as follows: If the null hypothesis is true, then the mean weight, $\bar{X}$, of the sample of 25 bottles should approximately equal 20 ounces. We say 'approximately equal' because we cannot expect a sample mean to equal exactly the population mean; some sampling error is anticipated. However, if the sample mean weight differs 'too much' from 20 ounces, we would be inclined to reject the null hypothesis and conclude that the alternative hypothesis is true. As we will see in part (d), we can use our knowledge of the sampling distribution of the sample mean to decide how much difference is 'too much.'

    c.   Since $n = 25$, $\sigma = 0.5$, and weights are normally distributed,

$$\mu_{\bar{X}} = \mu \; (unknown)$$
$$\sigma_{\bar{X}} = \frac{\sigma}{\sqrt{n}} = \frac{0.5}{\sqrt{25}} = 0.1$$
$$\bar{X} \; is \; normally \; distributed$$

Accordingly, for samples of size 25, the variable $\bar{X}$ is normally distributed with mean μ and standard deviation 0.1 ounces.

d. At 95% confidence, $z_{\alpha/2} = z_{0.025} = 1.96$. Following the procedures discussed in Chapter 8, at 95% confidence, the mean of the weight of Coke in these bottles should be between $20 - 1.96 \times 0.1$ and $20 + 1.96 \times 0.1$ or 19.804 and 20.196. In other words, if the mean weight of the sample is not within a 1.96 standard deviation (0.196) of the 20 ounces, we have evidence against the null hypothesis. This is because observing such a sample mean would occur by chance only 5% of the time if the null hypothesis is true (see Figure 9.9).

e. The mean of the sample weights is

$$\bar{X} = \frac{19 + 21 + 20 + \cdots + 19 + 20}{25} = 19.72$$

$$z = \frac{\bar{X} - \mu_o}{\sigma_{\bar{X}}} = \frac{19.72 - 20}{0.1} = -2.8$$

That is the sample mean of 19.72 ounces is a 2.8 standard deviation below the null-hypothesis population mean of 20 ounces. Thus, the data provides sufficient evidence to conclude that the bottling machine is not working properly.

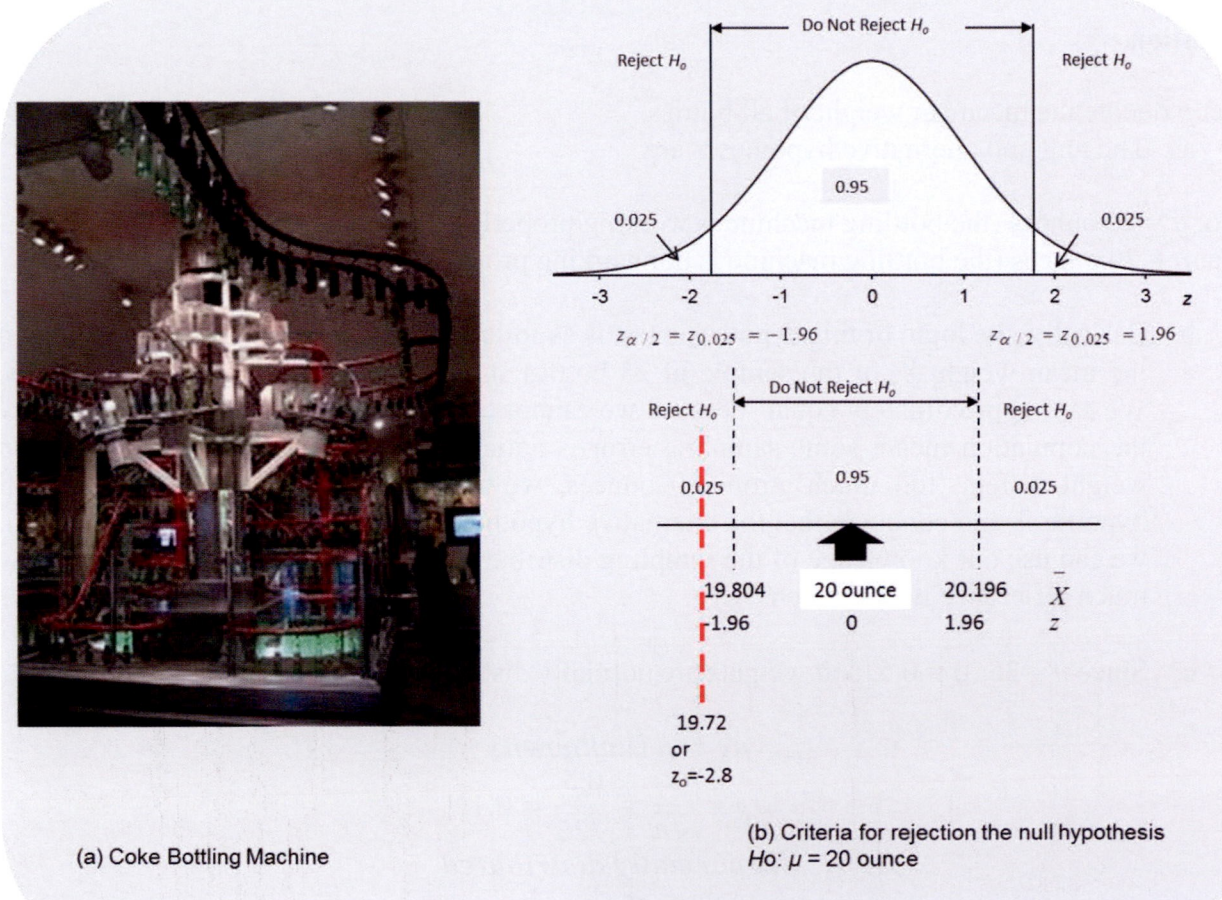

(a) Coke Bottling Machine

(b) Criteria for rejection the null hypothesis
H_o: $\mu = 20$ ounce

Figure 9.9 Criteria for testing the hypothesis associated with Coke bottle weight

Hypothesis tests for a population mean, μ, when σ is known (or for large samples, $n \geq 30$)
Basic Requirements:

1. The sample used is representative of the parent population-No outliers are allowed
2. The population from which the sample is selected is normally distributed or the sample size, n, is large ($n \geq 30$)
3. The population standard deviation, σ is known
4. The distribution of the sample mean, $\bar{X}$, is normal with mean μ_0 and standard deviation $\frac{\sigma}{\sqrt{n}}$

Step 1: *Identifying and defining the characteristic under consideration and stating the hypothesis*

Variable Category: Nominal-the-Best, Larger-the-Better, Smaller-the-Better

	Two-Tailed	Right-Tailed	Left-Tailed
Null hypothesis	$H_o: \mu = \mu_o$	$H_o: \mu \leq \mu_o$	$H_o: \mu \geq \mu_o$
Alternative hypothesis	$H_1: \mu \neq \mu_o$	$H_1: \mu > \mu_o$	$H_1: \mu < \mu_o$

Step 2: *Selecting a sample and determining sample statistics, $\bar{X}, \sigma$*
Step 3: *Selecting the level of significance or the extent of error*
$\alpha = P$ (type I error) $= P\{$reject $H_o \mid H_o$ is true$\}$, $\beta = P$ (type II error) $= P\{$fail to reject $H_o \mid H_o$ is false$\}$
Step 4: *Identify and use an appropriate test statistic* $z_0 = \frac{\bar{X} - \mu_o}{\frac{\sigma_x}{\sqrt{n}}}$

Step 5: *Follow appropriate decision rules to reject or accept the null hypothesis*

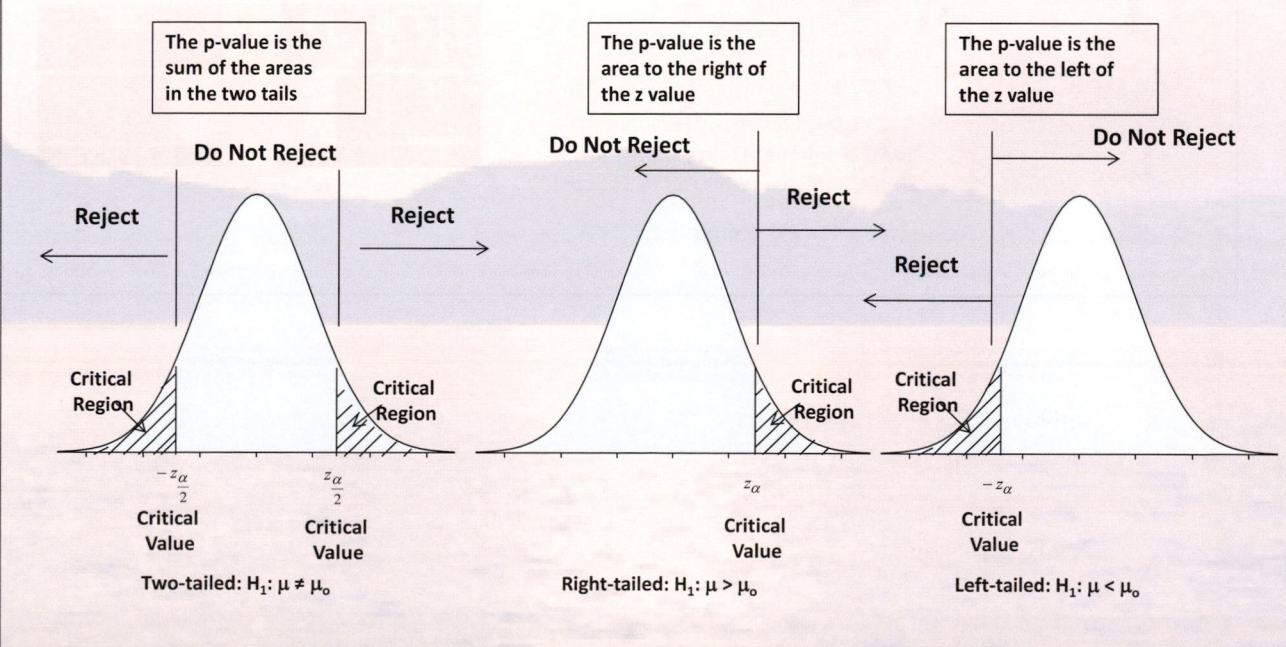

535

Working Problem 9.6: In 2010, the mean annual subscription for US Magazines was $55. Suppose that we want to perform a hypothesis test to decide whether this year's mean subscription price of US magazines has increased from the 2010 mean.

  a. Determine the null hypothesis for the hypothesis test.
  b. Determine the alternative hypothesis for the hypothesis test.
  c. Classify the hypothesis test as two tailed, left tailed, or right tailed.

Answer:
Let μ denote the 2010 mean subscription price of US magazines
a.   The null hypothesis is that this year's mean subscription price of US magazines equals the 2010 mean of $55; that is, Ho: μ = $55.
b. The alternative hypothesis is that this year's mean retail price of US magazines is *greater than* $55; that is, Ha: μ > $55
c. This hypothesis test is right tailed because a greater-than sign (>) appears in the alternative hypothesis

---

Working Problem 9.7: Given the following information:
The issue: the average area of ceramic tiles being greater than the nominal claimed area of 20 square inch
Information: n = 16,   sample mean = 20.1, population standard deviation = 0.20. Perform the hypothesis test using α = 0.05

  H_o: μ = 20
  H_1: μ > 20

Hypothesis Test: Mean vs. Hypothesized Value	
20.000	hypothesized value
20.100	mean Data
0.200	std. dev.
0.050	std. error
16	n
2.00	z
.0228	p-value (one-tailed, upper)
20.002	confidence interval 95.% lower
20.198	confidence interval 95.% upper
0.098	margin of error

,

Working problem 9.8:

A retail store selling bed sheets allows customers to purchase products using a store credit. On average, the store likes to maintain an average unpaid balance of $100 per month to be able to manage customer's credit. Using a random sample of 40 unpaid balances, it was found that the average unpaid balance was $105 and the standard deviation was $25. Should the store conclude the population mean is greater than $100, or it is reasonable that the difference of $5 is due to chance? Use $a = 0.05$.

Answer:
The null and alternate hypotheses are:

H_0: $\mu \leq \$100$
H_1: $\mu > \$100$

Because the alternate hypothesis states a direction, a one-tailed test is applied. The critical value of z is 1.65.

$$z_o = \frac{\overline{X} - \mu}{s/\sqrt{n}} = \frac{105 - 100}{25/\sqrt{40}} = 1.265$$

The decision rule is portrayed graphically in the following chart. Because the computed value of the test statistic (1.265) is smaller than the critical value (1.65), the null hypothesis cannot be rejected. The store can conclude the mean unpaid balance is not greater than $100.

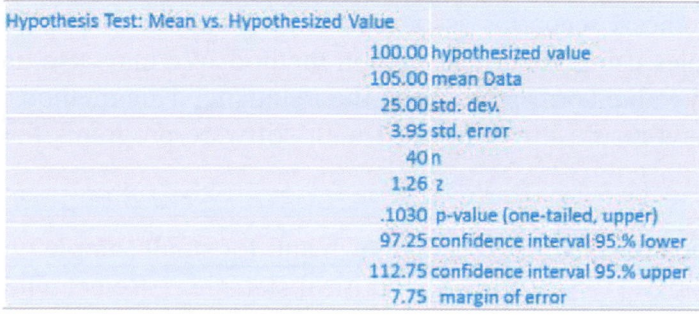

Hypothesis Test: Mean vs. Hypothesized Value

100.00	hypothesized value
105.00	mean Data
25.00	std. dev.
3.95	std. error
40	n
1.26	z
.1030	p-value (one-tailed, upper)
97.25	confidence interval 95.% lower
112.75	confidence interval 95.% upper
7.75	margin of error

$z_o = 1.265$

Working problem 9.9:

A retail store selling electronics allows customers to purchase products using a store credit. On average, the store likes to maintain an average unpaid balance of $600 per month to be able to manage customer's credit. Using a random sample of 300 unpaid balances, it was found that the average unpaid balance was $605 and the standard deviation was $35. Should the store conclude the population mean is greater than $600, or it is reasonable that the difference of $5 is due to chance? Use $a = 0.05$.

Answer:
The null and alternate hypotheses are:

H_0: $\mu \leq \$600$
H_1: $\mu > \$600$

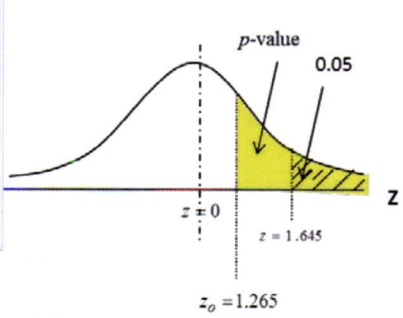

$$z = \frac{\overline{X} - \mu}{s/\sqrt{n}} = \frac{605 - 600}{35/\sqrt{300}} = 2.474$$

Because the alternate hypothesis states a direction, a one-tailed test is applied. The critical value of z is 1.65.
The decision rule is portrayed graphically in the following chart.
Because the computed value of the test statistic (2.474) is larger than the critical value (1.65), the null hypothesis is rejected. The store can conclude the mean unpaid balance is greater than $600.

Hypothesis Test: Mean vs. Hypothesized Value

600.00	hypothesized value
605.00	mean Stat
35.00	std. dev.
2.02	std. error
300	n
2.47	z
.0067	p-value (one-tailed, upper)

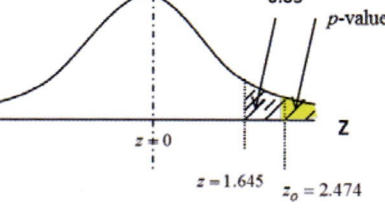

$z = 1.645$ $z_o = 2.474$

537

9.5 Hypothesis tests for a population mean, μ, when σ is unknown (or for small samples, n < 30)

Hypothesis tests can also be performed for situations where the population standard deviation is unknown or when small samples are withdrawn from populations with no knowledge of their standard deviations. In this case, we use the t statistic as the test statistic:

$$t_o = \frac{\bar{X} - \mu_o}{\frac{s}{\sqrt{n}}} \qquad (9.2)$$

where $\bar{X}$ = sample mean, μ_o = the claimed population mean, s = sample standard deviation, and n = sample size

Table 9.5 illustrates the different hypothesis scenarios associated with situations of populations of unknown variances and small samples using the critical region method. We may also use the p-value by determining the probability value corresponding to the t-statistic. This method is not accurate when it is done manually. As a result, it can be used with software programs that can determine the area more accurately.

Table 9.5 Hypothesis tests for population mean when σ is unknown and for small sample

Test	Null hypothesis	Alternative hypothesis	Test statistic	Critical statistic	Reject when
Two-sided	$H_o: \mu = \mu_o$	$H_1: \mu \neq \mu_o$		$t_{df,\alpha/2}$	$t < -t_{\alpha/2}$ or $t > t_{\alpha/2}$
One-sided-left	$H_o: \mu \geq \mu_o$	$H_1: \mu < \mu_o$	$t_o = \frac{\bar{X} - \mu_o}{\frac{s}{\sqrt{n}}}$	$t_{df,\alpha}$	$t < -t_\alpha$
One-sided-right	$H_o: \mu \leq \mu_o$	$H_1: \mu > \mu_o$		$t_{df,\alpha}$	$t > t_\alpha$

Example 9.11: Determine the t-statistic, the critical t value, and make appropriate decision for the hypothesis test for the following cases:

(a) $\bar{X} = 80, s = 5, n = 10, Claimed\ value = 82, \alpha = 0.05, H_o: \mu = \mu_o,\ H_1: \mu \neq \mu_o$
(b) $\bar{X} = 50, s = 8, n = 20, Claimed\ value = 52,, \alpha = 0.01, H_o: \mu = \mu_o,\ H_1: \mu > \mu_o$
(c) $\bar{X} = 17.57, s = 2.9522, n = 10, Claimed\ value = 20,, \alpha = 0.01, H_o: \mu = \mu_o,\ H_1: \mu < \mu_o$

Solution:

(a) $\bar{X} = 80, s = 5, n = 10, Claimed\ value = 82, \alpha = 0.05, H_o: \mu = \mu_o,\ H_1: \mu \neq \mu_o$

$$H_o: \mu = 82,\ H_1: \mu \neq 82$$

538

$$t_o = \frac{\bar{X} - \mu_o}{\frac{s_x}{\sqrt{n}}} = \frac{80 - 82}{\frac{5}{\sqrt{10}}} = -1.265,$$

$at\ \alpha = 0.05, \quad and\ df = n - 1 = 10 - 1 = 9, t_{\frac{\alpha}{2}} = 2.262, -2.262$

Conclusion: Using the criteria in Table 9.5, we reject when $t_o < -t_{\alpha/2}$. Accordingly, H_o should not be rejected. As illustrated below, at $\alpha = 0.05$, $\alpha/2 = 0.025$, $df = n-1 = 10-1 = 9$, $t = 2.262$ or -2.262 we fail to reject the null hypothesis since t_o of -1.265 is in the no-reject region ($t_o < t_{\alpha/2}$). Note that following the procedures discussed in Chapter 8 ($\bar{X} - t_{\alpha/2}s_{\bar{X}} < \mu < \bar{X} + t_{\alpha/2}s_{\bar{X}}$), we can also determine the confidence interval to verify our conclusion. In this case, the confidence interval is from 76.42 to 83.58. This means that the claimed value is within this range and we should not reject the null hypothesis. Also note that the p-value being 0.2377 >> 0.05 confirms the no-rejection of H_o. It is important to point out that the p-value for the t-distribution is best obtained using technology as it will be difficult to obtain it manually.

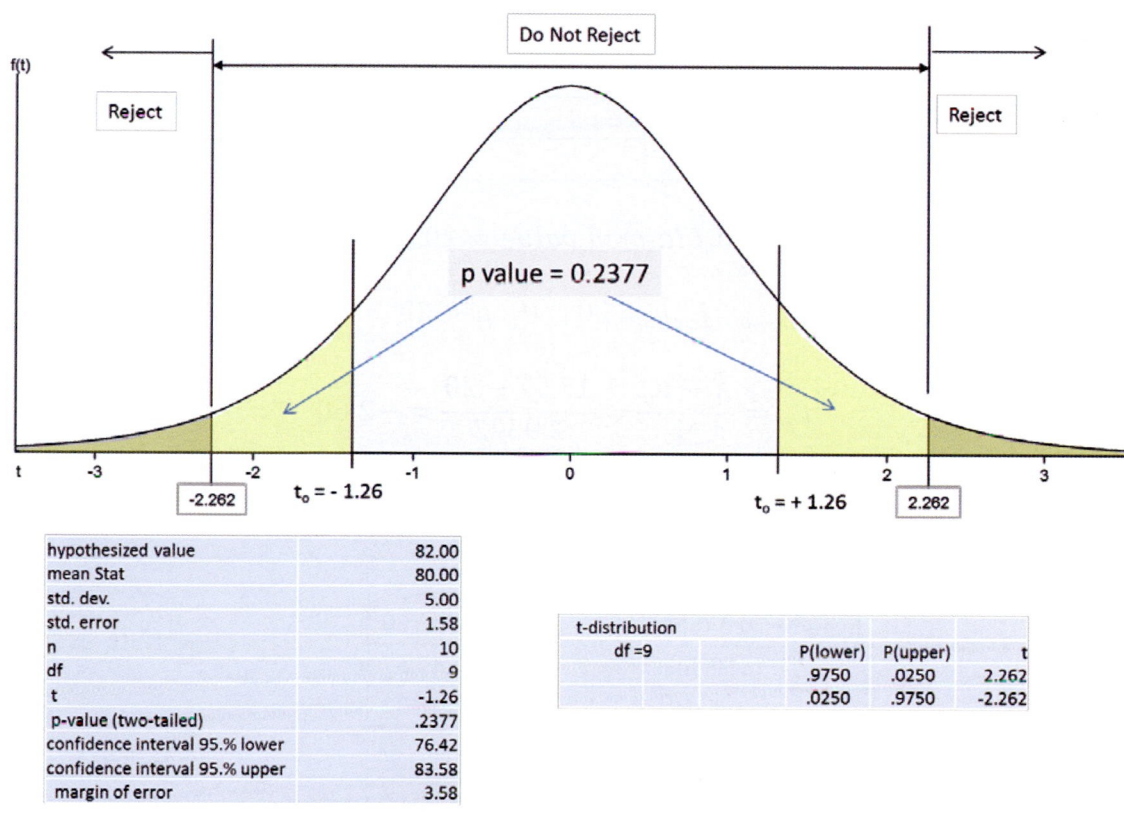

hypothesized value ... 82.00
mean Stat ... 80.00
std. dev. ... 5.00
std. error ... 1.58
n ... 10
df ... 9
t ... -1.26
p-value (two-tailed) ... .2377
confidence interval 95.% lower ... 76.42
confidence interval 95.% upper ... 83.58
margin of error ... 3.58

t-distribution			P(lower)	P(upper)	t
df =9			.9750	.0250	2.262
			.0250	.9750	-2.262

$(b)\ \bar{X} = 50, s = 8, n = 20, Claimed\ value = 52,, \alpha = 0.01, H_o: \mu = \mu_o,\ \ H_1: \mu > \mu_o$

$$H_o: \mu = 52,\ \ H_1: \mu > 52$$

$$t_o = \frac{\bar{X} - \mu_o}{\frac{S_x}{\sqrt{n}}} = \frac{50 - 52}{\frac{8}{\sqrt{20}}} = -1.12,$$

$at\ \alpha = 0.01, df = n - 1 = 20 - 1 = 19, t_\alpha = 2.539$

Conclusion: Using the criteria in Table 9.5, we reject when $t_o > t_\alpha$. Accordingly, H_o should not be rejected.

Hypothesis Test: Mean vs. Hypothesized Value	
hypothesized value	52
mean Stat	50
std. dev.	8
n	20
df	19
t	-1.12
p-value (one-tailed, upper)	0.8613
confidence interval 99.% lower	44.88
confidence interval 99.% upper	55.12
margin of error	5.12

$(c)\ \bar{X} = 17.57, s = 2.9522, n = 10, Claimed\ value = 20,, \alpha = 0.01, H_o: \mu = \mu_o,\ \ H_1: \mu < \mu_o$

$$H_o: \mu = 20,\ \ H_1: \mu < 20$$

$$t_o = \frac{\bar{X} - \mu_o}{\frac{S_x}{\sqrt{n}}} = \frac{17.57 - 20}{\frac{2.9522}{\sqrt{10}}} = -2.60$$

$at\ \alpha = 0.01, df = n - 1 = 10 - 1 = 9, t_\alpha = -2.821$

Hypothesis Test: Mean vs. Hypothesized Value	
hypothesized value	20
mean Stat	17.57
std. dev.	2.9522
n	10
df	9
T	-2.6
p-value (one-tailed, lower)	0.0143
confidence interval 99.% lower	14.5361
confidence interval 99.% upper	20.6039
margin of error	3.0339

Conclusion: We reject when $t_o < -t_\alpha$. Accordingly, we fail to reject the null hypothesis.

Example 9.12: A manufacturer of wooded boards used for making office desks has started to use a new surface finish treatment, which is believed to have minimum absorption of water in case of water or liquid spill incidents. The provider of the surface treatment claims that on average the absorption rate of surfaces using this treatment is 1.2%. The manufacturer decided to test this claim by testing a sample of 26 wooded boards selected randomly and treated with the new surface finish. Values of the absorption rate of the wooded boards of this sample are listed in Table 9.6. Using hypothesis testing at 99% confidence, determine whether the manufacturer should consider using this surface treatment in his operation?

Table 9.6 Values of absorption rate of treated wooded boards

Specimen number	Absorption rate (%)	Specimen number	Absorption rate (%)
1	0.91	14	1.28
2	1.16	15	1.83
3	0.97	16	0.96
4	1.48	17	1.17
5	0.59	18	1.58
6	1.18	19	1.18
7	0.90	20	0.67
8	1.42	21	1.20
9	1.41	22	0.93
10	0.89	23	0.94
11	0.70	24	0.91
12	1.15	25	0.41
13	1.30	26	0.98

Solution:

In order to address the question of this example, we assume that the absorption rate belongs to the category of nominal-the-best variable and we set the following hypothesis:

$$H_o: \mu = 1.2$$
$$H_1: \mu \neq 1.2$$

We calculate the mean and standard deviation of the sample data shown in Table 9.5.

$$\bar{X} = 1.08, n = 26, df = 25, s = 0.32$$

We calculate the test-statistic:

$$t_o = \frac{\bar{X} - \mu_o}{\frac{s}{\sqrt{n}}} = \frac{1.08 - 1.2}{\frac{0.32}{\sqrt{26}}} = -1.91$$

We now determine whether the t_o value falls in the rejection region by finding the value of $t_{n-1, \alpha/2}$ from Table I, Appendix 8.A. (for demonstration, see below). As shown in this table, the value of $t_{n-1, \alpha/2,} = t_{25, 0.005} = 2.787$.

Table I: t-Distribution Table

$\gamma \backslash \alpha$	0.4	0.25	0.1	0.05	0.025	0.01	0.005	0.0025	0.001	0.0005
1	0.325	1	3.078	6.314	12.706	31.821	63.657	127.32	318.31	636.62
2	0.289	0.816	1.886	2.92	4.303	6.965	9.925	1.4.089	23.326	31.598
..	..	..	..	..	..	..	..	..	..	..
25	0.256	0.684	1.316	1.708	2.06	2.485	**2.787**	3.078	3.45	3.725
26	0.256	0.684	1.315	1.706	2.056	2.479	2.779	3.067	3.435	3.707

The value of t_o (-1.91) falls in the 'Do Not Reject' region. This means that we cannot reject the null hypothesis and we conclude that the sample used indicates that the claim of 1.2% absorption rate is correct.

Note that as a way to verify your answer, you can always perform estimation on the mean value of the population, as discussed in Chapter 8, and see whether it agrees with your conclusion. In this example, we can use the following equation:

$$\mu = \bar{X} \pm t_{df, \alpha/2} \frac{s}{\sqrt{n}}$$

$$or \ \mu = 1.08 \pm 2.787 \frac{0.32}{\sqrt{26}}$$

$$0.905 < \mu < 1.26$$

The above estimation reveals that a value of μ_o of 1.2 falls within the estimated range of μ. For this reason, we fail to reject the null hypothesis $H_o: \mu = 1.2$

Hypothesis tests for a population mean, μ, when σ is Unknown

Basic Requirements:

- The sample used is representative of the parent population-No outliers are allowed
- The population from which the sample is drawn is normally distributed
- The population standard deviation, σ is unknown

Step 1: *Identifying and defining the characteristic under consideration and stating the hypothesis*

Variable Category: *Nominal-the-Best, Larger-the-Better, Smaller-the-Better*

	Two-Tailed	Right-Tailed	Left-Tailed
Null hypothesis	$H_o: \mu = \mu_o$	$H_o: \mu \leq \mu_o$	$H_o: \mu \geq \mu_o$
Alternative hypothesis	$H_1: \mu \neq \mu_o$	$H_1: \mu > \mu_o$	$H_1: \mu < \mu_o$

Step 2: *Selecting a sample and determining sample statistics $\bar{X}, s, n$*
Step 3: *Selecting the level of significance or the extent of error*
$\alpha = P$ (type I error) $= P\{$reject $H_o \mid H_o$ is true$\}$, $\beta = P$ (type II error) $= P\{$fail to reject $H_o \mid H_o$ is false$\}$
Step 4: *Identify and use an appropriate test statistic* $t_o = \dfrac{\bar{X} - \mu_o}{\frac{s}{\sqrt{n}}}$

Step 5: *Follow appropriate decision rules to reject or accept the null hypothesis*

For two-tailed H_1: The critical values are $t_{\alpha/2}$, which has area $\alpha/2$ to its right, and $-t_{\alpha/2}$, which has area $\alpha/2$ to its left
Reject H_o: if $t_o \geq t_{\alpha/2}$ or $t_o \leq -t_{\alpha/2}$

For right-tailed H_1: The critical value is t_α, which has area α to its right.
Reject H_o: if $t_o \geq t_\alpha$

For left-tailed H_1: The critical values is $-t_\alpha$, which has area α to its left
Reject H_o: if $t_o \leq -t_{\alpha/2}$

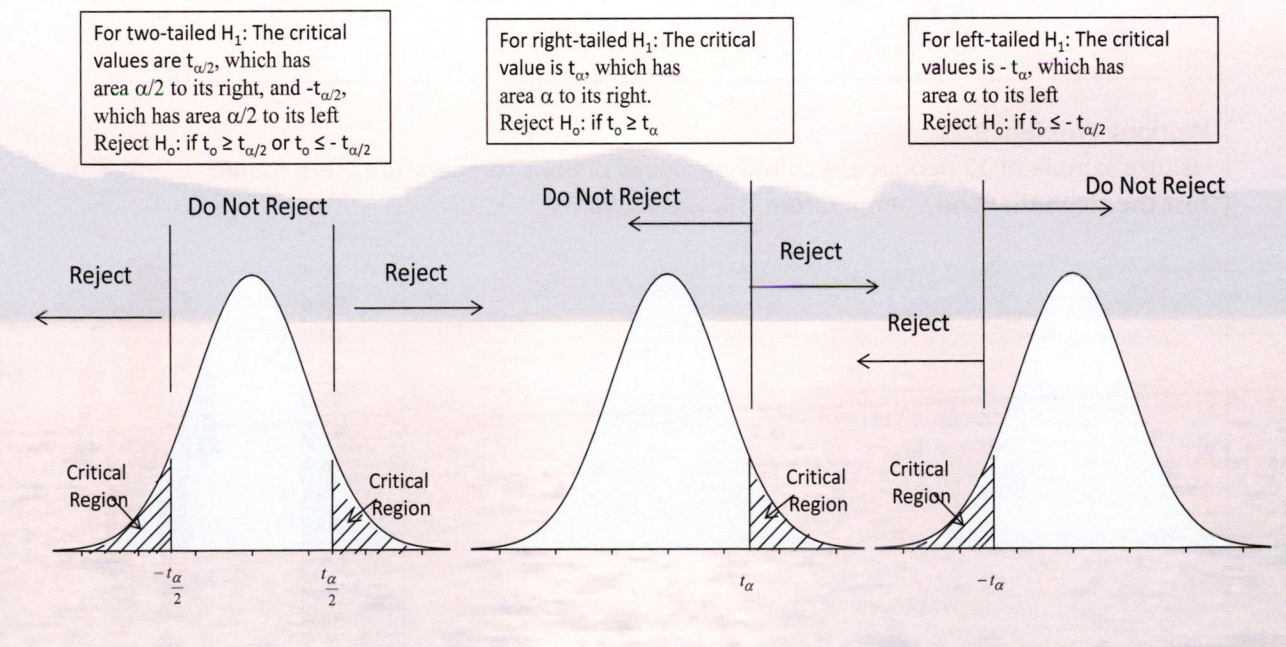

Working problem 9.10.:

Use a t-test to test the claim about the population mean, μ:

(a)$H_o : \mu = 80$, Sample mean = 77, Std.Dev = s = 4.5, $\alpha = 0.01$, n = 25

(b)$H_o : \mu = 15$, Sample mean = 13.9, Std.Dev. = s = 3.23, $\alpha = 0.01$, n = 6

(c)$H_1 : \mu < 100$, Sample mean = 105, Std.Dev = s = 8, $\alpha = 0.05$, n = 30

(d)$H_1 : \mu < 8000$, Sample mean = 7700, Std.Dev = s = 450, $\alpha = 0.01$, n = 25

Answer: See the outputs below and try to work out the problems yourself to reach the solutions given below. Make your conclusions.

(a)		(b)	
hypothesized value	80.00	hypothesized value	15.000
mean Stat	77.00	mean Stat	13.900
std. dev.	4.50	std. dev.	3.230
n	25	n	6
df	24	df	5
t	-3.33	t	-0.83
p-value (two-tailed)	.0028	p-value (two-tailed)	.4422
confidence interval 99.% lower	74.48	confidence interval 99.% lower	8.583
confidence interval 99.% upper	79.52	confidence interval 99.% upper	19.217
margin of error	2.52	margin of error	5.317

(c)		(d)	
hypothesized value	100.00	hypothesized value	8,000.00
mean Stat	105.00	mean Stat	7,700.00
std. dev.	8.00	std. dev.	450.00
n	30	n	25
df	29	df	24
t	3.42	t	-3.33
p-value (one-tailed, lower)	.9991	p-value (one-tailed, lower)	.0014
confidence interval 95.% lower	102.01	confidence interval 99.% lower	7,448.28
confidence interval 95.% upper	107.99	confidence interval 99.% upper	7,951.72
margin of error	2.99	margin of error	251.72

Working Problem 9.11:

Using a sample of 12 people, the following values of body temperature were found:
Test the claim that body temperature is less than 98.6°F.

Answer: See the outputs below and try to work out the problems yourself to reach the solutions given below. Make your conclusions

Hypothesis Test: Mean vs. Hypothesized Value

    98.60000 hypothesized value
    98.39000 mean Temp F
     0.53404 std. dev.
     0.15416 std. error
        12 n
        11 df

     -1.36 t
     .1002 p-value (one-tailed, lower)

Temp°F
99.4
98.4
98.8
98.6
97.6
97.5
98.6
98
98.68
98
98.5
98.6

Working Problem 9.12:

Acid rain is a rain or any other form of precipitation that is unusually acidic. This occurs at elevated levels of hydrogen ions (or low pH levels). It can have harmful effects on plants, aquatic animals, and infrastructure through the process of wet deposition. Acid rain is caused by emissions of sulfur dioxide and nitrogen oxides which react with the water molecules in the atmosphere to produce acids. Governments have made efforts since the 1970s to reduce the release of sulfur dioxide into the atmosphere with positive results. Nitrogen oxides can also be produced naturally by lighting strikes and sulfur dioxide is produced by volcanic eruptions. Many lakes around the globe have become acidic under the burning of fossil fuels. In general, a lake is classified as non-acidic if it has a pH level greater than 6. The data below shows the pH levels obtained using a sample of 15 lakes. Can you conclude that there is a sufficient evidence that on average the lakes are non-acidic? Use a 5% type I error.

Answer: See the outputs below and try to work out the problems yourself to reach the solutions given below. Make your conclusions

pH
7.1
6.9
7.3
7.3
6.3
6.9
6.2
6.3
7.9
5.2
7.2
7.3
6.1
6.6
6.7

$$H_o : \mu = 6$$
$$H_1 : \mu > 6$$

$$t_o = \frac{\bar{X} - \mu_o}{s/\sqrt{n}} = \frac{6.7533 - 6}{0.6632/\sqrt{15}} = 4.4$$

$$t_{0.05} = 1.761 \ at \ df = 14$$

$$t_o > t_{0.05}$$

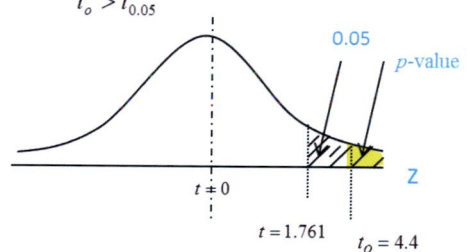

Hypothesis Test: Mean vs. Hypothesized Value

6.0000 hypothesized value
6.7533 mean pH
0.6632 std. dev.
0.1712 std. error
15 n
14 df

4.40 t
.0003 p-value (one-tailed, upper)

6.3861 confidence interval 95.% lower
7.1206 confidence interval 95.% upper
0.3673 margin of error

9.6 Hypothesis tests for a population proportion

Using a similar procedure to the one described in the previous sections, we can also perform a test of hypothesis for proportion using one of the following forms:

Null hypothesis	$H_o: p = p_o$	$H_o: p \leq p_o$	$H_o: p \geq p_o$
Alternative hypothesis	$H_1: p \neq p_o$	$H_1: p > p_o$	$H_1: p < p_o$

For large n, and p not too near 0 or 1 (around the center between 0 and 1), p is approximately normally-distributed with $\mu_p = p$ and $\sigma^2_p = p(1-p)/n$. This means that testing a proportion p can be made in a similar way to that of the mean value using the z-statistic.

The rule of thumb:

If $np \geq 5$ and $nq \geq 5$ for a variable following a binomial distribution, we can assume that the sampling distribution of $\hat{p}$ is normal with $\mu_p = p$ and $\sigma_p^2 = p(1-p)/n$.

In light of the above assumption, the test-statistic for proportion will be as follows:

$$z_o = \frac{\hat{p} - p}{\sqrt{\frac{p(1-p)}{n}}} \qquad (9.3)$$

where $\hat{p}$ = sample proportion, $\mu_p = p$ = the hypothesized proportion of population, n = sample size, and σ_p = population standard deviation (Note: if the value of population standard deviation σ_p is known from historical data, it should be used in the above equation).

Example 9.13: Recall in example 9.8 that a company of a large number of employees was thinking about providing transportation means for its employee who live within some distances from the company's headquarter. Also recall that we failed to reject the null hypothesis that the mean distance is less than or equal 80 miles. This conclusion should give a green signal to the company to go ahead with providing transportation to its employees. However, there was one catch! The company would charge the employees a cost-share of $50 per month for providing this service. If at least 80% of employees accepted this fee, the company would offer the service. Using a sample of 800 employees, 520 employees agreed to pay the fee for using this service, what should be the company's decision in this case?

Solution:

As you can see there are many factors that should be considered before making the costly decision of providing company transportation. Our concern in this example is about the percent of people that would be willing to pay the fee for using the service. The key questions in this regard are: what is the format of the test of hypothesis under these circumstances and what is the conclusion at 99% confidence?

The appropriate hypothesis test in this case is:

$$H_o: p \geq 0.8 \ (hope)$$

$$H_1: p < 0.8$$

Since out of 800 employees, 520 employees agreed to use the service, $\hat{p} = \frac{n_i}{n} = \frac{520}{800} = 0.65$. The products $np = 800(0.8) = 640$ and $nq = 800(0.2) = 160$ are both greater than 5, which allows the use of normal approximation. The test-statistic is:

$$z_o = \frac{\hat{p} - p}{\sqrt{\frac{p(1-p)}{n}}} = \frac{0.65 - 0.8}{\sqrt{\frac{0.8(0.2)}{800}}} = -10.6$$

At a type I error of 0.01, $z_\alpha = z_{0.01} = -2.33$. You can see that the z_o is in rejection region, which means we have to reject the null hypothesis that 80% or more employees will use the transportation service. In line of recommendation, we should recommend that the company does not offer this service at the price of $50 per month as it will not get the 80% of employees that justifies its decision.

Example 9.14: Suppose the company in the above example negotiated the transportation service with an independent company and was able to reduce the cost share by employee down to only $40 per month. At this rate, the company surveyed a random sample of 100 employees and found that 78 employees agreed to pay for using the service. How does this outcome change the above analysis and the company's decision?

Solution:

Again, the appropriate hypothesis test in this case is:

$$H_o: p \geq 0.8 \; (hope)$$
$$H_1: p < 0.8$$

Since out of 100 employees, 78 employees agreed to pay for using the service, $\hat{p} = \frac{n_i}{n} = \frac{78}{100} = 0.78$. The product $np = 100(0.8) = 80$ and $nq = 100(0.2) = 20$ are both greater than 5, which allows the use of normal approximation. The test-statistic is:

$$z_o = \frac{\hat{p} - p}{\sqrt{\frac{p(1-p)}{n}}} = \frac{0.78 - 0.8}{\sqrt{\frac{0.8(0.2)}{100}}} = -0.5$$

At a significance level = 0.01, $z_\alpha = z_{0.01} = -2.33$. You can see that the z_o is now in the 'Do Not Reject' region, which means we cannot reject the null hypothesis that 80% or more employees will use the transportation service. Accordingly, with the reduction in transportation cost, we should recommend that the company offers this service at this new rate of $40 per month as 80% of employees or more will use it.

We should point out that using the new proportion of 0.78, a two-sided confidence interval of the proportion of the population at 99% confidence will be:

$$\hat{p} - z_{\alpha/2}\sigma_p < p < \hat{p} + z_{\alpha/2}\sigma_p$$

$$\hat{p} - z_{\alpha/2}\sqrt{\frac{\hat{p}(1-\hat{p})}{n}} < p < \hat{p} + z_{\alpha/2}\sqrt{\frac{\hat{p}(1-\hat{p})}{n}}$$

$$0.78 - 2.58\sqrt{\frac{0.78(0.22)}{100}} < p < 0.78 + 2.58\sqrt{\frac{0.78(0.22)}{100}}$$

$$0.673 < p < 0.887$$

547

As you can see, an acceptance rate of 80% employees falls within the estimated range of 99% confidence, which supports the above conclusion.

Working Problem 9.13:

Find the critical *z values for each of the following alternative hypotheses* (assuming that the normal distribution can be used to approximate the binomial distribution):

a. H_1: $P \neq 0.20$ (the critical region is in *both tails of the normal distribution)*
b. H_1: $P < 0.20$ (the critical region is in the *left tail of the normal distribution)*
c. H_1: $P > 0.20$ (the critical region is in the *right tail of the normal distribution)*
Use a significance level *a* of 0.05

Answer:
$(a) \quad -1.96 < z < 1.96 \quad (b) \quad z = -1.645 \quad (c) \quad z = 1.645$

Working Problem 9.14 :

Assume that we are conducting a hypothesis test of the claim that p > 0.7 using the following format:

$$H_o{:}p = 0.7 \qquad H_1{:}p > 0.7$$

Identify:
a. Type I error.
b. Type II error.

Answer: Do it yourself

Working Problem 9.15:

Suppose we have the following null and alternative hypotheses, significant level, and sample data:

$$H_o{:}p = 0.5 \qquad H_1{:}p > 0.5$$

Sample size: n = 100
Sample proportion: = $\hat{p} = 0.57$

Significance level: $\alpha = 0.05$

Conduct a complete hypothesis test

Answer:
See the output and try to work out the problem yourself to reach the solutions. Make your conclusions

Observed	Hypothesized	
0.57	0.5	p (as decimal)
57/100	50/100	p (as fraction)
57.	50.	X
100	100	n
	1.40	z
	.0808	p-value (one-tailed, upper)
	0.473	confidence interval 95.% lower
	0.667	confidence interval 95.% upper
	0.097	margin of error

Hypothesis tests for a population proportion

Basic Requirements:
- The sample used is representative of the parent population-No outliers are allowed
- The sample is random
- The individuals in the population are divided into two categories (e.g. Yes or NO, Pass or Fail, Agree or Disagree, etc)
- The values $np \geq 5$ and $nq \geq 5$

Step 1: *Identifying and defining the characteristic under consideration and stating the hypothesis*
Variable Category: Nominal-the-Best, Larger-the-Better, Smaller-the-Better

Null hypothesis	$H_o: p = p_o$	$H_o: p \leq p_o$	$H_o: p \geq p_o$
Alternative hypothesis	$H_1: p \neq p_o$	$H_1: p > p_o$	$H_1: p < p_o$

Step 2: *Selecting a sample and determining sample statistics,* $\hat{p} = \frac{n_i}{n}$

Step 3: *Selecting the level of significance or the extent of error*
$\alpha = P$ (type I error) $= P\{$reject $H_o \mid H_o$ is true$\}$, $\beta = P$ (type II error) $= P\{$fail to reject $H_o \mid H_o$ is false$\}$

Step 4: *Identify and use an appropriate test statistic*

$$z_o = \frac{\hat{p} - p}{\sqrt{\dfrac{p(1-p)}{n}}}$$

Step 5: *Follow appropriate decision rules to reject or accept the null hypothesis*

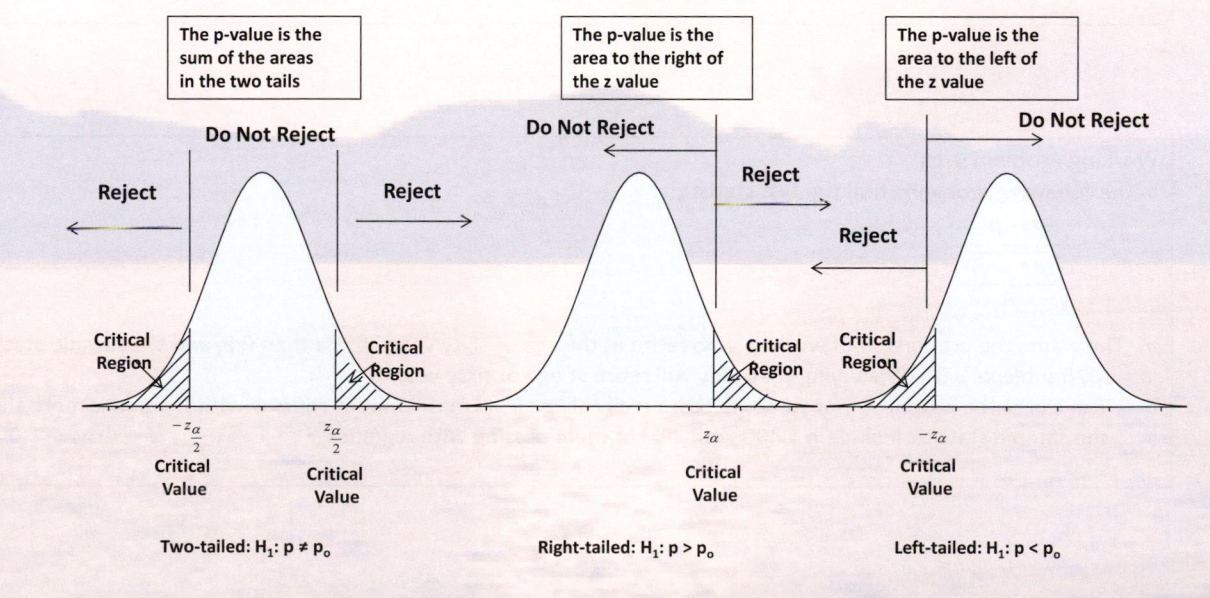

Two-tailed: $H_1: p \neq p_o$ Right-tailed: $H_1: p > p_o$ Left-tailed: $H_1: p < p_o$

549

Working Problem 9.16.

Election expert in an African Country suggested it is necessary for the new candidate for president to receive at least 80 percent of the vote in the eastern part of the country. The incumbent president wishes to know his chances of remaining as the president of the country. Using a sample of 2,000 registered voters in the eastern part of the country, it was found that 1,550 planned to vote for the incumbent president. Is the sample proportion close enough to 0.80 to conclude that the difference is due to sampling error?

Answer: See the output and try to work out the problem
yourself to reach the solutions. Make your conclusions

Observed	Hypothesized
0.775	0.8 p (as decimal)
1550/2000	1600/2000 p (as fraction)
1550.	1600. X
2000	2000 n
	0.0089 std. error
	-2.80 z
	.0026 p-value (one-tailed, lower)
	0.7567 confidence interval 95.% lower
	0.7933 confidence interval 95.% upper
	0.0183 margin of error

Working Problem 9.17:

In the following problems, identify H_o and H_1:

a. The mean annual income of employees who graduate from business schools is greater than $50,000
b. More than one-half of people who got married last month will either separate or divorced next year
c. Women's heights have a standard deviation less than 2.8 in, which is the standard deviation for men's heights
d. The mean weight of a soda bottle is at least 12 ounce.

Answer:

$(a) H_o: \mu = \$50,000$ $H_1: \mu > \$50,000$ (b) Do it yourself $(c) H_o: \sigma = 2.8$ $H_1: \sigma < 2.8$ (d) Do it yourself

Working Problem 9.18.:

In the following problems find the test statistic z:

$$z_o = \frac{\hat{p} - p}{\sqrt{\frac{p(1-p)}{n}}}$$

a. The claim: the proportion of workers who retire at the age of sixty years is less than 0.5, and the sample statistics include $n = 1025$ subjects with 29% saying that they will retire at age of sixty years
b. The claim: the proportion of students passing all college level mathematics courses with A grade is more than 0.25, and the sample statistic include n = 400 with 29% of them passing with A grades

Answer: (a) z = -13.45, (b) z = 1.85

Working Problem 9.19.:

In the following problem find the confidence interval and the margin of error at 95%:

a. The claim: the proportion of workers who retire at the age of sixty years is less than 0.5, and the sample statistics include n = 1025 subjects with 29% saying that they will retire at age of sixty years

b. The claim: the proportion of students passing all college level mathematics courses with A grade is more than 0.25, and the sample statistic include n = 400 with 29% of them passing with A grades

Answer: (a)

0.2622	confidence interval 95.% lower
0.3178	confidence interval 95.% upper
0.0278	margin of error

(b)

0.2455	confidence interval 95.% lower
0.3345	confidence interval 95.% upper
0.0445	margin of error

Working Problem 9.20:

Dioxin is the name generally given to a class of super-toxic chemicals, the chlorinated dioxins and furans, formed as a by-product of the manufacture, molding, or burning of organic chemicals and plastics that contain chlorine. It is the nastiest, most toxic man-made organic chemical; its toxicity is second only to radioactive waste. Dioxin made headlines several years ago at places such as Love Canal, where hundreds of families needed to abandon their homes due to dioxin contamination, and Times Beach, Missouri, a town that was abandoned as a result of dioxin. Based on a sample by the U.S. Environmental Protection Agency in the air surrounding the site of the World Trade Center, the amounts of dioxin in nano-grams per cubic meter were as follow:

a. Calculate the mean, median, variance, and range of the data of this sample.

f. Construct a 95% confidence interval estimate of the population mean.

g. The EPA uses 0.16 ng/m³ as its "screening level," which is "set to protect against significantly increased risks of cancer and other adverse health effects." Use a 0.05 significance level to test the claim that this sample comes from a population with a mean less than 0.16 ng/m³.

h. Is there any important characteristic of the data not addressed by the preceding results? If so, what is it?

Dioxin (ng/m3)
0.161
0.175
0.176
0.032
0.0524
0.044
0.018
0.0281
0.0268

Answer:

Dioxin (ng/m3)	
Mean	0.0793
Median	0.0440
Standard Deviation	0.0694
Sample Variance	0.0048
Range	0.1580
Minimum	0.0180
Maximum	0.1760

Confidence interval - mean	
95%	confidence level
0.0793	mean
0.0694	std. dev.
9	n
2.306	t (df = 8)
0.0533	half-width
0.1326	upper confidence limit
0.0260	lower confidence limit

Hypothesis Test: Mean vs. Hypothesized Value	
0.1600000	hypothesized value
0.0792556	mean Dioxin (ng/m3)
0.0693962	std. dev.
8	df
-3.49	t
.9959	p-value (one-tailed, upper)
0.0259129	confidence interval 95.% lower
0.1325982	confidence interval 95.% upper
0.0533426	margin of error

9.7 Hypothesis tests for a population variance

In Chapter 8, we introduced the concept of confidence interval on variance or standard deviation. In this regard, the key sampling distribution was the Chi-square χ^2 distribution. We also pointed out that the key condition for establishing confidence on the population variance is the assumption of normality; that is the characteristic in the parent population follows a normal distribution. The simplest way to establish confidence on the variance is to collect a random sample of size, n, calculate the sample variance, s^2, and find the critical values, $\chi^2_{1-\alpha/2}$ and , $\chi^2_{\alpha/2}$ using the χ^2 distribution with $n-1$ degrees of freedom. Given these values, we computed the confidence intervals on the population variance or standard deviation using the following expressions:

$$\frac{(n-1)s^2}{\chi^2_{\frac{\alpha}{2}}} < \sigma^2 < \frac{(n-1)s^2}{\chi^2_{1-\frac{\alpha}{2}}}$$

Or

$$\sqrt{\frac{(n-1)s^2}{\chi^2_{\frac{\alpha}{2}}}} < \sigma < \sqrt{\frac{(n-1)s^2}{\chi^2_{1-\frac{\alpha}{2}}}}$$

where n = sample size, s^2 = sample variance, σ^2 = population variance

The lower and upper $(1-\alpha)$ % confidence interval on the variance is given by:

$$\frac{(n-1)s^2}{\chi^2_{\alpha}} < \sigma^2$$

$$\sigma^2 < \frac{(n-1)s^2}{\chi^2_{1-\alpha}}$$

where χ^2_{α} and $\chi^2_{1-\alpha}$ are the percentage points of the chi-square distribution.

Using the above concepts, we can also perform a test of hypothesis on population variance or standard deviation. Table 9.7 shows a list of tests of hypothesis for variances. The examples given below illustrate the use of these tests. Figure 9.10 illustrates the criteria for rejecting the null hypothesis H_o.

Table 9.7 Different types of hypothesis testing for variances of normal distributions

Hypothesis testing	Test statistic	Reject when
H_o: $\sigma^2 = \sigma_o^2$ H_1: $\sigma^2 \neq \sigma_o^2$		$\chi_o^2 \geq \chi^2_{n-1,\alpha/2}$ or $\chi_o^2 \leq \chi^2_{n-1,1-\alpha/2}$
H_o: $\sigma^2 \geq \sigma_o^2$ H_1: $\sigma^2 < \sigma_o^2$	$\chi_o^2 = \dfrac{(n-1)s^2}{\sigma_o^2}$	$\chi_o^2 \leq \chi^2_{n-1,1-\alpha}$
H_o: $\sigma^2 \leq \sigma_o^2$ H_1: $\sigma^2 > \sigma_o^2$		$\chi_o^2 \geq \chi^2_{n-1,\alpha}$

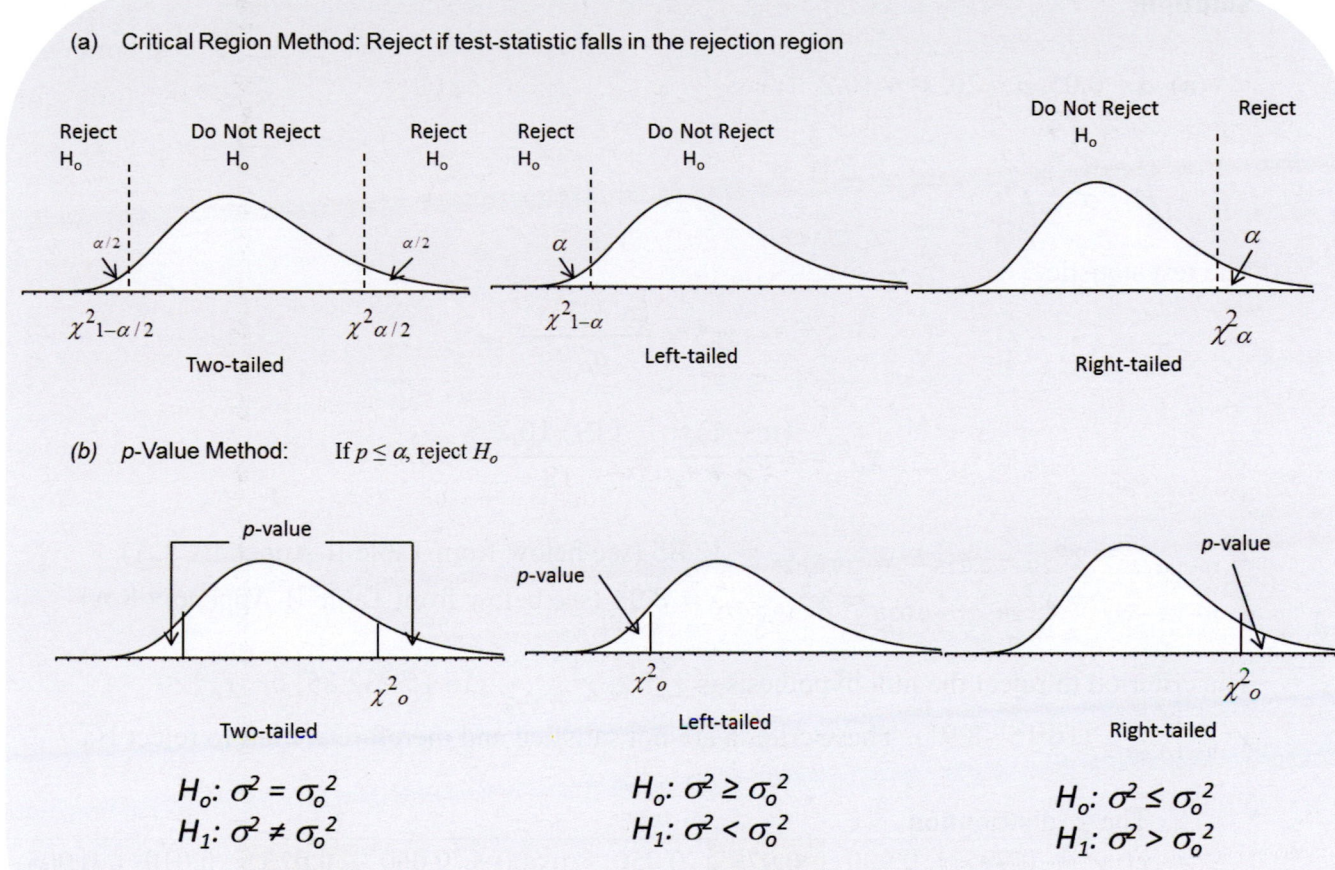

(a) Critical Region Method: Reject if test-statistic falls in the rejection region

(b) p-Value Method: If $p \leq \alpha$, reject H_o

Figure 9.10 Criteria for Rejection of Null Hypothesis of Variance

Example 9.15: For the following cases, determine the test-statistics, the critical values, and make the decision of rejecting or failing to reject the null hypothesis:

(a) $\alpha = 0.05$, $n = 20$, $s^2 = 10.2$

$$H_o: \sigma^2 = 12$$
$$H_1: \sigma^2 \neq 12$$

(b) $\alpha = 0.01$, $n = 16$, , $s^2 = 9.5$

$$H_o: \sigma^2 \geq 10$$
$$H_1: \sigma^2 < 10$$

Solution:

(a) $\alpha = 0.05$, $n = 20$, $s^2 = 10.2$

$H_o: \sigma^2 = 12$
$H_1: \sigma^2 \neq 12$

The test statistic

$$\chi_o{}^2 = \frac{(n-1)s^2}{\sigma_o{}^2}$$

$$\chi_o{}^2 = \frac{(n-1)s^2}{\sigma_o{}^2} = \frac{(19)\,10.2}{12} = 16.15$$

$\chi^2{}_{n-1,\alpha/2} = \chi^2{}_{20-1,0.025} = \chi^2{}_{19,0.025} = 32.85$ (see below from Table II-Appendix 8.A).
$\chi^2{}_{n-1,1-\alpha/2} = \chi^2{}_{20-1,1-0.025} = \chi^2{}_{19,0.975} = 8.91$ (see below from Table II-Appendix 8.A).

The criterion to reject the null hypothesis is $\chi_o{}^2 \geq \chi^2{}_{n-1,\frac{\alpha}{2}}$ ($16.15 \geq 32.85$) or $\chi_o{}^2 \leq \chi^2{}_{n-1,1-\alpha/2}$ ($16.15 \leq 8.91$). These criteria are not satisfied and therefore we fail to reject H_o.

The χ^2 distribution

γ	0.995	0.990	**0.975**	0.950	0.500	0.050	**0.025**	0.010	0.005
1	0.00	0.00	0.00	0.00	0.45	3.84	5.02	6.63	7.88
2	0.01	0.02	0.05	0.10	1.39	5.99	7.38	9.21	10.60
...	...	...	...	...	...	...	...	...	...
18	6.26	7.01	8.23	9.39	17.34	28.87	31.53	34.81	37.16
19	6.84	7.63	**8.91**	10.12	18.34	30.14	**32.85**	36.19	38.58
20	7.43	8.26	9.59	10.85	19.34	31.41	34.17	37.57	40.00
25	10.52	11.52	13.12	14.61	24.34	37.65	40.65	44.31	46.93
...	...	...	...	...	...	...	...	...	...
100	67.33	70.06	74.22	77.93	99.33	124.34	129.56	135.81	140.17

One way to verify the answer is to determine the confidence interval on σ^2 as discussed in Chapter 8 using the expression:

$$\frac{(n-1)s^2}{\chi^2{}_{\frac{\alpha}{2}}} < \sigma^2 < \frac{(n-1)s^2}{\chi^2{}_{1-\frac{\alpha}{2}}}$$

We will let the student perform the analysis. The final results should yield a confidence interval from 5.899 to 21.751 at $\alpha = 0.05$. Note that $\sigma^2 = 12$ falls within this range. Therefore, we fail to reject H_o.

(b) $\alpha = 0.01$, $n = 16$, $s^2 = 9.5$

H_o: $\sigma^2 \geq 10$
H_1: $\sigma^2 < 10$

The test statistic

$$\chi_o{}^2 = \frac{(n-1)s^2}{\sigma_o{}^2}$$

$$\chi_o{}^2 = \frac{(n-1)s^2}{\sigma_o{}^2} = \frac{(15)\,9.5}{10} = 14.25$$

$\chi^2{}_{n-1,1-\alpha} = \chi^2{}_{16-1,1-0.01} = \chi^2{}_{15,0.99} = 5.23$ (see below from Table II-Appendix 8.A).

The criterion to reject the null hypothesis is $\chi_o{}^2 \leq \chi^2{}_{n-1,1-\alpha}$. Since this criterion is not satisfied, we fail to reject H_o.

The χ^2 distribution

γ	0.995	**0.990**	0.975	0.950	0.500	0.050	0.025	0.010	0.005
1	0.00	0.00	0.00	0.00	0.45	3.84	5.02	6.63	7.88
....	....	....	....	....	....	....	....	....	....
14	4.07	4.66	5.63	6.57	13.34	23.68	26.12	29.14	31.32
15	4.60	**5.23**	6.27	7.26	14.34	25.00	27.49	30.58	32.80
16	5.14	5.81	6.91	7.96	15.34	26.30	28.85	32.00	34.27
17	5.70	6.41	7.56	8.67	16.34	27.59	30.19	33.41	35.72
....	....	....	....	....	....	....	....	....	....
100	67.33	70.06	74.22	77.93	99.33	124.34	129.56	135.81	140.17

Example 9.16: A company producing glazed porcelain Tile 13 in. × 13 in. is very concerned about variation in tile dimensions as this could mean total rejection of tiles due to mismatch. As a result, the most important parameter considered is the standard deviation of the tile area. An acceptable standard deviation is less than 0.25 inch (< 0.25). Table 9.8 shows the values of tile area of a sample of 12 tiles selected randomly. Test the hypothesis that the standard deviation is less than 0.25 inch at $\alpha = 0.05$.

Table 9.8 Ceramic tile area of 20 randomly-selected tiles

Tile #	Tile areas (inch^2)
1	169.09
2	169.18
3	168.82
4	169.75
5	168.58
6	169.03
7	169.09
8	168.93
9	169.25
10	168.72
11	168.86
12	169.03

Solution:

The hypothesis test in this case is:

$$H_o: \sigma \geq 0.25$$
$$H_1: \sigma < 0.25$$

Note that if the null hypothesis can be rejected, the company would be happy as this means that variation in tile area will be acceptable.

Descriptive statistics of ceramic tile area of 20 randomly-selected tiles

Mean ($\bar{X}$)	169.028
Standard deviation (s)	0.298
Variance (s^2)	0.089

The above hypothesis can also be expressed in terms of variance as follows:

$$H_o: \sigma^2 \geq \sigma_o{}^2 \qquad \text{or } H_o: \sigma^2 \geq 0.0625$$
$$H_1: \sigma^2 < \sigma_o{}^2 \qquad \text{or } H_1: \sigma^2 < 0.0625$$

The test statistic

$$\chi_o{}^2 = \frac{(n-1)s^2}{\sigma_o{}^2}$$

$$\chi_o{}^2 = \frac{(n-1)s^2}{\sigma_o{}^2} = \frac{(11)0.089}{0.0625} = 15.664$$

The criteria of rejection is $\chi_o{}^2 < \chi^2{}_{n-1,1-\alpha}$

$\chi^2{}_{n-1,1-\alpha} = \chi^2{}_{12-1,0.05} = \chi^2{}_{11,0.95} = 4.57$ (see below from Table II-Appendix 8.A).

The χ^2 distribution

γ/α	0.995	0.99	0.975	**0.95**	0.5	0.05	0.005
2	0.01	0.02	0.05	0.1	1.39	..	10.6
..	..	..	..	..	..	..	..
9	1.73	2.09	2.7	3.33	8.34	..	23.59
10	2.16	2.56	3.25	3.94	9.34	..	25.19
11	2.6	3.05	3.82	**4.57**	10.34	..	26.76
12	3.07	3.57	4.4	5.23	11.34	..	28.3

Since $\chi_o{}^2$ is not less than $\chi^2{}_{n-1,1-\alpha}$ we fail to reject the null hypothesis $H_o: \sigma^2 \geq 0.0625$ and conclude that there may be a problem with the variability in the ceramic tiles dimension.

Working problem 9.21:

Find the test statistic and critical value or values

of χ^2 based on the given information.

$H_1: \sigma < 20$, $n = 12$, $\alpha = 0.05$, $s^2 = 18$

Answer: 9.9, 4.57

Chi-square Variance Test

20.00 hypothesized variance
18.00 observed variance of stat
12 n
11 df
9.90 chi-square

.4606 p-value (one-tailed, lower)

Hypothesis tests for a population variance

Basic Requirements:

- The sample used is representative of the parent population-No outliers are allowed
- The sample is random
- The sample comes from a normal distribution

Step 1: *Identifying and defining the characteristic under consideration and stating the hypothesis*
Variable Category: *In case of variance, the focus is typically on Smaller-the-Better category since the smaller the variance the smaller the variability. As a result, the alternative hypothesis* H_1: $\sigma^2 < \sigma_o^2$ *is of special practical interest.*

Hypothesis testing	Test statistic	Reject when
H_o: $\sigma^2 = \sigma_o^2$ H_1: $\sigma^2 \neq \sigma_o^2$		$\chi_o^2 \geq \chi^2_{n-1,\alpha/2}$ or $\chi_o^2 \leq \chi^2_{n-1,1-\alpha/2}$
H_o: $\sigma^2 \geq \sigma_o^2$ H_1: $\sigma^2 < \sigma_o^2$	$\chi_o^2 = \dfrac{(n-1)s^2}{\sigma_o^2}$	$\chi_o^2 \leq \chi^2_{n-1,1-\alpha}$
H_o: $\sigma^2 \leq \sigma_o^2$ H_1: $\sigma^2 > \sigma_o^2$		$\chi_o^2 \geq \chi^2_{n-1,\alpha}$

Step 2: *Selecting a sample and determining variance s^2 or standard deviation s*
Step 3: *Selecting the level of significance or the extent of error*
$\alpha = P$ (type I error) = P\{reject H_o | H_o is true\}, $\beta = P$ (type II error) = P\{fail to reject H_o |H_o is false\}
Step 4: *Identify and use an appropriate test statistic*

$$\chi_o^2 = \frac{(n-1)s^2}{\sigma_o^2}$$

Step 5: *Follow appropriate decision rules to reject or accept the null hypothesis*

Left-tailed: H_1: $\sigma^2 < \sigma_o^2$ *Reject if* $\chi_o^2 \leq \chi^2_{n-1,1-\alpha}$
Right-tailed: H_1: $\sigma^2 > \sigma_o^2$ *Reject if* $\chi_o^2 \geq \chi^2_{n-1,\alpha}$
Two-tailed: H_1: $\sigma^2 \neq \sigma_o^2$ *Reject if* $\chi_o^2 \geq \chi^2_{n-1,\frac{\alpha}{2}}$ *or* $\chi_o^2 \leq \chi^2_{n-1,1-\alpha/2}$

Working Problem 9.22: For the following cases, determine the test-statistics, the critical values, and make the decision of rejecting or failing to reject the null hypothesis:

$a = 0.01$, $n = 18$, $s^2 = 15.7$
$H_o: \sigma^2 = 12$
$H_1: \sigma^2 \neq 12$

Chi-square Variance Test		
(a)	12.000	hypothesized variance
	15.700	observed variance of Stat
	18	n
	17	df
	22.24	chi-square
	.3512	p-value (two-tailed)
	7.472	confidence interval 99.% lower
	46.847	confidence interval 99.% upper

$a = 0.01$, $n = 14$, , $s^2 = 7.2$
$H_o: \sigma^2 \geq 10$
$H_1: \sigma^2 < 10$

Chi-square Variance Test		
(b)	10.000	hypothesized variance
	7.200	observed variance of Stat
	14	n
	13	df
	9.36	chi-square
	.2548	p-value (one-tailed, lower)
	3.139	confidence interval 99.% lower
	26.255	confidence interval 99.% upper

$a = 0.05$, $n = 11$, $s^2 = 1.5$
$H_o: \sigma^2 \leq 1.2$
$H_1: \sigma^2 > 1.2$

Answer:
Summary of the calculations for each problem is Shown to the right.
Perform the analysis manually and make the decisions.

Chi-square Variance Test		
(c)	1.200	hypothesized variance
	1.500	observed variance of Stat
	11	n
	10	df
	12.50	chi-square
	.2530	p-value (one-tailed, upper)
	0.732	confidence interval 95.% lower
	4.620	confidence interval 95.% upper

9.8 Review Exercises

P9.1: Suppose the average grade of a biology course in a college is claimed to be 80%. What is the hypothesis test format that you would use to test this parameter? Explain how type I or type II error may occur for this hypothesis. What would be a reasonable type I error you would select to test this hypothesis?
Answer: $H_o: \mu = \mu_o = 80$, $H_1: \mu \neq \mu_o \neq 80$, 5% or 1%

P9.2: Suppose the average annual property tax in a large city is claimed to be less than $8,000. What is the hypothesis test format that you would use to test this parameter? Explain how type I or type II error may occur for this hypothesis. What would be a reasonable type one error you would select to test this hypothesis?

P9.3: A technical-support service center claims the mean time of technical support calls is less than 20 minutes. Which of the following null and alternative hypotheses is the correct one?

(a) $H_0: \mu = 20$ $H_1: \mu < 20$, (b) $H_0: \mu < 20$ $H_1: \mu = 20$,

(c) $H_0: \mu = 20$ $H_1: \mu > 20$, (d) $H_0: \mu > 20$ $H_1: \mu = 20$

Answer: (a)

559

P9.4: The critical value for a right-tailed test regarding a population mean with σ known at $\alpha = 0.1$ level of significance is:

(a) $z = 1.645$, (b) $z = -1.28$, (c) $z = 1.28$, (d) $z = -1.645$

P9.5: Determine whether the following hypothesis test is left-tailed, right-tailed, two-tailed, or invalid.

$$H_0: \mu = 0.43 \quad H_1: \mu > 0.43$$

(a) Left-tailed   (b) Right-tailed   (c) Two-tailed   (d) Invalid

Answer: (b)

P9.6: To test $H_0: \mu = 120$ versus $H_1: \mu > 120$, a random sample of size $n = 22$ is obtained from a population that is known to be normally distributed with $\sigma = 6$. If the sample mean is determined to be $\bar{X} = 117$, the test statistic is:

(a) $z = 1.28$, (b) $z = -2.35$, (c) $z = 2.35$, (d) $z = -1.28$

P9.7: To test student's grade hypothesis: $H_0: \mu = 80$ versus $H_1: \mu > 80$, a random sample of size $n = 25$ students is obtained from a population of students that is known to have a normally distributed grade with $\sigma = 5$. If the sample mean is determined to be $\bar{X} = 78$, the test statistic is

(a) $z = 2.0$, (b) $z = -2.0$, (c) $z = 1.96$, (d) $z = -1.96$
Answer: (b)-Find out why

P9.8: To test $H_0: \mu = 120$ versus $H_1: \mu > 120$, a random sample of size $n = 22$ is obtained from a population that is known to be normally distributed with $\sigma = 6$. If the sample mean is determined to be $\bar{X} = 117$, compute the P- value in the right tail.

(a) 0.9905   (b) 0.9897   (c) 0.0095   (d) 0.0103   (e) none of the above

P9.9: To test student's grade hypothesis: $H_0: \mu = 80$ versus $H_1: \mu > 80$, a random sample of size $n = 25$ students is obtained from a population of students that is known to have a normally distributed grade with $\sigma = 5$. If the sample mean is determined to be $\bar{X} = 78$, compute the P- value in the right tail.

(a) 0.0228   (b) 0.9772   (c) 0.9950   (d) 0.005   (e) none of the above

Answer: (b)-Find out why

P9.10: Suppose we are testing the hypotheses: $H_0: \mu = 120$ versus $H_1: \mu > 120$ and we find the P-value to be 0.0125. Would you reject the null hypothesis at $\alpha = 0.05$ level of significance? Why?

(a) Yes   (b) No

P9.11: In testing H_0: $\mu = 53$ versus H_1: $\mu \neq 53$ at $\alpha = 0.05$ level of significance, you found a 95% confidence interval about μ to be 51.40 and 54.20). Will you reject the null hypothesis?

(a) Yes (b) No

Answer: (b)-Find out why

P9.12: Calcium is the most plentiful mineral found in the human body. The teeth and bones contain the most calcium (about 99%). Nerve cells, body tissues, blood, and other body fluids contain the remaining calcium. Most dietary and health organizations recommend adequate intake of calcium with an average of 1000 milligrams per day for adults. An International health organization working as a consultant for the United Nation wanted to perform a hypothesis test to decide whether the average adult in East Africa gets less than the anticipated average of calcium content of 1000 mg.

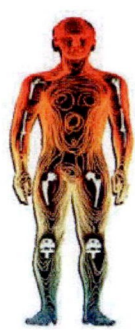

a. Format the null hypothesis for the hypothesis test.
b. Format the alternative hypothesis for the hypothesis test.
c. Classify the hypothesis test as two tailed, left tailed, or right tailed.

P9.13: To test H_0: $\mu = 152$ versus H_1: $\mu > 152$, a simple random sample of size $n = 20$ is obtained from a population that is known to be normally distributed with $\sigma = 8$. The mean of the sample was found to be 154. If the researcher decides to test this hypothesis at $\alpha = 0.05$ level of significance, the test statistic is:

(a) 1.12 (b) 1.96 (c) 1.64 (d) 2.58 (e) none of the above

Answer: (a)

P9.14: Consider the following information:
The claim: the average age of workers in an organization is 50 years
Sample information: $\mu_{\bar{x}} = \mu$ (unknown), $n = 36$, $\sigma_x = population\ standard\ deviation = 5$, $\bar{X} = 49$. Format the test of hypothesis using $\alpha = 0.05$

P9.15: According to AT&T, the mean monthly cell phone bill was $120 in 2008. If you suspects this mean monthly cell phone bill is different today, format the hypothesis test. Is this a two-tailed or one-tailed test? Explain how a type I and type II errors can be committed.
Answer: One possible answer is H_o: $\mu = \$120$; H_1: $\mu \neq \$120$

P9.16: Consider the following information:
The claim: A manufacturer of an automobile water-pump claims that the service life of the water pump is 60,000 miles of car driving
Sample information: $\mu_{\bar{x}} = \mu$ (unknown), $n = 48$, $\sigma_x = population\ standard\ deviation = 5,000\ mile$, $\bar{X} = 59,500\ miles$.
Perform the hypothesis test using $\alpha = 0.05$

P9.17: Consider the following information:

The claim: the average distance to drive to work by workers is less than 6.8 miles

Sample information: $\mu_{\bar{x}} = \mu$ (*unknown*), $n = 36$, $\sigma_x = $ *population standard deviation* $= 0.5$, $\bar{X} = 6.2$

Perform the hypothesis test using $\alpha = 0.05$

Answer: *Ho*: $\mu \geq 6.8$ miles, *Ha*: $\mu < 6.8$ miles (the claimed distance).

One-tailed, We reject H_o when z-statistic $< z_\alpha = $ -1.65, $z = \frac{\bar{X} - \mu}{\sigma_x/\sqrt{n}} = \frac{6.2 - 6.8}{0.5/\sqrt{36}} = -7.2$. Reject H_o at $\alpha = 0.05$. $P = 0$

P9.18: A human resource manager in a large company claimed that during working hours, employees spend on average about 13 minutes every hour talking on their cell phones or using text messaging in work-unrelated issues. Being concerned about this significant waste of time which amounts to over two hours per day, the company's top management hired a consultant to test this claim. Using a random sample of 150 employees, the consultant found that the average time spent per hour using cell phones or text messaging is about 14.5 minutes with a standard deviation of 2.65 minutes. Using this sample statistics and a 2% type I error, test the claim by the human resource manager that the time wasted is 13 minutes. Assume that minutes used talking on their cell phones or using text messaging follow a normal distribution.

P9.19: A company claimed that the hold time before responding to customer tech-support calls is on average less than 30 minutes. A random sample of 36 people revealed that they were put on hold for an average of 29 minutes. However, the standard deviation of this sample was 4 minutes. Would you support the company's claim at $\alpha = 0.01$? Assume that holding time follows a normal distribution.

P 9.20: A new Soda bottle is designed to have 20 ounce of Coke. Although the actual net weights may deviate slightly from 20 ounce and vary from one bottle to another, the company insists that the mean net weight of the bottles is 20 ounce. As a result, the quality assurance department periodically performs a hypothesis test to decide whether the bottling machines is working properly, that is, to decide whether the mean net weight of all bottles is 20 ounce. Using a sample of 25 bottles, values of bottle weight were found to be as shown in the table below.

Data of weight of coke in ounce

20.5	20.0	19.0	20.5	20.0
21.0	20.0	20.0	20.0	20.0
20.0	21.0	20.0	20.5	20.5
20.0	20.0	20.0	20.0	19.0
20.0	19.5	20.0	19.0	20.0

Assuming that the net weights are normally distributed and that the population standard deviation of weight is 0.5 ounce, do the data provide sufficient evidence to conclude that the bottling machine is not working properly?

a. State the null and alternative hypotheses for the hypothesis test.
b. Discuss the logic of this hypothesis test.

c. Identify the distribution of the variable $\bar{X}$, that is, the sampling distribution of the sample mean for samples of size 25.
d. Obtain a precise criterion for deciding whether to reject the null hypothesis in favor of the alternative hypothesis.
e. Apply the criterion in part (d) to the sample data and state the conclusion.

P9.21: According to a labor-force organization, the mean net annual income of starting engineers in the U.S. is $45,000 and the standard deviation is $3000. Using a sample of 120 engineers who recently graduated and found jobs, the mean net annual income was found to be $45,500. Assuming that the net income follows a normal distribution and using a 0.10 significance level, is it reasonable to conclude that the mean net annual income is not equal $45,000? Determine the p value.
Answer: The null and alternative hypotheses are Ho: μ = $45,000 (Claimed), Ha: $\mu \neq$ $45,000
z_o = 1.83, P-value = 0.0672.

P 9.22: A weight-loss practice claims that on average, customers can lose about 10 pound per month following their weight-watching program with a standard deviation of 2.8 pounds. Based on a random sample of 50 people who joined the program, the average weight loss per month was found to be 9 pounds. At the 0.05significance level, can we conclude that those joining the program will lose less than 10 pound.

P 9.23: The mean annual income of engineers who have earned their Professional Engineering Certificate (PE) is greater than $50,000. State the hypothesis test. Is this a two-tailed or one-tailed test? If the maximum tolerance is $5000, and the population standard deviation is $2000, what is the minimum sample size you would take to test this hypothesis? Select a confidence level of 95%.
Answer: Ho: μ = $50,000, Ha: $\mu >$ $50,000. Complete the answer.

P9.24: A construction company in Dubai sends its people to a construction site located in a desert area. The average travel time required to travel with normal trucks is 90 minutes. Recently the company purchased new and more durable trucks to transport its people, material, and equipment. The construction project leader wants to find if the average time to travel using the new trucks will be different from 90 minutes. A sample of 20 trips with the new trucks was monitored and the result showed that the average travel time was 85 minutes. If it is known that the travel time is normally distributed with a population standard deviation of 7 minutes, test the hypothesis that the new trucks will be associated with travel time different from 90 minutes at α = 0.01?

P9.25: A retailer placed a complaint to an appliance manufacturer claiming that on average the defect rate of the manufacturer's dishwasher has reached 10%. In an attempt to test this claim, the manufacturer took a random sample of 36 dishwashers, inspected them and found that the defect rate is actually 9.0%. If the population standard deviation of defect rate is known to be 2%, test the claim placed by the retailer at 95% confidence.
Answer: z_o = -3.0, P-value = 0.0013, 8.35 to 9.65 at 95%

P9.26: To test H_0: $\mu = 152$ versus H_1: $\mu > 152$, a simple random sample of size $n = 20$ is obtained from a population that is known to be normally distributed with $\sigma = 8$. The mean of the sample was found to be 154. If the researcher decides to test this hypothesis at $\alpha = 0.05$ level of significance, the p-value is:

(a) 0.1318   (b) 0.2636   (c) 0.8682   (d) 1.0034   (e) none of the above

P9.27: To test H_0: $\mu = 152$ versus H_1: $\mu > 152$, a simple random sample of size $n = 20$ is obtained from a population that is known to be normally distributed with $\sigma = 8$. The mean of the sample was found to be 154. If the researcher decides to test this hypothesis at $\alpha = 0.05$ level of significance, the decision is:

(a) Reject H_o (b) Fail to reject H_o

Answer: (b)-Explain why.

P9.28: In order to test student's grade hypothesis: H_0: $\mu = 80$ versus H_1: $\mu > 80$, a random sample of size $n = 25$ students is obtained from a population of students that is known to have a normally distributed grade. If the sample mean is determined to be $\overline{X} = 78$, and the standard deviation, $s = 5$, the test statistic is

(a) $t = 2.0$, (b) $t = -2.0$, (c) $t = 1.96$, (d) $t = -1.96$ (e) none of the above

P9.29: In order to test H_0: $\mu = 80$ versus H_1: $\mu \neq 80$, a simple random sample of size $n = 8$ is obtained from a population that is known to be normally distributed. If you decide to test this hypothesis at $\alpha = 0.05$ level of significance, the critical values will be

(a) $t_{0.025} = -1.96$; $t_{0.025} = 1.960$

(b) $t_{0.025} = -2.306$; $t_{0.025} = 2.306$

(c) $t_{0.025} = -1.895$; $t_{0.025} = 1.895$

(d) $t_{0.025} = -2.365$; $t_{0.025} = 2.365$

(e) None of the above

Answer: (d)

P9.30: Find the critical value(s) for the following cases:

(a) $\alpha = 0.05$, $n = 3$, H_1: $\mu \neq \mu_o$, (b) $\alpha = 0.05$, $n = 3$, H_1: $\mu > \mu_o$, (c) $\alpha = 0.01$, $n = 10$, H_1: $\mu > \mu_o$, (d) $\alpha = 0.01$, $n = 20$, H_1: $\mu > \mu_o$, (e) $\alpha = 0.10$, $n = 25$, H_1: $\mu \neq \mu_o$, (f) $\alpha = 0.10$, $n = 16$, H_1: $\mu < \mu_o$, (g) $\alpha = 0.02$, $n = 14$, H_1: $\mu \neq \mu_o$, (h) $\alpha = 0.001$, $n = 19$, H_1: $\mu > \mu_o$

P9.31: The data below represent statistics and hypothesis test format for a sample of students' grades:

Mean $\bar{X}$	80
Standard deviation s	5
Sample Size, n	20
α	0.05
Hypothesis Test	
H_o	$\mu = 78$
H_1	$\mu \neq 78$

The test statistic, t_o is:

(a) 2.08   (b) -1.79   (c) 1.79   (d) -2.08   (e) none of the above

P9.32: The data below represent statistics and hypothesis test format for a sample of house prices:

	House prices
Mean $\bar{X}$	$480,000
Std. dev., s	$14,000
Sample size, n	20
α	0.01
Hypothesis test	
H_o	$\mu = \$475,000$
H_1	$\mu < \$475000$

The test statistic, t_o is:

(a) 1.08   (b) -1.60   (c) 1.60   (d) -1.08   (e) none of the above

P9.33: The data below represent statistics and hypothesis test format for a sample of property tax:

	Property tax
Mean $\bar{X}$	$7,000
Std. dev., s	$800
Sample size, n	18
α	0.01
H_o	$\mu = \$7,200$
H_1	$\mu > \$7,200$

The test statistic, t_o is:

    (a) 1.09   (b) -1.06   (c) -1.09   (d) 1.06   (e) none of the above

P9.34: The data below represent statistics and hypothesis test format for a sample of annual income of newly engineering graduates:

	Annual Income of newly engineering graduates
Mean $\bar{X}$	$62,000
Std. Dev., s	$4,000
Sample Size, n	24
α	0.1
H_o	$\mu = \$61,500$
H_1	$\mu < \$61,500$

The test statistic, t_o is:

    (a) - 1.09   (b) 1.09   (c) -0.61   (d) 0.61   (e) none of the above

P9.35: The data below represent statistics and hypothesis test format for a sample of students' grades:

Students Grades	
Mean $\bar{X}$	80
Standard deviation s	5
Sample size, n	20
α	0.05
Hypothesis Test	
H_o	$\mu = 78$
H_1	$\mu \neq 78$

The lower and upper confidence interval at 95% confidence level is:

    (a) 77.66 & 85.23
    (b) 72.16 & 82.03
    (c) 77.66 & 82.34
    (d) 77.00 & 82.34
    (e) none of the above
Answer (c)-Show how to reach this answer

P9.36: The data below represent statistics and hypothesis test format for a sample of house prices:

	House Prices
Mean $\bar{X}$	$480,000
Std. dev., s	$14,000
Sample size, n	20
α	0.01
Hypothesis Test	
H_o	$\mu = \$475,000$
H_1	$\mu < \$475000$

The lower and upper confidence interval at 99% confidence level is:

(a) 471,043.86 & 482,923.11
(b) 472,042.36 & 488,956.14
(c) 479,022.16 & 482,923.11
(d) 471,043.86 & 488,956.14
(e) None of the above

P9.37: The data below represent statistics and hypothesis test format for a sample of property tax:

	Property Tax
Mean $\bar{X}$	$7,000
Std. dev., s	$800
Sample size, n	18
α	0.01
Hypothesis Test	
H_o	$\mu = \$7,200$
H_1	$\mu > \$7,200$

The lower and upper confidence interval at 99% confidence level is:
(a) 6,500.05 & 7,200.12
(b) 6,512.20 & 7,546.50
(c) 6,453.50 & 7,546.50
(d) 6,543.50 & 7,865.20
Answer (c)-Show how to reach this answer

567

P9.38: The data below represent statistics and hypothesis test format for a sample of annual income of newly engineering graduates:

	Annual Income of newly engineering graduates
Mean $\bar{X}$	$62,000
Std. dev., s	$4,000
Sample size, n	24
α	0.1
Hypothesis Test	
H_o	$\mu = \$61,500$
H_1	$\mu < \$61,500$

The lower and upper confidence interval at 90% confidence level is:

(a) 61,500.43 & 63,233.45
(b) 60,600.63 & 63,100.20
(c) 59,200.13 & 63,399.37
(d) 60,600.63 & 63,399.37

P9.39: The data below represent statistics and hypothesis test format for a sample of students' grades:

	Students Grades
Mean $\bar{X}$	80
Standard deviation s	5
Sample size, n	20
α	0.05
Hypothesis Test	
H_o	$\mu = 78$
H_1	$\mu \neq 78$

The null hypothesis should be:
   (a) Rejected   (b) Accepted
Answer (b)-Show how to reach this answer

P9.40: The data below represent statistics and hypothesis test format for a sample of house prices:

	House Prices
Mean $\bar{X}$	$480,000
Std. dev., s	$14,000
Sample size, n	20
α	0.01
Hypothesis Test	
H_o	$\mu = \$475,000$
H_1	$\mu < \$475,000$

The null hypothesis should be:
   (a) Rejected   (b) Accepted

P9.41: The data below represent statistics and hypothesis test format for a sample of property tax:

	Property Tax
Mean $\bar{X}$	$7,000
Std. dev., s	$800
Sample size, n	18
α	0.01
Hypothesis Test	
H_o	$\mu = \$7,200$
H_1	$\mu > \$7,200$

The null hypothesis should be:

   (a) Rejected   (b) Accepted
Answer (b)-Show how to reach this answer

P9.42: The data below represent statistics and hypothesis test format for a sample of annual income of newly engineering graduates:

	Annual Income of newly engineering graduates
Mean $\bar{X}$	$62,000
Std. dev., s	$4,000
Sample size, n	24
α	0.1
Hypothesis Test	
H_o	$\mu = \$61,500$
H_1	$\mu < \$61,500$

The null hypothesis should be:

(a) Rejected   (b) Accepted

P9.43: Consider the following information:

The issue: the average age of children in the fourth grade is less than or equal 10 years
Sample information: $\mu_{\bar{x}} = \mu$ (*unknown*), $n = 10$, $s = sample\ standard\ deviation = 3$,
$\bar{X} = 12$. Perform the hypothesis test using $\alpha = 0.05$:

(a) State the decision rule, (b) compute the value of the test statistic, (c) Decide on H_o.
Answer: $Ho: \mu \leq 10$ years (Claimed), $Ha: \mu > 10$, $t_\alpha = 1.833$, $t_o = 2.108$. Decide on H_o at $\alpha = 0.05$-explain why

P9.44: According to the Economist World in Figures (http://www.signonsandiego.com), the average number of hours per week spent by people in the U.S.A. watching television is 18.1 hours. Do adults in the age from 18 to 25 watch television less than the general population weekly? If a random sample of 40 adults in the age from 18 to 25 revealed that the Average number of hours per week spent watching television is 16.8 hours and a standard deviation of 4.7 hours. Is there sufficient evidence at the $\alpha = 0.1$ of significance to conclude that adults in the age from 18 to 25 watch television less than the general population weekly?

P9.45: A car dealer claims that the sales representatives make an average of 40 contacts per month with customers. In an attempt to justify a basic non-commission pay, many sales agents say that this estimate is too low. To investigate, a random sample of 28 sales agents reveals that the mean number of contacts made last month was 42. The standard deviation of the sample was 2.1 contacts. Using the .05 type I error, can we conclude that the mean number of contacts per salesperson per month is more than 40?
Answer: $Ho: \mu \leq 40$ contacts (Claimed), $Ha: \mu > 40$, $t_\alpha = 1.703$, $t_o = 5.040$. Make the decision.

P9.46: A manufacturer of transfer belts claimed that its belts have a mean service life in excess of 22,100 machine working hours. Assume the life of the transfer belt follows a normal distribution. In a sample of 18 belts used to verify this claim revealed an average of 23,400 hours, and a standard deviation of 1,500 hours. Is there enough evidence to substantiate the manufacturer's claim at the 0.05 significance level?

P9.47: A sport club claims that club members have an average age of less than 20 years. A random sample of five members resulted in the following values: 18, 15, 12, 19, and 21. Using the 0.01 significance level, can we conclude the population mean of the age of the club members is less than 20?

State the decision rule, compute the value of the test statistic, what is your decision regarding the null hypothesis?, estimate the p-value
Answer: $Ho: \mu \geq 20$ year , $Ha: \mu < 20$ year (Claimed), $t_\alpha = -3.747$, $\bar{X} = 17$, $s = 3.536$, $t_o = -1.90$

P9.48: A packaging company of rice sets its machine to produce a nominal average weight of 4.35 pound in each rice bag. With the intention to increase this weight, a new machine setting was made and the company selected a random sample of 10 bags and weighed each bag to find the following values:

Bag #	1	2	3	4	5	6	7	8	9	10
Weight (pound)	4.39	4.41	4.4	4.37	4.33	4.38	4.36	4.3	4.39	4.35

Given that the weight follows a normal distribution, and using a 0.01 significance level, has the new setting resulted in an increase in the mean rice bag weight?

P9.49: A tech support service records indicate that the average time used for phone calls is 12 minutes. If a sample of 18 phone calls was monitored and it was found that the average time used for the call was 13 minutes with a standard deviation of 2 minutes. Test the hypothesis that the population average time is 12 minutes at a significant level of 1%?

Answer: $\bar{X} = 13, df = 17, s = 2, H_o: \mu = \mu_o = 12, H_1: \mu \neq \mu_o \neq 12, t_o = \frac{\bar{X} - \mu_o}{\frac{s}{\sqrt{n}}} = \frac{13 - 12}{\frac{2}{\sqrt{18}}} = 2.12, t_{0.005} = 2.898$

P9.50: In the above problem, verify the answer by establishing confidence interval on the mean time of phone calls at 1% significance level.

P9.51: A textile company claims that the mean cost per carpet unit is $60. Some retailers showed that this cost is larger than the cost encountered by most carpet makers. As a result, the company implemented some cost cutting measures. At the end of this implementation, the company collected data of 26 different carpets selected randomly and found that the average cost per unit was $58.34 and the standard deviation was 10.22. At a 99% confidence, would it be reasonable to say that the mean cost per carpet unit has become less than $60?

Answer: $t_o = -0.83$, p = 0.2086

P9.52: In the above problem, verify the answer by establishing confidence interval on the mean cost at 1% significance level.

P9.53: Determine the test statistic z_0 for the following situation:

$H_0: p = 0.28$ versus $H_1: p \neq 0.28$
$n = 400$; $x = 125$ at 95% confidence
   (a) $z_o = 1.78$ (b) $z_o = -1.96$ (c) $z_o = 1.45$ (d) $z_o = -1.45$ (e) None of the above

Answer: (c)-Show how this is calculated.

$$\hat{p} = \frac{125}{400} = 0.3125$$

$$z_o = \frac{\hat{p} - p}{\sqrt{\frac{p(1-p)}{n}}} = \frac{0.3125 - 0.28}{\sqrt{\frac{0.28(1-0.28)}{400}}} = 1.45$$

P9.54: Determine the test statistic z_0 for the following situation:
$H_0: p = 0.85$ versus $H_1: p \neq 0.85$
$n = 600$; $x = 530$ at 99% confidence

$(a)\ z_o = 2.58\ (b)\ z_o = -2.58\ (c)\ z_o = 2.29\ (d)\ z_o = -1.87$ (e) None of the above

P9.55: A survey found 190 of 380 randomly selected Americans prefer staying home in the weekend in winter time. Construct a 95% confidence interval for the proportion of all Americans who prefer staying home in the weekend in winter time.

(a) (0.450, 0.550)   (b) (0.434, 566)   (c) (0.458, 0.542)   (d) (0.440, 0.560)
Answer: (a)-Show how you obtain these values.

P9.56: A survey found 190 of 380 randomly selected Americans prefer staying home in the weekend in winter time. Construct a 99% confidence interval for the proportion of all Americans who prefer staying home in the weekend in winter time.

(a) (0.450, 0.550)   (b) (0.434, 566)   (c) (0.458, 0.542)   (d) (0.440, 0.560)

P9.57: More than 80% of all Amazon.com visitors buy books. State the hypothesis test
Answer: Ho: $p = 0.8$, Ha: $p > 0.8$

P9.58: A government consultant claims that less than 20% of married couples in the United States actually end up with divorce within the first year of marriage. In a random sample of 100 couples, it was found that 15% of them actually filed for divorce within the first year of marriage. Using a 99% confidence, can this sample be used to support the claim? Calculate z_o and z_a and perform hypothesis test.

P9.59: An organization affiliated with the United Nation claims that 44% of Europeans are likely to refuse immigration of citizens of non-European nations to Europe. In order to test this claim, a sample of 1165 Europeans was surveyed and 556 refused immigration of citizens of non-European nations to Europe. Can you reject this claim at $\alpha = 0.05$?
Answer:Ho: $p = 0.44$ (Claimed), Ha: $p \neq 0.44$, $z_{\alpha/2} = \pm 1.96$, $z = 2.544$. Make a decision

P9.60: Given the following information:

The issue: the average proportion of people in the U.S. voting for a National Health Care program is claimed to exceed 70%
Sample information: $\mu_{\bar{x}} = P = \mu\ (unknown)$, $n = 100$, $\hat{p} = 0.75$
Perform the hypothesis test using $\alpha = 0.05$:

   (a) State the decision rule
   (b) Compute the value of the test statistic
   (c) Make a decision regarding the null hypothesis

P9.61: A study by an environmental organization reported that more than 52% of Americans prefers hybrid cars over traditional cars. A sample of 300 cars traveling on State Highway-85 last week revealed that 170 of the cars were hybrid. At the 0.01 significance level, can we conclude that a larger proportion of hybrid cars were driven than the national statistics indicate?

Answer: *Ho: $p \leq 0.52$, Ha: $p > 0.52$* (Claimed), $\hat{p} = 0.5667$, $z_o = 1.62$

P9.62: A tech-support of a large telecommunication company claims that 90% of the phone calls to tech-support are answered directly within 10 minutes of the time the call is made. A sample of 100 calls revealed that 82 were answered directly within 10 minutes. At the 0.1 significance level, can we conclude that less than 90% of the calls are answered within 10 minutes?

P9.63: In a survey by a major TV Network, 66% of the viewers like to watch morning talk shows. Another TV Network who wanted to verify this claim took a sample of 1000 viewers and found that 700 viewers indeed like to watch morning talk shows. Can we conclude that this sample confirms what the first TV Network claimed is true at 5% significance level? Use the equal/not equal hypothesis test for this problem.

Answer: The appropriate hypothesis test in this case is: *Ho: $p = 0.66$* (claim), *Ha: $p \neq 0.66$*, $\hat{p} = \frac{700}{1000} = 0.70$

$z_o = \frac{0.7 - 0.66}{\sqrt{(0.66 \times 0.34)/1000}} = 2.67$. Make the decision

P9.64: According to the U.S. Census Bureau, 10.2% of registered births in the United States in 2005 were to teenage mothers. If you believe that this percentage has increased since then, how would you format the hypothesis?

P9.65: To test $H_0: \mu = 152$ versus $H_1: \mu > 152$, a simple random sample of size $n = 20$ is obtained from a population that is known to be normally distributed with $\sigma = 8$. If the researcher decides to test this hypothesis at $\alpha = 0.05$ level of significance, compute the probability of making a Type II error if the true population mean is 154.

(a) 0.7123, (b) 0.8686, (c) 0.9535, (d) 0.5590

Answer: (a)-See Chapter Appendix

P9.66: For the following case, determine the test-statistics, the critical values, and make the decision of rejecting or failing to reject the null hypothesis:
$\alpha = 0.01$, $n = 19$, $s^2 = 3.0$, $H_o: \sigma^2 = 12$, $H_1: \sigma^2 \neq 12$

P9.67: For the following case, determine the test-statistics, the critical values, and make the decision of rejecting or failing to reject the null hypothesis:
$\alpha = 0.05$, $n = 12$, $s^2 = 25$, $H_o: \sigma^2 = 55$, $H_1: \sigma^2 < 55$

P9.68: For the following case, determine the test-statistics, the critical values, and make the decision of rejecting or failing to reject the null hypothesis:
$\alpha = 0.05$, $n = 12$, $s^2 = 2$, H_o: $\sigma^2 = 13$, H_1: $\sigma^2 > 13$

P9.69: For the following case, determine the test-statistics, the critical values, and make the decision of rejecting or failing to reject the null hypothesis:
$\alpha = 0.05$, $n = 13$, $s^2 = 1.3$, H_o: $\sigma^2 \leq 1.2$, H_1: $\sigma^2 > 1.2$
Answer: We fail reject H_o. Perform the analysis to verify this answer

P9.70: A company producing metal rods claims that the variance of diameter of a certain brand is 0.2. Test this claim using the data shown in the table below at $\alpha = 0.05$.

Diameter values (cm)

Observation No.	Rod diameter (cm)
1	7.86
2	7.43
3	8.11
4	8.57
5	8.54
6	8.78
7	7.02
8	7.89
9	8.49
10	7.51

APPENDIX 9.A: The Power of a Hypothesis Test

This subject is typically outside an introduction to statistics chapter but it is important to cover it for both the instructors and students who are interested on how the power of a hypothesis test is calculated.

Earlier in this chapter, we discussed the chances of committing two types of error:

TYPE I ERROR: If the null hypothesis H_o is rejected when it is true, then a type I error has occurred. This type of error may result in taking actions that are not necessary (over-control thinking), or in incorrectly it may result in modifying a process.

TYPE II ERROR: If the null hypothesis H_o is not rejected when it is false, then a type II error has occurred. This may lead to an opposite action to that of type I error or under-control.

In statistical terms, we define the probabilities of these two types of errors as follows:

- $\alpha = P$ (type I error) $= P\{$reject $H_o \mid H_o$ is true$\}$
- $\beta = P$ (type II error) $= P\{$fail to reject $H_o \mid H_o$ is false$\}$

The dynamics of these two types of errors are displayed below. In view of these dynamics, a good hypothesis test is the one in which we have a small probability of rejecting H_o when it is true and a large probability of rejecting H_o when it is false.

Decision	Reality	
	H_o True	H_o False
Reject H_o	Type I error (α)	Correct decision
Don't reject H_o	Correct decision	Type II error (β)

The power of a test is the probability of not committing a type II error, or the probability of rejecting H_o when it is false. This is the complimentary probability of β or:

$$Power = 1 - \beta$$

The goal of a successful test of hypothesis is twofold:

(1) Small type I error-This is achieved by using a small value of α.
(2) Large power (or large 1- β value)-This achieved by increasing sample size n.

In practice, the sequence of action is to first use an appropriate α and n values. As we increase the sample size the power will increase. Values of β of 0.2 and 0.1, or values of power of 0.8 and 0.9 are considered to be acceptable values.

In order to compute the power $1-\beta$ we follow these steps:

Step 1: We specify a value μ_o of the population mean that satisfies the alternative hypothesis H_1. $H_o: \mu = \mu_o$, $H_1: \mu \neq \mu_o$

Step 2: Determine the critical value z_α (one-tailed test) and $z_{\alpha/2}$ (two-tailed test) and compute the test statistic. The power is determined by the probability that the test statistic z_o or t_o falls in the critical region when μ_o is the true value of the population mean.

Step 3: For one-tailed test, determine the value of $\bar{X}$ whose z-score is equal to the critical value. This can be labeled, $\bar{X}^*$. This can be found as follows:

For one-tailed test:
Left-tailed: $H_1: \mu < \mu_o$

$$\bar{X}^* = \mu_o - z_\alpha \frac{\sigma_x}{\sqrt{n}}$$

Right-tailed: $H_1: \mu > \mu_o$

$$\bar{X}^* = \mu_o + z_\alpha \frac{\sigma_x}{\sqrt{n}}$$

For two-tailed test, we will have two values of $\bar{X}^*$:

$$\bar{X}^*_{lower} = \mu_o - z_{\alpha/2} \frac{\sigma_x}{\sqrt{n}}$$
$$\bar{X}^*_{upper} = \mu_o + z_{\alpha/2} \frac{\sigma_x}{\sqrt{n}}$$

Step 4: We let μ_1 be a specific value that satisfies the alternative hypothesis. At this point, it is preferable to sketch a normal curve with mean value μ_1.

Step 5: The power is an area under the normal curve (sketched in step 4). This area will depend on the form of the alternative hypothesis, as follow:

Left-tailed: $H_1: \mu < \mu_o$ Area to the left of $\bar{X}^*$.
Right-tailed: $H_1: \mu > \mu_o$ Area to the right of $\bar{X}^*$.
Two-tailed: $H_1: \mu \neq \mu_o$ Sum of the area to the left of $\bar{X}^*_{lower}$.and the area to the right of $\bar{X}^*_{upper}$

Example: The average American family's net worth was about $64,300 in 2010. The standard deviation was $15,000. Some economists believe that this net worth was less in 2012. An economist took a random sample of 15 families to test the hypothesis:

$$H_o: \mu = 64,300$$
$$H_1: \mu < 64,300$$

At a = 0.05 level. Assume the population standard deviation remains at $15,000 in 2012. Find the power of the test against the alternative $\mu_1 = \$55,000$

Solution:

This is a one-tailed test at $\alpha = 0.05$. In this case, $z_\alpha = 1.645$
Left-tailed: $H_1: \mu < \mu_o$

$$\bar{X}^* = \mu_o - z_\alpha \frac{\sigma_x}{\sqrt{n}} = 64,300 - (1.645)\frac{15000}{\sqrt{15}} = \$57,928.942$$

We now sketch a normal distribution with the average being μ_1 or $55,000 and place the $\bar{X}^* = 57,928.942$ value and standard deviation $\frac{\sigma_x}{\sqrt{n}} = \frac{15000}{\sqrt{15}} = \$3872.98$.

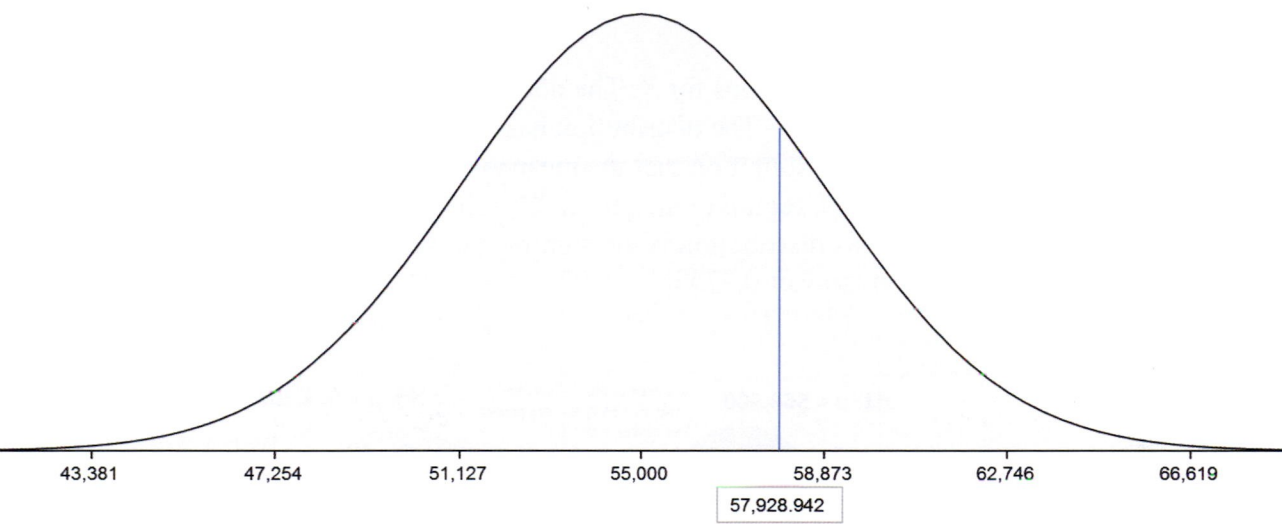

| 43,381 | 47,254 | 51,127 | 55,000 | 58,873 | 62,746 | 66,619 |

57,928.942

Since this is a left-tailed test, so the power is the area to the left of $\bar{X}^* = 57,928.942$. To find this area we use the z-score:

$$z_o = \frac{\bar{X} - \mu_1}{\frac{\sigma_x}{\sqrt{n}}} = \frac{57,928.942 - 55,000}{15000/\sqrt{15}} = \frac{2928.942}{3872.983} = 0.756$$

The power is the area under the normal curve to the left of 0.756. Using the standard normal table (Chapter 6, APPENDIX A), this area is as shown below and it is 0.7753 or 77.53%.

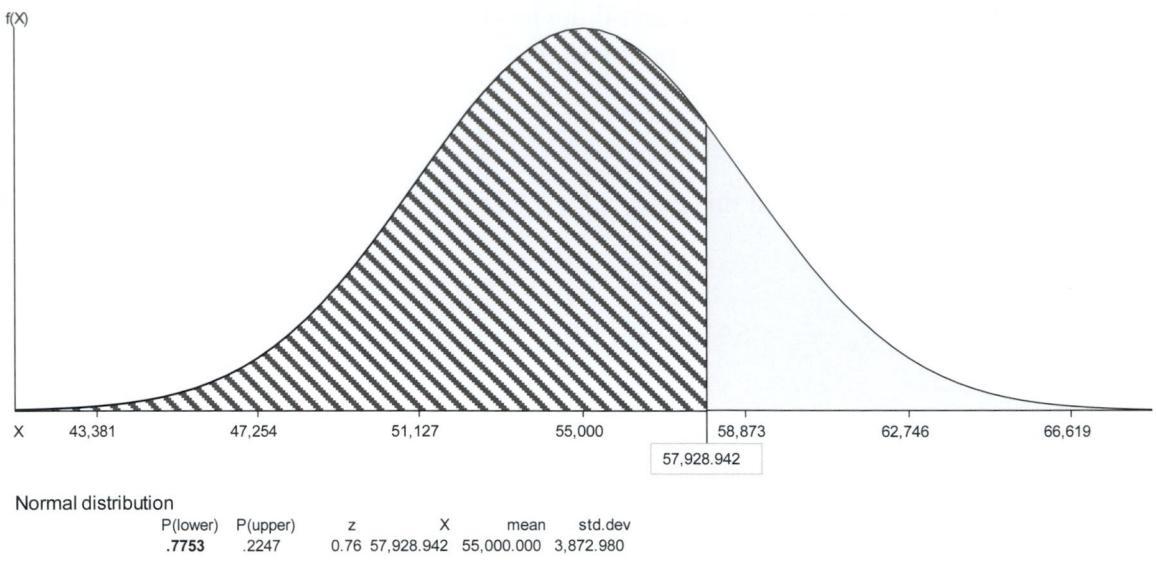

Normal distribution

	P(lower)	P(upper)	z	X	mean	std.dev
	.7753	.2247	0.76	57,928.942	55,000.000	3,872.980

The figure below shows two distributions for $\bar{X}$. The normal curve on the right is the distribution under the assumption that H_o is true. The distribution has mean $\mu_o = \$64,300$. The curve on the left is the distribution under the assumption that the mean is equal to the alternative value $\mu_1 = \$55,000$. The critical region is the region to the left of $\bar{X}^* = 57,928.942$. The area of the critical region under the null hypothesis distribution is the significance level $\alpha = 0.05$. The area under the alternate distribution is the power 0.7753.

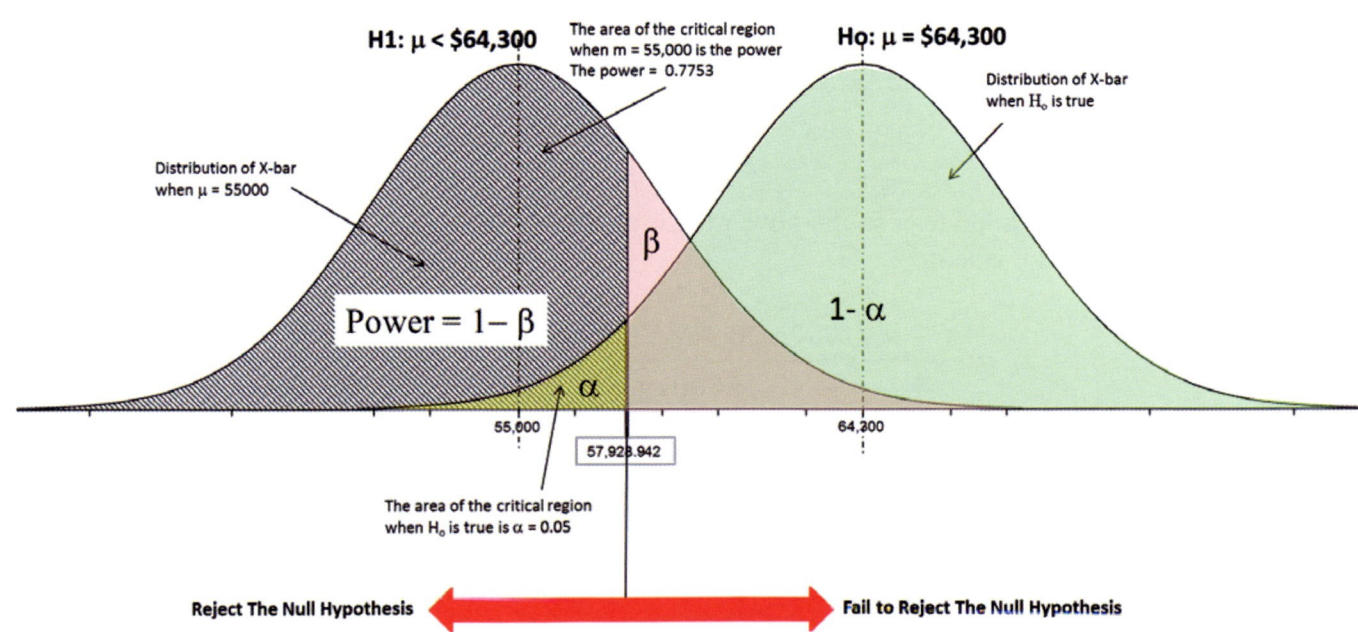

Example (same example above at different sample size): The average American family's net worth was about $64,300 in 2010. The standard deviation was $15,000. Some economists believe that this net worth was less in 2012. An economist took a random sample of 40 families to test the hypothesis:

$H_o: \mu = 64{,}300$
$H_1: \mu < 64{,}300$

At a = 0.05 level. Assume the population standard deviation remains $15,000 at 2012. Find the power of the test against the alternative $\mu_1 = \$55{,}000$.

Solution:

This is a one-tailed test at $\alpha = 0.05$. In this case, $z_\alpha = 1.645$
Left-tailed: $H_1: \mu < \mu_o$

$$\bar{X}^* = \mu_o - z_\alpha \frac{\sigma_x}{\sqrt{n}} = 64{,}300 - (1.645)\frac{15000}{\sqrt{40}} = \$61{,}928.291$$

We now sketch a normal distribution with the average being μ_1 or $55{,}000$ and place the $\bar{X}^* = \$61{,}928.291$ value and standard deviation $\frac{\sigma_x}{\sqrt{n}} = \frac{15000}{\sqrt{40}} = \$2371.708$

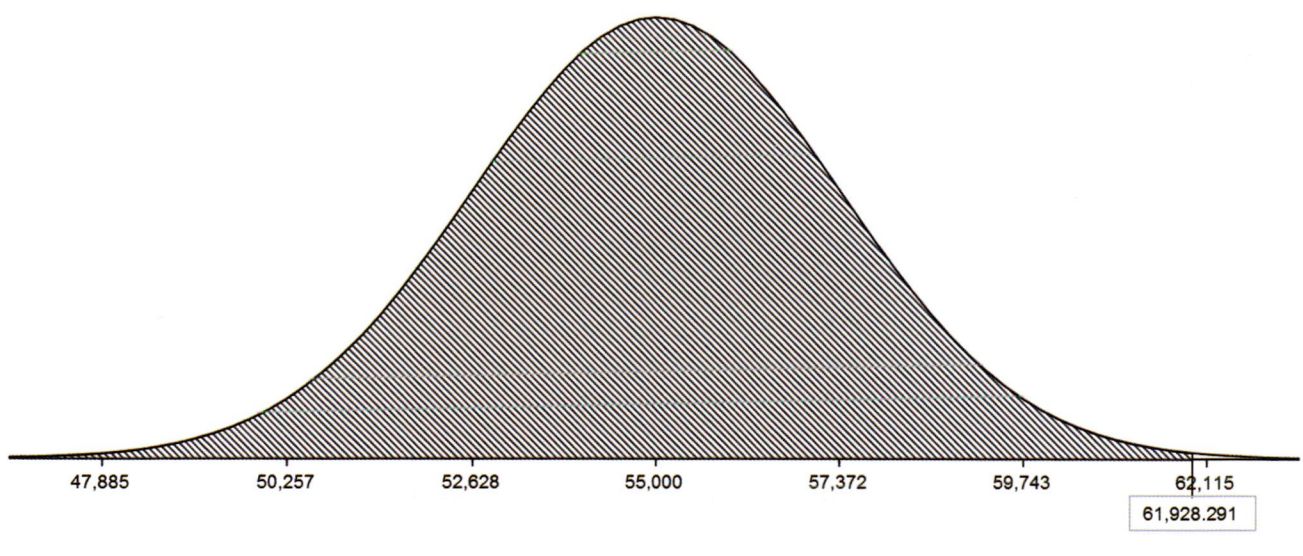

Normal distribution			P(lower)	P(upper)	z	X	mean	std.dev
			.9983	.0017	2.92	61,928.291	55,000.000	2,371.700

Since this is a left-tailed test, so the power is the area to the left of $\bar{X}^* = \$61,928.291$. To find this area we use the z-score:

$$z_o = \frac{\bar{X} - \mu_1}{\frac{\sigma_x}{\sqrt{n}}} = \frac{61,928.291 - 55,000}{15000/\sqrt{40}} = \frac{6928.291}{2371.7082} = 2.921$$

The power is the area under the normal curve to the left of 2.921. Using the standard normal table (Chapter 6, APPENDIX A), this area is as shown above and it is 0.9983

Note that as a result of increasing the sample size from 15 to 40, the power was increased from 0.7753 to 0.9983. Accordingly, increasing the sample size will result in increasing the power or reducing the chance of failing to reject H_o when it is false.

The figure below shows two distributions for $\bar{X}$. The normal curve on the right is the distribution under the assumption that H_o is true. The distribution has mean $\mu_o = \$64,300$. The curve on the left is the distribution under the assumption that the mean is equal to the alternative value $\mu_1 = \$55,000$. The critical region is the region to the left of $\bar{X}^* = \$61,928.291$. The area of the critical region under the null hypothesis distribution is the significance level $\alpha = 0.05$. The area under the alternate distribution is the power 0.9983.

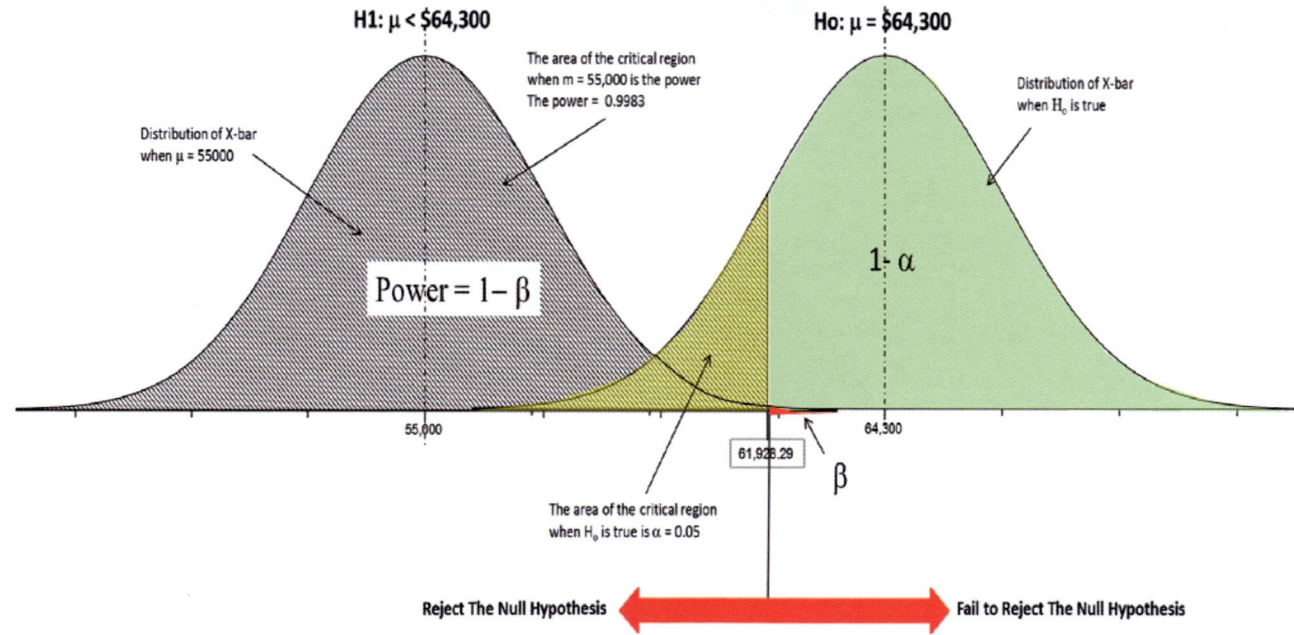

CHAPTER 10

Inferential Statistics: Hypothesis testing using two populations/two samples

LEARNING OBJECTIVES

After completing this chapter, students will be able to:

- Compare between Means of Two Independent Populations
- The z-test and the t-test
- Compare between Two dependent Populations- the paired t-test
- Compare between Two populations proportions
- Compare between Two populations variances

CHAPTER 10

In Chapter 9, we introduced the concept of hypothesis testing and we focused on situations where we only dealt with one population from which we draw a sample to assist us examining a hypothesis about the parent population. In many practical situations, we are often concerned about comparing two populations. This chapter focuses on performing hypothesis testing on the difference between two population means, proportions, and variances.

CHAPTER CONTENTS

10.1 Hypothesis Tests for Comparison between Means of Two Independent Populations- Standard Deviations Known- The z-Test

The comparison between means of two independent populations represents a common situation which is typically driven by a question regarding a potential difference between the two populations. Examples will include:

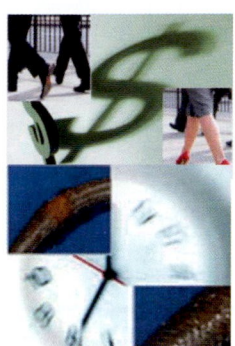

1. Is there a difference in the mean value of sick-leave time taken by male employees and female employees in a certain company?
2. Is there a difference in income between males and females in the U.S.?
3. Is there a difference in the number of defects found in products manufactured in the third shift from those manufactured in the first shift?

In order to perform hypothesis tests for comparison between the means of two populations, we follow the same steps discussed in Chapter 9 but using the two populations:

Step 1: *Identify and define the characteristic under consideration and state the hypothesis*
Step 2: *Select a sample from each population and determine sample statistics*
Step 3: *Select the level of significance or the extent of error*
Step 4: *Identify and use an appropriate test statistic*
Step 5: *Follow appropriate decision rules to reject or accept the null hypothesis*

The common form of hypothesis test to compare two populations is as follows:

$$H_o: \mu_1 = \mu_2$$
$$H_1: \mu_1 \neq \mu_2$$

Other forms of hypothesis testing are shown in Table 10.1 for situations where population variances are known. These tests assume that the samples are from independent populations, and the standard deviations for both populations are known. When population variances are known, the test statistic for mean difference is:

$$z_o = \frac{(\bar{X}_1 - \bar{X}_2) - (\mu_1 - \mu_2)}{\sqrt{\dfrac{\sigma_1^2}{n_1} + \dfrac{\sigma_2^2}{n_2}}} \qquad (10.1)$$

where $\bar{X}_1$ = the mean of the sample from the first population, $\bar{X}_2$ = the mean of the sample from the second population, n_1 = the size of the sample from the first population, n_2 = the size of the sample from the second population, σ_1^2 = variance of the first population, and σ_2^2 = variance of the second population.

Note that the term $\sqrt{\frac{\sigma_1^2}{n_1} + \frac{\sigma_2^2}{n_2}}$ is the standard error of the difference, $\sigma_{\bar{X}_1 - \bar{X}_2}$. Also note that the test statistic is defined as:

$$z_o = \frac{(sample\ mean\ difference) - (hypothesized\ difference)}{standard\ error}$$

Table 10.1 Hypothesis tests for comparison of means of two populations- σ is known or $n \geq 30$

Test	Null hypothesis	Alternative hypothesis	Test statistic	Critical statistic	Reject when
Two-sided	$H_o: \mu_1 = \mu_2$	$H_1: \mu_1 \neq \mu_2$		$z_{\alpha/2}$	
One-sided-left	$H_o: \mu_1 \geq \mu_2$	$H_1: \mu_1 < \mu_2$	$z_o = \frac{(\bar{X}_1 - \bar{X}_2) - (\mu_1 - \mu_2)}{\sqrt{\frac{\sigma_1^2}{n_1} + \frac{\sigma_2^2}{n_2}}}$	z_α	z_o is in the rejection region
One-sided-right	$H_o: \mu_1 \leq \mu_2$	$H_1: \mu_1 > \mu_2$		z_α	

Example 10.1: The statistics summarized below represent two random samples of student ages taken from two different colleges. The issue to be evaluated is whether the average of student ages in these two colleges is the same. The standard deviations of student's age in the two colleges are known to be 2.0 and 3.0, respectively.

  (a) Calculate the standard error of difference
  (b) Calculate the critical z-value,
  (c) Calculate the z-statistic
  (d) Test the hypothesis on whether the difference between the two populations means is zero at $\alpha = 0.01$.

Table 10.2 Summary of key statistics of two colleges

Statistic	College A	College B
Mean	$\bar{X}_A = 20$	$\bar{X}_B = 22$
Population standard deviation, σ	$\sigma_A = 2.0$	$\sigma_B = 3$
n	$n_1 = 36$	$n_2 = 36$

Solution:

The hypothesis form is:

$$H_o: \mu_A = \mu_B$$
$$H_1: \mu_A \neq \mu_B$$

The standard error of difference is:

$$\sqrt{\frac{\sigma_1^2}{n_1} + \frac{\sigma_2^2}{n_2}} = \sqrt{\frac{4}{36} + \frac{9}{36}} = 0.600$$

The test-statistic in this case is

$$z_0 = \frac{(\bar{X}_1 - \bar{X}_2) - (\mu_1 - \mu_2)}{\sqrt{\frac{\sigma_1^2}{n_1} + \frac{\sigma_2^2}{n_2}}}$$

Accordingly,

$$z_0 = \frac{(\bar{X}_A - \bar{X}_B) - (\mu_A - \mu_B)}{\sqrt{\frac{\sigma_A^2}{n_A} + \frac{\sigma_A^2}{n_B}}} = \frac{(20 - 22)}{\sqrt{\frac{2.0^2}{36} + \frac{3.0^2}{36}}} = -3.33$$

At $\alpha = 0.01$, $z_{0.005} = 2.58$. As can be seen in the figure below, z_0 falls in the rejection region. This means that we should reject the null hypothesis $H_0: \mu_A = \mu_B$ and conclude that the two colleges have different student ages.

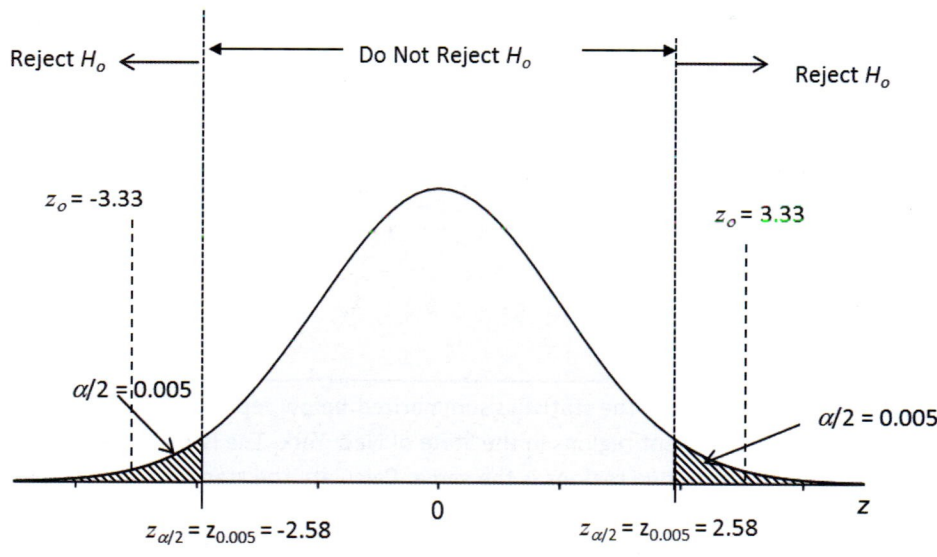

As we discussed in Chapter 9, we can verify the results of the hypothesis test of the difference between two means by establishing the confidence interval on the difference. Following the procedure discussed in Chapter 8 to determine the confidence interval on the difference between two means, the mean difference between the two samples (the point estimate) is $\bar{X}_A - \bar{X}_B = 20 - 22 = -2$

The confidence interval on the difference between two means is determined as follows:

$$\mu_A - \mu_B = (\bar{X}_A - \bar{X}_B) \pm z_{\frac{\alpha}{2}}\sqrt{\frac{\sigma_A^2}{n_A} + \frac{\sigma_B^2}{n_B}} = -2 \pm 2.58\sqrt{\frac{4.0}{36} + \frac{9.0}{36}} = -2.0 \pm 1.55$$

$$-3.55 < \mu_A - \mu_B < -0.45$$

As you can see the hypothesized difference of zero does not fall in the above range. As a result we reject H_o.

Working Problem 10.1: The statistics summarized below represent two random samples of student grades taken from two different classes The issue to be evaluated is whether the average grade in these two classes is the same. The standard deviations of student's grade in the two classes are known to be 4 and 6, respectively.

(a) Calculate the standard error of difference
(b) Calculate the critical z-value,
(c) Calculate the z-statistic
(d) Test the hypothesis on whether the
difference between the two populations means is zero at a = 0.05.

	Class A	Class B
Mean	80	79
Population Standard Deviation	4	6
Sample Size	30	30

Answer: Verify the values in the output below and make the decision

Hypothesis Test: Independent Groups (z-test)	Class A	Class B
mean	80	79
std. dev.	4	6
n	30	30
difference (Class A - C;ass B)	1.000	
standard error of difference	1.317	
hypothesized difference	0	
z	0.76	
p-value (two-tailed)	.4475	
confidence interval 95.% lower	-1.580	
confidence interval 95.% upper	3.580	
margin of error	2.580	

Working Problem 10.2: The statistics summarized below represent two random samples of house property tax taken from two different regions in the State of New York. The issue to be evaluated is whether the average of property tax in these two regions is the same. Calculate the standard error of difference.

Statistic	Region A	Region B
Mean	$7,200	$7,350
Standard deviation, σ	$8,00	$1,650
n	50	50
Variance	640000	2722500

Answer: 259.326

Working Problem 10.3: The statistics summarized below represent two random samples of house property tax taken from two different regions in the State of New York. The issue to be evaluated is whether the average of property tax in these two regions is the same.
(a) Calculate the critical z-value
(b) Calculate the z-statistic
(c) Test the hypothesis on whether the difference between the two populations means is zero at $\alpha = 0.05$.

Statistic	Region A	Region B
Mean	$7,200	$7,350
Standard deviation, σ	$8,00	$1,650
n	50	50
Variance	640000	2722500

Answer: Verify the output below and make the decision

Hypothesis Test: Independent Groups (z-test)

Region A	Region B	
7200	7350	mean
800	1650	std. dev.
50	50	n
	-150.000	difference (Region A - Region B)
	259.326	standard error of difference
	0	hypothesized difference
	-0.58	z
	.5630	p-value (two-tailed)
	-817.980	confidence interval 99.% lower
	517.980	confidence interval 99.% upper
	667.980	margin of error

Working Problem 10.4:

The statistics summarized below represent two random samples of weight loss values taken from two groups of people undergoing weight-loss programs. The issue to be evaluated is whether the average weight loss in these two groups is the same. The standard deviations of weight loss in the two groups are known to be 4 and 4, respectively.

(a) Calculate the standard error of difference
(b) Calculate the critical z-value at $\alpha = 0.01$
(c) Calculate the z-statistic
(d) Test the hypothesis on whether the difference between the two populations means is zero

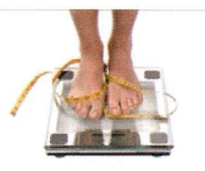

	Weight-Loss Program A	Weight-Loss Program B
Mean	30	36
Population Standard Deviation, σ	4	4
Sample Size	26	33

Answer: Verify the output below and make the decision

Hypothesis Test: Independent Groups (z-test)	Weight-Loss Program A	Weight-Loss Program B
mean	30	36
std. dev.	4	4
n	26	33
difference (Weight-Loss Program A - Weight-Loss Program B)		-6.000
standard error of difference		1.049
hypothesized difference		0
z		-5.72
p-value (two-tailed)		1.06E-08
confidence interval 99.% lower		-8.702
confidence interval 99.% upper		-3.298
margin of error		2.702

10.2 Hypothesis Tests for Comparison between Means of Two Independent Populations- Standard Deviations Unknown-The t-Test

As we did in the case of hypothesis tests about a single population of unknown standard deviation, we can use the t-test for the comparison between two populations with unknown standard deviations. In this case, we typically assume the populations have equal but unknown standard deviations. This assumption allows us to combine or 'pool' the variances of the samples withdrawn from the two populations (as discussed earlier in Chapter 8). The pooled variance is obtained from the following formula:

$$S_p{}^2 = \frac{(n_1 - 1)s_1{}^2 + (n_2 - 1)s_2{}^2}{n_1 + n_2 - 2} \qquad (10.2)$$

where n_1= the size of the sample from the first population, n_2= the size of the sample from the second population, $s_1{}^2$ = variance of the first sample, and $s_2{}^2$ = variance of the second sample

The formula for calculating the t-statistic is as follows:

$$t_o = \frac{(\bar{X}_1 - \bar{X}_2) - (\mu_1 - \mu_2)}{S_p\sqrt{\dfrac{1}{n_1} + \dfrac{1}{n_2}}} \qquad (10.3)$$

where $\bar{X}_1$ = the mean of the sample from the first population, $\bar{X}_2$ = the mean of the sample from the second population, n_1 = the size of the sample from the first population, n_2 = the size of the sample from the second population, S_p = pooled standard deviation

Again, basic requirements for performing this hypothesis test are:

1. The characteristic of the parent populations follow a normal distribution
2. Parent populations are independent
3. The standard deviations of the two populations are equal

Table 10.3 shows the different formats of hypothesis tests, the test-statistic, and the rejection criteria. Note that the critical t value is found at a degree of freedom $df = n_1 + n_2$ -2.

Table 10.3 Hypothesis tests for comparison between means of two populations when σ is unknown and small samples

Test	Null hypothesis	Alternative hypothesis	Test statistic	Critical statistic	Reject when
Two-sided	$H_o: \mu_1 = \mu_2$	$H_1: \mu_1 \neq \mu_2$		$t_{(n_1+n_2-2,\frac{\alpha}{2})}$	
One-sided-left	$H_o: \mu_1 \geq \mu_2$	$H_1: \mu_1 < \mu_2$	$t_o = \dfrac{(\bar{X}_1 - \bar{X}_2) - (\mu_1 - \mu_2)}{S_p\sqrt{\dfrac{1}{n_1} + \dfrac{1}{n_2}}}$	$t_{(n_1+n_2-2,\alpha)}$	t_o in the rejection region
One-sided-right	$H_o: \mu_1 \leq \mu_2$	$H_1: \mu_1 > \mu_2$	$S_p{}^2 = \dfrac{(n_1 - 1)s_1{}^2 + (n_2 - 1)s_2{}^2}{n_1 + n_2 - 2}$	$t_{(n_1+n_2-2,\alpha)}$	

Example 10.2: A weight-loss clinic has received some criticisms regarding the effectiveness of its weight loss treatment. As a result, the clinic has begun an experiment with a new weight loss treatment with the hope that it will result in more significant weight loss. Using two random samples of people, one from the previous treatment and the second from the new treatment, the clinic produced the results of the amount of weight loss shown in Table 10.4. Test the hypothesis that the new weight-loss treatment is different from the previous one? Use $\alpha = 0.05$.

Table 10.4 Weight reduction values (lbs) for two weight-loss treatments

Weight loss (lbs) using previous treatment (A)	Weight loss (lbs) using new treatment (B)
12	13
14	17
19	15
13	18
12	14
	13

Solution:

In this example, the appropriate test of hypothesis is:

$$H_o: \mu_A = \mu_B$$
$$H_1: \mu_A \neq \mu_B$$

Note that the samples sizes here are small and no information about population standard deviation is provided. Indeed, the population associated with the experimental new treatment did not exist yet as this only a trial experiment. Accordingly, we need to perform a t-test to compare the two populations. For the data of Table 10.4, we calculate the statistics as shown in Table 10.5.

Table 10.5 Statistics of weight reduction values for two weight-loss treatments

	Weight loss (lbs) using previous treatment	Weight loss (lbs) using new treatment
Mean	$\bar{X}_A = 14$	$\bar{X}_B = 15$
Standard Deviation	$s_A = 2.92$	$s_B = 2.1$
Sample Variance	$s_A^2 = 8.53$	$s_B^2 = 4.4$
n	$n_A = 5$	$n_B = 6$

Using the above statistics:

$$S_p^2 = \frac{(n_1 - 1)s_1^2 + (n_2 - 1)s_2^2}{n_1 + n_2 - 2} = \frac{(5 - 1)8.53 + (6 - 1)4.4}{5 + 6 - 2} = 6.24$$

This yields a $S_p = 2.497$. The t-statistic is calculated follows:

$$t_o = \frac{(\bar{X}_1 - \bar{X}_2) - (\mu_1 - \mu_2)}{S_p\sqrt{\frac{1}{n_1} + \frac{1}{n_2}}} = \frac{(14 - 15)}{2.497\sqrt{\frac{1}{5} + \frac{1}{6}}} = -0.6614$$

At $\alpha = 0.05$, and a degree of freedom $n_1 + n_2$ - 2, $t_{\alpha/2} = t_{9, 0.025} = 2.262$ (see below)

$\gamma \backslash \alpha$	0.4	0.1	0.05	0.025	0.01	0.001	0.0005
1	0.325	3.078	6.314	12.706	31.821	318.31	636.62
..	..	..	..	..	..	..	..
8	0.262	1.397	1.86	2.306	2.896	4.501	5.041
9	0.261	1.383	1.833	2.262	2.821	4.297	4.781
..	..	..	..	..	..	..	..

The t_o falls within the 'Do-Not-Reject' region as shown below. As a result, we fail to reject $H_o: \mu_A = \mu_B$ and we conclude that the two treatments are the same or have the same effect on weight loss.

As discussed in the previous example, we can verify the results of the hypothesis test of the difference between two means by establishing the confidence interval on the difference. Following the procedure discussed in Chapter 8 to determine the confidence interval on the difference between two means, the mean difference between the two samples (the point estimate) is

$$\bar{X}_A - \bar{X}_B = 14 - 15 = -1.0.$$

The confidence interval on the difference between two means is determined as follows:

$$(\bar{X}_1 - \bar{X}_2) - t_{(df,\frac{\alpha}{2})} \; S_p \sqrt{\frac{1}{n_1} + \frac{1}{n_2}} < \mu_1 - \mu_2 < (\bar{X}_1 - \bar{X}_2) + t_{(df,\frac{\alpha}{2})} \; S_p \sqrt{\frac{1}{n_1} + \frac{1}{n_2}}$$

$$(-1) - 2.262 \; (2.497) \sqrt{\frac{1}{5} + \frac{1}{6}} < \mu_1 - \mu_2 < (-1) + 2.262 \; (2.497) \sqrt{\frac{1}{5} + \frac{1}{6}}$$

$$-4.42 < \mu_1 - \mu_2 < 2.42$$

As you can see the hypothesized difference of zero falls in the above range. As a result we fail to reject H_o.

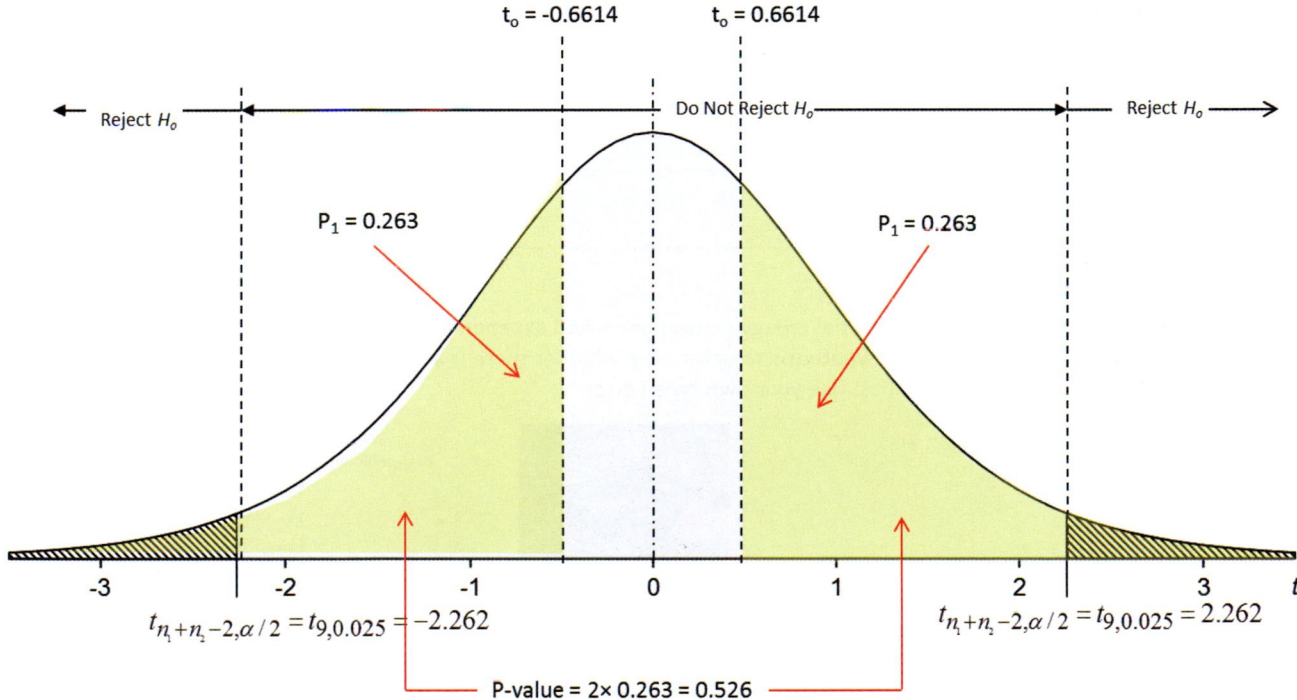

Working Problem 10.5:

The following data represents residential energy consumption and expenditures in two different cities in the U.S.A. in millions of BTUs. Calculate the mean, mode, median, range, standard deviation, and variance for each city. Compare the two cities energy consumption. Do you see a difference between the two cities?

Answer:

	BTU(millions)-City A	BTU(millions)-City B
Mean	106.15	67.3
Median	Do it yourself	67.5
Mode	111	45
Standard Deviation	Do it yourself	Do it yourself
Sample Variance	Do it yourself	Do it yourself
Range	106	Do it yourself

#	BTU(millions)-City A	#	BTU(millions)-City B
1	102	1	76
2	151	2	45
3	111	3	111
4	78	4	55
5	54	5	54
6	129	6	58
7	130	7	70
8	45	8	45
9	112	9	58
10	111	10	80
11	102	11	75
12	111	12	66
13	120	13	54
14	108	14	69
15	113	15	71
16	129	16	80
17	135	17	59
18	145	18	83
19	87	19	87
20	50	20	50

Working Problem 10.6:

The following data represents residential energy consumption and expenditures in two different cities in the U.S.A. in millions of BTUs. Perform a test of hypothesis to determine whether there is a significant difference in BTU consumption between the two cities. Use your own type I error.

Answer: One Possible answer at 5% error

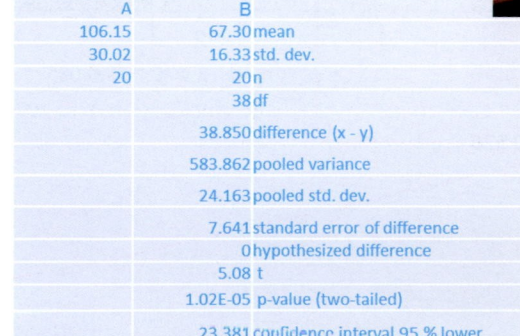

A	B	
106.15	67.30	mean
30.02	16.33	std. dev.
20	20	n
	38	df
	38.850	difference (x - y)
	583.862	pooled variance
	24.163	pooled std. dev.
	7.641	standard error of difference
	0	hypothesized difference
	5.08	t
	1.02E-05	p-value (two-tailed)
	23.381	confidence interval 95.% lower
	54.319	confidence interval 95.% upper
	15.469	margin of error

#	BTU(millions)-City A	#	BTU(millions)-City B
1	102	1	76
2	151	2	45
3	111	3	111
4	78	4	55
5	54	5	54
6	129	6	58
7	130	7	70
8	45	8	45
9	112	9	58
10	111	10	80
11	102	11	75
12	111	12	66
13	120	13	54
14	108	14	69
15	113	15	71
16	129	16	80
17	135	17	59
18	145	18	83
19	87	19	87
20	50	20	50

Working Problem 10.7:

Different countries may have different life expectancy depending on many factors including: life style, crime rate, medical care, and human services. The data in the table represents 2004 data. Use this data to perform descriptive statistics and answer the following question:

- Perform a test of hypothesis on the difference in life expectance between males
- and females at $\alpha = 0.01$.
- Determine the standard error, test statistics, ?
- Make a decision

Answer:

t-Test: Two-Sample Assuming Equal Variances		
	Male	Female
Mean	74.90333	80.98
Variance	17.51068	7.900276
Observations	30	30
Pooled Variance	12.70548	
Hypothesized Mean Difference	0	
df	58	
t Stat	-6.60261	
P(T<=t) one-tail	6.79E-09	
t Critical one-tail	2.392377	
P(T<=t) two-tail	1.36E-08	
t Critical two-tail	2.663287	

Life Expectance(yrs)

Country	Male	Female
Japan	78.6	85.6
Israel	77.9	82.2
Switzerland	78.6	83.7
Hong Kong	79	84.7
Costa Rica	76.4	80.7
England and Wales	76.8	81.1
Canada	77.8	82.6
Sweden	78.4	82.7
Germany	75.7	81.4
Northern Ireland	76	80.8
Scotland	74.2	79.3
Bulgaria	69.1	76.3
Romania	68.3	75.6
Czech Republic	72.6	79
Puerto Rico	74.1	82.3
United States	75.2	80.4
Denmark	75.2	79.9
Austria	76.4	82.1
Spain	77.2	83.7
Australia	78.1	83
Finland	75.3	82.3
Portugal	74.5	81
Poland	70.7	79.2
Hungary	68.6	76.9
Belgium	75.6	81.5
France	76.7	83.8
Greece	76.6	81.5
Norway	77.5	82.3
Netherlands	76.9	81.4
Russian Federation	59.1	72.4

(From *Deaths: Final Data for 2006*, by Melonie Heron, Donna L. Hoyert, Sherry L. Murphy, Jiaquan Xu, Kenneth D. Kochanek, and Betzaida Tejada. Division of Vital Statistics-National-Vital Statistics Reports, Volume 57, Number 14, April 17, 2009)

10.3 Hypothesis Tests for Comparison between Means of Two Dependent Populations- The Case of Paired Data

The case of paired data represents bivariate data of one-to-one correspondence. This type of data requires a special kind of hypothesis test that reflects the source parity. The example below illustrates this type of testing.

Example 10.3: In the weight loss case of Example 10.2, we assumed that the two samples are independent. In other words, individuals in the sample that have undergone the first treatment were not the same people picked in the second sample. This may raise doubts about the effectiveness of the comparison between the two treatments as a result of the difference in people's reaction to the weight loss treatment. To overcome this problem one approach is to test the same people for both treatments. In other words, an individual who has undergone the first treatment will also undergo the new one and the weight difference in each treatment is calculated. This approach is called *paired testing* and it results in *paired data*. For the sake of demonstration, suppose the weight-loss clinic picked 10 people randomly who used the previous weight-loss treatment but were not satisfied and tried the new treatment on each one of them. Table 10.6 lists the weight loss data for each person under the previous and the new treatment.

Table 10.6 Weight reduction values (lbs) for ten participants

Person	Weight loss (lbs) using previous treatment	Weight loss (lbs) using new treatment
A	18.8	19.7
B	11.3	17.2
C	14.3	14.9
D	16.8	17.6
E	16.2	14.1
F	15.1	17.8
G	10.4	16.6
H	11.7	18.0
I	12.9	14.6
J	11.2	16.7

Solution:

In this situation, our concern should be about the differences in weight loss for different participants. These differences are shown in Table 10.7. We also need to calculate the mean and the standard deviation of differences as shown in Table 10.7.

Table 10.7 Differences in weight reduction values (lbs) for participants

Person	Weight loss (lbs) using previous treatment	Weight loss (lbs) using new treatment	Differences
A	18.8	19.7	-0.9
B	11.3	17.2	-5.9
C	14.3	14.9	-0.6
D	16.8	17.6	-0.8
E	16.2	14.1	2.1
F	15.1	17.8	-2.7
G	10.4	16.6	-6.2
H	11.7	18	-6.3
I	12.9	14.6	-1.7
J	11.2	16.7	-5.5
			$\bar{X}_d = \bar{d} = -2.85$
			$s_d = 2.95$

The test of hypothesis for paired data is about whether the difference is zero. This leads to:

$$H_o: \mu_d = 0$$
$$H_1: \mu_d \neq 0$$

The test statistic is the *t*-statistic defined by:

$$t_o = \frac{\bar{d}}{\frac{s_d}{\sqrt{n}}} \qquad (10.4)$$

where $\bar{d}$ = the mean of the differences, s_d= the standard deviation of differences, and n = the sample size (the number of pairs).

Using the statistics of Table 10.7, the t-statistic is calculated as follows:

$$t_o = \frac{\bar{d}}{\frac{s_d}{\sqrt{n}}} = \frac{-2.85}{\frac{2.95}{\sqrt{10}}} = -3.05$$

This t_o value of -3.05 should be compared with $t_{n-1,\alpha/2}$ at the desired significance level. Suppose 0.01 is the significance level used, then $t_{9,0.005}$= ± 3.25. This means that t_o value is in the 'Do-Not-Reject' region, and we fail to reject the null hypothesis $H_o: \mu_d = 0$; meaning there is no difference between the two treatments.

Working Problem 10.8:
The data shown below represents the gas price ($/gallon) for the same states in 2008 and 2009. Conduct a hypothesis test at $\alpha = 0.01$ to determine whether the gas price was significantly different in 2009 in comparison with 2008.

Answer:

The output below was produced using Excel data analysis (paired test)
Carry out the analysis manually and make the decision at $\alpha = 0.01$.

	Year 2009	Year 2008
Mean	2.636	3.775
Variance	0.065	0.010
Observations	9	9
Pearson Correlation	-0.121	
Hypothesized Mean Difference	0	
df	8	
t Stat	-11.988	
P(T<=t) one-tail	0.00000108	
t Critical one-tail	2.896	
P(T<=t) two-tail	0.0000022	
t Critical two-tail	3.355	

State	Sept- 2009	Sep-2008
California	3.099	3.750
Colorado	2.480	3.732
Florida	2.527	3.893
Massachusetts	2.597	3.582
Minnesota	2.452	3.765
New York	2.811	3.805
Ohio	2.411	3.933
Texas	2.404	3.729
Washington	2.947	3.785

Working Problem 10.9:

A retired couple plans to tour around big cities in the U.S.A. They prepared a list of the price per night of two preferred hotels in a sample of 10 cities. The two hotels are Ramada Inn and Holiday Inn This list is shown below.

(a) Use descriptive statistics to compare the price of the two hotels in the different cities.
(b) Test the claim that Ramada Inn Hotels are priced differently than Holiday Inn Hotels at the $\alpha = 0.01$ level of significance

Answer: See outputs below. Determine the statistics manually and interpret the results

City	Ramada Inn	Holiday Inn
Atlanta	89	78
Newark	105	115
Orlando	170	165
New Orleans	99	105
Birmingham	72	79
Atlantic City	56	75
Las Vegas	48	55
San Diego	152	165
Tampa Bay	80	95
Chicago	180	175

	Ramada Inn	Holiday Inn
Mean	105.1	110.7
Median	94	100
Standard Deviation	46.8033	43.1793
Sample Variance	2190.5444	1864.4556
Range	132	120
Minimum	48	55
Maximum	180	175
Sum	1051	1107
Count	10	10

t-Test: Paired Two Sample for Means	Ramada Inn	Holiday Inn
Mean	105.1	110.7
Variance	2190.544	1864.456
Observations	10	10
Pearson Correlation	0.979982	
Hypothesized Mean Difference	0	
df	9	
t Stat	-1.82609	
P(T<=t) one-tail	0.050561	
t Critical one-tail	2.821438	
P(T<=t) two-tail	0.101122	
t Critical two-tail	3.249836	

10.4 Hypothesis Tests for Comparison between Proportions of Two Independent Populations

A hypothesis test for comparison between proportions of two independent populations will take the following form:

$$H_o: p_1 = p_2$$

$$H_1: p_1 \neq p_2$$

To conduct this test, take a sample from each population and determine the sample proportion of the characteristic of interest. We should also assume each sample is large enough that the normal distribution will serve as a good approximation of the binomial distribution. This allows us to use a test statistic, which follows the standard normal distribution. In this case, the test-statistic is:

$$z_o = \frac{\hat{p}_1 - \hat{p}_2}{\sqrt{\frac{P_p(1 - P_p)}{n_1} + \frac{P_p(1 - P_p)}{n_2}}} \qquad (10.5)$$

where $\hat{p}_1 =$ the mean of the sample proportion from the first population, $\hat{p}_2 =$ the mean of the sample proportion from the second population, $n_1 =$ the size of the sample from the first, population, $n_2 =$ the size of the sample from the second population, and $P_p =$ the pooled estimate of the population proportion calculated as follows:

$$P_p = \frac{X_1 + X_2}{n_1 + n_2} \qquad (10.6)$$

where X_1 and X_2 are the success events in the samples taken from the first population and the second population, respectively.

Example 10.4: A company producing video games made a claim that a new game would be equally liked by males and females in the age range from 15 to 22 years. To test this claim a sales agent surveyed two samples one of females and the other of males, each of 100 people. These samples revealed that 70% of males and 55% of females liked the game. Using test of hypothesis, assist the agent in making a decision of whether gender is an issue in the interest in video games at $\alpha = 0.01$.

Solution:

The test of hypothesis in this case is:

$$H_o: p_m = p_f$$

$$H_1: p_m \neq p_f$$

The test-statistic:

$$z_o = \frac{\hat{p}_1 - \hat{p}_2}{\sqrt{\frac{P_p(1 - P_p)}{n_1} + \frac{P_p(1 - P_p)}{n_2}}} = \frac{0.70 - 0.55}{\sqrt{\frac{P_p(1 - P_p)}{100} + \frac{P_p(1 - P_p)}{100}}}$$

The pooled estimate of proportion p_p is calculated as follows:

$$P_p = \frac{X_1 + X_2}{n_1 + n_2} = \frac{70 + 55}{100 + 100} = 0.625$$

Accordingly,

$$z_o = \frac{\hat{p}_1 - \hat{p}_2}{\sqrt{\frac{P_p(1 - P_p)}{n_1} + \frac{P_p(1 - P_p)}{n_2}}} = \frac{0.70 - 0.55}{\sqrt{\frac{0.625(1 - 0.625)}{100} + \frac{0.625(1 - 0.625)}{100}}} = 2.19$$

At $\alpha = 0.01$, $z_{\alpha/2} = 2.58$

As we can see below, the z_o value falls in the 'Do-Not-Reject' region, which means that it is likely that equal proportions of male and female will like the new video game. This conclusion is valid at $\alpha = 0.01$. Also note that the p-value corresponding to z_o of 2.19 is 0.028 (2×0.014), which is greater than 0.01. This supports the failure to reject the null hypothesis.

Students are encouraged to repeat this problem at a 5% risk and see the difference in results.

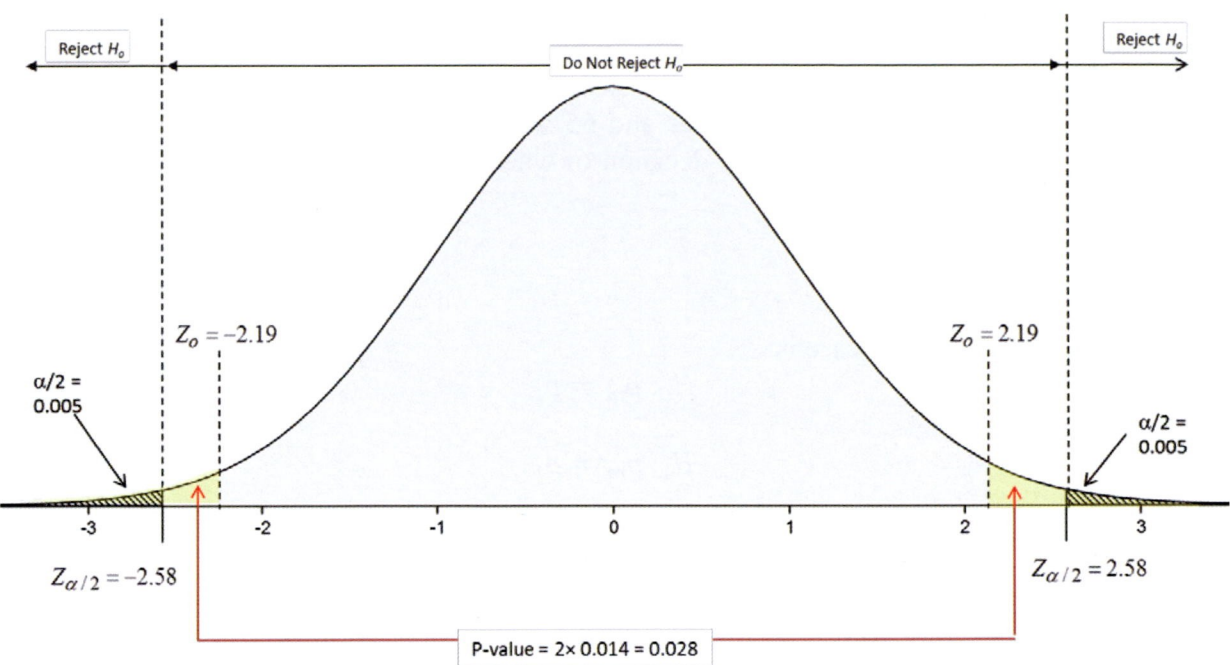

Working Problem 10.10:

In November, 2012, Apple® introduced the new e-tablet called 'iPad mini' after its classic iPad, which sold by the end of its first year introduction (2010) nearly 15 million iPads, generating about $9.5 billion in revenue. The idea of the iPad mini is to create the smallest possible iPad that could still deliver the full iPad experience. The iPad mini is 23 percent thinner, 53 percent lighter, and fits in one hand , yet according to Apple® it can do everything an iPad can do. A sales consultant who conducted a survey in 2010 regarding consumer's appeal to iPad conducted another survey in October 2012 for the iPad mini. The results of the two surveys were as follows:

	2010 Survey	2012 Survey
n	1000	1000
X	820	833

Using test of hypothesis, and $\alpha = 0.01$, can you determine if the iPad mini will have a better attraction by consumers than the classic iPad?

Answer:
- See the answer outputs and try to perform the analysis manually.
- Determine if the iPad mini will have a better attraction by consumers than the classic iPad

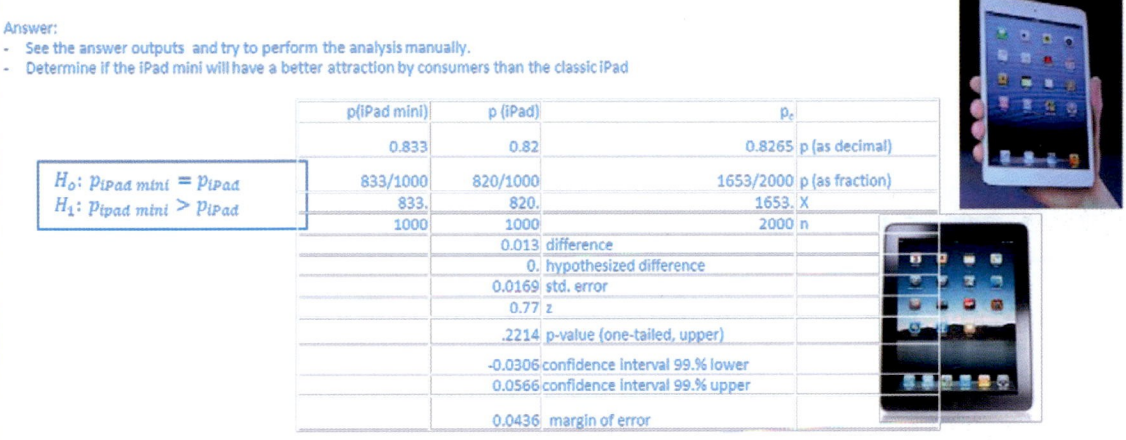

	p(iPad mini)	p (iPad)		p_c	
	0.833	0.82		0.8265	p (as decimal)
$H_o: p_{iPad\ mini} = p_{iPad}$	833/1000	820/1000		1653/2000	p (as fraction)
$H_1: p_{iPad\ mini} > p_{iPad}$	833.	820.		1653.	X
	1000	1000		2000	n
		0.013	difference		
		0.	hypothesized difference		
		0.0169	std. error		
		0.77	z		
		.2214	p-value (one-tailed, upper)		
		-0.0306	confidence interval 99.% lower		
		0.0566	confidence interval 99.% upper		
		0.0436	margin of error		

Working Problem 10.11:

An education expert believes that the percentage of students earning an Associate Degree from a Community College are the same for rural areas and urban areas. Using a sample 1100 , he found that 338 came from urban area; using another sample of 1600, he found that 692 came from Rural area. Test the expert's claim at the $\alpha = 0.05$ level of significance.

Answer:		Urban	Rural
	n	1100	1600
	X	338	692
	p_i	0.307273	0.4325

	p1	p2	p_c	
Hypothesis test for two independent proportions	0.3073	0.4325	0.3815	p (as decimal)
	338/1100	692/1600	1030/2700	p (as fraction)
	338.	692.	1030.	X
	1100	1600	2700	n
		-0.1252	difference	
		0.	hypothesized difference	
		0.019	std. error	
		-6.58	z	
		4.64E-11	p-value (two-tailed)	
		-0.1617	confidence interval 95.% lower	
		-0.0887	confidence interval 95.% upper	
		0.0365	margin of error	

10.5 Using Software Programs to perform Hypothesis Tests for Comparison between Means of Two Populations

Microsoft Excel® Data Analysis allows performing many tests for comparison between population means. Four key tests can be performed as shown in Figure 10.1. In order to perform these tests, data should be available (input ranges). In addition, we should specify the significance level. The key outputs in these tests are: the critical z or t values obtained for the one-sided and the two-sided tests, the test-statistic (z_o or t_o), and the p-values.

Example 10.5: Consider the data of students ages in two different colleges listed in Table 10.8 and use Excel® Data Analysis to evaluate whether the average age of students in College A is the same as that in College B. Test this hypothesis at $\alpha = 0.01$.

Solution:

Before we begin performing this analysis in Excel®, we should establish the hypothesis test format appropriate for this evaluation. In this case, we use a double-sided test:

$$H_o: \mu_A = \mu_B$$
$$H_1: \mu_A \neq \mu_B$$

We should then find out what test to use. Recall that the z-test is used when the population variances are known. When the variances are unknown, we can still use the z-test provided that the sample size is large as in this example ($n = 36$). In this case, the variances of the samples will be used to roughly estimate the population variances. Figures 10.1 and 10.2 demonstrate the main steps to perform this test. Note that the two data sets are arranged side-by-side in two columns in the spreadsheet. Also note that in addition to the two input ranges used, we have to specify the variance of each population. In this case, you should perform descriptive statistics to calculate the variance of each data set and input these variances in the z-test menu.

Table 10.8 Students' ages in two different colleges

Observation #	Student Ages in College A	Student Ages in College B	Observation #	Student Ages in College A	Student Ages in College B
1	20.6	24.2	19	22	18.3
2	16.9	25.5	20	22.1	21.8
3	20.2	23.7	21	21.7	20.8
4	18.8	20.9	22	18.4	24.6
5	20.9	25	23	17.6	19.1
6	19.5	22.8	24	18.7	20.4
7	24.3	20.2	25	20.4	17.4
8	19.7	19	26	21.2	25.2
9	23.9	24.9	27	19.2	25.6
10	17.3	23.7	28	22.8	19.1
11	18.9	21.1	29	22	18.3
12	19.3	21.2	30	19.5	22.8
13	20.8	23.8	31	24.3	20.2
14	19.5	20.8	32	19.7	19
15	19.3	22	33	23.9	24.9
16	21.2	25.2	34	17.3	23.7
17	19.2	25.6	35	18.9	21.1
18	22.8	19.1	36	19.3	21.2

Table 10.9 Descriptive statistics of the two colleges are shown below

	Student Ages in College A	*Student Ages in College B*
Mean	20.336	22.006
Median	19.7	21.5
Mode	19.5	23.7
Standard Deviation	2.0067	2.4905
Sample Variance	4.0269	6.2028
Range	7.4	8.2
Minimum	16.9	17.4
Maximum	24.3	25.6

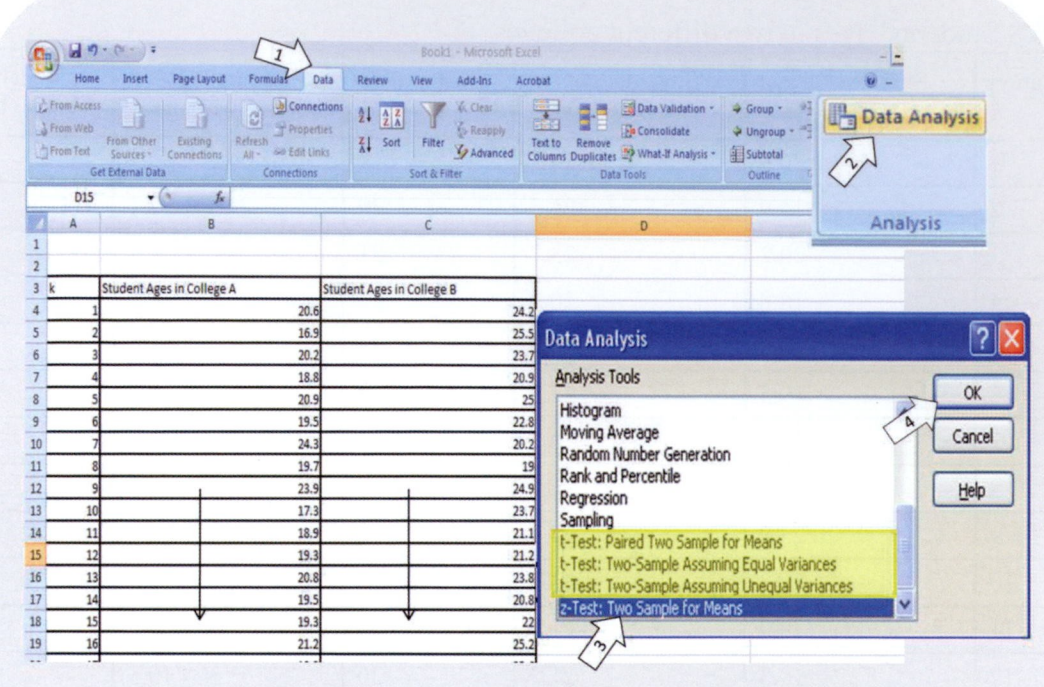

Figure 10.1 Using Excel® to Perform a z-Hypothesis Test: Steps 1 through 4

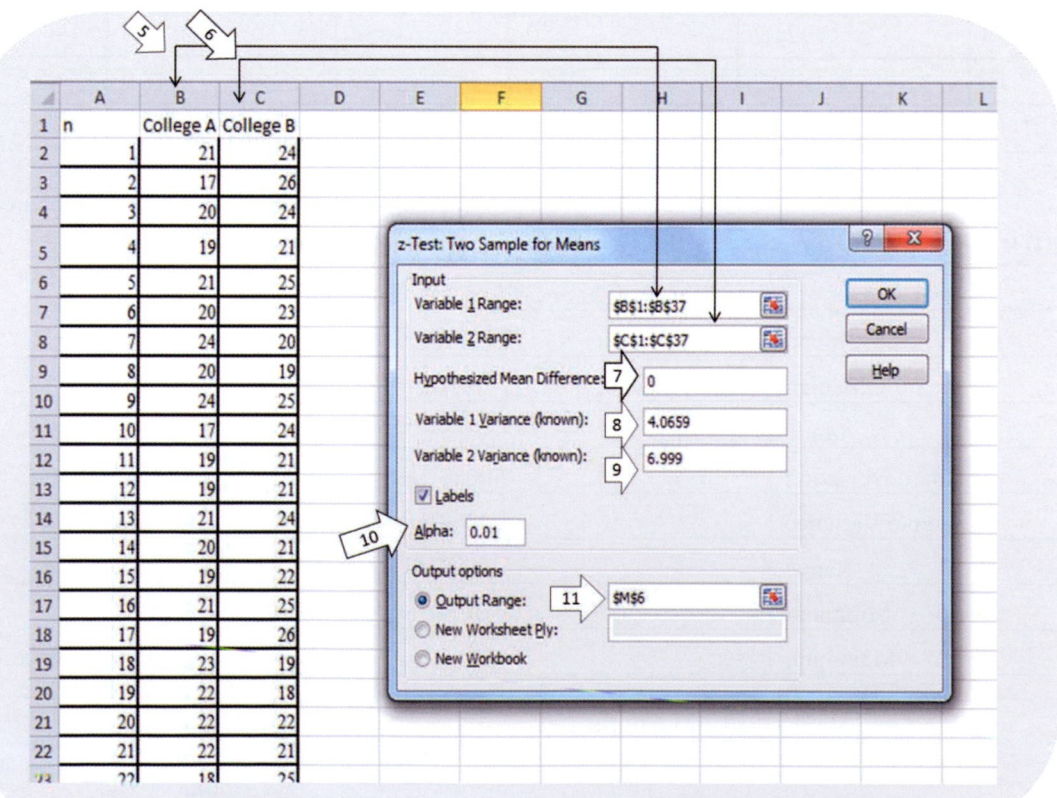

Figure 10.2 Using Excel® to Perform a z-Hypothesis Test: Steps 5 to 11

The output of the z-test analysis is shown in Table 10.10. In this output, Excel® provides the mean and variance for each sample. It also provides the value of the test-statistic, z_o (-3.132), and the critical z values for one-tail and two-tail tests. For our test of hypothesis, we only consider the two-tail critical z value ($z_{\alpha/2}$ or 2.576) and the two-tail p-value (0.002). Interpretations of these values are now left to the student to make.

Table 10.10 Output of Excel® z-test

z-Test: Two Sample for Means		
	Student Ages in College A	*Student Ages in College B*
Mean	20.336	22.006
Known Variance	4.027	6.203
Observations	36	36
Hypothesized Mean Difference	0	
z	-3.132	
P(Z<=z) one-tail	0.001	
z Critical one-tail	2.326	
P(Z<=z) two-tail	0.002	
z Critical two-tail	2.576	

Since population variances are not given in the above example, we can also use the t-test. In this case, we assume equal variances in Excel® Data Analysis. Figure 10.3 shows Excel® t-test menu assuming equal variances. The output of this analysis is shown in Table 10.11. Again, interpretations of these values are now left to the student to make.

Table 10.11 Output of Excel® t-test-equal variances

t-Test: Two-Sample Assuming Equal Variances		
	Student ages in College A	*Student ages in College B*
Mean	20.336	22.006
Variance	4.027	6.203
Observations	36	36
Pooled Variance	5.115	
Hypothesized Mean Difference	0.000	
df	70.000	
t Stat	-3.132	
P(T<=t) one-tail	0.001	
t Critical one-tail	2.381	
P(T<=t) two-tail	0.003	
t Critical two-tail	2.648	

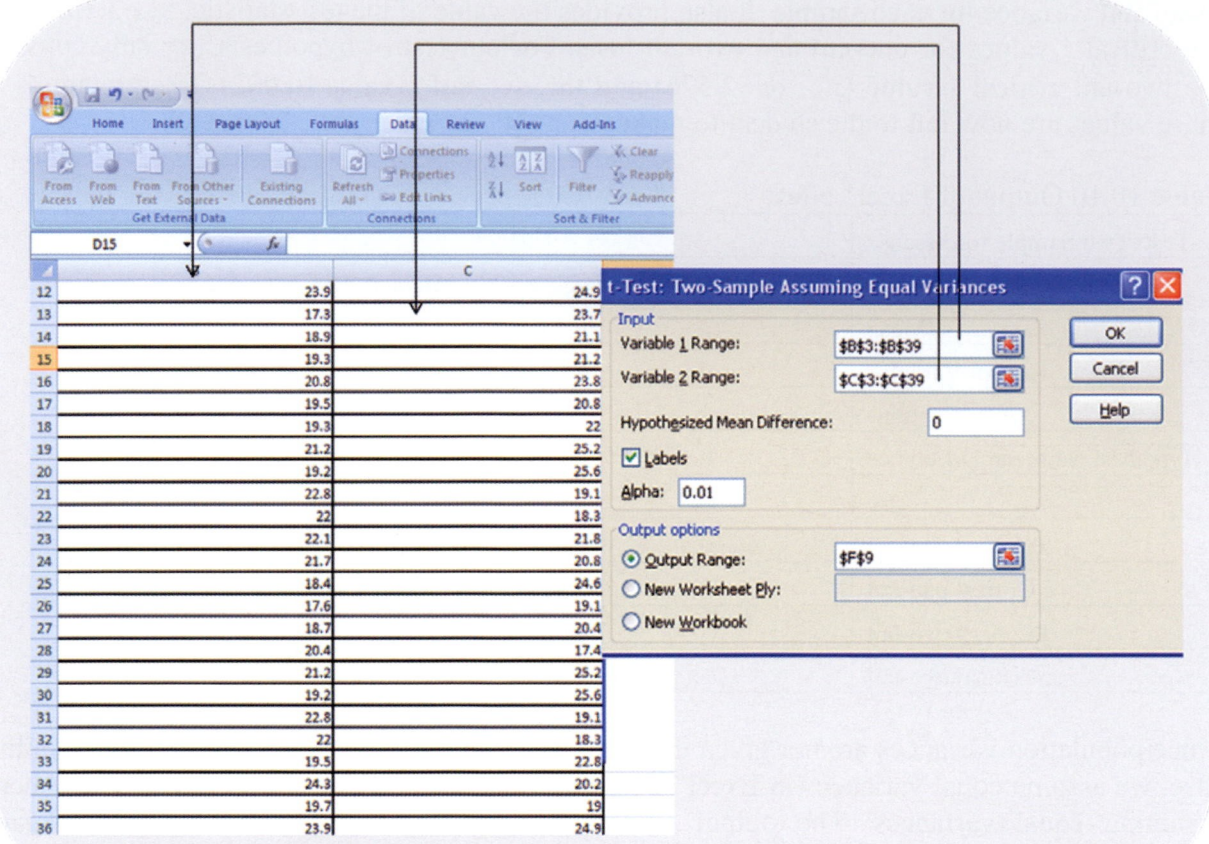

Figure 10.3 Using Excel® to Perform a *t*-Hypothesis Test for Two Populations Assuming Equal Variances

Example 10.6: For the weight loss example in which paired data were used (Table 10.6), perform the test of hypothesis for the difference using Excel® Data Analysis.

Solution:

Figures 10.4 and 10.5 illustrate the basic steps to perform test of hypothesis for paired data using Excel® Data Analysis. The output of this analysis is shown in Table 10.12. Interpretations of these values are now left to the student to make.

Table 10.12 Excel® output-paired test

t-Test: Paired Two Sample for Means	Weight loss (lb) using previous treatment	Weight loss (lb) using new treatment
Mean	13.87	16.72
Variance	7.938	3.042
Observations	10	10
Hypothesized Mean Difference	0	
df	9	
t Stat	-3.054	
P(T<=t) one-tail	0.007	
t Critical one-tail	2.821	
P(T<=t) two-tail	0.014	
t Critical two-tail	3.250	

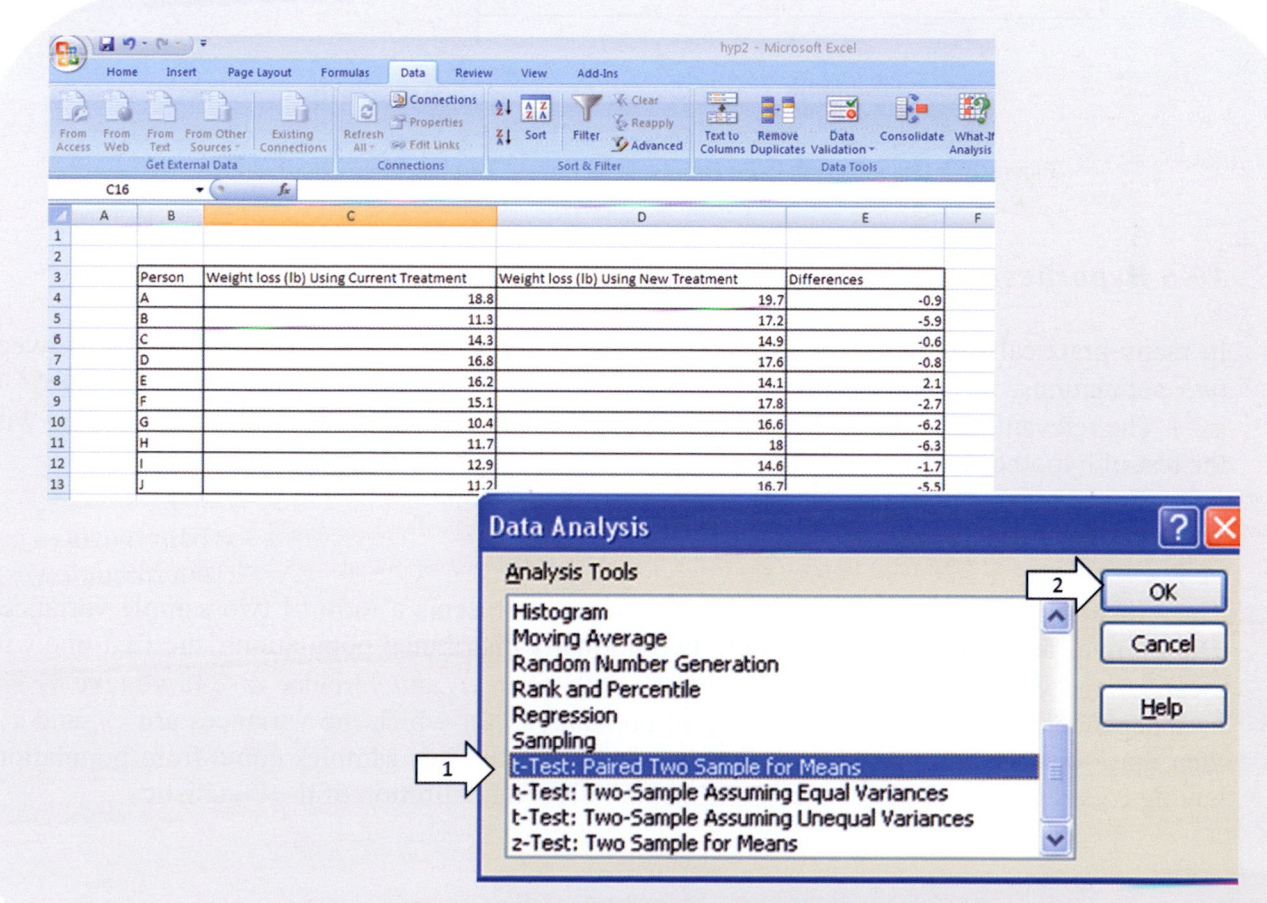

Figure 10.4 Using Excel® to Perform t-test for Paired Two Samples: Step 1 and 2

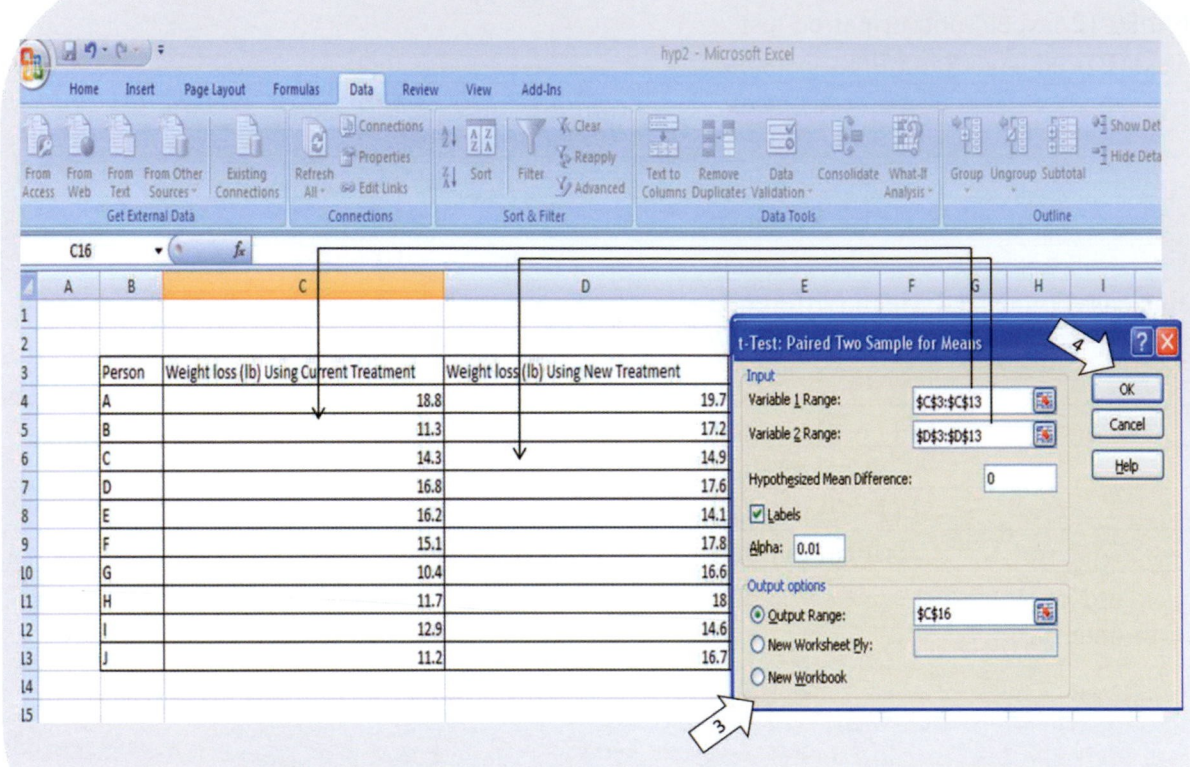

Figure 10.5 Using Excel® to Perform *t*-test for Paired Two Samples: Step 3 and 4

10.6 Hypothesis Tests for comparison of Two Populations Variances

In many practical situations, the primary concern is about the difference in variability between two populations. In this case, we may have to test the hypothesis of variance equality ($\sigma_1^2 = \sigma_2^2$). The relevant sampling distribution in this case is the *F*-distribution. Before proceeding with the test of hypothesis, it will be important to discuss the *F*-distribution.

10.6.1 The F Distribution

The *F*-distribution is a sampling distribution which represents a ratio of two sample variances. The samples are assumed to come from two normally distributed populations; the first one with mean μ_1 and variance σ_1^2 and the second one with mean μ_2 and variance σ_2^2. If we take n_1 and n_2 independent samples from two different populations for which the variances are s_1^2 and s_2^2, then the *F*-distribution provides evaluation of whether the two samples come from populations having equal variances. This concept yields the following definition of the F-statistic:

$$F_{[\gamma_1, \gamma_2]} = \frac{s_1^2}{s_2^2}$$

where γ_1 and γ_2 are the degrees of freedom associated with the two samples, $\gamma_1 = n_1 - 1$ and $\gamma_2 = n_2 - 1$.

606

Theoretically, the F-distribution describes a ratio of two independent chi-square χ^2 random variables with u and v degrees of freedom. This leads to the general expression:

$$F_{u,v} = \frac{\chi_u^2/u}{\chi_v^2/v}$$

where u is the numerator degree of freedom and v is the denominator degree of freedom.

In this case the relative frequency distribution (or density function) of F is:

$$\phi(F) = \frac{\Gamma\left(\frac{u+v}{2}\right)\left(\frac{u}{v}\right)^{u/2} F^{\frac{u}{2}-1}}{\Gamma\left(\frac{u}{2}\right)\Gamma\left(\frac{v}{2}\right)\left[\frac{u}{v}F+1\right]^{(u+v)/2}} \qquad 0 < F < \infty$$

Figure 10.6 illustrates three F-distributions with three different degrees of freedom. Critical F values and corresponding areas can be found in Appendix 10.A. The example below illustrates how to determine these values.

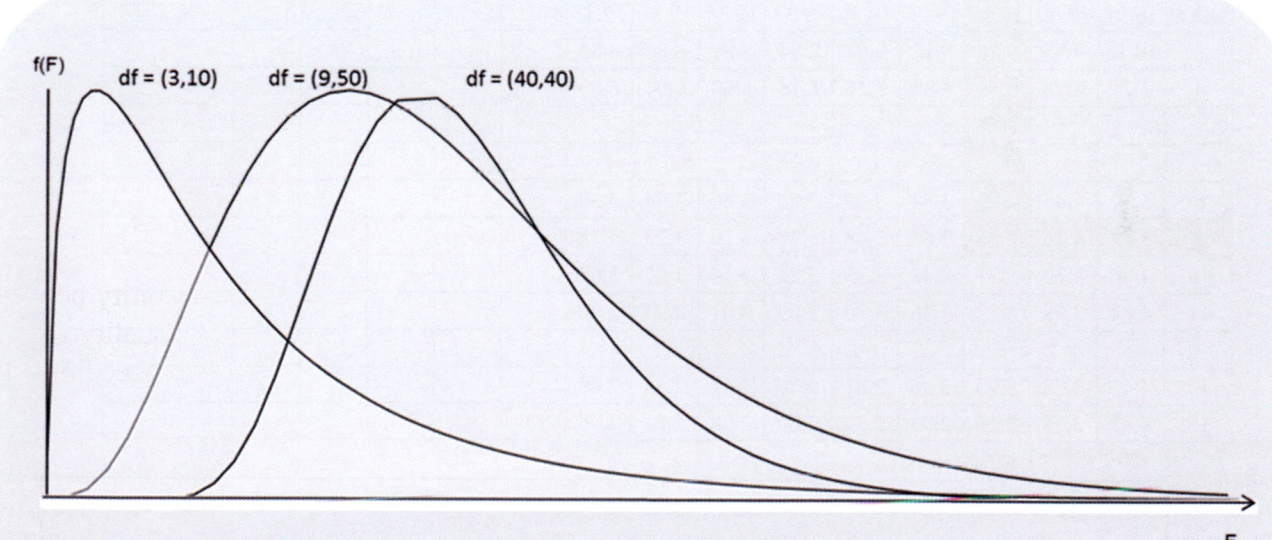

Figure 10.6 F-distributions at different degrees of freedom

Example 10.7: Determine the F value at $\alpha = 0.05$ and degree of freedom 3 and 9.

Solution:

The table below represents a portion of the F table (Appendix 10.A) at $\alpha = 0.05$. In order to find $F_{3,9}$ we find the column corresponding to 3 degrees of freedom for the numerator, and the row corresponding to 9 degrees of freedom for the denominator. This yields the critical value of 3.86.

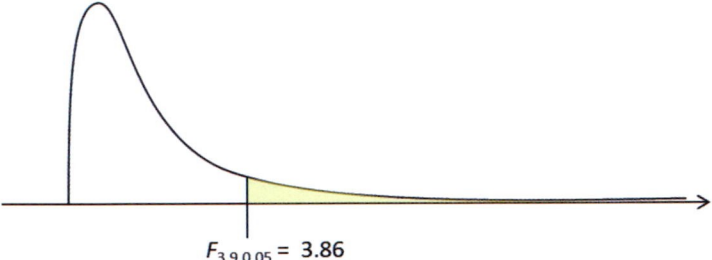

$F_{3,9,0.05} = 3.86$

Critical Values of the F distribution - $[F_{0.05,\gamma1,\gamma2}]$ degree of freedom: $\gamma_1 = n_1-1$, $\gamma_2 = n_2-1$

						Numerator Degrees of Freedom									
$\gamma2 \backslash \gamma1$	1	2	3	4	5	6	7	8	9	10	12	15	20	24	30
1	161.4	199.5	215.7	224.6	230.2	234.0	236.8	238.9	240.5	...	...	...	...	...	...
2	18.51	19.00	19.16	19.25	19.30	19.33	19.35	19.37	19.38	...	...	...	...	...	...
3	10.13	9.55	9.28	9.12	9.01	8.94	8.89	8.85	8.81	...	...	...	...	...	...
4	7.71	6.94	6.59	6.39	6.26	6.16	6.09	6.04	6.00	...	...	...	...	...	...
...	...	...	...	...	...	...	...	...	...	...	...	...	...	...	...
...	...	...	...	...	...	...	...	...	...	...	...	...	...	...	...
8	5.32	4.46	4.07	3.84	3.69	3.58	3.50	3.44	3.39	...	...	...	...	...	...
9	5.12	4.26	3.86	3.63	3.48	3.37	3.29	3.23	3.18	...	...	...	...	...	...
10	4.96	4.10	3.71	3.48	3.33	3.22	3.14	3.07	3.02	...	...	...	...	...	...
11	4.84	3.98	3.59	3.36	3.20	3.09	3.01	2.95	2.90	...	...	...	...	...	...
...	...	...	...	...	...	...	...	...	...	...	...	...	...	...	...
17	4.45	3.59	3.20	2.96	2.81	2.70	2.61	2.55	2.49	...	...	...	...	...	...
18	4.41	3.55	3.16	2.93	2.77	2.66	2.58	2.51	2.46	...	...	...	...	...	...

Working Problem 10.12:

Determine the F value at $a = 0.01$ and degree of freedom 6 and 10.

Answer:
Do it yourself using tables in Appendix 10.A

Working Problem 10.13:

Determine the F value at $1-a = 0.9$ and degree of freedom 7 and 9.

Answer:
Do it yourself using tables in Appendix 10.A

10.6.2 Key Steps for Performing a Hypothesis Test for two population variances

Table 10.13 shows a list of tests of hypothesis involving two variances and the criteria for rejection associated with these tests. The examples given below illustrate the use of these tests.

Table 10.13 Different types of hypothesis testing for variances of normal distributions

Hypothesis testing	Test statistic	Reject when
$H_o: \sigma_1^2 = \sigma_2^2$ $H_1: \sigma_1^2 \neq \sigma_2^2$	$F_o = \dfrac{Larger\ of\ s_1^2\ and\ s_2^2}{Smaller\ of\ s_1^2\ and\ s_2^2}$	$F_o > F_{\frac{\alpha}{2}, n_1-1, n_2-1}$
$H_o: \sigma_1^2 \leq \sigma_2^2$ $H_1: \sigma_1^2 > \sigma_2^2$	$F_o = \dfrac{Larger\ of\ s_1^2\ and\ s_2^2}{Smaller\ of\ s_1^2\ and\ s_2^2}$	$F_o > F_{a, n_1-1, n_2-1}$

Example 10.8: Find the critical F-value:

a) For a right-tailed test with $\alpha = 0.1$, degrees of freedom in the numerator = 8 and degrees of freedom in the denominator = 4.

b) For a two-tailed test with $\alpha = 0.05$, degrees of freedom in the numerator = 20 and degrees of freedom in the denominator = 15.

Solution:

(a) $F_{0.1, 8, 4} = 3.95$

Critical Values of the F distribution - $[F_{0.10, \gamma1, \gamma2}]$

v2 \ v1	1	2	3	4	5	6	7	8	9	10	12	15	20	24	30	40	60	120	∞
1	39.86	49.50	53.59	55.83	57.24	58.20	58.91	59.44	59.86	60.19	60.71	61.22	61.74	62.00	62.26	62.53	62.79	63.06	63.33
3	5.54	5.46	5.39	5.34	5.31	5.28	5.27	5.25	5.24	5.20	5.22	5.20	5.18	5.18	5.17	5.16	5.15	5.14	5.13
4	4.54	4.32	4.19	4.11	4.05	4.01	3.98	**3.95**	3.94	3.92	3.90	3.87	3.84	3.83	3.82	3.80	3.79	3.78	3.76
5	4.06	3.78	3.62	3.52	3.45	3.40	3.37	3.34	3.32	3.30	3.27	3.24	3.21	3.19	3.17	3.16	3.14	3.12	3.10

Note: $F_{0.90, \gamma1, \gamma2} = 1/ F_{0.10, \gamma2, \gamma1}$

(b) $F_{.025, 20, 15} = 2.76$;

$$F_{0.975, 20, 15} = \frac{1}{F_{0.025, 15, 20}} = \frac{1}{2.57} = 0.39$$

Critical Values of the F distribution $[F_{0.025,\gamma1,\gamma2}]$

v2 \ v1	1	2	3	4	5	6	7	8	9	10	12	15	20	24	30	40	60	120	∞
1	647.8	799.5	864.2	899.6	921.8	937.1	948.2	956.7	963.3	968.6	976.7	984.9	993.1	997.2	1001	1006	1010	1014	1018
...	...	...	...	...	...	...	...	...	...	...	...	..	...	...	...	...	...	...	...
14	6.30	4.86	4.24	3.89	3.66	3.50	3.38	3.29	3.21	3.15	3.05	2.95	2.84	2.79	2.73	2.67	2.61	2.55	2.49
15	6.20	4.77	4.15	3.80	3.58	3.41	3.29	3.20	3.12	3.06	2.96	2.86	2.76	2.70	2.64	2.59	2.52	2.46	2.40
...	...	...	...	...	...	...	...	...	...	...	...	...	...	...	...	...	...	...	...
19	5.92	4.51	3.90	3.56	3.33	3.17	3.05	2.96	2.88	2.82	2.72	2.62	2.51	2.45	2.39	2.33	2.27	2.20	2.13
20	5.87	4.46	3.86	3.51	3.29	3.13	3.01	2.91	2.84	2.77	2.68	2.57	2.46	2.41	2.35	2.29	2.22	2.16	2.09
21	5.83	4.42	3.82	3.48	3.25	3.09	2.97	2.87	2.80	2.73	2.64	2.53	2.42	2.37	2.31	2.25	2.18	2.11	2.04
...	...	...	...	...	...	...	...	...	...	...	...	...	...	...	...	...	...	...
120	5.15	3.80	3.23	2.89	2.67	2.52	2.39	2.30	2.22	2.16	2.05	1.94	1.82	1.76	1.69	1.61	1.53	1.43	1.31
∞	5.02	3.69	3.12	2.79	2.57	2.41	2.29	2.19	2.11	2.05	1.94	1.83	1.71	1.64	1.57	1.48	1.39	1.27	1.00

Note: $F_{0.975,\gamma1,\gamma2} = 1/ F_{0.025,\gamma2,\gamma1}$

Example 10.9: The data below illustrates two samples of the ages of employees in two software programming companies: Company A and Company B. The two companies claim that the variability in their employees' ages is the same. Test this claim at $\alpha = 0.1$.

Table 10.14 Ages of employees of two different companies

Company A	Company B
42	41
44	43
41	41
38	41
44	43
44	41
40	42
41	44
42	43
42	42
45	41
42	43
43	42
	42
	43
	43
	40
	41

Solution:

Perform descriptive statistics to obtain sample statistics

	Company A	Company B
Mean	42.154	42.000
Median	42	42
Mode	42	41
Standard Deviation	1.908	1.085
Sample Variance	3.641	1.176
Range	7	4
Minimum	38	40
Maximum	45	44
Count	13	18

The test of hypothesis for variance comparison is

$$H_o: \sigma^2_1 = \sigma^2_2$$
$$H_1: \sigma^2_1 \neq \sigma^2_2$$

The test-statistic is:

$$F_o = \frac{s_1{}^2}{s_2{}^2} = \frac{3.641}{1.176} = 3.096$$

The critical F value is obtained from the table in Appendix 10.A (also see below a portion of this table), $F_{\alpha/2, n1-1, n2-1} = F_{0.05, 12, 17} = 2.38$. Since $F_o \geq F_{\alpha/2}$, we reject $H_o: \sigma^2_1 = \sigma^2_2$ and conclude there is a difference between the two variances.

Critical Values of the F distribution - $[F_{0.05, \gamma1, \gamma2}]$

v2 \ v1	1	2	3	4	5	6	7	8	9	10	12	15	20	24	30	40	60	120	∞
1	161.4	199.5	215.7	224.6	230.2	234.0	236.8	238.9	240.5	241.9	243.9	245.9	248.0	249.1	250.1	251.1	252.2	253.3	254.0
2	18.51	19.00	19.16	19.25	19.30	19.33	19.35	19.37	19.38	19.40	19.41	19.43	19.45	19.45	19.46	19.47	19.48	19.49	19.50
...	...	...	...	...	...	...	...	...	...	...	...	...	...	...	...	...	...	...	...
...	...	...	...	...	...	...	...	...	...	...	...	...	...	...	...	...	...	...	...
...	...	...	...	...	...	...	...	...	...	...	...	...	...	...	...	...	...	...	...
16	4.49	3.63	3.24	3.01	2.85	2.74	2.66	2.59	2.54	2.49	2.42	2.35	2.28	2.24	2.19	2.15	2.11	2.06	2.01
17	4.45	3.59	3.20	2.96	2.81	2.70	2.61	2.55	2.49	2.45	2.38	2.31	2.23	2.19	2.15	2.10	2.06	2.01	1.96
18	4.41	3.55	3.16	2.93	2.77	2.66	2.58	2.51	2.46	2.41	2.34	2.27	2.19	2.15	2.11	2.06	2.02	1.97	1.92
...	...	...	...	...	...	...	...	...	...	...	...	...	...	...	...	...	...	...	...
...	...	...	...	...	...	...	...	...	...	...	...	...	...	...	...	...	...	...	...

Note: $F_{0.95, \gamma1, \gamma2} = 1/ F_{0.05, \gamma2, \gamma1}$

10.7 Review Exercises

P10.1: When two independent samples are compared for a hypothesis test, and the variances of populations are known, the standard error of the difference between the means of the two populations is:

A) $\sqrt{\frac{\sigma_1^2}{n_1} + \frac{\sigma_2^2}{n_2}}$,   B) $\sqrt{\frac{P_p(1-P_p)}{n_1} + \frac{P_p(1-P_p)}{n_2}}$,   C) $S_p\sqrt{\frac{1}{n_1} + \frac{1}{n_2}}$,   D) $\frac{S_d}{\sqrt{n}}$

Answer: (A)

P10.2: The statistics summarized below represent two random samples of student ages taken from two different colleges.

Statistic	College A	College B
Standard deviation	$\sigma_A = 2.0$	$\sigma_B = 3.0$
n	$n_1 = 40$	$n_2 = 40$

The standard error of difference is:

A) 0.230   B) 0.570   C) 0.289   D) 0.750

P10.3: When two independent samples are compared for a certain variable, and the variances of the populations variables are known, the significance of their difference is determined by the following test statistic:

A) $S_p^2 = \frac{(n_1-1)s_1^2 + (n_2-1)s_2^2}{n_1+n_2-2}$ B) $z_o = \frac{(\bar{X}_1-\bar{X}_2)-(\mu_1-\mu_2)}{\sqrt{\frac{\sigma_1^2}{n_1}+\frac{\sigma_2^2}{n_2}}}$

C) $t_o = \frac{(\bar{X}_1-\bar{X}_2)-(\mu_1-\mu_2)}{S_p\sqrt{\frac{1}{n_1}+\frac{1}{n_2}}}$ D) $t_o = \frac{\bar{d}}{\frac{S_d}{\sqrt{n}}}$

Answer: (B)

P10.4: The statistics summarized below represent two random samples of student ages taken from two different colleges. The issue to be evaluated is whether the average of student ages in these two colleges is the same. Test this hypothesis at $\alpha = 0.01$. Calculate the standard error of difference, the test statistics, and decide whether to reject the null hypothesis that the ages of students in the two colleges are the same.

Statistic	College A	College B
Mean	$\bar{X}_A = 20$	$\bar{X}_B = 23$
Standard deviation	$s_A = 2.0$	$s_B = 3.0$
Variance	4.0	9.0
n	$n_1 = 40$	$n_2 = 40$

P10.5: The statistics summarized below represent two random samples of property tax taken from two different regions in the State of New Jersey. The issue to be evaluated is whether the average property tax in these two regions is the same. Test this hypothesis at $\alpha = 0.05$.

Statistic	Region A	Region B
Mean	$7,000	$7,800
n	60	60
Variance	810000	883600

Answer:

difference (Region A - Region B)	-800	p-value (two-tailed)	1.92E-06
standard error of difference	168.008	confidence interval 95.% lower	-1,129.29
hypothesized difference	0	confidence interval 95.% upper	-470.71
z	-4.76	margin of error	329.29

P10.6: The following data represents residential energy consumption and expenditures in two different cities in the U.S.A. in millions of BTUs. Compare the two cities energy consumption. Do you see a difference between the two cities? Use test of hypothesis at $\alpha = 0.01$ given that the variances of the two populations are 900 and 300.

#	BTU(millions)-City A	#	BTU(millions)-City B
1	102	1	76
2	151	2	45
3	111	3	111
4	78	4	55
5	54	5	54
6	129	6	58
7	130	7	70
8	45	8	45
9	112	9	58
10	111	10	80
11	102	11	75
12	111	12	66
13	120	13	54
14	108	14	69
15	113	15	71
16	129	16	80
17	135	17	59
18	145	18	83
19	87	19	87
20	50	20	50

P10.7: The table below shows data of two random samples of employees, wages taken from two small business firms providing the same service. The issue to be evaluated is whether the average wage in these two firms is the same. Test this hypothesis at $\alpha = 0.05$.

Wages from two small business firms

Observation #	Wages in Firm A ($)	Wages in Firm B ($)	Observation #	Wages in Firm A ($)	Wages in Firm B ($)
1	29363	34035	19	39034	35606
2	39535	31466	20	33363	33632
3	38587	31027	21	29784	37682
4	36103	29679	22	29864	35320
5	34304	38730	23	34093	29587
6	43698	33258	24	39914	30293
7	32119	33979	25	40139	29658
8	37081	32870	26	22099	30544
9	40069	33578	27	37759	36973
10	44344	33946	28	35928	32826
11	36377	28985	29	36832	37557
12	43284	33640	30	30786	25704
13	43229	35110	31	33870	29079
14	29988	34993	32	35884	32816
15	32308	31458	33	40703	30827
16	37747	32321	34	28414	31136
17	32830	30939	35	30870	34792
18	26695	31492	36	34301	34860

Answer: Standard error = 979.492, $z_o = 2.58$, p-value = 0.0099

P10.8: The statistics below describe the mean of the household income (people of income up to $250,000) for US households based on samples taken from New York State and New Jersey State. Test the hypothesis that the mean household income in NY State is less than that in NJ at $\alpha = 0.01$. Use the z-test.

Stat	New York	New Jersey	USA
Mean	$55,603	$69,811	$51,914
SD	5000	7000	
n	40	40	

http://quickfacts.census.gov/qfd/index.html

P10.9: Singapore is one of the countries that have the lowest rate of infant mortality in the world. Based on two samples one from Singapore and the other from the USA, the statistics in the table below were determined. The variable in question is deaths per 1000 live births. Given the fact that infant mortality is considered an important indicator of the health of a nation, test the hypothesis that the average mortality rate in the USA is greater than that of Singapore at $\alpha = 0.01$.

	USA	Singapore
Mean	6.9	2.1
SD	1.2	0.8
n	400	450

Answer: Standard error = 0.0709, z_o = 67.73, p-value = 0.00E+00

P10.10: When two independent populations are compared for a certain variable, and the variances of the populations' variable are unknown, the standard error of the difference is:

A) $\sqrt{\dfrac{\sigma_1{}^2}{n_1} + \dfrac{\sigma_2{}^2}{n_2}}$
B) $\sqrt{\dfrac{P_p(1 - P_p)}{n_1} + \dfrac{P_p(1 - P_p)}{n_2}}$

C) $S_p\sqrt{\dfrac{1}{n_1} + \dfrac{1}{n_2}}$
D) $\dfrac{S_d}{\sqrt{n}}$

P10.11: The statistics summarized in the table below represent two small random samples of people ages among those who are 60 years or older in two different cities: Winchester, Virginia, and Gainesville, GA. These two cities are known to be good places to retire.

Statistic	Winchester, Virginia	Gainesville, GA
Standard deviation	6	5
n	22	26

The standard error of difference is:

A) 1.587 B) 1.218   C) 1.878   D) 1.236

Answer: (A) Explain why

P10.12: When two independent populations are compared for a certain variable, and the variances of the populations' variable are unknown, the significance of their difference is determined by the following test statistic:

A) $S_p{}^2 = \frac{(n_1-1)s_1{}^2+(n_2-1)s_2{}^2}{n_1+n_2-2}$

B) $z_o = \frac{(\bar{X}_1-\bar{X}_2)-(\mu_1-\mu_2)}{\sqrt{\frac{\sigma_1{}^2}{n_1}+\frac{\sigma_2{}^2}{n_2}}}$

C) $t_o = \frac{(\bar{X}_1 - \bar{X}_2) - (\mu_1 - \mu_2)}{S_p\sqrt{\frac{1}{n_1} + \frac{1}{n_2}}}$

D) $t_o = \frac{\bar{d}}{\frac{S_d}{\sqrt{n}}}$

P10.13: The statistics summarized below represent two small random samples of people ages among those who are 60 years or older in two different cities: Winchester, Virginia, and Gainesville, GA. These two cities are known to be good places to retire. The issue to be evaluated is whether the average age of elder people in these two cities is the same. Test this hypothesis at $\alpha = 0.05$.

Statistic	Winchester, Virginia	Gainesville, GA
Mean	72	76
Standard deviation	6	5
n	22	26
Variance	36	25

Answer: Standard error = 1.587, t_o = -2.52, p-value = 0.0153

P10.14: We wish to test the hypothesis that the values of the mean thickness (mm) of two types of steel plates are equal. Using samples of 20 plates from each type, we obtain the thickness results shown below. Test the hypothesis using $\alpha = 0.05$.

Values of thickness

Plate Type I	Plate Type II	Plate Type I	Plate Type II
103	95	101	87
99	92	97	100
105	93	97	95
109	93	100	92
109	86	101	95
111	90	96	86
95	98	102	100
103	94	102	84
108	97	105	91
100	91	103	108

P10.15: In the above problem, test the hypothesis that the mean thickness of Type I steel plates is smaller than that of Type II steel plates.
Answer: Standard error = 1.620, t_o = 5.53, p-value (one-tailed lower) = 0.999999999.

616

P10.16: The statistics below describe wood board thickness of boards produced by two different companies. Test the hypothesis that the average thicknesses of the wood board populations produced by the two companies are the same at $\alpha = 0.01$.

Stat	Company A	Company B
Mean	5	4.6
Standard deviation	1.4	0.8
n	50	30

P10.17: The statistics below describe the mean travel time to work (minutes) for workers of age 16+ based on samples taken from New York State and New Jersey State. Test the hypothesis that the mean travel time to work is the same for the populations of workers in the two States at $\alpha = 0.01$.

Stat	New York	New Jersey	USA
Mean	31.3	29.8	25.2
SD	5	4	
n	30	25	

(http://quickfacts.census.gov/qfd/index.html)

Answer: Standard error = 1.2387, $t_o = 1.21$, p-value = 0.2313

P10.18: Literacy tests have become common in many Nations including the U.S.A. Typically, adults age 16 or older are assessed in three types of literacy (prose, document, and quantitative). *Prose literacy* is the knowledge and skills needed to perform prose tasks (i.e., to search, comprehend, and use information from continuous texts, such as paragraphs from stories); *document literacy* is the knowledge and skills needed to perform document tasks (i.e., to search, comprehend, and use information from non-continuous texts in various formats, such as bills or prescription labels); and *quantitative literacy* is the knowledge and skills required to perform quantitative tasks (i.e., to identify and perform computations, either alone or sequentially, using numbers embedded in printed materials). Results are reported in terms of average scores on a 0–500 scale. Using two random samples one male and the other female adults age 16 or older, the following statistics were determined:

Sex	Male	Female
Average (Prose, Document, Quantitative)	278	276
Standard deviation	14	15
n	120	120

Test the hypothesis that males and females in the U.S.A. have the same literacy level. Use $\alpha = 0.01$.

P10.19: In evaluating the literacy test score, using two random samples from two groups of adults age 16 or older, the following statistics were determined:

Group	Group A	Group B
Average (Prose, Document, Quantitative)	289	239.7
Standard deviation	16	12
n	80	80

Test the hypothesis that adults of Group A have better literacy level than adults of Group B. Use $\alpha = 0.01$.
Answer: Standard error = 2.236, t_o = 22.06, p-value (one-tailed upper)= 2.05E-50

P10.20: In evaluating the literacy test score, using two random samples one from adults of age from 16 to 18 and the other of age from 19 to 24, the following statistics were determined:

Age Group	Age Range: 16-18	Age Range: 19-24
Average (Prose, Document, Quantitative)	267.3	277.3
Standard deviation	18	20
n	46	48

Test the hypothesis that adults of age 16-18 have less literacy level than adults of age 19-24. Use $\alpha = 0.01$.

P10.21: In evaluating the literacy test score, using two random samples one from adults of age from 19 to 24 and the other of age from 25 to 39, the following statistics were determined:

Age Group	Age Range: 19-24	Age Range: 25-39
Average (Prose, Document, Quantitative)	277.3	285.7
Standard deviation	20	19
n	48	36

Test the hypothesis that adults of age 19-24 have less literacy level than adults of age 25-39. Use $\alpha = 0.01$.

Answer: Hypothesis Test: Independent Groups (t-test, pooled variance)

df	82		t	-1.93
difference (19-24 - 25-39)	-8.333	p-value (one-tailed, lower)		0.0285
pooled std. dev.	19.579	confidence interval 99.% lower		-19.717416
standard error of difference	4.3169	confidence interval 99.% upper		3.0507492
hypothesized difference	0	margin of error		11.384083

P10.22: In evaluating the literacy test score, using two random samples one from adults of age from 50 to 64 and the other of age from 65 or older, the following statistics were determined:

Age Group	Age Group: 50-64	Age Group: 65 or older
Average (Prose, Document, Quantitative)	279	246.7
Standard deviation	20	26
n	26	26

Test the hypothesis that adults of age 50-64 have less literacy level than adults of age 65 or older. Use $\alpha = 0.01$.

P10.23: In evaluating the literacy test score, using two random samples one from high-school graduates and the other from the population of adults who earned an Associate degree, the following statistics were determined:

Age Group	High school graduate	Associate's/2-year degree
Average (Prose, Document, Quantitative)	263	298
Standard deviation	29	22
n	80	46

Test the hypothesis that adults of from high-school graduates have less literacy level than adults who earned an Associate degree. Use $\alpha = 0.05$.
Answer: Standard error = 4.936, t_o = -7.09, p-value (one-tailed, lower) = 4.45E-11

P10.24: In evaluating the literacy test score, using two random samples one from the population of adults who earned an Associate degree, and the other from the population of adults who graduated from four-year college the following statistics were determined:

Age Group	Associate's/2-year degree	College graduate
Average (Prose, Document, Quantitative)	298	313
Standard deviation	22	18
n	46	49

Test the hypothesis that adults who earned an Associate degree have less literacy level than those who graduated from four-year College. Use $\alpha = 0.05$.

P10.25: Two samples are selected randomly and come from populations that are normal. Find the pooled variance to test the null hypothesis that $\mu_1 = \mu_2$.

	Sample A	Sample B
$\bar{X}$	10	11
S	2.5	2.8
n	14	12

A) 6.979   B) 5.890   C) -6.980   D) – 4.589   (E) None of the above

619

Answer: (A) Explain why

P10.26: Two samples are selected randomly and come from populations that are normal. Find the standard error of difference to test the null hypothesis that $\mu_1 = \mu_2$.

	Sample A	Sample B
$\bar{X}$	10	11
S	2.5	2.8
n	14	12

A) – 2.65   B) 1.039   C) -2.230   D) 1.222   (E) None of the above

P10.27: Two samples are selected randomly and come from populations that are normal. Find the standardized test statistic, t_o, to test the null hypothesis that $\mu_1 = \mu_2$.

	Sample A	Sample B
$\bar{X}$	10	11
S	2.5	2.8
n	14	12

A) - 0.962   B) -0.915   C) -1.558   D) -0.909   (E) None of the above
Answer: A

P10.28: Two samples are selected randomly and come from populations that are normal. Find the standard error of difference to test the alternative hypothesis that $\mu_1 > \mu_2$. The sample statistics are given below.

	Sample A	Sample B
$\bar{X}$	680	665
s	40	25
n	18	13

A) 12.82   B) 32.71   C) 12.59   D) 11.86   (E) None of the above

P10.29: Two samples are selected randomly and come from populations that are normal. Find the test statistic and make a decision about the alternative hypothesis that $\mu_1 > \mu_2$. at $\alpha = 0.01$. The sample statistics are given below.

	Sample A	Sample B
$\bar{X}$	680	665
S	40	25
n	18	13

A) 1.58; reject H_o
B) - 2.58; fail to reject H_o
C) - 1.48; reject H_o
D) 1.19; fail to reject H_o
Answer: (D. Explain why

620

P10.30: According to Centers for Medicare & Medicaid Services (http://www.cms.gov/), health care expenditures in the United States were nearly $2.6 trillion in 2010. Using two samples one was taken at 2000 and the other at 2011, the statistics of health care expenditure per person was found to be:

	Year 2000	Year 2011
Mean	$7210	$8402
SD	$1000	$1400
n	30	26

Find the test statistic and make a decision about the null hypothesis that the average at 2000 was less than that at 2011 using $\alpha = 0.01$.

A) 2.9; reject H_o
B) – 3.1; fail to reject H_o
C) - 3.7; reject H_o
D) 3.1; fail to reject H_o

P10.31: Two samples are selected randomly and come from populations that are normal. Find the pooled standard deviation, to test the null hypothesis that $\mu_1 = \mu_2$. The sample statistics are given below.

	Sample A	Sample B
$\bar{X}$	19	17
s	1.5	1.9
n	25	30

A) 2.12   B) -1.40   C) 1.73   D) 1.98   (E) None of the above
Answer: (C) Explain why

P10.32: Two samples are selected randomly and come from populations that are normal. Find the test statistic to test the null hypothesis that $\mu_1 = \mu_2$. The sample statistics are given below.

	Sample A	Sample B
$\bar{X}$	19	17
s	1.5	1.9
n	25	30

A) 4.366   B) - 3.999   C) 4.27   D) 2.58   (E) None of the above

P10.33: Two samples are selected randomly and come from populations that are normal. Find the test statistic, test the alternative hypothesis that $\mu_1 > \mu_2$ and make the decision at $\alpha = 0.05$ and make a decision. The sample statistics are given below.

	Sample A	Sample B
$\bar{X}$	160	157
S	6.5	8.2
n	20	19

A) -2.33, fail to reject H_o B) -2.33, reject H_o C) 1.27, fail to reject H_o D) 1.66 reject H_o
        (E) None of the above
Answer: (C) Explain why

P10.34: Classify the two given samples as independent or dependent.
        Sample 1: Smoking rate by 20 people before undergoing a stop-smoking program
        Sample 2: Smoking rate by the same 20 people after undergoing a stop-smoking program

A) Dependent   B) Independent   (C) None of the above

P10.35: Classify the two given samples as independent or dependent.
        Sample1: The weight of 20 players of the Florida State Football team
        Sample2: The weight of 20 players of the University of Alabama Football team

A) Independent   B) Dependent   (C) None of the above

Answer: (A)

P10.36: Classify the two given samples as independent or dependent.
Sample1: The scores of 40 students who took a developmental math final
Sample2: The scores of 40 different students who took a biology course final

A) Independent   B) Dependent   (C) None of the above

P10.37: If the potential team members selected for a sample have no influence upon which team members are selected for a second sample, then the samples are said to be

A) Independent   B) Dependent   C) Paired   D) Equal   (E) None of the above
Answer: (A)

P10.38: When two dependent populations are compared for a certain variable, and the variances of the populations' variable are unknown known, the standard error of the difference is:

A) $\sqrt{\dfrac{\sigma_1^2}{n_1} + \dfrac{\sigma_2^2}{n_2}}$ B) $\sqrt{\dfrac{(n_1-1)s_1^2+(n_2-1)s_2^2}{n_1+n_2-2}}$ C) $\sqrt{\dfrac{P_p(1-P_p)}{n_1} + \dfrac{P_p(1-P_p)}{n_2}}$ D) $\dfrac{s_d}{\sqrt{n}}$
(E) None of the above

622

P10.39: When two dependent populations are compared for a certain variable, and the variances of the populations' variable are unknown, the significance of their difference is determined by the following test statistic:

A) $S_p{}^2 = \dfrac{(n_1-1)s_1{}^2+(n_2-1)s_2{}^2}{n_1+n_2-2}$

B) $z_o = \dfrac{(\bar{X}_1-\bar{X}_2)-(\mu_1-\mu_2)}{\sqrt{\frac{\sigma_1{}^2}{n_1}+\frac{\sigma_2{}^2}{n_2}}}$

C) $t_o = \dfrac{(\bar{X}_1-\bar{X}_2)-(\mu_1-\mu_2)}{S_p\sqrt{\frac{1}{n_1}+\frac{1}{n_2}}}$

D) $t_o = \dfrac{\bar{d}}{\frac{s_d}{\sqrt{n}}}$

(E) None of the above

Answer: (D)

P10.40: Two samples are said to be dependent if

A) The individuals in one sample are used to determine the individuals in a second sample.
B) The individuals in one sample have no influence over the selection of the individuals in a second sample.
C) The individuals in one sample are a segment of the individuals in a second sample.
D) The individuals in one sample are twice as much as the individuals in a second sample.

P10.41: Data sets A and B are dependent. Find $\bar{d}$

.

A	38	40	50	55	40
B	41	40	40	33	34

Assume that the paired data came from a population that is normally distributed.

A) 14   B) -7   C) -12   D) – 20   (E) None of the above
Answer: (B) Explain why
P10.42: Data sets A and B are dependent. Find s_d:

.

A	38	40	50	55	40
B	41	40	40	33	34

Assume that the paired data came from a population that is normally distributed.
A) 8.410   B) -7.500   C) – 9.798   D) 9.798   (E) None of the above

P10.43: Data sets A and B are dependent. Test the hypothesis $\mu_d = 0$

.

A	38	40	50	55	40
B	41	40	40	33	34

Assume that the paired data came from a population that is normally distributed.
1) The t-statistic is

A) 3.444   B) 2.577   C) – 3.211   D) 1.960   (E) None of the above
Answer: (B) Explain why

2) The decision at $\alpha = 0.05$ is:
A) Reject H_o
B) Fail to reject H_o
C) No decision can be taken
D) Type I error is zero
E) None of the above
Answer: (B) Explain why

t-Test: Paired Two Sample for Means

	A	B
Mean	37.8	28.8
Variance	73.7	25.7
Observations	5	5
Pearson Correlation	0.441165	
Hypothesized Mean Difference	0	
df	4	
t Stat	2.576693	
P(T<=t) one-tail	0.030771	
t Critical one-tail	2.131847	
P(T<=t) two-tail	0.061542	
t Critical two-tail	2.776445	

P10.44: A textile quality control department is in the process to determine whether a new testing instrument of fiber strength should be purchased to replace an existing one. In other words, the quality control department wishes to determine whether the two instruments yield the same average tensile strength values. Eight specimens of fiber were randomly selected and each specimen was split into halves. A sub-specimen from one half was tested on the existing instrument and a sub-specimen from the other half was tested on the new instrument, which was leased for the purpose of evaluation. This sampling process was continued until all 8 specimens were tested. The data obtained are shown in the table below. Assist the QC department in making the decision using $\alpha = 0.05$.

Tensile strength data

Test No.	Old Instrument	New Instrument	Difference
1	74	78	4
2	76	79	3
3	74	75	1
4	69	66	-3
5	58	63	5
6	71	70	-1
7	66	66	0
8	65	67	2

P10.45: The data below represent people weight before and after a weight-loss treatment given to the same participants. Test the hypothesis that people will significantly experience weight loss after the treatment at $\alpha = 0.01$.

	Before Weight Loss (lb)	After Weight Loss (lb)
Participant #1	180	178
Participant #2	195	180
Participant #3	200	188
Participant #4	175	172
Participant #5	160	150
Participant #6	170	152

Answer: $t_o = 3.816$, t(one-tailed) = 3.365

P10.46: Data sets A and B are dependent. Test the claim that $\mu_d = 0$. Use $\alpha = 0.05$.

A	111	105	162	150	114
B	105	93	96	126	87

Assume that the paired data came from a population that is normally distributed.

P10.47: 10 students took a literacy test. Their scores are listed below prior to any test practice. After some practice they retake the test. Their new scores are listed below. Test the claim that the practice had no effect on their scores. Use $\alpha = 0.05$. Assume that the distribution is normally distributed.

Student	1	2	3	4	5	6	7	8	9
Scores before practice	223	220	300	315	287	300	250	260	300
Scores after practice	253	260	305	305	280	322	260	255	306

Answer: Claim: $\mu_d = 0$; critical values t = ±2.306; standardized test statistic t = -1.75, fail to reject H_o

P10.48: A cosmetic company wishes to test a new facial treatment with the expectation of reducing skin wrinkles. Ten subjects are randomly selected and pretested. The results are expressed in area occupied by wrinkle (cm^2) and they are listed below. The subjects were then treated for a period of 3 months, after which their facial wrinkles were tested again. The results are listed below. Test the company's claim that the treatment lowers facial wrinkles. Use $\alpha = 0.01$.

Before Treatment	22	21	30	25	26	28	22
After Treatment	18	19	22	24	28	22	18

P10.49: When two independent samples are compared for a certain variable, the standard error of the difference between proportions of the two populations is:

A) $\sqrt{\dfrac{\sigma_1^2}{n_1} + \dfrac{\sigma_2^2}{n_2}}$
B) $\sqrt{\dfrac{P_p(1-P_p)}{n_1} + \dfrac{P_p(1-P_p)}{n_2}}$
C) $S_p\sqrt{\dfrac{1}{n_1} + \dfrac{1}{n_2}}$
D) $\dfrac{s_d}{\sqrt{n}}$

(E) None of the above
Answer: (B)

P10.50: Find the standard error to test the hypothesis that $p_1 = p_2$. Use $\alpha = 0.05$. The sample statistics listed below are from independent samples

n	50	60
x	35	40

A) 0.074   B) 0.0892   C) 1.028   D) 2.361   (E) None of the above

P10.51: When two independent samples are compared for proportion, the significance of the difference is determined by the following test statistic:

A) $S_p^2 = \dfrac{(n_1-1)s_1^2 + (n_2-1)s_2^2}{n_1+n_2-2}$

B) $z_o = \dfrac{(\bar{X}_1 - \bar{X}_2) - (\mu_1 - \mu_2)}{\sqrt{\dfrac{\sigma_1^2}{n_1} + \dfrac{\sigma_2^2}{n_2}}}$

C) $t_o = \dfrac{(\bar{X}_1 - \bar{X}_2) - (\mu_1 - \mu_2)}{S_p\sqrt{\dfrac{1}{n_1} + \dfrac{1}{n_2}}}$

D) $z_o = \dfrac{\hat{p}_1 - \hat{p}_2}{\sqrt{\dfrac{P_p(1-P_p)}{n_1} + \dfrac{P_p(1-P_p)}{n_2}}}$

(E) None of the above

Answer: (D)

P10.52: Find the standardized test statistic, z to test the hypothesis that $p_1 = p_2$. Use $\alpha = 0.05$. The sample statistics listed below are from independent samples

n	50	60
x	35	40

A) 0.374   B) 0.982   C) 1.328   D) 2.361   (E) None of the above

P10.53: Find the standardized test statistic, z to test the hypothesis that $p_1 = p_2$. Use $\alpha = 0.05$. The sample statistics listed below are from independent samples

n	100	140
x	38	50

A) 0.362   B) 2.116   C) 1.324   D) 0.638   (E) None of the above

Answer: (A)

P10.54: The data below represent the percentage of people who live below poverty level in two different states based on a random sample from each state. Test the hypothesis that the proportion of people who live below poverty level in NY State is greater than that in NJ State at $\alpha = 0.01$.

Stat	New York	New Jersey	USA
Mean	14.20	9.10	13.80
n	400	500	

P10.55: The data below represent the percentage of people who drive alone to work in two different states based on a random sample from each state. Test the hypothesis that the proportion of people who drive alone in NY State is less than that in NJ State at $\alpha = 0.01$.

Stat	New York	New Jersey	USA
P	53.90%	71.80%	76.40%
n	490	560	

Answer: Standard error = 0.0298, z_0 = -6.01, p-value (one-tailed, lower) = 9.35E-10

P10.56: Since the Children's Health Insurance Program (CHIP, http://www.chipcoverspakids.com/) was created in 1997, the percentage of children ages 0-17 with health insurance has increased from 86% to 93% (Source: National Center for Health Statistics, http://www.cdc.gov/nchs/, December 2011) . To test if this trend is persistent, two samples were taken: one in 2000 and the other in 2011 to determine whether indeed the percentage of children ages 0-17 with health insurance has increased. Test this hypothesis at $\alpha = 0.01$.

Year 2000	Year 2011
$p = 0.83$	$p = 0.85$
$n = 400$	$n = 420$

P10.57: Two conditions are required to test a claim about two population standard deviations. What are they?

A) The samples are independent and the population is normal.
B) The samples are mutually exclusive and the population is normal.
C) The samples are independent and the populations are randomly selected.
D) The samples are mutually exclusive and the populations are randomly selected.
(E) None of the above
Answer: (A)

P10.58: Find the critical F-value:

 (a) For a right-tailed test with $\alpha=0.05$, degrees of freedom in the numerator $= 10$ and degrees of freedom in the denominator $= 5$.
 (b) For a two-tailed test with $\alpha=0.05$, degrees of freedom in the numerator $= 24$ and degrees of freedom in the denominator $= 15$.

P10.59: Find the right hand critical value F_o for a two-tailed test using $\alpha = 0.05$ degrees of freedom in the numerator $= 5$, and degrees of freedom in the denominator $= 10$.

A) 4.24 B) 4.07 C) 4.47 D) 6.62 (E) None of the above
Answer: (A)

P10.60: Find the critical value F_o for a two-tailed test using $\alpha = 0.01$ degrees of freedom in the numerator $= 3$, and degrees of freedom in the denominator $= 20$.

A) 4.94 B) 25.58 C) 5.82 D) 3.09 (E) None of the above

P10.61: Find the critical value F_o for a two-tailed test using $\alpha = 0.05$ degrees of freedom in the numerator $= 6$, and degrees of freedom in the denominator $= 16$.

A) 0.255 B) 2.74 C) 2.66 D) 0.365 (E) None of the above

P10.62: Find the left hand critical value F_o for a two-tailed test using $\alpha = 0.02$ degrees of freedom in the numerator $= 5$, and degrees of freedom in the denominator $= 10$.

A) 0.099 B) 10.05 C) 5.64 D) 0.177 (E) None of the above

P10.63: Test the hypothesis that $\sigma_1 \neq \sigma_2$ at $\alpha = 0.1$ level of significance for the given sample data.

Sample	From Population 1	From Population 2
n	31	25
s	5.23	4.62

A) Test statistic: $F = 1.28$. Critical value $= 0.529, 1.94$. Do not reject Ho

628

B) Test statistic: $F = 1.28$. Critical value $= 0.515, 1.94$. Do not reject Ho
C) Test statistic: $F = 1.13$. Critical value $= 0.529, 1.94$. Do not reject Ho
D) Test statistic: $F = 1.13$. Critical value $= 0.515, 1.94$. Do Reject Ho
(E) None of the above
Answer: (A) Explain why

P10.64: Test the hypothesis that the variances of yarn strength of the two yarns given below are the same at $\alpha = 0.05$.

Statistic	Yarn A (100% Cotton)	Yarn B (75%Cotton/25% Polyester)
Mean strength	104	93
Standard deviation	3.97	4.36
n	20	20

P10.65: Test the hypothesis that $\sigma_1 > \sigma_2$ at $\alpha = 0.01$ level of significance for the given sample data.

	Population 1	Population 2
n	61	31
s	27.5	26.3

A) Test statistic: $F = 1.09$. Critical value $= 2.21$. Do not reject Ho
B) Test statistic: $F = 1.09$. Critical value $= 2.03$. Reject Ho
C) Test statistic: $F = 28.75$. Critical value $= 2.03$. Reject Ho
D) Test statistic: $F = 1.05$. Critical value $= 2.21$. Do not reject Ho
(E) None of the above
Answer: (A) Explain why

P10.66: Test the hypothesis that the variances in absorption rate of two wood materials are the same at $\alpha = 0.05$.

Descriptive statistics of two samples of yarns

Statistic	Wood A	Wood B
Standard deviation	2	3.4
Variances	4	11.56
n	16	21

P10.67: Test the alternative hypothesis that $\sigma_1 > \sigma_2$ at $\alpha = 0.01$ level of significance for the given sample data.

	Population 1	Population 2
n	25	17
s	5.76	2.21

A) Test statistic: $F = 6.79$. Critical value $= 3.18$. Reject Ho
B) Test statistic: $F = 6.79$. Critical value $= 3.18$. Do not reject Ho
C) Test statistic: $F = 2.61$. Critical value $= 1.87$. Reject Ho

D) Test statistic: $F = 2.61$. Critical value = 3.18. Do not reject Ho
(E) None of the above
Answer: (A) Explain why

P10.68: Test the hypothesis that the variances of yarn strength of the two yarns given in the table below are the same at $\alpha = 0.05$.

Descriptive statistics of two samples of yarns

Statistic	Yarn A (100% Cotton)	Yarn B (75%Cotton/25% Polyester)
Mean strength	104	93
Standard deviation	3.97	4.36
Variances	15.8	19
n	20	20

P10.69: Test the hypothesis that $\sigma_1 < \sigma_2$ at $\alpha = 0.01$ level of significance for the given sample data.

	Population 1	Population 2
n	9	10
s	0.0782	0.2079

A) Test statistic: $F = 0.14$. Critical value = 0.295. Reject Ho
B) Test statistic: $F = 0.14$. Critical value = 0.310. Reject Ho
C) Test statistic: $F = 0.14$. Critical value = 0.318. Do not reject Ho
D) Test statistic: $F = 0.14$. Critical value = 0.295. Do not reject Ho
(E) None of the above
Answer: (A) Explain why

APPENDIX 10
Table 10.A The F-distribution

If the number of degrees of freedom is not found in the table, we follow the practice of choosing the degrees of freedom closest to that desired. If the degrees of freedom are exactly between two values, find the mean of the values.

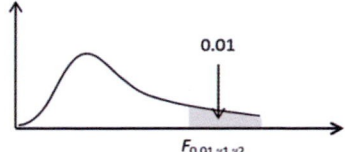

Critical Values of the F distribution $[F_{0.01,\gamma1,\gamma2}]$

$\gamma2 \backslash \gamma1$	1	2	3	4	5	6	7	8	9	10	12	15	20	24	30	40	60	120	∞
1	4052	5000	5403	5625	5764	5859	5928	5982	6022	6056	6106	6157	6209	6235	6261	6287	6313	6339	6366
2	98.50	99.00	99.17	99.25	99.30	99.33	99.36	99.37	99.39	99.40	99.42	99.43	99.45	99.46	99.47	99.47	99.48	99.49	99.50
3	34.12	30.82	29.46	28.71	28.24	27.91	27.67	27.49	27.35	27.23	27.05	26.87	26.69	26.00	26.50	26.41	26.23	26.22	26.13
4	21.20	18.00	16.69	15.98	15.52	15.21	14.98	14.80	14.66	14.55	14.37	14.20	14.02	13.93	13.84	13.75	13.65	13.56	13.46
5	16.26	13.27	12.06	11.39	10.97	10.67	10.46	10.29	10.16	10.05	9.89	9.72	9.55	9.47	9.38	9.29	9.20	9.11	9.02
6	13.75	10.92	9.78	9.15	8.75	8.47	8.26	8.10	7.98	7.87	7.72	7.56	7.40	7.31	7.23	7.14	7.06	6.97	6.88
7	12.25	9.55	8.45	7.85	7.46	7.19	6.99	6.84	6.72	6.62	6.47	6.31	6.16	6.07	5.99	5.91	5.82	5.74	5.65
8	11.26	8.65	7.59	7.01	6.63	6.37	6.18	6.03	5.91	5.81	5.67	5.52	5.36	5.28	5.20	5.12	5.03	4.95	4.86
9	10.56	8.02	6.99	6.42	6.06	5.80	5.61	5.47	5.35	5.26	5.11	4.96	4.81	4.73	4.65	4.57	4.48	4.40	4.31
10	10.04	7.56	6.55	5.99	5.64	5.39	5.20	5.06	4.94	4.85	4.71	4.56	4.41	4.33	4.25	4.17	4.08	4.00	3.91
11	9.65	7.21	6.22	5.67	5.32	5.07	4.89	4.74	4.63	4.54	4.40	4.25	4.10	4.02	3.94	3.86	3.78	3.69	3.60
12	9.33	6.93	5.95	5.41	5.06	4.82	4.64	4.50	4.39	4.30	4.16	4.01	3.86	3.78	3.70	3.62	3.54	3.45	3.36
13	9.07	6.70	5.74	5.21	4.86	4.62	4.44	4.30	4.19	4.10	3.96	3.82	3.66	3.59	3.51	3.43	3.34	3.25	3.17
14	8.86	6.51	5.56	5.04	4.69	4.46	4.28	4.14	4.03	3.94	3.80	3.66	3.51	3.43	3.35	3.27	3.18	3.09	3.00
15	8.68	6.36	5.42	4.89	4.36	4.32	4.14	4.00	3.89	3.80	3.67	3.52	3.37	3.29	3.21	3.13	3.05	2.96	2.87
16	8.53	6.23	5.29	4.77	4.44	4.20	4.03	3.89	3.78	3.69	3.55	3.41	3.26	3.18	3.10	3.02	2.93	2.84	2.75
17	8.40	6.11	5.18	4.67	4.34	4.10	3.93	3.79	3.68	3.59	3.46	3.31	3.16	3.08	3.00	2.92	2.83	2.75	2.65
18	8.29	6.01	5.09	4.58	4.25	7.01	3.84	3.71	3.60	3.51	3.37	3.23	3.08	3.00	2.02	2.84	2.75	2.66	2.57
19	8.18	5.93	5.01	4.50	4.17	3.94	3.77	3.63	3.52	3.43	3.30	3.15	3.00	2.92	2.84	2.76	2.67	2.58	2.59
20	8.10	5.85	4.94	4.43	4.10	3.87	3.70	3.56	3.46	3.37	3.23	3.09	2.94	2.86	2.78	2.69	2.61	2.52	2.42
21	8.02	5.78	4.87	4.37	4.04	3.81	3.64	3.51	3.40	3.31	3.17	3.03	2.88	2.80	2.72	2.64	2.55	2.46	2.36
22	7.95	5.72	4.82	4.31	3.99	3.76	3.59	3.45	3.35	3.26	3.12	2.98	2.83	2.75	2.67	2.58	2.50	2.40	2.31
23	7.88	5.66	4.76	4.26	3.94	3.71	3.54	3.41	3.30	3.21	3.07	2.93	2.78	2.70	2.62	2.54	2.45	2.35	2.26
24	7.82	5.61	4.72	4.22	3.90	3.67	3.50	3.36	3.26	3.17	3.03	2.89	2.74	2.66	2.58	2.49	2.40	2.31	2.21
25	7.77	5.57	4.68	4.18	3.85	3.63	3.46	3.32	3.22	3.13	2.99	2.85	2.70	2.62	2.54	2.45	2.36	2.27	2.17
26	7.72	5.53	4.64	4.14	3.82	3.59	3.42	3.29	3.18	3.09	2.96	2.81	2.66	2.58	2.50	2.42	2.33	2.23	2.13
27	7.68	5.49	4.60	4.11	3.78	3.56	3.39	3.26	3.15	3.06	2.93	2.78	2.63	2.55	2.47	2.38	2.29	2.20	2.10
28	7.64	5.45	4.57	4.07	3.75	3.53	3.36	3.23	3.12	3.03	2.90	2.75	2.60	2.52	2.44	2.35	2.26	2.17	2.06
29	7.60	5.42	4.54	4.04	3.73	3.50	3.33	3.20	3.09	3.00	2.87	2.73	2.57	2.49	2.41	2.33	2.23	2.14	2.03
30	7.56	5.39	4.51	4.02	3.70	3.47	3.30	3.17	3.07	2.98	2.84	2.70	2.55	2.47	2.39	2.30	2.21	2.11	2.01
40	7.31	5.18	4.31	3.83	3.51	3.29	3.12	2.99	2.89	2.80	2.66	2.52	2.37	2.29	2.20	2.11	2.02	1.92	1.80
60	7.08	4.98	4.13	3.65	3.34	3.12	2.95	2.82	2.72	2.63	2.50	2.35	2.20	2.12	2.03	1.94	1.84	1.73	1.60
120	6.85	4.79	3.95	3.48	3.17	2.96	2.79	2.66	2.56	2.47	2.34	2.19	2.03	1.95	1.86	1.76	1.66	1.53	1.38
∞	6.63	4.61	3.78	3.32	3.02	2.80	2.64	2.51	2.41	2.32	2.18	2.04	1.88	1.79	1.70	1.59	1.47	1.32	1.00

Note: $F_{0.99,\gamma1,\gamma2}=1/ F_{0.01,\gamma2,\gamma1}$

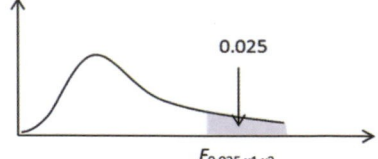

Critical Values of the F distribution $[F_{0.025,\gamma 1,\gamma 2}]$

$\gamma 2 \setminus \gamma 1$	1	2	3	4	5	6	7	8	9	10	12	15	20	24	30	40	60	120	∞
1	647.8	799.5	864.2	899.6	921.8	937.1	948.2	956.7	963.3	968.6	976.7	984.9	993.1	997.2	1001	1006	1010	1014	1018
2	38.51	39.00	39.17	39.25	39.30	39.33	39.36	39.37	39.39	39.40	39.41	39.43	39.45	39.46	39.46	39.47	39.48	39.49	39.50
3	17.44	16.04	15.44	15.10	14.88	14.73	14.62	14.54	14.47	14.42	14.34	14.25	14.17	14.12	14.08	14.04	13.99	13.95	13.90
4	12.22	10.65	9.98	9.60	9.36	9.20	9.07	8.98	8.90	8.84	8.75	8.66	8.56	8.51	8.46	8.41	8.36	8.31	8.26
5	10.01	8.43	7.76	7.39	7.15	6.98	6.85	6.76	6.68	6.62	6.52	6.43	6.33	6.28	6.23	6.18	6.12	6.07	6.02
6	8.81	7.26	6.60	6.23	5.99	5.82	5.70	5.60	5.52	5.46	5.37	5.27	5.17	5.12	5.07	5.01	4.96	4.90	4.85
7	8.07	6.54	5.89	5.52	5.29	5.12	4.99	4.90	4.82	4.76	4.67	4.57	4.47	4.42	4.36	4.31	4.25	4.20	4.14
8	7.57	6.06	5.42	5.05	4.82	4.65	4.53	4.43	4.36	4.30	4.20	4.10	4.00	3.95	3.89	3.84	3.78	3.73	3.67
9	7.21	5.71	5.08	4.72	4.48	4.32	4.20	4.10	4.03	3.96	3.87	3.77	3.67	3.61	3.56	3.51	3.45	3.39	3.33
10	6.94	5.46	4.83	4.47	4.24	4.07	3.95	3.85	3.78	3.72	3.62	3.52	3.42	3.37	3.31	3.26	3.20	3.14	3.08
11	6.72	5.26	4.63	4.28	4.04	3.88	3.76	3.66	3.59	3.53	3.43	3.33	3.23	3.17	3.12	3.06	3.00	2.94	2.88
12	6.55	5.10	4.47	4.12	3.89	3.73	3.61	3.51	3.44	3.37	3.28	3.18	3.07	3.02	2.96	2.91	2.85	2.79	2.72
13	6.41	4.97	4.35	4.00	3.77	3.60	3.48	3.39	3.31	3.25	3.15	3.05	2.95	2.89	2.84	2.78	2.72	2.66	2.60
14	6.30	4.86	4.24	3.89	3.66	3.50	3.38	3.29	3.21	3.15	3.05	2.95	2.84	2.79	2.73	2.67	2.61	2.55	2.49
15	6.20	4.77	4.15	3.80	3.58	3.41	3.29	3.20	3.12	3.06	2.96	2.86	2.76	2.70	2.64	2.59	2.52	2.46	2.40
16	6.12	4.69	4.08	3.73	3.50	3.34	3.22	3.12	3.05	2.99	2.89	2.79	2.68	2.63	2.57	2.51	2.45	2.38	2.32
17	6.04	4.62	4.01	3.66	3.44	3.28	3.16	3.06	2.98	2.92	2.82	2.72	2.62	2.56	2.50	2.44	2.38	2.32	2.25
18	5.98	4.56	3.95	3.61	3.38	3.22	3.10	3.01	2.93	2.87	2.77	2.67	2.56	2.50	2.44	2.38	2.32	2.26	2.19
19	5.92	4.51	3.90	3.56	3.33	3.17	3.05	2.96	2.88	2.82	2.72	2.62	2.51	2.45	2.39	2.33	2.27	2.20	2.13
20	5.87	4.46	3.86	3.51	3.29	3.13	3.01	2.91	2.84	2.77	2.68	2.57	2.46	2.41	2.35	2.29	2.22	2.16	2.09
21	5.83	4.42	3.82	3.48	3.25	3.09	2.97	2.87	2.80	2.73	2.64	2.53	2.42	2.37	2.31	2.25	2.18	2.11	2.04
22	5.79	4.38	3.78	3.44	3.22	3.05	2.93	2.84	2.76	2.70	2.60	2.50	2.39	2.33	2.27	2.21	2.14	2.08	2.00
23	5.75	4.35	3.75	3.41	3.18	3.02	2.90	2.81	2.73	2.67	2.57	2.47	2.36	2.30	2.24	2.18	2.11	2.04	1.97
24	5.72	4.32	3.72	3.38	3.15	2.99	2.87	2.78	2.70	2.64	2.54	2.44	2.33	2.27	2.21	2.15	2.08	2.01	1.94
25	5.69	4.29	3.69	3.35	3.13	2.97	2.85	2.75	2.68	2.61	2.51	2.41	2.30	2.24	2.18	2.12	2.05	1.98	1.91
26	5.66	4.27	3.67	3.33	3.10	2.94	2.82	2.73	2.65	2.59	2.49	2.39	2.28	2.22	2.16	2.09	2.03	1.95	1.88
27	5.63	4.24	3.65	3.31	3.08	2.92	2.80	2.71	2.63	2.57	2.47	2.36	2.25	2.19	2.13	2.07	2.00	1.93	1.85
28	5.61	4.22	3.63	3.29	3.06	2.90	2.78	2.69	2.61	2.55	2.45	2.34	2.23	2.17	2.11	2.05	1.98	1.91	1.83
29	5.59	4.20	3.61	3.27	3.04	2.88	2.76	2.67	2.59	2.53	2.43	2.32	2.21	2.15	2.09	2.03	1.96	1.89	1.81
30	5.57	4.18	3.59	3.25	3.03	2.87	2.75	2.65	2.57	2.51	2.41	2.31	2.20	2.14	2.07	2.01	1.94	1.87	1.79
40	5.42	4.05	3.46	3.13	2.90	2.74	2.62	2.53	2.45	2.39	2.29	2.18	2.07	2.01	1.94	1.88	1.80	1.72	1.64
60	5.29	3.93	3.34	3.01	2.79	2.63	2.51	2.41	2.33	2.27	2.17	2.06	1.14	1.88	1.82	1.74	1.67	1.58	1.48
120	5.15	3.80	3.23	2.89	2.67	2.52	2.39	2.30	2.22	2.16	2.05	1.94	1.82	1.76	1.69	1.61	1.53	1.43	1.31
∞	5.02	3.69	3.12	2.79	2.57	2.41	2.29	2.19	2.11	2.05	1.94	1.83	1.71	1.64	1.57	1.48	1.39	1.27	1.00

Note: $F_{0.975,\gamma 1,\gamma 2} = 1/ F_{0.025,\gamma 2,\gamma 1}$

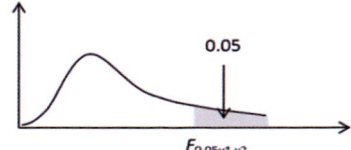

0.05

$F_{0.05,\gamma1,\gamma2}$

Critical Values of the F distribution - $[F_{0.05,\gamma1,\gamma2}]$

$\gamma2 \backslash \gamma1$	1	2	3	4	5	6	7	8	9	10	12	15	20	24	30	40	60	120	∞
1	161.4	199.5	215.7	224.6	230.2	234.0	236.8	238.9	240.5	241.9	243.9	245.9	248.0	249.1	250.1	251.1	252.2	253.3	254.0
2	18.51	19.00	19.16	19.25	19.30	19.33	19.35	19.37	19.38	19.40	19.41	19.43	19.45	19.45	19.46	19.47	19.48	19.49	19.50
3	10.13	9.55	9.28	9.12	9.01	8.94	8.89	8.85	8.81	8.79	8.74	8.70	8.66	8.64	8.62	8.59	8.57	8.55	8.53
4	7.71	6.94	6.59	6.39	6.26	6.16	6.09	6.04	6.00	5.96	5.91	5.86	5.80	5.77	5.75	5.72	5.69	5.66	5.63
5	6.61	5.79	5.41	5.19	5.05	4.95	4.88	4.82	4.77	4.74	4.68	4.62	4.56	4.53	4.50	4.46	4.43	4.40	4.36
6	5.99	5.14	4.76	4.53	4.39	4.28	4.21	4.15	4.10	4.06	4.00	3.94	3.87	3.84	3.81	3.77	3.74	3.70	3.67
7	5.59	4.74	4.35	4.12	3.97	3.87	3.79	3.73	3.68	3.64	3.57	3.51	3.44	3.41	3.38	3.34	3.30	3.27	3.23
8	5.32	4.46	4.07	3.84	3.69	3.58	3.50	3.44	3.39	3.35	3.28	3.22	3.15	3.12	3.08	3.04	3.01	2.97	2.93
9	5.12	4.26	3.86	3.63	3.48	3.37	3.29	3.23	3.18	3.14	3.07	3.01	2.94	2.90	2.86	2.83	2.79	2.75	2.71
10	4.96	4.10	3.71	3.48	3.33	3.22	3.14	3.07	3.02	2.98	2.91	2.85	2.77	2.74	2.70	2.66	2.62	2.58	2.54
11	4.84	3.98	3.59	3.36	3.20	3.09	3.01	2.95	2.90	2.85	2.79	2.72	2.65	2.61	2.57	2.53	2.49	2.45	2.40
12	4.75	3.89	3.49	3.26	3.11	3.00	2.91	2.85	2.80	2.75	2.69	2.62	2.54	2.51	2.47	2.43	2.38	2.34	2.30
13	4.67	3.81	3.41	3.18	3.03	2.92	2.83	2.77	2.71	2.67	2.60	2.53	2.46	2.42	2.38	2.34	2.30	2.25	2.21
14	4.60	3.74	3.34	3.11	2.96	2.85	2.76	2.70	2.65	2.60	2.53	2.46	2.39	2.35	2.31	2.27	2.22	2.18	2.13
15	4.54	3.68	3.29	3.06	2.90	2.79	2.71	2.64	2.59	2.54	2.48	2.40	2.33	2.29	2.25	2.20	2.16	2.11	2.07
16	4.49	3.63	3.24	3.01	2.85	2.74	2.66	2.59	2.54	2.49	2.42	2.35	2.28	2.24	2.19	2.15	2.11	2.06	2.01
17	4.45	3.59	3.20	2.96	2.81	2.70	2.61	2.55	2.49	2.45	2.38	2.31	2.23	2.19	2.15	2.10	2.06	2.01	1.96
18	4.41	3.55	3.16	2.93	2.77	2.66	2.58	2.51	2.46	2.41	2.34	2.27	2.19	2.15	2.11	2.06	2.02	1.97	1.92
19	4.38	3.52	3.13	2.90	2.74	2.63	2.54	2.48	2.42	2.38	2.31	2.23	2.16	2.11	2.07	2.03	1.98	1.93	1.88
20	4.35	3.49	3.10	2.87	2.71	2.60	2.51	2.45	2.39	2.35	2.28	2.20	2.12	2.08	2.04	1.99	1.95	1.90	1.84
21	4.32	3.47	3.07	2.84	2.68	2.57	2.49	2.42	2.37	2.32	2.25	2.18	2.10	2.05	2.01	1.96	1.92	1.87	1.81
22	4.30	3.44	3.05	2.82	2.66	2.55	2.46	2.40	2.34	2.30	2.23	2.15	2.07	2.03	1.98	1.94	1.89	1.84	1.78
23	4.28	3.42	3.03	2.80	2.64	2.53	2.44	2.37	2.32	2.27	2.20	2.13	2.05	2.01	1.96	1.91	1.86	1.81	1.76
24	4.26	3.40	3.01	2.78	2.62	2.51	2.42	2.36	2.30	2.25	2.18	2.11	2.03	1.98	1.94	1.89	1.84	1.79	1.73
25	4.24	3.39	2.99	2.76	2.60	2.49	2.40	2.34	2.28	2.24	2.16	2.09	2.01	1.96	1.92	1.87	1.82	1.77	1.71
26	4.23	3.37	2.98	2.74	2.59	2.47	2.39	2.32	2.27	2.22	2.15	2.07	1.99	1.95	1.90	1.85	1.80	1.75	1.69
27	4.21	3.35	2.96	2.73	2.57	2.46	2.37	2.31	2.25	2.20	2.13	2.06	1.97	1.93	1.88	1.84	1.79	1.73	1.67
28	4.20	3.34	2.95	2.71	2.56	2.45	2.36	2.29	2.24	2.19	2.12	2.04	1.96	1.91	1.87	1.82	1.77	1.71	1.65
29	4.18	3.33	2.93	2.70	2.55	2.43	2.35	2.28	2.22	2.18	2.10	2.03	1.94	1.90	1.85	1.81	1.75	1.70	1.64
30	4.17	3.32	2.92	2.69	2.53	2.42	2.33	2.27	2.21	2.16	2.09	2.01	1.93	1.89	1.84	1.79	1.74	1.68	1.62
40	4.08	3.23	2.84	2.61	2.45	2.34	2.25	2.18	2.12	2.08	2.00	1.92	1.84	1.79	1.74	1.69	1.64	1.58	1.51
60	4.00	3.15	2.76	2.53	2.37	2.25	2.17	2.10	2.04	1.99	1.92	1.84	1.75	1.70	1.65	1.59	1.53	1.47	1.39
120	3.92	3.07	2.68	2.45	2.29	2.17	2.09	2.02	1.96	1.91	1.83	1.75	1.66	1.61	1.55	1.55	1.43	1.35	1.25
∞	3.84	3.00	2.60	2.37	2.21	2.10	2.01	1.94	1.88	1.83	1.75	1.67	1.57	1.52	1.46	1.39	1.32	1.22	1.00

Note: $F_{0.95,\gamma1,\gamma2} = 1/F_{0.05,\gamma2,\gamma1}$

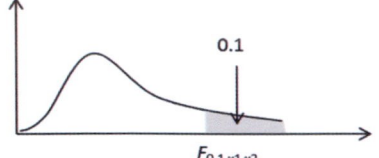

Critical Values of the F distribution - $[F_{0.10,\gamma1,\gamma2}]$

$\gamma2 \backslash \gamma1$	1	2	3	4	5	6	7	8	9	10	12	15	20	24	30	40	60	120	∞
1	39.86	49.50	53.59	55.83	57.24	58.20	58.91	59.44	59.86	60.19	60.71	61.22	61.74	62.00	62.26	62.53	62.79	63.06	63.33
2	8.53	9.00	9.16	9.24	9.29	9.33	9.35	9.37	9.38	9.39	9.41	9.42	9.44	9.45	9.46	9.47	9.47	9.48	9.49
3	5.54	5.46	5.39	5.34	5.31	5.28	5.27	5.25	5.24	5.20	5.22	5.20	5.18	5.18	5.17	5.16	5.15	5.14	5.13
4	4.54	4.32	4.19	4.11	4.05	4.01	3.98	3.95	3.94	3.92	3.90	3.87	3.84	3.83	3.82	3.80	3.79	3.78	3.76
5	4.06	3.78	3.62	3.52	3.45	3.40	3.37	3.34	3.32	3.30	3.27	3.24	3.21	3.19	3.17	3.16	3.14	3.12	3.10
6	3.78	3.46	3.29	3.18	3.11	3.05	3.01	2.98	2.96	2.94	2.90	2.87	2.84	2.82	2.80	2.78	2.76	2.74	2.72
7	3.59	3.26	3.07	2.96	2.88	2.83	2.78	2.75	2.72	2.70	2.67	2.63	2.59	2.58	2.56	2.54	2.51	2.49	2.47
8	3.46	3.11	2.92	2.81	2.73	2.67	2.62	2.59	2.56	2.54	2.50	2.46	2.42	2.40	2.38	2.36	2.34	2.32	2.29
9	3.36	3.01	2.81	2.69	2.61	2.55	2.51	2.47	2.44	2.42	2.38	2.34	2.30	2.28	2.25	2.23	2.21	2.18	2.16
10	3.29	2.92	2.73	2.61	2.52	2.46	2.41	2.38	2.35	2.32	2.28	2.24	2.20	2.18	2.16	2.13	2.11	2.08	2.06
11	3.23	2.86	2.66	2.54	2.45	2.39	2.34	2.30	2.27	2.25	2.21	2.17	2.12	2.10	2.08	2.05	2.03	2.00	1.97
12	3.18	2.81	2.61	2.48	2.39	2.33	2.28	2.24	2.21	2.19	2.15	2.10	2.06	2.04	2.01	1.99	1.96	1.93	1.90
13	3.14	2.76	2.56	2.43	2.35	2.28	2.23	2.20	2.16	2.14	2.10	2.05	2.01	1.98	1.96	1.93	1.90	1.88	1.85
14	3.10	2.73	2.52	2.39	2.31	2.24	2.19	2.15	2.12	2.10	2.05	2.01	1.96	1.94	1.91	1.89	1.86	1.83	1.80
15	3.07	2.70	2.49	2.36	2.27	2.21	2.16	2.12	2.09	2.06	2.02	1.97	1.92	1.90	1.87	1.85	1.82	1.79	1.76
16	3.05	2.67	2.46	2.33	2.24	2.18	2.13	2.09	2.06	2.03	1.99	1.94	1.89	1.87	1.84	1.81	1.78	1.75	1.72
17	3.03	2.64	2.44	2.31	2.22	2.15	2.10	2.06	2.03	2.00	1.96	1.91	1.86	1.84	1.81	1.78	1.75	1.72	1.69
18	3.01	2.62	2.42	2.29	2.20	2.13	2.08	2.04	2.00	1.98	1.93	1.89	1.84	1.81	1.78	1.75	1.72	1.69	1.66
19	2.99	2.61	2.40	2.27	2.18	2.11	2.06	2.02	1.98	1.96	1.91	1.86	1.81	1.79	1.76	1.73	1.70	1.67	1.63
20	2.97	2.59	2.38	2.25	2.16	2.09	2.04	2.00	1.96	1.94	1.89	1.84	1.79	1.77	1.74	1.71	1.68	1.64	1.61
21	2.96	2.57	2.36	2.23	2.14	2.08	2.02	1.98	1.95	1.92	1.87	1.83	1.78	1.75	1.72	1.69	1.66	1.62	1.59
22	2.95	2.56	2.35	2.22	2.13	2.06	2.01	1.97	1.93	1.90	1.86	1.81	1.76	1.73	1.70	1.67	1.64	1.60	1.57
23	2.94	2.55	2.34	2.21	2.11	2.05	1.99	1.95	1.92	1.89	1.84	1.80	1.74	1.72	1.69	1.66	1.62	1.59	1.55
24	2.93	2.54	2.33	2.19	2.10	2.04	1.98	1.94	1.91	1.88	1.83	1.78	1.73	1.70	1.67	1.64	1.61	1.57	1.53
25	2.92	2.53	2.32	2.18	2.09	2.02	1.97	1.93	1.89	1.87	1.82	1.77	1.72	1.69	1.66	1.63	1.59	1.56	1.52
26	2.91	2.52	2.31	2.17	2.08	2.01	1.96	1.92	1.88	1.86	1.81	1.76	1.71	1.68	1.65	1.61	1.58	1.54	1.50
27	2.90	2.51	2.30	2.17	2.07	2.00	1.95	1.91	1.87	1.85	1.80	1.75	1.70	1.67	1.64	1.60	1.57	1.53	1.49
28	2.89	2.50	2.29	2.16	2.06	2.00	1.94	1.90	1.87	1.84	1.79	1.74	1.69	1.66	1.63	1.59	1.56	1.52	1.48
29	2.89	2.50	2.28	2.15	2.06	1.99	1.93	1.89	1.86	1.83	1.78	1.73	1.68	1.65	1.62	1.58	1.55	1.51	1.47
30	2.88	2.49	2.28	2.14	2.03	1.98	1.93	1.88	1.85	1.82	1.77	1.72	1.67	1.64	1.61	1.57	1.54	1.50	1.46
40	2.84	2.44	2.23	2.09	2.00	1.93	1.87	1.83	1.79	1.76	1.71	1.66	1.61	1.57	1.54	1.51	1.47	1.42	1.38
60	2.79	2.39	2.18	2.04	1.95	1.87	1.82	1.77	1.74	1.71	1.66	1.60	1.54	1.51	1.48	1.44	1.40	1.35	1.29
120	2.75	2.35	2.13	1.99	1.90	1.82	1.77	1.72	1.68	1.65	1.60	1.55	1.48	1.45	1.41	1.37	1.32	1.26	1.19
∞	2.71	2.30	2.08	1.94	1.85	1.77	1.72	1.67	1.63	1.60	1.55	1.49	1.42	1.38	1.34	1.30	1.24	1.17	1.00

Note: $F_{0.90,\gamma1,\gamma2} = 1/\ F_{0.10,\gamma2,\gamma1}$

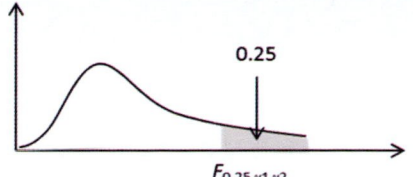

0.25

$F_{0.25,\gamma1,\gamma2}$

Critical Values of the F distribution - $[F_{0.25,\gamma1,\gamma2}]$

$\gamma2 \backslash \gamma1$	1	2	3	4	5	6	7	8	9	10	12	15	20	24	30	40	60	120	∞
1	5.83	7.50	8.20	8.58	8.82	8.98	9.10	9.19	9.26	9.32	9.41	9.49	9.58	9.63	9.67	9.71	9.76	9.80	9.85
2	2.57	3.00	3.15	3.23	3.28	3.31	3.34	3.35	3.37	3.38	3.39	3.41	3.43	3.43	3.44	3.45	3.46	3.47	3.48
3	2.02	2.28	2.36	2.39	2.41	2.42	2.43	2.44	2.44	2.44	2.45	2.46	2.46	2.46	2.47	2.47	2.47	2.47	2.47
4	1.81	2.00	2.05	2.06	2.07	2.08	2.08	2.08	2.08	2.08	2.08	2.08	2.08	2.08	2.08	2.08	2.08	2.08	2.08
5	1.69	1.85	1.88	1.89	1.89	1.89	1.89	1.89	1.89	1.89	1.89	1.89	1.88	1.88	1.88	1.88	1.87	1.87	1.87
6	1.62	1.76	1.78	1.79	1.79	1.78	1.78	1.78	1.77	1.77	1.77	1.76	1.76	1.75	1.75	1.75	1.74	1.74	1.74
7	1.57	1.70	1.72	1.72	1.71	1.71	1.70	1.70	1.70	1.69	1.68	1.68	1.67	1.67	1.66	1.66	1.65	1.65	1.65
8	1.54	1.66	1.67	1.66	1.66	1.65	1.64	1.64	1.63	1.63	1.62	1.62	1.61	1.60	1.60	1.59	1.59	1.58	1.58
9	1.51	1.62	1.63	1.63	1.62	1.61	1.60	1.60	1.59	1.59	1.58	1.57	1.56	1.56	1.55	1.54	1.54	1.53	1.53
10	1.49	1.60	1.60	1.59	1.59	1.58	1.57	1.56	1.56	1.55	1.54	1.53	1.52	1.52	1.51	1.51	1.50	1.49	1.48
11	1.47	1.58	1.58	1.57	1.56	1.55	1.54	1.53	1.53	1.52	1.51	1.50	1.49	1.49	1.48	1.47	1.47	1.46	1.45
12	1.46	1.56	1.56	1.55	1.54	1.53	1.52	1.51	1.51	1.50	1.49	1.48	1.47	1.46	1.45	1.45	1.44	1.43	1.42
13	1.45	1.55	1.55	1.53	1.52	1.51	1.50	1.49	1.49	1.48	1.47	1.46	1.45	1.44	1.43	1.42	1.42	1.41	1.40
14	1.44	1.53	1.53	1.52	1.51	1.50	1.49	1.48	1.47	1.46	1.45	1.44	1.43	1.42	1.41	1.41	1.40	1.39	1.38
15	1.43	1.52	1.52	1.51	1.49	1.48	1.47	1.46	1.46	1.45	1.44	1.43	1.41	1.41	1.40	1.39	1.38	1.37	1.36
16	1.42	1.51	1.51	1.50	1.48	1.47	1.46	1.45	1.44	1.44	1.43	1.41	1.40	1.39	1.38	1.37	1.36	1.35	1.34
17	1.42	1.51	1.50	1.49	1.47	1.46	1.45	1.44	1.43	1.43	1.41	1.40	1.39	1.38	1.37	1.36	1.35	1.34	1.33
18	1.41	1.50	1.49	1.48	1.46	1.45	1.44	1.43	1.42	1.42	1.40	1.39	1.38	1.37	1.36	1.35	1.34	1.33	1.32
19	1.41	1.49	1.49	1.47	1.46	1.44	1.43	1.42	1.41	1.41	1.40	1.38	1.37	1.36	1.35	1.34	1.33	1.32	1.30
20	1.40	1.49	1.48	1.47	1.45	1.44	1.43	1.42	1.41	1.40	1.39	1.37	1.36	1.35	1.34	1.33	1.32	1.31	1.29
21	1.40	1.48	1.48	1.46	1.44	1.43	1.42	1.41	1.40	1.39	1.38	1.37	1.35	1.34	1.33	1.32	1.31	1.30	1.28
22	1.40	1.48	1.47	1.45	1.44	1.42	1.41	1.40	1.39	1.39	1.37	1.36	1.34	1.33	1.32	1.31	1.30	1.29	1.28
23	1.39	1.47	1.47	1.45	1.43	1.42	1.41	1.40	1.39	1.38	1.37	1.35	1.34	1.33	1.32	1.31	1.30	1.28	1.27
24	1.39	1.47	1.46	1.44	1.43	1.41	1.40	1.39	1.38	1.38	1.36	1.35	1.33	1.32	1.31	1.30	1.29	1.28	1.26
25	1.39	1.47	1.46	1.44	1.42	1.41	1.40	1.39	1.38	1.37	1.36	1.34	1.33	1.32	1.31	1.29	1.28	1.27	1.25
26	1.38	1.46	1.45	1.44	1.42	1.41	1.39	1.38	1.37	1.37	1.35	1.34	1.32	1.31	1.30	1.29	1.28	1.26	1.25
27	1.38	1.46	1.45	1.43	1.42	1.40	1.39	1.38	1.37	1.36	1.35	1.33	1.32	1.31	1.30	1.28	1.27	1.26	1.24
28	1.38	1.46	1.45	1.43	1.41	1.40	1.39	1.38	1.37	1.36	1.34	1.33	1.31	1.30	1.29	1.28	1.27	1.25	1.24
29	1.38	1.45	1.45	1.43	1.41	1.40	1.38	1.37	1.36	1.35	1.34	1.32	1.31	1.30	1.29	1.27	1.26	1.25	1.23
30	1.38	1.45	1.44	1.42	1.41	1.39	1.38	1.37	1.36	1.35	1.34	1.32	1.30	1.29	1.28	1.27	1.26	1.24	1.23
40	1.36	1.44	1.42	1.40	1.39	1.37	1.36	1.35	1.34	1.33	1.31	1.30	1.28	1.26	1.25	1.24	1.22	1.21	1.19
60	1.35	1.42	1.41	1.38	1.37	1.35	1.33	1.32	1.31	1.30	1.29	1.27	1.25	1.24	1.22	1.21	1.19	1.17	1.15
120	1.34	1.40	1.39	1.37	1.35	1.33	1.31	1.30	1.29	1.28	1.26	1.24	1.22	1.21	1.19	1.18	1.16	1.13	1.10
∞	1.32	1.39	1.37	1.35	1.33	1.31	1.29	1.28	1.27	1.25	1.24	1.22	1.19	1.18	1.16	1.14	1.12	1.08	1.00

Note: $F_{0.75,\gamma1,\gamma2} = 1/ F_{0.25,\gamma2,\gamma1}$

CHAPTER 11

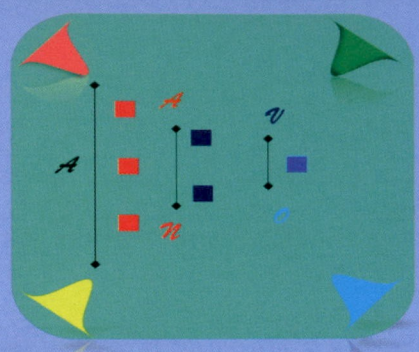

Analysis of Variance (ANOVA)

LEARNING OBJECTIVES

After completing this chapter, students will be able to:

- Understand the basic concepts of conducting an experiment
- Examine the effect of one factor on a certain response variable
- Compare multiple means
- Formulate models for designed experiments
- Examine the significances of the effects of multiple factors on a certain response variable

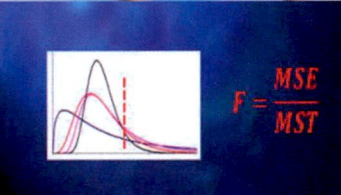

$$F = \frac{MSE}{MST}$$

CHAPTER 11

In the previous chapters, we dealt with data that were collected using observational sampling approaches. In other words, there was no particular design to select the samples. In addition, the effect(s) of the values of one or more variables on a variable of interest was not addressed. When specific control is required on how samples are selected, and when we need to examine the effect(s) of levels of one or more variables on a variable of interest, we have to use designed experiments. The analysis of variance (ANOVA) represents a key statistical tool in dealing with these situations. Using analysis of variance, we can determine the significance of the effect of a certain factor on a response variable. We can also compare the effects of many factors on a response variable.

CHAPTER CONTENTS

11.1 What is an analysis of variance (ANOVA)?

The analysis of variance is a critical statistical tool that is commonly used to evaluate a process or a system performance. In Chapter 1 of this book, we introduced two key terms: a process and a system. A process implies one or more of five basic elements: machine, material, methodology, people, and environment. A system is an entity that has inputs and outputs. Examples of systems and processes were introduced in Chapter 1.

In evaluating a system or a process, the analysis of variance determines the significance of the effect of any factor on a process or a system variable by the amount of noise caused by the factor. This noise is determined by the variance in the variable under study due to the effect of the factor. To explain this point, let us take a simple example.

Example 11.1: Suppose an economist is attempting to determine the effects of a number of factors on household expenses. How can we use the analysis of variance to assist in achieving this objective?

Solution:

Budgeting for household expenses is often a complex task, and almost every family will incur different expenses and different priorities. This complexity is increased by the increase in the gross income of a household as a result of the increase in spending options. The key variable in this question is the *monthly household expenses*. In the analysis of variance, this variable is called '*the response variable*.' The main objective of the analysis of variance is to determine the significances of the effects of relevant '*factors*' on the response variable. Therefore, it is important to determine which factors are likely to influence the monthly

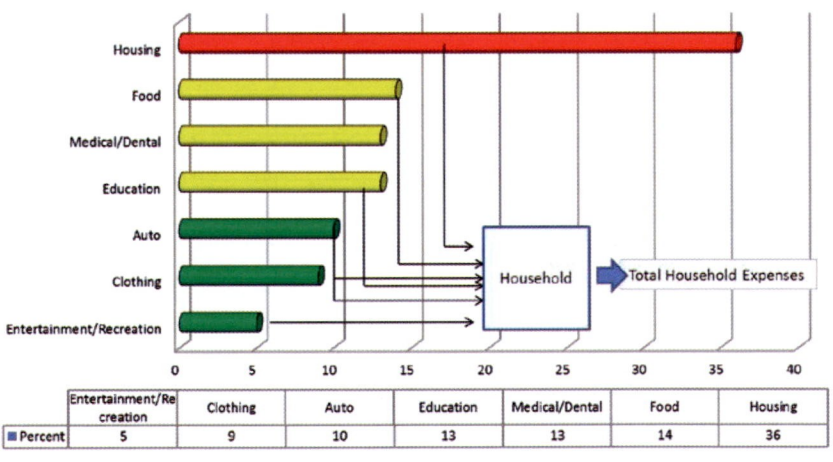

	Entertainment/Recreation	Clothing	Auto	Education	Medical/Dental	Food	Housing
■ Percent	5	9	10	13	13	14	36

household expenses. In this regard, it should be pointed out that the more factors involved in the study, the more complicated the analysis of variance will become. Therefore, we should attempt to reduce the number of factors to the most critical ones.

In this example, potential key expense-related factors that can influence the monthly household expenses include: housing, food, medical/dental, education, automobile, clothing, and entertainment. In order to determine the significance of the effects of these factors, it will be important to select different levels of each factor. These levels may be quantitative or qualitative. For example, low, medium, and high food expenses, or high and low medical expenses are considered quantitative levels. On the other hand, education level may be classified as K-12 education and college education, which represent qualitative factor levels. In the analysis of variance, these are called *'factor levels.'* The response variable is examined by determining its values at different levels of each factor. We may also repeat this process using replicates of the same factor levels. The outcome of the analysis of variance will represent variance components associated with each factor as will be discussed later.

11.2 Single-Factor Experiment (One-Way Classification)

As indicated in the example above, four key components should be identified in the analysis of variance:

1. *Response variable*- this is the characteristic that we wish to study.
2. *Factors*- these are the variables influencing the response variable.
3. *Levels*- these are the levels associated with each factor.
4. *Replicates*- these are the number of times a factor level is tested.

The simplest case in which the analysis of variance is used is the single-factor experiment. In this experiment, we are interested in investigating the effect of one factor on a certain response variable. The experiment in one-way analysis of variance should be made using completely randomized design. This type of design was discussed in Chapter 7.

Examples of applications in which single-factor ANOVA can be used include:

- Among the many factors that affect student's performance, we are interested in determining the significance of the effect of the number of hours a student studies (factor) on the test grade (response variable) they achieve
- Among the many factors that affect people's gross income, we are interested in determining the significance of the effect of the number of years of working experience (factor) on the annual gross income (response variable)

- Among the many factors that affect fuel efficiency during driving, we are interested in determining the significance of the effect of driving speed (factor) on the miles per gallon (response variable)

- Among the many factors that affect total household monthly expenses, we are interested in determining the significance of the effect of food expenses (factor) on the total monthly expenses (response variable)

Example 11.2: In the previous example of household expenses, suppose the economist conducting the study seeks households that have more or less the same housing expenses, the same food expenses, and the same education expenses with the main difference being medical expenses. This will reduce the study to a single-factor study in which the factor is medical expenses and the response variable is the household's total monthly expenses. Suppose an experiment was conducted in which three groups of households earning the same annual gross income were selected: Group A (premium family health insurance), Group B (premium family health insurance plus dental), and Group C (special insurance package). The key question in this study is whether medical expenses will have a significant impact on the total expenses of a household.

Solution:

In carrying out the analysis of variance, it will be useful to construct a table summarizing the experiment associated with the analysis. This experiment is summarized in Table 11.1.

Table 11.1 Summary of the single-factor ANOVA experiment

Title	Effect of medical expenses on the total household monthly expenses
Objective	To determine whether differences in medical expenses will lead to differences in the total household monthly expenses
Response variable	Household monthly expenses ($/month)
Factor	Single-factor experiment (medical expenses). Other factors such as housing, education, and food expenses are kept constant
Levels (a)	3 health insurance groups (Group A-premium family health insurance, Group B-premium family health insurance plus dental, and Group C-special insurance package)
Replicates (n)	10 monthly expenses selected randomly for each group
Total Number of Experimental Runs	$N = a \times n = 3 \times 10 = 30$ experimental runs
Type of Experiment	Random trials

It is important to discuss the role of randomization in the analysis of variance. When we perform an experiment for comparing the effects of several factor levels or treatments, our estimates for these effects may be biased because of an improper choice of samples leading to the existence of factors favoring some treatments more than others. To eliminate this bias, experimental runs should be assigned randomly. In this example, randomization may be achieved by assigning numbers for the experimental runs as shown in Table 11.2.

Table 11.2 Randomization of Experiment

Insurance group	Experimental Run number									
Group A	1	2	3	4	5	6	7	8	9	10
Group B	11	12	13	14	15	16	17	18	19	20
Group C	21	22	23	24	25	26	27	28	29	30

After assigning sequential numbers to the experimental runs (Table 11.2), we then select the test sequence by randomly selecting numbers from the experimental runs between 1 and 30 as shown in Table 11.3 (second column). As you can see in this table, suppose the first randomly selected number is 5 (i.e. at Group A). Then a random value of monthly household expenses for Group A is selected first. If the second number is 2, then another random value of monthly household expenses for Group A is selected. If the third number is 20, then a random value of monthly household expenses for Group B is selected. If the next number is 13, then a random value of monthly household expenses for Group B is selected. This process is repeated until all 30 experimental runs are exhausted as shown in Table 11.3. The only restriction on randomization here is that if the same number is drawn again it should be discarded.

Table 11.3 Sequence of experimental runs

Test sequence	Experimental run #	Factor level	Test sequence	Experimental run #	Factor level
1	5	Group A	16	24	Group C
2	2	Group A	17	22	Group C
3	20	Group B	18	19	Group B
4	13	Group B	19	16	Group B
5	12	Group B	20	28	Group C
6	15	Group B	21	4	Group A
7	21	Group C	22	17	Group B
8	26	Group C	23	1	Group A
9	14	Group B	24	3	Group A
10	7	Group A	25	8	Group A
11	6	Group A	26	9	Group A
12	30	Group C	27	10	Group A
13	23	Group C	28	11	Group B
14	18	Group B	29	27	Group C
15	25	Group C	30	29	Group C

After selecting the random experimental runs, we collect data of monthly expenses corresponding to each run. Table 11.4 shows the values of monthly household expenses (the values of the response variable) collected from within each group.

Table 11.4 Values of the response variables at different experimental runs

Test sequence	Run #	Factor level	Total monthly expenses (Y)	Test sequence	Run #	Factor level	Total monthly expenses (Y)
1	5	Group A	5465	16	24	Group C	5920
2	2	Group A	5752	17	22	Group C	5600
3	20	Group B	5400	18	19	Group B	5289
4	13	Group B	5600	19	16	Group B	5565
5	12	Group B	5524	20	28	Group C	5389
6	15	Group B	5400	21	4	Group A	5880
7	21	Group C	6100	22	17	Group B	5320
8	26	Group C	6102	23	1	Group A	5900
9	14	Group B	5777	24	3	Group A	5489
10	7	Group A	5550	25	8	Group A	5800
11	6	Group A	5700	26	9	Group A	5720
12	30	Group C	5990	27	10	Group A	5640
13	23	Group C	5550	28	11	Group B	5488
14	18	Group B	5280	29	27	Group C	5400
15	25	Group C	5800	30	29	Group C	5800

Before illustrating how the analysis of variance is performed, let us perform descriptive statistics to compare between the response variable values for different groups. Table 11.5 shows the mean and the standard deviation for each group.

Table 11.5 Descriptive statistics for different groups

Levels	y_1	y_2	y_3	y_4	y_5	y_6	y_7	y_8	y_9	y_{10}	Total $\sum y_i$	Mean $\bar{y}_i = \dfrac{\sum y_i}{n}$	Variance $s_i^2 = \dfrac{\sum(y_i - \bar{y})^2}{n-1}$
Group A	5900	5752	5489	5880	5465	5700	5550	5800	5720	5640	56896	5689.6	23363.16
Group B	5488	5524	5600	5777	5400	5565	5320	5280	5289	5400	54643	5464.3	24916.68
Group C	6100	5600	5550	5920	5800	6102	5400	5389	5800	5990	57651	5765.1	72327.21

The contents of Table 11.5 are critical for understanding the underlying concepts of the analysis of variance (ANOVA). This table reveals the following important information:

- The table shows that Group C had the highest total ($57,651), the highest mean value ($5,765.1), and the highest variance (72327.21). This is an initial indication that households using this group insurance incur the highest monthly expenses. In other words, the special insurance package was not very beneficial to the overall household monthly expenses.

- Group B had the lowest total and the lowest mean value. This is an initial indication that households using this group insurance incur the lowest monthly expenses. However, in comparison with Group A, it has higher variance (24916.68 vs. 23363.16); what does this mean? Well, it simply means we are not sure if there is a significant difference between Group A and Group B. One of the benefits of ANOVA is to help us determine this significance.

- Figure 11.1 illustrates how the mean values of household monthly expenses are compared. As can be seen in this figure, Group B households incur the lowest monthly expenses. This conclusion relies totally on the average values for each group.

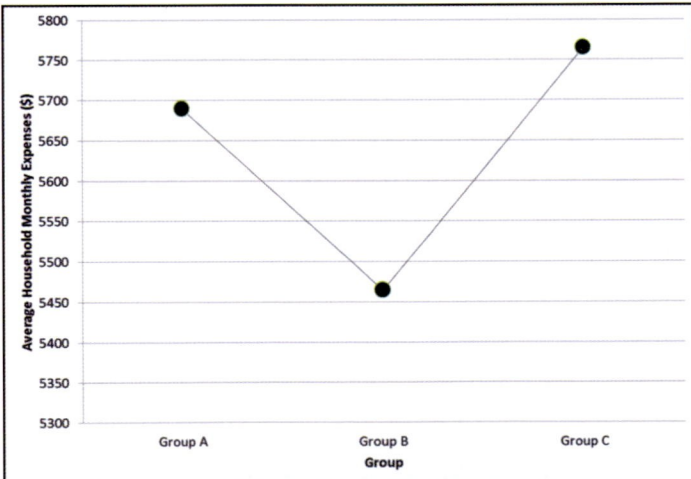

Figure 11.1 Comparison between Group Means

- Now, let us plot the individual values of monthly household expenses as shown in Figure 11.2 in which the individual observations are also included in the graph along with the mean values.

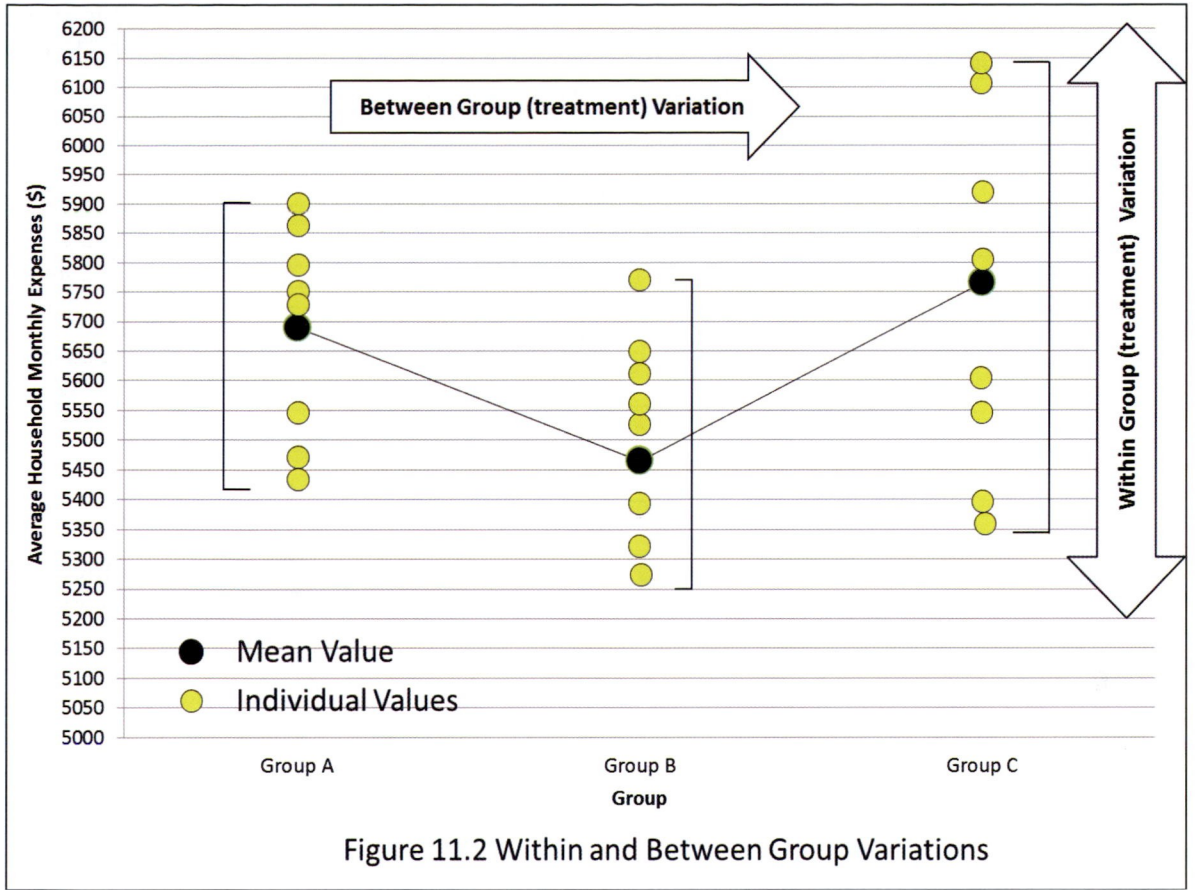

Figure 11.2 Within and Between Group Variations

- As shown in Figure 11.2, there is a great deal of variation between values within each group. Indeed, one can see many points (monthly household expenses) under Group B that are higher than those under Group C.

- In light of the observations of Figures 11.1 and 11.2, the key issue now is which source of variation is bigger: the between-group variation or the within-group variation. This question can be answered using the analysis of variance as will be shown shortly.

- It should be pointed out that if the between-group variation is greater than the within-group variation we will be able to conclude that Group B indeed incurs the lowest cost. On the other hand, if the within-group variation is greater than the between-group variation, we will not be able to conclude that Group B incurs the lowest cost as a result of the high variations within groups. This point will be discussed in the context of the analysis of variance.

Working Problem 11.1:

The system under study is metal rod manufacturing. The response variable of concern is the metal rod strength. The factors that are likely to influence the strength are: (1) cross-sectional shape, (2) rod length, and (3) rod diameter or thickness. Suggest different levels for the factors considered. If the thickness of metal rods was the only factor under consideration. List a summary of the experiment.

Answer:
- See the different proposed factor levels (you may suggest other levels)
- Fix two factors and use the levels of the third factor

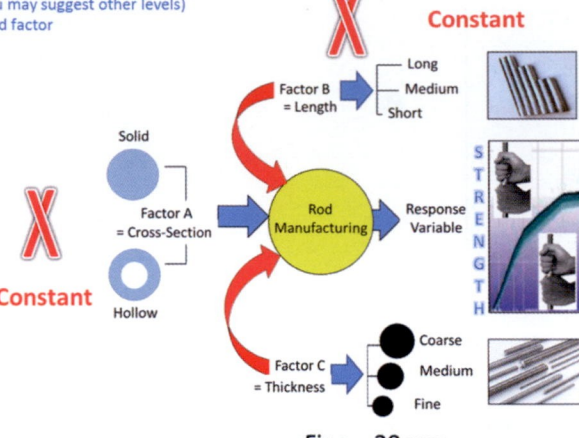

Fine = 20 mm
Medium = 30 mm
High = 50 mm

Working Problem 11.2:

The system under study is automobile performance. The response variable of concern is fuel efficiency (miles/gallon). Recommend a number of factors that are likely to influence fuel efficiency and suggest associated factor levels.

Answer:

Fuel efficiency is essentially a form of thermal efficiency and it is best represented by the efficiency of a system that converts chemical potential energy contained in an automobile fuel into work or kinetic energy. There are many factors that can influence fuel efficiency. The best way to realize some of these factors is to consider the different common ways to improve fuel efficiency. A list of these ways is given below (http://eartheasy.com/move_fuel_efficient_driving.html):

- **Avoid aggressive driving.** "Jack-rabbit" starts and hard braking can increase fuel consumption by as much as 40%.
- **Drive steadily at posted speed limits.** Statistics suggests that increasing your highway cruising speed from 55mph (90km/h) to 75mph (120km/h) can raise fuel consumption as much as 20%. You can improve your gas mileage 10 - 15% by driving at 55mph rather than 65mph (104km/h).

- **Avoid idling your vehicle, in both summer and winter.** Idling wastes fuel, gets you nowhere and produces unnecessary greenhouse gases. If you're going to be stopped for more than 30 seconds, except in traffic, turn off the engine. In winter, don't idle a cold engine for more than 30 seconds before driving away. (Older vehicles, however, may need more idling time when first started). In severe cold, vehicles may need more idling time to warm up and ensure the windshield is fully defogged.

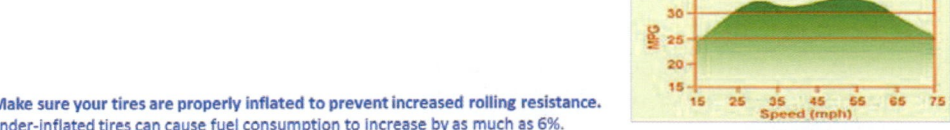

- **Make sure your tires are properly inflated to prevent increased rolling resistance.** Under-inflated tires can cause fuel consumption to increase by as much as 6%.
- **Use the cruise control.** On long stretches of highway driving, cruise control can save fuel by helping your car maintain a steady speed. However, this efficiency is lost on steep hills where the cruise control tries to maintain even speeds. In hilly terrain, it is best to turn off the cruise control.
- **Choose the octane fuel which best suits your car.** Premium, high-octane fuels aren't necessarily the best choice for your car; higher price doesn't guarantee better performance. In fact, such fuels don't provide any greater fuel efficiency. Many cars are designed to use regular low-octane fuel. Check your owner's manual to see what your car requires.

11.3 ANOVA Table for Single-Factor Experiment

The analysis of variance for a single-factor is performed by determining the sums of squares and corresponding mean squares of the values of the response variable at different factor levels. The analysis is commonly summarized in a table called the ANOVA table. The general format of the ANOVA Table is shown in Table 11.6. The symbols used in this table are defined as follows:

a = number of levels of the factor under study
N = total number of observations
SS = Sum of squares of deviation from the mean
MSB = mean square between treatment
MSE = mean square within (or error mean square)
F_o = F-statistic as defined in the ANOVA table

Table 11.6 ANOVA Table

Source of Variation	Sum of Squares	Degree of Freedom	Mean Square	F_o
Between-Treatment	$SS_{between}$	a-1	$MSB = SS_{between} / a$-1	$F_o = \dfrac{MSB}{MSE}$
Residuals (Error) or Within-Treatment	$SS_{within(error)}$	N-a	$MSE = SS_{within(error)} / N$-$a$	
Total	SS_{total}	N-1		

The example below illustrates how the different components of the ANOVA Table are calculated.

Example 11.3: For the previous example of household expenses, the data and associated statistics are as shown in Table 11.7. (a) Calculate all the components of the ANOVA Table. (b) Determine which component is higher: the between group variation or the within group variation. (c) What is the meaning of the value of the F-statistic?

Table 11.7 Values of household monthly expenses and associated statistics

Levels	y1	y2	...	...	y9	y10	Total	Mean	Variance
Group A	5900	5752	...	...	5720	5640	56896	5690	23363
Group B	5488	5524	...	...	5289	5400	54643	5464	24917
Group C	6100	5600	...	...	5800	5990	57651	5765	72327
							Overall Total= $y_{..}$ = 169190	Grand Average= 5639.667	
Variance (between)	97381.3	13477.3	...	...	75547	88033.3			

Solution:

Before proceeding with the calculations of the different components of the ANOVA Table, it will be important to understand that the analysis of variance is based on the additive sum of all different sources of variability. In this regard, the general form of the analysis of variance is:

$$SS_{total} = SS_{Factor\ A} + SS_{Factor\ B} + SS_{Factor\ C} + \ldots + SS_{Error} \qquad (11.1)$$

where SS is the sum of squares.

Each factor is represented in the analysis of variance by the sum of squares in the response variable, y, associated with the factor. Since there is no way to account for all the factors affecting a response variable, we should always account for an error term, or an error sum of squares, which is determined by the total sum of squares minus the sum of squares due to factors.

The case of a single factor is a unique case since it only has one factor at different levels or treatments. In this case, the focus is on the variability between levels (treatments or groups) and within each level (or each treatment). As we noticed in Figure 11.2, it was difficult to draw a reliable conclusion of the effect of medical group on the household monthly expenses. This was a result of the high variability between points within each group. In the context of the analysis of variance, the appropriate expression to reveal the between- and within-treatment components is:

$$SS_{total} = SS_{Between\ treatments} + SS_{within\ treatment(or\ error)} \qquad (11.2)$$

The total variance or, the total mean square is determined by:

$$MS_{total} = MSB_{Between\ treatments} + MSE_{within\ treatment(or\ error)} \qquad (11.3)$$

The F-statistic in this case is

$$F_o = \frac{MSB}{MSE} \qquad (11.4)$$

Note that for the between treatments effects (or the effects of factor levels) to be highly significant, we should have a value of between treatment variation that is much higher than that of within treatment variation or error (i.e. MSB >> MSE).

Steps of calculating different components of the ANOVA Table:

Refer to Table 11.7 as you examine the calculations below.

(1) The total sum of squares:

$$SS_{total} = \sum_{1}^{N}(y_i - \bar{y})^2$$

$$= (5900 - 5639.667)^2 + (5752 - 5639.667)^2 + \cdots + (5990 - 5639.667)^2$$
$$= 1575267$$

(2) The between-treatment sum of squares:

$$SS_{treatment} = n \sum_{1}^{n}(\bar{y}_{i.} - \bar{y}_{..})^2$$

$$= 10[(5690 - 5639.667)^2 + (5464 - 5639.667)^2 + (5765 - 5639.667)^2]$$
$$= 489803.3$$

(3) The error sum of squares is calculated as follows:

$$SS_{error} = SS_{total} - SS_{treatment} = 1575267 - 489803.3 = 1085463.7$$

(4) The mean squares for both the treatment and the error are calculated by dividing the sum of squares by their respective degrees of freedom:

$$Mean\ Square\ (Between\ treatments) = \frac{SS_{tretament}}{a-1} = \frac{489803.3}{3-1} = 244901.65$$

$$Mean\ Square\ (Within\ treatments) or\ Mean\ Square\ Error = \frac{SS_{error}}{N-a} = \frac{1085463.7}{30-3}$$
$$= 40202.359$$

The F-statistic is calculated from:

$$F_o = \frac{MSB}{MSE} = \frac{244901.65}{40202.359} = 6.09$$

The F-statistic shown in the ANOVA Table is a result of a null hypothesis test that all treatments are alike, and none of them has a significant effect on the response variable:

$$H_o: \tau_1 = \tau_2 = \cdots = \tau_a$$

$$H_1: \tau_i \neq 0\ for\ at\ least\ one\ i$$

The ANOVA Table for this example is illustrated below. This table was produced using Excel® data analysis as will be described shortly.

Table 11.8 The ANOVA Table for household monthly expenses

ANOVA: Single Factor						
SUMMARY						
Groups	*Count*	*Sum*	*Average*	*Variance*		
Group A	10	56896	5689.6	23363.16		
Group B	10	54643	5464.3	24916.68		
Group C	10	57651	5765.1	72327.21		
ANOVA						
Source of Variation	*SS*	*df*	*MS*	*F*	*P-value*	*F crit*
Between Groups	489803.3	2	244901.6	6.091725	0.006554	3.354131
Within Groups	1085463	27	40202.35			
Total	1575267	29				

The results of the ANOVA Table can be interpreted as follows:

- As shown in Table 11.8, the $MSB_{treatments}$ (between-treatment) is 244901.6. This value is larger than 40202.35, which is the MSE (or within- treatment). This resulted in a value of F-ratio (MSB/MSE) of 6.0917. As we learned in the test of hypothesis for comparison between two variances (Chapter 10), this statistic should be compared with the F-Table at a certain α value (say 0.05) and degree of freedom $a-1$, and $N-a$ *(or 2 and 27)*. The rejection condition is $F_o > F_{\alpha/2, a-1, N-a}$, or if $6.0917 > F_{0.05, 2, 27}$. *Since* $F_{0.05, 2, 27} = 3.35$, we reject the null hypothesis that all treatments or insurance groups yield the same household monthly expenses.
- This means that differences in treatments (differences in delivery speed) lead to significant differences in the response variable.

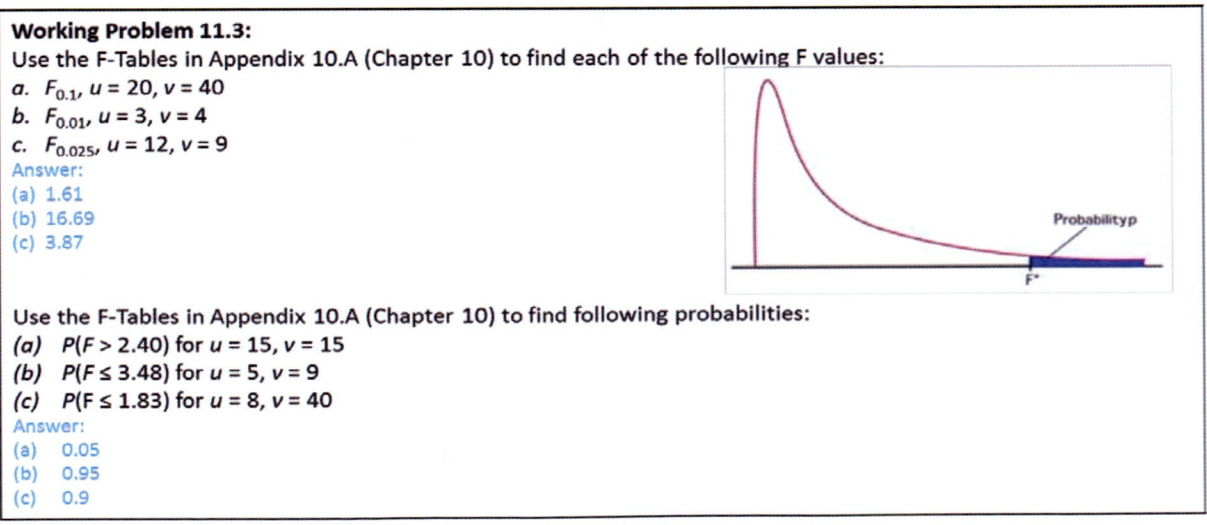

Working Problem 11.3:
Use the F-Tables in Appendix 10.A (Chapter 10) to find each of the following F values:
a. $F_{0.1}$, $u = 20$, $v = 40$
b. $F_{0.01}$, $u = 3$, $v = 4$
c. $F_{0.025}$, $u = 12$, $v = 9$
Answer:
(a) 1.61
(b) 16.69
(c) 3.87

Use the F-Tables in Appendix 10.A (Chapter 10) to find following probabilities:
(a) $P(F > 2.40)$ for $u = 15$, $v = 15$
(b) $P(F \le 3.48)$ for $u = 5$, $v = 9$
(c) $P(F \le 1.83)$ for $u = 8$, $v = 40$
Answer:
(a) 0.05
(b) 0.95
(c) 0.9

Working Problem 11.4:

A partially completed ANOVA Table for a completely randomized design is shown here

a. Complete the ANOVA Table
b. How many treatments are involved in the experiment?
c. Do the data provide sufficient evidence to indicate a difference among population means? Test, using $\alpha = 0.05$.

ANOVA						
Source of Variation	SS	df	MS	F	P-value	F crit
Between Groups	40470.17	2	20235.08	....	0.553107	4.256495
Within Groups	....	....	....			
Total	328200.9	11				

Working Problem 11.5:

A partially completed ANOVA Table for a completely randomized design is shown here

a. Complete the ANOVA Table
b. How many treatments are involved in the experiment?
c. Do the data provide sufficient evidence to indicate a difference among population means? Test, using $\alpha = 0.05$.

ANOVA						
Source of Variation	SS	df	MS	F	P-value	F crit
Between Groups	....	2	82246.06	....	0.127699	6.358873
Within Groups	520949.5	15	....			
Total	685441.6	....				

Working Problem 11.6:
For the following experiment in which a completely randomized design was performed to determine weight loss using three different weight loss treatments, perform ANOVA at $\alpha = 0.01$ and determine if the treatments are significantly different. What is your conclusion?

ANOVA: Single Factor

SUMMARY						
Groups	Count	Sum	Average	Variance		
18	2	30	15	2		
20	2	41	20.5	0.5		
27	2	55	27.5	12.5		
ANOVA						
Source of Variation	SS	df	MS	F	P-value	F crit
Between Groups	157	2	78.5	15.7	0.025754	30.81652
Within Groups	15	3	5			
Total	172	5				

Factor Level	y₁	y₂	y₃
A	18	16	14
B	20	21	20
C	27	30	25

11.4 Using Microsoft Excel® to Perform Single-Factor Experiment (One-Way Classification)

The analysis discussed above can be performed using many statistical software programs. The example below illustrates how Excel®-Data Analysis is used to perform the analysis of variance.

Example 11.4: Factors such as raw material properties, delivery speed, air pressure and total draft typically influence the strength of a textile yarn produced from an air-jet spinning machine. Suppose that the yarn manufacturer only wishes to determine the optimum delivery speed at which yarn strength is at its maximum level. In this case, the manufacturer keeps all other factors at constant levels and only changes the delivery speed (see Figure 11.3). This is a single-factor experiment, with the factor examined being the speed and the response variable being the strength of output material.

Since the practical range of delivery speed is between 150 *m/min* and 190 *m/min*, the manufacturer decided to use three levels of delivery speed within this practical range, namely; 160 *m/min*, 170 *m/min*, and 180 *m/min*. At each level, 3 test replicates of yarn strength were made. Perform analysis of variance using Excel®-Data Analysis to assist the manufacturer in evaluating the effect of spinning speed on yarn strength.

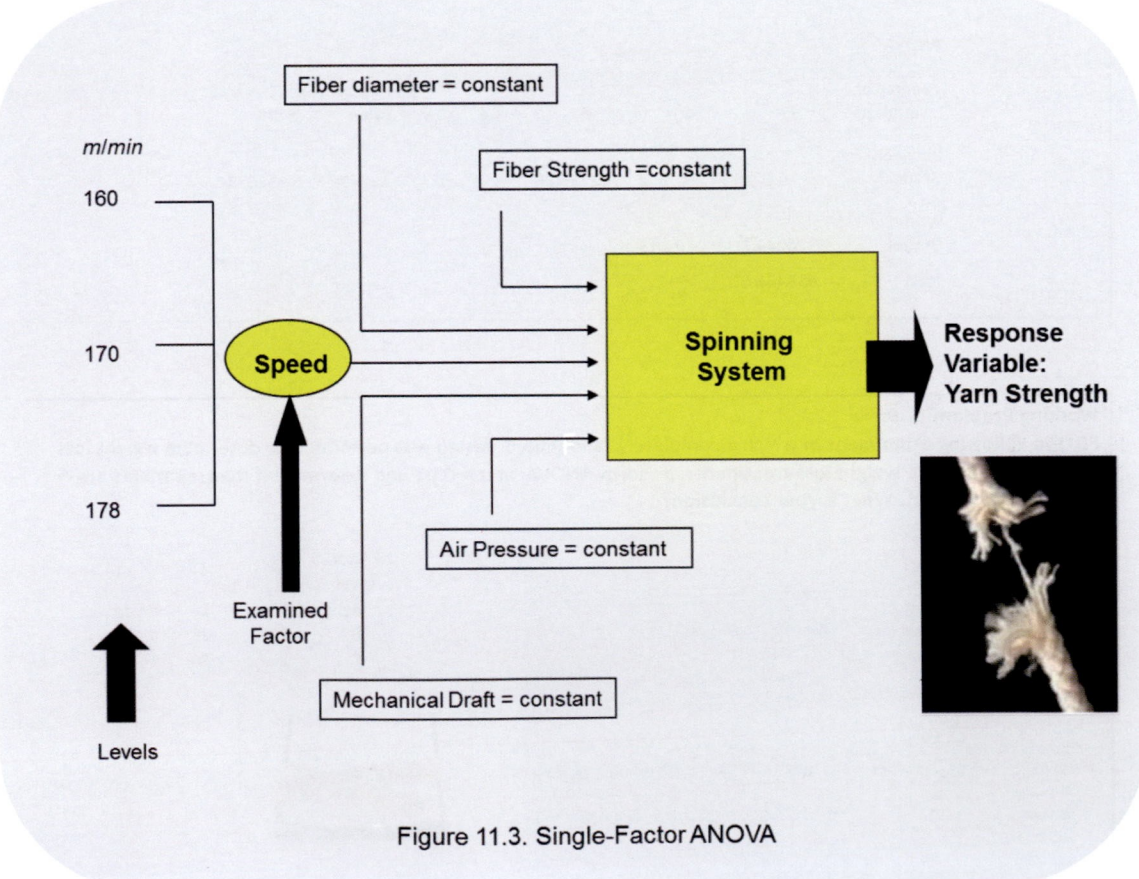

Figure 11.3. Single-Factor ANOVA

Before using Excel®-Data Analysis, it will be important that you construct a table summarizing the experiment associated with the analysis (see Table 11.9).

Table 11.9 Summary of the single-factor ANOVA

Title	Effect of delivery speed of air-jet spinning on yarn strength
Objective	To determine whether differences in delivery speed will lead to differences in yarn strength or to determine which delivery speed will produce a maximum strength
Response variable	Yarn strength (pound-force)
Factor	Single-factor experiment (delivery speed, *m/min*) Other factors are kept constant
Levels (*a*)	3 (160 *m/min*., 170 *m/min*., and 180 *m/min*)
Replicates (*n*)	3
Total Number of Experimental Runs	$N = a \times n = 3 \times 3 = 9$
Type of Experiment	Random trials

It is also important to consider the role of randomization in the analysis of variance as discussed earlier. When we perform an experiment for comparing the effects of several factor levels or treatments, our estimates for these effects may be biased due to an improper choice of samples, leading to the existence of factors favoring some treatments more than others. To eliminate this bias, experimental runs should be assigned randomly. In this example, randomization may be achieved by assigning numbers for the experimental runs as shown in Table 11.10.

Table 11.10 Randomization of Experiment

Deliver speed (*m/min*)	Experimental run number
160	1 2 3
170	4 5 6
180	7 8 9

After assigning numbers to the experimental runs, we then select a random number between 1 and 9. Suppose this number is 6 (i.e. at speed = 170 *m/min*). Then the speed level 170 *m/min* is run first. This process is then repeated until all 9 observations have been assigned in the test sequence. Table 11.11 illustrates a possible test sequence. The only restriction on randomization here is that if the same number is drawn again it is discarded. We can then carry out the experiments and report the values of the response variable as shown in Table 11.11.

Table 11.11 Sequence of experimental runs

Test sequence	Run number	Speed (*m/min*)	Yarn strength (*lbs.Ne*)[*]
1	6	170	2486
2	8	180	2387
3	1	160	2453
4	4	170	2395
5	9	180	2401
6	5	170	2357
7	2	160	2354
8	3	160	2244
9	7	180	2354

Before performing the analysis using Excel®-Data Analysis, we should arrange the data in the way described in Table 11.12.

Table 11.12 Excel® data arrangement for ANOVA

Speed (m/min)	y_1	y_2	y_3
160	2453	2354	2244
170	2486	2395	2357
180	2387	2401	2354

Step 1, 2, and 3: Go to Data, Data Analysis, and ANOVA: Single Factor
Step 4: Press Ok

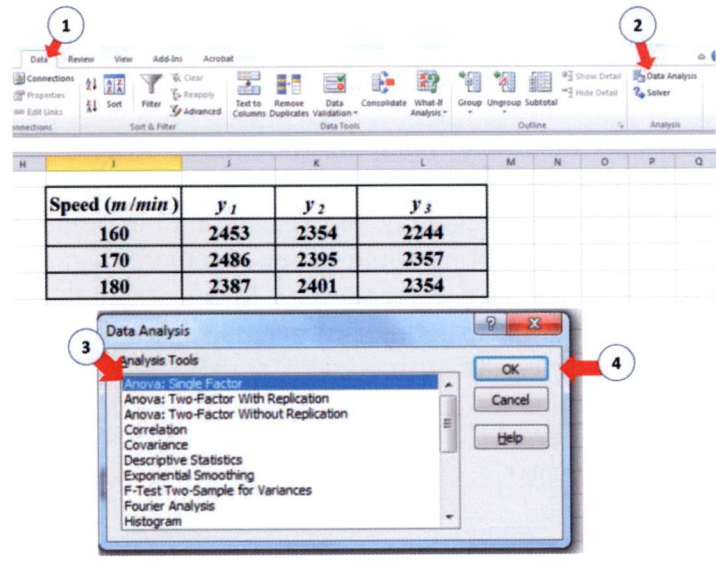

Step 5: Specify the cells covering the numerical values as the input range
Step 6: Group the data by rows since this specifies the levels used
Step 7: Specify the significance level. In this case $\alpha = 0.01$
Step 8: Specify the output as described in previous chapters
Step 9: Click ok to display the ANOVA output shown below

Speed (m/min)	y_1	y_2	y_3
160	2453	2354	2244
170	2486	2395	2357
180	2387	2401	2354

652

The above steps produce the ANOVA output below.

As can be seen in the output display, the format of the results is similar to those obtained earlier by manual calculations. In addition, Excel® displays the values of F-statistics and the F-value from the F-Table (F critical). We can see here that the F-statistic is too low (0.5497) in comparison with the $F_{critical}$(10.925). For this reason, we fail to reject the null hypothesis,

$$H_o: \tau_1 = \tau_2 = \cdots = \tau_a$$

$$H_1: \tau_i \neq 0 \; for \; at \; least \; one \; i$$

and conclude that there is not enough evidence to indicate that the different speed levels have a significant effect on yarn strength.

The p-value displayed in the output indicates the probability associated with our decision to accept the null hypothesis. Normally, the lower the p-value (approaching zero), the more reliable our conclusion will be to reject the null hypothesis as discussed in Chapter 10. As you can see in the output, the p-value is 0.603, which is much greater than the critical area α of 0.01. The next example will illustrate this point.

A good way to confirm the ANOVA results is by plotting the values of yarn strength at different speed levels on a scatter graph. This is shown in Figure 11.4. As one can easily see, the data scatter at each level is so large that it makes the within-treatment variation overwhelmingly larger than between-treatment variation.

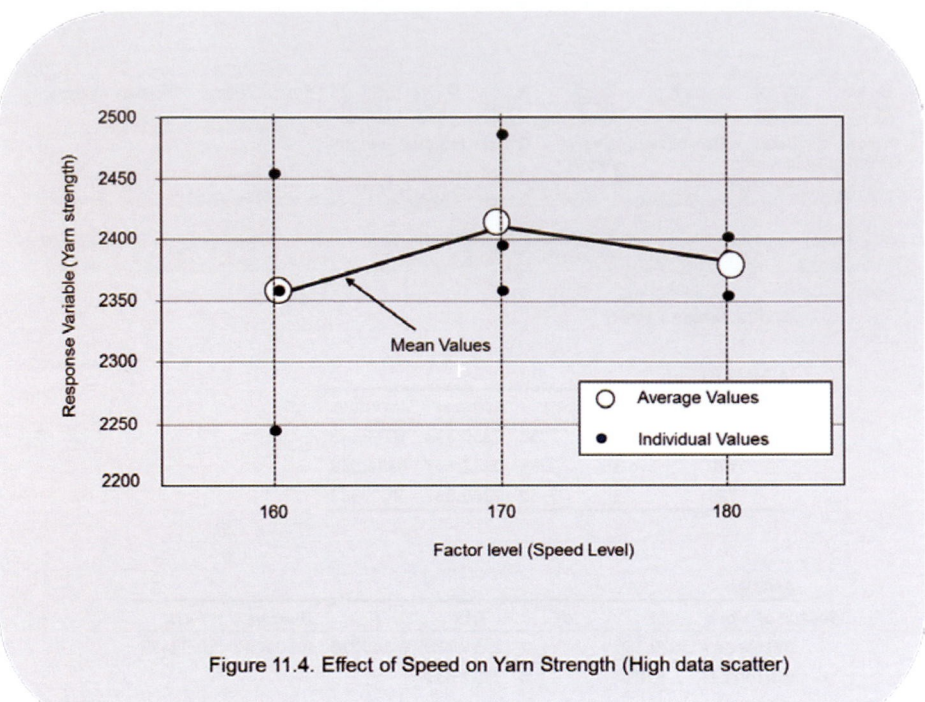

Figure 11.4. Effect of Speed on Yarn Strength (High data scatter)

Example 11.5: Suppose some errors were found in the data of Example 11.4 (Table 11.12) and the experiment was repeated. Suppose the new data was as shown in Table 11.13. Perform ANOVA for this new set of data using Excel® data analysis. Compare the results in this example with those of Example 11.4.

Table 11.13 Excel Data Arrangement for ANOVA

Speed (*m/min*)	y_1	y_2	y_3
160	2453	2458	2455
170	2588	2591	2589
180	2387	2399	2381

Solution:

The data in Table 11.13 shows a great deal of consistency in the values of the response variable (yarn strength) within each treatment (speed level). The reader can easily see that by comparing these values with those of Table 11.12, or comparing Figure 11.4 with Figure 11.5, which displays the new results.

Using the same procedure discussed above, the Excel®-Data Analysis yields the output of Table 11.14.

654

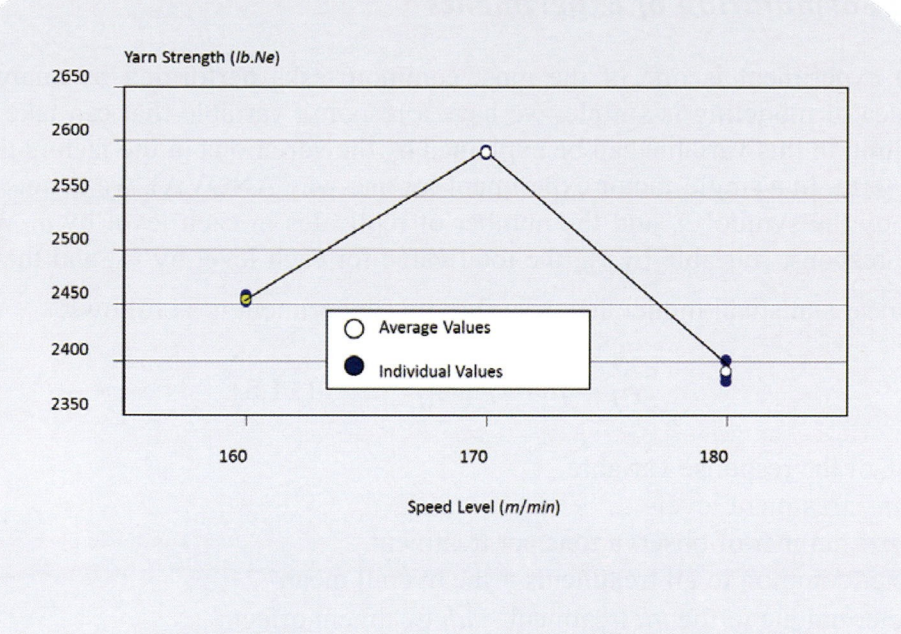

Figure 11.5. Effect of Speed on Yarn Strength (low data scatter)

Table 11.14 Excel® Output for Example 11.5
ANOVA: Single Factor

Anova: Single Factor ($\alpha = 1\%$)						
SUMMARY						
Groups	*Count*	*Sum*	*Average*	*Variance*		
160	3	7366	2455.333	6.333333		
170	3	7768	2589.333	2.333333		
180	3	7167	2389	84		
ANOVA						
Source of Variation	*SS*	*Df*	*MS*	*F*	*P-value*	*F crit*
Between Groups	62489.56	2	31244.78	1011.522	2.59E-08	10.925
Within Groups	185.3333	6	30.88889			
Total	62674.89	8				

As can be seen in Table 11.14, there is a dramatic change in this output in comparison with that obtained in the previous example. Here you see a value of *MS* for treatments (between treatment variability) of 31244.78, which is overwhelmingly higher than the value of MSE (or the mean square error) of 30.889. This indicates a significant effect of the treatment or the speed on yarn strength enhanced by a small within-treatment or error variability. The *F*-statistic of 1011.522 is much higher than the critical $F_{0.01,2,6}$ value of 10.925, and the *p* value is approximately zero. This means that we must reject the null hypothesis, and conclude that the treatment has a significant effect on the response variable. On the basis of the ANOVA output, we can now conclude that the speed level 170 m/min yields the maximum value of yarn strength.

11.5 Model Formulation of Experiments

Modeling an experiment is one of the most common tasks performed by analysts in various fields. The idea of modeling is simple; we have a response variable that can take many random values. Variation in this variable can be explained by the variations in the factors that influence it plus an error term. In a single-factor experiment (or one-way ANOVA), we denote the number of factor levels by the symbol a, and the number of replicates in each level by n. We also denote values of the response variable by y_{ij}, the total value for each level by $y_{i.}$, and the average value by $\bar{y}_i$. The linear statistical model that describes this experiment is as follows:

$$y_{ij} = \mu + \tau_i + \epsilon_{ij} \qquad (11.5)$$

where
y_{ij} = the value of the response variable
$i = 1, 2, \ldots, a$ = treatment levels
$j = 1, 2, \ldots, n$ = number of observations per treatment
μ = a parameter common to all treatments = the overall mean
τ_i = a parameter unique to the *ith* treatment = *ith* treatment effect
ε_{ij} = a random error component

The above model summarizes the outcome of an experiment. If the treatment has no effect ($\tau_i = 0$), and no error is encountered ($\varepsilon_{ij} = 0$), then the observation y_{ij} will perfectly estimate the overall mean μ. This model is commonly called a one-way ANOVA model because only one factor is considered. The use of this model requires that the experiment be performed in random order (a completely randomized design) as discussed in examples 11.2 and 11.4.

When the treatments are selected specifically by the experimenter with the intention to investigate only the factor levels representing these treatments, the model is called a '*fixed effects model.*' For example, the selection of 3 levels of speed described in Examples 11.4 and 11.5 to evaluate yarn strength represents a case of fixed effects model. In this case, we test the hypotheses about the treatment means (the average yarn strength at each speed level). Conclusions drawn from fixed effects model only apply to the specific factor levels considered in the experiment. In other words, no conclusion can be drawn about yarn strength at a level of speed not specified in the experiment.

In theory, the following form represents the *fixed-effects model*:

$$y_{ij} = \mu + \varphi_i + \epsilon_{ij} \qquad (11.6)$$

where y_{ij} = the value of the response variable; $i = 1, 2, \ldots, a$ = treatment levels; $j = 1, 2, \ldots, n$ = number of observations/treatment; μ = a parameter common to all treatments = the overall mean; ϕ_i = a parameter unique to the *ith* treatment = *ith* treatment effect; ε_{ij} = a random error component $\sim N(0, \sigma^2)$; and $\mu + \phi_i = \mu_i$

In words, the fixed-effects model indicates that any observed value, y_{ij}, in the experiment is the sum of three parts: (i) an overall mean μ, (ii) a treatment or class deviation, ϕ_i, and (iii) a random element, ε_{ij}, from a normally distributed population with mean 0 and variance σ^2. The effects of the treatments or classes, measured by the parameter ϕ_i, are regarded as fixed but unknown quantities to be estimated. The random element, ε_{ij}, in the model represents the combined contribution of other influences that are not considered in the model.

When the treatments represent a random sample from a large population of treatments, the model is called a '***random-effects model.***' For example, suppose that the quality characteristic is the absorption capacity of soil material. Since we suspect variations within and between soil particles, we may select at random a sample of soil out of a large amount. In this case, we can extend our conclusion to all treatments in the population whether they were explicitly considered in the analysis or not. In this case, ϕ_i are random variables and we test hypotheses about their variability.

In theory, the following form represents the ***random-effects model***:

$$y_{ij} = \mu + A_i + \epsilon_{ij} \qquad (11.7)$$

where
y_{ij} = the value of the response variable
$i = 1, 2, \ldots, a$ = treatment levels
$j = 1, 2, \ldots, n$ = number of observations/treatment
μ = a parameter common to all treatments = the overall mean
A_i = a parameter unique to the *ith* treatment = *ith* treatment effect of $N(0, \sigma_A^2)$
ε_{ij} = a random error component of $N(0, \sigma^2)$

In words, the random-effects model indicates that any observed value, y_{ij}, in the experiment is the sum of three parts: (i) an overall mean μ, (ii) a random variable representing treatment or class deviation, A_i, that is the difference between the treatment mean value and the population mean ($A_i = \mu_i - \mu$), and (iii) a random element, ε_{ij}, from a normally distributed population with mean 0 and variance σ^2. The effects of the treatments or classes, measured by the parameter A_i, are regarded as random and unknown quantities to be estimated. The random element, ε_{ij}, in the model represents the combined contribution of other influences that are not considered in the model. The following example represents a random-effects model.

Example 11.6: Consider an experiment in which the carbon content in steel is investigated. Five different batches are selected at random from a large population of steel. These batches are labeled: batch *I*, batch *II*, batch *III*, batch *IV*, and batch *V*. For each steel batch, 10 carbon content tests were made. The results of these tests are shown in Table 11.15. Suppose that all tests were performed by the same analyst and in a randomized fashion as discussed earlier. The purpose of this experiment can be stated in two different ways:

- *Do all steel batches exhibit the same carbon content?*
- *Which batch has the least carbon content, and which has the highest?*

Table 11.15 Carbon content in 5 steel batches

Batch I	Batch II	Batch III	Batch IV	Batch V
0.30	0.35	0.37	0.31	0.39
0.31	0.35	0.37	0.31	0.39
0.32	0.33	0.33	0.31	0.39
0.30	0.31	0.36	0.30	0.42
0.30	0.33	0.35	0.30	0.42
0.31	0.34	0.35	0.30	0.43
0.32	0.35	0.35	0.30	0.41
0.31	0.33	0.37	0.30	0.44
0.30	0.32	0.38	0.30	0.41
0.30	0.35	0.38	0.30	0.43

Using Excel® data analysis, we can perform ANOVA using the procedures shown below.

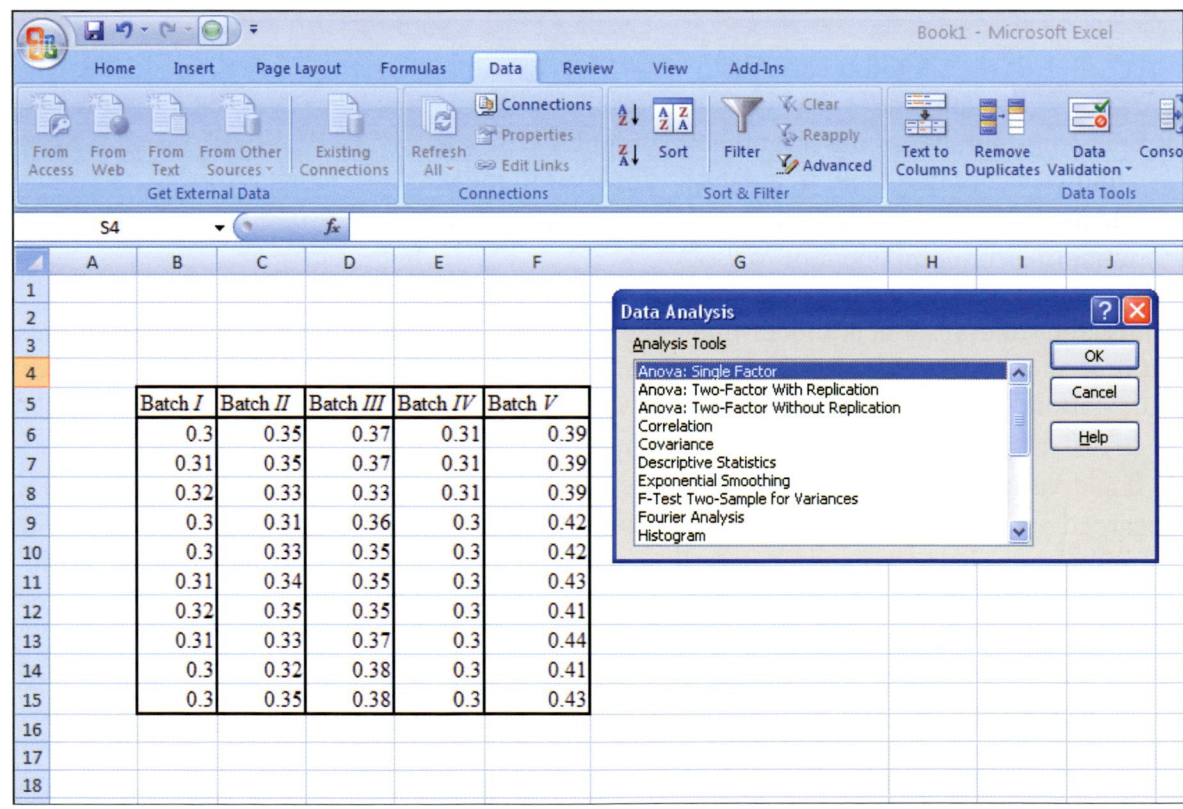

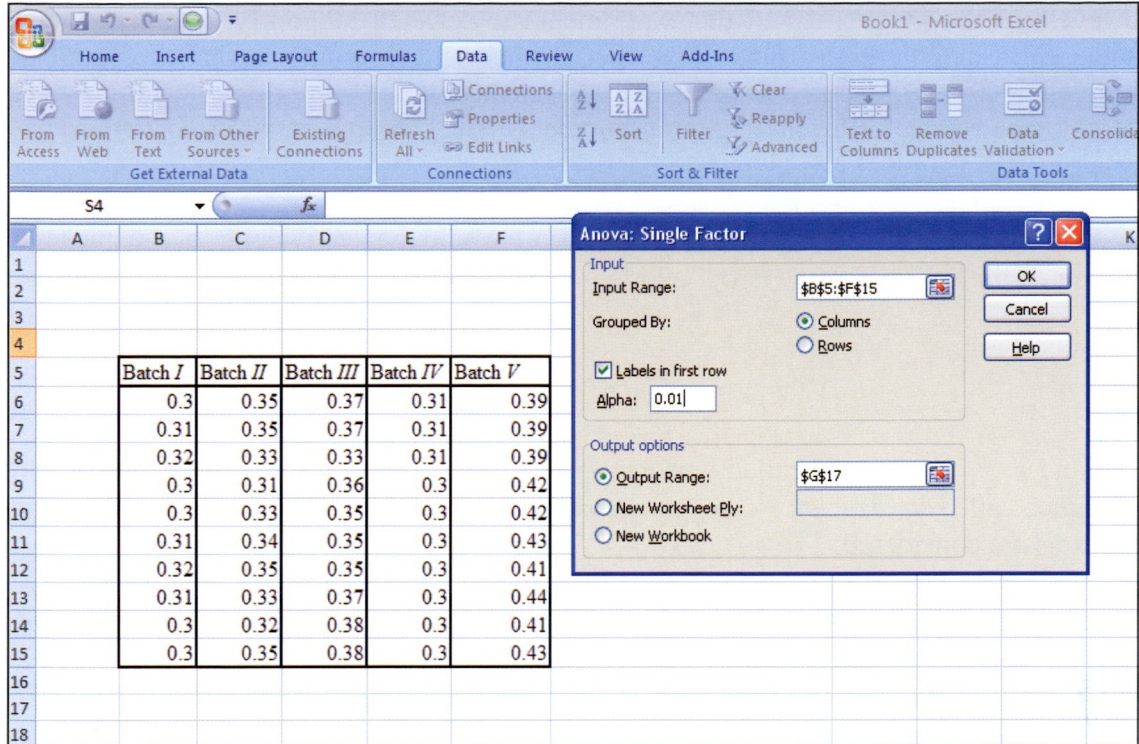

The output of the ANOVA is as shown in Table 11.16. This output indicates that treatments do have effects on the carbon content of steel. In other words, different batches may have different carbon contents. This is immediately revealed by the high value of $MS_{treatments}$ (or between-group MS) compared to that of MSE. Also note the high F-value. This means that we reject the null hypothesis that all treatments are the same or all steel batches are alike. More elaboration on this example is given below.

Table 11.16 ANOVA Output of steel content experiment

ANOVA: Single Factor						
SUMMARY						
Groups	*Count*	*Sum*	*Average*	*Variance*		
Batch I	10	3.07	0.307	6.78E-05		
Batch II	10	3.36	0.336	0.000204		
Batch III	10	3.61	0.361	0.000254		
Batch IV	10	3.03	0.303	2.33E-05		
Batch V	10	4.13	0.413	0.000334		
ANOVA						
Source of Variation	*SS*	*df*	*MS*	*F*	*P-value*	*F crit*
Between Groups	0.08164	4	0.02041	115.3832	4.74E-23	3.767427
Within Groups	0.00796	45	0.000177			
Total	0.0896	49				

Since levels of the factor used in the experiment are selected randomly, inferences are made about the entire population of factor levels. It is important to point out that the population of factor levels is usually assumed to be infinite. In practice, this assumption is valid provided that the total number of factor levels (e.g. total number of steel components to select from) is large. The random effects model was given by equation 11.7.

If the treatment had no effect the y_{ij} observation would be equivalent to the mean of the population. If the variance of A_i is σ_A^2 and is independent of ε_{ij}, the variance of any observation y_{ij} is

$$V(y_{ij}) = \sigma_A^2 + \sigma^2 \qquad (11.8)$$

The variances σ_A^2 and σ^2 are called *variance components*. Therefore, the random effects model is sometimes called *the variance components model*. In order to make inferences, the following assumptions are considered:

(i) The error terms ε_{ij} are assumed to follow a normal distribution with mean = 0, and variance σ^2.
(ii) The terms A_i follow a normal distribution with mean = 0 and variance σ_A^2.
(ii) A_i and ε_{ij} are independent.

As we did with the fixed effects model, the total sum of squares can be partitioned into treatment sum of squares and error sum of squares:

$$SS_T = SS_{treatment} + SS_E$$

Recall that $SS_{treatment}$ represents the between treatment (between steel batches) variation, and SS_E represents the within treatment variation. These sums of squares are obtained from the analysis of variance (Table 11.16).

Since no specific treatments have been made on the steel, instead each steel batch is considered as a treatment as it stands on its own with the hope that all batches are alike, the usual test of hypothesis of treatment effects becomes meaningless. Instead, we are interested in evaluating the variability resulting from using different steel batches. The suitable test of hypothesis in this case is:

$$H_o : \sigma_A^2 = 0$$

$$H_1 : \sigma_A^2 > 0$$

If the null hypothesis H_o is accepted, we conclude that all treatments are identical (or all steel batches have the same carbon content) and if it is rejected we conclude that variability exists between batches. The term SS_E/σ^2 follows a Chi-square distribution with degree of freedom, $df = N-a$. The term $SS_{treatments}/\sigma^2$ follows a Chi-square with degree of freedom, $df = a-1$. If the assumption that A_i and ε_{ij} are independent is valid, we can use the F-statistic to test the null hypothesis $\sigma^2_A = 0$. Thus,

$$F_o = \frac{\dfrac{S_{treatment}}{a - 1}}{\dfrac{SS_E}{N - a}} = \frac{MS_{treatment}}{MSE}$$

is distributed as F with a-1 and N-a degrees of freedom. This F value is 115.383 as shown in Table 11.16. Since this value is much greater than the $F_{critical}$ of 3.767, we reject H_o. Thus, we conclude that some of the steel batches differ significantly.

Working Problem 11.7:

Consider an experiment in which five groups of students from a large population of students were selected to take a standard test (with a maximum score of 500). Ten students were randomly picked for each group. The results of these tests are shown in the Table below. Suppose that all tests were performed by the same examiner and in a randomized fashion. The purpose of this experiment can be stated in two different ways:

Do all students groups exhibit the same scores?
Which group has the least test scores, and which has the highest?

Address the above questions using ANOVA. Use a = 0.01.

Test 1	Test 2	Test 3	Test 4	Test 5
300	350	370	310	390
310	350	370	310	390
320	330	330	310	390
300	310	360	300	420
300	330	350	300	420
310	340	350	300	430
320	350	350	300	410
310	330	370	300	440
300	320	380	300	410
300	350	380	300	430

Answer:

Anova: Single Factor

SUMMARY

Groups	Count	Sum	Average	Variance
Test 1	10	3070	307	67.778
Test 2	10	3360	336	204.444
Test 3	10	3610	361	254.444
Test 4	10	3030	303	23.333
Test 5	10	4130	413	334.444

ANOVA

Source of Variation	SS	df	MS	F	P-value	F crit
Between Groups	81640	4	20410	115.383	4.74E-23	3.767
Within Groups	7960	45	176.889			
Total	89600	49				

11.6 Mean Multiple Comparisons

In reference to the above example, the question now is which steel batch has the highest and which has the lowest carbon content. For this example, this question can be answered through comparison of the mean values of carbon content shown in Table 11.16. These values indicate that steel batch V has the highest carbon content, and batch IV has the lowest. Figure 11.6 shows little scatter within each steel batch, making the comparison more valid.

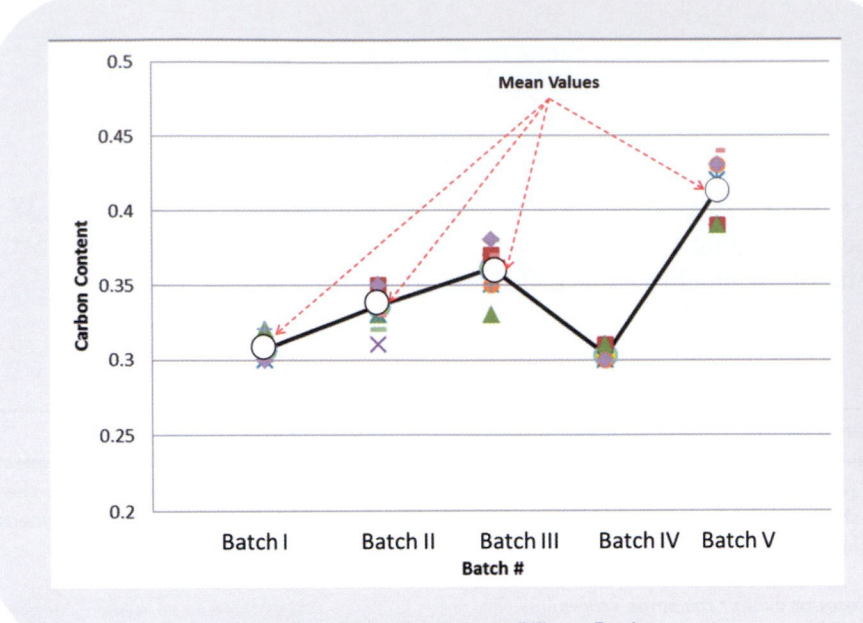

Figure 11.6. Comparison between Different Batches

The above comparison will be more difficult, perhaps invalid, if each treatment exhibits a high level of variability or scatter about the mean value. In addition, the simple comparison does not reveal whether other steel batches differ greatly in carbon content from the selected highest or lowest batches. The answer to this question requires statistical analysis for mean comparison. We can perform multiple comparisons of different treatment means as demonstrated below.

11.7 Multiple Comparisons Methods

When the conclusion of an ANOVA is to conclude that at least one treatment mean is different from the others, it is often important to compare different means to determine which means differ significantly. The procedures for making these comparisons are called multiple comparison methods. One of the multiple comparison methods is the so-called 'least significance difference, LSD, method'

In this method, we use the following t-value:

$$t_o = \frac{\bar{y}_{i.} - \bar{y}_{j.}}{\sqrt{MSE\left(\frac{1}{n_i} + \frac{1}{n_j}\right)}} \qquad (11.9)$$

Assuming a two-sided alternative, the pair of means μ_i and μ_j are significantly different if the following condition is satisfied:

$$\left|\bar{y}_{i.} - \bar{y}_{j.}\right| > t_{\frac{\alpha}{2}, N-a}\sqrt{MSE\left(\frac{1}{n_i} + \frac{1}{n_j}\right)} \qquad (11.10)$$

662

The least significant difference is given by:

$$LSD = t_{\frac{\alpha}{2},N-a}\sqrt{MSE\left(\frac{1}{n_i}+\frac{1}{n_j}\right)} \qquad (11.11)$$

When all a treatments have the same number of observations (n), the design is called a *balanced design*. In this case, the least significant difference LSD is given by:

$$LSD = t_{\frac{\alpha}{2},N-a}\sqrt{\frac{2MSE}{n}} \qquad (11.12)$$

Example 11.7: Using the LSD compare the means of carbon content of the five steel batches of

Solution:

In order to solve this problem, the first step is to perform the ANOVA. From that we need the *MSE* value so that we can calculate the *LSD*. As shown in Table 11.16, the Mean Square Error is 0.000177. We also need to determine the value $t_{\alpha/2,\ N-a,}$ or $t_{0.005,45}$. From the *t*-Table (Appendix 8.A, Chapter 8), the t-value is about 2.7. Thus,

$$LSD = t_{\frac{\alpha}{2},N-a}\sqrt{\frac{2MSE}{n}} = 2.7\sqrt{\frac{2(0.000177)}{10}} = 0.0160644$$

For any pair of treatment means, if their absolute difference is greater than 0.0160644 (*LSD*), we conclude that this difference is significant. Absolute values of mean differences are shown in Table 11.17. It follows that only batch *I*, and batch *IV* exhibit no significant difference. This is also illustrated in Figure 11.6.

Table 11.17 Difference in treatment means

Compared Batches	Absolute difference	Comparison with LSD	Decision
Y_I-Y_{II}	0.029	>LSD	Significant
Y_I-Y_{III}	0.054	>LSD	Significant
Y_I-Y_{IV}	0.004	<LSD	Insignificant
Y_I-Y_V	0.106	>LSD	Significant
Y_{II}-Y_{III}	0.025	>LSD	Significant
Y_{II}-Y_{IV}	0.033	>LSD	Significant
Y_{II}-Y_V	0.077	>LSD	Significant
Y_{III}-Y_{IV}	0.058	>LSD	Significant
Y_{III}-Y_V	0.052	>LSD	Significant
Y_{IV}-Y_V	0.11	>LSD	Significant

Two problems may be encountered with the use of the LSD method:

- As the number of factor levels or treatments, *a*, increases, the Type *I* error of the experiment becomes large.
- Occasionally, the overall *F*-statistic in the analysis of variance is significant but the LSD method fails to find any significant pairwise differences. This situation is a result of the fact that the *F*-test simultaneously considers all possible comparisons between the treatment means, not just pair wise comparisons.

There are other statistical techniques such as the Scheffé's test, Tukey's w procedure, S-N-K test, and Duncan's test. Theoretical discussion of these techniques is outside the scope of this book. However, the student can find the details of these different tests in numerous statistics books.

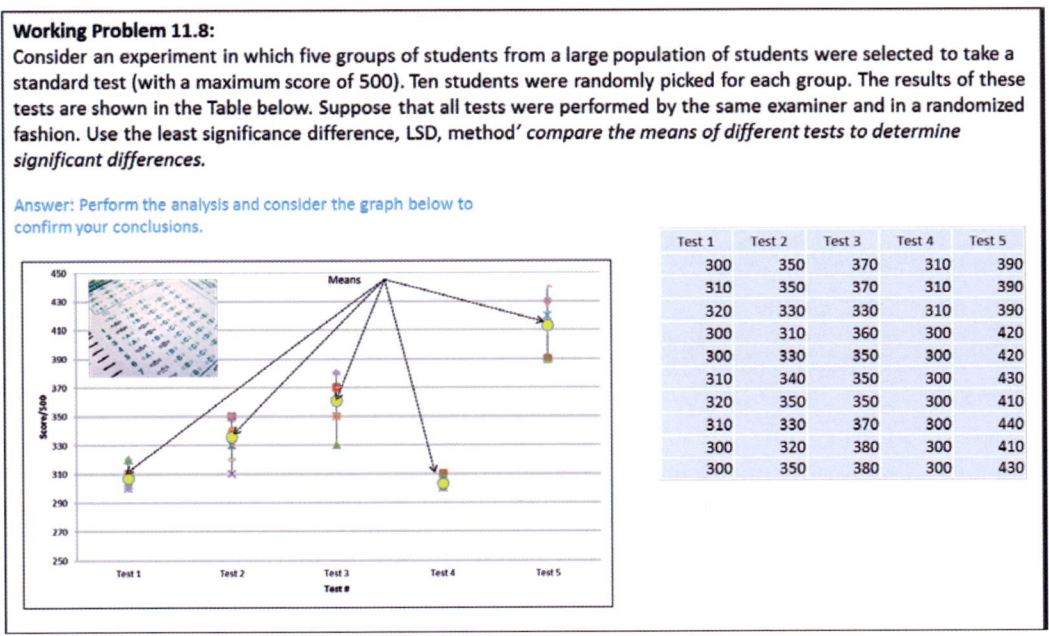

Working Problem 11.8:
Consider an experiment in which five groups of students from a large population of students were selected to take a standard test (with a maximum score of 500). Ten students were randomly picked for each group. The results of these tests are shown in the Table below. Suppose that all tests were performed by the same examiner and in a randomized fashion. Use the least significance difference, LSD, method' *compare the means of different tests to determine significant differences.*

Answer: Perform the analysis and consider the graph below to confirm your conclusions.

Test 1	Test 2	Test 3	Test 4	Test 5
300	350	370	310	390
310	350	370	310	390
320	330	330	310	390
300	310	360	300	420
300	330	350	300	420
310	340	350	300	430
320	350	350	300	410
310	330	370	300	440
300	320	380	300	410
300	350	380	300	430

11.8 Two-Way Analysis of Variance

When two factors are considered in an experiment, the concepts discussed above are extended to examine the significances of the effects of these factors' levels. In this case, the analysis tool is useful when data can be classified along two different dimensions. For example, in the experiment of the household monthly expenses, we can consider two factors: education expenses and food expenses. Using the analysis of variance, we can test:

- Whether high and low food expenses can influence the household monthly expenses significantly
- Whether high and low education expenses can influence the household monthly expenses significantly

The experiment in two-way analysis of variance should be made using randomized block design. This type of design was discussed in Chapter 7.

In this case, the general ANOVA model is:

$$SS_{total} = SS_{Food\ expenses} + SS_{education\ expenses} + SS_{Error}$$

If three levels are selected for each factor, the six samples representing these levels should be drawn from the same population. The null and alternative hypotheses used in this case are:

$$H_o: \tau_{food} = \tau_{education}$$
$$H_1: \tau_i \neq 0\ for\ at\ least\ one\ i$$

Example 11.8: In the previous example of household expenses, suppose the social organization conducting the study seeks households that have more or less the same housing expenses, and the same medical expenses. This makes food expenses and education expenses the two factors of interest that we can study to determine their influences on the household total monthly expenses. Using two levels of food expenses and three levels of education expenses (2x3 factorial) and using one replicate, the results of household monthly expenses are as shown in Table 11.8. The key question in this problem is whether food and education expenses have significant effects on the total expenses of a household.

Table 11.18 Total expenses at all factor levels- Two-way treatments data

		Education		
	Level	low	Medium	High
	Low	4000	4200	4900
Food	High	4700	5150	5588

Solution

In carrying out the analysis of variance, it will be useful to construct a table summarizing the experiment associated with the analysis. This experiment is summarized in Table 11.19.

Table 11.19 Summary of the single-factor ANOVA

Title	Effect of food and education expenses on the total household monthly expenses
Objective	To determine whether differences in food expenses and education expenses will lead to differences in the total household monthly expenses
Response variable	Household monthly expenses ($/month)
Factor	Two-factor experiment (food and education expenses). Other factors such as housing and medical expenses are kept constant
Levels (a)	3 levels for education expenses and two levels for food expenses.
Replicates (n)	No replicates
Total Number of Experimental Runs	$N = 2 \times 3 = 6$
Type of Experiment	Random trials

The question of this experiment requires two-way ANOVA analysis, which can be performed using Excel® data analysis as will be shown shortly. Before proceeding with this analysis, we may use descriptive statistics and see what information it may reveal. Using the statistics in Table 11.20, the following points can be made:

- With regard to the food expenses factor, we can see that at the higher level of food expenses, the total monthly household expenses are higher (from $4366. 7 to $5146 per month) and this is to be expected. However, the variances at the two levels of food expenses are quite different (low = 223333.3, and high = 197148). This raises doubt on whether indeed higher food expenses can always lead to higher total household expenses.
- With regard to the education expenses factor, we can see that as education expenses increases, the total household monthly expenses also increase. However, the variance components associated with the three levels of education expenses are quite different (low = 245000, medium = 451250, and high = 236672).

Now, let us see how the two-way analysis of variance will resolve these issues.

Table 11.20 Descriptive statistics of the two-way data

			Education					
	Level	Low	Medium	High	**Total**	**Mean**	**Std. dev.**	**Variance**
	Low	4000	4200	4900	**13100**	**4366.667**	**472.5816**	**223333.3**
Food	High	4700	5150	5588	**15438**	**5146**	**444.0135**	**197148**
	Total	**8700**	**9350**	**10488**				
	Mean	**4350**	**4675**	**5244**				
	Std. dev.	**494.9747**	**671.7514**	**486.4895**				
	variance	**245000**	**451250**	**236672**				

In order to perform a Two-Way ANOVA using Excel® Data Analysis we follow the steps shown in the figures below. Please note that we select ANOVA: Two-Factor without replication since we do not have any replicates in this experiment. Also note the shaded area representing the input range for this type of analysis, which includes the levels and the response variable data. These steps yield the ANOVA-Two-Way results in Table 11.21.

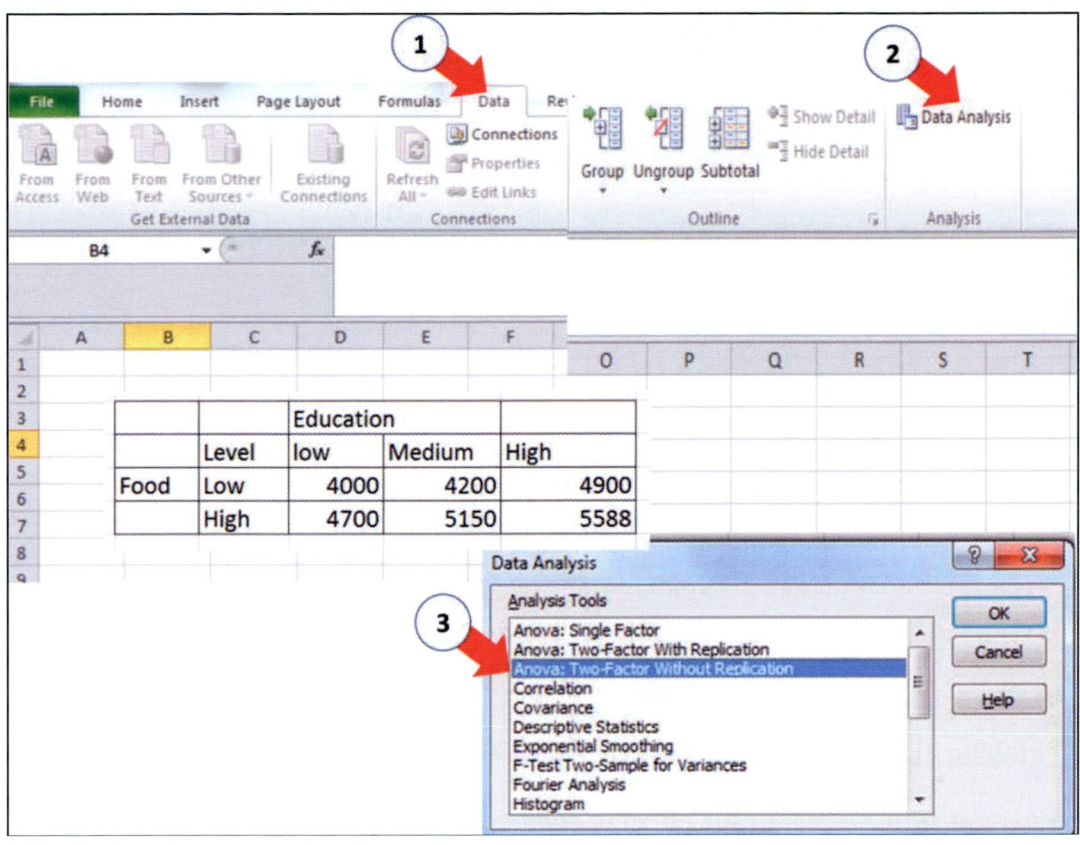

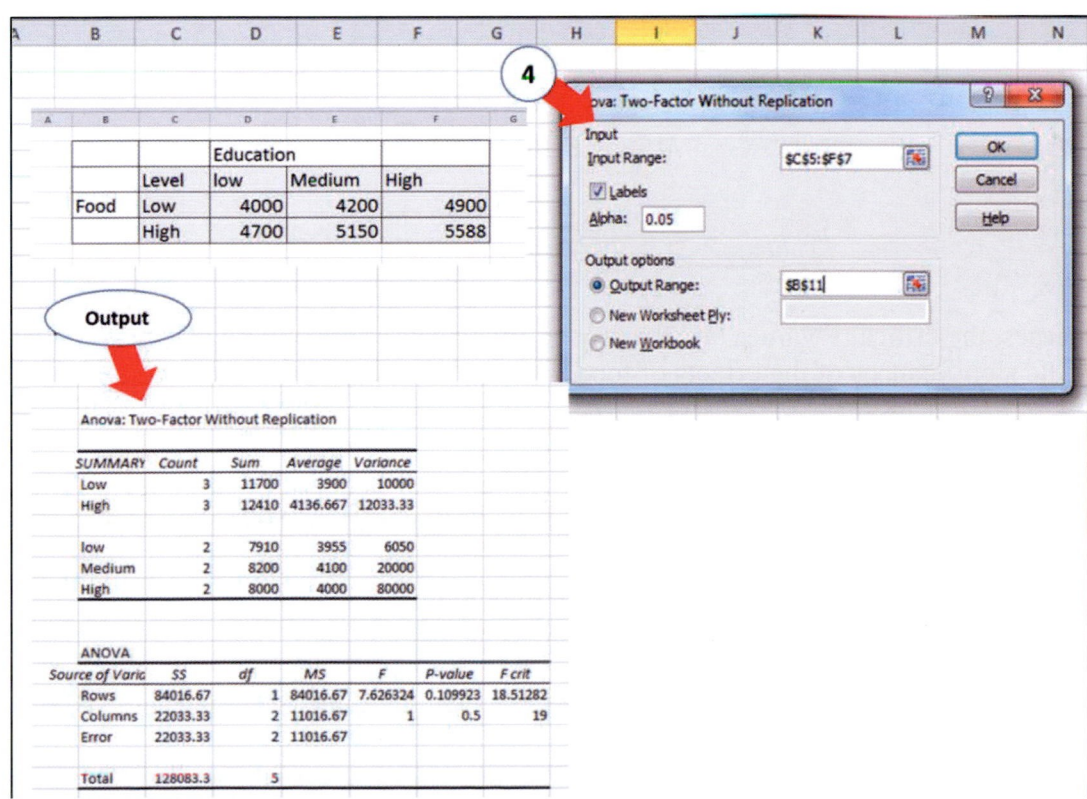

Table 11.21 Two-Way ANOVA Table

ANOVA: Two-Factor Without Replication						
SUMMARY	Count	Sum	Average	Variance		
Food expenses						
Low	3	13100	4366.666	223333.33		
High	3	15438	5146	197148		
Education expenses						
Low	2	8700	4350	245000		
Medium	2	9350	4675	451250		
High	2	10488	5244	236672		
ANOVA						
Source of Variation	SS	df	MS	F	P-value	F crit
Rows	911040.66	1	911040.666	83.2710377	0.0118	18.513
Columns	819081.33	2	409540.666	37.4328803	0.0260	19
Error	21881.333	2	10940.666			
Total	1752003.3	5				

Important points to interpret the two-way ANOVA are as follows:

- The term 'Rows' refer to the effect of food expenses and the term 'Columns' refers to the effect of education expenses.
- The F-values are as defined earlier but are calculated for each factor:

$$F_{Row} = \frac{MS_{Row}}{MSE} = \frac{911040.666}{10940.666} = 83.271$$

$$F_{Column} = \frac{MS_{Column}}{MSE} = \frac{409540.666}{10940.666} = 37.432$$

In both cases, the critical F values and the probability values corresponding to the F-statistic support the significances of the effects of food and education expenses on the household monthly expenses.

Example 11.9: The system under study is automobile performance. The response variable of concern is fuel efficiency (miles/gallon). Suppose the following two factors were considered:

- *Vehicle idling* with two levels: short and long idling
- *Driving speed* with three levels: 50 miles/hr, 60 miles/hr, and 70 miles/hr.

Each factor level was associated with replicates as shown in Table 11.22, and same type and model of automobiles was used.

Table 11.22 Data of miles per gallon at different driving speed and different idling period

		Driving Speed		
		Low	Medium	High
Vehicle idling	Short	32	28	26
	Short	31	29	25
	Short	30	26	24
	Long	30	29	26
	Long	29	27	25
	Long	29	28	25

Table 11.23 ANOVA Table for Fuel Efficiency

ANOVA: Two-Factor With Replication						
SUMMARY	Low	Medium	High	Total		
Short						
Count	3	3	3	9		
Sum	93	83	75	251		
Average	31	27.667	25.000	27.889		
Variance	1	2.333	1.000	7.861		
Long						
Count	3	3	3	9		
Sum	88	84	76	248		
Average	29.33333	28	25.333	27.556		
Variance	0.333333	1	0.333	3.528		
Total						
Count	6	6	6			
Sum	181	167	151			
Average	30.167	27.833	25.167			
Variance	1.367	1.367	0.567			
ANOVA						
Source of Variation	*SS*	*df*	*MS*	*F*	*P-value*	*F crit*
Sample	0.5	1	0.5	0.5	0.493	4.747
Columns	75.111	2	37.556	37.556	6.83E-06	3.885
Interaction	4	2	2	2	0.178	3.885
Within	12	12	1			
Total	91.611	17				

Important points to interpret the two-way ANOVA are as follows:

- The term '*Sample*' refers to the effect of idling time samples and the term '*Columns*' refers to the effect of driving speed.
- The F-values are as defined earlier but are calculated for each factor:

$$F_{Sample=Vehicle\ idling} = \frac{MS_{Sample}}{MSE} = \frac{0.5}{1} = 0.5$$

$$F_{Column=driving\ speed} = \frac{MS_{Column}}{MSE} = \frac{37.556}{1} = 37.556$$

$$F_{Sample \times Column=interaction} = \frac{MS_{interaction}}{MSE} = \frac{2}{1} = 2.0$$

By comparison with the critical F values and by examining the probability values, the factor that seems to be significantly influencing the fuel efficiency is the column factor or the driving speed.

Working Problem 11.9: In a weight loss program, two approaches were taken simultaneously: diet program, and exercise program. The results of weight loss (lb) at the different levels of these two factors are as shown below. Perform ANOVA and make conclusions about the effects of each factor on weight loss.

			Food Package	
	Level	Light diet	Medium diet	Strict diet
Excerise Level	Low	28	26	22
	High	16	14	13

Answer: The ANOVA table is shown below. Interpret the results and make conclusions.

Anova: Two-Factor Without Replication

SUMMARY	Count	Sum	Average	Variance
Low	3	76	25.333	9.333
High	3	43	14.333	2.333
Light diet	2	44	22	72
Medium diet	2	40	20	72
Srict diet	2	35	17.5	40.5

ANOVA

Source of Variation	SS	df	MS	F	P-value	F crit
Rows	181.5	1	181.5	121	0.0082	18.5128
Columns	20.333	2	10.1667	6.7778	0.1286	19
Error	3	2	1.5			
Total	204.833	5				

Working Problem 11.10: In a weight loss program, two approaches were taken simultaneously: diet program, and exercise program. The results of weight loss (lb) at the different levels and for different replicates of these two factors are as shown below. Perform ANOVA and make conclusions about the effects of each factor on weight loss.

	Food Package		
Level	Light diet	Medium diet	Strict diet
Low	28	26	22
Low	27	25	24
Low	29	26	23
Low	26	24	23
High	20	18	17
High	19	16	15
High	21	14	14
High	16	14	13

Excerise Level

Answer: The ANOVA table is shown below.
Interpret the results and make conclusions.

ANOVA: Two-Factor With Replication

SUMMARY	Light diet	Medium diet	Srict diet	Total
Low				
Count	4	4	4	12
Sum	110	101	92	303
Average	27.5	25.25	23	25.25
Variance	1.6667	0.9167	0.6667	4.5682
High				
Count	4	4	4	12
Sum	76	62	59	197
Average	19	15.5	14.75	16.41667
Variance	4.6667	3.6667	2.9167	6.8106
Total				
Count	8	8	8	
Sum	186	163	151	
Average	23.25	20.375	18.875	
Variance	23.35714	29.125	20.98214	

ANOVA

Source of Variation	SS	df	MS	F	P-value	F crit
Sample	468.1667	1	468.17	193.72	4.48E-11	4.41
Columns	79.0833	2	39.54	16.36	8.92E-05	3.55
Interaction	2.5833	2	1.29	0.53	0.59	3.55
Within	43.5000	18	2.417			
Total	593.3333	23				

11.9 Review Exercises

P11.1: In an experiment of one factor and three levels, how many experimental runs would you need if there are 3 replicated at each level?
 Answer: 3×3 = 9

P11.2: In an experiment of two factors and three levels each, how many experimental runs would you need if there are 3 replicated at each level?

P11.3: In an experiment of three factors and three levels each, how many experimental runs would you need if there are 3 replicated at each level?
Answer: 3×3×3 = 27

P11.4: In comparing two means, what is the test statistic to use?

P11.5: In comparing multiple means, what is the key test statistic to use?
Answer: LSD

P11.6: In a single-factor experiment, what is the practical meaning of within-treatment variation? How it is determined in ANOVA?

P11.7: In a single-factor experiment, what is the practical meaning of between-treatment variation? How it is determined in ANOVA?
Answer: To determine the significance of the effect(s) of factor(s) on the response variable. It is determined by the $SS_{treatment}$ and the F-statistic.

P11.8: In a single-factor experiment, what is the practical meaning of total variation? How it is determined in ANOVA?

P11.9: Suppose we want to compare the taste preferences of consumers for three different orange juice brands (JA, JB, and JC). If 9 consumers were selected randomly, and asked to evaluate the taste using a 5-point scale (1 to 5), summarize the different components of this experiment using a single-factor ANOVA.
Answer: complete

Title	Effect of orange juice type on human taste
Objective	To determine whether differences in juice brands will lead to differences in people favorable taste
Response variable	Juice taste (5-point scale, 1 = least favorable, and 5 = most favorable
Factor	Single-factor experiment (juice brand). Other factors such as previous experience with the juice brand, gender (male or female), age (old or young) are maintained constant.
Levels (a)	3 orange juice brands (JA, JB, and JC)
Replicates (n)	Three groups of people
Total Number of Experimental Runs	$N = a \times n = 3 \times 9 = 27$
Type of Experiment	Random trials

P11.10: Suppose we want to compare the taste preferences of consumers for three different orange juice brands (JA, JB, and JC). If 9 consumers were selected randomly, and asked to evaluate the taste using a 5-point scale (1 to 5), set up a completely randomized design for this purpose (assign the treatments to the experimental units for this design).

P11.11: Suppose we want to compare the taste preferences of consumers for three different orange juice brands (JA, JB, and JC). If 9 consumers were selected randomly, and asked to evaluate the taste using a 5-point scale (1 to 5), the results of this experiment are shown below. Perform analysis of variance at $\alpha = 0.05$ to address the following questions:

(a) Does the brand of orange juice make a difference in people taste?
(b) Which juice brand was most favorable and which was least favorable
(c) Was the problem conducted properly, or it can be improved? Explain.

Results of juice taste experiment (1-5 scale)

Orange Juice group	Experimental Run number		
JA	2	4	3
JB	1	1	4
JC	2	3	2

Answer: Interpret the ANOVA Table

ANOVA						
Source of Variation	SS	df	MS	F	P-value	F crit
Between Groups	1.556	2	0.778	0.538	0.609	5.143
Within Groups	8.667	6	1.444			
Total	10.222	8				

P11.12: In the above problem, another experiment revealed the following results. Perform analysis of variance at $\alpha = 0.05$ to address the following questions:

(a) Does the brand of orange juice make a difference in people taste?
(b) Which juice brand was most favorable and which was least favorable
(c) Was the problem conducted properly, or it can be improved? Explain

Results of juice taste experiment (1-5 scale)

Orange Juice group	Experimental Run number		
JA	1	1	2
JB	4	5	5
JC	3	3	2

P11.13: Compare the results of the analysis of variance of the above two problems and explain the reasons of the differences in results.

P11.14: Suppose we want to evaluate the effects of student weekly activities on school study performance. In this regard, the response variable of interest is the student grade-point GPA. Factors that may influence student's GPA include: (1) attendance, (2) number of hours of studying, (3) student's background, (4) social factors, etc. 15 students were randomly selected. Propose the different components of this experiment using a single-factor ANOVA.

P11.15: Suppose we want to evaluate the effects of student weekly activities on school study performance. In this regard, the response variable of interest is the student grade-point GPA. The only factor examined is the number of hours of studying and three levels of this factor were considered (1 hours, 3 hours, and 5 hours/week). 15 students were randomly selected and the results were as shown below. Perform analysis of variance at $\alpha = 0.05$ to address the following question: Does the number of studying hours make a difference in student's GPA?

Results of student's GPA at different levels of studying time

Studying Hour Level (hours)	GPA				
1	2.2	2.1	2	2.6	2.8
3	3.6	4	3.2	4	3.7
5	3	2.8	2.2	3.6	2.2

Answer: Interpret the ANOVA Table

ANOVA						
Source of Variation	*SS*	*df*	*MS*	*F*	*P-value*	*F crit*
Between Groups	4.849	2	2.425	12.628	0.001	3.885
Within Groups	2.304	12	0.192			
Total	7.153	14				

P11.16: Suppose we want to evaluate the effects of student weekly activities on school study performance. In this regard, the response variable of interest is the student grade-point GPA. The only factor examined is the number of hours of studying and three levels of this factor were considered (1 hours, 3 hours, and 5 hours/week). 15 students were randomly selected and the results were as shown below. Perform analysis of variance at $\alpha = 0.01$ to address the following question: Does the number of studying hours make a difference in student's GPA?

P11.17: Compare the results in problems 11.15 and 11.16 and interpret the differences if any.

P11.18: For the following results of students' grades using three different classes, perform the analysis of variance and interpret the results (use $\alpha = 0.01$).

Levels	GPA									
A	80	89	95	66	80	88	78	89	90	92
B	70	77	90	72	87	80	82	99	80	88
C	72	70	86	84	80	88	86	92	93	95

P11.19: For the following results of students' grades using three different classes, perform the analysis of variance and interpret the results (use $\alpha = 0.01$)

Levels	GPA									
A	88	89	95	82	80	88	88	89	90	92
B	70	77	80	74	80	80	78	82	77	77
C	66	70	66	74	79	80	69	77	66	65

Answer: Interpret the ANOVA Table

ANOVA						
Source of Variation	*SS*	*df*	*MS*	*F*	*P-value*	*F crit*
Between Groups	1458.866667	2	729.4333	33.66615	4.63E-08	5.488118
Within Groups	585	27	21.66667			
Total	2043.866667	29				

P11.20: Complete the missing values in the following ANOVA Table. What is the total number of observations examined in this experiment? How many treatment levels examined?

ANOVA						
Source of Variation	SS	df	MS	F	P-value	F crit
Between Groups	4.849333	2	....		0.001116	3.885294
Within Groups	....	12	0.192	....		
Total	7.153333	....				

P11.21: Complete the missing values in the following ANOVA Table. What is the total number of observations examined in this experiment? How many treatment levels examined?

ANOVA						
Source of Variation	SS	df	MS	F	P-value	F crit
Between Groups	....	2	....	....	4.63E-08	5.488118
Within Groups	585	27	21.66667			
Total	2043.866667	....				

P11.22: Complete the missing values in the following ANOVA Table. What is the total number of observations examined in this experiment? How many treatment levels examined?

ANOVA						
Source of Variation	SS	df	MS	F	P-value	F crit
Between Groups	....	2	8.444444	....	0.001187	5.143253
Within Groups	2	6	....			
Total	18.88889	....				

P11.23: The data in the table below represent observations of grades of a Pre-Calculus course offered in three different ways: (1) Face-to-face teaching, (2) On-line (distance) learning, and (3) hybrid or combination of the face-to-face and distance learning. Construct an ANOVA summary table in which you identify the factors, levels, replicates, and response variable.

Students' grades of Pre-Calculus course offered in three different ways

Levels	y1	y2	y3	y4	y5	y6	y7	y8	y9	y10
Face-to-Face Class	80	82	55	65	99	90	80	50	45	90
Distance-Learning Class	77	70	65	90	80	88	60	50	70	75
Combination Class	90	80	75	99	80	88	40	43	55	83

Answer: Do it yourself

P11.24: In the above problem, calculate the total, mean, and variance for each level and interpret the results.

P11.25: Perform ANOVA for the data in problem 11.23 and interpret the results.

Students' grades of Pre-Calculus course offered in three different ways

Levels	y1	y2	y3	y4	y5	y6	y7	y8	y9	y10
Face-to-Face Class	80	82	55	65	99	90	80	50	45	90
Distance-Learning Class	77	70	65	90	80	88	60	50	70	75
Combination Class	90	80	75	99	80	88	40	43	55	83

Answer: Interpret the ANOVA Table

ANOVA						
Source of Variation	SS	df	MS	F_o	P-value	F crit
Between Groups	7.113	2	3.556667	0.01302	0.98707	5.390346
Within Groups	8195	30	273.1667			
Total	8202.113	32				

P11.26: The data in the table below represent observations of property value in three different residential areas in a large city classified as: (1) Area A, (2) Area B, and (3) Area C. Perform ANOVA to determine whether the area a property located in will make a difference in the property value in this city.

Property values in three different areas (in thousands)

Levels	y1	y2	y3	y4	y5	y6	y7	y8	y9	y10
Area A	380	445	500	385	405	445	420	390	400	500
Area B	200	210	230	175	210	280	250	289	120	180
Area C	110	250	180	160	150	88	90	95	110	120

P11.27: The data in the table below represent the amount of weight loss resulting from five weight-loss systems. Using ANOVA, test the hypothesis that all treatments result in the same weight loss. Which system yielded the lowest weight lost and which one yielded the highest weigh loss?

Weight loss values of five different weight-loss systems

Group A	Group B	Group C	Group D	Group E
15	33	10	14	28
19	32	12	12	28
19	35	11	11	25
22	33	10	17	26
20	28	8	15	27
21	24	12	18	22
22	26	11	16	23
25	31	13	12	25
21	33	9	18	25
20	30	7	15	25

Answer: Interpret the ANOVA Table

ANOVA						
Source of Variation	*SS*	*df*	*MS*	*F*	*P-value*	*F crit*
Between Groups	2603.08	4	650.77	99.27	1E-21	3.767427
Within Groups	295	45	6.555556			
Total	2898.08	49				

P11.28: Perform ANOVA at $\alpha = 0.01$ to compare between the following groups of students taking a standard test. The data in the table represent the test scores. Use multiple comparison method to compare the different means and determine which group had the lowest score and which had the highest score.

Group A	Group B	Group C	Group D
450	280	490	300
400	300	488	299
488	360	475	320
390	340	460	299
400	400	444	310
410	380	399	316
440	360	489	325
420	400	472	310
389	320	470	290
390	400	468	333
380	410	478	340
440	360	480	330

P11.29: Perform ANOVA at $\alpha = 0.01$ to compare between the following samples of rod diameters produced by the same machines but at different times and taken from different shipments for inspection purposes. Use multiple comparison method to compare the different means and determine which shipment had the lowest score and which had the highest score.

Shipment 1	Shipment 2	Shipment 3	Shipment 4
1.13	0.70	1.23	0.75
1.00	0.75	1.22	0.75
1.22	0.90	1.19	0.80
0.98	0.85	1.15	0.75
1.00	1.00	1.11	0.78
1.03	0.95	1.00	0.79
1.10	0.90	1.22	0.81
1.05	1.00	1.18	0.78
0.97	0.80	1.18	0.73
0.98	1.00	1.17	0.83
0.95	1.03	1.20	0.85
1.10	0.90	1.20	0.83

Answer: Interpret the ANOVA Table

ANOVA						
Source of Variation	SS	df	MS	F	P-value	F crit
Between Groups	1.006326	3	0.335442	57.78459	2.65E-15	4.261
Within Groups	0.255422	44	0.005805			
Total	1.261748	47				

P11.30: Perform ANOVA to compare between the following samples of students' grades of a course assessment test taken in four consecutive semesters. Perform ANOVA at $\alpha = 0.05$, and use multiple comparison method to compare the different means and determine which student group had the lowest score and which had the highest score.

Student's group A	Student's group B	Student's group C	Student's group D
90	56	98	60
80	60	97.6	59.8
97.6	72	95	64
78	68	92	59.8
80	80	88.8	62
82	76	79.8	63.2
88	72	97.8	65
84	80	94.4	62
77.8	64	94	58
78	80	93.6	66.6
76	82	95.6	68
88	72	96	66

P11.31: In a weight loss program, two approaches were taken simultaneously: diet program, and exercise program. The results of weight loss (lb) at the different levels of these two factors are as shown below. Use ANOVA at $\alpha = 0.05$ to examine the effects of each factor on weight loss.

		Food Package		
	Level	Light diet	Medium diet	Strict diet
Exercise Level	Low	17	14	12
	High	16	13	12

Answer: Interpret the ANOVA Table

ANOVA						
Source of Variation	SS	df	MS	F	P-value	F crit
Rows	0.6667	1	0.6667	4	0.1835	18.5128
Columns	21	2	10.500	63	0.0156	19
Error	0.3333	2	0.1667			
Total	22	5				

P11.32: Perform ANOVA to evaluate the effects of the number of hours of studying and the number of absences on student's grade in the course of statistics using the data shown below. Use ANOVA at a = 0.05 to examine the effects of each factor on student's grade.

		Hours of Studying		
	Level	Low	Medium	High
Number of absences	Low	70	77	89
	Low	80	82	80
	Low	70	77	89
	Low	80	82	88
	Low	88	79	92
	High	66	74	85
	High	80	81	80
	High	77	72	81
	High	80	81	81
	High	80	79	83

P11.33: Complete the missing values in the following ANOVA Table. What is the total number of observations examined in this experiment? How many treatment levels examined? How many replicates? What is your interpretation of the effects of factors of the study at $\alpha = 0.05$?

ANOVA						
Source of Variation	SS	df	MS	F	P-value	F crit
Rows	……..	1	……..	……..	0.001885	18.51282
Columns	420.3333	2	210.1667	……..	0.000792	19
Error	0.333333	2	0.166667			
Total	508.8333	5				

P11.34: Complete the missing values in the following ANOVA Table. What is the total number of observations examined in this experiment? How many treatment levels examined? How many replicates? What is your interpretation of the effects of factors of the study at $\alpha = 0.05$?

ANOVA						
Source of Variation	SS	df	MS	F	P-value	F crit
Rows	1.5	1	1.5	0.75	0.477767	18.51282
Columns	……	2	……	……	0.0075	19
Error	4	……	2			
Total	534.8333	5				

P11.35: Complete the missing values in the following ANOVA Table. What is the total number of observations examined in this experiment? How many treatment levels examined? How many replicates? What is your interpretation of the effects of factors of the study at $\alpha = 0.05$?

ANOVA						
Source of Variation	SS	df	MS	F	P-value	F crit
Sample	……..	……..	……..	……..	0.1215	4.2597
Columns	84.95	2	42.4750	7.1038	0.0038	3.4028
Interaction	7.316667	2	3.6583	……..	0.5506	3.4028
Within	143.5	24	5.9792			
Total	251.175	29				

P11.36: Complete the missing values in the following ANOVA Table. What is the total number of observations examined in this experiment? How many treatment levels examined? How many replicates? What is your interpretation of the effects of factors of the study at $\alpha = 0.05$?

ANOVA						
Source of Variation	SS	df	MS	F	P-value	F crit
Sample	420.5000	1	420.5000	26.4650	0.0002	4.7472
Columns	……..	2	……..	……..	0.0000	3.8853
Interaction	272.3333	2	……..	……..	0.0049	3.8853
Within	190.6667	12	……..			
Total	6731.6111	17				

P11.37: Complete the missing values in the following ANOVA Table. What is the total number of observations examined in this experiment? How many treatment levels examined? How many replicates? What is your interpretation of the effects of factors of the study at $\alpha = 0.05$?

ANOVA						
Source of Variation	SS	df	MS	F	P-value	F crit
Sample	1.33	1	……..	0.571	0.478	5.987
Columns	2433.50	2	……..	……..	0.000	5.143
Interaction	10.17	2	……..	……..	0.194	5.143
Within	14	6	……..			
Total	2459	11				

CHAPTER 12

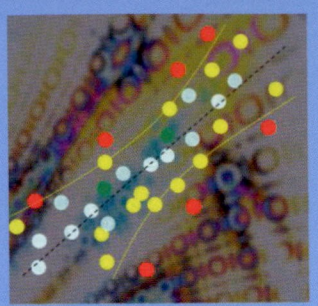

Correlation and Regression Analysis

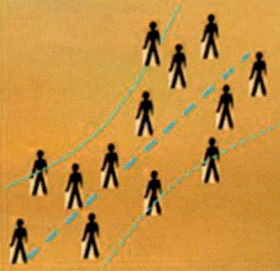

After completing this Chapter, students will be able to:

- Identify variables appropriate for a regression model
- Develop simple linear regression equation
- Develop multiple regression equations
- Compute the coefficient of correlation and the coefficient of determination
- Interpret the F-test for a regression model
- Construct residual plots
- Understand the effects of adding new variables to a regression model

CHAPTER 12

This chapter discusses the methods of developing relationships between variables using regression analysis. The chapter begins with a discussion of the different types of relationships between variables. This discussion will lead to the concept of linear models and how they are fit to data relating dependent and independent variables using the common method of 'least squares'. This will lead to understanding the method of developing a simple regression equation. The chapter then moves to a more advanced topic, which is multiple regression analysis. In this topic a dependent variable is related to two or more independent variables. The analysis of variance associated with both simple and multiple regression analysis will be discussed by examples.

CHAPTER CONTENTS

12.1 Simple View of x-y Relationships

Correlation and linear regression analyses are commonly used for investigating the relationships between quantitative variables. The main goal of correlation analysis is to determine whether two variables are related (one of the two variables varies when the other one does), and to quantify the strength of the relationship. Regression analysis is used to develop an equation describing the relationship between variables.

Most students who had courses in basic mathematics are familiar with the so-called '*curve fitting*.' This is a process of finding a curve which matches a series of data points and possibly other constraints. It is most often used by scientists, social researchers, economists, and engineers to visualize and plot the curve that best describes the shape and behavior of their data.

Mathematically, curve fitting involves collection of data of the variables under consideration. For example, suppose x denotes an independent variable that has some influence on a dependent variable y. Then a sample of n individual observations of x would be represented by x_1, x_2, ..., x_n. Corresponding y observations would be y_1, y_2, ..,y_n. The next step is to plot the points (x_1, y_1), (x_2, y_2), ..., (x_n, y_n) on an x-y coordinate system as shown in Figure 12.1.

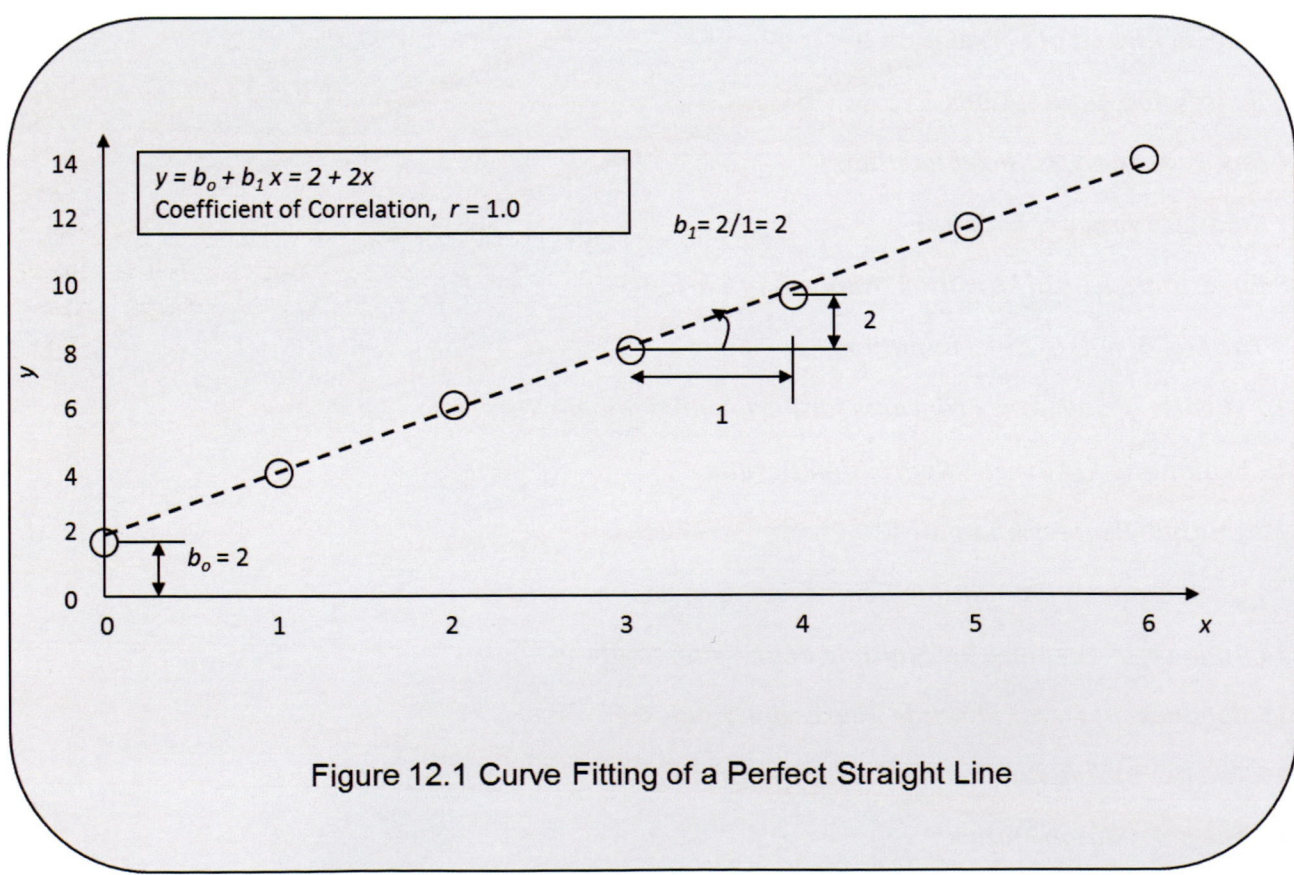

Figure 12.1 Curve Fitting of a Perfect Straight Line

Mathematical curve fitting aims at determining the values of the parameters controlling the x-y relationship. For example, suppose that a set of x and y values can be represented by the following linear form:

$$y = b_o + b_1 x \qquad (12.1)$$

In this case, we should determine the parameters b_o and b_1 which govern the linear x-y relationship. Mathematically, this task is quite easy. As shown in Figure 12.1, the values of b_o and b_1 directly represent the intercept and the slope of the straight line. In this example, $b_o = 2$, and $b_1 = 2$, and the linear relationship is:

$$y = 2 + 2x$$

The case of Figure 12.1 represents a situation where no scatter of the y values is observed at each value of the variable x. In other words, at each value of x, we get a constant value of y no matter how many observations we take at that level. This situation is very seldom in practice as it is often the case that we obtain multiple y values for every x value. This point leads us to 'statistical curve fitting' in which a 'smooth' function is constructed that approximately fits the data. The resulting graph is commonly called a *scatter plot*. This plot provides the first visualization of the nature of the relationship between two variables.

Normally, at each level of the variable x, we obtain a scatter of random values of y. Figure 12.2 shows the same x-y relationship as that represented in Figure 12.1 but with data scatter at each level of x. If the average value of the y-variable at each level of x is exactly the same as the corresponding single value shown in Figure 12.1, the linear relationship will keep the same form (i.e. $y = 2 + 2x$). However, the strength of the x-y relationship will be weakened by the presence of the scatter. This strength is measured by the so-called *coefficient of correlation*, r, between x and y. A value of one of the coefficient of correlation, r indicates a perfect linear relationship. A value of r slightly less than one indicates a less-than-perfect linear relationship. A positive value of r will indicate a positive relationship (an increase in x results in an increase in y), and a negative value of r will indicate a negative relationship (an increase in x results in a decrease y). Later in this chapter, we will discuss the underlying concepts of the coefficient of correlation.

When all points in an x-y plot seem to lie near a line, as in Figure 12.2, the relationship between two variables x and y is said to be linear. The strength of a linear relationship can be visualized by simply examining the trend and the cluster of points around the straight line. In this regard, there are three distinguished situations that one may observe as shown in Figure 12.3:

- A strong positive linear correlation. This means y increases as x increases in linear fashion (Figure 12.3.a)
- A strong negative linear correlation. This means that y decreases as x increases (Figure 12.3.b)
- A weak relationship. This means that points do not show any correlation between x and y, or a change in x does not result in a corresponding change of a particular pattern in the values of y (Figure 12.3.c)

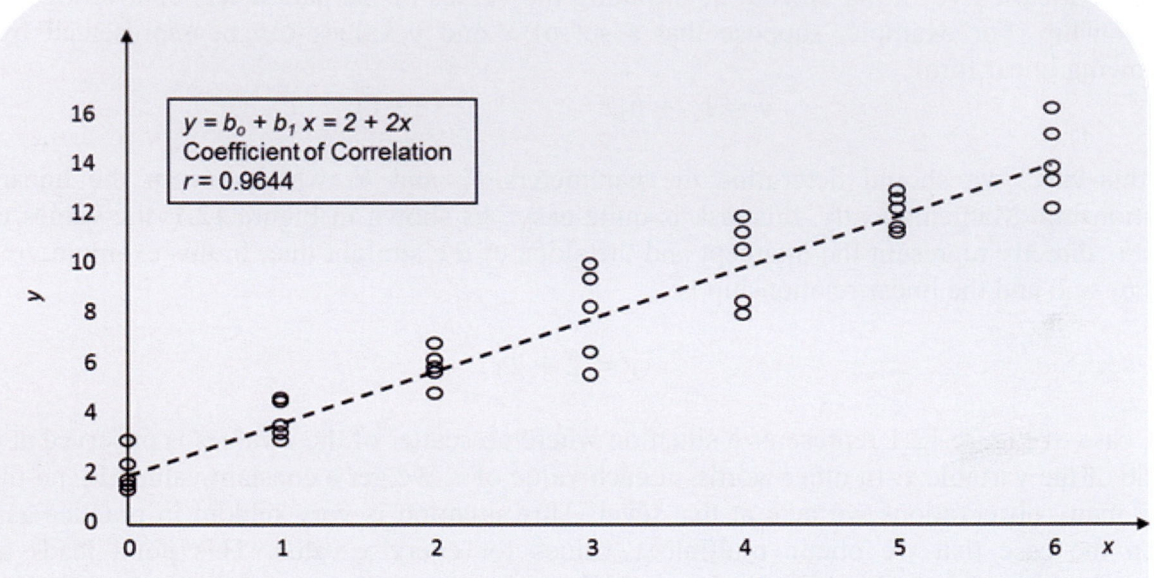

Figure 12.2 The Concept of Data Scatter

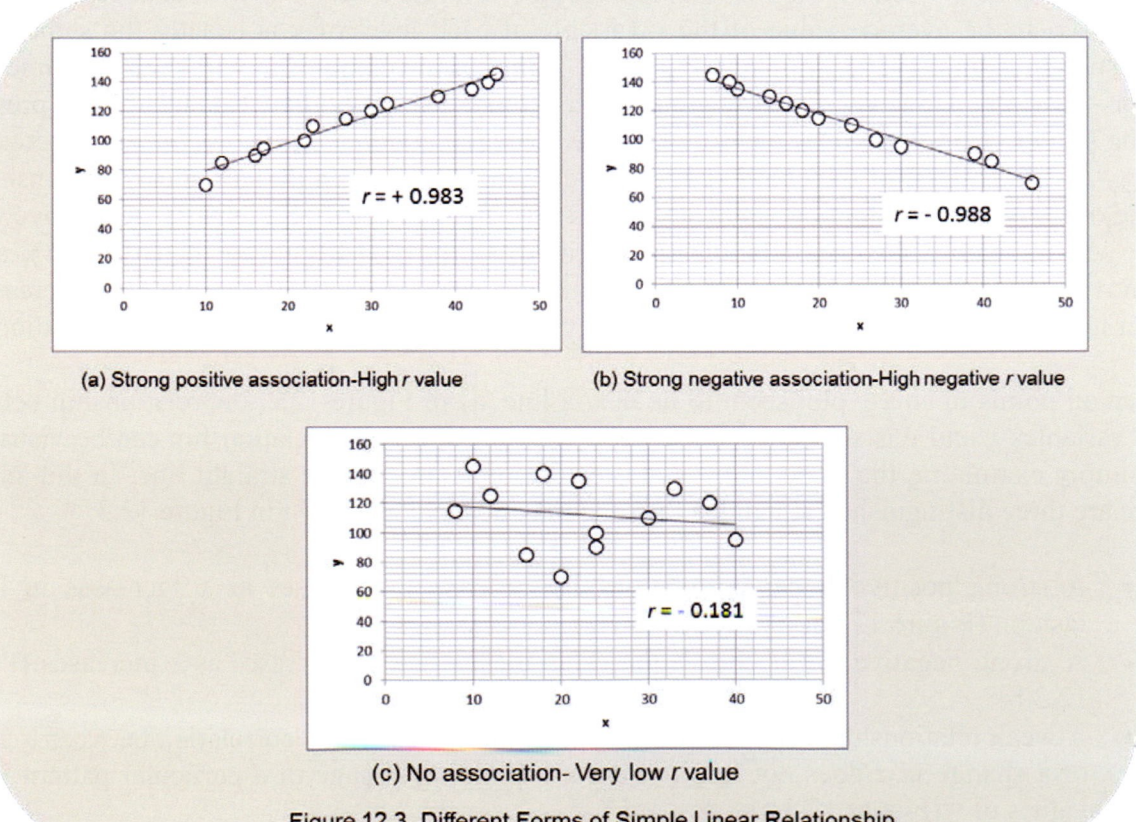

(a) Strong positive association-High r value

(b) Strong negative association-High negative r value

(c) No association- Very low r value

Figure 12.3. Different Forms of Simple Linear Relationship

As you can see in Figure 12.3, the strength of the relationship between the x and y variables is determined by the coefficient of correlation. Key characteristics of the coefficient of correlation are:

- The value of r varies from -1 to +1 and it is a dimensionless quantity, i.e. it is independent of the units of the variable used.
- The closer the value of r to -1 or +1 the more linear the association between x and y.
- If r is close to zero, we conclude that there is a very weak linear association between x and y.

In describing the relationship between two variables, one should keep in mind two important points:

- The relationship should be described in view of the range of values of the independent variable used.
- A poor linear relationship does not mean a poor overall relationship between variables; in other words, a strong nonlinear relationship may exist.

With regard to the first point, it is important to specify the range of the independent variable x over which the relationship is developed. This is because of the fact that different ranges of data may be associated with different forms of the x-y relationship. To illustrate this point consider the relationship between the cost and the revenue of a certain business shown in Figure 12.4. Over the entire range of cost, the relationship is nonlinear. However, if we partition the range into three cost regions, namely: < $50,000, between $50,000 and $90,000, and > $90,000, we will note the following observations:

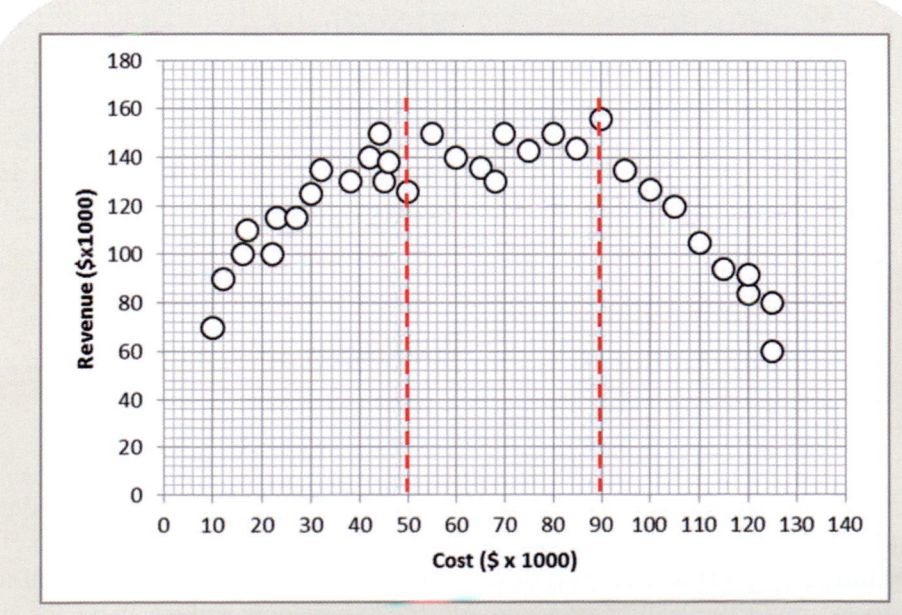

Figure 12.4. Nonlinear x-y relationship over the entire range of data

- Initially, as the cost increases the revenue increases. This trend continues until a cost of about $50,000.
- In the range of cost from $50,000 to about $90,000, revenues seem to respond randomly and without any particular pattern.
- Above $90,000 in costs, the increase in cost results in a decrease in revenues.

These regional changes are associated with different values of the coefficient of correlation as shown in Figure 12.5. The first region results in a positive coefficient of correlation of 0.924, which is considerably high given that a perfect positive r value is +1; the second region results in a small value of the coefficient of correlation of 0.324, which is considerably low given the least r value is zero; and the third region results in a negative coefficient of correlation of -0.977, which is considerably high given a perfect negative r value is -1.

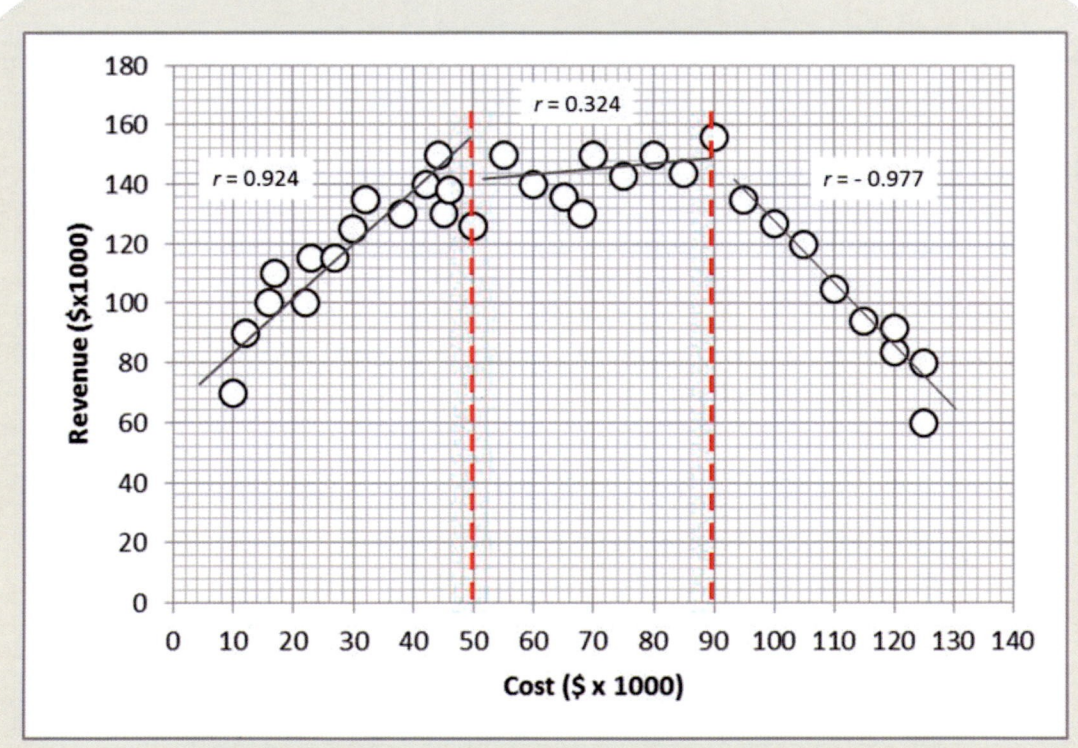

Figure 12.5. Regional trends at partitioned ranges of the x-y relationship

In light of the above example, it is important that we use the plausible range of data that reflects the entire nature of the relationship. If we are certain that the relationship is likely to be linear over the entire range of x values; we can develop it using a narrower range of values and rely on extrapolation to estimate the values of y outside the range of x values used for developing the relationship.

With regard to the second point, initial observations often indicate whether the relationship is linear or non-linear. In the example shown in Figure 12.4, the relationship is a nonlinear one over the entire range of data. Indeed, it can be modeled by a good polynomial function as shown in Figure 12.6.

The polynomial function shown in Figure 12.6 can easily be generated provided the availability of the data of cost and the corresponding data of revenue. Recall in Chapter 3, we demonstrated how you can produce a scatter graph using Excel® graph tools. Following the same procedure discussed in Chapter 3 and adding a trend line of polynomial type can result in the graph of Figure 12.6.

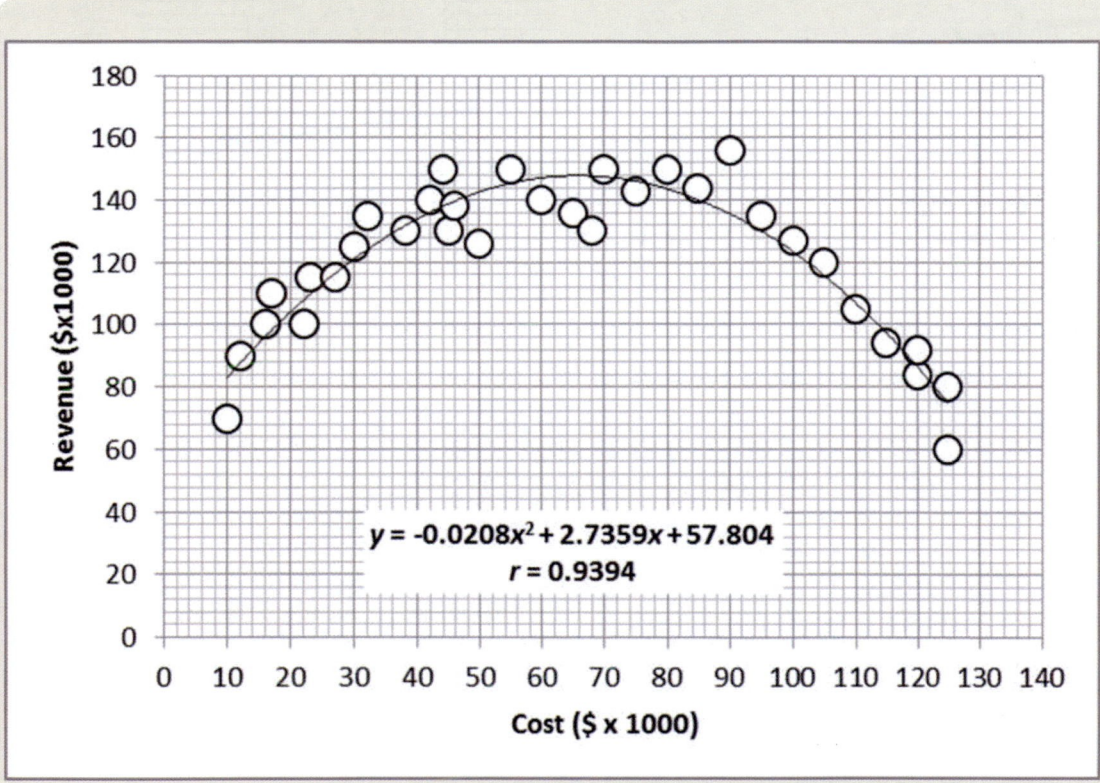

Figure 12.6. Fitting the Revenue-Cost data with a polynomial function

Working problem 12.1

In order to develop an x-y relationship, it is important to identify key system inputs and key system outputs. Suggest key input variables and key output variables that can be related for the following systems:

(a) An education program

(b) Football game

(c) Weight-loss system

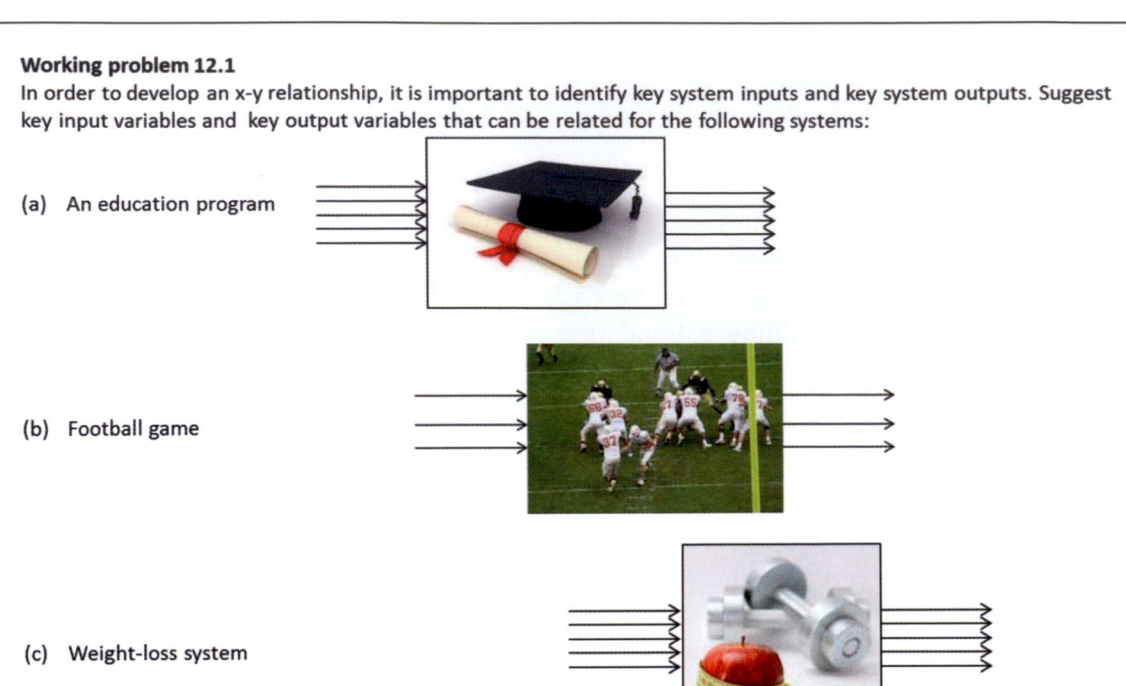

Working problem 12.2:

Visualize the following x-y relationships and describe them in terms of direction and linearity

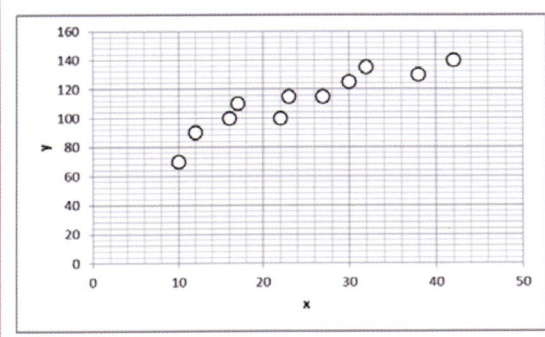

(a) Positive ..... Negative ..... No trend ......
Linear ...... Nonlinear ....

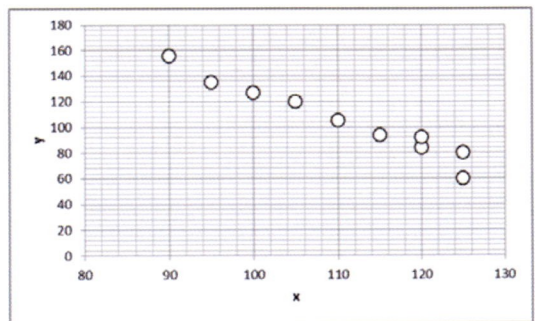

(b) Positive ..... Negative ..... No trend ....
Linear ...... Nonlinear ....

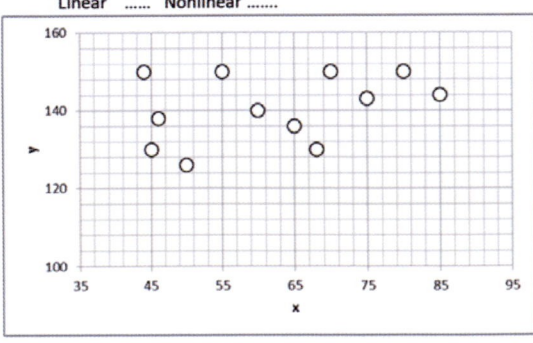

(c) Positive ..... Negative ..... No trend ....
Linear ...... Nonlinear ....

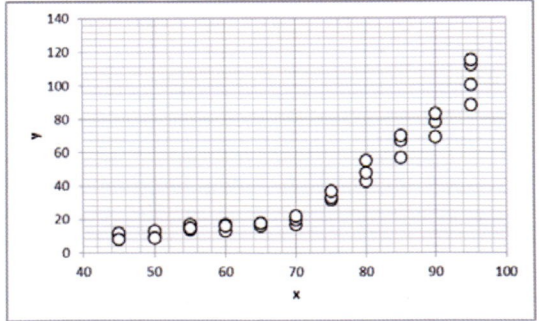

(d) Positive ..... Negative ..... No trend ......
Linear ...... Nonlinear ....

Working problem 12.3:

The following data represents household annual income and the corresponding amount of money spent annually in eating
outside homes
(a) What is the dependent variable, and what is the independent variable?
(b) Plot the scatter diagram relating annual income to annual eating expenses?

Household Annual Income ($10,000s)	Annual expenses of eating outside ($100s)
6	9
4	8
2	4.5
5	9.5
3	6
4	5

Answer:

(a) Dependent variable = Annual expenses of eating outside
Independent Variable = Household annual income,
Use Excel® Graph Features

12.2 The Linear Model: Simple regression

An x-y relationship can be represented by the following simple linear model:

$$y = \beta_o + \beta_1 x + \varepsilon \qquad (12.2)$$

where β_o and β_1 are called parameter estimates, and ε is an error term stemming from the fact that the change in x may not fully explain the change in y.

The equation derived from the above model through estimating the parameters β_o and β_1 and minimizing the error effect is called the simple regression equation:

$$y = b_o + b_1 x \qquad (12.3)$$

where b_o and b_1 are the estimates of β_o and β_1.

The method used for fitting a linear relationship is called the *least squares method*. This method is discussed below.

12.3 The Concept of Least Squares

The best-fitting line determined by the least squares method is the line which minimizes the sum of squares of the distances from the observed data points on the scatter plot to the fitted line (see Figure 12.7). The smaller the deviations of observed values from this line, the smaller the sum of squares of these deviations of the observed values from the line and, consequently, the closer the best-fitting line will be to the data. The least squares method solution is based on finding the values of b_0 and b_1 (the estimates of β_0 and β_1) for which the sum of squares of the deviations is minimal.

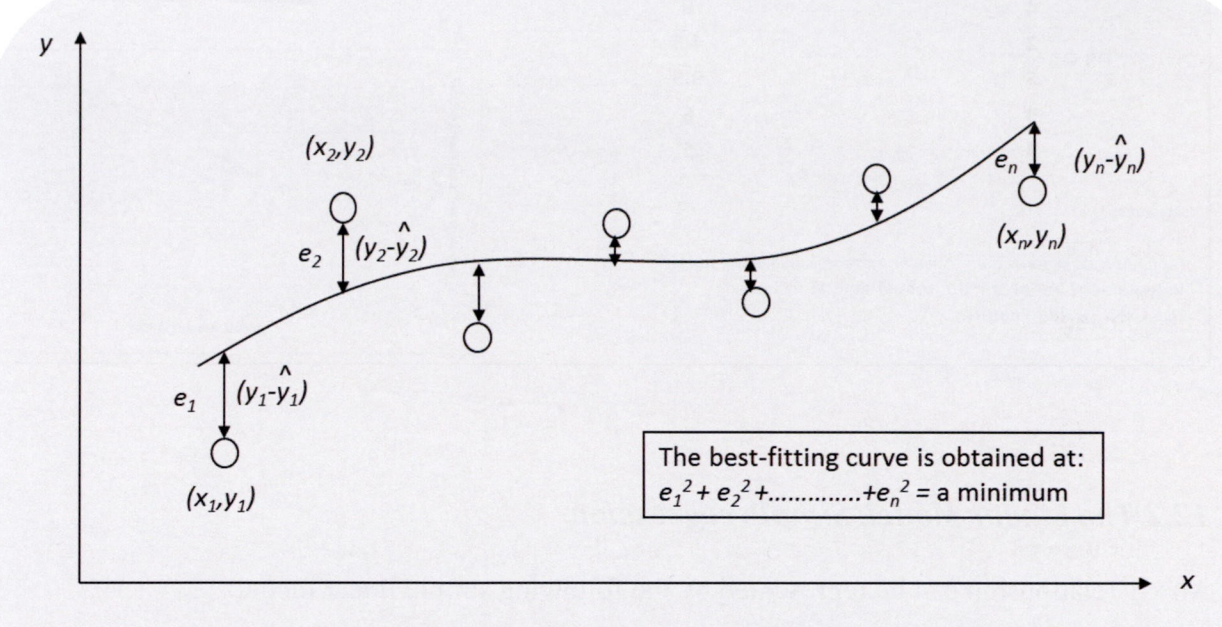

Figure 12.7. The Concept of Least Squares

The minimum sum of squares corresponding to the least-squares estimates, b_0 and b_1, is usually called *the sum of squares about the regression line, the residual sum of squares,* or *the sum of squares due to error (SSE)*. This measure is critically important in determining the quality of the straight-line fit. If $SSE = 0$, the straight line fits perfectly, and every observed point lies on the fitted line. As the fit gets worse, SSE becomes larger indicating larger deviation from the regression line. In general, two possible factors can influence the SSE: (1) large variation in data, or large σ^2, and (2) inappropriate assumption of a straight-line model.

Using the least squares method, the constants b_o and b_1 in Equation 12.3 are determined from the x and y data by solving the following equations simultaneously:

$$\sum y = b_o n + b_1 \sum x \qquad (12.4.a)$$

$$\sum xy = b_o \sum x + b_1 \sum x^2 \qquad (12.4.b)$$

The above equations are called the *normal equations for least square line*. Note that division of both sides of the first normal equation by n yields:

$$\bar{Y} = b_o + b_1 \bar{X} \qquad (12.5)$$

Where $\bar{Y}$ and $\bar{X}$ are the average values of y and x observations, respectively.

The constants b_o and b_1 are determined from equations 12.4 as follows:

$$b_o = \frac{(\sum y)(\sum x^2) - (\sum x)(\sum xy)}{n \sum x^2 - (\sum x)^2} \qquad b_1 = \frac{n(\sum xy) - (\sum x)(\sum y)}{n \sum x^2 - (\sum x)^2} \qquad (12.6)$$

Another way to obtain the values of the constants b_o and b_1 is to use the following expressions:

$$b_o = \bar{Y} - b_1 \bar{X} \qquad (12.7.a)$$

$$b_1 = \frac{\sum (X - \bar{X})(Y - \bar{Y})}{\sum (X - \bar{X})^2} \qquad (12.7.b)$$

Example 12.1: The data in Table 12.1 represent values of cost of a retail business and corresponding values of revenue. Assume a linear model relating revenue to cost and develop a simple regression equation (estimate b_o and b_1) to predict revenues.

Table 12.1 Data of Cost and Revenue of a retail business

n	X = Cost ($\times$1000)	Y = Revenue ($\times$1000)	n	X = Cost ($\times$1000)	Y = Revenue ($\times$1000)
1	10	70	8	30	120
2	12	85	9	32	125
3	16	90	10	38	130
4	17	95	11	42	135
5	22	100	12	44	140
6	23	110	13	45	145
7	27	115			

Solution:

The procedure for fitting a least square line to this set of data can be summarized as follows:

- We assume a linear model relating the dependent variable y to the independent variable x
- We denote the independent variable (costs) by x and the dependent variable (revenues) by y.
- We calculate the sum terms Σx, Σy, Σx^2, and Σxy
- Using Equation 12.6, we calculate the constants b_o and b_1.

The best linear model representing the relationship between cost and revenue is expressed by the following equation:
$$y = \beta_o + \beta_1 x + \varepsilon$$

Or $\quad Revenue = \beta_o + \beta_1(Cost) + \varepsilon$

The corresponding regression equation is: $Revenue = b_o + b_1(Cost)$

The values of the constants b_o and b_1 will be calculated from the following equations:

$$b_o = \frac{(\Sigma y)(\Sigma x^2) - (\Sigma x)(\Sigma xy)}{n\Sigma x^2 - (\Sigma x)^2}$$

$$b_1 = \frac{n(\Sigma xy) - (\Sigma x)(\Sigma y)}{n\Sigma x^2 - (\Sigma x)^2}$$

The calculations used to find b_o and b_1 are illustrated in Table 12.2.

The resulting regression equation is: $\quad Revenue = 60.844 + 1.869(Cost)$

where the value $b_o = 1.869$ is the slope of the linear relationship and $b_1 = 60.844$ is the intercept.

694

Table 12.2 Calculations for determining b_0 and b_1

n	x = Cost (\$x1000)	y = Revenue (\$x1000)	x^2	xy
1	10	70	100	700
2	12	85	144	1020
3	16	90	256	1440
4	17	95	289	1615
5	22	100	484	2200
6	23	110	529	2530
7	27	115	729	3105
8	30	120	900	3600
9	32	125	1024	4000
10	38	130	1444	4940
11	42	135	1764	5670
12	44	140	1936	6160
13	45	145	2025	6525
Sum	$\sum x_i = 358$	$\sum y_i = 1460$	$\sum x_i^2 = 11624$	$\sum xy = 43505$
Mean	$\bar{X} = \sum \dfrac{x_i}{n} = \dfrac{358}{13} = 27.54$	$\bar{Y} = \sum \dfrac{y_i}{n} = \dfrac{1460}{13}$ $= 112.308$		
	$b_0 = \dfrac{(\sum y)(\sum x^2) - (\sum x)(\sum xy)}{n \sum x^2 - (\sum x)^2}$ $= \dfrac{1460 \times 11624 - 358 \times 43505}{13 \times 11624 - 358^2}$ $= 60.844$			
	$b_1 = \dfrac{n(\sum xy) - (\sum x)(\sum y)}{n \sum x^2 - (\sum x)^2}$ $= \dfrac{13 \times 43505 - 358 \times 1460}{13 \times 11624 - 358^2}$ $= 1.869$			

Example 12.2: Construct the scatter graph for the data in Example 12.1 and superimpose the fit line.

Solution:

Using Excel® graphing, you can construct the scatter plot shown below. We will illustrate how the coefficient of correlation, r, is calculated shortly. For now, note how high the coefficient is (0.983), indicating a very strong positive relationship between cost and revenue.

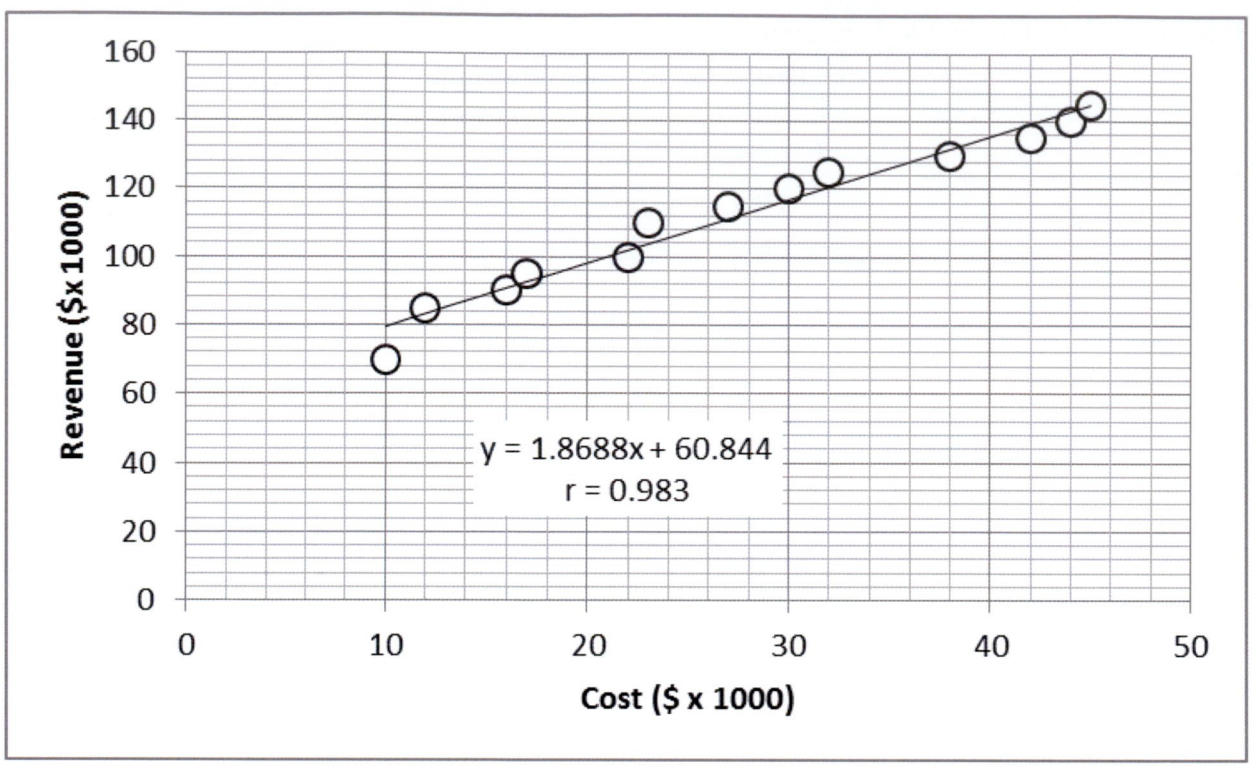

Example 12.3: Using the regression equation developed in Example 12.1 predict the value of revenue at a cost of $48,000.

Solution:

$$Revenue = 60.844 + 1.869(Cost) = 60.844 + 1.869 \times 48 = 150.556$$

Thus, at a cost of $48,000, the predicted revenue is $150,556.

Example 12.4: Table 12.3 shows values of number of working hours and corresponding wages in a small business firm for different employees. Assume a linear model relating wages to working hours and develop a simple regression equation (estimate b_o and b_1) to predict wages.

Table 12.3 Values of number of working hours and corresponding wages in a small business firm

Number of working hours	Wages ($)
20.0	309
24.0	334
25.4	344
28.0	402
30.0	458

The procedure for fitting a least square line to this set of data can be summarized as follows:

- We assume a linear model relating the dependent variable y to the independent variable x.
- We denote the independent variable (number of working hours) by x and the dependent variable (wages) by y.
- We calculate the sum terms Σx, Σy, Σx^2, and Σxy.
- Using Equation 12.6, we calculate the constants b_o and b_1.

The best linear model representing the relationship between working hours and wages is expressed by the following equation:

$$y = \beta_o + \beta_1 x + \varepsilon$$

Or

$$Wages = \beta_o + \beta_1 (Number\ of\ Working\ Hours) + \varepsilon$$

The corresponding regression equation is:

$$Wages = b_o + b_1 (Working\ Hours)$$

The calculations procedures of b_o and b_1 are illustrated in Table 12.4.

Table 12.4 Calculations of terms used for determining b_o and b_1

Working hours, x	Wages, y	x^2	xy	y^2
20.0	309	400.00	6180.0	95481
24.0	334	576.00	8016.0	111556
25.4	344	645.16	8737.6	118336
28.0	402	784.00	11256.0	161604
30.0	458	900.00	13740.0	209764
$\Sigma x = 127.4$	$\Sigma y = 1847$	$\Sigma x^2 = 3305.2$	$\Sigma xy = 47929$	$\Sigma y^2 = 696741$

The values of the constants b_o and b_1 will be calculated from the following equations:

$$b_o = \frac{(\Sigma y)(\Sigma x^2) - (\Sigma x)(\Sigma xy)}{n \Sigma x^2 - (\Sigma x)^2} = \frac{(1847)(3305.16) - (127.4)(47929.6)}{5(3305.16) - (127.4)^2} = -5.4$$

$$b_1 = \frac{n(\Sigma xy) - (\Sigma x)(\Sigma y)}{n \Sigma x^2 - (\Sigma x)^2} = \frac{5(47929.6) - (127.4)(1847)}{5(3305.16) - (127.4)^2} = 14.7105$$

The linear equation: $y = -5.4 + 14.71x$ $\;or\; wages(\$) = -5.4 + 14.71(working\; hours)$

The above relationship is plotted in the figure below. Note that the fitted line is passing through the actual points (i.e. at minimum distances from the actual points). This is the basis for the least-squares method.

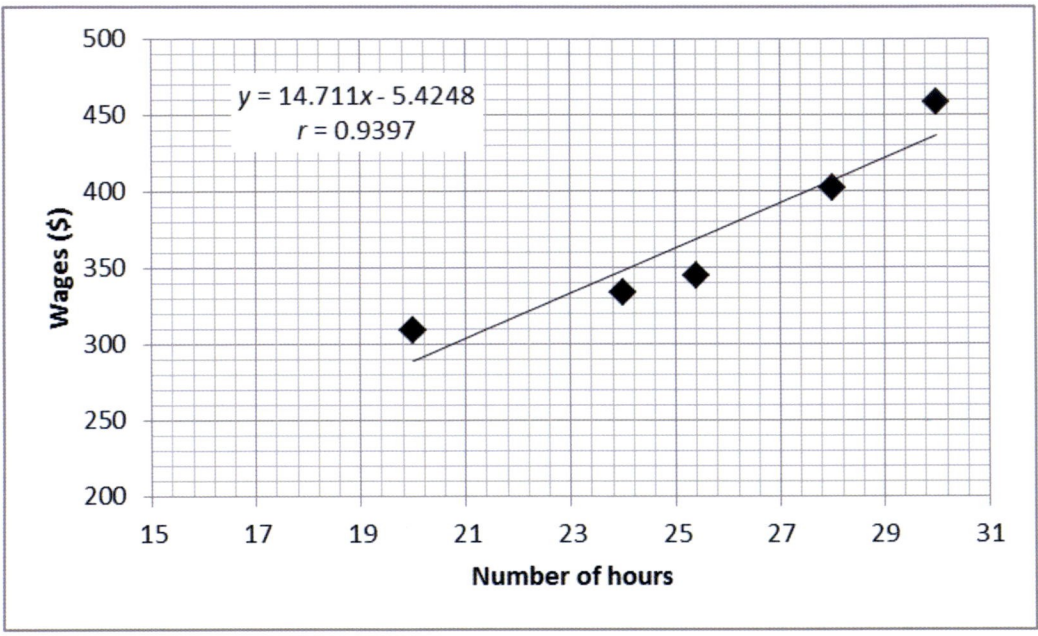

12.4 The Coefficient of Correlation (r)

In Chapter 2, we learned about basic descriptive statistics of a sample data. In particular, we learned how to determine the variance of a set of data. In Chapter 11, we used the concept of variance to partition the different sources of variability using the Analysis of Variance (*ANOVA*). Here, we use the concept of variance again; this time to determine the strength of the *x-y* relationship.

For the x and y data used for developing an *x-y* relationship, the variances of x and y values are defined by:

$$Var(x) = s_x{}^2 = \frac{\Sigma(x_i - \bar{X})^2}{n} \qquad (12.8.\,a)$$

$$Var(y) = s_y{}^2 = \frac{\Sigma(y_i - \bar{Y})^2}{n} \qquad (12.8.\,b)$$

The concept of variance can be extended to two or more variables having some joint correspondence. In this case, the term used is called '*covariance*' and is defined by:

$$Cov(x, y) = s_{xy} = \frac{\Sigma(x_i - \bar{X})(y_i - \bar{Y})}{n} \qquad (12.9)$$

Note that if x and y are independent, then $Cov(x,y) = 0$. On the other hand, if x and y are completely dependent, say if $x = y$, then $Cov(x,y) = s_{xy} = s_x.s_y$. This simple concept leads us to a useful measure of the extent of correlation between the variables x and y, called '*the coefficient of correlation, r*' defined by:

$$r = \frac{s_{xy}}{s_x s_y} \qquad (12.10)$$

In light of the above discussion, the coefficient of correlation r is zero when the variables x and y are uncorrelated. The other extreme value of r is ± 1, which indicates complete dependence or perfect correlation. This means that $-1 \leq r \leq 1$.

Example 12.5: Referring to Table 12.3, which shows values of number of working hours and corresponding wages in a small business firm for different employees. Determine the coefficient of correlation between number of working hours and wages.

Solution:

Table 12.5 Calculations of the coefficient of correlation, r

n	Working hours, x	Wages, y	$x - \bar{X}$	$y - \bar{Y}$	$(x - \bar{X})(y - \bar{Y})$	$(x - \bar{X})^2$	$(y - \bar{Y})^2$
1	20	309	-5.48	-60.4	330.992	30.0304	3648.16
2	24	334	-1.48	-35.4	52.392	2.1904	1253.16
3	25.4	344	-0.08	-25.4	2.032	0.0064	645.16
4	28	402	2.52	32.6	82.152	6.3504	1062.76
5	30	458	4.52	88.6	400.472	20.4304	7849.96
Sum	127.4	1847			868.04	59.008	14459.2
Mean	25.48	369.4				14.752	3614.8
Std. dev.	3.84	60.12				3.840833	60.12321
					$Cov(x,y) = s_{xy}$ $= \frac{\Sigma(x_i - \bar{X})(y_i - \bar{Y})}{n-1}$ $= 217.01$	s_x $= \sqrt{\frac{\Sigma(x_i - \bar{X})}{n-1}}$ $= \sqrt{\frac{59.008}{4}}$ $= 3.84$	s_x $= \sqrt{\frac{\Sigma(y_i - \bar{Y})^2}{n-1}}$ $= \sqrt{\frac{14459.2}{4}}$ $= 60.12$

$$Cov(x, y) = s_{xy} = \frac{\Sigma(x_i - \bar{X})(y_i - \bar{Y})}{n-1} = 217.01$$

$$r = \frac{s_{xy}}{s_x s_y} = \frac{217.01}{(3.84)(60.12)} = 0.939$$

Example 12.6: Referring to the data in Table 12.1, which represent values of cost of a retail business and corresponding values of revenue, determine the coefficient of correlation, r between revenue and cost.

Solution:

Table 12.6 Calculations of the coefficient of correlation, r

n	x = Cost ($x1000)	y = Revenue ($x1000)	$x - \bar{X}$	$y - \bar{Y}$	$(x - \bar{X})(y - \bar{Y})$
1	10	70	-17.54	-42.31	742.01
2	12	85	-15.54	-27.31	424.32
3	16	90	-11.54	-22.31	257.40
4	17	95	-10.54	-17.31	182.40
5	22	100	-5.54	-12.31	68.17
6	23	110	-4.54	-2.31	10.47
7	27	115	-0.54	2.69	-1.45
8	30	120	2.46	7.69	18.93
9	32	125	4.46	12.69	56.63
10	38	130	10.46	17.69	185.09
11	42	135	14.46	22.69	328.17
12	44	140	16.46	27.69	455.86
13	45	145	17.46	32.69	570.86
Sum	358	1460			3298.846
Mean	27.538	112.308			
Std. dev.	12.13	23.06			

$$Cov(x, y) = s_{xy} = \frac{\Sigma(x_i - \bar{X})(y_i - \bar{Y})}{n - 1} = \frac{3298.846}{12} = 274.9$$

$$r = \frac{s_{xy}}{s_x s_y} = \frac{274.9}{(12.13)(23.06)} = 0.98278$$

Working problem 12.4:

The following data represents household annual income of some families and the amount of money they spend annually in eating outside their homes

(a) Find the values of the regression coefficients of the relationship between the household annual income and the amount of money families spend annually in eating outside their homes

(b) Write the regression equation with the values of the regression coefficients

(c) Find the value of the coefficient of correlation between the household annual income and the amount of money families spend annually in eating outside their homes

Household Annual Income ($10,000s)	Annual expenses of eating outside ($100s)
6	9
4	8
2	4.5
5	9.5
3	6
4	5

Answer:

$$y = b_o + b_1 x = 2.0 + 1.25x$$

0.833307

Working problem 12.5:

The following data represents household annual income of some families and the amount of money they spend annually in eating outside their homes. Using the regression equation relating the household annual income and the amount of money families spend annually in eating outside their homes,

(a) Estimate the annual expenses of eating outside for a household annual income of $80,000

(b) Estimate the annual expenses of eating outside for a household annual income of $70,000

Household Annual Income ($10,000s)	Annual expenses of eating outside ($100s)
6	9
4	8
2	4.5
5	9.5
3	6
4	5

(a) $1200

(b) Try it yourself

701

Working Problem 12.6:

A teacher decided to evaluate whether the number of hours a student study every week would actually make a difference in grade. At the end of the course, he asked different students about how many hours they study per week. He then recorded the hours and the corresponding grades of the students and the data below show the results.

(a) What is the dependent variable, and what is the independent variable?
(b) Plot the scatter diagram relating the numbers of hours a student study per week and the student grade
(c) Estimate the regression coefficients and develop the regression equation
(d) Determine the coefficient of correlation

Answer:
(a) Dependent Variable = Grade (%)
Independent Variable = Number of hours of study
(b) Use Excel® Graphing

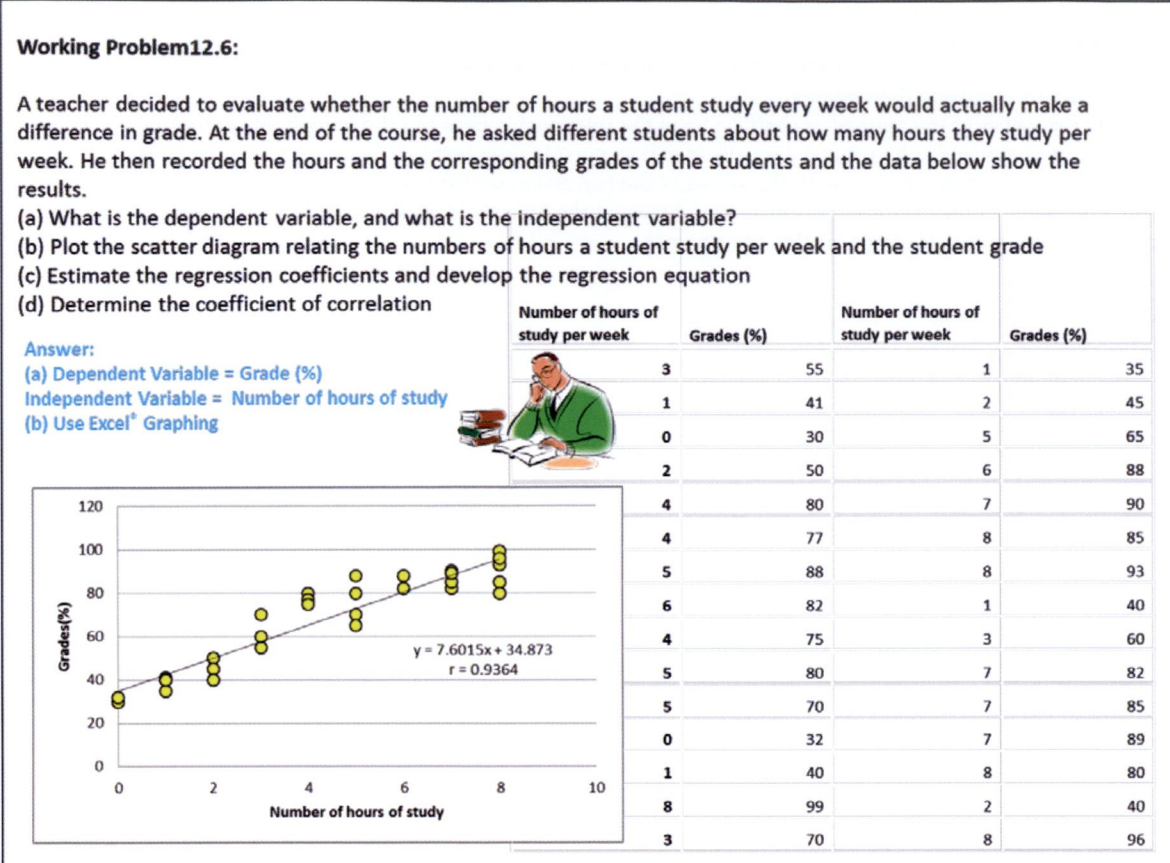

Number of hours of study per week	Grades (%)	Number of hours of study per week	Grades (%)
3	55	1	35
1	41	2	45
0	30	5	65
2	50	6	88
4	80	7	90
4	77	8	85
5	88	8	93
6	82	1	40
4	75	3	60
5	80	7	82
5	70	7	85
0	32	7	89
1	40	8	80
8	99	2	40
3	70	8	96

$y = 7.6015x + 34.873$
$r = 0.9364$

12.5 Regression Assumptions

In order to perform regression analysis, a number of basic assumptions are commonly made. These are discussed below.

Existence: For a fixed value of the variable x, the variable y is a random variable with certain probability distribution having finite mean (μ_{yx}) and variance (σ^2_{yx}). The symbol yx indicates the dependence of y on x. This assumption applies to any regression model (linear or non-linear). Figure 12.8 illustrates this assumption.

Linearity: The mean value of y, (μ_{yx}) is a linear function of x. This assumption may be described as follows:

$$\mu_{y|x} = \beta_o + \beta_1 x$$

where β_o and β_1 are the intercept and slope of the population straight line, respectively.

Independence: In regression analysis, the values of the random variable y are assumed to be independent of one another. This assumption applies to almost any regression model. When observations are not independent, special procedures such as multivariate linear modeling, and weighted least squares techniques may be utilized. These are outside the scope of this book.

Homoscedasticity: This assumption implies that the variance of *y* is the same for any *x* value. The term '*Homo*' means '<u>same</u>', and '*scedastic*' is a Greek term meaning '*to scatter.*' The opposite term is called '*hetroscedasticity.*' Different spreads in the distribution of *y* values at different values of *x* indicate a violation of the homoscedasticity assumption.

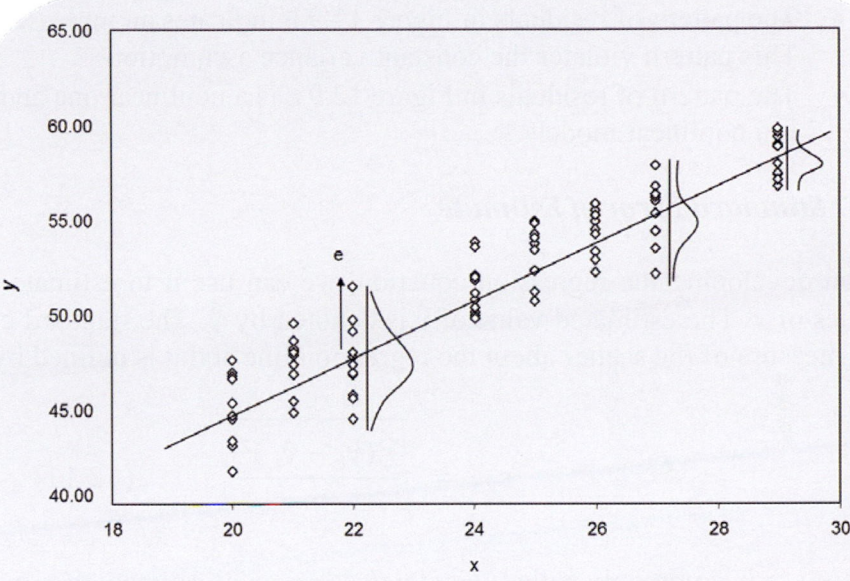

Figure 12.8 *y-x* Relationship (Existence & Linearity)

Normality: This assumption implies that for any fixed value of *x*, *y* has a normal distribution. This assumption is important for statistical inferences of regression parameters (e.g. confidence intervals and test of hypothesis). Normally, the assumption of normality is satisfactory for cases in which distributions are only approximately normal. On the other hand, if the normality assumption is deemed unsatisfactory the observations may be transformed by using a log, square root, or other function to see if the new set of observations is approximately normal. Such procedure requires that other assumptions should remain satisfactory after the transformation.

12.6 Residual Analysis (Residual Plots)

Residuals are the differences between actual *y* values and predicted *y* values. The most important assumptions about a regression model are those about the error terms. These are:

1. Errors are independent
2. Errors are normally distributed
3. Errors have a mean of zero
4. Errors have a constant variance

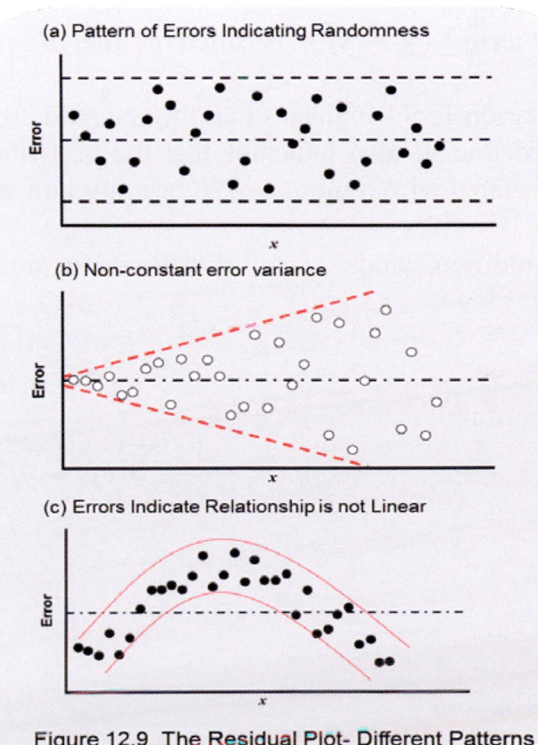

Figure 12.9 The Residual Plot- Different Patterns

Violations of these assumptions are detected using the so-called residual plot as shown in Figures 12.9. In this regard, the following points are important:

- The pattern of residuals in a residual plot is typically random (see Figure 12.9.a)
- The pattern of residuals in Figure 12.9.b indicates an increase in errors as x increases This pattern violates the constant variance assumption
- The pattern of residuals in Figure 12.9.c is a nonlinear one and it indicates that the model is a nonlinear model

12.7 Standard Error of Estimate

Upon developing the regression equation, we can use it to estimate the values of y at different values of x. The estimated value of y is denoted by $\hat{y}$. The standard error of this estimated value is a measure of the scatter about the regression line and it is defined by the quantity:

$$s_{y.x} = \sqrt{\frac{\Sigma(y_i - \hat{y}_i)^2}{n}} \qquad (12.11)$$

where $s_{y.x}$ is commonly called *the standard error of estimate of y on x*, and the estimate of y is given by:

$$\hat{y}_i = b_o + b_1 x_i$$

The term $\Sigma(y_i - \hat{y}_i)^2$ is called *the sum of squared error (SSE)*.

Equation 12.11 indicates that the standard error of estimate is a measure of the scatter around the fitted line. It also indicates that the best line or curve fitted to a set of data is the one that is associated with minimum *SSE* or minimum standard error.

A modified standard error of estimate for small samples is given by:

$$\hat{s}_{y.x} = \sqrt{\frac{n}{n-2}}\, s_{yx}$$

Accordingly,

$$s_{y.x}^2 = \frac{1}{n-2}\sum(y_i - \hat{y}_i)^2 = \frac{1}{n-2}SSE \qquad (12.12)$$

The standard error calculated for the estimate may be used to construct confidence intervals on the population y-value (95% or 99% confidence). For example, suppose that we wish to construct two lines parallel to the regression line produced from the data of Table 12.3, and having vertical distance $s_{y.x}$ from it. At a distance $\pm 3\ s_{y.x}$, more than 99% of the data will lie between these two lines (see Figure 12.10).

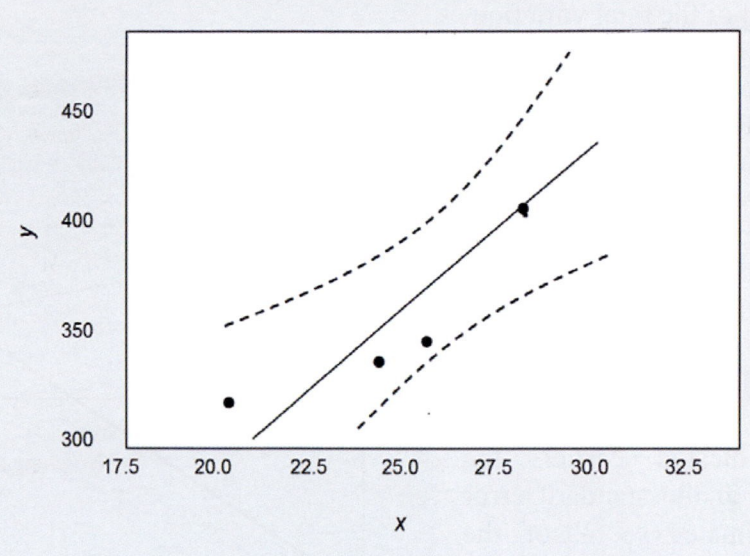

Figure 12.10 Regression Confidence Interval

When n is large, $s_{y.x}$ can be calculated from:

$$s_{y.x}^2 = \frac{\sum y_i^2 - b_o \sum y_i - b_1 \sum x_i y_i}{n} =$$

$$\frac{\sum (y_i - \bar{y})^2 - b_1 \sum (x_i - x)(y_i - \bar{y})}{n} \qquad (12.13)$$

12.8 Partitioning Total Variation: Analysis of Variance

The total variation of the response variable y is defined by:

$$\sum (y_i - \bar{y})^2$$

This represents the sum of squares of the deviations of the y values from their mean. Using the analysis of variance concept discussed in Chapter 11, this amount can be resolved into two terms as follows:

$$\sum (y_i - \bar{y})^2 = \sum (\hat{y}_i - \bar{y})^2 + \sum (y_i - \hat{y}_i)^2 \qquad (12.14)$$

or

Total variation = variation due to regression + error or residual variation

705

Equation 12.14 is often called the *fundamental equation of regression analysis*. The partitioning concept of the total variation is illustrated in Figure 12.11. The second term in the right hand-side of the equation is the sum of squares of error (*SSE*), which is also called the unexplained error (or residual) variation because the deviations involved in it behave in a random or unpredictable manner.

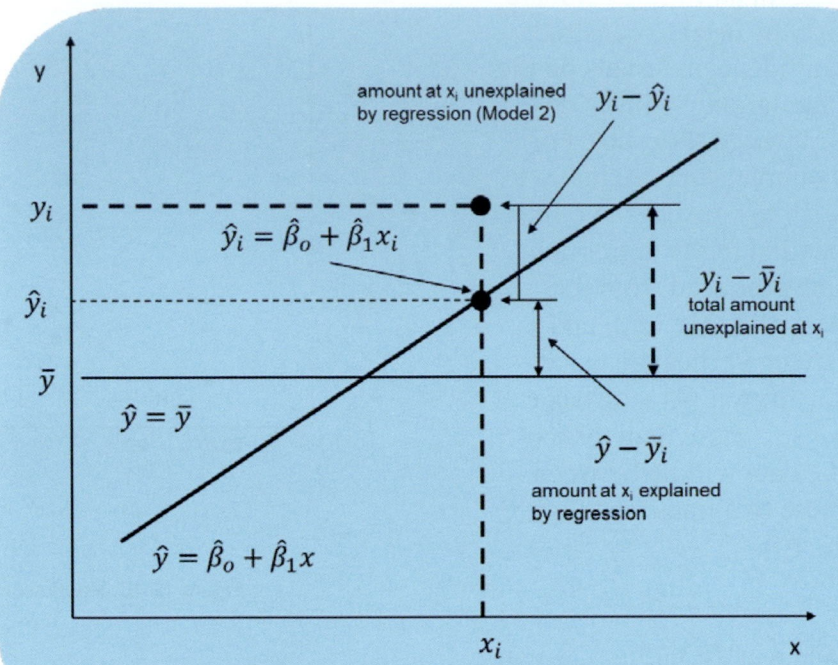

Figure 12.11. Different Sources of Variation Associated with Regression

As indicated earlier, the square of the standard error of estimate (s_{yx}^2), or the mean-square error (*MSE*), is defined by the *SSE* divided by (*n-2*). If the true regression model is a straight line, s_{yx}^2 will be an estimate of σ^2 (the variance of the response variable *y*). The first term is called the *variation due to regression* expressed by (*SSY* - *SSE*). *SSY* is sum of squares of *Y* deviation. This term is often called the *explained variation* because the deviations involved in it have a definite pattern. The corresponding mean-square regression provides an estimate of σ^2 only if the variable *x* does not help to predict the response variable *y* (that is if the slope, β_1, of the straight line is zero). If, in fact, the slope β_1 is not zero, the mean-square regression term will be inflated in proportion to the magnitude of β_1 and will correspondingly overestimate σ^2.

12.9 The Coefficient of Determination, R^2 (or r^2)

Earlier in this chapter, we indicated that the coefficient of correlation, *r,* is a measure of the strength of the *x-y* relationship. This coefficient was defined by the following equation:

$$r = \frac{s_{xy}}{s_x s_y}$$

We also showed evidence that *r* is a measure of the scatter about the fitted line. Recall that the standard error of estimate is also a measure of the scatter about the regression line. For the least-squares line, the two statistics are related by the following equation:

$$s_{y.x}^2 = s_y^2(1 - r^2) \qquad (12.15)$$

706

The term r^2, or R^2 (as the capital letter represents the standard way of denoting it) is called the coefficient of determination, and it is of special significance. To understand the significance of this term, we rewrite the above equation as follows:

$$r^2 = 1 - \frac{s_{y.x}^2}{s_y^2} = 1 - \frac{\sum(y_i - \hat{y}_i)^2}{\sum(y_i - \bar{y})^2} \qquad (12.16)$$

From Equations 12.14 and 12.16,

$$r^2 = \frac{\sum(\hat{y}_i - \bar{y})^2}{\sum(y_i - \bar{y})^2} = \frac{variation\ due\ to\ regression}{total\ variation} = \frac{explained\ variation}{total\ variation}$$

or

$$r^2 = \frac{SSY - SSE}{SSY} \qquad (12.17)$$

In view of Equation 12.17, the coefficient of determination, r^2, can be interpreted as *the proportion of total variation which is explained by the least-squares regression line.* The r^2 value ranges from zero to 1. A value of r^2 of one indicates that 100% of the total variation of the variable y is explained by the least-squares regression line.

The coefficient of determination, r^2 is commonly used to measure the prediction power or the strength of the linear relationship between x and y. To clarify this point, suppose that x is not in use. In this case, the best predictor of y would simply be the mean value of y, or the sample mean of the y observations. The variation in y is expressed by, $SSY = \sum(y_i - \bar{y})^2$. If the variable x is of any value in predicting the variable y, the residual or error sum of squares or $SSE = \sum(y_i - \hat{y}_i)^2$ should be considerably less than SSY. In this case, we say that the linear model $\hat{y}_i = b_o + b_1 x$ fits the data better than the horizontal line, $\hat{y} = \bar{y}$ as demonstrated in Figure 12.11. Accordingly, r^2 is a quantitative measure of the improvement in the fit obtained by using x.

In summary, we can see that the larger the value of r^2, the greater the reduction in SSE relative to SSY, and the stronger the relationship between x and y. The largest value that r^2 can have is one. This value occurs when b_1 is nonzero and when $SSE = 0$, which indicates perfect linear relationship. An intermediate value of r^2 of, say 0.60 means that about 60% of the variation in the response variable, y, is explained by the variable x.

We should also point out that the r^2 value is not a measure of the magnitude of the slope of the regression line. In other words, if r^2 is close to one that does not necessarily mean that b_1 is large. Accordingly, you may have two correlations each equal to one, yet the slopes of the two relationships are quite different.

12.10 The Use of Software Programs for Performing Simple Regression Analysis

In this section, we illustrate how to use Excel® Spreadsheet Data Analysis to perform simple regression analysis.

Example 12.7: The data of Table 12.7 represents original annual salary in thousands and the annual salary after a merit-raise decided by the company's top management. Using Excel® Spreadsheet, develop a regression equation relating the two variables. Evaluate the statistics associated with this relationship.

Table 12.7 Data of salary increases based on merits (thousands $)

Original annual salary (x)	Salary after merit raise (y)
62	66
63	66
66	65
64	65
68	69
71	70
70	68
67	67
68	71
69	68
67	68
65	68

The procedure for performing regression analysis using Excel® Spreadsheet is shown in Figures 12.12 and 12.13. In the data analysis menu, go to regression. The regression menu will ask you to enter the input y and x values as shown in Figure 12.13. It will also ask you to specify where you want your output to be displayed. In addition, you will get to select a number of options such as residuals, standard residuals, residual plots, line fit plots, etc. These options allow complete evaluation of the x-y relationship. For this example, Excel® regression output results are shown in Tables 12.8 and 12.9. Figure 12.17 shows the line fit resulting from this regression analysis.

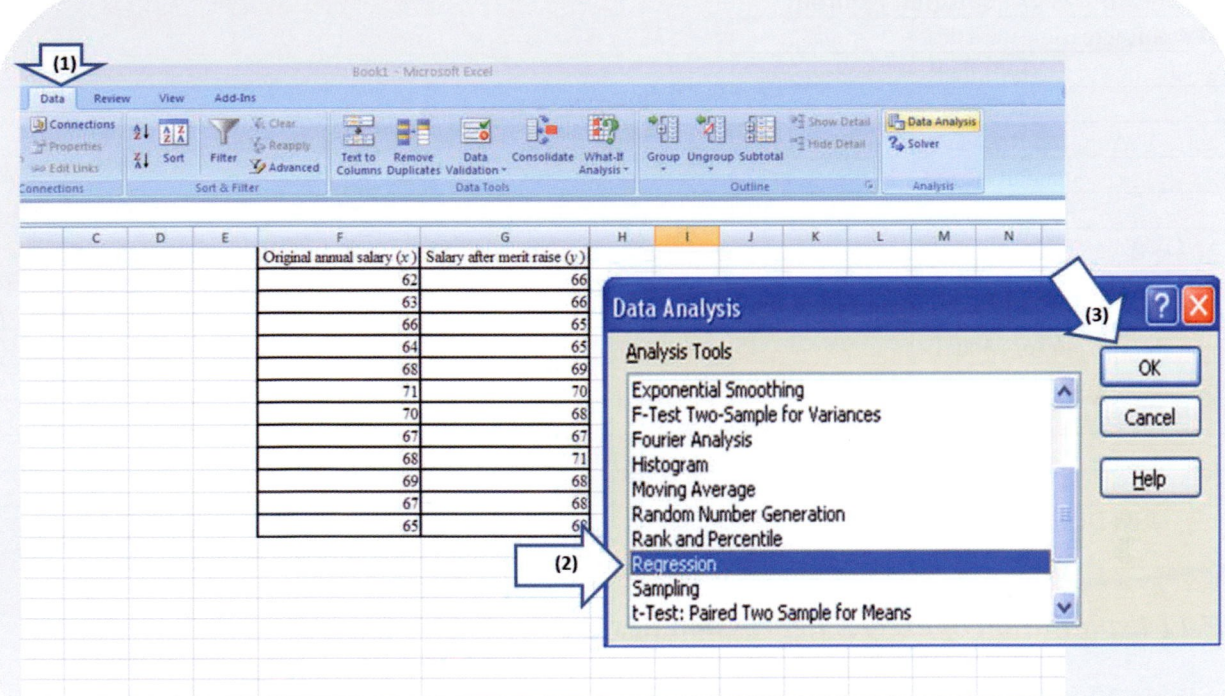

Figure 12.12. Using Excel® Data Analysis for Performing Regression Analysis: Steps 1-3

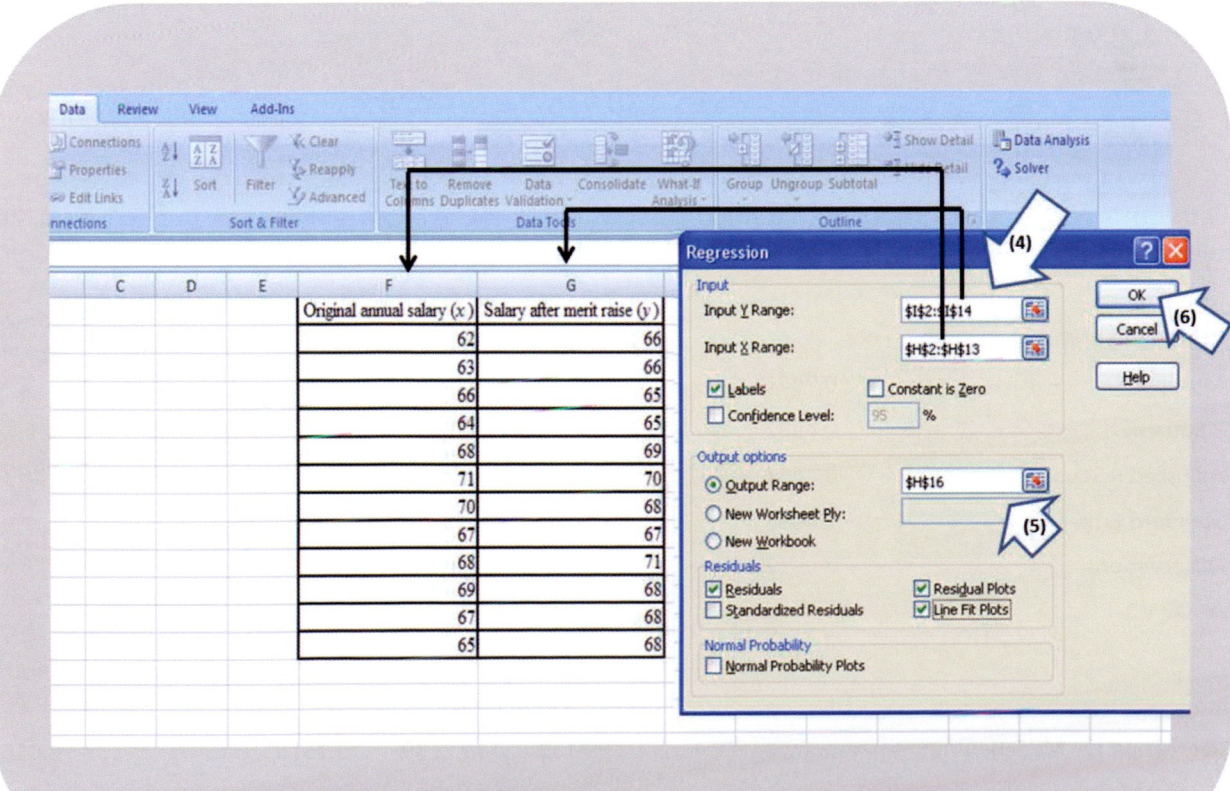

Figure 12.13. Using Excel® Data Analysis for Performing Regression Analysis: Steps 4-6

Table 12.8 Excel® summary output

Regression statistics	
Multiple R	0.7027
R Square	0.4937
Adjusted R Square	0.4431
Standard Error	1.4037
Observations	12

ANOVA

	df	SS	MS	F	Significance F (or Prob >F)
Regression (or Model)	1	19.2139	19.2139	9.7519	0.0108
Residual (or error)	10	19.7028	1.9703		
Total	11	38.9167			
	Coefficients	*Standard Error*	*t Stat*	*P-value*	
Intercept	35.8248	10.1780	3.52	0.0055	
Rod Diameter Before Treatment (x)	0.4764	0.1525	3.12	0.0108	

12.11 Explanation of Excel® Regression Results

In Table 12.8, the first output is the coefficient of correlation, *r* (or *Multiple R*), between the two variables *x* and *y* which is 0.7027. The corresponding coefficient of determination, R^2, is 0.4937. This means that out of the total variation in the dependent variable *Y*, about 49.37% is explained by this relationship and 50.63% is unexplained. Recall that this value is calculated from the following equation:

$$r^2 or R^2 = \frac{SSY - SSE}{SSY} = \frac{38.9167 - 19.7028}{38.9167} = 0.4937$$

The terms *SSY* and *SSE* can be obtained directly from the ANOVA Table associated with the regression analysis as shown in Table 12.8. Note that *SSY* is equal to the total sum of squares.

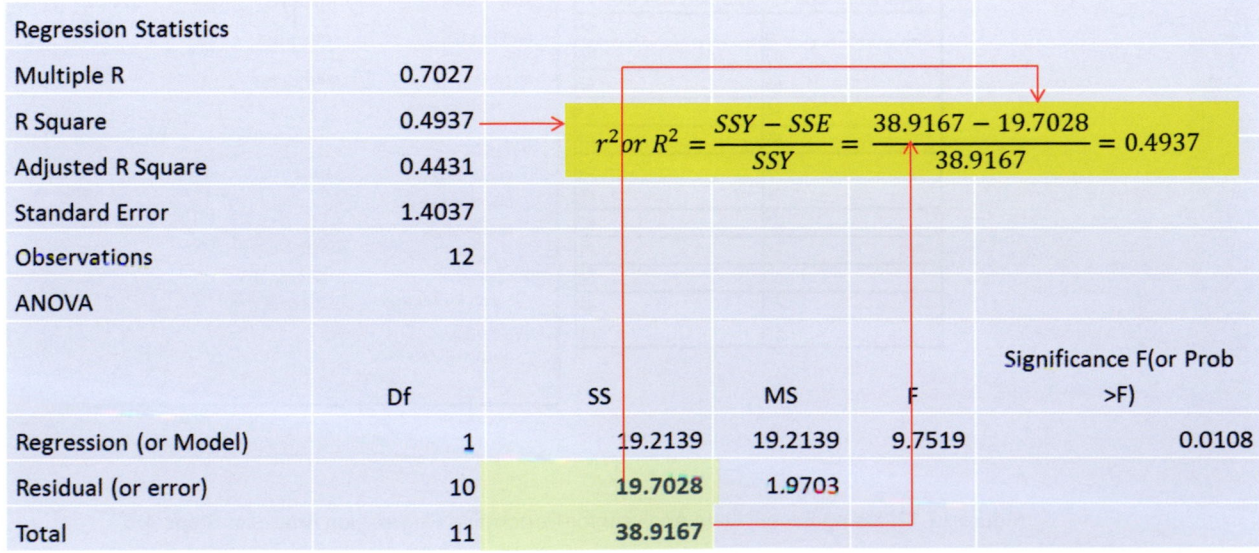

710

The adjusted R-square has a better meaning in multiple regression analysis. It is the coefficient of determination after adjusting for the number of parameters in the model so that models of different numbers of parameters can be compared. In this case, we use the mean squares (sum of squares/degrees of freedom) to determine the value of adjusted R square:

$$Adjusted\ R^2 = \frac{MSY - MSE}{MSY} = \frac{\frac{38.9167}{11} - 1.97028}{\frac{38.9167}{11}} = 0.4431$$

The value of the standard error of estimate shown in Table 12.8 is calculated from Equation 12.12 discussed earlier. This calculation is performed as follows:

$$s_{y.x}{}^2 = \frac{1}{n-2}\sum(y_i - \hat{y}_i)^2 = \frac{1}{n-2}SSE$$

$$s_{y.x} = \sqrt{\frac{1}{n-2}\sum(y_i - \hat{y}_i)^2} = \sqrt{\frac{1}{n-2}SSE} = \sqrt{MSE} = \sqrt{1.9703} = 1.4037$$

The F value of Table 12.8 can be interpreted in similar fashion to that discussed in Chapter 11 in the context of the analysis of variance. In this case, the F-value of the $ANOVA$ Table is calculated using the following equation:

$$F = \frac{MSR}{MSE} = \frac{19.2139}{1.9703} = 9.75$$

Accordingly, the F-value is the ratio of mean square for lack of fit (MSR) to mean square for pure error (MSE).

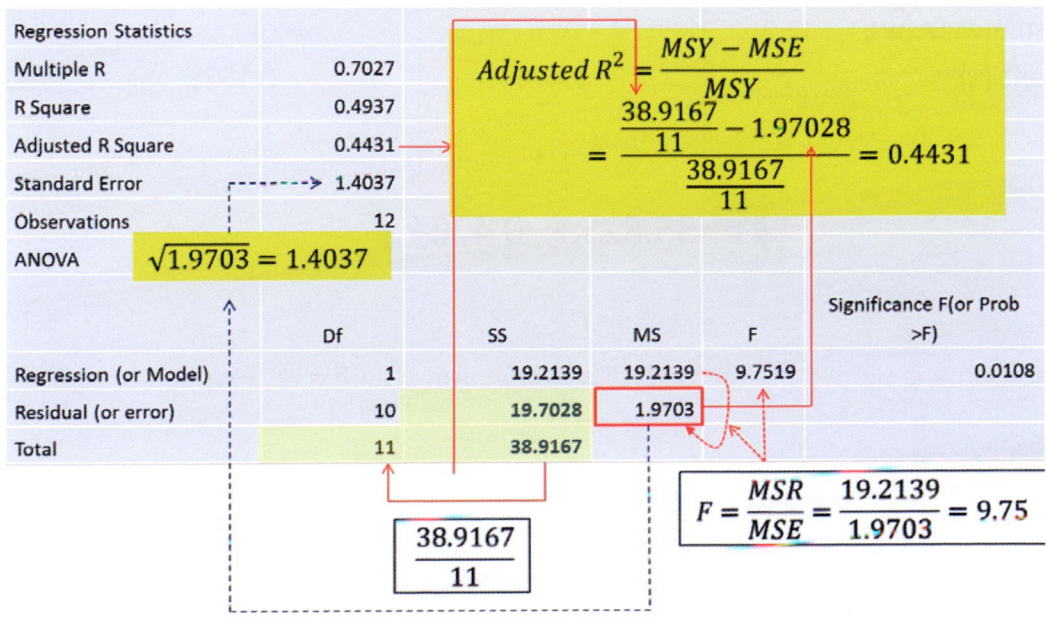

711

Basically, this F-value tests the following hypothesis:

H_o: 'No significant straight-line relationship of y on x'
or
H_o: $\beta_1 = 0$, or H_o: $r = 0$

In other words, the F-value tests whether the x-y relationship occurs by chance. In general, when the F-value is higher than the critical F-value (or $F_{1,10,0.95}$), determined from the F-distribution (Appendix 8.A Table III, Chapter 8), we reject the null hypothesis H_o. The term labeled significance F (or Prob $> F$) is the probability associated with the computed F-value. Typically, the smaller the Prob $> F$-value, the better the indication that the linear fit to the y variable is significantly better than the horizontal line that fits the sample mean to the data.

Using the values of the coefficients b_o and b_1 of Table 12.8, which are 35.825 and 0.4764, respectively, we can write the regression equation as follows:

$$y = 35.825 + 0.4764\,x$$

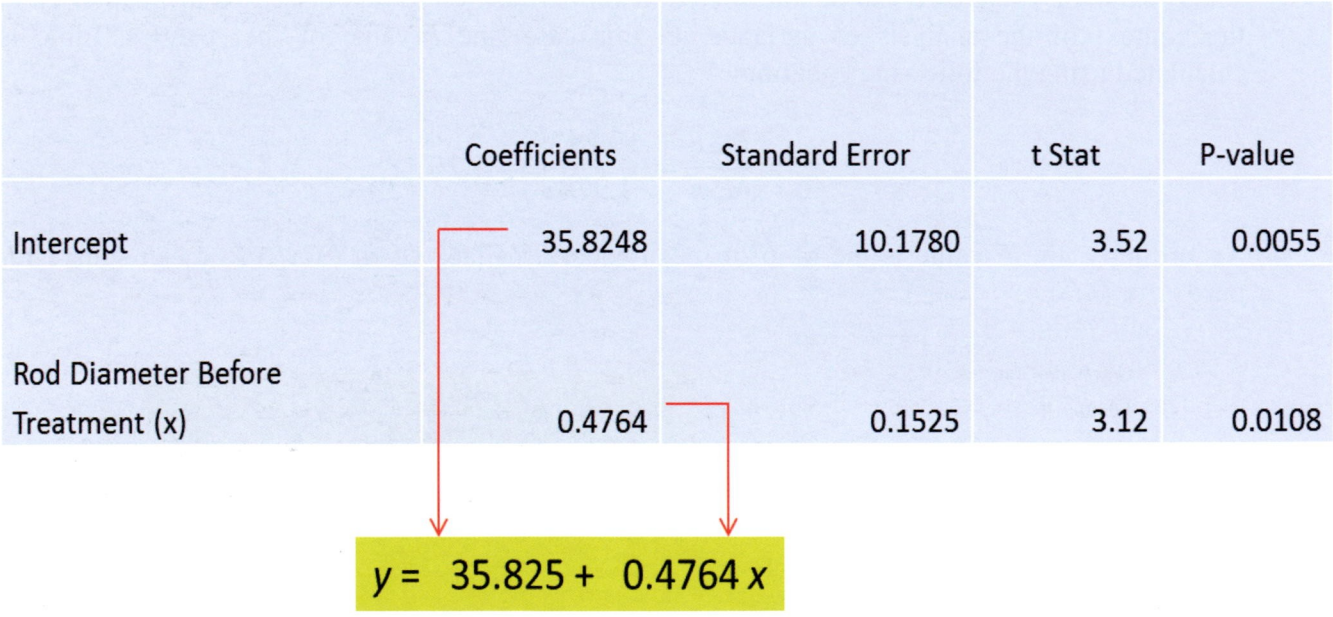

	Coefficients	Standard Error	t Stat	P-value
Intercept	35.8248	10.1780	3.52	0.0055
Rod Diameter Before Treatment (x)	0.4764	0.1525	3.12	0.0108

$$y = 35.825 + 0.4764\,x$$

This relationship is plotted in Figure 12.14.a, which is also an Excel® output.

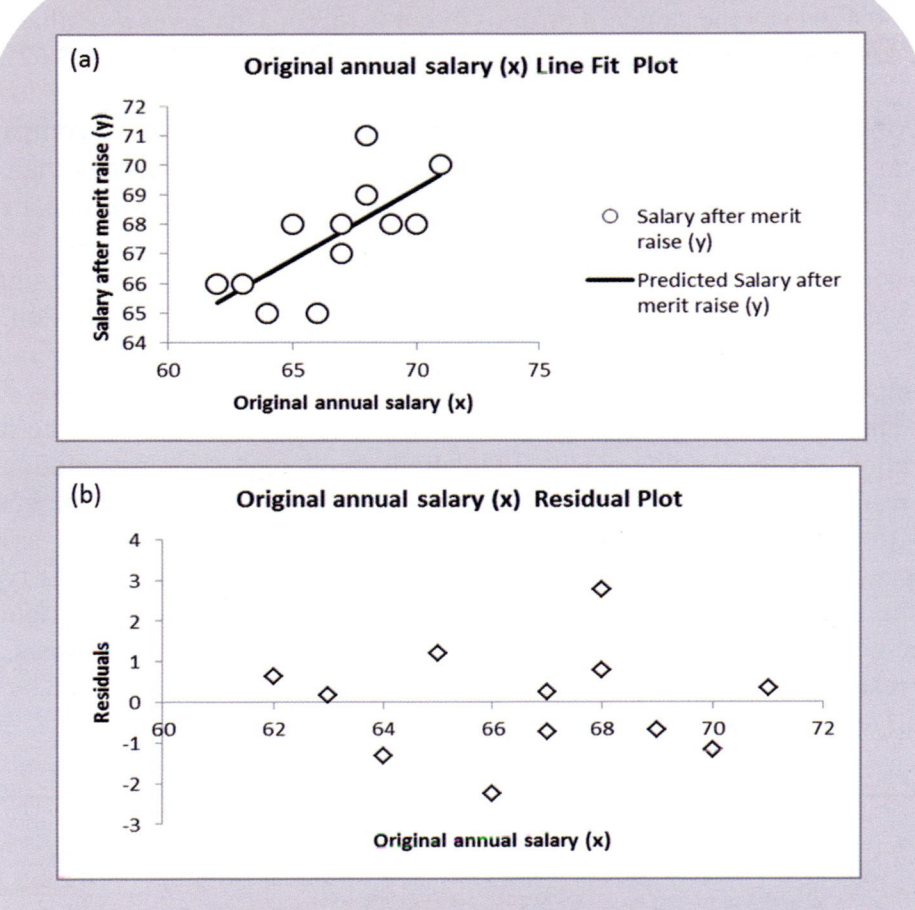

Figure 12.14 Line Fit and Residual Plot

The coefficients b_o and b_1 are also tested using a t-test. Basically, we can determine whether a significant relationship between the variables x and y exists by testing whether the coefficient β_1 (the true slope) is equal to zero. If we reject this hypothesis, we could conclude that there is evidence of a linear relationship between x and y variables. The format of this test of hypothesis is as follows:

$$H_o: \beta_1 = 0 \qquad \textit{There is no linear Relationship}$$
$$H_o: \beta_1 \neq 0 \qquad \textit{There is a linear Relationship}$$

The t-statistic is

$$t = \frac{b_1 - \beta_1}{s_{b_1}} \qquad (12.18)$$

where the term s_{b_1} is the standard error of the slope.

713

From the output of Table 12.8, and Equation 12.18, the t-statistic is calculated by dividing the value of b_1 (or 0.4764) by the standard error of b_1 (or 0.1525). This gives a t-value of about 3.12. Similarly, we can calculate the t-value for the intercept b_o (35.8248/10.1780 = 3.52).

The t-statistic follows a t-distribution with n-2 degrees of freedom. Thus, we compare the t-value with the critical value $t_{n-2,\alpha/2}$ or $t_{10, .025}$ or 2.2281. Since the t-statistic is greater than the critical t-value, we reject the null hypothesis and conclude that there is an evidence of linear relationship.

The p-values corresponding to the t-values of Table 12.8 indicate the levels of significance; the smaller the p-value the better the significance of the coefficient under consideration.

One of the important elements of regression modeling is the residual analysis. This analysis evaluates the appropriateness of the regression model that has been fitted to the data. Residual analysis also allows us to examine potential violations in the regression assumptions. Table 12.9 provides the residuals values or the differences between the predicted and the actual y values. Another way to analyze residuals is by plotting the residuals on the vertical axis against the corresponding x_i values of the independent variable on the horizontal axis. This type of plots is produced in the Excel® output (see Figure 12.14.b). If the fitted line is appropriate for the data, we should see no apparent pattern in the residuals-x_i plot. Table 12.9 also shows values of the standardized residuals. This quantity is determined by dividing each residual by the standard deviation of all residuals.

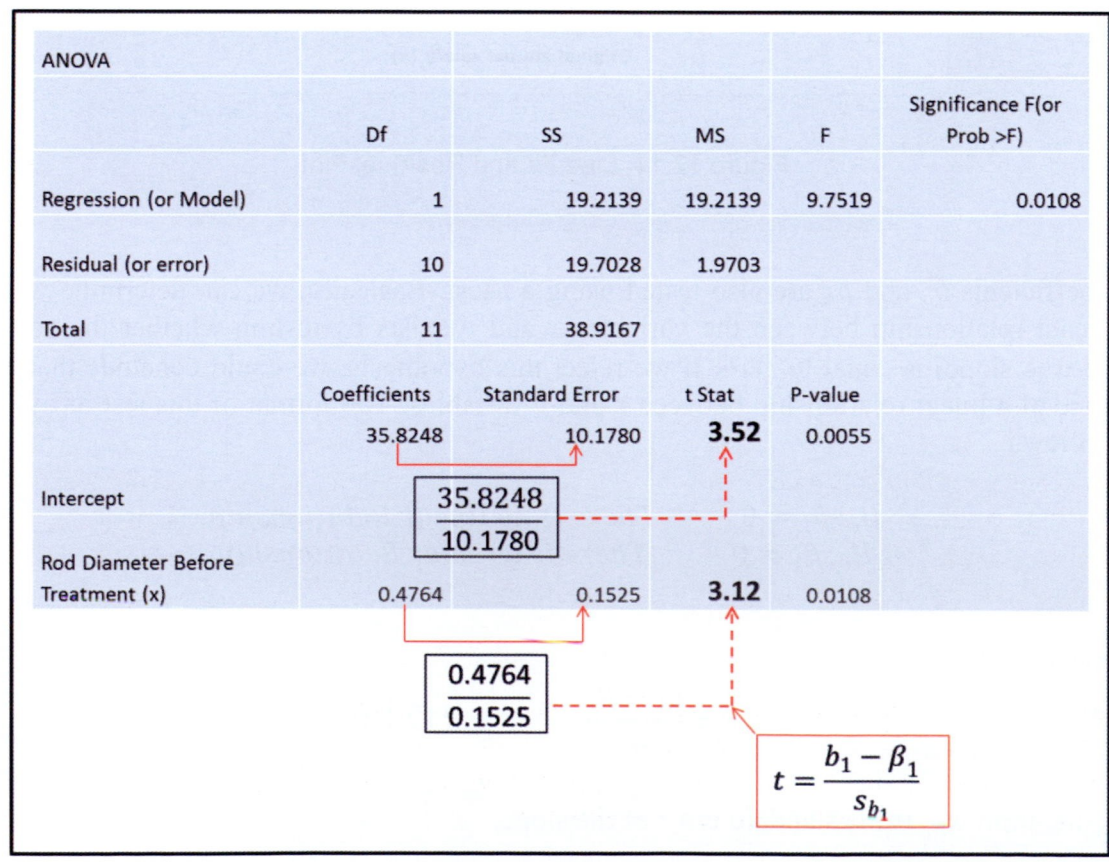

ANOVA					
	Df	SS	MS	F	Significance F(or Prob >F)
Regression (or Model)	1	19.2139	19.2139	9.7519	0.0108
Residual (or error)	10	19.7028	1.9703		
Total	11	38.9167			
	Coefficients	Standard Error	t Stat	P-value	
	35.8248	10.1780	**3.52**	0.0055	
Intercept	$\dfrac{35.8248}{10.1780}$				
Rod Diameter Before Treatment (x)	0.4764	0.1525	**3.12**	0.0108	

$$\dfrac{0.4764}{0.1525}$$

$$t = \frac{b_1 - \beta_1}{s_{b_1}}$$

Table 12.9 Excel® residual output

Observation	Predicted y	Residuals	Standard Residuals
1	65.3602	0.6398	0.4780
2	65.8366	0.1634	0.1221
3	67.2657	-2.2657	-1.6930
4	66.3130	-1.3130	-0.9811
5	68.2185	0.7815	0.5839
6	69.6476	0.3524	0.2633
7	69.1713	-1.1713	-0.8752
8	67.7421	-0.7421	-0.5545
9	68.2185	2.7815	2.0783
10	68.6949	-0.6949	-0.5192
11	67.7421	0.2579	0.1927
12	66.7894	1.2106	0.9046

12.12 Multiple Regression Analysis

A logical expansion of the simple x-y relationship discussed in the previous sections is the multiple- variable relationship in which two or more independent variables are related to a response variable. Multiple regression analysis is used for handling such relationships. Computations involved in multiple regression analyses are quite lengthy and often complicated. However, the availability of computers and powerful statistical software programs has made it possible to carry out these computations accurately and more efficiently. Therefore, our focus will be on the general concepts underlying multiple regression analysis and different applications.

A multiple regression model may take one of the following forms:

$$Y = \beta_o + \beta_1 x + \beta_2 x^2 + \cdots + \beta_k x^k + \varepsilon \qquad (12.19.a)$$

$$Y = \beta_o + \beta_1 x_1 + \beta_2 x_2 + \cdots + \beta_k x_k + \varepsilon \qquad (12.19.b)$$

where x^i or x_j are the independent variables, $\beta_o, \beta_1, \beta_2, \ldots . \beta_k$ are the regression coefficients, and ε is a random error.

The polynomial model (Equation 12.19.a) is considered a linear regression model since the term linear refers to linearity in the parameters (β's) and not the independent variable x. As indicated earlier, we assume that the random error ε is normally distributed with a mean of 0 and a variance of σ^2. Polynomial models are often useful when a simple x-y relationship seems to be nonlinear.

The assumptions associated with simple regression, namely; existence, independence, linearity, homoscedasticity, and normality, are also used in multiple regression analysis. An expansion of the linearity assumption means that the mean value of Y for each specific combination of x_1, $x_2, \ldots, x_k$ is a linear function of these x variables:

$$\mu_{Y|x_1,x_2,x_3,...,x_k} = \beta_o + \beta_1 x + \beta_2 x^2 + \cdots + \beta_k x^k + \varepsilon$$

or

$$\mu_{Y|x_1,x_2,x_3,...,x_k} = \beta_o + \beta_1 x_1 + \beta_2 x_2 + \cdots + \beta_k x_k + \varepsilon$$

Recall that in simple regression, the *x-y* relationship was easily described graphically using the points (x_i,y_i) in a two-dimensional graph. In this graph, the regression equation was defined as the path described by the mean values of the distribution of *y* as *x* was allowed to vary. Graphs of this sort become more complex as more independent variables (*k* variables) enter the regression model. The resultant graph in this case will be a hyper surface in ($k+1$) dimensional space.

Example 12.8: Using the data in Table 12.10, construct a scatter graph relating the number of accidents per week and the driving speed on a highway and propose an appropriate regression model to represent the relationship.

Table 12.10 Data of number of accidents per week and corresponding driving speeds

Driving Speed (miles/hr)	Number of Accidents per Week	Driving Speed (miles/hr)	Number of Accidents per Week
45	12	70	24
45	20	75	18
45	18	75	19
50	18	75	45
50	30	80	37
50	17	80	65
55	20	80	45
55	15	85	70
55	32	85	67
60	21	85	60
60	28	90	70
60	18	90	80
65	18	90	65
65	32	95	140
65	18	95	180
70	40	95	190
70	16	95	200

Solution:

Using Excel® Graph tools (discussed in Chapter 3), the scatter graph of the relationship between the driving speed and the number of accidents is shown in Figure 12.15. This relationship indicates that as the driving speed increases, the number of car accidents increase. In general, this is expected. The key question, however, is whether we can propose a linear model to represent this relationship or a nonlinear model (polynomial) will be more suitable. This question can be

716

addressed using Excel® Graph tools by adding two types of trend lines: linear and polynomial and then observing the equations and the coefficient of correlation in each case. Figure 12.16 shows both the linear and the polynomial fit and associated equations and R-square values.

The linear fit yields the following simple regression equation:

$$y = 2.375x - 116.59$$

and the coefficient of correlation r is 0.759.

The nonlinear fit yields the following multiple-regression equation (polynomial):

$$y = 0.1116x^2 - 13.358x + 409.05$$

and the coefficient of correlation r is 0.908.

The above results indicate that a non-linear polynomial fit is more appropriate to represent the relationship between driving speed and accidents than a linear fit.

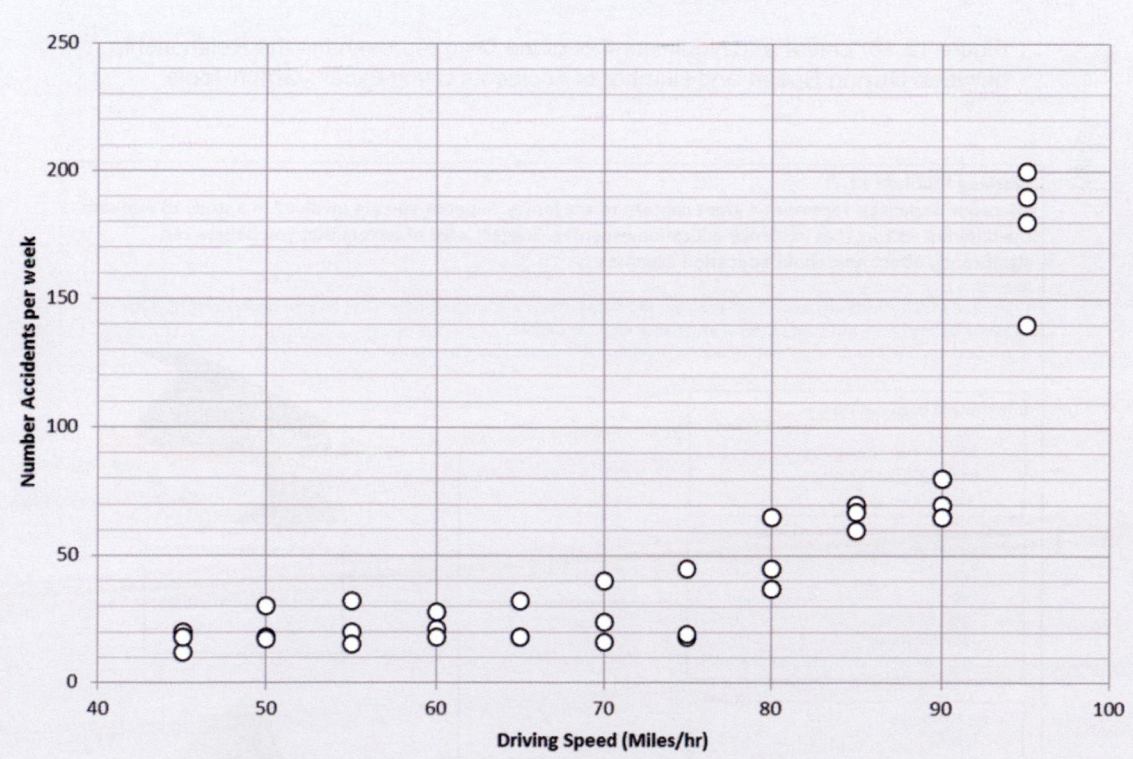

Figure 12.15. Scatter Graph of the Relationship between Driving Speed and Number of Accidents Using Excel® Graph Tools

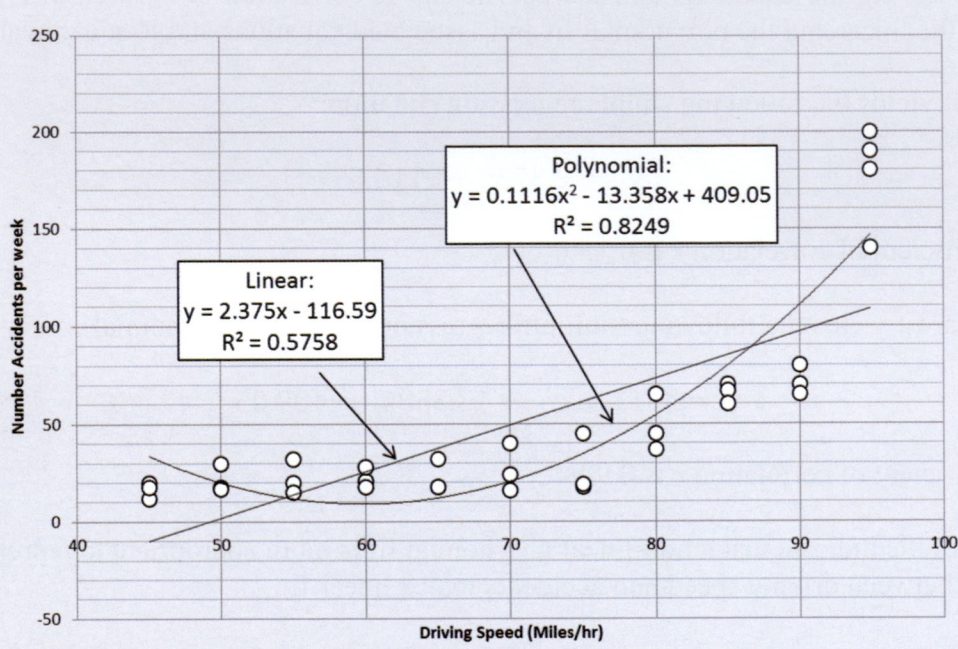

Figure 12.16. Linear and Nonlinear Fits of the Data representing the Relationship between Driving Speed and Number of Accidents Using Excel® Graph Tools

Working Problem 12.7:

Education expenses represent a great concern to any family. Suppose you are involved in a study to evaluate the different factors that influence education expenses. Suggest a list of factors that you believe can significantly affect household education expenses.

Answer:

This question represents an open-ended problem and it may have many answers depending on your understanding of the issue of education expenses and your personal experience with the subject.

Given below is one list. You may modify, add, or eliminate to produce your own answer

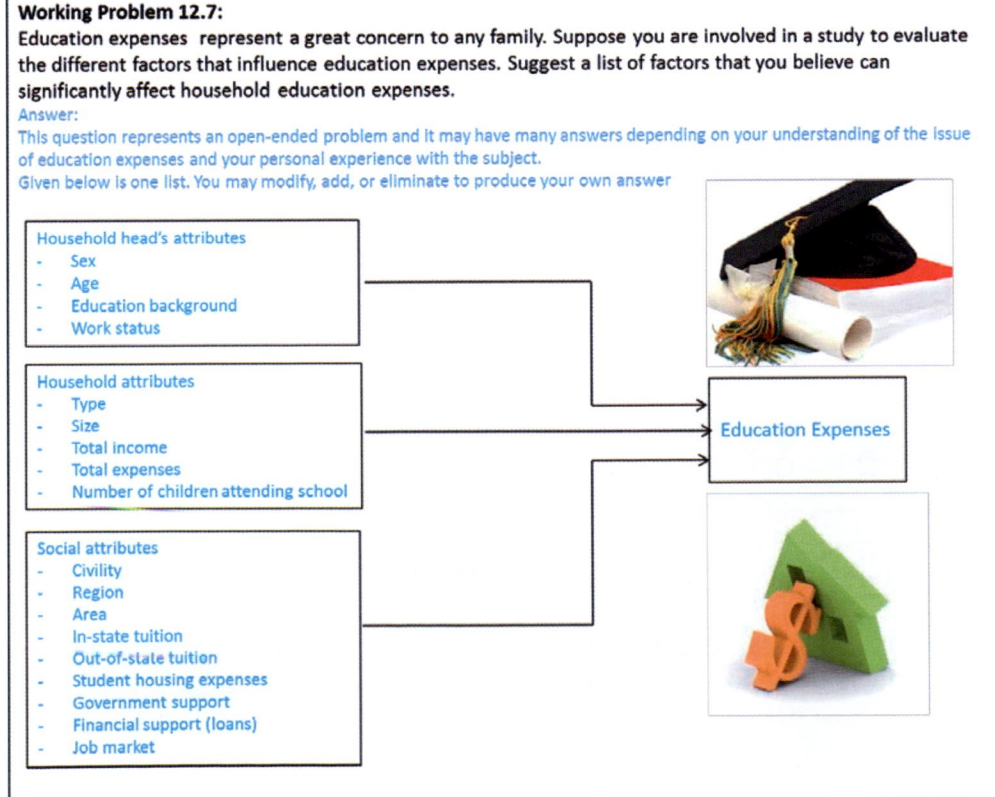

Working Problem 12.8
The data given below represent the number of hours a student study per week and the corresponding grades for a random sample of students. Develop a linear and a polynomial relationship between the two variables and compare the relationships using the coefficient of determination.

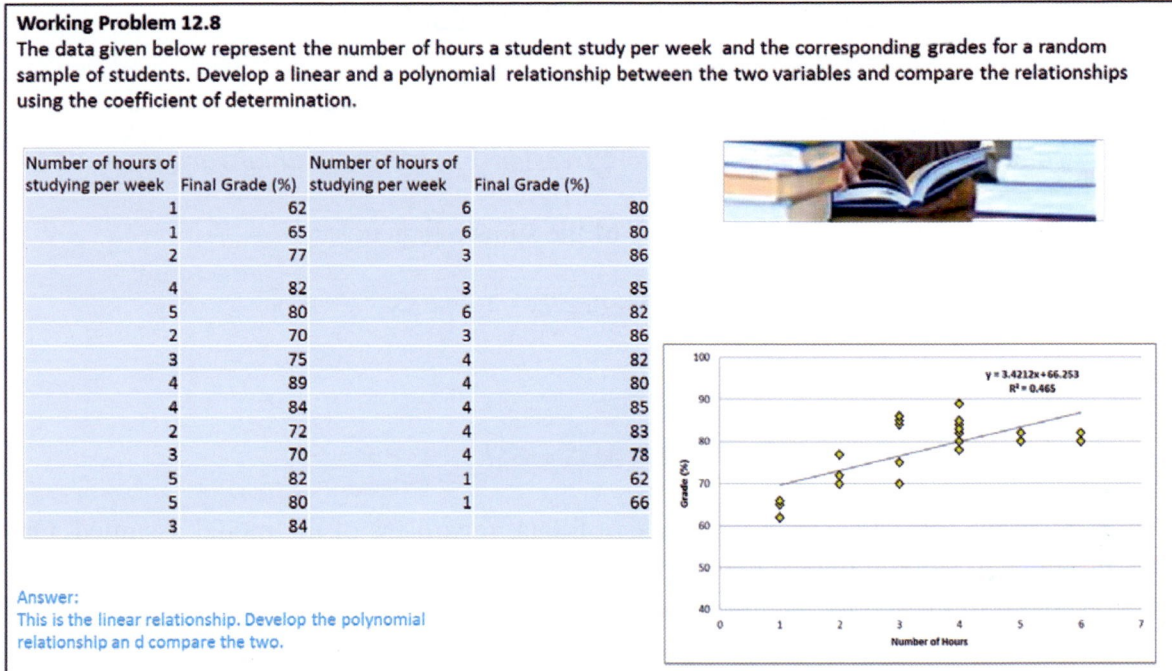

Number of hours of studying per week	Final Grade (%)	Number of hours of studying per week	Final Grade (%)
1	62	6	80
1	65	6	80
2	77	3	86
4	82	3	85
5	80	6	82
2	70	3	86
3	75	4	82
4	89	4	80
4	84	4	85
2	72	4	83
3	70	4	78
5	82	1	62
5	80	1	66
3	84		

Answer:
This is the linear relationship. Develop the polynomial relationship an d compare the two.

12.13 Least-Squares for Multiple Regression Analysis

The least-squares method discussed earlier is also used for multiple regression analysis. In this case, the least-squares solution giving the best-fitting plane is determined by minimizing the sum of squares of the distances between the observed values Y_i and the corresponding predicted values:

$$\hat{Y}_i = \hat{\beta}_o + \hat{\beta}_1 x_{1i} + \hat{\beta}_2 x_{2i} + \cdots$$

The sum of squares

$$\sum \left(Y_i - \hat{Y}_i \right)^2 = \sum (Y_i - \hat{\beta}_o - \hat{\beta}_1 x_{1i} - \hat{\beta}_2 x_{2i} + \cdots)^2$$

is minimized to determine the least-squares estimates.

12.14 Analysis of Variance for Multiple Regression Analysis

As indicated earlier, the total variation of the response variable y is defined by $\sum (y_i - \bar{y})^2$. This represents the sum of squares of the deviations of the y values from their mean. It was also indicated that the total sum of squares can be resolved into two terms: (a) unexplained residual variation or the sum of squared deviations from the observed y values to the regression line, and (b) variation due to regression or the sum of squared deviations from the regression line to the overall mean:

$$\sum (y_i - \bar{y})^2 = \sum (\hat{y}_i - \bar{y})^2 + \sum (y_i - \hat{y}_i)^2$$

or

Total variation = variation due to regression + error or residual variation

The above equation expresses the partitioning of the sums of squares:

$$\text{Total } SS = \text{Model } SS + \text{Error } SS$$

or

$$SSY = MSS + SSE$$

SSY always has the same value for a given set of data, regardless of the model assumed. On the other hand, the partitioning into *SSE* and *MSS* will depend on the proposed model. When a new x variable is added to the model, the *MSS* will generally increase. This will result in a reduction in the *SSE*. Using the matrix notation, the *SSE* is expressed as follows:

$$SSE = Y'(X'X)^{-1}X'Y = Y'Y - Y'X(X'X)^{-1}X'Y = Y'Y - \hat{\beta}X'Y \qquad (12.20)$$

For inferences about regression estimates, we calculate the error mean square:

$$s^2 = MSE = \frac{\text{Error } SS}{(n - k - 1)} \qquad (12.21)$$

where s^2 is an unbiased estimate of σ^2, the variance of the ε_i, n is the number of observations, and k is the number of independent variables in the model.

The ANOVA Table for multiple regression analysis is shown in Table 12.11. Notice the similarity of this table with that discussed earlier for simple regression analysis.

Table 12.11 Analysis of variance table

Source	df	SS	MS	F-Value	Prob > F
Model	k	SSY-SSE	SSM/k		
Error	n-k-1	SSE	SSE/(n-k-1)		
Total	n-1	SSY			

As shown in Table 12.11, the 'SS' column contains the various sums of squares. The 'df' column gives the corresponding degrees of freedom. For the model sum of squares, the degree of freedom is k, which is the number of independent variables in the model. The residual degree of freedom is $n-k-1$, and the total degree of freedom is $n-1$. The 'MS' column contains the mean-square terms, obtained by dividing the sum-of-squares terms by their corresponding degrees-of-freedom values. The *F*-value is obtained by dividing the mean square for model (regression *MS*) by the mean-square residual or error (*MSE*).

As indicated earlier, the coefficient of determination measures how well the fitted model is. In multiple regression analysis, the coefficient of determination is determined in the same way as in simple regression. In this case, we normally use the capital letter R^2 to denote the coefficient of determination:

$$R^2 = \frac{SSY - SSE}{SSY}$$

where R^2 lies between 0 and 1.

12.15 Goodness of Fit for Multiple Regression Analysis

Regression analysis provides many techniques by which a regression model can be tested. The most common technique is the test of hypothesis. This test is designed to answer some questions about the contributions of various independent variables to the prediction of the response variable *Y*. These questions include:

- Does the entire set of independent variables (or, equivalently, the fitted model itself) contribute significantly to the prediction of *Y*? The answer to this question requires an '*overall test.*'

- Does the addition of one particular independent variable of interest add significantly to the prediction of *Y* above that achieved by other independent variables already present in the model? The answer to this question requires '*test for addition of a single variable.*'

The tests of hypothesis used to answer the above questions involve the use of *F*-statistic and/or equivalent *t*-statistic. In the following discussion, we will illustrate these tests.

12.15.1 Overall Test

For the general model:

$$Y = \beta_o + \beta_1 x_1 + \beta_2 x_2 + \cdots + \beta_k x_k + \varepsilon$$

The null hypothesis for an overall test can be stated as follows:

H_o: '*all k independent variables considered together do not explain a significant amount of the variation in Y.*'

Equivalently,

H_o: '*there is no significant overall regression using all k independent variables in the model*' or

$$H_o: \beta_o = \beta_1 = \beta_2 = \cdots = \beta_k = 0$$

To test this hypothesis we use the F-statistic obtained from the analysis of variance:

$$F = \frac{MSR}{MSE} = \frac{\dfrac{SSY - SSE}{k}}{\dfrac{SSE}{n - k - 1}} \qquad (12.22)$$

where SSY is the total sum of squares and SSE is the error sum of squares.

The computed F-statistic can then be compared with the critical point $F_{k,n-k-1,1-\alpha}$. This value can be obtained from tables of F-Distributions (Appendix 8.A Table III, Chapter 8). We would reject H_o if the computed F is greater than $F_{k,n-k-1,1-\alpha}$. We also compute the p-value for this test as the area under the curve to the right of the computed F-statistic (*Prob >F* in the ANOVA Table).

The computed F-statistic can be expressed in terms of R^2 as follows:

$$F = \frac{R^2/k}{(1 - R^2)/(n - k - 1)} \qquad (12.23)$$

12.15.2 Test for Addition of a New Variable

In this case, we consider the null hypothesis H_o: $\beta_l = 0$, where β_l is the coefficient of the variable added last, x_l, to the regression model:

$$Y = \beta_o + \beta_1 x_1 + \beta_2 x_2 + \cdots + \beta_k x_k + \varepsilon$$

The t-statistic in this case is:

$$t = \frac{\hat{\beta}_l}{s_{\beta_l}} \qquad (12.24)$$

where $\hat{\beta}_l$ is the corresponding estimated coefficient and s_{β_l} is the estimate of the standard error of $\hat{\beta}_l$.

In performing this test, we reject H_o: $\beta_l = 0$, if:

$|t| > t_{n-p-2,\ \alpha/2}$ (two-sided test, H_a: $\hat{\beta}_l \neq 0$)
$t > t_{n-p-2,\ 1-\alpha}$ (upper one-sided test, H_a: $\beta_l > 0$)
$t < - t_{n-p-2,\ 1-\alpha}$ (lower one-sided test, H_a: $\beta_l < 0$)

The critical t-value can be obtained from the t-table (Appendix 8.A Table I, Chapter 8).

The examples below will illustrate how the goodness of fit test is performed.

Example 12.9: The data in Table 12.12 represents three independent variables, namely: sales ($), S, salesman expenses ($), E, and years of service (Yr). The response or dependent variable is the commission ($), C. Develop a regression equation relating commission to sales ($).

Table 12.12 Values of sales, expenses, years in service, and sales commission

Sales ($), S	Expenses ($), E	Year of Service, Yr	Commission($) C	Sales ($), S	Expenses ($), E	Year of Service, Yr	Commission($) C
282137	22838	7	14107	299341	19129	6	22122
328685	21328	12	24620	282338	20273	6	11294
339633	24954	14	28350	286152	19221	4	5723
347385	19141	15	29851	288332	17615	8	14417
288613	24438	6	11545	298019	23341	13	26321
289716	19253	7	14486	298374	27458	16	30442
293356	20709	12	23643	299127	27038	17	30029
294166	21734	12	24676	316016	14777	12	25404
324810	24504	8	16241	316128	20003	10	18968
324911	20510	11	22744	318094	24572	8	12724
326343	21754	10	19581	322804	19411	6	9684
300923	26240	15	27752	323216	21417	13	24649
305644	21547	10	18339	320846	23796	12	22083
306264	19360	8	15313	324061	25438	16	28679
306991	21550	11	18419	307530	23913	15	26988
307392	22330	6	15370	309901	26752	7	9297
299184	23830	10	23164	314470	24152	8	15724

Solution:

The relationship between sales ($) and commission ($) is a case of simple regression for developing an x-y relationship. In this case, the proposed model is in the following form:

$$C = \beta_o + \beta_1 S + \varepsilon$$

The independent variable is the sales, S, and the dependent variable is the commission, C. The population of data is represented by the above linear model in which the slope is β_1 and the intercept is β_o with an error term ε.

If the true relationship between the sales ($) and the sales commission ($) is essentially linear over the given data range, then the parameter β_1 will measure the actual change in sales commission, C, corresponding to a unit change in sales, S. On the other hand, the practical value of the parameter β_o generally depends on the nature of the variables under consideration. In this example, the value of C corresponding to S of zero has no practical meaning since a value of $S = 0$ does not exist. The scatter graph representing this relationship is shown in Figure 12.17.

Using Excel® data analysis, the output of the regression analysis is as shown in Table 12.13. Explanation of the output is given below.

Table 12.13 Excel® Regression Output ($\alpha = 0.05$): Model $C = \beta_o + \beta_1 S + \varepsilon$

SUMMARY OUTPUT						
Regression Statistics						
Multiple R	0.3593					
R Square	0.1291					
Adjusted R Square	0.1019					
Standard Error	6469.2					
Observations	34					
ANOVA						
	df	*SS*	*MS*	*F*	*Significance F*	
Regression	1	198530515.3	198530515.26	4.74	0.0368	
Residual	32	1339197578.3	41849924.32			
Total	33	1537728093.6				
	Coefficients	*Standard Error*	*t Stat*	*P-value*	*Lower 95%*	*Upper 95%*
Intercept	-26219.635	21286.726	-1.232	0.227	-69579.28	17140
S($)	0.150	0.069	2.178	0.037	0.010	0.290

Summary of Fit:

The value R-Square shown in Table 12.13 is calculated from:

$$R^2 = \frac{SSY - SSE}{SSY} = \frac{1537728093.586 - 1339197578.322}{1537728093.586} = 0.129$$

As indicated earlier, the coefficient of determination R^2, represents an estimate of the fraction of the total variation in the values of the dependent variable explained by its linear relationship to the independent variable. Thus, we may conclude that based on the given data set only 13% of the variation in sales commission is explained by the variation in sales ($) and 87% is due to other factors not explained by the model. The value standard error in the table is the square root of the error mean square ($\sqrt{41849924.32} = 6469.152$).

Recall that the standard error is obtained from the following equation:

$$s_{y.x} = \sqrt{\frac{1}{n-2}\sum(y_i - \hat{y}_i)^2} = \sqrt{\frac{1}{n-2}SSE} = \sqrt{MSE} = \sqrt{\frac{1}{32}(1339197578.322)}$$
$$= 6469.152$$

ANOVA Table:

The analysis of variance (*ANOVA* Table) associated with this simple regression model is also shown in Table 12.13. In this case, the model involves one independent variable, *S*. Thus, the model degrees of freedom (df_{Model} = the number of independent variables in the model) is 1. The total degrees of freedom is n-1 = 34-1 = 33. The error (or residual) degrees of freedom is $n - k - 1 = 34 - 1 - 1 = 32$. The term *k* is the number of independent variables in the model, which is one in this case.

The values of sum of squares corresponding to different sources of variation are given in the third column of the ANOVA Table. Recall that these sums of squares are based on the partitioning rule (*Total SS = Model SS + Error SS*). Usually, good models result in the model *SS* being a large fraction of the total *SS*. The mean squares values are given in the fourth column of the ANOVA Table. As indicated earlier, these values are obtained by dividing *SS* by *df*. For example, the error or residual mean square *MSE* = (*Error SS*)/df_{Error} = 1339197578.322/32 = 41849924.323. This value represents an unbiased estimate of σ^2, provided the model is correctly specified.

The F-value is calculated from the ratio of the Model *MS* and the Error *MS* (or 198530515.26/41849924.32 = 4.744). As mentioned earlier, this value can be used to perform the following overall test:

H_o: 'there is no significant overall regression using the independent variable, *S*, in the model' or

$$H_o: \beta_1 = 0$$

As indicated earlier, the computed F-statistic can then be compared with the critical point $F_{k,n-k-1, 1-\alpha}$ or $F_{1,33,0.95}$. From the *F*-Distribution (Appendix 8.A Table III, Chapter 8), $F_{1, 33, 0.95}$ is 0.239. We would reject H_o if the computed, F_o is greater than $F_{k,n-k-1,1-\alpha}$. Accordingly, we reject H_o and conclude that the variable *S* helps to predict the sales commission *C*. Alternatively, we could compute the *p*-value for this test as the area under the curve of the $F_{k,n-k-1}$ ($F_{1,33}$) distribution to the right of the computed *F*-statistic (*Significance F* in the ANOVA Table). This area is shown in the ANOVA Table as 0.0368. This area is smaller than 0.05 yielding the same conclusion that the β_1 coefficient is significant.

Parameter Estimates:

In the bottom portion of the output table, the parameter estimates are given. The terms 'Intercept' and '*S*' identify the coefficient estimates. The values of parameter estimates being β_o = -26219.635 and β_1 = 0.1501 indicate that the regression equation is in the following linear form:

$$C = -26219.635 + 0.1501\,S$$

This equation may be used to predict the value of sales commission at a given value of sales ($), provided a number of criteria have been met.

The value of standard error corresponding to each parameter estimate is calculated in the same way as discussed earlier. These values are 21286.726 for β_o, and 0.0689 for β_1. We can use these values to construct confidence intervals for the model parameters as shown in the output at 95%.

Example 12.10: For the data in Table 12.12, develop a regression equation relating commission to sales ($) and sales expenses ($).

Solution:

The proposed model in this case is a two-variable model as shown by the following form:

$$C = \beta_o + \beta_1 S + \beta_2 E + \varepsilon$$

The Excel® output of regression analysis is given in Table 12.14. Different values shown in this table are explained below.

Table 12.14 Excel® Regression Output ($\alpha = 0.05$): Model $C = \beta_o + \beta_1 S + \beta_2 E + \varepsilon$

SUMMARY OUTPUT						
Regression Statistics						
Multiple R	0.4266					
R Square	0.1820					
Adjusted R Square	0.1292					
Standard Error	6370.0123					
Observations	34					
ANOVA						
	df	*SS*	*MS*	*F*	*Significance F*	
Regression	2	279839333	139919666	3.45	0.044	
Residual	31	1257888761	40577057			
Total	33	1537728094				
	Coefficients	*Standard Error*	*t Stat*	*P-value*	*Lower 95%*	*Upper 95%*
Intercept	-37232	22358	-1.665	0.106	-82831	8367
S($)	0.147	0.068	2.166	0.038	0.009	0.285
E($)	0.539	0.381	1.416	0.167	-0.237	1.315

Summary of Fit:

As shown in Table 12.14, the addition of another variable to the model has resulted in a slight increase in the R value (from 0.3593 to 0.4266). The standard error or root mean square error for this two-variable model is slightly smaller than that of the one-variable model (from 6469.2 to 6370.01).

ANOVA Table:

As can be seen in the *ANOVA* Table, the model involves two independent variables, *S* and *E*. Thus, the model degree of freedom (df_{Model} = the number of independent variables in the model) is 2. The error (or residual) degree of freedom is $n - k - 1 = 34 - 2 - 1 = 31$, and the total degree of freedom = $34 - 1 = 33$.

Also note that as a result of adding expenses, *E*, to the model, a larger value of the model *SS* is obtained (compare *ANOVA* of Tables 12.13 and 12.14). With the total *SS* being the same, this leads to a higher value of R^2.

The *F*-value (Model MS/Error MS = 139919666/40577057= 3.45) can again be used to perform the overall test:

H_o: 'there is no significant overall regression using all k independent variables in the model' or

$$H_o: \beta_1 = \beta_2 = 0$$

We reject H_o since *Prob>F* of 0.04 is less than 0.05, and we conclude that the variables *S* and *E* help to predict the sales commission, *C*. However, note that the F-value for this two-variable model is slightly less than that of the one-variable model (Table 12.13). The probability value is also slightly higher than that of the one-variable model. In general, this indicates that the addition of sales expenses, *E*, to the model did not reveal additional goodness of fit. In other words, the increase in the Prob > F value and the reduction in the *F*-value of the two-variable model indicates that the addition of the variable *E* to the model, although slightly improves the R^2 value, upsets the overall significance of the model. The overall test simply indicates that rejection of the null hypothesis means that some of the β's are not zero. But it does not mean that every single coefficient is not approximately equal to zero.

The above point indicates that addition of variables to the model leads to an increase in the R^2 value. If the added variable is superfluous the improvement in fit will not be real. To overcome this problem, the adjusted R^2 is introduced:

$$Adjusted\ R^2 = 1 - (1 - R^2)\left[\frac{(n-1)}{(n-k-1)}\right] = 1 - (1 - 0.1820)[\frac{33}{31}] = 0.129$$

The adjusted R^2 tends to stabilize to a certain value when an adequate set of variables is included in the model. This point is better illustrated when at least a two-variable model is compared with another model of larger number of independent variables as will be shown in the next example. The adjusted R^2 value of this example is the same as the R^2 value of the one-variable model, or slightly better. This again indicates no improvement as a result of the addition of the new variable.

The above observations indicate that the addition of the new variable (sales expenses) did not add much to the overall model of sales commission. This can also be revealed by observing the simple relationship between sales expenses and sales commission as shown in Figure 12.18. This relationship reveals a weak effect of sales expenses on commission.

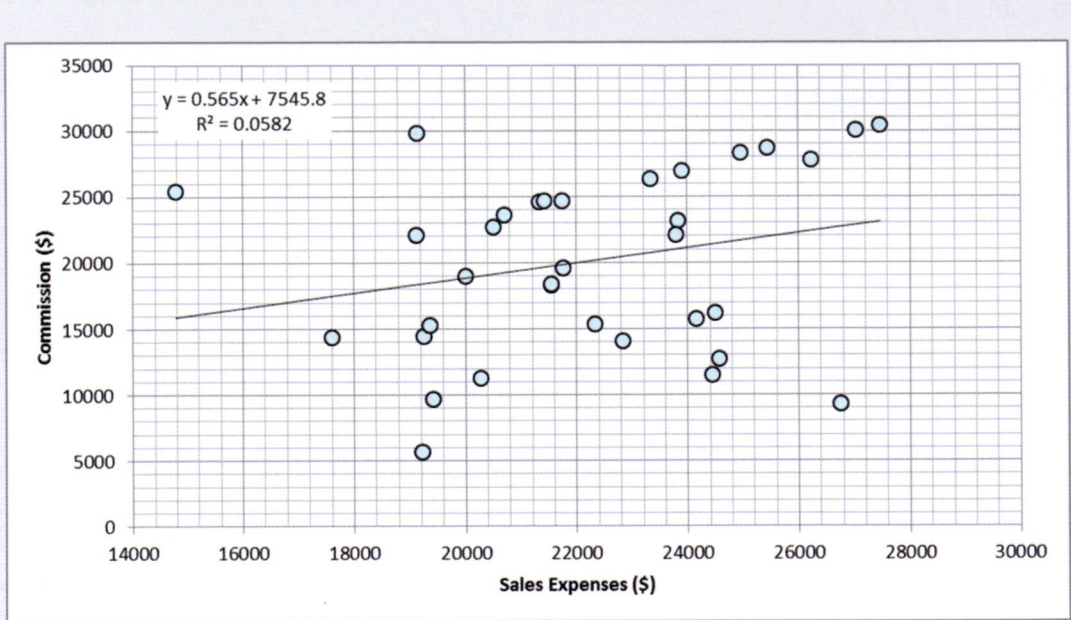

Figure 12.18. Linear Fit of the Data representing the Relationship between Sales Expenses and Commission Using Excel® Graph Tools

Parameter Estimates:

The parameter estimates given in Table 12.14 yield the following equation:

$$C = -37232 + 0.147S + 0.539E$$

Example 12.11: For the data in Table 12.12, develop a regression equation relating commission to sales ($), sales expenses ($), and years of service, Yr.

Solution:
The proposed model in this case is a three-variable model as shown in the following form:

$$C = \beta_o + \beta_1 S + \beta_2 E + \beta_3 Yr + \varepsilon$$

The Excel® output of regression analysis is given in Table 12.15. This output can be explained in similar fashion to that of the one- or two-variable models. Different values shown in this table are explained below.

Table 12.15 Excel® Regression Output ($\alpha = 0.05$): Model $C = \beta_o + \beta_1 S + \beta_2 E + \beta_3 Yr + \varepsilon$

Regression Statistics						
Multiple R	0.935					
R Square	0.874					
Adjusted R Square	0.861					
Standard Error	2544.126					
Observations	34					
ANOVA						
	df	SS	MS	F	Sig. F	
Regression	3	1.34E+09	4.48E+08	69.19009	1.3922E-13	
Residual	30	1.94E+08	6472577			
Total	33	1.54E+09				
	Coefficients	Std. Error	t Stat	P-value	Lower 95%	Upper 95%
Intercept	6335.253	9554.326	0.6631	0.512344	-13177.285	25847.8
Sales ($), S	0.0015	0.0294	0.0501	0.960350	-0.0585	0.0615
Expenses ($), E	-0.2736	0.1647	-1.6614	0.107051	-0.6100	0.0627
Years of Serv, Yr	1875.519	146.303	12.819	0.000000	1576.7274	2174.31

Summary of Fit: The addition of a third variable to the model has resulted in a substantial increase in the R value (from 0.4266 for the two-variable model to 0.935 for the three-variable model). The standard error or root mean square error for this three-variable model is smaller than that of the two-variable model (from 6370.0123 to 2544.13). These are signs that the added variable has a significant effect on the response or dependent variable. This can also be revealed by observing the simple relationship between years of service and sales commission as shown in Figure 12.19. This relationship reveals a very strong effect of years of service on commission. An R^2 value of 0.874 indicates that about 87% of the variation in the response variable is explained by the variables in the model and 13% is unexplained.

ANOVA **Table:**

Since the model involves three independent variables, S, E, and Yr, the model degrees of freedom (df_{Model} = the number of independent variables in the model) is 3. The error (or residual) degree of freedom is $n - k - 1 = 34 - 3 - 1 = 30$. The total degree of freedom is $n - 1 = 33$.

As a result of adding the variable years of service to the model, a much larger value of the model SS is obtained. Model SS for the two-variable model was 279839333 and Model SS for the three-variable model is 1.34×10^9. With the total SS being the same, this leads to a much higher value of R^2 (0.874 for the three variable model compared to 0.1820 for the two variable model).

The three-variable model showed a much higher F-value (Model MS/Error $MS = 4.48 \times 10^8$ /6472577 = 69.19) than the two-variable model or the one-variable model. This value can again be used to perform the overall test:

H_o: 'there is no significant overall regression using all k independent variables in the model' or

$$H_o: \beta_1 = \beta_2 = \beta_3 = 0$$

We reject H_o since $Prob > F$ of 1.3922×10^{-13} is much less than 0.05, and we conclude that the variables S, E, and Yr help to predict sales commission.

Parameter Estimates:

The parameter estimates given in Table 12.15 yield the following equation:

$$C = 6335.253 + 0.0015\,S - 0.2736\,E + 1875.52\,Yr$$

Note how high the t-statistic associated with the years of service variable (12.819) as compared to those of sales and expenses. Also note how low its corresponding probability (0 value).

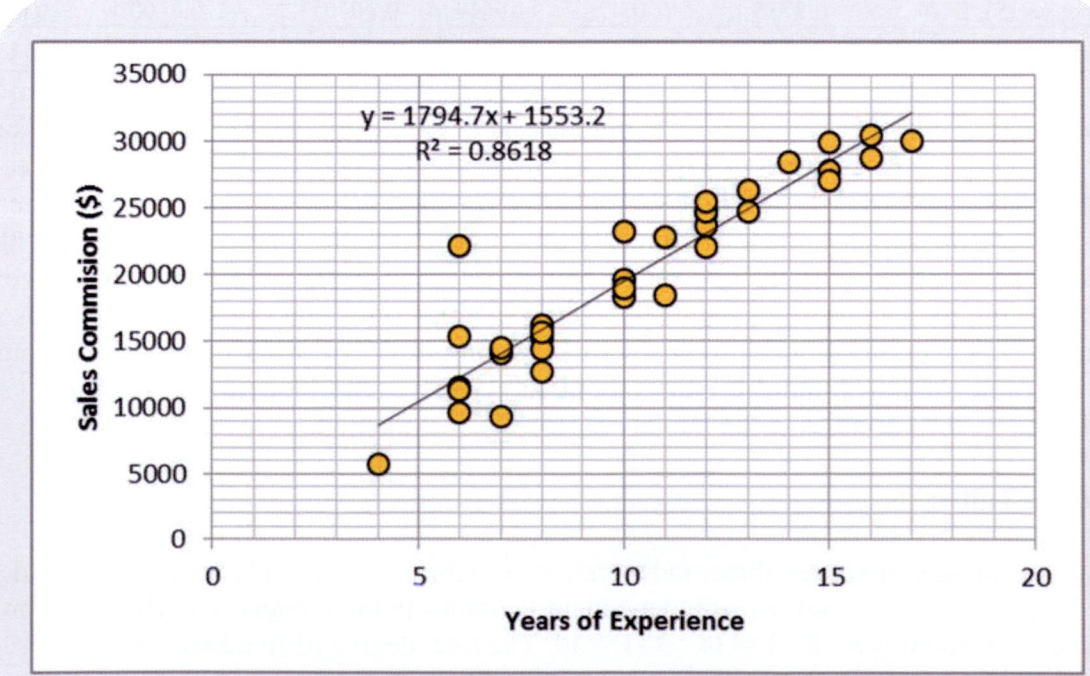

Figure 12.19. Linear Fit of the Data representing the Relationship between Years of Service and Commission Using Excel® Graph Tools

In addition to the above analysis, it is also important to perform residual analysis for each variable used in the regression model. Figure 12.20 shows these residual plots. Note that these plots reveal random patterns, which is the desirable pattern of residual plots.

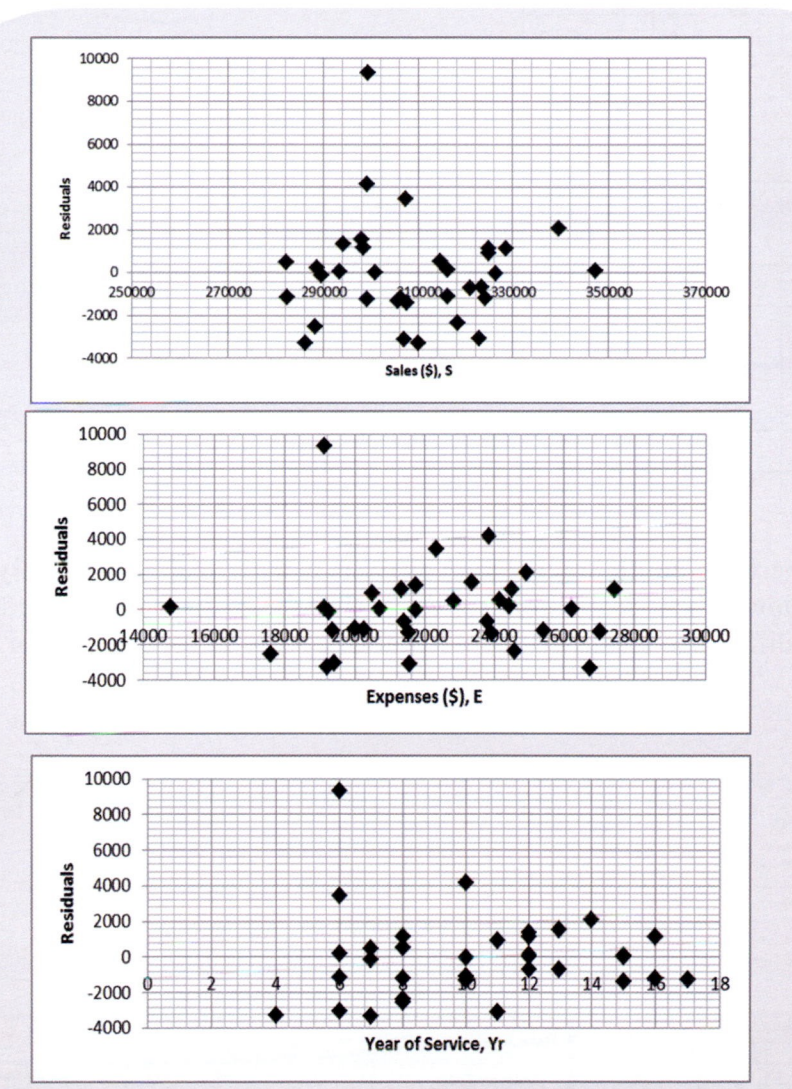

Figure 12.20. Residual Plots of Different Variables in the Model
$$C = \beta_o + \beta_1 S + \beta_2 E + \beta_3 Yr + \varepsilon$$

12.16 The Use of Software Programs for Performing Multiple Regression Analysis

Example 12.12: For the data in Table 12.16, perform multiple regression analysis to relate y to the variables x_1, x_2, and x_3 using Excel® Data Analysis.

Table 12.16

x_1	x_2	x_3	y
2	12	5	7
1.4	10.5	3	8
1.6	9	6	11
3.2	8.2	7	14
4	6.8	8	19
4.3	7	5	21
5.8	5.8	4	27
6.3	7	6	28
7.5	6.2	8	25
8.4	4.6	3	32
8.2	3.8	6	33
9.4	4	5	35

The steps used to perform multiple regression analysis using Excel® Data Analysis are shown in the two Figures below. These steps are identical to those used for performing simple regression analysis. The only difference is that the Input X Range covers all the columns of the x variables.

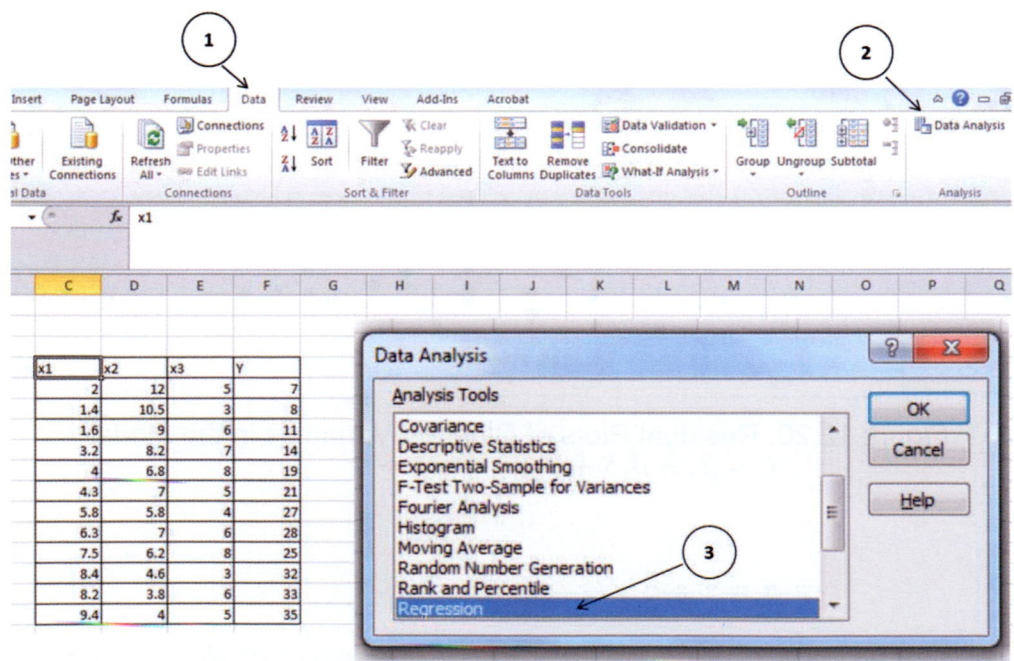

Using Excel® to perform Multiple Regression Analysis: Step 1, 2 & 3

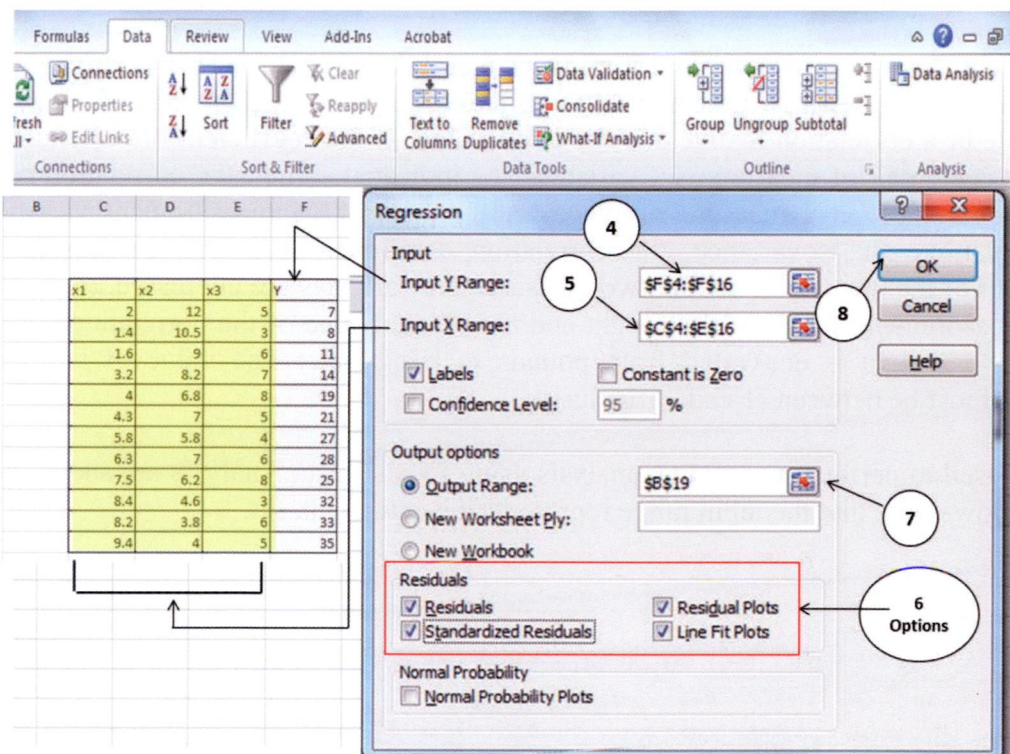

Using Excel® to perform Multiple Regression Analysis: Steps 4 through 8

The output of the above steps is similar to those is shown in Table 12.17 and it is similar to those shown in Tables 12.13, 12.4, and 12.15 discussed earlier.

Table 12.17 Output of multiple regression analysis of the relationship between x_1, x_2, x_3, and y

Regression Statistics								
Multiple R	0.9869							
R Square	0.9739							
Adjusted R Square	0.9642							
Standard Error	1.8709							
Observations	12							
ANOVA	df	SS	MS	F	Significance F			
Regression	3	1046.665	348.888	99.676	1.12E-06			
Residual	8	28.002	3.500					
Total	11	1074.667						
	Coefficients	Standard Error	t Stat	P-value	Lower 95%	Upper 95%	Lower 95.0%	Upper 95.0%
Intercept	25.9630	6.7602	3.8406	0.0049	10.3740	41.5520	10.3740	41.5520
x1	1.9723	0.4841	4.0743	0.0036	0.8560	3.0886	0.8560	3.0886
x2	-1.7543	0.5439	-3.2255	0.0121	-3.0085	-0.5001	-3.0085	-0.5001
x3	-0.3802	0.3396	-1.1195	0.2954	-1.1634	0.4030	-1.1634	0.4030

12.17 The Correlation Matrix

Excel® data analysis can also be used to produce a correlation matrix. This is particularly useful when there are more than two measurement variables for each of the n subjects. It provides an output table or a correlation matrix that shows the value of the coefficient of correlation applied to each possible pair of measurement variables. As indicated earlier, the correlation coefficient, like the covariance, is a measure of the extent to which two measurement variables 'vary together.' Unlike the covariance, the correlation coefficient is scaled so that its value is independent of the units in which the two measurement variables are expressed. (For example, if the two measurement variables are weight and height, the value of the correlation coefficient is unchanged if weight is converted from pounds to kilograms.) The value of any correlation coefficient must be between -1 and +1 inclusive.

The steps used to perform correlation analysis using Excel® Data Analysis are shown in the two Figures below. Note that the input range represents the entire data set.

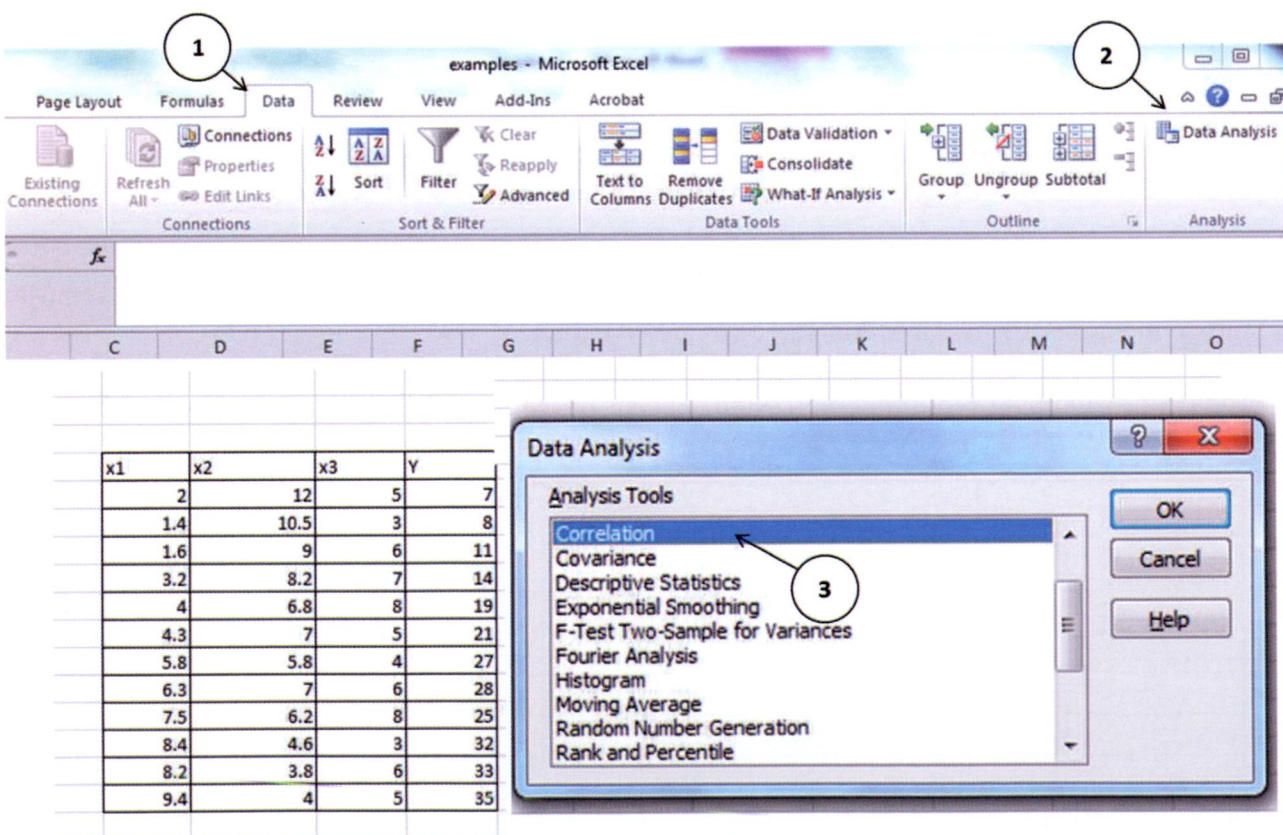

Using Excel® to perform Correlation Analysis : Steps 1 through 3

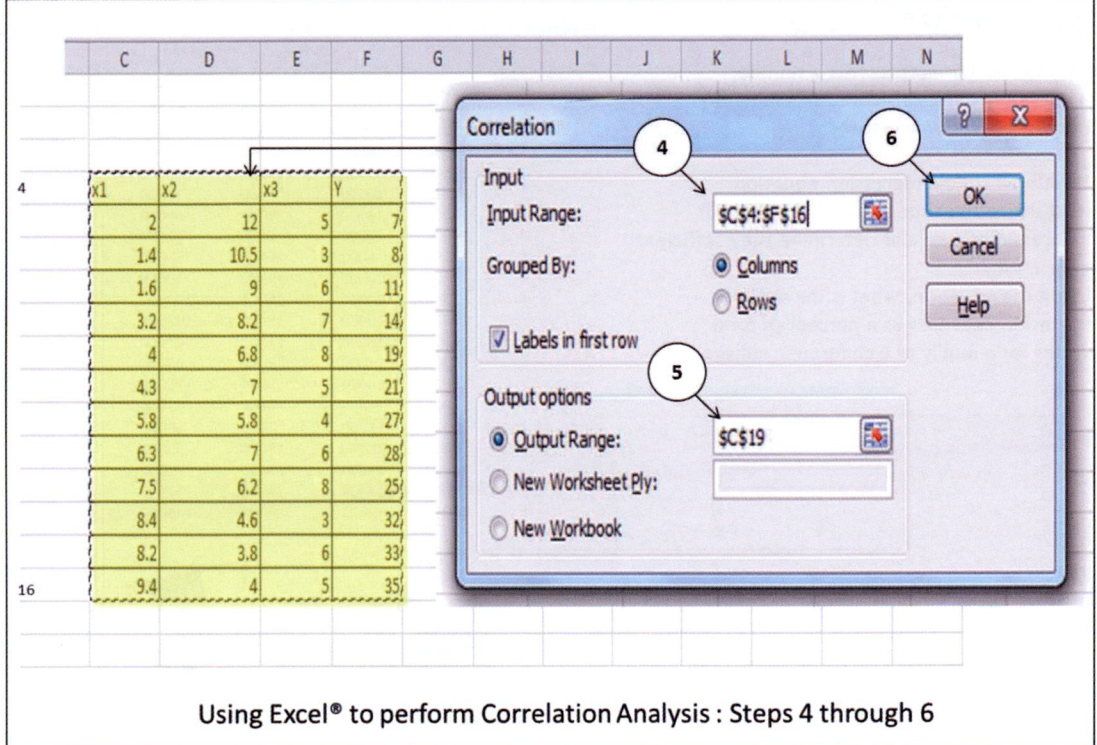

Using Excel® to perform Correlation Analysis : Steps 4 through 6

The output of the above steps is shown in Table 12.18. You can use the correlation analysis tool to examine each pair of measurement variables to determine whether the two measurement variables tend to move together; that is, whether large values of one variable tend to be associated with large values of the other (positive correlation), whether small values of one variable tend to be associated with large values of the other (negative correlation), or whether values of both variables tend to be unrelated (correlation near 0 (zero)). Also, note how some correlation coefficients are close to 1 or -1 implying high correlation and how some are near zero implying low correlation.

Table 12.18 Correlation matrix of the variables x_1, x_2, x_3, and y

	x_1	x_2	x_3	Y
x_1	1			
x_2	-0.9092	1		
x_3	0.0106	-0.0699	1	
Y	0.9688	-0.9545	-0.0274	1

Working Problem 12.9:

The data given here represents a number of factors that were considered in evaluating household education expenses:

(a) Develop a simple regression equation relating education expenses and the number of children in college and determine the coefficient of correlation

(c) Using the equation, what is the percent of education expenses as a percent of total expenses for a family of 6 children in college?

Number of children in College	Federal Aid ($)	Tuition ($)	Student Housing expenses ($)	Household income ($)	Education Expenses as a percent of Total Expenses (%)
3	8000	19000	16000	112000	12
4	10000	24000	13000	90000	14
2	11000	12000	12000	80000	12
4	6000	18000	20000	140000	16
2	18000	9000	6000	44000	7
1	24000	10000	4000	11000	9
2	16000	14000	8000	60000	12
3	14000	22000	8000	62000	10
3	12000	18000	10000	65000	13
4	9000	22000	14000	90000	12
4	8000	24000	16000	110000	14
3	7000	20000	18000	132000	14
3	9000	18000	14000	102000	12
4	14000	28000	8000	60000	10
2	18000	14000	6000	55000	8
2	22000	11000	5000	42000	6
2	16000	11000	7000	60000	8
3	10000	18000	13000	85000	14
3	12000	15000	12000	75000	12
2	14000	17000	9000	62000	12
1	18000	12000	6000	45000	10

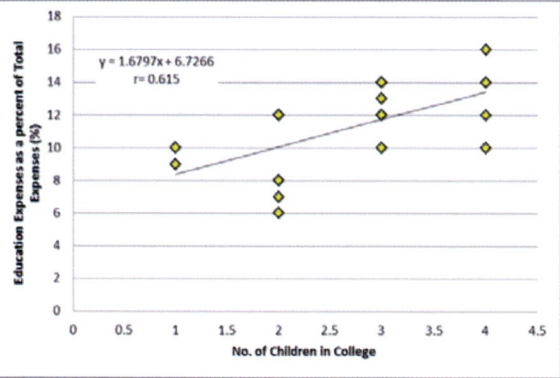

$y = 1.6797x + 6.7266$
$r = 0.615$

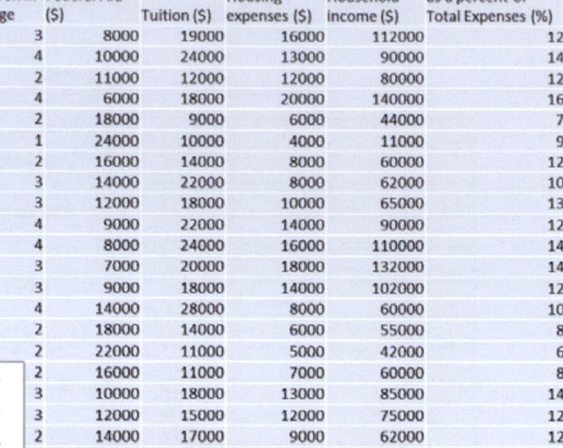

Working Problem 12.10:

The data given here represents a number of factors that were considered in evaluating household education expenses:
(a) Develop a simple regression equation relating education expenses and the amount of financial aid and determine the coefficient of correlation
(c) Using the equation, what is the percent of education expenses as a percent of total expenses for an amount of financial aid of $20,000?

Number of children in College	Federal Aid ($)	Tuition ($)	Student Housing expenses ($)	Household income ($)	Education Expenses as a percent of Total Expenses (%)
3	8000	19000	16000	112000	12
4	10000	24000	13000	90000	14
2	11000	12000	12000	80000	12
4	6000	18000	20000	140000	16
2	18000	9000	6000	44000	7
1	24000	10000	4000	11000	9
2	16000	14000	8000	60000	12
3	14000	22000	8000	62000	10
3	12000	18000	10000	65000	13
4	9000	22000	14000	90000	12
4	8000	24000	16000	110000	14
3	7000	20000	18000	132000	14
3	9000	18000	14000	102000	12
4	14000	28000	8000	60000	10
2	18000	14000	6000	55000	8
2	22000	11000	5000	42000	6
2	16000	11000	7000	60000	8
3	10000	18000	13000	85000	14
3	12000	15000	12000	75000	12
2	14000	17000	9000	62000	12
1	18000	12000	6000	45000	10

$y = -0.0004x + 17.173$
$r = 0.848$

Working Problem 12.11:

The data given here represents a number of factors that were considered in evaluating household education expenses:

(a) Develop a multiple regression equation relating education expenses and both the number of children in college and federal aid
(b) What is the coefficient of correlation
(c) What is the coefficient of determination
(d) Discuss the significance of the overall model
(e) Discuss the significance of each independent variable

Number of children in College	Federal Aid ($)	Tuition ($)	Student Housing expenses ($)	Household income ($)	Education Expenses as a percent of Total Expenses (%)
3	8000	19000	16000	112000	12
4	10000	24000	13000	90000	14
2	11000	12000	12000	80000	12
4	6000	18000	20000	140000	16
2	18000	9000	6000	44000	7
1	24000	10000	4000	11000	9
2	16000	14000	8000	60000	12
3	14000	22000	8000	62000	10
3	12000	18000	10000	65000	13
4	9000	22000	14000	90000	12
4	8000	24000	16000	110000	14
3	7000	20000	18000	132000	14
3	9000	18000	14000	102000	12
4	14000	28000	8000	60000	10
2	18000	14000	6000	55000	8
2	22000	11000	5000	42000	6
2	16000	11000	7000	60000	8
3	10000	18000	13000	85000	14
3	12000	15000	12000	75000	12
2	14000	17000	9000	62000	12
1	18000	12000	6000	45000	10

Regression Statistics	
Multiple R	0.8506
R Square	0.7236
Adjusted R Square	0.6928
Standard Error	1.4467
Observations	21

ANOVA	df	SS	MS	F
Regression	2	98.6108	49.3054	23.5567
Residual	18	37.6749	2.0931	
Total	20	136.2857		

	Coefficients	Standard Error	t Stat	P-value
Intercept	18.4817	2.6635	6.9390	0.0000
Number of children in College	-0.2795	0.5342	-0.5232	0.6072
Federal Aid ($)	-0.0005	0.0001	-4.7397	0.0002

Working Problem 12.12:

The data given below represents a number of factors that were considered in evaluating household education expenses:
(a) Develop a simple regression equation relating education expenses to tuition ($) using a linear model
(b) Develop a simple regression equation relating education expenses to tuition ($) using a polynomial model
(c) Compare the above two models and determine which model is more suitable.

Number of children in College	Federal Aid ($)	Tuition ($)	Student Housing expenses ($)	Household income ($)	Education Expenses as a percent of Total Expenses (%)
3	8000	19000	16000	112000	12
4	10000	24000	13000	90000	14
2	11000	12000	12000	80000	12
4	6000	18000	20000	140000	16
2	18000	9000	6000	44000	7
1	24000	10000	4000	11000	9
2	16000	14000	8000	60000	12
3	14000	22000	8000	62000	10
3	12000	18000	10000	65000	13
4	9000	22000	14000	90000	12
4	8000	24000	16000	110000	14
3	7000	20000	18000	132000	14
3	9000	18000	14000	102000	12
4	14000	28000	8000	60000	10
2	18000	14000	6000	55000	8
2	22000	11000	5000	42000	6
2	16000	11000	7000	60000	8
3	10000	18000	13000	85000	14
3	12000	15000	12000	75000	12
2	14000	17000	9000	62000	12
1	18000	12000	6000	45000	10

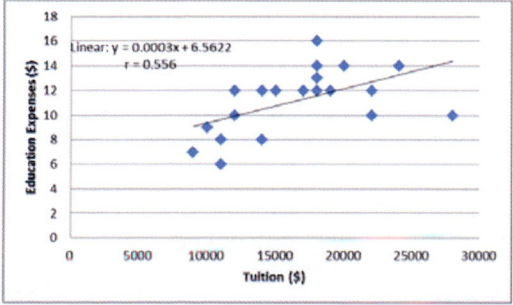

Linear: $y = 0.0003x + 6.5622$
$r = 0.556$

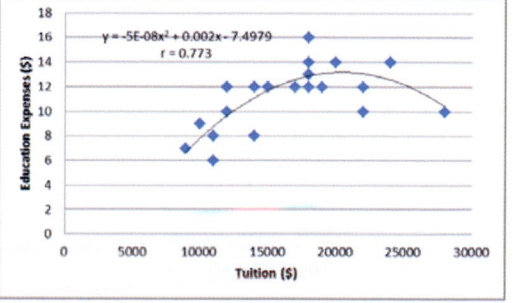

$y = -5E-08x^2 + 0.002x - 7.4979$
$r = 0.773$

Working Problem 12.13:

The data given here represents a number of factors that were considered in evaluating household education expenses:

(a) Develop a simple regression equation relating education expenses to student housing expenses ($) using a linear model
(b) Develop a simple regression equation relating education expenses to student housing expenses ($) using a polynomial model
(c) Compare the above two models and determine which model is more suitable.

Number of children in College	Federal Aid ($)	Tuition ($)	Student Housing expenses ($)	Household income ($)	Education Expenses as a percent of Total Expenses (%)
3	8000	19000	16000	112000	12
4	10000	24000	13000	90000	14
2	11000	12000	12000	80000	12
4	6000	18000	20000	140000	16
2	18000	9000	6000	44000	7
1	24000	10000	4000	11000	9
2	16000	14000	8000	60000	12
3	14000	22000	8000	62000	10
3	12000	18000	10000	65000	13
4	9000	22000	14000	90000	12
4	8000	24000	16000	110000	14
3	7000	20000	18000	132000	14
3	9000	18000	14000	102000	12
4	14000	28000	8000	60000	10
2	18000	14000	6000	55000	8
2	22000	11000	5000	42000	6
2	16000	11000	7000	60000	8
3	10000	18000	13000	85000	14
3	12000	15000	12000	75000	12
2	14000	17000	9000	62000	12
1	18000	12000	6000	45000	10

Linear model: $y = 0.0005x + 6.0431$, $r = 0.853$

Polynomial model: $y = -2E\text{-}08x^2 + 0.001x + 3.7514$, $r = 0.867$

Working Problem 12.14:

The data given here represents a number of factors that were considered in evaluating household education expenses:

(a) Develop a simple regression equation relating education expenses and annual household income
(b) What is the coefficient of correlation
(c) Using the equation, what is the percent of education expenses as a percent of total expenses for an amount of annual household income of $150,000?

Number of children in College	Federal Aid ($)	Tuition ($)	Student Housing expenses ($)	Household income ($)	Education Expenses as a percent of Total Expenses (%)
3	8000	19000	16000	112000	12
4	10000	24000	13000	90000	14
2	11000	12000	12000	80000	12
4	6000	18000	20000	140000	16
2	18000	9000	6000	44000	7
1	24000	10000	4000	11000	9
2	16000	14000	8000	60000	12
3	14000	22000	8000	62000	10
3	12000	18000	10000	65000	13
4	9000	22000	14000	90000	12
4	8000	24000	16000	110000	14
3	7000	20000	18000	132000	14
3	9000	18000	14000	102000	12
4	14000	28000	8000	60000	10
2	18000	14000	6000	55000	8
2	22000	11000	5000	42000	6
2	16000	11000	7000	60000	8
3	10000	18000	13000	85000	14
3	12000	15000	12000	75000	12
2	14000	17000	9000	62000	12
1	18000	12000	6000	45000	10

$y = 6E\text{-}05x + 6.4093$, $r = 0.783$

738

Working Problem 12.15:

The data given here represents a number of factors that were considered in evaluating household education expenses:
(a) Develop a multiple regression equation relating education expenses to the number of children in college, federal aid, and tuition.
(b) What is the coefficient of correlation
(c) What is the coefficient of determination
(d) Discuss the significance of the overall model
(e) Discuss the significance of each independent Variable

Number of children in College	Federal Aid ($)	Tuition ($)	Student Housing expenses ($)	Household income ($)	Education Expenses as a percent of Total Expenses (%)
3	8000	19000	16000	112000	12
4	10000	24000	13000	90000	14
2	11000	12000	12000	80000	12
4	6000	18000	20000	140000	16
2	18000	9000	6000	44000	7
1	24000	10000	4000	11000	9
2	16000	14000	8000	60000	12
3	14000	22000	8000	62000	10
3	12000	18000	10000	65000	13
4	9000	22000	14000	90000	12
4	8000	24000	16000	110000	14
3	7000	20000	18000	132000	14
3	9000	18000	14000	102000	12
4	14000	28000	8000	60000	10
2	18000	14000	6000	55000	8
2	22000	11000	5000	42000	6
2	16000	11000	7000	60000	8
3	10000	18000	13000	85000	14
3	12000	15000	12000	75000	12
2	14000	17000	9000	62000	12
1	18000	12000	6000	45000	10

SUMMARY OUTPUT

Regression Statistics	
Multiple R	0.8568
R Square	0.7341
Adjusted R Square	0.6871
Standard Error	1.4601
Observations	21

ANOVA

	df	SS	MS	F	Significance F
Regression	3	100.0432	33.3477	15.6422	0.0000
Residual	17	36.2425	2.1319		
Total	20	136.2857			

	Coefficients	Standard Error	t Stat	P-value	Lower 95%	Upper 95%	Lower 95.0%	Upper 95.0%
Intercept	18.227	2.706	6.736	0.000	12.518	23.936	12.518	23.936
Number of children in College	-0.782	0.817	-0.958	0.352	-2.505	0.941	-2.505	0.941
Federal Aid ($)	-0.0005	0.0001	-4.749	0.0002	-0.0007	-0.0003	-0.0007	-0.0003
Tuition ($)	0.0001	0.0001	0.820	0.4237	-0.0002	0.0004	-0.0002	0.0004

Working Problem 12.16:

The data given here represents a number of factors that were considered in evaluating household education expenses. (y). The factors considered are:
- The number of children in college (x1)
- Federal aid (x2)
- Tuition (x3)
- Student housing expenses (x4)
- Household annual income (x5)
Construct a Correlation Matrix of the pairs of these variables and interpret the results.

Number of children in College	Federal Aid ($)	Tuition ($)	Student Housing expenses ($)	Household income ($)	Education Expenses as a percent of Total Expenses (%)
3	8000	19000	16000	112000	12
4	10000	24000	13000	90000	14
2	11000	12000	12000	80000	12
4	6000	18000	20000	140000	16
2	18000	9000	6000	44000	7
1	24000	10000	4000	11000	9
2	16000	14000	8000	60000	12
3	14000	22000	8000	62000	10
3	12000	18000	10000	65000	13
4	9000	22000	14000	90000	12
4	8000	24000	16000	110000	14
3	7000	20000	18000	132000	14
3	9000	18000	14000	102000	12
4	14000	28000	8000	60000	10
2	18000	14000	6000	55000	8
2	22000	11000	5000	42000	6
2	16000	11000	7000	60000	8
3	10000	18000	13000	85000	14
3	12000	15000	12000	75000	12
2	14000	17000	9000	62000	12
1	18000	12000	6000	45000	10

	x1	x2	x3	x4	x5	y
x1	1					
x2	-0.7738	1				
x3	0.8602	-0.6385	1			
x4	0.7156	-0.9494	0.5286	1		
x5	0.7073	-0.9416	0.5309	0.9755	1	
y	0.6153	-0.8481	0.5561	0.8531	0.7828	1

Working Problem 12.17:

The data given below represents a number of factors that can affect students grades.
These include:
- Number of studying hours
- Number of class absences

The dependent variable is the student's grade (%).

Construct a Correlation Matrix of the pairs of these variables and interpret the results.

Student Number n	Number of studying hours	number of class absences	Grade/100 %
1	1	1	70
2	1	0	81
3	1.5	1	78
4	2	2	77
5	2	0	88
6	3	1	92
7	1	0	65
8	1	0	77
9	1.5	1	78
10	1.5	0	80
11	2	0	89
12	2	1	80
13	3	0	94
14	3	2	87
15	1	0	90
16	1	2	76
17	2	4	78
18	3	1	89

	Number of studying hours	number of class absences	Grade/100%
Number of studying hours	1		
number of class absences	0.2205	1	
Grade/100%	0.6902	-0.1867	1

12.18 Review Exercises

P12.1: Identify independent and dependent variables for the following systems
   (a) Hospital data system
   (b) Class teaching/learning system
   (c) Weight loss system
   (d) Drug rehabilitation system
Answer:
   (a) Independent variables: Patient's name, age, insurance, initial routine tests, etc.
       Dependent variables: cost, diagnostic report, medicine prescription, etc.
   (b) Attempt it yourself
   (c) Attempt it yourself
   (d) Attempt it yourself

P12.2: When the residuals (errors) are plotted after a regression line is found, the errors should follow:
   a. a random pattern
   b. a linear pattern
   c. a nonlinear quadratic pattern
   d. constant values

P12.3: When using regression, an error is also called
   a. slope
   b. regression coefficient
   c. residual
   d. a response variable

Answer: (c)

P12.4: One of the assumptions in regression analysis is that
   a. the errors have a mean of 1
   b. the errors have a mean of 0
   c. the observations (Y) have a mean of 1
   d. the observations (Y) have a mean of 0

P12.5: When using regression,
   a. the errors have a mean of 1
   b. the errors have a mean of 0
   c. the observations (Y) have a mean of 1
   d. the observations (Y) have a mean of 0

Answer: (b)

P12.6: What is the correct answer?
The regression line is a method used to
   -   summarize the association between two numerical variables
   -   estimate the standard deviation in Y values
   -   determine the median of observations to develop a distribution of an independent variable

P12.7: A residual is
   a. an error of calculating the mean value of dependent variable
   b. the difference between the coefficient of correlation and the coefficient of determination
   c. the difference between the actual (observed) y-value and the predicted y-value that lies on the line
   d. the mean of observations (Y)

Answer: (c)

P12.8: Which of the following conditions must hold for the linear model to be a valid description of the data?
   a. Normality: the residuals must be $N(0, \sigma)$
   b. Constant standard deviation
   c. Independence
   d. All of the above

P12.9: A residual plot is a scatterplot that has
   a. the residuals on the vertical axis and the original y-values on the horizontal axis
   b. the residuals on the vertical axis and the original x-values on the horizontal axis
   c. the residuals on the horizontal axis and the original x-values on the vertical axis

741

    d. none of the above
Answer: (b)

P12.10: When performing a hypothesis test on the slope, the null hypothesis should be
    a. H_0: The slope equals 0
    b. H_0: There is no linear association
    c. H_0: The correlation is 0
    d. All of the above

P12.11: When performing a hypothesis test on the slope, the alternative hypothesis should be
    a. H_a: The slope does not equal 0
    b. H_a: There is a linear association
    c. H_a: The correlation is not 0
    d. All of the above
Answer: (d)

P12.12: Describe the following correlations between two variables x and y as positive linear, negative Linear, no Pattern, nonlinear, or no scatter

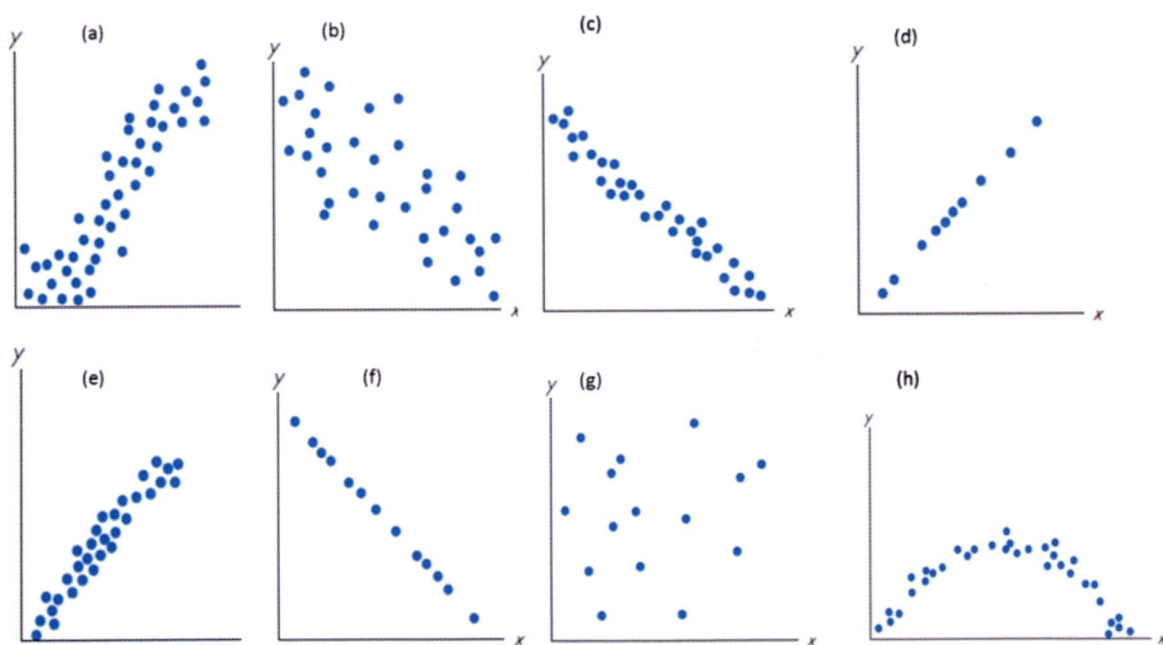

P12.13: What is the difference between the coefficient of correlation, r, and the coefficient of determination, r^2?

Answer: The coefficient of determination (r^2) is the square of the coefficient of correlation (r). Both of these give an indication of how well a regression model fits a particular set of data. r^2 value of 1 would indicate a perfect fit of the regression model to the points. It specifies the extent of contribution of independent variables to the dependent variable. The coefficient of correlation, r, will range from –1 or +1. It indicates the strength of the relationship.

P12.14: For a value of coefficient of correlation of 0.67, the coefficient of determination is

   a. 0.4489
   b. 0.4578
   c. 0.6734
   d. 0.4444
   e. None of the above

P12.15: How can a scatter plot help in determining the type of regression model to use.
Answer: A scatter diagram is a plot of the data. This graphical image helps to determine if a linear relationship is present, or if another type of relationship would be more appropriate.

P12.16: What is the SSE? How is related to SST and SSR?

P12.17: Explain the merits of the F-test in regression analysis.

Answer: The F-test is used to determine if the overall regression model is helpful in predicting the value of the independent variable (Y). If the F-value is large and the p-value or significance level is low, then we can conclude that there is a linear relationship and the model is useful, as these results would probably not occur by chance. If the significance level is high, then the model is not useful and the results in the sample could be due to random variations.

P12.18: What are the benefits of residual plots?

P12.19: What is the expected shape of a residual plot?

Answer: When the residuals (errors) are plotted after a regression line is found, the errors should be random and should not show any significant pattern. If a pattern does exist, regression assumptions may not be met or another model (perhaps nonlinear) would be more appropriate.

P12.20: The following regression model is used to determine the greenhouse gas emission (GHG) in g/mile of cars of different engine size (liter).

GHG = 70.26 Engine Size + 89.307

   (a) Estimate the value of GHG at Engine size of 1.5 L
   (b) Estimate the value of GHG at Engine size of 2.5 L

P12.21: The following relationship between the price of a house and the area in square foot was developed for a certain area in Alabama:
$$\hat{Y} = 72\,x + 14{,}000$$

The coefficient of correlation for the model was 0.72.

   (a) Predict the price of a house that is 2000 square feet
   (b) Predict the price of a house that is 4000 square feet
   (c) What other independent variables would you add to this model if you can use multiple regression analysis?
   (d) What is the coefficient of determination for this model?
Answer (show the method of calculation): (a) $158,000, (b) $302,000, (c) Try it yourself, (d) 0.5184.

P12.22: Given the following data of the hours of daily exercise and the corresponding weight loss after 6 month period, develop a simple regression equation and determine the coefficient of correlation.

Hours of daily exercise	1	1	1	2	2	2	3	3	3	4	4	4	4
Weight loss (lbs)	12	8	15	10	18	22	16	19	24	22	24	26	21

P12.23: The data in the table below represent the depth of a hole in a construction site and the time needed to drill

Depth of drilling	20	40	31	30	20	40	20	30	33	40	20	41
Time to drill (minutes)	15	32	21	22	14	29	16	22	20	33	13	30

    (a) Develop a regression equation relating time to depth
    (b) Determine the coefficient of correlation
    (c) Construct a scatter plot
    (d) Construct a residual plot
Answer: Time = -1.9592 + 0.7959 (Depth) r = 0.9613

P12.24: For the following pair of observations, the regression equation is:

x	1	2	3	4	5	6
y	2	4	6	8	10	12

    a. $y = 3x + 2$, $r = 0.8$
    b. $y = 2x$, $r = 1.0$
    c. $y = x + 12$, $r = 0.7$
    d. $y = 7x$, $r = 0.9$
    e. *None of the above*

P12.25: For the following pair of observations, the regression equation is:

x	3	3	8	5	5	6
y	2	4	10	8	10	12

    a. $y = 2x + 12$, $r = 0.815$
    b. $y = 1.67x - 0.667$, $r = 0.6637$
    c. $y = 1.67x - 0.667$, $r = 0.815$
    d. $y = 7x - 1$, $r = 0.880$
    e. *None of the above*
Answer: (c)

P12.26: Given that the value of the linear correlation coefficient, r, is -0.521, the coefficient of determination is
    a. 0.2215
    b. 0.3637
    c. 0.2714
    d. 0.2180
    e. None of the above

P12.27: For the following dataset of X_1, X_2, X_3, and Y, where X_1 = house square foot area, X_2 = number of bedrooms, X_3 = house age (years), *and Y* = selling price ($)

Y = Selling Price ($)	X_1 = Square Footage	X_2 = Bedrooms	X_3 =Age (Years)
192000	2505	3	15
177000	2008.5	3	13
184500	2568	4	15
237000	2760	4	20
262500	3450	4	9
277500	3351	4	15
285000	3466.5	4	10
339000	3565.5	4	4

(I)   The coefficient of determination, R^2, is

(a) 0.8681
(b) 0.9317
(c) 0.7692
(d) 0.9888
(e) None of the above

(II)   The standard error is

(a) 38814.741
(b) 27511.23
(c) 96576.575
(d) 2963.857
(e) None of the above

(III)   The regression equation is in the following form:

(a) $Y = 20723.044 + 88.876 \, X_1 + 1504.737 \, X_2 + 1180.054 \, X_3$
(b) $Y = 39739.077 + 12.677 \, X_1 + 3594.666 \, X_2 + 2160.334 \, X_3$
(c) $Y = 29733.244 + 82.877 \, X_1 - 1514.727 \, X_2 - 1980.054 \, X_3$
(d) $Y = 28733.664 + 44.777 \, X_1 - 1414.797 \, X_2 - 1960.054 \, X_3$
(e) None of the above

(IV)   For X_1 = house square foot area = 4000, X_2 = number of bedrooms = 4 , X_3 = house age (years) = 18, predict the selling price of the house Y ($)

(a) $250,000
(b) $319,540
(c) $965,762
(d) $296,385
(e) None of the above

(V)   For X_1 = house square foot area = 2800, X_2 = number of bedrooms = 5 , X_3 = house age (years) = 10, predict the selling price of the house Y ($)

(a) $220,000
(b) $309,510
(c) $365,782
(d) $234,414
(e) None of the above

(VI)   For X_1 = house square foot area = 1000, X_2 = number of bedrooms = 2 , X_3 = house age (years) = 5, predict the selling price of the house Y ($)

(a) $120,000
(b) $109,510
(c) $65,782
(d) $99,680
(e) None of above

Answer (perform calculations to verify the answers): I (a), II (b), III (c), IV (b), V (d), VI (d)

P12.28: If the model mean square is 7006 and the error mean square is 505, the F-value is

(a) 18.76
(b) 13.87
(c) 0.072
(d) 0.067
(e) None of the above

P12.29: The table below shows house values ($) and corresponding property tax in Jersey City, NJ ($).

(a) Develop a regression line relating these two variables
(b) Determine the coefficient of correlation, r
(c) Determine the standard error

Values of house values and corresponding property tax in Jersey City, NJ

n	House value ($)	Property tax ($)	n	House value ($)	Property tax ($)
1	401086	4428	16	612030	5470
2	412549	4665	17	626423	6144
3	436879	3719	18	634248	7060
4	442763	6882	19	654634	5800
5	443947	4979	20	655000	5900
6	445839	3808	21	679025	6790
7	459401	4474	22	691195	7230
8	487515	3361	23	704074	6921
9	492056	4271	24	713242	7672
10	505216	4932	25	716843	8000
11	519596	5736	26	718442	6534
12	540580	5946	27	770348	7053
13	546892	5349	28	770971	6000
14	597699	5327	29	775268	7753
15	603302	6033	30	780969	7810

Answer: Property Tax = 780.629 + 0.009 (house price), r = 0.8066, SE = 781.493

P12.30: For a sedan car claimed to operate at up to 30 miles per gallon gasoline, the following data of speed (miles per hour) and corresponding miles per gallon were reported:

Data of driving speed and fuel economy in miles per gallon

Speed (mph)	Fuel economy (mpg)	Speed (mph)	Fuel economy (mpg)	Speed (mph)	Fuel economy (mpg)
5	10	24	30	45	22
5	11	26	30	45	24
5	9	28	30	45	28
10	15	30	28	50	22
10	18	32	28	55	25
12	18	35	27	55	24
12	22	25	28	60	26
14	25	25	27	60	19
15	25	30	28	60	22
15	30	30	26	65	21
18	27	35	26	65	23
20	25	35	25	65	20
20	24	40	24	20	27
				40	26

(a) Develop a simple regression model of the following form:

$$Miles\ Per\ Gallon = \beta_o + \beta_1 Miles/hr$$

(b) Develop a multiple regression model of the following form:

$$Miles\ Per\ Gallon = \beta_o + \beta_1(Miles\ per\ hr) + \beta_2\ (Miles\ per\ hr)^2$$

(c) Compare the r and r^2 of the two models
(d) Which model is more suitable to predict the miles per gallon from the car speed (miles/hour).

P12.31: The data given below represents a number of factors that can affect students' grades. These include:
- Number of studying hours
- Number of class absences

The dependent variable is the student's grade (%).

(a) Develop a simple regression equation relating the number of studying hours to the grade
(b) According to the above regression equation, what is the maximum number of hours that a student can study to earn a full grade of 100%
(c) Develop a multiple regression equation in which both number of studying hours and number of absences are related to student's grade
(d) Did the addition of number of absences provide better explanation of student's performance as judged by the grade?

Student #	Number of studying hours	number of class absences	Grade/100%
1	1	1	70
2	1	0	81
3	1.5	1	78
4	2	2	77
5	2	0	88
6	3	1	92
7	1	0	65
8	1	0	77
9	1.5	1	78
10	1.5	0	80
11	2	0	89
12	2	1	80
13	3	0	94
14	3	2	87
15	1	0	90
16	1	2	76
17	2	4	78
18	3	1	89

Answer (do the calculations to verify the answers below):
  (a) Grade (%) = 68.9448 + 7.0152 Number of hours to study, r = 0.6902, SE = 5.8349
  (b) 4.3 hours
  (c) Grade (%) = 69.7999 + 7.8132 × Number of hours to study + -2.5830 × Number of absences, r = 0.7727, SE = 5.2864
  (d) The two independent variables are significant but the number of hours to study is more significant than the number of absences

P12.32: The cost of travel, Y ($) is related to the number of days on the road (X_1) and distance traveled (X_2) by the following regression equation:

$$\hat{Y} = \$90.00 + \$48.50X_1 + \$0.40X_2$$

The coefficient of correlation is 0.68
  (a) What is the expected cost ($) for a distance of 300 miles and 5 days on the road?
  (b) What percent of the variation in cost of travel is explained by the independent variables used?
  (c) Comment on the validity of the model. Should any other variables be included? Which ones and why?

P12.33: The data in the table below represent values of fuel price, average miles per gallon, years owning a car, annual fuel cost, and total fuel cost.

(a) Using Excel® data analysis, develop a regression equation relating total fuel cost during the time you own the car to fuel price and miles per galloon
(b) Interpret the regression output
(c) If you have a car that makes 35 miles per gallon and if the price per gallon is $3.5, what would be your total fuel cost during the time you own the car?
(d) If you have a car that makes 35 miles per gallon and if the price per gallon is $5.0, what would be your total fuel cost during the time you own the car?

Data of fuel price, average miles per gallon, and annual fuel cost

Fuel price ($/gallon)	Average MPG	Annual driving distance	Years owning the car	Annual fuel cost	Total cost during the time you own the car ($\approx$ 5 years)
3.87	15	15000	5	3870	19350
3.87	18	15000	5	3225	16125
3.95	18	15000	5	3292	16460
4	18	15000	5	3333	16665
5	18	15000	5	4167	20835
3.65	25	15000	5	2190	10950
3.65	30	15000	5	1825	9125
3	30	15000	5	1500	7500
3.65	40	15000	5	1369	6845
3.5	40	15000	5	1313	6565
3.5	22	15000	5	2386	11930

Answer: Do it yourself using Excel Data Analysis as described in the Chapter contents

P12.34: The data in the table below represent three independent variables, namely: sales ($), S, salesman expenses ($), E, and years of service (Yr). The response or dependent variable is the commission ($), C.

(a) Develop a regression equation relating the commission to sales ($).
(b) Develop a regression equation relating commission to expenses ($).
(c) Develop a regression equation relating commission to years of service ($).
(d) Compare the above equations
(e) Develop a regression equation relating commission to sales, expenses, and years of service ($). Interpret the outcome of the regression model.

Data of Sales ($), expenses ($), years of service, and sales commission ($)

Annual Sales ($), S	Annual Expenses ($), E	Year of Service, Yr	Annual Commission($) C	Annual Sales ($), S	Annual Expenses ($), E	Year of Service, Yr	Annual Commission($) C
282137	285	7	12000	299341	300	6	12000
328685	330	12	14000	282338	300	6	11000
339633	345	14	14000	286152	300	4	11500
347385	355	15	14000	288332	290	8	12000
288613	290	6	12000	298019	300	13	13000
289716	290	7	12000	298374	300	16	15000
293356	300	12	11000	299127	302	17	15000
294166	300	12	12000	316016	325	12	12800
324810	330	8	13000	316128	325	10	12800
324911	330	11	13000	318094	340	8	13000
326343	330	10	13000	322804	325	6	13000
300923	300	15	14000	323216	330	13	14000
305644	310	10	12500	320846	320	12	12900
306264	305	8	12250	324061	330	16	15000
306991	310	11	12300	307530	312	15	16000
307392	310	6	13000	309901	310	7	12400
299184	300	10	12000	314470	315	8	12600

P12.35: The following data represent the values of Systolic-Blood Pressure for a random sample of people that exhibit different characteristics of smoking intensity (number of cigarettes per day), weight (lbs), alcohol consumption (ounce/day), and age (years). Using the data of this sample, construct a correlation matrix and interpret the results.

Number of cigarettes per day	Weight (lbs)	Alcohol consumption (ounce/day)	Age	Systolic-blood pressure
10	144	0	55	130
10	136	0	50	120
10	140	20	50	125
10	148	18	45	130
15	155	0	56	120
15	155	30	47	140
15	147	26	55	129
15	160	30	52	120
20	180	12	50	120
20	144	12	45	135
20	165	36	44	168
20	170	46	60	177
30	165	40	62	170
30	165	28	58	155
30	170	32	56	168
30	155	18	60	170
40	145	12	62	155
40	180	36	62	180
40	177	40	58	180

Answer:

	Number of Cigarettes per Day	Weight (lb)	Alcohol Consumption (oz/day)	Age	Systolic-Blood Pressure
Number of Cigarettes per Day	1				
Weight (lb)	0.577	1			
Alcohol Consumption (oz/day)	0.446	0.644	1		
Age	0.678	0.342	0.255	1	
Systolic-Blood Pressure	0.784	0.591	0.722	0.553	1

P12.36: The following data represent the values of Systolic-Blood Pressure for a random sample of people that exhibit different characteristics of smoking intensity (number of cigarettes per day), weight (lb), alcohol consumption (oz/day), and age (years). Develop multiple regression equations in stepwise approach, by increasing the number of independent variables by one consecutively and determine if the added variable has added to the reliability of the model. You may choose to begin with any variable. You may also use the correlation matrix obtained in the above problem as a guideline to which variable you need to begin with.

Number of cigarettes/ day	Weight (lbs)	Alcohol Consumption (ounce/day)	Age	Systolic-Blood Pressure
10	144	0	55	130
10	136	0	50	120
10	140	20	50	125
10	148	18	45	130
15	155	0	56	120
15	155	30	47	140
15	147	26	55	129
15	160	30	52	120
20	180	12	50	120
20	144	12	45	135
20	165	36	44	168
20	170	46	60	177
30	165	40	62	170
30	165	28	58	155
30	170	32	56	168
30	155	18	60	170
40	145	12	62	155
40	180	36	62	180
40	177	40	58	180

P12.37: The data given below represents a number of factors that were considered in evaluating household education expenses. Construct a correlation matrix between variables and interpret the results.

Number of children in college	Federal aid ($)	Tuition ($)	Student housing expenses ($)	Household income ($)	Education expenses as a percent of total expenses (%)
3	8000	19000	16000	112000	12
4	10000	24000	13000	90000	14
2	11000	12000	12000	80000	12
4	6000	18000	20000	140000	16
2	18000	9000	6000	44000	7
1	24000	10000	4000	11000	9
2	16000	14000	8000	60000	12
3	14000	22000	8000	62000	10
3	12000	18000	10000	65000	13
4	9000	22000	14000	90000	12
4	8000	24000	16000	110000	14
3	7000	20000	18000	132000	14
3	9000	18000	14000	102000	12
4	14000	28000	8000	60000	10
2	18000	14000	6000	55000	8
2	22000	11000	5000	42000	6
2	16000	11000	7000	60000	8
3	10000	18000	13000	85000	14
3	12000	15000	12000	75000	12
2	14000	17000	9000	62000	12
1	18000	12000	6000	45000	10

Answer:

	Number of children in College	Federal Aid ($)	Tuition ($)	Student Housing expenses ($)	Household income ($)	Education Expenses as a percent of Total Expenses (%)
Number of children in College	1					
Federal Aid ($)	-0.774	1				
Tuition ($)	0.860	-0.639	1			
Student Housing expenses ($)	0.716	-0.949	0.529	1		
Household income ($)	0.707	-0.942	0.531	0.976	1	
Education Expenses as a percent of Total Expenses (%)	0.615	-0.848	0.556	0.853	0.783	1

P12.38: The data given below represents a number of factors that were considered in evaluating household education expenses:

(a) Develop a multiple regression equation relating education expenses to the number of children in college, federal aid, and tuition.
(b) What is the coefficient of correlation?
(c) What is the coefficient of determination?
(d) Discuss the significance of the overall model
(e) Discuss the significance of each independent variable

Number of children in college	Federal aid ($)	Tuition ($)	Student housing expenses ($)	Household income ($)	Education expenses as a percent of total expenses (%)
3	8000	19000	16000	112000	12
4	10000	24000	13000	90000	14
2	11000	12000	12000	80000	12
4	6000	18000	20000	140000	16
2	18000	9000	6000	44000	7
1	24000	10000	4000	11000	9
2	16000	14000	8000	60000	12
3	14000	22000	8000	62000	10
3	12000	18000	10000	65000	13
4	9000	22000	14000	90000	12
4	8000	24000	16000	110000	14
3	7000	20000	18000	132000	14
3	9000	18000	14000	102000	12
4	14000	28000	8000	60000	10
2	18000	14000	6000	55000	8
2	22000	11000	5000	42000	6
2	16000	11000	7000	60000	8
3	10000	18000	13000	85000	14
3	12000	15000	12000	75000	12
2	14000	17000	9000	62000	12
1	18000	12000	6000	45000	10

CHAPTER 13

Statistical Tests with Qualitative Data

After completing this chapter, students will be able to:

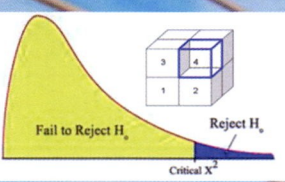

- Understand the difference between parametric and non-parametric statistics
- Calculate expected frequencies of qualitative variables.
- Use the χ^2 distribution to find the critical values of χ^2 at a certain degree of freedom and confidence area.
- Perform goodness-of-fit-tests
- Perform independence tests
- Perform homogeneity tests

CHAPTER 13

Chapters 8 through 10 dealt exclusively with hypothesis tests and confidence intervals for quantitative population parameters, such as population means, population variances, and population proportions. In this chapter, we deal with a different type of inferential statistics in which qualitative parameters (defined in words) are described by their frequencies or number of occurrences. For these qualitative data, we may wish to perform a hypothesis test about the frequency distribution of a qualitative (categorical) variable that has only finitely many possible values. In this regard, we perform the so-called 'goodness-of-fit' test, which is an inferential procedure used to determine whether a frequency distribution follows a specific pattern or fit a previously claimed distribution. We also discuss the relationships between qualitative or categorical variables that are described by cross frequencies in the form of a contingency table. The analysis used for handling contingency tables is called 'independence tests', which is essentially a hypothesis test of the null hypothesis that the row and column variables are independent of each other. We also use the so-called 'homogeneity test' in which we consider the case of samples that are obtained from different populations, and test whether those populations have the same proportions of the characteristics being considered.

CHAPTER CONTENTS

13.1 Parametric vs. Nonparametric Statistical Procedures

In Chapters 8 through 10, we discussed inferential statistics and how to establish confidence intervals or perform hypothesis tests for variables described by interval or ratio measurement levels such as ages, weights, incomes, or years of service. These are known as parametric statistical procedures and they rely mostly on the assumption that the variable can be approximated by a normal distribution.

Nonparametric statistical procedures are inferential procedures that make no assumptions about the underlying distribution of the data. In these procedures, there are tests available in which no assumption regarding the shape of the population distribution is necessary. There are also tests exclusively for data of nominal scale of measurement in which data are classified into categories where there is no natural order. Examples include opinions of taste or comfort as good and bad, gender, country of birth, or brand of cereal purchased. For this type of data, the chi-square statistic is widely used.

13.2 Summary of the Characteristics of Chi-Square, χ^2, Distribution

When we construct a frequency distribution of variances of many samples (a sampling distribution), we are essentially producing a chi-squared distribution. This distribution was discussed earlier in Chapter 8, but it will be useful to review it again in the context of the subject of this chapter. The symbol χ is the Greek letter chi (pronounced 'kigh'). The chi-squared distribution is an asymmetrical distribution that has a shape determined by the degrees of freedom or the sample size. As the number of degrees of freedom increases, the chi-square distribution becomes more nearly symmetric (see Figure 13.1). The chi-squared distribution can be used in many practical applications including confidence interval estimation for a population variance (see chapter 8), chi-squared tests for goodness of fit of an observed distribution to a theoretical one, and the independence of two criteria of classification of qualitative variables. The last two applications are the subjects of this chapter. The examples given below assist students in practicing how to find the critical values of χ^2 at different degrees of freedom and different areas under the curve. Other key characteristics of the Chi-square probability function include:

- The total area under a χ^2-curve equals 1.
- A χ^2-curve starts at 0 on the horizontal axis and extends indefinitely to the right, approaching, but never touching, the horizontal axis as it does so.
- A χ^2-curve is right skewed.

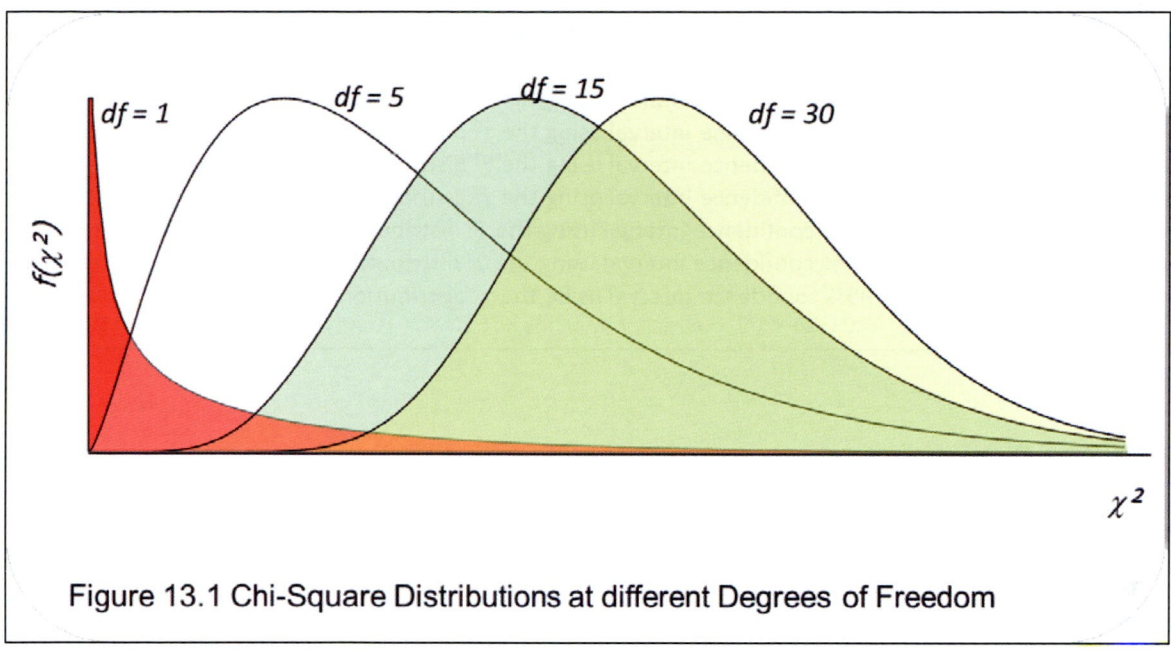

Figure 13.1 Chi-Square Distributions at different Degrees of Freedom

Example 13.1: Find the critical values of χ^2 that separate the middle 95% of the chi-square distribution from the 2.5% area in each tail, assuming 12 degrees of freedom.

Solution:

See the way this value is found from the χ^2 table (Chapter 8, Appendix-Table 8.A.II).

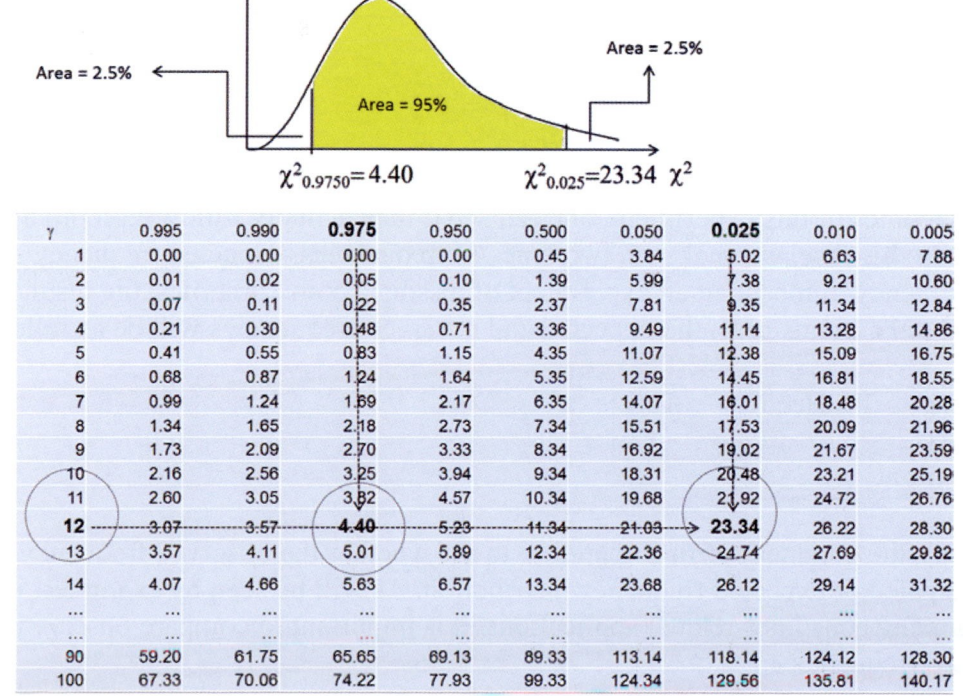

γ	0.995	0.990	**0.975**	0.950	0.500	0.050	**0.025**	0.010	0.005
1	0.00	0.00	0.00	0.00	0.45	3.84	5.02	6.63	7.88
2	0.01	0.02	0.05	0.10	1.39	5.99	7.38	9.21	10.60
3	0.07	0.11	0.22	0.35	2.37	7.81	9.35	11.34	12.84
4	0.21	0.30	0.48	0.71	3.36	9.49	11.14	13.28	14.86
5	0.41	0.55	0.83	1.15	4.35	11.07	12.38	15.09	16.75
6	0.68	0.87	1.24	1.64	5.35	12.59	14.45	16.81	18.55
7	0.99	1.24	1.69	2.17	6.35	14.07	16.01	18.48	20.28
8	1.34	1.65	2.18	2.73	7.34	15.51	17.53	20.09	21.96
9	1.73	2.09	2.70	3.33	8.34	16.92	19.02	21.67	23.59
10	2.16	2.56	3.25	3.94	9.34	18.31	20.48	23.21	25.19
11	2.60	3.05	3.82	4.57	10.34	19.68	21.92	24.72	26.76
12	3.07	3.57	4.40	5.23	11.34	21.03	23.34	26.22	28.30
13	3.57	4.11	5.01	5.89	12.34	22.36	24.74	27.69	29.82
14	4.07	4.66	5.63	6.57	13.34	23.68	26.12	29.14	31.32
...	...	...	...	...	...	...	...	...	...
...	...	...	...	...	...	...	...	...	...
90	59.20	61.75	65.65	69.13	89.33	113.14	118.14	124.12	128.30
100	67.33	70.06	74.22	77.93	99.33	124.34	129.56	135.81	140.17

Working problem 13.1:
This working problem will help students practicing finding the values of χ^2 at different areas and different degrees of freedom.
Q1: Find the critical values for a 95% confidence interval using the χ^2 distribution with 18 degrees of freedom.
Q2: Find the critical values for a 99% confidence interval using the χ^2 distribution with 25 degrees of freedom.
Q3: Find the critical values for a 95% confidence interval using the χ^2 distribution with 2 degrees of freedom.
Q4: Find the critical values for a 95% confidence interval using the χ^2 distribution with 100 degrees of freedom.
Q5: Find the critical values for a 99% confidence interval using the χ^2 distribution with 2 degrees of freedom.
Q6: Find the critical values for a 99% confidence interval using the χ^2 distribution with 80 degrees of freedom.
Q7: Find the critical values for a 99% confidence interval using the χ^2 distribution with 90 degrees of freedom.
Answer: Q1: 8.23, 31.53, Q2: 10.52, 46.93, Q3: 0.05, 7.38, Q4: 74.22, 129.56, Q5: 0.01, 10.60, Q6: 51.17, 116.32, Q7: 59.20, 128.30

13.3 Goodness of Fit

In practice, we often wish to perform a hypothesis test about the distribution of a qualitative (categorical) variable or a discrete quantitative variable that has only finitely many possible values. A goodness-of-fit test is a procedure used to determine whether a frequency distribution follows a specific pattern or fits a previously claimed distribution.

One classic example to illustrate the goodness of fit is the tossing of a coin experiment. If we wish to determine whether a coin is fair, one way to do that is to toss the coin a number of times and count the number of heads and tails revealed. This will lead to a sample proportion, $\hat{p}$, say for the head outcome. The hypothesis test in this case is:

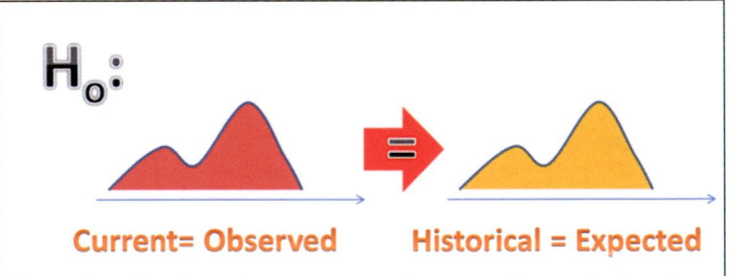

Current= Observed   **Historical = Expected**

$$H_o: p = 0.5$$
$$H_1: p \neq 0.5$$

Using the outcomes of this experiment, one can see if they actually follow a binomial distribution. In this case, we deal with two types of frequencies, expected frequency and observed frequency. Suppose in an experiment of tossing a coin 100 times, the results were 47 heads and 53 tails. In this case, the expected and observed frequencies will be as follows:

Outcome	Head	Tail
Observed	47	53
Expected	50	50

The essence of the goodness of fit is therefore to see whether the observed frequency distribution fits the anticipated or expected frequency distribution. As will be seen by examples, in social science and many consumer-related applications, it is important to compare observed frequencies with expected frequencies.

Example 13.2: Historical reports revealed that there is no significant difference in the relative frequency between different psychological problems. This means that a psychologist should expect to treat a nearly equal number of people exhibiting the different categories of psychological problems. These categories are shown in the box below.

Common Psychological Problems

• Depression- This category describes the various types of depression, including major depression, dysthymic disorder, non-specific depression, adjustment disorder with depression and bi-polar depression.

• Anxiety disorder- This category describes different anxiety problems including panic disorder, post-traumatic stress, social anxiety, agoraphobia, generalized anxiety, obsessive compulsive disorder and specific phobias.

• Schizophrenia- This category is a chronic, severe, and disabling brain disease. People with schizophrenia often suffer terrifying symptoms such as hearing internal voices not heard by others, or believing that other people are reading their minds, controlling their thoughts, or plotting to harm them. These symptoms may leave them fearful and withdrawn.

• Childhood disorder- This category is related to behavioral control problems, including attention deficit hyperactivity disorder (ADHD), conduct disturbance, and oppositional behavior are discussed.

• Impulse control disorders- This category involves loss of control modes such as intermittent explosive disorder, domestic violence, pathological gambling, kleptomania, pyromania, and trichotillomania

• Family problems- This category deals strictly with family conflicts resulting from one or more family members having a psychological disorder, such as those described above. However, family conflicts also arise because of communication problems, parenting issues, school problems and sibling conflict.

In a study by a medical consulting organization, a random sample of people, who have some form of disorder, was surveyed. The results of the survey are listed in Table 13.1.

Table 13.1 Observed frequencies of different categories of psychological problems

Psychological problems	Observed frequency (O)
Depression	360
Anxiety disorder	330
Schizophrenia	70
Childhood disorder	130
Impulse control disorders	140
Family problems	170
Total	1200

As can be seen in the above results, there is a disagreement between the observed frequencies and the anticipated expected frequency, which should be equal for all psychological problems if historical reports are still valid. Both observed and expected values of frequency are listed in Table 13.2.

Table 13.2 Observed and expected frequencies of different categories of psychological problems

Psychological problems	Observed frequency (O)	Expected frequency (E)
Depression	360	200
Anxiety disorder	330	200
Schizophrenia	70	200
Childhood disorder	130	200
Impulse control disorders	140	200
Family problems	170	200
Total	1200	1200

- We first state the null hypothesis and the alternate hypothesis.

The null hypothesis, *H_o: there is no difference between the set of observed frequencies and the set of expected frequencies*; that is, any difference between the two sets of frequencies can be attributed to sampling error or chance.

The alternate hypothesis, *H_1: there is a difference between the observed and expected sets of frequencies.*

- If H_o is rejected and H_1 is accepted, it means that psychological problems are not equally distributed among the six categories.

We then select the level of significance, say 0.05 significance level. This means that the probability is 0.05 that a true null hypothesis will be rejected.

- We select the test statistic, which follows the chi-square distribution,

$$\chi^2 = \sum_{1}^{k}(O - E)^2/E \qquad (13.1)$$

where O = observed frequency and E = expected frequency. When H_o is true, the χ^2 statistic has approximately a χ^2 distribution, provided that all the expected frequencies are 5 or more.

- We now formulate the decision rule. The decision rule in hypothesis testing requires finding a number that separates the region where we do not reject from the region of rejection. This number is called the *critical value*. As discussed above, the chi-square distribution is a family of distributions, each of slightly different shape depending on the number of degrees of freedom. The number of degrees of freedom in this type of problem is found by *k-1*, where *k* is the number of categories. In this particular problem, we have six categories leading to 5 degrees of freedom. At this degree of freedom, and a 95% confidence, the critical χ^2 value is 11.07, as shown below.

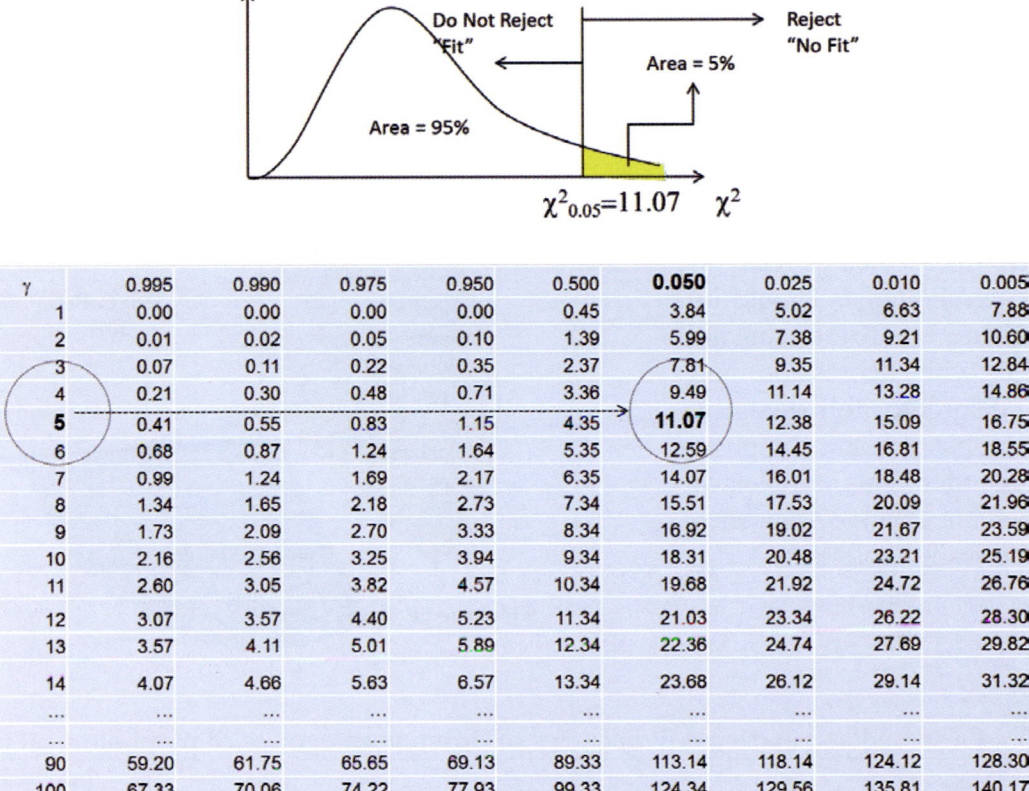

γ	0.995	0.990	0.975	0.950	0.500	**0.050**	0.025	0.010	0.005
1	0.00	0.00	0.00	0.00	0.45	3.84	5.02	6.63	7.88
2	0.01	0.02	0.05	0.10	1.39	5.99	7.38	9.21	10.60
3	0.07	0.11	0.22	0.35	2.37	7.81	9.35	11.34	12.84
4	0.21	0.30	0.48	0.71	3.36	9.49	11.14	13.28	14.86
5	0.41	0.55	0.83	1.15	4.35	**11.07**	12.38	15.09	16.75
6	0.68	0.87	1.24	1.64	5.35	12.59	14.45	16.81	18.55
7	0.99	1.24	1.69	2.17	6.35	14.07	16.01	18.48	20.28
8	1.34	1.65	2.18	2.73	7.34	15.51	17.53	20.09	21.96
9	1.73	2.09	2.70	3.33	8.34	16.92	19.02	21.67	23.59
10	2.16	2.56	3.25	3.94	9.34	18.31	20.48	23.21	25.19
11	2.60	3.05	3.82	4.57	10.34	19.68	21.92	24.72	26.76
12	3.07	3.57	4.40	5.23	11.34	21.03	23.34	26.22	28.30
13	3.57	4.11	5.01	5.89	12.34	22.36	24.74	27.69	29.82
14	4.07	4.66	5.63	6.57	13.34	23.68	26.12	29.14	31.32
...	...	...	...	...	...	...	...	...	...
...	...	...	...	...	...	...	...	...	...
90	59.20	61.75	65.65	69.13	89.33	113.14	118.14	124.12	128.30
100	67.33	70.06	74.22	77.93	99.33	124.34	129.56	135.81	140.17

In order to make a decision of whether we reject the null hypothesis or not, we calculate the test statistics $\chi_o{}^2$ as shown in Table 13.3.

Table 13.3 Calculations of Chi-Squared

Psychological problems	Observed frequency (O)	Expected Frequency (E)	Difference (O-E)	Square of difference $(O-E)^2$	Chi-Square Subtotal $(O-E)^2/E$
Depression	360	200	160	25600	128
Anxiety disorder	330	200	130	16900	84.5
Schizophrenia	70	200	-130	16900	84.5
Childhood disorder	130	200	-70	4900	24.5
Impulse control disorders	140	200	-60	3600	18
Family problems	170	200	-30	900	4.5
Total	1200	1200		68800	$\chi_o{}^2 = 344$

- The decision rule indicates that if there are large differences between the observed and expected frequencies, resulting in a computed χ_o^2 of more than the critical value of 11.070, the null hypothesis should be rejected. This is the case in this example $\chi_o^2 = 344 \gg 11.07$. The decision, therefore, is to reject the null hypothesis H_0 at the 0.05 level and to accept H_1. The difference between the observed and the expected frequencies is not due to chance. Instead, we have sufficient evidence to conclude that the differences between O and E are large enough to be considered significant. The chance these differences are due to sampling error is very small. So we conclude that it is unlikely that these psychological problems have equal frequencies.

If the medical consulting organization believes that the newly observed frequencies are more accurate than the expected (reported) ones, their advice to different psychologists should be to anticipate more treatments associated with depression and anxiety disorder; followed by family problems and impulse control disorder. This is revealed by the percent relative frequency values shown in Table 13.4.

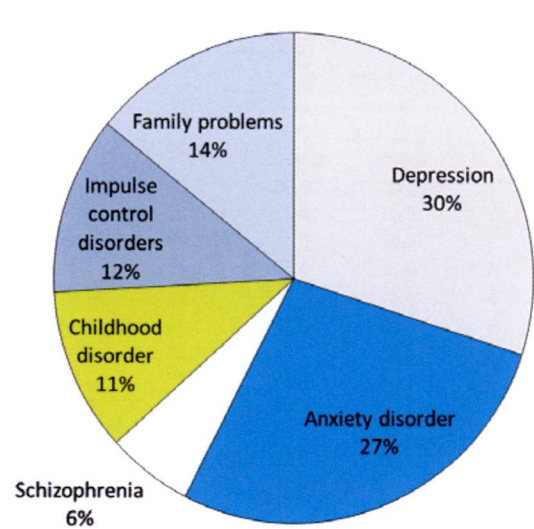

Table 13.4 Observed and expected frequencies of different categories of psychological problems

Psychological problems	Observed frequency (O)	Observed relative frequency (O)	Observed percent relative frequency ($O\%$)
Depression	360	0.300	30.0
Anxiety disorder	330	0.275	27.5
Schizophrenia	70	0.058	5.8
Childhood disorder	130	0.108	10.8
Impulse control disorders	140	0.117	11.7
Family problems	170	0.142	14.2
Total	1200	1	100

Example 13.3: A fair die has 6 outcomes: 1, 2, 3, 4, 5, and 6. Suppose we want to determine whether a die is fair. We rolled the die 60 times and obtained the frequency corresponding to each outcome given below:

Table 13.5 Actual outcome of rolling a die

Outcome	Observed Frequency
1	4
2	16
3	20
4	9
5	5
6	6

(a) Format the hypothesis to determine whether the die is fair
(b) Calculate the expected frequencies
(c) Test the goodness-of-fit

Solution:

(a)

H_o: $P_1 = P_2 = P_3 = P_4 = P_5 = P_6 = 1/6$
H_1: Not all $P_i = 1/6$

(b) The expected frequencies in this case are 10 for each outcome.

Goodness of Fit Test

observed	expected	O - E	$(O - E)^2 / E$	% of χ_o^2
4	10.000	-6.000	3.600	16.82
16	10.000	6.000	3.600	16.82
20	10.000	10.000	10.000	46.73
9	10.000	-1.000	0.100	0.47
5	10.000	-5.000	2.500	11.68
6	10.000	-4.000	1.600	7.48
			$\chi_o^2 =$	
60	60.000	0.000	21.400	100.00

21.40 chi-square
5 df
.0007 p-value

As you can see the area calculated by technology is 0.0007. This is in the rejection region at 0.05 confidence. The critical chi-square value is 11.07 as shown below. Thus, the test statistic being

21.4 is in the 'Reject' area implying a no good fit. In other words, we reject the null hypothesis and conclude that the observed frequencies support the use of an unfair die.

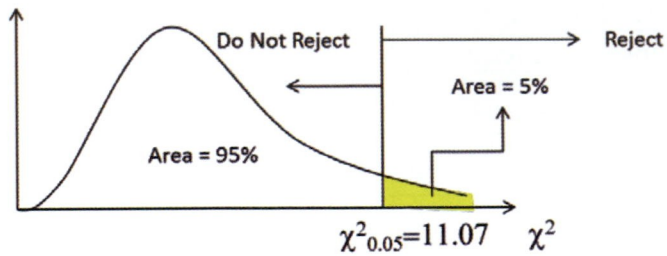

$$\chi^2_{0.05}=11.07 \quad \chi^2$$

γ	0.995	0.990	0.975	0.950	0.500	0.050	0.025	0.010	0.005
1	0.00	0.00	0.00	0.00	0.45	3.84	5.02	6.63	7.88
2	0.01	0.02	0.05	0.10	1.39	5.99	7.38	9.21	10.60
3	0.07	0.11	0.22	0.35	2.37	7.81	9.35	11.34	12.84
4	0.21	0.30	0.48	0.71	3.36	9.49	11.14	13.28	14.86
5	0.41	0.55	0.83	1.15	4.35	11.07	12.38	15.09	16.75
6	0.68	0.87	1.24	1.64	5.35	12.59	14.45	16.81	18.55
7	0.99	1.24	1.69	2.17	6.35	14.07	16.01	18.48	20.28
8	1.34	1.65	2.18	2.73	7.34	15.51	17.53	20.09	21.96
9	1.73	2.09	2.70	3.33	8.34	16.92	19.02	21.67	23.59
10	2.16	2.56	3.25	3.94	9.34	18.31	20.48	23.21	25.19
11	2.60	3.05	3.82	4.57	10.34	19.68	21.92	24.72	26.76
12	3.07	3.57	4.40	5.23	11.34	21.03	23.34	26.22	28.30
13	3.57	4.11	5.01	5.89	12.34	22.36	24.74	27.69	29.82
14	4.07	4.66	5.63	6.57	13.34	23.68	26.12	29.14	31.32
...	...	...	...	...	...	...	...	...	...
...	...	...	...	...	...	...	...	...	...
90	59.20	61.75	65.65	69.13	89.33	113.14	118.14	124.12	128.30
100	67.33	70.06	74.22	77.93	99.33	124.34	129.56	135.81	140.17

Example 13.4: Suppose four political candidates are running for the presidency. A survey conducted prior to the election using a sample of 1600 people revealed the following results:

Table 13.6 Actual survey voting frequencies

Candidate	Survey Results (O)
A	380
B	440
C	380
D	400
Total	1600

Suppose we wish to decide whether the voters have a preference for any one of the candidates. Form the necessary hypothesis and test the hypothesis to address the voters' preferences.

Solution:

$$H_0: p_1 = p_2 = p_3 = p_4 = \frac{1}{4} \quad (no\ preference)$$

$$H_1: At\ least\ one\ of\ the\ proportions\ exceeds \frac{1}{4} \quad (a\ preference\ exists)$$

If the null hypothesis is true and $H_0: p_1 = p_2 = p_3 = p_4 = \frac{1}{4}$, then the expected value (mean value) of the number of voters who prefer candidate A is given by: $E_A = np_A = 1600 \times \frac{1}{4} = 400$. Similarly, $E_B = E_C = E_D = 400$ if the null hypothesis is true and no preference exists.

Table 13.7 Chi-Square Calculations

Candidate	Survey Results (O)	Expected Frequency (E)	Difference $(O\text{-}E)$	Square of difference $(O\text{-}E)2$	Chi-Square Subtotal $(O\text{-}E)^2/E$
A	380	400	-20	400	1
B	440	400	40	1600	4
C	380	400	-20	400	1
D	400	400	0	0	0
	1600	1600			$\chi_o^2 = 6$

The computed χ^2 is 6. The critical χ^2 value is 7.81 as shown below. This means that the computed χ^2 is in the no-rejection region. Thus, we fail to reject the null hypothesis and conclude that the survey revealed no preference to any candidate.

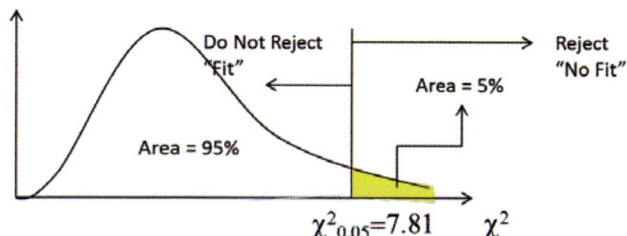

$\chi^2_{0.05}=7.81$

γ	0.995	0.990	0.975	0.950	0.500	0.050	0.025	0.010	0.005
1	0.00	0.00	0.00	0.00	0.45	3.84	5.02	6.63	7.88
2	0.01	0.02	0.05	0.10	1.39	5.99	7.38	9.21	10.60
3	0.07	0.11	0.22	0.35	2.37	7.81	9.35	11.34	12.84
4	0.21	0.30	0.48	0.71	3.36	9.49	11.14	13.28	14.86
5	0.41	0.55	0.83	1.15	4.35	11.07	12.38	15.09	16.75
6	0.68	0.87	1.24	1.64	5.35	12.59	14.45	16.81	18.55
7	0.99	1.24	1.69	2.17	6.35	14.07	16.01	18.48	20.28

Working Problem 13.2

Historical reports revealed that there is no significant difference in the relative frequency between the types of complaints expressed by consumers regarding a power outage in case of stormy sever weather. This means that the power company should expect to treat nearly equal number of people having different categories of complaints. These categories are shown in the box below. In a study by a consumer advocate, a random sample of people who have complaints directed to the power company was surveyed. The results of the survey are listed in the table below .

Complaint Category	Observed frequency (O)
Very lengthy time to get to a customer-support personnel	180
Inappropriate reaction and attitude by Customer-support personnel	298
Lack of specificity on when the Power Company will act	402
Poor answering-machine menu and poor channeling to proper helper	120

Using the goodness of fit analysis:

(a) Calculate the expected frequency of complaint categories
(b) Test the hypothesis that there is no difference between the set of observed frequencies and the set of expected frequencies at 5% risk

Answer: See calculations below and find the critical c at 0.05 to make the decision. The decision should be to reject the null hypothesis and conclude that different complaints have different frequencies

Complaint Category	Observed frequency (O)	Expected frequency E	$(O-E)^2/E$
Very lengthy time to get to a customer-support personnel	180	250	19.6
Inappropriate reaction and attitude by Customer-support personnel	298	250	9.216
Lack of specificity on when the Power Company will act	402	250	92.416
Poor answering-machine menue and poor channeling to proper helper	120	250	67.6
Total	1000	1000	$\chi_o^2 = 188.832$

Working Problem 13.3:

In a factory setting, it's a priority that clothing promote employee comfort and safety, yet still convey a positive image. Suppose a company making electronics wishes to establish a uniform dress to all its employees. Based on a nationwide survey conducted by an independent organization 5 years ago, it was found that 50% of the workers prefer no dress uniform, 40% prefer a simple shirt of unified color with company logo, 5% prefer an overall with logo, and 5% have no opinion. The company decided to survey its own workers using a random sample of 500 workers. The results of this survey were as shown below:

Dress Code	Observed Frequency (O)
No Uniform Dress	575
Simple Shirt with Logo	225
Overall with logo	100
No opinion	100
Total	1000

Test at $\alpha = 0.01$ level to see whether these data indicate that the distribution of opinion differs significantly from proportions of the old survey. Format your hypot

Answer: see the Table below and make your conclusion

Dress Code	Observed Frequency (O)	p-values	Expected frequencies (E)	$(O-E)^2$	$(O-E)^2/E$
No Uniform Dress	575	0.5	500	5625	11.25
Simple Shirt with Logo	225	0.4	400	30625	76.5625
Overall with logo	100	0.05	50	2500	50
No opinion	100	0.05	50	2500	50
Total	1000	1	1000	41250	187.8125

Working Problem 13.4:

Upon electing President Obama for a second term in November 2012, the first challenge facing the president was the so-called 'Fiscal Cliff'. This is a term that was used by the U.S. government to describe a bundle of momentous U.S. federal tax increases and spending cuts that were due to take effect at the end of 2012 and early 2013. In total, the measures were set to automatically slash the federal budget deficit by $503 billion between FY 2012 and FY 2013. One of the most debatable issues associated with the fiscal cliff was whether an increase in tax rate should be applied on the wealthy people in the U.S, or alternative ways to generate revenues should be followed. Economical analysts suggested that the probability of U.S. citizens to accept increase in tax rate on the wealthy people is 0.50, the probability that the entire society shares in generating revenues via all pay increased income tax is 0.25, the probability that budget cuts and reduction of tax deductions are the only way to generate revenues is 0.10, and the probability of no opinion is 0.15. An independent organization conducted a poll using a random sample of 1000 representing various financial levels found the following frequencies:

Opinion on Fiscal Cliff	Observed Frequency (O)
Increase in tax rate on the wealthy people	640
Entire society shares in generating revenues via all pay increased income tax	200
Budget cuts and reduction of tax deductions	120
No opinion	40
Total	1000

Test the hypothesis that the observed distribution is similar to the expected one.

Answer: Show how to reach the value of the statistic given below, find the critical chi-square value and make your conclusion

$\chi_o^2 = 91.2$

Working Problem 13.5:

The American people have little or no knowledge of how the wealth of over $55 trillion of the great U.S.A. is distributed among different classes of people from very poor to poor, to below-middle, to middle, to above-middle, to rich, to wealthy, and to very wealthy. Suppose we divided the American classes from the poorest to the very wealthy into percentiles, with each class of 10%. A survey of 1000 people of socialist orientation estimated that the U.S. wealth should be distributed as shown in Table A. This is the expected distribution by this group. The actual observed distribution is shown in Table B. Use the goodness of fit test to test the hypothesis that the expected distribution is equal to the actual (observed) distribution.

Table A (EXPECTED)

Percentile Groups from poorest to Richest	Socialist Group
0-10	10
10-20	10
20-30	10
30-40	10
40-50	10
50-60	10
60-70	10
70-80	10
80-90	10
90-100	10
Total	100
Percent difference between bottom 10% and top 10%	0

Table B: http://www.youtube.com/watch?v=QPKKQnijnsM

Percentile Groups from poorest to Richest	Actual (%)
0-10	0.2
10-20	0.3
20-30	0.4
30-40	0.7
40-50	0.9
50-60	1.2
60-70	1.5
70-80	1.8
80-90	20
90-100	73
Total	100
Percent difference between bottom 10% and top 10%	36400%

Answer:

4737.52	chi-square
9	df
0.00E+00	p-value

Goodness of Fit Test

observed	expected	O - E	(O - E)² / E	% of chisq
2	100.000	-98.000	96.040	2.03
3	100.000	-97.000	94.090	1.99
4	100.000	-96.000	92.160	1.95
7	100.000	-93.000	86.490	1.83
9	100.000	-91.000	82.810	1.75
12	100.000	-88.000	77.440	1.63
15	100.000	-85.000	72.250	1.53
18	100.000	-82.000	67.240	1.42
200	100.000	100.000	100.000	2.11
730	100.000	630.000	3969.000	83.78
1000	1000.000	0.000	4737.520	100.00

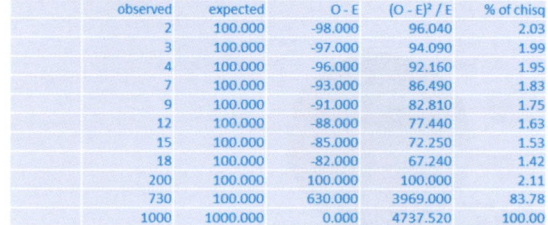

Working Problem 13.6:

The American people have little or no knowledge of how the wealth of over $55 trillion of the great U.S.A. is distributed among different classes of people from very poor to poor, to below-middle, to middle, to above-middle, to rich, to wealthy, and to very wealthy. Suppose we divided the American classes from the poorest to the very wealthy into percentiles, with each class of 10%. A survey of a random sample of 1000 people with the question being "what is the ideal wealth distribution?" the results were as shown in Table A. This is the expected distribution by this group. The actual observed distribution is shown in Table B. Use the goodness of fit test to test the hypothesis that the expected distribution is equal to the actual (observed) distribution.

Table A

Percentile Groups from poorest to Richest	Ideal (Expected)
0-10	90
10-20	93
20-30	94
30-40	96
40-50	98
50-60	102
60-70	104
70-80	106
80-90	107
90-100	110
Total	1000
Percent difference between bottom 10% and top 10%	22.22

Table B: http://www.youtube.com/watch?v=QPKKQnijnsM

Percentile Groups from poorest to Richest	Actual (%)
0-10	0.2
10-20	0.3
20-30	0.4
30-40	0.7
40-50	0.9
50-60	1.2
60-70	1.5
70-80	1.8
80-90	20
90-100	73
Total	100
Percent difference between bottom 10% and top 10%	36400%

Answer:

4226.66	chi-square
9	df
0.00E+00	p-value

Goodness of Fit Test

observed	expected	O - E	(O - E)² / E	% of chisq
2	90.000	-88.000	86.044	2.04
3	93.000	-90.000	87.097	2.06
4	94.000	-90.000	86.170	2.04
7	96.000	-89.000	82.510	1.95
9	98.000	-89.000	80.827	1.91
12	102.000	-90.000	79.412	1.88
15	104.000	-89.000	76.163	1.80
18	106.000	-88.000	73.057	1.73
200	107.000	93.000	80.832	1.91
730	110.000	620.000	3494.545	82.68
1000	1000.000	0.000	4226.657	100.00

Working Problem 13.7:

The American people have little or no knowledge of how the wealth of over $55 trillion of the great U.S.A. is distributed among different classes of people from very poor to poor, to below-middle, to middle, to above-middle, to rich, to wealthy, and to very wealthy. Suppose we divided the American classes from the poorest to the very wealthy into percentiles, with each class of 10%. A survey of a random sample of 1000 people with the question being "what do you think is the wealth distribution?" the results were as shown in Table A. This is the expected distribution by this group. The actual observed distribution is shown in Table B. Use the goodness of fit test to test the hypothesis that the expected distribution is equal to the actual (observed) distribution.

Table A

Percentile Groups from poorest to Richest	Most people think (Expected)
0-10	72
10-20	83
20-30	84
30-40	86
40-50	88
50-60	92
60-70	104
70-80	116
80-90	131
90-100	144
Total	1000
Percent difference between bottom 10% and top 10%	100

Table B: http://www.youtube.com/watch?v=QPKKQnijnsM

Percentile Groups from poorest to Richest	Actual (%)
0-10	0.2
10-20	0.3
20-30	0.4
30-40	0.7
40-50	0.9
50-60	1.2
60-70	1.5
70-80	1.8
80-90	20
90-100	73
Total	100
Percent difference between bottom 10% and top 10%	36400%

Answer:

3014.40	chi-square
9	df
.00	p-value

Goodness of Fit Test

observed	expected	O - E	(O - E)² / E	% of chisq
2	72.000	-70.000	68.056	2.26
3	83.000	-80.000	77.108	2.56
4	84.000	-80.000	76.190	2.53
7	86.000	-79.000	72.570	2.41
9	88.000	-79.000	70.920	2.35
12	92.000	-80.000	69.565	2.31
15	104.000	-89.000	76.163	2.53
18	116.000	-98.000	82.793	2.75
200	131.000	69.000	36.344	1.21
730	144.000	586.000	2384.694	79.11
1000	1000.000	0.000	3014.404	100.00

Working Problem 13.8:

The American people have little or no knowledge of how the wealth of over $55 trillion of the great U.S.A. is distributed among different classes of people from very poor to poor, to below-middle, to middle, to above-middle, to rich, to wealthy, and to very wealthy. Suppose we divided the American classes from the poorest to the very wealthy into percentiles, with each class of 10%. A survey of a random sample of 1000 expert people with the question being "what do you think is the wealth distribution?" the results were as shown in Table A. This is the expected distribution by this group. The actual observed distribution is shown in Table B. Use the goodness of fit test to test the hypothesis that the expected distribution is equal to the actual (observed) distribution.

Table A

Percentile Groups from poorest to Richest	Expert Opinions
0-10	1
10-20	2
20-30	3
30-40	9
40-50	11
50-60	13
60-70	16
70-80	17
80-90	199
90-100	729
Total	1000
Percent difference between bottom 10% and top 10%	72800

Table B: http://www.youtube.com/watch?v=QPKKQnijnsM

Percentile Groups from poorest to Richest	Actual (%)
0-10	0.2
10-20	0.3
20-30	0.4
30-40	0.7
40-50	0.9
50-60	1.2
60-70	1.5
70-80	1.8
80-90	20
90-100	73
Total	100
Percent difference between bottom 10% and top 10%	36400%

2.85 chi-square
9 df
.9701 p-value

Answer:

Goodness of Fit Test

observed	expected	O - E	(O - E)² / E	% of chisq
2	1.000	1.000	1.000	35.14
3	2.000	1.000	0.500	17.57
4	3.000	1.000	0.333	11.71
7	9.000	-2.000	0.444	15.62
9	11.000	-2.000	0.364	12.78
12	13.000	-1.000	0.077	2.70
15	16.000	-1.000	0.063	2.20
18	17.000	1.000	0.059	2.07
200	199.000	1.000	0.005	0.18
730	729.000	1.000	0.001	0.05
1000	1000.000	0.000	2.846	100.00

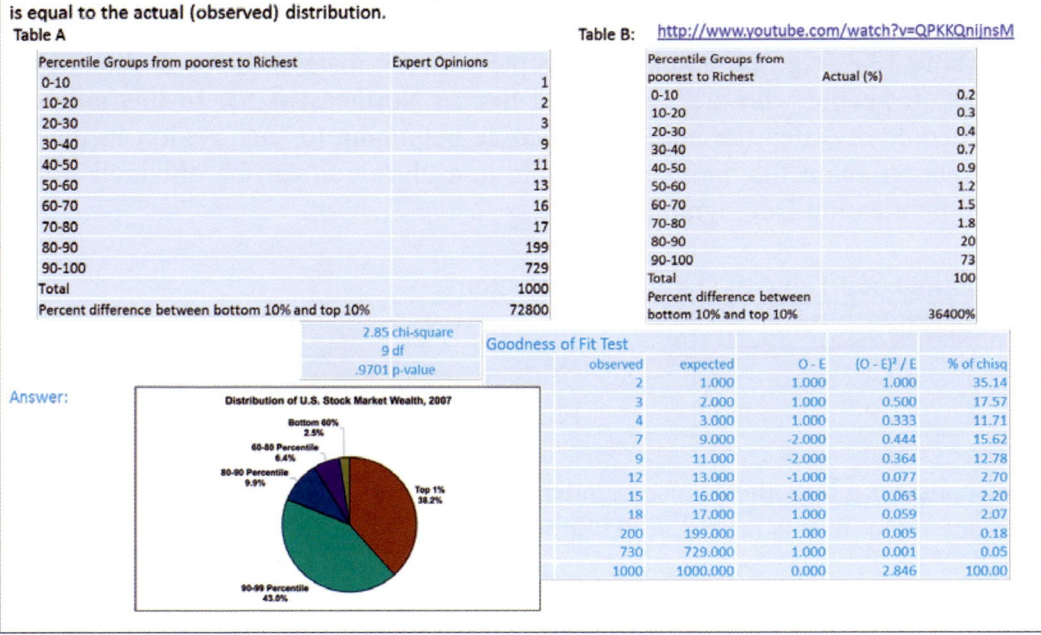

Distribution of U.S. Stock Market Wealth, 2007

Working Problem 13.9:

Review your answers of working problems 13.5 to 13.8 and interpret the results

Answer:

The different results are shown below

- This actual distribution is very disturbing as it indicates that the top 10 % of Americans have about 73% of the total U.S. wealth, and that the top 20% have about 93% of the total wealth of America.
- Indeed, the top 1% of Americans have 40% of all American Wealth and the bottom 80% only have 7% of the wealth between them..

Percentile Groups from poorest to Richest	The Dreaded Socialism	Ideal	Most people think	Actual	Expert Opinions
0-10	10.0	9.0	7.2	0.2	0.1
10-20	10.0	9.3	8.3	0.3	0.2
20-30	10.0	9.4	8.4	0.4	0.3
30-40	10.0	9.6	8.6	0.7	0.9
40-50	10.0	9.8	8.8	0.9	1.1
50-60	10.0	10.2	9.2	1.2	1.3
60-70	10.0	10.4	10.4	1.5	1.6
70-80	10.0	10.6	11.6	1.8	1.7
80-90	10.0	10.7	13.1	20.0	19.9
90-100	10.0	11.0	14.4	73.0	72.9
Total	100	100	100	100	100
Percent difference between bottom 10% and top 10%	0.00	22.22	100.00	36400.00	72800

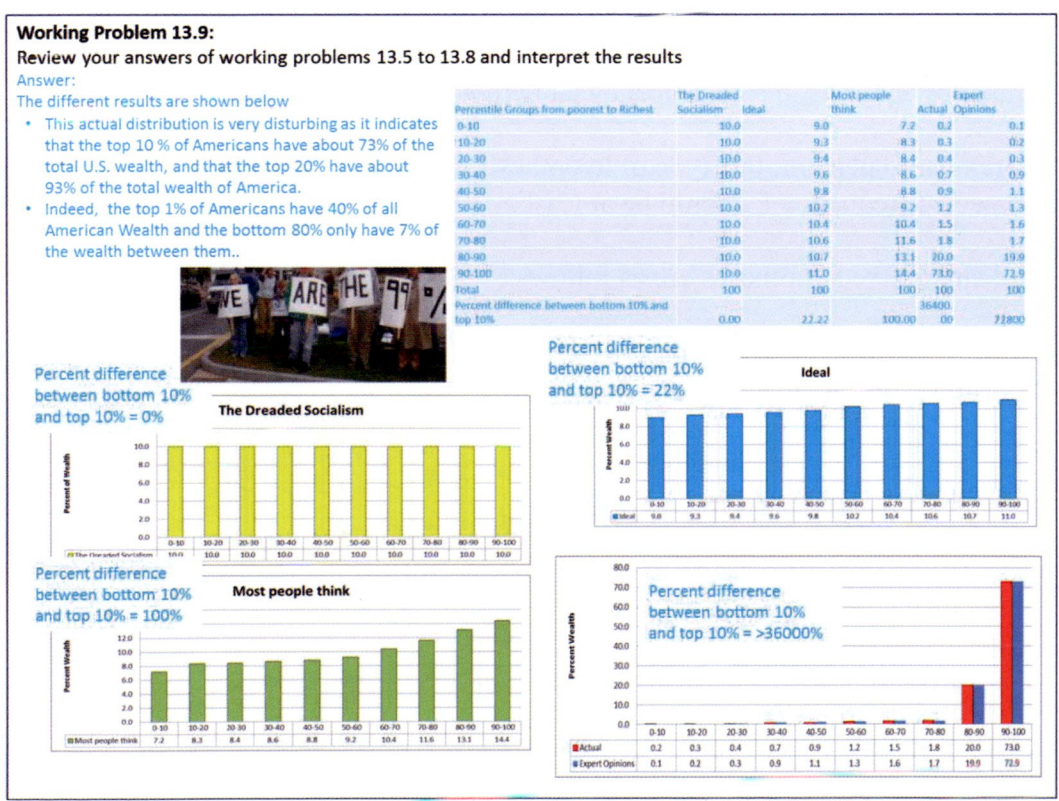

Percent difference between bottom 10% and top 10% = 0%

The Dreaded Socialism

Percent difference between bottom 10% and top 10% = 22%

Ideal

Percent difference between bottom 10% and top 10% = 100%

Most people think

Percent difference between bottom 10% and top 10% = >36000%

13.4 Contingency Tables and Tests for Independence

A contingency table (or two-way frequency table) is a table in which frequencies corresponding to two variables are listed. One variable is used to categorize rows, and a second variable is used to categorize columns. The cells of the table contain cross frequencies as shown in the contingency Table 13.8 (e.g. the number of people who are male and live in the Northeast is 5, and the number of people who are female and live in Northeast is 9). In this table, a random sample of 60 people revealed the number of people belonging to each region in the U.S. More accurate information about the number of people in each region can be obtained from the U.S. Census Bureau publication Demographic Profiles.

Table 13.8 Contingency Table of Genders and Regions

	Northeast	Midwest	South	West
Male	5	6	8	9
Female	9	3	12	8

We will now consider a hypothesis test of independence between the row and column variables in a contingency table. In this regard, it is important to introduce the following terms:

O = the *observed frequency* in a cell of a contingency table.
E = the *expected frequency* in a cell, found by assuming that the row and column variables are independent.
r = the number of rows in a contingency table (not including labels).
c = the number of columns in a contingency table (not including labels).

A key requirement to perform this type of hypothesis test is that for every cell in the contingency table, the expected frequency E should be at least 5.

The null and alternative hypotheses are as follows:

H_o: The row and column variables are independent
H_a: The row and column variables are dependent

Test Statistic for a Test of Independence

$$\chi_o{}^2 = \Sigma(O - E)^2/E$$

$$E = \frac{(row\ total)(column\ total)}{(grand\ total)}$$

Critical Values: χ^2 value at $df = (r\text{-}1)(c\text{-}1)$

Note that Tests of independence with a contingency table are always *right-tailed*.

Some of the key points that should be taken into consideration in performing the hypothesis test of independence are:

- The purpose of the test is essentially to determine the extent of disagreement between the observed frequencies and those that we would theoretically expect when the two variables are independent.
- Large values of the test statistic χ_o^2 are in the rightmost region of the chi-square distribution, and they reflect significant differences between observed and expected frequencies.
- The distribution of the test statistic can be approximated by the chi-square distribution, provided that all expected frequencies are at least 5.

Example 13.5: In this example, we refer to Table 13.8 obtained from a random sample of 60 people, which reveals the number of people belonging to each region in the U.S.

	Northeast	Midwest	South	West
Male	5	6	8	9
Female	9	3	12	8

Test the hypothesis that the number of people in different U.S. regions (columns) is independent of the gender (rows) at a confidence of 0.05.

Solution:

It will be useful that we first calculate the totals of each row and column and the grand total.

Table 13.9 Calculations of total category values (observed values)

	Northeast	Midwest	South	West	Total
Male	5	6	8	9	28
Female	9	3	12	8	32
Total	14	9	20	17	60

The expected values of the above frequencies are calculated using the expression:

$$E = \frac{(row\ total)(column\ total)}{(grand\ total)}$$

Table 13.10 Calculations of Expected Values

	Northeast	Midwest	South	West	Total
Male	(28*14/60 = 6.533)	(28*9/60 = 4.200)	(28*20/60 = 9.333)	(28*17/60 = 7.933)	28
Female	(32*14/60 = 7.467)	(32*9/60 = 4.800)	(32*20/60 = 10.667)	(32*17/60 = 9.067)	32
Total	14	9	20	17	60

773

We now calculate the test Statistic, $\chi_o{}^2$ for the test of independence:

$$\chi_o{}^2 = \sum (O - E)^2/E$$

Table 13.11 Calculations of χ^2 Values (use Table 13.9 1nd 13.10)

	Northeast	Midwest	South	West	Total
Male	$(5-6.533)^2/6.533$ $= 0.360$	$(6-4.2)^2/4.2$ $= 0.771$	$(8-9.333)^2/9.333$ $= 0.190$	$(9-7.933)^2/7.933$ $= 0.143$	1.465
Female	$(9-7.467)^2/7.467$ $= 0.315$	$(3-4.8)^2/4.8$ $= 0.675$	$(12-10.667)^2/10.667$ $= 0.167$	$(8-9.067)^2/9.067$ $= 0.125$	1.282
Total	0.675	1.446	0.357	0.269	$\chi_o{}^2 = 2.747$

The critical χ^2 value is determined at degrees of freedom $df = (r-1)(c-1) = (2-1)(4-1) = 3$. As shown below, this value is 7.81. Since the test statistic $\chi_o{}^2$ of 2.747 is less than the critical value of 7.81, we do not reject the hypothesis and conclude that the number of people in a U.S. region is independent of gender.

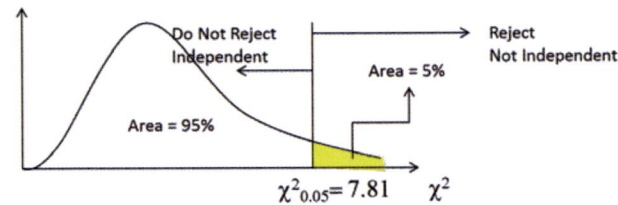

γ	0.995	0.990	0.975	0.950	0.500	0.050	0.025	0.010	0.005
1	0.00	0.00	0.00	0.00	0.45	3.84	5.02	6.63	7.88
2	0.01	0.02	0.05	0.10	1.39	5.99	7.38	9.21	10.60
3	0.07	0.11	0.22	0.35	2.37	7.81	9.35	11.34	12.84
4	0.21	0.30	0.48	0.71	3.36	9.49	11.14	13.28	14.86
5	0.41	0.55	0.83	1.15	4.35	11.07	12.38	15.09	16.75
6	0.68	0.87	1.24	1.64	5.35	12.59	14.45	16.81	18.55
7	0.99	1.24	1.69	2.17	6.35	14.07	16.01	18.48	20.28
8	1.34	1.65	2.18	2.73	7.34	15.51	17.53	20.09	21.96
9	1.73	2.09	2.70	3.33	8.34	16.92	19.02	21.67	23.59
10	2.16	2.56	3.25	3.94	9.34	18.31	20.48	23.21	25.19
11	2.60	3.05	3.82	4.57	10.34	19.68	21.92	24.72	26.76
12	3.07	3.57	4.40	5.23	11.34	21.03	23.34	26.22	28.30
13	3.57	4.11	5.01	5.89	12.34	22.36	24.74	27.69	29.82
14	4.07	4.66	5.63	6.57	13.34	23.68	26.12	29.14	31.32
...	...	...	...	...	...	...	...	...	...
...	...	...	...	...	...	...	...	...	...
90	59.20	61.75	65.65	69.13	89.33	113.14	118.14	124.12	128.30
100	67.33	70.06	74.22	77.93	99.33	124.34	129.56	135.81	140.17

Working Problem 13.10:

Do people views on government approaches in the U.S. depend on the political parties the people are affiliated with?

A random sample of 3000 people representing different political affiliations were asked about their views on solving budget deficits in the U.S. The Contingency Table below represents the results of this survey. Perform a hypothesis test to conclude whether U.S. people views will depend on their political affiliations. Use $\alpha = 0.01$.

Answer: Show how the χ^2 value is determined and make your conclusion

Political Affiliations	Budge Cut Method			
	Agree to increase tax rate on the Wealthy	Agree to increase in tax rate on the entire society	Raising Revenue via budget cuts	Reduce U.S. foreign support & increase tax on U.S. Business Abroad
Republican	200	280	400	180
Democart	700	220	260	170
Independent	100	200	150	140

421.48 chi-square
6 df
6.72E-88 p-value

Working Problem 13.11:

In most governments, male has the lion share in governments' jobs. One solution to this problem is to establish a quota by which male and female are represented in governments' jobs using a proportional weight allocation; meaning in proportion to their percent in the population. A sample of 1690 people was asked about this important issue and the results are shown below.

Opinion Category	Gender	
	Male	Female
Prefer Quota in State/Federal Government Positions	350	620
Disagree with Quota in State/Federal Government Positions	600	120

Perform a hypothesis test to conclude whether the opinion regarding gender share in proportional weight allocation will depend on the gender. Use $\alpha = 0.05$.

Answer: Show how to reach the value of the statistic given below, find the critical chi-square value and make your conclusion

$\chi_0^2 = 374.847$

13.5 Contingency Tables and Tests for Homogeneity

In the previous section, we focused on the test of independence between the row and column variables in a contingency table. In this case, the sample data was obtained from the same population. When samples are obtained from different populations, and we want to determine whether those populations have the same proportions of the characteristics being considered, we should use the test of **homogeneity** in which we test the claim that different populations have the same proportions of some characteristics. In performing a test of homogeneity, we use the same procedure discussed above but instead of testing the null hypothesis of *independence* between the row and column variables, we test the null hypothesis that the different populations have the same proportions of some characteristics.

Example13.6: Many treatments are available commercially to assist people to stop smoking. Three of these treatments are:

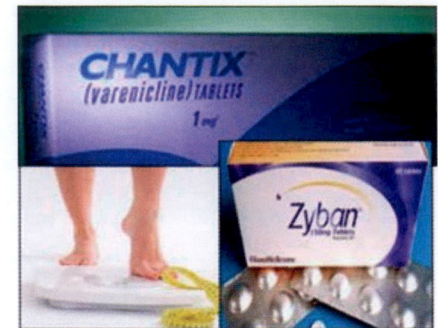

- Zyban (bupropion) is a prescription anti-depressant medication marketed under the brand names Wellbutrin (for depression) and Zyban (for smoking cessation). Zyban does not contain nicotine and is thought to affect chemicals in the brain that are related to nicotine craving. Zyban can be used either alone or in conjunction with nicotine replacement therapy.

- Chantix (varenicline) was developed solely to help people quit smoking and is one of the newest medication approaches available. Chantix works by interfering with nicotine receptors in the brain. This interference decreases the pleasurable effects of the nicotine and reduces the unpleasant symptoms of nicotine withdrawal.

- Sugar pills (placebo) are glucose tablets that are known to help smokers to quit. If the recent ex-smoker takes some glucose tablets, it will satiate their craving for carbohydrates, and also help the person feel less severe overall cravings.

Many studies suggested that these three treatments, if successful can result in a significant weight gain as a side effect. A medical consulting company conducted a research in this area using three different groups of people who used these three treatments and found the results shown in Table 13.12.

Table 13.12 Observed frequencies of people who gained weight and those who did not at different anti-smoking treatments

	Group I: Chantix (varenicline)	Group II: Zyban (bupropion)	Group III: Sugar pills (placebo)
Number of people who gained weight upon the treatment	300	290	210
Number of people who did not gain weight upon the treatment	180	150	120

Is there evidence to indicate that the proportion of subjects in each group who experienced weight gain is different at the level of significance of 0.01?

Solution:

The null hypothesis is a statement of 'no difference,' so the proportions of subjects in each group who experienced weight gain are equal. We state the hypothesis as follows:

H_o: $p_I = p_{II} = p_{III}$
H_1: At least one of the proportions in groups I, II, and III is different from the other

Table 13.13 Calculations of Totals

	Group I: Chantix (varenicline)	Group II: Zyban (bupropion)	Group III: Sugar pills (placebo)	Total
Number of people who gained weight upon the treatment	300	290	210	800
Number of people who did not gain weight upon the treatment	180	150	120	450
Total	480	440	330	1250

Table 13.14 Calculations of Expected Values (same procedure as that in Table 13.10)

	Group I: Chantix (varenicline)	Group II: Zyban (bupropion)	Group III: Sugar pills (placebo)	Total
Number of people who gained weight upon the treatment	307.2	281.6	211.2	800
Number of people who did not gain weight upon the treatment	172.8	158.4	118.8	450
Total	480	440	330	1250

Table 13.15 Calculations of Expected Values ($\chi_o{}^2 = \sum (O - E)^2 / E$)

Chi-Square Values				
	Group I: Chantix (varenicline)	Group II: Zyban (bupropion)	Group III: Sugar pills (placebo)	Total
Number of people who gained weight upon the treatment	$(300-307.2)^2 /$ $307.2 = 0.169$	0.251	0.007	0.426
Number of people who did not gain weight upon the treatment	0.300	0.445	0.012	0.758
Total	0.469	0.696	0.019	$\chi_o{}^2 = 1.184$

The critical χ^2 value is determined at degrees of freedom $df = (r\text{-}1)(c\text{-}1) = (2\text{-}1)(3\text{-}1) = 2$. As shown below, this value is 9.21. Since the test statistic $\chi_o{}^2$ of 1.184 is less than the critical value of 9.21, we do not reject the hypothesis test and conclude that $p_I = p_{II} = p_{III}$.

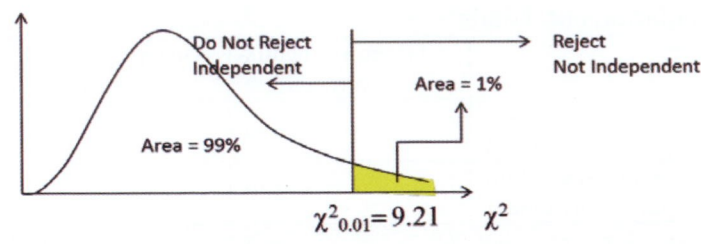

γ	0.995	0.990	0.975	0.950	0.500	0.050	0.025	**0.010**	0.005
1	0.00	0.00	0.00	0.00	0.45	3.84	5.02	6.63	7.88
2	0.01	0.02	0.05	0.10	1.39	5.99	7.38	9.21	10.60
3	0.07	0.11	0.22	0.35	2.37	7.81	9.35	11.34	12.84
4	0.21	0.30	0.48	0.71	3.36	9.49	11.14	13.28	14.86
5	0.41	0.55	0.83	1.15	4.35	11.07	12.38	15.09	16.75
6	0.68	0.87	1.24	1.64	5.35	12.59	14.45	16.81	18.55
7	0.99	1.24	1.69	2.17	6.35	14.07	16.01	18.48	20.28
8	1.34	1.65	2.18	2.73	7.34	15.51	17.53	20.09	21.96
9	1.73	2.09	2.70	3.33	8.34	16.92	19.02	21.67	23.59
10	2.16	2.56	3.25	3.94	9.34	18.31	20.48	23.21	25.19
11	2.60	3.05	3.82	4.57	10.34	19.68	21.92	24.72	26.76
12	3.07	3.57	4.40	5.23	11.34	21.03	23.34	26.22	28.30
13	3.57	4.11	5.01	5.89	12.34	22.36	24.74	27.69	29.82
14	4.07	4.66	5.63	6.57	13.34	23.68	26.12	29.14	31.32
...	...	...	...	...	...	...	...	...	...
...	...	...	...	...	...	...	...	...	...
90	59.20	61.75	65.65	69.13	89.33	113.14	118.14	124.12	128.30
100	67.33	70.06	74.22	77.93	99.33	124.34	129.56	135.81	140.17

13.6 Review Exercises

P13.1: In a factory setting, it's a priority that clothing promotes employee comfort and safety, yet still conveys a positive image. Suppose a company making electronics wishes to establish a uniform dress for all its employees. Based on a nationwide survey conducted by an independent organization 5 years ago, it was found that 50% of the workers prefer no dress uniform, 40% prefer a simple shirt of unified color with company logo, 5% prefer an overall with logo, and 5% displayed no opinion. The company decided to survey its own workers using a random sample of 500 workers. The results of this survey were as shown below:

Dress code	Observed frequency (O)
No Uniform Dress	245
Simple Shirt with Logo	205
Overall with logo	20
No opinion	30
Total	500

Test at $\alpha = 0.01$ level to see whether these data indicate that the distribution of opinion differs significantly from proportions of the old survey.
Answer: $\chi_o^2 = 2.225$, $\chi^2_{0.01} = 11.3449$.

P13.2: Upon electing President Obama for a second term in November 2012, the first challenge facing the president was the so-called 'Fiscal Cliff.' This is a term that was used by the U.S. government to describe a bundle of momentous U.S. federal tax increases and spending cuts that were due to take effect at the end of 2012 and early 2013. In total, the measures were set to automatically slash the federal budget deficit by $503 billion between FY 2012 and FY 2013. One of the most debatable issues associated with the fiscal cliff was whether an increase in tax rate should be applied on the wealthy people in the U.S, or alternative ways to generate revenues should be followed. Economical analysts suggested that the probability of U.S. citizens to accept increase in tax rate on the wealthy people is 0.50, the probability that the entire society shares in generating revenues via all pay increased income tax is 0.25, the probability that budget cuts and reduction of tax deductions are the only way to generate revenues is 0.10, and the probability of no opinion is 0.15. An independent organization conducted a poll using a random sample of 1000 representing various financial levels found the following frequencies:

Opinion on fiscal cliff	Observed frequency (O)
Increase in tax rate on the wealthy people	500
Entire society shares in generating revenues via all pay increased income tax	270
Budget cuts and reduction of tax deductions	140
No opinion	90
Total	1000

Test at $\alpha = 0.01$ level to see whether these data indicate that the distribution of opinion differs significantly from proportions of the analysts suggestions.

P13.3: Causes of student's failure in college has been the subject of many studies. Every year more than 380,000 students fail out of college in the United States. The impact of college failure can cause lasting damage to self-esteem, and the consequences can influence one for an entire lifetime. In studying the complexities of the failure problem, a higher-education organization determined that the primary causes of student's failure are as follows:

1. Lack of work expectation
2. Distraction by other activities
3. Poor time management
4. Poor language skills
5. Lack of vision of long-term goals
6. Inappropriate choice of a major
7. Poor mathematics skills

The table below gives a relative-frequency distribution for causes of student's failure reported in the last 20 years. For instance, 5% of the students fail due to inappropriate choice of a major.

Reported relative frequency values of the causes of student's failure

n	Cause of Failure	Relative Frequency
1	Lack of work expectation	0.32
2	Distraction by other activities	0.18
3	Poor time management	0.17
4	Poor language skills	0.13
5	Lack of vision of long-term goals	0.12
6	Inappropriate choice of a major	0.05
7	Poor mathematics skills	0.03

A recent random sample of 850 college students was taken to decide whether the previously reported distribution of causes of student's failure has changed from the new distribution associated with this sample. This distribution is shown in the table below.

Observed frequency values of the causes of student's failure

n	Cause of failure	Frequency
1	Lack of work expectation	165
2	Distraction by other activities	200
3	Poor time management	150
4	Poor language skills	100
5	Lack of vision of long-term goals	130
6	Inappropriate choice of a major	65
7	Poor mathematics skills	40

Use the chi-square goodness-of-fit test to test the hypothesis that the frequency distribution of reported causes of student's failure is the same as the recently observed frequency distribution of student's failure

Answer: $\chi_o^2 = 85.58$, $\chi_{0.05}^2 = 12.59$

P13.4: Suppose three political candidates are running for the presidency. A survey conducted prior to the election using a sample of 1600 people revealed the following results:

Candidate	Survey Results (O)
A	490
B	550
C	460
Total	1500

Suppose we wish to decide whether the voters have a preference for any one of the candidates. Form the necessary hypothesis and test the hypothesis to address the voters' preferences.

P13.5: Developmental math is perhaps the biggest stumbling block in higher education. Approximately 60% of incoming community college students are unprepared for college-level work, typically in math and English, and place into developmental courses (the preferred term among academics). Success rates are the worst for math, and only a small portion of remedial math students ever complete a single college-level math course. Many get frustrated at their lack of progress and drop out, a major impediment in the push to get more Americans into and out of higher education with a credential. Some higher-education reports suggest the following opinion's frequencies of developmental math courses:

Opinion	Reported relative frequency
Developmental Math in College helps students doing better in advanced math classes	0.54
Developmental Math in College is a burden on Tax-payers	0.08
Developmental Math in College does not help students doing better in advanced math classes	0.25
Developmental Math should be made at the high school only	0.13

In a survey of 1000 students, the following results were obtained:

Opinion	Survey results
Developmental Math in College helps students doing better in advanced math classes	0.5
Developmental Math in College is a burden on Tax-payers	0.1
Developmental Math in College does not help students doing better in advanced math classes	0.3
Developmental Math should be made at the high school only	0.1

Test the hypothesis that the survey results agree with the reported results.
Answer: $\chi_o^2 = 24.89$

P13.6: On the issue of same-sex marriage in one of the European Countries, the following data was reported:

Opinion	Expected
Citizens Against	0.18
Citizens Favoring	0.07
Citizens favoring waiting for more research	0.65
Citizens of no opinion	0.1

A survey of a sample of 500 people revealed the following opinions:

Opinion	Observed
Citizens Against	100
Citizens Favoring	40
Citizens favoring waiting for more research	330
Citizens of no opinion	30

Test the hypothesis that the survey results agree with the reported results.

P13.7: Following are observed frequencies of students opinions of food service offered on campus:

Category	Poor	Fair	Good	Very Good	Excellent	Total
Observed (O)	50	200	65	20	3	338

The expected values are:

$$H_o: p_{poor} = 0.2, p_{fair} = 0.4, p_{good} = 0.2, p_{v.good} = 0.09, p_{excellent} = 0.11$$

(a) Compute the values of χ^2
(b) How many degrees of freedom are there?
(c) Find the level $\alpha = 0.05$ critical value of χ^2
(d) What is your conclusion about the null hypothesis at $\alpha = 0.05$
(e) Find the level $\alpha = 0.01$ critical value of χ^2
(f) What is your conclusion about the null hypothesis at $\alpha = 0.01$
Answer: χ^2= 70.73155, 4, 9.49, Reject, 13.28, Reject

P13.8: Do some courses require more studying than other? A sample of 2000 students was chosen, and the number of students in each category is presented below.

Hours studying per week	History	Calculus	Chemistry	Biology	Total
0-2	136	212	262	80	690
2-4	238	206	254	162	860
more then 4	140	104	102	104	450
Total	514	522	618	346	2000

Perform a hypothesis test to conclude whether the number of hours of studying was dependent on the course. Use $\alpha = 0.01$.

P13.9: Attendance of college under the era of economic pressure is a subject of great interest. A college decided to conduct a survey among potential students of male and female. The sample size was 1000 potential students. Perform a hypothesis test to conclude whether the opinion regarding college attendance will depend on the gender. Use $a = 0.05$.

Opinion	Male	Female
Part-time college attendance is preferred	250	400
Full-Time college attendance is preferred	150	200

Answer: χ_o^2 = 1.831502, find the critical chi-square value and make the decision

P13.10: A college is planning to increase the letter-grade thresholds at all levels so that an *A* letter grade would be associated with a 95% or more; a *B* letter grade would be associated with a 85% or more; a *C* letter grade would be associated with a 75% or more; a *D* letter grade would be associated with a 65% or more; and a *F* letter grade would be associated with any value less than 65%. A sample of 300 students was surveyed from three different categories of students: (a) A to B average students, (b) C to B average students, and (c) C to D average students. The results of the survey were as follow:

		Student Opinion		
		Dissatisfied	Undecided	Very Satisfied
	A-B Average	15	50	120
Student's Performance	*B-C* Average	10	50	80
	D-C Average	110	55	10

(a) Construct a bar graph of opinions at different student levels.
(b) Based on your observation of the bar graph, would you conclude that student's satisfaction level was dependent on student's performance level?
(c) Perform a hypothesis test to conclude whether student's satisfaction level was dependent on student's performance level. Use $\alpha = 0.05$.
(d) What is your final conclusion regarding the dependence of the two categories?

P 13.11: The table below is obtained from a survey of a random sample of 300 college students asked about their opinions in weekend classes. Test the hypothesis that student's opinion is independent of gender. Use $\alpha = 0.05$.

	Disagree	Undecided	Agree
Male	80	45	30
Female	41	44	60

Answer: $\chi_o^2 = 22.27$, find the critical chi-square value and make the decision

P 13.12: The table below is obtained from a random sample of 196 children (under 11) to evaluate overweight and obesity. Test the hypothesis that children obesity is independent of the ethnic background. Use $\alpha = 0.05$.

	Non-Hispanic White	Non-Hispanic Black	Hispanic	Asian
Overweight	27	41	41	18
Obese	13	24	23	9

CHAPTER 14

Forecasting

After completing this chapter, students will be able to:

- Understand and know why we do forecasting
- Know the different applications in which forecasting can be useful
- Understand how to smooth time-series data to minimize random patterns
- Understand the difference between trend, seasonal, cyclical, and random time-series patterns
- Understand how to decompose time-series patterns
- Know how to forecast future events

CHAPTER 14

Forecasting is another way of developing relationships for the purpose of making statements about events whose outcomes have not yet been observed and it may happen in the future. Similar to the regression analysis discussed in Chapter 12, forecasting analysis requires the use of historic data to predict the direction of future trends. The independent variable used in forecasting analysis is always the time, t, or a function of time. The dependent variable is the parameter of interest, which can be of numerous types as discussed in this chapter. Key subjects discussed in this chapter include: the basic concepts of forecasting, measures of forecasting accuracy, time-series models, and decomposition procedures.

CHAPTER CONTENTS

14.1 Introduction

In chapter 12, we discussed regression analysis in the context of developing *x-y* relationships for the purpose of predicting values of a response variable from given values of one or more independent variables. Forecasting is another way of developing relationships for the purpose of making statements about events whose outcomes have not yet been observed and it may happen in the future. Forecasting analysis requires the use of historic data to predict the direction of future trends. In practice, forecasting is used in numerous applications including:

- A business firm needs to forecast the demand for certain goods and services it offers, compared to the cost of producing them so that the firm can determine how to allocate their budgets for an upcoming period of time.

- Investors utilize forecasting to determine if events affecting a company, such as sales expectations, will increase or decrease the price of shares in that company in the marketplace.
- Stock analysts use various forecasting methods to determine how a stock's price will perform in the future.
- Economists use forecasting to extrapolate how key economic parameters, such as Gross Domestic Product (GDP) or unemployment rate, will change in the coming quarter or year.
- Manufacturers use forecasting in supply-chain management to make sure that the right product is at the right place and at the right time.

- Retailers use forecasting to predict inventory and therefore reduce storage and carrying costs.
- Weather forecasters use science and technology to predict the state of the atmosphere for a given location and in a given period of time. They collect quantitative data about the current state of the atmosphere and use scientific understanding of environmental processes to project how the atmosphere will evolve.
- All telecommunications service providers perform forecasting calculations to assist them in planning their networks.

The basic steps of most forecasting methods are as follows:

1. **Objectives**- Determine the reason for forecasting
2. **Variables**- Determine what to forecast
3. **Time**- Determine the time horizon of the forecast
4. **Modeling**- Propose a forecasting model
5. **Data**- Collect historic data needed to make the forecast
6. **Validation**- Verify the reliability of the forecasting model
7. **Implementation**- Make the forecast
8. **Utilization**- Use forecasting results

Organizations using forecasting follow the above steps regularly over time. Data is collected routinely and calculations are performed automatically using capable forecasting software programs. The modeling process may vary depending on the application and data availability. Different organizations may use different techniques depending on which tool works best for the organization.

Many quantitative techniques can be used to perform forecasting analysis. In this chapter, the following techniques will be discussed:

(a) *Moving averages*
(b) *Exponential smoothing*
(c) *Trend projections*
(d) *Least squares regression analysis*

14.2 Begin with a Scatter Diagram

In performing forecasting analysis, it will always be useful to begin by examining a scatter diagram of the data in hand. In this case, the horizontal axis will always represent time periods and the vertical axis will be the variable to be forecast (such as volume of sales, sales value, revenues, profits, etc.).

Example 14.1: A retailer selling house appliances wants to forecast the sales volumes for three different products: (a) microwaves, (b) coffee makers, and (c) food processors. Table 14.1 shows these volumes over the last 10 years. Construct scatter diagrams for these three products and forecast sales volume for year 11.

Solution:

Table 14.1 Sales volumes of three products sold by a retailer

YEAR	Microwaves	Coffee makers	Food processors
1	3250	3300	1650
2	3250	3410	1500
3	3250	3520	1800
4	3250	3630	2100
5	3250	3740	2550
6	3250	3850	2250
7	3250	3960	2400
8	3250	4070	2850
9	3250	4180	3000
10	3250	4290	2850

The scatter diagrams for the three products are shown in Figure 14.1. The following important points can be revealed from these diagrams:

(a) Sales appear to be constant over time at 3250 units annually. Good forecast of year 11 is 3250 microwaves

(b) Sales appear to be increasing at a constant rate of 110 coffee makers each year. A reasonable forecast of year 11 is 4400 coffee makers as obtained from the straight line equation in Figure14.1.b ($Sales = 110(Year) + 3190 = 110(11) + 3190 = 4400$).

(c) Sales appear to be scattered due to variation from year to year, but following a linear upward trend (sales appear to be increasing). A reasonable forecast would probably be a larger volume each year, with year 11 being roughly 3200 food processors ($Sales = 164.55(Year) + 1390 = 164.55(11) + 1390 = 3200$)

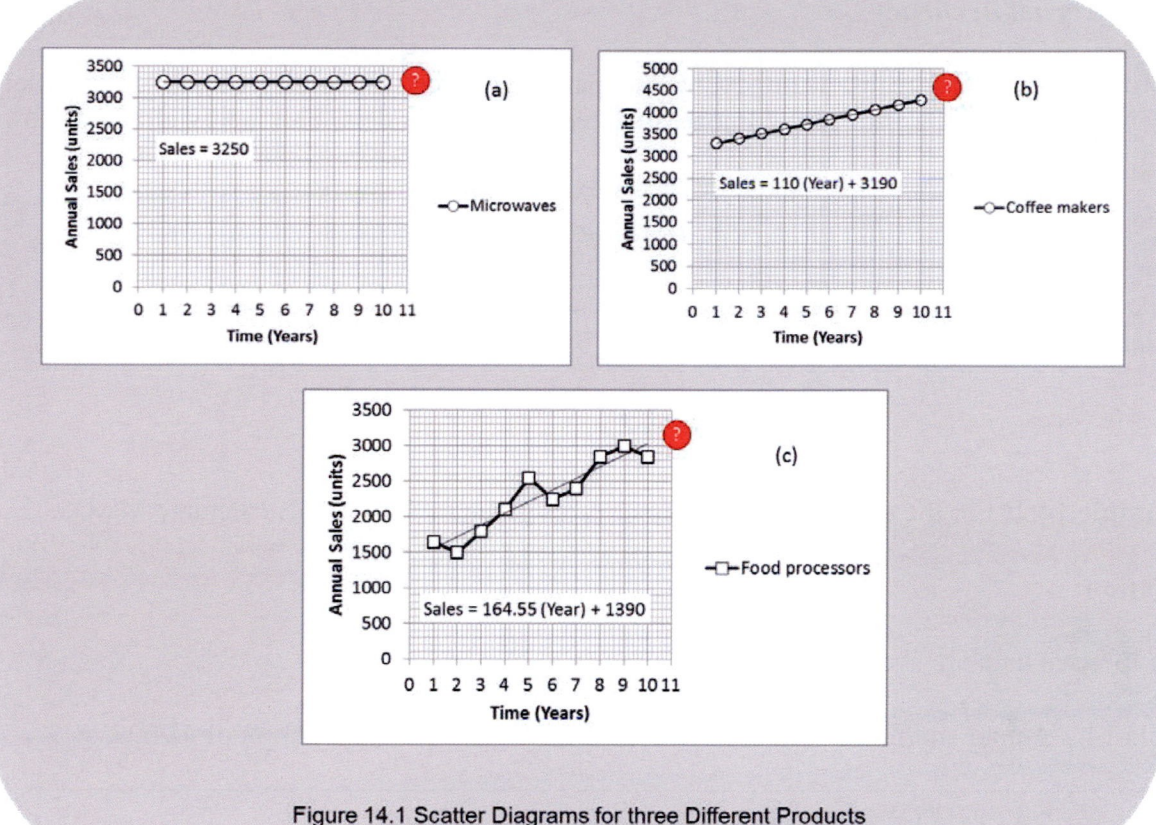

Figure 14.1 Scatter Diagrams for three Different Products

Working Problem 14.1 An electronic retailer selling different electronics wants to forecast the sales volumes for three different products: (a) computers, (b) cell phones, and (c) printers. The table below shows these volumes over the last 10 years. Construct scatter diagrams for these three products and forecast sales volume for year 11.

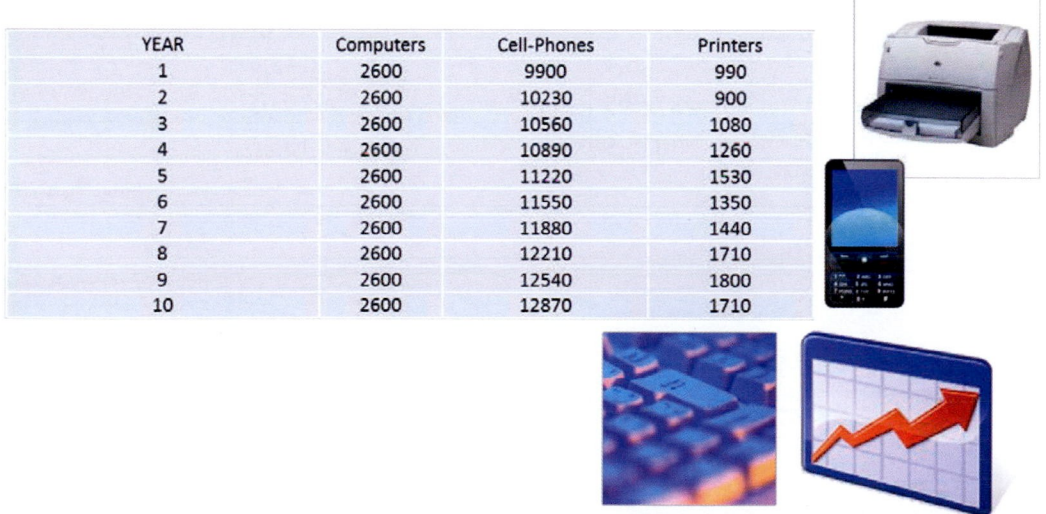

YEAR	Computers	Cell-Phones	Printers
1	2600	9900	990
2	2600	10230	900
3	2600	10560	1080
4	2600	10890	1260
5	2600	11220	1530
6	2600	11550	1350
7	2600	11880	1440
8	2600	12210	1710
9	2600	12540	1800
10	2600	12870	1710

Follow the procedure in Example 14.1 to solve this problem.

14.3 Forecast Accuracy

In order to measure forecast accuracy, we compare forecasted values with actual values to see how well one model works or to compare different forecast models. This will yield the following equation:

$$Forecast\ Error = Actual\ Value - Forecast\ Value \qquad (14.1)$$

Since forecast error can be positive or negative, we can use the so-called ***mean absolute deviation (MAD)***:

$$MAD = \frac{\sum|forecsat\ error|}{n} \qquad (14.2)$$

Example 14.2: For the data of food processor sales given in Table 14.1, calculate MAD.

Solution:

The forecast data are shown in Table 14.2.

Table 14.2 Actual and forecast data of food processor sales and calculation of *MAD*

Year	Actual number of food processors	Forecast values	Error or difference	Absolute error
1	1650	1554.55	1554.55- 1650 = -95.45	95.45
2	1500	1719.1	1719.1- 1500 = 219.1	219.1
3	1800	1883.65	83.65	83.65
4	2100	2048.2	-51.8	51.8
5	2550	2212.75	-337.25	337.25
6	2250	2377.3	127.3	127.3
7	2400	2541.85	141.85	141.85
8	2850	2706.4	-143.6	143.6
9	3000	2870.95	-129.05	129.05
10	2850	3035.5	185.5	185.5
				Sum = 1514.55
				$MAD = \frac{\sum|forecsat\ error|}{n}$ $= \frac{1514.55}{10} = 151.455$

Other ways to calculate forecast accuracy are listed below:

The mean square error (MSE):

$$MSE = \frac{\sum (error)^2}{n} \qquad (14.3)$$

The ***mean absolute percent error (MAPE)***:

$$MAPE(\%) = \frac{\sum \left| \frac{error}{actual} \right|}{n} \times 100 \qquad (14.4)$$

The bias: This is the average error

Example 14.3: For the data of food processor sales given in Table 14.1, forecast data are shown in Table 14.3. Calculate *MSE,* and *MAPE* (%).

Solution:

Table 14.3 Actual and forecast data of food processor sales and calculations of *MSE* and *MAPE*

Year	Food processors	Forecast values	Error	(Error)^2	|Error/Actual|
1	1650	1554.55	1554.55- 1650 = -95.45	9110.703	0.057848
2	1500	1719.1	1719.1- 1500 = 219.1	48004.81	0.146067
3	1800	1883.65	83.65	6997.323	0.046472
4	2100	2048.2	-51.8	2683.24	0.024667
5	2550	2212.75	-337.25	113737.6	0.132255
6	2250	2377.3	127.3	16205.29	0.056578
7	2400	2541.85	141.85	20121.42	0.059104
8	2850	2706.4	-143.6	20620.96	0.050386
9	3000	2870.95	-129.05	16653.9	0.043017
10	2850	3035.5	185.5	34410.25	0.065088
				Sum =288545.5	Sum = 0.681481
				MSE= $$MSE = \frac{\sum (error)^2}{n}$$ $$= \frac{288545.5}{10}$$ $$= 28854.55$$	$MAPE(\%)$ $$= \frac{\sum \left\| \frac{error}{actual} \right\|}{n} \times 100$$ $$= \frac{0.681481}{10} \times 100$$ $$= 6.82\%$$

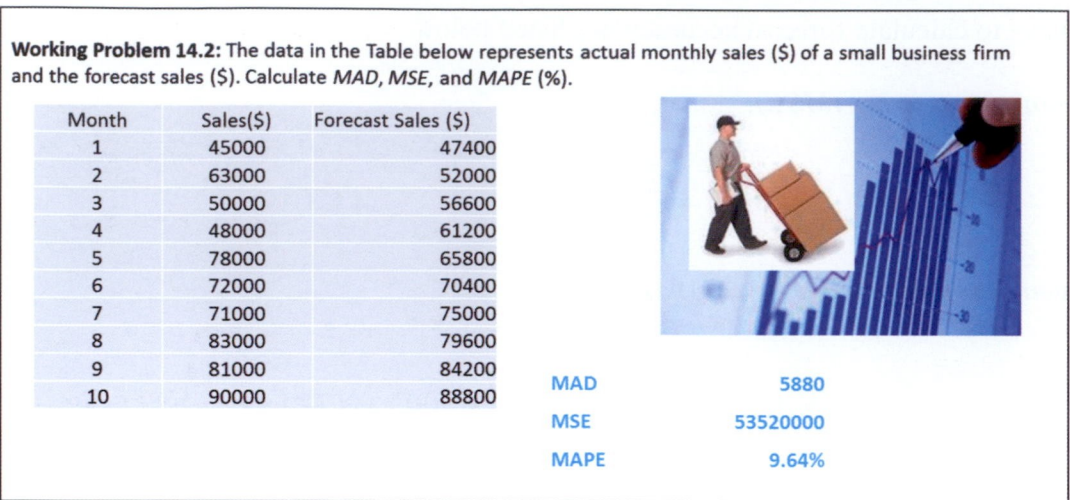

Working Problem 14.2: The data in the Table below represents actual monthly sales ($) of a small business firm and the forecast sales ($). Calculate *MAD*, *MSE*, and *MAPE* (%).

Month	Sales($)	Forecast Sales ($)
1	45000	47400
2	63000	52000
3	50000	56600
4	48000	61200
5	78000	65800
6	72000	70400
7	71000	75000
8	83000	79600
9	81000	84200
10	90000	88800

MAD	5880
MSE	53520000
MAPE	9.64%

14.4 Time-Series Forecasting Models

A time series is a sequence of evenly spaced data points, measured typically at successive time instants. Time-series forecasts predict the future based solely on the past values of the variable.

In practice, time series data often arise under the following conditions:

- When monitoring business data (sales, revenues, costs, market share, etc.) over time periods
- When monitoring quality parameters of manufactured products (shipments, returns, rejects, etc.) over time
- When tracking social changes (ethnic distribution, poverty, divorce, etc.) annually

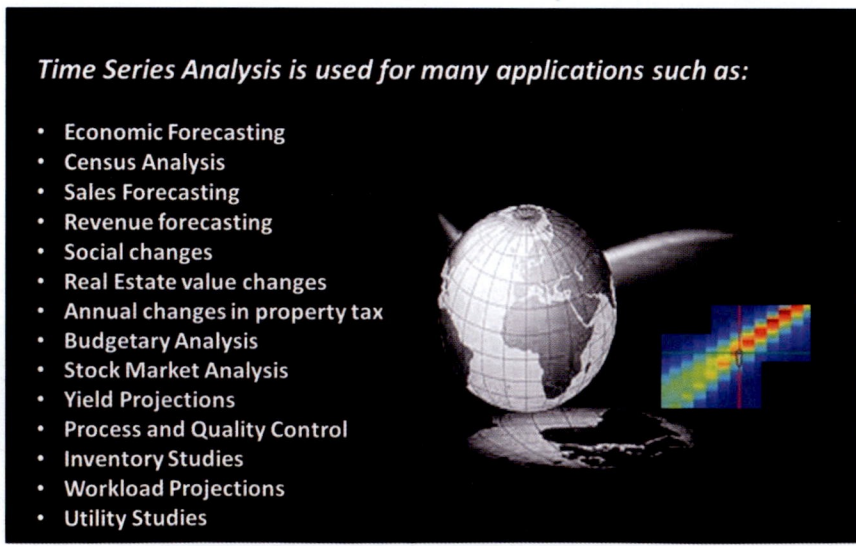

Time Series Analysis is used for many applications such as:

- Economic Forecasting
- Census Analysis
- Sales Forecasting
- Revenue forecasting
- Social changes
- Real Estate value changes
- Annual changes in property tax
- Budgetary Analysis
- Stock Market Analysis
- Yield Projections
- Process and Quality Control
- Inventory Studies
- Workload Projections
- Utility Studies

In performing time-series analysis, it is important to anticipate a number of possible common components that may occur over time. These components are as follows (see Figure 14.2):

(1) **Trend (T)**: a gradual upward or downward movement of the data over time.
(2) **Seasonality (S)**: a pattern of fluctuations above or below the trend line that repeats at regular intervals.
(3) **Cycles (C)**: a pattern in annual data that occurs every several days, months, or years.
(4) **Random variations (R)**: a nonsystematic pattern in the data caused only by chance.

These components are commonly decomposed using two common models:

The multiplicative model:

$$Variable = T \times S \times C \times R \qquad (14.5)$$

The additive model:

$$Variable = T + S + C + R \qquad (14.6)$$

Time-series models may be represented by combinations of these two forms. In addition, forecasters often assume errors are normally distributed with a mean of zero. This is similar to the case of regression analysis.

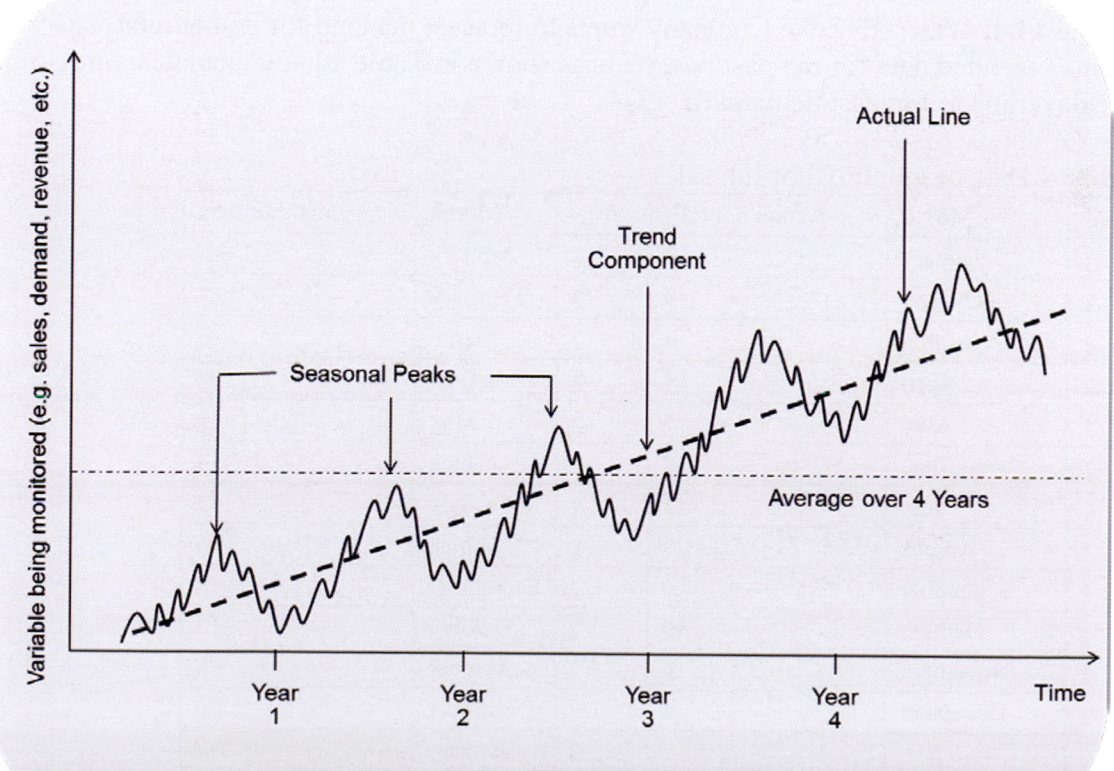

Figure 14.2 Different Components of Time Series

793

14.5 Moving Averages

Random variations represent an inherent aspect in all data collected over time. These variations often mask other patterns in a time series. It is important, therefore, to use techniques by which random variations can be reduced or largely eliminated. In practice, these are called smoothing techniques. When properly applied, smoothing techniques can reveal the underlying trend, seasonal and cyclic components in a time series. Moving averages and exponential smoothing are two of the most commonly used smoothing techniques in real-world forecasting applications. In this section, we focus on moving averages. Moving averages can be used when the **variable considered is relatively steady over time**. A moving average is calculated using the following equation:

$$Moving\ average\ forecast = \frac{Sum\ of\ points\ in\ pervious\ n\ periods}{n}$$

Or

$$F_{t+1} = \frac{Y_t + Y_{t-1} + Y_{t-2} + \cdots + Y_{t-n-1}}{n} \qquad (14.7)$$

where: F_{t+1} = forecast for time period $t + 1$, Y_t = actual value in time period t, n = number of periods to average.

The above equation can be used to smooth out short-term irregularities in the data series.

Example 14.4: Waterfall Zeko Company wants to forecast demand for its hot tubs. The company collected data for the past two years as shown in Table 14.4. Calculate a three-month moving average to forecast demand ($n = 3$).

Table 14.4 Data of monthly hot-tub sales

Year	Month	Actual hot tubs	Year	Month	Actual hot tubs
1	January	3	2	January	3
1	February	9	2	February	7
1	March	4	2	March	6
1	April	15	2	April	20
1	May	7	2	May	9
1	June	28	2	June	34
1	July	41	2	July	45
1	August	29	2	August	36
1	September	6	2	September	8
1	October	10	2	October	12
1	November	6	2	November	8
1	December	4	2	December	6
			3	January	?????

Solution:

The calculations of the moving averages are shown in Figure 14.3. Figure 14.4 shows the effect of smoothing on the time series at different values n. You can easily see here that the removal of the random variations via moving averages has resulted in a great deal of smoothing particularly at $n = 6$. Therefore, it is important to use some judgment of the value of n to avoid masking important information.

Month	Actual Hot Tubs	Moving Average (n=3)
January	3	...
February	9	...
March	4	...
April	15	(3+9+4)/3 = 5.333
May	7	(9+4+15)/3 = 9.333
June	28	8.667
July	41	16.667
August	29	25.333
September	6	32.667
October	10	25.333
November	6	15.000
December	4	7.333
January	3	6.667
February	7	4.333
March	6	4.667
April	20	5.333
May	9	11.000
June	34	11.667
July	45	21.000
August	36	29.333
September	8	38.333
October	12	29.667
November	8	18.667
December	6	9.333
January		8.667

Figure 14.3 Calculations of the Moving Average of Hot Tubs

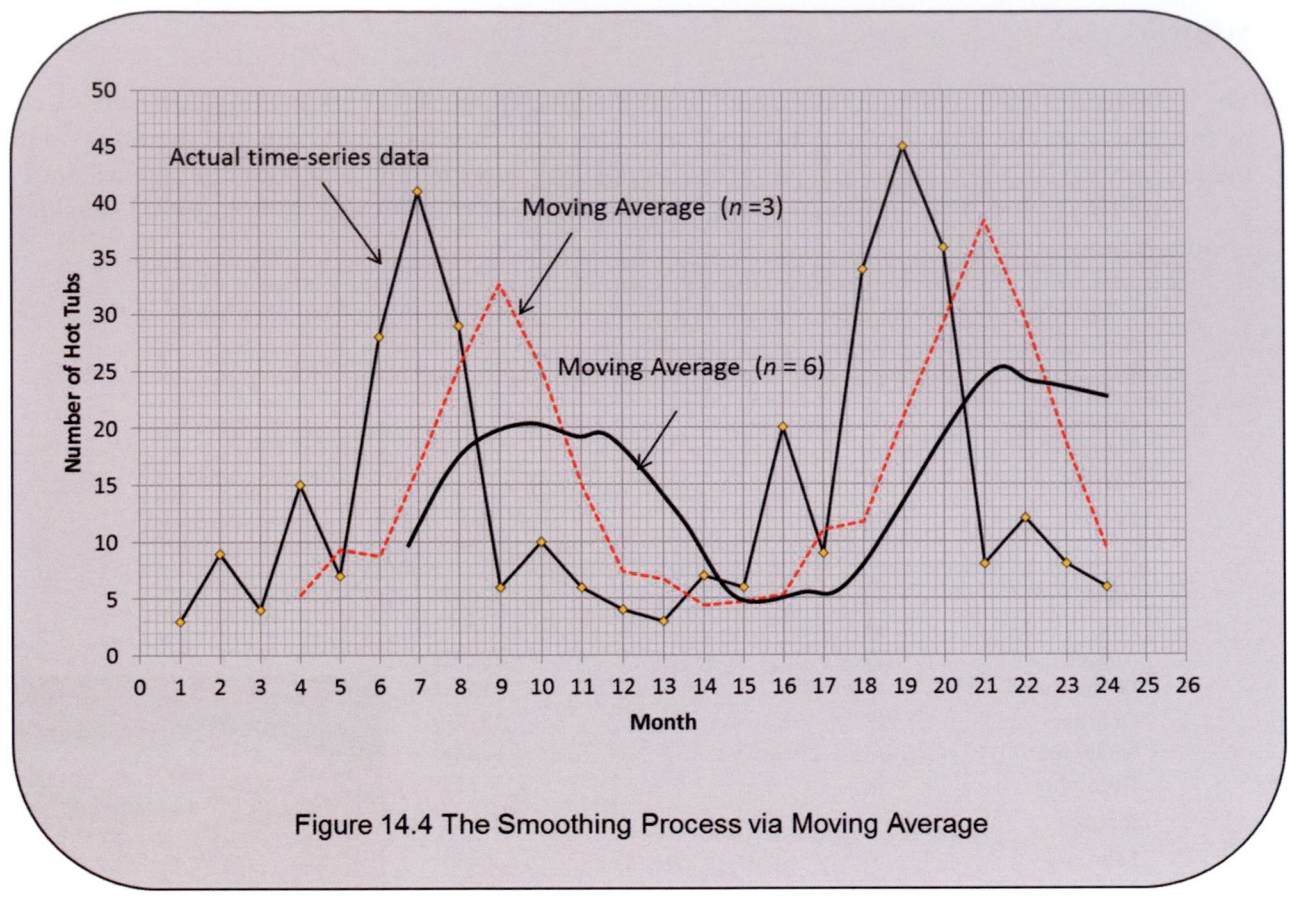

Figure 14.4 The Smoothing Process via Moving Average

Example 14.5: For the time series in Table 14.4, calculate *MAD*, *MSE*, and *MAPE* (%).

Solution:
The calculations for this problem are shown in Table 14.5.

Table 14.5 Calculations of *MAD*, *MSE*, and *MAPE* (%)

Period	Demand	Forecast-moving average (*n*=3)	Error	Absolute error	Squared error	Abs Pct error
month 1	3	......	......	......	......	......
month 2	9	......	......	......	......	......
month 3	4	......	......	......	......	......
month 4	15	5.333	9.667	9.667	93.444	64.44%
month 5	7	9.333	-2.333	2.333	5.444	33.33%
month 6	28	8.667	19.333	19.333	373.778	69.05%
month 7	41	16.667	24.333	24.333	592.111	59.35%
month 8	29	25.333	3.667	3.667	13.444	12.64%
month 9	6	32.667	-26.667	26.667	711.111	444.44%
month 10	10	25.333	-15.333	15.333	235.111	153.33%
month 11	6	15.000	-9.000	9.000	81.000	150.00%
month 12	4	7.333	-3.333	3.333	11.111	83.33%
month 13	3	6.667	-3.667	3.667	13.444	122.22%
month 14	7	4.333	2.667	2.667	7.111	38.10%
month 15	6	4.667	1.333	1.333	1.778	22.22%
month 16	20	5.333	14.667	14.667	215.111	73.33%
month 17	9	11.000	-2.000	2.000	4.000	22.22%
month 18	34	11.667	22.333	22.333	498.778	65.69%
month 19	45	21.000	24.000	24.000	576.000	53.33%
month 20	36	29.333	6.667	6.667	44.444	18.52%
month 21	8	38.333	-30.333	30.333	920.111	379.17%
month 22	12	29.667	-17.667	17.667	312.111	147.22%
month 23	8	18.667	-10.667	10.667	113.778	133.33%
month 24	6	9.333	-3.333	3.333	11.111	55.56%
		Total	4.333	253.000	4834.333	2200.84%
		Average	0.206	12.048	230.206	104.80%
		Bias	MAD	MSE	MAPE
			SE	15.951	
Next period	8.66666667					

Another type of moving averages is the so called '***Weighted Moving Averages***' in which we use weights to place more emphasis on data of previous periods based on our judgment. This is often used when a trend or other patterns is emerging.

$$F_{t+1} = \frac{\sum(Weight\ in\ period\ i)(Actual\ value\ in\ period)}{\sum(Weights)}$$

Or

$$F_{t+1} = \frac{w_1 Y_t + w_2 Y_{t-1} + Y_{t-2} + \cdots + w_n Y_{t-n-1}}{w_1 + w_2 + \cdots + w_n} \qquad (14.8)$$

Where w_i = weight for the ith observation.

Example 14.6: Waterfall Zeko Company wants to forecast demand for its hot tubs. The company collected data for the past year as was shown in Table 14.4. Calculate a three-month weighted moving average to forecast demand ($n = 3$).

Solution:

This is an open-end problem in which it will be left up to the student to decide on the weights. Suppose you selected the following weighing scheme:

Table 14.6 Moving average weighing scheme

Weights applied	Period
3	Last month
2	Two months ago
1	Three months ago
Sum of weights = $\sum w_i = 3 + 2 + 1 = 6$	

In this case, the calculations will be as demonstrated in Table 14.7. Figure 14.5 shows the weighted moving averages superimposed on the actual data.

Table 14.7 Calculation of weighted moving average

Month	Actual hot tubs	Moving average (n=3)	Moving averages (n=3) weights 1,2,3	Moving averages (n=3) weights 1,2,3
January	3			
February	9			
March	4			
April	15	5.333	$(3{\times}1 + 9{\times}2 + 4{\times}3)/6 = 33/6$	5.500
May	7	9.333	$(9{\times}1 + 4{\times}2 + 15{\times}3)/6 = 62/6$	10.333
June	28	8.667		9.167
July	41	16.667		18.833
August	29	25.333		31.000
September	6	32.667		32.833
October	10	25.333		19.500
November	6	15.000		11.833
December	4	7.333		7.333
January	3	6.667	$(10{\times}1 + 6{\times}2 + 4{\times}3)/6 = 34/6$	5.667
February	7	4.333		3.833
March	6	4.667		5.167
April	20	5.333		5.833
May	9	11.000		13.167
June	34	11.667		12.167
July	45	21.000		23.333
August	36	29.333		35.333
September	8	38.333		38.667
October	12	29.667		23.500
November	8	18.667		14.667
December	6	9.333		9.333
January		8.667		7.667

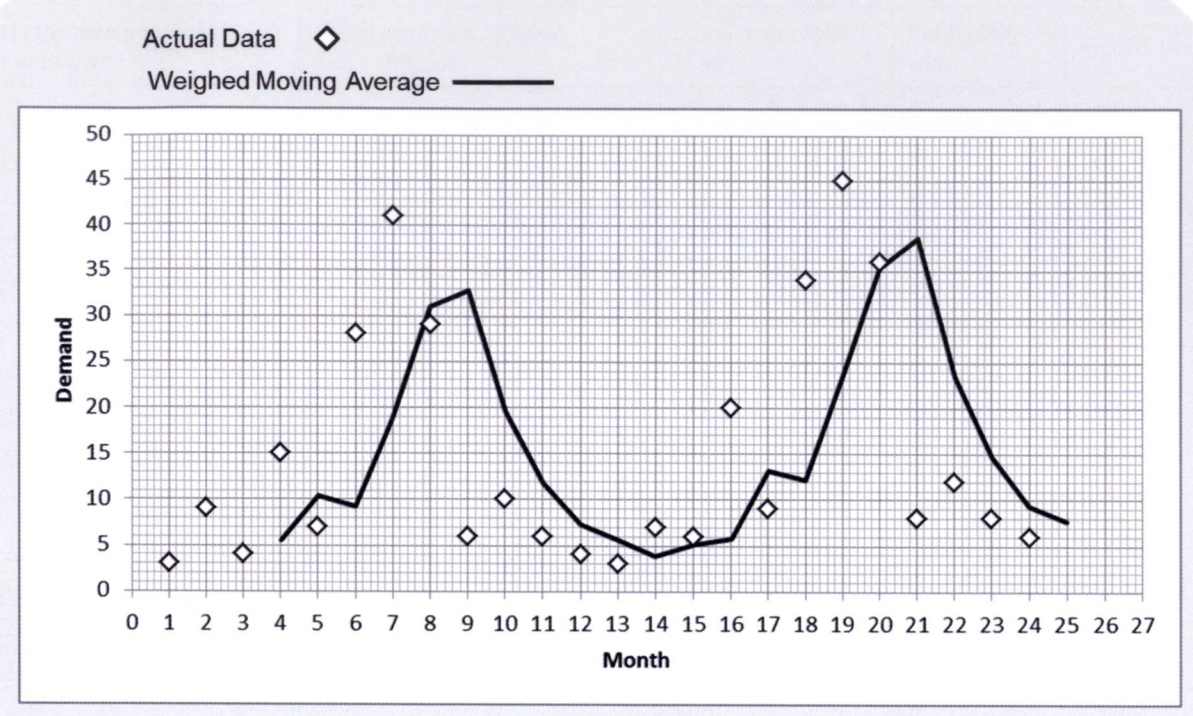

Figure 14.5 Weighed Moving Average of Hot Tubs at *n* = 3, and 1,2, and 3 Weights

Working Problem 14.3

The data in the Table represents actual monthly demand for large-screen TVs over 2 year period. Calculate moving average at n =4, and determine *MAD, MSE,* and *MAPE* (%).

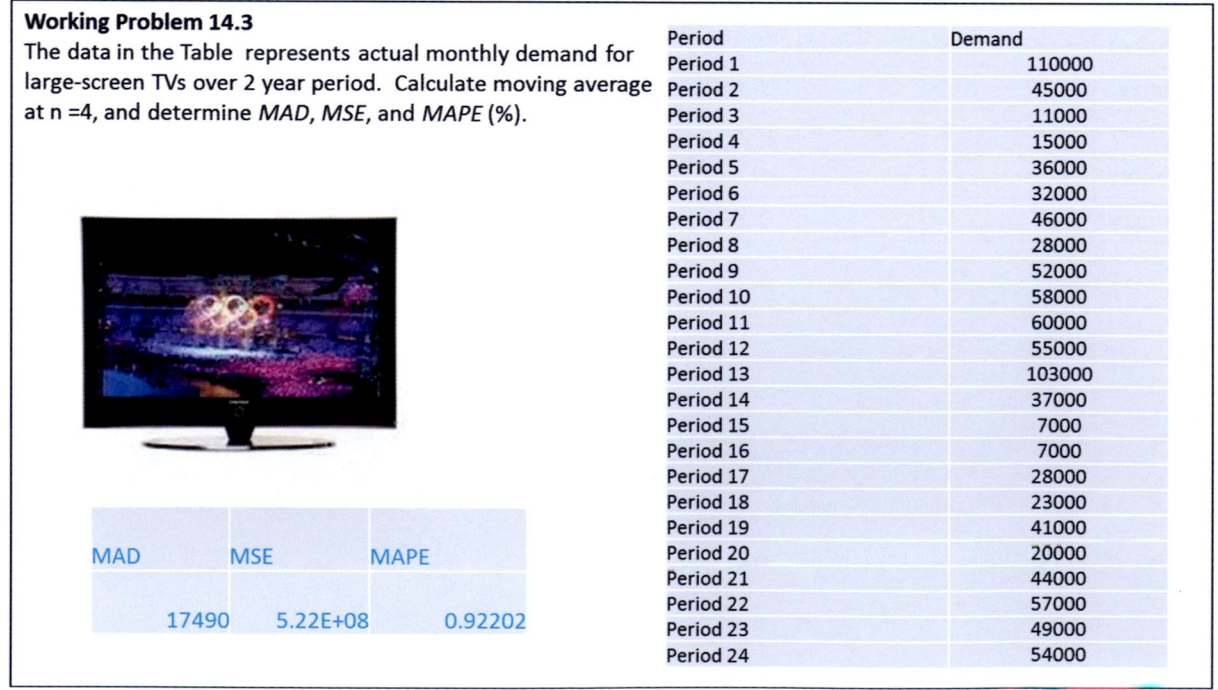

MAD	MSE	MAPE
17490	5.22E+08	0.92202

Period	Demand
Period 1	110000
Period 2	45000
Period 3	11000
Period 4	15000
Period 5	36000
Period 6	32000
Period 7	46000
Period 8	28000
Period 9	52000
Period 10	58000
Period 11	60000
Period 12	55000
Period 13	103000
Period 14	37000
Period 15	7000
Period 16	7000
Period 17	28000
Period 18	23000
Period 19	41000
Period 20	20000
Period 21	44000
Period 22	57000
Period 23	49000
Period 24	54000

Example 14.7: For the time series in Table 14.4, and using a three-month weighted moving average to forecast demand ($n = 3$), calculate *MAD*, *MSE*, and *MAPE* (%).

Calculations of *MAD*, *MSE*, and *MAPE* (%) are shown in Table 14.8.

Table 14.8 Calculations of *MAD*, *MSE*, and *MAPE* (%) for weighed moving average

Period	Demand	Weights	Forecast	Error	Absolute	Squared	Abs Pct Err
Period 1	3	1					
Period 2	9	2					
Period 3	4	3					
Period 4	15		5.500	9.500	9.500	90.250	63.33%
Period 5	7		10.333	-3.333	3.333	11.111	47.62%
Period 6	28		9.167	18.833	18.833	354.694	67.26%
Period 7	41		18.833	22.167	22.167	491.361	54.07%
Period 8	29		31.000	-2.000	2.000	4.000	06.90%
Period 9	6		32.833	-26.833	26.833	720.028	447.22%
Period 10	10		19.500	-9.500	9.500	90.250	95.00%
Period 11	6		11.833	-5.833	5.833	34.028	97.22%
Period 12	4		7.333	-3.333	3.333	11.111	83.33%
Period 13	3		5.667	-2.667	2.667	7.111	88.89%
Period 14	7		3.833	3.167	3.167	10.028	45.24%
Period 15	6		5.167	0.833	0.833	0.694	13.89%
Period 16	20		5.833	14.167	14.167	200.694	70.83%
Period 17	9		13.167	-4.167	4.167	17.361	46.30%
Period 18	34		12.167	21.833	21.833	476.694	64.22%
Period 19	45		23.333	21.667	21.667	469.444	48.15%
Period 20	36		35.333	0.667	0.667	0.444	01.85%
Period 21	8		38.667	-30.667	30.667	940.444	383.33%
Period 22	12		23.500	-11.500	11.500	132.250	95.83%
Period 23	8		14.667	-6.667	6.667	44.444	83.33%
Period 24	6		9.333	-3.333	3.333	11.111	55.56%
			Total	3.000	222.667	4117.556	1959.37%
			Average	0.143	10.603	196.074	93.30%
				Bias	MAD	MSE	MAPE
					SE	14.721	
Next period	7.667						

801

Working Problem 14.4

The data in the Table represents actual monthly demand for large-screen TVs over 2 year period.

Calculate weighed moving average at n = 4, and determine *MAD*, *MSE*, and *MAPE* (%).

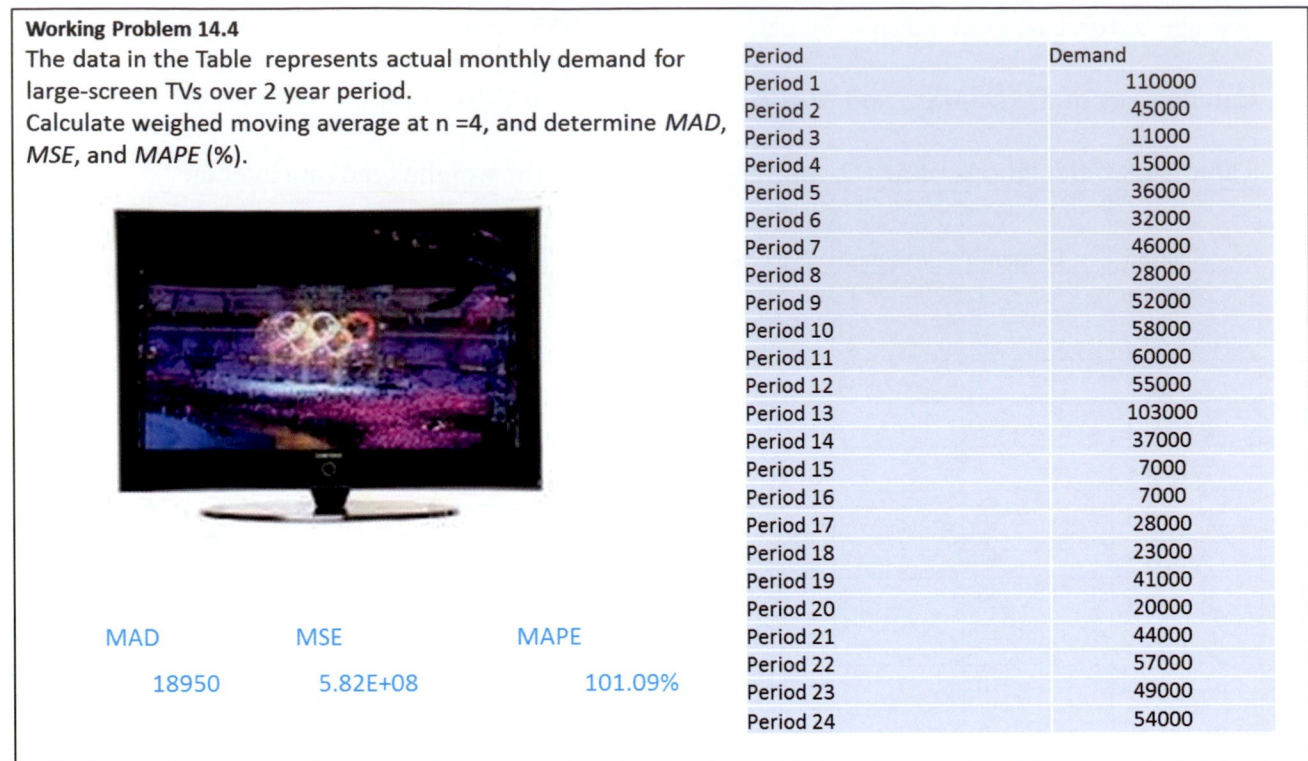

Period	Demand
Period 1	110000
Period 2	45000
Period 3	11000
Period 4	15000
Period 5	36000
Period 6	32000
Period 7	46000
Period 8	28000
Period 9	52000
Period 10	58000
Period 11	60000
Period 12	55000
Period 13	103000
Period 14	37000
Period 15	7000
Period 16	7000
Period 17	28000
Period 18	23000
Period 19	41000
Period 20	20000
Period 21	44000
Period 22	57000
Period 23	49000
Period 24	54000

MAD	MSE	MAPE
18950	5.82E+08	101.09%

14.6 Exponential Smoothing

Exponential smoothing is a very popular scheme to produce a smoothed Time Series. In essence, exponential smoothing is another type of weighted moving average that is easy to use and requires little record keeping of data. It is more like the weighed moving average in that it assigns weights or coefficients to past observations used in forecasting. These weights are decreasing as the data get older. In other words, recent observations are given relatively more weight in forecasting than the older observations.

The general formula of exponential smoothing is:

$$F_{t+1} = \alpha A_t + (1 - \alpha)F_t$$

- A_t is the actual value
- F_t is the forecasted value
- α is the weighting factor, which ranges from 0 to 1
- t is the current time period.

Typically,

New Forecast = Last period's forecast
+ α (Last period's actual demand − Last period's forecast)

Where α is a weight (or *smoothing constant*) with $0 \leq \alpha \leq 1$.

Or

$$F_{t+1} = F_t + \alpha(Y_t - F_t) \qquad (14.9)$$

where:

$\quad F_{t+1}$ = new forecast (for time period $t + 1$)
$\quad F_t$ = previous forecast (for time period t)
$\quad \alpha$ = smoothing constant $(0 \leq \alpha \leq 1)$
$\quad Y_t$ = pervious period's actual demand

Note that the smoothed value becomes the forecast for period $t + 1$. A small α provides a detectable and visible smoothing. While a large α provides a fast response to the recent changes in the time series but provides a smaller amount of smoothing. Notice that the exponential smoothing and simple moving average techniques will generate forecasts having the same average age of information if moving average of order n is the integer part of $(2-\alpha)/\alpha$ (e.g. at $\alpha = 0.5$, $n = (2-0.5)/0.5 = 3$).

Example 14.8: In June, July's demand for outdoor hot tubs was predicted to be 600. Actual July demand was 612 hot tubs. Using a smoothing constant of $\alpha = 0.20$, what is the forecast for August?

Solution:

$$F_{t+1} = F_t + \alpha(Y_t - F_t)$$

New forecast (for August demand) $= 600 + 0.2(612 - 600) = 602.4$ or about 602 hot tubs

Example 14.9: In the hot tub example discussed above, if actual demand in August was 580 hot tubs, what is the September forecast?

Solution:

New forecast (for September demand) $= 602.4 + 0.20(580 - 602.4) = 597.92$

It should be noted that the key factor of good forecast using exponential smoothing is determining the value of α, or the smoothing constant. The general approach is to develop trial forecasts with different values of α and select the value of α, which results in the lowest *MAD*. The value of α can be changed to give more weight to recent data when the value is high or more weight to past data when it is low.

Example 14.10: For the following demand data of shipments of clothing, use exponential smoothing for estimating period 9(the ninth quarter) at values of α of 0.1, 0.2, 0.3, and 0.5. Begin at forecast of 17500.

Table 14.9 Exponential smoothing of shipment data at different values of α

Quarter	Actual Number of Shipments
1	20000
2	18600
3	15000
4	17500
5	19000
6	20500
7	18000
8	18200
9	?

Solution:

Table 14.10 Exponential smoothing of shipment data at different values of α

Quarter	Actual number of shipments	Forecast (at $\alpha = 0.1$)	$\alpha = 0.1$	$\alpha = 0.2$	$\alpha = 0.3$	$\alpha = 0.5$
1	20000	17500	17500	17500	17500	17500
2	18600	17750 = 17500 + 0.10(20000 − 17500)	17750.00	18000.00	18250.00	18750.00
3	15000	17835 = 17750 + 0.10(18600 − 17750)	17835.00	18120.00	18355.00	18675.00
4	17500	173.18 = 174.75 + 0.10(159 − 174.75)	17551.50	17496.00	17348.50	16837.50
5	19000	173.36 = 173.18 + 0.10(175 − 173.18)	17546.35	17496.80	17393.95	17168.75
6	20500	175.02 = 173.36 + 0.10(190 − 173.36)	17691.72	17797.44	17875.77	18084.38
7	18000	178.02 = 175.02 + 0.10(205 − 175.02)	17972.54	18337.95	18663.04	19292.19
8	18200	178.22 = 178.02 + 0.10(180 − 178.02)	17975.29	18270.36	18464.12	18646.09
9		**178.60 = 178.22 + 0.10(182 − 178.22)**	**17997.76**	**18256.29**	**18384.89**	**18423.05**

Example 14.11: Using the demand data of shipments of clothing of the previous example, which coefficient would you use for exponential smoothing; $\alpha = 0.1, 0.2, 0.3,$ or 0.5?

Solution:

This problem requires calculations of MAD, MSE, and MAPE (%) and select α at the lowest values. Based on the calculations of table 14.11, exponential smoothing at $\alpha = 0.1$ exhibits the lowest errors. Figure 14.6 shows forecast values at different values of α.

Table 14.11 Values of MAD, MSE, and MAPE(%) at different α values

Quarter	Actual data	$\alpha = 0.1$	$\alpha = 0.2$	$\alpha = 0.3$	$\alpha = 0.5$
1	20000	17500	17500	17500	17500
2	18600	17750	18000	18250	18750
3	15000	17835	18120	18355	18675
4	17500	17551.5	17496	17348.5	16837.5
5	19000	17546.35	17496.8	17393.95	17168.75
6	20500	17691.72	17797.44	17875.77	18084.38
7	18000	17972.54	18337.95	18663.04	19292.19
8	18200	17975.29	18270.36	18464.12	18646.09
9		17997.76	18256.29	18384.89	18423.05
MAD		1343.83	1354.76	1439.24	1621.58
MSE		3132899	3253377	3453358	3909313
MAPE(%)		7.38	7.49	8.00	9.08

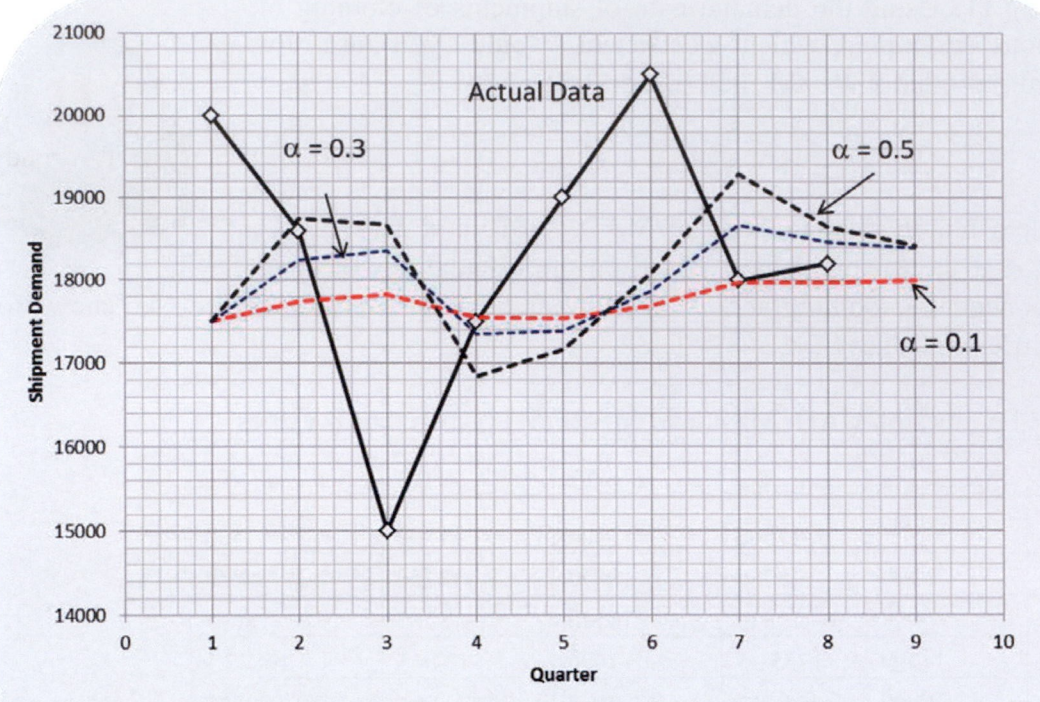

Figure 14.6 Exponential Smoothing at Different Values of α for Quarterly Shipment Demand

---

Working Problem 14.5

The data in the Table below represents actual yearly sales ($) made by a fast food corner in a large Mall. Use exponential smoothing for estimating year 11(the eleventh year) at values of *a* of 0.1, and 0.3. Calculate Bias, MAD, MSE, and MAPE (%) at each *a* value.

Year	Sales ($)
1	200000
2	218000
3	215000
4	260000
5	253000
6	305000
7	316000
8	311700
9	322700
10	304700

Alpha	Year 11	Bias	MAD	MSE	MAPE
0.1	253716.7	53716.68	53716.68	3.93E+09	18.34%
0.3	298568.3	32856.11	32856.11	1.61E+09	0.1146376

806

14.7 Exponential Smoothing with Trend Adjustment

One of the problems with classic exponential smoothing is that it does not respond to trends. In this case, a more complex model should be used to adjust for trends. One of the common approaches is to develop an exponential smoothing forecast, and then adjust it for the trend.

In this case, the forecast model will be as follow:

Forecast Including Trend = Smoothed Forecast + Smoothed Trend

Or

$$FIT_{t+1} = F_{t+1} + T_{t+1} \qquad (14.10)$$

where

$$F_{t+1} = FIT_t + \alpha(Y_t - FIT_t) \qquad (14.11)$$

and

$$T_{t+1} = T_t + \beta(F_{t+1} - FIT_t) \qquad (14.12)$$

T_t = smoothed trend for time period t (must be given or estimated)
F_t = smoothed forecast for time period t
FIT_t = forecast including trend for time period t
α = smoothing constant for forecasts
β = smoothing constant for trend

It should be noted that a high value of β makes the forecast more responsive to changes in trend. A low value of β gives less weight to the recent trend and tends to smooth out the trend. Again, values are generally selected using a trial-and-error approach based on the value of the *MAD* for different values of β.

Example 14.12: The data in Table 14.12 shows the demand for a 12x16 Oval White Vinyl Gazebo over the last 7 years from C-ZAK Gazebo store.

Use exponential smoothing with trend adjustment to forecast the demands for a 12x16 Oval White Vinyl Gazebo

Table 14.12 Demand for a 12x16 Oval White Vinyl Gazebo

Time (t)	Demand (Y_t)
1	50
2	60
3	77
4	98
5	90
6	105
7	111

Solution:

To forecast demand, we assume:
F_1 is perfect
$T_1 = 0$
$\alpha = 0.3$
$\beta = 0.4$

The key steps to perform exponential smoothing with trend adjustment are:

For time period 2:

Step 1: Compute F_{t+1} using the equation

$$F_{t+1} = FIT_t + \alpha(Y_t - FIT_t)$$

$$F_2 = FIT_1 + \alpha(Y_1 - FIT_1) = 50 + 0.3(50 - 50) = 50$$

Step 2: Update the trend T_{t+1} using the equation

$$T_{t+1} = T_t + \beta(F_{t+1} - FIT_t)$$
$$T_2 = T_1 + \beta(F_2 - FIT_1) = 0 + 0.4(50 - 50) = 0$$

Step 3: Calculate the trend adjusted exponential smoothing forecast (FIT_{t+1}) using the equation

$$FIT_{t+1} = F_{t+1} + T_{t+1}$$
$$FIT_2 = F_2 + T_2 = 50 + 0 = 50$$

For time period 3:

Step 1: Compute F_{t+1} using the equation

$$F_{t+1} = FIT_t + \alpha(Y_t - FIT_t)$$

$$F_3 = FIT_2 + \alpha(Y_2 - FIT_2) = 50 + 0.3(60 - 50) = 53$$

Step 2: Update the trend T_{t+1} using the equation

$$T_{t+1} = T_t + \beta(F_{t+1} - FIT_t)$$
$$T_3 = T_2 + \beta(F_3 - FIT_2) = 0 + 0.4(53 - 50) = 1.2$$

Step 3: Calculate the trend adjusted exponential smoothing forecast (FIT_{t+1}) using the equation

$$FIT_{t+1} = F_{t+1} + T_{t+1}$$
$$FIT_3 = F_3 + T_3 = 53 + 1.2 = 54.2$$

You then continue the calculations as shown in Table 14.13.

Table 14.13 calculations of Exponential Smoothing with Trend Adjustment

Time (t)	Demand (Y_t)	F_{t+1} $= FIT_t + \alpha(Y_t - FIT_t)$	T_{t+1} $= T_t + \beta(F_{t+1} - FIT_t)$	FIT_{t+1} $= F_{t+1} + T_{t+1}$
1	50	50	0	50
2	60	50 =50+0.3(50-50)	0 = 0+0.4(50-50)	50 = 50+0
3	77	53=50+0.3(60-50)	1.2 = 0+0.4(53-50)	54.2 =53+1.2
4	98	61.04 =54.2 +0.3(77-54.2)	3.936 = 1.2+0.4(61.04-54.2)	64.976 = 61.04 +3.936
5	90	74.8832=64.976+0.3(98-64.976)	7.8988 = 3.936+0.4(74.88-64.976)	82.782 = 74.883 + 7.8988
6	105	84.947=82.78+0.3(90-82.78)	8.765 = 7.8988+0.4(84.947-82.782)	93.712 = 84.947 + 8.765
7	111	97.0987=93.712+ 0.3(105-93.712)	10.1195 = 8.765+0.4(97.0987-93.712)	107.218 = 97.098 + 10.119
8		108.35=107.218+0.3(111-107.218)	10.573 = 10.1195+0.4(108.3527 - 107.218)	118.926 = 108.3527 + 10.5733

Figure 14.7 shows the actual demand data and the corresponding exponential smoothing forecast with trend adjustment. Also included in the Figure is the exponential smoothing forecast without trend adjustment. Comparing these two forecasts reveals how the adjustment made resulted in a forecast that is highly sensitive to the data trend.

It is also important to see the differences between the forecast accuracy measures *MAD*, *MSE*, *MAPE*, and *Bias* for exponential smoothing forecast without trend adjustment and that with trend adjustment. Tables 14.14 and 14.15 show the calculations of these measures. The results of these calculations indicate that all error measures of exponential smoothing forecast with trend adjustment are lower than those of exponential smoothing forecast without trend adjustment.

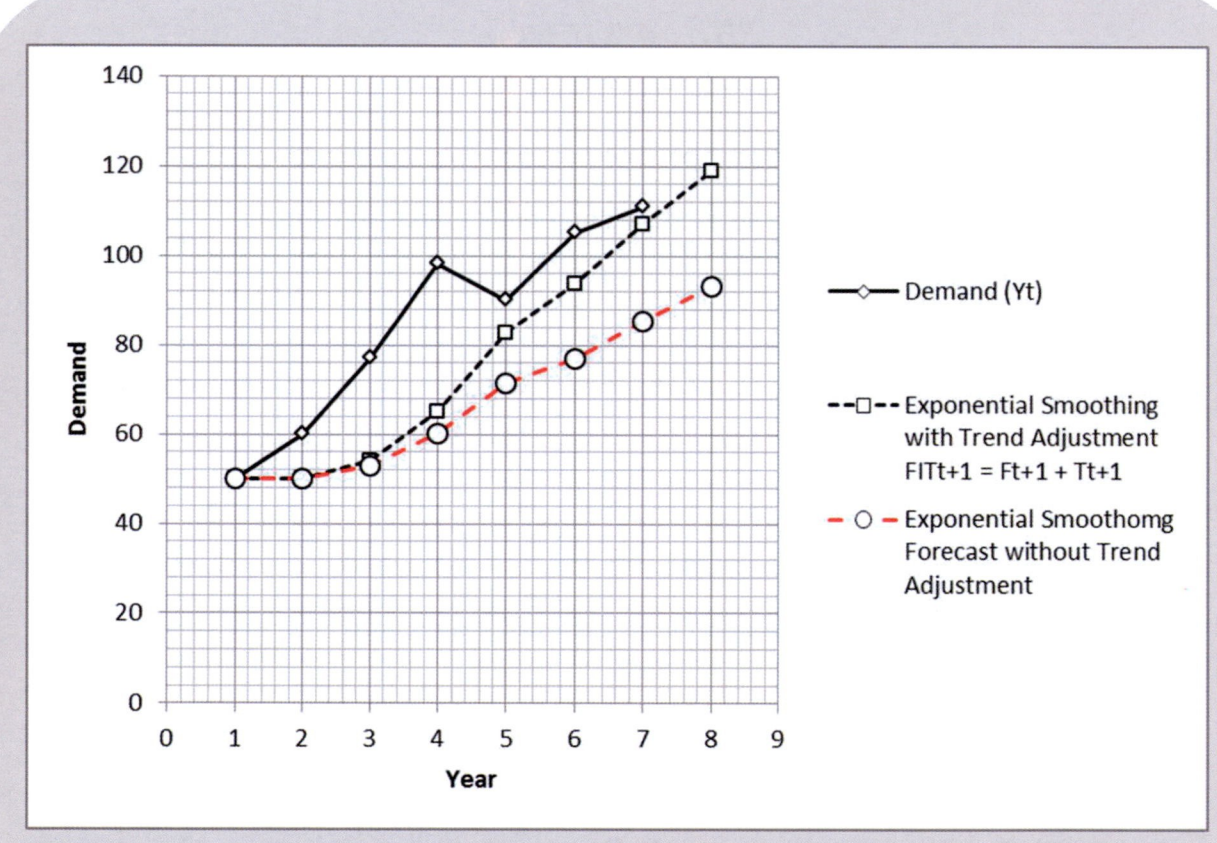

Figure 14.7 Exponential Smoothing with Trend Adjustment for Demand for Oval White Vinyl Gazebo

Table 14.14 Forecast accuracy measures for exponential smoothing without trend adjustment

Alpha	0.3					
Data		Forecasts and rrror analysis				
Period	Demand	Forecast	Error	Absolute	Squared	Abs % error
1	50	50	0	0	0	0
2	60	50	10	10	100	0.167
3	77	53	24	24	576	0.312
4	98	60.2	37.8	37.800	1428.840	0.386
5	90	71.54	18.46	18.460	340.772	0.205
6	105	77.078	27.922	27.922	779.638	0.266
7	111	85.455	25.545	25.545	652.567	0.230
		Total	143.727	143.727	3877.817	1.565
		Average	20.532	20.532	553.974	22.4%
			Bias	MAD	MSE	MAPE

Table 14.15 Forecast accuracy measures for exponential smoothing with trend adjustment

Alpha	0.3							
Beta	0.4							
Data		Forecasts and Error Analysis						
Period	Demand	Smoothed Forecast, Ft	Smoothed Trend, Tt	Forecast Including Trend, FITt	Error	Absolute	Squared	Abs % error
1	50	50	0	50	0	0	0	0
2	60	50	0	50	10	10	100	0.167
3	77	53	1.2	54.2	22.8	22.8	519.840	0.296
4	98	61.04	3.936	64.976	33.024	33.024	1090.585	0.337
5	90	74.883	7.899	82.782	7.218	7.218	52.098	0.080
6	105	84.947	8.765	93.712	11.288	11.288	127.408	0.108
7	111	97.099	10.120	107.218	3.782	3.782	14.301	0.034
	Next period	108.353	10.573	118.926				
		Total			88.111	88.111	1904.232	1.022
		Average			12.587	12.587	272.033	14.6%
					Bias	MAD	MSE	MAPE

Working Problem 14.6

The data in the Table below represents actual yearly sales ($) made by a fast food corner in a large Mall. Use exponential smoothing with trend adjustment for estimating year 11(the eleventh year) at values of α of 0.1, and $\beta = 0.4$. Calculate Bias, MAD, MSE, and MAPE (%).

Year	Sales ($)
1	200000
2	218000
3	215000
4	260000
5	253000
6	305000
7	316000
8	311700
9	322700
10	304700

Alpha	Beta	Year 11	Bias	MAD	MSE	MAPE
0.1	0.4	313355.3	39019.66	39019.66	2.27E+09	13.57%

14.8 Trend Projection

In Chapter 12, we discussed regression analysis as an appropriate technique to develop relationships between variables. We can also use this technique to fit a trend line to a series of historical data points. This line can be projected into the future for medium to long-term forecasts.

Recall that an *x-y* relationship can be represented by the following simple linear model:

$$y = \beta_o + \beta_1 x + \varepsilon$$

where β_o and β_1 are called parameter estimates, and ε is an error term stemming from the fact that x may not fully explain the change in y.

The equation derived from the above model through estimating the parameters β_o and β_1 and minimizing the error effect is called the simple regression equation:

$$y = b_o + b_1 x$$

where b_o and b_1 are the estimates of β_o and β_1.

In case of time-series data, the above equation can be rewritten in the following form:

$$y = b_o + b_1 t \qquad (14.13)$$

Example 14.13: Use simple regression analysis to develop a forecast equation of demand for the 12x16 Oval White Vinyl Gazebo in Example 14.12. The data of the demand is shown in Table 14.12.

Solution:

The regression line of the demand data for the 12x16 Oval White Vinyl Gazebo is shown in Figure 14.8. Forecast accuracy measures are calculated in Table 14.16.

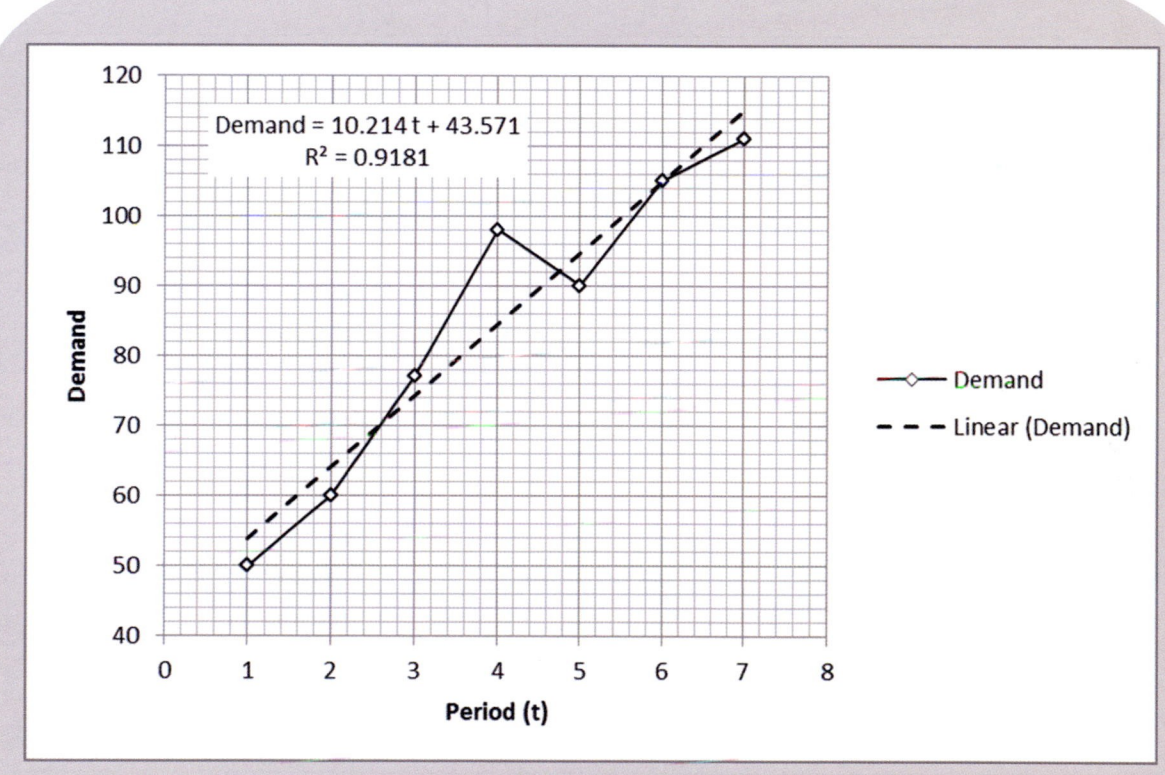

Figure 14.8 Line Trend Projection of Demand for 12x16 Oval White Vinyl Gazebo

Table 14.16 Values of MAD, MSE, Bias and MAPE for the linear forecast of demand for the 12x16 Oval White Vinyl Gazebo

Period(x)	Demand (y)	Forecast	Error	Absolute	Squared	Abs % error
1	50	53.786	-3.786	3.786	14.332	0.076
2	60	64	-4	4	16	0.067
3	77	74.214	2.786	2.786	7.760	0.036
4	98	84.429	13.571	13.571	184.184	0.138
5	90	94.643	-4.643	4.643	21.556	0.052
6	105	104.857	0.143	0.143	0.020	0.001
7	111	115.071	-4.071	4.071	16.577	0.037
		Total	0.000	33.000	260.429	0.407
		Average	0.000	4.714	37.204	5.800%
			Bias	MAD	MSE	MAPE

Working Problem 14.7

The data in the Table below represents actual monthly demand for car batteries sold by an Auto part chain. Use trend projections to forecast the following three months. Calculate Bias, MAD, MSE, and MAPE (%)

Forecast	15722.7273	13
	16710.8392	14
	17698.951	15
Bias	MAD	MSE	MAPE
3.0316E-13	1027.38928	1466649	0.158396

Month	Demand
January	4800
February	3000
March	6000
April	8000
May	5500
June	10000
July	9800
August	12000
September	13000
October	11600
Novemeber	14000
December	13900

14.9 Seasonal Data

When a time-series pattern shows periodic changes, this indicates the existence of seasonal data. In this regard, a seasonal index is used to determine the extent of seasonality. This index indicates how a particular season (e.g. month or quarter) compares with an average season. In the absence of trend in the data, the seasonal index is calculated by dividing the average value for a particular season by the average of all the data. An index of one means the particular season is an average season. For example, if the average demand for July was 600 and the average demand of all months was 300, the seasonal index for July would be 600/300 = 2.0. This means that July is above average. If seasonal data is superimposed with a trend line, seasonal adjustment in the trend line will be required. The examples below will explain these points.

Example 14.14: The data in Table 14.17 represents actual monthly sales ($) made by a famous Ice Cream Place over a 12 month period and for two years.
   (a) Calculate the average sales per month
   (b) Calculate the overall monthly sales
   (c) Calculate the average seasonal index
   (d) If total sales in the third year are expected to be 279633, forecast every month in the third year using the average seasonal index.

Table 14.17 Sales of ice cream in two years

Month	Sales ($) Year 1 (Y1)	Year 2 (Y2)
January	4800	4889
February	6000	7399
March	9000	9290
April	15000	17000
May	19000	21000
June	23000	24300
July	21600	24230
August	26000	26890
September	12000	14300
October	8000	10200
November	9000	98900
December	3890	43578

Solution:

Different calculations required to solve this problem are shown in Table 14.18. The calculations are straightforward and can be easily followed as shown in the different columns of the table. Figure 14.9 shows actual sales data and forecast for the third year using seasonally index adjustment.

Table 14.18 Calculations of Seasonal Indexes

Month	Sales ($) Year 1 (Y1)	Year 2 (Y2)	Average-two-year [AVG 1 = (Y1 + Y2)/2]	Average monthly (AVG2)	Average seasonal index (AVG1/AVG2)	Adjustment of third year avg. (ASI*EAVG)
January	4800	4889	4844.5	13793.125	0.351	6307.94
February	6000	7399	6699.5	13793.125	0.486	8723.3
March	9000	9290	9145	13793.125	0.663	11907.5
April	15000	17000	16000	13793.125	1.160	20833.3
May	19000	21000	20000	13793.125	1.450	26041.7
June	23000	24300	23650	13793.125	1.715	30794.3
July	21600	24230	22915	13793.125	1.661	29837.2
August	26000	26890	26445	13793.125	1.917	34433.6
September	12000	14300	13150	13793.125	0.953	17122.4
October	8000	10200	9100	13793.125	0.660	11849
November	9000	9890	9445	13793.125	0.685	12298.2
December	3890	4357	4123.5	13793.125	0.299	5369.14
			Total = 165517.5			Expected third year Sales (ETD) = 215517.5
			Average = AVG1= 13793.125			Expected third year monthly average Sales (EAVG) = 17959.79

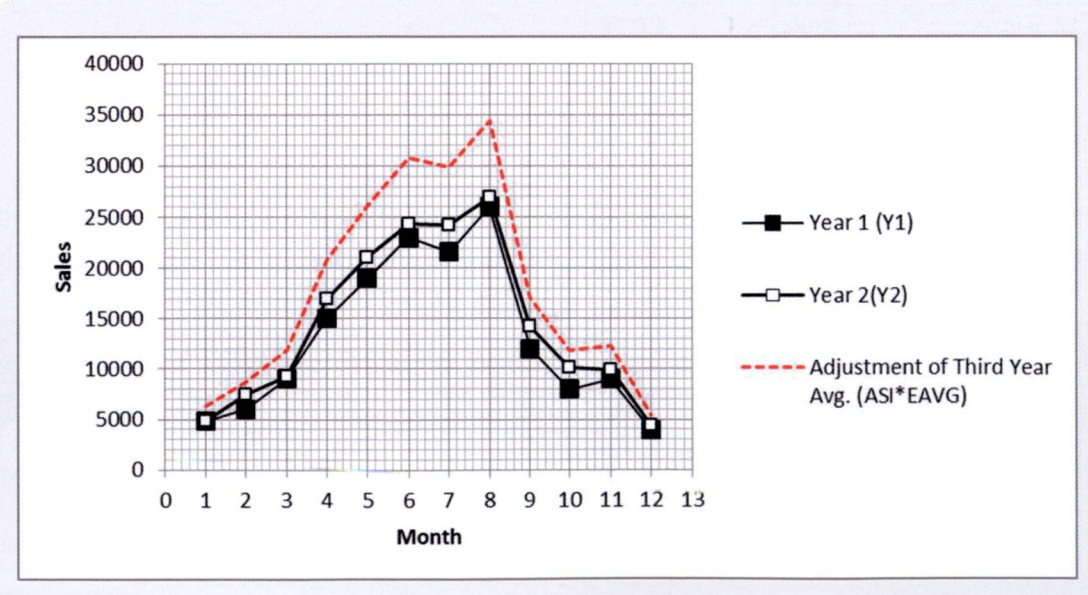

Figure 14.9 Forecast of Ice Cream Sales Using Seasonality Indexes

Working Problem 14.8

The data in the Table below represents actual monthly sales ($) made by an auto parts chain of windshield wiper blades over a 12 month period and for two years.

(a) Calculate the average sales per month
(b) Calculate the overall monthly sales
(c) Calculate the average seasonal index
(d) If total sales in the third year are expected to be 16759, forecast every month in the third year using the average seasonal index.

Month	Sales ($) Year 1 (Y1)	Sales ($) Year 2(Y2)
January	480	499
February	600	740
March	900	929
April	1500	1700
May	1900	2100
June	2300	2430
July	2160	2423
August	2600	2689
September	1200	1430
October	800	1020
November	900	989
December	389	440

Seasonal Adjustment of Third Year Avg.												
$495.4	$678.1	$925.5	$1,619.3	$2,024.2	$2,393.6	$2,319.2	$2,676.4	$1,330.9	$921.0	$955.9	$419.5

14.10 Seasonal Data with Trend

When both trend and seasonal components coexist, the forecasting task becomes more complex. In this case, seasonal indices should be computed using a *centered moving average* (*CMA*) approach.

There are four steps in computing CMAs:

    a. *Compute the CMA for each observation (where possible)*
    b. *Compute the seasonal ratio = Observation/CMA for that observation.*
    c. *Average seasonal ratios to get seasonal indices.*
    d. *If seasonal indices do not add to the number of seasons, multiply each index by (Number of seasons)/(Sum of indices).*

Example 14.15: The data in Table 14.19 represents actual quarterly demands for water dispensers sold by a hardware store.

    (a) Calculate CMAs
    (b) Calculate seasonal ratios
    (c) Calculate quarterly seasonal indices
    (d) Construct a scatterplot and CMA values and interpret the results

Table 14.19 Quarterly demands for water dispensers sold by a hardware store

Quarter	Year 1	Year 2	Year 3
1	300	317	420
2	350	390	520
3	600	730	890
4	310	480	520

Solution:

Close examination of the data in Table 14.19 reveals that there are two key features of this set of data:

- Seasonal within a year
- Trend from one year to the next

These features can easily be revealed by calculating the averages of the quarters in each year (column 5, Table 14.20) and also the average of each year (row 6, Table 14.20). They can also be revealed by sketching a scatter diagram of the data as shown in Figure 14.10. Note how the first quarter is always associated with the lowest demand and the third quarter is always associated with the highest demand from year to year. Also note how the demand increases from one year to the next.

Table 14.20 Average values of quarterly and yearly demands

Quarter	Year 1	Year 2	Year 3	Average
1	300	317	420	345.667
2	350	390	520	420.000
3	600	730	890	740.000
4	310	480	520	436.667
Average	390.00	479.25	587.50	485.58

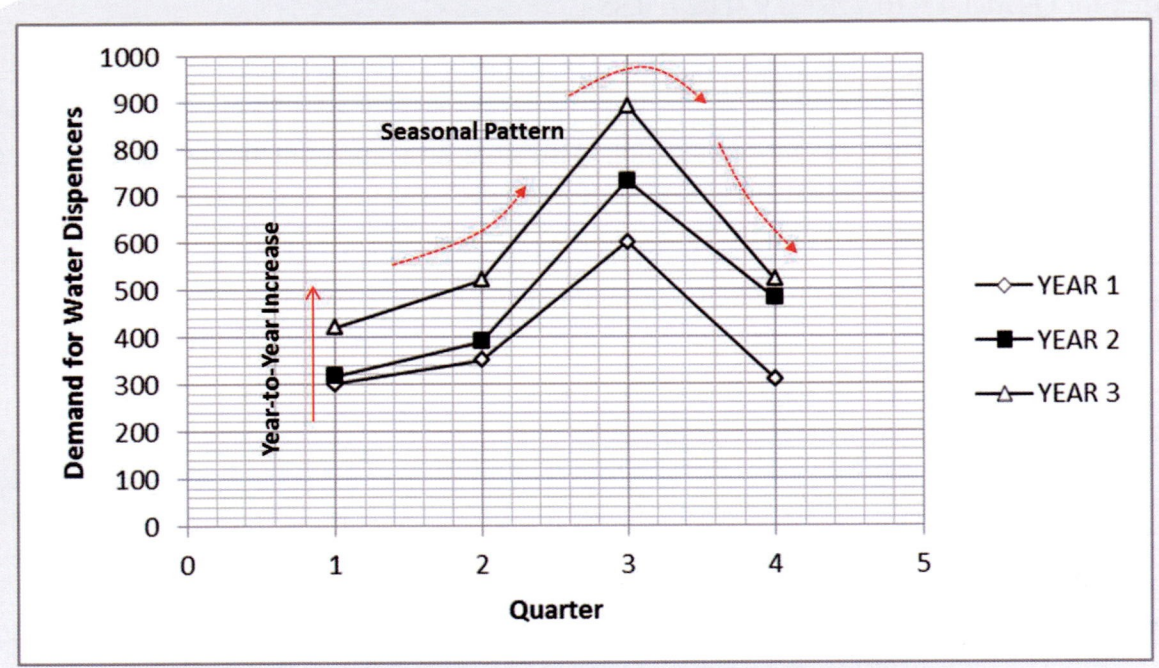

Figure 14.10 Quarterly and Yearly Demand for Water Dispensers

In order to calculate the seasonal indices for this series, we may consider say quarter 3 of year 1. The actual demands in that quarter were 600. To determine the magnitude of the seasonal variations, we should compare this with an average quarter centered at that time period (*centered moving average, CMA*). Thus, we should have a total of four quarters (one year of data) with an equal number of quarters before and after quarter 3 so the trend is averaged out. Thus, we need 1.5 quarters before quarter 3 and 1.5 quarters after it.

To calculate the *CMA*, we take quarters 2, 3, and 4 of year 1, plus one-half of quarter 1 for year 1 and one-half of quarter 1 for year 2. The average will be:

$$CMA \ (quarter \ 3 \ of \ year \ 1) = \frac{0.5(300) + 350 + 600 + 310 + 0.5(317)}{4} = 392.125$$

We then calculate the *seasonal ratio* in this quarter by comparing actual demand to the *CMA*:

$$Seasonal \ Ratio = \frac{Demand \ in \ Quarter \ 3}{CMA} = \frac{600}{392.125} = 1.53$$

Since there are two seasonal ratios for each quarter, we average these to obtain the seasonal index for the quarter:

Index for Quarter 1 = (0.754+ 0.753)/2 = 0.75
Index for Quarter 2 = (0.852+ 0.893)/2 = 0.87
Index for Quarter 3 = (1.53+ 1.483)/2 = 1.51

Index for Quarter 4 = (0.776+ 0.921)/2 = 0.85

Table 14.21 shows the above calculations. Note that some numbers were rounded off. Figure 14.11 shows a scatterplot of the quarterly data and the values of the *CMA*. Note how smooth the *CMA* curve is compared to the scatter plot. Also note how apparent the trend is in the *CMA* curve.

Table 14.21 Calculations of *CMA* and seasonal indices

Year	Quarter	Demand (number of units)	CMA	Seasonal Ratio	Seasonal Index
1	1	300			(0.754+ 0.753)/2 = 0.7535
	2	350			(0.852+ 0.893)/2 = 0.8725
	3	600	$MA\ (q3\ of\ Y1)$ $= \dfrac{0.5(300) + 350 + 600 + 310 + 0.5(317)}{4}$ $= 392.125$	600/392.125 = \$1.530	(1.53+ 1.483)/2 = 1.51
	4	310	$MA\ (q4\ of\ Y1)$ $= \dfrac{0.5(350) + 600 + 310 + 317 + 0.5(390)}{4}$ $= 399.25$	310/399.25 = \$0.776	(0.776+ 0.921)/2 = 0.85
2	1	317	$MA\ (q1\ of\ Y2)$ $= \dfrac{0.5(600) + 310 + 317 + 390 + 0.5(730)}{4}$ $= 420.5$	\$0.754	0.75
	2	390	$MA\ (q2\ of\ Y2)$ $= \dfrac{0.5(310) + 317 + 390 + 730 + 0.5(480)}{4}$ $= 458$	\$0.852	0.87
	3	730	$MA\ (q3\ of\ Y3)$ $= \dfrac{0.5(317) + 390 + 730 + 480 + 0.5(420)}{4}$ $= 492.125$	\$1.483	1.51
	4	480	$MA\ (q4\ of\ Y2)$ $= \dfrac{0.5(390) + 730 + 480 + 420 + 0.5(520)}{4}$ $= 521.250$	\$0.921	0.85
3	1	420	$MA\ (q1\ of\ Y3)$ $= \dfrac{0.5(730) + 480 + 420 + 520 + 0.5(890)}{4}$ $= 557.50$	\$0.753	0.75
	2	520	$MA\ (q2\ of\ Y3)$ $= \dfrac{0.5(480) + 420 + 520 + 890 + 0.5(520)}{4}$ $= 582.50$	\$0.893	0.87
	3	890			1.51
	4	520			0.85

820

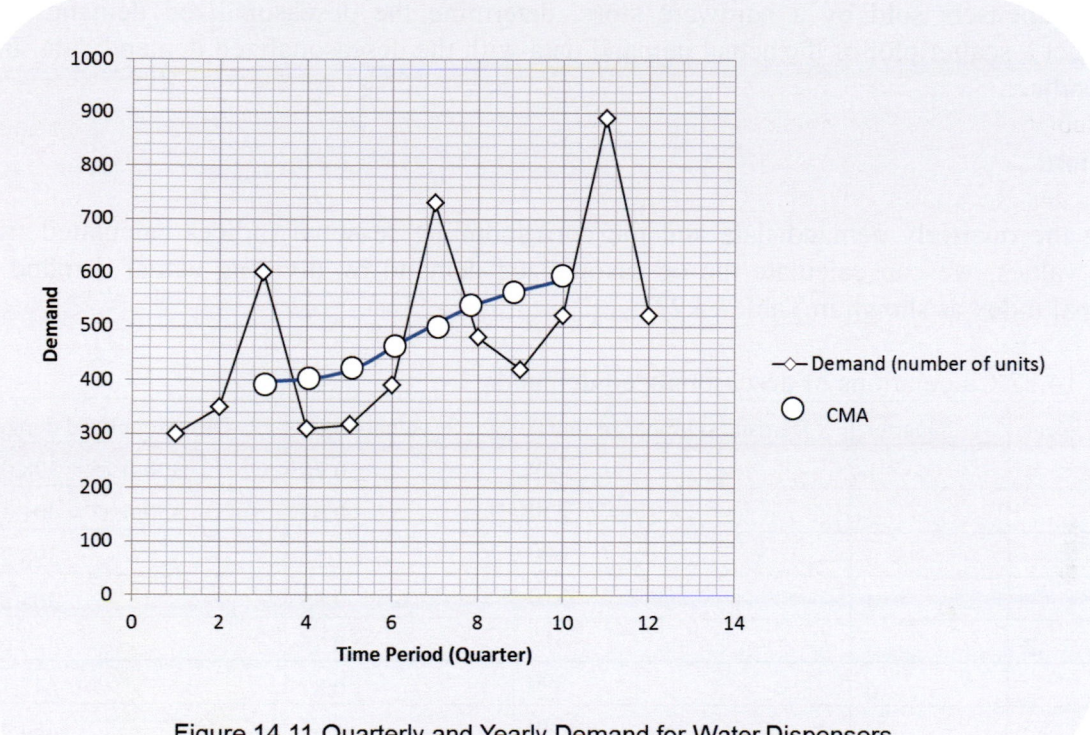

Figure 14.11 Quarterly and Yearly Demand for Water Dispensers

14.11 The Decomposition Method of Forecasting with Trend and Seasonal Components

When we have both seasonal and trend data combined in a time series, it will be important to isolate linear trend and seasonal factors so that a more accurate forecast can be made. This procedure is called '*decomposition of time series.*' We first compute seasonal indices for each season as we did earlier. We then deseasonalize the data by dividing each number by its seasonal index. Finally, a trend line is developed using the deseasonalized data.

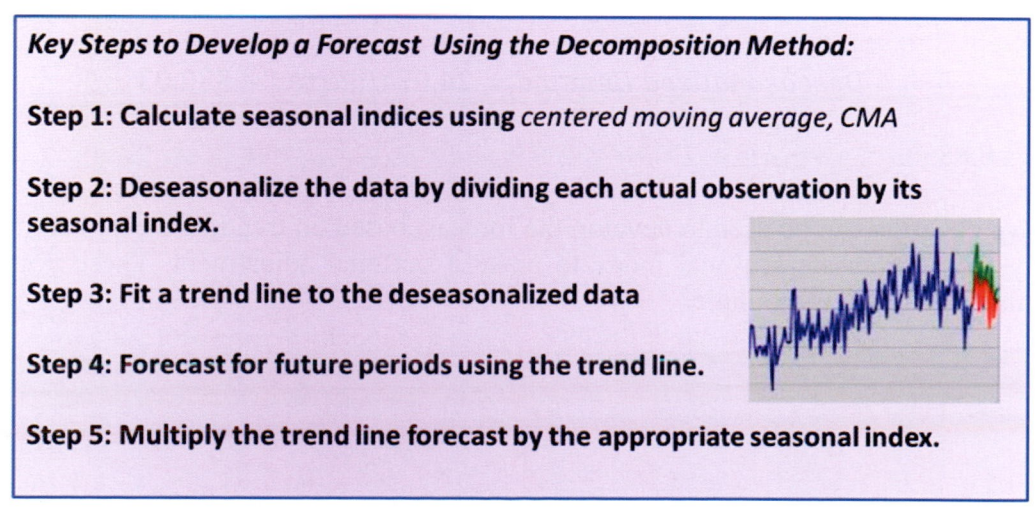

Key Steps to Develop a Forecast Using the Decomposition Method:

Step 1: Calculate seasonal indices using *centered moving average, CMA*

Step 2: Deseasonalize the data by dividing each actual observation by its seasonal index.

Step 3: Fit a trend line to the deseasonalized data

Step 4: Forecast for future periods using the trend line.

Step 5: Multiply the trend line forecast by the appropriate seasonal index.

Example 14.16: Using the data in Table 14.22, which represent actual quarterly demands for water dispensers sold by a hardware store, determine the deseasonalized demand data and construct a scatter plot of the actual demand data with the deseasonalized demand data. Interpret the results.

Solution:

Using the quarterly demand data and the corresponding seasonal indices calculated from the *CMA* values, we can calculate the deseasonalized demand by dividing actual demand by the seasonal index as shown in Table 14.22.

Table 14.22 Calculations of deseasonalized demands

Year	Quarter	Demand (number of units)	Seasonal index	Deseasonalized demand
1	1	300	0.75	300/0.75 = 398.082
	2	350	0.87	350/0.87 = 401.323
	3	600	1.51	398.210
	4	310	0.85	365.282
2	5	317	0.75	420.640
	6	390	0.87	447.188
	7	730	1.51	484.489
	8	480	0.85	565.598
3	9	420	0.75	557.315
	10	520	0.87	596.251
	11	890	1.51	590.678
	12	520	0.85	612.731

Figure 14.12 shows both actual demand data and the deseasonalized demand. Note how deseasonalization resulted in removal of seasonal data and highlighted the trend data.

We can also fit a line to the deseasonalized data. This will result in the following equation:

$$Deseasonalized\ Demand = 24.07\ Quarter + 330.03$$

with $R^2 = 0.8856$.

The above equation can be used to develop the forecast based on trend. We can then multiply the result by the appropriate seasonal index to make a seasonal adjustment. These points will be demonstrated in the next example.

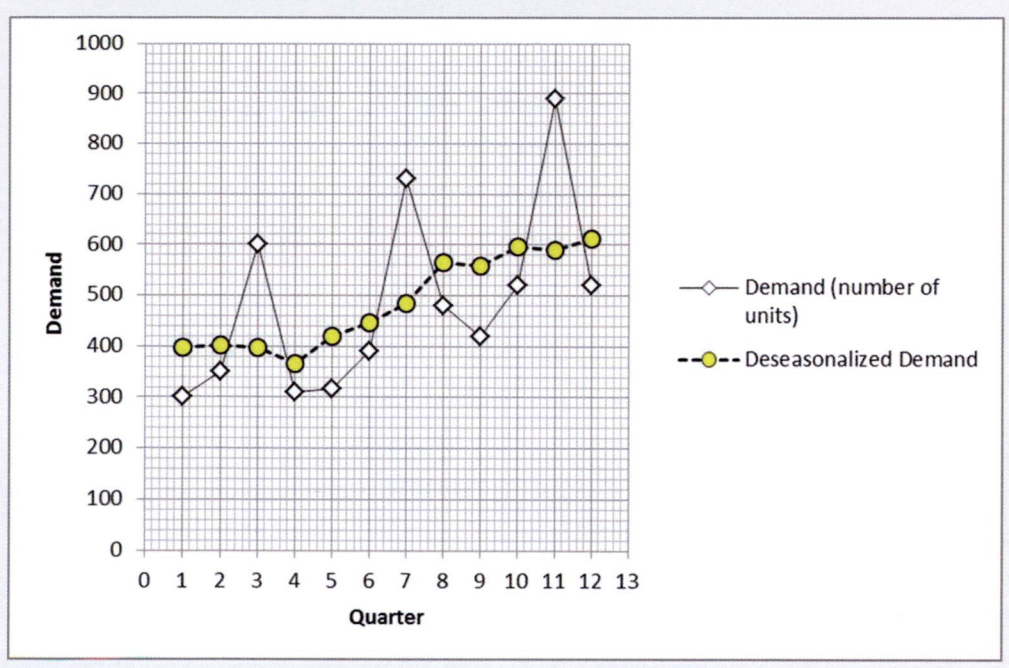

Figure 14.12 Quarterly Demand for Water Dispensers and Corresponding Deseasonalized Demands

Example 14.17: Using the data in Table 14.22, forecast the deseasonalized demands in the four quarters of year 4.

Solution:

$$Deseasonalized\ Demand = 24.07\ Quarter + 330.03$$

For the four quarters of year 4, estimated demand values are as shown in Table 14.23. Figure 14.13 shows the forecasts for quarters 13, 14, 15, and 16 of year 4. If we multiply a forecast deseasonalized demand by the seasonal index, this will yield a seasonalized forecast as shown in Table 14.23 and Figure 14.14.

Table 14.23 Calculations of deseasonalized and sesaonalized demand forecasts for year 4

Quarter	Deseasonalized Demand (Unadjusted)	Seasonal Index	Seasonalized Forecast (Adjusted)
13	*Deseasonalized Demand =* 24.07 (13) + 330.03 = 642.94	0.75	0.75× 642.94= 482.205
14	*Deseasonalized Demand =* 24.07 (14) + 330.03 =667.01	0.87	0.87× 667.01= 580.299
15	*Deseasonalized Demand =* 24.07 (15) + 330.03 =691.08	1.51	1.51× 691.08= 1043.53
16	*Deseasonalized Demand =* 24.07 (16) + 330.03 =715.15	0.85	0.85× 715.15= 607.88

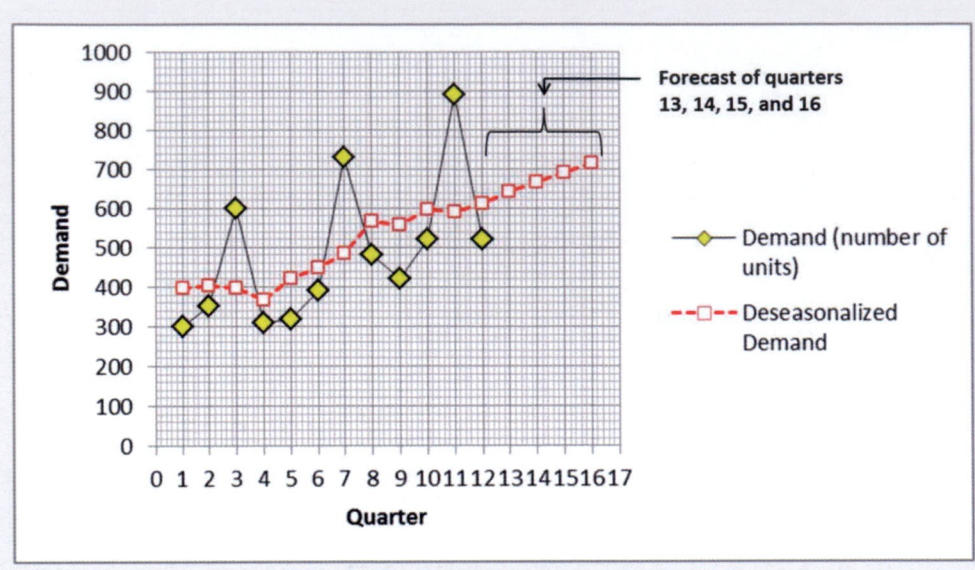

Figure 14.13 Forecast for Quarterly Demands of Quarters 13,14,15, and 16

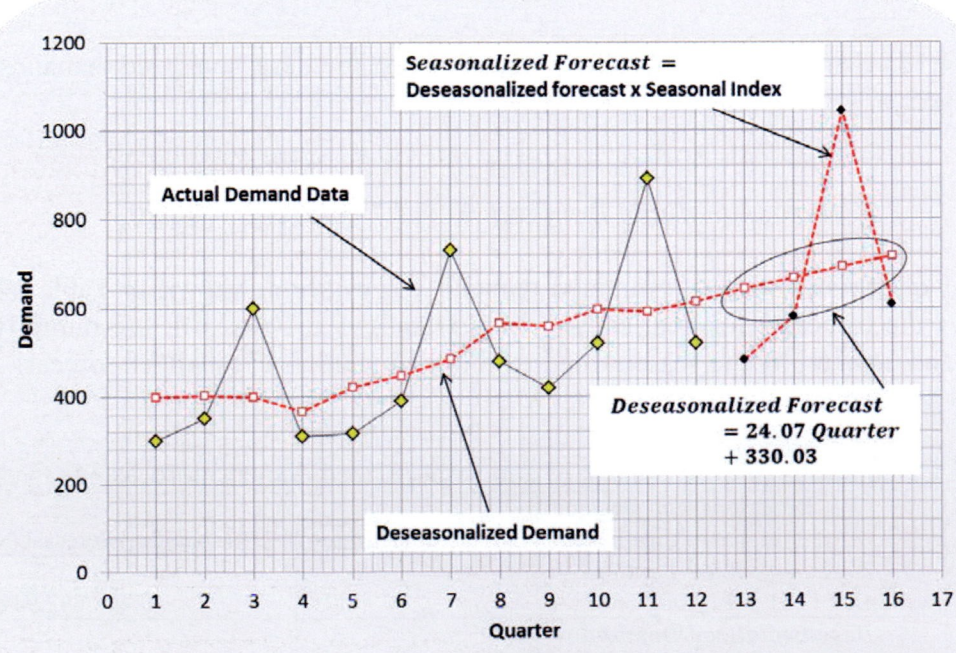

Figure 14.14 Seasonalized Forecast for Quarterly Demands of Quarters 13,14,15, and 16

Working Problem 14.9 : The data in the Table below represents actual quarterly sales ($) of washer/dryer sets made by a large appliance store. Using Decomposition method

(a) Calculate Seasonal Ratios
(b) Calculate Seasonal Indices
(c) Calculate Smoothed Forecast
(d) Calculate Unadjusted Forecast
(e) Calculate Adjusted Forecast
(f) Calculate Bias, MAD, MSE, and MAPE (%)

Quarter	Sales ($)	Quarter	Sales ($)
1	300000	9	420000
2	350000	10	520000
3	600000	11	890000
4	310000	12	520000
5	317000		
6	390000		
7	730000		
8	480000		

Data Period	Demand (y)	Time (x)		Average	Ratio	Seasonal	Smoothed	Unadjusted	Adjusted	Error	[Error]	Error^2	Abs Pct Err
Period 1	300000	1				0.754	398081.9	354098.2	266853.3	33146.7	33146.7	1.1E+09	11.05%
Period 2	350000	2				0.872	401322.7	378168	329806.4	20193.6	20193.6	4.08E+08	05.77%
Period 3	600000	3	390000	392125	1.530	1.507	398209.7	402237.8	606069.2	-6069.22	6069.22	36835428	01.01%
Period 4	310000	4	394250	399250	0.776	0.849	365281.9	426307.6	361790	-51790	51790.01	2.68E+09	16.71%
Period 5	317000	5	404250	420500	0.754	0.754	420639.8	450377.4	339410.6	-22410.6	22410.62	5.02E+08	07.07%
Period 6	390000	6	436750	458000	0.852	0.872	447188.2	474447.2	413773	-23773	23773.02	5.65E+08	06.10%
Period 7	730000	7	479250	492125	1.483	1.507	484488.5	498517	751137.3	-21137.3	21137.26	4.47E+08	02.90%
Period 8	480000	8	505000	521250	0.921	0.849	565597.8	522586.8	443498.3	36501.74	36501.74	1.33E+09	07.60%
Period 9	420000	9	537500	557500	0.753	0.754	557314.6	546656.6	411967.9	8032.057	8032.057	64513946	01.91%
Period 10	520000	10	577500	582500	0.893	0.872	596250.9	570726.3	497739.7	22260.35	22260.35	4.96E+08	04.28%
Period 11	890000	11	587500			1.507	590677.8	594796.1	896205.3	-6205.31	6205.309	38505855	00.70%
Period 12	520000	12				0.849	612731	618865.9	525206.5	-5206.51	5206.509	27107733	01.00%
									Total	-16457.5	256726.4	7.7E+09	66.09%
				Average		Intercept	330028.4			-1371.46	21393.87	6.41E+08	05.51%
						Slope	24069.8			Bias	MAD	MSE	MAPE

Forecasts and Error Analysis

Working Problem 14.10 : The data in the Table below represents actual quarterly sales ($) of washer/dryer sets made by a large appliance store. Using Decomposition method

(a) Forecast year 4 quarters 1, 2, 3, and 4.
(b) Construct a scatter diagram of actual sales, smoothed forecast, unadjusted forecast, and adjusted forecast.

Quarter	Sales ($)	Quarter	Sales ($)
1	300000	9	420000
2	350000	10	520000
3	600000	11	890000
4	310000	12	520000
5	317000		
6	390000		
7	730000		
8	480000		

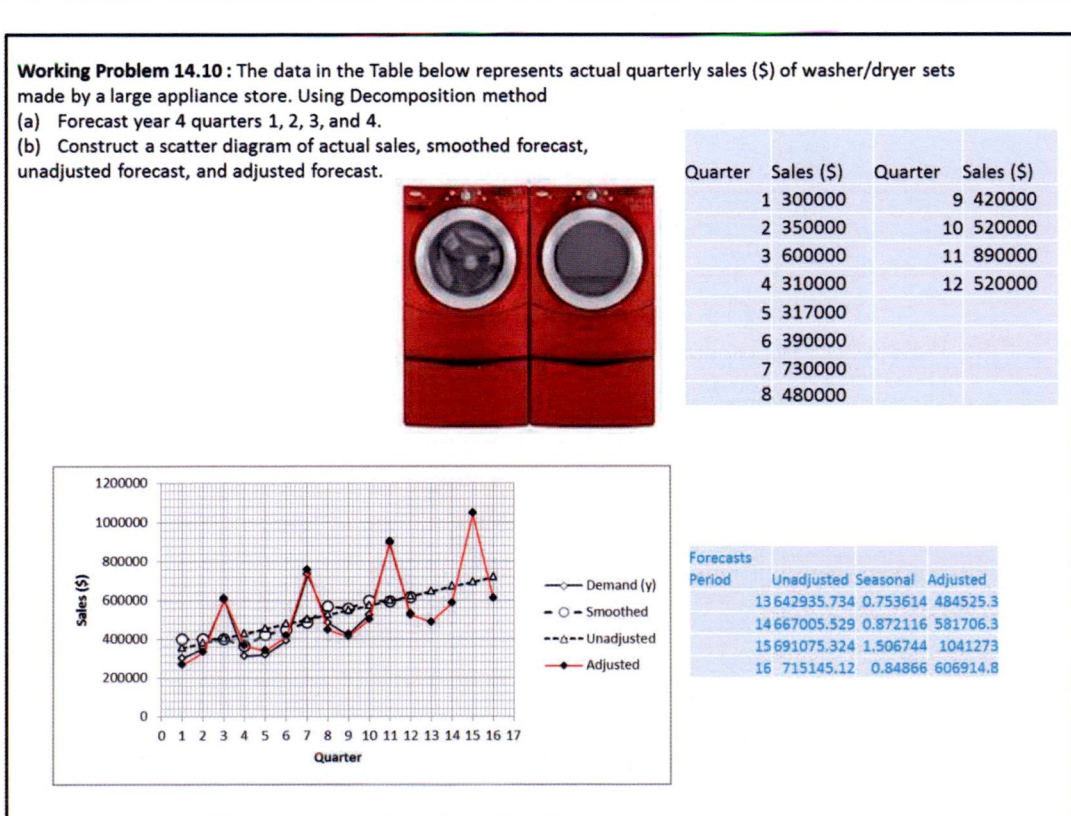

Forecasts

Period	Unadjusted	Seasonal	Adjusted
13	642935.734	0.753614	484525.3
14	667005.529	0.872116	581706.3
15	691075.324	1.506744	1041273
16	715145.12	0.84866	606914.8

14.12 Using Regression Analysis with Trend and Seasonal Components

Multiple regression analysis can be used to forecast time series data containing both trend and seasonal components. In this case, the independent variable is time period. In addition, we use dummy independent variables to represent different seasons. In this case, the model is an additive one of the following form:

$$\hat{Y} = a + b_1 X_1 + b_2 X_2 + b_3 X_3 + b_4 X_4$$

where

X_1 = time period
X_2 = 1 if quarter 2, 0 otherwise
X_3 = 1 if quarter 3, 0 otherwise
X_4 = 1 if quarter 4, 0 otherwise

Example 14.18: Using the data in Table 14.24 which represents actual quarterly demands for water dispensers sold by a hardware store, develop a regression equation in which both trend and seasonality are accounted for.

Table 14.24 Regression analysis with trend and seasonality

Year	Quarter	Demand	Time Period	X2-Q2	X3-Q3	X4-Q4
1	1	300	1	0	0	0
	2	350	2	1	0	0
	3	600	3	0	1	0
	4	310	4	0	0	1
2	5	317	5	0	0	0
	6	390	6	1	0	0
	7	730	7	0	1	0
	8	480	8	0	0	1
3	9	420	9	0	0	0
	10	520	10	1	0	0
	11	890	11	0	1	0
	12	520	12	0	0	1

Solution:

The output of the regression analysis is shown in Table 14.25.

The resultant equation is:

$$Demand = 222.229 + 24.688\, X + 49.646\, X_2 + 344.958\, X_3 + 16.938\, X_4$$

Table 14.25 Regression output

Regression Statistics					
Multiple R	0.982				
R Square	0.964				
Adjusted R Square	0.943				
Standard Error	43.567				
Observations	12				
ANOVA	df	SS	MS	F	Significance F
Regression	4	351008.1	87752.02	46.23104	4.05E-05
Residual	7	13286.83	1898.119		
Total	11	364294.9			
	Coefficients	Standard Error	t Stat	P-value	
Intercept	222.229	31.677	7.015	0.000	
Time Period	24.688	3.851	6.411	0.000	
X2-Quarter 2	49.646	35.780	1.388	0.208	
X3-Quarter 3	344.958	36.397	9.478	0.000	
X4-Quarter 4	16.938	37.402	0.453	0.664	

Table 14.26 Regression Forecasts

Year	Quarter	Demand	Time Period	X2-Quarter 2	X3-Quarter 3	X4-Quarter 4	Forecast
1	1	300	1	0	0	0	246.917
	2	350	2	1	0	0	321.251
	3	600	3	0	1	0	641.251
	4	310	4	0	0	1	337.919
2	5	317	5	0	0	0	345.669
	6	390	6	1	0	0	420.003
	7	730	7	0	1	0	740.003
	8	480	8	0	0	1	436.671
3	9	420	9	0	0	0	444.421
	10	520	10	1	0	0	518.755
	11	890	11	0	1	0	838.755
	12	520	12	0	0	1	535.423
4	13			0	0	0	543.173
	14			1	0	0	617.507
	15			0	1	0	937.507
	16			0	0	1	634.175
5	17			0	0	0	641.925
	18			1	0	0	716.259
	19			0	1	0	1036.259
	20			0	0	1	732.927

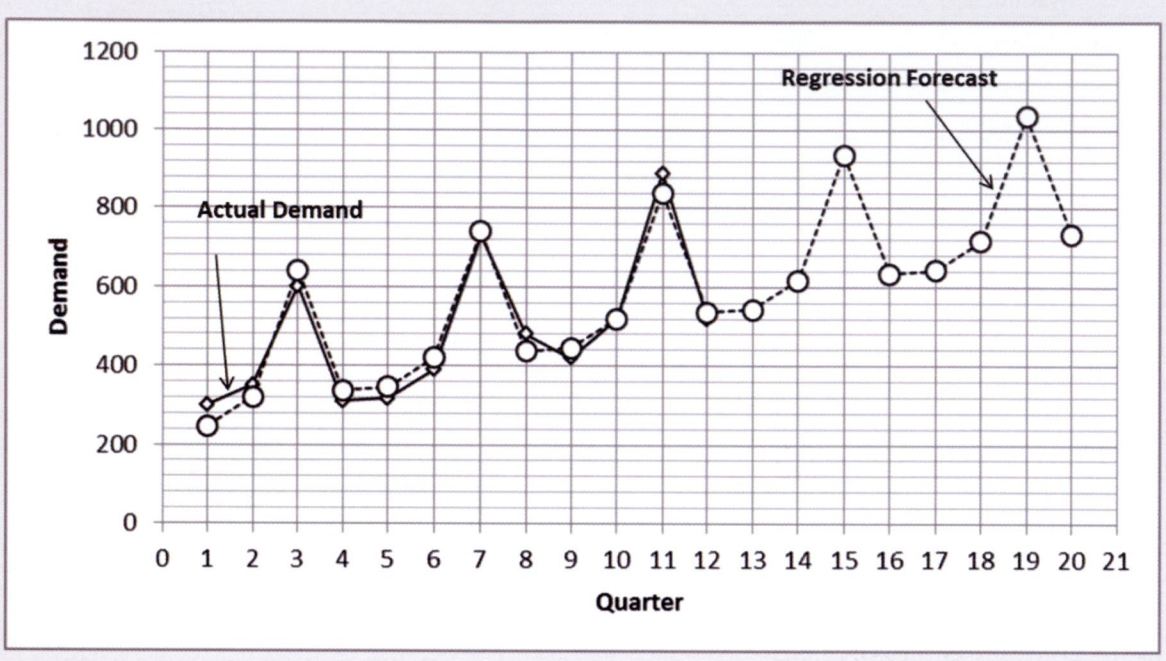

Figure 14.15 Regression Forecast with Trend and Seasonal Components

Working Problem 14.11 : Demands for Sport-Utility vehicles (SUVS) in an SUV sales facility were monitored over the last three years. The Table below shows these quarterly demands .
Using Regression Analysis with Trend and Seasonal Components forecast the demands for the next two years.

Year	Quarter	Demand
1	1	500
	2	550
	3	900
	4	600
2	5	380
	6	439
	7	840
	8	480
3	9	269
	10	379
	11	791
	12	410

$$Demand = 492.5313 - 21.9063X + 94.90625\,X_2 + 504.4792\,X_3 + 179.3854\,X_4$$

14.13 Review Exercises

P14.1: The table below shows demand in square foot for three different types of floor covers: ceramic tiles, carpets, and hardwood. Develop a scatter plot for each product and describe the results.

Year	Ceramic tiles (Square Foot)	Carpets (Square Foot)	Hardwood (Square Foot)
1	325000000	330000000	165000000
2	325000000	341000000	150000000
3	325000000	352000000	180000000
4	325000000	363000000	210000000
5	325000000	374000000	255000000
6	325000000	385000000	225000000
7	325000000	396000000	240000000
8	325000000	407000000	285000000
9	325000000	418000000	300000000
10	325000000	429000000	285000000

P14.2: The table below shows monthly demand in square foot for hardwood flooring over the last three years. Develop a scatter plot and describe the results.

Month	Hardwood (Square Foot)	Month	Hardwood (Square Foot)	Month	Hardwood (Square Foot)
1	133000	13	118000	25	103000
2	137500	14	122500	26	107500
3	130000	15	115000	27	100000
4	140000	16	125000	28	110000
5	200000	17	185000	29	170000
6	205000	18	190000	30	175000
7	200000	19	185000	31	170000
8	215000	20	200000	32	185000
9	150000	21	135000	33	120000
10	142500	22	127500	34	112500
11	144500	23	129500	35	114500
12	143500	24	128500	36	113500

P14.3: The data in the table below represents actual monthly sales ($) of a small business firm and the corresponding forecast sales ($). Calculate *MAD*, *MSE*, and *MAPE* (%).

Month	Sales($)	Forecast Values
1	585000	568800
2	819000	624000
3	650000	679200
4	624000	734400
5	1014000	789600
6	936000	844800
7	923000	900000
8	1079000	955200
9	1053000	1010400
10	1170000	1065600

Answer:

MAD =	MSE =	MAPE (%)
96020	13857060000	=10.757

P14.4: The data in the table below represents actual monthly sales ($) of a small business firm and the corresponding forecast sales ($). Calculate *MAD*, *MSE*, and *MAPE* (%).

Month	Sales($)	Forecast Values
1	450000	437538.4615
2	630000	480000.0000
3	500000	522461.5385
4	480000	564923.0769
5	780000	607384.6154
6	720000	649846.1538
7	710000	692307.6923
8	830000	734769.2308
9	810000	777230.7692
10	900000	819692.3077

P14.5: The table below gives the average monthly exchange rate between the U.S. Dollar and the Euro for 2011 and part of 2012 (http://www.x-rates.com/d/USD/EUR/hist2011.html) . It shows that 1 Euro was equivalent to 1.33 dollars in April 2012 while in April 2011, 1 Euro was equivalent to 1.44 dollars. Economists attribute this drop to economic problems in Greece. Using Moving Average (n = 4):

    (a) Forecast the exchange rate for the following 4 months
    (b) Calculate *Bias*, *MAD*, *MSE*, and *MAPE* (%)

Year	Month	Month	Exchange Rate
2011	January	1	1.33654
2011	February	2	1.36452
2011	March	3	1.39992
2011	April	4	1.44484
2011	May	5	1.43486
2011	June	6	1.43884
2011	July	7	1.42643
2011	August	8	1.43432
2011	September	9	1.377
2011	October	10	1.381955
2011	November	11	1.35622
2011	December	12	1.315827
2012	January	13	1.290128
2012	February	14	1.323908
2012	March	15	1.321165
2012	April	16	1.330373

Answer:

MAD	MSE	MAPE
0.03188	0.001582	02.33%

P 14.6: The table below shows monthly demand in square foot for hardwood flooring over the last three years. Using Moving Average ($n = 4$):

(a) Forecast the demand for the following 4 months

(b) Calculate *Bias*, *MAD*, *MSE*, and *MAPE* (%)

Month	Hardwood (Square Foot)	Month	Hardwood (Square Foot)	Month	Hardwood (Square Foot)
1	133000	13	118000	25	103000
2	137500	14	122500	26	107500
3	130000	15	115000	27	100000
4	140000	16	125000	28	110000
5	200000	17	185000	29	170000
6	205000	18	190000	30	175000
7	200000	19	185000	31	170000
8	215000	20	200000	32	185000
9	150000	21	135000	33	120000
10	142500	22	127500	34	112500
11	144500	23	129500	35	114500
12	143500	24	128500	36	113500

P14.7: The table below shows the monthly demand for Lexus ES 350 Sedan cars sold by a car dealer in Atlanta, GA. Use a 3-month moving average determine the corresponding forecasts and the forecast for the thirteenth month. Calculate Bias, MSE, and MAPE (%). Construct a scatter plot of the demands and the forecasts.

Month	Demand for Lexus ES 350 Sedan
January	18
February	19
March	24
April	30
May	45
June	43
July	56
August	44
September	33
October	24
November	21
December	19
January	—

Answer:

Bias	MAD	MSE	MAPE
-0.185	12.852	194.704	40.73%

P14.8: The table below shows the monthly demand for Sofa Beds sold by a furniture store. Use a 4-month moving average; determine the corresponding forecasts and the forecast for the thirteenth month. Calculate Bias, MSE, and MAPE (%). Construct a scatter plot of the actual demands and the corresponding forecasts.

Month	Demand for Sofa Beds
January	18
February	23
March	19
April	22
May	26
June	23
July	29
August	25
September	33
October	30
November	34
December	32
January	----

P14.9: The data in the table below represents actual monthly demand for large-screen TVs over 2 year period. Calculate moving average at $n = 3$, and determine *MAD*, *MSE*, and *MAPE* (%).

Period	Demand	Period	Demand
Period 1	110000	Period 13	103000
Period 2	45000	Period 14	37000
Period 3	11000	Period 15	7000
Period 4	15000	Period 16	7000
Period 5	36000	Period 17	28000
Period 6	32000	Period 18	23000
Period 7	46000	Period 19	41000
Period 8	28000	Period 20	20000
Period 9	52000	Period 21	44000
Period 10	58000	Period 22	57000
Period 11	60000	Period 23	49000
Period 12	55000	Period 24	54000

Answer:

Bias	MAD	MSE	MAPE
1333.333	20222.22	6.26E+08	112.08%

P14.10: The table below gives the average monthly exchange rate between the U.S. Dollar and the Euro for 2011 and part of 2012 (http://www.x-rates.com/d/USD/EUR/hist2011.html) . It shows that 1 Euro was equivalent to 1.33 dollars in April 2012 while in April 2011, 1 Euro was equivalent to 1.44 dollars. Economists attribute this drop to economic problems in Greece. Using Weighted Moving Average ($n = 4$):

        (a) Forecast the demand for the following 4 months
        (b) Calculate *Bias*, *MAD*, *MSE*, and *MAPE* (%)

Year	Month	Month	Exchange Rate	Year	Month	Month	Exchange Rate
2011	January	1	1.33654	2011	September	9	1.377
2011	February	2	1.36452	2011	October	10	1.381955
2011	March	3	1.39992	2011	November	11	1.35622
2011	April	4	1.44484	2011	December	12	1.315827
2011	May	5	1.43486	2012	January	13	1.290128
2011	June	6	1.43884	2012	February	14	1.323908
2011	July	7	1.42643	2012	March	15	1.321165
2011	August	8	1.43432	2012	April	16	1.330373

P14.11: The data in the table below represents actual monthly demand for large-screen TVs over 2 year period. Calculate weighted moving average at $n = 3$, and determine *MAD*, *MSE*, and *MAPE* (%).

Period	Demand	Period	Demand
Period 1	110000	Period 13	103000
Period 2	45000	Period 14	37000
Period 3	11000	Period 15	7000
Period 4	15000	Period 16	7000
Period 5	36000	Period 17	28000
Period 6	32000	Period 18	23000
Period 7	46000	Period 19	41000
Period 8	28000	Period 20	20000
Period 9	52000	Period 21	44000
Period 10	58000	Period 22	57000
Period 11	60000	Period 23	49000
Period 12	55000	Period 24	54000

Answer:

	Bias	MAD	MSE	MAPE
	1722.222	18404.76	5.29E+08	94.27%

P14.12: The data in the table below represents actual monthly demand for Air Conditioning Units over one year period. Calculate weighted moving average at $n = 3$, and determine *MAD*, *MSE*, and *MAPE* (%).

Month	Air conditioning units
January	54
February	69
March	57
April	66
May	78
June	69
July	87
August	75
September	99
October	90
November	102
December	96
January	----

P14.13: The table below gives the average monthly exchange rate between the U.S. Dollar and the Euro for 2011 and part of 2012 (http://www.x-rates.com/d/USD/EUR/hist2011.html) . It shows that 1 Euro was equivalent to 1.33 dollars in April 2012 while in April 2011, 1 Euro was equivalent to 1.44 dollars. Economists attribute this drop to economic problems in Greece. Use exponential smoothing for estimating year 11(the eleventh year) at values of α of 0.1 and 0.3. Calculate Bias, MAD, MSE, and MAPE (%) at each α value.

Year	Month	Month	Exchange rate	Year	Month	Month	Exchange rate
2011	January	1	1.33654	2011	September	9	1.377
2011	February	2	1.36452	2011	October	10	1.381955
2011	March	3	1.39992	2011	November	11	1.35622
2011	April	4	1.44484	2011	December	12	1.315827
2011	May	5	1.43486	2012	January	13	1.290128
2011	June	6	1.43884	2012	February	14	1.323908
2011	July	7	1.42643	2012	March	15	1.321165
2011	August	8	1.43432	2012	April	16	1.330373

Answer:

	Bias	MAD	MSE	MAPE
Alpha = 0.1	0.010874	0.046232	0.003014	03.34%
Alpha = 0.3	-0.00098	0.036539	0.001949	02.66%

P14.14: The data in the table below represents actual yearly sales ($) made by a Mexican Restaurant in downtown San Diego, California. Use exponential smoothing for estimating year 11(the eleventh year) at values of α of 0.1 and 0.3. Calculate Bias, MAD, MSE, and MAPE (%) at each α value.

Year	Sales ($)
1	180000
2	196200
3	193500
4	234000
5	227700
6	274500
7	284400
8	280530
9	290430
10	274230

P14.15: The data in the table below represents actual yearly demands for a new laptop. Use exponential smoothing to estimate year 11(the eleventh year) at value of α of 0.1. Calculate Bias, MAD, MSE, and MAPE (%) at each α value.

Year	Demand
1	12000
2	13080
3	12900
4	15600
5	15180
6	18300
7	18960
8	18702
9	19362
10	18282

Answer:

Bias	MAD	MSE	MAPE
3223.001	3223.001	14164950	18.34%

P14.16: The table below gives the average monthly exchange rate between the U.S. Dollar and the Euro for 2011 and part of 2012 (http://www.x-rates.com/d/USD/EUR/hist2011.html) . It shows that 1 Euro was equivalent to 1.33 dollars in April 2012 while in April 2011, 1 Euro was equivalent to 1.44 dollars. Economists attribute this drop to economic problems in Greece. Use exponential smoothing with trend adjustment for estimating year 11(the eleventh year) at values of α of 0.1, and $\beta = 0.4$. Calculate Bias, MAD, MSE, and MAPE (%).

Year	Month	Month	Exchange rate
2011	January	1	1.33654
2011	February	2	1.36452
2011	March	3	1.39992
2011	April	4	1.44484
2011	May	5	1.43486
2011	June	6	1.43884
2011	July	7	1.42643
2011	August	8	1.43432
2011	September	9	1.377
2011	October	10	1.381955
2011	November	11	1.35622
2011	December	12	1.315827
2012	January	13	1.290128
2012	February	14	1.323908
2012	March	15	1.321165
2012	April	16	1.330373

P14.17: The data in the table below represents actual yearly sales ($) made by a fast food corner in a large Mall. Use exponential smoothing with trend adjustment for estimating year 11(the eleventh year) at values of α of 0.1, and $\beta = 0.4$. Calculate Bias, MAD, MSE, and MAPE (%).

Year	1	2	3	4	5	6	7	8	9	10
Sales ($)	1000000	1090000	1075000	1300000	1265000	1525000	1580000	1558500	1613500	1523500

Answer:

Bias	MAD	MSE	MAPE
195098.3	195098.3	5.67E+10	13.57%

P14.18: The data in the table below represents actual monthly demands for storage sheds reported by a storage shed dealer. Use exponential smoothing with trend adjustment for estimating the thirteenth month at values of α of 0.1, and $\beta = 0.4$. Calculate Bias, MAD, MSE, and MAPE (%).

Year	1	2	3	4	5	6	7	8	9	10	11	12
Demand	384	419	413	500	487	587	608	599	621	586	520	500

P14.19: The data in the table below represents actual monthly demand for car batteries sold by an Auto parts chain. Use trend projections to forecast the following three months. Calculate Bias, MAD, MSE, and MAPE (%)

Month	Jan	Feb	Mar	Apr	May	June	July	August	Sep	Oct	Nov	Dec
Demand	2400	1500	3000	4000	2750	5000	4900	6000	6500	5800	7000	6950

Answer: Bias = 1.52E-13, MAD = 513.6946, MSE =366662.3, MAPE = 15.84%

P14.20: The data in the table below represents actual new monthly subscriptions for a cable service. Use trend projections to forecast the following three months. Calculate Bias, MAD, MSE, and MAPE (%)

Month	Jan	Feb	Mar	Apr	May	June	July	August	Sept	Oct	Nov	Dec
Demand	27	16	28	36	28	48	47	53	62	55	65	70

P14.21: The table below gives the average monthly exchange rate between the U.S. Dollar and the Euro for 2011 and part of 2012 (http://www.x-rates.com/d/USD/EUR/hist2011.html) . It shows that 1 Euro was equivalent to 1.33 dollars in April 2012 while in April 2011, 1 Euro was equivalent to 1.44 dollars. Economists attribute this drop to economic problems in Greece. Use trend projections to forecast the following three months. Calculate Bias, MAD, MSE, and MAPE (%)

Year	Month	Month	Exchange Rate
2011	January	1	1.33654
2011	February	2	1.36452
2011	March	3	1.39992
2011	April	4	1.44484
2011	May	5	1.43486
2011	June	6	1.43884
2011	July	7	1.42643
2011	August	8	1.43432
2011	September	9	1.377
2011	October	10	1.381955
2011	November	11	1.35622
2011	December	12	1.315827
2012	January	13	1.290128
2012	February	14	1.323908
2012	March	15	1.321165
2012	April	16	1.330373

Answer: Bias = 000, MAD = 0.033, MSE = 0.002, MAPE = 02.37%

P14.22: The data in the table below represents actual monthly sales ($) made by an auto parts chain of Water Pumps over a 12 month period and for three years.
(a) Calculate the average sales per month
(b) Calculate the overall monthly sales
(c) Calculate the average seasonal index
(d) If total sales in the fourth year are expected to be 1300, forecast every month in the fourth year using the average seasonal index.

Month	Year 1 (Y1)	Year 2(Y2)	Year 3 (Y3)
January	80	100	97
February	85	75	72
March	80	90	87
April	110	90	87
May	115	131	128
June	120	110	107
July	100	110	107
August	110	90	87
September	85	95	92
October	75	85	82
November	85	75	72
December	80	80	77

P14.23: Given the data of sales ($×1000) of a clothing store, answer the following questions:

Month	Year 1	Year 2	Year 3	Year 4
Jan	300	330	333	420
Feb	188	188	212	240
Mar	192	192	202	196
Apr	229	259	262	349
May	329	359	362	449
Jun	440	470	473	560
Jul	560	590	593	680
Aug	540	570	573	660
Sep	340	370	373	460
Oct	370	400	403	490
Nov	570	600	603	690
Dec	600	630	633	720

(a) Calculate the average seasonal index for every month
(b) If the expected fifth year sales (× 1000) = $5300, using the average index for every month, forecast the Adjusted fifth year average sales
(c) Construct a scatterplot for every year including the forecasts of the fifth year.
Answer: Expected Fifth year monthly average Sales (EAVG×1000) = $441.6667

P 14.24: The data in the table below represents actual quarterly sales ($) of Large-Screen TVs made by a large Electronic Company. Using Decomposition method

    (a) Calculate Seasonal Ratios
    (b) Calculate Seasonal Indices
    (c) Calculate Smoothed Forecast
    (d) Calculate Unadjusted Forecast
    (e) Calculate Adjusted Forecast
    (f) Calculate Bias, MAD, MSE, and MAPE (%)

Quarter	Sales ($)	Quarter	Sales ($)
1	30000	9	42000
2	35000	10	52000
3	60000	11	89000
4	31000	12	52000
5	31700		
6	39000		
7	73000		
8	48000		

P14.25: Demands for Sport-Utility vehicles (SUVS) in an SUV sales facility were monitored over the last three years. The table below shows these quarterly demands. Using Regression Analysis with Trend and Seasonal Components forecast the demands for the next two years.

Year	Quarter	Demand
1	1	333
	2	383
	3	633
	4	343
2	5	350
	6	423
	7	763
	8	513
3	9	453
	10	553
	11	923
	12	553

Answer:

	Coefficients
Intercept	255.2292
Time Period	24.6875
X2-Quarter 2	49.64583
X3-Quarter 3	344.9583
X4-Quarter 4	16.9375

P14.26: The data in the table below represents a time series with the time zone being a month and the variable being sales commissions in thousands of dollars paid by a company to its sales personnel.

(a) Use exponential smoothing at a of 0.1, 0.2, 0.4, and 0.5 and determine the optimum *Bias, MAD, MSE,* and *MAPE* (%)
(b) At the optimum values of forecasting error, construct a scatterplot of the actual data and the forecast values.

t	X(t)	t	X(t)	t	X(t)	t	X(t)	t	X(t)
1	50.8	6	48.1	11	50.8	16	53.1	21	49.7
2	50.3	7	50.1	12	52.8	17	51.6	22	50.3
3	50.2	8	48.7	13	53	18	50.8	23	49.9
4	48.7	9	49.2	14	51.8	19	50.6	24	51.8
5	48.5	10	51.1	15	53.6	20	49.7	25	51

P14.27: The data in the table below represents a time series with the time zone being a month and the variable being sales commissions in thousands of dollars paid by a company to its sales personnel. Use exponential smoothing with trend adjustment for estimating the thirteenth month at values of α of 0.6, and $\beta = 0.4$. Calculate Bias, MAD, MSE, and MAPE (%).

t	X(t)	t	X(t)	t	X(t)	t	X(t)	t	X(t)
1	50.8	6	48.1	11	52.8	16	55.1	21	51.7
2	50.3	7	50.1	12	54.8	17	53.6	22	52.3
3	50.2	8	48.7	13	55	18	52.8	23	51.9
4	48.7	9	49.2	14	53.8	19	52.6	24	53.8
5	48.5	10	51.1	15	55.6	20	51.7	25	53

Answer:

Bias	MAD	MSE	MAPE
0.052	1.017	1.796	01.94%

CHAPTER 15

The World of Statistics:

Critical Thinking & Writing Assignments

LEARNING OBJECTIVES

After completing this chapter, students will be able to:

- Understand the importance of expressing statistics in words
- Write a statistical report
- Practice critical thinking
- Understand how to report on case studies and practical application

CHAPTER 15

Throughout the different chapters of this book, we emphasized the importance of interpretation and rationalization of results. Indeed, no matter how simple or complicated an analysis can be, without good interpretation of results and knowledge-based rationalization, the efforts made will yield little benefits. In this chapter, we focus on the subject of '*Writing-to-Learn*' in statistics and introduce general guidelines for good writing and evaluation rubrics. We also discuss **critical thinking** as a key component of writing-to-learn. Finally, many case studies of writing assignments are presented to assist students on how to approach different subjects and applications in the context of statistics.

CHAPTER CONTENTS

15.1 The importance of expressing statistics in words

In chapter 1 of this book, we introduced statistics as:

> *"The <u>science</u> and <u>art</u> of reading, describing, and manipulating <u>data</u>, which represents <u>variables</u> so that practical observations about a <u>population</u> can be made from a <u>sample</u> drawn from the population, and guidelines can be established to allow making conclusions with high levels of <u>precision</u> and <u>accuracy</u> about a certain <u>process</u> or a given <u>system</u>"*

This definition indicates that the essence of a statistical analysis is to explore populations' characteristics via measures of small samples selected from those populations. In most writing reports that involve statistics, one or more of ten basic terms of statistics are normally used: (1) process, (2) system, (3) variable, (4) data, (5) population, (6) parameter, (7) sample, (8) statistic, (9) interpretation, and (10) conclusion. These terms, defined earlier in Chapter 1, represent important components of statistics and when statistical analyses are used in a certain project, these components may collectively be used in what is commonly called *'project cycle.'* An example of a project cycle is shown in Figure 15.1.

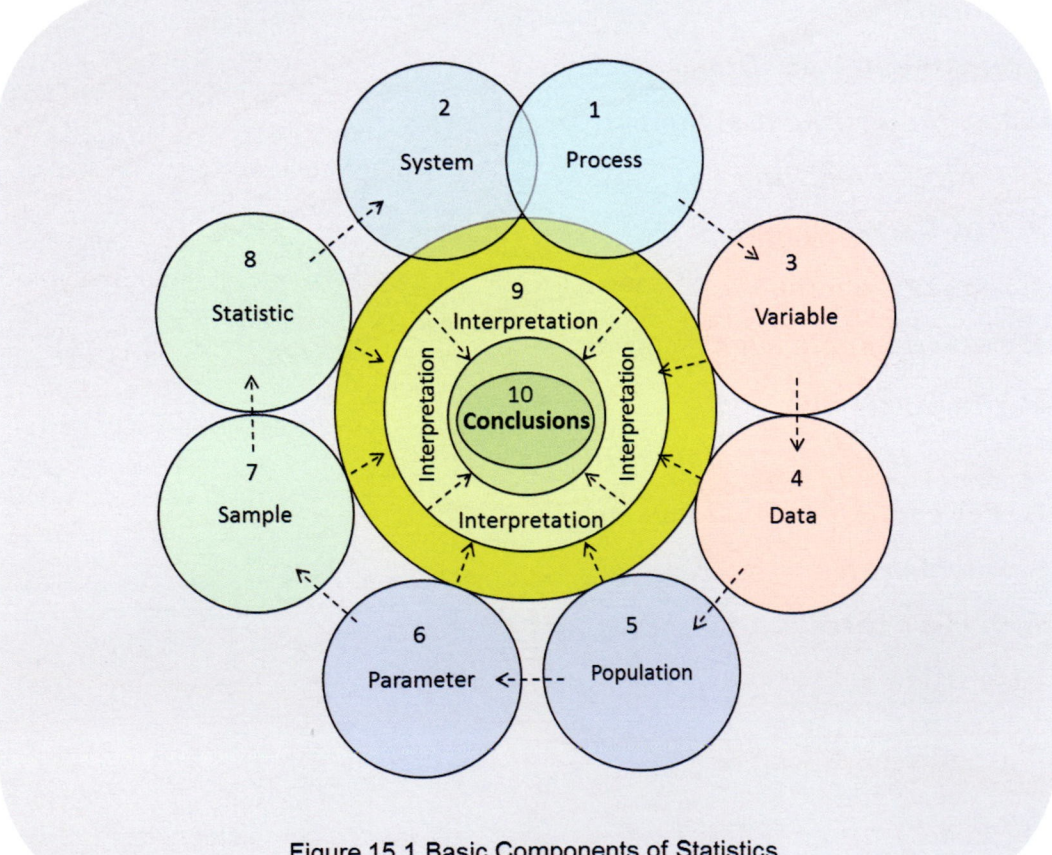

Figure 15.1 Basic Components of Statistics

According to the project cycle, the objective of any project is commonly to explore a ***system*** or a ***process*** and perhaps solve particular problem(s) associated with the system or the process under consideration. The system may be education, health, or even a machine with well-defined inputs and outputs. A process may be education, health, welfare, or business with well-defined components such as people, methods, machines, materials, or environment. Upon defining the system or the process, we start by identifying the ***variable*** of interest (say, the rate of student failure, monthly income, property tax, etc.). A variable is identified by the concern or the problem associated with it (say, high rate of student failure, low income, or high property tax). The next step is to seek quantitative methods to measure the variable (say, number of students, income in dollar, or property tax in dollar). This effort should yield ***data*** that can be analyzed using various statistical tools. In the process of identifying the variable and the data describing it, we should not lose sight of the fact that we are analyzing a ***population*** or a measure of the population. This is called a ***parameter***. Since evaluation of the whole population is virtually impossible and even if it is possible it will be cost or time prohibited, we should rely on a representative ***sample*** from the population. Once a representative sample is selected from the population, and measures of the variable(s) are converted into useful data, it becomes important to then begin with descriptive analysis of the sample data to produce sample descriptive ***statistics***.

The steps discussed above are common to all types of statistical analyses. As indicated in Chapters 2 and 3, descriptive statistics represent initial steps in any statistical analysis as not only they provide an overall exploration of the nature of data but also assist in detecting any data abnormality or outliers. Upon completion of this initial analysis, further analysis may be required depending on the ultimate objective(s) of the project. Regardless the type of analysis, the objective will always be to explore the populations' parameters using sample measures or 'statistics.' This may be carried out via the different techniques discussed in this book. Examples of these techniques include:

- Explore and simulate all possible outcomes of an experiment via probability analysis and probability distributions (Chapters 4, 5, and 6)
- Estimate the populations' parameters from sample statistics using confidence intervals at particular confidence levels (Chapter 8)
- Test claims made about populations' parameters using test of hypothesis (Chapter 9 and 10)
- Compare multiple means to examine the significances of the effects of some factors on a response variable using analysis of variance (Chapter 11)
- Develop relationships between a response variable and a number of independent variables using regression analysis (Chapter 12)
- Evaluate the fitability of observed frequency distributions with expected frequency distributions of qualitative parameters (Chapter 13)
- Evaluate the independence or the homogeneity of two categorical variables (Chapter 13)
- Forecast future data over a given period of time (Chapter 14)

Upon completion of any type of analysis, it will be important to complete the project cycle via two key steps:

- *Interpretation:* explain the outcomes of the statistical analysis with respect to the objectives of the study.
- *Conclusion:* summarize the practical outcomes of the analysis with respect to the objectives of the study so that decisions regarding these outcomes can be made.

With the above common aspects in mind and in the sequence presented, a successful statistical report can be produced. In the following sections of this chapter, we will review a number of important applications in which statistics represent a critical tool. The idea of this chapter is to assist students in improving their technical writing skills particularly in applications where statistics can be used.

15.2 Writing-to-learn

In classic writing assignments, the focus is typically on the linguistic ability and the command of the language. ***Writing-to-learn is a tool to promote learning and critical thinking***. Indeed, writing-to-learn should be perceived as '*learning to express what you have learned and display your thoughts in writing.*' The idea of writing-to-learn is to involve students in an active learning process in which they can learn key concepts and understand material more fully while also practicing effective communication skills.

The following general guidelines will be useful for both students and teachers who are involved in writing-to-learn assignments in statistics:

- Writing-to-learn in statistics is considered as a form of writing in the discipline (WID) assignment. In this regard, the assignment provides the student with a great opportunity to practice with the language conventions associated with statistics particularly in interpreting the outcomes of statistical analyses.
- Teachers should comment primarily on the substance of these assignments. They should also expect students to meet professional standards of layout and proofreading (format and mechanical correctness).
- Writing assignments can be implemented for individual students or as a collaborative effort (team writing assignment).
- Not all writing assignments should be implemented in a team format; only when the subject requires multiple coordinated efforts.
- Collaborative groups draw upon the strengths of all their members; one student may be stronger in organization, another may be better in critical thinking skills, and another may excel in interpretation skills. By working in groups, students learn from each other while they complete assigned tasks.
- When writing assignments are given to students, it is important that teachers articulate the task to all students. Good writing assignments always start with clear goals and objectives.
- Good writing assignments often begin by asking the question, 'what do I want to read at the end of the assignment?' By working from what they anticipate the final product to look like, teachers can give students detailed guidelines about both the writing task and the final report.

The contents of a typical writing-to-learn document in statistics are shown below.

Basic Contents of Statistical Writing Report

1. Abstract or report summary
2. Introduction
3. Objectives
4. System or process considered
5. Variables under consideration
6. Population and parameters
7. Samples and statistics
8. Suggested analyses
9. Analyses' outcomes
10. Interpretation
11. Conclusions
12. References

Key criteria to evaluate a writing assignment are described by the suggested rubric in Table 15.1. It should be pointed out that these criteria only represent general guidelines for evaluating a writing-to-learn report. Different instructors may use different criteria depending on the subject at hand and/or their own style of writing, provided no fundamental criteria are overlooked. Teachers should also share the rubric with the students prior to giving the writing-to-learn assignment. This will assure common understanding and consistency of reporting and grading.

Table 15.1 Suggested rubric: criteria for writing-to-learn assignments

Criteria	Rubric Scale				Rubric Score
	4	3	2	1	1, 2, 3, or 4
(1) Title	Title is clear and draw reader attention	Title is clear	Title is unclear	No title or meaningless title	
(2) Problem definition	The problem is well defined	The problem lacks clarity	The problem is ill-defined	No problem was addressed	
(3) Objective of writing report	Objectives are related to problem and they are clearly and orderly listed	Objectives are listed but key objectives are overlooked	Unclear objectives	No objectives listed	
(4) Claim or key issue	The student makes a good claim and explains why it is worth discussing	The student makes a claim but overlooks important reasons as to why it is worth discussing	The student makes a claim but fails to address reasons as to why it is worth discussing	The student makes no claim and does not address key issues	
(5) Organization	Compelling introduction, informative body, and satisfying conclusion	The report has introduction, body, and conclusion but not compelling	A great deal of deviation from subject in the introduction, body, and conclusion	The report is missing one of the three key organization elements: introduction, body, or conclusion	
(6) Word choice	These are the student words and quotations were clearly specified and cited	These are the student words but lack clarity and correctness	The student relied totally on copying other people words	Words are disconnected and often meaningless	
(7) Sentence Structure	Sentences are clear, complete, and of correct grammar	Too many repeated sentences	Fragmented sentences or inappropriate grammar	Difficult to read sentences (scattered, fragmented, incoherent, misspelling, and improper grammar)	
(8) Credible sources (References)	Information sources are reliable and clearly specified in a reference list or within the text body	Many facts were mentioned without references	Use of unreliable references	No references specified	
(9) Conclusion	The conclusion revealed an answer to the claim	The conclusion only addressed the objectives	The conclusion was disconnected with the objectives	no conclusion	
A= Rubric Average					Sum of Scores divided by 9
Rubric Average Score/100%					100*(A/4)

15.3 Critical thinking in statistics

A key aspect of writing-to-learn is 'critical thinking.' In reference to the rubric of Table 15.1, critical thinking should be implemented in defining the problem, making the claim, and in the conclusion of the writing-to-learn report.

The National Council for Excellence in Critical Thinking (http://www.criticalthinking.org) defines critical thinking as

'the intellectually disciplined process of actively and skillfully conceptualizing, applying, analyzing, synthesizing, and/or evaluating information gathered from, or generated by, observation, experience, reflection, reasoning, or communication, as a guide to belief and action.'

Most advocates of critical thinking agree that critical thinking is **_self-guided_**, **_self-disciplined thinking_** which attempts to reason at the highest level of quality in a fair-minded way.

In the context of applying statistics in the real world, critical thinkers should exhibit the following attributes:

Attributes of Critical Thinker

- *A critical thinker should know the differences between goals and objectives*
- *A critical thinker should know the differences between deductive and inductive reasoning*
- *A critical thinker may not be the person with best memory- What counts is reflection*
- *A critical thinker represents pieces of knowledge in an interesting and unique way*
- *A critical thinker should make efforts to improve the existing thinking process*
- *A critical thinker asks why, and not just how*
- *A critical thinker should look for possible bias*

15.3.1 A critical thinker should know the differences between goals and objectives

In a given study, it is important to specify the goals and the objectives of the study. Figure 15.2 illustrates the difference between goals and objectives. Table 15.2 gives examples of goals and objectives.

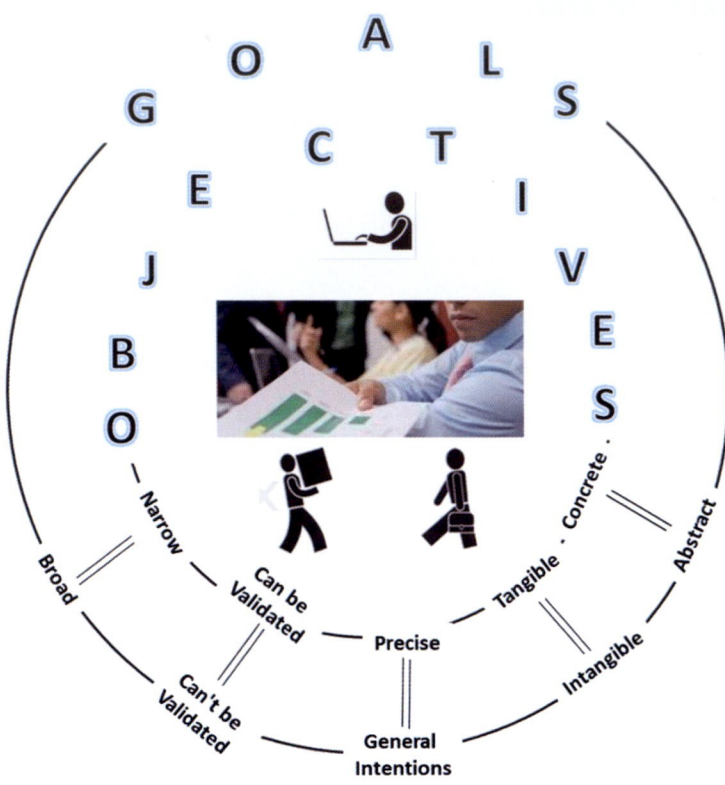

Figure 15.2 Goals and Objectives

Table 15.2 Examples of goals and objectives

Application	Goals	Objectives
Education	Improving student's performance in college algebra	Standardizing course contents
		Standardizing student's evaluation process
		Achieving precise course assessment process
Hospital Operation	Increasing the efficiency in handling patients' care	Assuring immediate responses in the emergency room
		Assuring staff intensity in accommodation to anticipated patent's intensity
		Improving task distribution among hospital staff
College	Increasing student's enrollment over the next five years	Widen the diversity of education programs
		Establishing a good first-year program for good retention
		Improving student's counseling and advising
Business	Improving a corporate's competitive position in the marketplace	Reducing operational cost
		Assuring customer's satisfaction
		Improving quality
		Widening market recognition

As a follow up on the above discussion, other terms that are commonly used are '*mission*' and '*strategy.*' The term mission is more general than the term 'goals.' It implies long-term and unchangeable aspects. An organization mission is more of an organization identity in the way of introducing the organization to consumers and societies. For example, a college may set a mission that states, '*our mission is to provide quality and affordable education to all students.*' A hospital, on the other hand, may state its mission as, '*providing quality medical care with comfort.*' As one can see these are very general statements that can be understood by all people. A strategy, on the other hand, is how to achieve objectives, goals, or even missions. It represents the course of actions ranging from the general actions to the more specific actions. For example, exhibiting a good attitude toward customers is a general strategy which requires educating employees on better ways to deal with customers and delivering services in a timely fashion.

The distinction between missions, goals, objectives, and strategies is a key aspect in preparing a critical thinker. A critical thinker cannot discuss one of these terms as a substitute for another. Indeed, an initial critical thinking process begins with clear descriptions of these terms in the context of the subject being addressed.

15.3.2 A critical thinker should know the differences between deductive and inductive reasoning

A critical thinker should clearly know the difference between deductive reasoning and inductive reasoning. In statistics, both approaches are used but the inductive reasoning appears to be most prominent. In the context of statistics, the use of inductive or deductive reasoning will depend on the objective and the type of analysis used. The following points represent general guidelines in this regard:

Deductive reasoning happens when an analyst works from the more general information to the more specific details. This is essentially a 'top-down' approach because we start at the top with a very broad spectrum of information and then work our way down to reach a specific conclusion. Example: we know from general knowledge that many students entering college do not do well in mathematics as a result of math anxiety. Taking samples of students entering college and testing them to verify this general hypothesis is a form of deductive reasoning.

Inductive reasoning works in an opposite way to that of deductive reasoning, moving from specific observations to broader generalizations and theories, or a bottom-up approach. Example: In the inspection of a new car model, we find from testing few cars that there is a problem of the design of engine start due to electric shortage, speculating that this could mean a significant return of this car model with a great deal of customer's dissatisfaction is an inductive reasoning.

- When you begin with a small sample, and then analyze its observations to reach information that you can then use to make more general observations, or draw conclusions about the population from which the sample was drawn, you are in essence performing inductive reasoning.
- When you assume that most frequency distributions (histograms) of large data will follow a normal distribution then you try to verify this by analyzing large data sets to determine if your assumption is true or false, you are in essence performing deductive reasoning.
- When you determine the confidence intervals for a population parameter from a small sample data, you are in essence performing inductive reasoning.
- When you challenge the fact that the chance of any number (1, 2, 3, 4, 5, 6) in rolling a fair die is 1/6 by rolling a die 6000 times to see if each number showed up 1000 times, you are in essence performing deductive reasoning.
- When you challenge the claim that there are equal proportions of people sharing the U.S. total wealth, you are in essence performing deductive reasoning.

15.3.3 A critical thinker may not be the person with best memory- What counts is reflection

A critical thinker should be able to engage in reflective and independent thinking. This is the most critical attribute of a critical thinker. Critical thinking is not merely a matter of collecting information. A person with an excellent memory may be able to present a lot of facts, but this does not necessarily make him/her a critical thinker. Only when this person deduces consequences from what he/she knows can he/she be considered critical in their thinking. It is how to make use of information to solve problems or address issues.

Given the facts presented to a critical thinker, he/she should do the following:

- Examine the facts
- Detect inconsistencies in information or opinions
- Connect ideas logically
- Suggest ideas or solutions

15.3.4 A critical thinker represents pieces of knowledge in an interesting and unique way

As indicated earlier, knowledge tends to be specific to the context in which it is presented. Good learning involves making use of a knowledge piece in a more meaningful sense and integrating new knowledge with existing knowledge. The examples below provide simple cases of how a piece of knowledge can be evaluated in a nontraditional fashion.

Example 15.1: Suppose the question to be addressed is, 'What can we learn from the arithmetic mean beyond the fact that it reflects a measure of the data center?'

Solution:

To provide one possible answer, consider the 10 numbers given below. A piece of knowledge is how to calculate the mean value of these numbers as shown below:

0, 1, 2, 3, 4, 5, 6, 7, 8, 9

$$\bar{X} = \frac{\sum x_i}{n} = \frac{0+1+2+3+4+5+6+7+8+9}{10} = 4.5$$

The way the average is calculated represents a piece of knowledge, which is valid for any set of data, large or small.

A reflection on what you can learn from this calculation can take different forms depending on your own view of the meaning of the mean value of a data set. For example, you may think of the mean value as a representation of the center of the data. This means that if we subtract each number from the mean value and determine the sum of the differences, we will have a sum of zero as shown below:

$$\sum_{1}^{n}(x_i - \bar{X}) = 0 \quad or \quad (0-4.5)+(1-4.5)+(2-4.5)+(3-4.5)+(4-0.5)+(5-4.5)+(5-4.5)$$

$$+ (6-4.5)+(7-4.5)+(8-4.5)+(9-4.5) = 0$$

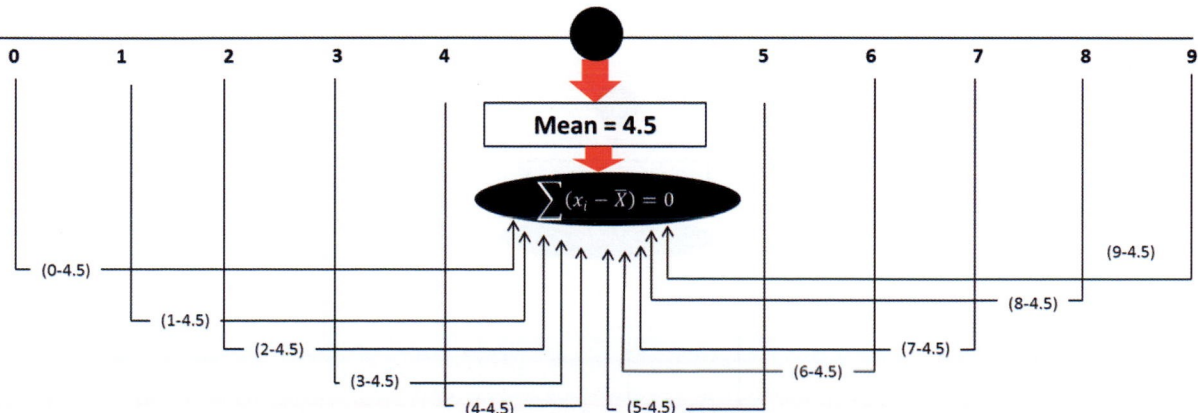

Learning the above concept will lead one to conclude that for this symmetrical set of data, if we eliminate the lowest number, 0, and the maximum number 9, the mean value will remain the same. It also lead us to learn that if we continue to eliminate the highest number and the lowest number and consecutively calculate the mean, we will always obtain the same mean value of 4.5 as shown below.

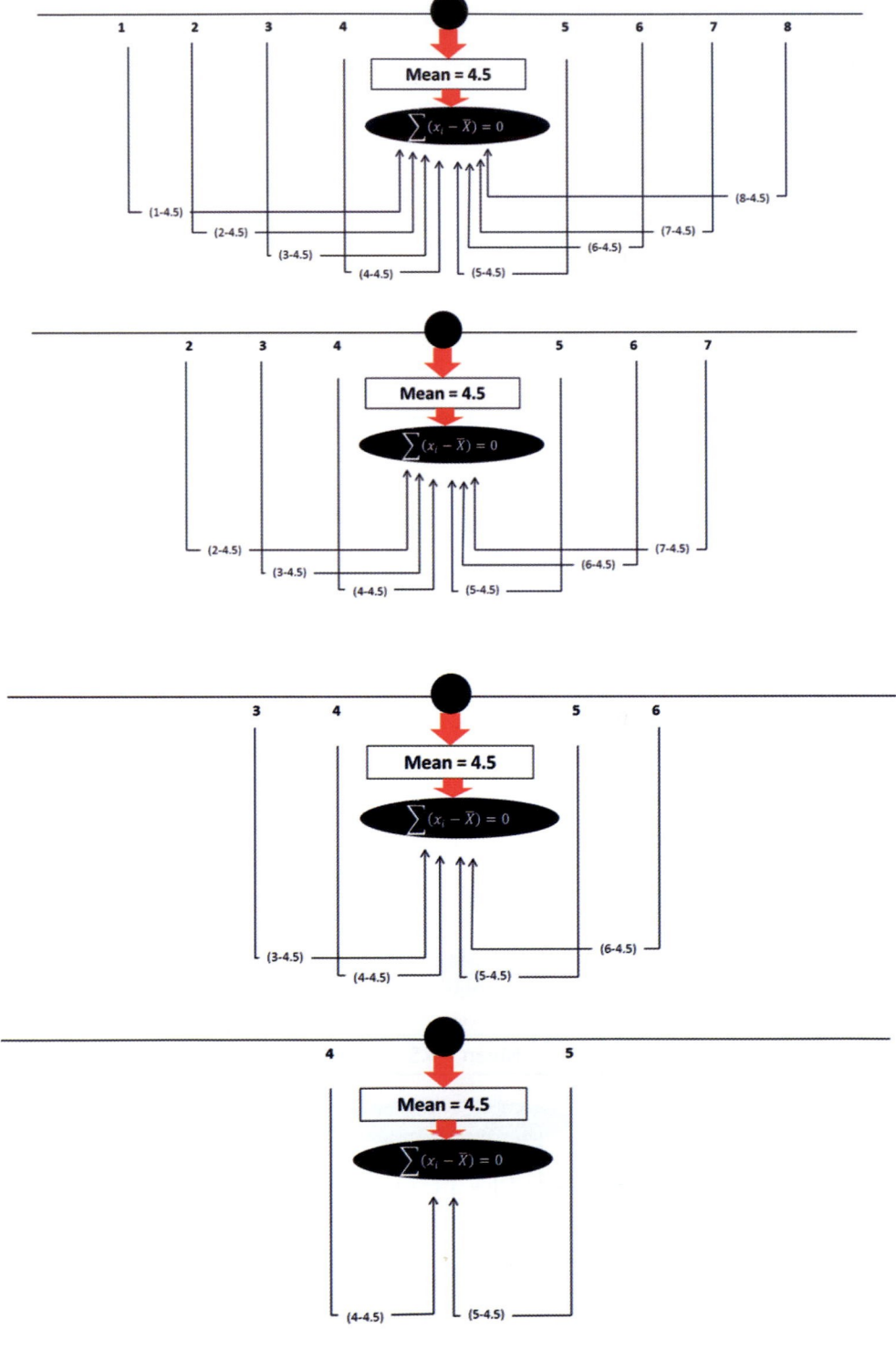

854

The above concept will ultimately lead us to understand why describing a set of data using only the mean value may be misleading as we may obtain the same mean value for different sets of data that exhibit different variability levels (different ranges). As one can see, the first set has a range of 9, the second set has a range of 7, and the ranges of the other sets are 5, 3, and 1 respectively. It follows that what began as a piece of knowledge, in which we learned how to calculate a mean value of a data set, led us to learn other aspects on our own. Conceptually, this means that we cannot rely on the mean value as the only descriptor of a data set and that a measure of variability must associate a measure of the center to completely describe the data.

0	1	2	3	4	5	6	7	8	9
	1	2	3	4	5	6	7	8	
		2	3	4	5	6	7		
			3	4	5	6			
				4	5				

Mean	Range	Std. Dev.
4.5	9	3.0
4.5	7	2.4
4.5	5	1.9
4.5	3	1.3
4.5	1	0.7

Example 15.2: In the subject of descriptive statistics, we discussed two measures of variability: the standard deviation (σ) and the variance (σ^2). A critical thinker should question the reason of why using these two measures to describe variability, and why not only one of the two measures, particularly since one of the two measures is the square of the other.

Solution:

The answer to this question cannot be satisfactory without understanding the conceptual differences between the two measures. Mathematically, one measure is the square of the other. If all values of standard deviation are greater than one, this would make the variance a magnified measure of variability. However, this is not true since the values of standard deviation can be less than one, which makes the variance a shrinking measure of variability.

As one look at the use of the standard deviation and the variance throughout this book, one will find that there are unique utilizations of each measure that cannot be substituted for using the other measure. For example, the empirical rule uses factors of the standard deviation to determine the areas under the normal curve (see Chapter 3 and 6). The standard deviation is also used in establishing confidence intervals as a key factor in

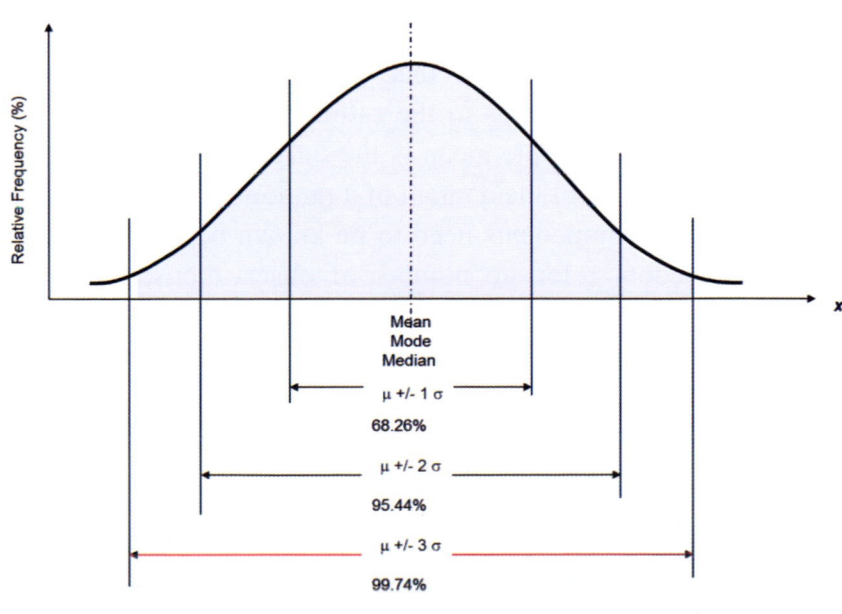

The Empirical Rule

determining the standard error (see chapter 6 and 8). The variance, on the other hand has a very unique utilization, particularly in dealing with various sources of variability as discussed in Chapter 11 under the topic of analysis of variance. In this regard, it is well known that variability cannot be subtracted; it can only be added. The addition of different variability sources can only be achieved through an addition of the variance components associated with these sources. Another important difference between the standard deviation and the variance is that the standard deviation is expressed in the same units as the mean is, whereas the variance is expressed in squared units.

Example 15.3: In Chapter 2, the quantity '*n*-1' was used instead of the quantity '*n*' in calculating the standard deviation or variance for small sample size ($n < 30$). In Chapter 8 and 9, the value of '*n*-1'was used as the degree of freedom associated with the variable. The question is 'what is the significance of the value of '*n*-1?'

Solution:

Recall that sample variance is calculated from

$$s^2 = \frac{\sum_1^n (x_i - \bar{X})^2}{n-1}$$

A simple answer to this question is that using a divisor n instead of n-1 will tend to produce an underestimate of the population variance σ^2. Since the sample variance s^2 is primarily used to estimate population variance σ^2, (n-1) is preferred to n in determining sample variance, particularly when the sample is small.

The quantity '*n*-1' is called the degree of freedom. In statistics, the number of degrees of freedom is the number of values in the final calculation of a statistic that are free to vary. In general, the degrees of freedom of an estimate of a parameter is equal to the number of independent scores that go into the estimate minus the number of parameters used as intermediate steps in the estimation of the parameter itself (which, in sample variance, is one, since the sample mean is the only intermediate step. Mathematically, degree of freedom is the dimension of the domain of a random vector, or essentially the number of 'free' components: how many components need to be known before the vector is fully determined. When the degree of freedom refers to number of observations, this means that the first '*n*-1' observations have freedom to be whatever value they wish, but the nth value has no freedom. It must be whatever value forces the sum of deviation from the mean to equal zero.

Another way to address this question is through the expected value of the sample variance. This point is illustrated mathematically below:

We learned from the central limit theorem (Chapter 7) that the expected value of the sample average is $E(\bar{X}) = \mu$ and the variance of sample means is $V(\bar{X}) = \frac{\sigma^2}{n}$.

From the analysis of variance (Chapter 11), the variance of a sample is derived from the sum of squares of the deviations of individual values $x_1, x_2, \ldots\ldots, x_n$ from the sample mean $\bar{X}$:

$$s^2 = \sum_{1}^{n} (x_i - \bar{X})^2$$

A simple manipulation of the above expression yields:

$$s^2 = \sum_{1}^{n} [(x_i - \mu) - (\bar{X} - \mu)]^2$$

$$s^2 = \sum_{1}^{n} [(x_i - \mu)^2 - 2(x_i - \mu)(\bar{X} - \mu) + (\bar{X} - \mu)^2]$$

$$s^2 = \sum_{1}^{n} [(x_i - \mu)^2 - 2(x_i - \mu)(\bar{X} - \mu) + (\bar{X} - \mu)^2]$$

$$= \sum (x_i - \mu)^2 - 2n(\bar{X} - \mu) \sum_{1}^{n} (x_i - \mu) + n(\bar{X} - \mu)^2$$

$$= \sum (x_i - \mu)^2 - 2n(\bar{X} - \mu)^2 \times 0 + n(\bar{X} - \mu)^2$$

$$s^2 = \sum (x_i - \mu)^2 - n(\bar{X} - \mu)^2$$

Accordingly, the expected value of the sample variance is:

$$E(s^2) = \sum_{1}^{n} Var(x_i) - nVar(\bar{X})$$

$$E(s^2) = n\sigma^2 - n.\frac{\sigma^2}{n} = (n-1)\sigma^2$$

Or

$$\sigma^2 = E\left(\frac{s^2}{n-1}\right)$$

Example 15.4: In Chapter 2, the threshold between a small sample and a large sample was 30 observations. A small sample was considered as the sample that has less than 30 observations ($n < 30$) and a sample of 30 or more was considered a large sample. The question is 'why is 30 the "magic number" for sample size?'

Solution:

A simple answer to this question is that as the sample size approaches 30, the confidence limits on the variance and the margins of error in estimating population mean begin to stabilize. To elaborate further on the question, let us take two examples:

Example 1: In this example, we will attempt to estimate the variance of a population using the sample variance and the critical value of χ^2 (section 8.6.2, Chapter 8) given the following sample statistics:

Sample variance $= s^2 = 25$, $\alpha = 0.05$

In this case, the level $100(1-\alpha)\%$ confidence interval for σ^2 is

$$\frac{(n-1)s^2}{\chi^2_{\frac{\alpha}{2}}} < \sigma^2 < \frac{(n-1)s^2}{\chi^2_{1-\frac{\alpha}{2}}}$$

$$\frac{(n-1)(25)}{\chi^2_{\frac{\alpha}{2}}} < \sigma^2 < \frac{(n-1)(25)}{\chi^2_{1-\frac{\alpha}{2}}}$$

In the above inequality, the confidence interval is calculated using the values of $\chi^2_{\frac{\alpha}{2}}$ and $\chi^2_{1-\frac{\alpha}{2}}$. These values will vary with the value of degree of freedom (n-1) at $\alpha = 0.05$. Table 15.3 shows the confidence limits at different values of n or degrees of freedom (df). A close examination of these values indicates that as n or df increases, the rate of change in the values of the confidence limits decreases significantly. This is particularly true for values of n greater than 30. This point is also illustrated in Figure 15.3.

Table 15.3 Values of lower and upper limits of estimated variance at different values of sample size (n), $s^2 = 25$, and $\alpha = 0.05$

n	Df	s^2	confidence	$\chi^2_{1-\frac{\alpha}{2}}$	$\chi^2_{\frac{\alpha}{2}}$	Lower Limit (LL)	Upper Limit (UL)	Difference (UL-LL)
4	3	25	0.95	0.22	9.35	8.02	340.91	332.89
5	4	25	0.95	0.48	11.14	8.98	208.33	199.36
6	5	25	0.95	0.83	12.38	10.10	150.60	140.51
7	6	25	0.95	1.24	14.45	10.38	120.97	110.59
...	...	...	...	...	...	...	...	...
...	...	...	...	...	...	...	...	...
...	...	...	...	...	...	...	...	...
20	19	25	0.95	8.91	32.85	14.46	53.31	38.85
25	24	25	0.95	9.59	34.17	17.56	62.57	45.01
30	29	25	0.95	13.12	40.65	17.84	55.26	37.42
40	39	25	0.95	16.79	46.98	20.75	58.07	37.32
...	...	...	...	...	...	...	...	...
80	79	25	0.95	48.76	95.02	20.79	40.50	19.72
90	89	25	0.95	57.15	106.63	20.87	38.93	18.07
100	99	25	0.95	65.65	118.14	20.95	37.70	16.75
101	100	25	0.95	74.22	129.56	19.30	33.68	14.39

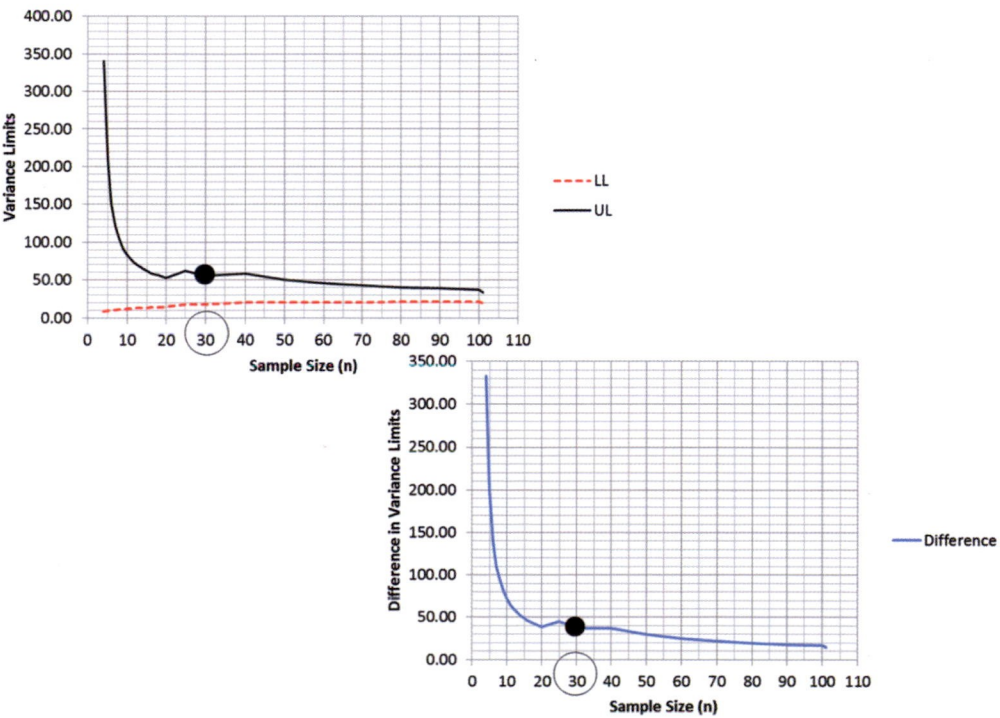

Figure 15.3 Stabilization of Variance Confidence Limits at about n = 30

859

Example 2: In this example, we will attempt to estimate the mean of a population of unknown standard deviation from a small sample.

Sample statistics are as follows: mean = $\bar{X} = 20$, standard deviation = s = 2, and $\alpha = 0.05$

In this case, the mean of the population is estimated as follows (section 8.3.3.2, Chapter 8):

$$\mu = \bar{X} \pm t \frac{s}{\sqrt{n}}$$

Or

$$\mu = 20 \pm t \frac{2}{\sqrt{n}}$$

The margin of error $t \frac{2}{\sqrt{n}}$ will vary with the value of the t statistic, which depends on the values of the degree of freedom (n -1) at $\alpha = 0.05$. Table 15.4 shows the values of the margin of error at different values of n or degrees of freedom (df). A close examination of these values indicates that as n or df increases, the rate of change in the values of the margin of error decreases significantly. This is particularly true for values of n greater than 30. This point is also illustrated in Figure 15.5.

Table 15.4 Values of margin of error at different values of sample size (n), s = 2, and $\alpha = 0.05$

n	df	t at 95%	t at 99%	E (95%)	E (99%)
4	3	3.18	5.84	3.18	5.84
5	4	2.78	4.60	2.48	4.12
6	5	2.57	4.03	2.10	3.29
....	....	....	....	....	....
....	....	....	....	....	....
....	....	....	....	....	....
25	24	2.06	2.80	0.83	1.12
26	25	2.06	2.79	0.81	1.09
27	26	2.06	2.78	0.79	1.07
28	27	2.05	2.77	0.78	1.05
29	28	2.05	2.76	0.76	1.03
30	29	2.05	2.76	0.75	1.01
31	30	2.04	2.75	0.73	0.99
41	40	2.02	2.70	0.63	0.84

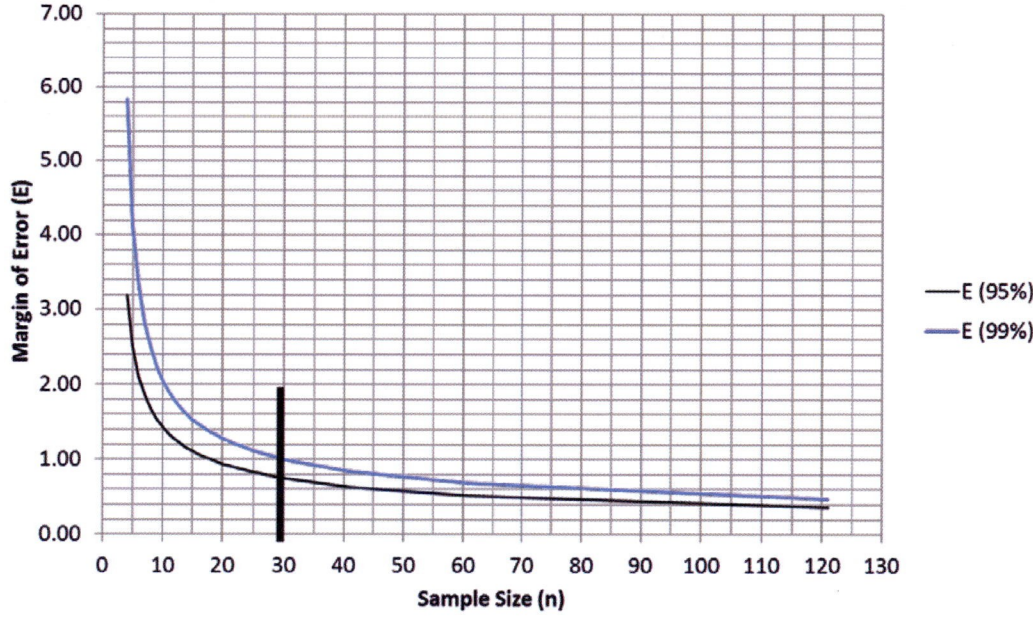

Figure 15.4 Stabilization of the Margin of Error at about n = 30

In light of the above examples, the agreement on the threshold of *n* = 30 is largely attributed to the stabilization of the rate of change in confidence limits and margin of errors for sample sizes above 30.

Working Problem 15.1:
In previous chapters, you learned about the standard deviation and the standard
Error? What is the difference between these two statistics? Which one is more
Useful in practical applications and why?

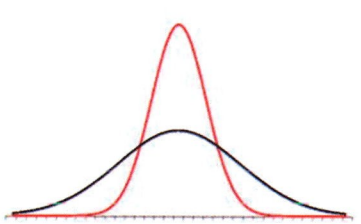

Working Problem 15.2:
In order to apply the Empirical Rule in the real world, you need to know the mean and the standard deviation. Suppose you were trying to use the Empirical rule to estimate the grades of the population of students taking a biology course in a college. You asked about the population mean grade, and the answer was 80%. You asked about the population standard deviation, but the person you asked did not know what do you mean by a standard deviation. You then Indicated that it is a measure of variability. The person then answered: if you mean variability the range of grades is from 20% to 100%. Can you still use the Empirical Rule? Explain how.

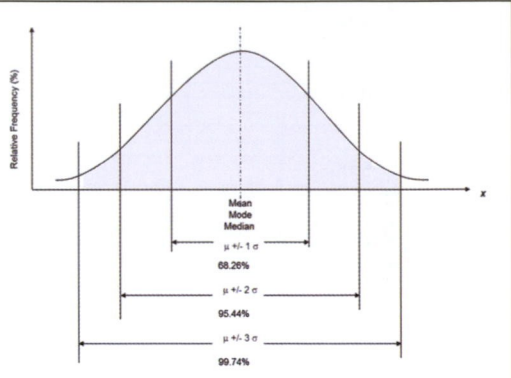

Working Problem 15.3:
In correlation and regression analysis, we use two important statistics: (1) the coefficient of correlation, r, and (2) the coefficient of determination, r^2. As you can see, one is the square of the other. Discuss the conceptual differences between these two statistics?

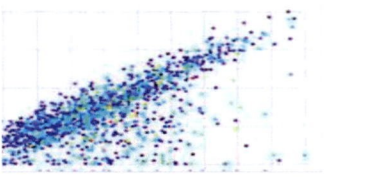

15.3.5 A critical thinker should make efforts to improve the existing thinking process

When a critical thinker reads an article, it will always be useful to play the role of the writer or the researcher and see if the information can be presented in a better format. In other words, to be a reliable critic you have to imagine assuming the task and see how it can be done differently. The following questions represent good guidelines in this regard:

- Is the problem being studied clearly identified?
- Are the variables being listed in the study measurable (quantitative) or are they of qualitative nature?
- Are the analyses suggested in the study appropriate?
- Are there additional analyses to the ones suggested in the study?
- Are there additional interpretive aspects of the analysis outcomes?
- Are the conclusions meaningful? Do they relate to the objectives of the study?
- Can decisions be made or further studies should be performed?

15.3.6 A critical thinker asks why, and not just how

Some experts believe that the problems that some students have in learning mathematics is the focus on 'how' and the negligence of 'why.' When the mathematical branch is statistics, learning 'why' should come before learning 'how.' In this regard, the objectives of the analysis should be clearly stated before analytical steps are used. It is also important to emphasize the fact that statistics may not reveal causes and effects and human judgment is critical. Indeed, not every correlation proves causation. You may find a high positive correlation between the hours a student spend studying and the student's grade, but this does not mean that every student who studies many hours will likely earn a high grade.

Working Problem 15.4:
One correlation analysis yielded a very high correlation coefficient of 0.95 between the consumption of ice cream in Myrtle Beach, South Carolina in the summer time and the rate of crime in Atlanta, Georgia during summer. Can you explain the cause of this high correlation?

15.3.7 A critical thinker should look for bias

In some situations the analyst may have a pre-bias to certain opinions or findings even before performing the analysis. In these situations, the analyst may not change the findings but rather emphasize the findings that support his/her bias or inclined views. A critical thinker should be able to look for this bias, detect it, and explore it. This aspect is critical in today's world of business and politics as many organizations conduct studies for promotional or campaigning purposes and not necessarily for the sake of finding facts. Consideration of bias is even more critical in lawsuits where there are two sides to a story, with each providing supporting evidences to make a favorable case. In these situations, the winner is often the expert witness that uses critical thinking to make the case.

15.4 Case studies for writing assignments in statistics

In practice, there are numerous applications in which statistics represent the central task and the driving force to yield meaningful conclusions and make critical decisions. In this section, we provide few examples to encourage the reader to look for more applications and sources of data. In today's information era, students and researchers can find numerous sources of data that are produced and updated periodically. Examples of these sources are listed below.

- Bureau of Economic Analysis (http://www.bea.gov/)

- Bureau of Justice Statistics (http://bjs.ojp.usdoj.gov/)

- Bureau of Labor Statistics (http://www.bls.gov/)

- Bureau of Transportation Statistics (http://www.rita.dot.gov/bts/)

- Census Bureau (http://www.census.gov/)

- Economic Research Service (http://www.ers.usda.gov/)

- Energy Information Administration (http://www.eia.gov/)

- National Agricultural Statistics Service (http://www.nass.usda.gov/)

- National Center for Education Statistics (http://nces.ed.gov/)

- National Center for Health Statistics (http://www.cdc.gov/nchs/Default.htm)

- Statistics of Income (IRS) (http://www.irs.gov/)

- Labor Market Information Agencies (http://www.bls.gov/bls/ofolist.htm)

- Health and Safety Executive (http://www.hse.gov.uk/statistics/sources.htm)

- Online resources for education and social science librarians

  (http://crln.acrl.org/content/71/1/16.full)

Case Study 1: Traffic congestion

A recent report conducted by the United States Treasury Department in 2011 has found that traffic congestion wastes 1.9 billion gallons of gasoline annually. The report shows that, in 90 percent of American households, one out every seven dollars goes towards transportation costs, with the average American family spending roughly $7,600 annually on transportation. Interestingly, this is more than is spent on food and double what it is spent towards out-of-pocket health care costs. The report also found that the average city motorist pays more than $400 per year in additional vehicle maintenance due to poor roads. Some motorists in major urban areas such as Los Angeles and New York pay upwards of $756 annually. Perhaps even more interesting — and not that surprising — in the Treasury Department findings is the number of gross domestic product spent on the nation's transportation infrastructure. The U.S spends about 2 percent of the gross domestic product on infrastructure. Compared to China's 9 percent, India's 8 percent, and Europe at 5 percent, that isn't exactly stellar. Another report by the Texas Transportation Institute estimates that congestion cost the national economy $87 billion per year. This is less than 1% of the US GNP ($14 trillion per year). While the Treasury Department was hard at work further establishing why we all hate traffic so much, it also took the time to point out one positive: during the past fifteen years, the amount of people taking to mass transit systems, like heavy and light rail, has increased from nearly 8 billion in 1996 to 10.4 billion in 2011.

Write an essay about traffic congestion in the U.S. in which you propose a statistical procedure to analyze the problem of traffic congestion.

Case Study 2: Retirement planning

As we get older, we should plan for retirement. There are many ways to plan for the golden years of retirement. These include:

- Start saving, keep saving, and adhere to your goals
- Know your retirement needs
- Contribute to your employer's retirement savings plan
- Learn about your employer's pension plan
- Plan on where to live during your golden years

The focus of this assignment is places to retire in the U.S.A.

According to an MSNBC News survey in 2012(http://www.msn.com/ &TopRetirements.com), the 10 worst States to retire in the U.S.A. are as illustrated below. Write a statistical report on some of the main reasons these States were considered as the top 10 worst States to retire. Key questions that you may choose to address include:

No. 1: Connecticut   No. 2: Illinois   No. 3: Rhode Island   No. 4: Vermont   No. 5: Massachusetts

- What are the factors determining the quality of living for a retired person or a retired couple?
- What type of data would you select about different states in the context of retirement?

No. 6: New Jersey   No. 7: Minnesota   No. 8: New York   No. 9: Maine   No. 10: Wisconsin

- Given the fact that most retirees are likely to have lower income than what they were making prior to retirement, how do you see the effect of the living cost on determining the 10 worst States to retire?

Case Study 3: Global warming

Global warming represents a continuing scientific debate. It began with data that suggests a rising in the average temperature of Earth's atmosphere and oceans, which started to increase in the late 19th century. This temperature rising is projected to continue by the estimates and the prediction models of some statisticians. Since the early 20th century, Earth's average surface temperature has increased by about 0.8 °C (1.4 °F), with about two thirds of the increase occurring since 1980. Many scientists believe that the primary cause of global warming is the increase in the concentrations of greenhouse gases produced by human activities. Discuss whether you agree with the published causes of global warming. Use data from various sources to support your views.

How can global warming be real when there's so much snow?

It has nothing to do with the heavy snow that you see outside your windows. This heavy snow is merely a snapshot of a much bigger picture.

Planet warming is all about trend lines, and you will understand trend lines when you learn statistics.

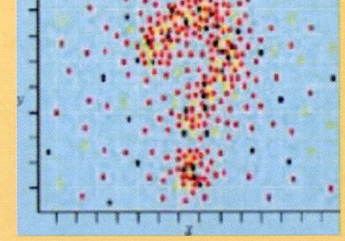  

Case Study 4: Detecting politicians' claims

Politicians tend to use data to support their views on many issues during political debates, and to reflect their knowledge of the state of the Nation. Some politicians, however, manipulate data to serve their political agenda. For example, during the Obama-Romney U.S. presidential debates and party conventions in 2012, the candidates made many claims that analysts investigated very carefully. Examples of these claims are listed below:

Do politicians lie?

This is a Rhetorical question; very much like "Is the Pope Catholic"? Or "will you die someday"? We live in a world where the thorniest policy issues increasingly boil down to arguments over what the source of data used in making the argument. If we don't understand statistics, we don't know what's going on, and we may be misled. When it comes to politics, it is important that you can't tell when you're being lied to.

- Romney claimed that 'the median income in the U.S. has declined 10 percent from 2009 to 2010. Analysts found out that between 2007 and 2010, the median income declined by 6.3 percent, while between 2006 and 2010, the median declined by 5.1 percent, according to the U.S. Census Bureau.

- Obama claimed that after a decade of decline, the U.S. created over half a million manufacturing jobs in the last two and half years. Analysts turned to data from the Bureau of Labor Statistics, the federal government's official source for employment numbers. They used seasonally adjusted statistics for manufacturing jobs. During the period Obama chose - from January 2010 to July 2012- manufacturing jobs began to rise again, by 532,000. That's 'over half a million manufacturing jobs," as Obama put it.

- During the debate, Obama claimed that 'Right now, American oil production is the highest that it's been in eight years.' Analysts looked at crude oil extracted from U.S. territory, rather than natural gas or other petroleum products, using data from the Energy Information Administration, the federal government's official office for energy statistics. They found that in 2003, the U.S. produced 2,073,453,000 barrels of oil. In 2010, the most recent year available when Obama made the claim, the U.S. produced 1,998,137,000 barrels of oil. U.S. oil production was not as high between 2004 and 2009.

- Romney claimed that, 'In the richest country in the history of the world, Obama's economy has crushed the middle class,...family income has fallen by $4,000, but health insurance premiums are higher, food prices are higher, utility bills are higher and gasoline prices have doubled.' Analysts found that under Obama, electricity, heating oil, propane and water-sewer-trash prices did rise, as Romney indicated. But natural gas and telephone prices fell.' Analysts also noted that the phenomenon is not unique to Obama. In the comparable three years of the Bush presidency, three of the six utility prices also rose.

Write a report about '*checking the facts on politicians' claims about different issues*' in which you explain how reliable statistics can assist detecting political claims.

Case Study 5: Life expectancy

Life expectancy from birth is a frequently utilized and analyzed component of demographic data for the countries of the world. It represents the average life span of a newborn and is an indicator of the overall health of a country. Life expectancy can fall due to problems like poor health care, high crime rates, wars, diseases, and poor life style. In general, improvements in health and welfare increase life expectancy. The higher the life expectancy, the better shape a country is in. Examples of data by country, gender, and year are listed below.

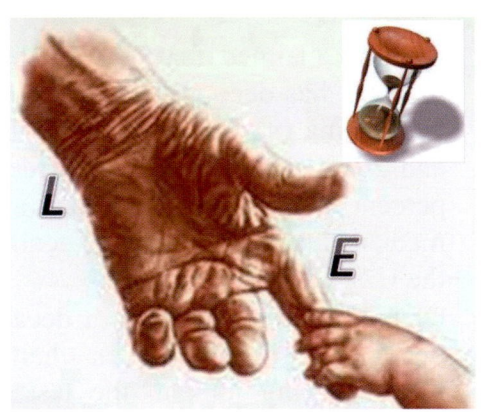

Life expectancy at birth: selected countries and territories, selected years 1980–2004

Country	Male						Female					
	1980	1990	1995	2000	2002	2004	1980	1990	1995	2000	2002	2004
Japan	73.4	75.9	76.4	77.7	78.3	78.6	78.8	81.9	82.9	84.6	85.2	85.6
Israel	72.2	75.1	75.5	76.7	77.5	77.9	75.8	78.5	79.5	80.9	81.5	82.2
Switzerland	72.8	74	75.3	76.9	77.8	78.6	79.6	80.7	81.7	82.6	83	83.7
Hong Kong	71.6	74.6	76	78	78.6	79	77.9	80.3	81.5	83.9	84.5	84.7
Costa Rica	71.9	74.7	74	75.4	76.2	76.4	77	79.1	78.6	80.2	81	80.7
England and Wales	70.8	73.1	74.3	75.6	76.1	76.8	76.8	78.6	79.5	80.3	80.7	81.1
Canada	71.7	74.4	75.1	76.7	77.2	77.8	78.9	80.8	81.1	81.9	82.1	82.6
Sweden	72.8	74.8	76.2	77.4	77.7	78.4	78.8	80.4	81.4	82	82.1	82.7
Germany	69.6	72	73.3	75	75.4	75.7	76.1	78.4	79.7	81	81.2	81.4
Northern Ireland	68.3	72.1	73.5	74.8	75.6	76	75	78	78.9	79.8	80.4	80.8
Scotland	69	71.1	72.1	73.1	73.5	74.2	75.2	76.7	77.7	78.6	78.9	79.3
Bulgaria	68.5	68.3	67.4	68.5	68.9	69.1	73.9	75	74.9	75.1	75.6	76.3
Romania	66.6	66.6	65.5	67.8	67.4	68.3	71.9	73.1	73.5	74.8	74.8	75.6
Czech Republic	66.8	67.6	69.7	71.6	72.1	72.6	73.9	75.4	76.6	78.4	78.7	79
Puerto Rico	70.8	69.1	69.6	72.3	73.7	74.1	76.9	77.2	78.9	81	82	82.3
United States	70	71.8	72.5	74.1	74.5	75.2	77.4	78.8	78.9	79.5	79.9	80.4
Denmark	71.2	72	72.7	74.5	74.8	75.2	77.3	77.7	77.8	79.3	79.5	79.9

Table (Cont'd)

Country	Male						Female					
	1980	1990	1995	2000	2002	2004	1980	1990	1995	2000	2002	2004
Austria	69	72.2	73.3	75.1	75.8	76.4	76.1	78.8	79.9	81.1	81.7	82.1
Spain	72.5	73.3	74.3	75.8	76.1	77.2	78.6	80.3	81.5	82.5	82.9	83.7
Australia	71	73.9	75	76.6	77.4	78.1	78.1	80.1	80.8	82	82.6	83
Finland	69.2	70.9	72.8	74.2	74.9	75.3	77.6	78.9	80.2	81	81.5	82.3
Portugal	67.7	70.4	71.6	73.2	73.8	74.5	75.2	77.4	78.7	80	80.5	81
Poland	66	66.2	67.6	69.7	70.4	70.7	74.4	75.2	76.4	78	78.7	79.2
Hungary	65.5	65.1	65.3	67.4	68.4	68.6	72.7	73.7	74.5	75.9	76.7	76.9
Belgium	70	72.7	73.4	74.6	75.1	75.6	76.8	79.4	80.7	80.9	81.7	81.5
France	70.2	72.8	73.9	75.3	75.8	76.7	78.4	80.9	81.8	82.7	83	83.8
Greece	72.2	74.6	75	75.5	76.2	76.6	76.8	79.5	80.3	80.5	81.1	81.5
Norway	72.3	73.4	74.8	76	76.4	77.5	79.2	79.8	80.8	81.4	81.5	82.3
Netherlands	72.5	73.8	74.6	75.5	76	76.9	79.2	80.9	80.4	80.5	80.7	81.4
Russian Federation	61.4	63.8	58.3	59.2	58.9	59.1	73	74.4	71.7	72.4	72	72.4

Write an essay about life expectancy using the data listed above (From *Deaths: Final Data for 2006, by Melonie Heron, Donna L. Hoyert, Sherry L. Murphy, Jiaquan Xu, Kenneth D. Kochanek, and Betzaida Tejada. Division of Vital Statistics-National- Vital Statistics Reports, Volume 57, Number 14, April 17, 2009*) or other relevant data in which you address key questions related to life expectancy such as:

- What are the key factors influencing life expectancy?
- In addition to those in the tables above, what other data that you believe are relevant to the subject of life expectancy?
- Does Nation's wealth automatically lead to high life expectancy?

Case Study 6: Gross domestic product (GDP)

The data below represents the Gross Domestic Product (GDP) of 8 different countries in 2010 and annual salaries of the presidents of these countries http://www.economist.com/node/16525240

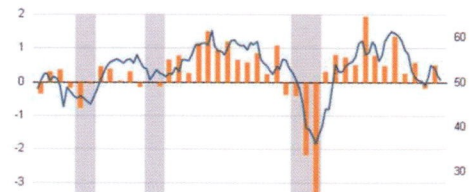

Country	President	GDP	Year	Annual Salary
Singapore	Lee Hsien Loong	$291,900,000,000.00	2010	$2,460,000
U.S.A.	Barack Obama	$14,660,000,000,000.00	2010	$400,000
Australia	Kevin Rudd	$882,400,000,000	2010	$286,752
Germany	Angela Merkel	$2,940,000,000,000	2010	$283,608
France	Nicolas Sarkozy	$2,145,000,000,000	2010	$304,800
Canada	Stephen Harper	$1,330,000,000,000	2010	$296,400
UK	Gordon Brown	$2,173,000,000,000	2010	$215,390
Russia	Vladimir Putin	$2,223,000,000,000	2010	$115,000

Write a short essay about Gross Domestic Product (GDP) in relation to president's salary in which you may address the following points:

(a) Why do different countries have different GDP?

(b) Why do different presidents have different salaries?

(c) Verify whether the annual salary of Lee Hsien Loong was true or not. If it was true, explain why it is substantially higher than other presidents' salaries.

(d) Excluding Lee Hsien Loong salary (as an outlier) calculate the mean, the median, the range, and standard deviation of president salary.

(e) The overall average of the basic salary of president excluding the president of Singapore's basic salary is $221,244 and the standard deviation is $137,157 (from the chart below) compare the salaries of the presidents in the table below excluding the president of Singapore using the z-score.

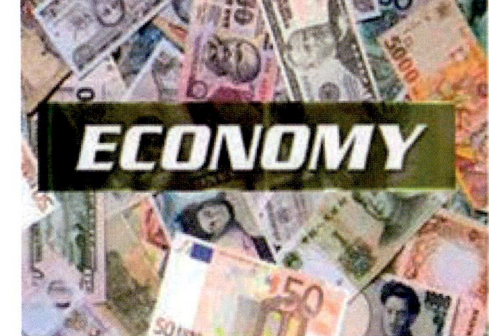

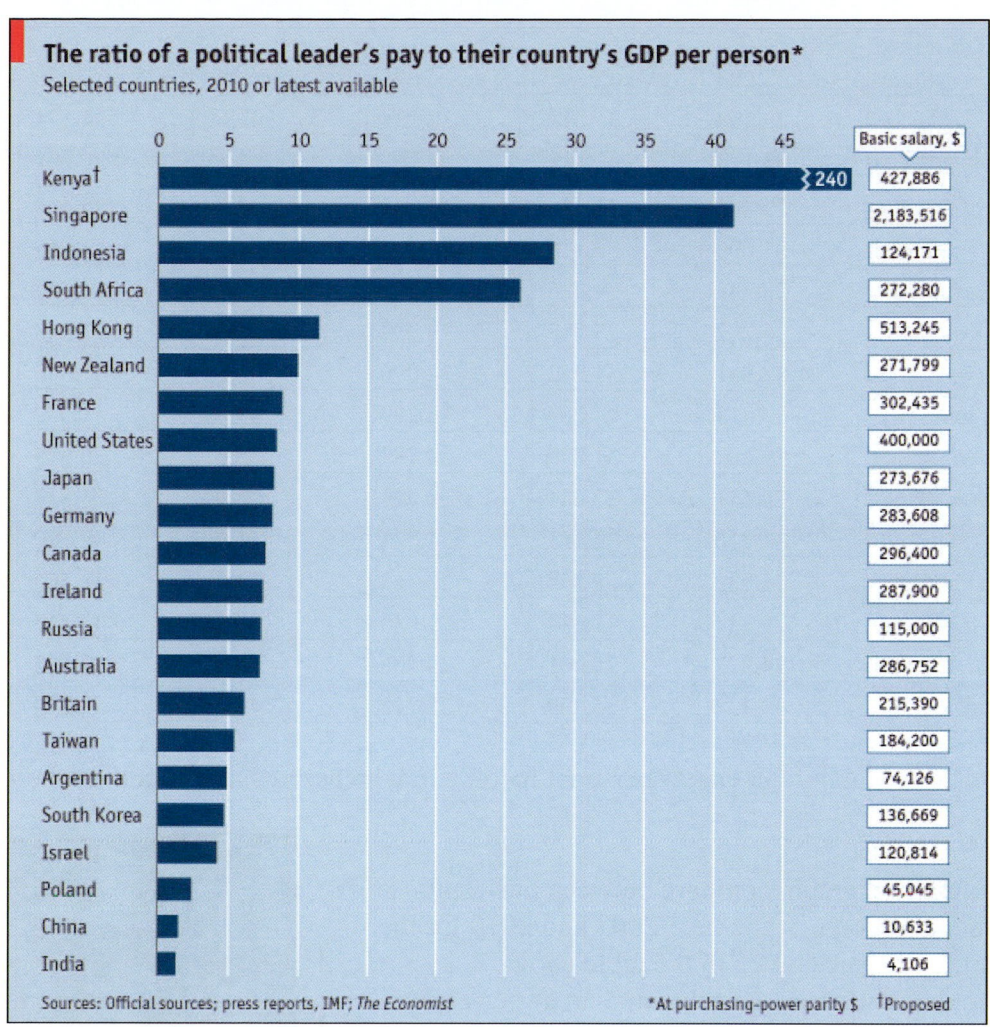

The ratio of a political leader's pay to their country's GDP per person*
Selected countries, 2010 or latest available

Country	Ratio	Basic salary, $
Kenya†	240	427,886
Singapore	41	2,183,516
Indonesia	28	124,171
South Africa	26	272,280
Hong Kong	11	513,245
New Zealand	10	271,799
France	8	302,435
United States	8	400,000
Japan	8	273,676
Germany	8	283,608
Canada	7	296,400
Ireland	7	287,900
Russia	6	115,000
Australia	7	286,752
Britain	6	215,390
Taiwan	5	184,200
Argentina	5	74,126
South Korea	5	136,669
Israel	4	120,814
Poland	3	45,045
China	1	10,633
India	1	4,106

Sources: Official sources; press reports, IMF; *The Economist*   *At purchasing-power parity $ †Proposed

Case Study 7: Per capita personal income

The data below represents five-year of per capita personal income of a sample of U.S. States computed using midyear population estimates of the Bureau of the Census. The source is U.S. Department of Commerce, Bureau of Economic Analysis, Survey of Current Business (Per Capita Personal Income by State —
Infoplease.com http://www.infoplease.com/ipa/A0104652.html#ixzz1hTnKgy87)

State	Year 2003	Year 2005	Year 2006	Year 2009	Year 2010
Alaska	33,568	35,612	38,138	42,603	44,174
Connecticut	43,173	47,819	50,762	54,397	56,001
Georgia	29,442	31,121	32,095	33,786	35,490
Illinois	33,690	36,120	38,409	41,411	43,159
Indiana	28,783	31,276	32,288	33,725	34,943
Kentucky	26,252	28,513	29,729	31,883	33,348
Maine	28,831	31,252	32,095	36,745	37,300
Massachusetts	39,815	44,289	46,299	49,875	51,552
Missouri	29,252	31,899	32,789	35,676	36,979
New Mexico	25,541	27,644	29,929	32,992	33,837
Rhode Island	31,916	36,153	37,523	41,003	42,579
South Carolina	26,132	28,352	29,767	31,799	33,163
South Dakota	29,234	31,614	32,030	36,935	33,865
Utah	24,977	28,061	29,406	30,875	32,595
Washington	33,332	35,409	38,212	41,751	43,564

Write a short essay about per capita personal income in which you should include the following points:

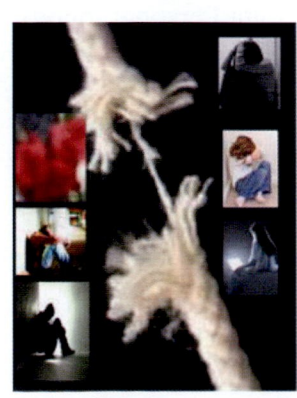

(a) Using a line graph, compare between per-capita personal income of the year 2003 and 2010 for the sample of States given in the table above.
(b) Calculate the mean, and the median of per-capita personal income of the year 2003 and 2010.
(c) Calculate the range, the standard deviation, and the variance of per-capita personal income of the year 2003 and 2010.
(d) Do you see a difference in per-capita personal income between the 2003 and the 2010 year?

Case Study 8: Suicide rates

Suicide is the act of deliberately killing oneself. In 2009, the average world suicide rate was 10.07 per 100,000 people (about 0.01%). This small percent translates to roughly one million suicides worldwide each year and 60% increase in worldwide suicide rates in the last 45 years according to the World Health Organization. Data on suicide rates are always available and can be obtained from many sources. One of the main sources is the World Health Organization ('Suicide rates per 100,000 by country, year and sex (table).' World Health Organization.

2011. http://www.who.int/mental_health/prevention/suicide_rates/en/. Retrieved 2012-01-26).

Suicides per 100,000 people per year

Rank	Country	Male	Female	Average	Year
1	Lithuania[2] (more info)	54.6	11.6	31.6	2011
2	South Korea[3] (more info)	41.4	21.0	31.2	2010
3	Guyana (more info)	39.0	13.4	26.4	2006
4	Kazakhstan (more info)	43.0	9.4	25.6	2008
5	Belarus[4][5]			25.3	2010
6	Hungary[6]	37.4	8.5	21.7	2009
7	Japan (more info)[7]	33.5	14.6	23.8	2011
8	Latvia	33.8	4.0	17.5	2009
9	People's Republic of China[8] (more info)			22.23	2011
10	Slovenia	29.3	3.0	17.2	2010
11	Sri Lanka[9] (more info)			21.6	1996
12	Russia[10]			21.4	2011
13	Ukraine (more info)	37.8	7.0	21.2	2009
14	Serbia and Montenegro	28.4	11.1	19.5	2006
15	Estonia	20.6	7.3	18.1	2008
16	Switzerland	15.7	6.5	11.1	2007
17	Croatia[11]	30.2	10.0	19.7	2002
18	Belgium[note 1][6]	26.5	9.3	17.6	2009
19	Finland[12]	25.7	8.1	16.8	2010
20	Moldova	30.1	5.6	17.4	2008
21	France (more info)	23.5	7.5	15.0	2009
22	Uruguay	26.0	6.3	15.8	2004
23	South Africa[13]	25.3	5.6	15.4	2005
24	Austria	20.9	5.7	12.8	2009
25	Poland	28.0	3.8	15.4	2010
26	Hong Kong	19.0	10.7	14.6	2009
27	Suriname	23.9	4.8	14.4	2005
28	Czech Republic	22.1	4.1	12.8	2010
29	New Zealand[14]	20.3	6.5	13.2	2008
30	Sweden[15]	21.4	9.2	15.3	2011
31	Cuba	19.0	5.5	12.3	2008
32	Bulgaria	18.8	6.2	12.3	2008
33	Romania	21.0	3.5	12.0	2009
34	Norway	17.3	6.5	11.9	2009
35	Denmark	17.5	6.4	11.9	2006
36	Ireland	19.0	4.7	11.8	2009
37	Bosnia and Herzegovina[16]	20.3	6.3	13.3	2011
38	United States[17] (more info)	19.2	5.0	12.0	2009
39	Canada	17.3	5.4	11.3	2004
40	Iceland[18]	17.9	4.5	11.3	2009
41	Chile	18.2	4.2	11.1	2007
42	Trinidad and Tobago	17.9	3.8	10.7	2006
43	India (more info)	13.0	7.8	10.5	2009
44	Singapore	12.9	7.7	10.3	2006
45	Slovakia[6]	19.8	1.9	10.3	2009
46	Australia[19]	14.9	4.5	9.7	2009
47	Germany[6]	15.6	4.7	9.9	2009
48	Kyrgyzstan	14.1	3.6	8.8	2009
49	Turkmenistan	13.8	3.5	8.6	1998
50	Netherlands[6]	12.0	5.0	8.5	2009
51	Republic of Macedonia[6]	12.6	3.9	8.0	2009
52	El Salvador	12.9	3.6	8.0	2008
53	Portugal[6]	13.2	3.4	7.9	2008
54	Zimbabwe	10.6	5.2	7.9	1990
55	Luxembourg[6]	13.2	2.9	7.8	2008
56	Thailand	12.0	3.8	7.8	2002
57	Argentina	12.6	3.0	7.7	2008
58	Spain	11.9	3.4	7.6	2008
59	Puerto Rico	13.2	2.0	7.4	2005
60	Ecuador	10.5	3.6	7.1	2009
61	United Kingdom	10.9	3.0	6.9	2009
62	Mauritius	11.8	1.9	6.8	2008
63	Iran[20]	7.6	5.1	6.4	2001
64	Italy	10.0	2.8	6.3	2007
65	Costa Rica	10.2	1.9	6.1	2009
66	Israel[21]	9.9	2.1	5.8	2007
67	Nicaragua	9.0	2.6	5.8	2006
68	Panama	9.0	1.9	5.5	2008
69	Colombia	7.9	2.0	4.9	2007
70	Brazil	7.7	2.0	4.8	2008
71	Uzbekistan	7.0	2.3	4.7	2005

72	Seychelles	8.9	0.0	4.6	2008	93	The Bahamas	1.9	0.6	1.2	2005
73	Georgia	7.1	1.7	4.3	2009	94	Jordan	0.0	0.0	1.1	2009
74	Albania[22]	4.7	3.3	4.0	2003	95	Peru	1.1	0.6	0.9	2000
75	Mexico	6.8	1.3	4.0	2008	96	São Tomé and Príncipe	0.0	1.8	0.9	1987
76	Turkey[23]	5.36	2.50	3.94	2008	96	São Tomé and Príncipe	0.0	1.8	0.9	1987
77	Bahrain	4.0	3.5	3.8	2006	97	Pakistan [24]	3.4	0.5	0.88	2012
78	Belize	6.6	0.7	3.7	2008	98	Azerbaijan	1.0	0.3	0.6	2007
79	Saint Vincent and the Grenadines	5.4	1.9	3.7	2008	98	Azerbaijan	1.0	0.3	0.6	2007
80	Paraguay	5.1	2.0	3.6	2008	99	Maldives	0.7	0.0	0.3	2005
81	Cyprus[8]	5.9	1.3	3.6	2009	99	Maldives	0.7	0.0	0.3	2005
82	Guatemala	5.6	1.7	3.6	2008	100	Jamaica	0.3	0.0	0.1	1990
83	Barbados	7.3	0.0	3.5	2006	101	Syria	0.2	0.0	0.1	1985
84	Greece	6.1	1.0	3.5	2009	101	Syria	0.2	0.0	0.1	1985
85	Malta	5.9	1.0	3.4	2008	102	Egypt	0.1	0.0	0.1	2009
86	Venezuela	5.3	1.2	3.2	2007	103	Grenada	0.0	0.0	0.0	2008
87	Tajikistan	2.9	2.3	2.6	2001	103	Grenada	0.0	0.0	0.0	2008
88	Saint Lucia	4.9	0.0	2.4	2005	104	Honduras	0.0	0.0	0.0	1978
89	Dominican Republic	3.9	0.7	2.3	2005	105	Saint Kitts and Nevis	0.0	0.0	0.0	1995
90	Philippines	2.5	1.7	2.1	1993	106	Antigua and Barbuda	0.0	0.0	0.0	1995
91	Armenia	2.8	1.1	1.9	2008	106	Antigua and Barbuda	0.0	0.0	0.0	1995
92	Kuwait	1.9	1.7	1.8	2009	107	Haiti	0.0	0.0	0.0	2003

Write a short essay about suicide rates in which you may include the following points:

(a) What are the primary causes of suicide?
(b) Do the reasons for suicide vary with the country or the culture?

Case Study 9: Divorce rates

In the 2000s, many reports indicated that the U.S. national divorce rate was approximately 50%. This value was based on various forms of surveys made by specialized organizations (e.g. http://www.divorcereform.org/real.html). Some of these surveys are entirely subjective, and others are based on evaluation of available data. In either case, it is safe to consider this probability as highly subjective since most experts do not make these projections over time using consistent methods. Different people may interpret this value in many different ways. Some may see it as an alarming indication that the chance of marriage success is now about 50%; some may conclude that every 100 couples getting married today will likely to separate next year; and other may simply conclude that today's marriage is like coin tossing, with failure having an equal probability to success.

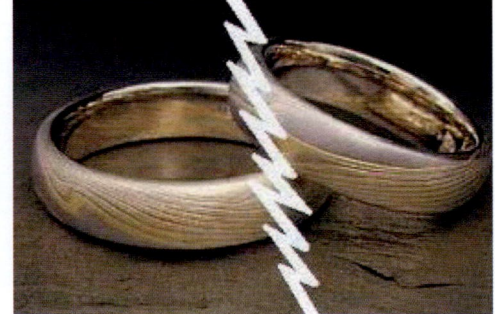

Different reasons why these probability values of divorce may be overestimated include:

- Divorce rate will likely depend on the background and culture of people
- Annual income can influence divorce rate
- Religion can be a factor
- Younger people are likely to get divorced faster than older people
- The initial reason for marriage can have a great effect on divorce
- There is high chance of long marriage survival for people that are educated, have good income, religious, twenty five years of age or older, and not having a baby prior to marriage

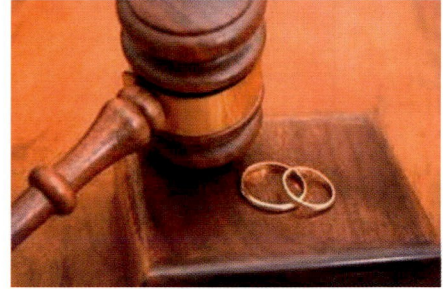

The point here is that when probability is subjective, it should be examined carefully and in the context of its sources. One should also consider all the surrounding factors associated with subjective probability. Using data from various sources of your choice, write a short essay about the current rate(s) of divorce or separation in the U.S., statistics associated with these rates; and possible causes of divorce or separation.

Case Study 10: Purchasing a stock

The decision to purchase a stock in the marketplace can't be made solely from a review of financial ratios. You should also evaluate other factors including subjective factors, such as the quality of management, prospects for the company's industry, and where the company stands in relation to competitors. Key points to consider in deciding to purchase a stock are: (a) behind every winning stock is a good company with a history of making money, (b) stocks that have produced good returns in the past are good candidates, (c) a formal stock selection

process ensures that you perform all the relevant checks, and (d) check the most important things first and leave nothing to chance. Analytically, there are many tools that can be used to purchase stocks. These include (http://www.stock-market-college.com/how-to-pick-winning-stocks.html): (1) stock screening tools, (2) key performance indicators, (3) stock charts, (4) profitability analysis, (5) financial health, (6) management assessment, (7) industry analysis, (8) company valuation, (9) portfolio analysis, and (10) investment decision tools.

Using reliable statistical tools, one can determine which stock to purchase based on payoff analysis. The illustrations below provide examples that can be useful in making stock purchasing decisions. Write an essay about the factors that should be taken into consideration in the decision making of stock purchasing. Focus on statistical tools that can be useful in this regard.

Can you make a wise stock purchase decision?

You have $1000 to invest. After searching for a number of stocks, you decided on considering three stocks: X-L Electronics, Ag-Commodity, and Soft-Tech. In a strong 'Bull' market (when stock prices increase significantly), your $1000 is estimated to become $1800, $1400, or $2500 at the end of the year with these three stocks, respectively. In a weak 'Bear' market (when stock prices decline), your $1000 is estimated to become $900, $1280, or $950 at the end of the year with these three stocks, respectively. A summary of these outcomes is listed in the so-called payoff table shown below. A payoff table consists of the so-called decision alternatives or acts. In this case, there are three alternatives S_1, S_2, and S_3. The estimated outcomes are called the states of nature as they represent uncontrolled future events. Let the bull market be represented by B_1 and the bear market by B_2.

Purchase	Bull Market (B_1)	Bear Market (B_2)
X-L Electronics (S_1)	$1800	$1050
Ag-Commodity (S_2)	$1400	$1000
Soft-Tech (S_3)	$2500	$800

If the payoff values were the only information available, what is the best choice that you would make?

Solution:

- You may make a conservative choice by selecting X-L Electronics. In this case, you will either make a big gain of $800 ($1800-$1000) in a Bull market, or a small gain of $50 ($1050-$1000) in a Bear market.

- If you have no fear, you may want to make a risky choice and select Soft-Tech, which allows you to more than doubling your $1000 investment in a year if the market is a Bull one, but there is a risk of a $200 loss in a Bear market. The third choice would be the Ag-Commodity in which you either make a $400 profit or make no gain.

Can you make a wise stock purchase decision?

Now, suppose you learned that the probability of a market rise next year is 0.40 and the probability of a market decline is 0.60. Assuming these speculations are largely realistic, combine the payoff table and the probability estimates (0.40 and .60) to arrive at the expected values of payoff of buying each of the three stocks. Note that expected payoff is also called expected monetary value, shortened to EMV. It can also be described as the mean payoff. An EMV is calculated as follows:

$$EMV(S_i) = \sum \left[P(B_j) \times V(S_i, B_j) \right]$$

EMV for X-L Electronics (S_1):

$$EMV(S_1) = \sum \left[P(B_j) \times V(S_1, B_j) \right] = 0.4 \times 1800 + 0.6 \times 1050 = \$1350$$

EMV for Ag-Commodity (S_2):

$$EMV(S_2) = \sum \left[P(B_j) \times V(S_2, B_j) \right] = 0.4 \times 1400 + 0.6 \times 1000 = \$1160$$

EMV for Soft-Tech (S_3):

$$EMV(S_3) = \sum \left[P(B_j) \times V(S_3, B_j) \right] = 0.4 \times 2500 + 0.6 \times 800 = \$1480$$

Purchase	Bull Market (B_1), $P =$ 0.4	Bear Market (B_2), $P =$ 0.6	Expected Payoff
X-L Electronics (S_1)	$1,800	$1,050	1350
Ag-Commodity (S_2)	$1,400	$1,000	1160
Soft-Tech (S_3)	$2,500	$800	1480

To explain one expected monetary value calculation, note that if you had purchased Soft-Tech and the market prices declined, the value of the stock would be only $800 at the end of the year. However, speculations revealed that this event (a market decline) occurred only 60 percent of the time. In the long run, therefore, a market decline would contribute $480 to the total expected payoff from the stock, found by $800 × 0.60. Adding the $480 to the $1000 expected under rising market (0.4×2500) conditions gives $1,480, the "expected" payoff in the long run.

Case Study 11: How many miles can a car drive?

For most cost-conscious consumers, keeping a car running for as long as possible is a financial decision. Statistics suggest that it's usually cheaper to repair a car that's still in serviceable condition than it is to make payments on a new one. Obviously, no matter which model a motorist ultimately chooses, only a well-maintained car or truck will last long enough to go the distance. The road to 200,000 miles begins with following the automaker's maintenance schedule to the letter, particularly during the first few years of ownership to prevent voiding the vehicle's warranty. Key tasks to prolong car life include: (a) change oil and filter periodically, (b) inspect the hoses and belts regularly and have them replaced whenever they appear cracked,

brittle, frayed, become loose or show signs of excessive wear, (c) check the level of fluid in the battery at least once a month; and keep the battery terminals clear of corrosion to ensure a good connection, (d) check the air pressure in the tires – including the spare weekly, (e) check the tire tread depth periodically by placing a penny head first into the tread; if any part of Lincoln's head is visible it's time for new tires, and (f) have the tires rotated once a year, or sooner if they begin to show signs of uneven wear.

If you wonder about how many miles a car can go, there are few incredible examples that in the context of statistics will certainly be considered as outliers. A man by the name Joe LoCicero kept his 1990 Honda Accord running through a whopping 1,000,000 miles. While Joe was getting plenty of media attention as he approached that milestone (and a brand new Accord from Honda once he passed it), a New York man, Irv Gordon of East Patchogue, was quietly racking up even more miles, almost 3,000,000, in a beautiful red 1966 Volvo P1800. Gordon now holds the Guinness world record for racking up the highest mileage in the same vehicle.

Write an essay about the typical miles that most cars can run and the factors that contribute to prolonging car life. You may consider the following factors:

- Car model
- City versus highway driving
- Frequency of oil change
- Frequency of tire change
- People life style

Case Study 12: Are common frustrating issues to the boss equally weighted?

Frustrating issues to your boss represent categorical variables that can be analyzed using classic goodness of fit tests. Unfortunately, your manager may not always tell you that your behavior is driving him up the wall but you will get the message sooner or later. Here are some of these issues:

(a) Keeping your boss in the dark. Bosses don't like to have to confront problems either, but they also don't want them to be neglected until it's too late. Speak up when there's a problem that's too big to ignore.

(b) Constantly asking for help. Taking ownership of your tasks and work without constantly needing guidance or positive reinforcement is a key attribute in a dependable worker. Though you should ask for help when you're truly unsure about how to proceed with a project, be careful not to monopolize your manager's time and attention.

(c) Make mountains out of molehills and manufacture conflict.

(d) Promising big things that you cannot deliver.

(e) Deflecting criticism- when you drop the ball be ready to admit your mistakes.

Think of other frustrating issues to address and look for data to support your points. Write an essay about typical aspects that are not appropriate or acceptable in the working place in which you may attempt to seek ways to analyze them and propose corrective tasks.

Case Study 13: Sky Rocketing college costs in the context of the extent of delivering quality education

College tuitions soar each year, advancing far in excess of the inflation rate. The overall inflation rate from 1986 to 2011 increased 115.06%, which is why we pay more than double for everything we buy. On the other hand, during the same time, tuition increased a whopping 498.31%. For example, if the cost of college tuition was $10,000 in 1986, it would cost in 2011 the same student over $21,500 if education had increased as much as the average inflation rate but instead education is $59,800 or over 2½ times the inflation rate. Economists predict the cost of attending state colleges will soar to an average of $100,000 by 2020.

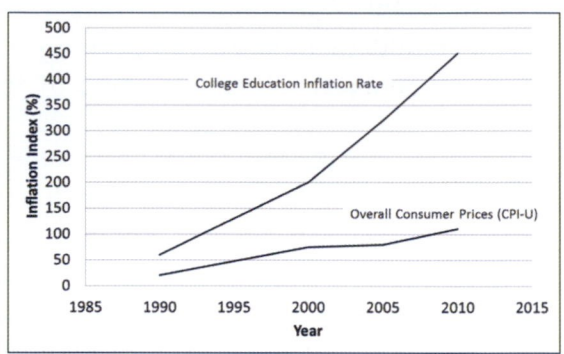

No. 1: Harvard University
2011 endowment funds: $31,728,080,000
Change from previous year: 15.1%
Students, fall 2011: 21,000
Undergraduate tuition: $52,652 for tuition, room and board for the 2011-12 school year

No. 2: Yale University
2011 endowment funds: $19,374,000,000
Change from previous year: 16.3%
Students, fall 2011: 11,875
Undergraduate tuition: $52,700 for tuition, room and board for the 2011-12 academic year

No. 5: Stanford University
2011 endowment funds: $16,502,606,000
Change from previous year: 19.1%
Students, fall 2011: 19,945
Undergraduate tuition: $52,860 for tuition, room and board for the 2011-12 academic year

No. 6: Massachusetts Institute of Technology
2011 endowment funds: $9,712,628,000
Change from previous year: 16.8%
Students, fall 2011: 10,894
Undergraduate tuition: $40,460 for tuition only for the 2011-2012 academic year

No. 3: The University of Texas
2011 endowment funds: $17,148,649,000
Change from previous year: 22%
Students, fall 2011: 51,112 for the main Austin Campus Undergraduate tuition: $9,816 for residents, $32,594 for nonresidents, covering tuition only for the 2011-12 school year

No. 4: Princeton University
2011 endowment funds: $17,109,508,000
Change from previous year: 18.9%
Students, fall 2011: 7,859
Undergraduate tuition: $54,780 for the estimated cost of attendance in the 2012-13 academic year, including tuition, room and board.

No. 7: University of Michigan
2011 endowment funds: $7,834,752,000
Change from previous year: 19.4%
Students, fall 2011: 42,716 for the main Ann Arbor campus
Undergraduate tuition: $25,204 for tuition, room and board for on-campus residents for the 2011-2012 school year.

No. 8: Columbia University
2011 endowment funds: $7,789,578,000
Change from previous year: 19.5%
Students, fall 2011: 28,221
Undergraduate tuition: $59,208 for tuition, room and board for the 2011-12 academic year for New York residents

No. 9: Northwestern University
2011 endowment funds: $7,182,745,000
Change from previous year: 20.8%
Students, fall 2011: 20,284
Undergraduate tuition: $40,223 for tuition, room and board

No. 10: Texas A&M University
2011 endowment funds: $6,999,517,000
Change from previous year: 22%
Students, fall 2011: 49,861
Undergraduate tuition: $19,035 (estimated cost of attendance for Texas residents for one year at the main campus)

The country that led the world in higher education is now leading its youngest generations into a deep hole. According to the Federal Reserve Bank of New York, Americans owe some $914 billion in student loans; other estimates say the total tops $1 trillion. That's more than the nation's entire credit-card debit. On average, a college degree still pays for itself (and then some) over the course of a career. But about 40% of students at four-year colleges do not manage to get that degree within six years. Regardless, student loans have to be repaid; unlike other kinds of debt, they generally cannot be shed in bankruptcy. The government can withhold tax refunds and garnish paychecks until it gets its money back.

Colleges argue the significant increase in tuition on the basis of higher overhead costs, rising utility and labor costs, many older college buildings are in need of renovation or replacement, and the demand for expanded libraries and new research and computer labs. On the other hand, one can see some colleges in the U.S. that have net worth in billions of dollars.

One may question the fact that as tuition costs continue to mount at universities across the nation, some colleges are sitting on mountains of cash. While some of that cash goes to regular campus operations or scholarships for students with financial need, many schools don't really use it at all, investing the money to fund big future projects and sometimes, when the economy tanks, the money simply gets lost in the market. Private schools rely on alumni and corporate sponsors to raise funds for the school's endowment fund, and while some endowments are quite restricted (so they can be spent only after a certain amount of time, or they can only be invested so as to use the profits), many leading universities have taken criticism for collecting the money and sitting on it while raising costs for students. The most recent comprehensive endowment study from the National Association of College and University Business Owners, which evaluated the 2011 endowment funds for 839 institutions in the U.S., found 75 higher education institutions with more than $1 billion in the bank.

Write an essay about your views on tuition increases and their impacts on student's ability to earn a degree. You may make some efforts to find data on tuitions, financial aids, and total students' costs in different universities in an attempt to make recommendations on the best cost-efficient universities that students should join.

Case Study 14: College dropout rate

Based on a 2011 study by Harvard Graduate School of Education, only 56% of college students complete a four-year degree within six years. If you're graduating from college this year, consider yourself lucky. To make news even worse, among the 18 developed countries in the Organization for Economic Co-operation and Development, the U.S. was dead last for the percentage of students who completed college once they started it, behind even Slovakia. College dropouts tend to be male, and they give reasons such as cost, not feeling prepared, and not being able to juggle family, school and jobs, according to the Harvard study. An American Institutes for Research report last year estimated that college dropouts cost the nation $4.5 billion in lost earnings and taxes. One factor in these disappointing statistics is America's

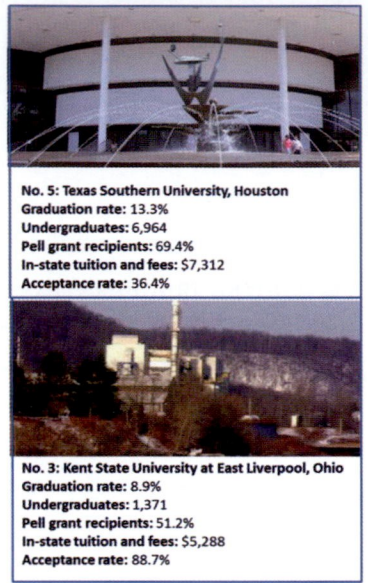

No. 5: Texas Southern University, Houston
Graduation rate: 13.3%
Undergraduates: 6,964
Pell grant recipients: 69.4%
In-state tuition and fees: $7,312
Acceptance rate: 36.4%

No. 3: Kent State University at East Liverpool, Ohio
Graduation rate: 8.9%
Undergraduates: 1,371
Pell grant recipients: 51.2%
In-state tuition and fees: $5,288
Acceptance rate: 88.7%

No. 4: Rogers State University, Claremore, Okla.
Graduation rate: 11.5%
Undergraduates: 4,486
Pell grant recipients: 40.5%
In-state tuition and fees: $4,820
Acceptance rate: 50.4%

No. 1: Southern University at New Orleans
Graduation rate: 4%
Undergraduates: 2,590
Pell grant recipients: 75.8%
In-state tuition and fees: $3,906
Acceptance rate: 48.4%

for-profit schools, which have garnered plenty of recent media attention. Such schools are sometimes accused of being 'dropout factories' that send students out into the workforce with major debt and few skills. But there are a number of four-year public universities, funded at least in part by taxpayer dollar, that have graduation rates that are just as bad as, or even worse than their for-profit counterparts. Some of the worst colleges in dropout rates in 2010 are shown in the figure to the right (the Chronicle of Higher Education-2010). Write an essay about the different causes of student's dropout using actual data from some colleges.

Case Study 15: The job market in the U.S.A. in comparison with the rest of the world

All governments around the world see unemployment rate as the number one economic challenge. Indeed, no other single number reveals at a glance the strength of the economy more than the unemployment rate. In the U.S.A. an 8% or more unemployment rate has been the alerting threshold for most governments over the years. In 2012, this meant about 12 million people remain unemployed or cannot find the kind of work they want. Some economists use unemployment rate as a measure to compare different countries economic stands. For example, in 2012, the U.S.A. had about 7.9% unemployment rate; 4.2% in Japan; 5.5% in Germany and Netherlands, 7.4% in Canada, 7.9% in United Kingdom, 10.8% in France and Italy, 25.1% in Greece, and 25.8% in Spain. As one can see from this comparison, the U.S. job market is weaker than in a few developed nations, but better than in many others. And that's true even though many European nations have strong unions and job protections that make it far harder for companies to lay off workers and streamline. Germany, for example, has a government-backed policy that encourages companies to pursue work-sharing arrangements instead of laying people off during tough times. If the United States had such a policy, it's fair to assume the U.S. unemployment rate would be considerably lower. Japan, meanwhile, may have low

unemployment, but it also has an economy that's been stuck in a deflationary rut for more than a decade. People have jobs, but living standards are declining for many, because wages are falling and there's a strong disincentive to spend money. China's economy is obviously an up-and-comer, yet the official unemployment rate of about 4 percent probably excludes factors to which the communist government prefers not to draw attention. In addition, China has its own problems, including a worrisome economic slowdown, millions of disgruntled rural workers, and a property bubble that may foretell a coming crash.

Write an essay about the different causes of unemployment and how these causes may differ from one country to another. You may attempt to address key questions such as:

- Can the unemployment rate be used as a prime index in comparing different countries economic performance?
- What other factors associated with unemployment should be taken into consideration?

Case Study 16: What are the booming jobs in the U.S.A.?

The job market, '*what and where*' is perhaps the most important issue that concerns many economic analysts. It also concerns all people as it touches upon their daily survival and their planning for careers. Although the correlation is not perfect, students typically select education majors that have opportunities in the marketplace, even if they do not meet their personal interest or their true qualifications. In the context of statistics, numerous data can be collected regarding job markets. Examples of these include, job growth rates,

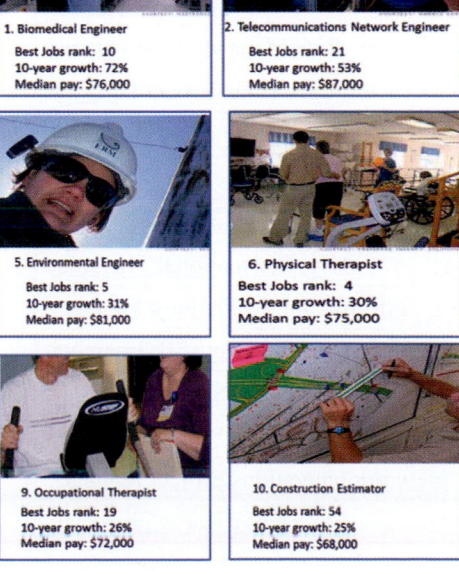

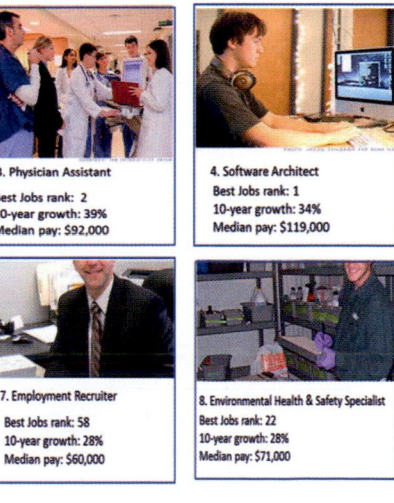

1. Biomedical Engineer
Best Jobs rank: 10
10-year growth: 72%
Median pay: $76,000

2. Telecommunications Network Engineer
Best Jobs rank: 21
10-year growth: 53%
Median pay: $87,000

3. Physician Assistant
Best Jobs rank: 2
10-year growth: 39%
Median pay: $92,000

4. Software Architect
Best Jobs rank: 1
10-year growth: 34%
Median pay: $119,000

5. Environmental Engineer
Best Jobs rank: 5
10-year growth: 31%
Median pay: $81,000

6. Physical Therapist
Best Jobs rank: 4
10-year growth: 30%
Median pay: $75,000

7. Employment Recruiter
Best Jobs rank: 58
10-year growth: 28%
Median pay: $60,000

8. Environmental Health & Safety Specialist
Best Jobs rank: 22
10-year growth: 28%
Median pay: $71,000

9. Occupational Therapist
Best Jobs rank: 19
10-year growth: 26%
Median pay: $72,000

10. Construction Estimator
Best Jobs rank: 54
10-year growth: 25%
Median pay: $68,000

Booming Jobs in the U.S.A. 2011-2012

demographic aspects, regional factors, etc. Given below are examples of key job-related information collected in 2011 and 2012.

Write an essay about the job market in the U.S.A. in which you may wish to address the following points:

- What are the factors that made you select your education major?
- Do you anticipate finding a job upon graduation? In case of yes or no explain why?
- Would you consider relocation to get a job that is appropriate to you?
- What trends do you see the job market exhibit?
- What suggestions would you make to others in terms of major selection and job searching?

Top 50 jobs by growth rate
(**http://money.cnn.com/magazines/moneymag/bestjobs/2010/full_list/index.html**)

Rank	Job title	Job growth (10-year forecast)
1	Software Architect	34%
2	Physician Assistant	39%
3	Management Consultant	24%
4	Physical Therapist	30%
5	Environmental Engineer	31%
6	Civil Engineer	24%
7	Database Administrator	20%
8	Sales Director	15%
9	Certified Public Accountant	22%
10	Biomedical Engineer	72%
11	Actuary	21%
12	Dentist	15%
13	Nurse Anesthetist	13%
14	Risk Management Manager	24%
15	Product Management Director	12%
16	Healthcare Consultant	24%
17	Information Systems Security Engineer	23%
18	Software Engineering / Development Director	17%
19	Occupational Therapist	26%
20	Information Technology Manager	17%
21	Telecommunications Network Engineer	53%
22	Environmental Health & Safety Specialist	28%
23	Construction Project Manager	17%
24	Network Operations Project Manager	23%
25	Emergency Room Physician	22%

Top 50 jobs by growth rate (cont'd)

Rank	Job title	Job growth (10-year forecast)
26	Information Technology Business Analyst	20%
27	Director of Nursing	16%
28	Information Technology Consultant	17%
29	Psychiatrist	24%
30	Test Software Development Engineer	20%
31	Information Technology Network Engineer	23%
32	Senior Sales Executive	15%
33	Information Technology Program Manager	17%
34	Primary Care Physician	22%
35	Computer and Information Scientist	24%
36	Hospital Administrator	16%
37	Programmer Analyst	20%
38	Applications Engineer	34%
39	Research & Development Manager	15%
40	Regional Sales Manager	15%
41	Project Engineer	24%
42	Training Development Director	23%
43	Human Resources Consultant	21%
44	Speech-Language Pathologist	19%
45	Business Development Analyst	24%
46	Physical Therapy Director	16%
47	Structural Engineer	24%
48	Nursing Home Director	16%
49	Systems Engineer	13%
50	Healthcare Services Program Director	13%

Case Study 17: Where to do you go to find jobs in the U.S.A.?

After a significant drop in the job market in the U.S.A. in the years from 2008 to 2012, it appeared that the job market may be getting some relief that is determined by the particular region in the U.S. According to a 2012 survey, the recovery was in full swing in America's largest cities. In the early summer of 2012, Gallup released results of its Job Creation Index for the 50 largest metropolitan regions in the United States. The results showed that companies in every city were hiring more often than they were firing (24/7/2012 Wall Street Journal). An examination of these cities suggests that workers have reason to be confident. The vast majority had among the best employment conditions in the country. Nearly every city had either excellent current employment rates, major declines in unemployment rates in the past year, or both (http://www.foxbusiness.com/economy/2012/04/02/nine-us-cities-where-jobs-are-booming/#ixzz2FtDK1Lfb). The Job Creation Index scores assigned by Gallup reflect the difference between the number of workers reporting their businesses were hiring compared to those who believed people were being let go. According to the report, these nine cities received Job Creation Index scores of 20 or better, meaning the percentage of employees who believed their companies were hiring was at least 20% more than those who believed their employers were looking to makes cuts to the payroll.

1. Oklahoma City, Okla.
> Job creation index: 25
> Unemployment rate (Jan. 2012): 5.9%
> Change in unemployment (Jan. 2011 – Jan. 2012): -3.3%

2. Pittsburgh, Pa.
> Job creation index: 22
> Unemployment rate (Jan. 2012): 7.6%
> Change in unemployment (Jan 2011 – Jan. 2012): -6.2%

3. Richmond, Va.
> Job creation index: 22
> Unemployment rate (Jan. 2012): 6.6%
> Change in unemployment (Jan. 2011 – Jan. 2012): -13.2%

4. Nashville-Davidson-Murfreesboro-Franklin, Tenn.
> Job creation index: 22
> Unemployment rate (Jan. 2012): 7.2%
> Change in unemployment (Jan, 2011 – Jan. 2012): -18.2%

5. Orlando-Kissimmee, Fla.
> Job creation index: 21
> Unemployment rate (Jan. 2012): 9.5%
> Change in unemployment (Jan. 2011 – Jan. 2012): -15.2%

6. Atlanta-Sandy Springs-Marietta, Ga.
> Job creation index: 20
> Unemployment rate (Jan. 2012): 9.2%
> Change in unemployment (Jan, 2011 – Jan. 2012): -10.7%

7. Houston-Sugar Land-Baytown, Tex.
> Job creation index: 20
> Unemployment rate (Jan. 2012): 7.6%
> Change in unemployment (Jan. 2011 – Jan. 2012): -12.6%

8. San Antonio, Tex.
> Job creation index: 20
> Unemployment rate (Jan. 2012): 7.3%
> Change in unemployment (Jan. 2011 – Jan. 2012): -6.4%

9. San Jose-Sunnyvale-Santa Clara, Calif.
> Job creation index: 20
> Unemployment rate (Jan. 2012): 9.1%
> Change in unemployment (Jan. 2011 – Jan. 2012): -15.7%

Write an essay about the job market in which you may address the following points:

- What are the effects of the presence of having a government institution such as college, capital or university in your city on creating stable workforces with relatively-decent salaries?
- What are the effects of having strong regional industries on the job market?
- What are the effects of having strong regional health care industry on the job market? Health care is traditionally a recession-robust industry.
- What are the effects of having strong regional tourist industry on the job market?

Case Study 18: How stressful is your job?

The ability to deal with job stress can mean the difference between success or failure. While some workplace stress is normal, excessive stress can interfere with one's productivity and impact one's physical and emotional health. You can't control everything in your work environment, but that doesn't mean you're powerless—even when you're stuck in a difficult situation. Finding ways to manage workplace stress isn't about making huge changes or rethinking career ambitions, but rather about focusing on the one thing that's always within your control (http://www.helpguide.org/mental/work_stress_management.htm). For workers everywhere, the troubled economy may feel like an emotional roller coaster. 'Layoffs' and 'budget cuts' have become bywords in the workplace, and the result is increased fear, uncertainty, and higher levels of stress. Since job and workplace stress increase in times of economic crisis, it's important to learn new and better ways of coping with the pressure.

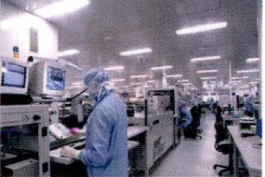

1. Biomedical Engineer
Best Jobs rank: 10
% who say the job is low stress: 70%

2. Transportation Engineer
Best Jobs rank: 51
% who say the job is low stress: 69%

3. Statistician
Best Jobs rank: 64
% who say the job is low stress: 64%

4. Web Developer
Best Jobs rank: 67
% who say the job is low stress: 58%

5. Geographic Information Systems Analyst
Best Jobs rank: 97
% who say the job is low stress: 55.6%

6. Technical Writer
Best Jobs rank: 88
% who say the job is low stress: 55%

Some statistics suggest that some jobs are less stressful than other based on surveys among workers in different jobs (see below, **http://money.cnn.com/galleries/2010/pf/jobs/**).

Write an essay about job stress in which you may consider the following points:

- What are the best ways to measure job stress?
- Suggest an analysis of variance in which different sources of job stress can be separated and their relative contributions can be determined

- Suggest ways to reduce or eliminate job stress

Case Study 19: How good is your community college?

According to CNNMoney (http://money.cnn.com/pf/college/community-colleges/) - Not all community colleges are created equal. Figuring out which school will give you the best chance of transferring to a four-year college or university can be difficult, especially since there is so little standardized information out there. In order to overcome this challenge, a joint venture of the American Institutes of Research and Matrix Knowledge Group, has created a chart for CNNMoney to help students find the best options. Based on the percentage of students that graduated within three years or transferred to four-year colleges, they compiled a 'success' rating for each community college in the U.S.

Write an essay about the 'quality of education in community colleges.' You may consider the following key points

    a. Should transferability rating be considered as the primary criteria for ranking community colleges?

    b. How do other factors such as the quality of the college feeder high schools, and state rules governing transfer credits influence the ranking process?

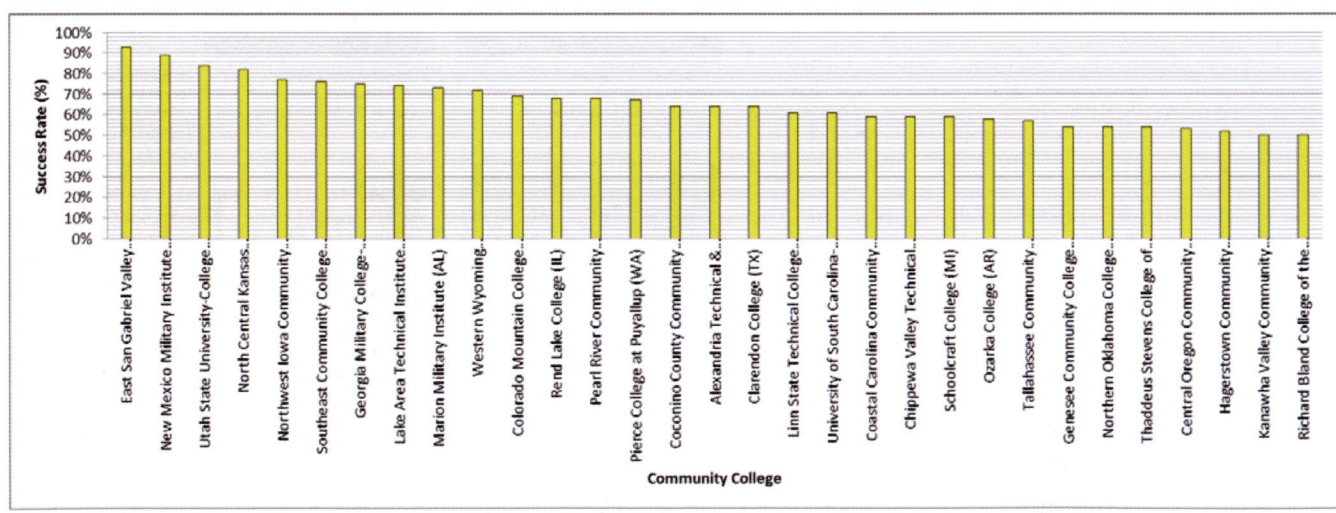

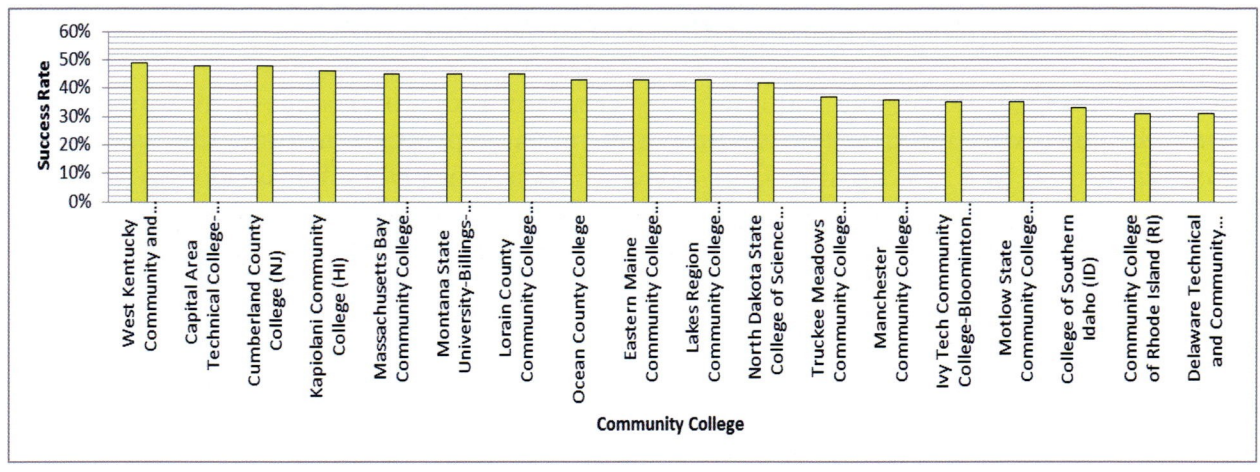

Case Study 20: Factors influencing the success of a community college

The CNNMoney (http://money.cnn.com/pf/college/community-colleges/) success rating of community colleges has only considered one factor of success, which is the rate of student's transferability. The problem with using this measure as the only index of success is that:

-   Not all community colleges aim only at transferability as many colleges offer Associate degrees for the purpose of transferring  students to four-year colleges but also other degrees such as AAS (Associate in Applied Sciences) designed with the options of being entirely terminal degrees.
-   Community colleges have full-time and part-time students. They also have a diverse group of students such as older students, housewives, currently-working students, temporary unemployed students, etc. These students may have different goals of education depending on their reasoning to obtain more education.
-   Community colleges provide continuing education to the surrounding community.
-   Community colleges participate effectively to the community in many aspects.

Write an essay about better ways to value community colleges education using a matrix of different criteria that contribute to community colleges success. You may search through different colleges' websites to develop your own matrix.

Case Study 21: Online education: Upward or Downward?

On September 17, 2012 The Pakistani government shut down access to YouTube to block the anti-Muslim film trailer that was inciting protests around the world; the same film that led to killing Christopher Stevens, the U.S. ambassador to Libya in Benghazi. As a result, 215 Pakistani students suddenly lost their access to a massive, open online physics course (*Time*, October 29, 2012). This was a free course offered by a Silicon Valley start-up called Udacity to some 23,000 students from 125 countries worldwide. A Pakistani student was in the middle of a test when she encountered a curt message saying '*this site is unavailable.*' The same student posted a lament on the class discussion board: '*I am very angry, but I will not quit.*' Within an hour of this student anger, another student taking the same class in Malaysia began helping the Pakistani student by posting the test questions that came in each video. The professor teaching the class, who was from Portugal, tried to create a workaround so the Pakistani student could bypass YouTube; it did not work. From England, another student promised to help and warned the Pakistani student not to write anything too negative about her government online. None of these students had ever met one another in person, but together they'd found a passageway into a rigorous, free, college-level class, and they weren't about to let anyone lock it up. Oh, one thing that should be mentioned: those students were 10 to 12 years old.

The merit of the Time story is very obvious; the education's world is stunningly changing and yes, online education will not only be the way of the future but will bring the world together regardless of ethnic, religion, culture, and social background.

In the late 1990s, Cisco CEO John Chambers predicted that 'education over the Internet is going to be so big; it is going to make e-mail usage look like a rounding error.' Since this time, the flexibility, convenience and growing acceptance of online distance education has created a new trend in how college students attend classes and earn their degrees. Today, almost all public institutions in the United States offer some type of online coursework-either through fully online programs or blended courses where students attend classroom lectures and participate in online class activities. According to the National Center for Education Statistics (NCES, http://nces.ed.gov/), the number of students enrolled in at least one distance education course increased significantly between 2002 and 2006, from 1.1 million to 12.2 million-and the growth spurt doesn't seem to be slowing down. In fact, the research firm Ambient Institute expects this figure to skyrocket to 22 million within the next five years. By 2014, Ambient predicts that the number of students taking all of their classes online will increase to 3.55 million, while the number of students taking all of their courses in on-campus classrooms will drop to 5.14 million.

Research by the Sloan Consortium (http://sloanconsortium.org/) has found that online college enrollments have continued to grow faster than the total population of college students. This means that more and more students are taking advantage of online learning options at their colleges and universities-particularly at 2-year public universities and other schools offering associate's degree programs.

A survey of postsecondary institutions by the NCES revealed that a variety of factors influenced schools' decisions to increase distance education offerings in the 2006-7 academic year.

- 92% - Meeting student demand for more flexible schedules
- 89% - Providing access to college
- 82% - Seeking to increase enrollment
- 86% - Making more courses available
- 62% - Responding to needs of employers/business
- 55% - Making more degree programs available
- 47% - Meeting student demand for reduced seat time
- 34% - Making more certificate programs available

Now, different forces are coming together to take e-learning upstream and to the level that will be satisfactory by most students. These efforts are now reflected in the following achievements:

- New technology, from cloud computing to social media- This should dramatically lower the costs and increase the odds of creating a decent online education platform
- In 2011-2012, startups like Udacity, Coursera, and edX, each with an elite-university imprimatur have put 219 college-level courses online, free of charge.
- Many traditional colleges are offering classes and even entire degree programs online

Despite the steady growth of e-learning or online education, skeptical educators perceive e-learning, generally speaking, as ineffective and inefficient. Per *Time* article, 'To this day, most are dry, uninspired affairs, consisting of a patchwork of online readings, written Q&As and low-budget lecture videos.' Many students nevertheless pay hundreds of dollars for these classes. According to *Time* magazine 3 in 10 college students report taking at least one online course in 2012, up from 1 in 10 in 2003-but afterward, most are no better off than they would have been at their local community college campuses.

With the information given above, write an essay about the future of online education. You may gather recent data from the National Center for Education Statistics and other sources and suggest the best way to analyze the data and make useful statistical conclusions.

Case Study 22: Purchasing a new car

The choice of purchasing a car can be a frustrating experience. Different people may have different views of what attributes to consider in purchasing a new car. Write an essay about the criteria that should be used in purchasing a new car. Select quantitative and qualitative criteria and suggest ways to analyze each type. You may use the illustration below as a guideline in your discussion.

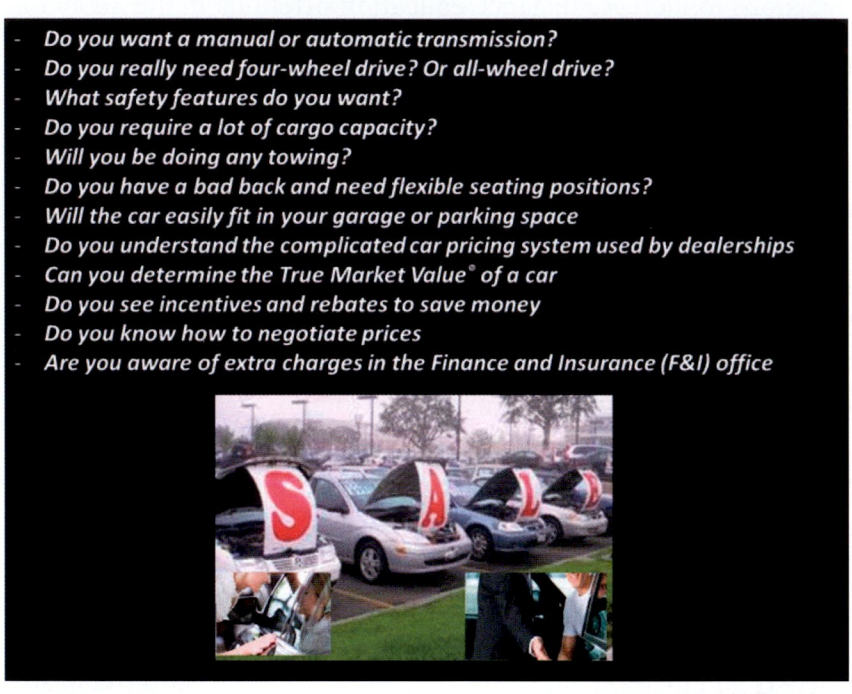

- *Do you want a manual or automatic transmission?*
- *Do you really need four-wheel drive? Or all-wheel drive?*
- *What safety features do you want?*
- *Do you require a lot of cargo capacity?*
- *Will you be doing any towing?*
- *Do you have a bad back and need flexible seating positions?*
- *Will the car easily fit in your garage or parking space*
- *Do you understand the complicated car pricing system used by dealerships*
- *Can you determine the True Market Value® of a car*
- *Do you see incentives and rebates to save money*
- *Do you know how to negotiate prices*
- *Are you aware of extra charges in the Finance and Insurance (F&I) office*

Case Study 23: IQ versus EQ

An IQ (*intelligence quotient*) is a score derived from one of several standardized tests designed to assess intelligence. IQ scores are used as predictors of educational achievement, special needs, job performance and income. EQ (*emotional intelligence*) refers to the ability to perceive, control, and evaluate emotions. Some researchers suggest that emotional intelligence can be learned and strengthened, while other claim it is an inborn characteristic. A number of testing instruments have been developed to measure emotional intelligence, although the content and approach of each test varies. Find data on both IQ and EQ and write an essay about your opinion of the reliability of these measures in determining people's intellectual ability.

Case Study 24: Math Anxiety

Math Anxiety has been a widely addressed issue among educators. More recent studies even suggested that math anxiety has Neurological Basis (http://psychcentral.com). One of the measures proposed to determine the extent of math anxiety is the so-called Mathematics Anxiety Rating Scale, MARS (Suinn RM, Winston EH, Psychol Rep., 2003 Feb;92,1:167-73). This measure has been used for research and clinical studies since 1972.

Mathematics Anxiety

- Mathematics anxiety has been defined as feelings of tension and anxiety that interfere with the manipulation of numbers and the solving of mathematical problems in a wide variety of ordinary life and academic situations. Math anxiety can cause one to forget and lose one's self-confidence (Tobias, S., 1993, *Overcoming math anxiety*. New York: W. W. Norton & Company).
- Math anxiety is very real and occurs among thousands of people. Much of this anxiety happens in the classroom due to the lack of consideration of different learning styles of students.
- Today, the needs of society require a greater need for mathematics.
- Math must be looked upon in a positive light to reduce math anxiety.
- Teachers must re-examine traditional teaching methods which often do not match students' learning styles and skills needed in society (Spikell, M. (1993). *Teaching mathematics with manipulatives: A resource of activities for the K-12 teacher.* New York: Allyn and Bacon)
- Lessons must be presented in a variety of ways. For instance, a new concept can be taught through play acting, cooperative groups, visual aids, hands on activities and technology.
- As a result once young children see math as fun, they will enjoy it, and, the joy of mathematics could remain with them throughout the rest of their lives.

Write an essay about math anxiety using data that support your views.

Case Study 25: Teen suicide

According to an annual survey published by The Centers for Disease Control and Prevention (2012), 16 percent of high school teens nationwide admitted they had considered suicide within the previous year. According to the survey, teens in Chicago are among the most depressed in the nation and that Chicago leads the Nation in teen suicide planning. Write an essay about measurable factors of teen suicide attempts or planning. You may attempt to address the issue of regional effects on teen suicide attempts or planning.

Case Study 26: Text messaging

According to reported statistics by MSNB (http://www.msnbc.msn.com/id/47723985/ns/health-health_care/#.T9G6rPJoVBk), nearly 60 percent of teens text while driving. A typical teen sends and receives about 100 text messages a day, and it's the most common way many kids communicate with their peers. Some teens indicated that 'if the car's not moving and I'm at a stoplight or I'm stuck in traffic, text messaging should be ok.' Other teens acknowledge they know it's not safe, but think it is safer if they hold the phone up so they can see the road and text at the same time. Based on data that you may collect

from highway departments, or Centers for Disease Control and Prevention, write an essay about the impacts of text messaging on teens safety. You may also suggest ways to solve this serious safety problem.

Case Study 27: Americans live in Poverty

The number of Americans living in poverty has been on the rise since the Great Recession, as many households have seen their incomes drop and their debts mount in the past few years. Some counties in the U.S. entirely live under poverty. The Census Bureau routinely reports data on the nation counties that have the highest poverty rates with the worst at or close to 50%. In total, more than 15% of the population lived in poverty in 2010, the highest percentage since 1993, according to the most recent data from the Census Bureau. To put that in perspective, that means more than 46 million people fell below the poverty line, defined as $22,314 for a family of four. If you factor in the income spent on expenses like medical costs, child care and mortgage payments, the number of Americans whose remaining income falls below the poverty line is closer to 50 million, or roughly 16% of

No. 15: Wilcox County, Ala.
Poverty rate: 39.6%
Poverty rate of children under 18: 52.5%
Median household income: $21,611

No. 14: Maverick County, Texas
Poverty rate: 39.9%
Poverty rate of children under 18: 53.2%
Median household income: $27,710

No. 13: Owsley County, Ky.
Poverty rate: 40.1%
Poverty rate of children under 18: 54.4%
Median household income: $22,335

No. 12: East Carroll Parish, La.
Poverty rate: 40.3%
Poverty rate of children under 18: 53.7%
Median household income: $25,442

the population. Write an essay about the problem of poverty in the Super Power Country of the world, the U.S.A.

Case Study 28: Why Median in determining household income?

Household income is typically expressed using the 'Median.' One has to wonder why not the mean or the mode. Write an essay about household income in the U.S., in which you explain why the median is the preferable measure and not the mean or the mode.

Case Study 29: Nation Wealth

In order to rank the world's wealthiest countries, Forbes looked at per capita gross domestic product adjusted for purchasing power for 182 nations. They use International Monetary Fund data from each year particularly the most recent available gross-domestic product. The purchasing power parity-adjusted GDP - preferred by economists when making international comparisons - takes into account the relative cost of living and inflation rates, rather than just exchange rates, which may distort real differences in worth. Using Forbes data or data from other sources write an essay on the main factors that contribute to nation wealth.

Case Study 30: Graying of baby boomers

Would the graying of the boomers (born 1946 and 1964) change the world (*Smart Money*, September 2012)? Steve Jobs was a boomer. So are George Clooney, Oprah and the Boss Bruce Springsteen. So are president Obama, Hillary Clinton, and Mitt Romney. About 70 million Americans are baby boomers. Are they happy now? How long would they work? During the stock market booms of the 1990s and the mid-2000s, many boomers undoubtedly thought their retirement would be safe and robust. But since the 2008 economic crash, many are coping with shriveled savings and diminished expectations. In summary, the money may not be there when they need it as the cost of Social Security and Medicare benefits for boomers is the angry elephant in the room in any debate over government spending. Are there silver linings in all of this? Yes, 45-to-64-year-olds composed 48% of all new entrepreneurs in 2011. In the context of social statistics, one way to examine the satisfaction of a certain age group is the so-called '*thriving index*' developed by the AARP. This organization formerly the American Association of Retired Persons, is a United States-based organization based in Washington, D.C. According to its mission statement, it is 'a nonprofit, nonpartisan membership organization for people age 50 and over ... dedicated to enhancing quality of life for all as we age,' which 'provides a wide range of unique benefits, special products, and services for our members.' The AARP Thriving index measures emotional well-being. This index suggests that people's happiness reaches its lowest point at ages 51 to 55 and start peaking after 65.

The Figure shown to the right represents the extent of happiness at different age groups (http://www.aarp.org/). Perform your own survey and see if it agrees with the AARP findings. You may use goodness of fit to assist you in your analysis. Write an essay about how happiness may change with grayness and the different factors that may contribute to this happiness.

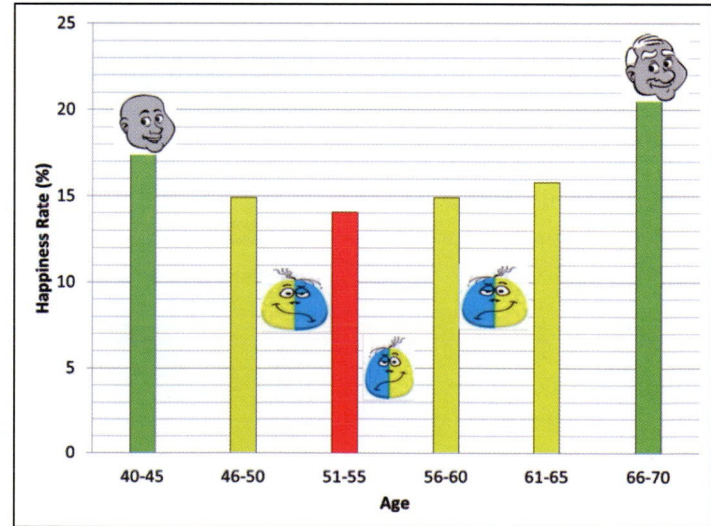

Case Study 31: Education iron triangle

The term *iron triangle* has been used frequently in politics. In the context of education, the iron triangle is used by education experts to describe the three big, interrelated problems facing America's colleges and universities. The 2012 statistics associated with this triangle are depressing (*Time*, October 29, 2012):

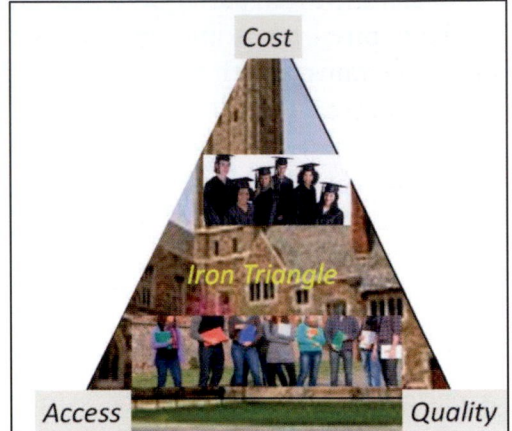

- Only 3% of the students at the top 146 colleges in the U.S. come from families in the bottom fourth of household income
- Fewer than 6 in 10 (60%) undergraduates finish four-year degrees within 6 years
- Student-loan debt has topped $900 billion
- Employers need workers with a college degree more than ever

Write an essay about the iron triangle of education in the U.S.A using data of cost, access, and quality.

Case Study 32: The Best- and Worst-Run States in America

Can you imagine California being the worst-run state in America? This was actually the second year in a row according to *24/7 Wall St – Tue, Nov 27, 2012*.

How well run are America's 50 states? The answer depends a lot on where you live.

Every year, 24/7 Wall St. conducts an extensive survey of all fifty states in America. Based on a review of data on financial health, standard of living and government services by state they determine how well each

state is managed. For the first time, North Dakota is the best run. California is the worst run for the second year in a row.

The successful management of a state is difficult to measure. Factors that affect its finances and population may be the result of decisions made years ago. A state's difficulties can be caused by poor governance or by external factors, such as extreme weather. A state with abundant natural resources should have an easier time balancing its budget than one starved for resources. Regional problems or the national decline of certain industries can destroy local economies. The subprime mortgage crisis, for example, disproportionately affected states with strong construction and real estate markets. Such factors can be easily identified and noted as possible causes for a state's poverty levels, unemployment, or strained coffers. Despite these factors, it is the responsibility of each state to deal with the resources at its disposal. Each government must anticipate economic shifts and diversify its industries and attract new business. A state should be able to raise enough revenue to ensure the safety of its citizens and minimize hardship without spending more than it can prudently afford. Some states have historically done this much better than others.

To determine how well the states are run, 24/7 Wall St. reviewed hundreds of data sets from dozens of sources. They looked at each state's debt, revenue, expenditure and deficit to determine how well it is managed fiscally. They reviewed taxes, exports, and GDP growth, including a breakdown by sector, to identify how each state is managing its resources. We looked at poverty, income, unemployment, high school graduation, violent crime and foreclosure rates to measure if residents are prospering. The best-run states have certain characteristics in common, as do the worst run.

- The high-ranking states all have well-managed budgets. Each of the top ten has a perfect, or near-perfect, credit rating from Standard & Poor's, Moody's, or both. Of the ten worst-ranked, only three received top scores from one agency, and none from both. California is currently the only state rated A- by S&P, the lowest score given to any state. These poor-ranked states have high debt relative to both income and expenditure.
- There is a strong correlation between well-educated populations and generally well-managed states. Of the ten best-scoring states on our list, nine have among the highest percentages of adults with high school diplomas.
- Employment is also closely correlated to how well a state is managed. The unemployment rates of most of the poorly ranked states are among the highest in the country. Nine of the ten best-ranked states had an unemployment rate of less than 7% in 2011. This includes North Dakota, which had the lowest rate in the country in 2011, at just 3.6%. The average unemployment rate nationwide was 8.9% in 2011.

Based on the information above, write an essay about the factors that determine how well a state is run using actual data from the best states and the worst states. Review the current methods of data analysis and express your opinion about the fairness of these methods.

Case Study 33: Gun-Violence Rates in the U.S.A.

On January 11th, 2013, and as he was preparing a legislative package for President Obama's review, Vice President Biden said that multiple approaches are needed to address the plague of gun violence. *'We know that there is no silver bullet ... no seat belt you can put on,'* Biden said before meeting with members of video game industry. It was the latest in a string of meetings Biden has held the week of January 7th, with guests ranging from gun-control advocates to gun rights supporters, hunters to retailers, mayors to governors, lawyers to doctors, and faith leaders to entertainment industry executives. This task was assigned by president Obama after the December 14th, 2012, shooting that killed 20 children and six adults at an elementary school in Newtown, Connecticut, which promoted the president to plan to make a major push for gun legislation in 2013. In Europe, most countries have on average less than 150 gun homicides annually; in Japan, it less than 50; in Canada, it is less than 200; but in the U.S.A. it is more than 10,000 (*IANSA (International Action Network on Small Arms of the United Nations,* http://www.iansa.org/).

More facts about gun violence are given below. Based on this information and other data that you can obtain from numerous sources, express your opinion about the relationship between gun ownership and gun violence and whether you would agree with gun ownership. You must support your opinion with data and statistics.

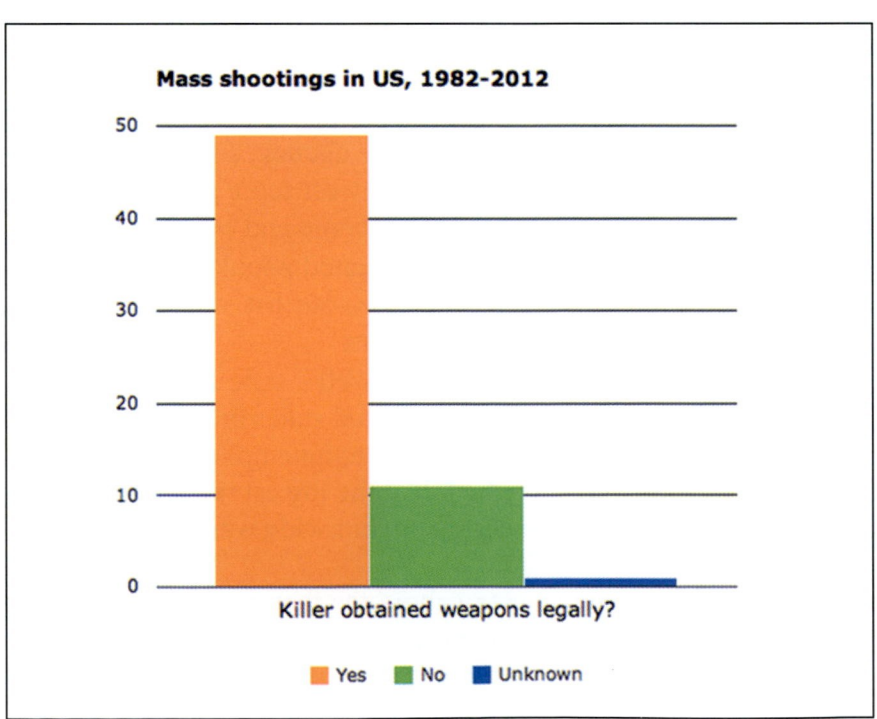

Facts (Source: *Injury Prevention (2007); ATF (2000); National Opinion Research Center (2008); Pew Research Center (2009)*

- In 2012, the US had an estimated 283 million guns in civilian hands
- Each year about 4.5 million firearms, including approximately 2 million handguns, are sold in the United States
- An estimated 2 million second hand firearms are sold each year
- The percentage of American households with a gun has been steadily declining (high of 54% in 1977 to 33% in 2009)
- The average number of guns per owner has increased from 4.1 in 1994 to 6.9 in 2004
- More than 30,000 people are killed by firearms each year in this country
- More than 30 people are shot and murdered each day
- 1/2 of them are between the ages of 18 and 35
- 1/3 of them are under the age of 20
- Homicide is the second leading cause of death among 15-24 year-olds and the primary cause of death among African Americans of that age group

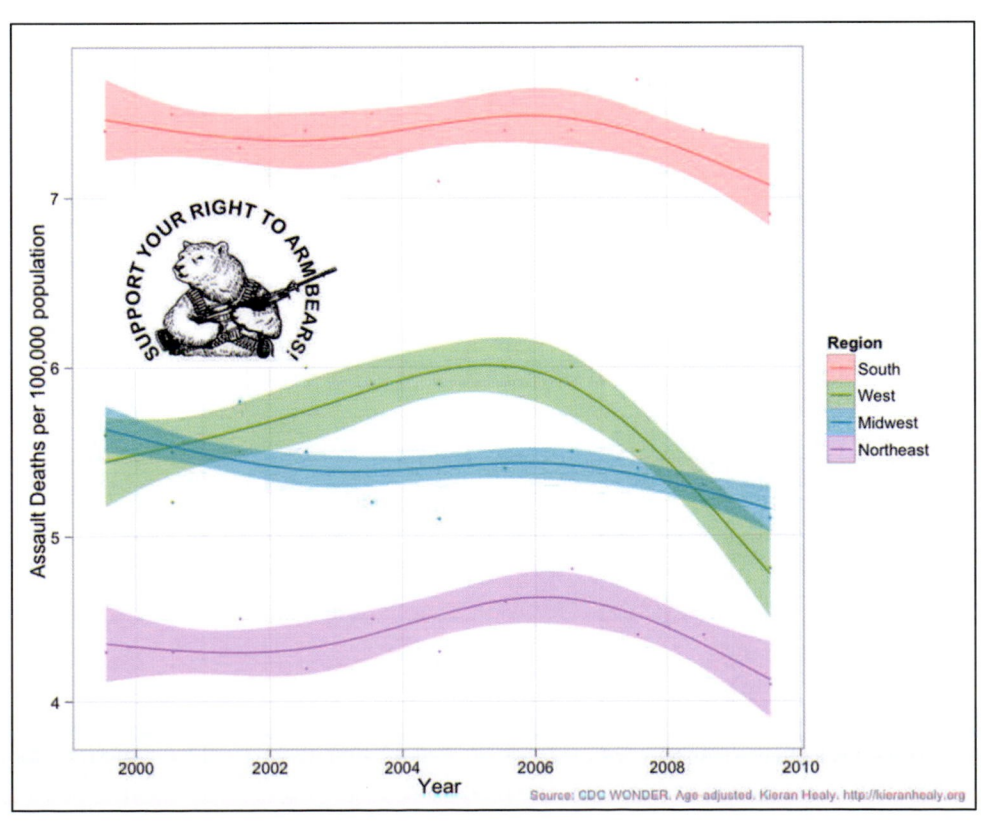

Case Study 34: The Importance of Quarterback in Football

What constitutes a successful quarterback in American Football? Is it the weight? height?, or brain?. The size of a football quarterback can vary. It depends on the style of offense that the team is running. If a team is running a pro offense, meaning that the quarterback stands in the pocket most of the time, a typical quarterback is between 6'3" and 6'5", 220 pounds to 270 pounds. Examples include famous quarterbacks such as Peyton Manning and Tom Brady. In a spread offense, seen in colleges now, quarterbacks range from 6' to 6'9" and 200 pounds to 250 pounds. The most important thing for these quarterbacks is speed. They are expected to be able to pass the ball and to make plays with their feet. Examples include famous quarterbacks such as Pat White and Michael Vick. In all cases, it is important that a quarterback has the ability to make timely decisions. The data below illustrates some of the key attributes of NFL quarterbacks. Using this data and other sources, write an essay about the importance of a Quarterback in Football. Support your views with statistical outcomes.

Best NFL quarterbacks going into 2012-13 season (http://www.nflen.com/2012/07/best-nfl-quarterbacks-going-into-2012.html) - H = height, W = Weight (lb), Age = Experience, PY = Passing yards, TD = Touchdowns, INT = intercept, RTD = Rushing Touchdown

						2012-Season			Career Stat			
QB	Team	H	W	Age	Years	PY	TD	INT	PY	TD	INT	RTD
Aaron Rodgers	Green Bay Packers	6' 2"	225	28	8	4643	45	6	17366	132	38	16
Drew Brees	New Orleans Saints	6'	209	33	12	5476	46	14	40742	281	146	8
Tom Brady	New England Patriots	6' 4"	225	35	13	5235	39	12	39979	300	115	10
Peyton Manning	Denver Broncos	6' 5"	230	36	15	4700	33	17	54828	399	198	17
Ben Roethlisberger	Pittsburgh Steelers	6' 5"	241	30	9	4077	21	14	26579	165	100	14
Eli Manning	New York Giants	6' 4"	218	31	9	4933	29	16	27579	185	129	8
Philip Rivers	San Diego Chargers	6' 5"	228	30	9	4624	27	20	24285	163	78	3
Tony Romo	Dallas Cowboys	6' 2"	228	32	10	4184	31	10	20834	149	72	4
Matt Ryan	Atlanta Falcons	6' 4"	217	27	5	4177	29	12	14238	95	46	4
Matthew Stafford	Detroit Lions	6' 2"	232	24	4	5038	41	16	7840	60	37	3
Joe Flacco	Baltimore Ravens	6' 6"	245	27	5	3610	20	12	13816	80	46	4
Matt Schaub	Houston Texans	6' 5"	241	31	9	2479	15	6	17936	98	58	4
Michael Vick	Philadelphia Eagles	6'	215	32	11	3303	18	14	17912	111	72	33
Jay Cutler	Chicago Bears	6' 3"	220	29	7	2319	13	7	18283	117	86	6
Cam Newton	Carolina Panthers	6' 5"	248	23	2	4051	21	17	4051	21	17	14

Subject Index

APPENDIX A
Statistical Tables

Cumulative Normal Distribution

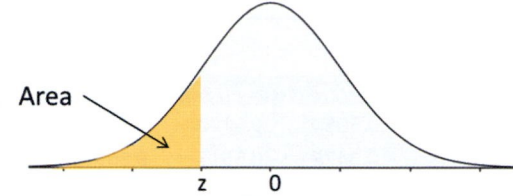

Area

z   0

z	0	0.01	0.02	0.03	0.04	0.05	0.06	0.07	0.08	0.09
-3.6	0.0002	0.0002	0.0001	0.0001	0.0001	0.0001	0.0001	0.0001	0.0001	0.0001
-3.5	0.0002	0.0002	0.0002	0.0002	0.0002	0.0002	0.000	0.000	0.0002	0.0002
-3.4	0.0003	0.0003	0.0003	0.0003	0.0003	0.0003	0.0003	0.0003	0.0003	0.0002
-3.3	0.0005	0.0005	0.0005	0.0004	0.0004	0.0004	0.0004	0.0004	0.0004	0.0003
-3.2	0.0007	0.0007	0.0006	0.0006	0.0006	0.0006	0.0006	0.0005	0.0005	0.0005
-3.1	0.0010	0.0009	0.0009	0.0009	0.0008	0.0008	0.0008	0.0008	0.0007	0.0007
-3.0	0.0013	0.0013	0.0013	0.0012	0.0012	0.0011	0.0011	0.0011	0.0010	0.0010
-2.9	0.0019	0.0018	0.0018	0.0017	0.0016	0.0016	0.0015	0.0015	0.0014	0.0014
-2.8	0.0026	0.0025	0.0024	0.0023	0.0023	0.0022	0.0021	0.0021	0.0020	0.0019
-2.7	0.0035	0.0034	0.0033	0.0032	0.0031	0.0030	0.0029	0.0028	0.0027	0.0026
-2.6	0.0047	0.0045	0.0044	0.0043	0.0041	0.0040	0.0039	0.0038	0.0037	0.0036
-2.5	0.0062	0.0060	0.0059	0.0057	0.0055	0.0054	0.0052	0.0051	0.0049	0.0048
-2.4	0.0082	0.0080	0.0078	0.0075	0.0073	0.0071	0.0069	0.0068	0.0066	0.0064
-2.3	0.0107	0.0104	0.0102	0.0099	0.0096	0.0094	0.0091	0.0089	0.0087	0.0084
-2.2	0.0139	0.0136	0.0132	0.0129	0.0125	0.0122	0.0119	0.0116	0.0113	0.0110
-2.1	0.0179	0.0174	0.0170	0.0166	0.0162	0.0158	0.0154	0.0150	0.0146	0.0143
-2.0	0.0228	0.0222	0.0217	0.0212	0.0207	0.0202	0.0197	0.0192	0.0188	0.0183
-1.9	0.0287	0.0281	0.0274	0.0268	0.0262	0.0256	0.0250	0.0244	0.0239	0.0233
-1.8	0.0359	0.0351	0.0344	0.0336	0.0329	0.0322	0.0314	0.0307	0.0301	0.0294
-1.7	0.0446	0.0436	0.0427	0.0418	0.0409	0.0401	0.0392	0.0384	0.0375	0.0367
-1.6	0.0548	0.0537	0.0526	0.0516	0.0505	0.0495	0.0485	0.0475	0.0465	0.0455
-1.5	0.0668	0.0655	0.0643	0.0630	0.0618	0.0606	0.0594	0.0582	0.0571	0.0559
-1.4	0.0808	0.0793	0.0778	0.0764	0.0749	0.0735	0.0721	0.0708	0.0694	0.0681
-1.3	0.0968	0.0951	0.0934	0.0918	0.0901	0.0885	0.0869	0.0853	0.0838	0.0823
-1.2	0.1151	0.1131	0.1112	0.1093	0.1075	0.1056	0.1038	0.1020	0.1003	0.0985
-1.1	0.1357	0.1335	0.1314	0.1292	0.1271	0.1251	0.1230	0.1210	0.1190	0.1170
-1.0	0.1587	0.1562	0.1539	0.1515	0.1492	0.1469	0.1446	0.1423	0.1401	0.1379
-0.9	0.1841	0.1814	0.1788	0.1762	0.1736	0.1711	0.1685	0.1660	0.1635	0.1611
-0.8	0.2119	0.2090	0.2061	0.2033	0.2005	0.1977	0.1949	0.1922	0.1894	0.1867
-0.7	0.2420	0.2389	0.2358	0.2327	0.2296	0.2266	0.2236	0.2206	0.2177	0.2148
-0.6	0.2743	0.2709	0.2676	0.2643	0.2611	0.2578	0.2546	0.2514	0.2483	0.2451
-0.5	0.3085	0.3050	0.3015	0.2981	0.2946	0.2912	0.2877	0.2843	0.2810	0.2776
-0.4	0.3446	0.3409	0.3372	0.3336	0.3300	0.3264	0.3228	0.3192	0.3156	0.3121
-0.3	0.3821	0.3783	0.3745	0.3707	0.3669	0.3632	0.3594	0.3557	0.3520	0.3483
-0.2	0.4207	0.4168	0.4129	0.4090	0.4052	0.4013	0.3974	0.3936	0.3897	0.3859
-0.1	0.4602	0.4562	0.4522	0.4483	0.4443	0.4404	0.4364	0.4325	0.4286	0.4247
0.0	0.5000	0.4960	0.4920	0.4880	0.4840	0.4801	0.4761	0.4721	0.4681	0.4641

Cumulative Normal Distribution

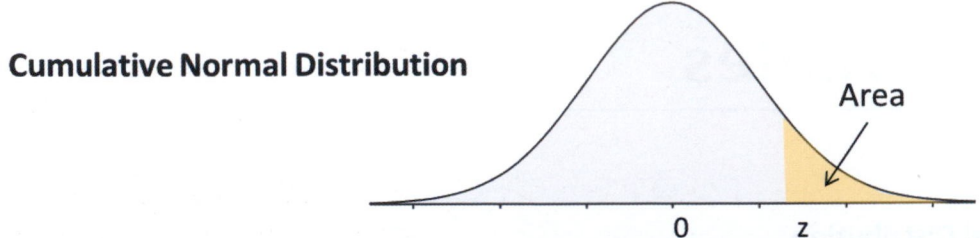

Area

0   z

z	0	0.01	0.02	0.03	0.04	0.05	0.06	0.07	0.08	0.09
0.0	0.5000	0.5040	0.5080	0.5120	0.5160	0.5199	0.5239	0.5279	0.5319	0.5359
0.1	0.5398	0.5438	0.5478	0.5517	0.5557	0.5596	0.5636	0.5675	0.5714	0.5753
0.2	0.5793	0.5832	0.5871	0.5910	0.5948	0.5987	0.6026	0.6064	0.6103	0.6141
0.3	0.6179	0.6217	0.6255	0.6293	0.6331	0.6368	0.6406	0.6443	0.6480	0.6517
0.4	0.6554	0.6591	0.6628	0.6664	0.6700	0.6736	0.6772	0.6808	0.6844	0.6879
0.5	0.6915	0.6950	0.6985	0.7019	0.7054	0.7088	0.7123	0.7157	0.7190	0.7224
0.6	0.7257	0.7291	0.7324	0.7357	0.7389	0.7422	0.7454	0.7486	0.7517	0.7549
0.7	0.7580	0.7611	0.7642	0.7673	0.7704	0.7734	0.7764	0.7794	0.7823	0.7852
0.8	0.7881	0.7910	0.7939	0.7967	0.7995	0.8023	0.8051	0.8078	0.8106	0.8133
0.9	0.8159	0.8186	0.8212	0.8238	0.8264	0.8289	0.8315	0.8340	0.8365	0.8389
1.0	0.8413	0.8438	0.8461	0.8485	0.8508	0.8531	0.8554	0.8577	0.8599	0.8621
1.1	0.8643	0.8665	0.8686	0.8708	0.8729	0.8749	0.8770	0.8790	0.8810	0.8830
1.2	0.8849	0.8869	0.8888	0.8907	0.8925	0.8944	0.8962	0.8980	0.8997	0.9015
1.3	0.9032	0.9049	0.9066	0.9082	0.9099	0.9115	0.9131	0.9147	0.9162	0.9177
1.4	0.9192	0.9207	0.9222	0.9236	0.9251	0.9265	0.9279	0.9292	0.9306	0.9319
1.5	0.9332	0.9345	0.9357	0.9370	0.9382	0.9394	0.9406	0.9418	0.9429	0.9441
1.6	0.9452	0.9463	0.9474	0.9484	0.9495	0.9505	0.9515	0.9525	0.9535	0.9545
1.7	0.9554	0.9564	0.9573	0.9582	0.9591	0.9599	0.9608	0.9616	0.9625	0.9633
1.8	0.9641	0.9649	0.9656	0.9664	0.9671	0.9678	0.9686	0.9693	0.9699	0.9706
1.9	0.9713	0.9719	0.9726	0.9732	0.9738	0.9744	0.9750	0.9756	0.9761	0.9767
2.0	0.9772	0.9778	0.9783	0.9788	0.9793	0.9798	0.9803	0.9808	0.9812	0.9817
2.1	0.9821	0.9826	0.9830	0.9834	0.9838	0.9842	0.9846	0.9850	0.9854	0.9857
2.2	0.9861	0.9864	0.9868	0.9871	0.9875	0.9878	0.9881	0.9884	0.9887	0.9890
2.3	0.9893	0.9896	0.9898	0.9901	0.9904	0.9906	0.9909	0.9911	0.9913	0.9916
2.4	0.9918	0.9920	0.9922	0.9925	0.9927	0.9929	0.9931	0.9932	0.9934	0.9936
2.5	0.9938	0.9940	0.9941	0.9943	0.9945	0.9946	0.9948	0.9949	0.9951	0.9952
2.6	0.9953	0.9955	0.9956	0.9957	0.9959	0.9960	0.9961	0.9962	0.9963	0.9964
2.7	0.9965	0.9966	0.9967	0.9968	0.9969	0.9970	0.9971	0.9972	0.9973	0.9974
2.8	0.9974	0.9975	0.9976	0.9977	0.9977	0.9978	0.9979	0.9979	0.9980	0.9981
2.9	0.9981	0.9982	0.9982	0.9983	0.9984	0.9984	0.9985	0.9985	0.9986	0.9986
3.0	0.9987	0.9987	0.9987	0.9988	0.9988	0.9989	0.9989	0.9989	0.9990	0.9990
3.1	0.9990	0.9991	0.9991	0.9991	0.9992	0.9992	0.9992	0.9992	0.9993	0.9993
3.2	0.9993	0.9993	0.9994	0.9994	0.9994	0.9994	0.9994	0.9995	0.9995	0.9995
3.3	0.9995	0.9995	0.9995	0.9996	0.9996	0.9996	0.9996	0.9996	0.9996	0.9997
3.4	0.9997	0.9997	0.9997	0.9997	0.9997	0.9997	0.9997	0.9997	0.9997	0.9998
3.5	0.9998	0.9998	0.9998	0.9998	0.9998	0.9998	0.9998	0.9998	0.9998	0.9998
3.6	0.9998	0.9998	0.9999	0.9999	0.9999	0.9999	0.9999	0.9999	0.9999	0.9999

Critical Values for the t-distribution

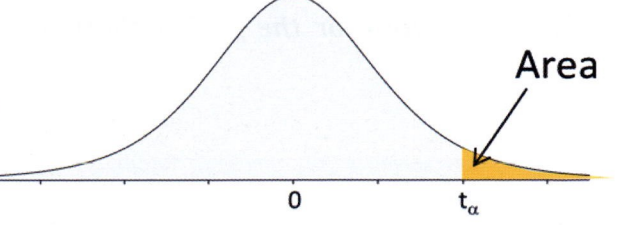

Area

				Area in the Right Tail						
γ \ α	0.40	0.25	0.10	0.05	0.025	0.01	0.005	0.0025	0.001	0.0005
1	0.325	1.000	3.078	6.314	12.706	31.821	63.657	127.32	318.31	636.62
2	0.289	0.816	1.886	2.920	4.303	6.965	9.925	1.4.089	23.326	31.598
3	0.277	0.765	1.638	2.353	3.182	4.541	5.841	7.453	10.213	12.924
4	0.271	0.741	1.533	2.132	2.776	3.747	4.604	5.598	7.173	8.610
5	0.267	0.727	1.476	2.015	2.571	3.365	4.032	4.773	5.893	6.869
6	0.265	0.727	1.440	1.943	2.447	3.143	3.707	4.317	5.208	5.959
7	0.263	0.711	1.415	1.895	2.365	2.998	3.499	4.019	4.785	5.408
8	0.262	0.706	1.397	1.860	2.306	2.896	3.355	3.833	4.501	5.041
9	0.261	0.703	1.383	1.833	2.262	2.821	3.250	3.690	4.297	4.781
10	0.260	0.700	1.372	1.812	2.228	2.764	3.169	3.581	4.144	4.587
11	0.260	0.697	1.363	1.796	2.201	2.718	3.106	3.497	4.025	4.437
12	0.259	0.695	1.356	1.782	2.179	2.681	3.055	3.428	3.930	4.318
13	0.259	0.694	1.350	1.771	2.160	2.650	3.012	3.472	3.852	4.221
14	0.258	0.692	1.345	1.761	2.145	2.624	2.977	3.326	3.787	4.140
15	0.258	0.691	1.341	1.753	2.131	2.602	2.947	3.286	3.733	4.073
16	0.258	0.690	1.337	1.746	2.120	2.583	2.921	3.252	3.686	4.015
17	0.257	0.689	1.333	1.740	2.110	2.567	2.898	3.222	3.646	3.965
18	0.257	0.658	1.330	1.734	2.101	2.552	2.878	3.197	3.610	3.922
19	0.257	0.688	1.328	1.729	2.093	2.539	2.861	3.174	3.579	3.883
20	0.257	0.687	1.325	1.725	2.086	2.528	2.845	3.153	3.552	3.850
21	0.257	0.686	1.323	1.721	2.080	2.518	2.831	3.135	3.527	3.819
22	0.256	0.686	1.321	1.717	2.074	2.508	2.819	3.119	3.505	3.792
23	0.256	0.685	1.419	1.714	2.069	2.500	2.807	3.104	3.485	3.767
24	0.256	0.685	1.318	1.711	2.064	2.492	2.797	3.091	3.467	3.745
25	0.256	0.684	1.316	1.708	2.060	2.485	2.787	3.078	3.450	3.725
26	0.256	0.684	1.315	1.706	2.056	2.479	2.779	3.067	3.435	3.707
27	0.256	0.684	1.314	1.703	2.052	2.473	2.771	3.057	3.421	3.690
28	0.256	0.683	1.313	1.701	2.048	2.467	2.763	3.047	3.408	3.674
29	0.256	0.683	1.311	1.699	2.045	2.462	2.756	3.038	0.330	3.659
30	0.256	0.683	1.310	1.697	2.042	2.457	2.750	3.030	3.385	3.646
40	0.255	0.681	1.303	1.684	2.021	2.423	2.704	2.971	3.307	3.551
60	0.254	0.679	1.296	1.671	2.000	2.390	2.660	2.915	3.232	3.460
120	0.254	0.677	1.289	1.658	1.980	2.358	2.617	2.860	3.160	3.373
∞	0.253	0.674	1.282	1.645	1.960	2.326	2.576	2.807	3.090	3.291

Critical Values for the χ^2-distribution

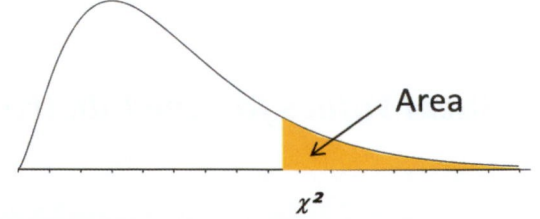

				Area in Right Tail				
DF = γ	0.995	0.990	0.975	0.950	0.500	0.050	0.025	0.010	0.005
1	0.00	0.00	0.00	0.00	0.45	3.84	5.02	6.63	7.88
2	0.01	0.02	0.05	0.10	1.39	5.99	7.38	9.21	10.60
3	0.07	0.11	0.22	0.35	2.37	7.81	9.35	11.34	12.84
4	0.21	0.30	0.48	0.71	3.36	9.49	11.14	13.28	14.86
5	0.41	0.55	0.83	1.15	4.35	11.07	12.38	15.09	16.75
6	0.68	0.87	1.24	1.64	5.35	12.59	14.45	16.81	18.55
7	0.99	1.24	1.69	2.17	6.35	14.07	16.01	18.48	20.28
8	1.34	1.65	2.18	2.73	7.34	15.51	17.53	20.09	21.96
9	1.73	2.09	2.70	3.33	8.34	16.92	19.02	21.67	23.59
10	2.16	2.56	3.25	3.94	9.34	18.31	20.48	23.21	25.19
11	2.60	3.05	3.82	4.57	10.34	19.68	21.92	24.72	26.76
12	3.07	3.57	4.40	5.23	11.34	21.03	23.34	26.22	28.30
13	3.57	4.11	5.01	5.89	12.34	22.36	24.74	27.69	29.82
14	4.07	4.66	5.63	6.57	13.34	23.68	26.12	29.14	31.32
15	4.60	5.23	6.27	7.26	14.34	25.00	27.49	30.58	32.80
16	5.14	5.81	6.91	7.96	15.34	26.30	28.85	32.00	34.27
17	5.70	6.41	7.56	8.67	16.34	27.59	30.19	33.41	35.72
18	6.26	7.01	8.23	9.39	17.34	28.87	31.53	34.81	37.16
19	6.84	7.63	8.91	10.12	18.34	30.14	32.85	36.19	38.58
20	7.43	8.26	9.59	10.85	19.34	31.41	34.17	37.57	40.00
25	10.52	11.52	13.12	14.61	24.34	37.65	40.65	44.31	46.93
30	13.79	14.95	16.79	18.49	29.34	43.77	46.98	50.89	53.67
40	20.71	22.16	24.43	26.51	39.34	55.76	59.34	63.69	66.77
50	27.99	29.71	32.36	34.76	49.33	67.50	71.42	76.15	79.49
60	35.53	37.48	40.48	43.19	59.33	79.08	83.30	88.38	91.95
70	43.28	45.44	48.76	51.74	69.33	90.53	95.02	100.42	104.22
80	51.17	53.54	57.15	60.39	79.33	101.88	106.63	112.33	116.32
90	59.20	61.75	65.65	69.13	89.33	113.14	118.14	124.12	128.30
100	67.33	70.06	74.22	77.93	99.33	124.34	129.56	135.81	140.17

Critical Values for the F-distribution

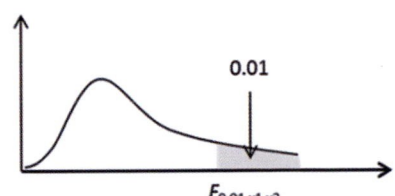

If the number of degrees of freedom is not found in the table, we follow the practice of choosing the degrees of freedom closest to that desired. If the degrees of freedom are exactly between two values, find the mean of the values.

Note: $F_{0.99,\gamma 1,\gamma 2}=1/F_{0.01,\gamma 2,\gamma 1}$

0.01

$F_{0.01,\gamma 1,\gamma 2}$

Critical Values of the F distribution $[F_{0.01,\gamma 1,\gamma 2}]$

γ2 / γ1	1	2	3	4	5	6	7	8	9	10	12	15	20	24	30	40	60	120	∞
1	4052	5000	5403	5625	5764	5859	5928	5982	6022	6056	6106	6157	6209	6235	6261	6287	6313	6339	6366
2	98.50	99.00	99.17	99.25	99.30	99.33	99.36	99.37	99.39	99.40	99.42	99.43	99.45	99.46	99.47	99.47	99.48	99.49	99.50
3	34.12	30.82	29.46	28.71	28.24	27.91	27.67	27.49	27.35	27.23	27.05	26.87	26.69	26.00	26.50	26.41	26.23	26.22	26.13
4	21.20	18.00	16.69	15.98	15.52	15.21	14.98	14.80	14.66	14.55	14.37	14.20	14.02	13.93	13.84	13.75	13.65	13.56	13.46
5	16.26	13.27	12.06	11.39	10.97	10.67	10.46	10.29	10.16	10.05	9.89	9.72	9.55	9.47	9.38	9.29	9.20	9.11	9.02
6	13.75	10.92	9.78	9.15	8.75	8.47	8.26	8.10	7.98	7.87	7.72	7.56	7.40	7.31	7.23	7.14	7.06	6.97	6.88
7	12.25	9.55	8.45	7.85	7.46	7.19	6.99	6.84	6.72	6.62	6.47	6.31	6.16	6.07	5.99	5.91	5.82	5.74	5.65
8	11.26	8.65	7.59	7.01	6.63	6.37	6.18	6.03	5.91	5.81	5.67	5.52	5.36	5.28	5.20	5.12	5.03	4.95	4.86
9	10.56	8.02	6.99	6.42	6.06	5.80	5.61	5.47	5.35	5.26	5.11	4.96	4.81	4.73	4.65	4.57	4.48	4.40	4.31
10	10.04	7.56	6.55	5.99	5.64	5.39	5.20	5.06	4.94	4.85	4.71	4.56	4.41	4.33	4.25	4.17	4.08	4.00	3.91
11	9.65	7.21	6.22	5.67	5.32	5.07	4.89	4.74	4.63	4.54	4.40	4.25	4.10	4.02	3.94	3.86	3.78	3.69	3.60
12	9.33	6.93	5.95	5.41	5.06	4.82	4.64	4.50	4.39	4.30	4.16	4.01	3.86	3.78	3.70	3.62	3.54	3.45	3.36
13	9.07	6.70	5.74	5.21	4.86	4.62	4.44	4.30	4.19	4.10	3.96	3.82	3.66	3.59	3.51	3.43	3.34	3.25	3.17
14	8.86	6.51	5.56	5.04	4.69	4.46	4.28	4.14	4.03	3.94	3.80	3.66	3.51	3.43	3.35	3.27	3.18	3.09	3.00
15	8.68	6.36	5.42	4.89	4.36	4.32	4.14	4.00	3.89	3.80	3.67	3.52	3.37	3.29	3.21	3.13	3.05	2.96	2.87
16	8.53	6.23	5.29	4.77	4.44	4.20	4.03	3.89	3.78	3.69	3.55	3.41	3.26	3.18	3.10	3.02	2.93	2.84	2.75
17	8.40	6.11	5.18	4.67	4.34	4.10	3.93	3.79	3.68	3.59	3.46	3.31	3.16	3.08	3.00	2.92	2.83	2.75	2.65
18	8.29	6.01	5.09	4.58	4.25	7.01	3.84	3.71	3.60	3.51	3.37	3.23	3.08	3.00	2.02	2.84	2.75	2.66	2.57
19	8.18	5.93	5.01	4.50	4.17	3.94	3.77	3.63	3.52	3.43	3.30	3.15	3.00	2.92	2.84	2.76	2.67	2.58	2.59
20	8.10	5.85	4.94	4.43	4.10	3.87	3.70	3.56	3.46	3.37	3.23	3.09	2.94	2.86	2.78	2.69	2.61	2.52	2.42
21	8.02	5.78	4.87	4.37	4.04	3.81	3.64	3.51	3.40	3.31	3.17	3.03	2.88	2.80	2.72	2.64	2.55	2.46	2.36
22	7.95	5.72	4.82	4.31	3.99	3.76	3.59	3.45	3.35	3.26	3.12	2.98	2.83	2.75	2.67	2.58	2.50	2.40	2.31
23	7.88	5.66	4.76	4.26	3.94	3.71	3.54	3.41	3.30	3.21	3.07	2.93	2.78	2.70	2.62	2.54	2.45	2.35	2.26
24	7.82	5.61	4.72	4.22	3.90	3.67	3.50	3.36	3.26	3.17	3.03	2.89	2.74	2.66	2.58	2.49	2.40	2.31	2.21
25	7.77	5.57	4.68	4.18	3.85	3.63	3.46	3.32	3.22	3.13	2.99	2.85	2.70	2.62	2.54	2.45	2.36	2.27	2.17
26	7.72	5.53	4.64	4.14	3.82	3.59	3.42	3.29	3.18	3.09	2.96	2.81	2.66	2.58	2.50	2.42	2.33	2.23	2.13
27	7.68	5.49	4.60	4.11	3.78	3.56	3.39	3.26	3.15	3.06	2.93	2.78	2.63	2.55	2.47	2.38	2.29	2.20	2.10
28	7.64	5.45	4.57	4.07	3.75	3.53	3.36	3.23	3.12	3.03	2.90	2.75	2.60	2.52	2.44	2.35	2.26	2.17	2.06
29	7.60	5.42	4.54	4.04	3.73	3.50	3.33	3.20	3.09	3.00	2.87	2.73	2.57	2.49	2.41	2.33	2.23	2.14	2.03
30	7.56	5.39	4.51	4.02	3.70	3.47	3.30	3.17	3.07	2.98	2.84	2.70	2.55	2.47	2.39	2.30	2.21	2.11	2.01
40	7.31	5.18	4.31	3.83	3.51	3.29	3.12	2.99	2.89	2.80	2.66	2.52	2.37	2.29	2.20	2.11	2.02	1.92	1.80
60	7.08	4.98	4.13	3.65	3.34	3.12	2.95	2.82	2.72	2.63	2.50	2.35	2.20	2.12	2.03	1.94	1.84	1.73	1.60
120	6.85	4.79	3.95	3.48	3.17	2.96	2.79	2.66	2.56	2.47	2.34	2.19	2.03	1.95	1.86	1.76	1.66	1.53	1.38
∞	6.63	4.61	3.78	3.32	3.02	2.80	2.64	2.51	2.41	2.32	2.18	2.04	1.88	1.79	1.70	1.59	1.47	1.32	1.00

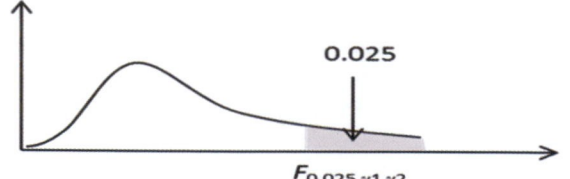

0.025

$F_{0.025,\gamma1,\gamma2}$

Note: $F_{0.975,\gamma1,\gamma2}=1/\ F_{0.025,\gamma2,\gamma1}$

Critical Values of the F distribution [$F_{0.025,\gamma1,\gamma2}$]

$\gamma2\,/\,\gamma1$	1	2	3	4	5	6	7	8	9	10	12	15	20	24	30	40	60	120	∞
1	647.8	799.5	864.2	899.6	921.8	937.1	948.2	956.7	963.3	968.6	976.7	984.9	993.1	997.2	1001	1006	1010	1014	1018
2	38.51	39.00	39.17	39.25	39.30	39.33	39.36	39.37	39.39	39.40	39.41	39.43	39.45	39.46	39.46	39.47	39.48	39.49	39.50
3	17.44	16.04	15.44	15.10	14.88	14.73	14.62	14.54	14.47	14.42	14.34	14.25	14.17	14.12	14.08	14.04	13.99	13.95	13.90
4	12.22	10.65	9.98	9.60	9.36	9.20	9.07	8.98	8.90	8.84	8.75	8.66	8.56	8.51	8.46	8.41	8.36	8.31	8.26
5	10.01	8.43	7.76	7.39	7.15	6.98	6.85	6.76	6.68	6.62	6.52	6.43	6.33	6.28	6.23	6.18	6.12	6.07	6.02
6	8.81	7.26	6.60	6.23	5.99	5.82	5.70	5.60	5.52	5.46	5.37	5.27	5.17	5.12	5.07	5.01	4.96	4.90	4.85
7	8.07	6.54	5.89	5.52	5.29	5.12	4.99	4.90	4.82	4.76	4.67	4.57	4.47	4.42	4.36	4.31	4.25	4.20	4.14
8	7.57	6.06	5.42	5.05	4.82	4.65	4.53	4.43	4.36	4.30	4.20	4.10	4.00	3.95	3.89	3.84	3.78	3.73	3.67
9	7.21	5.71	5.08	4.72	4.48	4.32	4.20	4.10	4.03	3.96	3.87	3.77	3.67	3.61	3.56	3.51	3.45	3.39	3.33
10	6.94	5.46	4.83	4.47	4.24	4.07	3.95	3.85	3.78	3.72	3.62	3.52	3.42	3.37	3.31	3.26	3.20	3.14	3.08
11	6.72	5.26	4.63	4.28	4.04	3.88	3.76	3.66	3.59	3.53	3.43	3.33	3.23	3.17	3.12	3.06	3.00	2.94	2.88
12	6.55	5.10	4.47	4.12	3.89	3.73	3.61	3.51	3.44	3.37	3.28	3.18	3.07	3.02	2.96	2.91	2.85	2.79	2.72
13	6.41	4.97	4.35	4.00	3.77	3.60	3.48	3.39	3.31	3.25	3.15	3.05	2.95	2.89	2.84	2.78	2.72	2.66	2.60
14	6.30	4.86	4.24	3.89	3.66	3.50	3.38	3.29	3.21	3.15	3.05	2.95	2.84	2.79	2.73	2.67	2.61	2.55	2.49
15	6.20	4.77	4.15	3.80	3.58	3.41	3.29	3.20	3.12	3.06	2.96	2.86	2.76	2.70	2.64	2.59	2.52	2.46	2.40
16	6.12	4.69	4.08	3.73	3.50	3.34	3.22	3.12	3.05	2.99	2.89	2.79	2.68	2.63	2.57	2.51	2.45	2.38	2.32
17	6.04	4.62	4.01	3.66	3.44	3.28	3.16	3.06	2.98	2.92	2.82	2.72	2.62	2.56	2.50	2.44	2.38	2.32	2.25
18	5.98	4.56	3.95	3.61	3.38	3.22	3.10	3.01	2.93	2.87	2.77	2.67	2.56	2.50	2.44	2.38	2.32	2.26	2.19
19	5.92	4.51	3.90	3.56	3.33	3.17	3.05	2.96	2.88	2.82	2.72	2.62	2.51	2.45	2.39	2.33	2.27	2.20	2.13
20	5.87	4.46	3.86	3.51	3.29	3.13	3.01	2.91	2.84	2.77	2.68	2.57	2.46	2.41	2.35	2.29	2.22	2.16	2.09
21	5.83	4.42	3.82	3.48	3.25	3.09	2.97	2.87	2.80	2.73	2.64	2.53	2.42	2.37	2.31	2.25	2.18	2.11	2.04
22	5.79	4.38	3.78	3.44	3.22	3.05	2.93	2.84	2.76	2.70	2.60	2.50	2.39	2.33	2.27	2.21	2.14	2.08	2.00
23	5.75	4.35	3.75	3.41	3.18	3.02	2.90	2.81	2.73	2.67	2.57	2.47	2.36	2.30	2.24	2.18	2.11	2.04	1.97
24	5.72	4.32	3.72	3.38	3.15	2.99	2.87	2.78	2.70	2.64	2.54	2.44	2.33	2.27	2.21	2.15	2.08	2.01	1.94
25	5.69	4.29	3.69	3.35	3.13	2.97	2.85	2.75	2.68	2.61	2.51	2.41	2.30	2.24	2.18	2.12	2.05	1.98	1.91
26	5.66	4.27	3.67	3.33	3.10	2.94	2.82	2.73	2.65	2.59	2.49	2.39	2.28	2.22	2.16	2.09	2.03	1.95	1.88
27	5.63	4.24	3.65	3.31	3.08	2.92	2.80	2.71	2.63	2.57	2.47	2.36	2.25	2.19	2.13	2.07	2.00	1.93	1.85
28	5.61	4.22	3.63	3.29	3.06	2.90	2.78	2.69	2.61	2.55	2.45	2.34	2.23	2.17	2.11	2.05	1.98	1.91	1.83
29	5.59	4.20	3.61	3.27	3.04	2.88	2.76	2.67	2.59	2.53	2.43	2.32	2.21	2.15	2.09	2.03	1.96	1.89	1.81
30	5.57	4.18	3.59	3.25	3.03	2.87	2.75	2.65	2.57	2.51	2.41	2.31	2.20	2.14	2.07	2.01	1.94	1.87	1.79
40	5.42	4.05	3.46	3.13	2.90	2.74	2.62	2.53	2.45	2.39	2.29	2.18	2.07	2.01	1.94	1.88	1.80	1.72	1.64
60	5.29	3.93	3.34	3.01	2.79	2.63	2.51	2.41	2.33	2.27	2.17	2.06	1.14	1.88	1.82	1.74	1.67	1.58	1.48
120	5.15	3.80	3.23	2.89	2.67	2.52	2.39	2.30	2.22	2.16	2.05	1.94	1.82	1.76	1.69	1.61	1.53	1.43	1.31
∞	5.02	3.69	3.12	2.79	2.57	2.41	2.29	2.19	2.11	2.05	1.94	1.83	1.71	1.64	1.57	1.48	1.39	1.27	1.00

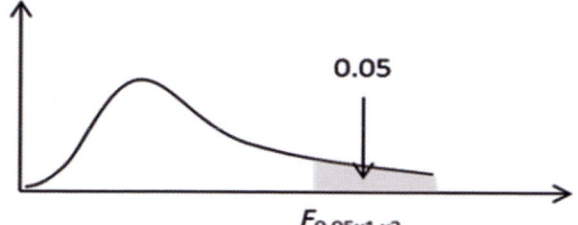

0.05

$F_{0.05\gamma1,\gamma2}$

Note: $F_{0.95,\gamma1,\gamma2}=1/ F_{0.05,\gamma2,\gamma1}$

Critical Values of the F distribution - [$F_{0.05,\gamma1,\gamma2}$]

γ2 /γ1	1	2	3	4	5	6	7	8	9	10	12	15	20	24	30	40	60	120	∞
1	161.4	199.5	215.7	224.6	230.2	234.0	236.8	238.9	240.5	241.9	243.9	245.9	248.0	249.1	250.1	251.1	252.2	253.3	254.0
2	18.51	19.00	19.16	19.25	19.30	19.33	19.35	19.37	19.38	19.40	19.41	19.43	19.45	19.45	19.46	19.47	19.48	19.49	19.50
3	10.13	9.55	9.28	9.12	9.01	8.94	8.89	8.85	8.81	8.79	8.74	8.70	8.66	8.64	8.62	8.59	8.57	8.55	8.53
4	7.71	6.94	6.59	6.39	6.26	6.16	6.09	6.04	6.00	5.96	5.91	5.86	5.80	5.77	5.75	5.72	5.69	5.66	5.63
5	6.61	5.79	5.41	5.19	5.05	4.95	4.88	4.82	4.77	4.74	4.68	4.62	4.56	4.53	4.50	4.46	4.43	4.40	4.36
6	5.99	5.14	4.76	4.53	4.39	4.28	4.21	4.15	4.10	4.06	4.00	3.94	3.87	3.84	3.81	3.77	3.74	3.70	3.67
7	5.59	4.74	4.35	4.12	3.97	3.87	3.79	3.73	3.68	3.64	3.57	3.51	3.44	3.41	3.38	3.34	3.30	3.27	3.23
8	5.32	4.46	4.07	3.84	3.69	3.58	3.50	3.44	3.39	3.35	3.28	3.22	3.15	3.12	3.08	3.04	3.01	2.97	2.93
9	5.12	4.26	3.86	3.63	3.48	3.37	3.29	3.23	3.18	3.14	3.07	3.01	2.94	2.90	2.86	2.83	2.79	2.75	2.71
10	4.96	4.10	3.71	3.48	3.33	3.22	3.14	3.07	3.02	2.98	2.91	2.85	2.77	2.74	2.70	2.66	2.62	2.58	2.54
11	4.84	3.98	3.59	3.36	3.20	3.09	3.01	2.95	2.90	2.85	2.79	2.72	2.65	2.61	2.57	2.53	2.49	2.45	2.40
12	4.75	3.89	3.49	3.26	3.11	3.00	2.91	2.85	2.80	2.75	2.69	2.62	2.54	2.51	2.47	2.43	2.38	2.34	2.30
13	4.67	3.81	3.41	3.18	3.03	2.92	2.83	2.77	2.71	2.67	2.60	2.53	2.46	2.42	2.38	2.34	2.30	2.25	2.21
14	4.60	3.74	3.34	3.11	2.96	2.85	2.76	2.70	2.65	2.60	2.53	2.46	2.39	2.35	2.31	2.27	2.22	2.18	2.13
15	4.54	3.68	3.29	3.06	2.90	2.79	2.71	2.64	2.59	2.54	2.48	2.40	2.33	2.29	2.25	2.20	2.16	2.11	2.07
16	4.49	3.63	3.24	3.01	2.85	2.74	2.66	2.59	2.54	2.49	2.42	2.35	2.28	2.24	2.19	2.15	2.11	2.06	2.01
17	4.45	3.59	3.20	2.96	2.81	2.70	2.61	2.55	2.49	2.45	2.38	2.31	2.23	2.19	2.15	2.10	2.06	2.01	1.96
18	4.41	3.55	3.16	2.93	2.77	2.66	2.58	2.51	2.46	2.41	2.34	2.27	2.19	2.15	2.11	2.06	2.02	1.97	1.92
19	4.38	3.52	3.13	2.90	2.74	2.63	2.54	2.48	2.42	2.38	2.31	2.23	2.16	2.11	2.07	2.03	1.98	1.93	1.88
20	4.35	3.49	3.10	2.87	2.71	2.60	2.51	2.45	2.39	2.35	2.28	2.20	2.12	2.08	2.04	1.99	1.95	1.90	1.84
21	4.32	3.47	3.07	2.84	2.68	2.57	2.49	2.42	2.37	2.32	2.25	2.18	2.10	2.05	2.01	1.96	1.92	1.87	1.81
22	4.30	3.44	3.05	2.82	2.66	2.55	2.46	2.40	2.34	2.30	2.23	2.15	2.07	2.03	1.98	1.94	1.89	1.84	1.78
23	4.28	3.42	3.03	2.80	2.64	2.53	2.44	2.37	2.32	2.27	2.20	2.13	2.05	2.01	1.96	1.91	1.86	1.81	1.76
24	4.26	3.40	3.01	2.78	2.62	2.51	2.42	2.36	2.30	2.25	2.18	2.11	2.03	1.98	1.94	1.89	1.84	1.79	1.73
25	4.24	3.39	2.99	2.76	2.60	2.49	2.40	2.34	2.28	2.24	2.16	2.09	2.01	1.96	1.92	1.87	1.82	1.77	1.71
26	4.23	3.37	2.98	2.74	2.59	2.47	2.39	2.32	2.27	2.22	2.15	2.07	1.99	1.95	1.90	1.85	1.80	1.75	1.69
27	4.21	3.35	2.96	2.73	2.57	2.46	2.37	2.31	2.25	2.20	2.13	2.06	1.97	1.93	1.88	1.84	1.79	1.73	1.67
28	4.20	3.34	2.95	2.71	2.56	2.45	2.36	2.29	2.24	2.19	2.12	2.04	1.96	1.91	1.87	1.82	1.77	1.71	1.65
29	4.18	3.33	2.93	2.70	2.55	2.43	2.35	2.28	2.22	2.18	2.10	2.03	1.94	1.90	1.85	1.81	1.75	1.70	1.64
30	4.17	3.32	2.92	2.69	2.53	2.42	2.33	2.27	2.21	2.16	2.09	2.01	1.93	1.89	1.84	1.79	1.74	1.68	1.62
40	4.08	3.23	2.84	2.61	2.45	2.34	2.25	2.18	2.12	2.08	2.00	1.92	1.84	1.79	1.74	1.69	1.64	1.58	1.51
60	4.00	3.15	2.76	2.53	2.37	2.25	2.17	2.10	2.04	1.99	1.92	1.84	1.75	1.70	1.65	1.59	1.53	1.47	1.39
120	3.92	3.07	2.68	2.45	2.29	2.17	2.09	2.02	1.96	1.91	1.83	1.75	1.66	1.61	1.55	1.55	1.43	1.35	1.25
Infin	3.84	3.00	2.60	2.37	2.21	2.10	2.01	1.94	1.88	1.83	1.75	1.67	1.57	1.52	1.46	1.39	1.32	1.22	1.00

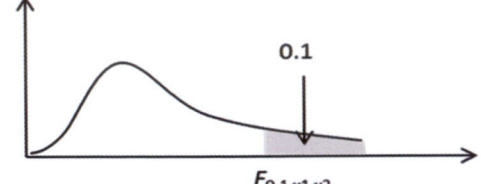

0.1

$F_{0.1,\gamma1,\gamma2}$

Note: $F_{0.90,\gamma1,\gamma2}=1/ F_{0.10,\gamma2,\gamma1}$

Critical Values of the F distribution - [$F_{0.10,\gamma1,\gamma2}$]

γ2/γ1	1	2	3	4	5	6	7	8	9	10	12	15	20	24	30	40	60	120	∞
1	39.86	49.50	53.59	55.83	57.24	58.20	58.91	59.44	59.86	60.19	60.71	61.22	61.74	62.00	62.26	62.53	62.79	63.06	63.33
2	8.53	9.00	9.16	9.24	9.29	9.33	9.35	9.37	9.38	9.39	9.41	9.42	9.44	9.45	9.46	9.47	9.47	9.48	9.49
3	5.54	5.46	5.39	5.34	5.31	5.28	5.27	5.25	5.24	5.20	5.22	5.20	5.18	5.18	5.17	5.16	5.15	5.14	5.13
4	4.54	4.32	4.19	4.11	4.05	4.01	3.98	3.95	3.94	3.92	3.90	3.87	3.84	3.83	3.82	3.80	3.79	3.78	3.76
5	4.06	3.78	3.62	3.52	3.45	3.40	3.37	3.34	3.32	3.30	3.27	3.24	3.21	3.19	3.17	3.16	3.14	3.12	3.10
6	3.78	3.46	3.29	3.18	3.11	3.05	3.01	2.98	2.96	2.94	2.90	2.87	2.84	2.82	2.80	2.78	2.76	2.74	2.72
7	3.59	3.26	3.07	2.96	2.88	2.83	2.78	2.75	2.72	2.70	2.67	2.63	2.59	2.58	2.56	2.54	2.51	2.49	2.47
8	3.46	3.11	2.92	2.81	2.73	2.67	2.62	2.59	2.56	2.54	2.50	2.46	2.42	2.40	2.38	2.36	2.34	2.32	2.29
9	3.36	3.01	2.81	2.69	2.61	2.55	2.51	2.47	2.44	2.42	2.38	2.34	2.30	2.28	2.25	2.23	2.21	2.18	2.16
10	3.29	2.92	2.73	2.61	2.52	2.46	2.41	2.38	2.35	2.32	2.28	2.24	2.20	2.18	2.16	2.13	2.11	2.08	2.06
11	3.23	2.86	2.66	2.54	2.45	2.39	2.34	2.30	2.27	2.25	2.21	2.17	2.12	2.10	2.08	2.05	2.03	2.00	1.97
12	3.18	2.81	2.61	2.48	2.39	2.33	2.28	2.24	2.21	2.19	2.15	2.10	2.06	2.04	2.01	1.99	1.96	1.93	1.90
13	3.14	2.76	2.56	2.43	2.35	2.28	2.23	2.20	2.16	2.14	2.10	2.05	2.01	1.98	1.96	1.93	1.90	1.88	1.85
14	3.10	2.73	2.52	2.39	2.31	2.24	2.19	2.15	2.12	2.10	2.05	2.01	1.96	1.94	1.91	1.89	1.86	1.83	1.80
15	3.07	2.70	2.49	2.36	2.27	2.21	2.16	2.12	2.09	2.06	2.02	1.97	1.92	1.90	1.87	1.85	1.82	1.79	1.76
16	3.05	2.67	2.46	2.33	2.24	2.18	2.13	2.09	2.06	2.03	1.99	1.94	1.89	1.87	1.84	1.81	1.78	1.75	1.72
17	3.03	2.64	2.44	2.31	2.22	2.15	2.10	2.06	2.03	2.00	1.96	1.91	1.86	1.84	1.81	1.78	1.75	1.72	1.69
18	3.01	2.62	2.42	2.29	2.20	2.13	2.08	2.04	2.00	1.98	1.93	1.89	1.84	1.81	1.78	1.75	1.72	1.69	1.66
19	2.99	2.61	2.40	2.27	2.18	2.11	2.06	2.02	1.98	1.96	1.91	1.86	1.81	1.79	1.76	1.73	1.70	1.67	1.63
20	2.97	2.59	2.38	2.25	2.16	2.09	2.04	2.00	1.96	1.94	1.89	1.84	1.79	1.77	1.74	1.71	1.68	1.64	1.61
21	2.96	2.57	2.36	2.23	2.14	2.08	2.02	1.98	1.95	1.92	1.87	1.83	1.78	1.75	1.72	1.69	1.66	1.62	1.59
22	2.95	2.56	2.35	2.22	2.13	2.06	2.01	1.97	1.93	1.90	1.86	1.81	1.76	1.73	1.70	1.67	1.64	1.60	1.57
23	2.94	2.55	2.34	2.21	2.11	2.05	1.99	1.95	1.92	1.89	1.84	1.80	1.74	1.72	1.69	1.66	1.62	1.59	1.55
24	2.93	2.54	2.33	2.19	2.10	2.04	1.98	1.94	1.91	1.88	1.83	1.78	1.73	1.70	1.67	1.64	1.61	1.57	1.53
25	2.92	2.53	2.32	2.18	2.09	2.02	1.97	1.93	1.89	1.87	1.82	1.77	1.72	1.69	1.66	1.63	1.59	1.56	1.52
26	2.91	2.52	2.31	2.17	2.08	2.01	1.96	1.92	1.88	1.86	1.81	1.76	1.71	1.68	1.65	1.61	1.58	1.54	1.50
27	2.90	2.51	2.30	2.17	2.07	2.00	1.95	1.91	1.87	1.85	1.80	1.75	1.70	1.67	1.64	1.60	1.57	1.53	1.49
28	2.89	2.50	2.29	2.16	2.06	2.00	1.94	1.90	1.87	1.84	1.79	1.74	1.69	1.66	1.63	1.59	1.56	1.52	1.48
29	2.89	2.50	2.28	2.15	2.06	1.99	1.93	1.89	1.86	1.83	1.78	1.73	1.68	1.65	1.62	1.58	1.55	1.51	1.47
30	2.88	2.49	2.28	2.14	2.03	1.98	1.93	1.88	1.85	1.82	1.77	1.72	1.67	1.64	1.61	1.57	1.54	1.50	1.46
40	2.84	2.44	2.23	2.09	2.00	1.93	1.87	1.83	1.79	1.76	1.71	1.66	1.61	1.57	1.54	1.51	1.47	1.42	1.38
60	2.79	2.39	2.18	2.04	1.95	1.87	1.82	1.77	1.74	1.71	1.66	1.60	1.54	1.51	1.48	1.44	1.40	1.35	1.29
120	2.75	2.35	2.13	1.99	1.90	1.82	1.77	1.72	1.68	1.65	1.60	1.55	1.48	1.45	1.41	1.37	1.32	1.26	1.19
Infin	2.71	2.30	2.08	1.94	1.85	1.77	1.72	1.67	1.63	1.60	1.55	1.49	1.42	1.38	1.34	1.30	1.24	1.17	1.00

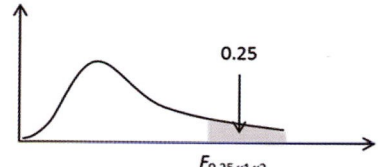

$F_{0.25,\gamma 1,\gamma 2}$

Note: $F_{0.75,\gamma 1,\gamma 2}=1/\ F_{0.25,\gamma 2,\gamma 1}$

Critical Values of the F distribution - [$F_{0.25,\gamma 1,\gamma 2}$]

γ2 / γ1	1	2	3	4	5	6	7	8	9	10	12	15	20	24	30	40	60	120	∞
1	5.83	7.50	8.20	8.58	8.82	8.98	9.10	9.19	9.26	9.32	9.41	9.49	9.58	9.63	9.67	9.71	9.76	9.80	9.85
2	2.57	3.00	3.15	3.23	3.28	3.31	3.34	3.35	3.37	3.38	3.39	3.41	3.43	3.43	3.44	3.45	3.46	3.47	3.48
3	2.02	2.28	2.36	2.39	2.41	2.42	2.43	2.44	2.44	2.44	2.45	2.46	2.46	2.46	2.47	2.47	2.47	2.47	2.47
4	1.81	2.00	2.05	2.06	2.07	2.08	2.08	2.08	2.08	2.08	2.08	2.08	2.08	2.08	2.08	2.08	2.08	2.08	2.08
5	1.69	1.85	1.88	1.89	1.89	1.89	1.89	1.89	1.89	1.89	1.89	1.89	1.88	1.88	1.88	1.88	1.87	1.87	1.87
6	1.62	1.76	1.78	1.79	1.79	1.78	1.78	1.78	1.77	1.77	1.77	1.76	1.76	1.75	1.75	1.75	1.74	1.74	1.74
7	1.57	1.70	1.72	1.72	1.71	1.71	1.70	1.70	1.70	1.69	1.68	1.68	1.67	1.67	1.66	1.66	1.65	1.65	1.65
8	1.54	1.66	1.67	1.66	1.66	1.65	1.64	1.64	1.63	1.63	1.62	1.62	1.61	1.60	1.60	1.59	1.59	1.58	1.58
9	1.51	1.62	1.63	1.63	1.62	1.61	1.60	1.60	1.59	1.59	1.58	1.57	1.56	1.56	1.55	1.54	1.54	1.53	1.53
10	1.49	1.60	1.60	1.59	1.59	1.58	1.57	1.56	1.56	1.55	1.54	1.53	1.52	1.52	1.51	1.51	1.50	1.49	1.48
11	1.47	1.58	1.58	1.57	1.56	1.55	1.54	1.53	1.53	1.52	1.51	1.50	1.49	1.49	1.48	1.47	1.47	1.46	1.45
12	1.46	1.56	1.56	1.55	1.54	1.53	1.52	1.51	1.51	1.50	1.49	1.48	1.47	1.46	1.45	1.45	1.44	1.43	1.42
13	1.45	1.55	1.55	1.53	1.52	1.51	1.50	1.49	1.49	1.48	1.47	1.46	1.45	1.44	1.43	1.42	1.42	1.41	1.40
14	1.44	1.53	1.53	1.52	1.51	1.50	1.49	1.48	1.47	1.46	1.45	1.44	1.43	1.42	1.41	1.41	1.40	1.39	1.38
15	1.43	1.52	1.52	1.51	1.49	1.48	1.47	1.46	1.46	1.45	1.44	1.43	1.41	1.41	1.40	1.39	1.38	1.37	1.36
16	1.42	1.51	1.51	1.50	1.48	1.47	1.46	1.45	1.44	1.44	1.43	1.41	1.40	1.39	1.38	1.37	1.36	1.35	1.34
17	1.42	1.51	1.50	1.49	1.47	1.46	1.45	1.44	1.43	1.43	1.41	1.40	1.39	1.38	1.37	1.36	1.35	1.34	1.33
18	1.41	1.50	1.49	1.48	1.46	1.45	1.44	1.43	1.42	1.42	1.40	1.39	1.38	1.37	1.36	1.35	1.34	1.33	1.32
19	1.41	1.49	1.49	1.47	1.46	1.44	1.43	1.42	1.41	1.41	1.40	1.38	1.37	1.36	1.35	1.34	1.33	1.32	1.30
20	1.40	1.49	1.48	1.47	1.45	1.44	1.43	1.42	1.41	1.40	1.39	1.37	1.36	1.35	1.34	1.33	1.32	1.31	1.29
21	1.40	1.48	1.48	1.46	1.44	1.43	1.42	1.41	1.40	1.39	1.38	1.37	1.35	1.34	1.33	1.32	1.31	1.30	1.28
22	1.40	1.48	1.47	1.45	1.44	1.42	1.41	1.40	1.39	1.39	1.37	1.36	1.34	1.33	1.32	1.31	1.30	1.29	1.28
23	1.39	1.47	1.47	1.45	1.43	1.42	1.41	1.40	1.39	1.38	1.37	1.35	1.34	1.33	1.32	1.31	1.30	1.28	1.27
24	1.39	1.47	1.46	1.44	1.43	1.41	1.40	1.39	1.38	1.38	1.36	1.35	1.33	1.32	1.31	1.30	1.29	1.28	1.26
25	1.39	1.47	1.46	1.44	1.42	1.41	1.40	1.39	1.38	1.37	1.36	1.34	1.33	1.32	1.31	1.29	1.28	1.27	1.25
26	1.38	1.46	1.45	1.44	1.42	1.41	1.39	1.38	1.37	1.37	1.35	1.34	1.32	1.31	1.30	1.29	1.28	1.26	1.25
27	1.38	1.46	1.45	1.43	1.42	1.40	1.39	1.38	1.37	1.36	1.35	1.33	1.32	1.31	1.30	1.28	1.27	1.26	1.24
28	1.38	1.46	1.45	1.43	1.41	1.40	1.39	1.38	1.37	1.36	1.34	1.33	1.31	1.30	1.29	1.28	1.27	1.25	1.24
29	1.38	1.45	1.45	1.43	1.41	1.40	1.38	1.37	1.36	1.35	1.34	1.32	1.31	1.30	1.29	1.27	1.26	1.25	1.23
30	1.38	1.45	1.44	1.42	1.41	1.39	1.38	1.37	1.36	1.35	1.34	1.32	1.30	1.29	1.28	1.27	1.26	1.24	1.23
40	1.36	1.44	1.42	1.40	1.39	1.37	1.36	1.35	1.34	1.33	1.31	1.30	1.28	1.26	1.25	1.24	1.22	1.21	1.19
60	1.35	1.42	1.41	1.38	1.37	1.35	1.33	1.32	1.31	1.30	1.29	1.27	1.25	1.24	1.22	1.21	1.19	1.17	1.15
120	1.34	1.40	1.39	1.37	1.35	1.33	1.31	1.30	1.29	1.28	1.26	1.24	1.22	1.21	1.19	1.18	1.16	1.13	1.10
Infin	1.32	1.39	1.37	1.35	1.33	1.31	1.29	1.28	1.27	1.25	1.24	1.22	1.19	1.18	1.16	1.14	1.12	1.08	1.00

APPENDIX B
SUMMARY of FORMULA

Summary of Formula

$$Mean = \bar{X} = \frac{sum\ of\ all\ values}{number\ of\ observations} = \sum_{1}^{n} x_i / n$$

$$Standard\ Deviation = s = \sqrt{\frac{\Sigma_1^n (x_i - \bar{X})^2}{n}}$$

$$Variance = s^2 = \frac{\Sigma_1^n (x_i - \bar{X})^2}{n}$$

$$The\ z-score = z = \frac{x - \bar{X}}{s} \quad or \quad z = \frac{x - \mu}{\sigma}$$

$$Skewness\ Index = \frac{n}{(n-1)(n-2)} \sum_{1}^{n} \left(\frac{x_i - \bar{X}}{s} \right)^3$$

$$Kurtosis\ Index = \frac{n(n+1)}{(n-1)(n-2)(n-3)} \sum_{1}^{n} \left(\frac{x_i - \bar{X}}{s} \right)^4 - \frac{3(n-1)^2}{(n-2)(n-3)}$$

$$Box\ Plot\ Parameters: l_p = \frac{p}{100}(n+1)$$

$$P(A) = \frac{number\ of\ favorable\ outcomes}{total\ number\ of\ outcomes} = \frac{m}{n}$$

$$P(A') = q(A) = P(not\ A) = \frac{(n-m)}{n} = 1 - p(A) = 1 - \frac{m}{n}$$

$$0 \le P(A) \le 1$$

$$\sum P(A_i) = 1$$

Conditional Probability $= P(B|A) = \frac{P(A\&B)}{P(A)}$

$$P(A\ and\ B) = P(A)P(B|A)$$

Counting Rules:

$$m! = m(m-1)(m-2) \cdots 2 \cdot 1$$
$$0! = 1\ and\ 1! = 1.$$
$$n^P r = \frac{n!}{(n-r)!}$$

$$n^C r = \frac{n!}{r!\,(n-r)!}$$

Bayes Theorem:

$$P(A_i|B) = \frac{P(A_i)P(B|A_i)}{P(A_1)P(B|A_1) + P(A_2)P(B|A_2)}$$

Binomial distribution:

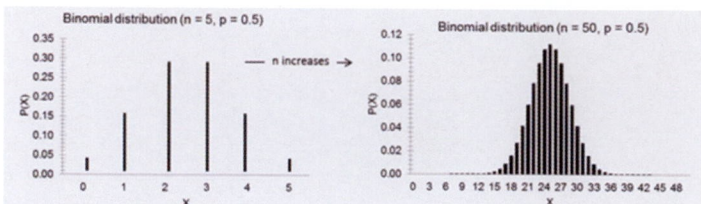

$$P(x) = f(x|n) = \binom{n}{x}p^x(1-p)^{n-x}$$

Or

$$P(x) = \frac{n!}{x!(n-x)!} \, p^x \, (1-p)^{n-x}$$

$$x = 0,1,2,3,4,\dots,n$$

$$\mu = np$$
$$\sigma^2 = np(1-p)$$

Poisson distribution:

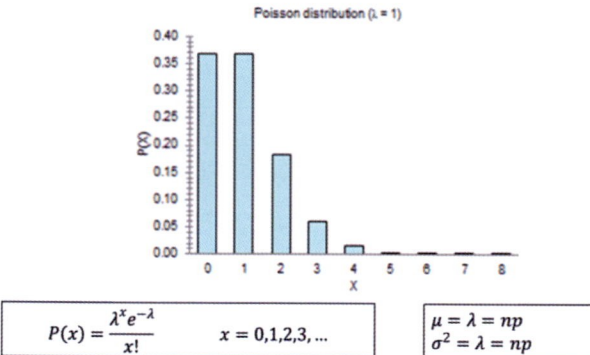

$$P(x) = \frac{\lambda^x e^{-\lambda}}{x!} \qquad x = 0,1,2,3,\dots$$

$$\mu = \lambda = np$$
$$\sigma^2 = \lambda = np$$

Uniform distribution:

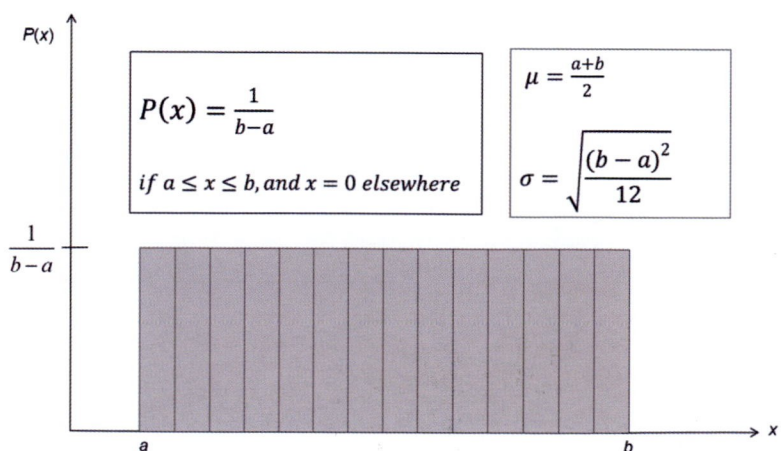

$$P(x) = \frac{1}{b-a}$$

$$if \; a \leq x \leq b, and \; x = 0 \; elsewhere$$

$$\mu = \frac{a+b}{2}$$

$$\sigma = \sqrt{\frac{(b-a)^2}{12}}$$

Normal distribution:

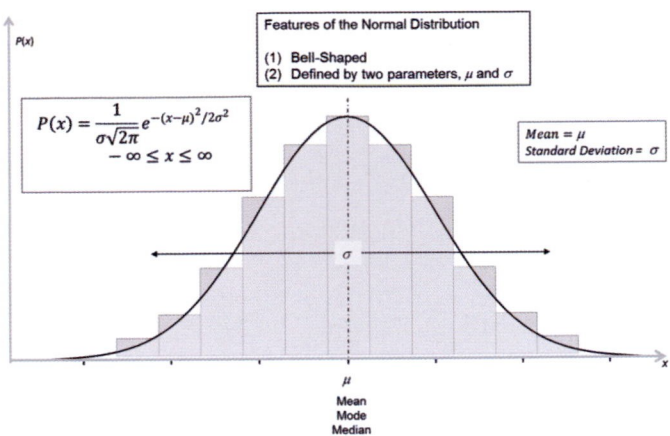

$$Sampling\ error = \bar{X} - \mu$$

The Central Limit theorem

$$\mu_{\bar{X}} = \mu_x \quad , \quad \sigma_{\bar{X}} = \frac{\sigma_x}{\sqrt{n}}$$

Estimation of population mean: Special conditions
Condition I: Large sample (n ≥ 30) or population standard deviation, σ, is known
Two-Sided Interval Estimate:

$$\bar{X} - z_{\frac{\alpha}{2}}\sigma_{\bar{X}} < \mu < \bar{X} + z_{\frac{\alpha}{2}}\sigma_{\bar{X}} \quad or\ \mu = \bar{X} \pm z_{\alpha/2}\sigma_{\bar{X}}$$

$$\sigma_{\bar{X}} = \frac{\sigma_x}{\sqrt{n}}\ is\ called\ the\ standard\ error$$

One-Sided Interval Estimate:

$$\bar{X} - z_{\alpha}\sigma_{\bar{X}} < \mu \quad or \quad \mu < \bar{X} + z_{\alpha}\sigma_{\bar{X}}$$

The minimum sample size (n)

$$n = \left(\frac{z \cdot \sigma_x}{E}\right)^2$$

Condition II: Small Sample (n < 30) - Population Standard Deviation, σ is Unknown
Two-Sided Confidence Interval
$$\bar{X} - t_{df,\frac{\alpha}{2}}s_{\bar{X}} < \mu < \bar{X} + t_{df,\frac{\alpha}{2}}s_{\bar{X}}$$

$$or\ \mu = \bar{X} \pm t_{df,\frac{\alpha}{2}}s_{\bar{X}}$$

$$or\ \mu = \bar{X} \pm t_{df,\alpha/2}\frac{s}{\sqrt{n}}$$

One-sided Interval Estimate:

$$\bar{X} - t_{df,\alpha}s_{\bar{X}} < \mu\ \&\ \mu < \bar{X} + t_{df,\alpha}s_{\bar{X}}$$

Estimation of Population Proportion

Two-sided confidence interval for the proportion, p, of a population:

$$\hat{p} - z_{\alpha/2}\sigma_p < p < \hat{p} + z_{\alpha/2}\sigma_p$$

$$p = \hat{p} \pm z_{\alpha/2}\sigma_p$$

$$\hat{p} - z_{\alpha/2}\sqrt{\frac{\hat{p}(1-\hat{p})}{n}} < p < \hat{p} + z_{\alpha/2}\sqrt{\frac{\hat{p}(1-\hat{p})}{n}}$$

One-sided confidence interval for the proportion, p, of a population:

$$\hat{p} - z_{\alpha}\sqrt{\frac{\hat{p}(1-\hat{p})}{n}} < p \quad \& \quad p < \hat{p} + z_{\alpha}\sqrt{\frac{\hat{p}(1-\hat{p})}{n}}$$

The minimum sample size for proportion inspection is obtained from the following formula:

$$n = \hat{p}(1-\hat{p})\left(\frac{z}{E}\right)^2$$

Hypothesis Testing:

Condition I: Large sample ($n \geq 30$) or population standard deviation, σ, is known-Using the p-Value

Test	Null hypothesis	Alternative hypothesis	Test statistic	Reject when
Two-sided	$H_o: \mu = \mu_o$	$H_1: \mu \neq \mu_o$		
One-sided-left	$H_o: \mu \geq \mu_o$	$H_1: \mu < \mu_o$	$z_o = \dfrac{\bar{X} - \mu_o}{\dfrac{\sigma_x}{\sqrt{n}}}$	p-value $< \alpha$
One-sided-right	$H_o: \mu \leq \mu_o$	$H_1: \mu > \mu_o$		

Condition II: Small Sample ($n < 30$) - Population Standard Deviation, σ is Unknown

Test	Null hypothesis	Alternative hypothesis	Test statistic	Critical statistic	Reject when
Two-sided	$H_o: \mu = \mu_o$	$H_1: \mu \neq \mu_o$		$t_{df,\alpha/2}$	
One-sided-left	$H_o: \mu \geq \mu_o$	$H_1: \mu < \mu_o$	$t_o = \dfrac{\bar{X} - \mu_o}{\dfrac{s}{\sqrt{n}}}$	$t_{df,\alpha}$	t_o is in the rejection region
One-sided-right	$H_o: \mu \leq \mu_o$	$H_1: \mu > \mu_o$		$t_{df,\alpha}$	

Hypothesis tests for a population proportion

Null hypothesis	$H_o: p = p_o$	$H_o: p \leq p_o$	$H_o: p \geq p_o$
Alternative hypothesis	$H_1: p \neq p_o$	$H_1: p > p_o$	$H_1: p < p_o$

$$z_o = \frac{\hat{p} - p}{\sqrt{\frac{p(1-p)}{n}}}$$

Variance Testing:

Hypothesis testing	Test statistic	Reject when
[1] $H_o: s^2 = s_o^2$ $H_1: s^2 \neq s_o^2$		$\chi_o^2 \geq \chi^2_{n-1,\alpha/2}$ or $\chi_o^2 \leq \chi^2_{n-1,1-\alpha/2}$
[2] $H_o: s^2 \geq s_o^2$ $H_1: s^2 < s_o^2$	$\chi_o^2 = \dfrac{(n-1)s^2}{\sigma_o^2}$	$\chi_o^2 \leq \chi^2_{n-1,1-\alpha}$
[3] $H_o: s^2 \leq s_o^2$ $H_1: s^2 > s_o^2$		$\chi_o^2 \geq \chi^2_{n-1,\alpha}$

Condition I: Hypothesis Tests for Comparison between Means of Two Independent Populations- Standard Deviations Known- The z-Test:

Test	Null hypothesis	Alternative hypothesis	Test statistic	Critical statistic	Reject when
Two-sided	$H_o: \mu_1 = \mu_2$	$H_1: \mu_1 \neq \mu_2$		$z_{\alpha/2}$	
One-sided-left	$H_o: \mu_1 \geq \mu_2$	$H_1: \mu_1 < \mu_2$	$z_o = \dfrac{(\bar{X}_1 - \bar{X}_2) - (\mu_1 - \mu_2)}{\sqrt{\dfrac{\sigma_1^2}{n_1} + \dfrac{\sigma_2^2}{n_2}}}$	z_α	z_o is in the rejection region
One-sided-right	$H_o: \mu_1 \leq \mu_2$	$H_1: \mu_1 > \mu_2$		z_α	

Condition II: Hypothesis Tests for Comparison between Means of Two Independent Populations- Standard Deviations Unknown-The t-Test:

Test	Null hypothesis	Alternative hypothesis	Test statistic	Critical statistic	Reject when
Two-sided	$H_o: \mu_1 = \mu_2$	$H_1: \mu_1 \neq \mu_2$		$t_{(n_1+n_2-2,\frac{\alpha}{2})}$	
One-sided-left	$H_o: \mu_1 \geq \mu_2$	$H_1: \mu_1 < \mu_2$	$t_o = \dfrac{(\bar{X}_1 - \bar{X}_2) - (\mu_1 - \mu_2)}{S_p\sqrt{\dfrac{1}{n_1} + \dfrac{1}{n_2}}}$	$t_{(n_1+n_2-2,\alpha)}$	t_o in the rejection region
One-sided-right	$H_o: \mu_1 \leq \mu_2$	$H_1: \mu_1 > \mu_2$	$S_p^2 = \dfrac{(n_1-1)s_1^2 + (n_2-1)s_2^2}{n_1 + n_2 - 2}$	$t_{(n_1+n_2-2,\alpha)}$	

Hypothesis Tests for Comparison between Means of Two Dependent Populations- The Case of Paired Data:

The test of hypothesis for paired data is about whether the difference is zero. This leads to:

$H_o: \mu_d = 0$
$H_1: \mu_d \neq 0$

B-6

The test statistic is the t-statistic defined by:

$$t_o = \frac{\bar{d}}{\frac{s_d}{\sqrt{n}}}$$

Hypothesis Tests for Comparison between Proportions of Two Independent Populations

$H_o: p_1 = p_2$

$H_1: p_1 \neq p_2$

$$z_o = \frac{\hat{p}_1 - \hat{p}_2}{\sqrt{\frac{P_p(1 - P_p)}{n_1} + \frac{P_p(1 - P_p)}{n_2}}}$$

$$P_p = \frac{X_1 + X_2}{n_1 + n_2}$$

Hypothesis Tests for comparison of Two Populations Variances

Hypothesis testing	Test statistic	Reject when
[1] $H_o: \sigma_1^2 = \sigma_2^2$ $H_1: \sigma_1^2 \neq \sigma_2^2$		$F_0 < F_{1-\alpha/2, n_1-1, n_2-1}$ or $F_0 > F_{\alpha/2, n_1-1, n_2-1}$
[2] $H_o: \sigma_1^2 \geq \sigma_2^2$ $H_1: \sigma_1^2 < \sigma_2^2$	$F_o = \frac{s_1^2}{s_2^2}$	$F_o > F_{\alpha, n_1-1, n_2-1}$
[3] $H_o: \sigma_1^2 \leq \sigma_2^2$ $H_1: \sigma_1^2 > \sigma_2^2$		$F_o > F_{\alpha, n_1-1, n_2-1}$

The Coefficient of Correlation, r:

$$r = \frac{S_{xy}}{S_x S_y}$$

$$Cov(x, y) = s_{xy} = \frac{\sum(x_i - \bar{X})(y_i - \bar{Y})}{n}$$

$$S_x^2 = \frac{\sum(x_i - \bar{X})^2}{n}$$

$$S_y^2 = \frac{\sum(y_i - \bar{Y})^2}{n}$$

Standard error of estimate:

$$\hat{S}_{y.x} = \sqrt{\frac{n}{n-2}} \, S_{yx}$$

$$S_{y.x}^2 = \frac{1}{n-2}\sum(y_i - \hat{y}_i)^2 = \frac{1}{n-2}SSE$$

The Coefficient of Determination, R^2 & the F-Value

$$R^2 = \frac{SSY - SSE}{SSY}$$

Source	df	SS	MS	F-Value	Prob > F
Model	k	SSY-SSE	SSM/k		
Error	n-k-1	SSE	SSE/(n-k-1)		
Total	n-1	SSY			

$$F = \frac{MSR}{MSE} = \frac{\dfrac{SSY - SSE}{k}}{\dfrac{SSE}{n - k - 1}}$$

Goodness of Fit:

H_o: there is no difference between the set of observed frequencies and the set of expected frequencies;

H_1: there is a difference between the observed and expected sets of frequencies.

$$\chi^2 = \sum_{1}^{k} (O - E)^2 / E$$

Contingency Tables and Tests for Independence:

H_o: The row and column variables are independent

H_a: The row and column variables are dependent

Test Statistic for a Test of Independence

$$\chi_o^2 = \sum (O - E)^2 / E$$

$$E = \frac{(row\ total)(column\ total)}{(grand\ total)}$$

Critical Values: χ^2 value at $df = (r\text{-}1)(c\text{-}1)$
$df = (r\text{-}1)(c\text{-}1) = (2\text{-}1)(4\text{-}1) = 3$

Forecast Accuracy:

Forecast Error = Actual Error − Forecast Value

Since forecast error can be positive or negative, we can use the so-called *mean absolute deviation (MAD)*:

$$MAD = \frac{\sum |forecsat\ error|}{n}$$

The mean square error (MSE):

$$MSE = \frac{\sum (error)^2}{n}$$

The *mean absolute percent error (MAPE):*

$$MAPE\,(\%) = \frac{\sum \left|\frac{error}{actual}\right|}{n} \times 100$$

The bias: This is the average error

Moving Average:

$$Moving\ average\ forecast = \frac{Sum\ of\ points\ in\ pervious\ n\ periods}{n}$$

Or $F_{t+1} = \frac{Y_t + Y_{t-1} + Y_{t-2} + \cdots + Y_{t-n-1}}{n}$

F_{t+1} = forecast for time period t + 1

Y_t = actual value in time period t

n = number of periods to average

Exponential Smoothing:

The general formula of exponential smoothing is:

$$F_{t+1} = \alpha A_t + (1 - \alpha) F_t$$

- A_t is the actual value
- F_t is the forecasted value
- α is the weighting factor, which ranges from 0 to 1
- t is the current time period.